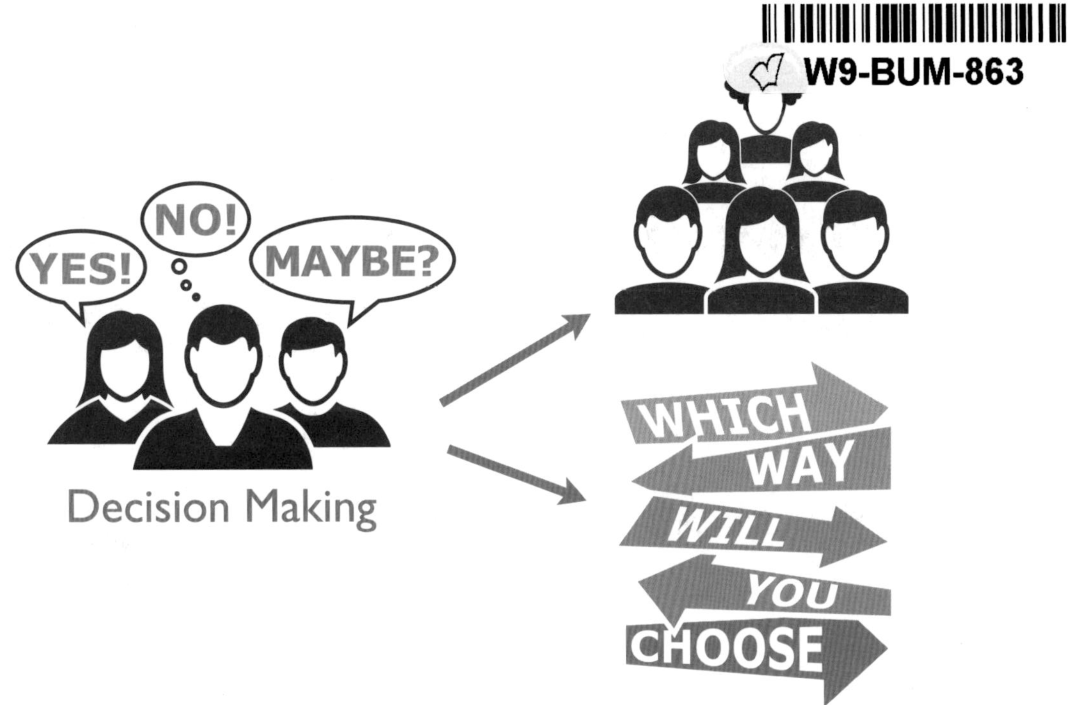

- **Decision making simulations** – place your students in the role of a key decision-maker where they are asked to make a series of decisions. The simulation will change and branch based on the decisions students make, providing a variation of scenario paths. Upon completion of each simulation, students receive a grade, as well as a detailed report of the choices they made during the simulation and the associated consequences of those decisions.

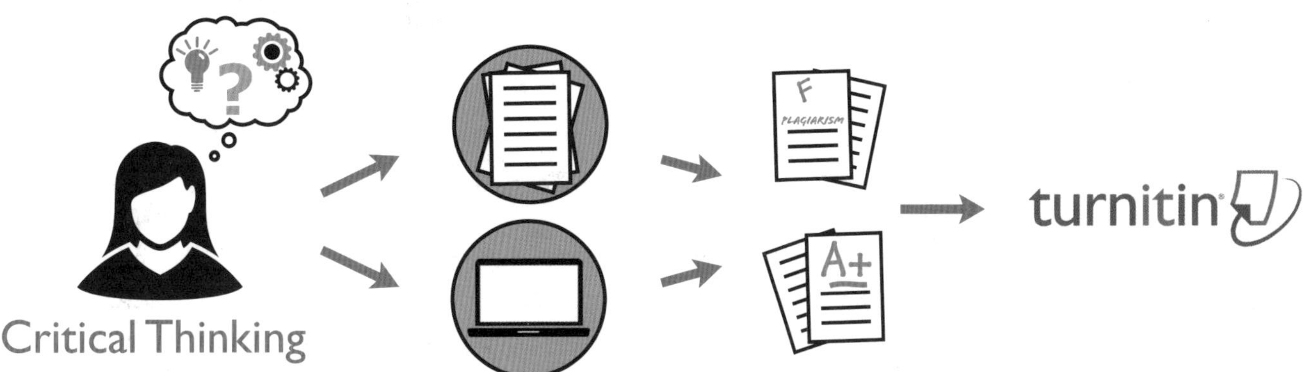

- **Writing Space** – better writers make great learners—who perform better in their courses. Providing a single location to develop and assess concept mastery and critical thinking, the Writing Space offers automatic graded, assisted graded and create your own writing assignments; allowing you to exchange personalized feedback with students quickly and easily.

  Writing Space can also check students' work for improper citation or plagiarism by comparing it against the world's most accurate text comparison database available from **Turnitin**.

http://www.pearsonmylabandmastering.com

PEARSON

Human Resource Management

Human Resource Management

Fourteenth Edition

GARY DESSLER
Florida International University

PEARSON

Boston Columbus Indianapolis New York San Francisco Upper Saddle River
Amsterdam Cape Town Dubai London Madrid Milan Munich Paris Montréal Toronto
Delhi Mexico City São Paulo Sydney Hong Kong Seoul Singapore Taipei Tokyo

Editor in Chief: Stephanie Wall
Senior Acquisitions Editor: Kris Ellis-Levy
Program Manager Team Lead: Ashley Santora
Program Manager: Sarah Holle
Editorial Assistant: Bernard Ollila
Director of Marketing: Maggie Moylan
Senior Marketing Manager: Erin Gardner
Marketing Assistant: Gianna Sandri
Project Manager Team Lead: Judy Leale
Project Manager: Kelly Warsak
Operations Specialist: Michelle Klein
Creative Director: Jayne Conte
Cover Designer: Bruce Kenselaar
Cover Photo: Comstock/Getty Images
VP, Director of Digital Strategy & Assessment: Paul Gentile
Digital Editor: Brian Surette
Digital Development Manager: Robin Lazrus
Digital Project Manager: Alana Coles
Digital Production Project Manager: Lisa Rinaldi
MyLab Product Manager: Joan Waxman
Full-Service Project Management: Lori Bradshaw/S4Carlisle Publishing Services
Composition: S4Carlisle Publishing Services
Printer/Binder: R.R. Donnelley/Roanoke
Cover Printer: Lehigh-Phoenix Color/Hagerstown
Text Font: Times LT Std

Credits and acknowledgments borrowed from other sources and reproduced, with permission, in this textbook appear on the appropriate page within text.

Library of Congress Cataloging-in-Publication Data

Dessler, Gary
Human resource management/Gary Dessler, Florida International University.—14th ed.
pages cm
Includes index.
ISBN 978-0-13-354517-3
1. Personnel management. I. Dessler, Gary, Essentials of human resource management. II. Title.
HF5549.D4379 2013b
658.3—dc23

2013024012

10 9 8 7 6 5 4 3

ISBN 10: 0-13-354517-2
ISBN 13: 978-0-13-354517-3

DEDICATED TO SAMANTHA AND TAYLOR

BRIEF CONTENTS

CONTENTS

PREFACE

Human Resource Management, 14th edition, provides students in human resource management courses and practicing managers with a full and practical introduction to human resource management concepts and techniques, with a focus on how to use those techniques to improve performance, productivity, and profitability at work. As this new edition goes to press, I feel even more strongly than I did when I wrote the first that all managers—not just HR managers—need a strong foundation in HR/personnel management concepts and techniques to do their jobs effectively. You will therefore find an emphasis here on practical material you need to perform your day-to-day management responsibilities, even if you never spend a day as a human resource manager.

I focused this edition on performance, productivity, and profitability for two reasons. First, companies must be competitive, and at the end of the day, competitiveness requires improved performance, productivity, and profitability.

Second, as I write this preface, the remnants of 2008's global recession continue to impede economic growth. For example, America's gross domestic product rose only about 1% on average from 2008 to 2013, well below the roughly 3% average for similar earlier periods. To boost performance, productivity, and profitability in the face of such weak demand, employers turned in part to human resource management. Many first instituted headcount cost controls. That helps explain why America's 59% employment-to-population ratio is down to where it was in the early 1980s, the 7+% unemployment rate is at least 2% too high, and the ratio of wages to gross domestic product (about 44%) is well below average. But headcount cost controls did help employers keep both after-tax profit margins (9.3%) and profits as a share of gross domestic product (about 11%) higher than in the past 50 years.

And as we'll see in this book, those headcount controls were just one of hundreds of HR techniques employers used to reduce costs and improve performance, productivity, and profitability, often while maintaining or improving employee relations, morale and engagement. A skill-based pay program at JLG Industries led to lower overall staffing levels, higher minimum hiring qualifications, increased productivity, and expanded plant capacity. One forest products company saved over $1 million over 5 years by investing about $50,000 in safety improvements and employee safety training. GE Medical used recruiting metrics such as "percentage interviews that lead to offers" to lower recruiting costs by 17%. In staffing its call centers, Xerox Corp. long hired applicants with call center experience. But after using special *HR data analytics* tools to analyze call center performance, it discovered that operator personality, not experience was the key. It now keeps hiring costs down and performance up by using special software to screen for its almost 40,000 call center jobs.

CHANGES AND NEW FEATURES

In addition to thoroughly updating all chapters, and streamlining the book, I used the following features and changes to help implement this edition's new focus on performance, productivity, and profitability.

First, **Improving Performance** features demonstrate real-world human resource management tools and practices that managers actually use to improve performance. The discussion questions within each of the three boxed Improving Performance features are also in the accompanying MyManagementLab®.

IMPROVING PERFORMANCE: HR as a Profit Center

Controlling Sick Leave

Sick leave often gets out of control because employers don't measure it. In one survey, only 57% of employers formally tracked sick days for their exempt employees.[22] Three-fourths of the employers couldn't provide an estimate of what sick pay was costing them. Therefore, the employer should first have a system in place for monitoring sick leaves and for measuring their financial impact.[23]

Improving Performance: HR as a Profit Center contains actual examples of how human resource management practices add value by reducing costs or boosting revenues.

Improving Performance: HR Tools for Line Managers and Entrepreneurs explains that many line managers and entrepreneurs are "on their own" when it comes to human resource management, and describes work sampling tests and other straightforward HR tools that line managers and entrepreneurs can create and safely use to improve performance.

IMPROVING PERFORMANCE: HR Tools for Line Managers and Entrepreneurs

How to Conduct an Effective Interview

You may not have the time or inclination to create a structured situational interview. However, there is still much you can do to make your interviews systematic and productive.

Step 1: **First, make sure you know the job.** Do not start the interview unless you understand the job's duties and what human skills you're looking for. Study the job description.

Step 2: **Structure the interview.** *Any* structuring is better than none. If pressed for time, you can still do several things to ask more consistent and job-relevant questions, without developing a full-blown structured interview.[75] They include:[76]

- Base questions on *actual job duties.* This will minimize irrelevant questions.
- Use *job knowledge, situational, or behavioral questions,* and know enough about the job to be able to evaluate the interviewee's answers. Questions that simply ask for opinions and attitudes, goals and aspirations, and self-descriptions and self-evaluations

IMPROVING PERFORMANCE: HR Practices Around the Globe

Safety at Saudi Petrol Chemical

The industrial safety and security manager for the Saudi Petrol Chemical Co., in Jubail City, Saudi Arabia, says that his company's excellent safety record results from the fact that "our employees are champions of safety." Employees are involved in every part of the safety process. They serve on safety committees, develop and lead daily and monthly safety meetings, and conduct job safety analyses, for instance.

Improving Performance: HR Practices Around the Globe shows how actual companies around the globe use HR practices to improve their teams' and companies' performance, while illustrating the challenges managers face in managing internationally.

Improving Performance Through HRIS are embedded features that demonstrate how managers use human resource technology to improve performance.

KNOW YOUR EMPLOYMENT LAW

Employee Incentives and the Law

Various laws affect incentive pay. Under the Fair Labor Standards Act, if the incentive the worker receives is in the form of a prize or cash award, the employer generally must *include the value of that award* when calculating the worker's overtime pay for that pay period.[15] So, unless you structure the incentive bonuses properly, the bonus itself becomes part of the week's wages. For

Know Your Employment Law boxed features within each chapter discuss the practical implications of the employment laws that apply to that chapter's topics, such as the laws relating to recruitment (Chapter 5), selection (Chapter 6), training (Chapter 8), and safety (Chapter 16).

Diversity Counts features provide practical insights for managing a diverse work force, for instance regarding gender bias in selection decisions, bias in performance appraisal, and "hidden" gender bias in some bonus plans (Chapter 12).

Fully Integrated Strategy Case and Strategy Maps provide the most comprehensive treatment of strategic human resource management in any HR survey text.

- Chapter 1 introduces and Chapter 3 presents the concepts and techniques of human resource strategy.
- Each chapter starting with Chapter 3 contains a continuing "Hotel Paris" case, written to help make strategic human resource management come alive for readers. The continuing case shows how this hotel company's HR director uses that chapter's human resource management concepts and techniques to create HR policies and practices that produce the employee skills and behaviors that the Hotel Paris needs to improve its service and thereby achieve its strategic goals.
- An overall strategy map for the Hotel Paris on the book's inside back cover, as well as chapter-specific Hotel Paris strategy maps in the accompanying MyManagementLab, help readers understand and follow the strategic implications of the hotel's HR decisions.
- "Eiffel Tower" callouts in each chapter draw students' attention to the Hotel Paris case.

Social Media and HR features in each chapter demonstrate how employers use social media to improve their human resource processes.

Knowledge Base icons in each chapter highlight coverage of the HR Certification Institute's (HRCI) Knowledge Base topics for which the HRCI certification exams test mastery. This book explicitly addresses the HR Certification Institute's Knowledge Base topics including topics other textbooks often neglect, such as ethics, employee rights, and employee relations. Chapter opening Learning Objectives align to the HRCI Knowledge Base as well. The HR Certification Institute is an independent certifying organization for human resource professionals (see www.hrci.org/). The HRCI "PHR and SPHR Knowledge Base" is in Appendix A of this book (see pp. 580–588) and lists about 91 specific "Knowledge of" subject areas within its main topic area groups.

A revised Chapter 14, now titled **Ethics, Employee Relations, and Fair Treatment at Work,** includes—unique to this book—detailed coverage of employee relations, including what it means, why it is important, and how to measure and influence it. HRCI's knowledge base includes the topic of employee relations.

Video Title: Motivation (TWZ Role-Play)

SYNOPSIS

During a rough economy, companies struggle with rewarding employees when they can't afford to give raises. This video examines some incentives that employees may accept in lieu of money, at least temporarily. In this video, David is meeting with his supervisor, Linda, to discuss a potential raise. Their company could not afford to give raises the previous year and David understood that since it was a bad economy; as a company, they needed to pull together. Since the company has seemed to be doing better, David feels the time is right to ask for a raise. While Linda agrees that David is a valuable employee and she appreciates everything he has done for the company, she is not able to increase his salary. Linda does suggest some other options to David other than a raise, such as a flexible sched-

Video Title: Motivating Employees Through Company Culture (Zappos)

SYNOPSIS

Zappos is an online store that sells shoes, clothing, accessories, housewares, and beauty products. They are known throughout the industry for excellent customer service. Zappos CEO Tony Hsieh is also committed to making Zappos a fun loving and energetic place to work. Hsieh's passion is to create a culture where he would be excited about going to work every day. He aims to motivate and inspire his employees with a commitment to 10 Core Values, including create fun and a little weirdness; be adventurous, creative, and open-minded; and build positive and family spirit.

Video Cases selected by the author with accompanying discussion questions are now integrated into the end of each chapter and can be found online for students to watch at any time on MyManagementLab.

Assisted-Graded Writing Questions found in the boxed feature at the end of each chapter are also available in the Writing Space in MyManagementLab. Also available in MyManagementLab are Auto-Graded Writing Questions. Writing Space includes plagiarism detection powered by TurnItIn.com and greatly simplifies the submission and grading process.

Don't usually cover all 18 chapters? Available for enrollments of 25 or more, **Pearson Custom Library** allows you to easily create your own custom book. Include only the chapters you want to cover, in the order you want to cover them, or just change chapter order to match how you cover the topics. Minimized cross-referencing between chapters facilitates customization. *To begin building your custom text, visit* www.pearsoncustomlibrary.com or contact your Pearson representative.

INSTRUCTOR SUPPLEMENTS

At www.pearsonhighered.com/irc, instructors can download a variety of digital resources available with this text.

- Instructor's Manual
- Test Item File—Questions are tagged to reflect AACSB Learning Standards
- TestGen
- PowerPoint Presentation

Registration is easy; contact your Pearson sales representative, who will provide your login and password information. If you need assistance, our dedicated technical support team is ready to help with the media supplements that accompany this text. **Visit 247pearsoned.custhelp.com** for answers to frequently asked questions and toll-free user support phone numbers.

VIDEO LIBRARY

Videos illustrating the most important subject topics are available in two formats:

- DVD–available for in classroom use by instructors, includes videos mapped to Pearson textbooks.
- MyLab–available for instructors and students, provides round the clock instant access to videos and corresponding assessment and simulations for Pearson textbooks.

Contact your local Pearson representative to request access to either format.

ACKNOWLEDGMENTS

Everyone involved in creating this book is proud of what we've achieved. *Human Resource Management* is one of the top-selling books in this market, and, as you read this, students and managers around the world are using versions translated into about a dozen languages, including Thai, French, Spanish, Indonesian, Russian, and Chinese.

Although I am responsible for *Human Resource Management*, I want to thank several people for their assistance. They include, first, the faculty who carefully reviewed the 13th edition, and who made many useful and insightful suggestions:

Kyle Stone, *Fort Hayes State University*
George Wynn, *University of Tampa*
Edward Ward, *Saint Cloud State University*
Daniel Grundmann, *Indiana University*
Clare Francis, *University of North Dakota*
John Durboraw, *Columbia College*
Mary Kern, *Baruch College*
Lucy Ford, *St. Joseph's University*
Tom Zagenczyk, *Clemson University*
Leonard Bierman, *Texas A&M University*
Thomas J. Zagenczyk, *Clemson University*
Itoe Valentine, *Albany Technical College*
Pravin Kamdar, *College of Business and Management Cardinal Stritch University*
Craig J. Russell, *Price College of Business, University of Oklahoma*
Matthew S. Rodgers, *The Ohio State University*
Carol Heeter, *Ivy Tech Community College*
Magdalem Upshaw, *Richland College Dallas*
C. Darren Brooks, *Florida State University*
Brian D. Lyons, *Wright State University*

Thank you also to the supplement authors for the 14th edition for their hard work on updating and improving the supplements. They include Donna Gala: American Public University; Lisa Moeller: Beckfield College; Angela Boston: University of Texas-Arlington.

At Pearson, thank you for the support and dedicated assistance of all involved. This 14th edition had the benefit of a new editorial team, and I particularly appreciate the insights, suggestions, and personal involvement of Editor in Chief Stephanie Wall and Senior Acquisitions Editor Kris Ellis-Levy. Thank you again to my outstanding production team, with whom I've worked for many years, Judy Leale, Project Manager Team Lead, and Kelly Warsak, Project Manager. Thanks to Erin Gardner, Senior Marketing Manager, and the Pearson sales staff, without whose efforts this book would languish on the shelf, and to Sarah Holle, Program Manager, and Bernie Ollila IV, Editorial Assistant. I want to thank everyone at Pearson International for successfully managing *Human Resource Management's* internationalization. Development editor Kerri Tomasso was extraordinarily helpful, and thank you to Lori Bradshaw at S4Carlisle.

At home, I want to acknowledge and thank my wife, Claudia, for her support during the many hours I spent working on this edition. My son, Derek, always a source of enormous pride, was very helpful. Lisa, Samantha, and Taylor are always in my thoughts. My parents were always a great source of support and encouragement and would have been very proud to see this book.

Gary Dessler

Human Resource Management

PART ONE

Introduction

1 Introduction to Human Resource Management

Source: Ryan McVay/Getty Images

MyManagementLab®

Improve Your Grade!

When you see this icon, visit **www.mymanagementlab.com** for activities that are applied, personalized, and offer immediate feedback.

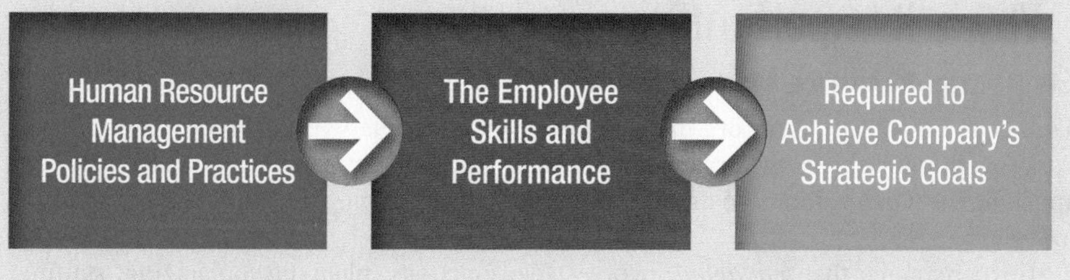

For a bird's eye view of how managers formulate human resource management policies and practices that produce the employee skills and performance the company needs to achieve its strategic goals, we will use the Hotel Paris continuing case starting in Chapter 3 as an applied example.

WHERE ARE WE NOW . . .

This chapter's purpose is to explain what human resource management is, and why it is important to all managers. We'll see that human resource management responsibilities such as hiring, training, appraising, compensating, and developing employees are part of every manager's job. We will also see that human resource management is often a separate function, usually with its own human resource or "HR" manager, and what that manager's duties and challenges are. The main topics we'll cover include what is human resource management, and why is it important?; the trends shaping human resource management; the new human resource manager; the human resource manager's competencies; and the plan of this book. The three-box model above introduces each chapter and makes this point: That the firm's HR policies and practices should produce the employee skills and behaviors the company needs to achieve its strategic aims.

LEARNING OBJECTIVES

1 Explain what human resource management is and how it relates to the management process.

2 Briefly discuss and illustrate each of the important trends influencing human resource management.

3 List and briefly describe important traits of today's human resource managers.

4 Describe four important human resource manager competencies.

5 Outline the plan of this book.

The bank's president was excited as they threw the switch activating the new productivity software; she had told her board of directors that it would dramatically improve the customer service representatives' performance and boost bank profitability. And then she waited. And waited some more. But it was soon apparent that the service reps were no more productive than they'd been before. We'll see why.

What Is Human Resource Management, and Why Is it Important?

1 Explain what human resource management is and how it relates to the management process.

organization
People with formally assigned roles who work together to achieve the organization's goals.

manager
The person responsible for accomplishing the organization's goals, and who does so by managing (planning, organizing, staffing, leading, and controlling) the efforts of the organization's people.

management process
The five basic functions of planning, organizing, staffing, leading, and controlling.

human resource management (HRM)
The process of acquiring, training, appraising, and compensating employees, and of attending to their labor relations, health and safety, and fairness concerns.

What Is Human Resource Management?

This bank is an organization. An **organization** consists of people with formally assigned roles who work together to achieve the organization's goals. A **manager** is the person responsible for accomplishing the organization's goals, and who does so by managing the efforts of the organization's people.

Most experts agree that *managing* involves five functions: planning, organizing, staffing, leading, and controlling. In total, these functions represent the **management process**. Specific activities involved in each function include:

- ***Planning.*** Establishing goals and standards; developing rules and procedures; developing plans and forecasting.
- ***Organizing.*** Giving each subordinate a specific task; establishing departments; delegating authority to subordinates; establishing channels of authority and communication; coordinating subordinates' work.
- ***Staffing.*** Determining what type of people you should hire; recruiting prospective employees; selecting employees; training and developing employees; setting performance standards; evaluating performance; counseling employees; compensating employees.
- ***Leading.*** Getting others to get the job done; maintaining morale; motivating subordinates.
- ***Controlling.*** Setting standards such as sales quotas, quality standards, or production levels; checking to see how actual performance compares with these standards; taking corrective action, as needed.

In this book, we are going to focus on one of these functions—the staffing, personnel management, or *human resource management (HRM) function*. **Human resource management (HRM)** is the process of acquiring, training, appraising, and compensating employees, and of attending to their labor relations, health and safety, and fairness concerns. The topics we'll discuss should therefore provide you with the concepts and techniques you need to perform the "people" or personnel aspects of your management job. These include:

Conducting job analyses (determining the nature of each employee's job)
Planning labor needs and *recruiting job candidates*
Selecting job candidates
Orienting and training new employees
Managing wages and salaries (compensating employees)
Providing incentives and benefits
Appraising performance
Communicating (interviewing, counseling, disciplining)
Training and developing managers
Building employee commitment

And what a manager should know about:

Equal opportunity and affirmative action
Employee health and safety
Handling grievances and labor relations

Why Is Human Resource Management Important to All Managers?

Perhaps it's easier to answer this by listing some personnel mistakes you *don't* want to make while managing. For example, no manager wants to:

Hire the wrong person for the job
Experience high turnover
Have your people not doing their best

Waste time with useless interviews

Have your company taken to court because of your discriminatory actions

Have your company cited under federal occupational safety laws for unsafe practices

Have some employees think their salaries are unfair relative to others in the organization

Allow a lack of training to undermine your department's effectiveness

Commit any unfair labor practices

Carefully studying this book will help you avoid mistakes like these.

IMPROVING PERFORMANCE: HR AS A PROFIT CENTER More importantly, the human resource management concepts and techniques you'll learn in this book can help ensure that you get results—through people. Remember that you can do everything else right as a manager—lay brilliant plans, draw clear organization charts, set up world-class assembly lines, and use sophisticated accounting controls—but still fail, by hiring the wrong people or by not motivating subordinates. On the other hand, many managers—presidents, generals, governors, supervisors—have been successful even with inadequate plans, organization, or controls. They were successful because they had the knack of hiring the right people for the right jobs and motivating, appraising, and developing them. Remember as you read this book that *getting results* is the bottom line of managing, and that, as a manager, you will have to get those results through people. As one company president summed up:

> For many years, it has been said that capital is the bottleneck for a developing industry. I don't think this any longer holds true. I think it's the workforce and the company's inability to recruit and maintain a good work force that does constitute the bottleneck for production. I don't know of any major project backed by good ideas, vigor, and enthusiasm that has been stopped by a shortage of cash. I do know of industries whose growth has been partly stopped or hampered because they can't maintain an efficient and enthusiastic labor force, and I think this will hold true even more in the future.[1]

Because of global competition, technological advances, and the changing nature of work, that president's statement has never been truer than it is today. Human resource management methods like those in this book can help any line manager/supervisor (or HR manager) boost his or her team's and company's profits and performance. Here are a few of the actual examples we'll meet in this book:

At one Ball Corp. packaging plant, managers trained supervisors to set and communicate daily performance goals. Management tracked daily goal attainment with team scorecards. Employees received special training to ensure they had the skills. Within 12 months production was up 84 million cans, customer complaints dropped by 50%, and the plant's return on investment rose by $3,090,000.

To reduce recruiting costs, *GE Medical* managers met with 20 recruiters and said they would henceforth use only the 10 best. To implement this, managers developed measures—such as "% résumés lead to interviews," and "% interviews lead to offers." Because of what it learned from these measures, GE also boosted its intern program and its referrals program. Recruiting costs dropped 17%.

Department store Bon-Ton Stores Inc. had high turnover among its cosmetics sales associates. It used special statistical tools to identify high-performing cosmetics associates. The best associates, they discovered, were problem solvers who could figure out what the customer wants and needs, and solve the problem.

The call center. This center averaged 18.6 vacancies per year (about a 60% turnover rate). The researchers estimated the cost of a call-center operator leaving at about $21,500. They estimated total annual cost of agent turnover for the call center at $400,853. Cutting that rate in half would save this firm about $200,000 per year.

YOU MAY SPEND SOME TIME AS AN HR MANAGER Here is another reason to study this book's contents: You may make an unplanned stopover as a human resource manager. For example, Pearson Corporation (which publishes this book) promoted the head of one of its publishing divisions to chief human resource executive at its corporate headquarters. About one-third of the top HR managers in Fortune 100 companies moved there from other functional areas.[2] Reasons given include the fact that such people may give the firm's HR efforts a more strategic emphasis, and the possibility that they're sometimes better equipped to integrate the firm's human resource efforts with the rest of the business.[3]

However, most top human resource executives do have prior human resource experience. About 80% of those in one survey worked their way up within HR.[4] About 17% of these HR executives had earned the Human Resource Certification Institute's Senior Professional in Human Resources (SPHR) designation, and 13% were certified Professionals in Human Resources (PHR). The Society for Human Resource Management (SHRM) offers a brochure describing alternative career paths within human resource management. Find it at www.shrm.org/Communities/StudentPrograms/Documents/07-0971%20Careers%20HR%20Book_final.pdf.

HR FOR ENTREPRENEURS Finally, study this book because you might end up as your own human resource manager. More than half the people working in the United States—about 68 million out of 118 million—work for small firms. Small businesses as a group also account for most of the 600,000 or so new businesses created every year. Statistically speaking, therefore, most people graduating from college in the next few years either will work for small businesses or will create new small businesses of their own. Especially if you are managing your own small firm with no human resource manager, you should know the nuts and bolts of human resource management.[5] We will address HR for entrepreneurs in later chapters.

Line and Staff Aspects of Human Resource Management

All managers are, in a sense, human resource managers, because they all get involved in recruiting, interviewing, selecting, and training their employees. Yet most firms also have a human resource department with its own top manager. How do the duties of this human resource manager and department relate to the human resource duties of sales and production and other managers? Answering this requires a short definition of line versus staff authority. **Authority** is the right to make decisions, to direct the work of others, and to give orders. Managers usually distinguish between line authority and staff authority.

authority
The right to make decisions, direct others' work, and give orders.

line authority
The authority exerted by an HR manager by directing the activities of the people in his or her own department and in service areas (like the plant cafeteria).

staff authority
Staff authority gives the manager the right (authority) to advise other managers or employees.

line manager
A manager who is authorized to direct the work of subordinates and is responsible for accomplishing the organization's tasks.

staff manager
A manager who assists and advises line managers.

In organizations, having what managers call **line authority** traditionally gives managers the right to *issue orders* to other managers or employees. Line authority therefore creates a superior (order giver)–subordinate (order receiver) relationship. When the vice president of sales tells her sales director to "get the sales presentation ready by Tuesday," she is exercising her line authority. **Staff authority** gives a manager the right to *advise* other managers or employees. It creates an advisory relationship. When the human resource manager suggests that the plant manager use a particular selection test, he or she is exercising staff authority.

On the organization chart, managers with line authority are **line managers**. Those with staff (advisory) authority are **staff managers**. In popular usage, people tend to associate line managers with managing departments (like sales or production) that are crucial for the company's survival. Staff managers generally run departments that are advisory or supportive, like purchasing and human resource management. Human resource managers are usually staff managers. They assist and advise line managers in areas like recruiting, hiring, and compensation.

Line Managers' Human Resource Duties

However, line managers still have many human resource duties. This is because the direct handling of people has always been part of every line manager's duties, from president down to first-line supervisors. For example, one major company outlines its line supervisors' responsibilities for effective human resource management under these general headings:

1. Placing the right person in the right job
2. Starting new employees in the organization (orientation)
3. Training employees for jobs that are new to them
4. Improving the job performance of each person
5. Gaining cooperation and developing smooth working relationships
6. Interpreting the company's policies and procedures
7. Controlling labor costs
8. Developing the abilities of each person
9. Creating and maintaining department morale
10. Protecting employees' health and physical condition

Line authority gives the manager the right to issue orders.

iStockphoto/Thinkstock

In small organizations, line managers may carry out all these personnel tasks unassisted. But as the organization grows, they need the assistance, specialized knowledge, and advice of a separate human resource staff. The human resource department provides this specialized assistance.

Human Resource Manager's Duties

In providing this specialized assistance, the *human resource manager* carries out three distinct functions:

functional authority
The authority exerted by an HR manager as coordinator of personnel activities.

1. ***A line function.*** The human resource manager directs the activities of the people in his or her own department, and perhaps in related areas (like the plant cafeteria).
2. ***A coordinative function.*** The human resource manager also coordinates personnel activities, a duty often referred to as **functional authority** (or functional control). Here he or she ensures that line managers are implementing the firm's human resource policies and practices (for example, adhering to its sexual harassment policies).
3. ***Staff (assist and advise) functions.*** Assisting and advising line managers is the heart of the human resource manager's job. He or she *advises* the CEO so the CEO can better understand the personnel aspects of the company's strategic options. HR *assists* in hiring, training, evaluating, rewarding, counseling, promoting, and firing employees. It *administers* benefit programs (health and accident insurance, retirement, vacation, and so on). It helps line managers comply with equal employment and occupational safety laws, and plays an important role in handling grievances and labor relations. It carries out an *innovator* role, by providing up-to-date information on current trends and new methods for better utilizing the company's employees (or "human resources"). It plays an *employee advocacy* role, by representing the interests of employees within the framework of its primary obligation to senior management. Although human resource managers generally can't wield line authority (outside their departments), they are likely to exert *implied authority*. This is because line managers know the human resource manager has top management's ear in areas like testing and affirmative action.

Organizing the Human Resource Department's Responsibilities

The size of the human resource department reflects the company's size. For a very large employer, an organization chart like the one in Figure 1-1 would be typical, containing a full complement of specialists for each HR function.

Examples of human resource management specialties include:[6]

- ***Recruiters.*** Search for qualified job applicants.
- ***Equal employment opportunity (EEO) coordinators.*** Investigate and resolve EEO grievances, examine organizational practices for potential violations, and compile and submit EEO reports.
- ***Job analysts.*** Collect and examine information about jobs to prepare job descriptions.

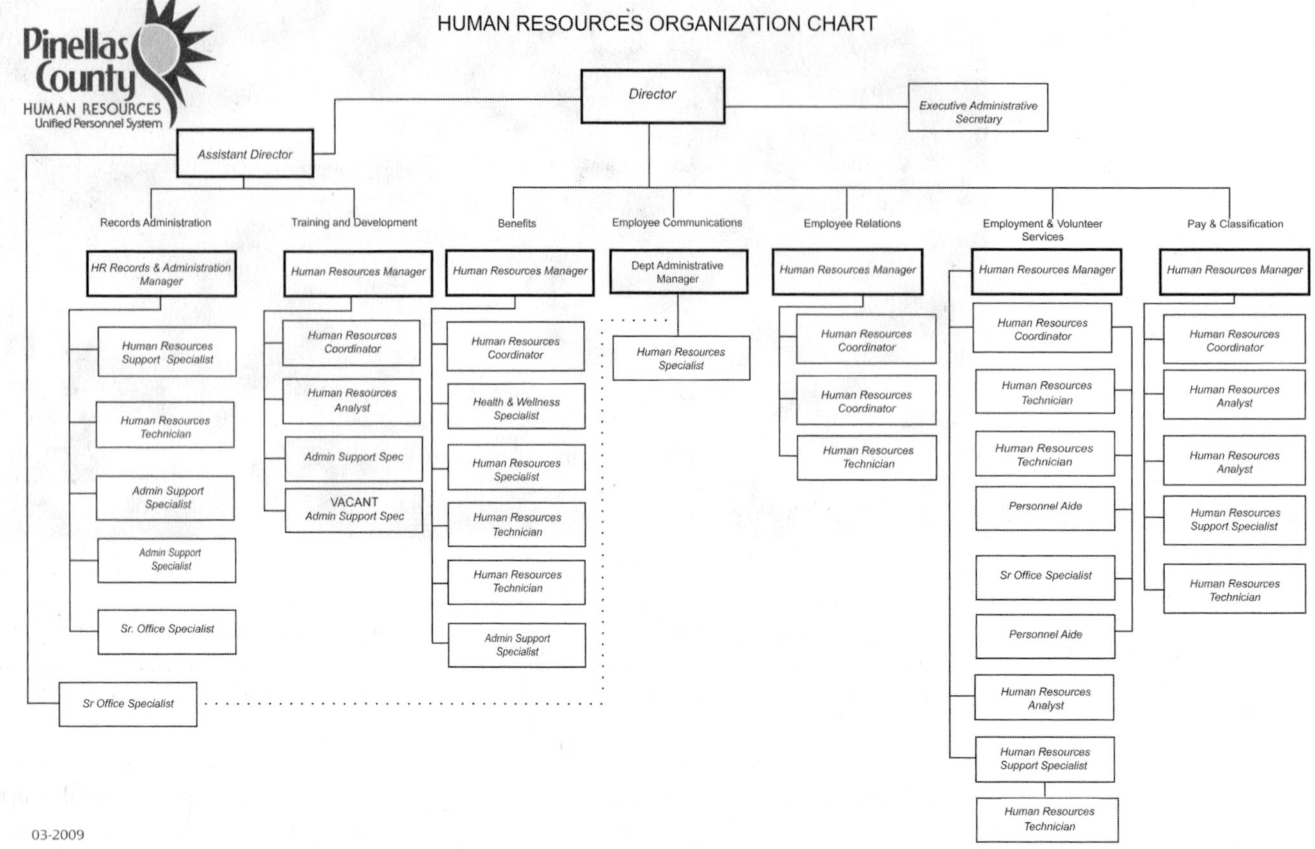

FIGURE 1-1 Human Resources Organization Chart Showing Typical HR Job Titles

Source: "Human Resources Organization Chart Showing Typical HR Job Titles," www.co.pinellas.fl.us/persnl/pdf/orgchart.pdf. Courtesy of Pinellas County Human Resources. Reprinted with permission.

- ***Compensation managers.*** Develop compensation plans and handle the employee benefits program.
- ***Training specialists.*** Plan, organize, and direct training activities.
- ***Labor relations specialists.*** Advise management on all aspects of union–management relations.

At the other extreme, the human resource team for a small manufacturer may contain just five or six (or fewer) staff, and have an organization similar to that in Figure 1-2. There is generally about one human resource employee per 100 company employees.

REORGANIZING THE HUMAN RESOURCE MANAGEMENT FUNCTION Many employers are changing how they organize their human resource functions. For one thing, the traditional human resource organization tends to divide HR activities into separate "silos" such as recruitment, training, and employee relations for the whole company. J. Randall MacDonald, IBM's senior vice president of human resources, took a different approach. He split IBM's 330,000 employees into three segments for HR purposes: executive and technical employees, managers, and rank and file. Now separate human resource management teams (consisting of recruitment, training, and pay specialists, for instance) focus on each employee segment. This helps to ensure that the employees in each segment get the specialized testing, training, and rewards they require.[7]

FIGURE 1-2 HR Organization Chart (Small Company)

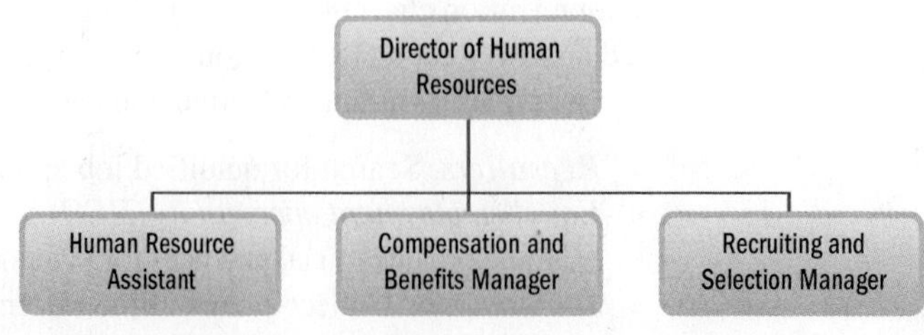

You may find other configurations.[8] For example, some employers create *transactional HR teams*. These teams provide specialized support in day-to-day HR activities (such as changing benefits plans), usually through centralized call centers and through outside vendors (such as benefits advisors). Specialized *corporate HR teams* assist top management in top-level issues such as developing the personnel aspects of the company's long-term strategic plan. *Embedded HR teams* have HR generalists (also known as "relationship managers" or "HR business partners") assigned to functional departments like sales and production. They provide the selection and other assistance the departments need. *Centers of expertise* are like specialized HR consulting firms within the company. For example, one might provide specialized advice in organizational change to the company's department managers.

Cooperative Line and Staff HR Management: An Example

Line managers and human resource managers share responsibility for most human resource management activities.[9] For example, in recruiting and hiring, the line manager describes the qualifications employees need to fill specific positions. Then the human resource team develops sources of qualified applicants and conducts initial screening interviews. They administer the appropriate tests. Then they refer the best applicants to the line manager, who interviews and selects the ones he or she wants. In training, the line manager again describes what he or she expects the employee to be able to do. Then the human resource team devises a training program, which the line manager may then administer.

Some activities are usually HR's alone. For example, 60% of firms assign HR the exclusive responsibility for preemployment testing, 75% assign it college recruiting, and 80% assign it insurance benefits administration. But employers split most activities, such as employment interviews, performance appraisal, skills training, job descriptions, and disciplinary procedures, between HR and line managers.[10]

So in summary, human resource management is part of every manager's job. Whether you are a first-line supervisor, middle manager, or president—or whether you're a production manager or county manager (or HR manager)—*getting results through people* is the name of the game. And to do this, you will need a good working knowledge of the human resource management concepts and techniques in this book.

The Trends Shaping Human Resource Management

2 Briefly discuss and illustrate each of the important trends influencing human resource management.

What human resource managers do and how they do it is changing. Some of the reasons for these changes are obvious. One is technology. For example, employers now use their intranets to let employees change their own benefits plans, something they obviously couldn't do years ago. Other trends shaping human resource management include globalization, deregulation, changes in demographics and the nature of work, and economic challenges (summarized in Figure 1-3). Let's look at these trends next.[11]

FIGURE 1-3 Trends Shaping Human Resource Management

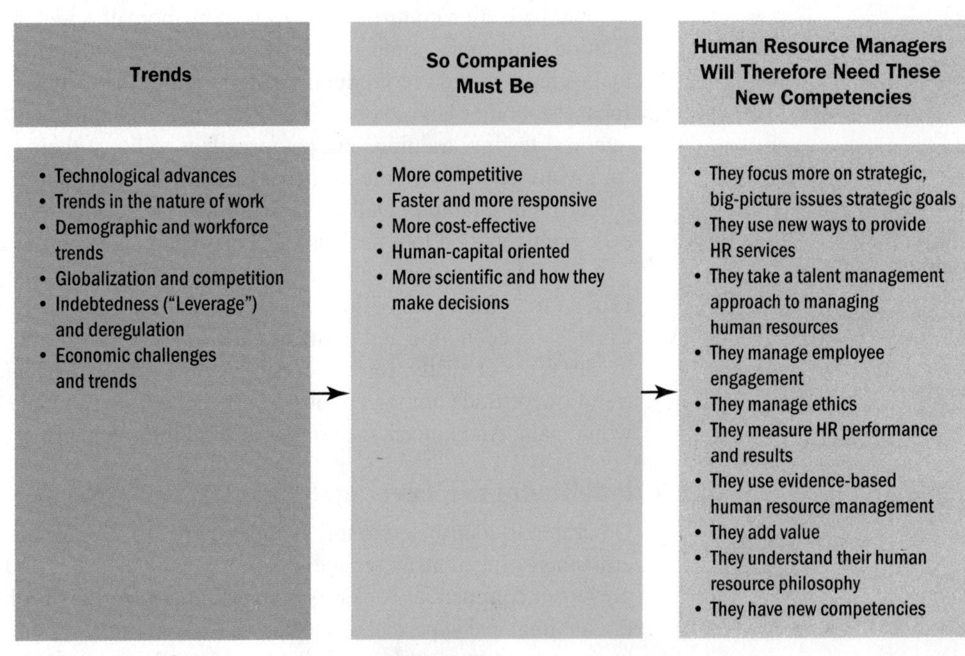

Technological Advances

For one thing, technology dramatically changed how human resource managers do their jobs. LinkedIn and Facebook recruiting are examples.[12] Employers can access candidates via Facebook's job board. This provides a seamless way to recruit and promote job listings from Facebook.[13] Then, after creating a job listing, the employer can advertise its job link using Facebook. Innovations like these have dramatically changed how human resource managers do things.[14] Another example, The HR Portal, follows.

Improving Performance Through HRIS: The HR Portal

HR portals, usually hosted on a company's intranet, provide employees with a single access point or "gateway" to HR information.[15] They let employees, managers, and executives interactively access and modify selected HR information. They thereby streamline the HR process, improve human resource management performance, and allow HR managers to focus more on strategic issues.

Some such portals are specialized. Anheuser-Busch used this approach for its annual benefits package enrollments. The firm's HR managers expected a large number of employee inquiries. It therefore replaced its manual inquiry process with an HR portal from Authoria, Inc. (www.authoria.com). Doing so let HR digitize and aggregate through a single source (the new portal) all the former paper benefits reports, electronic spreadsheets, and benefit summaries that the firm's benefits counselors had been using. That made it much easier for specialists in Anheuser-Busch's HR call center to answer employees' questions. The company expects to eventually allow employees to research and answer their own HR questions through a browser-based interface.[16]

Wells Fargo used an HR portal when it merged with Norwest Corporation. The merger meant moving 90,000 employees to a new benefits plan, which of course triggered numerous employee inquiries. As at Anheuser-Busch, Wells Fargo armed its HR call center counselors with a specialized portal; this helped them research and answer employees' inquiries.

NCR calls its HR portal HR eXpress. It contains three information areas: benefits and compensation, training and career growth, and NCR values and HR policies.[17] HR eXpress gives NCR employees a shortcut to all the information they need to manage HR tasks, such as those relating to company benefits and updating their personal information. A Forms Center gives them quick access to any HR forms they need.[18]

Globalization and Competition Trends

globalization
The tendency of firms to extend their sales, ownership, and/or manufacturing to new markets abroad.

Globalization refers to companies extending their sales, ownership, and/or manufacturing to new markets abroad. For example, Toyota builds Camrys in Kentucky, while Dell assembles PCs in China. Free-trade areas—agreements that reduce tariffs and barriers among trading partners—further encourage international trade. NAFTA (the North American Free Trade Agreement) and the EU (European Union) are examples.

Globalization compels employers to be more efficient. More globalization means more competition, and more competition means more pressure to be "world class"—to lower costs, to make employees more productive, and to do things better and less expensively. Thus, when the Japanese retailer Uniqlo opened its first store in Manhattan, many local competitors had to institute new testing, training, and pay practices to boost their employees' performance. The search for greater efficiencies prompts many employers to *offshore* (export jobs to lower-cost locations abroad). For example, Dell offshored some call-center jobs to India. Many employers offshore even highly skilled jobs such as sales managers, general managers—and HR managers.[19]

For 50 or so years, globalization boomed. For example, the total sum of U.S. imports and exports rose from $47 billion in 1960, to $562 billion in 1980, to about $4.7 *trillion* recently.[20] Changes in economic and political philosophies drove this boom. Governments dropped cross-border taxes or tariffs, formed economic free-trade areas, and took other steps to encourage the free flow of trade among countries. The economic rationale was that by doing so, all countries would gain. And indeed, economies around the world did grow quickly.

Indebtedness ("Leverage") and Deregulation

Other trends contributed to this economic growth. Deregulation was one. In many countries, governments stripped away regulations. In the United States and Europe, for instance, the rules that prevented commercial banks from expanding into stock brokering were relaxed. Giant, multinational "financial supermarkets" such as Citibank quickly emerged. As economies boomed, more businesses and consumers went deeply into debt. Homebuyers bought homes, often with little money down. Banks freely lent money to developers to build more homes. For almost 20 years, U.S. consumers spent more than they earned. On a grander scale, the United States itself increasingly became a debtor nation. Its balance of payments (exports minus imports) went from a healthy positive $3.5 billion in 1960, to a not-so-healthy *minus* $19.4 billion in 1980 (imports exceeded exports), to a huge $497 billion deficit recently.[21] The only way the country could keep buying more from abroad than it sold was by borrowing money. So, much of the boom was built on debt. A few years ago, Standard & Poor's lowered the ratings of U.S. sovereign (treasury) bonds, fearing Washington policymakers could not get a handle on the huge indebtedness. The United States (and much of the rest of the world) seemed to be heading for a financial cliff.

Trends in the Nature of Work

Technology has affected how people work, and therefore impacts the skills and training today's workers need.

HIGH-TECH JOBS For example, skilled machinist Chad Toulouse illustrates the modern blue-collar worker. After an 18-week training course, this former college student works as a team leader in a plant where about 40% of the machines are automated. In older plants, machinists would manually control machines that cut chunks of metal into things like engine parts. Today, Chad and his team spend much of their time keying commands into computerized machines that create precision parts for products, including water pumps.[22] As the U.S. government's *Occupational Outlook Quarterly* put it, "knowledge-intensive high-tech manufacturing in such industries as aerospace, computers, telecommunications, home electronics, pharmaceuticals, and medical instruments" is replacing factory jobs in steel, auto, rubber, and textiles.[23]

human capital
The knowledge, education, training, skills, and expertise of a firm's workers.

SERVICE JOBS Technology is not the only trend driving the change from "brawn to brains." Today, over two-thirds of the U.S. workforce is already employed in producing and delivering services, not products. By 2020, service-providing industries are expected to account for 131 million out of 150 million (87%) of wage and salary jobs overall. So in the next few years, almost all the new jobs added in the United States will be in services, not in goods-producing industries.[24]

Several things account for this.[25] With global competition, more manufacturing jobs have moved to low-wage countries. For example, Levi Strauss, one of the last major clothing manufacturers in the United States, closed the last of its American plants a few years ago.

Furthermore, higher productivity enables manufacturers to produce more with fewer workers. Just-in-time manufacturing techniques link daily manufacturing schedules more precisely to customer demand, reducing inventory needs. As manufacturers integrate Internet-based customer ordering with just-in-time manufacturing, scheduling becomes more precise. For example, when a customer orders a Dell computer, the same Internet message that informs Dell's factory to produce the order also signals the screen and keyboard makers to prepare for UPS to pick up their parts. The net effect is that manufacturers have been squeezing slack and inefficiencies out of production, enabling companies to produce more products with fewer employees. So, in America and much of Europe, manufacturing jobs are down, service jobs up, and the manufacturing jobs that remain are increasingly high-tech.

Digital Vision/Thinkstock

Many blue-collar workers no longer do physical labor with dangerous machinery like this. Instead, as explained in the text, Chad Toulouse spends most of his time as a team leader keying commands into computerized machines.

KNOWLEDGE WORK AND HUMAN CAPITAL In general, therefore, jobs require more education and more skills. For example, we saw that automation and just-in-time manufacturing mean that even manufacturing jobs require more reading, math, and communication skills.[26]

For employers, this means relying more on knowledge workers like Chad Toulouse, and therefore on *human capital*.[27] **Human capital** refers to the knowledge, skills, and abilities of a firm's workers.[28] Today, as management guru Peter Drucker predicted years ago, "the center of gravity in employment is moving fast from manual and clerical workers to knowledge workers."[29] Human resource managers now list "critical thinking/problem solving" and "information technology application" as the two skills most likely to increase in importance over the next few years.[30] The accompanying HR as a Profit Center feature illustrates how human resource management methods can boost profitability by building such employee skills.

IMPROVING PERFORMANCE: HR as a Profit Center

Improving a Bank's Customer Service

One bank installed special software that made it easier for its customer service representatives to handle customers' inquiries. However, the bank did not otherwise change the service reps' jobs or training in any way. Here, the new software system did help the service reps handle more calls. But otherwise, this bank saw no big performance gains.[31]

Interestingly, a second bank installed the same software. But, seeking to capitalize on how the new software freed up customer reps' time, this bank's human resource team also upgraded the customer service representatives' jobs. New training programs taught them how to sell more of the bank's services, new job descriptions gave them more authority to make decisions, and new pay policies raised their wages. Here, the new computer system did dramatically improve product sales and profitability, thanks to the newly trained and empowered customer service reps. Today's employers need human resource practices like these that improve employee performance and company profitability.[32]

Discussion Question 1-1: Discuss three more specific examples of what you believe this second bank's HR department could have done to improve the reps' performance.

Demographic and Workforce Trends

DEMOGRAPHIC TRENDS The U.S. workforce is also becoming older and more multiethnic.[33] Table 1-1 offers a bird's eye view. Between 1990 and 2020, the percent of the workforce that the U.S. Department of Labor classifies as "white, non-Hispanic" will have dropped from 77.7% to 62.3%. At the same time, the percent of the workforce that it classifies as Asian will have risen from 3.7% to 5.7%, and those of Hispanic origin from 8.5% to 18.6%. The percentages of younger workers will fall, while those over 55 years of age will leap from 11.9% of the workforce in 1990 to 25.2% in 2020.[34]

Demographic trends are making finding and hiring employees more challenging. In the United States, labor-force growth will lag job growth, with an estimated shortfall of about 14 million college-educated workers by 2020.[35] One study of 35 large global companies' senior human resource officers said "talent management"—the acquisition, development and retention of talent to fill the companies' employment needs—ranked as their top concern.[36]

"GENERATION Y" Furthermore, many younger workers may have different work values than did their parents.[37] These "Generation Y" employees (also called "Millennials") were born from roughly 1977 to 2002. They take the place of the labor force's previous new entrants, Generation X, those born roughly from 1965 to 1976 (themselves the children of the baby boomers, born roughly from 1946 to 1964). Based on one study, older employees are more likely to be work-centric (to focus more on work than on family with respect to career decisions). Gen Y workers tend to be more family-centric or dual-centric (balancing family and work life).[38]

Fortune magazine says that Millennial/Generation Y employees bring challenges and strengths. They may be "the most high maintenance workforce in the history of the world."[39] Employers like Lands' End and Bank of America are therefore teaching their managers to give

TABLE 1-1 Demographic Groups as a Percent of the Workforce, 1990–2020

Age, Race, and Ethnicity	1990	2000	2010	2020
Age: 16–24	17.9%	15.8%	13.6%	11.2%
25–54	70.2	71.1	66.9	63.7
55+	11.9	13.1	19.5	25.2
White, non-Hispanic	77.7	72.0	67.5	62.3
Black	10.9	11.5	11.6	12.0
Asian	3.7	4.4	4.7	5.7
Hispanic origin	8.5	11.7	14.8	18.6

Source: US Burean of Labor Statistics Economic News Release 2/1/12. http://www.bls.gov/news.release/ecopro.t01.htm

Millennials quick feedback and recognition.[40] But, their information technology skills will also make them the most high performing.[41]

RETIREES Many employers call "the aging workforce" their biggest demographic threat. The problem is that there aren't enough younger workers to replace the projected number of baby boom–era older workers retiring.[42] One survey found that 41% of surveyed employers are bringing retirees back into the workforce.[43]

NONTRADITIONAL WORKERS At the same time, work is shifting to nontraditional workers. Nontraditional workers are those who hold multiple jobs, or who are "temporary" or part-time workers, or those working in alternative arrangements (such as a mother–daughter team sharing one clerical job). Others serve as "independent contractors" on projects. Almost 10% of American workers—13 million people—fit this nontraditional workforce category.

Technology facilitates alternative work arrangements. For example, www.linkedin.com enables such professionals to promote their services. Thanks to information technology, about 17 million people now work from remote locations at least once per month. "Co-working sites" are springing up. These offer freelance workers and consultants office space and access to office equipment (and the opportunity to interact with other independents) for several hundred dollars per month.[44] We'll see that all this changes how employers manage their human resource systems.

WORKERS FROM ABROAD With projected workforce shortfalls, many employers are hiring foreign workers for U.S. jobs. The H-1B visa program lets U.S. employers recruit skilled foreign professionals to work in the United States when they can't find qualified American workers. U.S. employers bring in about 181,000 foreign workers per year under these programs. Particularly with high unemployment, such programs face opposition. One study concluded that many workers brought in under these programs actually filled jobs that didn't require specialized skills.[45]

Economic Challenges and Trends

All these trends are occurring in a context of economic upheaval. As shown in Figure 1-4, gross national product (GNP)—a measure of U.S. total output—boomed between 2001 and 2008. During this period, home prices leaped as much as 20% per year. (See Figure 1-5.) Unemployment remained at about 4.7%.[46] Then, around 2007–2008, all these measures seemingly fell off a cliff. GNP fell. Home prices dropped by 20% or more (depending on city). Unemployment nationwide rose to more than 9.1%.

Why did all this happen? It's complicated, but for one thing, all those years of accumulating excessive debt seems to have run their course. Banks and other financial institutions (such as hedge funds) found themselves with trillions of dollars of worthless loans on their books. Governments stepped in to try to prevent their collapse. Lending dried up. Many businesses and consumers simply stopped buying. The economy tanked.

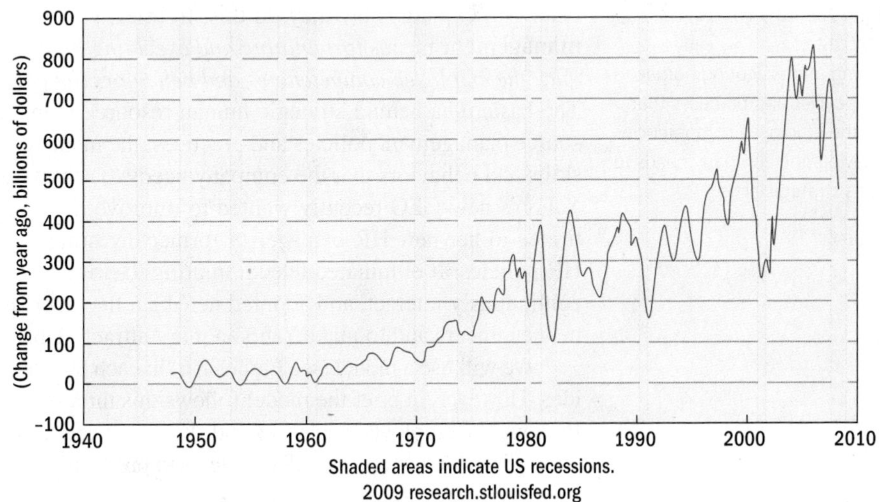

FIGURE 1-4 Gross National Product, 1940–2010

Source: "Gross National Product (GNP)," FRED Economic Data/St. Louis Fed., from Federal Reserve Bank of St. Louis.

FIGURE 1-5 Case-Shiller Home Price Indexes June 1988–June 2013

Source: S&P Dow Jones Indices LLC. Assessed September 30, 2013.

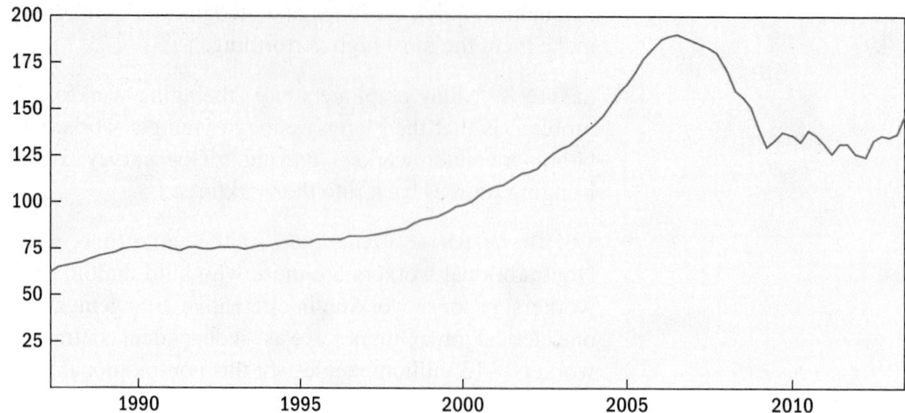

Economic trends will turn positive again, probably as you read these pages. However, they have certainly grabbed employers' attention. After what the world went through starting in 2007–2008, it's doubtful that the deregulation, leveraging, and globalization that drove economic growth for the previous 50 years will continue unabated. That may mean slower growth for many countries, perhaps for years. This means challenging times ahead for employers. The challenging times mean that for the foreseeable future—and even well after things turn positive—employers will be more frugal and creative in managing their human resources than perhaps they've been in the past.

The New Human Resource Manager

3 List and briefly describe important traits of today's human resource managers.

"Personnel" managers used to focus mostly on administrative activities. They took over hiring and firing from supervisors, ran the payroll department, and administered benefits plans. As expertise in testing emerged, the personnel department played a bigger role in employee selection and training.[47] New union laws in the 1930s added "Helping the employer deal with unions" to the list of duties. With new equal employment laws in the 1960s, employers relied on HR for avoiding discrimination claims.[48]

Today, employers face new challenges, such as squeezing more profits from operations. They expect their human resource managers to have what it takes to address these new challenges. Let's look how today's HR managers deal with these challenges.

They Focus More on Strategic, Big-Picture Issues

strategic human resource management
Formulating and executing human resource policies and practices that produce the employee competencies and behaviors the company needs to achieve its strategic aims.

First, human resource managers are more involved in helping their companies address longer-term, strategic "big-picture" issues. Chapter 3 (Human Resource Management Strategy and Analysis) explains how they do this. In brief, we will see there that **strategic human resource management** means *formulating and executing human resource policies and practices that produce the employee competencies and behaviors the company needs to achieve its strategic aims.* The basic idea behind strategic human resource management is this: In formulating human resource management policies and practices, the manager's aim should be to produce the employee skills and behaviors that the company needs to achieve its strategic aims. So, for example, when Yahoo's new CEO recently wanted to improve her company's innovation and productivity, she turned to her new HR manager (a former investment banker). Yahoo then instituted many new HR policies. It eliminated telecommuting to bring workers back to the office, where they could continuously interact, and adopted new benefits (such as 16 weeks' paid maternity leave) to lure new engineers and to make Yahoo a more attractive place in which to work.[49]

We will use a model (see Figure 1-6) in each chapter, starting with this chapter, to illustrate this idea. However, in brief the model follows this three-step sequence: Set the firm's strategic aims → Pinpoint the employee behaviors and skills we need to achieve these strategic aims → Decide what HR policies and practices will enable us to produce these necessary employee behaviors and skills.

They Focus on Improving Performance

Employers expect their human resource managers to help lead their companies' performance-improvement efforts. Human resource managers recognize this. Surveys of HR professionals list

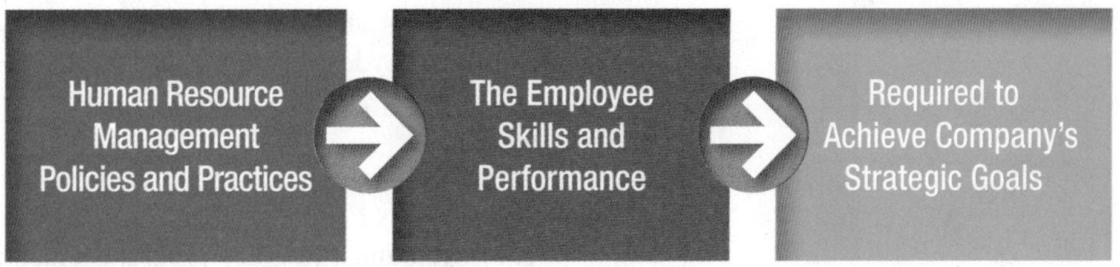

FIGURE 1-6

Strategic human resource management means formulating HR polices and practices that produce the employee skills and performance required to achieve the company's strategic goals.

competition for market share, price competition/price control, governmental regulations, need for sales growth, and need to increase productivity as top challenges HR managers face.[50]

Today's human resource manager is in a powerful position to improve the firm's performance and profitability, and uses three main levers to do so. The first is the *HR department lever*. He or she ensures that the human resource management function is delivering its services efficiently. For example, this might include outsourcing certain HR activities such as benefits management to more cost-effective outside vendors, controlling HR function headcount, and using technology such as portals and automated online employee prescreening to deliver its services more cost-effectively. The second is the *employee costs lever*. For example, the human resource manager takes a prominent role in advising top management about the company's staffing levels, and in setting and controlling the firm's compensation, incentives, and benefits policies. The third is the *strategic results lever*. Here the HR manager puts in place the policies and practices that produce the employee competencies and skills the company needs to achieve its strategic goals. For example, Yahoo's new employment policies helped to improve its innovation and competitiveness, and the bank's new software helped its customer service reps improve their performance, thanks to new human resource training and compensation practices. We'll encounter many similar examples in this book.

They Measure HR Performance and Results

This focus on performance requires measurability. Management expects HR to provide measurable, benchmark-based evidence for its current efficiency and effectiveness, and for the expected efficiency and effectiveness of new or proposed HR programs. In other words, management expects solid, quantified evidence that HR is contributing in a meaningful and positive way to achieving the firm's strategic aims.

For example, when IBM's MacDonald needed $100 million to reorganize its HR operations, he told top management, "I'm going to deliver talent to you that's skilled and on time and ready to be deployed. I will be able to measure the skills, tell you what skills we have, what [skills] we don't have [and] then show you how to fill the gaps or enhance our training."[51] Human resource managers use performance measures (or "metrics") to validate claims like these. For example, median HR expenses as a percentage of companies' total operating costs average just under 1%. On average, there is about 1 human resource staff person per 100 employees.[52]

To compare their own companies to others, human resource managers obtain customized benchmark comparisons from services such as the Society for Human Resource Management's Human Capital Benchmarking Service.[53] We'll look at this in later chapters.

They Use Evidence-Based Human Resource Management

Basing decisions on such evidence is the heart of *evidence-based human resource management*. This is the use of data, facts, analytics, scientific rigor, critical evaluation, and critically evaluated research/case studies to support human resource management proposals, decisions, practices, and conclusions.[54] Put simply, evidence-based human resource management means using the best-available evidence in making decisions about the human resource management practices you are focusing on.[55] The evidence may come from *actual measurements* (such as, how did the trainees like this program?). It may come from *existing data* (such as, what happened to company profits after we installed this training program?). Or, it may come from published *research studies* (such as, what does the research literature conclude about the best way to ensure that trainees remember what they learn?). We'll discuss this in Chapter 3.

They Add Value

The bottom line is that today's employers want their HR managers to *add value* by boosting profits and performance. Professors Dave Ulrich and Wayne Brockbank describe this as the "HR Value Proposition."[56] They say human resource programs (such as screening tests) are just a means to an end. The human resource manager's ultimate aim must be to add value. "Adding value" means helping the firm and its employees improve in a measurable way as a result of the human resource manager's actions.

We'll see in this book how human resource practices do this. For example, we'll use, in each chapter, "HR as a Profit Center" features like the one on page 12 to illustrate this.

They Use New Ways to Provide HR Services

To free up time for their new strategic duties and to deliver HR services cost-effectively, today's human resource managers deliver their traditional day-to-day HR services (such as benefits administration) in new ways. For example, they use technology such as *company portals* so employees can self-administer benefits plans, *Facebook recruiting* to recruit job applicants, *online testing* to prescreen job applicants, and *centralized call centers* to answer supervisors' HR-related inquiries. IBM's employees use its own internal social networking site to "create personal profiles similar to those on LinkedIn . . . share files, and gain knowledge from white papers, videos, and podcasts."[57] Table 1-2 illustrates how employers use technology to support delivering human resource management activities.[58]

They Take a Talent Management Approach to Managing Human Resources

talent management
The goal-oriented and integrated process of planning, recruiting, developing, managing, and compensating employees.

With employers pressing for improved performance, one survey of human resource executives found that "talent management issues" were among the most pressing ones they faced.[59] **Talent management** is the *goal-oriented* and *integrated* process of *planning, recruiting, developing, managing, and compensating* employees.[60] It involves putting in place a coordinated process for identifying, recruiting, hiring, and developing employees. For example, IBM split its employees into three groups to better coordinate how it serves the employees in each. We'll look at talent management methods in Chapter 4.

They Manage Employee Engagement

Improved performance requires engaged employees. The Institute for Corporate Productivity defines *engaged employees* "as those who are mentally and emotionally invested in their work and in contributing to an employer's success." Unfortunately, studies suggest that less than one-third of the U.S. workforce is engaged.[61] Today's human resource managers need skills to manage employee engagement. We'll look at employee engagement in later chapters.

They Manage Ethics

ethics
The standards someone uses to decide what his or her conduct should be.

Regrettably, news reports today are filled with managers' ethical misdeeds. For example, prosecutors filed criminal charges against several Iowa meatpacking plant human resource managers who allegedly violated employment law by hiring children younger than 16.[62] Behaviors like these risk torpedoing even otherwise competent managers and employers. **Ethics** means *the standards someone uses to decide what his or her conduct should be.* We will see that many serious workplace ethical issues—workplace safety and employee privacy, for instance—are human resource management related.[63]

TABLE 1-2 Some Technology Applications to Support Human Resource Activities

Technology	How Used by HR
Streaming desktop video	Used to facilitate distance learning and training or to provide corporate information to employees quickly and inexpensively
Internet- and network-monitoring software	Used to track employees' Internet and e-mail activities or to monitor their performance
Data warehouses and computerized analytical programs	Help HR managers monitor their HR systems. For example, they make it easier to assess things like cost per hire, and to compare current employees' skills with the firm's projected strategic needs

They Understand Their Human Resource Philosophy

People's actions are always based in part on the basic assumptions they make; this is especially true in regard to human resource management. The basic assumptions you make about people—Can they be trusted? Do they dislike work? Why do they act as they do? How should they be treated?—together comprise your philosophy of human resource management. And every personnel decision you make—the people you hire, the training you provide, your leadership style, and the like—reflects (for better or worse) this basic philosophy.

How do you go about developing such a philosophy? To some extent, it's preordained. There's no doubt that you will bring to your job an initial philosophy based on your experiences, education, values, assumptions, and background. But your philosophy doesn't have to be set in stone. It should evolve as you accumulate knowledge and experiences. For example, after a worker uprising in China at Apple's Foxconn plant, the personnel philosophy at Hon Hai's Foxconn plant softened in response to its employees' and Apple's discontent. In any case, no manager should manage others without first understanding the personnel philosophy that is driving his or her actions.

One of the things molding your own philosophy is that of your organization's top management. While it may or may not be stated, it is usually communicated by their actions and permeates every level and department in the organization. For example, here is part of the personnel philosophy of the founder of the Polaroid Corp., stated many years ago:

> To give everyone working for the company a personal opportunity within the company for full exercise of his talents—to express his opinions, to share in the progress of the company as far as his capacity permits, and to earn enough money so that the need for earning more will not always be the first thing on his mind. The opportunity, in short, to make his work here a fully rewarding and important part of his or her life.[64]

Current "best companies to work for" lists include many organizations with similar philosophies. For example, the CEO of software giant SAS has said, "We've worked hard to create a corporate culture that is based on trust between our employees and the company . . . a culture that rewards innovation, encourages employees to try new things and yet doesn't penalize them for taking chances, and a culture that cares about employees' personal and professional growth."[65]

Sometimes, companies translate philosophies like these into what management gurus call *high-performance work systems,* "sets of human resource management practices that together produce superior employee performance."[66] For example, at GE's assembly plant in Durham, North Carolina, highly trained self-directed teams produce high-precision aircraft parts. We'll discuss *high-performance work systems* in Chapter 3.

They Have New Competencies[67]

Tasks like formulating strategic plans and making data-based decisions require new human resource manager skills. HR managers can't just be good at traditional personnel tasks like hiring and training. Instead, they must "speak the CFO's language" by defending human resource plans in measurable terms (such as return on investment).[68] To create strategic plans, the human resource manager must understand strategic planning, marketing, production, and finance.[69] (Perhaps this is why about one-third of top HR managers in Fortune 100 companies moved there from other functional areas.[70]) He or she must be able to formulate and implement large-scale organizational changes, design organizational structures and work processes, and understand how to compete in and succeed in the marketplace.[71]

4 Describe four important human resource manager competencies.

The Human Resource Manager's Competencies

Figure 1-7 illustrates competencies today's HR managers need. Professor Dave Ulrich and his colleagues say that today's human resource managers need the knowledge, skills, and competencies to be:

Strategic positioners—for instance, by being able to help create the firm's strategy.

Credible activists—for instance, by exhibiting the leadership that make them "both *credible* (respected, admired, listened to) and *active* (offers a point of view, takes a position, challenges assumptions)."[72]

Capability builders—for instance, by creating a meaningful work environment and aligning strategy, culture, practices, and behavior.

Change champions—for instance, by initiating and sustaining change.

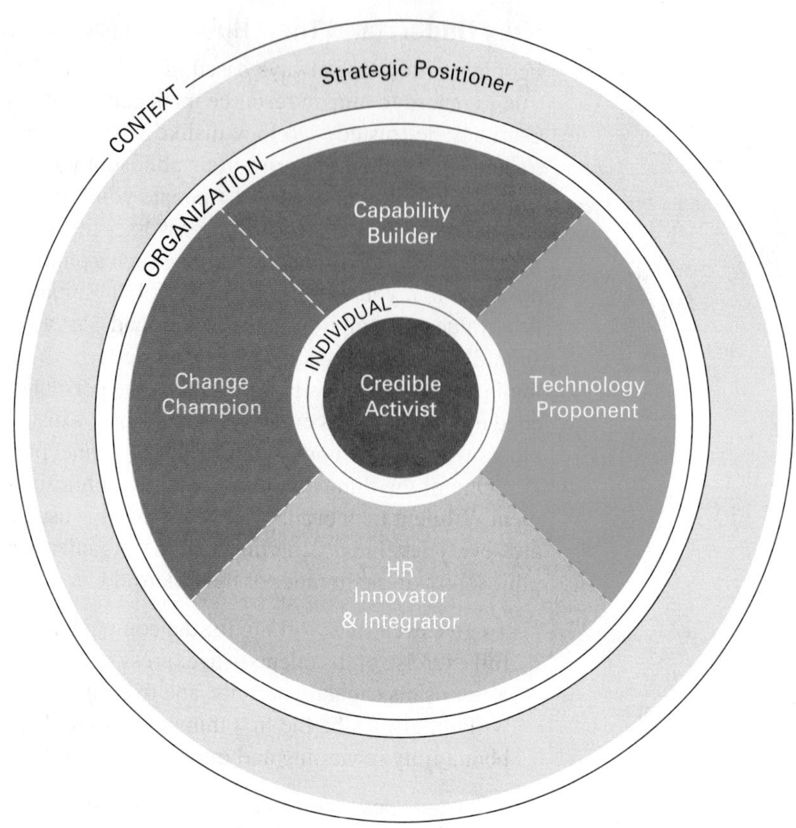

FIGURE 1-7 The Human Resource Manager's Competencies
Source: The RBL Group, © 2012.

HR innovators and integrators—for instance, by developing talent, and optimizing human capital through workforce planning and analytics.

Technology proponents—for instance, by connecting people through technology.

HRCI Certification

Many HR managers use certification to show their mastery of modern human resource management knowledge. The HR Certification Institute (HRCI) is an independent certifying organization for human resource professionals (see www.hrci.org). Through testing, HRCI awards several credentials, including Professional in Human Resources (PHR) and Senior Professional in Human Resources (SPHR). The evidence to date, while incomplete, generally suggests a positive relationship between human resource managers' competence, as reflected by PHR or SPHR certification, and the human resource managers' effectiveness (although of course it is the person's ability to apply what he or she knows, rather than just the knowledge, that ultimately determines one's success).[73] Managers can take an online HRCI practice quiz at www.hrci.org/AEP.aspx?id=2147483996&terms=practice%20quiz.[74]

The HRCI Knowledge Base

The HRCI body of knowledge devotes roughly the following percentages to its main topic areas (PHR exam %—SPHR exam %): Strategic Business Management, 12%—29%; Workforce Planning and Employment, 26%—17%; Human Resource Development, 17%—17%; Total Rewards, 16%—12%; Employee and Labor Relations, 22%—18%; Risk Management, 7%—7%; as well as certain Core Knowledge—for example, with respect to motivation and job analysis. The space this book devotes to these topics roughly follows these HRCI suggestions.

The Knowledge Base (see Appendix A of this book, pp. 580–588) lists about 91 specific "Knowledge of" subject areas within these main topic area groups with which those taking the test should be familiar; we use special icons starting in the following chapter to denote coverage of HRCI knowledge topics. Furthermore, most of this book's chapter-opening behavioral objectives follow the Knowledge Base's list of what test takers should be able to do.

The Plan of This Book

The Basic Themes and Features

5 Outline the plan of this book.

In this book, we'll use several themes and features to highlight particularly important issues, and to provide continuity from chapter to chapter.

PRACTICAL TOOLS FOR EVERY MANAGER First, human resource management is the *responsibility of every manager*—not just those in human resources. Throughout every page in this book, you'll therefore find an emphasis on practical material that you as a manager will need to perform your day-to-day management responsibilities, even if you never spend one day as an HR manager.

Second, managers use human resource management techniques to *improve performance, productivity, and profitability*. To highlight this, you will find special boxed features titled:

IMPROVING PERFORMANCE: HR TOOLS FOR LINE MANAGERS AND ENTREPRENEURS. These features highlight actual tools and practices any manager can use to improve performance at work.

IMPROVING PERFORMANCE: HR AS A PROFIT CENTER. We've seen that employers need human resource management practices that add value. To illustrate this throughout the book, each chapter contains illustrative IMPROVING PERFORMANCE: HR AS A PROFIT CENTER features. These show actual examples of how human resource management practices add measurable value—by reducing costs or boosting revenues.

IMPROVING PERFORMANCE: HR PRACTICES AROUND THE GLOBE. These features highlight how actual companies around the globe use effective HR practices to improve their teams' and companies' performance.

IMPROVING PERFORMANCE THROUGH HRIS. These features highlight how managers use human resource technology to improve performance.

DIVERSITY COUNTS. These features provide insights and guidelines for managing a diverse workforce.

SOCIAL MEDIA AND HR. These features explain how managers use social media to improve human resource performance.

Third, the employer's human resource management policies and practices should produce the employee skills and performance the company needs *to achieve its strategic aims*. Use the Hotel Paris continuing case starting in Chapter 3 to apply that idea.

Chapter Contents Overview

Following is a brief overview of the chapters and their content.

Part 1: Introduction

Chapter 1: Introduction to Human Resource Management. The manager's human resource management jobs; crucial global and competitive trends; how managers use technology and modern HR measurement systems to create high-performance work systems.

Chapter 2: Equal Opportunity and the Law. What you should know about equal opportunity laws; how these laws affect activities such as interviewing, selecting employees, and evaluating performance; *Know Your Employment Law* features highlight important laws in each chapter.

Chapter 3: Human Resource Management Strategy and Analysis. What is strategic planning; strategic human resource management; building high-performance HR practices; tools for evidence-based HR.

Part 2: Recruitment, Placement, and Talent Management

Chapter 4: Job Analysis and the Talent Management Process. How to analyze a job; how to determine the human resource requirements of the job, as well as its specific duties; and what is talent management.

Chapter 5: Personnel Planning and Recruiting. Human resource planning; determining what sorts of people need to be hired; recruiting them.

Chapter 6: Employee Testing and Selection. Techniques you can use to ensure that you're hiring the right people.

Chapter 7: Interviewing Candidates. How to interview candidates effectively.

Part 3: Training and Development

Chapter 8: Training and Developing Employees. Providing the training and development to ensure that your employees have the knowledge and skills needed to accomplish their tasks.

Chapter 9: Performance Management and Appraisal. Techniques you can use for appraising employee performance.

Chapter 10: Employee Retention, Engagement, and Careers. Coaching employees; managing careers; techniques such as career planning and promotion from within; talent management methods.

Part 4: Compensation

Chapter 11: Establishing Strategic Pay Plans. How to develop equitable pay plans for your employees.

Chapter 12: Pay for Performance and Financial Incentives. Pay-for-performance plans such as financial incentives, merit pay, and incentives that help tie performance to pay.

Chapter 13: Benefits and Services. Providing benefits that make it clear the firm views its employees as long-term investments and is concerned with their welfare.

Part 5: Enrichment Topics in Human Resource Management

Chapter 14: Ethics, Employee Relations, and Fair Treatment at Work. How to ensure positive employee relations and ethical and fair treatment through grievance and discipline processes.

Chapter 15: Labor Relations and Collective Bargaining. How to deal with unions, including the union organizing campaign; negotiating and agreeing upon a collective bargaining agreement between unions and management; and managing the agreement via the grievance process.

Chapter 16: Employee Safety and Health. How to make the workplace safe, including the causes of accidents; laws governing your responsibilities for employee safety and health.

Chapter 17: Managing Global Human Resources. Special topics in managing the HR side of multinational operations.

Chapter 18: Managing Human Resources in Small and Entrepreneurial Firms. Special topics for managing human resources in smaller firms.

The Topics Are Interrelated

In practice, do not think of each of this book's topics as being unrelated to the others. Each topic interacts with and affects the others, and all should align with the employer's strategic plan. For example, hiring people who don't have the potential to learn the job will doom their performance, regardless of how much training they get. As another example, how good a job you do selecting and training employees will affect how safely they do their jobs. Similarly, we will see throughout this book that each human resource management function, from job analysis to recruiting, selecting, training and rewarding employees, should aim to produce the employee behaviors and competencies that the company needs to achieve its strategic goals.

Review

MyManagementLab Go to **mymanagementlab.com** to complete the problems marked with this icon. 

Chapter Section Summaries

1. All managers should be able to answer, **What is human resource management, and why is it important?** Doing so helps managers avoid problems like hiring the wrong person for the job. And more important, it can help ensure that managers get results through people. Line managers' human resource duties include placing the right person on

the job, and orienting and training new employees. The human resource manager's duties include supervising his or her own employees, coordinating the company's overall personnel policies, and assisting and advising line managers in the areas of human resource management.

2. **The trends shaping human resource management** areinfluencing what human resource managers do and how they do it. Globalization means more competition, and more competition means more pressure to lower costs and to make employees more productive and quality conscious. Technology is requiring more employees to be technologically well informed and pressuring employers to improve their human resource processes by applying new technological tools. There is more emphasis on "knowledge work" and therefore on building "human capital," the knowledge, education, training, skills, and expertise of a firm's employees. Workforce and demographic changes mean that the workforce is becoming older and more diverse.
3. **The new human resource manager** faces new challenges. Traditionally, personnel/HR managers focused on administrative issues such as running the payroll department. Today, employers expect their human resource management teams to focus more on big-picture issues, including instituting human resource policies and practices that support the companies' strategic objectives; to find new, more efficient ways to provide transactional services; and to have new proficiencies, for instance, in terms of strategizing and creating high-performance work systems that produce superior employee performance.
4. To do so, **the human resource managers** need **new competencies.** They should be able to apply evidence-based human resource management, which means the use of data, facts, analytics, scientific rigor, critical evaluation, and critically evaluated research/case studies to support human resource management proposals, decisions, practices, and conclusions.
5. In understanding the overall **plan of this book,** keep several important themes in mind: that human resource management is the responsibility of every manager, that the workforce is increasingly diverse, that employers and their human resource managers face the need to manage in challenging economic times, and that human resource managers must be able to defend their plans and contributions in measurable terms—to use evidence-based management—to show they've added value.

Discussion Questions

✪ **1-2.** Explain what HR management is and how it relates to the management process.

1-3. Give examples of how HR management concepts and techniques can be of use to all managers.

✪ **1-4.** Illustrate the HR management responsibilities of line and staff managers.

1-5. Compare the authority of line and staff managers. Give examples of each.

Individual and Group Activities

1-6. Working individually or in groups, develop outlines showing how trends like workforce diversity, technological innovation, globalization, and changes in the nature of work have affected the college or university you are attending now. Present in class.

1-7. Working individually or in groups, contact the HR manager of a local bank. Ask the HR manager how he or she is working as a strategic partner to manage human resources, given the bank's strategic goals and objectives. Back in class, discuss the responses of the different HR managers.

1-8. Working individually or in groups, interview an HR manager. Based on that interview, write a short presentation regarding HR's role today in building competitive organizations.

1-9. Working individually or in groups, bring several business publications such as *Bloomberg Businessweek* and *The Wall Street Journal* to class, or access them in class via the Web. Based on their contents, compile a list titled "What HR Managers and Departments Do Today."

1-10. Based on your personal experiences, list 10 examples showing how you used (or could have used) human resource management techniques at work or school.

1-11. Laurie Siegel, senior vice president of human resources for Tyco International, took over her job just after numerous charges forced the company's previous board of directors and top executives to leave the firm. Hired by new CEO Edward Breen, Siegel had to tackle numerous difficult problems starting the moment she assumed office. For example, she had to help hire a new management team. She had to do something about what the outside world viewed as a culture of questionable ethics at her company. And she had to do something about the company's top-management compensation plan, which many felt contributed to the allegations by some that some former company officers had used the company as a sort of private ATM.

Siegel came to Tyco after a very impressive career. For example, she had been head of executive compensation at Allied Signal, and was a graduate of the Harvard Business School. But, as strong as her background was, she obviously had her work cut out for her when she took the senior vice president of HR position at Tyco.

Working individually or in groups, conduct an Internet search and library research to answer the following questions: What human resource management–related steps did

Siegel take to help get Tyco back on the right track? Do you think she took the appropriate steps? Why or why not? What, if anything, do you suggest she do now?

1-12. Appendix A, PHR and SPHR Knowledge Base, at the end of this book (pages 580–588) lists the knowledge someone studying for the HRCI certification exam needs to have in each area of human resource management (such as in Strategic Management, Workforce Planning, and Human Resource Development). In groups of four to five students, do four things: (1) review Appendix A; (2) identify the material in this chapter that relates to the required knowledge Appendix A lists; (3) write four multiple-choice exam questions on this material that you believe would be suitable for inclusion in the HRCI exam; and (4) if time permits, have someone from your team post your team's questions in front of the class, so that students in all teams can answer the exam questions created by the other teams.

Experiential Exercise

Helping "The Donald"

Purpose: The purpose of this exercise is to provide practice in identifying and applying the basic concepts of human resource management by illustrating how managers use these techniques in their day-to-day jobs.

Required Understanding: Be thoroughly familiar with the material in this chapter, and with at least several episodes of Donald Trump's *The Apprentice* or *The Celebrity Apprentice*.

How to Set Up the Exercise/Instructions:

- Divide the class into teams of three to four students.
- Read this: As you may know by watching "the Donald" as he organizes his business teams for *The Apprentice* and *The Celebrity Apprentice*, human resource management plays an important role in what Donald Trump and the participants on his separate teams need to do to be successful. For example, Donald Trump needs to be able to appraise each of the participants. And, for their part, the leaders of each of his teams need to be able to staff his or her team with the right participants, and then provide the sorts of training, incentives, and evaluations that help their companies succeed and that therefore make the participants themselves (and especially the team leaders) look like "winners" to Mr. Trump.
- Watch several of these shows (or reruns of the shows), and then meet with your team and answer the following questions:
  - 1-13. What specific HR functions (recruiting, interviewing, and so on) can you identify Donald Trump using on this show? Make sure to give specific examples based on the show.
  - 1-14. What specific HR functions (recruiting, selecting, training, etc.) can you identify one or more of the team leaders using to help manage their teams on the show? Again, please give specific answers.
  - 1-15. Provide a specific example of how HR functions (such as recruiting, selection, interviewing, compensating, appraising, and so on) contributed to one of the participants coming across as particularly successful to Mr. Trump. Can you provide examples of how one or more of these functions contributed to a participant being told by Mr. Trump, "You're fired"?
  - 1-16. Present your team's conclusions to the class.

Video Case

Video Title: Human Resource Management (Patagonia)

SYNOPSIS

The mission at Patagonia is to build the best product possible, cause no unnecessary environmental harm, and inspire solutions to the environmental crisis. The benefits to employees working for Patagonia are considerable. Although the pay is slightly below the industry average, employees are given time off work to try out the wetsuits the company produces, and employees are encouraged to put the needs of their families first. Employees can work flexible hours to accommodate this company value. Employees are also offered a period of 60 days in which they can work for a nonprofit environmental organization and still receive their full pay. Much thought is put into the hiring of new employees at Patagonia; ambitious, mission-driven people, with whom the core values of Patagonia resonate, are selected to fill open positions within this unique company.

Discussion Questions

1-17. How does the mission of Patagonia differ from most other companies?

1-18. Patagonia has often been selected as one of the country's best places to work. What Patagonia HR practices and employee benefits do you think help Patagonia earn this honor?

1-19. What characteristics would you use to describe a candidate likely to be hired by Patagonia? How do these characteristics reflect and support Patagonia's strategy?

Application Case

Jack Nelson's Problem

As a new member of the board of directors for a local bank, Jack Nelson was being introduced to all the employees in the home office. When he was introduced to Ruth Johnson, he was curious about her work and asked her what the machine she was using did. Johnson replied that she really did not know what the machine was called or what it did. She explained that she had only been working there for 2 months. However, she did know precisely how to operate the machine. According to her supervisor, she was an excellent employee.

At one of the branch offices, the supervisor in charge spoke to Nelson confidentially, telling him that "something was wrong," but she didn't know what. For one thing, she explained, employee turnover was too high, and no sooner had one employee been put on the job than another one resigned. With customers to see and loans to be made, she continued, she had little time to work with the new employees as they came and went.

All branch supervisors hired their own employees without communication with the home office or other branches. When an opening developed, the supervisor tried to find a suitable employee to replace the worker who had quit.

After touring the 22 branches and finding similar problems in many of them, Nelson wondered what the home office should do or what action he should take. The banking firm generally was regarded as being a well-run institution that had grown from 27 to 191 employees during the past 8 years. The more he thought about the matter, the more puzzled Nelson became. He couldn't quite put his finger on the problem, and he didn't know whether to report his findings to the president.

Questions

1-20. What do you think is causing some of the problems in the bank's home office and branches?

1-21. Do you think setting up an HR unit in the main office would help?

1-22. What specific functions should an HR unit carry out? What HR functions would then be carried out by supervisors and other line managers? What role should the Internet play in the new HR organization?

Source: GEORGE, SUPERVISION IN ACTION: ART MANAGING OTHERS, 4th, (c) 1985. Printed and Electronically reproduced by permission of Pearson Education, Inc., Upper Saddle River, New Jersey.

Continuing Case

Carter Cleaning Company

Introduction

A main theme of this book is that human resource management activities like recruiting, selecting, training, and rewarding employees is not just the job of a central HR group but rather a job in which every manager must engage. Perhaps nowhere is this more apparent than in the typical small service business. Here the owner/manager usually has no HR staff to rely on. However, the success of his or her enterprise (not to mention his or her family's peace of mind) often depends largely on the effectiveness through which workers are recruited, hired, trained, evaluated, and rewarded. Therefore, to help illustrate and emphasize the front-line manager's HR role, throughout this book we will use a continuing case based on an actual small business in the southeastern United States. Each chapter's segment of the case will illustrate how the case's main player—owner/manager Jennifer Carter—confronts and solves personnel problems each day at work by applying the concepts and techniques of that particular chapter. Here is background information that you will need to answer questions that arise in subsequent chapters. (We also present a second, unrelated "application case" case incident in each chapter.)

Carter Cleaning Centers

Jennifer Carter graduated from State University in June 2005, and, after considering several job offers, decided to do what she always planned to do—go into business with her father, Jack Carter.

Jack Carter opened his first laundromat in 1995 and his second in 1998. The main attraction of these coin laundry businesses for him was that they were capital- rather than labor-intensive. Thus, once the investment in machinery was made, the stores could be run with just one unskilled attendant and none of the labor problems one normally expects from being in the retail service business.

The attractiveness of operating with virtually no skilled labor notwithstanding, Jack had decided by 1999 to expand the services in each of his stores to include the dry cleaning and pressing of clothes. He embarked, in other words, on a strategy of "related diversification" by adding new services that were related to and consistent with his existing coin laundry activities. He added these for several reasons. He wanted to better utilize the unused space in the rather large stores he currently had under lease. Furthermore, he was, as he put it, "tired of sending out the dry cleaning and pressing work that came in from our coin laundry clients to a dry cleaner 5 miles away, who then took most of what should have been our profits." To reflect the new, expanded line of services, he renamed each of his two stores Carter Cleaning Centers and was sufficiently satisfied with their performance to open four more of the same type of stores over the next 5 years. Each store had its own on-site manager and, on average, about seven employees and annual revenues of about $500,000. It was this six-store chain that Jennifer joined after graduating.

Her understanding with her father was that she would serve as a troubleshooter/consultant to the elder Carter with the aim of both learning the business and bringing to it modern management concepts and techniques for solving the business's problems and facilitating its growth.

Questions

1-23. Make a list of five specific HR problems you think Carter Cleaning will have to grapple with.

1-24. What would you do first if you were Jennifer?

MyManagementLab

Go to **mymanagementlab.com** for Auto-graded writing questions as well as the following Assisted-graded writing questions:

1-25. Why is it important for companies today to make their human resources into a competitive advantage? Explain how HR can contribute to doing this. What are some examples of employers that do this?

1-26. Think of some companies that you are familiar with or that you've read about where you think the human resource managers have been successful in "adding value." What do the HR managers do to lead you to your conclusion?

1-27. MyManagementLab only—comprehensive writing assignment for this chapter.

Key Terms

organization, 4
manager, 4
management process, 4
human resource management (HRM), 4
authority, 6
line authority, 6
staff authority, 6
line manager, 6
staff manager, 6
functional authority, 7
globalization, 10
human capital, 11
strategic human resource management, 14
talent management, 16
ethics, 16

Endnotes

1. Quoted in Fred K. Foulkes, "The Expanding Role of the Personnel Function," *Harvard Business Review*, March–April 1975, pp. 71–84. See also www.bls.gov/oco/ocos021.htm, accessed October 3, 2011.
2. Adrienne Fox, "Do Assignments Outside HR Pay Off?" *HR Magazine*, November 2011, p. 32. See also Lorna Collier, "More CFOs Landing in HR Territory," *Workforce Management*, October 2011, p. 8.
3. Steve Bates, "No Experience Necessary? Many Companies Are Putting Non-HR Executives in Charge of HR with Mixed Results," *HR Magazine* 46, no. 11 (November 2001), pp. 34–41. See also Fay Hansen, "Top of the Class," *Workforce Management*, June 23, 2008, pp. 1, 25–30.
4. "A Profile of Human Resource Executives," *BNA Bulletin to Management*, June 21, 2001, p. S5.
5. This data comes from "Small Business: A Report of the President" (1998), www.SBA.gov/ADV/stats, accessed March 9, 2006. See also "Statistics of U.S. Businesses and Non-Employer Status," www.SBA.gov/ADV_oh/research/data.html, accessed March 9, 2006; and James Rosen, "Economists Credit Small Business 'Gazelles' with Job Creation," www.foxnews.com/us/2011/04/25/economists-credit-small-business-gazelles-job-creation/, accessed October 5, 2012.
6. Some employers, such as Google, are adding "chief sustainability officers" within human resource management who are responsible for fostering the company's environmental sustainability efforts. Nancy Woodward, "New Breed of Human Resource Leader," *HR Magazine*, June 2008, pp. 53–57.
7. Robert Grossman, "IBM's HR Takes a Risk," *HR Management,* April 2007, pp. 54–59.
8. See Dave Ulrich, "The New HR Organization," *Workforce Management,* December 10, 2007, pp. 40–44; and Dave Ulrich, "The 21st-Century HR Organization," *Human Resource Management* 47, no. 4 (Winter 2008), pp. 829–850. Some writers distinguish among three basic human resource management subfields: *micro HRM* (which covers the HR subfunctions such as recruitment and selection), *strategic HRM*, and *international HRM.* Mark Lengnick Hall et al., "Strategic Human Resource Management: The Evolution of the Field," *Human Resource Management Review* 19 (2009), pp. 64–85.
9. In fact, one study found that delegating somewhat more of the HR activities to line managers "had a positive effect on HR managers' perceptions of their units' reputation among line managers." Carol Kulik and Elissa Perry, "When Less Is More: The Effect of Devolution on HR as a Strategic Role and Construed Image," *Human Resource Management* 47, no. 3 (Fall 2008), pp. 541–558.
10. "Human Resource Activities, Budgets, and Staffs, 1999–2000," *BNA Bulletin to Management*, June 20, 2000.
11. For discussions of some other important trends, see, for example, Society for Human Resource Management, "Workplace Trends: An Overview of the Findings of the Latest SHRM Workplace Forecast," *Workplace Visions*, no. 3 (2008), pp. 1–8; and Ed Frauenheim, "Future View," *Workforce Management*, December 15, 2008, pp. 18–23.
12. See, for example, www.forbes.com/sites/jjcolao/2012/11/14/the-facebook-job-board-is-here-recruiting-will-never-look-the-same/, accessed May 9, 2013.
13. Ibid.
14. As another example, at one San Francisco–based company, employees use an online interactive game to set goals for exercising and to monitor each other's progress. Lisa Beyer, "Companies Are Turning to Technology to Help Keep Workers Well," *Workforce Management*, October 2011, p. 6. See also Bill Roberts, "The Grand Convergence," *HR Magazine,* October 2011, pp. 39–46.
15. Chris Pickering, "A Look Through the Portal," *Software Magazine* 21, no. 1 (February 2001), pp. 18–19.
16. Ibid., p. 19.
17. Jill Elswick, "How NCR Corp. Undertook an Intranet Makeover to Improve Access to HR Information," *Employee Benefit News*, January 1, 2001, item 01008001.
18. Sharon McDonnell, "More Out of ERP," *Computerworld*, October 2, 2000, p. 56.
19. "Study Predicts 4.1 Million Service Jobs Offshored by 2008," *BNA Bulletin to Management,* August 2, 2005, p. 247; and Patrick Thibodeau, "Offshoring Shrinks Number of IT Jobs, Study Says," *Computerworld*, March 21, 2012, www.computerworld.com/s/article/9225376/Offshoring_shrinks_number_of_IT_jobs_study_says_, accessed October 5, 2012.
20. www.census.gov/foreign-trade/statistics/historical/gands.pdf, accessed March 3, 2012.
21. Ibid.
22. Timothy Appel, "Better Off a Blue-Collar," *The Wall Street Journal*, July 1, 2003, p. B-1.
23. Roger Moncarz and Azure Reaser, "The 2000–10 Job Outlook in Brief," *Occupational Outlook Quarterly*, Spring 2002, pp. 9–44.
24. See "Charting the Projections: 2010–2020," *Occupational Outlook Quarterly* (Winter 2011). www.bls.gov/ooq/2011/winter/winter2011ooq.pdf, www.bls.gov/emp/optd/optd003.pdf, accessed July 29, 2012.
25. Ibid.
26. See, for example, "Engine of Change," *Workforce Management*, July 17, 2006, pp. 20–30.
27. Moncarz and Reaser, "The 2010 Job Outlook in Brief."
28. Richard Crawford, *In the Era of Human Capital* (New York: Harper Business, 1991), p. 26; Russell Crook et al., "Does Human Capital Matter? A Meta-Analysis of the Relationship

Between Human Capital and Firm Performance," *Journal of Applied Psychology* 96, no. 3 (2011), pp. 443–456.
29. Peter Drucker, "The Coming of the New Organization," *Harvard Business Review*, January–February 1998, p. 45. See also James Guthrie et al., "Correlates and Consequences of High Involvement Work Practices: The Role of Competitive Strategy," *International Journal of Human Resource Management*, February 2002, pp. 183–197.
30. Society for Human Resource Management, "Workforce Readiness and the New Essential Skills," *Workplace Visions*, no. 2 (2008), p. 5.
31. "Human Resources Wharton," www.knowledge.wharton.upe.edu, accessed January 8, 2006.
32. See, for example, Anthea Zacharatos et al., "High-Performance Work Systems and Occupational Safety," *Journal of Applied Psychology* 90, no. 1 (2005), pp. 77–93.
33. www.bls.gov/news.release/ecopro.t01.htm, accessed July 29. 2012.
34. "Percent Growth in Labor Force, Projected 1990–2020," www.bls.gov/news.release/ecopro.t01.htm, accessed July 29, 2012.
35. Tony Carnevale, "The Coming Labor and Skills Shortage," *Training and Development*, January 2005, p. 39.
36. "Talent Management Leads in Top HR Concerns," *Compensation & Benefits Review*, May/June 2007, p. 12.
37. For example, see Kathryn Tyler, "Generation Gaps," *HR Magazine*, January 2008, pp. 69–72.
38. Eva Kaplan-Leiserson, "The Changing Workforce," *Training and Development*, February 2005, pp. 10–11. See also S. A. Hewlett, et al., "How Gen Y & Boomers Will Reshape Your Agenda," *Harvard Business Review* 87, no. 7/8 (July/August 2009), pp. 71–76.
39. By one report, the economic downturn of 2008 made it more difficult for dissatisfied Generation Y employees to change jobs, and contributed to a buildup of "griping" among some of them. "Generation Y Goes to Work," *Economist*, January 3, 2009, p. 47.
40. Nadira Hira, "You Raised Them, Now Manage Them," *Fortune*, May 28, 2007, pp. 38–46; Katheryn Tyler, "The Tethered Generation," *HR Magazine*, May 2007, pp. 41–46; Jeffrey Zaslow, "The Most Praised Generation Goes to Work," *The Wall Street Journal*, April 20, 2007, pp. W1, W7; and Rebecca Hastings, "Millennials Expect a Lot from Leaders," *HR Magazine*, January 2008, p. 30.
41. To capitalize on this, more employers are using social networking tools to promote employee interaction and collaboration, particularly among Generation Y employees. "Social Networking Tools Aimed at Engaging Newest Employees," *BNA Bulletin to Management*, September 18, 2007, p. 303.
42. "Talent Management Leads in Top HR Concerns," *Compensation & Benefits Review*, May/June 2007, p. 12.
43. Jennifer Schramm, "Exploring the Future of Work: Workplace Visions," *Society for Human Resource Management* 2 (2005), p. 6; Rainer Strack, Jens Baier, and Anders Fahlander, "Managing Demographic Risk," *Harvard Business Review*, February 2008, pp. 119–128.
44. Adrienne Fox, "At Work in 2020," *HR Magazine*, January 2010, pp. 18–23.
45. Rita Zeidner, "Does the United States Need Foreign Workers?" *HR Magazine*, June 2009, pp. 42–44.
46. www.bls.gov/opub/ted/2006/may/wk2/art01.htm, accessed April 18, 2009.
47. For a book describing the history of human resource management see, for example, SHRM, *A History of Human Resources*, http://shrmstore.shrm.org/a-history-of-human-resources.html, accessed October 4, 2012.
48. "Human Capital Critical to Success," *Management Review*, November 1998, p. 9. See also "HR 2018: Top Predictions," *Workforce Management* 87, no. 20 (December 15, 2008), pp. 20–21, and Edward Lawler III, "Celebrating 50 Years: HR: Time for a Reset?" *Human Resource Management* 50, no. 2 (March–April 2011), pp. 171–173.
49. Lindsey Riddell, "Mayer Boosts Yahoo Parental Leave, Escalates Baby-Benefits Arms Race," www.bizjournals.com/sanfransiso/blog/2013/05/mayer-improves-yahoo-parental-leave.html, accessed May 9, 2013.
50. Philip Way, "HR/IR Professionals' Educational Needs and Master's Program Curricula," *Human Resource Management Review* (2002), p. 478.
51. Robert Grossman, "IBM's HR Takes a Risk," *HR Magazine*, April 1, 2007.
52. Chris Brewster et al., "What Determines the Size of the HR Function? A Cross National Analysis," *Human Resource Management* 45, no. 1 (Spring 2006), pp. 3–21.
53. Contact the Society for Human Resource Management, 703.535.6366.
54. See, for example, www.personneltoday.com/blogs/hcglobal-human-capital-management/2009/02/theres-no-such-thing-as-eviden.html, accessed April 18, 2009.
55. The evidence-based movement began in medicine. In 1996, in an editorial published by the *British Medical Journal*, David Sackett, MD, defined *evidence-based medicine* as "use of the best-available evidence in making decisions about patient care" and urged his colleagues to adopt its tenets. "Evidence-Based Training™: Turning Research into Results for Pharmaceutical Sales Training," An AXIOM White Paper © 2006 AXIOM Professional Health Learning LLC. All rights reserved.
56. Susan Wells, "From HR to the Top," *HR Magazine*, June 2003, p. 49. See also "HR Will Have More Opportunities to Demonstrate Value in 2012," *Bloomberg BNA Bulletin to Management*, January 17, 2012, p. 22.
57. Susan Ladika, "Socially Evolved," *Workforce Management*, September 2010, pp. 18–22.
58. Studies suggest that IT usage does support human resource managers' strategic planning. See Victor Haines III and Genevieve LaFleur, "Information Technology Usage and Human Resource Roles and Effectiveness," *Human Resource Management* 47, no. 3 (Fall 2008), pp. 525–540. See also R. Zeidner, "The Tech Effect on Human Resources," *HR Magazine* (2009 HR Trendbook suppl.), pp. 49–50, 52.
59. "Survey: Talent Management a Top Concern," *CIO Insight*, January 2, 2007; see also, Towers Watson, "The 2011/2012 Talent Management and Rewards Study," www.towerswatson.com/research/5563#MainTab2, accessed October 3, 2012.
60. www.talentmanagement101.com, accessed December 10, 2007.
61. Dean Smith, "Engagement Matters," *T+D* 63, no. 10 (October 2009), p. 14.
62. "Meatpacking Case Highlights HR's Liability," *Workforce Management*, September 20, 2008, p. 6.
63. Kevin Wooten, "Ethical Dilemmas in Human Resource Management," *Human Resource Management Review* 11 (2001), p. 161. See also Ann Pomeroy, "The Ethics Squeeze," *HR Magazine* 51, no. 3 (March 2006), pp. 48–55.
64. Fred Foulkes and Henry Morgan, "Organizing and Staffing the Personnel Function," *Harvard Business Review*, May–June 1977.
65. "Working at SAS: An Ideal Environment for New Ideas," SAS website, April 20, 2012. Copyright © 2011 by SAS Institute, Inc. Reprinted with permission. All rights reserved.
66. "Super Human Resources Practices Result in Better Overall Performance, Report Says," *BNA Bulletin to Management*, August 26, 2004, pp. 273–274. See also Wendy Boswell, "Aligning Employees with the Organization's Strategic Objectives: Out of Line of Sight, Out of Mind," *International Journal of Human Resource Management* 17, no. 9 (September 2006), pp. 1014–1041. A recent study found that some employers, which the researchers called *cost minimizers*, intentionally took a lower-cost approach to human resource practices, with mixed results. See Soo Min Toh et al., "Human Resource Configurations: Investigating Fit with the Organizational Context," *Journal of Applied Psychology* 93, no. 4 (2008), pp. 864–882.
67. Richard Vosburgh, "The Evolution of HR: Developing HR as an Internal Consulting Organization," *Human Resource Planning* 30, no. 3 (September 2007), pp. 11–24; and The RBL Group, "2012 Human Resource Competency Study," http://rbl.net/index.php/hrcs/index/overview, accessed October 4, 2012.
68. Dave Ulrich and Wayne Brockbank, *The HR Value Proposition* (Boston: Harvard Business School Publishing, 2005).
69. See, for example, "Employers Seek HR Executives with Global Experience, SOX Knowledge, Business Sense," *BNA Bulletin to Management*, September 19, 2006, pp. 297–298; and Robert Rodriguez, "HR's New Breed," *HR Magazine*, January 2006, pp. 67–71.
70. Fox, "Do Assignments Outside HR Pay Off?" p. 32. See also Collier, "More CFOs Landing in HR Territory," p. 8.
71. Fox, "Do Assignments Outside HR Pay Off?" p. 32.
72. "The State of the HR Profession," The RBL White Paper Series, The RBL Group © 2011, p. 8.
73. See for example, Gary Latham, "What We Know and What We Would Like to Know About Human Resource Management Certification," *Human Resource Management Review* 22, no. 4 (December 2012), pp. 269–270. Recently, 15.6% of sampled Web-based job openings for HR professionals listed PHR or SPHR certification, a low rate but about 11 times the percent found in 2005. See Brian Lyons et al., "A Reexamination of the Web-Based Demand for PHR and SPHR Certifications in the United States," *Human Resource Management* 51, no. 5 (September–October 2012), pp. 769–788.
74. SHRM and HRCI policies no longer make it possible for college graduates without HR experience to sit for one of the certification exams. However, the HRCI does provide an *SHRM Assurance of Learning Assessment Preparation Guidebook*. This helps students study for an SHRM exam that aims to verify that the student has acquired the knowledge required to enter the human resource management profession at the entry level. See www2.shrm.org/assuranceoflearning/StudentMaterials.html, accessed September 21, 2013.

2

Equal Opportunity and the Law

Source: Gustavo Toledo/Shutterstock

MyManagementLab®

Improve Your Grade!

When you see this icon, visit **www.mymanagementlab.com** for activities that are applied, personalized, and offer immediate feedback.

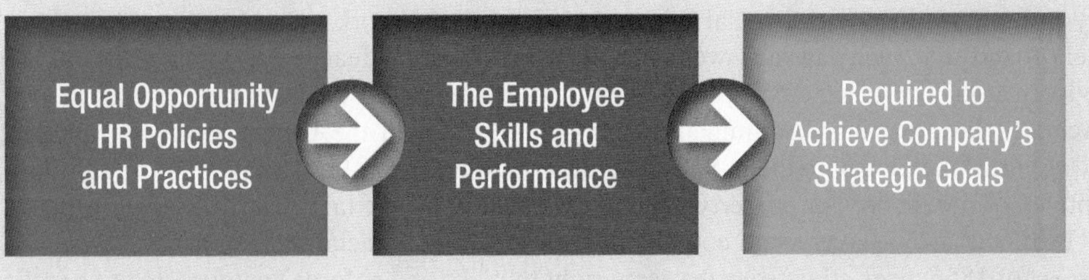

For a bird's eye view of how managers formulate human resource management policies and practices that produce the employee skills and performance the company needs to achieve its strategic aims, we will use the Hotel Paris continuing case starting in Chapter 3 as an applied example.

WHERE ARE WE NOW . . .

Every HR action you take as a manager, from interviewing applicants to training, appraising, and rewarding them, has equal employment implications. Therefore, the purpose of this chapter is to provide you with the knowledge to deal effectively with equal employment questions on the job. The main topics we cover are equal opportunity laws enacted from 1964 to 1991, the laws enacted from 1991 to the present, defenses against discrimination allegations, illustrative discriminatory employment practices, the EEOC enforcement process, and diversity management.

LEARNING OBJECTIVES

1. Explain the importance of and list the basic features of Title VII of the 1964 Civil Rights Act and at least five other equal employment laws.
2. Describe post-1990 employment laws including the Americans with Disabilities Act and how to avoid accusations of sexual harassment at work.
3. Illustrate two defenses you can use in the event of discriminatory practice allegations, and cite specific discriminatory personnel management practices in recruitment, selection, promotion, transfer, layoffs, and benefits.
4. List the steps in the EEOC enforcement process.
5. Discuss why diversity management is important and how to install a diversity management program.

It was an outrageous example of how to cost your employer millions of dollars in lost profits. The supervisor demoted a man from manager to janitor, and took other steps to humiliate him. The jury subsequently awarded the former manager $3.4 million. We'll see what employers can do to avoid such problems.

1 Explain the importance of and list the basic features of Title VII of the 1964 Civil Rights Act and at least five other equal employment laws.

Equal Opportunity Laws Enacted from 1964 to 1991

Hardly a day goes by without equal opportunity lawsuits at work.[1] One survey of corporate counsels found that such lawsuits were their biggest litigation fears.[2] Performing day-to-day supervisory tasks like hiring employees without understanding these laws is fraught with peril.

Actually, laws barring discrimination against minorities in the United States are nothing new. The Fifth Amendment to the U.S. Constitution (ratified in 1791) states that "no person shall be deprived of life, liberty, or property, without due process of the law." The Thirteenth Amendment (1865) outlawed slavery, and courts have held that it bars racial discrimination. The Civil Rights Act of 1866 gives all persons the same right to make and enforce contracts and to benefit from U.S. laws.[3] But as a practical matter, Congress and presidents avoided dramatic action on implementing equal employment until the early 1960s. At that point, civil unrest among minorities and women and changing traditions prompted them to act. Congress passed a multitude of new civil rights laws.

Title VII of the 1964 Civil Rights Act

Title VII of the 1964 Civil Rights Act
The section of the act that says an employer cannot discriminate on the basis of race, color, religion, sex, or national origin with respect to employment.

Title VII of the 1964 Civil Rights Act was one of the first of these laws. As amended by the 1972 Equal Employment Opportunity Act, Title VII states that an employer cannot discriminate based on race, color, religion, sex, or national origin. Specifically, it states that it shall be an unlawful employment practice for an employer:

1. To fail or refuse to hire or to discharge an individual or otherwise to discriminate against any individual with respect to his or her compensation, terms, conditions, or privileges of employment, because of such individual's race, color, religion, sex, or national origin.
2. To limit, segregate, or classify employees or applicants for employment in any way that would deprive or tend to deprive any individual of employment opportunities or otherwise adversely affect his or her status as an employee, because of such individual's race, color, religion, sex, or national origin.

WHO DOES TITLE VII COVER? Title VII bars discrimination on the part of most employers, including all public or private employers of 15 or more persons and most labor unions. It also covers all private and public educational institutions, the federal government, and state and local governments. It bars public and private employment agencies from failing or refusing to refer for employment any individual because of race, color, religion, sex, or national origin.

Equal Employment Opportunity Commission (EEOC)
The commission, created by Title VII, empowered to investigate job discrimination complaints and sue on behalf of complainants.

THE EEOC Title VII established the **Equal Employment Opportunity Commission (EEOC)** to administer and enforce the Civil Rights Act at work. It consists of five members appointed by the president with the advice and consent of the Senate. Each member serves a 5-year term. In popular usage, the EEOC also includes the thousands of staff the EEOC has around the United States. They receive and investigate job discrimination complaints from aggrieved individuals. When the EEOC finds reasonable cause that the charges are justified, it attempts (through conciliation) to reach an agreement.[4] If this fails, it can go to court. The EEOC may file discrimination charges on behalf of aggrieved individuals, or the individuals may file on behalf of themselves.[5] We'll discuss the EEOC procedure later in this chapter.

affirmative action
Steps that are taken for the purpose of eliminating the present effects of past discrimination.

Office of Federal Contract Compliance Programs (OFCCP)
This office is responsible for implementing the executive orders and ensuring compliance of federal contractors.

Executive Orders

Various U.S. presidents signed executive orders expanding equal employment in federal agencies. For example, the Johnson administration (1963–1969) issued Executive Orders 11246 and 11375. These required that government contractors with contracts of over $50,000 and 50 or more employees take **affirmative action** to ensure employment opportunities for those who may have suffered past discrimination. They also established the **Office of Federal Contract Compliance Programs (OFCCP)**. It implements the orders and ensures compliance.[6]

Equal Pay Act of 1963
The act requiring equal pay for equal work, regardless of sex.

Equal Pay Act of 1963

Under the **Equal Pay Act of 1963** (amended in 1972), it is unlawful to discriminate in pay on the basis of sex when jobs involve equal work; require equivalent skills, effort, and responsibility; and are performed under similar working conditions. Pay differences derived from seniority systems, merit systems, and systems that measure earnings by production quantity or quality or from any factor other than sex do not violate the act. **Unfortunately, this act notwithstanding, women still earn only about 70% as much as men in similar jobs; we'll address this inequity and how to deal with it in our chapter on establishing strategic pay plans.**

Age Discrimination in Employment Act of 1967

Age Discrimination in Employment Act of 1967 (ADEA)
The act prohibiting arbitrary age discrimination and specifically protecting individuals over 40 years old.

The **Age Discrimination in Employment Act of 1967 (ADEA)** made it unlawful to discriminate against employees or applicants who are between 40 and 65 years of age. Subsequent amendments effectively ended most mandatory retirement at age 65. Most states and local agencies, when acting as employers, must also adhere to the ADEA.[7]

You can't get around the ADEA by replacing employees who are, say, 60 with someone over 40. In one case the U.S. Supreme Court held that an employee who is over 40 years of age might sue for discrimination if a "significantly younger" employee replaces him or her, even if the replacement is also over 40. The Court didn't specify what "significantly younger" meant. Here the plaintiff was replaced by someone 16 years younger.[8]

Younger managers especially may have to guard against ageist prejudices. For example, a 54-year-old former manager alleged that Google fired him because his supervisor said he wasn't a "cultural fit." Such comments prompted the California Court of Appeals to let the manager's case proceed.[9]

Lawyers like the ADEA. It allows jury trials and double damages to those proving "willful" discrimination.[10]

Vocational Rehabilitation Act of 1973

Vocational Rehabilitation Act of 1973
The act requiring certain federal contractors to take affirmative action for disabled persons.

The **Vocational Rehabilitation Act of 1973** requires employers with federal contracts of more than $2,500 to take affirmative action in employing handicapped persons. It does not require hiring unqualified people. It does require an employer to take steps to accommodate a handicapped worker unless doing so imposes an undue hardship on the employer.

Pregnancy Discrimination Act of 1978

Pregnancy Discrimination Act
An amendment to Title VII of the Civil Rights Act that prohibits sex discrimination based on "pregnancy, childbirth, or related medical conditions."

The **Pregnancy Discrimination Act** of 1978 prohibits using pregnancy, childbirth, or related medical conditions to discriminate in hiring, promotion, suspension, or discharge, or in any term or condition of employment. Furthermore, under the act, if an employer offers its employees disability coverage, then it must treat pregnancy and childbirth like any other disability, and include it in the plan as a covered condition.[11]

More women are suing under this act, and progressive human resources notwithstanding, it's easy to see why.[12] As one example, an auto dealership fired an employee after she said she was pregnant. The reason? Allegedly, "In case I ended up throwing up or cramping in one of their vehicles. They said pregnant women do that sometimes, and I could cause an accident. . . ."[13] Managers therefore should base such decisions on "medical documentation, not on a manager's interpretation."[14]

Federal Agency Guidelines

The federal agencies charged with ensuring compliance with these laws and executive orders have their own implementing guidelines. These spell out recommended procedures for complying with the law.[15]

Uniform Guidelines
Guidelines issued by federal agencies charged with ensuring compliance with equal employment federal legislation explaining recommended employer procedures in detail.

The EEOC, Civil Service Commission, Department of Labor, and Department of Justice together issued **Uniform Guidelines.**[16] These set forth "highly recommended" procedures for things like employee selection and record keeping. As an example, they specify that employers must *validate* any employment selection devices (like tests) that screen out disproportionate numbers of women or minorities, and explain how to do so. (We explain this procedure in Chapter 6.) The EEOC and other agencies also periodically issue updated guidelines clarifying and revising their positions on matters such as sexual harassment. The American Psychological Association has its own (non–legally binding) Standards for Educational and Psychological Testing.

Early Court Decisions Regarding Equal Employment Opportunity

Several court decisions between 1964 and 1991 helped clarify courts' interpretations of equal employment opportunity (EEO) laws such as Title VII.

GRIGGS V. DUKE POWER COMPANY *Griggs* was a landmark case because the Supreme Court used it to define unfair discrimination. Lawyers sued the Duke Power Company on behalf of Wilie Griggs, an applicant for a job as a coal handler. The company required its coal handlers to be high school graduates. Griggs claimed this requirement was illegally discriminatory. He said it wasn't related to success on the job, and it resulted in more blacks than whites being rejected for these jobs. Griggs won the case. The Court's decision was unanimous. In his written opinion, Chief Justice Burger laid out three crucial guidelines affecting equal employment legislation.

- First, the Court ruled that the *discrimination does not have to be overt to be illegal.* The plaintiff does not have to show that the employer intentionally discriminated against the employee or applicant. Instead, the plaintiff just has to show that discrimination took place.
- Second, the Court held that an employment practice (in this case, requiring the high school degree) *must be job related* if it has an unequal impact on members of a **protected class.** (For example, if arithmetic is not required to perform the job, don't test for arithmetic.)
- Third, Chief Justice Burger's opinion placed the *burden of proof on the employer* to show that the hiring practice is job related. Thus, the employer must show that the employment practice (in this case, requiring a high school degree) is necessary for satisfactory job performance if the practice discriminates against members of a protected class. Said Justice Burger,

protected class
Persons such as minorities and women protected by equal opportunity laws, including Title VII.

> The act proscribes not only overt discrimination, but also practices that are fair in form, but discriminatory in operation. The touchstone is business necessity. If an employment practice which operates to exclude Negroes cannot be shown to be related to job performance, the practice is prohibited.[17]

For employers, *Griggs* established these five principles:

1. A test or other selection practice must be job related, and the burden of proof is on the employer.
2. An employer's intent not to discriminate is irrelevant.[18]
3. If a practice is "fair in form but discriminatory in operation," the courts will not uphold it.
4. *Business necessity* is the defense for any existing program that has adverse impact. The court did not define business necessity.
5. Title VII does not forbid testing. However, the test must be job related (valid), in that performance on the test must relate to performance on the job.

ALBEMARLE PAPER COMPANY V. MOODY In the *Albemarle* case, the Court provided more details on how employers could prove that tests or other screening tools relate to job performance.[19] For example, the Court said that if an employer wants to test candidates for a job, then the employer should first clearly document and understand the job's duties and responsibilities. Furthermore, the job's performance standards should be clear and unambiguous. That way, the employer can identify which employees are performing better than others. The Court's ruling also established the EEOC (now Federal) Guidelines on validation as the procedures for validating employment practices.

The Laws Enacted from 1991 to the Present

The Civil Rights Act of 1991

2 Describe post-1990 employment laws including the Americans with Disabilities Act and how to avoid accusations of sexual harassment at work.

Several subsequent Supreme Court rulings in the 1980s limited the protection of women and minority groups under equal employment laws. For example, they raised the plaintiff's burden of proving that the employer's acts were in fact discriminatory. This prompted Congress to pass a new Civil Rights Act. President George H. W. Bush signed the **Civil Rights Act of 1991 (CRA 1991)** into law in November 1991. The effect of CRA 1991 was to roll back equal employment law to where it stood before the 1980s decisions, and to place more responsibility on employers.

Civil Rights Act of 1991 (CRA 1991)
The act that places the burden of proof back on employers and permits compensatory and punitive damages.

BURDEN OF PROOF First, CRA 1991 addressed the issue of *burden of proof.* Burden of proof—what the plaintiff must show to establish possible illegal discrimination, and what the employer must show to defend its actions—plays a central role in equal employment cases.[20] Today, in brief, once an aggrieved applicant or employee demonstrates that an employment practice (such as "must lift 100 pounds") has an adverse impact on a particular group, then the burden of proof shifts to the employer, who must show that the challenged practice is job related.[21] For example, the employer has to show that lifting 100 pounds is required for performing the job in question, and that the business could not run efficiently without the requirement—that it is a business necessity.[22]

MONEY DAMAGES Before CRA 1991, victims of *intentional* discrimination (which lawyers call *disparate treatment*) who had not suffered financial loss and who sued under Title VII could not then sue for compensatory or punitive damages. All they could expect was to have their jobs reinstated (or to get a particular job). They were also eligible for back pay, attorneys' fees, and court costs.

CRA 1991 makes it easier to sue for *money damages* in such cases. It provides that an employee who is claiming intentional discrimination can ask for (1) compensatory damages and (2) punitive damages, if he or she can show the employer engaged in discrimination "with malice or reckless indifference to the federally protected rights of an aggrieved individual."[23]

"mixed-motive" case
A discrimination allegation case in which the employer argues that the employment action taken was motivated not by discrimination, but by some nondiscriminatory reason such as ineffective performance.

MIXED MOTIVES Some employers in **"mixed-motive" cases** had taken the position that even though their actions were discriminatory, other factors like the employee's dubious behavior made the job action acceptable. Under CRA 1991, an employer cannot avoid liability by proving it would have taken the same action—such as terminating someone—even without the discriminatory motive.[24] *If there is any such motive, the practice may be unlawful.*[25]

The Americans with Disabilities Act

Americans with Disabilities Act (ADA)
The act requiring employers to make reasonable accommodations for disabled employees; it prohibits discrimination against disabled persons.

The **Americans with Disabilities Act (ADA)** of 1990 prohibits employment discrimination against qualified disabled individuals.[26] It prohibits employers with 15 or more workers from discriminating against qualified individuals with disabilities, with regard to applications, hiring, discharge, compensation, advancement, training, or other terms, conditions, or privileges of employment.[27] It also says employers must make "reasonable accommodations" for physical or mental limitations unless doing so imposes an "undue hardship" on the business.

The ADA does not list specific disabilities. Instead, EEOC guidelines say someone is disabled when he or she has a physical or mental impairment that "substantially limits" one or more major life activity. Initially, impairments included any physiological disorder or condition, cosmetic disfigurement, or anatomical loss affecting one or more of several body systems, or any mental or psychological disorder, but the list is growing.[28] The act specifies conditions that it does *not* regard as disabilities, including homosexuality, compulsive gambling, pyromania, and certain disorders resulting from the current illegal use of drugs.[29]

MENTAL IMPAIRMENTS AND THE ADA Mental disabilities account for the greatest number of ADA claims.[30] Under EEOC ADA guidelines, "mental impairment" includes "any mental or psychological disorder, such as . . . emotional or mental illness." Examples include major depression, anxiety disorders, and personality disorders. The ADA also protects employees with intellectual disabilities, including those with IQs below 70–75.[31] The guidelines say employers should be alert to the possibility that traits normally regarded as undesirable (such as chronic lateness, hostility, or poor judgment) may reflect mental impairments. Reasonable accommodation might then include providing barriers between work spaces.

qualified individuals
Under ADA, those who can carry out the essential functions of the job.

QUALIFIED INDIVIDUAL Just being disabled doesn't qualify someone for a job, of course. Instead, the act prohibits discrimination against **qualified individuals**—those who, with (or without) a reasonable accommodation, can carry out the *essential functions* of the job. The individual must have the requisite skills, educational background, and experience. A job function is essential when, for instance, it is the reason the position exists, or it is so highly specialized that the employer hires the person for his or her expertise or ability to perform that particular function. For example, when an Iowa County highway worker had an on-the-job seizure, his driver's license was suspended and the court ruled he had no ADA claim because he couldn't perform the essential functions of the job.[32]

REASONABLE ACCOMMODATION If the individual can't perform the job as currently structured, the employer must make a "reasonable accommodation" unless doing so would present an

FIGURE 2-1 Examples of How to Provide Reasonable Accommodation

- Employees with *mobility or vision impairments* may benefit from voice-recognition software.
- Word-prediction software suggests words based on context with just one or two letters typed.
- Real-time translation captioning enables employees to participate in meetings.
- Vibrating text pagers notify employees when messages arrive.
- Arizona created a disability-friendly website to help link prospective employees and others to various agencies.

Huntstock/Thinkstock

Technology enables employers to accommodate disabled employees.

"undue hardship."[33] Reasonable accommodation might include redesigning the job, modifying work schedules, or modifying or acquiring equipment or other devices: widening door openings or permitting telecommuting are examples.[34] For example, about 70% of working age blind adults are unemployed or underemployed. Existing technologies such as screen-reading programs might enable most to work successfully.[35]

Attorneys, employers, and the courts continue to work through what "reasonable accommodation" means.[36] In one classic case, a Walmart door greeter with a bad back asked if she could sit on a stool while on duty. The store said no. The federal district court agreed door greeters must act in an "aggressively hospitable manner," which can't be done from a stool.[37] Standing was an essential job function. You can use technology and common sense to make reasonable accommodation (see Figure 2-1).

TRADITIONAL EMPLOYER DEFENSES Employers traditionally prevailed in almost all—96%—federal circuit court ADA decisions.[38] A U.S. Supreme Court decision typifies what plaintiffs faced. An assembly worker sued Toyota, arguing that carpal tunnel syndrome prevented her from doing her job.[39] The U.S. Supreme Court ruled that the ADA covers carpal tunnel syndrome only if her impairments affect not just her job performance, but also her daily living activities. The employee admitted that she could perform personal chores such as washing her face and fixing breakfast. The Court said the disability must be central to the employee's daily living (not just to his or her job).[40]

THE "NEW" ADA However, the ADA Amendments Act of 2008 (ADAAA) will make it easier for employees to show that their disabilities are influencing one of their "major life activities," such as reading and thinking.[41] For example, sensitivity to perfume might be considered a disability.[42] Employers must therefore redouble their efforts to ensure they're complying with the ADA.[43]

Many employers simply take a progressive approach. Common employer concerns about people with disabilities (for instance, that they are less productive, and have more accidents) are generally baseless.[44] For example, Walgreens tries to fill at least one-third of the jobs at its large distribution centers with people with disabilities.[45]

Figure 2-2 summarizes some important ADA guidelines for managers and employers.

FIGURE 2-2 ADA Guidelines for Managers and Employers

- *Do not* deny a job to a disabled individual if the person is qualified and able to perform the essential job functions.
- *Make* a reasonable accommodation unless doing so would result in undue hardship.
- *Know* what you can ask applicants. In general, you may *not* make preemployment inquiries about a person's disability before making an offer. However, you *may* ask questions about the person's ability to perform essential job functions.
- *Itemize* essential job functions on the job descriptions. In virtually any ADA legal action, a central question will be, what are the essential functions of the job?
- *Do not* allow misconduct or erratic performance (including absences and tardiness), even if that behavior is linked to the disability.

Uniformed Services Employment and Reemployment Rights Act

Under the Uniformed Services Employment and Reemployment Rights Act (1994), employers are generally required, among other things, to reinstate employees returning from military leave to positions comparable to those they had before leaving.[46]

Genetic Information Nondiscrimination Act of 2008 (GINA)

The Genetic Information Nondiscrimination Act (GINA) prohibits discrimination by health insurers and employers based on people's genetic information. Specifically, it prohibits the use of genetic information in employment, prohibits the intentional acquisition of genetic information about applicants and employees, and imposes strict confidentiality requirements.[47]

State and Local Equal Employment Opportunity Laws

In addition to federal laws, all states and many local governments prohibit employment discrimination. The state or local laws usually cover employers (like those with less than 15 employees) not covered by federal legislation.[48]

Employers ignore city and state EEO laws at their peril. In New York City, for instance, city law applies to employers with as few as 4 employees (not 15, as under Title VII).[49] Connecticut recently became the first state to require that employers provide paid sick leave to employees. Hawaii and Massachusetts prohibit employers from asking about criminal convictions on applications.[50]

State and local equal employment opportunity agencies (often called *Human Resources Commissions* or *Fair Employment Commissions*) also play a role in equal employment compliance. When the EEOC receives a discrimination charge, it usually defers it for a limited time to the state and local agencies that have comparable jurisdiction. If that doesn't achieve satisfactory remedies, the charges go back to the EEOC for resolution. Foreign laws are another matter, as the HR Practices Around the Globe feature illustrates.

IMPROVING PERFORMANCE: HR Practices Around the Globe

Employers' workforces are increasingly international, and this complicates dealing with employment law. As an example, the employer should consider the legal situation when relocating employees from one country to another. In one case, a German company moved an employee from Germany to New York, where he worked satisfactorily for 11 years. At that point, a problem arose at the New York subsidiary, and the German company fired several managers, including this employee. Objecting to his firing, the employee filed a lawsuit against the subsidiary in New York, and filed one against the parent company in Germany. The German firm had left his German employment contract in place all these years. It allowed disputes to be heard in Germany (where dismissals tend to be more strictly limited than in the United States). If the German company had terminated the German contract sometime during the previous 11 years, it could have avoided the considerable costs of fighting the case in Germany.[51]

Discussion Question 2-1: If you were the HR director at a company, what exactly would you do to avoid such problems in the future?

In Summary: Religious and Other Types of Discrimination[52]

The EEOC enforces laws prohibiting discrimination based on age, disability, equal pay/compensation, genetic information, national origin, pregnancy, race/color, religion, retaliation, sex, and sexual harassment. The EEOC has also held that discrimination against an individual because that person is transgender is discrimination because of sex and therefore covered under Title VII. The Commission has also found that sexual orientation claims by lesbian, gay, and bisexual individuals alleging sex-stereotyping have a sex discrimination claim under Title VII.

Religious discrimination involves treating someone unfavorably because of his or her religious beliefs. The law protects not only people who belong to traditional, organized religions, such as Buddhism, Christianity, Hinduism, Islam, and Judaism, but also others who have sincerely held religious, ethical, or moral beliefs. Unless it would be an undue hardship on the employer, an employer must reasonably accommodate an employee's religious beliefs or practices. This applies to schedule changes or leave for religious observances, as well as to such things as religious dress or grooming practices. These might include, for example, wearing particular head coverings or other religious dress (such as a Jewish yarmulke or a Muslim headscarf), or wearing certain hairstyles or facial hair (such as Rastafarian dreadlocks or Sikh uncut hair and beard). Table 2-1 summarizes selected equal employment opportunity laws, actions, executive orders, and agency guidelines.

Sexual Harassment

sexual harassment
Harassment on the basis of sex that has the purpose or effect of substantially interfering with a person's work performance or creating an intimidating, hostile, or offensive work environment.

Under Title VII, **sexual harassment** generally refers to harassment on the basis of sex when such conduct has the purpose or effect of substantially interfering with a person's work performance or creating an intimidating, hostile, or offensive work environment. In one recent year, the EEOC received 11,717 sexual harassment charges, about 15% of which were filed by men.[53] (The U.S. Supreme Court held, in *Oncale v. Sundowner Offshore Services Inc.*, that same-sex sexual harassment is also actionable under Title VII.[54]) One study found "women experienced more sexual harassment than men, minorities experienced more ethnic harassment than whites, and minority women experience more harassment overall than majority men, minority men, and majority women."[55]

Federal Violence Against Women Act of 1994
The act that provides that a person who commits a crime of violence motivated by gender shall be liable to the party injured.

Under EEOC guidelines, employers have an affirmative duty to maintain workplaces free of sexual harassment and intimidation. CRA 1991 permits victims of intentional discrimination, including sexual harassment, to have jury trials and to collect compensatory damages for pain and suffering and punitive damages, where the employer acted with "malice or reckless indifference" to the person's rights.[56] The **Federal Violence Against Women Act of 1994** further provides that a person "who commits a crime of violence motivated by gender and thus deprives another" of her rights shall be liable to the party injured.

TABLE 2-1 Summary of Important Equal Employment Opportunity Actions

Action	What It Does
Title VII of 1964 Civil Rights Act, as amended	Bars discrimination because of race, color, religion, sex, or national origin; instituted the EEOC.
Executive orders	Prohibit employment discrimination by employers with federal contracts of more than $10,000 (and their subcontractors); establish office of federal compliance; require affirmative action programs.
Federal agency guidelines	Indicate guidelines covering discrimination based on sex, national origin, and religion, as well as employee selection procedures; for example, require validation of tests.
Supreme Court decisions: *Griggs v. Duke Power Co.*, *Albemarle v. Moody*	Rule that job requirements must be related to job success; that discrimination need not be overt to be proved; that the burden of proof is on the employer to prove the qualification is valid.
Equal Pay Act of 1963	Requires equal pay for men and women for performing similar work.
Age Discrimination in Employment Act of 1967	Prohibits discriminating against a person age 40 or over in any area of employment because of age.
State and local laws	Often cover organizations too small to be covered by federal laws.
Vocational Rehabilitation Act of 1973	Requires affirmative action to employ and promote qualified handicapped persons and prohibits discrimination against handicapped persons.
Pregnancy Discrimination Act of 1978	Prohibits discrimination in employment against pregnant women, or related conditions.
Vietnam Era Veterans' Readjustment Assistance Act of 1974	Requires affirmative action in employment for veterans of the Vietnam War era.
Ward Cove v. Atonio	Made it more difficult to prove a case of unlawful discrimination against an employer.
Americans with Disabilities Act of 1990	Strengthens the need for most employers to make reasonable accommodations for disabled employees at work; prohibits discrimination.
Civil Rights Act of 1991	Reverses various U.S. Supreme Court decisions; places burden of proof back on employer and permits compensatory and punitive money damages for discrimination.
ADA Amendments Act of 2008	Makes it easier for employee to show that his or her disability "substantially limits" a major life function.
Genetic Information Nondiscrimination Act	Signed into law in May 2008, prohibits discriminating against employees and applicants based on their genetic information.

Source: The actual laws (and others) can be accessed via a search at www.usa.gov/Topics/Reference-Shelf/Laws.shtml, accessed September 21, 2013.

WHAT IS SEXUAL HARASSMENT? EEOC guidelines define *sexual harassment* as unwelcome sexual advances, requests for sexual favors, and other verbal or physical conduct of a sexual nature that takes place under any of the following conditions:

1. Submission to such conduct is made either explicitly or implicitly a term or condition of an individual's employment.
2. Submission to or rejection of such conduct by an individual is used as the basis for employment decisions affecting such individual.
3. Such conduct has the purpose or effect of unreasonably interfering with an individual's work performance or creating an intimidating, hostile, or offensive work environment.

PROVING SEXUAL HARASSMENT There are three main ways someone can prove sexual harassment:

1. ***Quid Pro Quo.*** The most direct is to prove that rejecting a supervisor's advances adversely affected what the EEOC calls a "tangible employment action," such as hiring, firing, promotion, demotion, and/or work assignment. In one case, the employee showed that continued job success and advancement were dependent on her agreeing to the sexual demands of her supervisors.
2. ***Hostile Environment Created by Supervisors.*** The harassment need not have tangible consequences such as demotion. For example, one court found that a male supervisor's behavior had substantially affected a female employee's emotional and psychological ability to the point that she felt she had to quit her job. Therefore, even though the supervisor made no direct threats or promises in exchange for sexual advances, his advances interfered with the woman's performance and created an offensive work environment. That was sufficient to prove sexual harassment. Courts generally do not interpret as sexual harassment sexual relationships that arise during the course of employment but that do not have a substantial effect on that employment.[57] The U.S. Supreme Court also held that sexual harassment law doesn't cover ordinary "intersexual flirtation." In his ruling, Justice Antonin Scalia said courts must carefully distinguish between "simple teasing" and truly abusive behavior.[58]
3. ***Hostile Environment Created by Coworkers or Nonemployees.*** Coworkers or nonemployees can trigger such suits. One court held that a mandatory sexually provocative uniform led to lewd comments by customers. When the employee refused to wear the uniform, they fired her. The employer couldn't show there was a job-related necessity for the uniform, and only female employees wore it. The court ruled that the employer, in effect, was responsible for the sexually harassing behavior. Such abhorrent client behavior is more likely when the clients are in positions of power, and when they think no one will penalize them.[59] Employers are also liable for the sexually harassing acts of nonsupervisory employees if the employer knew or should have known of the conduct.

WHEN IS THE ENVIRONMENT "HOSTILE"? Hostile environment sexual harassment generally means the intimidation, insults, and ridicule were sufficiently severe to alter the employee's working conditions. Courts look at several things. These include whether the discriminatory conduct is *frequent or severe*; whether it is *physically threatening* or humiliating, or a mere offensive utterance; and whether it unreasonably *interferes* with an employee's work performance.[60] Courts also consider whether the employee subjectively *perceives* the work environment as being abusive. For example, did he or she welcome the conduct or immediately complain?[61]

SUPREME COURT DECISIONS The U.S. Supreme Court used a case called *Meritor Savings Bank, FSB v. Vinson* to endorse broadly the EEOC's guidelines on sexual harassment. Two other Supreme Court decisions further clarified sexual harassment law.

In the first, *Burlington Industries v. Ellerth*, the employee accused her supervisor of *quid pro quo* harassment. She said her boss propositioned and threatened her with demotion if she did not respond. He did not carry out the threats, and she was promoted. In the second case, *Faragher v. City of Boca Raton*, the employee accused the employer of condoning a hostile work environment. She said she quit her lifeguard job after repeated taunts from other lifeguards. The Court ruled in favor of the employees in both cases.

The Court's written decisions have two implications for employers and managers. First, in *quid pro quo* cases it is *not* necessary for the employee to suffer a tangible job action (such as a demotion) to win the case. Second, the Court laid out an important defense against harassment suits. It said the employer must show that it took "reasonable care" to prevent and promptly correct any sexually harassing behavior *and* that the employee unreasonably failed to take advantage of the employer's policy.

Implications for Employers and Managers These decisions suggest an employer can defend itself against sexual harassment liability by showing two things:

- First, it must show "that the employer exercised reasonable care to *prevent* and *correct promptly* any sexually harassing behavior."[62]
- Second, it must demonstrate that the plaintiff "unreasonably *failed to take advantage* of any preventive or corrective opportunities provided by the employer." The employee's failure to use formal reporting systems would satisfy the second component.[63]

Prudent employer steps therefore include:[64]

- Take all complaints about harassment seriously.
- Issue a strong policy statement condemning such behavior. Describe the prohibited conduct, assure protection against retaliation, describe a confidential complaint process, and provide impartial investigation and corrective action.
- Take steps to prevent sexual harassment from occurring. For example, communicate to employees that the employer will not tolerate sexual harassment, and take immediate action when someone complains.
- Establish a management response system that includes an immediate reaction and investigation.
- Train supervisors and managers to increase their awareness of the issues, and discipline managers and employees involved in sexual harassment.

WHEN THE LAW ISN'T ENOUGH Unfortunately, two practical considerations often trump the legal requirements. First, "Women perceive a broader range of socio-sexual behaviors (touching, for instance) as harassing."[65] In one study, about 58% of employees reported experiencing potentially harassment-type behaviors at work. Overall, about 25% found it flattering and about half viewed it as benign. But on closer examination, about four times as many men as women found the behavior flattering or benign.[66] Sexual harassment training and policies can reduce this problem.[67]

A second problem is that employees often won't complain. For example, two Air Force generals recently appeared before the U.S. Congress' House Armed Services Committee to explain (among other things) how 23 instructors at an Air Force base could engage in unprofessional relationships or sexual assaults against 48 female trainees. The Air Force blamed both a climate of fear among female personnel (who believed that reporting the offenses to superior officers would be futile or counterproductive) and "a weak command structure."[68]

WHAT THE EMPLOYEE CAN DO First, complain. Remember that courts generally look to whether *the harassed employee used the employer's reporting procedures to file a complaint promptly.* If the employer has an effectively communicated complaint procedure, use it and then cooperate in the investigation.[69] In that context, steps an employee can take include:

1. File a verbal contemporaneous complaint with the harasser and the harasser's boss, stating that the unwanted overtures should cease because the conduct is unwelcome.
2. If the unwelcome conduct does not cease, file verbal and written reports regarding the unwelcome conduct and unsuccessful efforts to get it to stop with the harasser's manager and/or the human resource director.
3. If the letters and appeals to the employer do not suffice, contact the local office of the EEOC to file the necessary claim. In very serious cases, the employee can also consult an attorney about suing the harasser for assault and battery, intentional infliction of emotional distress, injunctive relief, and to recover compensatory and punitive damages.

Social Media and HR

Employees' increasing use of social media can be problematic for employers. Some states forbid employers from requiring or requesting employees' or applicants' passwords. Employers also must distinguish between illegal online harassment (that applying to race, religion, national origin, age, sex/gender, genetic information, and disability discrimination) and common personality conflicts. Yet some employees do use Facebook and other accounts to harass and bully coworkers (as with disparaging comments). Solutions aren't straightforward. At a minimum, employers should have a zero-tolerance policy on bullying.[70]

Defenses Against Discrimination Allegations

3 Illustrate two defenses you can use in the event of discriminatory practice allegations, and cite specific discriminatory personnel management practices in recruitment, selection, promotion, transfer, layoffs, and benefits.

To understand how employers defend themselves against employment discrimination claims, we should first briefly review some basic legal terminology.

Discrimination law distinguishes between disparate *treatment* and disparate *impact. Disparate treatment* means intentional discrimination. Disparate treatment "exists where an employer treats an individual differently because that individual is a member of a particular race, religion, gender, or ethnic group."[71] A rule that says "we don't hire drivers over 60 years of age" exemplifies this.

Disparate impact means that "an employer engages in an employment practice or policy that has a greater adverse impact (effect) on the members of a protected group under Title VII than on other employees, regardless of intent."[72] A rule that says "employees must have college degrees to do this particular job" exemplifies this (because more white males than some minorities earn college degrees).

Disparate impact claims do not require proof of discriminatory intent. Instead, the plaintiff must show that the apparently neutral employment practice (such as requiring a college degree) creates an adverse impact—a significant disparity—between the proportion of (say) minorities in the available labor pool and the proportion you hire. Thus, disparate impact allegations require a showing that the act produced an adverse impact. If it has, then the employer will probably have to defend itself (for instance, by arguing that there is a business necessity for the practice). Adverse impact "refers to the total employment process that results in a significantly higher percentage of a protected group in the candidate population being rejected for employment, placement, or promotion."[73] Then the burden of proof shifts to the employer.

adverse impact
The overall impact of employer practices that result in significantly higher percentages of members of minorities and other protected groups being rejected for employment, placement, or promotion.

The Central Role of Adverse Impact

Showing that one of the employer's employment practices or policies has an **adverse impact** therefore plays a central role in discriminatory practice allegations.[74] Under Title VII and

Maurice van der Velden/Getty Images

Employees who believe they are victims of harassment should have a mechanism for filing a complaint.

CRA 1991, a person who believes that (1) he or she was a victim of unintentional discrimination because of an employer's practices need only (2) establish a *prima facie* case of discrimination. This means showing, for instance, that the employer's selection procedures (like requiring a college degree for the job) did have an adverse impact on the protected minority group.

So, for example, if a minority applicant feels he or she was a victim of discrimination, the person need only show that the employer's selection process resulted in an adverse impact on his or her group. (For example, if 80% of the white applicants passed the test, but only 20% of the black applicants passed, a black applicant has a *prima facie* case proving adverse impact.) Then the burden of proof shifts to the employer. It becomes the employer's task to prove that its test (or application blank or the like) is a valid predictor of performance on the job (and that it applied its selection process fairly and equitably to both minorities and nonminorities).

In practice, an applicant or employee can use one of the following five methods to show that one of an employer's procedures (such as a selection test) has an adverse impact on a protected group.

disparate rejection rates
A test for adverse impact in which it can be demonstrated that there is a discrepancy between rates of rejection of members of a protected group and of others.

4/5ths rule
Federal agency rule that a minority selection rate less than 80% (4/5ths) of that for the group with the highest rate is evidence of adverse impact.

DISPARATE REJECTION RATES The **disparate rejection rate** method compares the rejection rates for a minority group and another group (usually the remaining nonminority applicants).[75]

Federal agencies use a **"4/5ths rule"** to assess disparate rejection rates: "A selection rate for any racial, ethnic, or sex group which is less than four-fifths or 80% of the rate for the group with the highest rate will generally be regarded as evidence of adverse impact, while a greater than four-fifths rate will generally not be regarded as evidence of adverse impact." For example, suppose the employer hires 60% of male applicants, but only 30% of female applicants. Four-fifths of the 60% male hiring rate would be 48%. Because the female hiring rate of 30% is less than 48%, adverse impact exists as far as these federal agencies are concerned.[76]

THE STANDARD DEVIATION RULE Similarly, the courts have used the *standard deviation rule* to confirm adverse impact. (The standard deviation is a statistical measure of variability. It is a measure of the dispersion of a set of data from its mean. Suppose we calculate the average height of students in your management class. In simplest terms, the standard deviation helps to describe, among other things, how wide a range there is in height between the shortest and tallest students and the class's average student height.) In selection, the standard deviation rule holds that, as a rule of thumb, the difference between the numbers of minority candidates we *would have expected* to hire and whom *we actually hired* should be less than two standard deviations.

Consider this example. Suppose 300 applicants apply for 20 openings; 80 of the applicants are women and the other 220 are men. We use our screening processes and hire 2 females and 18 males. Did our selection process have an adverse impact? To answer this, we can compute the standard deviation:

$$SD = \sqrt{\frac{\text{(Number of minority applicants)}}{\text{(Number of total applicants)}} \times \frac{\text{(Number of non-minority applicants)}}{\text{(Number of total applicants)}} \times \text{(Number of applicants selected)}}$$

In our case:

$$SD = \sqrt{\left(\frac{80}{300} \times \frac{220}{300} \times 20\right)} = \sqrt{(0.2667 \times 0.7333 \times 20)}$$

$$= \sqrt{3.911} = SD = 1.977$$

In our example, women are 26% (80/300) of the applicant pool. We should therefore *expect* to hire 26% of 20, or about 5 women. We *actually* hired 2 women. The difference between the numbers of women we would expect to hire and whom we actually hired is 5 − 2 = 3. We can use the standard deviation rule to gauge if there is adverse (disparate) impact. In our example, the standard deviation is 1.977. Again, the standard deviation rule holds that as a rule of thumb, the difference between the numbers of minority candidates we would have expected to hire and whom we actually hired should be less than two standard deviations. Two times 1.9777 is about 4. Since the difference between the number of women we would have expected to hire (5) and actually hired (2) is 3, the results suggest that our screening did not have adverse impact on women. (Put another way, in this case, hiring just 2 rather than 5 is not a highly improbable result.)[77]

restricted policy
Another test for adverse impact, involving demonstration that an employer's hiring practices exclude a protected group, whether intentionally or not.

RESTRICTED POLICY The **restricted policy** approach means demonstrating that the employer's policy intentionally or unintentionally excluded members of a protected group. Here the problem is usually obvious—such as policies against hiring guards less than 6 feet tall. Evidence of restricted policies such as these is enough to prove adverse impact and to expose an employer to litigation.

POPULATION COMPARISONS This approach compares (1) the percentage of minority/protected group and white workers in the organization with (2) the percentage of the corresponding group in the labor market.

"Labor market," of course, varies with the job. For some jobs, such as secretary, it makes sense to compare the percentage of minority employees with the percentage of minorities in the surrounding community, since they will come from that community. But determining whether an employer has enough black engineers might involve determining the number available nationwide, not in the surrounding community.

Employers use *workforce analysis* to analyze the data regarding the firm's use of protected versus nonprotected employees in various job classifications. The process of comparing the percentage of minority employees in a job (or jobs) at the company with the number of similarly trained minority employees available in the relevant labor market is *utilization analysis*.

MCDONNELL-DOUGLAS TEST Lawyers in disparate impact cases use the previous approaches (such as population comparisons) to test whether an employer's policies or actions have the effect of unintentionally screening out disproportionate numbers of women or minorities. Lawyers use the McDonnell-Douglas test for showing (intentional) disparate treatment, rather than (unintentional) disparate impact.

This test grew out of a case at the former McDonnell-Douglas Corporation. The applicant was qualified but the employer rejected the person and continued seeking applicants. Did this show that the hiring company intentionally discriminated against the female or minority candidate? The U.S. Supreme Court set four rules for applying the McDonnell-Douglas test:

1. that the person belongs to a protected class;
2. that he or she applied and was qualified for a job for which the employer was seeking applicants;
3. that, despite this qualification, he or she was rejected; and
4. that, after his or her rejection, the position remained open and the employer continued seeking applications from persons with the complainant's qualifications.

If the plaintiff meets all these conditions, then a *prima facie* case of disparate treatment is established. At that point, the employer must articulate a legitimate nondiscriminatory reason for its action, and produce evidence but not prove that it acted based on such a reason. If it meets this relatively easy standard, the plaintiff then has the burden of proving that the employer's articulated reason is merely a pretext for engaging in unlawful discrimination.

ADVERSE IMPACT EXAMPLE Assume you turn down a member of a protected group for a job with your firm. You do this based on a test score (although it could have been interview questions or something else). Further, assume that this person feels he or she was discriminated against due to being in a protected class, and decides to sue your company.

Basically, all he or she must do is show that your procedure (such as the selection test) had an adverse impact on members of his or her minority group. The plaintiff can apply five approaches here. These are disparate rejection rates, the standard deviation rule, restricted policy, population comparisons (or, for disparate *treatment* cases, the McDonnell-Douglas test). Once the person proves adverse impact (to the court's satisfaction), the burden of proof shifts to the employer. The employer must defend against the discrimination charges.

There is nothing in the law that says that because your procedure has an adverse impact on a protected group, you can't use it. In fact, it may well happen that some tests screen out disproportionately higher numbers of, say, blacks than they do whites. What the law does say is that once your applicant has made his or her case (showing adverse impact), the burden of proof shifts to you. Now the employer must defend use of the procedure.

There are then two basic defenses employers use to justify an employment practice that has an adverse impact on members of a minority group: the bona fide occupational qualification (BFOQ) defense and the business necessity defense.

Bona Fide Occupational Qualification

bona fide occupational qualification (BFOQ)
Requirement that an employee be of a certain religion, sex, or national origin where that is reasonably necessary to the organization's normal operation. Specified by the 1964 Civil Rights Act.

An employer can claim that the employment practice is a **bona fide occupational qualification (BFOQ)** for performing the job. Title VII specifically permits this defense. Title VII provides that "it should not be an unlawful employment practice for an employer to hire an employee . . . on the basis of religion, sex, or national origin *in those certain instances where religion, sex, or national origin is a bona fide occupational qualification* reasonably necessary to the normal operation of that particular business or enterprise."

However, courts usually interpret the BFOQ exception narrowly. It is usually a defense to a disparate treatment case based upon direct evidence of *intentional* discrimination, rather than to disparate impact (unintentional) cases. As a practical matter, employers use it mostly as a defense against charges of intentional discrimination based on age.

AGE AS A BFOQ The Age Discrimination in Employment Act (ADEA) permits disparate treatment in those instances when age is a BFOQ.[78] For example, age is a BFOQ when the Federal Aviation Agency sets a compulsory retirement age of 65 for commercial pilots.[79] Actors required for youthful or elderly roles suggest other instances when age may be a BFOQ. However, courts set the bar high: The reason for the age limit must go to the essence of the business. A court said a bus line's maximum-age hiring policy for bus drivers was a BFOQ. The court said the essence of the business was safe transportation of passengers, and, given that, the employer could strive to employ the most qualified persons available.[80]

RELIGION AS A BFOQ Religion may be a BFOQ in religious organizations or societies that require employees to share their particular religion. For example, religion may be a BFOQ when hiring persons to teach in a religious school. But again, courts construe this defense very narrowly.

GENDER AS A BFOQ Gender may be a BFOQ for positions like actor, model, and restroom attendant requiring physical characteristics possessed by one sex. However, for most jobs today, it's difficult to claim that gender is a BFOQ. For example, gender is not a BFOQ just because the position requires lifting heavy objects. A Texas man filed a complaint against Hooters of America alleging that one of its franchisees would not hire him as a waiter because it "merely wishes to exploit female sexuality as a marketing tool to attract customers and ensure profitability" and so was limiting hiring to females.[81] Hooters argued a BFOQ defense before reaching a confidential settlement.

NATIONAL ORIGIN AS A BFOQ A person's country of national origin may be a BFOQ. For example, an employer who is running the Chinese pavilion at a fair might claim that Chinese heritage is a BFOQ for persons to deal with the public.

Business Necessity

"Business necessity" is a defense created by the courts. It requires showing that there is an overriding business purpose for the discriminatory practice and that the practice is therefore acceptable.

It's not easy to prove business necessity.[82] The Supreme Court made it clear that business necessity does not encompass such matters as avoiding an employer inconvenience, annoyance, or expense. For example, an employer can't generally discharge employees whose wages have been garnished merely because garnishment (requiring the employer to divert part of the person's wages to pay his or her debts) creates an inconvenience. The Second Circuit Court of Appeals held that business necessity "must not only directly foster safety and efficiency," but also be essential to these goals.[83] Furthermore, "the business purpose must be sufficiently compelling to override any racial impact. . . ."[84]

However, many employers use the business necessity defense successfully. In an early case, *Spurlock v. United Airlines*, a minority candidate sued United Airlines. He said that its requirements that pilot candidates have 500 flight hours and college degrees were unfairly discriminatory. The court agreed that the requirements did have an adverse impact on members of the person's minority group. But it held that in light of the cost of the training program and the huge human and economic risks in hiring unqualified candidates, the selection standards were a business necessity and were job related.[85]

In general, when a job requires a small amount of skill and training, the courts closely scrutinize any preemployment standards or criteria that discriminate against minorities. There is a correspondingly lighter burden when the job requires a high degree of skill, and when the economic and human risks of hiring an unqualified applicant are great.[86]

Attempts by employers to show that their selection tests or other employment practices are *valid* are examples of the business necessity defense. Here the employer must show that the test or other practice is job related—in other words, that it is a valid predictor of performance on the job. Where the employer can establish such validity, the courts have generally supported using the test or other employment practice as a business necessity. In this context, *validity* means the degree to which the test or other employment practice is related to or predicts performance on the job; Chapter 6 explains validation. The following Know Your Employment law feature sums up how to apply all this.

KNOW YOUR EMPLOYMENT LAW

Examples of What You Can and Cannot Do

Before proceeding, we should review what federal fair employment laws allow (and do not allow) you to say and do.

Federal laws like Title VII usually don't expressly ban preemployment questions about an applicant's race, color, religion, sex, or national origin. In other words, "with the exception of personnel policies calling for outright discrimination against the members of some protected group," it's not the questions but their impact.[87] Thus, illustrative inquiries and practices like those on the next few pages are not illegal per se. For example, it isn't illegal to ask a job candidate about her marital status (although such a question might seem discriminatory). You can ask. However, be prepared to show either that you do not discriminate or that you can defend the practice as a BFOQ or business necessity.

But, in practice, there are two reasons to avoid such questions. First, although federal law may not bar such questions, many state and local laws do.

Second, the EEOC has said that it will disapprove of such practices, so just asking the questions may draw its attention. Such questions become illegal if a complainant can show you use them to screen out a greater proportion of his or her protected group's applicants, and you can't prove the practice is required as a business necessity or BFOQ.

Let's look now at some of the potentially discriminatory practices to avoid.[88]

Recruitment

Word of Mouth You cannot rely upon word-of-mouth dissemination of information about job opportunities when your workforce is all (or mostly all) white or all members of some other class such as all female, all Hispanic, and so on. Doing so reduces the likelihood that others will become aware of the jobs.

Misleading Information It is unlawful to give false or misleading information to members of any group, or to fail or refuse to advise them of work opportunities and the procedures for obtaining them.

Help-Wanted Ads "Help wanted—male" and "help wanted—female" ads are violations unless gender is a bona fide occupational qualification for the job. The same applies to ads that suggest age discrimination. For example, you cannot advertise for a "young" man or woman.

Selection Standards

Educational Requirements Courts have found educational qualifications to be illegal when (1) minority groups are less likely to possess the educational qualifications (such as a high school degree) and (2) such qualifications are also not job related. However, there may be jobs of course for which educational requirements (such as college degrees for pilot candidates) are a necessity.

Tests Courts deem tests unlawful if they disproportionately screen out minorities or women *and* they are not job related. According to a former U.S. Supreme Court Chief Justice,

> Nothing in the [Title VII] act precludes the use of testing or measuring procedures; obviously they are useful. What Congress has forbidden is giving these devices and mechanisms controlling force unless they are demonstrating a reasonable measure of job performance.

The employer must be prepared to show that the test results are job related—for instance, that test scores relate to on-the-job performance.

Preference to Relatives Do not give preference to relatives of current employees with respect to employment opportunities if your current employees are substantially nonminority.

Height, Weight, and Physical Characteristics Physical requirements such as minimum height are unlawful unless the employer can show they're job related. For example, a U.S. Appeals Court upheld a $3.4 million jury verdict against Dial Corp. Dial rejected 52 women for entry-level jobs at a meat-processing plant because they failed strength tests, although strength was not a job requirement.[89] *Maximum* weight rules generally don't trigger adverse legal rulings. To qualify for reasonable accommodation, obese applicants must be at least 100 pounds above their ideal weight or there must be a physiological cause for their disability. However, legalities aside, managers should be vigilant.[90] Studies show that obese individuals are less likely to be hired, less likely to receive promotions, more likely to get undesirable sales assignments, and more likely to receive poor customer service.[91]

Arrest Records Unless the job requires security clearance, do not ask an applicant whether he or she has been arrested or spent time in jail, or use an arrest record to disqualify a person automatically. Due to racial and ethnic disparities in arrest and prison rates, both the EEOC and the Office of Federal Contract Compliance Programs (OFCCP) recently set forth new guidance discouraging employers from using blanket exclusions against individuals with criminal records.[92]

Application Forms Employment applications generally shouldn't contain questions about applicants' disabilities, workers' compensation history, age, arrest record, or U.S. citizenship. It's generally best to collect personal information required for legitimate reasons (such as emergency contact) after you hire the person.[93]

Discharge Due to Garnishment Disproportionate numbers of minorities suffer garnishment procedures (in which creditors make a claim to some of the person's wages). Therefore, firing a minority member whose salary is garnished is illegal, unless you can show some overriding business necessity.

Sample Discriminatory Promotion, Transfer, and Layoff Practices

Fair employment laws protect not just job applicants but also current employees. For example, the Equal Pay Act requires that equal wages be paid for substantially similar work performed by men and women. Therefore, courts may hold that any employment practices regarding pay, promotion, termination, discipline, or benefits that

1. are applied differently to different classes of persons,
2. adversely impact members of a protected group, and
3. cannot be shown to be required as a BFOQ or business necessity are illegally discriminatory.

Personal Appearance Regulations and Title VII Employees sometimes file suits against employers' dress and appearance codes under Title VII. They usually claim sex discrimination, but sometimes claim racial or even religious discrimination. A sampling of court rulings follows:[94]

- **Dress.** In general, employers do not violate the Title VII ban on sex bias by requiring all employees to dress conservatively. For example, a supervisor's suggestion that a female attorney tone down her attire was permissible when the firm consistently sought to maintain a conservative dress style and counseled men to dress conservatively. However, Alamo Rent-A-Car lost a case when it tried to prevent a Muslim woman employee from wearing a headscarf.
- **Hair.** Here, courts usually favor employers. For example, employer rules against facial hair do not constitute sex discrimination because they discriminate only between clean-shaven and bearded men, discrimination not qualified as sex bias under Title VII. Courts have also rejected arguments that prohibiting cornrow hairstyles infringed on black employees' expression of cultural identification.
- **Uniforms.** When it comes to discriminatory uniforms and/or suggestive attire, however, courts frequently side with employees. For example, requiring female employees (such as waitresses) to wear sexually suggestive attire as a condition of employment has been ruled as violating Title VII in many cases.[95]
- **Tattoos and body piercings.** About 38% of Millennials in one survey had tattoos as compared with 15% of baby boomers. About 23% of Millennials had body piercings as compared with 1% of baby boomers. One case involved a waiter with religious tattoos on his wrists at a Red Robin Gourmet Burgers store. The company insisted he cover his tattoos at work; he refused. Red Robin settled the suit after the waiter claimed that covering the tattoos would be a sin based on his religion.[96]

Finally, keep three other things in mind:

1. *Good intentions are no excuse.* As the Supreme Court held in the *Griggs* case,
   Good intent or absence of discriminatory intent does not redeem procedures or testing mechanisms that operate as built-in headwinds for minority groups and are unrelated to measuring job capability.
2. One cannot claim that a *union agreement necessitates some discriminatory practice*. Equal employment opportunity laws prevail.[97]
3. A strong defense *is not your only recourse.* The employer can also respond by agreeing to eliminate the illegal practice and (when required) by compensating the people discriminated against.

The EEOC Enforcement Process

4 List the steps in the EEOC enforcement process.

Even careful employers eventually face employment discrimination claims and have to deal with the EEOC.[98] All managers (not just human resource managers) play roles in this process. Figure 2-3 provides an overview of this EEOC enforcement process.[99]

- *File Charge.* The process begins when someone files a claim with the EEOC. Either the aggrieved person or a member of the EEOC who has reasonable cause to believe that a violation occurred must file the claim in writing and under oath.[100] Under CRA 1991, the discrimination claim must be filed within 300 days (when there is a similar state law) or 180 days (where there is no similar state law) after the alleged incident took place (2 years for the Equal Pay Act).[101] The U.S. Supreme Court, in *Ledbetter v. Goodyear Tire & Rubber Company,* held that employees claiming Title VII pay discrimination must file their claims within 180 days of when they first receive the allegedly discriminatory pay. Congress then passed, and President Obama signed, the Lilly Ledbetter Fair Pay Act into law. Employees can now file such claims anytime, as long as they're still receiving an "infected" paycheck. (In fiscal year 2012, individuals filed 99,412 charges with the EEOC; the two largest categories were for retaliation [37,836 charges] and racial discrimination [33,512].[102]) One may obtain employment practices liability insurance against discrimination claims.[103]

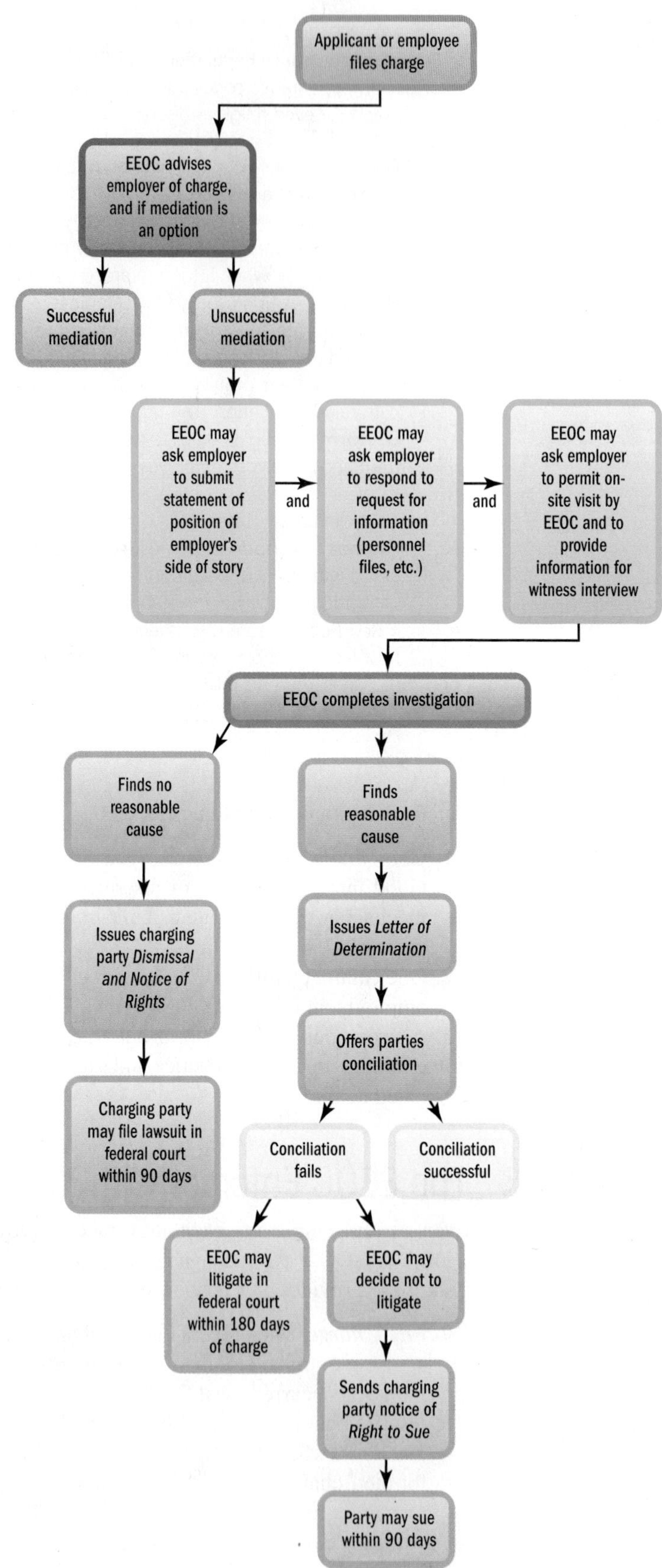

FIGURE 2-3 The EEOC Charge-Filing Process

Note: Parties may settle at any time.
Source: Based on information at www.eeoc.gov.

FIGURE 2-4 Questions to Ask When an Employer Receives Notice That the EEOC Has Filed a Bias Claim

Source: Bureau of National Affairs, Inc., "Fair Employment Practices: Summary of Latest Developments," January 7, 1983, p. 3; Kenneth Sovereign, *Personnel Law* (Upper Saddle River, NJ: Prentice Hall, 1999), pp. 36–37; and Equal Employment Opportunity Commission, "The Charge Handling Process," http://www.eeoc.gov/employers/process.cfm, accessed August 30, 2013.

1. Exactly what is the charge, and is your company covered by the relevant statutes? (For example, Title VII and the Americans with Disabilities Act generally apply only to employees with 15 or more employees.) Did the employee file his or her charge on time, and was it processed in a timely manner by the EEOC?
2. What protected group does the employee belong to?
3. Is the EEOC claiming disparate impact or disparate treatment?
4. Are there any obvious bases upon which you can challenge and/or rebut the claim? For example, would the employer have taken the action if the person did not belong to a protected group?
5. If it is a sexual harassment claim, are there offensive comments, calendars, posters, screensavers, and so on, on display in the company?
6. In terms of the practicality of defending your company against this claim, who are the supervisors who actually took the allegedly discriminatory actions, and how effective will they be as potential witnesses? Have you received an opinion from legal counsel regarding the chances of prevailing?

- ***Charge Acceptance.*** The EEOC's common practice is to accept a charge and orally refer it to the state or local agency on behalf of the charging party. If the agency waives jurisdiction or cannot obtain a satisfactory solution, the EEOC processes it upon the expiration of the deferral period.[104]
- ***Serve Notice.*** After a charge is filed (or the state or local deferral period has ended), the EEOC has 10 days to serve notice on the employer. Figure 2-4 lists some questions to ask after receiving a bias complaint from the EEOC.
- ***Investigation/Fact-Finding Conference.*** The EEOC then investigates the charge to determine whether there is reasonable cause to believe it is true; it has 120 days to decide.[105] Early in the investigation, the EEOC holds an initial *fact-finding conference.* The EEOC's focus here is often to find weak spots in each party's position. They use these to push for a settlement.
- ***Cause/No Cause.*** If it finds no reasonable cause, the EEOC must dismiss the charge, and must issue the charging party a Notice of Right to Sue. The person then has 90 days to file a suit on his or her own behalf.
- ***Conciliation.*** If the EEOC does find cause, it has 30 days to work out a conciliation agreement. The EEOC conciliator meets with the employee to determine what remedy would be satisfactory. It then tries to negotiate a settlement with the employer.
- ***Notice to Sue.*** If this conciliation is not satisfactory, the EEOC may bring a civil suit in a federal district court, or issue a Notice of Right to Sue to the person who filed the charge.

Voluntary Mediation

The EEOC refers about 10% of its charges to a voluntary mediation mechanism, "an informal process in which a neutral third party assists the opposing parties to reach a voluntary, negotiated resolution of a charge of discrimination."[106] If the parties don't reach agreement (or one of the parties rejects participation), the EEOC processes the charge through its usual mechanisms.[107]

Faced with an offer to mediate, the employer has three options: Agree to mediate the charge; make a settlement offer without mediation; or prepare a "position statement" for the EEOC. If the employer does not mediate or make an offer, the position statement is required. It should include a robust defense, including information relating to the company's business and the charging party's position; a description of any rules or policies and procedures that are applicable; and the chronology of the offense that led to the adverse action.[108]

Mandatory Arbitration of Discrimination Claims

Many employers, to avoid EEOC litigation, require applicants and employees to agree to arbitrate such claims. The EEOC does not favor mandatory arbitration. However, the U.S. Supreme Court's decisions (in *Gilmer v. Interstate/Johnson Lane Corp.* and similar cases) make it clear that "employment discrimination plaintiffs [employees] may be compelled to arbitrate their claims

FIGURE 2-5 Management Guidelines for Addressing EEOC Claims

Sources: "Tips for Employers on Dealing with EEOC Investigations," *BNA Fair Employment Practices*, October 31, 1996, p. 130; "Conducting Effective Investigations of Employee Bias Complaints," *BNA Fair Employment Practices*, July 13, 1995, p. 81; Commerce Clearing House, *Ideas and Trends*, January 23, 1987, pp. 14–15; http://eeoc.gov/employers/investigations.html, accessed October 4, 2009; and www.eeoc.gov/employers/process.cfm, accessed August 1, 2012.

During the EEOC Investigation:

Conduct your own investigation to get the facts.

Ensure that there is information in the EEOC's file *demonstrating lack of merit* of the charge.

Limit the information supplied to only those issues raised in the charge itself.

Get as much information as possible about the *charging party's claim*.

Meet with the employee who made the complaint to clarify all the relevant issues. For example, what happened? Who was involved?

Remember that *the EEOC can only ask (not compel) employers* to submit documents and ask for the testimony of witnesses under oath.

Give the EEOC a *position statement*. It should contain words to the effect that "the company has a policy against discrimination and would not discriminate in the manner charged in the complaint." Support the statement with documentation.

During the Fact-Finding Conference:

Because the only official record is the notes the EEOC investigator takes, *keep your own records*.

Bring an *attorney*.

Make sure you are *fully informed* of the charges and facts of the case.

Before appearing, *witnesses (especially supervisors) need to be aware* of the legal significance of the facts they will present.

During the EEOC Determination and Attempted Conciliation:

If there is a finding of cause, *review it carefully*, and point out inaccuracies in writing to the EEOC.

Use this letter to try again to convince the parties that the charge is *without merit*.

Conciliate prudently. If you have properly investigated the case, there may be no real advantage in settling at this stage.

Remember: It is likely that *no suit will be filed* by the EEOC.

under some circumstances."[109] Given this, employers "may wish to consider inserting a mandatory arbitration clause in their employment applications or employee handbooks."[110] To protect such a process against appeal, the employer should institute steps to protect against arbitrator bias, allow the arbitrator to offer a claimant broad relief (including reinstatement), and allow for a reasonable amount of prehearing fact finding.

alternative dispute resolution or ADR program
Grievance procedure that provides for binding arbitration as the last step.

Rockwell International has a grievance procedure that provides for binding arbitration as the last step. Called (as is traditional) an **alternative dispute resolution or ADR program**, Rockwell gradually extended the program to all nonunion employees at some locations. New hires at Rockwell must sign the agreement. Current employees must sign it prior to promotion or transfer. U.S. federal agencies must have ADR programs.[111] ADR plans are popular, although the EEOC generally prefers mediation for handling bias claims.[112]

diversity
The variety or multiplicity of demographic features that characterize a company's workforce, particularly in terms of race, sex, culture, national origin, handicap, age, and religion.

Figure 2-5 sums up guidelines employers should follow in addressing EEOC claims.

5 Discuss why diversity management is important and how to install a diversity management program.

Diversity Management

White males no longer dominate the labor force. Women and minorities will account for most labor force growth in the near future.[113] Employers today therefore often strive for diversity not just because the law says they must, but due to self-interest.[114] **Diversity** means being diverse or varied, and at work means having a workforce comprised of two or more groups of employees with various racial, ethnic, gender, cultural, national origin, handicap, age, and religious backgrounds.[115] We introduce diversity and diversity management here, and then address it in features throughout the book.

Potential Threats to Diversity

Workforce diversity produces both benefits and problems for employers. Unmanaged, it can produce behavioral barriers that reduce cooperation. Potential problems include:

stereotyping
Ascribing specific behavioral traits to individuals based on their apparent membership in a group.

- **Stereotyping**. Here someone ascribes specific behavioral traits to individuals based on their apparent membership in a group.[116] For example, "older people can't work hard."

Prejudice is a bias toward prejudging someone based on that person's traits, as in "we won't hire him because he's old."

- **Discrimination** is prejudice in action. It means taking specific actions toward or against the person based on the person's group.[117] Of course, it's generally illegal to discriminate at work based on someone's age, race, gender, disability, or national origin. But in practice, discrimination may be subtle. For example, many argue that a "glass ceiling," enforced by an "old boys' network" (friendships built in places like exclusive clubs), prevents women from reaching top management. Discrimination against Muslim employees is prohibited under Title VII. The number of such charges in rising quickly.[118]

discrimination
Taking specific actions toward or against a person based on the person's group.

- **Tokenism** means a company appoints a small group of women or minorities to high-profile positions, rather than more aggressively seeking full representation for that group.[119]
- **Ethnocentrism** is the tendency to view members of other social groups less favorably than one's own. Thus, in one study, managers attributed the performance of some minorities less to their abilities and more to help they received from others. The same managers attributed the performance of *non*minorities to their own abilities.[120]
- Discrimination against women goes beyond glass ceilings. Working women also confront **gender-role stereotypes**, the tendency to associate women with certain (frequently nonmanagerial) jobs.

tokenism
When a company appoints a small group of women or minorities to high-profile positions, rather than more aggressively seeking full representation for that group.

ethnocentrism
The tendency to view members of other social groups less favorably than members of one's own group.

gender-role stereotypes
The tendency to associate women with certain (frequently nonmanagerial) jobs.

Some Diversity Benefits

The key to deriving benefits is properly managing these potential problems. In one study, researchers examined the diversity climate in 654 stores of a large U.S. retail chain. They defined *diversity climate* as the extent to which employees in the stores said the firm promotes equal opportunity and inclusion. They found the highest sales growth in stores with the highest pro-diversity climate, and the lowest in stores where subordinates and managers reported less hospitable diversity climates.[121] Another study found racial discrimination to be related negatively to employee commitment, although organizational efforts to support diversity reduced such negative effects.[122]

Diversity Counts

Diversity can actually drive higher profits. For example, more than 50 of the largest U.S. companies, including GE, Microsoft, and Walmart, recently filed briefs with the U.S. Supreme Court arguing that affirmative action produces increased sales and profits. Thus, when Merck needed halal certification for one of its medicines, it turned to its Muslim employees. They helped Merck bring the product to market faster and helped ensure its acceptance among Muslims.[123]

Managing Diversity

Managing diversity means maximizing diversity's potential benefits while minimizing the potential problems—such as prejudice—that can undermine cooperation. In practice, diversity management involves both compulsory and voluntary actions. However, compulsory actions (particularly EEO compliance) can't guarantee cooperation. Managing diversity therefore usually relies on taking steps to encourage employees to work together productively.[124]

managing diversity
Maximizing diversity's potential benefits while minimizing its potential barriers.

Typically, this starts at the top. The employer institutes a *diversity management program*. A main aim is to make employees more sensitive to and better able to adapt to individual cultural differences.

Here one writer advocates a four-step "AGEM" diversity training process: Approach, Goals, Executive commitment, and Mandatory attendance. First, determine if diversity training is the solution or if some other approach is more advisable. If training is the solution, then set measurable program goals, for instance, having training participants evaluate their units' diversity efforts. Next, make sure a high-visibility executive commits to the program. Finally, make training mandatory.[125]

As an example, five sets of voluntary organizational activities often constitute such company-wide diversity management programs:[126]

Provide strong leadership. Companies with exemplary reputations in managing diversity typically have CEOs who champion the cause of diversity. Leadership means, for instance, becoming a role model for the behaviors required for the change.

Assess the situation. One study found that the most common tools for assessing a company's diversity include equal employment hiring and retention metrics, employee attitude surveys, management and employee evaluations, and focus groups.

Provide diversity training and education. The most common starting point for a diversity management effort is usually some type of employee education program.

Change culture and management systems. Combine education programs with other concrete steps aimed at changing the organization's culture and management systems. For example, change the performance appraisal procedure to appraise supervisors based partly on their success in reducing intergroup conflicts.

Evaluate the diversity management program. For example, do employee attitude surveys now indicate any improvement in employees' attitudes toward diversity?

One expert helps turn high-potential minority employees into senior leaders; he says employers tend to make four mistakes when cultivating minorities for higher positions. Rather than centralizing diversity management *they distribute diversity tasks* among various recruiting teams, while limiting their diversity departments primarily to retention and inclusiveness; the solution here is more central direction. They *focus on "inputs"* such as mentoring programs, rather than on outcomes such as the number of diversity candidates who gained promotions; goal setting is one solution. They focus on "*fixing the culture,*" which is typically a multiyear process; cultural change should be just one element of the process. Finally, they often staff their diversity departments with new minority employees; the solution is to rotate high-performance minority or nonminority line executives into diversity roles.[127]

Implementing the Affirmative Action Program

Equal employment opportunity aims to ensure that anyone, regardless of race, color, disability, sex, religion, national origin, or age, has an equal opportunity based on his or her qualifications. *Affirmative action* means taking actions (in recruitment, hiring, promotions, and compensation) to eliminate the current effects of past discrimination.

Affirmative action is still a significant workplace issue today. The incidences of major court-mandated affirmative action programs are down, but courts still use them. Furthermore, many employers must still engage in voluntary programs. For example, Executive Order (EO) 11246 (issued in 1965) requires federal contractors to take affirmative action to improve employment

Diversity management can blend a diverse workforce into a close-knit and productive community.

iStockphoto/Thinkstock

FIGURE 2-6 Steps in an Affirmative Action Program

1. Issue a written equal employment policy indicating that the firm is an equal employment opportunity employer and the employer's commitment to affirmative action.
2. Demonstrate top-management support for the equal employment policy—for instance, appoint a high-ranking EEO administrator.
3. Publicize internally and externally the equal employment policy and affirmative action commitment.
4. Survey current minority and female employment by department and job classification to determine where affirmative action programs are especially desirable.
5. Carefully analyze employer human resources practices to identify and eliminate hidden barriers.
6. Review, develop, and implement specific HR programs to improve female and minority utilization.
7. Use focused recruitment to find qualified applicants from the target group(s).
8. Establish an internal audit and reporting system to monitor and evaluate progress.
9. Develop support for the affirmative action program, inside the company and in the community.

opportunities for groups such as women and racial minorities. It covers about 22% of the U.S. workforce.[128]

Under guidelines such as EO 11246, the key aims of affirmative action programs are (1) to use numerical analysis to determine which (if any) target groups the firm is underutilizing relative to the relevant labor market, and (2) to eliminate the barriers to equal employment. Many employers pursue these aims with a **good-faith effort strategy**; this emphasizes identifying and eliminating the obstacles to hiring and promoting women and minorities, and increasing the minority or female applicant flow. Reasonable steps to take include those shown in Figure 2-6.

good-faith effort strategy
An affirmative action strategy that emphasizes identifying and eliminating the obstacles to hiring and promoting women and minorities, and increasing the minority or female applicant flow.

For example, place recruiting ads on online minority-oriented job sites. For example, Recruiting-Online.com lists dozens of online diversity candidate resources (www.recruiting-online.com/course55.html). Diversity candidate websites with job banks include the National Urban League, Hispanic Online, Latino Web, Society of Hispanic Engineers, Gay.com, Association for Women in Science, and Minorities Job Bank.

EMPLOYEE RESISTANCE Avoiding employee resistance to affirmative action programs is important. Here, studies suggest that current employees need to believe the program is fair. *Transparent selection procedures* (making it clear what selection tools and standards the company uses) help in this regard. *Communication* is also crucial. Show that the program doesn't involve preferential selection standards. Provide details on the qualifications of all new hires (both minority and nonminority). *Justifications* for the program should emphasize redressing past discrimination and the practical value of diversity, not underrepresentation.[129]

PROGRAM EVALUATION How can one tell if the diversity initiatives are effective? Some commonsense questions can be asked:

- Are there women and minorities reporting directly to senior managers?
- Do women and minorities have a fair share of the jobs that are the traditional steppingstones to successful careers in the company?
- Do women and minorities have equal access to international assignments?
- Is the employer taking steps that ensure that female and minority candidates will be in the company's career development pipeline?
- Are turnover rates for female and minority managers the same or lower than those for white males?
- Do employees report that they perceive positive behavior changes as a result of the diversity efforts?[130]

Reverse Discrimination

Reverse discrimination means discriminating against *non*minority applicants and employees. Many court cases addressed these issues, but until recently, few consistent answers emerged.

reverse discrimination
Claim that due to affirmative action quota systems, white males are discriminated against.

In one of the first such cases, *Bakke v. Regents of the University of California* (1978), the University of California at Davis Medical School denied admission to white student Allen Bakke, allegedly because of the school's affirmative action quota system, which required that a specific number of openings go to minority applicants. In a 5-to-4 vote, the U.S. Supreme Court struck down the policy that made race the only factor in considering applications for a certain number of class openings and thus allowed Bakke's admission.

Bakke was followed by many other cases. In June 2009, the U.S. Supreme Court ruled in an important reverse discrimination suit brought by Connecticut firefighters. In *Ricci v. DeStefano*, 19 white firefighters and one Hispanic firefighter said the city of New Haven should have promoted them based on their successful test scores. The city argued that certifying the tests would have left them vulnerable to lawsuits from minorities for violating Title VII.[131] The Court ruled in favor of the (predominantly white) plaintiffs. In New Haven's desire to avoid making promotions that might appear to adversely impact minorities, Justice Kennedy wrote that "The city rejected the test results solely because the higher scoring candidates were white." The consensus of observers was that the decision would make it much harder for employers to ignore the results obtained by valid tests, even if the results disproportionately impact minorities.[132]

The bottom line seems to be that employers should emphasize the external recruitment and internal development of better-qualified minority and female employees, "while basing employment decisions on legitimate criteria."[133] The HR Tools for Line Managers and Entrepreneurs feature sums up important EEO points line managers should keep in mind.

IMPROVING PERFORMANCE: HR Tools for Line Managers and Entrepreneurs

Human resource managers help employers navigate EEO problems, but the supervisor usually triggers the problem. Even telling a female candidate you're concerned about her safety on the job after dark might trigger a costly claim.

Keep three things in mind. First, knowing this chapter's contents (and particularly the Know Your Employment Law feature on pages 41–43) is important. For example, *understand the questions* you can and cannot ask when interviewing applicants, and know what *constitutes* sexual harassment. Avoiding EEO claims is one of the simplest things you can do to save your employer money.

Second, know that the courts may hold you (not just your employer) personally liable for your injudicious actions. *Management malpractice* is aberrant conduct on the part of the manager that has serious consequences for the employee's personal or physical well-being, or that "exceeds all bounds usually tolerated by society."[134] In one outrageous example noted earlier, the employer demoted a manager to janitor and took other steps to humiliate the person. The jury subsequently awarded the former manager millions. Supervisors who commit management malpractice may be personally liable for paying some of the judgment.

Third, *retaliation* is illegal under equal rights laws. To paraphrase the EEOC, "all of the laws we enforce make it illegal to fire, demote, harass, or otherwise 'retaliate' against people because they filed a charge, complained to their employer or other covered entity about discrimination, or because they participated in a discrimination investigation or lawsuit."[135] Retaliation charges are the most common charges filed with the EEOC.[136] In one U.S. Supreme Court case, the employee complained to a government agency that her employer paid her less than male counterparts. Soon after, the company fired her fiancé, who also worked for the firm. Finding for the employee, the U.S. Supreme Court decision said, "a reasonable worker might be dissuaded from engaging in protected activity" if she knew that her fiancé would be fired.[137]

Discussion Question 2-2: Check with the EEOC's website and compile a list of the biggest financial settlements this past year for retaliation claims. About how much was the average claim?

Review

MyManagementLab Go to **mymanagementlab.com** to complete the problems marked with this icon.

Chapter Section Summaries

1. Several of the most important **equal employment opportunity laws became law in the period from 1964 to 1991.**
   - Of these, Title VII of the 1964 Civil Rights Act was pivotal, and states that an employer cannot discriminate based on race, color, religion, sex, or national origin. This act established the Equal Employment Opportunity Commission, and covers most employees.
   - Under the Equal Pay Act of 1963 (amended in 1972), it is unlawful to discriminate in pay on the basis of sex when jobs involve equal work, skills, effort, and responsibility, and are performed under similar working conditions.
   - The Age Discrimination in Employment Act of 1967 made it unlawful to discriminate against employees or applicants who are between 40 and 65 years of age.
   - The Vocational Rehabilitation Act of 1973 requires most employers with federal contracts to take affirmative action when employing handicapped persons.
   - The Pregnancy Discrimination Act of 1978 prohibits using pregnancy, childbirth, or related medical conditions to discriminate in hiring, promotion, suspension, or discharge, or in any term or condition of employment.
   - The EEOC, Civil Service Commission, Department of Labor, and Department of Justice together issued Uniform Guidelines that set forth "highly recommended" procedures regarding HR activities like employee selection, record keeping, and preemployment inquiries.
   - One of the most important cases during this early period was *Griggs v. Duke Power Company.* Here, Chief Justice Burger held that in employment, discrimination does not have to be overt to be illegal, and an employment practice that discriminates must be job related.
2. Equal employment law continues to evolve, with important **new legislation being enacted since 1990–1991**.
   - The Civil Rights Act of 1991 reversed the effects of several Supreme Court rulings—for instance, underscoring that the burden of proof is the employer's once a plaintiff establishes possible illegal discrimination.
   - The Americans with Disabilities Act prohibits employment discrimination against qualified disabled individuals. It also says employers must make "reasonable accommodations" for physical or mental limitations unless doing so imposes an "undue hardship" on the business.
   - Although Title VII made sexual harassment at work illegal, the Federal Violence Against Women Act of 1994 provided women with another way to seek relief for (violent) sexual harassment. Basically, sexual harassment refers to unwelcome sexual advances, requests for sexual favors, and other verbal or physical conduct of a sexual nature that takes place, for instance, when such conduct is made either explicitly or implicitly a term or condition of an individual's employment. Three main ways to prove sexual harassment include *quid pro quo*, hostile environment created by supervisors, and hostile environment created by coworkers who are not employees.
3. Employers use various **defenses against discrimination allegations**. In defending themselves against discrimination allegations, employers need to distinguish between disparate treatment (intentional discrimination) and disparate impact (a policy that has an adverse impact regardless of intent). Plaintiffs show adverse impact by the standard deviation rule or by showing disparate rejection rates, restricted policy, or population comparisons, or by applying the McDonnell-Douglas test. Employers defend themselves by showing that the employment practice is a bona fide occupational qualification (for instance, gender is a BFOQ for a position such as model). Or they may defend themselves by using the business necessity defense, which requires showing that there is an overriding business purpose.

   Given this, it is useful to have a working knowledge of *discriminatory employment practices*. For example, in recruitment, employers no longer use "help wanted—male" ads and endeavor to ensure that educational requirements are necessary to do the job. Similarly, in promotion and transfer, the Equal Pay Act requires that equal wages be paid for substantially similar work performed by men and women.
4. All managers play an important role in **the EEOC enforcement process.** The basic steps in this process include filing the charge, charge acceptance by the

EEOC, serving notice on the employer, the investigation/fact-finding conference, a finding of cause/no cause, conciliation efforts, and (if necessary) a notice to sue. The EEOC refers about 10% of its charges to voluntary mediation mechanisms.

5. With an increasingly diverse workforce, **diversity management** is a key managerial skill. Managing diversity means maximizing diversity's potential benefits while minimizing the potential barriers. In one typical approach, the steps include providing strong leadership, assessing the situation, providing diversity training and education, changing the culture and management systems, and evaluating the diversity management program's results. Affirmative action generally means taking actions to eliminate the present effects of past discrimination. Many employers still pursue voluntary, good-faith effort strategies in identifying and eliminating the obstacles to hiring and promoting women and minorities, while some employers are under court-mandated requirement to do so.

Discussion Questions

✪ **2-3.** What important precedents were set by the *Griggs v. Duke Power Company* case? The *Albemarle v. Moody* case?

2-4. What is adverse impact? How can it be proved?

✪ **2-5.** What is sexual harassment? How can an employee prove sexual harassment?

2-6. What is the difference between disparate treatment and disparate impact?

Individual and Group Activities

2-7. Working individually or in groups, respond to these three scenarios based on what you learned in this chapter. Under what conditions (if any) do you think the following constitute sexual harassment? (a) A female manager fires a male employee because he refuses her requests for sexual favors. (b) A male manager refers to female employees as "sweetie" or "baby." (c) A female employee overhears two male employees exchanging sexually oriented jokes.

2-8. Working individually or in groups, discuss how you would set up an affirmative action program.

2-9. Compare and contrast the issues presented in *Bakke* with more recent court rulings on affirmative action. Working individually or in groups, discuss the current direction of affirmative action.

2-10. Working individually or in groups, write a one-page paper titled "What the Manager Should Know About How the EEOC Handles a Person's Discrimination Charge."

2-11. Explain the difference between affirmative action and equal employment opportunity.

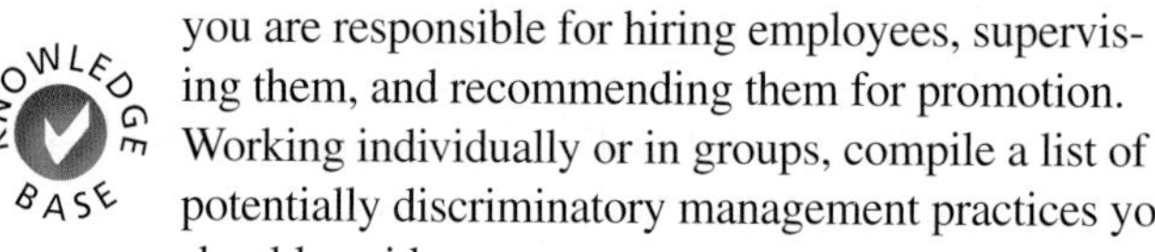

2-12. Assume you are the manager in a small restaurant; you are responsible for hiring employees, supervising them, and recommending them for promotion. Working individually or in groups, compile a list of potentially discriminatory management practices you should avoid.

2-13. Appendix A, PHR and SPHR Knowledge Base, at the end of this book (pages 580–588) lists the knowledge someone studying for the HRCI certification exam needs to have in each area of human resource management (such as in Strategic Management, Workforce Planning, and Human Resource Development). In groups of four to five students, do four things: (1) review Appendix A; (2) identify the material in this chapter that relates to the required knowledge Appendix A lists; (3) write four multiple-choice exam questions on this material that you believe would be suitable for inclusion in the HRCI exam; and (4) if time permits, have someone from your team post your team's questions in front of the class, so that students in all teams can answer the exam questions created by the other teams.

Experiential Exercise

"Space Cadet" or Victim?

Discrimination lawsuits are rarely simple, because the employer will often argue that the person was fired due to poor performance rather than discrimination. So, there's often a "mixed-motive" element to such situations. The facts of a case illustrate this (*Burk v. California Association of Realtors*, California Court of Appeals, number 161513, unpublished, 12/12/03). The facts were as follows. The California Association of Realtors maintained a hotline service to provide legal advice to real estate agents. One of the 12 lawyers who answered this hotline was a 61-year-old California attorney who worked there from 1989 to 2000. Until 1996 he received mostly good reviews. At that time, Association members began filing complaints about his advice. His supervisor told him to be more courteous.

Two years later, Association members were still complaining about this individual. Among other things, Association members who called in filed complaints referring to him as "a space cadet," and "incompetent." Subsequently, his supervisor contacted six Association members whom the 61-year-old lawyer had recently counseled; five of the six said they had had bad experiences. The Association fired him for mistreating Association members and providing inadequate legal advice.

The 61-year-old lawyer sued the Association, claiming that the firing was age related. To support his claim, he noted that one colleague had told him that he was "probably getting close to retirement" and that another colleague had told him he was "getting older." The appeals court had to decide whether the Association fired the 61-year-old lawyer because of his age or because of his performance.

Purpose: The purpose of this exercise is to provide practice in analyzing and applying knowledge of equal opportunity legislation to a real problem.

Required Understanding: Be thoroughly familiar with the material presented in this chapter. In addition, read the preceding "space cadet" case on which this experiential exercise is based.

How to Set Up the Exercise/Instructions:

- Divide the class into groups.
- Each group should develop answers to the following questions:
  - **2-14.** Based on what you read in this chapter, on what legal basis could the 61-year-old California attorney claim he was a victim of discrimination?
  - **2-15.** On what laws and legal concepts did the employer apparently base its termination of this 61-year-old attorney?
  - **2-16.** Based on what laws or legal concepts could you take the position that it is legal to fire someone for poor performance even though there may be a discriminatory aspect to the termination? (This is not to say that there necessarily was such a discriminatory aspect with this case.)
  - **2-17.** If you were the judge called on to make a decision on this case, what would your decision be, and why?
- The court's decision follows, so please do not read this until you've completed the exercise.

In this case, the California State Appeals court held that "the only reasonable inference that can be drawn from the evidence is that [plaintiff] was terminated because he failed to competently perform his job of providing thorough, accurate, and courteous legal advice to hotline callers."

Source: "On Appeal, Hotheaded Hotline Lawyer Loses Age, Disability Discrimination Claims," *BNA Human Resources Report*, January 12, 2004, p. 17.

Video Case

Video Title: Equal Employment (UPS)

SYNOPSIS

A former HR director for UPS, now the president of "The Virtual HR Director," gives some perspective on what diversity means, and what its value can be to a company. Employees of a wide variety of backgrounds are intrinsically valuable to a company in the varied perspectives that they bring to the table, and can help a company find creative solutions to new problems that it has not encountered before.

In a diverse workplace, where employees come from a variety of backgrounds and ethnicities, there is always the possibility of harassment between employees. This video addresses the value of diversity sensitivity training in its capacity to help prevent incidence of employee harassment. Effective and constructive corrective measures for incidents of harassment are also discussed.

Discussion Questions

2-18. What kinds of things does Gary Wheeler think a diverse workforce can contribute to a company?

2-19. What typical avenues are open to an employee who feels he or she is being harassed, in order to make sure it is dealt with properly?

2-20. What does Gary Wheeler report is most often the basis of reported claims of harassment, and how are these cases dealt with?

2-21. What else would you do to deal with employees who are hostile to the idea of diversity?

2-22. To what extent do you believe that harassment, such as sexual harassment, is usually primarily a communications problem? Why?

2-23. In this video, Mr. Wheeler focuses mostly on diversity and on sexual harassment. Discuss five other aspects of equal employment opportunity at work that are also important.

Application Case

An Accusation of Sexual Harassment in Pro Sports

The jury in a sexual harassment suit brought by a former high-ranking New York Knicks basketball team executive awarded her more than $11 million in punitive damages. Officials of Madison Square Garden (which owns the Knicks) said they would appeal the verdict. However, even if they were to win on appeal (which one University of Richmond Law School professor said was unlikely), the case still exposed the organization and its managers to a great deal of unfavorable publicity.

The federal suit pitted Anucha Browne Sanders, the Knicks' senior vice president of marketing and business operations (and former Northwestern University basketball star), against the team's owner, Madison Square Garden, and its president, Isiah Thomas. The suit charged them with sex discrimination and retaliation. Ms. Browne Sanders accused Mr. Thomas of verbally abusing and sexually harassing her over a 2-year period. She said the Garden fired her about a month after she complained to top management about the harassment. At the trial, the Garden cited numerous explanations for the dismissal, saying she had "failed to fulfill professional responsibilities." At a news conference,

Browne Sanders said that Thomas "refused to stop his demeaning and repulsive behavior and the Garden refused to intercede." Mr. Thomas vigorously insisted he was innocent. According to one report of the trial, her claims of harassment and verbal abuse had little corroboration from witnesses, but neither did the Garden's claims that her performance had been subpar. After the jury decision came in, Browne Sanders's lawyers said, "This [decision] confirms what we've been saying all along, that [Browne Sanders] was sexually abused and fired for complaining about it." The Garden's statement said, in part, "We look forward to presenting our arguments to an appeals court and believe they will agree that no sexual harassment took place."

Questions

2-24. Do you think Ms. Browne Sanders had the basis for a sexual harassment suit? Why?

2-25. From what you know of this case, do you think the jury arrived at the correct decision? If not, why not? If so, why?

2-26. Based on the few facts that you have, what steps could Garden management have taken to protect itself from liability in this matter?

2-27. Aside from the appeal, what would you do now if you were the Garden's top management?

2-28. "The allegations against Madison Square Garden in this case raise ethical questions with regard to the employer's actions." Explain whether you agree or disagree with this statement, and why.

Sources: "Jury Awards $11.6 Million to Former Executive of Pro Basketball Team in Harassment Case," *BNA Bulletin to Management*, October 9, 2007, p. 323; Richard Sandomir, "Jury Finds Knicks and Coach Harassed a Former Executive," *New York Times*, www.nytimes.com/2007/10/03/sports/basketball/03garden.html?em&ex=1191556800&en=41d47437f805290d&ei=5087%0A, accessed November 31, 2007; and "Thomas Defiant in Face of Harassment Claims," espn.com, accessed November 31, 2007.

Continuing Case

Carter Cleaning Company

A Question of Discrimination

One of the first problems Jennifer faced at her father's Carter Cleaning Centers concerned the inadequacies of the firm's current HR management practices and procedures.

One problem that particularly concerned her was the lack of attention to equal employment matters. Each store manager independently handled virtually all hiring; the managers had received no training regarding such fundamental matters as the types of questions they should not ask of job applicants. It was therefore not unusual for female applicants to be asked questions such as "Who's going to take care of your children while you are at work?" and for minority applicants to be asked questions about arrest records and credit histories. Nonminority applicants—three store managers were white males and three were white females—were not asked these questions, as Jennifer discerned from her interviews with the managers. Based on discussions with her father, Jennifer deduced two reasons for the laid-back attitude toward equal employment: (1) her father's lack of insight about the legal requirements and (2) the fact that, as Jack Carter put it, "Virtually all our workers are women or minority members anyway, so no one can come in here and accuse us of being discriminatory, can they?"

Jennifer decided to mull that question over, but before she could, she was faced with two serious equal rights problems. Two women in one store privately confided to her that their manager was making unwelcome sexual advances toward them. One claimed he had threatened to fire her unless she "socialized" with him after hours. And during a fact-finding trip to another store, an older gentleman—he was 73 years old—complained of the fact that although he had almost 50 years of experience, he was paid less than people half his age in the same job. Jennifer's review of the stores resulted in the following questions.

Questions

2-29. Is it true, as Jack Carter claims, that "Virtually all our workers are women or minority members anyway, so no one can come in here and accuse us of being discriminatory"?

2-30. How should Jennifer and her company address the sexual harassment charges and problems?

2-31. How should she and her company address the possible problems of age discrimination?

2-32. Given the fact that each of its stores has only a handful of employees, is her company covered by equal rights legislation?

2-33. And finally, aside from the specific problems, what other personnel management matters (application forms, training, and so on) have to be reviewed given the need to bring them into compliance with equal rights laws?

MyManagementLab

Go to **mymanagementlab.com** for Auto-graded writing questions as well as the following Assisted-graded writing questions:

2-34. Explain the main features of Title VII, the Equal Pay Act, the Pregnancy Discrimination Act, the Americans with Disabilities Act, and the Civil Rights Act of 1991.

2-35. What are the two main defenses you can use in the event of a discriminatory practice allegation, and what exactly do they involve?

2-36. MyManagementLab only—comprehensive writing assignment for this chapter.

Key Terms

Title VII of the 1964 Civil Rights Act, 28
Equal Employment Opportunity Commission (EEOC), 28
affirmative action, 28
Office of Federal Contract Compliance Programs (OFCCP), 28
Equal Pay Act of 1963, 28
Age Discrimination in Employment Act of 1967 (ADEA), 29
Vocational Rehabilitation Act of 1973, 29
Pregnancy Discrimination Act, 29
Uniform Guidelines, 29
protected class, 30
Civil Rights Act of 1991 (CRA 1991), 30
"mixed-motive" case, 31
Americans with Disabilities Act (ADA), 31
qualified individuals, 31
sexual harassment, 34
Federal Violence Against Women Act of 1994, 34
adverse impact, 37
disparate rejection rates, 38
4/5ths rule, 38
restricted policy, 39
bona fide occupational qualification (BFOQ), 40
alternative dispute resolution or ADR program, 46
diversity, 46
stereotyping, 46
discrimination, 47
tokenism, 47
ethnocentrism, 47
gender-role stereotypes, 47
managing diversity, 47
good-faith effort strategy, 49
reverse discrimination, 49

Endnotes

1. For example, see http://eeoc.gov/eeoc/newsroom/index.cfm. As another example, in a recent conciliation agreement between FedEx Corp. and the Department of Labor's Office of Federal Contract Compliance Programs, FedEx agreed to pay $3 million and amend its practices to settle charges that it discriminated against thousands of applicants. "FedEx to Pay $3 Million, Amend Practices to Settle OFCCP Charges of Bias in Hiring," *Bloomberg BNA Bulletin to Management*, March 27, 2012, p. 97.
2. Betsy Morris, "How Corporate America Is Betraying Women," *Fortune*, January 10, 2005, pp. 64–70.
3. Based on or quoted from International Association of Official Human Rights Agencies, *Principles of Employment Discrimination Law* (Washington, DC.). See also Bruce Feldacker, *Labor Guide to Labor Law* (Upper Saddle River, NJ: Prentice Hall, 2000); "EEOC Attorneys Highlight How Employers Can Better Their Nondiscrimination Practices," *BNA Bulletin to Management*, July 20, 2008, p. 233; and www.eeoc.gov, accessed August 4. 2013. Plaintiffs still bring equal employment claims under the Civil Rights Act of 1866. For example, in 2008 the U.S. Supreme Court held that the act prohibits retaliation against someone who complains of discrimination against others when contract rights (in this case, an employment agreement) are at stake. Charles Louderback, "U.S. Supreme Court Decisions Expand Employees' Ability to Bring Retaliation Claims," *Compensation & Benefits Review*, September/October 2008, p. 52. Employment discrimination law is a changing field, and the appropriateness of the rules, guidelines, and conclusions in this chapter may also be affected by factors unique to the employer's operation. They should be reviewed by the employer's attorney before implementation.
4. For a recent conciliation agreement, see "FedEx to Pay $3 Million, Amend Practices to Settle OFCCP Charges of Bias in Hiring," *Bloomberg BNA Bulletin to Management*, March 27, 2012, p. 97.
5. Individuals may file under the Equal Employment Act of 1972.
6. "The Employer Should Validate Hiring Tests to Withstand EEOC Scrutiny, Officials Advise," *BNA Bulletin to Management*, April 1, 2008, p. 107. President Obama's administration recently directed more funds and staffing to the OFCCP. "Restructured, Beefed Up OFCCP May Shift Policy Emphasis, Attorney Says," *BNA Bulletin to Management*, August 18, 2009, p. 257.
7. See, for example, "Divided EEOC Approves Draft of Rule Amending Age Discrimination Regulations," *BNA Bulletin to Management*, November 22, 2011, p. 369.
8. "High Court: ADEA Does Not Protect Younger Workers Treated Worse Than Their Elders," *BNA Bulletin to Management* 55, no. 10 (March 4, 2004), pp. 73–80. See also D. Aaron Lacy, "You Are Not Quite as Old as You Think: Making the Case for Reverse Age Discrimination Under the ADEA," *Berkeley Journal of Employment and Labor Law* 26, no. 2 (2005), pp. 363–403; Nancy Ursel and Marjorie Armstrong-Stassen, "How Age Discrimination in Employment Affects Stockholders," *Journal of Labor Research* 17, no. 1 (Winter 2006), pp. 89–99; and www.eeoc.gov/laws/statutes/adea.cfm, accessed October 3, 2011.
9. "Google Exec Can Pursue Claim," *BNA Bulletin to Management*, October 20, 2007, p. 342; and "Fired Google Manager May Proceed with Age Bias Suit, California Justices Rule," *BNA Bulletin to Management*, August 10, 2010, p. 249.
10. www.eeoc.gov/laws/statutes/adea.cfm, accessed October 3, 2011.
11. The U.S. Supreme Court ruled in *California Federal Savings and Loan Association v. Guerra* that if an employer offers no disability leave to any of its employees, it can (but need not) grant pregnancy leave to a woman disabled for pregnancy, childbirth, or a related medical condition.
12. John Kohl, Milton Mayfield, and Jacqueline Mayfield, "Recent Trends in Pregnancy Discrimination Law," *Business Horizons* 48, no. 5 (September 2005), pp. 421–429; and www.eeoc.gov/eeoc/statistics/enforcement/pregnancy.cfm, accessed October 3, 2011.
13. Nancy Woodward, "Pregnancy Discrimination Grows," *HR Magazine*, July 2005, p. 79.
14. "Pregnancy Claims Rising; Consistent Procedures Paramount," *BNA Bulletin to Management*, November 23, 2010, p. 375.
15. www.uniformguidelines.com/uniformguidelines.html, accessed November 23, 2007.
16. The EEOC and the OFCCP agreed to coordinate their efforts more closely and to share information on employers with federal contracts or subcontracts. "EEOC, OFCCP Issue Updated Agreement on Coordinated Enforcement, Data Sharing," *BNA Bulletin to Management*, November 22, 2011, p. 371.
17. *Griggs v. Duke Power Company*, 3FEP cases 175.
18. This is applicable only to Title VII and CRA 91; other statutes require intent.
19. James Ledvinka, *Federal Regulation of Personnel and Human Resources Management* (Boston: Kent, 1982), p. 41.
20. Bruce Feldacker, *Labor Guide to Labor Law* (Upper Saddle River, NJ: Prentice Hall, 2000), p. 513.
21. "The Eleventh Circuit Explains Disparate Impact, Disparate Treatment," *BNA Fair Employment Practices*, August 17, 2000, p. 102. See also Kenneth York, "Disparate Results in Adverse Impact Tests: The 4/5ths Rule and the Chi Square Test," *Public Personnel Management* 31, no. 2 (Summer 2002), pp. 253–262; and "Burden of Proof Under the Employment Non-Discrimination Act," www.civilrights.org/lgbt/enda/burden-of-proof.html, accessed August 8, 2011.

22. We'll see that the process of filing a discrimination charge goes something like this: The plaintiff (say, a rejected applicant) demonstrates that an employment practice (such as a test) has a disparate (or "adverse") impact on a particular group. *Disparate impact* means that an employer engages in an employment practice or policy that has a greater adverse impact (effect) on the members of a protected group under Title VII than on other employees, regardless of intent. (Requiring a college degree for a job would have an adverse impact on some minority groups, for instance.) Disparate impact claims do *not* require proof of discriminatory intent. Instead, the plaintiff's burden is to show two things. First, he or she must show that a significant disparity exists between the proportion of (say) women in the available labor pool and the proportion hired. Second, he or she must show that an apparently neutral employment practice, such as word-of-mouth advertising or a requirement that the jobholder "be able to lift 100 pounds," is causing the disparity. Then, once the plaintiff fulfills his or her burden of showing such disparate impact, the *employer* has the heavier burden of proving that the challenged practice is job related. For example, the employer has to show that lifting 100 pounds is actually required for effectively performing the position in question, and that the business could not run efficiently without the requirement—that it is a business necessity.
23. Commerce Clearing House, "House and Senate Pass Civil Rights Compromise by Wide Margin," *Ideas and Trends in Personnel*, November 13, 1991, p. 179.
24. Mark Kobata, "The Civil Rights Act of 1991," *Personnel Journal*, March 1992, p. 48.
25. Again, though, if the "employer shows that it would have taken the same action even absent the discriminatory motive, the complaining employee will not be entitled to reinstatement, back pay, or damages"; www.eeoc.gov/policy/docs/caregiving.html#mixed, accessed September 24, 2011.
26. Elliot H. Shaller and Dean Rosen, "A Guide to the EEOC's Final Regulations on the Americans with Disabilities Act," *Employee Relations Law Journal* 17, no. 3 (Winter 1991–1992), pp. 405–430; and www.eeoc.gov/ada, accessed November 20, 2007.
27. "ADA: Simple Common Sense Principles," *BNA Fair Employment Practices*, June 4, 1992, p. 63; and www.eeoc.gov/facts/ada17.html, accessed September 24, 2011.
28. Shaller and Rosen, "A Guide to the EEOC's Final Regulations," p. 408. Other specific examples include "epilepsy, diabetes, cancer, HIV infection, and bipolar disorder"; www1.eeoc.gov//laws/regulations/adaaa_fact_sheet, accessed October 3, 2011.
29. Shaller and Rosen, "A Guide to the EEOC's Final Regulations," p. 409. Thus, one court recently held that a worker currently engaging in illegal use of drugs was "not a qualified individual with a disability" under the ADA. "Drug Addict Lacks ADA Protection, Quarter Firms," *BNA Bulletin to Management*, April 26, 2011, p. 133.
30. James McDonald Jr., "The Americans with Difficult Personalities Act," *Employee Relations Law Journal* 25, no. 4 (Spring 2000), pp. 93–107; and Betsy Bates, "Mental Health Problems Predominate in ADA Claims," *Clinical Psychiatry News*, May 2003, http://findarticles.com/p/articles/mi_hb4345/is_5_31/ai_n29006702, accessed September 24, 2011. For a detailed discussion of dealing with this issue, see www.eeoc.gov/facts/intellectual_disabilities.html, accessed September 2, 2011.
31. "EEOC Guidance on Dealing with Intellectual Disabilities," *Workforce Management*, March 2005, p. 16.
32. "Driver Fired After Seizure on Job Lacks ADA Claim," *BNA Bulletin to Management*, January 4, 2011, p. 6.
33. www.ada.gov/reg3a.html#Anchor-Appendix-52467, accessed January 23, 2009.
34. See "EEOC Guidance on Telecommuting as ADA Accommodation Discussed," *Bloomberg BNA Bulletin to Management*, October 16, 2012, p. 335.
35. Martha Frase, "An Underestimated Talent Pool," *HR Magazine*, April 2009, pp. 55–58; and Nicole LaPorte, "Hiring the Blind, While Making a Green Statement," *New York Times*, March 25, 2012, p. b3.
36. M. P. McQueen, "Workplace Disabilities Are on the Rise," *The Wall Street Journal*, May 1, 2007, p. A1.
37. "No Sitting for Store Greeter," *BNA Fair Employment Practices*, December 14, 1995, p. 150. For more recent illustrative cases, see Tillinghast Licht, "Reasonable Accommodation and the ADA-Courts Draw the Line," at http://library.findlaw.com/2004/Sep/19/133574.html, accessed September 6, 2011.
38. For example, a U.S. circuit court recently found that a depressed former kidney dialysis technician could not claim ADA discrimination after the employer fired him for attendance problems. The court said he could not meet the essential job function of predictably coming to work. "Depressed Worker Lacks ADA Claim, Court Decides," *BNA Bulletin to Management*, December 18, 2007, p. 406. See also www.eeoc.gov/press/5-10-01-b.html, accessed January 8, 2008.
39. *Toyota Motor Manufacturing of Kentucky, Inc. v. Williams.* 534 U.S. 184 (2002).
40. "Supreme Court Says Manual Task Limitation Needs Both Daily Living, Workplace Impact," *BNA Fair Employment Practices*, January 17, 2002, p. 8.
41. "EEOC Issued Its Final Regulations for ADA Amendments Act," *Workforce Management*, June 2011, p. 12.
42. "Rise in ADA Cases Calls for Focus on Accommodations, Job Descriptions," *Bloomberg BNA Bulletin to Management*, September 25, 2012, p. 310.
43. Lawrence Postol, "ADAAA Will Result in Renewed Emphasis on Reasonable Accommodations," *Society for Human Resource Management Legal Report*, January 2009, pp. 1–3.
44. Mark Lengnick-Hall et al., "Overlooked and Underutilized: People with Disabilities Are an Untapped Human Resource," *Human Resource Management* 47, no. 2 (Summer 2008), pp. 255–273.
45. Susan Wells, "Counting on Workers with Disabilities," *HR Magazine*, April 2008, p. 45.
46. "Wachovia Violated USERRA by Failing to Reinstate Reservist to Comparable Job," *BNA Bulletin to Management*, September 20, 2011, p. 297.
47. www.eeoc.gov/press/2-25-09.html, accessed April 3, 2009; and Susan Hauser, "Sincerely Yours, Gina," *Workforce Management*, July 2011, pp. 16–18.
48. James Ledvinka and Robert Gatewood, "EEO Issues with Preemployment Inquiries," *Personnel Administrator* 22, no. 2 (February 1997), pp. 22–26.
49. "Employers More Vulnerable Under New York City Statute," *BNA Bulletin to Management*, July 31, 2012, p. 245.
50. Joanne Deshenaux and Dori Meinert, "States, Cities Go Beyond Federal Government," *HR Magazine*, February 2013, pp. 28–32.
51. Barbara Roth, "Multinationals, Multiple Claims," *HR Magazine*, August 2012, pp. 71–72.
52. Quoted or paraphrased from www.eeoc.gov/laws/types/index.cfm; www.eeoc.gov/laws/types/religion.cfm; www.eeoc.gov/eeoc/internal_eeo/index.cfm; and www.eeoc.gov/federal/otherprotections.cfm, all accessed May 9, 2013.
53. www.eeoc.gov/types/sexual_harassment.html, accessed April 24, 2009; and www.eeoc.gov/eeoc/statistics/enforcement/sexual_harassment.cfm, accessed October 3, 2011.
54. Richard Wiener et al., "The Fit and Implementation of Sexual Harassment Law to Workplace Evaluations," *Journal of Applied Psychology* 87, no. 4 (2002), pp. 747–764. Recently, for instance, a U.S. Court of Appeals told a male Walmart employee that he could proceed with his claim that a female supervisor had sexually harassed him. "Man's Harassment Claims Advanced," *BNA Bulletin to Management*, September 6, 2011, p. 285.
55. Jennifer Berdahl and Celia Moore, "Workplace Harassment: Double Jeopardy for Minority Women," *Journal of Applied Psychology* 91, no. 2 (2006), pp. 426–436.
56. Larry Drake and Rachel Moskowitz, "Your Rights in the Workplace," *Occupational Outlook Quarterly* (Summer 1997), pp. 19–29.
57. Patricia Linenberger and Timothy Keaveny, "Sexual Harassment: The Employer's Legal Obligations," *Personnel* 58 (November/December 1981), p. 64; and "Court Examines Workplace Flirtation," http://hr.blr.com/HR-news/Discrimination/Sexual-Harassment/Court-Examines-Workplace-Flirtation, accessed October 2, 2011.
58. Edward Felsenthal, "Justice's Ruling Further Defines Sexual Harassment," *The Wall Street Journal*, March 5, 1998, p. B5.
59. Hilary Gettman and Michele Gelfand, "When the Customer Shouldn't Be King: Antecedents and Consequences of Sexual Harassment by Clients and Customers," *Journal of Applied Psychology* 92, no. 3 (2007), pp. 757–770.
60. See the discussion in "Examining Unwelcome Conduct in a Sexual Harassment Claim," *BNA Fair Employment Practices*, October 19, 1995, p. 124. See also Michael Zugelder et al., "An Affirmative Defense to Sexual Harassment by Managers and Supervisors: Analyzing Employer Liability and Protecting Employee Rights in the U.S.," *Employee Responsibilities and Rights* 18, no. 2 (2006), pp. 111–122.
61. Ibid., "Examining Unwelcome Conduct in a Sexual Harassment Claim," p. 124.
62. For example, a server/bartender filed a sexual harassment claim against Chili's Bar & Grill. She claimed that her former boyfriend, also a restaurant employee, had harassed her. The court ruled that the restaurant's prompt response warranted ruling in favor of it.

"Ex-Boyfriend Harassed, But Employer Acted Promptly," *BNA Bulletin to Management*, January 8, 2008, p. 14.

63. See Mindy D. Bergman et al., "The (Un)reasonableness of Reporting: Antecedents and Consequences of Reporting Sexual Harassment," *Journal of Applied Psychology* 87, no. 2 (2002), pp. 230–242. See also www.eeoc.gov/policy/docs/harassment-facts.html, accessed October 2, 2011.
64. Adapted from *Sexual Harassment Manual for Managers and Supervisors* (Riverwood, IL: CCH Incorporated, a WoltersKluwer Company, 1991); www.eeoc.gov/types/sexual_harassment.html, accessed May 6, 2007; and www.eeoc.gov/policy/docs/harassment-facts.html, accessed October 2, 2011.
65. Maria Rotundo et al., "A Meta-Analytic Review of Gender Differences in Perceptions of Sexual Harassment," *Journal of Applied Psychology* 86, no. 5 (2001): 914–922. See also Nathan Bowling and Terry Beehr, "Workplace Harassment from the Victim's Perspective: A Theoretical Model and Meta Analysis," *Journal of Applied Psychology* 91, no. 5 (2006), pp. 998–1012.
66. Jennifer Berdahl and Karl Aquino, "Sexual Behavior at Work: Fun or Folly?" *Journal of Applied Psychology* 94, no. 1 (2009), pp. 34–47.
67. Jathan Janov, "Sexual Harassment and the Three Big Surprises," *HR Magazine* 46, no. 11 (November 2001), p. 123ff. California Mandates Sexual Harassment Prevention Training for Supervisors: see "California Clarifies Training Law; Employers Take Note," *BNA Bulletin to Management*, November 20, 2007, p. 375.
68. Ana Campoy and Julian Barnes, "Air Force Combats Sex Misconduct," *The Wall Street Journal*, November 15, 2012, p. A-8; and James Risen, "Air Force Leaders Testify on Culture That Led to Sexual Assaults of Recruits," *New York Times*, January 24, 2013, p. A-15.
69. Mary Rowe, "Dealing with Sexual Harassment," *Harvard Business Review*, May–June 1981, p. 43; the quoted material goes on to say that "The employer still bears the burden of proving that the employee's failure was unreasonable. If the employee had a justifiable fear of retaliation, his or her failure to utilize the complaint process may not be unreasonable," and is quoted from www.uiowa.edu/~eod/policies/sexual-harassment-guide/employer-liablity.htm, accessed October 3, 2011.
70. "Employers Should Address Inappropriate Behavior on Social Sites," *Bloomberg BNA*, February 19, 2013, p. 62.
71. John Moran, *Employment Law* (Upper Saddle River, NJ: Prentice Hall, 1997), p. 166.
72. "The Eleventh Circuit Explains Disparate Impact, Disparate Treatment," p. 102.
73. John Klinefelter and James Thompkins, "Adverse Impact in Employment Selection," *Public Personnel Management*, May/June 1976, pp. 199–204; and www.eeoc.gov/policy/docs/factemployment_procedures.html, accessed October 2, 2011.
74. Moran, *Employment Law*, p. 168.
75. Employers use several types of statistics in addressing adverse impact. (For a discussion, see Robert Gatewood and Hubert Feild, *Human Resource Selection* [Fort Worth, TX: The Dryden Press, 1994], pp. 40–42, and Jean Phillips and Stanley Gulley, *Strategic Staffing* [Upper Saddle River, NJ: Pearson, 2012], pp. 68–69.) For example, *stock statistics* might compare *at a single point in time* (1) the percentage of female engineers the company has, as a percentage of its total number of engineers, with (2) the number of trained female engineers in the labor force as a percentage of the total number of trained engineers in the labor force. Here, the question of relevant labor market is important. For example, the relevant labor market if you're hiring unskilled assemblers might be the local labor market within, say, 20 miles from your plant, whereas the relevant labor market for highly skilled engineers might well be national and possibly international. *Flow statistics* measure proportions of employees, in particular, groups at two points in time: before selection and after selection takes place. For example, when comparing the percentage of minority applicants who applied with the percentage hired, the employer is using flow statistics. An employer's company-wide minority hiring statistics may be defensible company-wide but not departmentally. The employer therefore may employ *concentration statistics* to drill down and determine the concentration of minorities versus nonminorities in particular job categories.
76. One study found that using the 4/5ths rule often resulted in false-positive ratings of adverse impact, and that incorporating tests of statistical significance could improve the accuracy of applying the 4/5ths rule. See Philip Roth, Philip Bobko, and Fred Switzer, "Modeling the Behavior of the 4/5ths Rule for Determining Adverse Impact: Reasons for Caution," *Journal of Applied Psychology* 91, no. 3 (2006), pp. 507–522.
77. The results must be realistic. In this example, hiring 2 out of 5 women suggests there is no adverse impact. But suppose we had hired only one woman. Then the difference between those we would be expected to hire (5) and whom we actually hired (1) would rise to 4. Hiring just one less woman might then trigger adverse impact issues, because twice the standard deviation is also about 4. However, realistically, it probably would not trigger such concerns, because with such small numbers, one person makes such a difference. The point is that tools like the 4/5ths rule and the standard deviation rule are only rules of thumb. They do not themselves determine if the employer's screening process is discriminatory. This fact may work both for and against the employer. As the Uniform Guidelines (www.uniformguidelines.com/qandaprint.html) put it, "Regardless of the amount of difference in selection rates, unlawful discrimination may be present, and may be demonstrated through appropriate evidence. . . ."
78. The ADEA does not just protect against intentional discrimination (disparate treatment). Under a Supreme Court decision (*Smith v. Jackson,* Miss., 2005), it also covers employer practices that seem neutral but that actually bear more heavily on older workers (disparate impact). "Employees Need Not Show Intentional Bias to Bring Claims Under ADEA, High Court Says," *BNA Bulletin to Management* 56, no. 14 (April 5, 2005), p. 105.
79. The Fair Treatment for Experienced Pilots Act raised commercial pilots' mandatory retirement age from 60 to 65 in 2008. Allen Smith, "Congress Gives Older Pilots a Reprieve," *HR Magazine*, February 2008, p. 24.
80. *Usery v. Tamiami Trail Tours*, 12FEP cases 1233. Alternatively, an employer faced with an age discrimination claim may raise the factors other than age (FOA) defense. Here, it argues that its actions were "reasonable" based on some factor other than age, such as the terminated person's poor performance.
81. www.foxnews.com/story/0,2933,517334,00.html, accessed January 7, 2010.
82. Howard Anderson and Michael Levin-Epstein, *Primer of Equal Employment Opportunity* (Washington, DC: The Bureau of National Affairs, 1982), pp. 13–14.
83. *U.S. v. Bethlehem Steel Company*, 3FEP cases 589.
84. *Robinson v. Lorillard Corporation*, 3FEP cases 653.
85. *Spurlock v. United Airlines*, 5FEP cases 17.
86. Anderson and Levin-Epstein, *Primer of Equal Employment Opportunity*, p. 14.
87. Ledvinka and Gatewood, "EEO Issues with Preemployment Inquiries," pp. 22–26.
88. Ibid.; http://www.eeoc.gov/laws/practices/index.cfm, accessed August 2, 2013.
89. "Eighth Circuit OKs $3.4 Million EEOC Verdict Relating to Pre-Hire Strength Testing Rules," *BNA Bulletin to Management*, November 28, 2006, p. 377.
90. Svetlana Shkolnikova, "Weight Discrimination Could Be as Common as Racial Bias," www.usatoday.com/news/health/weightloss/2008-05-20-overweight-bias_N.htm, accessed January 21, 2009.
91. Jenessa Shapiro et al., "Expectations of Obese Trainees: How Stigmatized Trainee Characteristics Influence Training Effectiveness," *Journal of Applied Psychology* 92, no. 1 (2007), pp. 239–249. See also Lisa Finkelstein et al., "Bias Against Overweight Job Applicants: Further Explanations of When and Why," *Human Resource Management* 46, no. 2 (Summer 2007), pp. 203–222. For an interesting study, see T. A. Judge and D. M. Cable, "When It Comes to Pay, Do the Thin Win? The Effect of Weight on Pay for Men and Women," *Journal of Applied Psychology,* January 2011.
92. "OFCCP Issues Criminal Records Directive, Cautions Contractors on Blanket Exclusions," *Bloomberg BNA Bulletin to Management*, February 12, 2013, p. 49; and "EEOC to Focus on Hiring, Pay and Harassment," *HR Magazine*, February 2013, p. 11.
93. See, for example, www.eeoc.gov/policy/docs/guidance-inquiries.html, accessed June 28, 2009.
94. This is based on *BNA Fair Employment Practices*, April 13, 1989, pp. 45–47; and "Crossed: When Religion and Dress Code Policies Intersect," www.mcguire_woods.com/news-resources/item.asp?item=3108, accessed October 2, 2011.
95. Eric Matusewitch, "Tailor Your Dress Codes," *Personnel Journal* 68, no. 2 (February 1989), pp. 86–91; Matthew Miklave, "Sorting Out a Claim of Bias," *Workforce* 80, no. 6 (June 2001), pp. 102–103, and "Laws and Cases Affecting Appearance," www.boardmanlawfirm.com/perspectives_articles/appearance.php, accessed September 8, 2011.

96. Rita Pyrillis, "Body of Work," *Workforce Management*, November 7, 2010, pp. 20–26.
97. This isn't ironclad, however. For example, the U.S. Supreme Court, in *Stotts*, held that a court cannot require retention of black employees hired under a court's consent decree in preference to higher-seniority white employees who were protected by a bona fide seniority system. It's unclear whether this decision also extends to personnel decisions not governed by seniority systems. *Firefighters Local 1784 v. Stotts* (*BNA*, April 14, 1985).
98. In its most recent plan, the EEOC said it would focus on hiring, and particularly enforcing its guidance on indiscriminate use of criminal conduct in background screening; on gender-based pay discrepancies; and on enforcing its requirements against harassment based on race, ethnicity, religion, age, and disability. "EEOC to Focus on Hiring, Pay and Assessment," p. 11.
99. Prudent employers often purchase employment practices liability insurance to insure against some or all of the expenses involved with defending against discrimination, sexual harassment, and wrongful termination–type claims. Antone Melton-Meaux, "Maximizing Employment Practices Liability Insurance Coverage," *Compensation & Benefits Review*, May/June 2008, pp. 55–59.
100. Litigants must watch the clock. In an equal pay decision, the U.S. Supreme Court held (in *Ledbetter v. Goodyear Tire & Rubber Company*) that the employee must file a complaint within 180 (or 300) days of the employer's decision to pay the allegedly unfair wage. The clock starts with that first pay decision, not with the subsequent paychecks that the employee receives. "Justices Rule 5–4 Claim-Filing Period Applies to Pay Decision, Not Subsequent Paycheck," *BNA Bulletin to Management* 58, no. 23 (June 5, 2007), pp. 177–184; and www.eeoc.gov/eeoc/statistics/enforcement/charges.cfm, accessed May 1, 2012. A recent U.S. Supreme Court case will make it more difficult for plaintiffs to file class-action claims for discrimination. See "Supreme Court Hands Wal-Mart Big Victory: Reverses Approval of Class-Action Claim," *BNA Bulletin to Management*, June 21, 2011, p. 193.
101. In 2007, the U.S. Supreme Court, in *Ledbetter v. Goodyear Tire & Rubber Company,* held that employees claiming Title VII pay discrimination must file their claims within 180 days of when they first receive the allegedly discriminatory pay. As of 2009, Congress was working to formulate new legislation enabling an employee to file a claim at any time, as long as the person is still receiving an "infected" paycheck.
102. www.eeoc.gov/eeoc/statistics/enforcement/charges.cfm, accessed March 20, 2013.
103. "EPLI Now Established Employer Litigation Strategy," *BNA Bulletin to Management*, November 29, 2011, p. 382.
104. If the charge was filed initially with a state or local agency within 180 days after the alleged unlawful practice occurred, the charge may then be filed with the EEOC within 30 days after the practice occurred or within 30 days after the person received notice that the state or local agency has ended its proceedings.
105. "EEOC Attorneys Stress the Importance of Cooperation During Investigations," *BNA Bulletin to Management*, March 8, 2011, p. 73.
106. www.eeoc.gov/mediate/facts.html, accessed June 29, 2009.
107. "EEOC's New Nationwide Mediation Plan Offers Option of Informal Settlements," *BNA Fair Employment Practices*, February 18, 1999, p. 21; and www.eeoc.gov/employees/mediation.cf, accessed October 2, 2011.
108. Timothy Bland, "Sealed Without a Kiss," *HR Magazine*, October 2000, pp. 85–92.
109. Stuart Bompey and Michael Pappas, "Is There a Better Way? Compulsory Arbitration of Employment Discrimination Claims After *Gilmer*," *Employee Relations Law Journal* 19, no. 3 (Winter 1993–1994), pp. 197–216, and www.eeoc.gov/policy/docs/mandarb.html, accessed September 5, 2011. The EEOC says here, for instance, that "the employer imposing mandatory arbitration is free to manipulate the arbitral mechanism to its benefit."
110. See Bompey and Pappas, pp. 210–211.
111. David Nye, "When the Fired Fight Back," *Across-the-Board*, June 1995, pp. 31–34; and www.eeoc.gov/federal/fed_employees/adr.cfm, accessed October 3, 2011.
112. "EEOC Opposes Mandatory Arbitration," *BNA Fair Employment Practices*, July 24, 1997, p. 85; and www.eeoc.gov/employees/mediation.cfm, accessed October 2, 2011.
113. See, for example, "Diversity Is Used as Business Advantage by Three Fourths of Companies, Survey Says," *BNA Bulletin to Management,* November 7, 2006, p. 355; and Claire Armstrong et al., "The Impact of Diversity and Equality Management on Firm Performance: Beyond High Performance Work Systems," *Human Resource Management* 49, no. 6 (November–December 2010), pp. 977–998.
114. Brian O'Leary and Bart Weathington, "Beyond the Business Case for Diversity in Organizations," *Employee Responsibilities and Rights* 18, no. 4 (December 2006), pp. 283–292.
115. See, for example, Michael Carrell and Everett Mann, "Defining Work-Force Diversity in Public Sector Organizations," *Public Personnel Management* 24, no. 1 (Spring 1995), pp. 99–111; Richard Koonce, "Redefining Diversity," *Training and Development Journal,* December 2001, pp. 22–33; and Kathryn Canas and Harris Sondak, *Opportunities and Challenges of Workplace Diversity* (Upper Saddle River, NJ: Pearson, 2008), pp. 3–27. Others list race and ethnicity diversity, gender diversity, age diversity, disability diversity, sexual diversity, and cultural and national origin diversity as examples. Lynn Shore et al., "Diversity in Organizations: Where Are We Now and Where Are We Going?" *Human Resource Management Review* 19 (2009), pp. 117–133.
116. Taylor Cox, Jr., *Cultural Diversity in Organizations* (San Francisco, CA: Berrett Kohler Publishers, Inc., 1993), p. 88; also see Stefanie Johnson et al., "The Strong, Sensitive Type: Effects of Gender Stereotypes and Leadership Prototypes on the Evaluation of Male and Female Leaders," *Organizational Behavior and Human Decision Processes* 106, no. 1 (May 2008), pp. 39–60.
117. Cox, ibid., p. 64.
118. "Workplace Bias Against Muslims Increasingly a Concern for Employers," *BNA Bulletin to Management*, October 26, 2010, p. 337. See also Robert Grossman, "Valuable But Vulnerable," *HR Magazine*, March 2011, pp. 22–27.
119. Cox, *Cultural Diversity in Organizations*, pp. 179–80.
120. J. H. Greenhaus and S. Parasuraman, "Job Performance Attributions and Career Advancement Prospects: An Examination of Gender and Race Affects," *Organizational Behavior and Human Decision Processes* 55 (July 1993), pp. 273–298. Much research here focuses on how ethnocentrism prompts consumers to avoid certain products based on their country of origin. See, for example, T. S. Chan et al., "How Consumer Ethnocentrism and Animosity Impair the Economic Recovery of Emerging Markets," *Journal of Global Marketing* 23, no. 3 (July/August 2010), pp. 208–225.
121. Patrick McKay et al., "A Tale of Two Climates: Diversity Climate from Subordinates' and Managers' Perspectives and Their Role in Store Unit Sales Performance," *Personnel Psychology* 62 (2009), pp. 767–791.
122. Maria del Carmen Triana, Maria Fernandez Garcia, and Adrian Colella, "Managing Diversity: How Organizational Efforts to Support Diversity Moderate the Effects of Perceived Racial Discrimination on Affective Commitment," *Personnel Psychology* 63 (2010), pp. 817–843.
123. "Selling the Supremes on Diversity," *Bloomberg Businessweek*, October 20–October 28, 2012, p. 38.
124. As another example, leaders who facilitated high levels of power sharing within their groups helped to reduce the frequently observed positive relationship between increased diversity and increased turnover. But leaders who were inclusive of only a select few followers "may actually exacerbate the relationship between diversity and turnover" (p. 1422). Lisa Nishii and David Mayer, "Do Inclusive Leaders Help to Reduce Turnover in Diverse Groups? The Moderating Role of Leader—Member Exchange in the Diversity to Turn Over Relationship," *Journal of Applied Psychology* 94, no. 6 (2009), pp. 1412–1426.
125. Faye Cocchiara et al., "A Gem for Increasing the Effectiveness of Diversity Training," *Human Resource Management* 49, no. 6 (November–December 2010), pp. 1089–1106.
126. For diversity management steps, see Cox, *Cultural Diversity in Organizations*, p. 236. See also Patricia Digh, "Creating a New Balance Sheet: The Need for Better Diversity Metrics," *Mosaics*, Society for Human Resource Management, September/October 1999, p. 1; and Richard Bucher, *Diversity Consciousness* (Upper Saddle River, NJ: Pearson Prentice Hall, 2004), pp. 109–137.
127. John Rice, "Why Make Diversity So Hard to Achieve?" *Harvard Business Review*, June 2012, p. 40.
128. David Harrison et al., "Understanding Attitudes Toward Affirmative Action Programs in Employment: Summary and Meta-Analysis of 35 Years of Research," *Journal of Applied*

Psychology 91, no. 5 (2006), pp. 1013–1036; and Margaret Fiester et al., "Affirmative Action, Stock Options, I-9 Documents," *HR Magazine*, November 2007, p. 31.

129. David Harrison et al., "Understanding Attitudes Toward Affirmative Action Programs in Employment: Summary and Meta-Analysis of 35 Years of Research," *Journal of Applied Psychology* 91, no. 5 (2006), pp. 1013–1036.
130. Bill Leonard, "Ways to Tell If a Diversity Program Is Measuring Up," *HR Magazine*, July 2002, p. 21; and Ye Yang Zheng and Brenda White, "The Evaluation of a Diversity Program at an Academic Library," *Library Philosophy and Practice*, 2007, http://unllib.unl.edu/LPP/yang.pdf, accessed October 2, 2011.
131. http://newsfeedresearcher.com/data/articles_n17/tests-city-court.html, accessed April 24, 2009.
132. Adam Liptak, "Supreme Court Finds Bias Against White Firefighters," *New York Times*, June 30, 2009, pp. A1, A13.
133. Ibid., p. 560.
134. Kenneth Sovereign, *Personnel Law*, 4th edition (Upper Saddle River, NJ: Prentice Hall, 1999), p. 220. Perhaps surprisingly, more senior managers than nonmanagers report suffering retaliation when reporting workplace misconduct. *Bloomberg BNA Bulletin to Management*, September 11, 2012, p. 294. This includes what one report calls "traceable retaliation," such as demotions, physical harm, and online harassment.
135. www.eeoc.gov/laws/types/retaliation.cfm, accessed August 19, 2011; and Adam Liptak, "Fiancé's Firing Is Ruled an Illegal Reaction to a Discrimination Claim," *New York Times*, January 25, 2011, p. A16.
136. See "Retaliation Becomes Most Common Charge," *HR Magazine*, March 2011, p. 16. For instance, there were recently 37,836 private-sector retaliation charges filed, 33,512 race discrimination charges, and 33,566 discrimination charges. "Retaliation Most Frequent EEOC Charge in Fiscal Year 2012," *Bloomberg BNA Bulletin to Management*, February 5, 2013, p. 45.
137. Liptak, "Fiancé's Firing," p. A16.

3

Human Resource Management Strategy and Analysis

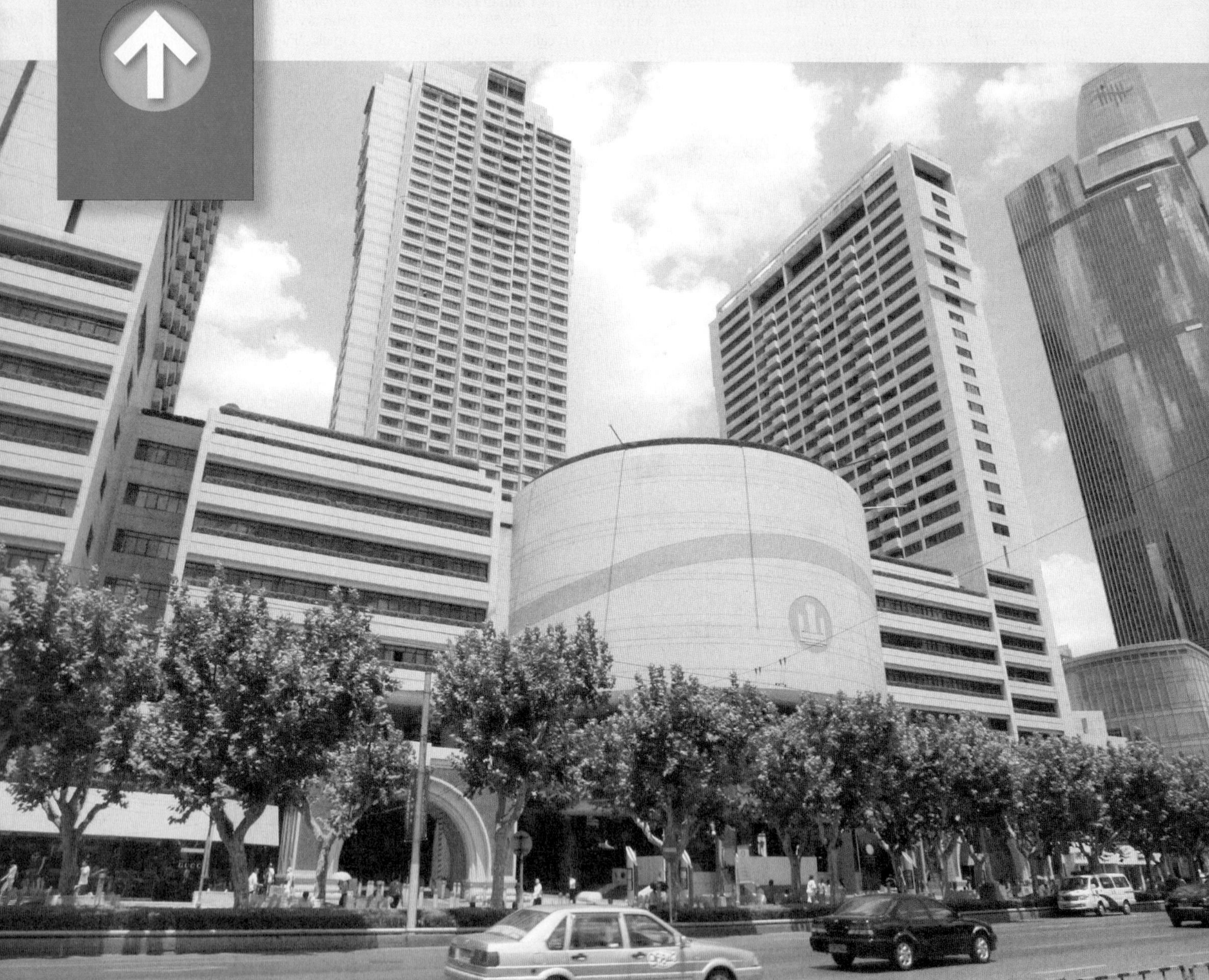

Source: Imaginechina/AP Images

MyManagementLab®

Improve Your Grade!

When you see this icon, visit **www.mymanagementlab.com** for activities that are applied, personalized, and offer immediate feedback.

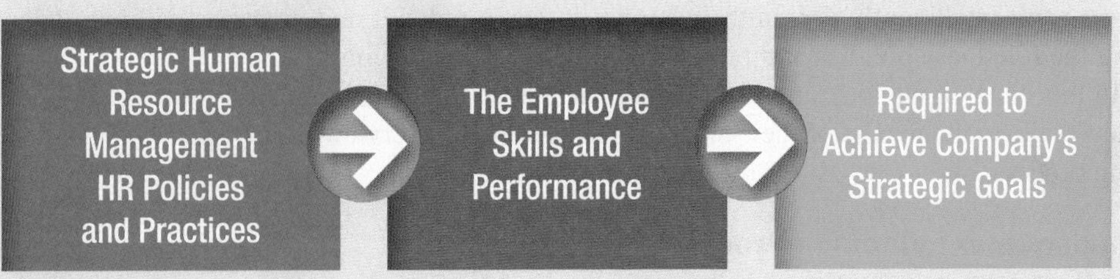

For a bird's eye view of how one company created a new human resource strategy to improve its strategic performance, read the Hotel Paris case on pages 82–83 and answer the questions after reading the chapter material.

WHERE ARE WE NOW . . .

This chapter's main purpose is to explain strategic human resource management, and in particular how to develop HR policies and practices that support the company's strategic goals. The topics we address include the strategic management process, types of strategies, strategic human resource management, HR metrics and benchmarking, and high-performance work systems. In the following part of this book, Part 2, we then turn to the nuts and bolts of human resource management, starting with how to analyze jobs and recruit and select employees.

LEARNING OBJECTIVES

1. Explain with examples each of the eight steps in the strategic management process.
2. List with examples the main types of strategies.
3. Define *strategic human resource management* and give an example of strategic human resource management in practice.
4. Give at least five examples of HR metrics.
5. Give five examples of what employers can do to have high-performance systems.

When the Ritz-Carlton Company took over managing the Portman Hotel in Shanghai, China, the hotel already had a fine reputation among business travelers. But many new luxurious hotels were opening there. To stay competitive, the Portman's new managers decided to reposition the hotel with a new strategy, one that emphasized top-notch customer service. But they knew that improving the service would require new employee selection, training, and pay policies and practices. We will see what they did.

The Strategic Management Process

1 Explain with examples each of the eight steps in the strategic management process.

Managers can't intelligently design their human resource policies and practices without understanding the role these policies and practices are to play in achieving their companies' strategic goals. In this chapter, we look at how managers design strategic and human resource plans, and how they evaluate the results of their plans. We start with an overview of the basic management planning process.

The Management Planning Process

The basic managerial planning process involves setting objectives, making basic planning forecasts, reviewing alternative courses of action, evaluating which options are best, and then choosing and implementing your plan. A *plan* shows the course of action for getting from where you are to the goal. *Planning* is always "goal-directed" (such as, "Double sales revenue to $16 million in fiscal year 2015").

THE HIERARCHY OF GOALS In companies, it is traditional to view the goals from the top of the firm down to front-line employees as a chain or *hierarchy of goals*. Figure 3-1 illustrates this. At the top, the president sets long-term or "strategic" goals (such as "double sales revenue to $16 million in fiscal year 2015"). His or her vice presidents then set goals for their units that flow from, and make sense in terms of accomplishing, the president's goal (see Figure 3-1). Then their own subordinates set goals, and so on down the chain.[1]

POLICIES AND PROCEDURES Policies and procedures provide day-to-day guidance employees need to do their jobs in a manner that is consistent with the company's plans and goals. Policies set broad guidelines delineating how employees should proceed. For example, "It is the policy of this company to comply with all laws, regulations, and principles of ethical conduct." *Procedures* spell out what to do if a specific situation arises. For example,

> Any employee who believes this policy has been violated must report this belief to the employee's immediate supervisor. If that is not practical, the employee should file a written report with the Director of Human Resources. There is to be no retaliation in any form.[2]

Employers write their own policies and procedures, or adapt ones from existing sources (or both). For example, most employers have an employee manual listing the company's policies and procedures regarding various HR matters. A Google search would produce vendors such as http://store.bizmanualz.com/Human-Resources-Policies-and-Procedures-p/abr41m.htm. These offer prepackaged HR policies manuals covering appraisal, compensation, equal employment compliance, and other policies and procedures.

FIGURE 3-1 Sample Hierarchy of Goals Diagram for a Company

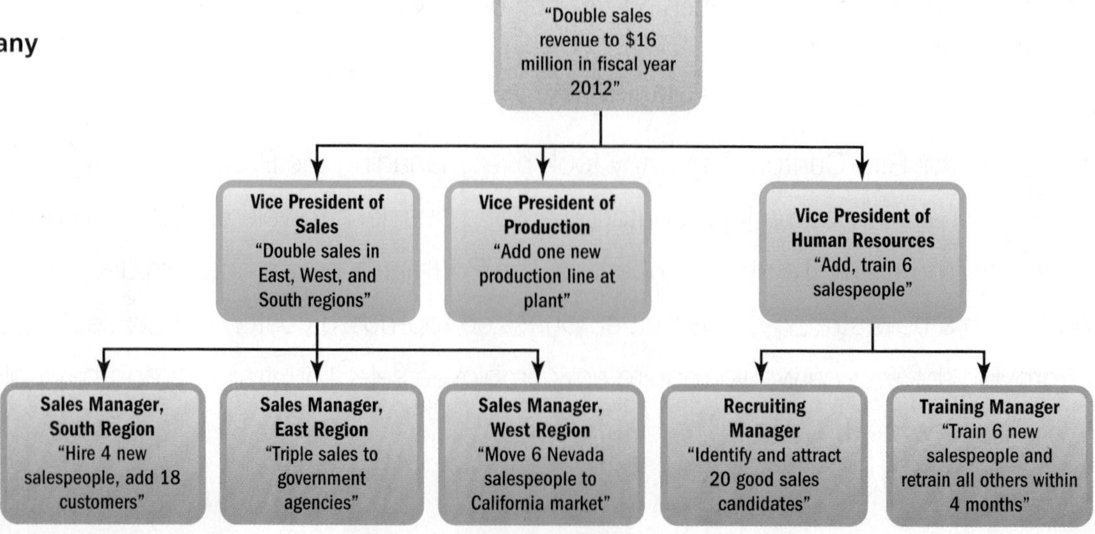

Strategic Planning

Before a hierarchy of goals can be set or policies and practices formulated, the manager should put in place a strategic plan. A **strategic plan** is the company's overall plan for how it will match its internal strengths and weaknesses with external opportunities and threats in order to maintain a competitive advantage. The strategic planner asks, "Where are we now as a business, and where do we want to be?" He or she then formulates a strategic plan to guide the company to the desired destination.[3] When Yahoo! tries to figure out whether to sell its search business to concentrate on offering more content, it is engaged in strategic planning.

strategic plan
The company's plan for how it will match its internal strengths and weaknesses with external opportunities and threats in order to maintain a competitive advantage.

The best strategic plans are usually customer focused. For example, several years ago, McDonald's found itself losing market share. Management decided that the solution was a new strategic plan, which they summed up as the Plan to Win. As their website says,

> McDonald's customer-focused Plan to Win provides a common framework for our global business yet allows for local adaptation. Through the execution of initiatives surrounding the five elements of our Plan to Win—People, Products, Place, Price and Promotion—we have enhanced the restaurant experience for customers worldwide and grown comparable sales and customer visits in each of the last eight years. This Plan, combined with financial discipline, has delivered strong results for our shareholders.[4]

In other words, management used the Plan to Win to improve their stores' layouts, extend their store-opening hours, offer an enhanced menu, and take other steps to make McDonald's an even more attractive place for its customers to visit.

Strategic plans are similar to but not quite the same as *business models*. Those investing in a business will ask top management, "What's your business model?" A business model "is a company's method for making money in the current business environment." It pinpoints who the company serves, what products or services it provides, what differentiates it, its competitive advantage, how it provides its product or service, and, most importantly, how it makes money.[5] For example, Google doesn't make money by requiring people to pay for searches; it makes money by offering targeted paid advertisements based on what you're searching for.

strategy
A course of action the company can pursue to achieve its strategic aims.

strategic management
The process of identifying and executing the organization's strategic plan by matching the company's capabilities with the demands of its environment.

A **strategy** is a course of action. If Yahoo!'s strategic plan is to focus more on applications like Yahoo! Finance, then one strategy might be to sell Yahoo! Search and put the money into those other applications. **Strategic management** is the process of identifying and executing the organization's strategic plan, by matching the company's capabilities with the demands of its environment.

Figure 3-2 sums up the strategic management process. Let's look at each step.

STEP 1 ASK, WHERE ARE WE NOW? The logical place to start is by asking, "Where are we now as a business?" Here the manager defines the company's current business and mission. Specifically, "What products do we sell, where do we sell them, and how do our products or services differ from our competitors'?" The manager will traditionally focus on four aspects of the current business. One is the firm's *product scope*, specifically its current range of products or services. For example, the WD-40 company offers one product line, a spray hardware lubricant called WD-40.

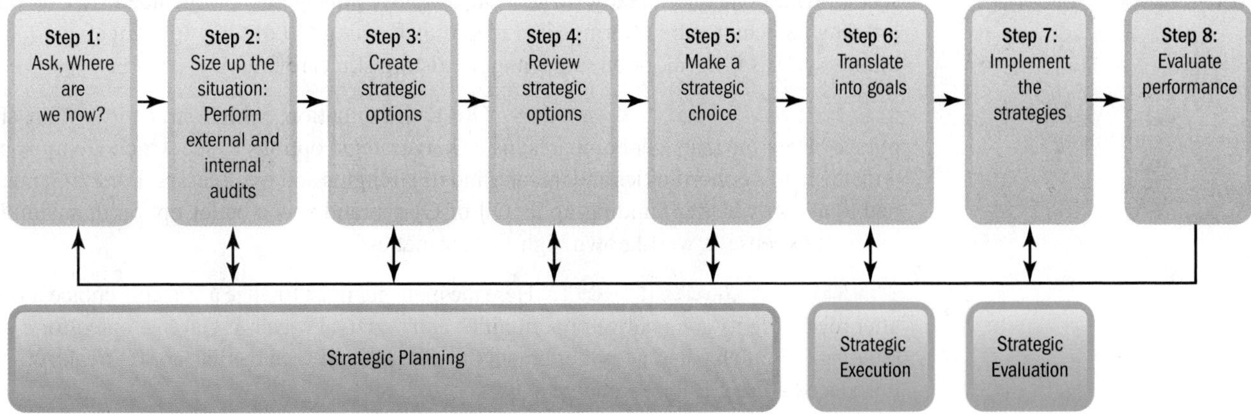

FIGURE 3-2 The Strategic Management Process

Apple offers a wider and growing product line, including (at the moment) computers, iPhones, iPods, and iPads.

Vertical integration is a second factor that distinguishes one business from another. Here the basic question is, "To what extent should we design, manufacture, and sell our own products?" For example, Apple designs and markets its products, but lets China's Foxconn manufacture them. It sells both through Apple stores and through stores like Best Buy.

Geographic range is a third distinguishing characteristic of a business. For example, the *New York Post* focuses on New York. *The New York Times* markets and distributes its paper worldwide.

Competitive advantage is the fourth (but by no means least important) feature that distinguishes one business from another. In other words, "On what basis do we compete? Do we compete based on *cost and price*, like Walmart? Do we compete based on some *difference* that customers value?" For example, people buy Volvos because of their relative safety. Or we might compete by focusing on a niche in the market. For example, the A Pea in the Pod chain specializes in offering stylish business-type maternity clothing for working pregnant women.

mission statement
Summarizes the answer to the question, "What business are we in?"

The manager will often sum up the essence of his or her business with a mission statement. The **mission statement** sums up the essence of what the company must do to compete in the marketplace, and provides the framework that guides managers and employees day-to-day. It helps them decide, for instance, "Should we expand into this new business or not?" Facebook's mission, in simple terms, is to help those who use the site to openly connect and share.[6] Several years ago, Ford Motor Company summed up its mission as, "Where Quality is Job One." Google's mission ". . . is to organize the world's information and make it universally accessible and useful."[7] PepsiCo's mission, in part, is "to be the world's premier consumer products company focused on convenient foods and beverages." PepsiCo managers would thus make product choice, expansion, and other strategic decisions based in part on adhering to the guidelines inherent in the firm's mission statement.[8]

STEP 2 SIZE UP THE SITUATION: PERFORM EXTERNAL AND INTERNAL AUDITS The next step is to ask, "Are we heading in the right direction given the challenges that we face?"

To answer this, managers need to study or "audit" the firm's environment, and its internal strengths and weaknesses. The environmental scan worksheet in Figure 3-3 is a guide for compiling information about the company's environment. It includes the economic, competitive, and political trends that may affect the company. Managers use a SWOT chart, such as the one in Figure 3-4, to compile and organize the company's **s**trengths, **w**eaknesses, **o**pportunities, and **t**hreats. The manager's aim is to create a strategic plan that makes sense in terms of balancing the company's strengths and weaknesses with its opportunities and threats.

STEP 3 CREATE STRATEGIC OPTIONS The situation may require that management consider strategic options for the company. Several years ago, for instance, Microsoft, facing a surging product lineup from Apple and competition from Google's cloud-based office programs, had to decide whether to change its mission and, if so, how. Should it continue to focus mostly on software for microcomputers? If not, then one strategic option was to expand into offering its own tablet computers. Several years ago, after reviewing its competitive opportunities and threats, Procter & Gamble (P&G) management decided to bulk up its offerings in the beauty-care sector.[9] The company already owned Oil of Olay. Management concluded that its options for growing its beauty-care offerings included transforming Oil of Olay to compete with higher-tier brands such as L'Oreal, or buying a major existing skincare brand.

STEP 4 REVIEW STRATEGIC OPTIONS Given the situation, which strategic option should we pursue? Here the manager compares his or her strategic options to see which are most consistent with the firm's opportunities and threats, and its strengths and weaknesses. For P&G, management had to assess whether building up its Oil of Olay brand was a better option than simply buying (at great expense) a well-known high-tier cosmetics brand.

STEP 5 MAKE A STRATEGIC CHOICE Here the manager must finalize a strategic choice. For example, after reviewing its competitive opportunities and threats, Procter & Gamble opted for a strategy of building Oil of Olay into a top-tier brand, one competitive with the likes of L'Oreal. And Microsoft introduced a line of tablet computers.

STEP 6 TRANSLATE INTO GOALS Next, management translates the new desired direction into actionable strategic goals. At P&G, for instance, strategic goals might have included "generate

FIGURE 3-3 Worksheet for Environmental Scanning

Economic Trends
(such as recession, inflation, employment, monetary policies)

____
____
____
____

Competitive and Market Trends
(such as market/customer trends, entry/exit of competitors, new products from competitors)

____
____
____
____

Political Trends
(such as legislation and regulation/deregulation)

____
____
____
____

Technological Trends
(such as introduction of new production/distribution technologies, rate of product obsolescence, trends in availability of supplies and raw materials)

____
____
____
____

Social Trends
(such as demographic trends, mobility, education, evolving values)

____
____
____
____

Geographic Trends
(such as opening/closing of new markets, factors affecting current plant/office facilities location decisions)

____
____
____
____

FIGURE 3-4 SWOT Matrix, with Generic Examples

Potential Strengths

- Market leadership
- Strong research and development
- High-quality products
- Cost advantages
- Patents

Potential Opportunities

- New overseas markets
- Failing trade barriers
- Competitors failing
- Diversification
- Economy rebounding

Potential Weaknesses

- Large inventories
- Excess capacity for market
- Management turnover
- Weak market image
- Lack of management depth

Potential Threats

- Market saturation
- Threat of takeover
- Low-cost foreign competition
- Slower market growth
- Growing government regulation

20% of corporate revenues from the Oil of Olay brand within 4 years," and "capture 18% of the top-tier beauty care market within 3 years." Ford breathed life into its "Quality is Job One" mission by setting goals such as "no more than 1 initial defect per 10,000 cars."

STEP 7 IMPLEMENT THE STRATEGIES Strategy execution means translating the strategies into action. This means actually hiring (or firing) people, building (or closing) plants, and adding (or eliminating) products and product lines. To do this, management uses the firm's new top-level strategic goals to formulate a hierarchy of goals, and policies and procedures. These guide action down the chain of command at lower organizational levels, and in the firm's various departments.

STEP 8 EVALUATE PERFORMANCE Things don't always turn out as planned. P&G soon built its Oil of Olay line into a world-class brand. However initially, at least, Microsoft's new tablets were off to a slow start. Microsoft soon cut their prices.

Improving Performance Through HRIS: Using Computerized Business Planning Software

Managers use business planning software packages for writing strategic plans. Business Plan Pro from Palo Alto Software contains all the information and planning aids required to create a business plan. For example, it contains 30 sample plans, step-by-step instructions (with examples) for creating each part of a plan (executive summary, market analysis, and so on), and financial planning spreadsheets. Other good options include BizPlan Builder (www.bizplan.com/tour/business-plan-builder) and My Strategic Plan (http://mystrategicplan.com/).

Types of Strategies

2 List with examples the main types of strategies.

In practice, managers engage in three types of strategic planning, *corporate-level* strategic planning, *business unit* (or *competitive*) strategic planning, and *functional* (or *departmental*) strategic planning (see Figure 3-5).

Corporate Strategy

corporate-level strategy Type of strategy that identifies the portfolio of businesses that, in total, comprise the company and the ways in which these businesses relate to each other.

For any business, the corporate strategy answers the question, "What businesses will we be in?" A company's **corporate-level strategy** identifies the portfolio of businesses that, in total, comprise the company and how these businesses relate to each other. For example, with a *concentration* (single-business) corporate strategy, the company offers one product or product line, usually in one market. WD-40 Company is one example. With one spray lubricant its product scope is narrow.

FIGURE 3-5 Type of Strategy at Each Company Level

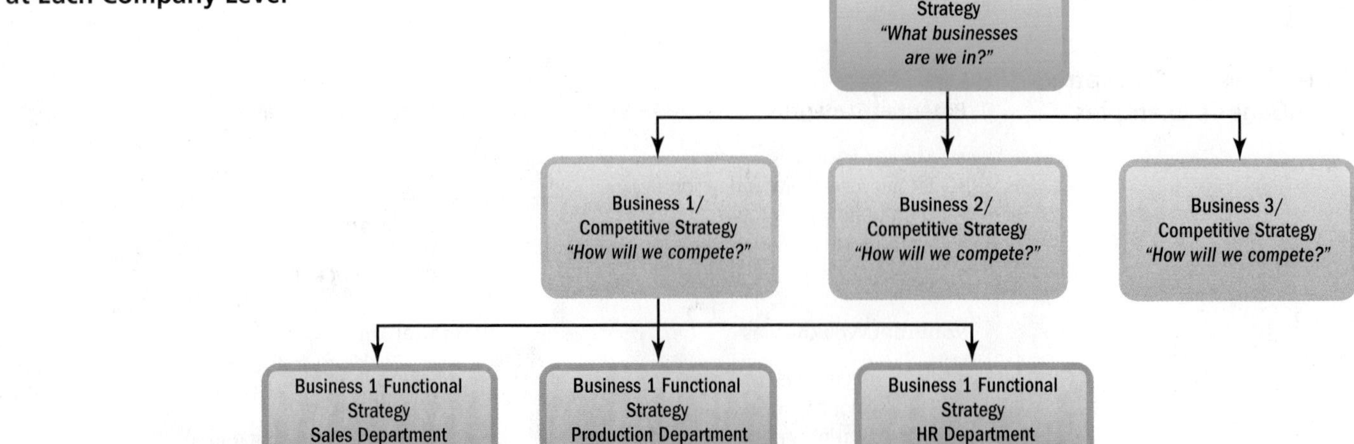

A *diversification* corporate strategy means the firm will expand by adding new product lines. PepsiCo is diversified. Thus, PepsiCo added Frito-Lay chips and Quaker Oats to its drinks businesses. Here product scope is wider. A *vertical integration* strategy means the firm expands by, perhaps, producing its own raw materials, or selling its products direct. Thus, Apple opened its own Apple stores. With a *consolidation* strategy, the company reduces its size. With *geographic expansion*, the company grows by entering new territorial markets, for instance, by taking the business abroad.

Competitive Strategy

competitive strategy
A strategy that identifies how to build and strengthen the business's long-term competitive position in the marketplace.

competitive advantage
Any factors that allow an organization to differentiate its product or service from those of its competitors to increase market share.

On what basis will each of our businesses compete? Within a company like PepsiCo, each business unit (such as Pepsi and Frito-Lay) needs a *business-level competitive strategy.* A **competitive strategy** identifies how to build and strengthen the business unit's long-term competitive position in the marketplace.[10] It shows, for instance, how Pizza Hut will compete with Papa John's, or how Walmart will compete with Target.

Managers hopefully build their competitive strategies around their businesses' competitive advantages. **Competitive advantage** means any factors that allow a company to differentiate its product or service from those of its competitors to increase market share. The competitive advantage needn't be tangible, such as high-tech machines. For example, at a GE airfoils plant in Greenville, South Carolina, teams of highly trained workers run computer-controlled machines, interview prospective team members, and adjust assembly lines themselves.[11] For GE, the workers' knowledge, skills, and dedication (their "human capital") produce the quality that makes GE an aerospace leader.

We saw that managers use several standard competitive strategies to achieve competitive advantage. *Cost leadership* means becoming the low-cost leader in an industry. Walmart is an example. *Differentiation* is a second possible competitive strategy. Here the firm seeks to be unique in its industry along dimensions that are widely valued by buyers.[12] Thus, Volvo stresses the safety of its cars, and Papa John's stresses fresh ingredients. *Focusers* carve out a market niche (like Bugatti cars). They offer a product or service that their customers cannot get from generalist competitors (such as Toyota).

Functional Strategy

functional strategy
A strategy that identifies the broad activities that each department will pursue in order to help the business accomplish its competitive goals.

Each department should operate within the framework of the business's strategic plan. **Functional strategies** identify what each department must do to help the business accomplish its strategic goals. Thus, for P&G to make Oil of Olay a top-tier brand, its product development, production, marketing, sales, and human resource departments had to engage in activities that were consistent with this unit's new high-quality mission. Inferior products and cheap packaging would not do, for instance.

Managers' Roles in Strategic Planning

Devising the company's overall strategic plan is top management's responsibility. However, few top executives formulate strategic plans without the input of lower-level managers. No one knows more about the firm's competitive pressures, vendor capabilities, product and industry trends, and employee capabilities and concerns than do the company's department managers.

For example, the human resource manager is in a good position to supply "competitive intelligence"—information on what competitors are doing. Details regarding competitors' incentive plans, employee opinion surveys about customer complaints, and information about pending legislation such as labor laws are examples. Human resource managers should also be the masters of information about their own firms' employees' strengths and weaknesses.

In practice, devising the firm's overall strategic plan involves frequent discussions among and between top and lower-level managers. The top managers then use this information to hammer out their strategic plan.

EXAMPLE: IMPROVING MERGERS AND ACQUISITIONS Mergers and acquisitions (M&A) are among the most important strategic decisions companies make. When mergers and acquisitions fail, it's often not due to financial issues but to personnel-related ones, such as employee resistance.[13] Prudent top managers therefore tap their human resource managers' input early in the merger process.

Critical human resource M&A tasks include choosing top management, communicating changes to employees, merging the firms' cultures, and retaining key talent.[14] Human resource consulting companies, such as Towers Perrin, assist firms with merger-related human resource management services. For example, they identify potential pension shortfalls, identify key talent and then develop suitable retention strategies, help clients plan how to combine payroll systems, and help determine which employee is best for which role in the new organization.[15]

3 Define *strategic human resource management* and give an example of strategic human resource management in practice.

Strategic Human Resource Management

Top managers design overall corporate strategies, and then design competitive strategies for each of the company's businesses. Then the departmental managers formulate functional strategies for their departments that support the business and company-wide strategic aims. The marketing department would have marketing strategies. The production department would have production strategies. The human resource management ("HR") department would have *human resource management strategies*.

HR in Practice at the Hotel Paris Starting as a single hotel in a Paris suburb in 1990, the Hotel Paris now comprises a chain of nine hotels, with two in France, one each in London and Rome, and others in New York, Miami, Washington, Chicago, and Los Angeles. To see how managers use strategic human resource management to improve performance, see the Hotel Paris Case on pages 82–83 and answer the questions.

strategic human resource management
Formulating and executing human resource policies and practices that produce the employee competencies and behaviors the company needs to achieve its strategic aims.

What Is Strategic Human Resource Management?

Every company needs its human resource management policies and activities to make sense in terms of its broad strategic aims. For example, a high-end retailer such as Neiman-Marcus will have different employee selection, training, and pay policies than will Walmart. **Strategic human resource management** means formulating and executing human resource policies and practices that produce the employee competencies and behaviors the company needs to achieve its strategic aims. The following HR Practices Around the Globe feature illustrates.

IMPROVING PERFORMANCE: HR Practices Around the Globe

When the Ritz-Carlton Company took over managing the Portman Hotel in Shanghai, China, the new management reviewed the Portman's strengths and weaknesses, and its fast-improving local competitors. They decided that to compete, they had to improve the hotel's level of service. Achieving that in turn meant formulating new human resource management plans for hiring, training, and rewarding hotel employees. It meant putting in place a new human resource strategy for the Portman Hotel, one aimed at improving customer service. Their HR strategy involved taking these steps:

- *Strategically*, they set the goal of making the Shanghai Portman outstanding by offering superior customer service.
- To achieve this, Shanghai Portman employees would have to exhibit new *skills and behaviors,* for instance, in terms of how they treated and responded to guests.
- To produce these employee skills and behaviors, management formulated new human resource management plans, policies, and procedures. For example, they introduced the Ritz-Carlton Company's *human resource system* to the Portman: "Our selection [now] focuses on talent and personal values because these are things that can't be taught . . . it's about caring for and respecting others."[16]

Management's efforts paid off. Their new human resource plans and practices helped to produce the employee behaviors required to improve the Portman's level of service, thus attracting new guests. Travel publications were soon calling it the "best employer in Asia," "overall best business hotel in Asia," and "best business hotel in China." Profits soared, in no small part due to effective strategic human resource management.

Discussion Question 3-1: Asian culture is different from that in the United States. For example, team incentives tend to be more attractive to people in Asia than are individual incentives. How do you think these cultural differences would have affected how the hotel's new management selected, trained, appraised, and compensated Portman employees?

The basic idea of strategic human resource management is this: In formulating human resource management policies and activities, the manager should aim to produce the employee skills and behaviors that the company needs to achieve its strategic goals.

FIGURE 3-6 The Practices Behaviors Strategy Pyramid

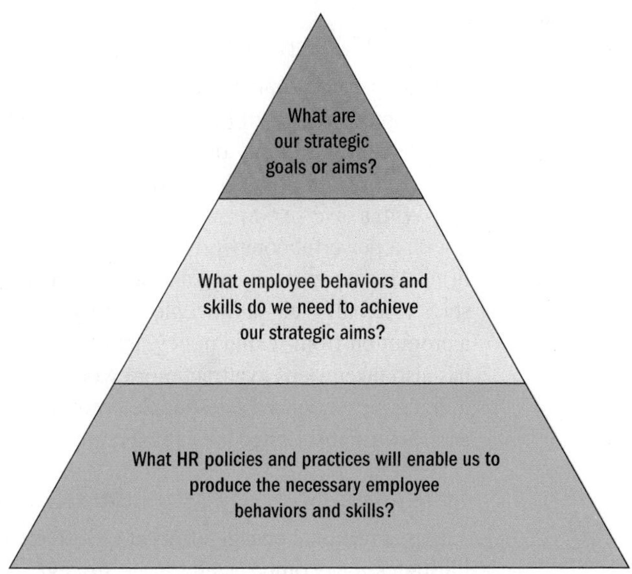

Figure 3-6 outlines this idea. First, the manager formulates *strategic plans* and goals. Next, he or she asks, "What *employee skills and behaviors* will we need to achieve these plans and goals?" And finally, he or she asks, "Specifically what recruitment, selection, training, and other *HR policies and practices* should we put in place so as to produce the required employee skills and behaviors." Managers often refer to their specific HR policies and practices as *human resource strategies*.[17]

Human Resource Strategies in Action

As one example of human resource strategy, consider Newell Rubbermaid. Several years ago, it changed its business from manufacturing and marketing housewares (such as Rubbermaid utensils and Levelor Blinds) to mostly just marketing them. They knew that implementing this change would require new employee skills and behaviors (for instance more advertising and sales employees and fewer manufacturing ones). The human resource management team began by benchmarking Newell's main marketing-oriented competitors to see what their best human resource practices were. Then the human resource team formulated new HR strategies—specific policies and practices addressing matters such as how to handle the winding down of the manufacturing staffing levels, how many new advertising and marketing employees to recruit and how to recruit them, what new training and development programs to implement, and how to compensate the new employees. Then they met with the head of each Newell Rubbermaid division to discuss how to implement the new human resource policies and practices.[18]

The HR Practices Around the Globe feature discussing the Shanghai Portman Hotel presented another example of human resource strategies in action, as does the following.

ALBERTSONS EXAMPLE Supermarket chain Albertsons competes with low-cost leader Walmart in part with a strategy of combining reasonably low costs with superior service. Albertsons' human resources team helps the company do this. For example, controlling personnel-related costs while improving customer service meant hiring customer-focused employees while reducing turnover, improving retention and eliminating time-consuming manual processes. Working with its information technology department, Albertsons' human resource team put in place an automated staffing system from Unicru. This collects and analyzes the information entered by applicants online and at kiosks. It ranks applicants based on whether they exhibit customer-focused traits, helps track candidates throughout the screening process, and tracks reasons for departure once applicants are hired. The Albertsons human resource managers were able to present a compelling business case for adopting the Unicru system, by showing its return on investment. The bottom line was that by working as a partner in Albertsons' strategy design and implementation process, the human resource team helped Albertsons control costs and improve customer service, and thereby achieve its strategic goals.[19]

Diversity Counts: Longo Builds Its Strategy on Diversity

Some experts assume that diverse workforces create conflicts and rising costs. But that argument is lost on the owners of Longo Toyota in El Monte, California.[20] Longo's business strategy is built on catering to a highly diverse customer base by hiring and developing salespeople who speak everything from Spanish and Korean to Tagalog.

With a diverse 60-person sales force that speaks more than 20 languages, Longo's staff provides it with a powerful competitive advantage for catering to an increasingly diverse customer base. The firm's HR department plays a central role in creating this competitive advantage. While other dealerships lose half their salespeople every year, Longo retains 90% of its staff, in part by emphasizing a promotion-from-within policy. In addition, more than two-thirds of its managers are minorities. It has also taken steps to attract more women, for instance by adding staff to spend time providing the training inexperienced salespeople need. In a business where competitors can easily imitate products and showrooms, Longo has built a competitive advantage based on employee diversity.

Translating Strategy into Human Resource Policies and Practices: An Example

An organizational change effort at the Albert Einstein Healthcare Network (Einstein Medical) also illustrates how companies translate strategic plans into human resource policies and practices.[21] In the 1990s, it was apparent to Einstein's new CEO that rising competition, technological changes, the growth of managed care (health maintenance organizations and preferred provider organizations), and significant cuts in Medicare and Medicaid meant that his company needed a new strategic plan. At the time, Einstein Medical was a single acute care hospital, treating the seriously ill.

NEW STRATEGY The essence of the CEO's new strategy was to change Einstein into a comprehensive health-care network of facilities providing a full range of high-quality services in multiple local markets. He knew that achieving this change in strategy within a fast-changing and uncertain health-care environment would require changing Einstein Medical's organization and employee behaviors. He felt that Einstein Medical would need a more flexible and fast-acting approach to delivering health-care services. Based on that, the CEO decided to summarize his change program's goals in three words: *initiate*, *adapt*, and *deliver*. Einstein Medical's HR and other departmental strategies would have to focus on helping the medical center and its employees to produce new services (initiate), capitalize on opportunities (adapt), and offer consistently high-quality services (deliver).

NEW EMPLOYEE COMPETENCIES AND BEHAVIORS For the human resource team, the question then became, "What specific employee skills and behaviors would Einstein Medical need to produce these three (initiate, adapt, and deliver) outcomes?" The CEO and the head of human resources chose four employee skills and behaviors: They said Einstein employees would need to be "*dedicated, accountable, generative,* and *resilient*." They would have to be *dedicated* to Einstein's goals of producing new services (initiating), capitalizing on opportunities (adapting), and offering consistently high-quality services (delivering). They would have to take personal *accountability* for their results. They would have to be *generative*, which means able and willing to apply new knowledge and skills in a constant search for innovative solutions. And they would have to be *resilient*, for instance, in terms of moving from job to job as the hospital's needs changed.

NEW HUMAN RESOURCE POLICIES AND PRACTICES Einstein Medical's human resource managers could now ask, "What specific HR policies and practices would help Einstein create a dedicated, accountable, generative, and resilient workforce?" The answer was to implement several new human resource programs. For example:

- New *training and communications programs* aimed at ensuring all employees understood the importance of the hospital's new strategy, and what it would require of all employees in terms of producing new services, capitalizing on opportunities, and offering high quality services.
- New *job enrichment programs* made employees more accountable for their results and more resilient in terms of moving from job to job.
- New *compensation and benefits programs* promoted personal growth and encouraged searching for innovative solutions.
- *Improved selection, orientation, and dismissal procedures* helped Einstein Medical attract and build a more dedicated, resilient, accountable, and generative workforce.

In sum, Einstein's managers knew they could not implement their new strategy without new employee skills and behaviors, (employees had to be "dedicated, accountable, generative, and resilient"). In turn, promoting these skills and behaviors meant implementing new human resource policies and practices.

Strategic Human Resource Management Tools

Managers use several tools to translate the company's broad strategic goals into human resource management policies and practices. Three important tools are the strategy map, the HR scorecard, and the digital dashboard.

strategy map
A strategic planning tool that shows the "big picture" of how each department's performance contributes to achieving the company's overall strategic goals.

STRATEGY MAP The **strategy map** summarizes how each department's performance contributes to achieving the company's overall strategic goals. It helps the manager and each employee visualize and understand the role his or her department plays in achieving the company's strategic plan. Management gurus sometimes say that the map clarifies employees' "line of sight." It does this by visually linking their efforts with the company's ultimate goals.[22]

Figure 3-7 presents a strategy-map example for Southwest Airlines. The top-level activity is achieving its strategic financial goals. Then the strategy map shows the chain of activities that help Southwest Airlines achieve these goals. Like Walmart, Southwest has a low-cost-leader strategy. So, for example, to boost revenues and profitability Southwest must fly fewer planes (to keep costs down), maintain low prices, and maintain on-time flights. In turn (further

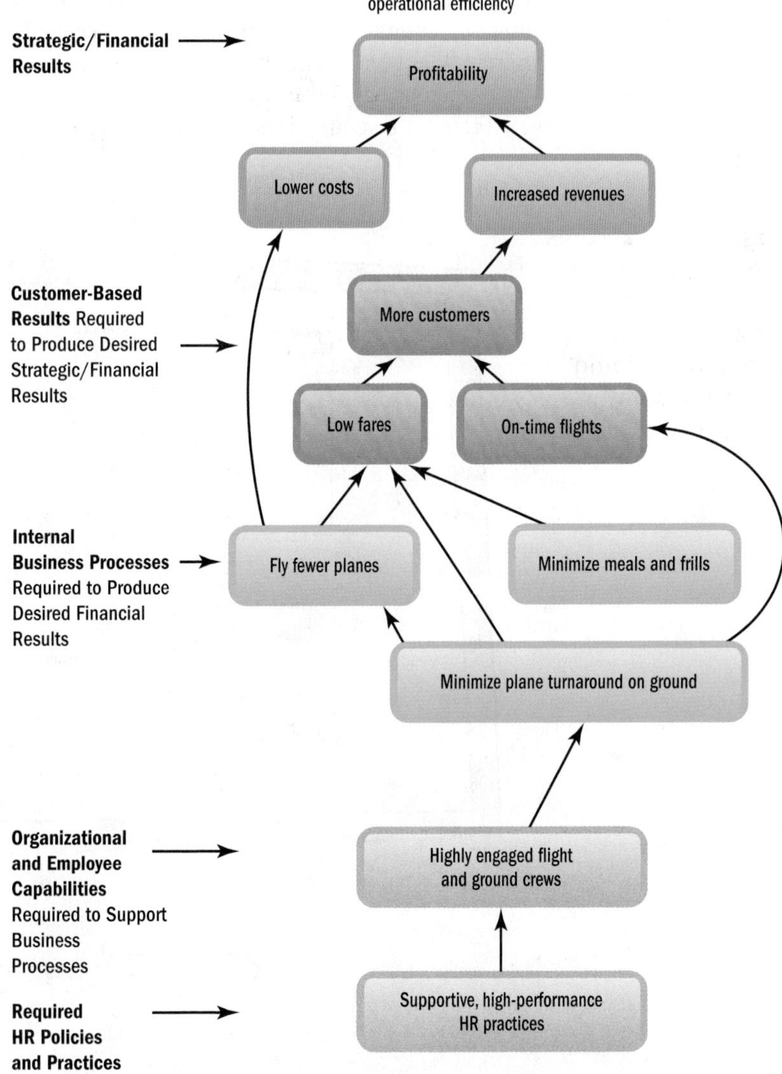

FIGURE 3-7 Strategy Map for Southwest Airlines
Source: Based on TeamCHRYSALIS.com, accessed July 2006; http://mcknightkaney.com/Strategy_Maps_Primer.html, accessed August 3, 2011; and www.strategymap.com.au/home/StrategyMapOverview.htm, accessed August 3, 2011.

down the strategy map), on-time flights and low prices require fast turnaround. This, in turn, requires motivated ground and flight crews. The strategy map thereby helps each department understand what it needs to do to support Southwest's low-cost strategy.[23] For example, what steps must Southwest's human resource team take to boost the motivation and dedication of its ground crews?

HR scorecard
A process for assigning financial and nonfinancial goals or metrics to the human resource management–related chain of activities required for achieving the company's strategic aims and for monitoring results.

THE HR SCORECARD Many employers quantify and computerize the strategy map's activities. The HR scorecard helps them to do so. The **HR scorecard** is not a scorecard. It refers to a process for assigning financial and nonfinancial goals or metrics to the human resource management–related strategy-map chain of activities required for achieving the company's strategic aims.[24] (Metrics for Southwest might include airplane turnaround time, percent of on-time flights, and ground crew productivity.) The idea is to take the strategy map and to quantify it.

Managers use special scorecard software to facilitate this. The computerized scorecard process helps the manager quantify the relationships between (1) the HR activities (amount of testing, training, and so forth), (2) the resulting employee behaviors (customer service, for instance), and (3) the resulting firm-wide strategic outcomes and performance (such as customer satisfaction and profitability).[25]

digital dashboard
Presents the manager with desktop graphs and charts, and so a computerized picture of where the company stands on all those metrics from the HR scorecard process.

DIGITAL DASHBOARDS The saying "a picture is worth a thousand words" explains the purpose of the digital dashboard. A **digital dashboard** presents the manager with desktop graphs and charts, showing a computerized picture of how the company is doing on all the metrics from the HR scorecard process. As in the accompanying illustration, a top Southwest Airlines manager's dashboard might display real-time trends for various strategy-map activities, such as fast turnarounds and on-time flights. This enables the manager to take corrective action. For example, if ground crews are turning planes around slower today, financial results tomorrow may decline unless the manager takes action.

Figure 3-8 summarizes the three strategic planning tools.

A digital dashboard presents the manager with desktop graphs and charts, showing a computerized picture of how the company is doing on all the metrics from the HR scorecard process.

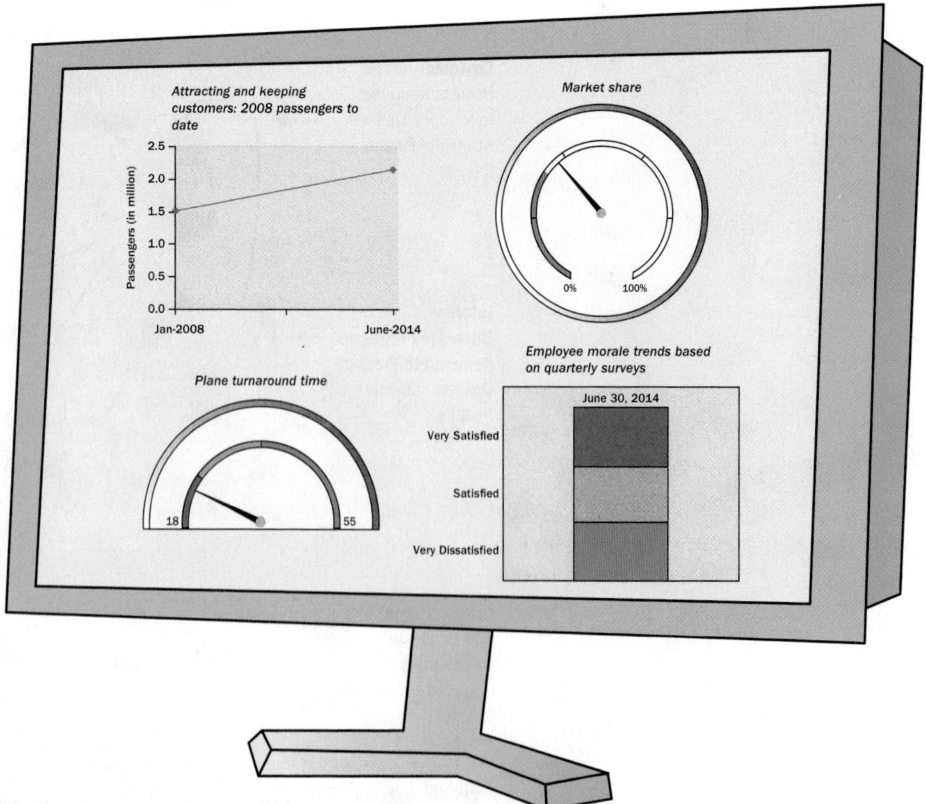

Strategy Map
Graphical tool that summarizes the chain of activities that contribute to a company's success, and so shows employees the "big picture" of how their performance contributes to achieving the company's overall strategic goals.

HR Scorecard
A process for assigning financial and nonfinancial goals or metrics to the human resource management-related chain of activities required for achieving the company's strategic aims and for monitoring results.

Digital Dashboard
Presents the manager with desktop graphs and charts, so he or she gets a picture of where the company has been and where it's going, in terms of each activity in the strategy map.

FIGURE 3-8 Three Important Strategic HR Tools

HR Metrics and Benchmarking

4 Give at least five examples of HR metrics.

We've seen that strategic human resource management means formulating HR policies and practices that produce the employee competencies and behaviors the company needs to achieve its strategic goals. Being able to measure results is essential to this process. For example, it would have been futile for the Ritz-Carlton Portman Shanghai's management to set "better customer service" as a goal if they couldn't measure customer service.[26] These measures might include, for instance, hours of training per employee, productivity per employee, and (via customer surveys) customer satisfaction.

Types of Metrics

Human resource managers use many such measures. For example, there is (on average) one human resource employee per 100 company employees for firms with 100–249 employees. The HR employee-to-employee ratio drops to about 0.79 for firms with 1,000–2,499 employees and to 0.72 for firms with more than 7,500 employees.[27] Figure 3-9 illustrates other human resource management metrics. They include employee tenure, cost per hire, and annual overall turnover rate.[28]

Improving Performance Through HRIS: Tracking Applicant Metrics for Improved Talent Management

As an example of why to use metrics, consider that most employers spend thousands of dollars (or more) recruiting employees, without measuring which hiring source produces the best candidates. The logical solution is to assess recruitment effectiveness using measures or metrics. Metrics here might include quality of new hires and which recruitment sources produce the most new hires.[29]

One way to track and analyze such data is by using a computerized applicant tracking system (ATS). ATS vendors include Authoria, PeopleFilter, Wonderlic, eContinuum, and PeopleClick. Regardless of the vendor, analyzing recruitment effectiveness using ATS software involves two basic steps:

- First, the employer (and vendor) decides how to measure the performance of new hires. For example, with Authoria's system, hiring managers input their evaluations of each new hire at the end of the employee's first 90 days, using a 1-to-5 scale.[30]
- Second, the applicant tracking system then enables the employer to track the recruitment sources that correlate with superior hires. It may show, for instance, that new employees hired through employee referrals stay longer and work better than those from newspaper ads do. Most applicant tracking systems enable hiring managers to track such hiring metrics on desktop dashboards.

For example, installing an Authoria ATS enabled the Thomson Reuters Company to identify the sources, candidate traits, and best practices that work best in each geographic area where the company does business.[31] This enabled Thomson Reuters to reduce recruiting costs, for instance, by shifting recruitment dollars from less effective to more effective sources.

Benchmarking and Needs Analysis

Measuring how one is doing (for instance, in terms of employee productivity) is rarely enough for deciding what to change. One must know "How are we doing?" *in relation to something*. For example, are our accident rates rising or falling? You may also want to *benchmark* your results—compare high-performing companies to your own, to understand what makes them better.[32]

Organizational Data

- Revenue
- Revenue per FTE
- Net Income Before Taxes
- Net Income Before Taxes per FTE
- Positions Included Within the Organization's Succession Plan

HR Department Data

- Total HR Staff
- HR-to-Employee Ratio
- Percentage of HR Staff in Supervisory Roles
- Percentage of HR Staff in Professional/Technical Roles
- Percentage of HR Staff in Administrative Support Roles
- Reporting Structure for the Head of HR
- Types of HR Positions Organizations Expect to Hire in 2011

HR Expense Data

- HR Expenses
- HR Expense to Operating Expense Ratio
- HR Expense to FTE Ratio

Compensation Data

- Annual Salary Increase
- Salaries as a Percentage of Operating Expense
- Target Bonus for Non-Executives
- Target Bonus for Executives

Tuition/Education Data

- Maximum Reimbursement Allowed for Tuition/Education Expenses per Year
- Percentage of Employees Participating in Tuition/Education Reimbursement Programs

Employment Data

- Number of Positions Filled
- Time-to-Fill
- Cost-Per-Hire
- Employee Tenure
- Annual Overall Turnover Rate
- Annual Voluntary Turnover Rate
- Annual Involuntary Turnover Rate

Expectations for Revenue and Organizational Hiring

- Percentage of Organizations Expecting Changes in Revenue in 2011 Compared to 2010
- Percentage of Organizations Expecting Changes in Hiring in 2011 Compared to 2010

Metrics for More Profitable Organizations

- Total HR Staff
- HR-to-Employee Ratio
- HR Expenses
- HR Expense to Operating Expense Ratio
- HR Expense to FTE Ratio
- Annual Salary Increase
- Target Bonus for Non-Executives
- Target Bonus for Executives
- Maximum Reimbursement Allowed for Tuition/Education Expenses per year
- Percentage of Employees Participating in Tuition/Education Reimbursement Programs
- Time-to-Fill
- Cost-Per-Hire
- Annual Overall Turnover Rate

Figure 3-9 Metrics for the SHRM® 2011–2012 Customized Human Capital Benchmarking Report

Source: Reprinted with permission from the Society for Human Resource Management.

The Society for Human Resource Management's (SHRM's) benchmarking service enables employers to compare their own HR metrics with those of other companies. The employer can request comparable (benchmark) figures not just by industry, but by employer size, company revenue, and geographic region. (See http://shrm.org/research/benchmarks/.)

Figure 3-10 illustrates one of the SHRM's many sets of comparable benchmark measures. It shows how much employers are spending for tuition reimbursement programs.

Strategy and Strategy-Based Metrics

Benchmarking provides only one perspective on how your company's human resource management system is performing.[33] It shows how your human resource management system's performance compares to the competition. However, it may *not* reveal the extent to which your firm's HR practices are supporting its strategic goals. For example, if the strategy calls for doubling profits by improving customer service, to what extent are our new training practices helping to improve customer service?

strategy-based metrics
Metrics that specifically focus on measuring the activities that contribute to achieving a company's strategic aims.

Managers use *strategy-based metrics* to answer such questions. **Strategy-based metrics** focus on measuring the activities that contribute to achieving a company's strategic aims.[34] Thus, for the Portman Shanghai, the strategic HR metrics might include 100% employee testing, 80% guest returns, incentive pay as a percent of total salaries, and sales up 50%. If changes in HR practices such as increased training and better incentives have their intended effects, then strategic metrics like guest returns and guest compliments should also rise.

FIGURE 3-10 SHRM Customized Human Capital Benchmarking Report

Source: "HR Expense Data," from *SHRM Customized Human Capital Benchmarking Report*. Reprinted with permission from the Society for Human Resource Management. www.shrm.org/Research/benchmarks/Documents/sample_humnba_capital_report.pdf.

Tuition/Education Data					
	n	25th Percentile	Median	75th Percentile	Average
Maximum reimbursement allowed for tuition/education expenses per year	32	$1,000	$5,000	$7,500	$6,000
Percentage of employees participating in tuition/education reimbursement programs	32	1.0%	3.0%	5.0%	4.0%

DATA MINING Such analyses often employ data-mining techniques. Data mining sifts through huge amounts of employee data to identify correlations that employers then use to improve their employee-selection and other practices. *Data mining* is "the set of activities used to find new, hidden, or unexpected patterns in data."[35] Data-mining systems use tools like statistical analysis to sift through data looking for relationships. Department stores often use data mining. For example, Macy's data mining reveals which customers come in to redeem "20% off" coupons.

Managers use data mining–based talent analytics to discover patterns and to make predictions. The Improving Performance Through HRIS feature presents examples.

Improving Performance Through HRIS: Workforce/Talent Analytics

Data such as cost-per-hire are interesting but relatively useless until converted to information. *Information* is data presented in a form that makes it useful for making decisions. Knowing your cost-per-hire is interesting. However, presenting cost-per-hire data in a way that shows you whether the cost is trending up or down, and how those costs compare with your competitors', provides information you can actually use to make decisions.

Most firms do not use HR data in this way. In one study, 83% of respondents said their human resource departments regularly report workplace metrics like cost-per-hire to senior managers, but only 10% said they use such data to actually analyze their workforce management practices' effectiveness. Only 7% use the data to change their workforce management practices.[36]

Managers use special workforce (or talent) analytics software tools to convert their workforce data into actionable information. For example, human resource consulting firms such as Aon Hewitt will compile a client's employee data. Its analytics engine then analyzes this data and presents it to the client through a Web-based portal. Dashboards then enable managers to identify workforce trends, and to answer questions such as "Are there trends we should further analyze in the turnover data?"

Analytics improves performance. For example, a talent analytics team at Google analyzed data on employee backgrounds, capabilities, and performance.[37] The team was able to identify the factors (such as an employee feeling underutilized) likely to lead to the employee leaving. In a similar project, Google analyzed data on things like employee survey feedback to identify the attributes of successful Google managers. Microsoft identified correlations among the schools and companies that the employees arrived from and the employees' subsequent performance. This enabled Microsoft to improve its recruitment and selection practices.[38] Software company SAS's employee-retention program sifts through employee data on traits like skills, tenure, performance, education, and friendships. The program can predict which high-value employees are more likely to quit in the near future.[39] Alliant Techsystems created a "flight risk model" to calculate the probability an employee would leave. This enabled it to predict high turnover and to take corrective action.[40] IBM uses workforce analytics to identify employees who are "idea leaders" to whom other employees frequently turn for advice (for instance, based on e-mail "mentions" by colleagues).[41] One study compared high- and low-performance organizations' use of HR analytics. Eighty-one percent of the high-performing organizations gave HR leaders such workforce data, compared with 33% of the low-performing ones.[42]

Employers are using talent analytics to answer six types of talent management questions:[43]

Human capital facts. For example, "What are the key indicators of my organization's overall health?" JetBlue found that one such key indicator was employee engagement, in that it correlated with financial performance.

Analytical HR. For example, "Which units, departments, or individuals need attention?" Lockheed Martin collects performance data in order to identify units needing improvement.

Human capital investment analysis. For example, "Which actions have the greatest impact on my business?" By monitoring employee satisfaction levels, Cisco was able to improve its employee-retention rate from 65% to 85%, saving the company nearly $50 million in recruitment, selection, and training costs.

Workforce forecasts. Dow Chemical uses a computerized model. This predicts future required headcount for each business unit based on predictions for things like sales trends.

Talent value model. For example, "Why do employees choose to stay with—or leave—my company?" For instance Google was able to anticipate when an employee felt underutilized and was preparing to quit, thus reducing turnover costs.

Talent supply chain. For example, "How should my workforce needs adapt to changes in the business environment?" Thus, retail companies can use special analytical models to predict daily store volume and release hourly employees early.

What Are HR Audits?

HR audit
An analysis by which an organization measures where it currently stands and determines what it has to accomplish to improve its HR functions.

Human resource managers often collect data on matters such as employee turnover and safety via *human resource audits*. One practitioner calls an **HR audit** "an analysis by which an organization measures where it currently stands and determines what it has to accomplish to improve its HR function."[44] The HR audit generally involves reviewing the company's human resource functions (recruiting, testing, training, and so on), usually using a checklist, as well as ensuring that the firm is adhering to regulations, laws, and company policies.

In conducting the HR audit, managers often benchmark their results to comparable companies'. Sample measures (metrics) might include the ratio of HR professionals per 100 company employees. HR audits vary in scope and focus. Typical areas audited include:[45]

1. Roles and headcount (including job descriptions, and employees categorized by exempt/nonexempt and full- or part-time)
2. Compliance with federal, state, and local employment-related legislation
3. Recruitment and selection (including use of selection tools, background checks, and so on)
4. Compensation (policies, incentives, survey procedures, and so on)
5. Employee relations (union agreements, performance management, disciplinary procedures, employee recognition)
6. Mandated benefits (Social Security, unemployment insurance, workers' compensation, and so on)
7. Group benefits (insurance, time off, flexible benefits, and so on)
8. Payroll (such as legal compliance)
9. Documentation and record keeping. For example, do our files contain information including résumés and applications, offer letters, job descriptions, performance evaluations, benefit enrollment forms, payroll change notices, and documentation related to personnel actions such as employee handbook acknowledgments?[46]
10. Training and development (new employee orientation, workforce development, technical and safety, career planning, and so on)
11. Employee communications (employee handbook, newsletter, recognition programs)
12. Termination and transition policies and practices

Evidence-Based HR and the Scientific Way of Doing Things

We've seen that decision making based on a measurable and objective review of the situation is important. Managers have a name for this. *Evidence-based human resource management* means using data, facts, analytics, scientific rigor, critical evaluation, and critically evaluated research/case studies to support human resource management proposals, decisions, practices, and conclusions.[47]

You may sense that being evidence based is similar to being scientific, and if so, you are correct. A recent *Harvard Business Review* article even argues that managers must become more scientific and "think like scientists" when making business decisions.[48]

HOW TO BE SCIENTIFIC But how can managers do this? Objectivity, experimentation, and prediction are the heart of science. In gathering evidence, scientists (or managers) first need to be *objective*, or there's no way to trust their conclusions. Recently, a medical school disciplined several professors. They had failed to reveal that they were on the payroll of the drug company that supplied the drugs, the results of which the doctors were studying. Who could trust their objectivity or conclusions?

Being scientific also requires *experimentation.* An experiment is a test one sets up in such a way as to ensure that he or she understands the reasons for the results obtained. For example, in their *Harvard Business Review* article, "A Step-by-Step Guide to Smart Business Experiments," the authors argue that if you want to judge a new incentive plan's impact on corporate profits, don't start by implementing the plan with all employees. Instead, implement it with an "experimental" group (which gets the incentive plan) *and* with a "control" group (a group that does *not* get the incentive plan). Doing so will help you gauge if any performance improvement stemmed from the incentive or from some other cause (such as a new company-wide training program).[49] And, it will enable you to *predict* how changing the incentive plan will affect performance.

For managers, the point of being "scientific" is to make better decisions by forcing you to gather the facts. "Is this sales incentive plan really boosting sales?" "We've spent $40,000 in the past 5 years on our tuition-refund plan; what (if anything) did we get out of it?" What's the evidence? The accompanying HR Tools for Line Managers and Entrepreneurs feature shows some examples.

IMPROVING PERFORMANCE: HR Tools for Line Managers and Entrepreneurs

Examples abound of human resource managers taking a scientific, evidence-based approach to making decisions. For example, an insurance firm was considering cutting costs by buying out senior underwriters, most of whom were earning very high salaries. But after analyzing the data, HR noticed that these underwriters also brought in a disproportionate share of the company's revenue. In fact, reviewing data on things such as employee salaries and productivity showed that it would be much more profitable to eliminate some low-pay call-center employees, replacing them with even less-expensive employees. As another example, the chemical company BASF Corp. analyzed data on the relationship among stress, health, and productivity in its 15,000 U.S. headquarters staff. Based on that analysis, the company instituted health programs that it calculated would more than pay for themselves in increased productivity by reducing stress.[50]

Discussion Question 3-2: If it is apparently so easy to do what BASF did to size up the potential benefits of health programs, why do you think more employers do not do so?

Throughout this book we will show examples of how managers use evidence to make better human resource management decisions. For example: Which recruitment source produces our best candidates? Does it pay to use this testing program? And, does our safety program really lead to fewer accidents?

High-Performance Work Systems

5 Give five examples of what employers can do to have high-performance systems.

high-performance work system (HPWS)
A set of human resource management policies and practices that promote organizational effectiveness.

One reason to measure, benchmark, and scientifically analyze human resource management practices is to promote high-performance work practices. A **high-performance work system (HPWS)** is a set of human resource management policies and practices that together produce superior employee performance.

One study looked at 17 manufacturing plants, some of which adopted high-performance work system practices. The high-performance plants paid more (median wages of $16 per hour compared with $13 per hour for all plants), trained more, used more sophisticated recruitment and hiring practices (tests and validated interviews, for instance), and used more self-managing work teams.[51] Thus those with the high-performance HR practices performed significantly better than did those without such practices. Because they are so dependent on customer service, service companies (such as hotels) particularly gain from having high-performance work systems and practices, by the way.[52]

High-Performance Human Resource Policies and Practices

What exactly are these high-performance work practices? Studies show that high-performance work systems' policies and practices do differ from less productive ones (see Table 3-1). For example, in terms of HR practices, high-performing companies recruit more job candidates, use more selection tests, and spend many more hours training employees.

Table 3-1 illustrates four things:

human resource metrics
The quantitative gauge of a human resource management activity, such as employee turnover, hours of training per employee, or qualified applicants per position.

- *First,* it presents examples of **human resource measures**, such as hours of training per employee, or qualified applicants per position. (In Table 3-1, the metric for "Number of qualified applicants per position" is 36.55 in the high-performing companies.) Managers use such metrics to assess their companies' HR performance and to compare one company's performance with another's.[53]

TABLE 3-1 Examples Selected from Several Studies of How Recruitment, Selection, Training, Appraisal, Pay, and Other Practices Differ in High-Performance and Low-Performance Companies

	Low-Performance Company HR System Averages (Bottom 10%, 42 Firms)	High-Performance Company HR System Averages (Top 10%, 43 Firms)
Sample HR Practices		
Number of qualified applicants per position (*Recruiting*)	8.24	36.55
Percentage hired based on a validated *selection* test	4.26	29.67
Percentage of jobs *filled from within*	34.90	61.46
Number of hours of *training* for new employees (less than 1 year)	35.02	116.87
Number of hours of *training* for experienced employees	13.40	72.00
Percentage of employees receiving a regular *performance appraisal*	41.31	95.17
Percentage of workforce whose *merit increase* or *incentive pay* is tied to performance	23.36	87.27
Percentage of workforce who received *performance feedback* from multiple sources (360)	3.90	51.67
Target percentile for total compensation (market rate = 50%)	43.03	58.67
Percentage of the workforce eligible for *incentive pay*	27.83	83.56
Percentage of the workforce routinely working in a self-managed, *cross-functional*, or *project team*	10.64	42.28
Percentage of HR budget spent on *outsourced activities* (e.g., recruiting, benefits, payroll)	13.46	26.24
Number of employees per HR professional	253.88	139.51
Percentage of the eligible workforce covered by a union contract	30.00	8.98
Firm Performance		
Employee turnover	34.09	20.87
Sales per employee	$158,101	$617,576
Market value to book value	3.64	11.06

Source: Based on "Comparison of HR Practices in High-Performance and Low-Performance Companies," by B.E. Becker, et al., from *The HR Scorecard: Linking People, Strategy and Performance* (Boston: Harvard Business School Press, 2001); Barry Macy, Gerard Farias, Jean-Francois Rosa, and Curt Moore, "Built To Change: High-Performance Work Systems and Self-Directed Work Teams—A Longitudinal Field Study," *Research in Organizational Change and Development*, V 16, pp. 339–418, 2007; James Gathrie, Wenchuan Liu, Patrick Flood, and Sarah MacCurtain, "High Performance Work Systems, Workforce Productivity, and Innovation: A Comparison of MNCs and Indigenous Firms," The Learning, Innovation and Knowledge (LINK) Research Centre Working Paper Series, WP 04-08, 2008.

- *Second,* it illustrates *what employers must do* to have high-performance systems. For example, hire based on validated selection tests, and extensively train employees.
- *Third,* the table shows that high-performance work practices usually *aspire to help workers to manage themselves*. The point of such recruiting, screening, training, and other human resources practices here is to foster an empowered and self-motivated workforce.[54]
- *Fourth,* Table 3-1 highlights *the measurable differences* between the human resource management systems in high-performance and low-performance companies. For example, high-performing companies have more than four times the number of qualified applicants per job than do low performers.

Review

MyManagementLab Go to **mymanagementlab.com** to complete the problems marked with this icon. 

Chapter Section Summaries

1. Because all managers operate within the framework of their company's overall plans, it's important for all managers to be familiar with **the strategic management process.**
   - The *management planning* process includes setting an objective, making forecasts, determining what your alternatives are, evaluating your alternatives, and implementing and evaluating your plan.
   - A *strategic plan* is the company's plan for how it will match its internal strengths and weaknesses with external opportunities and threats in order to maintain a competitive advantage. A strategy is a course of action.
   - *Strategic management* is the process of identifying and executing the organization's strategic plan. The 8 basic steps in the strategic management process include Ask, Where are we now?; Size Up the Situation: Perform external and internal audits; Create strategic options; Review strategic options; Make a strategic choice; Translate into goals; Implement the strategies; Evaluate performance.
2. We distinguished among three **types of strategies**, corporate-level, competitive-level, and functional strategies. Corporate strategies include, among others, diversification strategies, vertical integration, horizontal integration, geographic expansion, and consolidation. The main competitive strategies include cost leadership, differentiation, and focuser. Functional strategies reflect the specific departmental policies that are necessary for executing the business's competitive strategies.
   - Department managers play an important role in strategic planning in terms of devising the strategic plan, formulating supporting functional/departmental strategies, and, of course, executing the company's plans. Strategic planning is important to all managers. All managers' personnel and other decisions should be consistent with the goals that cascade down from the firm's overall strategic plan. Those goals form a hierarchy, starting with the president's overall strategic goals (such as "double sales revenue to $16 million") and filtering down to what each individual manager needs to do in order to support that overall company goal.
3. Each function or department in the business needs its own functional strategy, and **strategic human resource management** means formulating and executing human resource policies and practices that produce the employee skills and behaviors the company needs to achieve its strategic aims. Human resource strategies are the specific human resource management policies and practices managers use to support their strategic aims. The Shanghai Portman Hotel and Albertsons Markets are two examples of strategic human resource planning. Another is the use of HR consultants in improving mergers and acquisitions, for instance, with respect to managing the deal's costs and aligning the total rewards necessary for the new entity. Important and popular strategic human resource management tools include the strategy map, the HR scorecard, and digital dashboards.
4. The manager will want to use **HR metrics and benchmarking** prior to making decisions. Illustrative HR metrics include hours of training per employee, productivity per employee, and (via customer surveys) customer satisfaction. The manager may want to *benchmark* results—compare high-performing companies to your own, to understand what makes them better.
5. In answer to the question "What are **high-performance work systems,"** they are sets of human resource

management policies and practices that promote organizational effectiveness. Human resource metrics (quantitative measures of some human resource management activities, such as employee turnover) are critical in creating high-performance human resource policies and practices. This is because they enable managers to benchmark their own practices against those of successful organizations.

Discussion Questions

3-3. Give an example of hierarchical planning in an organization.

✪ **3-4.** What is the difference between a corporate strategy and a competitive strategy? Give one example of each.

3-5. Explain why strategic planning is important to all managers.

3-6. Explain with examples each of the eight steps in the strategic management process.

✪ **3-7.** Explain with examples how human resources management can be instrumental in helping a company create a competitive advantage.

Individual and Group Activities

3-8. With three or four other students, form a strategic management group for your college or university. Your assignment is to develop the outline of a strategic plan for the college or university. This should include such things as strategic goals; and corporate, competitive, and functional strategies. In preparing your plan, make sure to show the main strengths, weaknesses, opportunities, and threats the college faces, and which prompted you to develop your particular strategic plans.

3-9. Using the Internet or library resources, review the annual reports of five companies. Bring to class examples of how those companies say they are using their HR processes to help the company achieve its strategic goals.

3-10. Interview an HR manager and write a short report on "The Strategic Roles of the HR Manager at XYZ Company."

3-11. Using the Internet or library resources, bring to class and discuss at least two examples of how companies are using an HR scorecard to help create HR systems that support the company's strategic aims. Do all managers seem to mean the same thing when they refer to HR scorecards? If not, how do they differ?

3-12. In teams of four or five students, choose a company for which you will develop an outline of a strategic HR plan. What seem to be this company's main strategic aims? What is the firm's competitive strategy? What would the strategic map for this company look like? How would you summarize your recommended strategic HR policies for this company?

3-13. Appendix A, PHR and SPHR Knowledge Base, at the end of this book (pages 580–588) lists the knowledge someone studying for the HRCI certification exam needs to have in each area of human resource management (such as in Strategic Management, Workforce Planning, and Human Resource Development). In groups of four to five students, do four things: (1) review Appendix A; (2) identify the material in this chapter that relates to the required knowledge Appendix A lists; (3) write four multiple-choice exam questions on this material that you believe would be suitable for inclusion in the HRCI exam; and (4) if time permits, have someone from your team post your team's questions in front of the class, so that students in all teams can answer the exam questions created by the other teams.

KNOWLEDGE BASE

Experiential Exercise

Developing an HR Strategy for Starbucks

A few years ago, Starbucks was facing serious challenges. Sales per store were stagnant or declining, and its growth rate and profitability were down. Many believed that its introduction of breakfast foods had diverted its "baristas" from their traditional jobs as coffee-preparation experts. McDonald's and Dunkin' Donuts were introducing lower-priced but still high-grade coffees. Starbucks' former CEO stepped back into the company's top job. You need to help him formulate a new direction for his company.

Purpose: The purpose of this exercise is to give you experience in developing an HR strategy, in this case, by developing one for Starbucks.

Required Understanding: You should be thoroughly familiar with the material in this chapter.

How to Set Up the Exercise/Instructions: Set up groups of three or four students for this exercise. You are probably already quite familiar with what it's like to have a cup of coffee or tea in a Starbucks coffee shop, but if not, spend some time in one prior to this exercise. Meet in groups and develop an outline for an HR strategy for Starbucks Corp. Assume that for a corporate strategy Starbucks will remain primarily an international chain of coffee shops. Your outline should include four basic elements: a business/competitive strategy for Starbucks, the workforce requirements (in terms of employee competencies and behaviors) this strategy requires, specific HR policies and the activities necessary to produce these workforce requirements, and suggestions for metrics to measure the success of the HR strategy.

Video Case

Video Title: Strategic Management (Joie de Vivre Hospitality)

SYNOPSIS

Chip Conley is the founder of Joie de Vivre Hospitality (JDV), a collection of boutique hotels, restaurants, and spas in California. The kitschy atmosphere of the boutiques allows JDV to differentiate itself from both the luxury and the chain hotels. Customer loyalty is so great that JDV relies primarily on word-of-mouth advertising and spends little on traditional advertising methods.

Discussion Questions

3-14. How does Joie de Vivre Hospitality differentiate its boutique hotels from other hotel offerings in the area?

3-15. How did Chip Conley and Joie de Vivre Hospitality demonstrate great strategic flexibility during the dot-com crash and post-9/11 industry recession?

3-16. What is Joie de Vivre's philosophy on advertising for its hotels? How does this support the firm's strategic aims?

3-17. Similarly, list five specific human resource management practices that you would suggest JDV use in order to produce the employee behaviors required to achieve JDV's strategic aims.

CHAPTER 3

Application Case

Siemens Builds a Strategy-Oriented HR System

Siemens is a 150-year-old German company, but it's not the company it was even a few years ago. Until recently, Siemens focused on producing electrical products. Today the firm has diversified into software, engineering, and services. It is also global, with more than 400,000 employees working in 190 countries. In other words, Siemens became a world leader by pursuing a corporate strategy that emphasized diversifying into high-tech products and services, and doing so on a global basis.

With a corporate strategy like that, human resource management plays a big role at Siemens. Sophisticated engineering and services require more focus on employee selection, training, and compensation than in the average firm, and globalization requires delivering these services globally. Siemens sums up the basic themes of its HR strategy in several points. These include:

1. **A living company is a learning company.** The high-tech nature of Siemens' business means that employees must be able to learn on a continuing basis. Siemens uses its system of combined classroom and hands-on apprenticeship training around the world to help facilitate this. It also offers employees extensive continuing education and management development.
2. **Global teamwork is the key to developing and using all the potential of the firm's human resources.** Because it is so important for employees throughout Siemens to feel free to work together and interact, employees have to understand the whole process, not just bits and pieces. To support this, Siemens provides extensive training and development. It also ensures that all employees feel they're part of a strong, unifying corporate identity. For example, HR uses cross-border, cross-cultural experiences as prerequisites for career advances.
3. **A climate of mutual respect is the basis of all relationships—within the company and with society.** Siemens contends that the wealth of nationalities, cultures, languages, and outlooks represented by its employees is one of its most valuable assets. It therefore engages in numerous HR activities aimed at building openness, transparency, and fairness, and supporting diversity.

Questions

3-18. Based on the information in this case, provide examples for Siemens of at least four strategically required organizational outcomes, and four required workforce competencies and behaviors.

3-19. Identify at least four strategically relevant HR policies and activities that Siemens has instituted in order to help human resource management contribute to achieving Siemens' strategic goals.

3-20. Provide a brief illustrative outline of a strategy map for Siemens.

Continuing Case

Carter Cleaning Company

The High-Performance Work System

As a recent graduate and as a person who keeps up with the business press, Jennifer Carter is familiar with the benefits of programs such as total quality management and high-performance work systems.

Jack, her father, actually installed a total quality program of sorts at Carter, and it has been in place for about 5 years. This program takes the form of employee meetings. Jack holds employee meetings periodically, but particularly when there is a serious problem in a store—such as poor-quality work or machine breakdowns. When problems like these arise, instead of trying to diagnose them himself or with Jennifer, he contacts all the employees in that store and meets with them when the store closes. Hourly employees get extra pay for these meetings. The meetings have been useful in helping Jack to identify and rectify several problems. For example, in one store all the fine white blouses were coming out looking dingy. It turned out that the cleaner/spotter had been ignoring the company rule that required cleaning ("boiling down") the perchloroethylene cleaning fluid before washing items like these. As a result, these fine white blouses were being washed in cleaning fluid that had residue from other, earlier washes.

Jennifer now wonders whether these employee meetings should be expanded to give the employees an even bigger role in managing the Carter stores' quality. "We can't be everywhere watching everything all the time," she said to her father. "Yes, but these people only earn about $8 to $15 per hour. Will they really want to act like mini-managers?" he replied.

Questions

3-21. Would you recommend that the Carters expand their quality program? If so, specifically what form should it take?

3-22. Assume the Carters want to institute a high-performance work system as a test program in one of their stores. Write a one-page outline summarizing important HR practices you think they should focus on.

CHAPTER 3

Translating Strategy into HR Policies and Practices Case*,§

**The accompanying strategy map for this chapter is in the MyManagementLab, and the overall map on the inside back cover of this text outlines the relationships involved.*

IMPROVING PERFORMANCE at The Hotel Paris

The Hotel Paris International

Starting as a single hotel in a Paris suburb in 1990, the Hotel Paris now comprises a chain of nine hotels, with two in France, one each in London and Rome, and others in New York, Miami, Washington, Chicago, and Los Angeles. As a corporate strategy, the Hotel Paris's management and owners want to continue to expand geographically. They believe doing so will let them capitalize on their reputation for good service, by providing multicity alternatives for their satisfied guests. The problem is, their reputation for good service has been deteriorating. If they cannot improve service, it would be unwise for them to expand, since their guests might prefer other hotels after trying the Hotel Paris.

Several things are complicating their problem. Elected in 2012, French president Francois Hollande has been unable to halt or even slow the country's economic decline. His attempts to impose incremental tax rates of 75% on wealthy citizens are prompting many to contemplate leaving France. Furthermore, many tourists—faced with similar economic challenges elsewhere—are increasingly staying at short-term rental apartments in Paris, found on the Web, for a fraction of what a fine hotel stay might cost.

The Strategy

Top management, with input from the HR and other managers, and with the board of directors' approval, chooses a new competitive strategy and formulates new strategic goals. They decide: "The Hotel Paris International will use superior guest services to differentiate the Hotel Paris properties, and to thereby increase the length of stays and the return rate of guests, and thus boost revenues and profitability." All Hotel Paris managers—including the director of HR services—must now formulate strategies that support this competitive strategy.

§*Written by and copyright Gary Dessler, PhD.*

The Strategically Required Organizational Outcomes

The Hotel Paris's basic strategy is to use superior guest services to expand geographically. For HR director Lisa Cruz, reviewing the hotel's activities makes it clear that achieving the hotel's strategic aims means achieving a number of required organizational outcomes. For example, Lisa and her management colleagues must take steps that produce fewer customer complaints and more written compliments, more frequent guest returns and longer stays, and higher guest expenditures per visit.

The Strategically Relevant Workforce Competencies and Behaviors

The question facing Lisa, then, is this: What competencies and behaviors must our hotel's employees exhibit, if we are to produce required organizational outcomes such as fewer customer complaints, more compliments, and more frequent guest returns? Thinking through this question helps Lisa come up with an answer. For example, the hotel's required employee competencies and behaviors would include, "high-quality front-desk customer service," "taking calls for reservations in a friendly manner," "greeting guests at the front door," and "processing guests' room service meals efficiently." All require motivated, high-morale employees.

The Strategically Relevant HR Policies and Activities

The HR manager's task now is to identify and specify the HR policies and activities that will enable the hotel to produce these crucial workforce competencies and behaviors. For example, "high-quality front-desk customer service" is one such required behavior. From this, the HR director identifies HR activities to produce such front-desk customer service efforts. For example, she decides to *institute practices to improve the disciplinary fairness and justice in the company*, with the aim of *improving employee morale*. Her assumption is that enhanced fairness will produce higher morale and that higher morale will produce improved front-desk service.

The Strategy Map

Next, Lisa, working with the hotel's chief financial officer (CFO), outlines a strategy map for the hotel. This outlines the cause-and-effect links among the HR activities, the workforce behaviors, and the organizational outcomes (the figure on this book's inside back cover shows the overall map; you'll find detailed maps for each HR function in each chapter's related MyManagementLabs page).

This map and its linkages reflect certain assumptions on Lisa's part. For example, based on experience and discussions with the firm's other managers, she formulates the following *hypothesis* about how HR affects hotel performance: Improved grievance procedures cause improved morale, which leads to improved front-desk service, which leads to increased guest returns, which leads to improved financial performance. The HR director then chooses metrics to measure each of these factors. For example, she decides to measure "improved disciplinary procedures" in terms of how many grievances employees submit each month. She measures "improved morale" in terms of "scores on our hotel's semiannual attitude survey," and measures "high-quality front-desk customer service" in terms of "customer complaints per month."

She moves on to quantifying the cause-and-effect links among these measures. For example: "Can we show top management that there is a measurable, sequential link between improved disciplinary procedures, high morale, improved front-desk service, number of guest return visits, and hotel financial performance (revenues and profits)?" If she can show such links, she has a persuasive case that shows HR's measurable contribution to the hotel's bottom-line financial performance.

In practice, the HR manager may well just rely on a largely subjective but logical argument to make the case for such cause-and-effect linkages. But ideally, she will use statistical methods such as correlation analysis to determine if measurable links exist, and (if so) what their magnitudes are. In this way, she might find, for instance, that a 10% improvement in grievance rates is associated with an almost 20% improvement in morale. Similarly, a 20% improvement in morale is associated with a 30% reduction in customer front-desk complaints. Furthermore, a 30% reduction in complaints is associated with a 20% increase in guest return visits, and a 20% increase in return rate is associated with a 6% rise in hotel revenues. It would appear that a relatively small HR effort in reducing grievances might have a big effect on this hotel's bottom-line performance!

Several things complicate this measurement process. For example, it's risky to draw cause–effect conclusions from correlation measures like these (do fewer grievances lead to higher morale, or vice versa?). Furthermore, it's rare that a single factor (such as grievance rates) will have such effects alone, so we may want to measure the effects of several HR policies and activities on morale simultaneously.

As explained in this chapter, computerization could enable Lisa to build a more comprehensive HR scorecard process, one that might handle links among dozens of cause-and-effect metrics. (Several vendors supply such "scorecarding" software.) If not, then she will rely more on the logic and common sense underlying the strategy map to make her case.

How We Will Use the Hotel Paris Case

A Hotel Paris case in each chapter will show how Lisa, the Hotel Paris's HR director, uses that chapter's concepts and techniques to: (1) create HR policies and practices that help the Hotel Paris (2) produce the employee competencies and behaviors the company needs (3) to produce the customer service the Hotel Paris needs to achieve its strategic goals.

For example, she will endeavor to improve workforce competencies and behaviors by instituting improved recruitment processes (Chapter 5), and measure improved recruitment in terms of "number of qualified applicants per position." Similarly, she will recommend to management that they change the company's pay policies, so that the "target percentile for total compensation is in the top 25%." She could argue, based on competitors' experience, that doing so will translate into improved customer service behavior, more satisfied customers, and improved hotel performance. In practice, all the human resource management functions we discuss in this book influence employee competencies and behaviors, and thereby organizational performance.

You will find the strategy map for each chapter's topic in the chapter's MyManagementLab; the summary map on the inside back cover of this book outlines the overall relationships involved for the Hotel Paris.

Questions

3-23. Draw a more simplified and abbreviated strategy map for the Hotel Paris. Specifically, summarize in your own words an example of the hierarchy of links among the hotel's *HR practices*, necessary *workforce competencies* and behaviors, and required *organizational outcomes.*

3-24. Using Table 3-1, and Figure 3-9, list at least 15 metrics the Hotel Paris could use to measure its HR practices.

MyManagementLab

Go to **mymanagementlab.com** for Auto-graded writing questions as well as the following Assisted-graded writing questions:

3-25. Define and give at least two examples of the cost-leadership competitive strategy and the differentiation competitive strategy.

3-26. What is a high-performance work system? Provide several specific examples of the typical components in a high-performance work system.

3-27. MyManagementLab only—comprehensive writing assignment for this chapter.

Key Terms

strategic plan, 63
strategy, 63
strategic management, 63
mission statement, 64
corporate-level strategy, 66
competitive strategy, 67
competitive advantage, 67
functional strategies, 67
strategic human resource management, 68
strategy map, 71
HR scorecard, 72
digital dashboard, 72
strategy-based metrics, 74
HR audit, 76
high-performance work system (HPWS), 77
human resource metric, 78

Endnotes

1. For a good discussion of aligning goals, see, for example, Eric Krell, "Change Within," *HR Magazine,* August 2011, pp. 43–50.
2. James Jenks, *The Hiring, Firing (And Everything in Between) Personnel Forms Book* (Round Lake Publishing Co., 1994).
3. For perspectives on strategic planning, see, for example, Donald Sull and Kathleen Eisenhardt, "Simple Rules for a Complex World," *Harvard Business Review*, September 2012, pp. 69–75; and Martin Reeves, Claire Love, and Philipp Tillmann, "Your Strategy Needs a Strategy," *Harvard Business Review*, September 2012, pp. 76–83.
4. www.aboutmcdonalds.com/mcd/investors/company_profile.html, accessed March 23, 2013.
5. Thomas Wheelen and J. David Hunger, *Strategic Management and Business Policy* (Upper Saddle River, NJ: Pearson Education, 2010), pp. 142–143.
6. www.facebook.com/Facebook?v=info, accessed March 23, 2013.
7. www.google.com/about/company/, accessed March 23, 2013.
8. For the full mission statement, see http://www.pepsico.com/Company/Our-Mission-and-Vision.html, accessed September 6, 2013.
9. For a discussion of this, see A. G. Lafley et al., "Bringing Science to the Art of Strategy," *Harvard Business Review*, September 2012, pp. 58–59.
10. Paul Nutt, "Making Strategic Choices," *Journal of Management Studies*, January 2002, pp. 67–96.
11. Peter Coy, "A Renaissance in U.S. Manufacturing," *Bloomberg Businessweek*, May 9–15, 2011, pp. 11–13.
12. Michael Porter, *Competitive Strategy* (New York: The Free Press, 1980), p. 14. See also Chris Zook and James Allen, "The Great Repeatable Business Model," *Harvard Business Review,* November 2011, pp. 107–112.
13. Andy Cook, "Make Sure You Get a Prenup," *European Venture Capital Journal*, December/January 2007, p. 76, www.accessmylibrary.com/coms2/summary_0286-29140938_ITM, accessed June 29, 2009.
14. www.towersPerrin.com, accessed December 4, 2007. See also Ingmar Bjorkman, "The HR Function in Large-Scale Mergers and Acquisitions: The Case of Nordea," *Personnel Review* 35, no. 6 (2006), pp. 654–671; Elina Antila and Anne Kakkonen, "Factors Affecting the Role of HR Managers in International Mergers and Acquisitions: A Multiple Case Study," *Personnel Review* 37, no. 3 (2008), pp. 280–299; Linda Tepedino and Muriel Watkins, "Be a Master of Mergers and Acquisitions," *HR Magazine*, June 2010, pp. 53–56; and Yaakov Weber and Yitzak Fried, "Guest Editor's Note: The Role of HR Practices in Managing Culture Clash During the Post Merger Integration Process," *Human Resource Management* 50, no. 5 (September–October 2011), p. 565.
15. This is paraphrased or quoted from "HR Services, Service Offerings: Mergers, Acquisitions and Restructuring," www.towersPerrin.com, accessed December 4, 2007.
16. See, for example, Evan Offstein, Devi Gnyawali, and Anthony Cobb, "A Strategic Human Resource Perspective of Firm Competitive Behavior," *Human Resource Management Review* 15 (2005), pp. 305–318.
17. Brian Hults, "Integrate HR with Operating Strategy," *HR Magazine,* October 2011, pp. 54–56. A recent review of strategic human resource management research in the United States concluded that "strategic human resource management researchers as a group deserve a D to F grade" when it comes to "development of a strategic human resource management theory with predictive accuracy, production of actionable and value-added managerial principles, and accurate portrayal of the historical origins and development of this area of management scholarship in practice." Bruce Couchman, "Strategic Human Resource Management Research in the United States: A Failing Grade After 30 Years?" *Academy of Management Perspectives*, May 2012, pp. 12–34. See also Janet Marler, "Strategic Human Resource Management in Context: A Historical and Global Perspective," *Academy of Management Perspectives*, May 2012, pp. 6–10.
18. Arthur Yeung, "Setting Up for Success: How the Portman Ritz-Carlton Hotel Gets the Best from Its People," *Human Resource Management* 45, no. 2 (Summer 2006), pp. 67–75.
19. "Automation Improves Retailer's Hiring Efficiency and Quality," *HR Focus* 82, no. 2 (February 2005), p. 3.
20. Based on Kevin Wallstein, "Diversity Pays Off in Big Sales for Toyota Dealership," *Workforce* 77, no. 9 (September 1998), pp. 91–93.
21. Richard Shafer et al., "Crafting a Human Resource Strategy to Foster Organizational Agility: A Case Study," *Human Resource Management* 40, no. 3 (Fall 2001), pp. 197–211.
22. Paul Buller and Glenn McEvoy, "Strategy, Human Resource Management and Performance: Sharpening Line of Sight," *Human Resource Management Review* 22 (2012), pp. 43–56.
23. Managers can access their companies' strategy maps while on the go. They can use the ActiveStrategy Company's *ActiveStrategy Enterprise* to create and automate their strategy maps, and to access them through iPhone or similar devices. See www.activestrategy.com/solutions/strategy_mapping.aspx, accessed March 24, 2009.
24. When focusing on HR activities, managers call this an *HR scorecard*. When applying the same process broadly to all of the company's activities, including, for example, sales, production, and finance, managers call it the "balanced scorecard process."
25. The idea for the HR scorecard derives from the broader measurement tool managers call the "balanced scorecard." This does for the company as a whole what the HR scorecard does for HR, summarizing instead the impact of various functions including HRM, sales, production, and distribution. The "balanced" in *balanced scorecard* refers to a balance of goals—financial and nonfinancial.
26. See, for example, "Using HR Performance Metrics to Optimize Operations and Profits," *PR Newswire*, February 27, 2008; and "How to 'Make Over' Your HR Metrics," *HR Focus* 84, no. 9 (September 2007), p. 3.
27. SHRM Human Capital Benchmarking Study: 2007 Executive Summary.
28. For additional information on HR metrics, see, for example, Karen M. Kroll, "Repurposing Metrics for HR: HR Professionals Are Looking Through a People-Focused Lens at the CFO's Metrics on Revenue and Income per FTE," *HR Magazine* 51, no. 7 (July 2006), pp. 64–69; and http://shrm.org/metrics/library_publishedover/measurementsystemsTOC.asp, accessed February 2, 2008.
29. Connie Winkler, "Quality Check: Better Metrics Improve HR's Ability to Measure—and Manage—the Quality of Hires," *HR Magazine* 52, no. 5 (May 2007), pp. 93–94, 96, 98.
30. Ibid.
31. Ibid.
32. See, for example, "Benchmarking for Functional HR Metrics," *HR Focus* 83, no. 11 (November 2006), p. 1; and John Sullivan, "The Last Word," *Workforce Management,* November 19, 2007, p. 42. SHRM makes various metrics calculators available to members at www.shrm.org/TemplatesTools/Samples/Metrics/Pages/GeneralHumanResources.aspx, accessed October 6, 2012.
33. See Brian Becker and Mark Huselid, "Measuring HR? Benchmarking Is Not the Answer!" *HR Magazine* 8, no. 12 (December 2003), www.charmed.org, accessed February 2, 2008.
34. Ibid.

35. George Marakas, *Decision Support Systems* (Upper Saddle River, NJ: Prentice Hall, 2003), p. 326.
36. "Executive Workplace Analytics," www.aon.com/human-capital-consulting/hrbpo, accessed March 19, 2013.
37. Ed Frauenheim, "Keeping Score with Analytics Software," *Workforce Management* 86, no. 10 (May 21, 2007), pp. 25–33. See also Andrew McAfee and Eric Brynjolfsson, "Big Data: The Management Revolution," *Harvard Business Review*, October 2012, pp. 61–68.
38. Steven Baker, "Data Mining Moves to Human Resources," *Bloomberg Businessweek*, March 12, 2009, www.BusinessWeek.com/magazine/, accessed April 13, 2011.
39. Baker, op cit. See also "HR Analytics," *Workforce Management*, August 2012, p. 24.
40. Ed Frauenheim, "Numbers Game," *Workforce Management* 90, no. 3 (March 2011), p. 21.
41. Thomas Davenport, Jeanne Harris, and Jeremy Shapiro, "Competing on Talent Analytics," *Harvard Business Review*, October 2010, pp. 52–58.
42. Cliff Stevenson, "Five Ways High Performance Organizations Use HR Analytics," www.i4cp.com/print/trendwatchers/2012/12/12/five-ways-high-performance-organizations-use-hr-analytics, accessed July 14, 2013.
43. Ibid., p. 54.
44. Lin Grensing-Pophal, "HR Audits: Know the Market, Land Assignments," SHRM Consultants Forum, December 2004, www.shrm.org/-hrdisciplines/consultants/Articles/Pages/CMS_010705.aspx, accessed July 7, 2010.
45. Grensing-Pophal, "HR Audits: Know the Market"; and Bill Coy, "Introduction to the Human Resources Audit," La Piana Associates, Inc., www.lapiana.org/consulting, accessed May 1, 2008.
46. Dana R. Scott, "Conducting a Human Resources Audit," *New Hampshire Business Review*, August 2007. See also Eric Krell, "Auditing Your HR Department," *HR Magazine*, September 2011, pp. 101–103.
47. See, for example, www.personneltoday.com/blogs/hcglobal-human-capital-management/2009/02/theres-no-such-thing-as-eviden.html, accessed October 2, 2012.
48. Eric Anderson and Duncan Simester, "A Step-by-Step Guide to Smart Business Experiments," *Harvard Business Review*, March 2011, pp. 98–105.
49. Ibid.
50. Bill Roberts, "How to Put Analytics on Your Side," *HR Magazine*, October 2009, pp. 43–46.
51. www.bls.gov/opub/ted/2006/may/wk2/art01.htm, accessed April 18, 2009; and "Super Human Resources Practices Result in Better Overall Performance, Report Says," *BNA Bulletin to Management*, August 26, 2004, pp. 273–274. See also Wendy Boswell, "Aligning Employees with the Organization's Strategic Objectives: Out of Line of Sight, Out of Mind," *International Journal of Human Resource Management* 17, no. 9 (September 2006), pp. 1014–1041. A study found that some employers, which the researchers called *cost minimizers*, intentionally took a lower-cost approach to human resource practices, with mixed results. See Soo Min Toh et al., "Human Resource Configurations: Investigating Fit with the Organizational Context," *Journal of Applied Psychology* 93, no. 4 (2008), pp. 864–882.
52. Samuel Aryee et al., "Impact of High Performance Work Systems on Individual—and Branch—Level Performance: Test of a Multilevel Model of Intermediate Linkages," *Journal of Applied Psychology* 97, no. 2 (2012), pp. 287–300.
53. See, for example, www.personneltoday.com/blogs/hcglobal-human-capital-management/2009/02/theres-no-such-thing-as-eviden.html, accessed October 2, 2012.
54. See for example, J. G. Messersmith, "Unlocking the Black Box: Exploring the Link Between High-Performance Work Systems and Performance," *Human Resource Management International Digest* 20, no. 3 (2012), pp. 1118–1132.

4 Job Analysis and the Talent Management Process

Source: Monty Rakusen/Getty Images

MyManagementLab®

Improve Your Grade!

When you see this icon, visit **www.mymanagementlab.com** for activities that are applied, personalized, and offer immediate feedback.

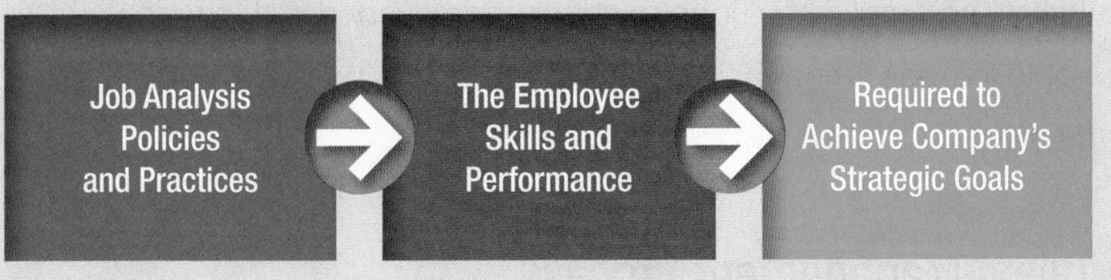

For a bird's eye view of how one company created a job analysis system to improve its strategic performance, read the Hotel Paris case on pages 117–118 and answer the questions after reading the chapter.

WHERE ARE WE NOW . . .

Managers should determine what a job entails before deciding who to recruit and select for the job. The main purpose of this chapter is to show you how to determine what a job entails, by analyzing a job and writing a job description for it. The main topics we address include the talent management process, the basics of job analysis, methods for collecting job analysis information, writing job descriptions, writing job specifications, and using models and profiles in talent management. Then, in Chapter 5 (Personnel Planning and Recruiting), we'll turn to the methods managers use to actually find the employees they need.

LEARNING OBJECTIVES

1 Define talent management and explain why it is important.

2 Discuss the process of job analysis, including why it is important.

3 Explain how to use at least three methods of collecting job analysis information, including interviews, questionnaires, and observation.

4 Explain how you would write a job description.

5 Explain how to write a job specification.

6 Explain competency-based job analysis, including what it means and how it's done in practice.

When Daimler opened its Mercedes-Benz assembly plant in Alabama, its managers had a dilemma. Their aim was to create an ultra high-performance plant, one Daimler could extend to its other plants in America, South Africa, Brazil, and Germany. The dilemma was that plant management could not hire, train, or pay their employees unless they knew what each employee was expected to do. But in this plant, self-managing teams would assemble the vehicles, so employees' jobs might change every day. How do you hire people for jobs when their job duties are a moving target?[1] We'll see what they did.

The Talent Management Process

1 Define talent management and explain why it is important.

For many, this portion of the book (Chapters 4–Chapter 13) represents the heart of human resource management—including recruitment, selection, training, appraisal, career planning, and compensation. The traditional way to view these activities is as a series of steps:

1. Decide what positions to fill, through job analysis, personnel planning, and forecasting.
2. Build a pool of job applicants, by recruiting internal or external candidates.
3. Have candidates complete application forms and perhaps have initial screening interviews.
4. Use selection tools like tests, interviews, background checks, and physical exams to identify viable candidates.
5. Decide to whom to make an offer.
6. Orient, train, and develop employees to provide them with the competencies they need to do their jobs.
7. Appraise employees to assess how they're doing.
8. Reward and compensate employees to maintain their motivation.

This linear view makes sense. For example, the employer needs job candidates before selecting whom to hire. The problem is that managers do not just, say, train employees (step 6 above) and then appraise how they're doing (step 7). Instead, the appraisals also loop back to shape the employee's subsequent training. The process is interactive. Recognizing this, the trend today is to view activities 1–8 above as part of a coordinated *talent management* effort.

"Talent management" means different things to different people. When many managers today say "talent management," they simply mean managing in such a way as to acquire, improve, and retain their best employees. For instance, "let's make sure we have retention practices in place so we don't lose valued talent." To be more precise, we will define **talent management** as *the goal oriented and integrated process of planning, recruiting, developing, managing, and compensating employees.*[2] (Figure 4-1 illustrates this.) By this definition, talent management has several distinguishing features. The manager who takes a talent management perspective:

talent management
The goal-oriented and integrated process of planning, recruiting, developing, managing, and compensating employees.

1. Treats talent management activities such as recruiting and training as interrelated. For example, having employees with the right skills depends as much on recruiting, training, and compensation as on applicant testing.
2. Makes sure all talent management decisions (such as staffing, training, and pay) are goal directed. In other words, ask, "What recruiting, testing, training, or pay action should I take to produce the employee competencies we need *to achieve our strategic goals*?"
3. Consistently uses the same "profile" of required human skills, knowledge, and behaviors ("competencies") for formulating a job's recruitment plans as for making selection, training, appraisal, and compensation decisions for it. For example, if "Design complex software applications" is one required software engineer skill, then ask interview questions to assess the candidate on this skill; train the new employee to improve this skill; and then appraise and compensate the person based on his or her skill proficiency.
4. Actively segments and manages employees. For example, Accenture recommends identifying the firm's "mission critical" employees, and then managing their development and rewards separately from the firm's other employees.
5. Actively coordinates or integrates the ongoing talent management functions such as recruiting and training. For example, HR managers meet to make sure they are using the same skills profile to recruit as to select, train, and appraise for a particular job, or use special talent management software to do so.

FIGURE 4-1 **Overview of Talent Management**

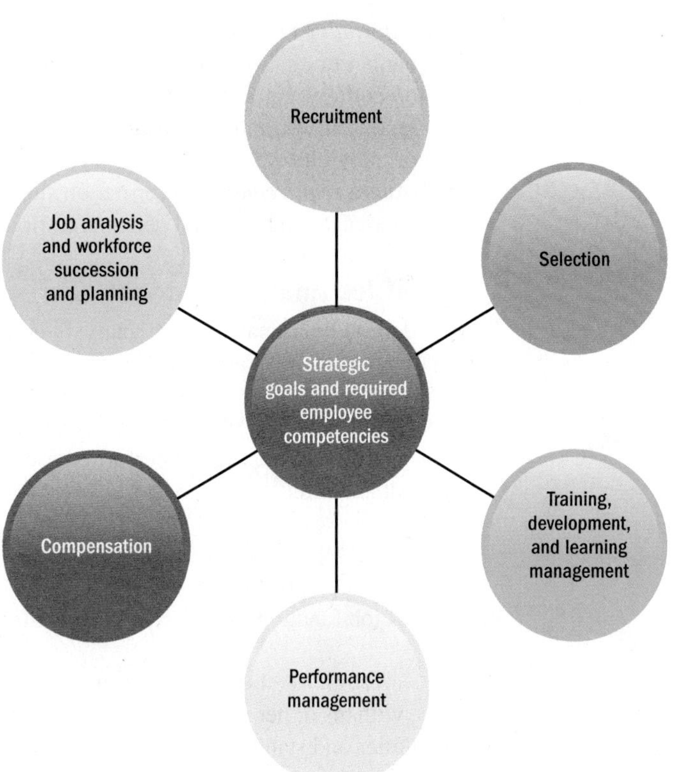

Improving Performance Through HRIS: Talent Management Software

Many employers adopt talent management software systems to coordinate their talent-related activities. For example, Talent Management Solutions' (www.talentmanagement101.com) *Talent Management Suite* includes recruiting software, employee performance management, a learning management system, and compensation management support. It "ensures that all levels of the organization are aligned—all working for the same goals."[3] SilkRoad Technology's Talent Management Solution includes applicant tracking, on boarding, performance management, compensation, and employee intranet support. Its Talent Management Life Suite "helps you recruit, manage, and retain your best employees."[4]

job analysis
The procedure for determining the duties and skill requirements of a job and the kind of person who should be hired for it.

2 Discuss the process of job analysis, including why it is important.

job descriptions
A list of a job's duties, responsibilities, reporting relationships, working conditions, and supervisory responsibilities—one product of a job analysis.

job specifications
A list of a job's "human requirements," that is, the requisite education, skills, personality, and so on—another product of a job analysis.

The Basics of Job Analysis

Talent management starts with understanding what jobs need to be filled, and the human traits and competencies employees need to do those jobs effectively. **Job analysis** is the procedure through which you determine the duties of the company's positions and the characteristics of the people to hire for them.[5] Job analysis produces information for writing **job descriptions** (a list of what the job entails) and **job** (or "person") **specifications** (what kind of people to hire for the job). Virtually every personnel-related action—interviewing applicants, and training and appraising employees, for instance—requires knowing what the job entails and what human traits one needs to do the job well.[6]

The supervisor or human resources specialist normally collects one or more of the following types of information via the job analysis:

- ***Work activities.*** Information about the job's actual work activities, such as cleaning, selling, teaching, or painting. This list may also include how, why, and when the worker performs each activity.
- ***Human behaviors.*** Information about human behaviors the job requires, like sensing, communicating, lifting weights, or walking long distances.
- ***Machines, tools, equipment, and work aids.*** Information regarding tools used, materials processed, knowledge dealt with or applied (such as finance or law), and services rendered (such as counseling or repairing).

- ***Performance standards.*** Information about the job's performance standards (in terms of quantity or quality levels for each job duty, for instance).
- ***Job context.*** Information about such matters as physical working conditions, work schedule, incentives, and, for instance, the number of people with whom the employee would normally interact.
- ***Human requirements.*** Information such as knowledge or skills (education, training, work experience) and required personal attributes (aptitudes, personality, interests).

Uses of Job Analysis Information

As Figure 4-2 summarizes, job analysis is important because it supports just about all human resource management activities.

RECRUITMENT AND SELECTION Information about what duties the job entails and what human characteristics are required to perform these activities helps managers decide what sort of people to recruit and hire.

EEO COMPLIANCE Job analysis is crucial for validating all major human resources practices. For example, to comply with the Americans with Disabilities Act, employers should know each job's essential job functions—which in turn requires a job analysis.

PERFORMANCE APPRAISAL A performance appraisal compares each employee's actual performance with his or her duties and performance standards. Managers use job analysis to learn what these duties and standards are.

COMPENSATION Compensation (such as salary and bonus) usually depends on the job's required skill and education level, safety hazards, degree of responsibility, and so on—all factors you assess through job analysis.

TRAINING The job description lists the job's specific duties and requisite skills—thus pinpointing what training the job requires.

Conducting a Job Analysis

There are six steps in doing a job analysis of a job, as follows.

STEP 1: DECIDE HOW YOU WILL USE THE INFORMATION Some data collection techniques—like interviewing the employee—are good for writing job descriptions. Other techniques, like the position analysis questionnaire we describe later, provide numerical ratings for each job; these can be used to compare jobs for compensation purposes.

FIGURE 4-2 Uses of Job Analysis Information

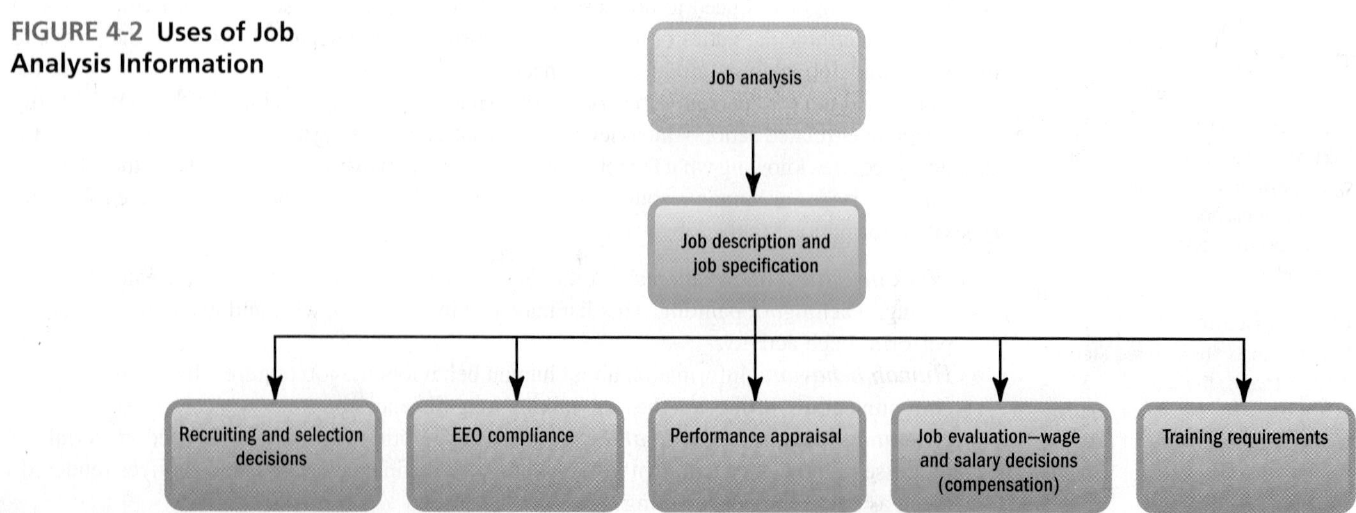

organization chart
A chart that shows the organization-wide distribution of work, with titles of each position and interconnecting lines that show who reports to and communicates with whom.

process chart
A workflow chart that shows the flow of inputs to and outputs from a particular job.

workflow analysis
A detailed study of the flow of work from job to job in a work process.

STEP 2: REVIEW RELEVANT BACKGROUND INFORMATION SUCH AS ORGANIZATION CHARTS AND PROCESS CHARTS[7] It is important to understand the job's context. For example, **organization charts** show the organizationwide division of work, and where the job fits in the overall organization. It should show the title of each position and, by means of interconnecting lines, who reports to whom, and with whom the job incumbent communicates. A **process chart** provides a detailed picture of the work flow. Thus, in the process chart in Figure 4-3, the quality control clerk should review components from suppliers, check components going to the plant managers, and give information regarding the components' quality to these managers. Finally, an existing job description may provide a starting point for revising the job description.

Workflow Analysis Reviewing the job's context helps the manager identify what a job's duties and demands are now. However, it does *not* answer questions like "Does how this job relates to other jobs make sense?" or "Should this job even exist?" To answer such questions, the manager may conduct a *workflow analysis*. **Workflow analysis** is a detailed study of the flow of work from job to job in a work process. Usually, the analyst focuses on one identifiable work process, rather than on how the company gets all its work done. The accompanying Profit Center feature illustrates workflow analysis.

IMPROVING PEFORMANCE: HR as a Profit Center

Boosting Productivity through Work Redesign

The Atlantic American insurance company in Atlanta conducted a workflow analysis to identify inefficiencies in how it processes its insurance claims. What did this involve? As the firm's HR director said, "We followed the life of a claim to where it arrived in the mail and where it eventually ended up" in order to find ways to improve the process.[8]

The workflow analysis prompted several performance-boosting redesigns of the insurance claim jobs. The firm reduced from four to one the number of people opening mail, replacing three people with a machine that does it automatically. A new date stamping machine lets staff stamp 20 pages at a time rather than 1. A new software program adds bar codes to each claim automatically, rather than manually. The new system lowered costs.

Discussion Question 4-1: Based on your experience, what would the workflow look like for the process a dry-cleaning store uses to accept and chronicle a new order of clothes from a customer? How might this process be improved?

In conducting a workflow analysis, the manager may use a *flow process chart*; this lists in order each step of the process. The manager may convert this step-by-step flow process chart into a diagrammatic process chart. This shows, with arrows and circles, each step in the process.

FIGURE 4-3 Process Chart for Analyzing a Job's Workflow

Source: Compensation Management: Rewarding Performance, 6th Edition, by Richard J. Henderson. Copyright © 1994 by Pearson Education, Inc. Reprinted and Electronically reproduced by permission of Pearson Education, Inc., Upper Saddle River, New Jersey.

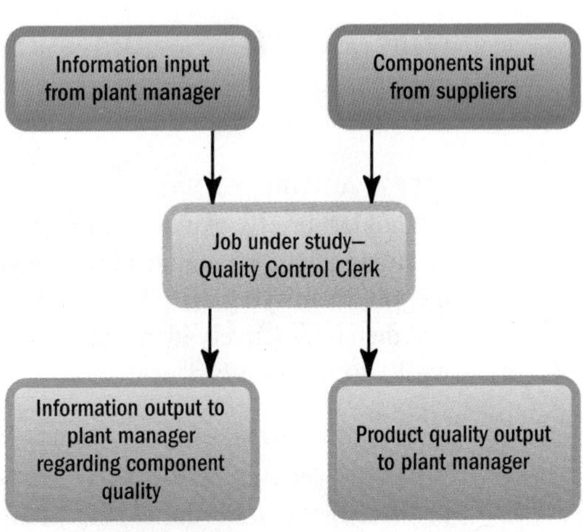

business process reengineering
Redesigning business processes, usually by combining steps, so that small multifunction process teams using information technology do the jobs formerly done by a sequence of departments.

Business Process Reengineering Business process reengineering means redesigning business processes, usually by combining steps, so that small multifunction teams, often using information technology, do the jobs formerly done by a sequence of departments. The workflow analysis at American Atlantic led to a reengineering of its claims processing operation. The basic reengineering approach is to

1. Identify a business process to be redesigned (such as processing an insurance claim)
2. Measure the performance of the existing processes
3. Identify opportunities to improve these processes
4. Redesign and implement a new way of doing the work
5. Assign ownership of sets of formerly separate tasks to an individual or a team who use new computerized systems to support the new arrangement

As at Atlantic American, reengineering usually requires *redesigning* individual jobs. For example, those doing date stamping must now know how to use the new date-stamping machine.

Job Redesign Early economists enthusiastically described why specialized jobs (doing the same small thing repeatedly) was more efficient (as in, "practice makes perfect"). But soon other writers were describing what they viewed as the "dehumanizing" aspects of pigeonholing workers into highly repetitive jobs. These workers weren't motivated, they said; they did their jobs well only when supervisors were closely watching them. Many of these writers proposed redesigning jobs using methods such as job enlargement, job rotation, and job enrichment. **Job enlargement** means assigning workers additional same-level activities. Thus, the worker who previously only bolted the seat to the legs might attach the back too. **Job rotation** means systematically moving workers from one job to another.

job enlargement
Assigning workers additional same-level activities.

job rotation
Systematically moving workers from one job to another.

job enrichment
Redesigning jobs in a way that increases the opportunities for the worker to experience feelings of responsibility, achievement, growth, and recognition.

Psychologist Frederick Herzberg argued that the best way to motivate workers is through job enrichment. **Job enrichment** means redesigning jobs in a way that increases the opportunities for the worker to experience feelings of responsibility, achievement, growth, and recognition—and therefore more motivation. It does this by *empowering* the worker—for instance, by giving the worker the skills and authority to inspect the work, instead of having supervisors do that. Herzberg said empowered employees would do their jobs well because they wanted to, and quality and productivity would rise. That philosophy, in one form or another, is the theoretical basis for the team-based self-managing jobs in many companies around the world today. As at Atlantic American, managers enrich jobs in several ways:[9]

1. ***Form natural work groups.*** For example, put a team in charge of an identifiable body of work, such as processing an entire claim.
2. ***Combine tasks.*** Let one person assemble a product from start to finish instead of having it go through separate operations performed by different people.
3. ***Establish client relationships.*** Let the worker have contact as often as possible with the client of that person's work.
4. ***Vertically load the job.*** Have the worker, rather than the supervisor, plan, schedule, troubleshoot, and control his or her job.
5. ***Open feedback channels.*** Find more and better ways for the worker to get quick feedback on performance.

STEP 3: SELECT REPRESENTATIVE POSITIONS The manager must at some point select particular positions to focus on. For example, to analyze an assembler's job, it is probably unnecessary to analyze the jobs of all the firm's 200 assembly workers; instead a sample of 10 jobs will do.

STEP 4: ACTUALLY ANALYZE THE JOB In brief, the job analysis process involves greeting each job holder; briefly explaining the job analysis process and the participants' roles in this process; spending about 15 minutes interviewing the employee to get agreement on a basic summary of the job; identifying the job's broad areas of responsibility, such as "calling on potential clients"; and then interactively identifying specific duties/tasks within each area using one of the methods we'll discuss shortly.[10]

STEP 5: VERIFY THE JOB ANALYSIS INFORMATION WITH THE WORKER PERFORMING THE JOB AND WITH HIS OR HER IMMEDIATE SUPERVISOR This will help confirm that the information (for instance on the job's duties) is factually correct and complete and help to gain their acceptance.

STEP 6: DEVELOP A JOB DESCRIPTION AND JOB SPECIFICATION The *job description* lists the duties, activities, and responsibilities of the job, as well as its important features, such as working conditions. The *job specification* summarizes the personal qualities, traits, skills, and background required for getting the job done.

Methods for Collecting Job Analysis Information

3 Explain how to use at least three methods of collecting job analysis information, including interviews, questionnaires, and observation.

There are many ways (interviews, or questionnaires, for instance) to collect job information. The basic rule is to use those that best fit your purpose. Thus, an interview might be best for creating a list of job duties. The more quantitative "position analysis questionnaire" method may be best for quantifying each job's relative worth for pay purposes. Before actually analyzing the job, keep several things in mind.

- Make the job analysis a *joint effort by a human resources manager, the worker, and the worker's supervisor.* The human resource manager might observe the worker doing the job, and have both the supervisor and worker fill out job questionnaires. Then he or she lists the job's duties and required human traits. The supervisor and worker then verify the HR manager's list of job duties.
- *Make sure the questions and the process are both clear* to the employees. (For example, some might not know what you mean when you ask about the job's "mental demands.")
- *Use several job analysis methods.* For example, a questionnaire might miss a task the worker performs just occasionally. Therefore it's prudent to follow up the questionnaire with a short interview.

The Interview

Job analysis interviews range from unstructured ("Tell me about your job") to highly structured ones containing hundreds of specific items to check off.

Managers may conduct individual interviews with each employee, group interviews with groups of employees who have the same job, and/or supervisor interviews with one or more supervisors who know the job. Use group interviews when a large number of employees are performing similar or identical work, since this can be a quick and inexpensive way to gather information. As a rule, the workers' immediate supervisor attends the group session; if not, you can interview the supervisor separately.

The interviewee should understand the reason for the interview. There's a tendency for workers to view such interviews, rightly or wrongly, as "efficiency evaluations." If so, interviewees may hesitate to describe their jobs accurately.

iStockphoto/Thinkstock

It is helpful to spend several minutes prior to collecting job analysis information explaining the process that you will be following.

TYPICAL QUESTIONS Typical interview questions include the following:

What is the job being performed?

What exactly are the major duties of your position?

What physical locations do you work in?

What are the education, experience, skill, and [where applicable] certification and licensing requirements?

In what activities do you participate?

What are the job's responsibilities and duties?

What are the basic accountabilities or performance standards that typify your work?

What are your responsibilities? What are the environmental and working conditions involved?

What are the job's physical demands? The emotional and mental demands?

What are the health and safety conditions?

Are you exposed to any hazards or unusual working conditions?

STRUCTURED INTERVIEWS Many managers use questionnaires to guide the interview. Figure 4-4 presents one example. It includes questions regarding matters like the general purpose of the job; supervisory responsibilities; job duties; and education, experience, and skills required.

Such structured lists are not just for interviews. Job analysts who collect information by personally observing the work or by using questionnaires—two methods explained later—can also use structured lists.[11]

PROS AND CONS The interview's wide use reflects its advantages. It's a simple and quick way to collect information. Skilled interviewers can also unearth important activities that occur only occasionally, or informal contacts that aren't on the organization chart. The employee can also vent frustrations that might otherwise go unnoticed.

Distortion of information is the main problem.[12] Job analysis often precedes changing a job's pay rate. Employees therefore may legitimately view it as pay-related, and exaggerate some responsibilities while minimizing others. In one study, researchers listed possible job duties either as simple task statements ("record phone messages and other routine information") or as ability statements ("ability to record phone messages and other routine information"). Respondents were more likely to report the ability-based versions of the statements. There may be a tendency for people to inflate their job's importance when abilities are involved, to impress the perceptions of others.[13] Employees will even puff up their job titles to make their jobs seem more important.[14]

INTERVIEWING GUIDELINES To get the best information possible:

- Establish rapport with the interviewee. Know the person's name, speak understandably, briefly review the interview's purpose, and explain how the person was chosen for the interview.
- Use a structured guide that lists questions and provides space for answers. This ensures you'll identify crucial questions ahead of time and that all interviewers (if more than one) cover all the required questions. (However, also ask, "Was there anything we didn't cover with our questions?")
- Make sure you don't overlook crucial but infrequently performed activities—like a nurse's occasional emergency room duties. Ask the worker to list his or her duties in order of importance and frequency of occurrence.
- After completing the interview, review the information with the worker's immediate supervisor and with the interviewee.

Questionnaires

Having employees fill out questionnaires to describe their job duties and responsibilities is another good way to obtain job analysis information.

FIGURE 4-4 Job Analysis Questionnaire for Developing Job Descriptions

Sources: Adapted from: http://www.tsu.edu/PDFFiles/Human%20Resources/HR%20Forms/JAQ%20FORM_rev%20100809%20a.pdf; http://www.delawarepersonnel.com/class/forms/jaq/jaq.shtml; www.uh.edu/human-resources/forms/JAQ.doc; www.tnstate.edu/hr/documents/.../Job%20Analysis%20Questionnaire.doc. All accessed July 24, 2013.

JOB ANALYSIS QUESTIONNAIRE*

PURPOSE AND INSTRUCTIONS

Because no one knows the job as well as the person doing it, we are asking you to complete this form. The purpose is to obtain current information on your job based on a review of job duties and responsibilities. We are not asking you about your job performance; only what your job requires you to do.

EMPLOYEE DATA (PLEASE PRINT):

Your Name: ______________________ Today's date ______________

Employee ID: ______________________

Location/Department: ______________________

Your Job Title: ______________________ Job Code: ______________

How long have you been in your current position: __________

Work Telephone Number: ______________

Supervisor's Name: ______________________ Supervisor's Title: ______________

SUMMARY OF DUTIES/RESPONSIBILITIES

Give a brief description of the main function/purpose of your job. This statement should be a brief summary of the responsibilities listed in the next section.

____

____

____

Listing of Job Duties

What do you do on your job? Please list your job's specific duties/responsibilities in the space below. In doing so:

Please list the most important duties/responsibilities first. Write a separate statement for each duty/responsibility.

At the end of each statement please indicate the approximate percent of your workday (25%, 7%, etc.) you spend on that duty.

Please place an asterisk (*) next to the duties that you consider to be absolutely essential to this job.

____

____

____

____

____

(Add additional duties as necessary)

Are there duties you are now performing that are not now in your job description? If so please list them on back of this page.

(Continued)

FIGURE 4-4 *Continued*

Minimum Level of Education (or Equivalent Experience) This Job Requires

What is the minimum level of education necessary to perform your job? Select only one please:

1. Elementary education.
2. Some high school.
3. A high school diploma or equivalent (G.E.D.)
4. A formal vocational training program (approximately one year), an apprenticeship, or some formal college education.
5. An Associate's degree (AA, AS)
6. A bachelor's degree (BA, BS)
7. A Master's degree (MA, MS, MBA, MPA) .
8. A doctorate degree (Ph.D., MD, JD, EED).
9. Are you required to be licensed or certified to perform your work?

[ ] Yes [ ] No List type ______________________

Required Training on Job

What is the level of on-the-job or classroom training someone requires to do your job? Please select one choice below:

1. No additional training required.
2. A day or two.
3. A week
4. A month
5. Several months
6. One year
7. Two years or more

SUPERVISORY RESPONSIBILITIES

Do you supervise others as part of your job? If so please briefly describe the nature of your supervisory responsibilities.

PHYSICAL JOB DEMANDS

Please briefly describe this job's main physical demands. For example, does it involve Sitting? Walking? Standing? Lifting? Detailed repetitive motions? Climbing? Etc.

Working Conditions: Environmental and Safety Job Demands

Please list this job's working conditions, such as: air-conditioned office work; outdoor or indoor extreme heat or cold; wet; noise; job hazards; working in elevated conditions; etc.

EMPLOYEE COMMENTS

Is there any other information that would be important in understanding your job? If so, please give us your comments below.

SUPERVISOR'S REVIEW

Based on your understanding of the job as it currently exists, please review the employee's response and provide your own comments in the space below. **Please do not change the employee's responses.**

Some questionnaires are structured checklists. Here each employee gets an inventory of perhaps hundreds of specific duties or tasks (such as "change and splice wire"). He or she must indicate if he or she performs each task and, if so, how much time is normally spent on each. At the other extreme, the questionnaire may simply ask, "describe the major duties of your job."

In practice, the best questionnaire often falls between these two extremes. As illustrated in Figure 4-4, a typical job analysis questionnaire might include several open-ended questions (such as "What is the job's overall purpose?") as well as structured questions (concerning, for instance, education required).

All questionnaires have pros and cons. A questionnaire is a quick and efficient way to obtain information from a large number of employees; it's less costly than interviewing hundreds of workers, for instance. However, developing the questionnaire and testing it (perhaps by making sure the workers understand the questions) can be time-consuming. And as with interviews, employees may distort their answers.

Observation

Direct observation is especially useful when jobs consist mainly of observable physical activities—assembly-line worker and accounting clerk are examples. However, observation is usually not appropriate when the job entails a lot of mental activity (lawyer, design engineer). Nor is it useful if the employee only occasionally engages in important activities, such as a nurse who handles emergencies. *Reactivity*—the worker's changing what he or she normally does because you are watching—is another problem.

Managers often use direct observation and interviewing together. One approach is to observe the worker on the job during a complete work cycle. (The *cycle* is the time it takes to complete the job; it could be a minute for an assembly-line worker or an hour, a day, or longer for complex jobs.) Here you take notes of all the job activities. Then, ask the person to clarify open points and to explain what other activities he or she performs that you didn't observe.

Participant Diary/Logs

diary/log
Daily listings made by workers of every activity in which they engage along with the time each activity takes.

Another method is to ask workers to keep a **diary/log**; here for every activity engaged in, the employee records the activity (along with the time) in a log.

Some firms give employees pocket dictating machines and pagers. Then at random times during the day, they page the workers, who dictate what they are doing at that time.

Quantitative Job Analysis Techniques

Qualitative methods like interviews and questionnaires are not always suitable. For example, if your aim is to compare jobs for pay purposes, a mere listing of duties may not suffice. You may need to say that, in effect, "Job A is twice as challenging as Job B, and so is worth twice the pay." To do this, it helps to have quantitative ratings for each job. The position analysis questionnaire and the Department of Labor approach are quantitative methods for doing this.

position analysis questionnaire (PAQ)
A questionnaire used to collect quantifiable data concerning the duties and responsibilities of various jobs.

POSITION ANALYSIS QUESTIONNAIRE The **position analysis questionnaire (PAQ)** is a very popular quantitative job analysis tool, consisting of a questionnaire containing 194 items (see Figure 4-5 for a sample).[15] The 194 items (such as "written materials") each represent a basic element that may play a role in the job. The items each belong to one of five PAQ basic activities: (1) having decision-making/communication/social responsibilities, (2) performing skilled activities, (3) being physically active, (4) operating vehicles/equipment, and (5) processing information (Figure 4-5 illustrates this last activity). The final PAQ "score" shows the job's rating on each of these five activities. The job analyst decides if each of the 194 items plays a role and, if so, to what extent. In Figure 4-5, for example, "written materials" received a rating of 4. Since the scale ranges from 1 to 5, a 4 suggests that written materials (such as books and reports) do play a significant role in this job. The analyst can use an online version of the PAQ (see www.paq.com) for each job he or she is analyzing.

The PAQ's strength is in assigning jobs to job classes for pay purposes. With ratings for each job's decision-making, skilled activity, physical activity, vehicle/equipment operation, and information-processing characteristics, you can quantitatively compare jobs relative to one another,[16] and then classify jobs for pay purposes.[17]

FIGURE 4-5 Portion of a Completed Page from the Position Analysis Questionnaire

The 194 PAQ elements are grouped into five activities, and this figure illustrates the "information input" questions or elements. Other PAQ pages contain questions regarding mental processes, work output, relationships with others, job context, and other job characteristics.

Information Input

1 Information Input

1.1 Sources of Job Information

Rate each of the following items in terms of the extent to which it is used by the worker as a source of information in performing his job.

	Extent of Use (U)
NA	Does not apply
1	Nominal/very infrequent
2	Occasional
3	Moderate
4	Considerable
5	Very substantial

1.1.1 Visual Sources of Job Information

1	4	Written materials (books, reports, office notes, articles, job instructions, signs, etc.)
2	2	Quantitative materials (materials which deal with quantities or amounts, such as graphs, accounts, specifications, tables of numbers, etc.)
3	1	Pictorial materials (pictures or picture-like materials used as *sources* of information, for example, drawings, blueprints, diagrams, maps, tracing, photographic films, x-ray films, TV pictures, etc.)
4	1	Patterns/related devices (templates, stencils, patterns, etc., used as *sources* of information when *observed* during use; do not include here materials described in item 3 above)
5	2	Visual displays (dials, gauges, signal lights, radarscopes, speedometers, clocks, etc.)
6	5	Measuring devices (rulers, calipers, tire pressure gauges, scales, thickness gauges, pipettes, thermometers, protractors, etc., used to obtain visual information about physical measurements; do not include here devices describe in item 5 above)
7	4	Mechanical devices (tools, equipment, machinery, and other mechanical devices which are *sources* of information when observed during use of operation)
8	3	Materials in process (parts, material, objects, etc., which are sources of information when being modified, worked on, or otherwise processed, such as bread dough being mixed, workpiece being turned in a lathe, fabric being cut, shoe being resoled, etc.)
9	4	Materials not in process (parts, materials, objects, etc., not in the process of being changed or modified, which are *sources* of information when being inspected, handled, packaged, distributed, or selected, etc., such as items or materials in inventory, storage, or distribution channels, items being inspected, etc.)
10	3	Features of nature (landscapes, fields, geological samples, vegetation, cloud formations, and other features of nature which are observed or inspected to provide information)
11	2	Man-made features of environment (structures, buildings, dams, highways, bridges, docks, railroads, and other "man-made" or altered aspects of the indoor environment which are observed or inspected to provide job information; do not consider equipment, machines, etc., that an individual uses in his work, as covered by item 7)

DEPARTMENT OF LABOR (DOL) PROCEDURE Experts at the U.S. Department of Labor did much of the early work developing job analysis.[18] They used their results to compile what was for many years the bible of job descriptions, the *Dictionary of Occupational Titles*. This mammoth book contained detailed information on virtually every job in America. Internet-based tools have largely replaced the *Dictionary*. However, the U.S. Department of Labor job analysis procedure remains a good example of how to quantitatively rate, classify, and compare jobs. As Table 4-1 shows, the DOL method uses a set of standard activities called *worker functions* to describe what a worker must do with respect to *data, people*, and *things*. With respect to data, for instance, the functions include synthesizing and copying. For people, they include mentoring and supervising. For things, basic functions include manipulating and handling.

Each worker function has an importance rating. Thus, "coordinating" is 1, whereas "copying" is 5. If you were analyzing the job of a receptionist/clerk, for example, you might label the job 5, 6, 7, to represent copying data, speaking/signaling people, and handling things. You might code a psychiatric aide in a hospital 1, 7, 5 in relation to data, people, and things. In practice, you would score each task that the worker performed as part of his or her job in terms of data, people, and things. Then you would use the highest combination (say 4, 6, 5) to rate the overall job, since this is the highest level that you would expect a successful job incumbent to attain. If you were selecting a worker for that 4, 6, 5 job, you'd expect him or her to be able to at least compute (4), speak/signal (6), and tend (5). If you were comparing jobs for pay purposes, then a 4, 6, 5 job should rank higher (see Table 4-1) than a 6, 8, 6 job. The manager can then present a summary of the job along with its 3-digit rating on a form such as in Figure 4-6.

Electronic Job Analysis Methods[19]

Employers increasingly rely on electronic or web-based job analysis methods. For example, the manager or job analyst may use the Web to review existing information about a job. Then, rather than collecting information about a job through direct interviews or questionnaires, the analyst uses online systems to send job questionnaires to job experts (often job incumbents) in remote locations. This also facilitates sharing responses and discussing them, for instance via Skype. Finally, the job analyst may convene the job experts to discuss and finalize the knowledge, skills, abilities, and other characteristics required for doing the job and its tasks.[20]

Conducting the job analysis via the Internet is often an obvious choice.[21] Most simply, the human resource department can distribute standardized job analysis questionnaires to geographically disbursed employees via their company intranets, with instructions to complete the forms and return them by a particular date.

TABLE 4-1 Basic Department of Labor Worker Functions

	Data	People	Things
Basic Activities	0 Synthesizing	0 Mentoring	0 Setting up
	1 Coordinating	1 Negotiating	1 Precision working
	2 Analyzing	2 Instructing	2 Operating/controlling
	3 Compiling	3 Supervising	3 Driving/operating
	4 Computing	4 Diverting	4 Manipulating
	5 Copying	5 Persuading	5 Tending
	6 Comparing	6 Speaking/signaling	6 Feeding/offbearing
		7 Serving	7 Handling
		8 Taking instructions/ helping	

Note: Determine employee's job "score" on data, people, and things by observing his or her job and determining, for each of the three categories, which of the basic functions illustrates the person's job. "0" is high; "6," "8," and "7" are lows in each column.

Another technique, *functional job analysis,* is similar to the DOL method. However, it rates the job not just on data, people, and things, but also on the extent to which performing the task requires four other things—specific instructions, reasoning and judgment, mathematical ability, and verbal and language facilities.

FIGURE 4-6 Sample Report Based on Department of Labor Job Analysis Technique

Job Analysis Schedule

1. Established Job Title: DOUGH MIXER
2. Ind. Assign: (bake prod.)
3. SIC Code(s) and Title(s): 2051 Bread and other bakery products

4. JOB SUMMARY:

Operates mixing machine to mix ingredients for straight and sponge (yeast) doughs according to established formulas, directs other workers in fermentation of dough, and curls dough into pieces with hand cutter.

5. WORK PERFORMED RATINGS:

	D	P	(T)
Worker Functions	Data	People	Things
	5	6	2

Work Field: Cooking, Food Preparing

6. WORKER TRAITS RATING (to be filled in by analyst):

Training time required
Aptitudes
Temperaments
Interests
Physical demands
Environment conditions

Of course, the instructions should be clear, and test the process first. Without a job analyst actually sitting there with the employee or supervisor, there's a chance that the employees won't cover important points or that misunderstandings will cloud the results.

U.S. NAVY EXAMPLE The U.S. Navy used Internet-based job analysis. The challenge was "to develop a system that would allow the collection of job-related information with minimal intervention and guidance, so that the system could be used in a distributed [long distance] manner."[22] To keep ambiguities to a minimum, they had the employees complete structured job analysis forms step-by-step and duty by duty, as follows:

- First, the online form *shows workers a set of work activities* (such as "Getting Information" and "Monitor the Process") from the Department of Labor online O*NET work activities list. (Figure 4-7 lists some of these activities, such as "Getting Information." You can access the site at www.onetcenter.org/content.html/4.A#cm_4.A.)
- Next, the form directs them to *select those work activities* that are important to their job.
- Then, the form asks them to *list actual duties* of their jobs that fit each of those selected work activities. For example, suppose an employee chose "Getting Information" as a work activity that was important to his or her job. Now he or she would list next to "Getting Information" one or more specific job duties from the job, perhaps such as "watch for new orders from our vendors and bring them to the boss's attention."

FIGURE 4-7 O*NET General Work Activities Categories

Note: The U.S. Navy employees were asked to indicate if their jobs required them to engage in work activities such as: Getting Information; Monitoring Processes; Identifying Objects; Inspecting Equipment; and Estimating Quantifiable Characteristics.
Source: Reprinted by permission of O*NET OnLine.

Print-friendly Version
(Outline View | **Description View**)

Generalized Work Activities — General types of job behaviors occurring on multiple jobs

- Information Input — Where and how are the information and data gained that are needed to perform this job?
  - Looking for and Receiving Job-Related Information — How is information obtained to perform this job?
    - **Getting Information** — Observing, receiving, and otherwise obtaining information from all relevant sources.
    - **Monitor Processes, Materials, or Surroundings** — Monitoring and reviewing information from materials, events, or the environment, to detect or assess problems.
  - Identify and Evaluating Job-Relevant Information — How is information interpreted to perform this job?
    - **Identifying Objects, Actions, and Events** — Identifying information by categorizing, estimating, recognizing differences or similarities, and detecting changes in circumstances or events.
    - **Inspecting Equipment, Structures, or Material** — Inspecting equipment, structures, or materials to identify the cause of errors or other problems or defects.
    - **Estimating the Quantifiable Characteristics of Products, Events, or Information** — Estimating sizes, distances, and quantities; or determining time, costs, resources, or materials needed to perform a work activity.

Again, the main issue with online job analysis is to strip the process of ambiguities. The Navy's method proved to be an effective way to collect job-related information online.[23]

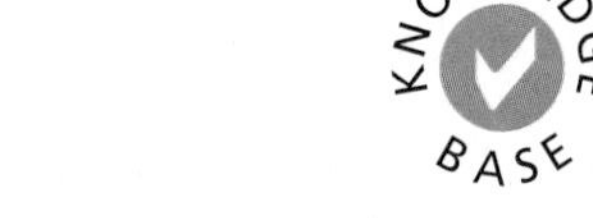

4 Explain how you would write a job description.

Writing Job Descriptions

The most important product of job analysis is the job description. A job description is a written statement of what the worker actually does, how he or she does it, and what the job's working conditions are. You use this information to write a job specification; this lists the knowledge, abilities, and skills required to perform the job satisfactorily.[24]

HR in Practice at the Hotel Paris In reviewing the Hotel Paris's employment systems, the HR manager was concerned that virtually all the company's job descriptions were out of date, and that many jobs had no descriptions at all. She knew that without accurate job descriptions, all her improvement efforts would be in vain. To see how they handled this, see the case on pages 117–118 of this chapter.

Diversity Counts

Most people assume that job descriptions are only of use in business settings, but that's not the case. In fact, for parents who want the best care for their kids, writing up a job description before hiring a child-care worker could be quite useful. For example, because what children learn when they're very young predicts their future academic and career success, facilitating early-childhood learning is a crucial task for many caregivers.[25] And yet few parents write a job description before recruiting their child-care workers. Many, therefore, hire this important person not clearly understanding what they want this person to do.

A well-thought-out job description might benefit everyone involved. The parent—knowing that supporting early-childhood learning is so important—might put more effort into finding and training her child's caregiver (95% of whom are women). The child might benefit from a more nurturing learning environment. And the caregiver would gain if, after recognizing how many challenging tasks she is responsible for, the parent would raise her salary from the current national average of about $19,000 per year—just about the poverty level for a family of three.

There is no standard format for writing a job description. However, most descriptions contain sections that cover:

1. Job identification
2. Job summary
3. Responsibilities and duties
4. Authority of incumbent
5. Standards of performance
6. Working conditions
7. Job specification

Figures 4-8 and 4-9 present two sample forms of job descriptions.

Job Identification

As in Figure 4-8, the job identification section (on top) contains several types of information.[26] The *job title* specifies the name of the job, such as supervisor of data processing operations, or inventory control clerk. The Fair Labor Standards Act (FLSA) status section identifies the job as exempt or nonexempt. (Under the FLSA, certain positions, primarily administrative and professional, are exempt from the act's overtime and minimum wage provisions.) *Date* is the date the job description was actually approved.

There may also be a space to indicate who approved the description and perhaps a space showing the location of the job in terms of its facility/division and department. This section might also include the immediate supervisor's title and information regarding salary and/or pay scale. There might also be space for the grade/level of the job, if there is such a category. For example, a firm may classify programmers as programmer II, programmer III, and so on.

Job Summary

The job summary should summarize the essence of the job, and include only its major functions or activities. Thus (in Figure 4-8), the telesales rep ". . . is responsible for selling college textbooks. . . ." For the job of mailroom supervisor, "the mailroom supervisor receives, sorts, and delivers all incoming mail properly, and he or she handles all outgoing mail including the accurate and timely posting of such mail."[27]

Some experts state unequivocally that "one item frequently found that should never be included in a job description is a 'cop-out clause' like 'other duties, as assigned,' "[28] since this leaves open the nature of the job. Finally, state in the summary that the employee is expected to carry out his or her duties efficiently, attentively, and conscientiously.

Relationships

There may be a "relationships" statement (not in Figure 4-8) that shows the jobholder's relationships with others inside and outside the organization. For a human resource manager, such a statement might say:[29]

> ***Reports to:*** Vice president of employee relations.
>
> ***Supervises:*** Human resource clerk, test administrator, labor relations director, and one secretary.
>
> ***Works with:*** All department managers and executive management.
>
> ***Outside the company:*** Employment agencies, executive recruiting firms, union representatives, state and federal employment offices, and various vendors.[30]

Responsibilities and Duties

This is the heart of the job description. It should present a list of the job's significant responsibilities and duties. As in Figure 4-8, list each of the job's major duties separately, and describe it in a few sentences. In the figure, for instance, the job's duties include "achieve quantitative sales

JOB TITLE: Telesales Respresentative	**JOB CODE:** 100001
RECOMMENDED SALARY GRADE:	**EXEMPT/NONEXEMPT STATUS:** Nonexempt
JOB FAMILY: Sales	**EEOC:** Sales Workers
DIVISION: Higher Education	**REPORTS TO:** District Sales Manager
DEPARTMENT: In-House Sales	**LOCATION:** Boston
	DATE: April 2013

SUMMARY (Write a brief summary of job.)

The person in this position is responsible for selling college textbooks, software, and multimedia products to professors, via incoming and outgoing telephone calls, and to carry out selling strategies to meet sales goals in assigned territories of smaller colleges and universities. In addition, the individual in this position will be responsible for generating a designated amount of editorial leads and communicating to the publishing groups product feedback and market trends observed in the assigned territory.

SCOPE AND IMPACT OF JOB

Dollar responsibilities (budget and/or revenue)

The person in this position is responsible for generating approximately $2 million in revenue, for meeting operating expense budget of approximately $4000, and a sampling budget of approximately 10,000 units.

Supervisory responsibilities (direct and indirect)

None

Other

REQUIRED KNOWLEDGE AND EXPERIENCE (Knowledge and experience necessary to do job)

Related work experience

Prior sales or publishing experience preferred. One year of company experience in a customer service or marketing function with broad knowledge of company products and services is desirable.

Formal education or equivalent

Bachelor's degree with strong academic performance or work equivalent experience.

Skills

Must have strong organizational and persuasive skills. Must have excellent verbal and written communications skills and must be PC proficient.

Other

Limited travel required (approx 5%)

(Continued)

FIGURE 4-8 Sample Job Description, Pearson Education

Source: Reprinted and Electronically reproduced by permission of Pearson Education, Inc., Upper Saddle River, New Jersey.

PRIMARY RESPONSIBILITIES (List in order of importance and list amount of time spent on task.)

Driving Sales (60%)

- Achieve quantitative sales goal for assigned territory of smaller colleges and universities.
- Determine sales priorities and strategies for territory and develop a plan for implementing those strategies.
- Conduct 15–20 professor interviews per day during the academic sales year that accomplishes those priorities.
- Conduct product presentations (including texts, software, and Web site); effectively articulate author's central vision of key titles; conduct sales interviews using the PSS model; conduct walk-through of books and technology.
- Employ telephone selling techniques and strategies.
- Sample products to appropriate faculty, making strategic use of assigned sampling budgets.
- Close class test adoptions for first edition products.
- Negotiate custom publishing and special packaging agreements within company guidelines.
- Initiate and conduct in-person faculty presentations and selling trips as appropriate to maximize sales with the strategic use of travel budget. Also use internal resources to support the territory sales goals.
- Plan and execute in-territory special selling events and book-fairs.
- Develop and implement in-territory promotional campaigns and targeted email campaigns.

Publishing (editorial/marketing) 25%

- Report, track, and sign editorial projects.
- Gather and communicate significant market feedback and information to publishing groups.

Territory Management 15%

- Track and report all pending and closed business in assigned database.
- Maintain records of customer sales interviews and adoption situations in assigned database.
- Manage operating budget strategically.
- Submit territory itineraries, sales plans, and sales forecasts as assigned.
- Provide superior customer service and maintain professional bookstore relations in assigned territory.

Decision-Making Responsibilities for This Position:

Determine the strategic use of assigned sampling budget to most effectively generate sales revenue to exceed sales goals.
Determine the priority of customer and account contacts to achieve maximum sales potential.
Determine where in-person presentations and special selling events would be most effective to generate the most sales.

Submitted By: Jim Smith, District Sales Manager	Date: April 10, 2013
Approval:	Date:
Human Resources:	Date:
Corporate Compensation:	Date:

FIGURE 4-8 ***Continued***

goal . . ." and "determine sales priorities. . . ." Typical duties for other jobs might include making accurate postings to accounts payable, maintaining favorable purchase price variances, and repairing production-line tools and equipment.

This section may also define the jobholder's authority limits. For example, the jobholder might have authority to approve purchase requests up to $5,000, grant time off or leaves of absence, discipline department personnel, recommend salary increases, and interview and hire new employees.

Usually, the manager's basic question here is, "How do I determine what the job's duties are and should be?" The answer first is, from the *job analysis*; this should reveal what the

FIGURE 4-9 Marketing Manager Description from Standard Occupational Classification

Source: U.S. Department of Labor, Bureau of Labor Statistics.

U.S. Department of Labor
Bureau of Labor Statistics
Standard Occupational Classification

www.bls.gov | Advanced Search | A-Z Index

BLS Home | Programs & Surveys | Get Detailed Statistics | Glossary | What's New | Find It! In DOL

11-2021 Marketing Managers

Determine the demand for products and services offered by a firm and its competitors and identify potential customers. Develop pricing strategies with the goal of maximizing the firm's profits or share of the market while ensuring the firm's customers are satisfied. Oversee product development or monitor trends that indicate the need for new products and services.

Standard Occupational Classification (SOC)
Classifies all workers into one of 23 major groups of jobs that are subdivided into minor groups of jobs and detailed occupations.

employees on each job are doing now. Second, you can review various sources of standardized job description information. For example, the **Standard Occupational Classification (SOC)** (www.bls.gov/soc/socguide.htm) classifies all workers into one of 23 major groups of jobs, such as "Management Occupations" and "Healthcare Occupations." These in turn contain 96 minor groups of jobs, which in turn include 821 detailed occupations, such as the marketing manager description in Figure 4-9. The employer can use standard descriptions like these to identify a job's duties and responsibilities, such as "Determine the demand for products." The employer may also use other popular sources of job description information, such as www.jobdescription.com. O*NET online, as noted, is another option for finding job duties. We present an example in the HR tools for line managers and entrepreneurs feature at the end of this section.

Writing clear job duties is an art. For a nurse, for example, one duty might be:[31]

Incorrect: Ensures that patients receive medical attention when needed.

Comment: This is not adequate. What the nurse does is ambiguous, and the expected process and results of the nurse's actions aren't clear.

Correct: Administers minor medical treatments or medication (taking temperatures, treating minor cuts and bruises, giving aspirin or cough syrup) to correct or treat residents' minor health problems using common first aid supplies and using own discretion to determine need following established institutional medical department procedures.

KNOW YOUR EMPLOYMENT LAW

Writing Job Descriptions That Comply with the ADA

The list of job duties is crucial to employers' efforts to comply with the Americans with Disabilities Act (ADA). Under the ADA, the individual must have the requisite skills, educational background, and experience to perform the job's essential functions. The EEOC says, "Essential functions are the basic job duties that an employee must be able to perform, with or without reasonable accommodation."[32] Factors to consider in determining if a function is essential include:

- Whether the position exists to perform that function,
- The number of other employees available to perform the function,
- The degree of expertise or skill required to perform the function.
- Whether employees in the position are actually required to perform the function?[33]
- What the degree of expertise or skill required to perform the function is.[34]

As an example, answering calls and directing visitors to the proper offices might be essential functions for a receptionist's job. The EEOC says it will consider the employer's judgment about which functions are essential, and a written job description prepared before advertising or interviewing for a job as evidence of essential functions. Other evidence includes the actual work experience of present or past employees in the job, the time spent performing a function, and the consequences of not requiring that an employee perform a function.

If the disabled individual can't perform the job as currently structured, the employer is required to make a "reasonable accommodation," unless doing so would present an "undue hardship." According to the EEOC, reasonable accommodation may include:

- acquiring or modifying equipment or devices,
- job restructuring,
- part-time or modified work schedules,
- reassignment to a vacant position,
- adjusting or modifying examinations, training materials, or policies,
- providing readers and interpreters, and
- making the workplace readily accessible to and usable by people with disabilities.

Standards of Performance and Working Conditions

A "standards of performance" section lists the standards the company expects the employee to achieve for each of the job description's main duties and responsibilities. One way to set standards is to finish the statement, "I will be completely satisfied with your work when. . . ." This sentence, if completed for each listed duty, should result in a usable set of performance standards. For example:

Duty: **Accurately Posting Accounts Payable**

1. Post all invoices received within the same working day.
2. Route all invoices to the proper department managers for approval no later than the day following receipt.
3. Commit an average of no more than three posting errors per month.

The job description may also list the job's working conditions, such as noise level, hazardous conditions, or heat.

IMPROVING PERFORMANCE: HR Tools for Line Managers and Entrepreneurs

Using O*NET

Without their own job analysts or even HR managers, many small business owners face two hurdles when doing job analyses. First, most need a more streamlined approach than those provided by questionnaires like that in Figure 4-4. Second is the concern that, in writing their job descriptions, they'll overlook duties that subordinates should be assigned. What they need is an encyclopedia listing all the possible positions they might encounter, including a list of the duties normally assigned to these positions.

The small business owner has at least three options. The *Standard Occupational Classification*, mentioned earlier, provides detailed descriptions of thousands of jobs and their human requirements. Web sites like www.jobdescription.com provide customizable descriptions by title and industry. And the Department of Labor's O*NET is a third alternative. We'll focus here on how to write a job description using O*NET (http://online.onetcenter.org).[35] It is free to use and highly cost effective.

O*NET

The U.S. Department of Labor's online occupational information network, called O*NET, is a popular tool. It enables users (not just managers, but workers and job seekers) to see the most important characteristics of various occupations, as well as the experience, education, and knowledge required to do each job well. Both the Standard Occupational Classification and O*NET list the specific duties associated with numerous occupations. O*NET also lists skills, including *basic skills* such as reading and writing, *process skills* such as critical thinking, and *transferable skills* such as persuasion and negotiation.[36] An O*NET job listing also includes information on worker requirements (required knowledge, for instance), occupation requirements (such as compiling, coding, and categorizing data, for instance), and experience requirements (including education and job training). Employers and career planers also use O*NET to check the job's labor market characteristics, such as employment projections and earnings data.[37]

The steps in using O*Net to facilitate writing a job description follow.

Step 1. **Review your Plan.** Ideally, the jobs you need should flow from your departmental or company plans. Do you plan to enter or exit businesses? What do you expect your sales to be in the next few years? What departments will have to be expanded or reduced? What kinds of new positions will you need?

Step 2. **Develop an Organization Chart.** Start with the organization as it is now. Then produce a chart showing how you want it to look in a year or two. Microsoft Word includes an organization charting function.[38]

Step 3. **Use a Job Analysis Questionnaire.** Next, gather information about each job's duties. (You can use job analysis questionnaires, such as those shown in Figure 4-4 and Figure 4-10).

FIGURE 4-10 Simple Job Description Questionnaire

Background Data for Job Description

Job Title ____________ Department ____________

Job Number ____________ Written by ____________

Today's Date ____________ Applicable DOT Codes ____________

I. Applicable DOT Definition(s):

II. Job Summary:
(List the more important or regularly performed tasks)

III. Reports To:

IV. Supervises: ____________

V. Job Duties: ____________
(Briefly describe, for each duty, what employee does and, if possible, how employee does it. Show in parentheses at end of each duty the approximate percentage of time devoted to duty.)

A. Daily Duties:

B. Periodic Duties:
(Indicate whether weekly, monthly, quarterly, etc.)

C. Duties Performed at Irregular Intervals:

Source: Reprinted by permission of O*NET OnLine.

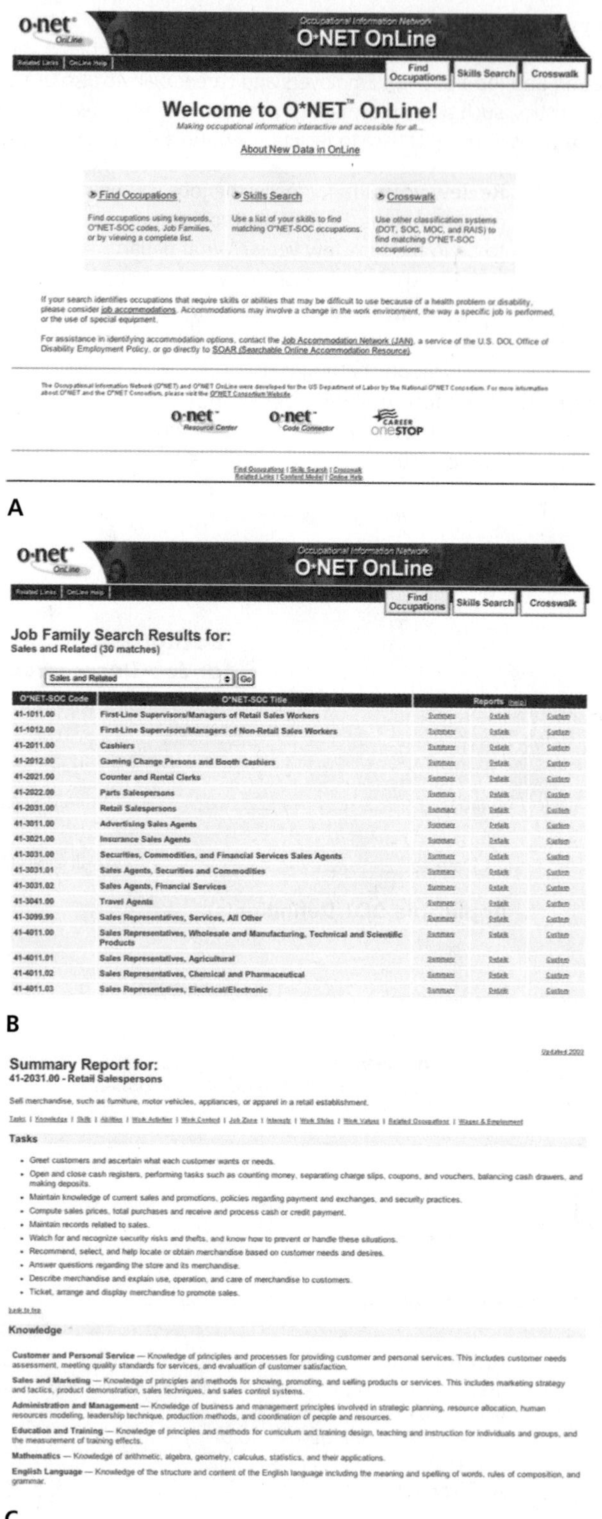

o·net® OnLine

Occupational Information Network

O·NET OnLine

Related Links | OnLine Help

Find Occupations | Skills Search | Crosswalk

Welcome to O*NET™ OnLine!

Making occupational information interactive and accessible for all...

About New Data in OnLine

» Find Occupations — Find occupations using keywords, O*NET-SOC codes, Job Families, or by viewing a complete list.

» Skills Search — Use a list of your skills to find matching O*NET-SOC occupations.

» Crosswalk — Use other classification systems (DOT, SOC, MOC, and RAIS) to find matching O*NET-SOC occupations.

If your search identifies occupations that require skills or abilities that may be difficult to use because of a health problem or disability, please consider job accommodations. Accommodations may involve a change in the work environment, the way a specific job is performed, or the use of special equipment.

For assistance in identifying accommodation options, contact the Job Accommodation Network (JAN), a service of the U.S. DOL Office of Disability Employment Policy, or go directly to SOAR (Searchable Online Accommodation Resource).

The Occupational Information Network (O*NET) and O*NET OnLine were developed for the US Department of Labor by the National O*NET Consortium. For more information about O*NET and the O*NET Consortium, please visit the O*NET Consortium Website.

o·net™ Resource Center | o·net™ Code Connector | CAREER oneSTOP

Find Occupations | Skills Search | Crosswalk
Related Links | Content Model | Online Help

A

o·net® OnLine

Occupational Information Network

O·NET OnLine

Related Links | OnLine Help

Find Occupations | Skills Search | Crosswalk

Job Family Search Results for:
Sales and Related (30 matches)

Sales and Related [Go]

O*NET-SOC Code	O*NET-SOC Title	Reports (help)		
41-1011.00	First-Line Supervisors/Managers of Retail Sales Workers	Summary	Details	Custom
41-1012.00	First-Line Supervisors/Managers of Non-Retail Sales Workers	Summary	Details	Custom
41-2011.00	Cashiers	Summary	Details	Custom
41-2012.00	Gaming Change Persons and Booth Cashiers	Summary	Details	Custom
41-2021.00	Counter and Rental Clerks	Summary	Details	Custom
41-2022.00	Parts Salespersons	Summary	Details	Custom
41-2031.00	Retail Salespersons	Summary	Details	Custom
41-3011.00	Advertising Sales Agents	Summary	Details	Custom
41-3021.00	Insurance Sales Agents	Summary	Details	Custom
41-3031.00	Securities, Commodities, and Financial Services Sales Agents	Summary	Details	Custom
41-3031.01	Sales Agents, Securities and Commodities	Summary	Details	Custom
41-3031.02	Sales Agents, Financial Services	Summary	Details	Custom
41-3041.00	Travel Agents	Summary	Details	Custom
41-3099.99	Sales Representatives, Services, All Other	Summary	Details	Custom
41-4011.00	Sales Representatives, Wholesale and Manufacturing, Technical and Scientific Products	Summary	Details	Custom
41-4011.01	Sales Representatives, Agricultural	Summary	Details	Custom
41-4011.02	Sales Representatives, Chemical and Pharmaceutical	Summary	Details	Custom
41-4011.03	Sales Representatives, Electrical/Electronic	Summary	Details	Custom

B

Updated 2003

Summary Report for:
41-2031.00 - Retail Salespersons

Sell merchandise, such as furniture, motor vehicles, appliances, or apparel in a retail establishment.

Tasks | Knowledge | Skills | Abilities | Work Activities | Work Context | Job Zone | Interests | Work Styles | Work Values | Related Occupations | Wages & Employment

Tasks

- Greet customers and ascertain what each customer wants or needs.
- Open and close cash registers, performing tasks such as counting money, separating charge slips, coupons, and vouchers, balancing cash drawers, and making deposits.
- Maintain knowledge of current sales and promotions, policies regarding payment and exchanges, and security practices.
- Compute sales prices, total purchases and receive and process cash or credit payment.
- Maintain records related to sales.
- Watch for and recognize security risks and thefts, and know how to prevent or handle these situations.
- Recommend, select, and help locate or obtain merchandise based on customer needs and desires.
- Answer questions regarding the store and its merchandise.
- Describe merchandise and explain use, operation, and care of merchandise to customers.
- Ticket, arrange and display merchandise to promote sales.

back to top

Knowledge

Customer and Personal Service — Knowledge of principles and processes for providing customer and personal services. This includes customer needs assessment, meeting quality standards for services, and evaluation of customer satisfaction.

Sales and Marketing — Knowledge of principles and methods for showing, promoting, and selling products or services. This includes marketing strategy and tactics, product demonstration, sales techniques, and sales control systems.

Administration and Management — Knowledge of business and management principles involved in strategic planning, resource allocation, human resources modeling, leadership technique, production methods, and coordination of people and resources.

Education and Training — Knowledge of principles and methods for curriculum and training design, teaching and instruction for individuals and groups, and the measurement of training effects.

Mathematics — Knowledge of arithmetic, algebra, geometry, calculus, statistics, and their applications.

English Language — Knowledge of the structure and content of the English language including the meaning and spelling of words, rules of composition, and grammar.

C

Step 4. Obtain Job Duties from O*NET. The list of job duties you uncovered through the job analysis in step 3 may or may not be complete. We'll therefore use O*NET to compile a more complete list. (Refer to the A, B, and C examples pictured just above.)

Start by going to http://online.onetcenter.org (A). Here, click on *Find Occupations*. Assume you want to create job descriptions for a retail salesperson. Key *Retail Sales* in the Keyword drop-down box. This brings you to the Occupations matching "retail sales" page (B).

Clicking on the *Retail Salespersons* summary produces the job summary and specific occupational duties for retail salespersons (C). For a small store, you might want to combine the duties of the "retail salesperson" with those of "first-line supervisors/managers of retail sales workers."

Step 5. **List the Job's Human Requirements from O*NET.** Next, return to the summary for *Retail Salesperson* (C). Here, click, for example, Knowledge, Skills, and Abilities. Use this information to help develop a job specification for your job. Use this information for recruiting, selecting, and training your employees.

Step 6. **Finalize the Job Description.** Finally, perhaps using Figure 4-10 as a guide, write an appropriate job summary for the job. Then use the information obtained previously in steps 4 and 5 to create a complete listing of the tasks, duties, and human requirements of each of the jobs you will need to fill.

Discussion Question 4-2: Pick out a job that someone with whom you are familiar is doing, such as a bus driver, mechanic, and so on. Review the O*NET information for that job. To what extent does the person seem to have what it takes to do that job, based on the O*NET information? How does that correspond to how he or she is actually doing?

Social Media and HR

Sometimes the easiest way to write a job description is just to use social media like LinkedIn to ask others what to put in it. For example, recently someone who says he recruits for all open positions in his company posted on LinkedIn: "I'm hoping some group members here can provide some insight on what makes for the best IT job descriptions. I've been recruiting for O*NET developers and Development Managers and I'd like to know what you all like to see in a job description. . . ." The first of many replies listed 12 tasks including (1) Does technical skills to match the desired job; (2) What technical problems were solved by the job seeker? and (3) Did job seeker know about Cloud Deployment?[39]

Writing Job Specifications

5 Explain how to write a job specification.

The job specification takes the job description and answers the question, "What human traits and experience are required to do this job effectively?" It shows what kind of person to recruit and for what qualities you should test that person. It may be a section of the job description, or a separate document. Often—as in Figure 4-8 on pages 103–104—it is part of the job description.[40]

Specifications for Trained versus Untrained Personnel

Writing job specifications for trained and experienced employees is relatively straightforward. Here job specifications tend to focus on factors such as length of previous service, quality of relevant training, and previous job performance.

The problems are more complex when you're filling jobs with untrained people (with the intention of training them on the job). Here you must specify qualities such as physical traits, personality, interests, or sensory skills that imply some potential for performing the job or for trainability. Thus, for a job that requires detailed manipulation in a circuit board assembly line, you might want someone who scores high on a test of finger dexterity. Employers identify the job's human requirements either through a subjective, judgmental approach or through statistical analysis (or both).

Specifications Based on Judgment

Most job specifications simply reflect the educated guesses of people like supervisors and human resource managers. The basic procedure here is to ask, "What does it take in terms of education, intelligence, training, and the like to do this job well?"

How does one make such "educated guesses"? You could simply review the job's duties, and deduce from those what human traits and skills the job requires. You can also choose human traits and skills from the competencies listed in Web-based job descriptions like those at www.jobdescription.com. (For example, a typical job description there lists competencies like "Generates creative solutions"

Filling jobs with untrained employees requires identifying the personal traits that predict performances.

Ingram Publishing/Getty Images

and "Manages difficult or emotional customer situations.") O*NET online is another option. Job listings there include lists of required education and other experience and skills.

In any case, use common sense when compiling your list. Don't ignore the behaviors that may apply to almost any job but that might not normally surface through a job analysis.

Industriousness is an example. Who wants an employee who doesn't work hard? One researcher collected supervisor ratings and other information from 18,000 employees in 42 different hourly entry-level mostly retail jobs.[41] Here are the work behaviors that he found to be important to all jobs:

Job-Related Behavior	Some Examples
Industriousness	Keeps working even when other employees are standing around talking; takes the initiative to find another task when finished with regular work.
Thoroughness	Cleans equipment thoroughly, creating a more attractive display; notices merchandise out of place and returns it to the proper area.
Schedule flexibility	Accepts schedule changes when necessary; offers to stay late when the store is extremely busy.
Attendance	Arrives at work on time; maintains good attendance.
Off-task behavior (reverse)	Uses store phones to make personal unauthorized calls; conducts personal business during work time; lets joking friends be a distraction and interruption to work.
Unruliness (reverse)	Threatens to bully another employee; refuses to take routine orders from supervisors; does not cooperate with other employees.
Theft (reverse)	(As a cashier) Under-rings the price of merchandise for a friend; cheats on reporting time worked; allows nonemployees in unauthorized areas.
Drug misuse (reverse)	Drinks alcohol or takes drugs on company property; comes to work under the influence of alcohol or drugs.

Job Specifications Based on Statistical Analysis

Basing job specifications on statistical analysis rather than only judgment is the more defensible approach, but it's also more difficult. The aim here is to determine statistically the relationship between (1) some *predictor* (human trait such as height, intelligence, or finger dexterity), and (2) some indicator or *criterion* of job effectiveness, such as performance as rated by the supervisor.

This procedure has five steps: (1) analyze the job and decide how to measure job performance; (2) select personal traits like finger dexterity that you believe should predict performance; (3) test candidates for these traits; (4) measure these candidates' subsequent job performance; and (5) statistically analyze the relationship between the human trait (finger dexterity) and job performance. Your aim is to determine whether the trait predicts performance.

This is more defensible than the judgmental approach. First, if the trait does not predict performance, why use it? Second, equal rights laws prohibit using traits that you can't prove distinguish between high and low job performers. Hiring standards that discriminate based on sex, race, religion, national origin, or age may have to be shown to predict job performance, as with the five-step approach just above. In practice, most employers rely on judgmental approaches.

The Job Requirements Matrix

Although most employers use job descriptions and specifications to summarize what their jobs entail, *the job requirements matrix* is also popular.[42] The matrix includes the job's *main duties*, each duty's *purpose*, and the *knowledge and skills* someone should have to do each duty.

task statement
Written item that shows *what* the worker does on one particular job task; *how* the worker does it; the *knowledge, skills, and aptitudes required* to do it; and the *purpose of the task*.

The first step in creating the job requirements matrix is to write *one task statement* for each of the job's, say, 12 tasks. Each **task statement** shows *what* the worker does on one particular job task; *how* the worker does it; the *knowledge, skills, and aptitudes required* to do it; and the *purpose of the task*.[43] For example, one task for a dry-cleaning store counter person might be "take in new orders." Its task statement might say, "Accepts an order of clothes from a customer and places it into a laundry bag and provides the customer with a receipt, in order to ensure that the customer's clothes items are together and identifiable and that the store and customer have an accurate record of the transaction." (In contrast, the traditional job duty might say, "accepts orders of clothes from customers and places them in laundry bags; gives customers receipts). For each task, also *identify the knowledge, skills, abilities*, and *other* characteristics (KSAOs) needed to do it. Thus, for "take in new orders" the counter person should know how to operate the computerized cash register, be skilled at identifying fabrics so proper prices can be charged, and have the ability (for instance, cognitive and physical ability) to perform arithmetic computations and lift heavy laundry bags. The task may also require certain "other" human characteristics, such as conscientiousness.

Second, the job analyst takes the resulting (in this case) 12 task statements for the job's 12 tasks, and groups them into four or five *main job duties*. Thus, the four main counter person job duties might include accepts and returns customer's clothes, handles the cash register, fills in for the cleaner/spotter when he or she is absent, and supervises the tailor and assistant counter person.

Finally, the job analyst compiles all this information in a *job requirements matrix* for this job. This matrix would list the following information, in 5 columns:

Column 1: Each of the four or five *main job duties*;

Column 2: The *task statements* associated with each main job duty;

Column 3: The relative *importance* of each main job duty;

Column 4: The *time spent* on each main job duty; and

Column 5: The *knowledge, skills, ability*, and other human characteristics related to each main job duty.[44]

job requirements matrix
A more complete description of what the worker does and how and why he or she does it; it clarifies each task's purpose and each duty's required knowledge, skills, abilities, and other characteristics.

Such a **job requirements matrix** provides a more complete picture of what the worker does on the job and how and why he or she does it than does a job description. (For instance, it specifies each task's purpose.) And, the list of each duty's required knowledge, skills, abilities, and other characteristics is useful for selection, training, and appraisal decisions.

Modeling or profiling, to which we turn next, is another way to compile information on the knowledge, skills, ability, and other characteristics a job requires of its incumbents.

6 Explain competency-based job analysis, including what it means and how it's done in practice.

Using Models and Profiles in Talent Management

Most people still think of a "job" as a set of specific duties someone carries out for pay, but the concept of job is changing. For example, teamwork often requires sharing jobs. In situations like these, the worker's "job" may change from day-to-day. Therefore, relying on a list of job duties that itemizes specific things you expect the worker to do can be meaningless.[45]

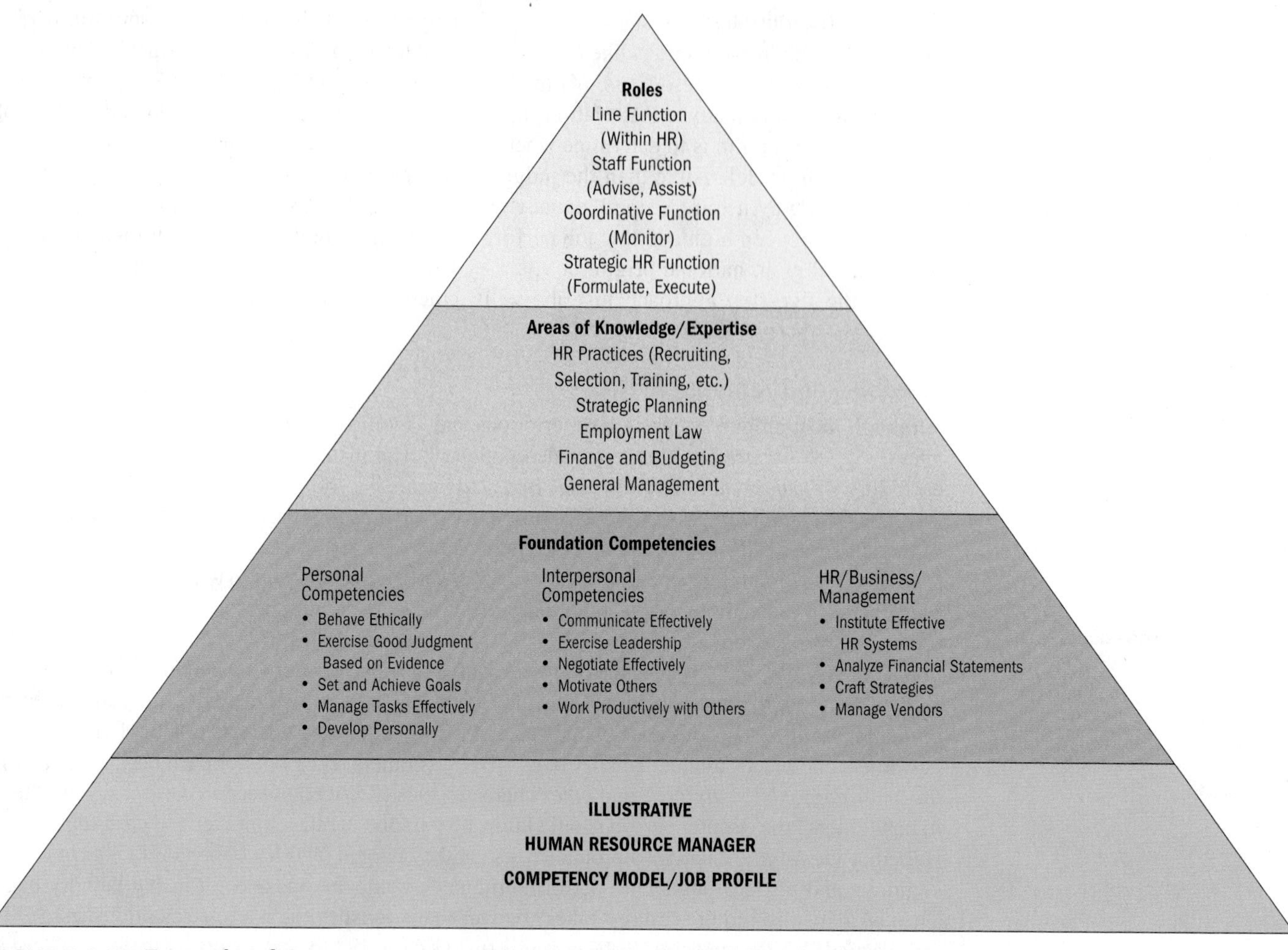

FIGURE 4-11 Example of Competency Model/Job Profile for Human Resource Manager

In such situations, it may be better to list what knowledge and skills someone needs to do the job in *competency models* or job profiles (we'll use the terms interchangeably). Such models or profiles (see Figure 4-11) list the knowledge, skills, and behaviors that employees must be able to exhibit to get their multiple jobs done.[46] The assumption is that if the new team member has the necessary skills and knowledge, he or she will be able to do whatever duties the job requires.

In general, the aim of writing a model or profile is to summarize what "competencies" a person requires for exceptional performance, for instance in terms of *skills* (such to analyze financial statements), *behaviors* (such as to behave ethically), *knowledge* (technical and/or professional), and *experience* (educational and work achievements). Figure 4-11 shows one way to present a competency model.

The model or profile then becomes the guidepost for recruiting, selecting, training, evaluating, and developing employees for each job.[47] For instance, the manager *hires* new employees using tests that measure the profile's list of competencies, *trains* employees with courses aimed to develop these competencies, and *appraises* performance by assessing the worker's competencies.

IMPROVING PERFORMANCE: HR Practices Around the Globe

Daimler Alabama Example

In planning its Alabama Mercedes-Benz factory, Germany-based Daimler's strategy was to design a high-tech factory.[48] The plant emphasizes *just-in-time* inventory methods, so inventories stay negligible due to the arrival "just in time" of parts. It also organizes employees into *work teams*, and emphasizes that all employees must dedicate themselves to *continuous improvement*.

Such production operations require certain employee competencies (skills and behaviors). For example, they require multiskilled and flexible employees.

Competencies-based job analysis played an important role in staffing this factory. Guidelines regarding who to hire and how to train them are based more on the competencies someone needs to do the job (such as "ability to work cooperatively on a team") than on lists of job duties. Because they don't have to follow detailed job descriptions showing what "my job" is, it's easier for employees to move from job to job within their teams.

Stressing competencies rather than duties also encourages workers to look beyond their own jobs to find ways to improve things. For instance, one team redesigned the racks that the assembly parts move on, saving assembly workers thousands of steps per year, thereby boosting performance and productivity.

Now that the new system, including the competencies-based job analysis, has proved itself in Alabama, Daimler plants in South Africa, Brazil, and Germany now use it.

Discussion Question 4-3: Are you surprised that Daimler could implement a team-based production system like this in places where the cultures are as disparate as Alabama, Germany, and Brazil? Why? What inter-country cultural differences would you think might have impeded Daimler's efforts?

A Closer Look at Competencies

Competencies are observable and measurable human characteristics that make performance possible. To determine what a job's required competencies are, ask, "In order to perform this job competently, what should the employee be able to do?" Competencies are typically skills. Competencies for the job of systems engineer might include the following:

- Design complex software applications, establish protocols, and create prototypes.
- Establish the necessary platform requirements to efficiently and completely coordinate data transfer.[49]

Competencies for a corporate treasurer might include, "recommend specific trades and when to make them."[50]

How to Write Competencies Statements

Uncovering the job's required competencies is similar to traditional job analysis. In other words, you might interview job incumbents and their supervisors, ask open-ended questions regarding job responsibilities and activities, and perhaps identify critical incidents that pinpoint success on the job.

However, instead of compiling lists of job duties, your aim is to finish the statement (as noted earlier), "*In order to perform this job competently, the employee should be able to. . . .*" Use your knowledge of the job to answer this, or the worker's or supervisor's insights, or use information from a source such as O*NET, or the Department of Labor's Office of Personnel Management (see www.opm.gov). Then for each competency write a *competency statement*.

A useful competency statement often includes three elements:[51] One is the *name and a brief description* of the competency, such as "project management: the art of creating accurate and effective schedules." The second is a *description of the observable behaviors* that represent proficiency in the competency, such as "personally accountable for the project's execution and invested in the success of the project; continuously manage project risks and dependencies by making timely decisions." Third are *proficiency levels.* For example (for project management):[52]

- ***Proficiency Level 1.*** Identifies project risks and dependencies and communicates routinely to stakeholders.
- ***Proficiency Level 2.*** Develops systems to monitor risks and dependencies and report changes.
- ***Proficiency Level 3.*** Anticipates changing conditions and impact to risks and dependencies and takes preventive action.
- ***Proficiency Level 4.*** Proactively identifies implications of related internal and external business conditions to risks and dependencies.

BP EXAMPLE British Petroleum's (BP's) exploration division executives decided their unit should be organized more efficiently.[53] To help accomplish this, they wanted to shift employees from a job duties–oriented "that's-not-my-job" attitude to one that motivated employees to obtain the skills required to accomplish their broader responsibilities.

Level 6	6	6	6	6	6
Level 5	5	5	5	5	5
Level 4	4	4	4	4	4
Level 3	3	3	3	3	3
Level 2	2	2	2	2	2
Level 1	1	1	1	1	1
	Technical Expertise/Skills	Decision Making and Problem Solving Skills	Interpersonal Skills	Leadership Skills	Commercial Awareness Skills

FIGURE 4-12 Skills Matrix

Note: This is an example of a skills matrix for technical/engineering product development employees. The light blue boxes show the level required for each skill for these product development employees. An accompanying key would provide specific examples for each level of each skill, with difficulty increasing for each skill level starting at Level 1. For example, Level 1 for Technical Expertise/Skills might say "has or is in process of acquiring the basic knowledge necessary to do this type of job," while Level 6 might say, "Capable of conducting and supervising highly complex analytical tasks requiring advanced technical know-how and skills."

Source: Copyright Gary Dessler PhD.

Competency-based job analysis
Describing the job in terms of measurable, observable, behavioral competencies (knowledge, skills, and/or behaviors) that an employee doing that job must exhibit to do the job well.

Their solution was what they called a skills matrix like that in Figure 4-12. There were skills matrices for each job or job family (such as drilling managers). As in Figure 4-12, each matrix listed (1) the types of skills required to do that job (such as technical expertise) and (2) the minimum skill required for proficiency at each level. The note beneath the Skills Matrix shows how to actually use the Matrix.

BP's solution also supported its talent management efforts. Talent management efforts in this unit could now focus on recruiting, hiring, training, appraising, and rewarding employees based on the set of skills employees need to perform the job in question.

Review

MyManagementLab Go to **mymanagementlab.com** to complete the problems marked with this icon. 

Chapter Section Summaries

1. Employers today often view all the staff–train–reward activities as part of a single integrated ***talent management* process**. We defined talent management as the *goal-oriented* and *integrated* process of *planning, recruiting, developing, managing, and compensating* employees. When a manager takes a talent management perspective, he or she should keep in mind that the talent management tasks are parts of a single interrelated talent management process; make sure talent management decisions such as staffing and pay are goal-directed; consistently use the same "profile" for formulating recruitment plans for a job as you do for making selection, training, appraisal, and payment decisions for it; actively segment and manage employees; and integrate/coordinate all the talent management functions.
2. All managers need to be familiar with **the basics of job analysis**.
   - Job analysis is the procedure through which you determine the duties of the department's positions and the characteristics of the people to hire for them.
   - Job descriptions are a list of what the job entails, while job specifications identify what kind of people to hire for the job.

- The job analysis itself involves collecting information on matters such as work activities; required human behaviors; and machines, tools, and equipment used.
- Managers use job analysis information in recruitment and selection, compensation, training, and performance appraisal.
- The basic steps in job analysis include deciding the use of the job analysis information, reviewing relevant background information including organization charts, analyzing the job, verifying the information, and developing job descriptions and job specifications.

3. There are various **methods for collecting job analysis information**. These include interviews, questionnaires, observation, participant diary/logs, and quantitative techniques such as position analysis questionnaires. Employers increasingly collect information from employees via the Internet.
4. Managers should be familiar with the process for **writing job descriptions**. While there is no standard format, most descriptions contain sections that cover job identification, a job summary, a listing of responsibilities and duties, the job incumbent's authority, and performance standards. The job description may also contain information regarding the job's working conditions, and the job specifications. Many employers use Internet sources such as www.jobdescription.com to facilitate writing job descriptions.
5. In **writing job specifications**, it's important to distinguish between specifications for trained versus untrained personnel. For trained employees, the process is relatively straightforward, because you're looking primarily for traits like experience. For untrained personnel, it's necessary to identify traits that might predict success on the job. Most job specifications come from the educated guesses of people like supervisors, and are based mostly on judgment. Some employers use statistical analyses to identify predictors or human traits that are related to success on the job.
6. Employers are using models and profiles in talent management, particularly creating "profiles" for each of their jobs. The aim of creating profiles is to create detailed descriptions of what is required for exceptional performance in a given role or job, in terms of required competencies, personal attributes, knowledge, and experience. Each job's profile then becomes the anchor for creating recruitment, selection, training, and evaluation and development plans for each job. **Competency-based job analysis** means describing the job in terms of measurable, observable, behavioral competencies (such as specific skills) that an employee doing the job must exhibit to do the job well. With the job of, say, a team member possibly changing daily, one should identify the skills the employee may need to move among jobs.

Discussion Questions

4-4. Why, in summary, should managers think of staffing, training, appraising, and paying employees as a talent management process?

✪ 4-5. What items are typically included in the job description?

4-6. We discussed several methods for collecting job analysis data—questionnaires, the position analysis questionnaire, and so on. Compare and contrast these methods, explaining what each is useful for and listing the pros and cons of each.

4-7. Describe the types of information typically found in a job specification.

✪ 4-8. Explain how you would conduct a job analysis.

4-9. Do you think all companies can really do without detailed job descriptions? Why or why not?

4-10. Explain how you would create a job requirements matrix for a job.

4-11. In a company with only 25 employees, is there less need for job descriptions? Why or why not?

Individual and Group Activities

4-12. Working individually or in groups, obtain copies of job descriptions for clerical positions at the college or university where you study, or the firm where you work. What types of information do they contain? Do they give you enough information to explain what the job involves and how to do it? How would you improve on the description?

4-13. Working individually or in groups, use O*NET to develop a job description for your professor in this class. Based on that, use your judgment to develop a job specification. Compare your conclusions with those of other students or groups. Were there any significant differences? What do you think accounted for the differences?

4-14. Appendix A, PHR and SPHR Knowledge Base, at the end of this book (pages 580–588) lists the knowledge someone studying for the HRCI certification exam needs to have in each area of human resource management (such as in Strategic Management, Workforce Planning, and Human Resource Development). In groups of four to five students, do four things: (1) review Appendix A; (2) identify the material in this chapter that relates to the required knowledge Appendix A lists; (3) write four multiple-choice exam questions on this material that you believe would be suitable for inclusion in the HRCI exam; and (4) if time permits, have someone from your team post your team's questions in front of the class, so that students in all teams can answer the exam questions created by the other teams.

Experiential Exercise

The Instructor's Job Description

Purpose: The purpose of this exercise is to give you experience in developing a job description, by developing one for your instructor.

Required Understanding: You should understand the mechanics of job analysis and be thoroughly familiar with the job analysis questionnaires. (See Figures 4-4 and 4-10.)

How to Set Up the Exercise/Instructions: Set up groups of four to six students for this exercise. As in all exercises in this book, the groups should be separated and should not converse with each other. Half of the groups in the class will develop the job description using the job analysis questionnaire (Figure 4-4), and the other half of the groups will develop it using the job description questionnaire (Figure 4-10). Each student should review his or her questionnaire (as appropriate) before joining his or her group.

4-15. Each group should do a job analysis of the instructor's job: Half of the groups will use the Figure 4-4 job analysis questionnaire for this purpose, and half will use the Figure 4-10 job description questionnaire.

4-16. Based on this information, each group will develop its own job description and job specification for the instructor.

4-17. Next, each group should choose a partner group, one that developed the job description and job specification using the alternate method. (A group that used the job analysis questionnaire should be paired with a group that used the job description questionnaire.)

4-18. Finally, within each of these new combined groups, compare and critique each of the two sets of job descriptions and job specifications. Did each job analysis method provide different types of information? Which seems superior? Does one seem more advantageous for some types of jobs than others?

Video Case

Video Title: Talent Management (The Weather Channel)

SYNOPSIS

This video discusses job analysis in some detail, including how employers use the job analysis, who contributes to a job analysis, and writing the job description and the job specification.

Discussion Questions

4-19. What job analysis tools would you suggest The Weather Channel use to supplement what it's doing now to analyze jobs?

4-20. What role do you think job analysis plays in talent management at The Weather Channel? What role should it play?

4-21. How is human resources at The Weather Channel involved in job analysis?

4-22. If Taylor asked you what strategic HR is, what would you tell her? Does The Weather Channel seem to be practicing strategic HR? Why or why not?

4-23. What indications, if any, are there that The Weather Channel takes a talent management approach?

Application Case

The Flood

In May 2011, Mississippi River flooding hit Vicksburg, Mississippi, and the Optima Air Filter Company. Many employees' homes were devastated. Optima found that it had to hire almost three completely new crews, one for each shift. The problem was that the "old-timers" had known their jobs so well that no one had ever bothered to draw up job descriptions for them. When about 30 new employees began taking their places, there was general confusion about what they should do and how they should do it.

The flood quickly became old news to the firm's out-of-state customers, who wanted filters, not excuses. Phil Mann, the firm's president, was at his wits' end. He had about 30 new employees,

10 old-timers, and his original factory supervisor, Maybelline. He decided to meet with Linda Lowe, a consultant from the local university's business school. She immediately had the old-timers fill out a job questionnaire that listed all their duties. Arguments ensued almost at once: Both Phil and Maybelline thought the old-timers were exaggerating to make themselves look more important, and the old-timers insisted that the lists faithfully reflected their duties. Meanwhile, the customers clamored for their filters.

Questions

4-24. Should Phil and Linda ignore the old-timers' protests and write the job descriptions as they see fit? Why? Why not? How would you go about resolving the differences?

4-25. How would you have conducted the job analysis? What should Phil do now?

Continuing Case

Carter Cleaning Company

The Job Description

Based on her review of the stores, Jennifer concluded that one of the first matters she had to attend to involved developing job descriptions for her store managers.

As Jennifer tells it, her lessons regarding job descriptions in her basic management and HR management courses were insufficient to convince her of the pivotal role job descriptions actually play in the smooth functioning of an enterprise. Many times during her first few weeks on the job, Jennifer found herself asking one of her store managers why he was violating what she knew to be recommended company policies and procedures. Repeatedly, the answers were either "Because I didn't know it was my job" or "Because I didn't know that was the way we were supposed to do it." Jennifer knew that a job description, along with a set of standards and procedures that specified what was to be done and how to do it, would go a long way toward alleviating this problem.

In general, the store manager is responsible for directing all store activities in such a way that quality work is produced, customer relations and sales are maximized, and profitability is maintained through effective control of labor, supply, and energy costs. In accomplishing that general aim, a specific store manager's duties and responsibilities include quality control, store appearance and cleanliness, customer relations, bookkeeping and cash management, cost control and productivity, damage control, pricing, inventory control, spotting and cleaning, machine maintenance, purchasing, employee safety, hazardous waste removal, human resource administration, and pest control.

The questions that Jennifer had to address follow.

Questions

4-26. What should be the format and final form of the store manager's job description?

4-27. Is it practical to specify standards and procedures in the body of the job description, or should these be kept separate?

4-28. How should Jennifer go about collecting the information required for the standards, procedures, and job description?

4-29. What, in your opinion, should the store manager's job description look like and contain?

Translating Strategy into HR Policies and Practices Case*,§

**The accompanying strategy map for this chapter is in the MyManagementLab, and the overall map on the inside back cover of this text outlines the relationships involved.*

IMPROVING PERFORMANCE at The Hotel Paris

The New Job Descriptions

The Hotel Paris's competitive strategy is "To use superior guest service to differentiate the Hotel Paris properties, and to thereby increase the length of stay and return rate of guests, and thus boost revenues and profitability." HR manager Lisa Cruz must now formulate functional policies and activities that support this competitive strategy and boost performance by eliciting the required employee behaviors and competencies.

As an experienced human resource director, the Hotel Paris's Lisa Cruz knew that recruitment and selection processes invariably influenced employee competencies and behavior and, through them, the company's bottom line. Everything about the workforce—its collective skills, morale, experience, and motivation—depended on attracting and then selecting the right employees.

In reviewing the Hotel Paris's employment systems, she was therefore concerned that virtually all the company's job descriptions were out of date, and that many jobs had no descriptions at all. She knew that without accurate job descriptions, all her improvement efforts would be in vain. After all, if you don't know a job's duties, responsibilities, and human requirements, how can you decide who to hire or how to train them? To create human resource policies and practices that would produce employee competencies and behaviors needed to achieve the hotel's strategic aims, Lisa's team first had to produce a set of usable job descriptions.

A brief analysis, conducted with her company's CFO, reinforced that observation. They chose departments across the hotel chain that did and did not have updated job descriptions. While they understood that many other factors might be influencing the results, they believed that the statistical relationships they observed did suggest that having job descriptions had a positive influence on various employee behaviors and competencies. Perhaps having the descriptions facilitated the employee selection process, or perhaps the departments with the descriptions just had better managers. In any case, Lisa received the go-ahead to design new job descriptions for the chain.

While the resulting job descriptions included numerous traditional duties and responsibilities, most also included several competencies

§Written by and copyright Gary Dessler, PhD.

CHAPTER 4

unique to each job. For example, job descriptions for the front-desk clerks included competencies such as "able to check a guest in or out in five minutes or less." Most service employees' descriptions included the competency, "able to exhibit patience and guest supportiveness even when busy with other activities." Lisa knew that including these competencies would make it easier for her team to devise useful employee selection, training, and evaluation processes.

Questions

In teams or individually:

4-30. Based on the hotel's stated strategy, list at least four more important employee behaviors important for the Hotel Paris's staff to exhibit.

4-31. If time permits, spend some time prior to class observing the front-desk clerk at a local hotel. In any case, create a job description for a Hotel Paris front-desk clerk.

MyManagementLab

Go to **mymanagementlab.com** for Auto-graded writing questions as well as the following Assisted-graded writing questions:

4-32. What is job analysis? How can you make use of the information it provides?

4-33. Explain to the head of a company how he or she could use the talent management approach to improve his or her company's performance.

4-34. MyManagementLab only—comprehensive writing assignment for this chapter.

Key Terms

talent management, 88
job analysis, 89
job description, 89
job specifications, 89
organization chart, 91
process chart, 91
workflow analysis, 91
business process reengineering, 92
job enlargement, 92
job rotation, 92
job enrichment, 92
diary/log, 97
position analysis questionnaire (PAQ), 97
Standard Occupational Classification (SOC), 105
task statement, 111
job-requirement matrix, 111
competency-based job analysis, 115

Endnotes

1. Daimler is now expanding this plant; see www.autoblog.com/2009/03/23/rumormill-mercedes-benz-expected-to-expand-alabama-plant, accessed March 25, 2009; and http://mbusi.com/ accessed August 20, 2011.
2. www.talent_management101.com, accessed December 10, 2007. Note that when many managers today say "talent management," they mean managing basic HR activities in such a way as to acquire, improve, and retain their best employees. For instance, "let's make sure we have retention practices in place so we don't lose valued talent."
3. Ibid.
4. www.silkRoadTech.com, accessed December 10, 2007.
5. For a good discussion of job analysis, see James Clifford, "Job Analysis: Why Do It, and How Should It Be Done?" *Public Personnel Management* 23, no. 2 (Summer 1994), pp. 321–340; and "Job Analysis," www.paq.com/index.cfm?FuseAction=bulletins.job-analysis, accessed February 3, 2009.
6. One writer calls job analysis, "The hub of virtually all human resource management activities necessary for the successful functioning organizations." See Parbudyal Singh, "Job Analysis for a Changing Workplace," *Human Resource Management Review* 18 (2008), p. 87.
7. Richard Henderson, *Compensation Management: Rewarding Performance* (Upper Saddle River, NJ: Prentice Hall, 1994), pp. 139–150. See also T. A. Stetz et al., "New Tricks for an Old Dog: Visualizing Job Analysis Results," *Public Personnel Management* 38, no. 1 (Spring 2009), pp. 91–100.
8. Ron Miller, "Streamlining Claims Processing," *eWeek* 23, no. 25 (June 19, 2006), pp. 33, 35.
9. J. Richard Hackman et al., "A New Strategy for Job Enrichment," *California Management Review* 17, no. 4, pp. 57–71.
10. Darin Hartley, "Job Analysis at the Speed of Reality," *Training & Development*, September 2004, pp. 20–22.
11. See Henderson, *Compensation Management*, pp. 148–152.
12. Wayne Cascio, *Applied Psychology in Human Resource Management* (Upper Saddle River, NJ: Prentice Hall, 1998), p. 142. Distortion of information is a potential with all self-report methods of gathering information. See, for example, http://apps.opm.gov/ADT/ContentFiles/AssessmentDecisionGuide071807.pdf, accessed October 1, 2011.
13. Frederick Morgeson et al., "Self Presentation Processes in Job Analysis: A Field Experiment Investigating Inflation in Abilities, Tasks, and Competencies," *Journal of Applied Psychology* 89, no. 4 (November 4, 2004), pp. 674–686; and Frederick Morgeson and Stephen Humphrey, "The Work Design Questionnaire (WDQ): Developing and Validating a Comprehensive Measure for Assessing Job Design and the Nature of Work," *Journal of Applied Psychology* 91, no. 6 (2006), pp. 1321–1339.
14. Arthur Martinez et al., "Job Title Inflation," *Human Resource Management Review* 18 (2008), pp. 19–27.
15. Note that the PAQ (and other quantitative techniques) can also be used for job evaluation, which is explained in Chapter 11.
16. We will see that job evaluation is the process through which jobs are compared to one another and their values determined. Although usually viewed as a job analysis technique, the PAQ, in practice, is actually as much or more of a job evaluation technique and could therefore be discussed in either this chapter or in Chapter 11.
17. Jack Smith and Milton Hakel, "Convergence Among Data Sources, Response Bias, and Reliability and Validity of a Structured Job Analysis Questionnaire," *Personnel Psychology* 32 (Winter 1979), pp. 677–692. See also Frederick Morgeson and Stephen Humphrey,

"The Work Design Questionnaire (WDQ): Developing and Validating a Comprehensive Measure for Assessing Job Design and the Nature of Work," *Journal of Applied Psychology* 91, no. 6 (2006), pp. 1321–1339; www.paq.com/index.cfm?FuseAction=bulletins.job-analysis, accessed February 3, 2009.
18. www.paq.com/index.cfm?FuseAction=bulletins.job-analysis, accessed February 3, 2009.
19. This is based on Dianna Stone et al., "Factors Affecting the Effectiveness and Acceptance of Electronic Selection Systems," *Human Resource Management Review* 23, 2013, pp. 53–54.
20. Ibid.
21. Roni Reiter-Palmon et al., "Development of an O*NET Web-Based Job Analysis and Its Implementation in the U.S. Navy: Lessons Learned," *Human Resource Management Review* 16 (2006), pp. 294–309.
22. Ibid., p. 295.
23. Digitizing the information also enables the employer to quantify, tag, and electronically store and access it more readily. Lauren McEntire et al., "Innovations in Job Analysis: Development and Application of Metrics to Analyze Job Data," *Human Resource Management Review* 16 (2006), pp. 310–323.
24. See, for example, Kathryn Tyler, "Job Worth Doing: Update Descriptions," *HR Magazine*, January 2013, pp. 47–49.
25. This feature is based on Rebecca Ruiz, "Care for the Caregivers: Child-Care Providers Have Long Been Thought of as Full-Time Baby Sitters. The Government Can Help Them Become Well-Paid Professionals." *The American Prospect* 21.8 (2010), A17+. *Academic OneFile*. Web. 26 Mar. 2013.
26. Regarding this discussion, see Henderson, *Compensation Management*, pp. 175–184. See also Louisa Wah, "The Alphabet Soup of Job Titles," *Management Review* 87, no. 6 (June 1, 1998), pp. 40–43.
27. For discussions of writing job descriptions, see James Evered, "How to Write a Good Job Description," *Supervisory Management*, April 1981, pp. 14–19; Roger J. Plachy, "Writing Job Descriptions That Get Results," *Personnel*, October 1987, pp. 56–58; and Jean Phillips and Stanley Gulley, *Strategic Staffing* (Upper Saddle River, New Jersey: Pearson Education, 2012), pp. 89–95.
28. Evered, op cit., p. 16.
29. Ibid.
30. Ibid.
31. http://academicaffairs.ucsd.edu/staffhr/classification/task-statements.html, accessed March 27, 2013.
32. http://www.eeoc.gov/facts/ada17.html, accessed July 17, 2013.
33. Deborah Kearney, *Reasonable Accommodations: Job Descriptions in the Age of ADA, OSHA, and Workers Comp* (New York: Van Nostrand Reinhold, 1994), p. 9. See also Paul Starkman, "The ADA's Essential Job Function Requirements: Just How Essential Does an Essential Job Function Have to Be?" *Employee Relations Law Journal* 26, no. 4 (Spring 2001), pp. 43–102; and Benjamin Wolkinson and Sarah Wolkinson, "The Pregnant Police Officer's Overtime Duties and Forced Leave Policies Under Title VII, the ADA, and FMLA," *Employee Relations Law Journal* 36, no. 1 (Summer 2010), pp. 3–20.
34. Kearney, op cit.
35. O*Net™ is a trademark of the U.S. Department of Labor, Employment, and Training Administration.
36. See, for example, Christelle Lapolice et al., "Linking O*NET Descriptors to Occupational Literacy Requirements Using Job Component Validation," *Personnel Psychology* 61 (2008), pp. 405–441.
37. Mariani, "Replace with a Database."
38. Jorgen Sandberg, "Understanding Competence at Work," *Harvard Business Review*, March 2001, p. 28. Other organization chart software vendors include Nakisa, Aquire, and HumanConcepts. See "Advanced Org Charting," *Workforce Management*, May 19, 2008, p. 34.
39. http://www.linkedin.com/groups/Best-job-descriptions-40949.S.201279941, accessed March 26, 2013.
40. Based on Ernest J. McCormick and Joseph Tiffin, *Industrial Psychology* (Upper Saddle River, NJ: Prentice Hall, 1974), pp. 56–61.
41. Steven Hunt, "Generic Work Behavior: An Investigation into the Dimensions of Entry-Level, Hourly Job Performance," *Personnel Psychology* 49 (1996), pp. 51–83.
42. Jean Phillips and Stanley Gulley, *Strategic Staffing* (Upper Saddle River, NJ: Pearson Education, 2012), pp. 96–102.
43. Ibid., p. 96. Note, some HR experts limit the task statement to the what, how, and why of the task, and then list the knowledge, skills, and aptitudes the task requires separately.
44. Ibid., p. 102.
45. Jeffrey Shippmann et al., "The Practice of Competency Modeling," *Personnel Psychology* 53, no. 3 (2000), p. 703.
46. Michael Campion et al., "Doing Competencies Well: Best Practices in Competency Modeling," *Personnel Psychology* 64 (2011), pp. 225–262.
47. Richard S. Wellins et al., "Nine Best Practices for Effective Talent Management," DDI Development Dimensions International, Inc. http://www.ddiworld.com/DDIWorld/media/white-papers/ninebestpracticetalentmanagement_wp_ddi.pdf?ext=pdf, accessed August 20, 2011. For a discussion of competency modeling, see Michael A. Campion, Alexis A. Fink, Brian J. Ruggeberg, Linda Carr, Geneva M. Phillips, and Ronald B. Odman, "Doing Competencies Well: Best Practices in Competency Modeling," *Personnel Psychology* 64, no. 1 (2011), pp. 225–262.
48. Lindsay Chappell, "Mercedes Factories Embrace a New Order," *Automotive News*, May 28, 2001. See also www.autoblog.com/2009/03/23/rumormillmercedes-benz-expected-to-expandalabama-plant, accessed March 25, 2009, http://mbusi.com, accessed August 20, 2011.
49. Adapted from Richard Mirabile, "Everything You Wanted to Know About Competency Modeling," *Training & Development* 51, no. 8 (August 1997), pp. 73–78. See also Campion et al., "Doing Competencies Well."
50. Mirabile, "Everything You Wanted to Know."
51. This is adapted from Michael Campion et al., "Doing Competencies Well."
52. Ibid.
53. See, for example, Carol Spicer, "Building a Competency Model," *HR Magazine*, April 2009, pp. 34–36.

5 Personnel Planning and Recruiting

Source: YinYang/Getty Images

MyManagementLab®

Improve Your Grade!

When you see this icon, visit **www.mymanagementlab.com** for activities that are applied, personalized, and offer immediate feedback.

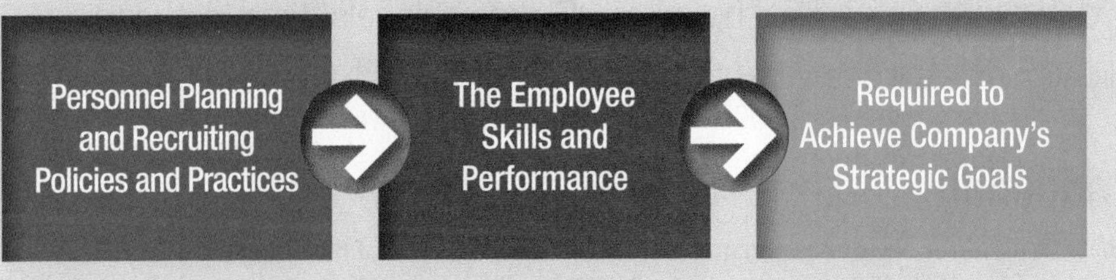

For a bird's eye view of how one company created a planning and recruiting system to improve its strategic performance, read the Hotel Paris case on page 152 and answer the questions after reading the chapter.

WHERE ARE WE NOW . . .

Having determined what the job entails, the next step is to recruit candidates for it. The purpose of Chapter 5 is to improve your effectiveness in recruiting candidates. The topics we discuss include workforce planning and forecasting, the need for effective recruiting, internal sources of candidates, outside sources of candidates, recruiting a more diverse workforce, and developing and using application forms. Then, in Chapter 6, we'll turn to how managers select who to hire from this applicant pool.

LEARNING OBJECTIVES

1 Explain the main techniques used in employment planning and forecasting.

2 Explain and give examples for the need for effective recruiting.

3 Name and describe the main internal sources of candidates.

4 List and discuss the main outside sources of candidates.

5 Explain how to recruit a more diverse workforce.

6 Discuss practical guidelines for obtaining application information.

Applying for jobs online is easy—just complete the online form, append your résumé, and click. But what's easy for applicants can be too much of a good thing for employers. Because the process is so easy, many firms are inundated with applications, some from applicants so far away they have no chance of being hired. For example, Starbucks recently got 7.6 *million* applications for about 65,000 jobs. California's Sutter Health gets over 300,000 applications for 10,000 job openings. They knew that if they didn't get this process under control, they'd waste thousands of hours of HR professionals' time just reading applications. We'll see what they did.

Introduction

Job analysis identifies the duties and human requirements for each of the company's jobs. The next step is to decide which of these jobs you need to fill, and to recruit and select employees for them. The traditional way to envision *recruitment and selection* is as a series of hurdles (Figure 5-1):

1. Decide what positions to fill, through *workforce/personnel planning and forecasting*.
2. Build a pool of candidates for these jobs, by *recruiting* internal or external candidates.
3. Have candidates complete *application forms* and perhaps undergo initial screening interviews.
4. Use *selection tools* like tests, background investigations, and physical exams to screen candidates.
5. Decide who to make an offer to, by having the supervisor and perhaps others *interview* the candidates.

We will see in this and the next two chapters that employers increasingly conduct activities 1 through 5 electronically. Applicants complete applications online or use interactive voice response systems. Employers conduct preliminary automated screens, and employees then take follow-up tests online. The interview is often videoconferenced or via online question/answer systems. Electronic selection decision software crunches multiple selection inputs (test results, interview results, references, and so on) to optimize selection decisions.[1] This chapter focuses on personnel planning and on recruiting employees. Chapters 6 and 7 address tests, background checks, physical exams, and interviews.

1 Explain the main techniques used in employment planning and forecasting.

workforce (or employment or personnel) planning
The process of deciding what positions the firm will have to fill, and how to fill them.

Workforce Planning and Forecasting

Workforce planning ideally precedes recruitment and selection. After all, if you don't know what your employment needs will be in the next few months or years, why should you be hiring?

Workforce (or employment or personnel) planning is the process of deciding what positions the firm will have to fill, and how to fill them. It embraces all future positions, from maintenance clerk to CEO. (However, most firms call the process of deciding how to fill executive jobs *succession planning*). We will see that workforce planners use various tools in their analyses. For example they scan employees' current skills based on employee biographical records, and conduct skills shortage analyses, succession planning, cross-training, and recruitment and mentoring programs.[2] However, analyses aside, judgment should play a big role in workforce planning Be prepared to modify any analysis based on subjective factors.

Improving Performance Through HRIS: Workforce Planning

Consultants Towers Watson offers a workforce planning solution that illustrates how employers manage their overall workforce planning process. The Towers Watson system ". . . helps your

FIGURE 5-1 Steps in Recruitment and Selection Process

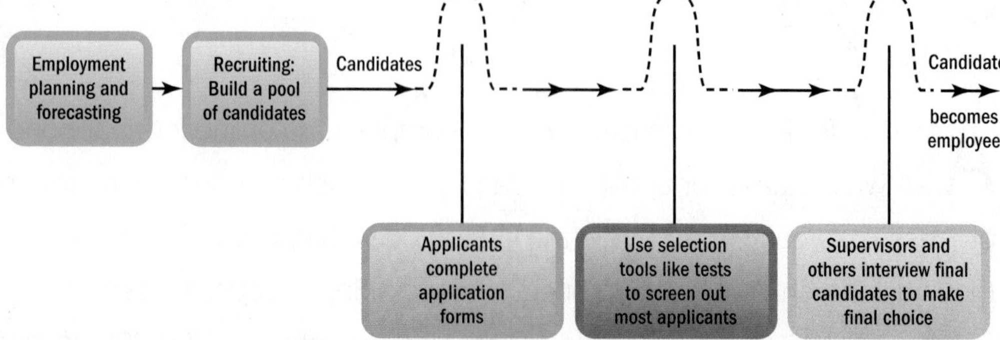

The recruitment and selection process is a series of hurdles aimed at selecting the best candidate for the job.

organization anticipate—and deliver—the talent component of your strategic business plans."[3] It answers critical workforce planning questions such as "Where are our talent risk areas, for instance, in terms of retirement and undesired talent loss?" "How will our new business strategy affect our staffing requirements?" And, "How can we manage the projected talent gaps (for instance, by seeking alternative sources for external talent)?"[4]

Using their system involves four steps. First, *review business plan and workforce data* (including historical workforce experience data) to project how business plan changes may influence headcount and skills requirements. Second, *identify gaps*, for instance by benchmarking against comparable employers the employer's current workforce composition, and by conducting workforce supply and demand projections. Third, develop a *workforce strategic plan and roadmap*, for instance by prioritizing key workforce gaps and identifying specific sources and methods for avoiding or filling those gaps. Finally, *execute and measure* the effects of the new workforce plan by implementing the changes (for instance, new recruiting sources and training and development programs), and by developing metrics and scorecards for monitoring the process.

Towers Watson's Internet software ("Towers Watson Workforce MAPS") helps clients manage this workforce planning process. It has *dashboards* (see the following four exhibits) for monitoring key metrics, for instance on recruiting and retention; a *workforce scan* that provides detailed analysis of the client's current workforce and historical workforce trends; a *workforce projection* showing projected employment and skill levels given the "status quo"; *scenario modeling* to let the employer compare "what if" scenarios; and an *external labor scan* for analyzing how the external labor market impacts the employer's workforce.

Strategy and Workforce Planning

Any workforce plans should, first, flow from the firm's strategic plans (see Figure 5-2). Thus, plans to enter new businesses or reduce costs all influence the types of positions you'll need to fill (or eliminate). For example, with IBM transitioning from supplying mostly computers to supplying software and consulting services, many current employees' skills will be obsolete.[5] At IBM, human resource executives review with finance and other executives "What sorts of skills and competencies will we need to execute our strategic plans?"[6] They can then put in place development and recruitment plans to address those needs.

The basic workforce planning process is to forecast the employer's demand for (need for) labor, and the supply of labor; then, identify supply–demand gaps, and develop action plans to fill the projected gaps. We'll start with forecasting personnel needs.

Forecasting Personnel Needs (Labor Demand)

How many people with what skills will we need? Managers consider several factors.[7] For example, when Dan Hilbert took over staffing at Valero Energy, he reviewed Valero's demographics, growth

The dashboards, which are part of Towers Watson's workforce planning Internet software, help clients manage the workforce planning process.

Workforce scan

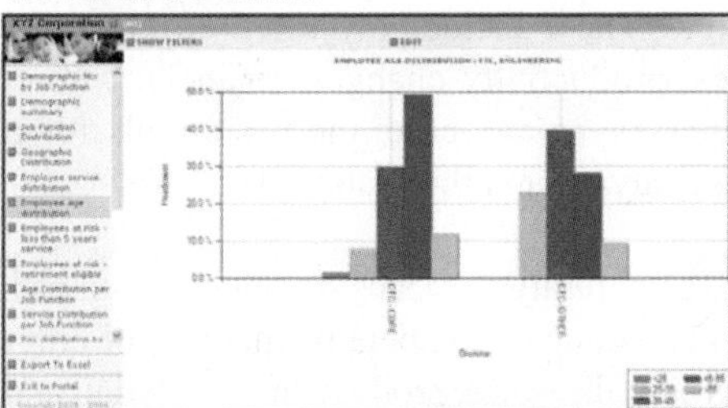

Dashboards

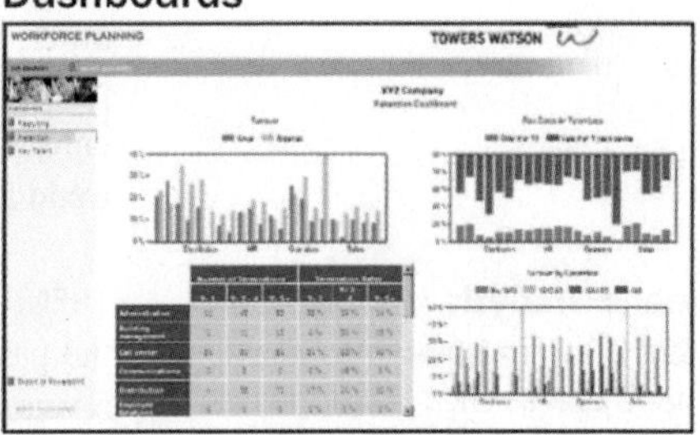

Workforce projection model

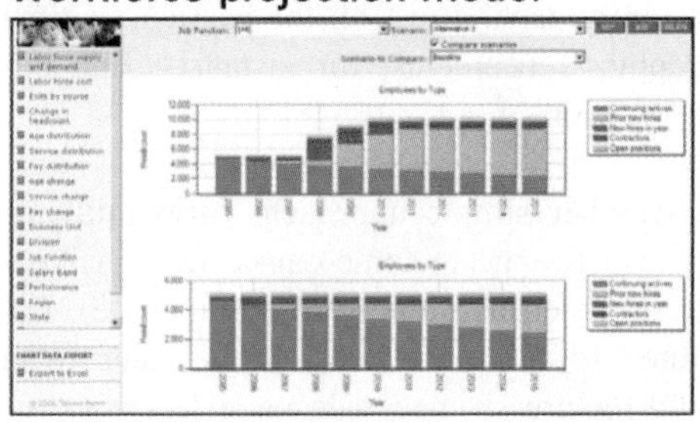

External labour scan

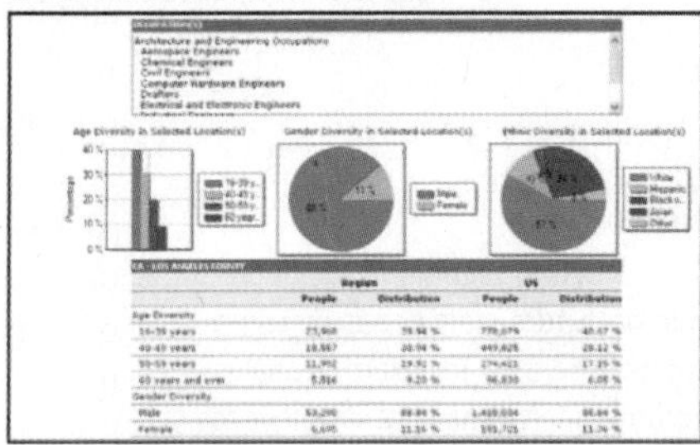

FIGURE 5-2 Linking Employer's Strategy to Personnel Plans

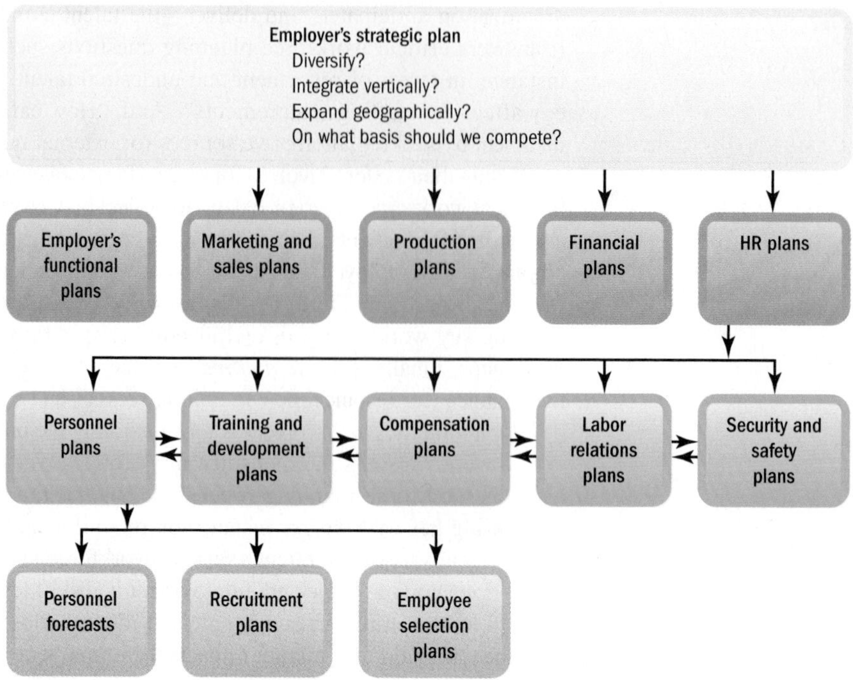

plans, and turnover history. He discovered that projected employment shortfalls were four times more than Valero could fill with its current recruitment procedures. He formulated new personnel plans for boosting employee retention and recruiting and screening more candidates.[8]

A firm's staffing needs reflect demand for its products or services, adjusted for changes the firm plans to make in its strategic goals and for changes in its turnover rate and productivity. Forecasting workforce demand therefore starts with estimating what the demand will be for your products or services. Short term, management should be concerned with daily, weekly, and seasonal forecasts.[9] For example, retailers track daily sales trends because they know, for instance, that Mother's Day produces a jump in business and a need for additional store staff. Seasonal forecasts are critical for retailers contemplating end-of-year holiday sales, and for many firms such as landscaping and air-conditioning vendors.

Longer term, managers will follow industry publications and economic forecasts closely, to try to get a sense for future demand. Such future predictions won't be precise, but should help you address the potential changes in demand.

The basic process for forecasting personnel needs is to forecast revenues first. Then estimate the size of the staff required to support this sales volume. However, managers must also consider other, strategic factors. These include projected turnover, decisions to upgrade (or downgrade) products or services, productivity changes, financial resources, and (as at IBM) decisions to enter or leave businesses. In any case, the basic tools for projecting personnel needs include trend analysis, ratio analysis, and the scatter plot.

trend analysis
Study of a firm's past employment needs over a period of years to predict future needs.

TREND ANALYSIS **Trend analysis** means studying variations in the firm's employment levels over the past few years. For example, compute the number of employees at the end of each of the last 5 years in each subgroup (like sales, production, secretarial, and administrative) to identify trends.

Trend analysis can provide an initial rough estimate of future staffing needs. However, employment levels rarely depend just on the passage of time. Other factors (like productivity, workforce demographics retirements, for instance), and changing skill needs will influence impending workforce needs.

ratio analysis
A forecasting technique for determining future staff needs by using ratios between, for example, sales volume and number of employees needed.

RATIO ANALYSIS Another simple approach, **ratio analysis**, means making forecasts based on the historical ratio between (1) some causal factor (like sales volume) and (2) the number of employees required (such as number of salespeople). For example, suppose a salesperson traditionally generates $500,000 in sales. If the sales revenue to salespeople ratio remains the same, you would require six new salespeople next year (each of whom produces an extra $500,000) to produce a hoped-for extra $3 million in sales.

Like trend analysis, ratio analysis assumes that things like productivity remain about the same. If sales productivity were to rise or fall, the ratio of sales to salespeople would change.

scatter plot
A graphical method used to help identify the relationship between two variables.

THE SCATTER PLOT A **scatter plot** shows graphically how two variables—such as sales and your firm's staffing levels—are related. If they are, then if you can forecast the business activity (like sales), you should also be able to estimate your personnel needs.

For example, suppose a 500-bed hospital expects to expand to 1,200 beds over the next 5 years. The human resource director wants to forecast how many registered nurses they'll need. The human resource director realizes she must determine the relationship between hospital size (in number of beds) and number of nurses required. She calls eight hospitals of various sizes and finds this:

Size of Hospital (Number of Beds)	Number of Registered Nurses
200	240
300	260
400	470
500	500
600	620
700	660
800	820
900	860

Figure 5-3's graph compares hospital size and number of nurses. If the two are related, then the points you plot (from the data above) will tend to fall on a straight line, as here. If you carefully draw in a line to minimize the distances between the line and each one of the plotted points, you will be able to estimate the number of nurses needed for each hospital size. Thus, for a 1,200-bed hospital, the human resource director would assume she needs about 1,210 nurses.

While simple, tools like scatter plots have drawbacks.[10]

1. Historical sales/personnel relationships assume that the firm's existing activities and skill needs will continue as is.
2. They tend to reward managers for adding employees, irrespective of the company's needs.
3. They tend to institutionalize existing ways of doing things, even in the face of change.

Improving Performance Through HRIS

COMPUTERIZED PERSONNEL FORECASTING *Computerized forecasts* enable managers to build more variables into their personnel projections.[11] Thus, at Chelan County Public Utility District, the development manager built a statistical model encompassing such things as age, tenure, turnover rate, and time to train new employees. This model helped them quickly identify five occupational "hotspots" among 33 occupational groups at their company. This in turn prompted them to focus more closely on creating plans to retain and hire, for instance, more systems operators.[12]

FIGURE 5-3 Determining the Relationship Between Hospital Size and Number of Nurses

Note: After fitting the line, you can project how many employees you'll need, given your projected volume.

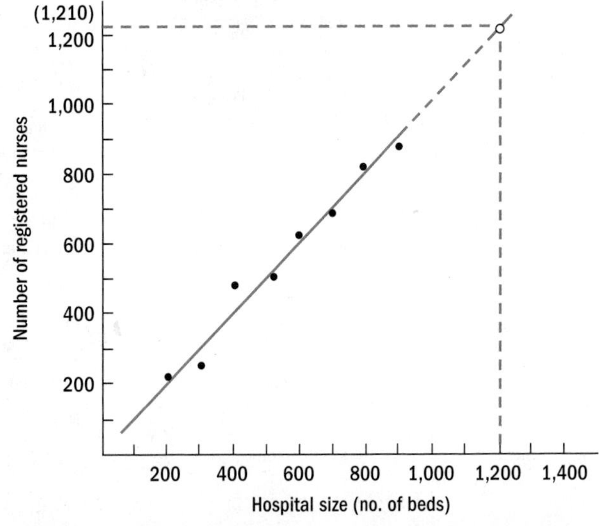

With such computerized programs, employers can more accurately translate projected productivity and sales levels into personnel needs. Many firms particularly use computerized employee forecasting systems for estimating short-term needs. Thus, labor scheduling systems help retailers estimate required staffing needs based on sales forecasts and estimated store traffic.[13]

Forecasting the Supply of Inside Candidates

Knowing your staffing *needs* satisfies only half the staffing equation.

Next, you must estimate the *supply* of inside and outside candidates. Most firms focus first on inside candidates. The main task here is determining which current employees might be qualified for the projected openings. Here, managers often turn to **qualifications (or skills) inventories**. These contain data on employees' performance records, educational background, and promotability. Whether manual or computerized, these help managers determine which employees are available for promotion or transfer.

qualifications (or skills) inventories
Manual or computerized records listing employees' education, career and development interests, languages, special skills, and so on, to be used in selecting inside candidates for promotion.

MANUAL SYSTEMS AND REPLACEMENT CHARTS Department managers or owners of smaller firms often use manual devices to track employee qualifications. Thus, a *personnel inventory and development record form* compiles qualifications information on each employee. The information includes education, company-sponsored courses taken, career and development interests, languages, desired assignments, and skills. **Personnel replacement charts** (Figure 5-4) are another option, particularly for the firm's top positions. They show the present performance and promotability for each position's potential replacement. As an alternative, you can develop a **position replacement card**. For this you create a card for each position, showing possible replacements as well as their present performance, promotion potential, and training.

personnel replacement charts
Company records showing present performance and promotability of inside candidates for the most important positions.

position replacement card
A card prepared for each position in a company to show possible replacement candidates and their qualifications.

COMPUTERIZED SKILLS INVENTORIES Larger firms obviously can't track the qualifications of hundreds or thousands of employees manually. They therefore computerize this information, using various packaged software systems such as SurveyAnalytics's Skills Inventory Software. Skills inventory systems such as one from Perceptyx (www.perceptyx.com/home/about/solutions/skills-inventories/) enables employers to collect and compile employee skills information in real time via online employee surveys. Such programs help management anticipate staffing and skills shortages, and thereby facilitate workforce planning, recruitment, and training plans.[14]

The usual process is for the employee, the supervisor, and human resource manager to enter information about the employee's background, experience, and skills via the system. Then, when a manager needs a person for a position, he or she uses key words to describe the position's specifications (for instance, in terms of education and skills). The computerized system then

FIGURE 5-4 Personnel or Management Replacement Chart Showing Development Needs of Potential Future Divisional Vice Presidents

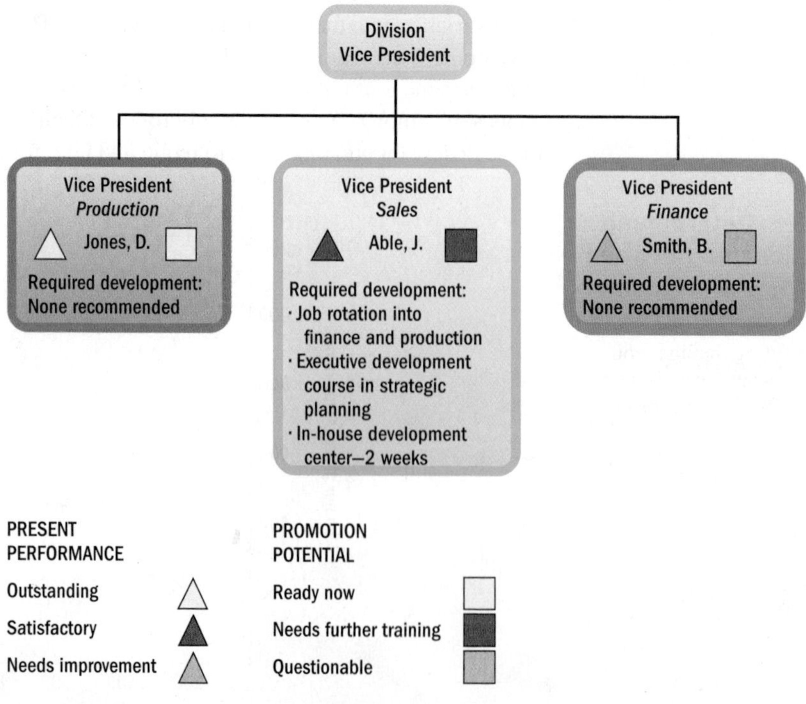

produces a list of qualified candidates. Computerized skills inventory data typically include items like *work experience codes, product knowledge*, the employee's *level of familiarity* with the employer's product lines or services, the person's *industry experience*, and *formal education*. As the user of one such system said, "The [SumTotal] platform allows us to track and assess the talent pool and promote people within the company. Our latest metrics show that 75% of key openings are fulfilled by internal candidates. The succession module helps us to identify who the next senior managers could be and build development plans to help them achieve their potential."[15]

The employer must secure all its employee data.[16] Legislation gives employees legal rights regarding who has access to information about them.[17] Internet access makes it relatively easy for more people to access the firm's computerized files.[18] Pfizer Inc. lost personal data on about 17,000 current and former employees this way.[19] One solution is to incorporate an access matrix in the database management system, to define the rights of users to various kinds of access. Figure 5-5 summarizes some guidelines for keeping employee data safe.

MARKOV ANALYSIS Employers also use a mathematical process known as *Markov analysis* (or "transition analysis") to forecast availability of internal job candidates. Markov analysis involves creating a matrix that shows the probabilities that employees in the chain of feeder positions for a key job (such as from junior engineer, to engineer, to senior engineer, to engineering supervisor, to director of engineering) will move from position to position and therefore be available to fill the key position.

Forecasting the Supply of Outside Candidates

If there won't be enough skilled inside candidates to fill the anticipated openings (or you want to go outside for another reason), you will turn to outside candidates.

Forecasting what the workforce availability will be depends first on the manager's own sense of what's happening in his or her industry and locale. For example, unemployment rates above 7% recently signaled to HR managers that finding good candidates would be easier.[20] He or she then supplements such observations with formal labor market analyses. For example, look for economic projections online, for instance, from the U.S. Congressional Budget Office (www.cbo.gov/) and the Bureau of Labor Statistics (www.bls.gov/news.release/ecopro.toc.htm). Your planning may also require forecasting specific occupations. O*NET (discussed in Chapter 4) reports projections for most occupations. The U.S. Bureau of Labor Statistics publishes annual occupational projections both online and in the *Monthly Labor Review* and in *Occupational Outlook Quarterly*.

The emphasis on technology means many applicants may lack basic skills such as math, communication, creativity, and teamwork.[21] Such needs, too, get factored into the employer's workforce plans.

Predictive Workforce Monitoring's Role in Talent Management

Most employers review their workforce plans every year or so, but this isn't always sufficient For instance, having failed to do much formal workforce planning, Valero Energy almost lacked sufficient time to implement a plan to address replacing employees who would soon retire.

In terms of best talent management practice, workforce planning therefore requires *paying continuous attention* to workforce planning issues. Managers call this *predictive workforce monitoring*. For example, Intel Corporation conducts semiannual "Organization Capability

FIGURE 5-5 Keeping Data Safe

Source: Taken from an interview with Linda Foley, co-founder of the ITRC. Published in "Safeguarding HR Information" by Dan Caternicchia, in *HR Magazine*, November 2005. Copyright © 2005 by Society for Human Resource Management, Alexandria, VA.

Since intruders can strike from outside an organization or from within, HR departments can help screen out potential identity thieves by following four basic rules:

- Perform background checks on anyone who is going to have access to personal information.
- If someone with access to personal information is out sick or on leave, don't hire a temporary employee to replace him or her. Instead, bring in a trusted worker from another department.
- Perform random background checks such as random drug tests. Just because someone passed 5 years ago doesn't mean their current situation is the same.
- Limit access to information such as SSNs, health information, and other sensitive data to HR managers who require it to do their jobs.

Assessments." The staffing department works with the firm's business heads twice a year to assess workforce needs—both immediate and up to 2 years in the future.[22] Amerada Hess has an Organizational Capability (OC) group to monitor and predict workforce attrition (such as retirement age, experience, education, etc.) and likely talent requirements. The group "considers how each line of business is evolving, examines what jobs at Hess will look like in the future, identifies sources for procuring the best talent, and assists in developing current and newly hired employees."[23] Boeing Corp. considers various factors when predicting talent gaps as part of its "workforce modeling" process. These include Boeing workforce demographic characteristics such as age, retirement eligibility for employees with various skills, economic trends, anticipated increases or decreases in staffing levels, and internal transfers and promotions.[24] The accompanying HR Practices Around the Globe feature shows another example.

IMPROVING PERFORMANCE: HR Practices Around the Globe

Predicting Labor Needs

Valero Energy created a "labor supply chain" for improving the efficiency of its workforce planning, recruiting, and hiring process. It includes an analytic tool that predicts Valero's labor needs based on past trends. And, it includes computer screen "dashboards" that show how components in the staffing chain, such as ads placed on job boards, are performing according to cost, speed, and quality. Before implementing the labor supply chain system, it took 41 pieces of paper to bring on board an employee and more than 120 days to fill a position; each hire cost about $12,000. The new system eliminated most of the paper forms needed to hire an employee, time-to-fill fell below 40 days, and cost per hire dropped to $2,300.[25]

Discussion Question 5-1: Explain how Valero might use the Towers Watson workforce planning process on pages 122–123.

Developing an Action Plan to Match Projected Labor Supply and Labor Demand

Workforce planning should logically culminate in a workforce plan. This lays out the employer's projected workforce and skills gaps, as well as staffing plans for filling these gaps. For example, the plan should identify the positions to be filled; potential internal and external sources for these positions; the training, development, and promotions moving people into the positions will entail; and the resources that implementing the plan will require, for instance in recruiter fees, estimated training costs, relocation costs, and interview expenses.[26]

Succession Planning

succession planning
The ongoing process of systematically identifying, assessing, and developing organizational leadership to enhance performance.

Succession planning involves developing workforce plans for the company's top positions. **Succession planning** is the ongoing process of systematically identifying, assessing, and developing organizational leadership to enhance performance.[27] It entails three steps: identify key needs, develop inside candidates, and assess and choose those who will fill the key positions.[28]

IDENTIFY KEY NEEDS First, based on the company's strategic and business plans, top management and the human resource director identify what the company's future key position needs will be. Matters to address here include defining key positions and "high potentials," reviewing the company's current talent, and creating (based on the company's strategy) skills profiles for the key positions.[29]

DEVELOP INSIDE CANDIDATES After identifying future key positions, management turns to creating candidates for these jobs. "Creating" means identifying inside or outside candidates and providing them with the developmental experiences they require to be viable candidates. Employers develop high-potential employees through internal training and cross-functional experiences, job rotation, external training, and global/regional assignments.[30]

ASSESS AND CHOOSE Finally, succession planning requires assessing these candidates and selecting those who will actually fill the key positions.[31]

Improving Performance Through HRIS: Succession Systems

At Dole Foods, the new president's strategy involved improving financial performance by reducing redundancies and centralizing certain activities, including succession planning.[32] Web technology helped Dole do this. Dole contracted with application system providers (ASPs) to handle things like payroll management.[33] For succession management, Dole chose software from Pilat NAI. The Pilat system keeps all the data on its own servers for a monthly fee. Dole's managers access the program via the Web using a password. They fill out online résumés for themselves, including career interests, and note special considerations such as geographic restrictions.

The managers also assess themselves on four competencies. Once the manager provides his or her input, the program notifies that manager's boss, who assesses his or her subordinate and indicates whether the person is promotable. This assessment and the online résumés then go automatically to the division head and the divisional HR director. Dole's senior vice president for human resources then uses the information to create career development plans for each manager, including seminars and other programs.[34]

Why Effective Recruiting Is Important

2 Explain and give examples for the need for effective recruiting.

employee recruiting
Finding and/or attracting applicants for the employer's open positions.

Assuming the company authorizes you to fill a position, the next step is to build up, through recruiting, an applicant pool. **Employee recruiting** means finding and/or attracting applicants for the employer's open positions.

It's hard to overemphasize the importance of effective recruiting. If only two candidates apply for two openings, you may have little choice but to hire them. But if 10 or 20 applicants appear, you can use techniques like interviews and tests to screen out all but the best.

Even with unemployment rates still high recently, many employers found getting qualified applicants challenging. One survey found that about two-thirds of the manufacturing executives surveyed faced a "moderate to severe shortage of skilled labor."[35] With manufacturing jobs increasingly high-tech, the available jobs require more math and science than most applicants possess.[36] A recent Lloyd's of London risk index listed "talent and skill shortages" as the number 2 risk facing businesses today ("loss of customers" was number 1).[37] The head of media at a Web design company with 85 employees in New York said he had 10 openings because he couldn't find enough qualified applicants.[38] He ended up hiring virtual independent contractors, who worked, for instance, from Greece. Other employers, such as a group of manufacturers near Fort Worth, Texas, banded together to create a 9-week course to train prospective employees in computer numeric control for machinists.[39]

Effective recruiting is not easy. First, some recruiting methods are superior to others, depending on the job. Second, recruiting depends on nonrecruitment issues such as pay scales.[40] Third, employment law prescribes what you can do.[41] See the accompanying Know Your Employment Law feature.

The Recruiting Yield Pyramid

recruiting yield pyramid
The historical arithmetic relationships between recruitment leads and invitees, invitees and interviews, interviews and offers made, and offers made and offers accepted.

Filling a relative handful of positions might require recruiting dozens or hundreds of candidates. Managers therefore use a staffing or **recruiting yield pyramid**, as shown in Figure 5-6, to gauge the staffing issues it needs to address. In Figure 5-6, the company knows it needs 50 new entry-level accountants next year. From experience, the firm also knows the following:

- The ratio of offers made to actual new hires is 2 to 1.
- The ratio of candidates interviewed to offers made is 3 to 2.

FIGURE 5-6 Recruiting Yield Pyramid

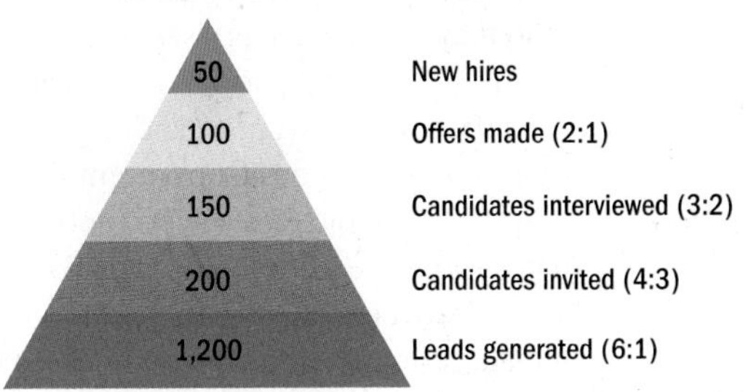

- The ratio of candidates invited for interviews to candidates interviewed is about 4 to 3.
- Finally, the firm knows that of six leads that come in from all its recruiting sources, it typically invites only one applicant for an interview—a 6-to-1 ratio.

Therefore, the firm must generate about 1,200 leads to be able to invite in 200 viable candidates of which it interviews about 150, and so on.

KNOW YOUR EMPLOYMENT LAW

Preemployment Activities

As we explained in Chapter 2, numerous federal, state, and local laws and court decisions restrict what employers can and cannot do when recruiting job applicants. For example, employers can't rely on word-of-mouth dissemination of information about job opportunities when its workforce is all, or substantially all, white or all members of some other class such as all female or all Hispanic. It is unlawful to give false or misleading information to members of any group, or to fail or to refuse to advise them of work opportunities and the procedures for obtaining them.

In practice, "the key question in all recruitment procedures is whether the method limits qualified applicants from applying."[42] So, for example, gender-specific ads that call for "busboy" or "firemen" would obviously raise red flags. Similarly, courts will often question word-of-mouth recruiting, because workers tend to nominate candidates of the same nationality, race, and religion.[43] The bottom line is that it is generally best to avoid limiting recruitment efforts to just one recruitment method; use multiple sources to reach out as widely as possible.

Organizing How You Recruit

Should you centralize your firm's recruitment efforts, or let each plant or office do their own recruiting? For many firms, it's simply much easier to recruit centrally now that so much recruiting is on the Web.[44] Accountants Deloitte Touche Tohmatsu Limited created a global recruitment site, thus eliminating the need to maintain 35 separate local recruiting websites.[45] Retailer 7-Eleven's site presents its worldwide job openings and lets prospective employees apply online.

THE SUPERVISOR'S ROLE The human resource manager charged with filling an open position is seldom very familiar with the job itself. So, for example, the recruiter will want to know from the supervisor what the job really entails and its job specifications, as well as informal things like the supervisor's leadership style and how the team gets along.

HR in Practice at the Hotel Paris As they reviewed the details of the Hotel Paris's current recruitment practices, Lisa Cruz and the firm's CFO became increasingly concerned. They found that the recruitment function was totally unmanaged. To see how they handled this, see the case on page 152 of this chapter.

3 Name and describe the main internal sources of candidates.

Internal Sources of Candidates

Recruiting typically brings to mind monster.com, LinkedIn, employment agencies, and classified ads, but internal sources—in other words, current employees or "hiring from within"—are often the best source of candidates. Internal recruiting is increasingly popular. For example, Cisco Systems uses its proprietary Talent Connection program to seek qualified internal Cisco employees who may not be actively seeking jobs.[46]

Filling open positions with inside candidates has several advantages. First, there is really no substitute for knowing a candidate's *strengths and weaknesses*, as you should after working with them for some time. Current employees may also be more *committed* to the company. *Morale* may rise if employees see promotions as rewards for loyalty and competence. And inside candidates should require *less orientation* and (perhaps) training than outsiders.

However, hiring from within can also backfire. Rejected applicants may become *discontented;* telling them why you rejected them and what remedial actions they might take is crucial.

It can also be a *waste of time*, since often the manager already knows whom he or she wants to hire. *Inbreeding* is another potential drawback, if new perspectives are required.

Finding Internal Candidates

job posting
Publicizing an open job to employees (often by literally posting it on bulletin boards) and listing its attributes, like qualifications, supervisor, working schedule, and pay rate.

In a perfect world, the employer will adhere to formal internal-recruitment policies and procedures. These typically rely heavily on job posting and on the firm's skills inventories. **Job posting** means publicizing the open job to employees (usually by literally posting it on company intranets or bulletin boards). These postings list the job's attributes, like qualifications, supervisor, work schedule, and pay rate. Qualifications skills inventories also play a role. For example, they may reveal to the company's recruiters those employees who have potential for further training or who have the right background for the open job. Ideally, the employer's system therefore matches the best inside candidate with the job. In practice, this doesn't always happen. For better or worse internal politics and having the right connections may well lead to placements they seem (and indeed may be) unfair and less than optimal.

REHIRING Rehiring someone who left your employ has pros and cons. Former employees are known quantities (more or less) and are already familiar with how you do things. On the other hand, employees who you let go may return with negative attitudes.[47]

Employers can reduce potential problems. Inquire (before rehiring) about what they did during the layoff and how they feel about returning. After a probationary period, credit them with the years of service they had accumulated before they left.[48]

4 List and discuss the main outside sources of candidates.

Outside Sources of Candidates

Employers can't always get all the employees they need from their current staff, and sometimes they just don't want to. We look at the sources firms use to find outside candidates next.

Informal Recruiting and the Hidden Job Market

Many (or most) job openings aren't publicized at all; jobs are created and become available when employers serendipitously come across the right candidates. The author of *Unlock the Hidden Job Market* estimates that perhaps half of all positions are filled informally (without formal recruiting).[49] Similarly, one survey found that 28% of those surveyed found their most recent job through word-of-mouth. Nineteen percent used online job boards, 16% direct approaches from employers and employment services, 7% print ads, and only 1% social media sites (although 22% used sites like LinkedIn to *search* for jobs).[50]

Recruiting via the Internet

U.S. employers' outlays on online recruitment could exceed $10 billion per year by 2016. For example, restaurant chain The Cheesecake Factory gets about a third of its management applicants via the Web.[51] Employers and vendors are therefore working hard to optimize online recruiting results.

Most employers recruit through their own websites, or use job boards (see Figure 5-7). The CareerBuilder.com iPhone application offers a way to search nearly 2 million jobs on CareerBuilder.com, the largest U.S. job site.[52] Users may search for jobs by key word, read job descriptions and salaries, save jobs to a list of favorites, and e-mail job links to anyone on their contact list. Users may direct it to search only for jobs near where they are located. Increasingly, employers are using niche job boards such as jobsinsports.com and vetjobs.com.[53]

Online recruiting is getting more sophisticated. One example is the *virtual office tour*.[54] In China the local office of Accountants Deloitte Touche Tohmatsu Limited posted a virtual office tour on Weibo, (similar to Twitter's messaging service). People visiting the site can virtually enter each of the company's offices in Asia, walking through meeting rooms and talking virtually with local employees, to get a feel for what working in that office is like.

Intelligent automated resúme screening is another trend. Employers have long used online applicant tracking software to identify likely candidates based on resúme key words or phrases

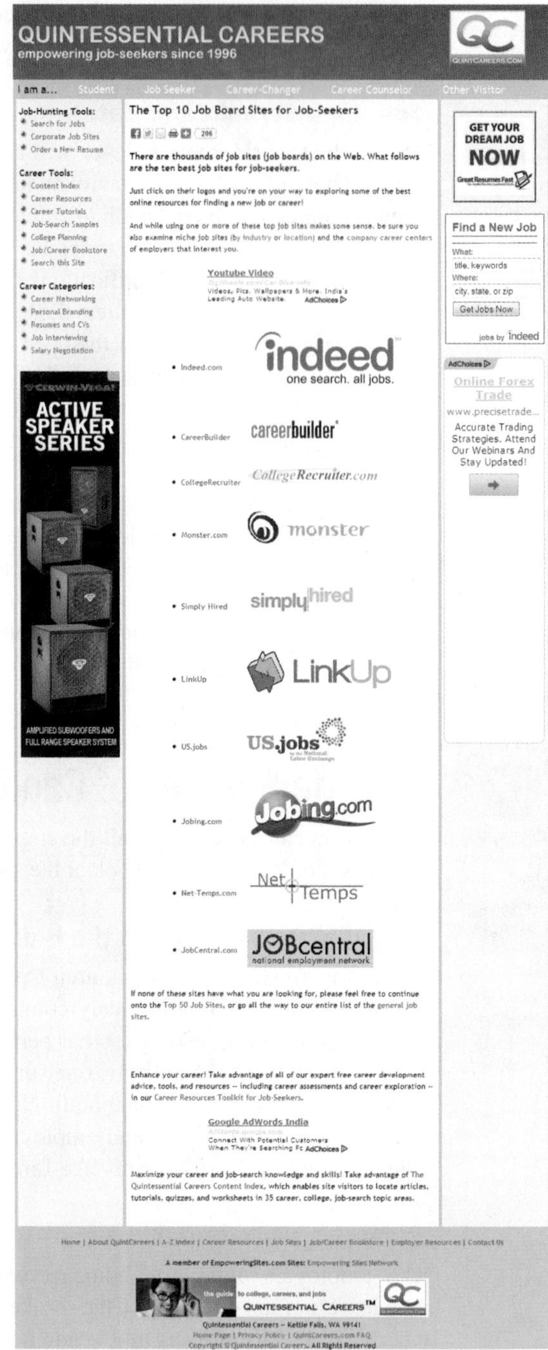

FIGURE 5-7 Some Top Online Recruiting Job Boards

Source: www.quintcareers.com/top_10_sites.html, accessed April 28, 2009. Used with permission of QuintCareers.com.

(such as "chemical engineer"). But basic key word screens like these won't necessarily zero in candidates who best fit the hiring employer and job. Vendors are therefore taking automated resúme screening to the next level. For example, rather than just trying to find a match based on key words, monster.com's new 6Sense resume search tool aims to better "understand" the applicant's job preferences (based on things like the person's job history) so as to better match the applicant with the available job. Other services, such as Jobfox, have applicants and employers complete detailed questionnaires so that (as with online dating sites) there's hopefully a better match, for instance in terms of work life preferences.

Social Media and HR

Recruiting is also shifting from online job boards to social networking sites such as Facebook and LinkedIn. In one survey, almost 90% of responding human resource and recruiting professionals planned to use social media recruiting tools for recruiting managers and professional.[55] The problem they aim to address is that many job applications received via job boards don't meet the job's qualifications. As one recruiter said, "recruiters had to put in all this extra time to read applications but we didn't get benefit from it." Instead, this company now hires recruiters who dig through social websites and competitors' publications to find applicants who may not even be looking for jobs.[56]

Recruiters are also seeking passive candidates (people not actively looking for jobs) by using social networking sites such as *LinkedIn Recruiter* to browse members' résumés and to find such passive candidates.[57] One Massachusetts staffing firm uses its Facebook and LinkedIn pages to announce openings. Other firms use Twitter to announce job openings to jobseekers who subscribe to their Twitter feeds.[58] Theladders.com's Pipeline™ networking tool lets recruiters maintain a dialogue with prospective job seekers even before they're interested in seeking a job. Others use Facebook's friend-finding search function, and Twitter, to learn more about prospective and actual candidates. TalentBin searches sites such as Pinterest to find qualified tech workers.[59] Employers such as the Mayo Clinic have social media strategies and career pages that establish an online presence highlighting the benefits of working for them.[60]

OTHER ONLINE RECRUITING PRACTICES There are many other such online tools. ResumePal, (see www.jobfox.com/), is one recruiting innovation. ResumePal is an online standard universal job application. Jobseekers submit it to participating employers, who can then use the standardized application's key words to identify viable candidates more easily.[61] McDonald's Corp. posted a series of employee testimonials on social networking sites like Second Life to attract applicants.[62] Other employers simply screen through job boards' résumé listings.[63]

Accountants Deloitte & Touche asked employees to make short videos describing their experiences with Deloitte, and put the best on YouTube.[64] Monster helps employers integrate streaming video into their job postings.[65] Facebook makes it easy to start a company networking site, which many employers use for recruiting.[66] At one diversity conference, consultants Hewitt Associates displayed posters asking attendees to text message *hewdiversity* to a specific 5-digit number. Each person texting then became part of Hewitt's "mobile recruiting network," periodically receiving text messages regarding Hewitt openings.[67] The *dot-jobs* domain gives job seekers a one-click conduit for finding jobs at the employers who register at www.goto.jobs. For example, applicants seeking a job at Disneyland can go to www.Disneyland.jobs. This takes them to Disney's Disneyland recruiting website.

Virtual (fully online) job fairs are another option. Here online visitors see a similar setup to a regular job fair. They can listen to presentations, visit booths, leave résumés and business cards, participate in live chats, and get contact information from recruiters and even hiring managers.[68] Fairs last about 5 hours. Specialist virtual fair website include Milicruit (for former military personnel) and Unicruit (for college students).

PROS AND CONS Online recruiting generates more responses quicker and for a longer time at less cost than just about any other method. But, it has two potential problems.

First, older people and some minorities are less likely to use the Internet, so online application gathering may inadvertently exclude disproportionate numbers of older applicants (and certain minorities). To prove they've complied with EEO laws, employers should keep track of each applicant's race, sex, and ethnic group. The EEO says that, to be an "applicant," he or she must meet three conditions: he or she must express interest in employment, the employer must have taken steps to fill a specific job, and the individual must have followed the employer's standard application procedure.[69]

applicant tracking systems
Online systems that help employers attract, gather, screen, compile, and manage applicants.

The second problem is Internet overload: Employers end up deluged with résumés. Self-screening helps: The Cheesecake Factory posts detailed job duties listings, so those not interested needn't apply. Another approach is to have job seekers complete a short online prescreening questionnaire, then use these to identify those who may proceed in the hiring process.[70]

Most employers also use applicant tracking systems, to which we now turn.

Improving Performance Through HRIS: Using Applicant Tracking

A deluge of applications means that just about all Fortune 500 companies and many others now use applicant tracking software to screen applications.[71] **Applicant tracking systems (ATS)** are online systems that help employers attract, gather, screen, compile, and manage applicants.[72] They also provide other services, including requisitions management (for monitoring the firm's open jobs), applicant data collection (for scanning applicants' data into the system), and reporting (to create various recruiting-related reports such as cost per hire and hire by source).[73] Most systems are from *application service providers* (ASPs). These basically redirect applicants from the employers to the ASP's site. Thus, applicants who log on to take a test at the employer are actually taking the test at the ASP's site.[74] Major suppliers of such e-recruiting services include Automatic Data Processing (ADP.com), HRSmart (hrsmart.com), Silkroad Technology (silkroad.com), and Monster (monster.com).[75]

As one example, a bank uses its ATS to bump applicants who don't meet the basic job requirements; it then e-mails them suggesting they review the bank's site for more appropriate positions. This bank then uses either phone interviews or automated interview systems to whittle down the applicant pool to a few candidates. Then its recruiters interview those at headquarters and send them through the final selection process.[76] One Ohio-based nursing care and assisted living facility company arranged to have the recruiting dashboard vendor jobs2Web integrate its dashboard with the employer's applicant tracking system. The recruiting manager now uses the dashboard to monitor visually recruitment data trends on things like which recruiting sources are doing the best job of attracting applications.[77]

SUTTER HEALTH EXAMPLE To deal with its 300,000 applications per year, Sutter Health contracted with Taleo Corporation, a recruiting applications service provider that is part of Oracle.[78] Taleo now does all the work of hosting Sutter Health's job site. Taleo doesn't just post Sutter Health job openings and collect its résumés; it also gives Sutter Health an automated way to evaluate, rank, and match IT and other job candidates with specific openings. For example, Taleo's system screens incoming résumés, compares them with Sutter's job requirements, and flags high-priority applicants. This helped Sutter cut its typical recruiting process from weeks to days.

IMPROVING ONLINE RECRUITING EFFECTIVENESS Planning the online effort is crucial. For example, one survey of Web-based recruiting uncovered these grad school alumni's objections:

- Job openings lacked relevant information (such as job descriptions).
- It was often difficult to format résumés and post them in the form required.
- They expressed concerns about privacy.
- Slow follow-up responses were annoying.[79]

Employers take several steps. Most firms place employment information one click away from their home pages.[80] Applicants can submit their résumés online at almost all *Fortune* 500 firms' websites. Fewer companies give job seekers the option of completing online applications, although that's what most applicants prefer.[81]

Furthermore, the best Web ads don't just transfer newspaper ads to the Web. As one specialist put it, "getting recruiters out of the 'shrunken want ad mentality' is a big problem." Figure 5-8 is an example of recycling a print ad to the Web. The ineffective Web ad has needless abbreviations, and doesn't say much about why the job seeker should want that job.[82]

Now look at the effective Web ad in Figure 5-8. It provides good reasons to work for this company. It starts with an attention-grabbing heading and uses the extra space to provide more specific job information. Many employers often include the entire job description.[83] Ideally, an ad also should provide a way (such as a checklist of the job's human requirements) for potential applicants to gauge if the job is a good fit.[84]

Finally, online recruiting requires caution for *applicants*. Many job boards don't check the legitimacy of the "recruiters" who place ads. Many applicants submit personal details, not realizing who is getting it.[85] U.S. laws generally do not prohibit job boards from sharing your data with other sources. One job board reportedly had personal information on more than 1 million subscribers stolen.[86]

Advertising

While Web-based recruiting is replacing traditional help wanted ads, a glance at almost any paper or business or professional magazine will confirm that print ads are still popular. To use such help wanted ads successfully, employers should address two issues: the advertising medium and the ad's construction.

FIGURE 5-8 Ineffective and Effective Web Ads

Ineffective Ad, Recycled from Magazine to the Web	Effective Web Ad (Space Not an Issue)
Process Engineer Pay: $65k–$85k/year Immediate Need in Florida for a Wastewater Treatment Process Engineer. Must have a min. 4–7 years Industrial Wastewater exp. Reply KimGD@ WatersCleanX.com	Do you want to help us make this a better world? We are one of the top wastewater treatment companies in the world, with installations from Miami to London to Beijing. We are growing fast and looking for an experienced process engineer to join our team. If you have at least 4–7 years' experience designing processes for wastewater treatment facilities and a dedication to make this a better world, we would like to hear from you. Pay range depending on experience is $65,000–$85,000. Please reply in confidence to KimGD@ WatersCleanX.com

THE MEDIA The best medium—the local paper, *The Wall Street Journal*, *The Economist*, for instance—depends on the positions for which you're recruiting. For example, the local newspaper is often a good source for local blue-collar help, clerical employees, and lower-level administrative employees. On the other hand, if recruiting for workers with special skills, such as furniture finishers, you'd probably want to advertise in places with many furniture manufacturers, such as the Carolinas, even if your plant is in Tennessee. The point is to target your ads where they'll reach your prospective employees.

For specialized employees, advertise in trade and professional journals like *American Psychologist, Sales Management, Chemical Engineering,* and *Women's Wear Daily*. Help wanted ads in papers like *The Wall Street Journal* can be good sources of middle- or senior-management personnel. Most of these print outlets now include online ads with the purchase of print help wanted ads.

Technology lets companies be more creative.[87] For example, the video-game publisher Electronic Arts (EA) uses its products to help solicit applicants. EA includes information about its internship program on the back of its video game manuals. Thanks to nontraditional techniques like these, EA has a database of more than 200,000 potential job candidates. It uses tracking software to identify potential applicants with specific skills, and to facilitate ongoing e-mail communications with everyone in its database.

CONSTRUCTING (WRITING) THE AD Experienced advertisers use the guide AIDA (attention, interest, desire, action) to construct ads. First, you must attract attention to the ad, or readers may ignore it. Why does the ad in Figure 5-9 attract attention? The phrase "next key player" helps.

Next, develop interest in the job. For instance, "are you looking to make an impact?"

Create desire by spotlighting words such as *travel* or *challenge*. As an example, having a graduate school nearby may appeal to engineers and professional people.

Finally, the ad should prompt action with a statement like "call today."

Job applicants view ads with more specific job information as more attractive and more credible.[88] If the job has big drawbacks, consider a realistic ad. When the New York City Administration for Children's Services was having problems with employee retention, it began using these ads: "Wanted: men and women willing to walk into strange buildings in dangerous neighborhoods, [and] be screamed at by unhinged individuals. . . ." Realism reduces applicants, but improves employee retention.[89] Finally, the ad should comply with equal employment laws, avoiding features like "man wanted."

Employment Agencies

There are three main types of employment agencies: (1) public agencies operated by federal, state, or local governments; (2) agencies associated with nonprofit organizations; and (3) privately owned agencies.

PUBLIC AND NONPROFIT AGENCIES Every state has a public, state-run employment service agency. The U.S. Department of Labor supports these agencies, through grants and through other

FIGURE 5-9 Help Wanted Ad That Draws Attention

Source: Giombetti Associates, Hampden, MA. Reprinted with permission.

Are You Our Next Key Player?

PLANT CONTROLLER **Northern New Jersey**

Are you looking to make an impact? Can you be a strategic business partner and team player, versus a classic, "bean counter"? Our client, a growing **Northern New Jersey** manufacturer with two locations, needs a high-energy, self-initiating, technically competent Plant Controller. Your organizational skills and strong understanding of general, cost, and manufacturing accounting are a must. We are not looking for a delegator, this is a hands-on position. If you have a positive can-do attitude and have what it takes to drive our accounting function, read oh!

Responsibilities and Qualifications:

- Monthly closings, management reporting, product costing, and annual budget.
- Accurate inventory valuations, year-end physical inventory, and internal controls.
- 4-year Accounting degree, with 5–8 years experience in a manufacturing environment.
- Must be proficient in Microsoft Excel and have general computer skills and aptitude.
- Must be analytical and technically competent, with the leadership ability to influence people, situations, and circumstances.

If you have what it takes to be our next key player, tell us in your cover letter, *"Beyond the beans, what is the role of a Plant Controller?"* Only cover letters addressing that question will be considered. Please indicate your general salary requirements in your cover letter and email or fax your resume and cover letter to:

Ross Giombetti
Giombetti Associates
2 Allen Street, P.O. Box 720
Hampden, MA 01036
Email: Rossgiombetti@giombettiassoc.com
Fax: (413) 566-2009

assistance such as a nationwide computerized job bank. The National Job Bank enables agency counselors to advise applicants about available jobs in other states as well.

Some employers have mixed experiences with public agencies. For one thing, applicants for unemployment insurance are required to register and to make themselves available for job interviews. Some of these people are not interested in returning to work, so employers can end up with applicants who have little desire for immediate employment. And fairly or not, employers probably view some of these local agencies as lethargic in their efforts to fill area employers' jobs.

Yet these agencies are useful. Beyond just filling jobs, counselors will visit an employer's work site, review the employer's job requirements, and even assist the employer in writing job descriptions. Most states have turned their local state employment service agencies into "one-stop" shops—neighborhood training/employment/career assessment centers.[90] At Oregon State's centers, job seekers can use "iMatch" skills assessment software, while employers can get up-to-date local economic news and use the center's online recruitment tools.[91] More employers should be taking advantage of these centers (formerly the "unemployment offices" in many cities).

Most (nonprofit) professional and technical societies, such as the Institute for Electrical and Electronic Engineers (IEEE), have units that help members find jobs. Many special public agencies place people who are in special categories, such as those who are disabled.

PRIVATE AGENCIES Private employment agencies are important sources of clerical, white-collar, and managerial personnel. They charge fees (set by state law and posted in their offices) for each applicant they place. Most are "fee-paid" jobs, in which the employer pays the fee. Use one if:

1. Your firm doesn't have its own human resources department and feels it can't do a good job recruiting and screening.
2. You must fill a job quickly.
3. There is a perceived need to attract more minority or female applicants.
4. You want to reach currently employed individuals, who might feel more comfortable dealing with agencies than with competing companies.
5. You want to reduce the time you're devoting to recruiting.[92]

Yet using employment agencies requires avoiding the potential pitfalls. For example, the employment agency's screening may let poor applicants go directly to the supervisors responsible for hiring, who may in turn naively hire them. Conversely, improper screening at the agency could block potentially successful applicants.

To help avoid problems:

1. Give the agency an accurate and complete job description.
2. Make sure tests, application blanks, and interviews are part of the agency's selection process.
3. Periodically review EEOC data on candidates accepted or rejected by your firm, and by the agency.
4. Screen the agency. Check with other managers to find out which agencies have been the most effective at filling the sorts of positions you need filled. Review the Internet and classified ads to discover the agencies that handle the positions you seek to fill.
5. Supplement the agency's reference checking by checking at least the final candidate's references yourself.

Temporary Workers and Alternative Staffing

Employers increasingly supplement their permanent workforces by hiring contingent or temporary workers, often through temporary help employment agencies. Also known as *part-time* or *just-in-time workers*, the contingent workforce is big and growing. In the recent recession, about 26% of all jobs private-sector employers added were temporary positions, two to three times the comparable figures for the last two recessions. The contingent workforce isn't limited to clerical or maintenance staff. It includes thousands of engineering, science, or management support occupations, such as temporary chief financial officers, human resource managers, and chief executive officers.[93]

Several things contribute to the trend toward using more temporary employees. One is continuing weak economic confidence among employers. Another is the trend toward organizing around short-term projects. For example, Makino, which manufactures machine tools, now outsources the installation of large machines to contract firms, who in turn hire temps to do the installations. Flexibility is another concern, with more employers wanting to quickly reduce employment levels if the economic turnaround proves short-lived.[94]

Employers can hire temp workers either through direct hires or through temporary staff agencies. Direct hiring involves simply hiring workers and placing them on the job. The employer

Ryan McVay/Thinkstock

The numbers of temporary and freelance workers are increasing all over the world.

usually pays these people directly, as it does all its employees, but classifies them separately, as casual, seasonal, or temporary employees, and often pays few if any benefits.[95] The other approach is to have a temp agency supply the employees. Here the agency handles all the recruiting, screening, and payroll administration for the temps. Thus, Nike hired Kelly Services to manage Nike's temp needs.

WHAT SUPERVISORS SHOULD KNOW ABOUT TEMPORARY EMPLOYEES' CONCERNS To make temporary relationships successful, those supervising temps should understand their concerns. In one survey, temporary workers said they were:

1. Treated by employers in a dehumanizing and ultimately discouraging way.
2. Insecure about their employment and pessimistic about the future.
3. Worried about their lack of insurance and pension benefits.
4. Misled about their job assignments and in particular about whether temporary assignments were likely to become full-time.
5. "Underemployed" (particularly those trying to return to the full-time labor market).[96]

PROS AND CONS Employers have long used "temps" to fill in for employees who were out sick or on vacation. But they have other advantages. Productivity in output per hour paid is higher, since temps are generally paid only when they're working—not for days off. If the economy sags, it may be easier to let temps go. Many firms also use temporary hiring to try out prospective employees.[97]

However, temps often cost employers more per hour than comparable permanent workers, since the agency gets a fee. And as noted, they can feel abused.[98]

When working with temporary agencies, understand their policies. For example, with temps, the time sheet is not just a verification of hours worked. Once the worker's supervisor signs it, it's usually an agreement to pay the agency's fees. What is the policy if the client wants to hire one of the agency's temps as a permanent employee? How does the agency plan to recruit employees? Checking a temporary agency's references and its listing with the Better Business Bureau is advisable.[99]

KNOW YOUR EMPLOYMENT LAW

Contract Employees

Several years ago, federal agents rounded up about 250 illegal "contract" cleaning workers in 60 Walmart stores. The raid underscores the need to understand the status of the contract employees who work on your premises handling activities like security or after-hours store cleaning.[100] The fact that they actually work for another, temp-type company is no excuse. For purposes of most employment laws, with certain limited exceptions, employees of temporary staffing firms working in an employer's workplace will be considered to be employees both of the agency and of the employer.[101] The employer's liability depends on the degree to which its supervisors control the temp employee's activities. The more the agency does the better. For example, ask the staffing agency to handle training. Let it negotiate and set pay rates and vacation/time-off policies with the temp.

Employers can take other steps to minimize risks. The employer should require the staffing agency to follow the employer's background checking process, and to assume the legal risks if the employer and agency are found to be jointly responsible. Carefully track how many temporary employees the company actually has. Screen and supervise temporary employees with care if they may have access to your firm's intellectual property and computer systems.[102]

alternative staffing
The use of nontraditional recruitment sources.

ALTERNATIVE STAFFING Temporary employees are examples of **alternative staffing**—basically, the use of nontraditional recruitment sources. Other alternative staffing arrangements include "in-house temporary employees" (people employed directly by the company, but on an explicit short-term basis) and "contract technical employees" (highly skilled workers like engineers, who are supplied for long-term projects under contract from an outside technical services firm).

Offshoring and Outsourcing Jobs

Rather than bringing people in to do the company's jobs, outsourcing and offshoring send the jobs out. *Outsourcing* means having outside vendors supply services (such as benefits management, market research, or manufacturing) that the company's own employees previously did in-house. *Offshoring* means having outside vendors or employees *abroad* supply services that the company's own employees previously did in-house.

Employees, unions, legislators, and even many business owners feel that "shipping jobs out" (particularly overseas) is ill-advised. That notwithstanding, employers are sending jobs out, and not just blue-collar jobs. For example, GE's transportation division announced that it was shifting 17 mid-level drafting jobs from Pennsylvania to India.[103]

Sending out jobs, particularly overseas, presents employers with special personnel challenges. One is the likelihood of cultural misunderstandings (such as between your home-based customers and the employees abroad). Others are security and information privacy concerns; the need to deal with foreign contract, liability, and legal systems issues; and the fact that the offshore employees need special training (for instance, in using pseudonyms like "Jim" without discomfort).

Rising wages in China and India, coupled with reputational issues and a desire to invest more in local communities, is prompting employers to bring jobs back. Several U.S. employers including Apple and Microsoft are shifting jobs back to the U.S.[104]

Executive Recruiters

Executive recruiters (also known as *headhunters*) are special employment agencies employers retain to seek out top-management talent for their clients. The percentage of your firm's positions filled by these services might be small. However, these jobs include key executive and technical positions. For executive positions, headhunters may be your only source of candidates. The employer always pays the fees.

There are contingent and retained executive recruiters. Members of the Association of Executive Search Consultants usually focus on executive positions paying $150,000 or more, and on "*retained* executive search." They are paid regardless of whether the employer hires the executive through the search firm's efforts. *Contingency-based recruiters* tend to handle junior- to middle-level management job searches in the $80,000 to $160,000 range. Recruiter fees are dropping from the usual 30% or more of the executive's first-year pay.[105] Top recruiters (all retained) include Heidrick and Struggles, Egon Zehnder International, Russell Reynolds, and Spencer Stuart.

The challenging part of recruiting has always been finding potential candidates. Not surprisingly, Internet-based databases now dramatically speed up such searches. Executive recruiters are also creating specialized units aimed at specialized functions (such as sales) or industries (such as oil products).

Recruiters bring a lot to the table. They have many contacts and are relatively adept at finding qualified candidates who aren't actively looking to change jobs. They can keep your firm's name confidential, and can save top management's time by building an applicant pool. The recruiter's fee might actually turn out to be small when you compare it to the executive time saved.

The big issue is ensuring that the recruiter really understands your needs and then delivers properly vetted candidates. It is essential that the employer explain completely what sort of candidate is required. Some recruiters also may be more interested in persuading you to hire a candidate than in finding one who will really do the job. And one or two of the "final candidates" may actually just be fillers to make the recruiter's one "real" candidate look better.

WORKING WITH RECRUITERS Retaining and working with executive recruiters requires some caution. In choosing and working with one, guidelines include:[106]

1. Make sure the firm can conduct a thorough search. Under their ethics code, a recruiter can't approach the executive talent of a former client for a period of 2 years after completing a search for that client. Since former clients are off limits for 2 years, the recruiter must search from a constantly diminishing pool.[107]
2. Meet the individual who will actually handle your assignment.
3. Make sure to ask how much the search firm charges. Get the agreement in writing.[108]
4. Make sure the recruiter and you agree on what sort of individual to hire for the position.
5. Ask if the recruiter has vetted the final candidates. Do not be surprised if the answer is, "No, I just get candidates—we don't really screen them."

6. *Never* rely solely on any recruiter do all the reference checking. Let them check the candidates' references, but get notes of these references in writing from the recruiter (if possible). Recheck at least the final candidate's references yourself.
7. Consider using a recruiter who has a special expertise in your specific industry—he or she may have the best grasp of who's available.

INTERNAL RECRUITING More employers are bringing management recruiting in house. They still call on executive recruiters such as Heidrick and Struggles and Korn/Ferry International to conduct top officer (CEO and president) and board member placements, and to conduct confidential searches. But employers ranging from General Electric to Sears, PepsiCo, and Campbell Soup now have their own internal executive recruiting offices handling most of their own management recruiting. (GE reports an internal recruiting staff of about 500 people). Time Warner reported saving millions of dollars per year using internal recruiting teams.[109] The accompanying HR Tools feature explains what small businesses can do.

IMPROVING PERFORMANCE: HR Tools for Line Managers and Entrepreneurs

Recruiting 101

There comes a time in the life of most small businesses when it dawns on the owner that new blood is needed to take the company to the next level. Should the owner personally recruit this person?

While most large firms don't think twice about hiring executive search firms, small-firm owners will understandably hesitate before committing to a fee that could reach $40,000 or more for a $120,000 marketing manager.

However, engaging in a search like this is not like seeking supervisors or data entry clerks. Chances are, you won't find a top manager by placing ads. He or she is probably not reading the want ads. You'll end up with résumés of people who are, for one reason or another, out of work, unhappy with their work, or unsuited for your job. Many may be capable. But you will have to ferret out the gem by interviewing and assessing them.

You won't know where to place or how to write the ads; or where to search, who to contact, or how to screen out the laggards who may appear to be viable candidates. Even if you do, this process will be time-consuming and will divert your attention from other duties.

If you do decide to do the job yourself, consider retaining an industrial psychologist to spend 4 or 5 hours assessing the problem-solving ability, personality, interests, and energy level of the two or three candidates in which you are most interested. The input can provide a valuable perspective on the candidates.

Exercise special care when recruiting applicants from competing companies. Always check to see if applicants are bound by noncompete or nondisclosure agreements. And (especially when recruiting other firms' higher-level employees) perhaps check with an attorney before asking certain questions—regarding patents or potential antitrust issues, for instance.[110]

If you're a manager with an open position to fill in a Fortune 500 company, even you may find you have a dilemma. You may find that your local HR office will do little recruiting, other than, perhaps, placing an ad on Monster.com. On the other hand, your firm almost surely will not let you place your own help wanted ads. What to do? Use word of mouth to "advertise" your open position within and outside your company. And contact your colleagues in other firms to let them know you are recruiting.

Discussion Question 5-2: You own a small chemical engineering company and want to hire a new president. Based on what you read in this chapter, how would you go about doing so, and why?

Referrals and Walk-Ins

Employee referral campaigns are a very important recruiting option. Here the employer posts announcements of openings and requests for referrals on its website, bulletin boards, and/or wallboards. It often offers prizes or cash awards for referrals that lead to hiring. For example, at health-care giant Kaiser Permanente, referring someone for one of its "award-eligible positions" can produce bonuses of $3,000 or more.[111] The Container Store trains employees to recruit candidates from among the firm's customers.

PROS AND CONS Referral's big advantage is that it tends to generate "more applicants, more hires, and a higher yield ratio (hires/applicants)."[112] Current employees tend to provide accurate information about their referrals because they're putting their own reputations on the line. And the new employees may come with a more realistic picture of what the firm is like. A SHRM survey found that of 586 employer respondents, 69% said employee referral programs are more cost-effective than other recruiting practices and 80% specifically said they are more cost-effective than employment agencies. On average, referral programs cost around $400–$900 per hire in incentives and rewards.[113]

If morale is low, address that prior to asking for referrals. And if you don't hire someone's referral, explain to your employee/referrer why you did not hire his or her candidate. In addition, remember that relying on referrals might be discriminatory where a workforce is already homogeneous.

WALK-INS Particularly for hourly workers, walk-ins—direct applications made at your office—are a big source of applicants. Sometimes, posting a "Help Wanted" sign outside the door may be the most cost-effective way of attracting good local applicants. Treat walk-ins courteously, for both the employer's community reputation and the applicant's self-esteem. Many employers give every walk-in a brief interview, even if it is only to get information on the applicant "in case a position should be open in the future." Employers also typically receive unsolicited applications from professional and white-collar applicants. Good business practice requires answering all applicants' letters of inquiry promptly.

On-Demand Recruiting Services

on-demand recruiting services (ODRS)
Services that provide short-term specialized recruiting to support specific projects without the expense of retaining traditional search firms.

On-demand recruiting services (ODRS) are recruiters who are paid by the hour or project, instead of a percentage fee, to support a specific project. For example, when the human resource manager for a biotech firm had to hire several dozen people with scientific degrees and experience in pharmaceuticals, she used an ODRS firm. A traditional recruiting firm might charge 20% to 30% of each hire's salary. The ODRS firm charged by time, rather than per hire. It handled recruiting and prescreening, and left the client with a short list of qualified candidates.[114]

College Recruiting

college recruiting
Sending an employer's representatives to college campuses to prescreen applicants and create an applicant pool from the graduating class.

College recruiting—sending an employer's representatives to college campuses to prescreen applicants and create an applicant pool from the graduating class—is an important source of management trainees and professional and technical employees. One study several years ago concluded, for instance, that new college graduates filled about 38% of all externally filled jobs requiring a college degree.[115]

The problem is that on-campus recruiting is expensive. Schedules must be set well in advance, company brochures printed, interview records kept, and much time spent on campus. And recruiters are sometimes ineffective. Some are unprepared, show little interest in the candidate, and act superior. Many don't screen candidates effectively. Employers need to train recruiters in how to interview candidates, how to explain what the company has to offer, and how to put candidates at ease. The recruiter should be personable and have a record of attracting good candidates.[116] GE hires 800 to 1,000 students each year from about 40 schools, and uses teams of employees and interns to build GE's brand at each school. Similarly, IBM has 10 recruiting staff who focus on improving the results of IBM's on-campus recruiting efforts.[117] Shell Oil reduced the list of schools its recruiters visit, using factors such as quality of academic program, number of students enrolled, and diversity of the student body.[118]

The campus recruiter has two main goals. One is to determine if a candidate is worthy of further consideration. Usual traits to assess include communication skills, education, experience, and technical and interpersonal skills. The other aim is to make the employer attractive to candidates. A sincere and informal attitude, respect for the applicant, and prompt follow-up letters can help sell the employer to the interviewee. And employers who build relationships with opinion leaders such as career counselors and professors have better recruiting results.[119] Building close ties with a college's career center provides recruiters with useful feedback regarding things like labor market conditions and the effectiveness of one's on- and offline recruiting ads.[120]

Employers generally invite good candidates for an on-site visit. The invitation should be warm but businesslike, and provide a choice of dates. Have a host meet the applicant, preferably at the airport or at his or her hotel. A package containing the applicant's schedule as well as other information—such as annual reports and employee benefits—should be waiting for the applicant at the hotel.

Plan the interviews and adhere to the schedule. Avoid interruptions; give the candidate the undivided attention of each person with whom he or she interviews. Have another recently hired graduate host the candidate's lunch. Make any offer as soon as possible, preferably at the time of the visit. Frequent follow-ups to "find out how the decision process is going" may help to tilt the applicant in your favor.

What else to do? A study of 96 graduating students provides some insights. Fifty-three percent said "on-site visit opportunities to meet with people in positions similar to those applied for, or with higher-ranking persons" had a positive effect. Fifty-one percent mentioned, "Impressive hotel/dinner arrangements and having well-organized site arrangements." "Disorganized, unprepared interviewer behavior, or uninformed, useless answers" turned off 41%.[121]

INTERNSHIPS Internships can be win–win situations. For students, they can mean being able to hone business skills, learn more about potential employers, and discover their career likes (and dislikes). And employers can use the interns to make useful contributions while evaluating them as possible full-time employees. A recent study found that about 60% of internships turned into job offers.[122]

Unfortunately, some internships turn into nightmares. Many interns, particularly in industries like high-fashion and media, report long unpaid days doing menial work. *The New York Times* recently quoted one company's manager as saying "we need to hire a 22—22—22," in other words a 22-year-old willing to work 22 hour days for $22,000 a year.[123]

Telecommuters

Telecommuters do all or most of their work remotely, often from home, using information technology. For example, JetBlue Airways uses at-home agents to handle its reservation needs. These JetBlue employee "crewmembers" live in the Salt Lake City area and work out of their homes. They use JetBlue-supplied computers and technology, and receive JetBlue training.[124]

Military Personnel

Returning and discharged U.S. military personnel provide an excellent source of trained and disciplined recruits. The military has programs to facilitate soldiers finding jobs. Thus the U.S. Army's Partnership for Youth Success enables someone entering the Army to select a post-army corporate partner as a way to help soldiers find a job after leaving the Army.[125]

Misconceptions about veterans (for instance, that posttraumatic stress disorders influence job performance) are generally not valid.[126] The U.S. Army's Warrior Transition Command website (http://www.wtc.army.mil/) discusses such misconceptions. Walmart has a 5-year program guaranteeing any honorably discharged veteran who left the service in the past year a job.[127] The website http://www.helmetstohardhats.org/ puts vets together with building trades employers.

Evidence-Based HR: Measuring Recruiting Effectiveness and Reducing Recruitment Costs

Even small employers may spend tens of thousands of dollars per year recruiting applicants, so it's important to control recruitment costs. These include internal recruitment costs, such as the time spent by the employer's HR professionals on recruiting, and related overhead costs such as office space. There are outside recruitment costs such as for employment agency fees, campus visits, and online ads. And there may be signing bonuses, if necessary to entice candidates to take the job.[128]

Controlling such costs requires first identifying and measuring them, and then analyzing them, for instance by assessing which recruitment method is the most cost effective.

Yet few firms assess their recruitment efforts' effectiveness, and so most firms are flying blind.[129] Is it more cost-effective for us to advertise for applicants on the Web or in Sunday's paper? Should we use this employment agency or that one?

In terms of recruitment effectiveness metrics, one is "How many applicants did we generate through each of our recruitment sources?"[130] Others include new hire job performance, new hire failure rate, new hire turnover, training success, and manager's satisfaction.[131] Also track your recruiting sources with measures showing how employees unearthed by these sources did after about a year on the job.

One problem here is that more applicants is not always better. Realistically, the manager looking to hire five engineers probably won't be twice as selective with 20,000 applicants as with 10,000. Furthermore, the employer needs *qualified, hirable* applicants. An Internet ad may

TABLE 5-1 Recruitment: Practical Applications for Managers

Recruitment Research Finding[a]	Practical Applications for Managers
The recruitment source affects the applicants you attract.	Use sources such as referrals from current employees that yield applicants more likely to be better performers.
Recruitment materials have a more positive impact if they contain more specific information.	Provide information on important aspects of the job, such as salary, location, and diversity.
Applicants with more job opportunities are more attentive to early recruitment activities.	First impressions are important. Review attractiveness of website, brochure, on-campus recruiting, and so on.
Realistic job previews that highlight both the advantages and the disadvantages of the job reduce subsequent turnover.	Provide applicants with a realistic picture of the job and organization, not just the positives.
Applicants will infer (perhaps erroneous) information about the job and company if the information is not clearly provided by the company.	Provide specific, and complete information in recruitment materials.
Recruiter warmth has a positive effect on applicants' decisions to accept a job.	Choose recruiters who have strong interpersonal skills.

[a]Selected research principles from M. S. Taylor and C. J. Collins (2000), Strategic Recruitment. In C. L. Cooper & E. A. Locke (Eds.), *I/O Psychology: Practice and Theory Book*. Oxford: Blackwell.

Sources: Adapted from Ann Marie Ryan and Nancy Tippins, "Attracting and Selecting: What Psychological Research Tells Us," *Human Resource Management* 43, no. 4 (Winter 2004), p. 311; and Ingo Weller et al., "Level and Time Effects of Recruitment Sources on Early Voluntary Turnover," *Journal of Applied Psychology* 94, no. 5 (2009), pp. 1146–1162 (1157). Reprinted by permission of Society for Human Resource Management via Copyright Clearance Center.

generate thousands of nonviable applicants. The applicant tracking system should help compare recruiting sources, as we said, but many lack the tools to do so.[132]

Research reveals several guidelines employers can use (see Table 5-1). For example, referrals from current employees yield applicants who are less likely to leave and more likely to perform better.[133] The accompanying HR as a Profit Center illustrates the role human resources can play.

IMPROVING PERFORMANCE: HR as a Profit Center

Cutting Recruitment Costs

GE Medical hires about 500 technical workers a year to design sophisticated medical devices such as CT scanners. It has cut its hiring costs by 17%, reduced time to fill the positions by 20% to 30%, and cut in half the percentage of new hires who don't work out.[134]

GE Medical's HR team accomplished this in part by applying its purchasing techniques to its dealings with recruiters. For example, it called a meeting and told 20 recruiters that it would work with only the 10 best. To measure "best," the company created measures inspired by manufacturing techniques, such as "percentage of résumés that result in interviews" and "percentage of interviews that lead to offers." Similarly, GE Medical discovered that current employees are very effective as references. For instance, GE Medical interviews just 1% of applicants whose résumés it receives, while 10% of employee referrals result in actual hires. So GE Medical took steps to double the number of employee referrals. It simplified the referral forms, eliminated bureaucratic submission procedures, and added a small reward like a Sears gift certificate for referring a qualified candidate. GE also upped the incentive—$2,000 if someone referred is hired, and $3,000 if he or she is a software engineer.

GE is also using more recruitment process outsourcers. *Recruitment process outsourcers* are special vendors that handle all or most of an employer's recruiting needs. They usually sign short-term contracts with the employer, and receive a monthly fee that varies with the amount of actual recruiting the employer needs done. This makes it easier for an employer to ramp up or ramp down its recruiting expenses, as compared with paying the relatively fixed costs of an in-house recruitment office.[135] Large RPO providers include Manpower Group Solutions, IBM, and Randstad Sourceright.[136]

Discussion Question 5-3: What other tools described in this chapter could GE Medical use to improve recruiting efficiency?

Recruiting a More Diverse Workforce

5 Explain how to recruit a more diverse workforce.

We saw in Chapter 2 that recruiting a diverse workforce isn't just socially responsible. Given the rapid rise in minority, older worker, and women candidates, it is a necessity. The recruiting tools we described to this point are certainly useful for minority and other applicants, too. However, diversity recruiting requires several special steps, to which we now turn.[137]

Recruiting Women

Given the progress women have made in getting and excelling in a wide range of professional, managerial, and military occupations, one might assume that employers need no special recruitment efforts to recruit women, but that's not necessarily the case. For example, women still face headwinds in certain male-dominated occupations such as engineering. Women also carry the heavier burden of child-rearing, fill proportionately fewer high-level managerial posts, and still earn only about 70% of what men earn for similar jobs. Many employers therefore focus particular efforts on recruiting qualified women.

The most effective strategy is top management driven.[138] Here the employer emphasizes the importance of recruiting women (as well as men), identifies gaps in the recruitment and retention of women, and puts in place a comprehensive plan to attract women applicants. The overall aim is to make it clear that the employer is the sort of place in which women want to work, and the details of any such plan needn't be complicated. For example, particularly for "nontraditional" jobs (like engineering) use the company Web site to highlight women now doing those jobs. Emphasize the effectiveness of the employer's mentoring program in moving women up. Offer real workplace flexibility; for example, not just flexible hours but the option of staying on a partner track even while working part-time. (For example, Yahoo recently implemented a generous 8-week paid maternity/paternity leave policy.) Focus a portion of the recruiting effort on women's organizations, women's employment websites, and career fairs at women's colleges. Make sure benefits cover matters such as family planning and prenatal care. Maintain a zero-tolerance sexual harassment policy.

Recruiting Single Parents

Recently, there were almost 10 million single parent families with children under 18 maintained by the mother, about two-thirds of whom were employed. There were about 1.25 million single parent families with children under 18 maintained by the father, three-fourths of whom were employed. Being a single parent isn't easy, and recruiting and keeping them requires understanding the problems they face.[139] (And keep in mind that many of these issues also apply to families in which both parents are struggling to make ends meet.) In one survey,

> Many described falling into bed exhausted at midnight without even minimal time for themselves. . . . They often needed personal sick time or excused days off to care for sick children. As one mother noted, "I don't have enough sick days to get sick."[140]

Given such concerns, the first step in attracting and keeping single parents is to make the workplace user friendly.[141] Surveys suggest that a supportive attitude on the supervisor's part can go far toward making the single parent's work–home balancing act more bearable.[142] Many firms have *flextime* programs that provide employees some schedule flexibility (such as 1-hour windows at the beginning or end of the day). Unfortunately, for many single parents this may not be enough. CNN even offered a "Work/Life Balance Calculator" (www.cnn.com/2008/LIVING/worklife/06/04/balance.calculator/) to assess how far out of balance one's life may be.[143] We'll discuss other options in the Chapter 13, Benefits and Services.

Mel Yates/Getty Images

Not just single parents, but also their children may occasionally need some extra support.

Older Workers

When it comes to hiring older workers, employers don't have much choice.[144] The fastest-growing labor force segment is those from 45 to 64 years old. On the positive side, a survey by AARP and SHRM concluded that older workers tend to have lower absenteeism rates, more reliability, and better work habits than younger workers.[145] Firms like Home Depot capitalize on this by hiring older employees, who "serve as a powerful draw to baby boomer shoppers by mirroring their knowledge and perspective."[146]

It therefore makes sense for employers to encourage older workers to stay (or to come to work at the company). The big draw is probably to provide opportunities for flexible (and often shorter) work schedules. One survey found that flexibility was the main concern for 71% of baby boomers, with those who continue working preferring to do so part time.[147] At one company, workers over 65 can progressively shorten their work schedules; another company uses "mini shifts" to accommodate those interested in working less than full time. Other suggestions include the following:

- Phased retirement that allows workers to ease out of the workforce.
- Portable jobs for "snowbirds" who wish to live in warmer climates in the winter.
- Part-time projects for retirees.
- Full benefits for part-timers.[148]

As always in recruiting, projecting the right image is crucial. For example, writing the ad so that it sends the message "we're older-worker friendly" is important. The most effective ads emphasize schedule flexibility, and accentuate the firm's equal opportunity employment statement, not "giving retirees opportunities to transfer their knowledge" to the new work setting.[149]

Diversity Counts

Older workers are good workers. A recent study focused on the validity of six common stereotypes about older workers: That they are less motivated, less willing to participate in training and career development, more resistant to change, less trusting, less healthy, and more vulnerable to work–family imbalance.[150] They actually found not a negative but a weakly positive relationship between age and motivation and job involvement (suggesting that as age goes up motivation actually rises). They did find a weak negative relationship between age and trainability. Age was weakly but positively related to willingness to change, and to being more trusting. Older workers were no more likely than younger ones to have psychological problems or day-to-day physical health problems, but were more likely to have heightened blood pressure and cholesterol levels. Older workers did not experience more work–family imbalance. So there was little support for the common age stereotypes.

What should employers do? First, raise employees', managers', and recruiters' consciousness about incorrect age stereotypes. And provide opportunities for more contacts with older people and for information flows between younger and older workers.[151]

Recruiting Minorities

Similar prescriptions apply to recruiting minorities.[152] First, *understand* the barriers that prevent minorities from applying. For example, some minority applicants won't meet the educational or experience standards for the job; many employers therefore offer remedial training. In one retail chain, a lack of role models stopped women from applying. Sometimes (as we saw) it's insufficient schedule flexibility.

After recognizing the impediments, one turns to formulating plans for remedying them and to attracting and retaining minorities and women. This may include, for instance, basic skills training, flexible work options, role models, and redesigned jobs.

Finally, implement these plans. For example, many job seekers check with friends or relatives when job hunting, so encouraging your minority employees to assist in your recruitment efforts makes sense. Diversity recruitment specialists include www.diversity.com, www.2trabajo.com, and http://recruitersnetwork.com/resources/diversity.htm.

Other firms collaborate with specialist professional organizations. These include the National Black MBA Association (www.nbmbaa.org/home.aspx?PageID=637&), the National Society of Hispanic MBAs (www.nshmba.org/), and the Organization of Chinese Americans (www.ocanational.org/).

Some employers experience difficulty in hiring and assimilating people previously on welfare. Applicants sometimes lack basic work skills, such as reporting for work on time, working in teams, and taking orders. The key to welfare-to-work seems to be the employer's pretraining program. Here, participants get counseling and basic skills training over several weeks.[153]

The Disabled

The research is quite persuasive regarding the fact that in terms of virtually all work criteria, employees with disabilities are capable workers. Thousands of employers in the United States and elsewhere have found that disabled employees provide an excellent and largely untapped source of competent, efficient labor for jobs ranging from information technology to creative advertising to receptionist.[154]

Employers can do several things to tap this huge potential workforce. The U.S. Department of Labor's Office of Disability Employment Policy offers several programs, including one that helps link disabled college undergraduates who are looking for summer internships with potential employers.[155] All states have local agencies (such as "Corporate Connections" in Tennessee) that provide placement services and other recruitment and training tools and information for employers seeking to hire the disabled. Employers also must use common sense. For example, employers who only post job openings in the paper may miss potential employees who are visually impaired.[156]

Developing and Using Application Forms

6 Discuss practical guidelines for obtaining application information.

application form
The form that provides information on education, prior work record, and skills.

Purpose of Application Forms

With a pool of applicants, the prescreening process can begin. The **application form** is usually the first step in this process (some firms first require a brief, prescreening interview or online test).

A filled-in application provides four types of information. First, you can make judgments on *substantive matters*, such as whether the applicant has the education and experience to do the job. Second, you can draw conclusions about the applicant's *previous progress* and growth, especially important for management candidates. Third, you can draw tentative conclusions about the applicant's *stability* based on previous work record (although years of downsizing suggest the need for caution here). Fourth, you may be able to use the data in the application to *predict* which candidates will succeed on the job. The HR Tools feature addresses practical guidelines.

IMPROVING PERFORMANCE: HR Tools for Line Managers and Entrepreneurs

Application Guidelines

Ineffective use of the application can cost the employer dearly. Managers should keep several practical guidelines in mind. In the "Employment History" section, request detailed information on each prior employer, including the name of the supervisor and his or her e-mail address and telephone number; this is essential for reference checking. In signing the application, the applicant should certify that falsified statements may be cause for dismissal, that investigation of credit and employment and driving record is authorized, that a medical examination and drug screening tests may be required, and that employment is for no definite period.

Estimates of how many applicants exaggerate their qualifications range from 40% to 70%.[157] The most common concern education and job experience. A majority of graduating seniors reportedly believe that employers expect a degree of exaggeration on résumés. Much of this exaggeration occurs on résumés, but may occur on application forms too. Therefore, make sure applicants complete the form and sign a statement on it indicating that the information is true. The court will almost always support a discharge for falsifying information when applying for work.[158]

Finally, doing a less-than-complete job of filling in the form may reflect poor work habits. Some applicants scribble "see résumé attached" on the application. This is not acceptable. You need the signed, completed form. Some firms no longer ask applicants for résumés at all, but instead request and then peruse Web presence links, such as Twitter or LinkedIn accounts.[159]

Discussion Question 5-4: Review several employers' online applications. Do they conform to the guidelines in this feature?

FIGURE 5-10 FBI Employment Application
Source: FBI Preliminary Application for Honors Internship Program.

FEDERAL BUREAU OF INVESTIGATION

Preliminary Application for Honors Internship Program (Please Type or Print in Ink)

Date: ____________

FIELD OFFICE USE ONLY
HP
Div: Program:

I. PERSONAL HISTORY

Name in Full (Last, First, Middle, Maiden) | List College(s) attended, Major, Degree (if applicable), Grade Point Average

Birth Date (Month, Day, Year)
Birth Place: | Social Security Number: (Optional)

Current Address

Street Apt. No. Home Phone Area Code Number

City State Zip Code Work Phone Area Code Number

Are you: Licensed Driver ☐ Yes ☐ No U. S. Citizen ☐ Yes ☐ No

Have you served on active duty in the Armed Forces of the United States? ☐ Yes ☐ No | Branch of military service and dates of active duty: | Type of Discharge

How did you learn or become interested in the FBI Honors Internship Program?

Do you have a foreign language background? ☐ Yes ☐ No List proficiency for each language on reverse side.

Have you ever been arrested or charged with any violation including traffic, but excluding parking tickets? ☐ Yes ☐ No If so, list all such matters even if found not guilty, not formally charged, no court appearance, or matter settled by payment of fine or forfeiture of collateral. Include date, place, charge, disposition, details, and police agency on reverse side.

II. EMPLOYMENT HISTORY

Identify your most recent three years FULL-TIME work experience, after high school (excluding summer, part-time and temporary employment).

From	To	Description of Work	Name/Location of Employer

III. PERSONAL DECLARATIONS

Persons with a disability who require an accommodation to complete the application process are required to notify the FBI of their need for the accommodation.

Have you used marijuana during the last three years or more than 15 times? ☐ Yes ☐ No

Have you used any illegal drug(s) or combination of illegal drugs, other than marijuana, more than 5 times or during the last 10 years? ☐ Yes ☐ No

All Information provided by applicants concerning their drug history will be subject to verification by a preemployment polygraph examination.

Do you understand all prospective FBI employees will be required to submit to an urinalysis for drug abuse prior to employment? ☐ Yes ☐ No

I am aware that willfully withholding information or making false statements on this application constitutes a violation of Section 1001, Title 18, U.S. Code and if appointed, will be the basis for dismissal from the Federal Bureau of Investigation. I agree to these conditions and I hereby certify that all statements made by me on this application are true and complete, to the best of my knowledge.

____
Signature of Applicant as usually written. **(Do Not Use Nickname)**

The Federal Bureau of Investigation is an equal opportunity employer.

Most employers need several application forms. For technical and managerial personnel, the form may require detailed answers to questions about education and training. The form for hourly factory workers might focus on tools and equipment. Figure 5-10 illustrates one employment application.

KNOW YOUR EMPLOYMENT LAW

Application Forms and EEO Law

Application forms must comply with equal employment laws. Items to be aware of include:

Education. A question on the dates of attendance and graduation from various schools is one potential violation, insofar as it may reflect the applicant's age.

Arrest record. The courts have usually held that employers violate Title VII by disqualifying applicants from employment because of an arrest. This item has an adverse impact on minorities, and employers usually can't show it's required as a business necessity.

Notify in case of emergency. It is generally legal to require the name, address, and phone number of a person to notify in case of emergency. However, asking the relationship of this person could indicate the applicant's marital status or lineage.

Membership in organizations. Some forms ask the applicant to list memberships in clubs, organizations, or societies. Employers should include instructions not to include organizations that would reveal race, religion, physical handicaps, marital status, or ancestry.

Physical handicaps. It is usually illegal to require the listing of an applicant's physical handicaps or past illnesses unless the application blank specifically asks only for those that "may interfere with your job performance." Similarly, it is generally illegal to ask whether the applicant has ever received workers' compensation.

Marital status. In general, the application should not ask whether an applicant is single, married, divorced, separated, or living with anyone, or the names, occupations, and ages of the applicant's spouse or children.

Housing. Asking whether an applicant *owns, rents*, or *leases* a house may also be discriminatory. It can adversely affect minority groups and is difficult to justify on business necessity.

Video Résumés. More candidates are submitting video résumés, a practice replete with benefits and threats. About half of employers in one survey thought video résumés might give employers a better feel for the candidate. The danger is that a video résumé makes it more likely that rejected candidates may claim discrimination.[160] To facilitate using video résumés, several websites compile multimedia résumés for applicants.[161]

Using Application Forms to Predict Job Performance

Some employers use analyses of application information ("biodata") to *predict* employee tenure and performance. In one study, the researchers found that applicants who had longer tenure with previous employers were less likely to quit, and also had higher performance within 6 months after hire.[162] Examples of predictive biodata items might include "quit a job without giving notice," "graduated from college," and "traveled considerably growing up."[163]

Choose biodata items with three things in mind. First, equal employment law limits the items you'll want to use (avoid age, race, or gender, for instance). And, noninvasive items are best. In one study, subjects perceived items such as "dollar sales achieved" and "grade point average in math" as not invasive. Items such as "birth order" and "frequent dates in high school" were more invasive. Finally, some applicants will fake biodata answers in an effort to impress the employer.[164]

KNOW YOUR EMPLOYMENT LAW

Mandatory Arbitration

Many employers, aware of the high costs of employment litigation, require applicants to agree on their applications to mandatory arbitration should a dispute arise.

Different federal courts have taken different positions on the enforceability of such "mandatory alternative dispute resolution" clauses. They are generally enforceable, with two caveats.

First, it must be a fair process.[165] For example, the agreement should be a signed and dated separate agreement. Use simple wording. Provide for reconsideration and judicial appeal if there is an error of law.[166] The employer must absorb most of the cost of the arbitration process. The process should be reasonably swift. Employees should be eligible to receive the full remedies that they would have had they if had access to the courts.

Second, mandatory arbitration clauses turn some candidates off. In one study, 389 MBA students read simulated employment brochures. Mandatory employment arbitration had a significantly negative impact on the attractiveness of the company as a place to work.[167]

Review

MyManagementLab Go to **mymanagementlab.com** to complete the problems marked with this icon. ✪

Chapter Section Summaries

1. The **recruitment and selection process** entails five main steps: decide what positions to fill; build a pool of candidates for these jobs; have candidates complete application forms; use selection tools; and decide to whom to make an offer, in part by having the supervisor and others interview the candidates.
2. Recruitment and selection starts with **workforce planning and forecasting**. Workforce planning is the process of deciding what positions the firm will have to fill, and how to fill them. This often starts by forecasting personnel needs, perhaps using trend analysis, ratio analysis, scatter plots, or computerized software packages. The other side of the equation is forecasting the supply of inside candidates. Here employers use manual systems and replacement charts, and computerized skills inventories. Forecasting the supply of outside candidates is important, particularly when entering periods of economic expansion where unemployment is low and good candidates are more difficult to come by.
3. All managers need to understand why **effective recruiting is important**. Without enough candidates, employers cannot effectively screen the candidates or hire the best. Some employers use a recruiting yield pyramid to estimate how many applicants they need to generate in order to fill predicted job openings.
4. Filling open positions with **internal sources of candidates** has several advantages. You are familiar with their strengths and weaknesses, and they require less orientation. Finding internal candidates often utilizes job posting. For filling the company's projected top-level positions, succession planning—the ongoing process of systematically identifying, assessing, and developing organizational leadership to enhance performance—is the process of choice.
5. Employers use a variety of **outside sources of candidates** when recruiting applicants.
   - Of these, recruiting via the Internet using job boards such as Monster.com represents a leading source. It is quick and cost-effective. One downside is too many applicants from too far away, but employers use applicant tracking software to screen online applicants.
   - Other sources include advertising and employment agencies (including public and nonprofit agencies, and private agencies).
   - Employers increasingly turn to temporary agencies and other alternative staffing methods to hire "alternative" types of employees, such as contract employees for special projects.
   - Executive recruiters, a special type of employment agency, are invaluable for finding and helping the employer hire top-level professionals and executives. However, the employer needs to ensure that the recruiter is conducting a thorough search and carefully checking references.
   - Other outside sources include college recruiting, referrals and walk-ins, and military personnel.
6. Understanding how to **recruit a more diverse workforce** is important. Whether the target is the single parent, older workers, or minorities, the basic rule is to understand their special needs and to create a set of policies and practices that create a more hospitable environment in which they can work.
7. The recruitment process inevitably includes **developing and using application forms** to collect essential background information about the applicant. The application should enable you to make judgments on substantial matters such as the person's education and to identify the person's job references and supervisors. Of course, it's important to make sure the application complies with equal employment laws, for instance with respect to questions regarding physical handicaps.

Discussion Questions

✪ **5-5.** Briefly outline the workforce planning process.

5-6. Briefly explain each step in the recruitment and selection process.

5-7. What are the four main types of information that application forms provide?

5-8. How, specifically, do equal employment laws apply to personnel recruiting activities?

✪ **5-9.** What are the five main things you would do to recruit and retain a more diverse workforce?

Individual and Group Activities

5-10. Bring to class several classified and display ads from the Web or the Sunday help wanted ads. Analyze the effectiveness of these ads using the guidelines discussed in this chapter.

5-11. Working individually or in groups, develop a 5-year forecast of occupational market conditions for five occupations such as accountant, nurse, and engineer.

5-12. Working individually or in groups, visit the local office of your state employment agency (or check out their site online). Come back to class prepared to discuss the following questions: What types of jobs seem to be available through this agency, predominantly? To what extent do you think this particular agency would be a good source of professional, technical, and/or managerial applicants? What sorts of paperwork are applicants to the state agency required to complete before their applications are processed by the agency? What other services does the office provide? What other opinions did you form about the state agency?

5-13. Working individually or in groups, find at least five employment ads, either on the Internet or in a local newspaper, that suggest that the company is family friendly and should appeal to women, minorities, older workers, and single parents. Discuss what they're doing to be family friendly.

5-14. Working individually or in groups, interview a manager between the ages of 25 and 35 at a local business who manages employees age 40 or older. Ask the manager to describe three or four of his or her most challenging experiences managing older employees.

5-15. Appendix A, PHR and SPHR Knowledge Base, at the end of this book (pages 580–588) lists the knowledge someone studying for the HRCI certification exam needs to have in each area of human resource management (such as in Strategic Management, Workforce Planning, and Human Resource Development). In groups of four to five students, do four things: (1) review Appendix A; (2) identify the material in this chapter that relates to the required knowledge Appendix A lists; (3) write four multiple-choice exam questions on this material that you believe would be suitable for inclusion in the HRCI exam; and (4) if time permits, have someone from your team post your team's questions in front of the class, so that students in all teams can answer the exam questions created by the other teams.

KNOWLEDGE BASE

Experiential Exercise

The Nursing Shortage

As of August 2013, U.S. unemployment was still disappointingly high, and employers were still holding back on their hiring. However, while many people were unemployed, that was not the case with nurse professionals. Virtually every hospital was aggressively recruiting nurses. Many were turning to foreign-trained nurses, for example, by recruiting nurses in the Philippines. Experts expect nurses to be in very short supply for years to come.

Purpose: The purpose of this exercise is to give you experience in creating a recruitment program.

Required Understanding: You should be thoroughly familiar with the contents of this chapter, and with the nurse recruitment program of a hospital such as Lenox Hill Hospital in New York (see http://lenoxhillhospital.org/careers_default.aspx).

How to Set Up the Exercise/Instructions: Set up groups of four to five students for this exercise. The groups should work separately and should not converse with each other. Each group should address the following tasks:

5-16. Based on information available on the hospital's website, create a hard-copy ad for the hospital to place in the Sunday edition of the *New York Times*. Which (geographic) editions of the *Times* would you use, and why?

5-17. Analyze the hospital's current online nurses' ad. How would you improve on it?

5-18. Prepare in outline form a complete nurses' recruiting program for this hospital, including all recruiting sources your group would use.

Video Case

Video Title: Recruiting (Hautelook)

SYNOPSIS

The online fashion retailer Hautelook is growing quickly and needs to recruit new employees at a rapid rate. The video discusses the company's methods for recruiting job applicants and for finding the best potential employees from among its applicants. Hautelook prefers to promote internal job candidates, but also to hire applicants who are most familiar with the company—ideally, previous customers.

Discussion Questions

5-19. Explain the importance of employee referrals to Hautelook's recruiting.

5-20. Based on the chapter, what other recruiting tools would you suggest a company like this use, and why?

5-21. How would you suggest Hautelook deal with the problem of receiving too many résumé applications?

5-22. Given that it loves to promote internally, what other steps would you suggest Hautelook take to facilitate this?

5-23. From what Hautelook says, is it really necessary for the company to use employment agencies? Why?

Video Title: Personnel Planning and Recruiting (Gawker Media)

SYNOPSIS

Gawker Media founder Nick Denton analyzes how his company responded to the 2007–2010 recession. A key was planning for staffing levels.

Discussion Questions

5-24. Based on what we discussed in Chapter 5, what advice would you give Gawker regarding how to improve its personnel planning?

5-25. How is it that some organizations succeed during a recession?

5-26. Evaluate Gawker Media's practice of recruiting new writers from the people who comment on its sites. How would you suggest the company improve its recruiting practices overall?

Application Case

Finding People Who Are Passionate About What They Do

Trilogy Enterprises Inc. of Austin, Texas, is a fast-growing software company, and provides software solutions to giant global firms for improving sales and performance. Many of its approaches to business practice are unusual, but in Trilogy's fast-changing and highly competitive environment, they seem to work.

There is no dress code and employees make their own hours, often very long. They tend to socialize together (the average age is 26), both in the office's well-stocked kitchen and on company-sponsored events and trips to places like local dance clubs and retreats in Las Vegas. Responsibility is heavy and comes early, with a "just do it now" attitude. New recruits get a few weeks of intensive training, described by participants as "more like boot camp than business school." Information is delivered as if with "a fire hose," and new employees are expected to commit their expertise and vitality to everything they do. Jeff Daniel, director of college recruiting, admits the intense and unconventional firm is not the employer for everybody.

The firm employs about 700 people. Trilogy's managers know the rapid growth they seek depends on having a staff of the best people they can find, quickly trained and given broad responsibility and freedom as soon as possible. CEO Joe Liemandt says, "At a software company, people are everything. . . . Of course, the leaders at every company say, 'People are everything.' But they don't act on it."

Trilogy makes finding the right people a company-wide mission. Recruiters actively scour college career fairs and computer science departments for talented overachievers with ambition and entrepreneurial instincts. Top managers conduct the first rounds of interviews. Employees take top recruits and their significant others out on the town when they fly into Austin for the standard, 3-day preliminary visit. A typical day might begin with grueling interviews but end with mountain biking.

One year, Trilogy reviewed 15,000 résumés, conducted 4,000 on-campus interviews, flew 850 prospects in for interviews, and hired 262 college graduates. The cost per hire was $13,000; Jeff Daniel believes it was worth every penny.

Questions

5-27. Identify some of the established recruiting techniques that apparently underlie Trilogy's unconventional approach to attracting talent.

5-28. What particular elements of Trilogy's culture most likely appeal to the kind of employees it seeks? How does it convey those elements to job prospects?

5-29. Would Trilogy be an appealing employer for you? Why? If not, what would it take for you to accept a job offer from Trilogy?

5-30. What suggestions would you make to Trilogy for improving its recruiting processes?

Sources: Chuck Salter, "Insanity, Inc.," *Fast Company*, January 1999, pp. 101–108; and www.trilogy.com/sections/careers/work, accessed August 24, 2007.

Continuing Case

Carter Cleaning Company

Getting Better Applicants

If you were to ask Jennifer and her father what the main problem was in running their firm, their answer would be quick and short: hiring good people. Originally begun as a string of coin-operated laundromats requiring virtually no skilled help, the chain grew to six stores, each heavily dependent on skilled managers, cleaner/spotters, and pressers. Employees generally have no more than a high school education, and the market for them is very competitive. Over a typical weekend, literally dozens of want ads for experienced pressers or cleaner/spotters can be found in area newspapers. All these people usually are paid around $15 per hour, and they change jobs frequently. Jennifer and her father thus face the continuing task of recruiting and hiring qualified workers out of a pool of individuals they feel are almost nomadic in their propensity to move from area to area and job to job. Turnover in their stores (as in the stores of many of their competitors) often approaches 400%. "Don't talk to me about human resources planning and trend analysis," says Jennifer. "We're fighting an economic war and I'm happy just to be able to round up enough live applicants to be able to keep my trenches fully manned."

In light of this problem, Jennifer's father asked her to answer the following questions:

Questions

5-31. First, how would you recommend we go about reducing the turnover in our stores?

5-32. Provide a detailed list of recommendations concerning how we should go about increasing our pool of acceptable job applicants so we no longer face the need to hire almost anyone who walks in the door. (Your recommendations regarding the latter should include completely worded online and hard-copy advertisements and recommendations regarding any other recruiting strategies you would suggest we use.)

Translating Strategy into HR Policies and Practices Case*,§

**The accompanying strategy map for this chapter is in the MyManagementLab, and the overall map on the inside back cover of this text outlines the relationships involved.*

IMPROVING PERFORMANCE at The Hotel Paris

The New Recruitment Process

The Hotel Paris's competitive strategy is "To use superior guest service to differentiate the Hotel Paris properties, and to thereby increase the length of stay and return rate of guests, and thus boost revenues and profitability." HR manager Lisa Cruz must now formulate functional policies and activities that support this competitive strategy and boost performance, by eliciting the required employee behaviors and competencies.

As a longtime HR professional, Lisa Cruz was well aware of the importance of effective employee recruitment. If the Hotel Paris didn't get enough applicants, it could not be selective about who to hire. And, if it could not be selective about who to hire, it wasn't likely that the hotels would enjoy the customer-oriented employee behaviors that the company's strategy relied on. She was therefore disappointed to discover that the Hotel Paris was paying virtually no attention to the job of recruiting prospective employees. Individual hotel managers slapped together help wanted ads when they had positions to fill, and no one in the chain had any measurable idea of how many recruits these ads were producing or which recruiting approaches worked the best (or worked at all). Lisa knew that it was time to step back and get control of the Hotel Paris's recruitment function.

As they reviewed the details of the Hotel Paris's current recruitment practices, Lisa Cruz and the firm's CFO became increasingly concerned. What they found, basically, was that the recruitment function was totally unmanaged. The previous HR director had simply allowed the responsibility for recruiting to remain with each separate hotel, and the hotel managers, not being HR professionals, usually just took the path of least resistance when a job became available by placing help wanted ads in their local papers. There was no sense of direction from the Hotel Paris's headquarters regarding what sorts of applicants the company preferred, what media and alternative sources of recruits its managers should use, no online recruiting, and, of course, no measurement at all of effectiveness of the recruitment process. The company totally ignored recruitment-source metrics that other firms used effectively, such as number of qualified applicants per position, percentage of jobs filled from within, the offer-to-acceptance ratio, acceptance by recruiting source, turnover by recruiting source, and selection test results by recruiting source. This despite the fact, as the CFO put it, "that high performance companies consistently score much higher than low performing firms on HR practices such as number of qualified applicants per position, and percentage of jobs filled from within."

It was safe to say that achieving the Hotel Paris's strategic aims depended largely on the quality of the people that it attracted to, and then selected for, employment at the firm. "What we want are employees who will put our guests first, who will use initiative to see that our guests are satisfied, and who will work tirelessly to provide our guests with services that exceed their expectations" said the CFO. Lisa and the CFO both knew this process had to start with better recruiting. The CFO gave her the green light to design a new recruitment process.

Lisa and her team had the firm's IT department create a central recruiting link for the Hotel Paris's website, with geographical links that each local hotel could use to publicize its openings. The HR team created a series of standard ads the managers could use for each job title. These standard ads emphasized the company's service-oriented values, and basically said (without actually saying it) that if you were not people oriented you should not apply. They emphasized what it was like to work for the Hotel Paris, and the excellent benefits (which the HR team was about to get started on) the firm provided. It created a new intranet-based job posting system and encouraged employees to use it to apply for open positions. For several jobs, including housekeeping crew and front-desk clerk, applicants must now first pass a short prescreening test to apply. The HR team analyzed the performance (for instance, in terms of applicants/source, and applicants hired/source) of the various local newspapers and recruiting firms the hotels had used in the past, and chose the best to be the approved recruiting sources in their local areas.

After 6 months with these and other recruitment function changes, the number of applicants was up on average 40%. Lisa and her team were now set to institute new screening procedures that would help them select the high-commitment, service-oriented, motivated employees they were looking for.

Questions

5-33. Given the hotel's required personnel skills, what recruiting sources would you have suggested they use, and why?

5-34. What would a Hotel Paris help wanted ad look like?

5-35. How would you suggest they measure the effectiveness of their recruiting efforts?

§Written by and copyright Gary Dessler, PhD.

CHAPTER 5

MyManagementLab

Go to **mymanagementlab.com** for Auto-graded writing questions as well as the following Assisted-graded writing questions:

5-36. What are the pros and cons of five sources of job candidates?

5-37. What should employers keep in mind when using Internet sites to find job candidates?

5-38. MyManagementLab only—comprehensive writing assignment for this chapter.

Key Terms

workforce (or employment or personnel) planning, 122

trend analysis, 124

ratio analysis, 124

scatter plot, 125

qualifications (or skills) inventories, 126

personnel replacement charts, 126

position replacement card, 126

succession planning, 128

employee recruiting, 129
recruiting yield pyramid, 129
job posting, 131
applicant tracking systems, 133
alternative staffing, 138
on-demand recruiting services (ODRS), 141
college recruiting, 141
application form, 146

Endnotes

1. Dianna Stone et al., "Factors Affecting the Effectiveness and Acceptance of Electronic Selection Systems," *Human Resource Management Review* 20 3, 2013, pages 50–70.
2. "Transforming Talent Management: Pursuing New Perspectives," 2013 Talent Management Conference & Exposition, Society for Human Resource Management, "Preparing for Tomorrow's Talent Gap: Five Strategies to Start Today" workshop, p. 4.
3. This section is quoted or paraphrased from, "Workforce Planning: Translating the Business Plan into the People Plan," Towers Watson, http://www.towerswatson.com/en-GB/Insights/IC-Types/Survey-Research-Results/2012/11/workforce-planning-translating-the-business-plan-into-the-people-plan?page=0, accessed March 29, 2013.
4. Ibid.
5. Spencer Ante and Joann Lublin, "IBM Crafts Succession Plan," *The New York Times*, June 13, 2011, pp. B1, B12.
6. "More Companies Turn to Workforce Planning to Boost Productivity and Efficiency," The Conference Board, press release/news, August 7, 2006; Carolyn Hirschman, "Putting Forecasting in Focus," *HR Magazine,* March 2007, pp. 44–49.
7. Jones Shannon, "Does HR Planning Improve Business Performance?" *Industrial Management*, January/February 2003, p. 20. See also Michelle Harrison et al., "Effective Succession Planning," *Training & Development*, October 2006, pp. 22–23.
8. Carolyn Hirschman, "Putting Forecasting in Focus," *HR Magazine*, March 2007, pp. 44–49.
9. Jean Phillips and Stanley Gully, *Strategic Staffing* (Upper Saddle River, NJ: Pearson Education, 2012), pp. 116–181.
10. Shannon, "Does HR Planning Improve Business Performance?" p. 16.
11. See, for example, Fay Hansen, "The Long View," *Workforce Management*, April 20, 2008, pp. 1, 14.
12. Bill Roberts, "Can They Keep Our Lights On?" *HR Magazine*, June 2010, pp. 62–68.
13. For an example of a computerized personnel planning system, see Dan Kara, "Automating the Service Chain," *Software Magazine* 20 (June 2000), pp. 3, 42. http://www.kronos.com/scheduling-software/scheduling.aspx, accessed October 2, 2011.
14. www.surveyanalytics.com/skills-inventory-software.html, accessed June 1, 2011.
15. www.sumtotalsystems.com/datasheets/sumt_succession_planning.pdf, accessed June 1, 2011.
16. For a recent discussion see, for example, "Pitfalls Abound for Employers Lacking Electronic Information Retention Policies," *BNA Bulletin to Management*, January 1, 2008, pp. 1–2.
17. The legislation includes the Federal Privacy Act of 1974 (applies to federal workers), the New York Personal Privacy Act of 1985, HIPAA (regulates use of medical records), and the Americans with Disabilities Act.
18. Ibid. See also Bill Roberts, "Risky Business," *HR Magazine,* October 2006, pp. 69–72.
19. "Traditional Security Insufficient to Halt File-Sharing Threat," *BNA Bulletin to Management*, January 20, 2008, p. 39.
20. See, for example, Society for Human Resource Management, "HR's Insight into the Economy," *Workplace Visions* 4 (2008), p. 5.
21. www.astd.org/NR/rdonlyres/CBAB6F0D-97FA-4B1F-920C-6EBAF98906D1/0/BridgingtheSkillsGap.pdf, accessed June 1, 2011.
22. "Next Generation Talent Management," www.hewittassociates.com/_MetaBasicCMAssetCache_/Assets/Articles/next_generation.pdf, accessed November 9, 2010.
23. Ibid.
24. "Boeing Soars Over Potential Talent Gaps with its Workforce Planning Strategies," *Bloomberg BNA*, bulletin to management, February 19, 2013, p. 57.
25. Ed Frauenheim, "Valero Energy," *Workforce Management,* March 13, 2006.
26. Phillips and Gully, *Strategic Staffing,* pp. 116–181.
27. Whereas *succession planning* aims to identify and develop employees to fill specific slots, talent management is a broader activity. *Talent management* involves identifying, recruiting, hiring, and developing high-potential employees. Soonhee Kim, "Linking Employee Assessments to Succession Planning," *Public Personnel Management* 32, no. 4 (Winter 2003), pp. 533–547. See also Michael Laff, "Talent Management: From Hire to Retire," *Training & Development*, November 2006, pp. 42–48.
28. See, for example, David Day, Developing Leadership Talent, SHRM Foundation, http://www.shrm.org/about/foundation/research/Documents/Developing%20Lead%20Talent-%20FINAL.pdf, accessed October 4, 2011.
29. Quoted in Susan Wells, "Who's Next," *HR Magazine*, November 2003, p. 43. See also Christee Atwood, "Implementing Your Succession Plan," *Training & Development*, November 2007, pp. 54–57; and David Day, op cit.
30. See "Succession Management: Identifying and Developing Leaders," *BNA Bulletin to Management* 21, no. 12 (December 2003), p. 15; and David Day, op cit.
31. Soonhee Kim, "Linking Employee Assessments to Succession Planning," *Public Personnel Management*, Winter 2003.
32. Bill Roberts, "Matching Talent with Tasks," *HR Magazine*, November 2002, pp. 91–96.
33. www.sumtotalsystems.com/datasheets/sumt_succession_planning.pdf, accessed June 1, 2011.
34. Ibid., p. 34.
35. Susan Ladika, "Manufacturers Enroll in Recruiting 101," *Workforce Management*, May 2012.
36. And David Ferris, "Ex-Factor for Factories is Factoring in Recruiting," *Workforce Management*, December 2012, page 8.
37. Susan Caminiti, "Leveraging Human Capital," Fortune.com/edit sections pp. 52 to 54, 2012.
38. Darren Dahl, "A Sea of Job Changers, but Some Companies Aren't Getting Any Bites," *The New York Times*, June 20 8, 2012, page B7.
39. Susan Ladika, op. cit.
40. Tom Porter, "Effective Techniques to Attract, Hire, and Retain 'Top Notch' Employees for Your Company," *San Diego Business Journal* 21, no. 13 (March 27, 2000), p. b36.
41. Jonathan Segal, "Land Executives, Not Lawsuits," *HR Magazine*, October 2006, pp. 123–130.
42. Kenneth Sovereign, *Personnel Law* (Upper Saddle River, NJ: Prentice Hall, 1999), pp. 47–49.
43. Ibid., p. 48.
44. Ibid.
45. Jessica Marquez, "A Global Recruiting Site Helps Far-Flung Managers at the Professional Services Company Acquire the Talent They Need—and Saves One Half-Million Dollars a Year," *Workforce Management*, March 13, 2006, p. 22.
46. Rachel Emma Silverman and Lauren Weber, "An Inside Job: More Firms Opt to Recruit from Within," *The Wall Street Journal*, May 30, 2012, page B1.
47. "Hiring Works the Second Time Around," *BNA Bulletin to Management*, January 30, 1997, p. 40; and Issie Lapowsky, "How to Rehire Former Employees," *INC.*, May 18, 2010, available at http://www.inc.com/guides/2010/05/rehiring-former-employees.html, accessed October 3, 2011.
48. Ibid.
49. Lauren Weber and Leslie Kwoh, "Beware the Phantom Job Listing," *The Wall Street Journal*, January 9, 2013, page B1.
50. "Many Workers Use Social Networking Sites in Job Hunt, Edit Own Content, Survey Finds," *BNA Bulletin to Management*, May 10, 2011, page 147.
51. See, for example, J. De Avila, "Beyond Job Boards: Targeting the Source," *The Wall Street Journal* (Eastern Edition), July 2, 2009, pp. D1, D5; and C. Fernandez-Araoz et al., "The Definitive Guide to Recruiting in Good Times and Bad" [Financial crisis spotlight], *Harvard Business Review* 87, no. 5 (May 2009), pp. 74–84.
52. Reprinted from www.careerbuilder.com/MarketingWeb/iPhone/CBJobsApplication.aspx?cbRecursionCnt=1&cbsid=7fd458dafd4a444fb192d9a24ceed771-291142537-wx-6&ns_siteid=ns_us_g_careerbuilder_iphone, accessed March 23, 2009.
53. Deborah Silver, "Niche Sites Gain Monster-Sized Following," *Workforce Management*, March 2011, pp. 10–11.
54. Except as noted, this *Online Recruiting* section is based on Lauren Weber, "Seeking Software Fix for Job-Search Game," *The Wall Street Journal*, June 6, 2012, page B8; and Juro Osawa and Paul Moser, "In China, Recruiting Gets Social," *The Wall Street Journal*, August 2, 2012, page B4.
55. "Social Recruiting in 2012, the Latter Is. com," Special Advertising Supplement to *Workforce Management*, 2012.

56. Joe Light, "Recruiters Rethink Online Playbook," online.wsj.com/article/SB1000142405 2748704307404576080492613858846.html, accessed May 17, 2011.
57. Aliah Wright, "Your Social Media Is Showing," *HR Magazine*, March 2012, page 16.
58. Jennifer Arnold, "Twittering at Face Booking While They Were," *HR Magazine*, December 2009, p. 54.
59. Ibid.
60. *Bloomberg BNA*, bulletin to management, "Certain Social Media Tools Are Helping HR Connect Swiftly with the Right Job Candidates," July 24, 2012, p. 233.
61. "ResumePal: Recruiter's Friend?" *Workforce Management*, June 22, 2009, p. 28.
62. "Innovative HR Programs Cultivate Successful Employees," *Nation's Restaurant News* 41, no. 50 (December 17, 2007), p. 74.
63. J. De Avila, "Beyond Job Boards: Targeting the Source," *The Wall Street Journal* (Eastern Edition), July 2, 2009, pp. D1, D5.
64. Josee Rose, "Recruiters Take Hip Path to Fill Accounting Jobs," *The Wall Street Journal*, September 18, 2007, p. 38.
65. Gina Ruiz, "Firms Tapping Web Videos to Lure Jobseekers," *Workforce Management*, October 8, 2007, p. 12.
66. Ed Frauenheim, "Social Revolution," *Workforce*, October 20, 2007, p. 30.
67. Jennifer Taylor Arnold, "Recruiting on the Run," February 2010, *HR Magazine*, pp. 65–67.
68. Elizabeth Agnvall, "Job Fairs Go Virtual," *HR Magazine*, July 2007, p. 85; Gary Stern, "Virtual Job Fairs Becoming More of a Reality," *Workforce Management*, February 2011, p. 11.
69. "EEOC Issues Much Delayed Definition of 'Applicant,'" *HR Magazine,* April 2004, p. 29; Valerie Hoffman and Greg Davis, "OFCCP's Internet Applicant Definition Requires Overhaul of Recruitment and Hiring Policies," *Society for Human Resources Management Legal Report*, January/February 2006, p. 2.
70. This carries legal risks, particularly if the device disproportionately screens out minority or female applicants. Lisa Harpe, "Designing an Effective Employment Prescreening Program," *Employment Relations Today* 32, no. 3 (Fall 2005), pp. 43–51.
71. Lauren Weber, "Your Resume Versus Oblivion," *The Wall Street Journal*, January 20 4, 2012, pp. B1, B6.
72. William Dickmeyer, "Applicant Tracking Reports Make Data Meaningful," *Workforce*, February 2001, pp. 65–67; and, as an example, http://www.icims.com/prelude/1101/3009?_vsrefdom=google_ppc&gclid=CPHki_nx1KsCFcPt7QodmkjLDA, accessed October 4, 2011.
73. Paul Gilster, "Channel the Resume Flood with Applicant Tracking Systems," *Workforce*, January 2001, pp. 32–34; William Dickmeyer, "Applicant Tracking Reports Make Data Meaningful," *Workforce*, February 2001, pp. 65–67; and, as an example, http://www.icims.com/prelude/1101/3009?_vsrefdom=google_ppc&gclid=CPHki_nx1KsCFcPt7QodmkjLDA, accessed October 4, 2011.
74. Note that the U.S. Department of Labor's Office of Federal Contract compliance programs recently announced it would review federal contractors' online application tracking systems to ensure they're providing equal opportunity to qualify prospective applicants with disabilities. "Feds Want a Look at Online Job Sites," *HR Magazine*, November 2008, p. 12.
75. "E-Recruiting Software Providers," *Workforce Management*, June 22, 2009, p. 14.
76. Lauren Weber, "Your Resume Versus Oblivion," *The Wall Street Journal*, January 20 4, 2012, pp. B1, B6.
77. Dave Zielinski, "Get to the Source," *HR Magazine*, November 2012, page 68.
78. Maria Seminerio, "E-Recruiting Takes Next Step," *eWeek*, April 23, 2001, pp. 49–51; http://www.sutterhealth.org/employment, accessed October 2, 2011.
79. Daniel Feldman and Brian Klaas, "Internet Job Hunting: A Field Study of Applicant Experiences with Online Recruiting," *Human Resource Management* 41, no. 2 (Summer 2002), pp. 175–192.
80. "Does Your Company's Website Click with Job Seekers?" *Workforce*, August 2000, p. 260.
81. "Study Says Career Web Sites Could Snare More Job Seekers," *BNA Bulletin to Management*, February 1, 2001, p. 36.
82. Sarah Gale, "Internet Recruiting: Better, Cheaper, Faster," *Workforce*, December 2001, p. 75.
83. "Help Wanted—and Found," *Fortune*, October 2, 2006, p. 40.
84. James Breaugh, "Employee Recruitment: Current Knowledge and Important Areas for Future Research," *Human Resource Management Review* 18 (2008), p. 114.
85. "Job Seekers' Privacy Has Been Eroded with Online Job Searchers, Report Says," *BNA Bulletin to Management*, November 20, 2003, p. 369.
86. James Breaugh, "Employee Recruitment."
87. Eric Krell, "Recruiting Outlook: Creative HR for 2003," *Workforce*, December 2002, pp. 40–44.
88. James Breaugh, "Employee Recruitment," p. 111.
89. James Breaugh, "Employee Recruitment," p. 113.
90. Find your nearest one-stop center at www.servicelocator.org.
91. Lynn Doherty and E. Norman Sims, "Quick, Easy Recruitment Help: From a State?" *Workforce*, May 1998, p. 36.
92. Ibid.
93. One "Wharton MBA and GE alum" manages short-term projects for major companies and served as interim CEO for one firm. See Jodi Greenstone Miller and Matt Miller, "The Best Executive and Professional Jobs May No Longer Be Full-Time Gigs," *Harvard Business Review*, May 2012, p. 51.
94. "As Hiring Falters, More Workers Are Temporary," *The New York Times*, December 20, 2010, pp. A1, A4.
95. Robert Bohner Jr. and Elizabeth Salasko, "Beware the Legal Risks of Hiring Temps," *Workforce*, October 2002, pp. 50–57. See also Fay Hansen, "A Permanent Strategy for Temporary Hires," *Workforce Management*, February 26, 2007, p. 27; and Robert Grossman, "Strategic Temp—Tations," *HR Magazine*, March 2012, pp. 24–34.
96. Daniel Feldman, Helen Doerpinghaus, and William Turnley, "Managing Temporary Workers: A Permanent HRM Challenge," *Organizational Dynamics* 23, no. 2 (Fall 1994), p. 49. See also Kathryn Tyler, "Treat Contingent Workers with Care," *HR Magazine*, March 2008, p. 75; and http://www.employment.oregon.gov/EMPLOY/ES/BUS/index.shtml, accessed October 4, 2011.
97. John Zappe, "Temp-to-Hire Is Becoming a Full-Time Practice at Firms," *Workforce Management*, June 2005, pp. 82–86.
98. Shari Cauldron, "Contingent Workforce Spurs HR Planning," *Personnel Journal*, July 1994, p. 60.
99. This is based on or quoted from Nancy Howe, "Match Temp Services to Your Needs," *Personnel Journal*, March 1989, pp. 45–51. See also Stephen Miller, "Collaboration Is Key to Effective Outsourcing," *HR Magazine* 58 (2008), pp. 60–61; and (as an example), http://www.bbb.org/shreveport/accredited-business-directory/employment-contractors-temporary-help/plain-dealing-la, accessed September 23, 2011.
100. Carolyn Hirschman, "Are Your Contractors Legal?" *HR Magazine*, March 2004, pp. 59–63. One staffing agency allegedly used 39 Filipino nationals to work 16-hour days at country clubs and golf courses, paying them little and allegedly treating them as "slaves." Dori Meinert, "Modern-Day Slavery," *HR Magazine*, May 2012, pp. 22–24.
101. Ibid.
102. Margaret Steen, "More Employers Take on Temps, But Planning Is Paramount," *Workforce Management*, May 2011, p. 14.
103. This section is based on Robyn Meredith, "Giant Sucking Sound," *Forbes* 172, no. 6 (September 29, 2003), p. 158; Jim McKay, "Inevitable Outsourcing, Offshoring Stirred Passions at Pittsburgh Summit," *Knight Ridder/Tribune Business News*, March 11, 2004; Peter Panepento, "General Electric Transportation to Outsource Drafting Jobs to India," *Knight Ridder/Tribune Business News*, May 5, 2004; Julie Harbin, "Recent Survey Charts Execs' Willingness to Outsource Jobs," *San Diego Business Journal* 25, no. 14 (April 5, 2004), pp. 8–10; and Pamela Babcock, "America's Newest Export: White-Collar Jobs," *HR Magazine* 49, no. 4 (April 2004), pp. 50–57.
104. Ed Frauenheim, "Homeward Bound," *Workforce Management*, February 2013, pp. 26–31.
105. Susan Wells, "Slow Times for Executive Recruiting," *HR Magazine*, April 2003, pp. 61–67.
106. Michelle Martinez, "Working with an Outside Recruiter? Get It in Writing," *HR Magazine*, January 2001, pp. 98–105.
107. See, for example, Stephenie Overman, "Searching for the Top," *HR Magazine*, January 2008, p. 49.
108. Bill Leonard, "Recruiting from the Competition," *HR Magazine*, February 2001, pp. 78–86. See also G. Anders, "Secrets of the Talent Scouts," *New York Times* (Late New York Edition) (March 15, 2009), pp. 1, 7 (Sec 3).
109. "Carol Hymowitz and Jeff Green, "These Days, Anybody Can Headhunt," *Bloomberg Business Week*, January 20 7, 2013, pp. 19–20; Joann Lublin, "More Executive Recruiting Ships in House," *The Wall Street Journal*, October 10, 2012, p. B8.
110. John Wareham, *Secrets of a Corporate Headhunter* (New York: Playboy Press, 1981), pp. 213–225; Chip McCreary, "Get the Most Out of Search Firms," *Workforce*, August 1997, pp. S28–S30.
111. www.kaiserpermanentejobs.org/employee-referral-program.aspx, accessed August 20, 2011.
112. James Breaugh, "Employee Recruitment," p. 109.
113. "Tell a Friend: Employee Referral Programs Earn High Marks for Low Recruiting Costs,"

BNA Bulletin to Management, June 28, 2001, p. 201.
114. Martha Frase-Blunt, "A Recruiting Spigot," *HR Magazine*, April 2003, pp. 71–79.
115. Sara Rynes, Marc Orlitzky, and Robert Bretz Jr., "Experienced Hiring Versus College Recruiting: Practices and Emerging Trends," *Personnel Psychology* 50 (1997), pp. 309–339. See also Lisa Munniksma, "Career Matchmakers: Partnering with Collegiate Career Centers Offers Recruiters Access to Rich Source of Applicants," *HR Magazine* 50, no. 2 (February 2005), p. 93.
116. See, for example, James Breaugh, "Employee Recruitment," p. 111.
117. "Recruiters Look to Be Big Man on Campus," *Workforce Management*, September 2010, p. 12.
118. Joe Mullich, "Finding the Schools That Yield the Best Job Applicant ROI," *Workforce Management*, March 2004, pp. 67–68.
119. Greet Van Hoye and Filip Lievens, "Tapping the Grapevine: A Closer Look at Word-of-Mouth as a Recruitment Source," *Journal of Applied Psychology* 94, no. 2 (2009), pp. 341–352.
120. Lisa Munniksma, "Career Matchmakers," *HR Magazine*, February 2005, pp. 93–96.
121. Wendy Boswell et al., "Individual Job Choice Decisions and the Impact of Job Attributes and Recruitment Practices: A Longitudinal Field Study," *Human Resource Management* 42, no. 1 (Spring 2003), pp. 23–37. See also James Breaugh, "Employee Recruitment," p. 115.
122. Hao Zhao Oh and Robert Liden, "Internship: A Recruitment and Selected Perspective," *Journal of Applied Psychology* 96, no. 1 (2011), pp. 221–229.
123. Teddy Wayne, "Then No Limits Job," *The New York Times*, March 3, 2013, Sunday styles p. 1.
124. Martha Frase-Blunt, "Call Centers Come Home," *HR Magazine*, January 2007, pp. 85–90.
125. Theresa Minton-Eversole, "Mission: Recruitment," *HR Magazine*, January 2009, pp. 43–45.
126. See, for example, Stephanie Castellano, "The Value of Veterans," *Training & Development*, February 2013, p. 16.
127. "Wal-Mart to Higher Projected 100,000 Deaths Over Five Years," *Bloomberg BNA Bulletin to Management*, January 20 2, 2013, p. 26, http://www.humanresourcemetrics.org/recruiting_cost_ratio.html.
128. See, for example, http://www.humanresourcemetrics.org/recruiting_cost_ratio.html, accessed July 17, 2013,.
129. Kevin Carlson et al., "Recruitment Evaluation: The Case for Assessing the Quality of Applicants Attracted," *Personnel Psychology* 55 (2002), pp. 461–490. For a recent survey of recruiting source effectiveness, see "The 2007 Recruiting Metrics and Performance Benchmark Report, 2nd ed.," Staffing.org, Inc., 2007.
130. Ibid., p. 466.
131. Phillips and Gully, *Strategic Staffing*, p. 180.
132. Gino Ruiz, "Special Report: Talent Acquisition," *Workforce Management*, July 23, 2007, p. 39.
133. Ann Marie Ryan and Nancy Tippins, "Attracting and Selecting: What Psychological Research Tells Us," *Human Resource Management* 43, no. 4 (Winter 2004), p. 311.
134. Thomas Stewart, "In Search of Elusive Tech Workers," *Fortune*, February 16, 1998, pp. 171–172; and http://www.outsourcing-center.com/2006-10-ge-looks-to-recruitment-process-outsourcer-to-find-meat-and-potatoes-candidates-as-well-as-the-purple-squirrel-article-37479.html, accessed October 5, 2011.
135. Robert Grossman, "How to Recruit a Recruitment Outsourcer," *HR Magazine*, July 2012, pp. 51–54; and Susan Ladika, "A Lot to Process," *Workforce Management*, July 2012, pp. 16–18.
136. "Recruitment Process Outsourcing Providers," *Workforce Management*, February 2013, p. 20.
137. "Internship Programs Help These Recruiters Toward Qualified Students with Disabilities," *BNA Bulletin to Management*, July 17, 2003, p. 225.
138. http://www.recruitingtrends.com/recruiting-women/; http://online.wsj.com/article/SB10001424127887323764804578314450063914388.html; http://www.theresumator.com/blog/how-to-recruit-women-for-your-workforce/; http://blogs.kenan-flagler.unc.edu/2012/06/12/the-new-business-imperative-recruiting-and-retaining-women-in-the-workplace/. All accessed May 9, 2013.
139. Judith Casey and Marcie Pitt-Catsouphes, "Employed Single Mothers: Balancing Job and Home Life," *Employee Assistance Quarterly* 9, no. 324 (1994), pp. 37–53; http://www.catalyst.org/publication/252/working-parents, accessed October 3, 2011.
140. Casey and Pitt-Catsouphes, op cit., p. 42.
141. "Barclaycard Helps Single Parents to Find Employment," *Personnel Today*, November 7, 2006.
142. Caroline Straub, "Antecedents and Organizational Consequences of Family Supportive Supervisor Behavior: A Multilevel Conceptual Framework for Research," *Human Resource Management Review* 22, 2012, pp. 15–26.
143. Susan Glairon, "Single Parents Need More Flexibility at Work, Advocate in Denver Says," *Daily Camera*, February 8, 2002; http://www.cnn.com/2008/LIVING/worklife/06/04/balance.calculator, accessed October 5, 2011.
144. Sandra Block and Stephanie Armour, "Many Americans Retire Years Before They Want To," *USA Today*, July 26, 2006, http://usatoday.com, accessed December 23, 2007.
145. Phaedra Brotherton, "Tapping into an Older Workforce," *Mosaics* (Society for Human Resource Management, March/April 2000). See also Thomas Ng and Daniel Feldman, "The Relationship of Age to Ten Dimensions of Job Performance," *Journal of Applied Psychology* 90, no. 2 (2008), pp. 392–423.
146. Sue Shellenbarger, "Gray Is Good: Employers Make Efforts to Retain Older, Experienced Workers," *The Wall Street Journal*, December 1, 2005.
147. Alison Wellner, "Tapping a Silver Mine," *HR Magazine*, March 2002, p. 29.
148. Sue Shellenbarger, "Gray Is Good." See also Robert Grossman, "Keep Pace with Older Workers," *HR Magazine*, May 2008, pp. 39–46.
149. Gary Adams and Barbara Rau, "Attracting Retirees to Apply: Desired Organizational Characteristics of Bridge Employment," *Journal of Organizational Behavior* 26, no. 6 (September 2005), pp. 649–660.
150. Thomas NG and Daniel Feldman, "Evaluating Six Common Stereotypes About Older Workers with Meta-analytical Data," *Personnel Psychology* 60 (6), 2012, pp. 821–858.
151. Ibid.
152. Abby Ellin, "Supervising the Graybeards," *The New York Times*, January 16, 2000, p. B16; Derek Avery and Patrick McKay, "Target Practice: An Organizational Impression Management Approach to Attracting Minority and Female Job Applicants," *Personnel Psychology* 59 (2006), pp. 157–189.
153. Herbert Greenberg, "A Hidden Source of Talent," *HR Magazine*, March 1997, pp. 88–91.
154. Linda Moore, "Firms Need to Improve Recruitment, Hiring of Disabled Workers, EEO Chief Says," *Knight Ridder/Tribune Business News*, November 5, 2003. See also "Recruiting Disabled More Than Good Deed, Experts Say," *BNA Bulletin to Management*, February 27, 2007, p. 71.
155. "Students with Disabilities Available," *HR Briefing*, June 15, 2002, p. 5.
156. Moore, "Firms Need to Improve Recruitment."
157. This paragraph is based on Jennifer L. Wood, James M. Schmidtke, and Diane L. Decker, "Lying on Job Applications: The Effects of Job Relevance, Commission, and Human Resource Management Experience," *Journal of Business and Psychology* 22 (2007), pp. 1–9.
158. Kenneth Sovereign, *Personnel Law* (Upper Saddle River, NJ: Pearson, 1999), p. 51. 132.
159. Rachel Emma Silverman, "No More Resumes, Say Some Firms," *The Wall Street Journal*, January 24, 2012, page B6.
160. Kathy Gurchiek, "Video Resumes Spark Curiosity, Questions," *HR Magazine*, May 2007, pp. 28–30; "Video Resumes Can Illuminate Applicants' Abilities, but Pose Discrimination Concerns," *BNA Bulletin to Management*, May 20, 2007, pp. 169–170.
161. As of May 2010, these companies included resumebook.tv, optimalresume.com, interviewstudio.com, and brightab.com. Alina Dizik, "Wooing Job Recruiters with Video Resumes," *The Wall Street Journal*, May 20, 2010, p. D4.
162. Murray Barrick and Ryan Zimmerman, "Hiring for Retention and Performance," *Human Resource Management* 48, no. 2 (March/April 2009), pp. 183–206.
163. James Breaugh, "The Use of Biodata for Employee Selection: Test Research and Future Directions," *Human Resource Management Review* 19 (2009), pp. 219–231. Utilizing biodata items of course presumes that the employer can show that the items predict performance. Biodata items such as "graduated from college" may have an adverse impact on minorities but studies suggest that employers can avoid that problem through judicious choice of biodata items (p. 229).
164. Fred Mael, Mary Connerley, and Ray Morath, "None of Your Business: Parameters of Biodata Invasiveness," *Personnel Psychology* 49 (1996), pp. 613–650; and Kenneth Law et al., "Impression Management and Faking in Biodata Scores Among Chinese Job-Seekers," *Asia Pacific Journal of Management* 19, no. 4 (December 2002), p. 541–556.
165. "Supreme Court Denies Circuit City's Bid for Review of Mandatory Arbitration," *BNA Bulletin to Management*, June 6, 2002, p. 177.
166. "Supreme Court Gives the Employers Green Light to Hold Most Employees to Arbitration Pacts," *BNA Bulletin to Management*, March 29, 2001, pp. 97–98.
167. Douglas Mahony et al., "The Effects of Mandatory Employment Arbitration Systems on Applicants Attraction to Organizations," *Human Resource Management* 44, no. 4 (Winter 2005), pp. 449–470; See also H. John Bernardin et al., "Mandatory and Binding Arbitration: Effects on Employee Attitudes and Recruiting Results," *Human Resource Management*, March–April 2011, 50, no. 2, pp. 175–200.

6 Employee Testing and Selection

Source: © Bob Pardue - Signs/Alamy

MyManagementLab®

Improve Your Grade!

When you see this icon, visit **www.mymanagementlab.com** for activities that are applied, personalized, and offer immediate feedback.

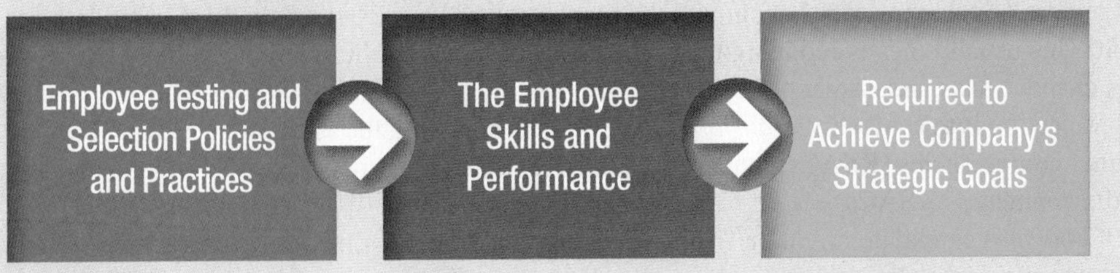

For a bird's eye view of how one company created an employee screening program to improve its strategic performance, read the Hotel Paris case on page 185 and answer the questions after reading the chapter.

WHERE ARE WE NOW . . .

Chapter 5 focused on building an applicant pool. The purpose of Chapter 6 is to explain how to use various tools to select the best candidates for the job. The main topics we'll cover are why employee selection is important, the basics of testing and selecting employees, types of tests, work samples and simulations, and background investigations and other selection methods.

LEARNING OBJECTIVES

1 Answer the question: Why is it important to test and select employees?

2 Explain what is meant by reliability and validity.

3 List and briefly describe the basic categories of selection tests, with examples.

4 Explain how to use two work simulations for selection.

5 Describe four ways to improve an employer's background checking process.

With many restaurants losing 100% or more of their workers every year, employee turnover is a hugely expensive problem in the business. It's not just the recruiting and training costs. It's also the hidden costs; for instance, when a customer vows to never return after receiving inept service from a newly hired server. So, when the young founders of Outback Steakhouse started their chain some years ago, they decided to minimize turnover. We'll see how they did it.

Why Employee Selection Is Important

1 Answer the question: Why is it important to test and select employees?

After reviewing the applicants' résumés, the manager turns to selecting the best candidate for the job. This usually means reducing the applicant pool by using the screening tools we discuss in this chapter: tests, assessment centers, and background and reference checks. The aim of employee selection is to achieve *person-job fit*. This means matching the knowledge, skills, abilities, and other competencies (KSACs) that are required for performing the job (based on job analysis) with the applicant's KSACs.

Of course, a candidate might be "right" for a job, but wrong for the organization.[1] For example, an experienced airline pilot might excel at American Airlines but perhaps not at Southwest, where the organizational values require that all employees help out, even if that means helping with baggage handling. Therefore, person-job fit is usually the main consideration, but *person-organization fit* is important too.

In any case, selecting the right employees is important for three main reasons: performance, costs, and legal obligations.

First, employees with the right skills will perform better for you and the company. Employees without these skills or who are abrasive or obstructionist won't perform effectively, and your own performance and the firm's profitability will suffer. The time to screen out undesirables is before they are in the door.

Second, effective selection is important because it's costly to recruit and hire employees. Hiring and training even a clerk can cost $5,000 or more in fees and supervisory time. The total cost of hiring a manager could easily be 10 times as high once you add search fees, interviewing time, reference checking, and travel and moving expenses.

negligent hiring
Hiring workers with questionable backgrounds without proper safeguards.

Third, it's important because inept hiring has legal consequences. For example (as we saw in Chapter 2), equal employment laws require nondiscriminatory selection procedures.[2] *Negligent hiring* is another such problem. **Negligent hiring** means hiring employees with criminal records or other problems who then use access to customers' homes (or similar opportunities) to commit crimes.[3] In one case, *Ponticas v. K.M.S. Investments*, an apartment manager entered a woman's apartment and assaulted her.[4] The court found the apartment complex's owner negligent for not checking the manager's background properly.[5] Similarly, the Employers Liability Act of 1969 holds employers responsible for their employees' health and safety at work.[6] Because personality traits may predict problems such as unsafe behaviors and bullying, this Act makes careful employee selection even more advisable.[7]

The Basics of Testing and Selecting Employees

2 Explain what is meant by reliability and validity.

In this chapter, we'll discuss several popular selection tools, starting with tests. A test is basically a sample of a person's behavior. Using any selection tool assumes the tool is both reliable and valid.

Reliability

reliability
The consistency of scores obtained by the same person when retested with the identical tests or with alternate forms of the same test.

Reliability is a selection tool's first requirement and refers to its consistency: "A reliable test is one that yields consistent scores when a person takes two alternate forms of the test or when he or she takes the same test on two or more different occasions."[8] If a person scores 90 on an intelligence test on a Monday and 130 when retested on Tuesday, you probably wouldn't have much faith in the test.

You can measure reliability in several ways. One is to administer a test to a group of people one day, re-administer the same test several days later to the same group, and then correlate the first set of scores with the second (called *test-retest reliability estimates*).[9] Or you could administer a test and then administer what experts believe to be an equivalent test later; this would be an *equivalent or alternate form estimate*. (The Scholastic Assessment Test (SAT) is one example.) Or, compare the test taker's answers to certain questions on the test with his or her answers to a separate set of questions on the same test aimed at measuring the same thing. This is an *internal comparison estimate*. For example, a psychologist includes 10 items on a test believing that they all measure interest in working outdoors. You administer the test and then statistically analyze the degree to which responses to these 10 items vary together.

Many things cause a test to be unreliable. These include physical conditions (quiet test conditions one day, noisy the next), differences in the test taker (healthy one day, sick the next), and differences in the person administering the test (courteous one day, curt the next). Or the questions may do a poor

FIGURE 6-1 Correlation Examples

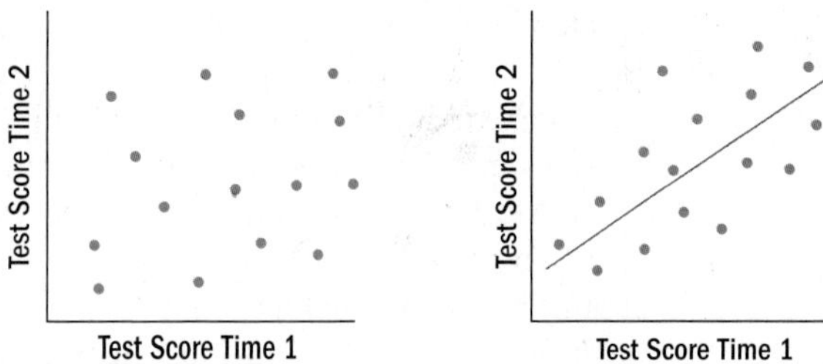

job of sampling the material; for example, test one focuses more on Chapters 1, 3, and 7, while test two focuses more on Chapters 2, 4, and 8.

Because measuring reliability generally involves comparing two measures that assess the same thing, it is typical to judge a test's reliability in terms of a *reliability coefficient*. This basically shows the degree to which the two measures (say, test score one day and test score the next day) are correlated.

Figure 6-1 illustrates correlation. In both the left and the right scatter plots, the psychologist compared each applicant's time 1 test score (on the *x*-axis) with his or her subsequent test score (on the *y*-axis). On the left, the scatter plot points (each point showing one applicant's test score and subsequent test performance) are dispersed. There seems to be no correlation between test scores obtained at time 1 and at time 2. On the right, the psychologist tried a new test. Here the resulting points fall in a predictable pattern. This suggests that the applicants' test scores correlate closely with their previous scores.

Validity

Reliability, while indispensable, only tells you that the test is measuring something consistently. *Validity* tells you whether the test is measuring what you think it's supposed to be measuring.[10] **Test validity** answers the question "Does this test measure what it's supposed to measure?" Put another way, it refers to the correctness of the inferences that we can make based on the test.[11] For example, if Jane's scores on mechanical comprehension tests are higher than Jim's, can we be sure that Jane possesses more mechanical comprehension than Jim?[12] With employee selection tests, *validity* often refers to evidence that the test is job related—in other words, that performance on the test accurately predicts subsequent performance on the job. A selection test must be valid since, without proof of validity, there is no logical or (under EEO law) legally permissible reason to continue using it to screen job applicants.

test validity
The accuracy with which a test, interview, and so on measures what it purports to measure or fulfills the function it was designed to fill.

A test, as we said, is a sample of a person's behavior, but some tests are more clearly representative of the behavior being sampled than others. A swimming test, for example, clearly corresponds to a lifeguard's on-the-job behavior. On the other hand, there may be no apparent relationship between the test and the behavior. Thus, in Figure 6-2, the psychologist asks the person

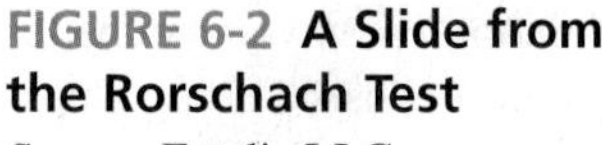

FIGURE 6-2 A Slide from the Rorschach Test
Source: Fotolia LLC.

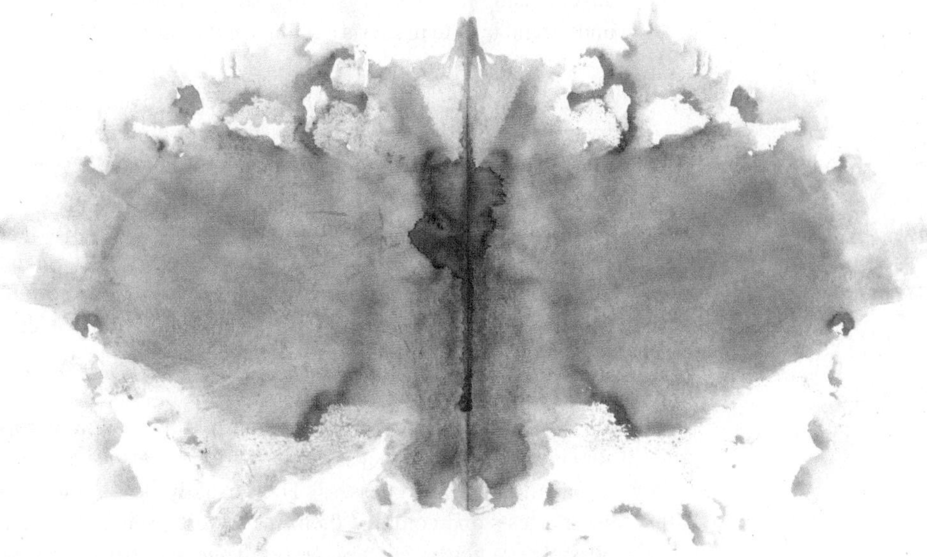

to interpret the picture, and then draws conclusions about the person's personality and behavior. Here it is more difficult to prove that the tests are measuring what they are said to measure, in this case, some trait of the person's personality—in other words, prove that they're valid. In employment testing, there are several ways to demonstrate a test's validity.[13]

criterion validity
A type of validity based on showing that scores on the test (predictors) are related to job performance (criterion).

Criterion validity involves demonstrating statistically a relationship between scores on a selection procedure and job performance of a sample of workers. For example, it means demonstrating that those who do well on the test also do well on the job, and that those who do poorly on the test do poorly on the job. The test has validity to the extent that the people with higher test scores perform better on the job. In psychological measurement, a *predictor* is the measurement (in this case, the test score) that you are trying to relate to a *criterion*, such as performance on the job. The term *criterion validity* reflects that terminology.

content validity
A test that is content valid is one that contains a fair sample of the tasks and skills actually needed for the job in question.

Content validity is a demonstration that the content of a selection procedure is representative of important aspects of performance on the job. For example, employers may demonstrate the *content validity* of a test by showing that the test constitutes a fair sample of the job's content. The basic procedure here is to identify job tasks that are critical to performance, and then randomly select a sample of those tasks to test. In selecting students for dental school, one might give applicants chunks of chalk, and ask them to carve something like a tooth. If the content you choose for the test is a representative sample of the job, then the test is probably content valid. Clumsy dental students need not apply. SMEs—subject matter experts (such as practicing dentists)—help choose the tasks.

construct validity
A test that is construct valid is one that demonstrates that a selection procedure measures a construct and that construct is important for successful job performance.

Construct validity means demonstrating that (1) a selection procedure measures a construct (an abstract idea such as morale or honesty) and (2) that the construct is important for successful job performance.

At best, invalid tests are a waste of time; at worst, they are discriminatory. Tests you buy "off the shelf" should include information on their validity.[14] But ideally, you should revalidate the tests for the job(s) at hand. In any case, tests rarely predict performance with 100% accuracy (or anywhere near it), so do not make tests your only selection tool; also use other tools like interviews and background checks.

Evidence-Based HR: How to Validate a Test

Employers often opt to demonstrate evidence of a test's validity using criterion validity. Here, in order for a selection test to be useful, you need evidence that scores on the test relate in a predictable way to performance on the job. Thus, other things being equal, students who score high on the graduate admissions tests also do better in graduate school. Applicants who score high on mechanical comprehension tests perform better as engineers. In other words, you validate the test before using it by ensuring that scores on the test are a good predictor of some *criterion* like job performance—thus demonstrating the test's *criterion validity*.[15]

An industrial psychologist usually conducts the validation study. The human resource department coordinates the effort. Strictly speaking, the supervisor's role is just to make sure that the job's human requirements and performance standards are clear to the psychologist. But in practice, anyone using tests (or test results) should know something about validation. Then you can better understand how to use tests and interpret their results. The validation process consists of five steps:

STEP 1: ANALYZE THE JOB The first step is to analyze the job and write job descriptions and job specifications. The aim here is to specify the human traits and skills you believe are required for job performance. For example, must an applicant be verbal, a good talker? These requirements become the *predictors,* the human traits and skills you believe predict success on the job. For an assembler's job, *predictors* might include manual dexterity and patience.[16]

In this first step, also define "success on the job," since it's this success for which you want predictors. The standards of success are *criteria*. You could use production-related criteria (quantity, quality, and so on), personnel data (absenteeism, length of service, and so on), or worker performance (reported by supervisors).

STEP 2: CHOOSE THE TESTS Once you know the predictors (such as manual dexterity) the next step is to decide how to test for them. Employers usually base this choice on experience, previous research, and "best guesses." They usually don't start with just one test. Instead, they choose several tests and combine them into a test battery. The test battery aims to measure an array of possible predictors, such as aggressiveness, extroversion, and numerical ability.

FIGURE 6-3 Examples of websites Offering Information on Tests or Testing Programs

- www.hr-guide.com/data/G371.htm
  Provides general information and sources for all types of employment tests.
- http://ericae.net
  Provides technical information on all types of employment and nonemployment tests.
- www.ets.org/testcoll
  Provides information on more than 20,000 tests.
- www.kaplan.com
  Information from Kaplan test preparation on how various admissions tests work.
- www.assessments.biz
  One of many firms offering employment tests.

What tests are available and where do you get them? Ideally, use a professional, such as an industrial psychologist. However, many firms publish tests.[17] Some tests are available to virtually any purchaser, others only to qualified buyers (such as with degrees in psychology). Wonderlic, Inc., publishes a well-known intellectual capacity test and other tests, including aptitude test batteries and interest inventories. G. Neil Company of Sunrise, Florida, offers employment testing materials including, for example, a clerical skills test, telemarketing ability test, service ability test, management ability test, team skills test, and sales abilities test. Figure 6-3 lists several websites that provide information about tests or testing programs.

However, do not let the widespread availability of tests blind you to this fact: You should use tests in a manner consistent with equal employment laws, and in a manner that is ethical and protects the test taker's privacy.

STEP 3: ADMINISTER THE TEST Next, administer the selected test(s). One option is to administer the tests to employees currently on the job. You then compare their test scores with their current performance; this is *concurrent (at the same time) validation*. Its advantage is that data on performance are readily available. The disadvantage is that current employees may not be representative of new applicants (who, of course, are really the ones for whom you are interested in developing a screening test). Current employees have already had on-the-job training and screening by your existing selection techniques.

Predictive validation is the second and more dependable way to validate a test. Here you administer the test to applicants before you hire them, then hire these applicants using only existing selection techniques, not the results of the new tests. After they have been on the job for some time, measure their performance and compare it to their earlier test scores. You can then determine whether you could have used their performance on the new test to predict their subsequent job performance.

STEP 4: RELATE YOUR TEST SCORES AND CRITERIA Here, ascertain if there is a significant relationship between test scores (the predictor) and performance (the criterion). The usual method is to determine the statistical relationship between (1) scores on the test and (2) job performance using correlation analysis, which shows the degree of statistical relationship.

expectancy chart
A graph showing the relationship between test scores and job performance for a group of people.

If there is a correlation between test and job performance, you can develop an **expectancy chart**. This presents the relationship between test scores and job performance graphically. To do this, split the employees into, say, five groups according to test scores, with those scoring the highest fifth on the test, the second highest fifth, and so on. Then compute the percentage of high job performers in each of these five test score groups and present the data in an expectancy chart like that in Figure 6-4.

In this case, someone scoring in the top fifth of the test has a 97% chance of being a high performer, while one scoring in the lowest fifth has only a 29% chance of being a high performer.[18]

STEP 5: CROSS-VALIDATE AND REVALIDATE Before using the test, you may want to check it by "cross-validating"—in other words, by again performing steps 3 and 4 on a new sample of employees. At a minimum, revalidate the test periodically.

WHO SCORES THE TEST? Some tests (such as the 16PF® Personality Profile) are professionally scored and interpreted. Thus Wonderlic, Inc., lets an employer administer the 16PF. The employer

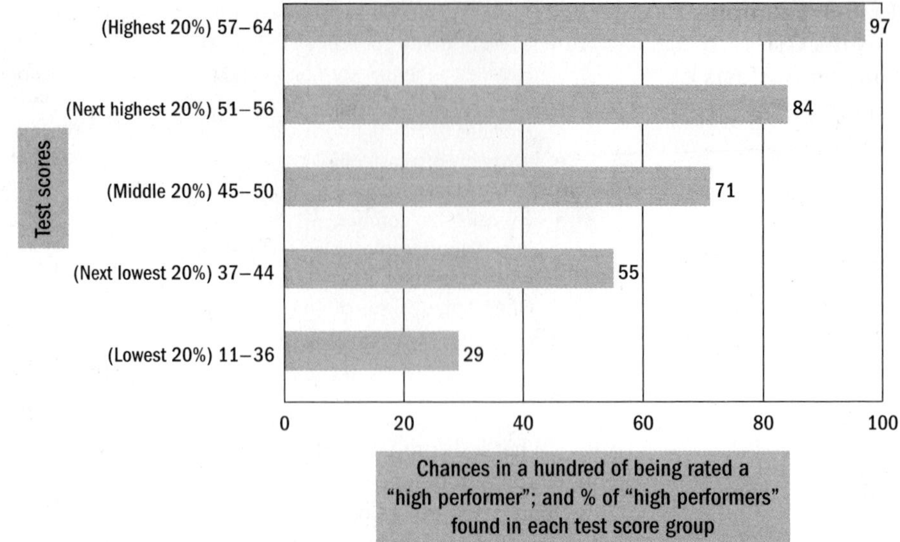

FIGURE 6-4 Expectancy Chart

Note: This expectancy chart shows the relation between scores made on the Minnesota Paper Form Board and rated success of junior draftspersons.

Example: Those who score between 37 and 44 have a 55% chance of being rated high performer and those scoring between 57 and 64 have a 97% chance.

then faxes (or scans) the answer sheet to Wonderlic, which scores the candidate's profile and faxes (or scans) back the interpretive report. Psychologists easily score many psychological tests online or using interpretive Windows-based software. However, managers can easily score many tests, like the Wonderlic Personnel Test, themselves.

Bias

Most employers know they should not use biased tests in the selection process.[19] As one example, there may be bias in how the test *measures the trait* it purports to measure. For example, a particular IQ test may provide a valid measure of cognitive ability for middle-class whites, but with minorities the score depends on whether they're familiar with middle-class culture.[20] Until recently, many industrial psychologists believed they were adequately controlling test bias, but today that issue is under review.[21] Employers should therefore redouble their efforts to ensure that the tests they're using aren't producing biased decisions.

Utility Analysis

Knowing that a test predicts performance may not be of practical use. For example, if it is going to cost the employer $1,000 per applicant for the test, and hundreds of applicants must be tested, the cost of the test may exceed the benefits derived from hiring a few more capable employees.

Answering the question, "Does it pay to use the test?" requires *utility analysis*. Two selection experts say, "Using dollar and cents terms, [utility analysis] shows the degree to which use of a selection measure improves the quality of individuals selected over what would have happened if the measure had not been used."[22] The information required for utility analysis generally includes, for instance, the validity of the selection measure, a measure of job performance in dollars, applicants' average test scores, cost of testing an applicant, and the number of applicants tested and selected.

Prudent employers endeavor to streamline their selection processes, for instance, to minimize how long it takes to fill a position. For example, with over 59,000 job applicants per day, the U.S. federal government was taking about 122 days to fill a position. By reviewing each step in its hiring process, it reduced time to hire to about 105 days by, for instance, eliminating the applicant essay.[23] The accompanying HR as a Profit Center feature shows how employers use tests to improve performance.

IMPROVING PERFORMANCE: HR as a Profit Center

Using Tests to Cut Costs and Boost Profits

Financial services firm KeyBank knew it needed a better way to screen and select tellers and call-center employees.[24] The company calculated it cost about $10,000 to select and train an employee, but it was losing

13% of new tellers and call-center employees within the first 90 days. That turnover number dropped to 4% after KeyBank implemented a *virtual job tryout candidate assessment screening tool*. "We calculated a $1.7 million cost savings in teller turnover in one year, simply by making better hiring decisions, reducing training costs and increasing quality of hires," said the firm's human resources director.

Outback Steakhouse Example

Outback Steakhouse has used preemployment tests almost from when the company started. The testing seems successful. While annual turnover rates for hourly employees may reach 200% in the restaurant industry, Outback's turnover ranges from 40% to 60%. Outback wants employees who are highly social, meticulous, sympathetic, and adaptable. They use a personality assessment test to screen out applicants who don't fit the Outback culture. This test is part of a three-step preemployment screening process. Applicants take the test, and managers then compare the candidates' results to the profile for Outback Steakhouse employees. Those who score low on certain traits (like compassion) don't move to the next step. Those who score high are interviewed by two managers, who ask behavioral questions such as "What would you do if a customer asked for a dish we don't have?"[25]

City Garage Example

City Garage, a 200-employee chain of 25 auto service and repair shops in Dallas–Fort Worth, implemented a computerized testing program to improve its operations' performance. The original hiring process consisted of a paper-and-pencil application and one interview, immediately followed by a hire/don't hire decision. The result was high turnover.

City Garage's solution was to purchase the Personality Profile Analysis online test from Thomas International USA. After a quick application and background check, candidates take the 10-minute, 24-question PPA. City Garage staff then enter the answers into the PPA Software system, with results available in less than 2 minutes. These show whether the applicant is high or low in four personality characteristics. It also triggers follow-up questions about potential problem areas. For example, "How did you handle a pushy person in the past?" If candidates answer those questions satisfactorily, they're asked back for all-day interviews, after which hiring decisions are made.

Discussion Question 6-1: Choose a position with which you are familiar, such as a counterperson at a McDonalds restaurant, and describe how you would create a selection process for it similar to those in this feature.

Validity Generalization

Many employers, particularly smaller ones, won't find it cost-effective to conduct validity studies for the selection tools they use. These employers must find tests and other screening tools that have been shown to be valid in other settings (companies), and then bring them in-house in the hopes that they'll be valid there, too.[26]

If the test is valid in one company, to what extent can we generalize those validity findings to our own company? *Validity generalization* "refers to the degree to which evidence of a measure's validity

Many employers administer online employment tests to job candidates.

obtained in one situation can be generalized to another situation without further study."[27] Factors to consider include existing validation evidence regarding using the test for various specific purposes, the similarity of the subjects with those in your organization, and the similarity of the jobs.[28]

Under the Uniform Guidelines, validation of selection procedures is desirable, but "the Uniform Guidelines require users to produce evidence of validity only when adverse impact is shown to exist. If there is no adverse impact, there is no validation requirement under the Guidelines."[29] Conversely, validating a test that suffers from adverse impact may not be enough. Under the Uniform Guidelines, the employer should also find an equally valid *but less adversely impacting* alternative.

KNOW YOUR EMPLOYMENT LAW

Testing and Equal Employment Opportunity

The federal agencies' "Uniform Guidelines" require users to produce evidence of validity when (and only when) adverse impact is shown to exist.[30]

If confronted by a legitimate discrimination charge, the burden of proof rests with the employer. Again, *adverse impact* is a significant discrepancy between rates of rejection of members of the protected groups and others. Once the plaintiff shows that one of your selection procedures has an adverse impact on his or her protected class, you must demonstrate the validity and selection fairness of the allegedly discriminatory test or item. With respect to testing, the EEO laws boil down to two things: (1) You must be able to prove that your tests are related to success or failure on the job, and (2) you must prove that your tests don't unfairly discriminate against either minority or nonminority subgroups.

The employer cannot avoid EEO laws by not using tests. The same burden of proving job relatedness falls on interviews and other techniques (including performance appraisals) that fall on tests.

Test Takers' Individual Rights and Test Security

Test takers have rights to privacy and feedback under the American Psychological Association's (APA) standard for educational and psychological tests; these guide psychologists but are *not* legally enforceable. Test takers have the following rights:

- To the confidentiality of test results.
- To informed consent regarding use of these results.
- To expect that only people qualified to interpret the scores will have access to them, or that sufficient information will accompany the scores to ensure their appropriate interpretation.
- To expect the test is fair. For example, no test taker should have prior access to the questions or answers.[31]

The Federal Privacy Act gives federal employees the right to inspect their personnel files, and limits the disclosure of personnel information without the employee's consent, among other things.[32] Common law provides employees some protection against disclosing information about them to people outside the company. The main application here involves defamation (either libel or slander), but there are privacy issues, too.[33] The bottom line is this:

1. Make sure you understand the need to keep employees' information confidential.
2. Adopt a "need to know" policy. For example, if an employee has been rehabilitated after a period of drug use, the new supervisor may not "need to know."

Diversity Counts: Gender Issues in Testing

Employers using selection tests should know that gender issues may distort results. Some parents and others socialize girls into traditionally female roles and boys into traditionally male roles. For example they may encourage young boys but not girls to make things with tools, or young girls but not boys to take care of their siblings. Such encouragement may in turn translate into differences in how males and females answer items on and score on, say, tests of vocational interests. And these test score differences may then in turn cause counselors and others to nudge men and women into what tend to be largely gender-segregated occupations, for instance male engineers and female nurses.

The bottom line is that employers and others need to interpret the results of various tests (including of interests, and aptitudes) with care. It may often be the case that such results say more about how the person was brought up and socialized than it does about the person's inherent ability to do some task.

FIGURE 6-5 Sample Test

Source: Based on a sample selection test from *The New York Times.*

CHECK YES OR NO	YES	NO
1. You like a lot of excitement in your life.		
2. An employee who takes it easy at work is cheating on the employer.		
3. You are a cautious person.		
4. In the past three years you have found yourself in a shouting match at school or work.		
5. You like to drive fast just for fun.		

Analysis: According to John Kamp, an industrial psychologist, applicants who answered no, yes, yes, no, no to questions 1, 2, 3, 4, and 5 are statistically likely to be absent less often, to have fewer on-the-job injuries, and, if the job involves driving, to have fewer on-the-job driving accidents. Actual scores on the test are based on answers to 130 questions.

How Do Employers Use Tests at Work?

About 41% of companies that the American Management Association surveyed tested applicants for basic skills (defined as the ability to read instructions, write reports, and do arithmetic).[34] About 67% of the respondents required employees to take job skills tests, and 29% required some form of psychological measurement.[35] To see what such tests are like, try the short test in Figure 6-5. It shows how prone you might be to on-the-job accidents.

Tests are not just for lower-level workers. In general, as work demands increase (in terms of skill requirements, training, and pay), employers tend to rely more on selection testing.[36] Employers don't use tests just to find good employees, but also to screen out bad ones.[37] For good reason: In retail, employers apprehended about one out of every 28 workers for stealing.[38]

HR in Practice at the Hotel Paris As she considered what to do next, Lisa Cruz, the Hotel Paris's HR director, knew that employee selection had to play a role. The Hotel Paris currently had an informal screening process in which local hotel managers obtained application forms, interviewed applicants, and checked their references. To see how she improved their system, see the case on page 185.

Types of Tests

3 List and briefly describe the basic categories of selection tests, with examples.

We can conveniently classify tests according to whether they measure cognitive (mental) abilities, motor and physical abilities, personality and interests, or achievement.[39] We'll look at each.

Tests of Cognitive Abilities

Cognitive tests include tests of general reasoning ability (intelligence) and tests of specific mental abilities like memory and inductive reasoning.

INTELLIGENCE TESTS Intelligence (IQ) tests are tests of general intellectual abilities. They measure not a single trait but rather a range of abilities, including memory, vocabulary, verbal fluency, and numerical ability. An adult's IQ score is a "derived" scored; it reflects the extent to which the person is above or below the "average" adult's intelligence score.

Intelligence is often measured with individually administered tests like the Stanford-Binet Test or the Wechsler Test. Employers can administer other IQ tests such as the Wonderlic

FIGURE 6-6 Type of Question Applicant Might Expect on a Test of Mechanical Comprehension

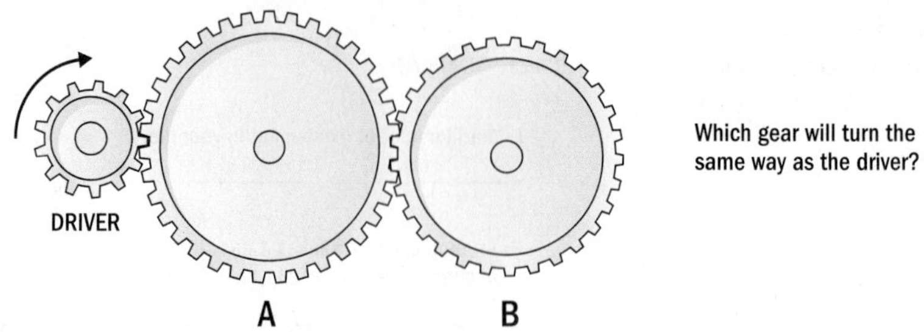

individually or to groups of people. Other intelligence tests include the Kaufman Adolescent and Adult Intelligence Test, and the Comprehensive Test of Nonverbal Intelligence. In a study of firefighter trainees' performance over 23 years, the researchers found that a measure of general intellectual ability and a physical ability assessment was highly predictive of trainee performance.[40]

SPECIFIC COGNITIVE ABILITIES There are also measures of specific mental abilities, such as deductive reasoning, verbal comprehension, memory, and numerical ability.

Psychologists often call such tests *aptitude tests*, since they purport to measure aptitude for the job in question. Consider the Test of Mechanical Comprehension illustrated in Figure 6-6, which tests applicants' understanding of basic mechanical principles. This may reflect a person's aptitude for jobs—like that of machinist or engineer—that require mechanical comprehension. Other tests of mechanical aptitude include the Mechanical Reasoning Test and the SRA Test of Mechanical Aptitude. The revised Minnesota Paper Form Board Test consists of 64 two-dimensional diagrams cut into separate pieces. It provides insights into an applicant's mechanical spatial ability; you'd use it for screening applicants for jobs such as designers or engineers.

Tests of Motor and Physical Abilities

You might also want to measure motor abilities, such as finger dexterity, manual dexterity, and (if hiring pilots) reaction time. Thus, the Crawford Small Parts Dexterity Test measures the speed and accuracy of simple judgment as well as the speed of finger, hand, and arm movements. Other tests include the Stromberg Dexterity Test and the Purdue Peg Board.

Tests of physical abilities may also be required. These include static strength (such as lifting weights), dynamic strength (pull-ups), body coordination (jumping rope), and stamina.[41] Applicants for the U.S. Marines must pass its Initial Strength Test (2 pull-ups, 35 sit-ups, and a 1.5 mile run).

Measuring Personality and Interests

A person's cognitive and physical abilities alone seldom explain his or her job performance. As one consultant put it, most people are hired based on qualifications, but most are fired because of attitude, motivation, and temperament.[42]

Personality tests measure basic aspects of an applicant's personality, such as introversion, stability, and motivation.

Some of these tests are *projective*. The psychologist presents an ambiguous stimulus (like an inkblot or clouded picture) and the person reacts. The person supposedly projects into the ambiguous picture his or her attitudes, such as insecurity. Other projective techniques include Make a Picture Story (MAPS) and the Forer Structured Sentence Completion Test.

Other personality tests are *self-reported*: applicants fill them out themselves, as in Figure 6-7. Thus, the Guilford-Zimmerman survey measures personality traits like emotional stability versus moodiness, and friendliness versus criticalness. Available online, the Myers-Briggs test provides a personality type classification useful for decisions such as career selection and planning.[43]

Industrial psychologists often focus on the "big five" personality dimensions: extraversion, emotional stability/neuroticism, agreeableness, conscientiousness, and openness to experience.[44]

> Neuroticism represents a tendency to exhibit poor emotional adjustment and experience negative effects, such as anxiety, insecurity, and hostility. Extraversion represents a tendency to be sociable, assertive, active, and to experience positive effects, such as energy and zeal. Openness to experience is the disposition to be imaginative, nonconforming, unconventional, and autonomous. Agreeableness is the tendency to be trusting, compliant, caring, and gentle. Conscientiousness is comprised of two related facets: achievement and dependability.[45]

FIGURE 6-7 Sample Online Personality Test Questions

Source: "Selection Assessment Methods: A Guide to Implementing Formal Assessments to Build a High-Quality Workforce" by Elaine Pulakos, from *SHRM Foundation's Effective Practice Guidelines*. Copyright © 2005 by SHRM Foundation. Reprinted with permission, all rights reserved.

HumanMetrics

Jung Typology Test™

After completing the questionnaire, you will obtain:

- Your type formula according to Carl Jung and Isabel Myers-Briggs typology along with the strengths of the preferences
- The description of your personality type
- The list of occupations and educational institutions where you can get relevant degree or training, most suitable for your personality type - **Jung Career Indicator™**

For Organizations and Professionals

Organizations and specialists interested in Jung personality assessments for team building, candidate assessment, leadership, career development, psychographics - visit **HRPersonality™** for practical and validated instruments and professional services.

1. You are almost never late for your appointments
   ○YES ○NO
2. You like to be engaged in an active and fast-paced job
   ○YES ○NO
3. You enjoy having a wide circle of acquaintances
   ○YES ○NO
4. You feel involved when watching TV soaps
   ○YES ○NO
5. You are usually the first to react to a sudden event: the telephone ringing or unexpected question
   ○YES ○NO
6. You are more interested in a general idea than in the details of its realization
   ○YES ○NO
7. You tend to be unbiased even if this might endanger your good relations with people
   ○YES ○NO
8. Strict observance of the established rules is likely to prevent a good outcome
   ○YES ○NO
9. It's difficult to get you excited
   ○YES ○NO
10. It is in your nature to assume responsibility
    ○YES ○NO
11. You often think about humankind and its destiny
    ○YES ○NO
12. You believe the best decision is one that can be easily changed
    ○YES ○NO
13. Objective criticism is always useful in any activity
    ○YES ○NO
14. You prefer to act immediately rather than speculate about various options
    ○YES ○NO
15. You trust reason rather than feelings
    ○YES ○NO
16. You are inclined to rely more on improvisation than on careful planning
    ○YES ○NO
17. You spend your leisure time actively socializing with a group of people, attending parties, shopping, etc.
    ○YES ○NO
18. You usually plan your actions in advance
    ○YES ○NO
19. Your actions are frequently influenced by emotions
    ○YES ○NO
20. You are a person somewhat reserved and distant in communication
    ○YES ○NO
21. You know how to put every minute of your time to good purpose
    ○YES ○NO
22. You readily help people while asking nothing in return
    ○YES ○NO
23. You often contemplate about the complexity of life
    ○YES ○NO
24. After prolonged socializing you feel you need to get away and be alone
    ○YES ○NO
25. You often do jobs in a hurry
    ○YES ○NO
26. You easily see the general principle behind specific occurrences
    ○YES ○NO
27. You frequently and easily express your feelings and emotions
    ○YES ○NO
28. You find it difficult to speak loudly
    ○YES ○NO

DO PERSONALITY TESTS PREDICT PERFORMANCE? Personality test results do often correlate with job performance. For example "in personality research, conscientiousness has been the most consistent and universal predictor of job performance."[46] In another study, neuroticism was negatively related to motivation.[47] Extraversion correlates with success in sales and management jobs.[48] The responsibility, socialization, and self-control scales of the California Psychological Inventory predicted dysfunctional job behaviors among law enforcement officers.[49] Emotional stability, extroversion, and agreeableness predicted whether expatriates would leave their overseas assignments early.[50]

There are four caveats. *First,* projective personality tests are particularly hard to interpret. An expert must analyze the test taker's interpretations and infer from them his or her personality.

Second, personality tests can trigger legal challenges. For example, one court held that the **Minnesota Multiphasic Personality Inventory (MMPI)** is a medical test (because it can screen out applicants with psychological impairments), and so might violate the ADA.[51]

Third, a panel of distinguished industrial psychologists said using *self-report* personality tests in selection "should be reconsidered [due to low validity]."[52] Other experts call such concerns "unfounded."[53]

Fourth, people can and will give fake responses to personality and integrity tests.[54] The bottom line: make sure the personality tests you use predict performance for the jobs you are testing for.

interest inventory
A personal development and selection device that compares the person's current interests with those of others now in various occupations so as to determine the preferred occupation for the individual.

INTEREST INVENTORIES **Interest inventories** compare one's interests with those of people in various occupations. Thus, the Strong-Campbell Interest Inventory provides a report comparing one's interests to those of people already in occupations like accounting or engineering. Someone taking the Self-Directed Search (SDS) (www.self-directed-search.com) uses it to identify likely high-potential occupations. Whether used for career planning or selection, someone will likely do better in occupations in which he or she is interested, and such inventories can predict employee performance and turnover.[55]

Achievement Tests

Achievement tests measure what someone has learned. Most of the tests you take in school are achievement tests. They measure your "job knowledge" in areas like economics, marketing, or human resources. Achievement tests are also popular at work. For example, the Purdue Test for Machinists and Machine Operators tests the job knowledge of experienced machinists with questions like "What is meant by 'tolerance'"? Some achievement tests measure the applicant's abilities; a swimming test is one example.

Improving Performance Through HRIS: Computerization, Online Testing, and Data Analytics

Computerized and/or online testing is increasingly replacing paper-and-pencil tests. For example, Timken Company recently began using online assessment for hourly position applicants in the United States. The online tests cover characteristics such as math skills and attention to detail.[56]

Such tests are also increasingly sophisticated. For example, SHL (www.shl.com/us/) offers online adaptive personality tests. As a candidate answers each question, these tests adapt the next question to the test taker's answers to the previous question. This improves test validity and may reduce cheating. For example, this approach makes it less likely that candidates can share test questions (since each candidate gets what amounts to a custom-made test).[57] Service firms like Unicru process and score online preemployment tests from employers' applicants. Most of the tests we describe are available in computerized form.

The applicant tracking systems we discussed in Chapter 5 often include online prescreening tests.[58] Vendors (as in www.iphonetypingtest.com) are making tests available for applicants to take via their smart phones.[59]

DATA ANALYTICS Data or workforce analysis is revolutionizing the employee selection process.[60] New numbers-crunching data analysis software enables employers to dig through their existing employee data to better identify what types of people succeed or fail, and also lets employers test more candidates more quickly on more aspects of their personal lives. For example, department store chain Bon-Ton Stores Inc. had very high turnover among its cosmetics sales associates. To analyze the problem, management worked with Kenexa, which supplies assessment tools.

They chose 450 current cosmetics associates who filled out anonymous surveys aimed at identifying employee traits. By using data mining techniques to analyze this and other data, the company identified cosmetics associates' traits that correlated with performance and tenure. Bon-Ton had assumed that the best associates were friendly and enthusiastic about cosmetics. However, the best were actually problem solvers. They take information about what the customer wants and needs, and solve the problem.[61] This helped Bon Ton formulate better selection tools.

Similarly, in staffing its call centers, Xerox Corp. long assumed that applicants with call center experience made the best candidates, but instead it turned out to be personality; creative personalities were successful, while inquisitive ones were not. Xerox now relies on its computerized software to hire for its almost 40,000 call center jobs.

Employers using such automated screening systems should remember that they are dealing with human beings. Ensure the rejection standards are valid, and respond quickly to applicants regarding their status.[62]

CROWD SOURCING Google found a way to foster the employee interaction its success depends on by using "crowd sourcing" for hiring decisions.[63]

When a prospective employee applies for a job, his or her information (such as school and previous employers) goes into Google's applicant-tracking system.[64] The ATS then matches the applicant's information with that of current Google employees. When it finds a match, it asks those Google employees to comment on the applicant's suitability for the position. This gives Google recruiters a valuable insight into how the employees actually doing the work think the applicant will do at Google. It also fosters a sense of community and interaction among Google employees.

COMPUTERIZED MULTIMEDIA CANDIDATE ASSESSMENT TOOLS Development Dimensions International developed a computerized multimedia skill test that Ford Motor Company uses for hiring assembly workers. "The company can test everything from how people tighten the bolt, to whether they followed a certain procedure correctly, to using a weight-sensitive mat on the floor that, when stepped on at the wrong time, will mark a candidate down in a safety category."[65]

Work Samples and Simulations

4 Explain how to use two work simulations for selection.

work samples
Actual job tasks used in testing applicants' performance.

With **work samples**, you present examinees with situations representative of the job for which they're applying, and evaluate their responses.[66] Experts consider these (and *simulations,* like the assessment centers we also discuss in this section) to be tests. However, they differ from most tests, because they measure job performance directly. For example, work samples for a cashier may include operating a cash register and counting money.[67]

Using Work Sampling for Employee Selection

work sampling technique
A testing method based on measuring performance on actual basic job tasks.

The **work sampling technique** tries to predict job performance by requiring job candidates to perform one or more samples of the job's tasks.

Work sampling has several advantages. It measures actual job tasks, so it's harder to fake answers. The work sample's content—the actual tasks the person must perform—is not as likely to be unfair to minorities (as might a personnel test that possibly emphasizes middle-class concepts and values).[68] Work sampling doesn't delve into the applicant's personality, so there's almost no chance of applicants viewing it as an invasion of privacy. Designed properly, work samples also exhibit better validity than do other tests designed to predict performance.

BASIC PROCEDURE The basic procedure is to select a sample of several tasks crucial to performing the job, and then to test applicants on them.[69] An observer monitors performance on each task, and indicates on a checklist how well the applicant performs. For example, in creating a work sampling test for maintenance mechanics, experts first listed all possible job tasks (like "install pulleys and belts"). Four crucial tasks were installing pulleys and belts, disassembling and installing a gearbox, installing and aligning a motor, and pressing a bushing into a sprocket. Since mechanics could perform each task in a slightly different way, the experts gave different weights to different approaches.

Figure 6-8 shows one of the steps required for the task *installing pulleys and belts*—"checks key before installing . . ." Here the examinee might choose to check the key against (1) the shaft, (2) the pulley, or (3) neither. The right of the figure lists the weights (scores) reflecting the worth

FIGURE 6-8 Example of a Work Sampling Question
Note: This is one step in installing pulleys and belts.

Checks key before installing against:

—shaft	score 3
—pulley	score 2
—neither	score 1

Note: This is one step in installing pulleys and belts.

of each method. The applicant performs the task, and the observer checks off and scores the approach used.

Situational Judgment Tests

Situational judgment tests are personnel tests "designed to assess an applicant's judgment regarding a situation encountered in the workplace."[70] For example:

> You are a sales associate at Best Buy in Miami, Florida. The store sells electronics, including smart phones. Competition comes from other neighborhood retailers, and from online firms. Many customers who come to your store check the product with you, and then buy it at Amazon for less. As a sales associate, you are responsible for providing exceptional customer service, demonstrating product knowledge, and maximizing sales. You get a weekly salary, with no sales incentive. How would you respond to this situation?
>
> **Situation:**
>
> A customer comes to you with a printout for a Samsung Galaxy phone from Amazon.com, and proceeds to ask you detailed questions about price, battery life, and how to work the phone, while mentioning that "the price at Amazon is $50 less than yours." You have been with this customer for almost an hour now, and there are other customers waiting. You would:
>
> 1. Tell the customer to go buy the phone at Amazon.
> 2. Tell the customer to wait 20 minutes while you take care of another customer.
> 3. Tell the customer to go to the Best Buy store about a 30-minute drive away, where they have a similar phone at a lower price.
> 4. Tell the customer that the local Sprint Mobility dealer has the phone for even less than Amazon.
> 5. Explain the advantages of similar phones you have that may better fulfill the buyer's requirements.
> 6. Ask your supervisor to come over and try to sell the customer on buying the Galaxy from you.

Management Assessment Centers

management assessment center
A simulation in which management candidates are asked to perform realistic tasks in hypothetical situations and are scored on their performance. It usually also involves testing and the use of management games.

A **management assessment center** is a 2- to 3-day simulation in which 10 to 12 candidates perform realistic management tasks (like making presentations) under the observation of experts who appraise each candidate's leadership potential. For example, The Cheesecake Factory created its Professional Assessment and Development Center to help select promotable managers. Candidates undergo 2 days of exercises, simulations, and classroom learning to see if they have the skills for key management positions.[71]

Typical simulated tasks include:

- ***The in-basket.*** The candidate gets reports, memos, notes of incoming phone calls, e-mails, and other materials collected in the actual or computerized in-basket of the simulated job he or she is about to start. The candidate must take appropriate action on each item. Trained evaluators review the candidate's efforts.
- ***Leaderless group discussion.*** Trainers give a leaderless group a discussion question and tell members to arrive at a group decision. They then evaluate each group member's interpersonal skills, acceptance by the group, leadership ability, and individual influence.
- ***Management games.*** Participants solve realistic problems as members of simulated companies competing in a marketplace.
- ***Individual oral presentations.*** Here trainers evaluate each participant's communication skills and persuasiveness.
- ***Testing.*** These may include tests of personality, mental ability, interests, and achievements.
- ***The interview.*** Most require an interview with a trainer to assess interests, past performance, and motivation.

Supervisor recommendations usually play a big role in choosing center participants. Line managers usually act as assessors and arrive at their ratings through consensus.[72] Assessment centers are expensive to develop, take longer than conventional tests, require managers acting as assessors, and often require psychologists. However, studies suggest they are worth it.[73]

IMPROVING PERFORMANCE: HR Practices Around the Globe

Testing in China

In the United States, testing for employee selection became popular after World War I, when the U.S. Army, to improve its selection processes, asked psychologists to develop tests for incoming army recruits. However, personnel testing goes back a bit further in China—about 3,000 years, to the beginnings of the Imperial Civil Service examination system.[74] By 1100 BC, the government was testing civil service candidates on topics like music, writing, and arithmetic.[75] By 206 BC they were using written test batteries covering law, agriculture, and taxation. By around 600 AD a national testing system was in place requiring candidates to memorize Confucian classics and compose poetry, among other tasks. By the 1300s, candidates receiving the highest marks went first to their provincial capital for further tests and then for more tests to the national capital. By 1832, Western companies, such as the British East India Company, were copying the system.

After 1949, the Chinese Communist Party adopted many Soviet Union management practices. The Soviet's Marxist philosophy emphasized one's social context rather than individual traits, so for a time testing for individual differences in China ceased to exist; China Communist Party committees selected civil servants using informal noncompetitive standards. As China entered a period of new openness in the 1970s, it reformed its civil service selection procedures. Soon, testing was reintroduced. The first book on psychological testing in China appeared in 1986.[76] Today, many enterprises in China use assessment centers to select employees. Civil service selection depends on factors including administrative ability, public speaking competitions, and psychological testing. Private employers use assessment-center tools including personnel tests, in-basket tests, and leaderless group discussions.

China's experience shows that the idea of using rigorous testing and selection tools to choose the people who will perform best in particular jobs is a global phenomenon. It also shows that China has a modern system of employee selection, although it really began 3,000 years ago.

Discussion Question 6-2: In what ways do you think the questions you put on a selection test in China might differ from those on a test in the USA, and why?

Situational Testing and Video-Based Situational Testing

situational test
A test that requires examinees to respond to situations representative of the job.

video-based simulation
A situational test in which examinees respond to video simulations of realistic job situations.

Situational tests require examinees to respond to situations representative of the job. Work sampling (discussed earlier) and some assessment center tasks (such as in-baskets) fall in this category. So do video-based tests and miniature job training (described next), and the situational interviews we address in Chapter 7.[77]

The **video-based simulation** presents the candidate with several online or computer video situations, each followed by one or more multiple-choice questions. For example, the scenario might depict an employee handling a situation on the job. At a critical moment, the scenario ends and the video asks the candidate to choose from several courses of action. For example:

(*A manager is upset about the condition of the department and takes it out on one of the department's employees.*)

MANAGER: Well, I'm glad you're here.

ASSOCIATE: Why?

MANAGER: I take a day off and come back to find the department in a mess. You should know better.

ASSOCIATE: But I didn't work late last night.

MANAGER: But there have been plenty of times before when you've left this department in a mess.

(*The scenario stops here.*)

If you were this associate, what would you do?

a. Let the other associates responsible for the mess know that you took the heat.
b. Straighten up the department, and try to reason with the manager later.
c. Suggest to the manager that he talk to the other associates who made the mess.
d. Take it up with the manager's boss.[78]

The Miniature Job Training and Evaluation Approach

miniature job training and evaluation
Training candidates to perform several of the job's tasks, and then evaluating the candidates' performance prior to hire.

Miniature job training and evaluation means training candidates to perform several of the job's tasks, and then evaluating the candidates' performance prior to hire. The approach assumes that

Issei Kato/Reuters Pictures - Americas

Employers such as Honda first train and then have applicants perform several of the job tasks, and then evaluate the candidates before hiring them.

a person who demonstrates that he or she can learn and perform the sample of tasks will be able to learn and perform the job itself. Like work sampling, *miniature job training and evaluation* tests applicants with actual samples of the job, so it's inherently content relevant and valid. The problem is the expense.

HONDA EXAMPLE Building a new plant in Alabama, Honda had to hire thousands of new employees. Its recruiting ad sought applicants for a free training program Honda was offering as a precondition for applying for jobs. Eighteen thousand people applied.

First Honda and the Alabama state employment agency screened the applicants by eliminating those who lacked the required education or experience. They then gave preference to applicants near the plant. About 340 applicants per 6-week session received special training at a new facility, two evenings a week. This included classroom instruction, videos of Honda employees in action, and actually practicing particular jobs. Some candidates who watched the videos dropped out after seeing the work's pace.

During training, Alabama state agency assessors scrutinized and rated the trainees. They then invited those who graduated to apply for plant jobs. Honda employees (from HR and departmental representatives) then interviewed the candidates, reviewed their training records, and decided who to hire. New employees then took a one-time drug test, but no other paper-and-pencil tests or credentials were required. New hires received a 3-day orientation. Then, assistant managers in each department coordinated their day-to-day training.[79]

Realistic Job Previews

Sometimes, a dose of realism makes the best screening tool. For example, when Walmart began explicitly explaining and asking about work schedules and work preferences, turnover improved.[80] In general, applicants who receive realistic job previews are more likely to turn down job offers, but their employers are more likely to have less turnover.[81]

Choosing a Selection Method

The employer needs to consider several things before choosing to use a particular selection tool (or tools). These include the tool's reliability and validity, its return on investment (in terms of utility analysis), applicant reactions, usability, adverse impact, and the tool's *selection ratio* (does it screen out, as it should, a high percentage of applicants or admit virtually all?).[82] Table 6-1 summarizes the validity, potential adverse impact, and cost of several popular assessment methods. The HR Tools feature shows how line managers may devise their own tests.

TABLE 6-1 Evaluation of Selected Assessment Methods

Assessment Method	Validity	Adverse Impact	Costs (Develop/ Administer)
Cognitive ability tests	High	High (against minorities)	Low/low
Job knowledge test	High	High (against minorities)	Low/low
Personality tests	Low to moderate	Low	Low/low
Integrity tests	Moderate to high	Low	Low/low
Structured interviews	High	Low	High/high
Situational judgment tests	Moderate	Moderate (against minorities)	High/low
Work samples	High	Low	High/high
Assessment centers	Moderate to high	Low to moderate, depending on exercise	High/high
Physical ability tests	Moderate to high	High (against females and older workers)	High/high

Source: Elaine Pulakos, *Selection Assessment Methods*, SHRM Foundation, 2005, p. 17. Reprinted by permission of Society for Human Resource Management via Copyright Clearance Center.

IMPROVING PERFORMANCE: HR Tools for Line Managers and Entrepreneurs

Employee Testing and Selection

One of the ironies of being a line manager in even the largest of companies is that, when it comes to screening employees, you're often on your own. Some large firms' HR departments may work with the hiring manager to design and administer the sorts of screening tools we discussed in this chapter. But the fact is that in many of these firms, the HR departments do little more than some preliminary prescreening (for instance, arithmetic tests for clerical applicants), and then follow up with background checks and drug and physical exams.

What should you do if you are, say, a marketing manager, and want to screen some of your job applicants more formally? It is possible to devise your own test battery, but caution is required. Purchasing and then using packaged intelligence tests or psychological tests or even tests of marketing ability could be a problem. Doing so may violate company policy, raise questions of validity, and even expose your employer to EEO liability if problems arise.

A preferred approach is to devise and use screening tools, the face validity of which is obvious. The work sampling test we discussed is one example. It's not unreasonable, for instance, for the marketing manager to ask an advertising applicant to spend half an hour designing an ad, or to ask a marketing research applicant to quickly outline a marketing research program for a hypothetical product. Similarly, a production manager might reasonably ask an inventory control applicant to spend a few minutes using a standard inventory control model to solve an inventory problem.

For small business owners, some tests' ease of use makes them particularly good for small firms. One is the *Wonderlic Personnel Test*; it measures general mental ability in about 15 minutes. The tester reads the instructions, and then keeps time as the candidate works through the 50 short problems on the two inside sheets. The tester scores the test by totaling the number of correct answers. Comparing the person's score with the minimum scores recommended for various occupations shows whether the person achieved the minimally acceptable score for the type of job in question. The *Predictive Index* measures work-related personality traits on a two-sided sheet. For example, there is the "social interest" pattern, for a person who is generally unselfish, congenial, and unassuming. This person would be a good personnel interviewer, for instance. A template makes scoring simple.

As many managers know, for some jobs past performance is a more useful predictor of performance than are formal selection tests. For example, one study of prospective NFL players concluded that collegiate performance was a significantly better predictor of NFL performance than were physical ability tests.[83]

Discussion Question 6-3: You own a small ladies' dress shop in a mall and want to hire a salesperson. Create a test for doing so.

Background Investigations and Other Selection Methods

5 Describe four ways to improve an employer's background checking process.

Testing is only part of an employer's selection process. Other tools may include background investigations and reference checks, preemployment information services, honesty testing, and substance abuse screening.

Why Perform Background Investigations and Reference Checks?

A few years ago, the newly hired CEO of Yahoo stepped down when critics discovered that his résumé contained incorrect college degree information.[84] One of the easiest ways to avoid such hiring mistakes is to check the candidate's background thoroughly. Doing so is inexpensive and (if done right) useful. There's usually no reason why even supervisors in large companies can't check the references of someone they're about to hire, as long as they know the rules.

Most employers check and verify the job applicant's background information and references. In one survey of about 700 human resource managers, 87% said they conduct reference checks, 69% conduct background employment checks, 61% check employee criminal records, 56% check employees' driving records, and 35% sometimes or always check credit.[85] Commonly verified data include legal eligibility for employment (in compliance with immigration laws), dates of prior employment, military service (including discharge status), education, identification (including date of birth and address to confirm identity), county criminal records (current residence, last residence), motor vehicle record, credit, licensing verification, Social Security number, and reference checks.[86] Some employers are checking executive candidates' civil litigation records, with the candidate's prior approval.[87] Massachusetts and Hawaii prohibit private employers from asking about criminal records on initial written applications.[88]

WHY CHECK? There are two main reasons to check backgrounds—to verify the applicant's information (name and so forth) and to uncover damaging information.[89] Lying on one's application isn't unusual. A survey found that 23% of 7,000 executive résumés contained exaggerated or false information.[90]

Even relatively sophisticated companies fall prey to criminal employees, in part because they haven't conducted proper background checks. In Chicago, a pharmaceutical firm discovered it had hired gang members in mail delivery and computer repair. The crooks were stealing computer parts, and using the mail department to ship them to their own nearby computer store.[91]

How deeply you search depends on the position. For example, a credit check is more important for hiring an accountant than a groundskeeper. In any case, also periodically check the credit ratings of employees (like cashiers) who have easy access to company assets, and the driving records of employees who use company cars.

EFFECTIVENESS Most managers don't view references as very useful. Few employers will talk freely about former employees. For example, in one poll, the Society for Human Resource Management (SHRM) found that 98% of 433 responding members said their organizations would verify dates of employment for current or former employees. However, 68% said they wouldn't discuss work performance; 82% said they wouldn't discuss character or personality; and 87% said they wouldn't disclose a disciplinary action.[92]

Many supervisors don't want to damage a former employee's chances for a job; others might prefer giving an incompetent employee good reviews if it will get rid of him or her.

Another reason is legal. Employers providing references generally can't be successfully sued for defamation unless the employee can show "malice"—that is, ill will, culpable recklessness, or disregard of the employee's rights.[93] But the managers and companies providing the references understandably still don't want the grief. The following feature explains this.

KNOW YOUR EMPLOYMENT LAW

Giving References

Federal laws that affect references include the Privacy Act of 1974, the Fair Credit Reporting Act of 1970, the Family Education Rights and Privacy Act of 1974 (and Buckley Amendment of 1974), and the Freedom of Information Act of 1966. They give individuals in general and students (the Buckley Amendment) the right to know the nature and substance of information in their credit files and files with government agencies, and (under the Privacy Act) to review records pertaining to them from any private business that contracts with a federal agency. The person may thus see your comments. If you seem to have given the bad reference to retaliate for the filing of an EEOC claim, you might be sued.[94]

Beyond that, common law (and in particular the tort of defamation) applies to any information you supply. Communication is defamatory if it is false and tends to harm the reputation of another by lowering the person in the estimation of the community or by deterring other persons from dealing with him or her.

Truth is not always a defense. In some states, employees can sue employers for disclosing to a large number of people true but embarrassing private facts about the employee. One case involved a supervisor shouting that the employee's wife had been having sexual relations with certain people. The jury found the employer liable for invasion of the couple's privacy and for the intentional infliction of emotional distress.[95]

The net result is that most employers and managers restrict who can give references, and what they can say. As a rule, only authorized managers should provide information. Other suggestions include "Don't volunteer information," "Avoid vague statements," and "Do not answer trap questions such as, 'Would you rehire this person?'" In practice, many firms have a policy of not providing any information about former employees except for their dates of employment, last salary, and position titles.[96]

(However, *not* disclosing relevant information can be dangerous, too. In one Florida case, a company fired an employee for allegedly bringing a handgun to work. After his next employer fired him for absenteeism, he returned to that company and shot several employees. The injured parties and their relatives sued the previous employer, who had provided the employee with a clean letter of recommendation allegedly because that first employer didn't want to anger the employee over his firing.)

The person alleging defamation has various legal remedies, including suing the source of the reference for defamation.[97] In one case, a court awarded a man $56,000 after a company turned him down for a job because, among other things, the former employer called him a "character." There are companies that, for a small fee, will call former employers on behalf of employees who believe they're getting bad references.[98] One supervisor hired BadReferences.com. This firm uses trained court reporters to record its investigations. It found that someone at the supervisor's previous company suggested that the employee was "a little too obsessive . . . and not comfortable with taking risks, or making big decisions." The former employee sued, demanding an end to defamation and $45,000 in compensation.[99]

How to Check a Candidate's Background

There are several things managers and employers can do to get better information.

Most employers at least try to verify an applicant's current (or former) position and salary with his or her current (or former) employer by phone (assuming you cleared doing so with the candidate). Others call the applicant's current and previous supervisors to try to discover more about the person's motivation, technical competence, and ability to work with others (although again, many employers have policies against providing such information). Figure 6-9 shows one form for phone references. Some employers get background reports from commercial credit rating companies for information about credit standing, indebtedness, reputation, character, and lifestyle. (Others check social network sites, as we will see in a moment.)

Automated online reference checking can improve the results. With a system such as pre-hire 360 (http://www.skillsurvey.com/pre-hire-360), the hiring employer inputs the applicant's name and e-mail address. Then the person's preselected references rate the applicant's skills anonymously, using a survey. The system then compiles these references into a report for the employer.[100]

Social Media and HR

More employers are Googling applicants or checking social networking sites. After doing so, some recruiters found that 31% of applicants had lied about their qualifications and 19% had posted information about their drinking or drug use.[101] One employer found that a candidate had described his interests on Facebook.com as smoking pot and shooting people. The student may have been kidding, but didn't get the job.[102] An article called "References You Can't Control" notes that you can use social networking sites to identify an applicant's former colleagues, and thus contact them.[103] And while applicants usually don't list race, age, disability or ethnic origin on their résumés, their Facebook pages may reveal such information, setting the stage for possible EEOC claims. Or, an over-eager supervisor might conduct his or her own Facebook page "background check."[104]

Googling is probably safe enough, but checking social networking sites raises legal issues. For example, it's probably best to get the candidate's prior approval for social networking searches.[105] And do not use a pretext or fabricate an identity.[106] A new Maryland law restricts employer demands for applicant usernames and passwords.[107] Other states will undoubtedly follow.

The solution isn't necessarily to prohibit the legitimate use of social media-based applicant and employee information (unless perusing such information is illegal under the law, as in Maryland). Instead, the employer should formulate and follow intelligent social media staffing policies and procedures. For example, inform employees and prospective employees ahead of time regarding what information the employer plans to review. Assign one or two specially trained human resource professionals to search social media sites. Prohibit unauthorized employees (such as the prospective supervisor) from accessing such information. Also, treat everyone equitably: don't permit accessing information on, say, LinkedIn job profiles unless all applicants have job profiles posted.[108]

Using Preemployment Information Services

It is easy to have employment screening services check out applicants. Major background checking providers include ADP, HireRight, LEXIS-NEXIS screening solutions, and TalentWise

FIGURE 6-9 Reference Checking Form

Source: Reprinted with permission from the Society for Human Resource Management.

(Verify that the applicant has provided permission before conducting reference checks.)

Candidate Name ______

Reference Name ______

Company Name ______

Dates of Employment
From: ______ To: ______

Position(s) Held ______

Salary History ______

Reason for Leaving ______

Explain the reason for your call and verify the above information with the supervisor (including the reason for leaving)

1. Please describe the type of work for which the candidate was responsible.

2. How would you describe the applicant's relationships with coworkers, subordinates (if applicable), and with superiors?

3. Did the candidate have a positive or negative work attitude? Please elaborate.

4. How would you describe the quantity and quality of output generated by the former employee?

5. What were his/her strengths on the job?

6. What were his/her weaknesses on the job?

7. What is your overall assessment of the candidate?

8. Would you recommend him/her for this position? Why or why not?

9. Would this individual be eligible for rehire? Why or why not?

Other comments?

solutions.[109] They use databases to access information about matters such as workers' compensation, credit histories, and conviction and driving records. For example, retail employers use First Advantage Corporation's Esteem Database to see if their job candidates have previously been involved in suspected retail thefts.[110] Another firm advertises that for less than $50 it will do a criminal history report, motor vehicle/driver's record report, and (after the person is hired) a workers' compensation claims report history, plus confirm identity, name, and Social Security number. There are thousands of databases, including sex offender registries and criminal and educational histories.

There are three reasons to use caution with such services.[111] First, EEO laws kick in. For example, the ADA prohibits employers from making preemployment inquiries into a disability, so asking about a candidate's previous workers' compensation claims before offering the person a job is usually unlawful. So be careful not to use the product of an unreasonable investigation.

Second, various federal and state laws govern how employers acquire and use applicants' and employees' background information. At the federal level, the Fair Credit Reporting Act is the main directive. In addition, at least 21 states impose their own requirements. Authorizing background reports while complying with these laws requires four steps, as follows:

Step 1: **Disclosure and authorization.** Before requesting reports, the employer must disclose to the applicant or employee that a report will be requested and that the employee/applicant may receive a copy. (Do this on the application form.)

Step 2: **Certification.** The employer must certify to the reporting agency that the employer will comply with the federal and state legal requirements—for example, that the employer obtained written consent from the employee/applicant.

Step 3: **Providing copies of reports.** Under federal law, the employer must provide copies of the report to the applicant or employee if adverse action (such as withdrawing a job offer) is contemplated.[112]

Step 4: **Notice after adverse action.** After the employer provides the employee or applicant with copies of the consumer and investigative reports and a "reasonable period" has elapsed, the employer may take an adverse action (such as withdrawing an offer). If the employer anticipates taking an adverse action, the employee/applicant must get an adverse action notice. This contains information such as the name of the consumer reporting agency. The employee/applicant then has various remedies under the laws.[113]

Third, the criminal background information may be flawed. Many return "possible matches" for the wrong person (who happens to be a criminal).[114] One such firm recently paid a $2.6 million penalty after the Federal Trade Commission sued it for such erroneous reporting.[115] The HR Tools feature offers some guidelines.

IMPROVING PERFORMANCE: HR Tools for Line Managers and Entrepreneurs

Making the Background Check More Valuable

Hiring a flawed candidate is expensive. At best you may have to write off the cost of the search and start again. At worst, the person could seriously damage your company. There are steps one can take to improve the usefulness of the background information being sought. Specifically:

- Include on the application form a statement for applicants to sign explicitly authorizing a background check, such as:

  > I hereby certify that the facts set forth in the above employment application are true and complete to the best of my knowledge. I understand that falsified statements or misrepresentation of information on this application or omission of any information sought may be cause for dismissal, if employed, or may lead to refusal to make an offer and/or to withdrawal of an offer. I also authorize investigation of credit, employment record, driving record, and, once a job offer is made or during employment, workers' compensation background if required.

- Telephone references tend to produce more candid assessments, so it's probably best to rely on telephone references. Use a form, such as Figure 6-9. Remember that you can get relatively accurate information regarding dates of employment, eligibility for rehire, and job qualifications. It's more difficult to get other background information (such as reasons for leaving a previous job).[116]

- Persistence and attentiveness to potential red flags improves results. For example, if the former employer hesitates or seems to qualify his or her answer, don't go on to the next question. Try to unearth what the applicant did to make the former employer pause. If he says, "Joe requires some special care," say, "Special care?"
- Compare the application to the résumé; people tend to be more imaginative on their résumés than on their application forms, where they must certify the information.
- Try to ask open-ended questions (such as, "How much structure does the applicant need in his/her work?") in order to get the references to talk more about the candidate.[117] But in asking for information:
  Only ask for and obtain information that you're going to use.
  Remember that using arrest information is highly suspect.
  Use information that is specific and job related.
  Keep information confidential.
- Ask the references supplied by the applicant to suggest other references. You might ask each of the applicant's references, "Could you give me the name of another person who might be familiar with the applicant's performance?" Then you begin getting information from references that may be more objective, because they did not come directly from the applicant.

Discussion Question 6-4: Evaluate Figure 6-9; what other questions would you ask, and why?

The Polygraph and Honesty Testing

The polygraph is a device that measures physiological changes like increased perspiration. The assumption is that such changes reflect changes in emotional state that accompany lying.

Complaints about offensiveness plus grave doubts about the polygraph's accuracy culminated in the Employee Polygraph Protection Act of 1988.[118] With a few exceptions, the law prohibits employers from conducting polygraph examinations of all job applicants and most employees. (Also prohibited are other mechanical or electrical devices that attempt to measure honesty or dishonesty, including voice stress analyzers.) Federal laws don't prohibit paper-and-pencil tests or chemical testing, as for drugs.

Local, state, and federal government employers (including the FBI) can use polygraphs for selection screening and other purposes, but state laws restrict many local and state governments. Private employers can use polygraph testing, but only under strictly limited circumstances.[119] They include those with

- National defense or security contracts
- Nuclear power-related contracts with the Department of Energy
- Access to highly classified information
- Counterintelligence-related contracts with the FBI or Department of Justice
- Private businesses (1) hiring private security personnel, (2) hiring persons with access to drugs, or (3) doing ongoing investigations involving economic loss or injury to an employer's business, such as a theft

However, even for ongoing investigations of theft, the law restricts employers' rights. To administer a polygraph test for an ongoing investigation, an employer must meet four standards:

1. It must show that it suffered an economic loss or injury.
2. It must show that the employee in question had access to the property.
3. It must have a reasonable suspicion before asking the employee to take the polygraph.
4. The person to be tested must receive the details of the investigation before the test, as well as the polygraph questions to be asked.

PAPER-AND-PENCIL HONESTY TESTS The Polygraph Protection Act triggered a burgeoning market for paper-and-pencil (or computerized or online) honesty tests. These are psychological tests designed to predict job applicants' proneness to dishonesty and other forms of counterproductivity.[120] Most measure attitudes regarding things like tolerance of others who steal, and admission of theft-related activities. Tests include the Phase II profile. London House, Inc., and Stanton Corporation publish similar tests.[121]

Psychologists were initially skeptical about paper-and-pencil honesty tests, but studies support these tests' validity.[122] One study involved 111 employees hired by a convenience store chain to work at store or gas station counters.[123] The firm estimated that "shrinkage" equaled 3% of sales, and believed that internal theft accounted for much of this. Scores on an honesty test successfully predicted theft here, as measured by termination for theft. At Hospital Management Corp., an integrity test is the first step in the hiring process, and those who fail go no further. It instituted the test after determining that such tests did weed out applicants with undesirable behaviors. For example, after several months using the test, workers compensation claims dropped among new hires.[124] The following HR Tools feature lists other techniques.

IMPROVING PERFORMANCE: HR Tools for Line Managers and Entrepreneurs

Testing for Honesty

Screening for dishonesty can obviously save employers money, and with or without testing, there's a lot a manager or employer can do to screen out dishonest applicants or employees. Specifically:

- **Ask blunt questions.**[125] Says one expert, there is nothing wrong with asking the applicant direct questions, such as, "Have you ever stolen anything from an employer?" "Have you recently held jobs other than those listed on your application?" "Is any information on your application misrepresented or falsified?"
- **Listen, rather than talk.** You want to learn as much about the person as possible.
- **Do a credit check.** Include a clause in your application giving you the right to conduct background checks, including credit checks and motor vehicle reports.
- **Check all employment and personal references.**
- **Use paper-and-pencil honesty tests and psychological tests.**
- **Test for drugs.** Devise a drug-testing program and give each applicant a copy of the policy.
- **Establish a search-and-seizure policy and conduct searches.** Give each applicant a copy of the policy and require each to return a signed copy. The policy should state, "All lockers, desks, and similar property remain the property of the company and may be inspected routinely."

Discussion Question 6-5: What other blunt questions do you think would be appropriate?

Honesty testing requires caution. Having just taken and "failed" what is fairly obviously an "honesty test," the candidate may leave the premises feeling mistreated. Some "honesty" questions also pose invasion-of-privacy issues. And some states such as Massachusetts and Rhode Island limit paper-and-pencil honesty testing.

Graphology

Graphology is the use of handwriting analysis to determine the writer's basic personality traits. It thus has some resemblance to projective personality tests, although graphology's validity is highly suspect. The handwriting analyst studies an applicant's handwriting and signature to discover the person's needs, desires, and psychological makeup. One graphologist says the writing in Figure 6-10 exemplifies "independence" and "isolation."

Virtually all scientific studies suggest graphology is not valid, or that when graphologists do accurately size up candidates, it's because they are also privy to other background information. Yet some firms swear by it.[126] One 325-employee firm uses profiles based on handwriting samples to design follow-up interviews.[127] Most experts shun it.

"Human Lie Detectors"

Some employers are using so-called "human lie detectors," experts who may (or may not) be able to identify lying just by watching candidates.[128] One Wall Street firm uses a former FBI agent. He sits in on interviews and watches for signs of candidate deceptiveness. Signs include pupils changing size (fear), irregular breathing (nervousness), crossing legs ("liars distance themselves from an untruth"), and quick verbal responses (scripted statements).

Physical Exams

Once the employer extends the person a job offer, a medical exam is often the next step in selection (although it may also occur after the new employee starts work).

There are several reasons for preemployment medical exams: to verify that the applicant meets the job's physical requirements, to discover any medical limitations you should consider

FIGURE 6-10 The Uptight Personality

Source: www.graphicinsight.co.za/writingsamples.htm#The%20Uptight%20Personality%2, accessed March 28, 2009. Used with permission of www.graphicinsight.co.za.

The Uptight Personality

From The Graphology Review No 17

The following sample shows several uptight tendencies. We see independence, a critical, rather severe attitude and an economy of feeling. Notice too, how the words are separated by large spaces indicating that the writer has a feeling of personal isolation.

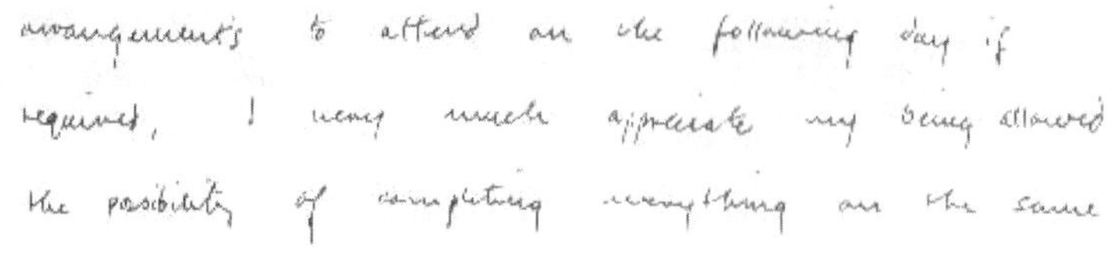

arrangements to attend on the following day if
required, I very much appreciate my being allowed
the possibility of completing everything on the same

Here are some of the handwriting indicators for the uptight personality as discussed in The Graphology Review No 17;

- Small to middle size handwriting
- Upright slant
- Narrow letters
- Angular connections
- Economical use of space on the page
- Although the words here are not extremely cramped they are certainly not expansive. The spacing between the letters is very economical.

in placement, and to establish a baseline for future workers compensation claims. Exams can also reduce absenteeism and accidents and detect communicable diseases.

Under the Americans with Disabilities Act, an employer cannot reject someone with a disability if he or she is otherwise qualified and can perform the essential job functions with reasonable accommodation. Recall that the ADA permits a medical exam during the period between the job offer and commencement of work if such exams are standard practice for all applicants for that job category.[129]

Substance Abuse Screening

Many employers conduct drug screenings. The most common practice is to test candidates just before they're formally hired. Many also test current employees when there is reason to believe they've been using drugs—after a work accident, or with obvious behavioral symptoms such as chronic lateness. Some firms routinely administer drug tests on a random or periodic basis, while others require drug tests when they transfer or promote employees to new positions.[130] Employers may use urine testing to test for illicit drugs, breath alcohol tests to determine amount of alcohol in the blood, blood tests to measure alcohol or drugs in the blood at the time of the test, hair analyses to reveal drug history, saliva tests for substances such as marijuana and cocaine, and skin patches to determine drug use.[131]

SOME PRACTICAL CONSIDERATIONS Drug testing, while ubiquitous, is neither as simple nor effective as it might appear. First, no drug test is foolproof. Some urine sample tests can't distinguish between legal and illegal substances; for example, Advil can produce positive results for marijuana. Furthermore, "there is a swarm of products that promise to help employees (both male and female) beat drug tests."[132] (Employers should view the presence of adulterants in a sample as a positive test.) One alternative, hair follicle testing, requires a small sample of hair, which the lab analyzes.[133] But here, too, classified ads advertise chemicals to rub on the scalp to fool the test.

There's also the question of what is the point.[134] Unlike roadside breathalyzers for DUI drivers, tests for drugs only show whether drug residues are present; they do not indicate impairment (or, for that matter, habituation or addiction).[135] Some therefore argue that testing is not justifiable on the grounds of boosting workplace safety.[136] Many feel the testing procedures themselves are degrading and intrusive. Many employers reasonably counter that they don't want drug-prone employees on their premises. Employers should choose the lab they engage to do the testing carefully.

KNOW YOUR EMPLOYMENT LAW

Drug Testing

Drug testing raises legal issues.[137] As one attorney writes, "It is not uncommon for employees to claim that drug tests violate their rights to privacy under common law or, in some states, a state statutory or constitutional provision."[138] Hair follicle testing is less intrusive than urinalysis but can actually produce more personal information: A 3-inch hair segment will record 6 months of drug use.

Several federal laws affect workplace drug testing. Under the Americans with Disabilities Act, a court would probably consider a former drug user (who no longer uses illegal drugs and has successfully completed or is participating in a rehabilitation program) as a qualified applicant with a disability.[139] Under the Drug Free Workplace Act of 1988, federal contractors must maintain a workplace free from illegal drugs. While this doesn't require contractors to conduct drug testing or rehabilitate affected employees, many do. Under the U.S. Department of Transportation workplace regulations, firms with over 50 eligible employees in transportation industries must conduct alcohol testing on workers with sensitive or safety-related jobs. These include mass transit workers, air traffic controllers, train crews, and school bus drivers.[140] Other laws, including the Federal Rehabilitation Act of 1973 and various state laws, protect rehabilitating drug users or those who have a physical or mental addiction.

What should an employer do when a job candidate tests positive? Most companies will not hire such candidates, and a few will immediately fire current employees who test positive. For example, 120 of the 123 companies responding to the question, "If test results are positive, what action do you take?" indicated that applicants testing positive are not hired. Current employees have more legal recourse; employers must tell them the reason for dismissal if the reason is a positive drug test.[141]

Particularly where sensitive jobs are concerned, courts tend to side with employers. In one case, a U.S. Court of Appeals ruled that Exxon acted properly in firing a truck driver who failed a drug test. Exxon requires random testing of employees in safety-sensitive jobs. The employee drove a tractor-trailer carrying 12,000 gallons of flammable motor fuel and tested positive for cocaine. The union representing the employee challenged the firing. An arbitrator reduced the penalty to a 2-month suspension, but the appeals court ruled that the employer acted properly in firing the truck driver.[142]

Complying with Immigration Law

Employees hired in the United States must prove they are eligible to work here. The requirement to verify eligibility does not provide any basis to reject an applicant just because he or she is a foreigner, not a U.S. citizen, or an alien residing in the United States, as long as that person can prove his or her identity and employment eligibility. To comply with this law, employers should follow procedures outlined in the so-called I-9 Employment Eligibility Verification form.[143] More employers are using the federal government's voluntary electronic employment verification program, E-Verify.[144] Federal contractors must use it.[145] Many employers now use automated I-9 verification systems with drop-down menus to electronically compile and submit applicants' I-9 data.[146] The latest I-9 forms contain a prominent "antidiscrimination notice."[147]

PROOF OF ELIGIBILITY Applicants can prove their eligibility for employment in two ways. One is to show a document (such as a U.S. passport or alien registration card with photograph) that proves both identity and employment eligibility. The other is to show a document that proves the person's identity, along with a second document showing his or her employment eligibility, such as a work permit.[148] In any case, it's always advisable to get two forms of proof of identity.

Identity theft—undocumented workers stealing and using an authorized worker's identity—is a problem even with E-Verify.[149] The federal government is tightening restrictions on hiring undocumented workers. Realizing that many documents are fakes, the government is putting the onus on employers to make sure whom they're hiring. The Department of Homeland Security files criminal charges against suspected employer violators.[150]

Employers can protect themselves in several ways. First, use E-Verify. Then, systematic preemployment checking should include employment verification, criminal record checks, drug screens, and reference checks. You can verify Social Security numbers by calling the Social Security Administration. Employers can avoid accusations of discrimination by verifying the documents of all applicants, not just those they may think suspicious.[151]

Review

MyManagementLab Go to **mymanagementlab.com** to complete the problems marked with this icon. 

Chapter Section Summaries

1. Careful **employee selection is important** for several reasons. Your own performance always depends on your subordinates; it is costly to recruit and hire employees; and mismanaging the hiring process has various legal implications including equal employment, negligent hiring, and defamation.
2. Whether you are administering tests or making decisions based on test results, managers need to understand several **basic testing concepts**. Reliability refers to a test's consistency, while validity tells you whether the test is measuring what you think it's supposed to be measuring. Criterion validity means demonstrating that those who do well on the test also do well on the job while content validity means showing that the test constitutes a fair sample of the job's content. Validating a test involves analyzing the job, choosing the tests, administering the test, relating your test scores and criteria, and cross-validating and revalidating. Test takers have rights to privacy and feedback as well as to confidentiality.
3. Whether administered via paper and pencil, by computer, or online, we discussed several main **types of tests**. Tests of cognitive abilities measure things like reasoning ability and include intelligence tests and tests of specific cognitive abilities such as mechanical comprehension. There are also tests of motor and physical abilities, and measures of personality and interests. With respect to personality, psychologists often focus on the "big five" personality dimensions: extroversion, emotional stability/neuroticism, agreeableness, conscientiousness, and openness to experience. Achievement tests measure what someone has learned.
4. With **work samples and simulations**, you present examinees with situations representative of the jobs for which they are applying. One example is the management assessment center, a 2- to 3-day simulation in which 10 to 12 candidates perform realistic management tasks under the observation of experts who appraise each candidate's leadership potential. Video-based situational testing and the miniature job training and evaluation approach are two other examples.
5. Testing is only part of an employer's selection process; you also want to conduct **background investigations and other selection procedures**.
   - The main point of doing a background check is to verify the applicant's information and to uncover potentially damaging information. However, care must be taken, particularly when giving a reference, that the employee not be defamed and that his or her privacy rights are maintained.
   - Given former employers' reluctance to provide a comprehensive report, those checking references need to do several things. Make sure the applicant explicitly authorizes a background check, use a checklist or form for obtaining telephone references, and be persistent and attentive to potential red flags.
   - Given the growing popularity of computerized employment background databases, many or most employers use preemployment information services to obtain background information.
   - For many types of jobs, honesty testing is essential and paper-and-pencil tests have proven useful.
   - Most employers also require that new hires, before actually coming on board, take physical exams and substance abuse screening. It's essential to comply with immigration law, in particular by having the candidate complete an I-9 Employment Eligibility Verification Form and submit proof of eligibility.

Discussion Questions

6-6. What is the difference between reliability and validity?

6-7. Explain why you think a certified psychologist who is specifically trained in test construction should (or should not) be used by a small business that needs an employment test.

6-8. Why is it important to conduct preemployment background investigations? How would you do so?

6-9. Explain how you would get around the problem of former employers being unwilling to give bad references on their former employees.

6-10. How can employers protect themselves against negligent hiring claims?

Individual and Group Activities

6-11. Write a short essay discussing some of the ethical and legal considerations in testing.

6-12. Working individually or in groups, develop a list of specific selection techniques that you would suggest your dean use to hire the next HR professor at your school. Explain why you chose each selection technique.

6-13. Working individually or in groups, contact the publisher of a standardized test such as the Scholastic Assessment Test and obtain from it written information regarding the test's validity and reliability. Present a short report in class discussing what the test is supposed to measure and the degree to which you think the test does what it is supposed to do, based on the reported validity and reliability scores.

KNOWLEDGE BASE

6-14. Appendix A, PHR and SPHR Knowledge Base, at the end of this book (pages 580–588) lists the knowledge someone studying for the HRCI certification exam needs to have in each area of human resource management (such as in Strategic Management, Workforce Planning, and Human Resource Development). In groups of four to five students, do four things: (1) review Appendix A; (2) identify the material in this chapter that relates to the required knowledge Appendix A lists; (3) write four multiple-choice exam questions on this material that you believe would be suitable for inclusion in the HRCI exam; and (4) if time permits, have someone from your team post your team's questions in front of the class, so that students in all teams can answer the exam questions created by the other teams.

Experiential Exercise

A Test for a Reservation Clerk

Purpose: The purpose of this exercise is to give you practice in developing a test to measure *one specific ability* for the job of airline reservation clerk for a major airline. If time permits, you'll be able to combine your tests into a test battery.

Required Understanding: Your airline has decided to outsource its reservation jobs to Asia. You should be fully acquainted with the procedure for developing a personnel test and should read the following description of an airline reservation clerk's duties:

> Customers contact our airline reservation clerks to obtain flight schedules, prices, and itineraries. The reservation clerks look up the requested information on our airline's online flight schedule systems, which are updated continuously. The reservation clerk must speak clearly, deal courteously and expeditiously with the customer, and be able to find quickly alternative flight arrangements in order to provide the customer with the itinerary that fits his or her needs. Alternative flights and prices must be found quickly, so that the customer is not kept waiting, and so that our reservations operations group maintains its efficiency standards. There may be a dozen or more alternative routes between the customer's starting point and destination.

You may assume that we will hire about one-third of the applicants as airline reservation clerks. Therefore, your objective is to create a test that is useful in selecting a third of those available.

How to Set Up the Exercise/Instructions: Divide the class into teams of five or six students. The ideal candidate will need to have a number of skills to perform this job well. Your job is to select a single skill and to develop a test to measure that skill. Use only the materials available in the room, please. The test should permit quantitative scoring and may be an individual or a group test.

Please go to your assigned groups. As per our discussion of test development in this chapter, each group should make a list of the skills relevant to success in the airline reservation clerk's job. Each group should then rate the importance of these skills on a 5-point scale. Then, develop a test to measure what you believe to be the top-ranked skill. If time permits, the groups should combine the various tests from each group into a test battery. If possible, leave time for a group of students to take the test battery.

Video Case

Video Title: Employee Testing and Selection (Patagonia)

SYNOPSIS

Patagonia strives to select employees whose values are in sync with the philosophies and values of the company. The interviewing process is a multi-faceted one, in which candidates take part in several group interviews. These interviews follow a very conversational style, in an attempt to reveal as much about a potential employee's interests, passions, and personality as possible. It is important that those hired by Patagonia not only have an interest in outdoor activities and the products the company produces, but also are passionate about preserving the environment, which is the mission of Patagonia.

Discussion Questions

6-15. If you had to create a talent management–type job profile for the average employee at Patagonia, what would the profile look like in terms of its specific contents?

6-16. What traits does Patagonia look for in its future employees during the interview process?

6-17. In what respects does Patagonia's employee selection process reflect a talent management approach to selection?

6-18. What is the employee turnover rate at Patagonia? Is this higher or lower than the industry average? What reason can you give for why Patagonia's turnover rate is as you described?

6-19. Describe the interview process used by Patagonia. How is this process similar to others in the industry? How does the process used by Patagonia differ?

Application Case

The Insider

A federal jury convicted a stock trader who worked for a well-known investment firm, along with two alleged accomplices, of insider trading. According to the indictment, the trader got inside information about pending mergers from lawyers. The lawyers allegedly browsed around their law firm picking up information about corporate deals others in the firm were working on. The lawyers would then allegedly pass their information on to a friend, who in turn passed it on to the trader. Such "inside" information reportedly helped the trader (and his investment firm) earn millions of dollars. The trader would then allegedly thank the lawyers, for instance, with envelopes filled with cash.

Things like that are not supposed to happen. Federal and state laws prohibit it. And investment firms have their own compliance procedures to identify and head off shady trades. The problem is that controlling such behavior once the firm has someone working for it who may be prone to engage in inside trading isn't easy. "Better to avoid hiring such people in the first place," said one pundit.

At lunch at the Four Seasons restaurant off Park Avenue in Manhattan, the heads of several investment firms were discussing the conviction, and what they could do to make sure something like that didn't occur in their firms. "It's not just compliance," said one, "we've got to keep out the bad apples." They ask you for your advice.

Questions

6-20. We want you to design an employee selection program for hiring stock traders. We already know what to look for as far as technical skills are concerned—accounting courses, economics, and so on. What we want is a program for screening out potential bad apples. To that end, please let us know the following: What screening test(s) would you suggest, and why? What questions should we add to our application form? Specifically how should we check candidates' backgrounds, and what questions should we ask previous employers and references?

6-21. What else (if anything) would you suggest?

Continuing Case

Carter Cleaning Company

HONESTY TESTING

Jennifer Carter, of the Carter Cleaning Centers, and her father have what the latter describes as an easy but hard job when it comes to screening job applicants. It is easy because for two important jobs—the people who actually do the pressing and those who do the cleaning/spotting—the applicants are easily screened with about 20 minutes of on-the-job testing. As with typists, Jennifer points out, "Applicants either know how to press clothes fast or how to use cleaning chemicals and machines, or they don't, and we find out very quickly by just trying them out on the job." On the other hand, applicant screening for the stores can also be frustratingly hard because of the nature of some of the other qualities that Jennifer would like to screen for. Two of the most critical problems facing her company are employee turnover and employee honesty. Jennifer and her father sorely need to implement practices that will reduce the rate of employee turnover. If there is a way to do this through employee testing and screening techniques, Jennifer would like to know about it because of the management time and money that are now being wasted by the never-ending need to recruit and hire new employees. Of even greater concern to Jennifer and her father is the need to institute new practices to screen out those employees who may be predisposed to steal from the company.

Employee theft is an enormous problem for the Carter Cleaning Centers, and not just cash. For example, the cleaner/spotter often opens the store without a manager present, to get the day's work started, and it is not unusual for that person to "run a route." Running a route means that an employee canvasses his or her neighborhood to pick up people's clothes for cleaning and then secretly cleans and presses them in the Carter store, using the company's supplies, gas, and power. It would also not be unusual for an unsupervised person (or his or her supervisor, for that matter) to accept a 1-hour rush order for cleaning or laundering, quickly clean and press the item, and return it to the customer for payment without making out a proper ticket for the item posting the sale. The money, of course, goes into the worker's pocket instead of into the cash register.

The more serious problem concerns the store manager and the counter workers who actually handle the cash. According to Jack Carter, "You would not believe the creativity employees use to get around the management controls we set up to cut down on employee theft." As one extreme example of this felonious creativity, Jack tells the following story: "To cut down on the amount of money my employees were stealing, I had a small sign painted and placed in front of all our cash registers. The sign said: YOUR ENTIRE ORDER FREE IF WE DON'T GIVE YOU A CASH REGISTER RECEIPT WHEN YOU PAY. CALL 552–0235. It was my intention with this sign to force all our cash-handling employees to give receipts so the cash register would record them for my accountants. After all, if all the cash that comes in is recorded in the cash register, then we should have a much better handle on stealing in our stores. Well, one of our managers found a way around this. I came into the store one night and noticed that the cash register this particular manager was using just didn't look right, although the sign was placed in front of it. It turned out that every afternoon at about 5:00 P.M. when the other employees left, this character would pull his own cash register out of a box that he hid underneath our supplies. Customers coming in would notice the sign and, of course, the fact that he was meticulous in ringing up every sale. But unknown to them, for about 5 months the sales that came in for about an hour every day went into his cash register, not mine. It took us that long to figure out where our cash for that store was going."

Here is what Jennifer would like you to answer:

Questions

6-22. What would be the advantages and disadvantages to Jennifer's company of routinely administering honesty tests to all its employees?

6-23. Specifically, what other screening techniques could the company use to screen out theft-prone and turnover-prone employees, and how exactly could these be used?

6-24. How should her company terminate employees caught stealing, and what kind of procedure should be set up for handling reference calls about these employees when they go to other companies looking for jobs?

Translating Strategy into HR Policies and Practices Case*,§

The accompanying strategy map for this chapter is in the MyManagementLab, and the overall map on the inside back cover of this text outlines the relationships involved.

IMPROVING PERFORMANCE at The Hotel Paris

The New Employee Testing Program

The Hotel Paris's competitive strategy is "To use superior guest service to differentiate the Hotel Paris properties, and to thereby increase the length of stay and return rate of guests, and thus boost revenues and profitability." HR manager Lisa Cruz must now formulate functional policies and activities that support this competitive strategy and boost performance, by eliciting the required employee behaviors and competencies.

As she considered what to do next, Lisa Cruz, the Hotel Paris's HR director, knew that employee selection had to play a role. The Hotel Paris currently had an informal screening process in which local hotel managers obtained application forms, interviewed applicants, and checked their references. However, a pilot project using an employment test for service people at the Chicago hotel had produced startling results. Lisa found consistent, significant relationships between test performance and a range of employee competencies and behaviors such as speed of check-in/out, employee turnover, and percentage of calls answered with the required greeting. She knew that such employee capabilities and behaviors translated into the improved guest service performance the Hotel Paris needed to execute its strategy. She therefore had to decide what selection procedures would be best.

Lisa's team, working with an industrial psychologist, designs a test battery that they believe will produce the sorts of high-morale, patient, people-oriented employees they are looking for. It includes a preliminary, computerized test in which applicants for the positions of front-desk clerk, door person, assistant manager, and security guard must deal with an apparently irate guest; a work sample in which front-desk clerk candidates spend 10 minutes processing an incoming "guest"; a personality test aimed at weeding out applicants who lack emotional stability; the Wonderlic test of mental ability; and the Phase II Profile for assessing candidate honesty. Their subsequent validity analysis shows that scores on the test batteries predict scores on the hotel's employee capabilities and behavior metrics. A second analysis confirmed that, as the percentage of employees hired after testing rose, so too did the hotel's employee capabilities and behaviors scores, for instance (see the strategy map), in terms of speed of check-in/out, and the percent of guests receiving the Hotel Paris required greeting.

Lisa and the CFO also found other measurable improvements apparently resulting from the new testing process. For example, it took less time to fill an open position, and cost per hire diminished, so the HR department became more efficient. The new testing program thus did not only contribute to the hotel's performance by improving employee capabilities and behaviors. It also did so by directly improving profit margins and profits.

Questions

6-25. Provide a detailed example of a security guard work sample test.

6-26. Provide a detailed example of two personality test items you would suggest they use, and why you would suggest using them.

6-27. What other tests would you suggest to Lisa, and why would you suggest them?

6-28. How would you suggest Lisa try to confirm that it is indeed the testig and not some other change that accounts for the improved importance.

§Written by and copyright Gary Dessler, PhD.

MyManagementLab

Go to **mymanagementlab.com** for Auto-graded writing questions as well as the following Assisted-graded writing questions:

6-29. Explain how you would go about validating a test. How can this information be useful to a manager?

6-30. Give some examples of how to use interest inventories to improve employee selection. In doing so, suggest several examples of occupational interests that you believe might predict success in various occupations, including college professor, accountant, and computer programmer.

6-31. MyManagementLab only—comprehensive writing assignment for this chapter.

Key Terms

negligent hiring, 158
reliability, 158
test validity, 159
criterion validity, 160
content validity, 160
construct validity, 160
expectancy chart, 161
interest inventory, 168
work samples, 169
work sampling technique, 169
management assessment center, 170
situational test, 171
video-based simulation, 171
miniature job training and evaluation, 171

Endnotes

1. See, for example, Jean Phillips and Stanley Gully, *Strategic Staffing* (Upper Saddle River, NJ: Pearson Education, 2012), pp. 234–235.
2. Even if they use a third party to prepare an employment test, contractors are "ultimately responsible" for ensuring the tests' job relatedness and EEO compliance. "DOL Officials Discuss Contractors' Duties on Validating Tests," *BNA Bulletin to Management*, September 4, 2007, p. 287. Furthermore, enforcement units are increasing their scrutiny of employers who rely on tests and screening. See "Litigation Increasing with Employer Reliance on Tests, Screening," *BNA Bulletin to Management*, April 8, 2008, p. 119. However, see also C. Tuna et al., "Job-Test Ruling Cheers Employers," *The Wall Street Journal*, July 1, 2009, p. B1–2.
3. See, for example, Ann Marie Ryan and Marja Lasek, "Negligent Hiring and Defamation: Areas of Liability Related to Pre-Employment Inquiries," *Personnel Psychology* 44, no. 2 (Summer 1991), pp. 293–319. See also Jay Stuller, "Fatal Attraction," *Across the Board* 42, no. 6 (November–December 2005), pp. 18–23.
4. For example, Ryan Zimmerman, "Wal-Mart to Toughen Job Screening," *The Wall Street Journal*, July 12, 2004, pp. B1–B8. See also Michael Tucker, "Show and Tell," *HR Magazine*, January 2012, pp. 51–52.
5. Negligent hiring highlights the need to think through what the job's human requirements really are. For example, "non-rapist" isn't likely to appear as a required knowledge, skill, or ability in a job analysis of an apartment manager, but in situations like this screening for such tendencies is obviously required. To avoid negligent hiring claims, "make a systematic effort to gain relevant information about the applicant, verify documentation, follow up on missing records or gaps in employment, and keep a detailed log of all attempts to obtain information, including the names and dates for phone calls or other requests." Fay Hansen, "Taking 'Reasonable' Action to Avoid Negligent Hiring Claims," *Workforce Management*, September 11, 2006, p. 31.
6. Bart Wille et al., "Expanding and Reconceptualizing Aberrant Personality at Work: Validity of Five Factor Model Aberrant Personality Tendencies to Predict Career Outcomes," *Personnel Psychology* 60, no. 6 (2013), pp. 173–223.
7. Ibid., p. 213.
8. Kevin Murphy and Charles Davidshofer, *Psychological Testing: Principles and Applications* (Upper Saddle River, NJ: Prentice Hall, 2001), p. 73.
9. Ibid., pp. 116–119.
10. W. Bruce Walsh and Nancy Betz, *Tests and Assessment* (Upper Saddle River, NJ: Prentice Hall, 2001).
11. Murphy and Davidshofer, *Psychological Testing*, p. 74.
12. Ibid.
13. See James Ledvinka, *Federal Regulation of Personnel and Human Resource Management* (Boston: Kent, 1982), p. 113; and Murphy and Davidshofer, *Psychological Testing*, pp. 154–165.
14. www.siop.org/workplace/employment%20testing/information_to_consider_when_cre.aspx, accessed March 22, 2009.
15. The procedure you would use to demonstrate content validity differs from that used to demonstrate criterion validity (as described in steps 1 through 5). Content validity tends to emphasize judgment. Here, you first do a careful job analysis to identify the work behaviors required. Then combine several samples of those behaviors into a test. A typing and computer skills test for a clerk would be an example. The fact that the test is a comprehensive sample of actual, observable, on-the-job behaviors is what lends the test its content validity.
16. Murphy and Davidshofer, *Psychological Testing*, p. 73. See also Chad Van Iddekinge and Robert Ployhart, "Developments in the Criterion-Related Validation of Selection Procedures: A Critical Review and Recommendations for Practice," *Personnel Psychology* 60, no. 1 (2008), pp. 871–925.
17. Psychological Assessment Resources, Inc., in Odessa, Florida, is typical.
18. Experts sometimes have to develop separate expectancy charts and cutting points for minorities and nonminorities if the validation studies indicate that high performers from either group (minority or nonminority) score lower (or higher) on the test.
19. In employment testing, bias has a precise meaning. Specifically, "bias is said to exist when a test makes systematic errors in measurement or prediction." Murphy and Davidshofer, *Psychological Testing*, p. 303.
20. Ibid., p. 305.
21. Herman Aguinis, Steven Culpepper, and Charles Pierce, "Revival of Test Bias Research in Preemployment Testing," *Journal of Applied Psychology* 95, no. 4 (2010), p. 648.
22. Robert Gatewood and Hubert Feild, *Human Resource Selection* (Mason, OH: South-Western, Cengage Learning, 2008), p. 243.
23. Bill Leonard, "Wanted: Shorter Time to Hire," *HR Magazine*, November 2011, pp. 49–52.
24. This is based on Dave Zielinski, "Effective Assessments," *HR Magazine*, January 2011, pp. 61–64.
25. Sarah Gale, "Three Companies Cut Turnover with Tests," *Workforce*, Spring 2002, pp. 66–69.
26. The Uniform Guidelines say, "Employers should ensure that tests and selection procedures are not adopted casually by managers who know little about these processes . . . no test or selection procedure should be implemented without an understanding of its effectiveness and limitations for the organization, its

appropriateness for a specific job, and whether it can be appropriately administered and scored."

27. Phillips and Gully, *Strategic Staffing*, p. 220.
28. Ibid., p. 220.
29. www.uniformguidelines.com/qandaprint.html, accessed July 19, 2013.
30. Ibid.
31. A complete discussion of the APA's "Ethical Principles of Psychologists and Code of Conduct" is beyond this book's scope. But points it addresses include competence, integrity, respect for people's dignity, nondiscrimination, and sexual harassment. From "Ethical Principles of Psychologists and Code of Conduct," *American Psychologist* 47 (1992), pp. 1597–1611; and www.apa.org/ethics/code/index.aspx, accessed September 9, 2011.
32. Mendelsohn and Morrison, "The Right to Privacy in the Work Place," p. 22.
33. Kenneth Sovereign, *Personnel Law* (Upper Saddle River, NJ: Prentice Hall, 1999), pp. 204–206.
34. "One-Third of Job Applicants Flunked Basic Literacy and Math Tests Last Year, American Management Association Survey Finds," *American Management Association*, www.amanet.org/press/amanews/bjp2001.htm, accessed January 11, 2008.
35. Ibid. See also Alison Wolf and Andrew Jenkins, "Explaining Greater Test Use for Selection: The Role of HR Professionals in a World of Expanding Regulation," *Human Resource Management Journal* 16, no. 2 (2006), pp. 193–213.
36. Steffanie Wilk and Peter Capelli, "Understanding the Determinants of Employer Use of Selection Methods," *Personnel Psychology* 56 (2003), p. 117.
37. Kevin Hart, "Not Wanted: Thieves," *HR Magazine*, April 2008, p. 119.
38. Sarah Needleman, "Businesses Say Theft by Their Workers Is Up," *The Wall Street Journal*, December 11, 2008, p. B8.
39. Except as noted, this is based on Laurence Siegel and Irving Lane, *Personnel and Organizational Psychology* (Burr Ridge, IL: McGraw-Hill, 1982), pp. 170–185. See also Cabot Jaffee, "Measurement of Human Potential," *Employment Relations Today* 17, no. 2 (Summer 2000), pp. 15–27; Maureen Patterson, "Overcoming the Hiring Crunch; Tests Deliver Informed Choices," *Employment Relations Today* 27, no. 3 (Fall 2000), pp. 77–88; Kathryn Tyler, "Put Applicants' Skills to the Test," *HR Magazine*, January 2000, p. 74; Murphy and Davidshofer, *Psychological Testing*, pp. 215–403; Elizabeth Schoenfelt and Leslie Pedigo, "A Review of Court Decisions on Cognitive Ability Testing, 1992–2004," *Review of Public Personnel Administration* 25, no. 3 (2005), pp. 271–287.
40. Norman Henderson, "Predicting Long-Term Firefighter Performance from Cognitive and Physical Ability Measures," *Personnel Psychology* 60, no. 3 (2010), pp. 999–1039.
41. As an example, results of meta-analyses in one study indicated that isometric strength tests were valid predictors of both supervisory ratings of physical performance and performance on work simulations. See Barry R. Blakley, Miguel Quinones, Marnie Swerdlin Crawford, and I. Ann Jago, "The Validity of Isometric Strength Tests," *Personnel Psychology* 47 (1994), pp. 247–274; and www.military.com/military-fitness/marine-corps-fitness-requirements/marine-corps-fitness-test, accessed October 4, 2011.
42. William Wagner, "All Skill, No Finesse," *Workforce*, June 2000, pp. 108–116. See also, for example, James Diefendorff and Kajal Mehta, "The Relations of Motivational Traits with Workplace Deviance," *Journal of Applied Psychology* 92, no. 4 (2007), pp. 967–977.
43. www.myersbriggsreports.com/?gclid=CK71m6rEh6ACFVZS2godDEjgkw, accessed February 22, 2010.
44. See, for example, Joyce Hogan et al., "Personality Measurement, Faking, and Employee Selection," *Journal of Applied Psychology* 92, no. 5 (2007), pp. 1270–1285; Colin Gill and Gerard Hodgkinson, "Development and Validation of the Five Factor Model Questionnaire (FFMQ): An Adjectival-Based Personality Inventory for Use in Occupational Settings," *Personnel Psychology* 60 (2007), pp. 731–766; and Lisa Penney and Emily Witt, "A Review of Personality and Performance: Identifying Boundaries, Contingencies, and Future Research Directions," *Human Resource Management Review* 20, no. 1 (2011), pp. 297–310.
45. Timothy Judge et al., "Personality and Leadership: A Qualitative and Quantitative Review," *Journal of Applied Psychology* 87, no. 4 (2002), p. 765.
46. L. A. Witt et al., "The Interactive Effects of Conscientiousness and Agreeableness on Job Performance," *Journal of Applied Psychology* 87, no. 1 (2002), pp. 164–169.
47. Timothy Judge and Remus Ilies, "Relationship of Personality to Performance Motivation: A Meta Analytic Review," *Journal of Applied Psychology* 87, no. 4 (2002), pp. 797–807.
48. Murray Barrick et al., "Personality and Job Performance: Test of the Immediate Effects of Motivation Among Sales Representatives," *Journal of Applied Psychology* 87, no. 1 (2002), p. 43.
49. Charles Sarchione et al., "Prediction of Dysfunctional Job Behaviors Among Law-Enforcement Officers," *Journal of Applied Psychology* 83, no. 6 (1998), pp. 904–912. See also W. A. Scroggins et al., "Psychological Testing in Personnel Selection, Part III: The Resurgence of Personality Testing," *Public Personnel Management* 38, no. 1 (Spring 2009), pp. 67–77.
50. Paula Caligiuri, "The Big Five Personality Characteristics as Predictors of Expatriate Desire to Terminate the Assignment and Supervisor Rated Performance," *Personnel Psychology* 53 (2000), pp. 67–68. For some other examples, see Ryan Zimmerman, "Understanding the Impact of Personality Traits on Individuals' Turnover Decisions: A Meta-Analytic Path Model," *Personnel Psychology* 60, no. 1 (2008), pp. 309–348.
51. Diane Cadrain, "Reassess Personality Tests After Court Case," *HR Magazine* 50, no. 9 (September 2005), p. 30.
52. Frederick Morgeson et al., "Reconsidering the Use of Personality Tests in Personnel Selection Contexts," *Personnel Psychology* 60 (2007), p. 683; and Frederick Morgeson et al., "Are We Getting Fooled Again? Coming to Terms with Limitations in the Use of Personality Tests for Personnel Selection," *Personnel Psychology* 60 (2007), p. 1046.
53. Robert Tett and Neil Christiansen, "Personality Tests at the Crossroads: A Response to Morgeson, Campion, Dipboye, Hollenbeck, Murphy, and Schmitt," *Personnel Psychology* 60 (2007), p. 967. See also Deniz Ones et al., "In Support of Personality Assessment in Organizational Settings," *Personnel Psychology* 60 (2007), pp. 995–1027.
54. See also Edwin A. J. van Hoot and Marise Ph. Born, "Intentional Response Distortion on Personality Tests: Using Eye Tracking to Understand Response Processes When Thinking," *Journal of Applied Psychology* 97, no. 2 (2012), pp. 301–316.
55. Chad H. Van Iddeking et al., "Are You Interested? A Meta-Analysis of Relations Between Vocational Interests and Employee Performance and Turnover," *Journal of Applied Psychology* 96, no 6 (2011), pp. 1167–1194.
56. Ed Frauenheim, "More Companies Go with Online Test to Fill in the Blanks," *Workforce Management*, May 2011, p. 12.
57. Ed Frauenheim, "Personality Tests Adapt to the Times," *Workforce Management*, February 2010, p. 4.
58. Requiring job seekers to complete prescreening questionnaires and screening selected applicants out on this basis carries legal and business consequences. See, for example, Lisa Harpe, "Designing an Effective Employment Prescreening Program," *Employment Relations Today* 32, no. 3 (Fall 2005), pp. 41–43.
59. www.iphonetypingtest.com, accessed March 23, 2009.
60. Based on Joseph Walker, "Meet the New Boss: Big Data," *The Wall Street Journal*, September 20, 2012, p. B1.
61. Bill Roberts, "Hire Intelligence," *HR Magazine*, May 2011, p. 64.
62. See, for example, Meg Breslin, "Can You Handle Rejection?" *Workforce Management*, October 2012, pp. 32–36.
63. Wright, "At Google, It Takes a Village to Hire an Employee."
64. Kevin Delaney, "Google Adjusts Hiring Process as Needs Grow," *The Wall Street Journal*, October 23, 2006, pp. B1, B8; http://googleblog.blogspot.com/2009/01/changes-to-recruiting.html, accessed March 25, 2009.
65. Except as noted, this is based on Dave Zielinski, "Effective Assessments," *HR Magazine*, January 2011, pp. 61–64.
66. Jeff Weekley and Casey Jones, "Video-Based Situational Testing," *Personnel Psychology* 50 (1997), p. 25.
67. Elaine Pulakos, *Selection Assessment Methods*, SHRM Foundation, 2005, p. 14.
68. However, studies suggest that blacks may be somewhat less likely to do well on work sample tests than are whites. See, for example, Philip Roth, Philip Bobko, and Lynn McFarland, "A Meta-Analysis of Work Sample Test Validity: Updating and Integrating Some Classic Literature," *Personnel Psychology* 58, no. 4 (Winter 2005), pp. 1009–1037; and Philip Roth et al., "Work Sample Tests in Personnel Selection: A Meta-Analysis of Black–White Differences in Overall and Exercise Scores," *Personnel Psychology* 60, no. 1 (2008), pp. 637–662.
69. Siegel and Lane, *Personnel and Organizational Psychology*, pp. 182–183.
70. Quoted from Deborah Whetzel and Michael McDaniel, "Situational Judgment Tests: An Overview of Current Research," *Human Resource Management Review* 19 (2009), pp. 188–202.

71. "Help Wanted—and Found," *Fortune*, October 2, 2006, p. 40. See also Brian Hoffman et al., "Exercises and Dimensions Are the Currency of Assessment Centers," *Personnel Psychology* 60, no. 4 (2011), pp. 351–395.
72. Annette Spychalski, Miguel Quinones, Barbara Gaugler, and Katja Pohley, "A Survey of Assessment Center Practices in Organizations in the United States," *Personnel Psychology* 50, no. 1 (Spring 1997), pp. 71–90. See also Winfred Arthur Jr. et al., "A Meta Analysis of the Criterion Related Validity of Assessment Center Data Dimensions," *Personnel Psychology* 56 (2003), pp. 124–154; and Brian Hoffman et al., "Exercises and Dimensions Are the Currency of Assessment Centers," *Personnel Psychology* 60, no. 4 (2011), pp. 351–395.
73. See, for example, John Meriac et al., "Further Evidence for the Validity of Assessment Center Dimensions: A Meta-Analysis of the Incremental Criterion-Related Validity of Dimension Ratings," *Journal of Applied Psychology* 93, no. 5 (2008), pp. 1042–1052.
74. This feature is based on Xiangdong Gu, Louise T. Higgins, Lixiang Weng, and Xiaoye Holt, "Civil Service Leadership Selection in China: Historical Evolution and Current Status," *Journal of Chinese Human Resources Management* 3, no. 1 (2012), pp. 67–78.
75. Ibid.
76. Ibid.
77. Weekley and Jones, "Video-Based Situational Testing," p. 26.
78. Ibid., p. 30.
79. Robert Grossman, "Made from Scratch," *HR Magazine*, April 2002, pp. 44–53.
80. Coleman Peterson, "Employee Retention, The Secrets Behind Wal-Mart's Successful Hiring Policies," *Human Resource Management* 44, no. 1 (Spring 2005), pp. 85–88. See also Murray Barrick and Ryan Zimmerman, "Reducing Voluntary, Avoidable Turnover Through Selection," *Journal of Applied Psychology* 90, no. 1 (2005), pp. 159–166.
81. James Breaugh, "Employee Recruitment: Current Knowledge and Important Areas for Future Research," *Human Resource Management Review* 18 (2008), pp. 106–107.
82. Phillips and Gully, *Strategic Staffing*, p. 223.
83. Brian J. Hoffman, John W. Michel, and Kevin J. Williams, "On the Predictive Efficiency of Past Performance and Physical Ability: The Case of the National Football League," *Human Performance* 24, no. 2 (2011), pp. 158–172.
84. "High Profile Example Shows Resume Fraud Is Still Major Problem HR Needs to Address," *BNA Bulletin to Management* 63, no. 23 (June 5, 2012), p. 177.
85. "Internet, E-Mail Monitoring Common at Most Workplaces," *BNA Bulletin to Management*, February 1, 2001, p. 34. See also "Are Your Background Checks Balanced? Experts Identify Concerns over Verifications," *BNA Bulletin to Management*, May 13, 2004, p. 153.
86. Merry Mayer, "Background Checks in Focus," *HR Magazine*, January 2002, pp. 59–62; and Carroll Lachnit, "Protecting People and Profits with Background Checks," *Workforce*, February 2002, p. 52.
87. Matthew Heller, "Special Report: Background Checking," *Workforce Management*, March 3, 2008, pp. 35–54.
88. Bill Roberts, "Close-up on Screening," *HR Magazine*, February 2011, pp. 23–29.
89. Seymour Adler, "Verifying a Job Candidate's Background: The State of Practice in a Vital Human Resources Activity," *Review of Business* 15, no. 2 (Winter 1993), p. 6.
90. Heller, "Special Report: Background Checking," p. 35.
91. This is based on Samuel Greengard, "Have Gangs Invaded Your Workplace?" *Personnel Journal*, February 1996, pp. 47–48.
92. Dori Meinert, "Seeing Behind the Mask," *HR Magazine* 56, no. 2 (February 2011), www.shrm.org/Publications/hrmagazine/EditorialContent/2011/0211/Pages/0211meinert.aspx, accessed August 20, 2011.
93. Ibid., p. 55.
94. For example, one U.S. Court of Appeals found that bad references might be grounds for a suit when they are retaliations for the employee having previously filed an EEOC claim. "Negative Reference Leads to Charge of Retaliation," *BNA Bulletin to Management*, October 21, 2004, p. 344.
95. *Kehr v. Consolidated Freightways of Delaware*, Docket No. 86–2126, July 15, 1987, U.S. Seventh Circuit Court of Appeals. Discussed in *Commerce Clearing House, Ideas and Trends*, October 16, 1987, p. 165.
96. James Bell, James Castagnera, and Jane Patterson Young, "Employment References: Do You Know the Law?" *Personnel Journal* 63, no. 2 (February 1984), pp. 32–36. In order to demonstrate defamation, several elements must be present: (a) the defamatory statement must have been communicated to another party; (b) the statement must be a false statement of fact; (c) injury to reputation must have occurred; and (d) the employer must not be protected under qualified or absolute privilege. For a discussion, see Ryan and Lasek, "Negligent Hiring and Defamation," p. 307. See also James Burns Jr., "Employment References: Is There a Better Way?" *Employee Relations Law Journal* 23, no. 2 (Fall 1997), pp. 157–168.
97. For additional information, see Lawrence E. Dube Jr., "Employment References and the Law," *Personnel Journal* 65, no. 2 (February 1986), pp. 87–91. See also Mickey Veich, "Uncover the Resume Ruse," *Security Management*, October 1994, pp. 75–76.
98. "Undercover Callers Tip Off Job Seekers to Former Employers' Negative References," *BNA Bulletin to Management*, May 27, 1999, p. 161.
99. Eileen Zimmerman, "A Subtle Reference Trap for Unwary Employers," *Workforce*, April 2003, p. 22.
100. Michelle Goodman, "Reference Checks Go Tech," *Workforce Management*, May 2012, pp. 26–28.
101. "Vetting via Internet Is Free, Generally Legal, but Not Necessarily Smart Hiring Strategy," *BNA Bulletin to Management*, February 20, 2007, pp. 57–58.
102. Alan Finder, "When a Risqué Online Persona Undermines a Chance for a Job," *The New York Times*, June 11, 2006, p. 1.
103. Anjali Athavaley, "Job References You Can't Control," *The Wall Street Journal*, September 27, 2007, p. B1.
104. "Practitioners Discuss Various Pitfalls of Using Social Media to Vet Job Applicants," *BNA Bulletin to Management*, November 1, 2011, pp. 345–346.
105. Rita Zeidner, "How Deep Can You Probe?" *HR Magazine*, October 1, 2007, pp. 57–62.
106. "Web Searches on Applicants Are Potentially Perilous for Employers," *BNA Bulletin to Management*, October 14, 2008, p. 335.
107. "Maryland Is First State to Restrict Employer Demands for Employee, Applicant Passwords," *BNA Bulletin to Management*, May 8, 2012, p. 145.
108. "Practitioners Discuss Various Pitfalls of Using Social Media to Vet Job Applicants," op cit.
109. "Background Checking Providers," *Workforce Management*, April 2012, p. 22.
110. Stephanie Clifford and Jessica Silver-Greenberg, "Retailers Track Employee Thefts in Vast Databases," *The New York Times*, April 4, 2013, pp. A1, A16.
111. Jeffrey M. Hahn, "Pre-Employment Information Services: Employers Beware?" *Employee Relations Law Journal* 17, no. 1 (Summer 1991), pp. 45–69. See also "Pre-Employment Background Screenings Have Evolved, But So Have Liability Risks," *BNA Bulletin to Management*, November 1, 2005, p. 345.
112. Under California law, applicants or employees must have the option of requesting a copy of the report regardless of action.
113. Teresa Butler Stivarius, "Background Checks: Steps to Basic Compliance in a Multistate Environment," *Society for Human Resource Management Legal Report*, March–April 2003, pp. 1–8.
114. See, for example, Dori Meinert, "Search and Verify," *HR Magazine*, December 2012, pp. 37–41.
115. "Background Check Firm Pays $2.6 Million Penalty," *Workforce Management*, October 2012, p. 12.
116. See Paul Taylor et al., "Dimensionality and the Validity of a Structured Telephone Reference Check Procedure," *Personnel Psychology* 57 (2004), pp. 745–772, for a discussion of checking other work habits and traits.
117. "Getting Applicant Information Difficult but Still Necessary," *BNA Bulletin to Management*, February 5, 1999, p. 63. See also Robert Howie and Laurence Shapiro, "Pre-Employment Criminal Background Checks: Why Employers Should Look Before They Leap," *Employee Relations Law Journal*, Summer 2002, pp. 63–77.
118. Polygraphs are still widely used in law enforcement and reportedly are quite useful. See, for example, Laurie Cohen, "The Polygraph Paradox," *The Wall Street Journal*, March 22, 2008, p. A1.
119. After a tragedy in Manhattan several years ago, more parents began turning to private investigators and industrial psychologists to conduct checks, including polygraph tests, on prospective nannies. Gabrielle Birkner, "Nanny Interviews Get More Aggressive," *The Wall Street Journal*, December 15–16, 2012, pp. A19, A21.
120. John Jones and William Terris, "Post-Polygraph Selection Techniques," *Recruitment Today*, May–June 1989, pp. 25–31.
121. Norma Fritz, "In Focus: Honest Answers—Post Polygraph," *Personnel*, April 1989, p. 8. See also Richard White Jr., "Ask Me No Questions, Tell Me No Lies: Examining the Uses and Misuses of the Polygraph," *Public Personnel Management* 30, no. 4 (Winter 2001), pp. 483–493.
122. A recent meta-analysis concluded that "relations between integrity tests and measures of job performance tend to be rather weak."

Chad H. Van Iddeking et al., "The Criterion Related Validity of Integrity Tests: An Updated Meta-Analysis," *Journal of Applied Psychology* 97, no. 3 (2012), pp. 499–530, a point disputed by a panel of test publishers. William G. Harris et al., "Test Publishers' Perspective on "An Updated Meta-Analysis": Comment on Van Iddeking, Ross, Raymark, and Odle-Dusseau (2012), *Journal of Applied Psychology* 97, no. 3, 2012, pp. 531–536.

123. John Bernardin and Donna Cooke, "Validity of an Honesty Test in Predicting Theft Among Convenience Store Employees," *Academy of Management Journal* 36, no. 5 (1993), pp. 1097–1108.
124. Bill Roberts, "Your Cheating Heart," *HR Magazine*, June 2011, pp. 55–57.
125. These are based on "Divining Integrity Through Interviews," *BNA Bulletin to Management*, June 4, 1987, p. 184; and *Commerce Clearing House, Ideas and Trends*, December 29, 1998, pp. 222–223. See also Bridget A. Styers and Kenneth S. Shultz, "Perceived Reasonableness of Employment Testing Accommodations for Persons with Disabilities," *Public Personnel Management* 38, no. 3 (Fall 2009), pp. 71–91.
126. Bill Leonard, "Reading Employees," *HR Magazine*, April 1999, pp. 67–73.
127. Ibid.
128. This is based on Kyle Stock, "Wary Investors Turn to Lie Pros," *The Wall Street Journal*, December 29, 2010, p. C3.
129. Mick Haus, "Pre-Employment Physicals and the ADA," *Safety and Health*, February 1992, pp. 64–65. See also Bridget A. Styers and Kenneth S. Shultz, "Perceived Reasonableness of Employment Testing Accommodations for Persons with Disabilities," *Public Personnel Management* 38, no. 3 (Fall 2009), pp. 71–91.
130. Scott MacDonald, Samantha Wells, and Richard Fry, "The Limitations of Drug Screening in the Workplace," *International Labor Review* 132, no. 1 (1993), p. 98. Not all agree that drug testing is worthwhile. See, for example, Veronica I. Luzzi et al., "Analytic Performance of Immunoassays for Drugs of Abuse Below Established Cutoff Values," *Clinical Chemistry* 50, 2004, pp. 717–722.
131. Rita Zeidner, "Putting Drug Screening to the Test," *HR Magazine*, November 2010, p. 26.
132. Diane Cadrain, "Are Your Employees' Drug Tests Accurate?" *HR Magazine*, January 2003, pp. 40–45.
133. Chris Berka and Courtney Poignand, "Hair Follicle Testing—An Alternative to Urinalysis for Drug Abuse Screening," *Employee Relations Today*, Winter 1991–1992, pp. 405–409; for an example, see www.americanscreeningcorp.com/default.aspx, accessed October 8, 2011.
134. MacDonald et al., "The Limitations of Drug Screening," pp. 102–104.
135. R. J. McCunney, "Drug Testing: Technical Complications of a Complex Social Issue," *American Journal of Industrial Medicine* 15, no. 5 (1989), pp. 589–600; discussed in MacDonald et al., "The Limitations of Drug Screening," p. 102.
136. MacDonald et al., "The Limitations of Drug Screening," p. 103.
137. This is based on Ann M. O'Neill, "Legal Issues Presented by Hair Follicle Testing," *Employee Relations Today*, Winter 1991–1992, pp. 411–415.
138. Ibid., p. 411.
139. Ibid., p. 413.
140. Richard Lisko, "A Manager's Guide to Drug Testing," *Security Management* 38, no. 8 (August 1994), p. 92. See also Randall Kesselring and Jeffrey Pittman, "Drug Testing Laws and Employment Injuries," *Journal of Labor Research*, Spring 2002, pp. 293–301.
141. Michael A. McDaniel, "Does Pre-Employment Drug Use Predict on-the-Job Suitability?" *Personnel Psychology* 41, no. 4 (Winter 1988), pp. 717–729.
142. *Exxon Corp. v. Esso Workers Union, Inc.*, CA1#96–2241, 7/8/97; discussed in *BNA Bulletin to Management*, August 7, 1997, p. 249.
143. For the form, see www.uscis.gov/files/form/i-9.pdf, accessed October 4, 2011.
144. "Conflicting State E-Verify Laws Troubling for Employers," *BNA Bulletin to Management*, November 4, 2008, p. 359.
145. "President Bush Signs Executive Order: Federal Contractors Must Use E-Verify," *BNA Bulletin to Management*, June 17, 2008, p. 193.
146. Davis Zielinski, "Automating I-9 Verification," *HR Magazine*, May 2011, pp. 57–60. Employees themselves can use E-Verify to confirm their U.S. work authorization status. "New Tools Will Aid Employers During Verification Process," *BNA Bulletin to Management*, March 15, 2011.
147. "As E-Verify, No Match Rules, I-9 Evolve, Employers Need to Stay on Top of Issues," *BNA Bulletin Management*, April 15, 2008, p. 121. For the latest I-9 form see www.uscis.gov/files/form/i-9.pdf, accessed September 7, 2013.
148. Note that the acceptable documents on page 3 of the previous I-9 form did not reflect the most current list of acceptable documents for confirming identity and eligibility. For the latest I-9 form see www.uscis.gov/files/form/i-9.pdf, accessed September 7, 2013.
149. "Identity Theft Remains Top Challenge for E-Verify," *BNA Bulletin to Management*, April 19, 2011, p. 121.
150. Susan Ladika, "Trouble on the Hiring Front," *HR Magazine*, October 2006, pp. 56–62.
151. Russell Gerbman, "License to Work," *HR Magazine*, June 2000, pp. 151–160; the I-9 form clearly states that the employer may not discriminate. See www.uscis.gov/files/form/i-9.pdf, accessed October 4, 2011.

7 Interviewing Candidates

Source: Keith Brofsky/Thinkstock

MyManagementLab®

Improve Your Grade!

When you see this icon, visit **www.mymanagementlab.com** for activities that are applied, personalized, and offer immediate feedback.

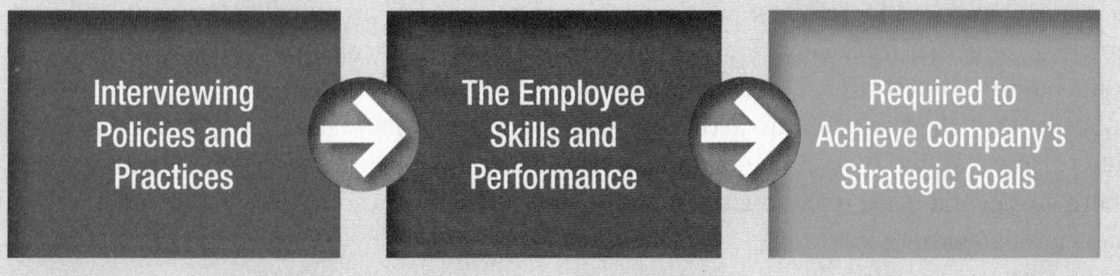

For a bird's eye view of how one company created a new interviewing program to improve its strategic performance, read the Hotel Paris case on pages 210–211 and answer the questions after reading the chapter.

WHERE ARE WE NOW . . .

Chapter 6 focused on the selection process and on important selection tools such as tests. The purpose of Chapter 7 is to explain how to improve one's effectiveness in using the most widely applied selection tool—the selection interview.[1] The main topics we'll cover include basic types of interviews, errors that can undermine an interview's usefulness, how to design and conduct an effective interview, and developing and extending the job offer. In Chapter 8, we'll turn to orienting and training the new employee.

LEARNING OBJECTIVES

1. List and give examples of the main types of selection interviews.
2. List and explain the main errors that can undermine an interview's usefulness.
3. Define a structured situational interview and give examples of situational questions, behavioral questions, and background questions that provide structure.
4. What are the main points to know about developing and extending the actual job offer?

Hiring customer service and teller employees in banks is never easy. Although the jobs entail significant responsibility and dealing with sometimes difficult customers, the positions are not highly paid. Turnover is high. The head of recruiting for Great Western Bank needed an interviewing system that could process large numbers of applicants quickly but effectively. We'll see what she did.

1 List and give examples of the main types of selection interviews.

Basic Types of Interviews

Managers use several interviews at work, such as performance appraisal interviews and exit interviews. A *selection interview* (the focus of this chapter) is a selection procedure designed to predict future job performance based on applicants' oral responses to oral inquiries.[2] Many techniques in this chapter (such as avoiding snap judgments) also apply to appraisal and exit interviews. However, we'll postpone discussions of those two interviews until later chapters.

There are several ways to conduct a selection interview. For example, we can classify selection interviews according to

1. How *structured* they are
2. Their "content"—the *types of questions* they contain
3. How the firm *administers* the interviews (for instance, one-on-one or via a committee)

Each has pros and cons. We'll look at each.

Structured versus Unstructured Interviews

unstructured (or nondirective) interview
An unstructured conversational-style interview in which the interviewer pursues points of interest as they come up in response to questions.

structured (or directive) interview
An interview following a set sequence of questions.

First, most interviews vary in the degree to which the interviewer structures or standardizes the interview process.[3] In **unstructured (or nondirective) interviews**, the manager follows no set format. A few questions might be specified in advance, but they're usually not, and there is seldom a formal guide for scoring "right" or "wrong" answers. Typical questions here might include, for instance, "Tell me about yourself," "Why do you think you'd do a good job here," and "What would you say are your main strengths and weaknesses." This type of interview could even be described as little more than a general conversation.[4] Most selection interviews probably fall in this category.

At the other extreme, in **structured (or directive) interviews**, the employer lists job-relevant questions ahead of time, and may even weight possible alternative answers for appropriateness.[5] McMurray's Patterned Interview was one early example. The interviewer followed a printed form to ask a series of questions, such as "How was the person's present job obtained?" Comments printed beneath the questions (such as "Has he/she shown self-reliance in getting his/her jobs?") then guide the interviewer in evaluating the answers. Some experts still restrict the term *structured interview* to interviews like these, which are based on carefully selected job-related questions with predetermined answers.

In practice, interview structure is a matter of degree. Sometimes the manager may just want to ensure he or she has a set list of questions to ask so as to avoid skipping any questions. Here, he or she might just choose questions from a list like that in Figure 7-3 (page 205). The structured interview guide in Figure 7-A1 (pages 214–216) illustrates a more structured approach. As another example, the Department of Homeland Security uses the structured guide in Figure 7-1 to help screen Coast Guard officer candidates. It contains a formal candidate rating procedure; it also enables geographically disbursed interviewers to complete the form via the Web.[6]

WHICH TO USE? Structured interviews are generally superior. In structured interviews, all interviewers generally ask all applicants the same questions. Partly because of this, these interviews tend to be more consistent, reliable, and valid. Having a standardized list of questions can also help even less talented interviewers conduct better interviews. Standardizing the interview also enhances job relatedness (because the questions chosen tend to provide insights into how the person will actually do the job), reduces overall subjectivity and thus the potential for bias, and may "enhance the ability to withstand legal challenge."[7] However, blindly following a structured format may not provide enough opportunity to pursue points of interest. The interviewer should always leave an opportunity to ask follow-up questions and pursue points of interest as they develop. We'll see how to write a structured interview later in this chapter.

Interview Content (What Types of Questions to Ask)

We can also classify interviews based on the "content" or the types of questions you ask. Many interviewers ask relatively unfocused questions, such as "What do you want to be doing in 5 years?" Questions like these generally do not provide much insight into how the person will do on the job. That is why *situational, behavioral*, and *job-related* questions are best.

FIGURE 7-1 Officer Programs Applicant Interview Form

Source: www.uscg.mil/forms/cg/CG5527.pdf, accessed September 8, 2013.

U.S. Department of Homeland Security CG-5527 (06-04)	**Officer Programs Applicant Interview Form**	1. Date:

2. Name of Applicant (Last, First, MI)

3. **Overall Impression:** Compare this applicant to others you have interviewed or known. (Note: Scores of 4 through 7 constitute a recommendation for selection.)

NOT RECOMMENDED			**RECOMMENDED**			
Unsatisfactory	Limited Potential	Fair Performer	Good Performer	Excellent Performer	Exceptional Performer	Distinguished Performer
1☐	2☐	3☐	4☐	5☐	6☐	7☐

Comments:

4. **Performance of Duties:** Measures an applicant's ability to manage and to get things done.

Unsatisfactory	Limited Potential	Fair Performer	Good Performer	Excellent Performer	Exceptional Performer	Distinguished Performer
1☐	2☐	3☐	4☐	5☐	6☐	7☐

Comments:

5. **Communication Skills:** Measures an applicant's ability to communicate in a positive, clear, and convincing manner.

Unsatisfactory	Limited Potential	Fair Performer	Good Performer	Excellent Performer	Exceptional Performer	Distinguished Performer
1☐	2☐	3☐	4☐	5☐	6☐	7☐

Comments:

6. **Names of Board Members**	7. **Rank**	8. **Command/Unit**	9. **Signature**	10. **Career Total of Interviews Conducted**

PREVIOUS EDITIONS ARE OBSOLETE

CONTINUED ON REVERSE

Reset

situational interview
A series of job-related questions that focus on how the candidate would behave in a given situation.

behavioral interview
A series of job-related questions that focus on how the candidate reacted to actual situations in the past.

SITUATIONAL QUESTIONS In a **situational interview**, you ask the candidate what his or her behavior *would be* in a given situation.[8] For example, ask a supervisory candidate how he or she would act in response to a subordinate coming to work late 3 days in a row.

BEHAVIORAL QUESTIONS Whereas situational interviews ask applicants to describe how they would react to a hypothetical situation today or tomorrow, **behavioral interviews** ask applicants to describe *how they reacted* to actual situations in the past.[9] *Situational* questions start with phrases such as, "Suppose you were faced with the following situation. . . . What would do?" *Behavioral* questions start with phrases like, "Can you think of a time when. . . you do?"[10] In one variant, Vanguard uses an interviewing technique they call S managers ask interviewees about a particular situation (S), or task (T) he or she

FIGURE 7-1 *Continued*

Page 2 - CG-5527 (06-04)

11. **Leadership Skills:** Measures an applicant's ability to support, develop, direct, and influence others in performing work.

Unsatisfactory	Limited Potential	Fair Performer	Good Performer	Excellent Performer	Exceptional Performer	Distinguished Performer
1☐	2☐	3☐	4☐	5☐	6☐	7☐

Comments:

12. **Personal and Professional Qualities:** Measures qualities which illustrate the applicant's character.

Unsatisfactory	Limited Potential	Fair Performer	Good Performer	Excellent Performer	Exceptional Performer	Distinguished Performer
1☐	2☐	3☐	4☐	5☐	6☐	7☐

Comments:

Reset

INSTRUCTIONS

The Officer Programs Applicant Interview Form is designed to help Officer Programs selection panels select applicants to be Coast Guard officers. The form is heavily based on the Officer Evaluation Report (OER) and the scale for each category is based on OER performance standards. While it should be remembered that applicants are not yet Coast Guard officers, they should have had opportunities to exhibit qualities that show they possess the character and potential necessary to be successful officers. Provide written comments in support of numeric markings for each category. Base these comments on what you observe during the interview or see in the supporting documentation in the applicant's package. Much like an OER, both the numerical evaluation and written comments are used by selection panels. Officer interview boards should review Article 4.B.2 of the Recruiting Manual, COMDTINST M1100.2 (series) and Articles 1.B.8 and 1.B.9 of the Personnel Manual, COMDTINST M1000.6 (series), which provide guidance on officer interviews.

1. Date of interview.
2. Self-explanatory.
3. Marks in the **Overall Impression** block should summarize the interview board's recommendation of the applicant's suitability for service as a Coast Guard Officer, and therefore should be completed last. Scores of 4 through 7 constitute a recommendation for selection.

4-5. Self-explanatory.

6. Last name, first name, and middle initial.

7-9. Self-explanatory.

10. Interviewer's career total of officer applicant interview boards.

11-12. Self-explanatory.

PREVIOUS EDITIONS ARE OBSOLETE

uncover the actions (A) the candidates took, and the result (R) of his or her actions.[11] Behavioral interviews are increasingly used.[12]

When Citizen's Banking Corporation in Flint, Michigan, found that 31 of the 50 people in its call center quit in one year, Cynthia Wilson, the center's head, switched to behavioral interviews. Many who left did so because they didn't enjoy irate questions from clients. So Wilson no longer tries to predict how candidates will act based on asking them if they want to work with angry clients. Instead, she asks behavioral questions like, "Tell me about a time you were speaking with an irate person, and how you turned the situation around." This makes it harder to fool the interviewer; only four people left in the following year.[13]

job-related interview
A series of job-related questions that focus on relevant past job-related behaviors.

OTHER TYPES OF QUESTIONS In a **job-related interview**, the interviewer asks applicants questions about job-relevant past experiences. The questions here don't revolve around hypothetical or actual situations or scenarios. Instead, the interviewer asks job-related questions such as, "Which courses did you like best in business school?" The aim is to draw conclusions about, say, the candidate's ability to handle the financial aspects of the job the employer seeks to fill.

stress interview
An interview in which the applicant is made uncomfortable by a series of often rude questions. This technique helps identify hypersensitive applicants and those with low or high stress tolerance.

There are other, lesser-used types of questions. In a **stress interview**, the interviewer seeks to make the applicant uncomfortable with occasionally rude questions. The aim is supposedly to spot sensitive applicants and those with low (or high) stress tolerance. Thus, a candidate for a customer relations manager position who obligingly mentions having had four jobs in the past 2 years might be told that frequent job changes reflect irresponsible and immature behavior. If the applicant then responds with a reasonable explanation of why the job changes were necessary, the interviewer might pursue another topic. On the other hand, if the formerly tranquil applicant reacts explosively, the interviewer might deduce that the person has a low tolerance for stress.

Stress interviews may help unearth hypersensitive applicants who might overreact to mild criticism with anger and abuse. However, the stress interview's invasive and ethically dubious nature demands that the interviewer be both skilled in its use and sure the job really calls for a thick skin and an ability to handle stress. This is definitely not an approach for amateur interrogators or for those without the skills to keep the interview under control.

Puzzle questions are popular. Recruiters see how candidates think under pressure. For example, an interviewer at Microsoft asked a tech service applicant this: "Mike and Todd have $21 between them. Mike has $20 more than Todd does. How much money has Mike, and how much money has Todd?"[14] (The answer is one paragraph below.)

HR in Practice at the Hotel Paris As an experienced HR professional, Lisa knew that the company's new testing program would go only so far. To see how the Hotel Paris created a new interview process, see the case on pages 210–211.

How Should We Conduct the Interview?

Employers also administer interviews in various ways: *one-on-one or by a panel of interviewers, sequentially or all at once*, and *computerized or personally.*

Most selection interviews are *one-on-one* and *sequential.* In a one-on-one interview, two people meet alone, and one interviews the other by seeking oral responses to oral inquiries. Employers tend to schedule these interviews *sequentially.* In a *sequential (or serial) interview*, several persons interview the applicant, in sequence, one-on-one, and then make their hiring decision. In an **unstructured sequential interview**, each interviewer generally just asks questions as they come to mind. In a **structured sequential interview**, each interviewer rates the candidates on a standard evaluation form, using standardized questions. The hiring manager then reviews these ratings before deciding whom to hire.[15] (Answer: Mike had $20.50, Todd $0.50.)

unstructured sequential interview
An interview in which each interviewer forms an independent opinion after asking different questions.

structured sequential interview
An interview in which the applicant is interviewed sequentially by several persons; each rates the applicant on a standard form.

panel interview
An interview in which a group of interviewers questions the applicant.

mass interview
A panel interviews several candidates simultaneously.

PANEL INTERVIEWS A **panel interview**, also known as a board interview, is an interview conducted by a team of interviewers (usually two to three), who together question each candidate and then combine their ratings of each candidate's answers into a final panel score. This contrasts with the *one-on-one interview* (in which one interviewer meets one candidate) and a *serial interview* (where several interviewers assess a single candidate one-on-one, sequentially).[16]

The panel format enables interviewers to ask follow-up questions, much as reporters do in press conferences. This may elicit more meaningful responses than a series of one-on-one interviews. On the other hand, some candidates find panel interviews more stressful, so they may actually inhibit responses. (An even more stressful variant is the **mass interview**. Here a panel interviews several candidates simultaneously. The panel poses a problem, and then watches to see which candidate takes the lead in formulating an answer.)

Whether panel interviews are more or less reliable and valid than sequential interviews depends on how the employer actually does the panel interview. For example, *structured* panel interviews in which members use scoring sheets with descriptive scoring examples for sample answers are more reliable and valid than those that don't. Training the panel interviewers may boost the interview's reliability.[17]

PHONE INTERVIEWS Employers occasionally conduct some interviews via phone. Somewhat counter-intuitively, these can actually be more useful than face-to-face interviews for judging one's conscientiousness, intelligence, and interpersonal skills. Because they needn't worry about appearance or handshakes, each party can focus on answers. And perhaps candidates—somewhat surprised by an unplanned call from the recruiter—give more spontaneous answers.[18] In one study, interviewers tended to evaluate applicants more favorably in telephone versus face-to-f interviews, particularly where interviewees were less physically attractive. (The interviewers came to about the same conclusions regarding the interviewees whether the interview was face-to-face or by videoconference). The applicants preferred the face-to-face interviews.[19]

Improving Performance Through HRIS: Web-Based Interviews

Firms have long used the Web for selection interviews (particularly the prescreening interviews). Now, with tablet video functionalities, FaceTime, and Skype™, their use is growing. Cisco Systems, Inc., recruiters conduct preliminary interviews online. Applicants use their own camera-supported PC or tablets. Then, at the appointed time, they link to Cisco via Web video for the prescreening interview. Video interviews of course reduce travel and recruiting expenses.[20] Several employers such as Microsoft and Hewlett-Packard use the online virtual community Second Life to conduct job interviews. Job seekers create avatars to represent themselves in the interviews.[21]

InterviewStream, Inc. (www.InterviewStream.com) offers employer clients prerecorded and live video interview management systems for prescreening candidates and interviewing remote talent. For prerecorded interviews, candidates use a Webcam to record responses to the client's tailored, prerecorded questions, which the client can review at its convenience. Or, the client and candidate use InterviewStream's live videoconference platform for a live interview. Consider the firm's InterviewStream 360 Video Practice Interview System. College career centers and outplacement firms use it to have students or jobseekers record interviews, for their own development and to make available to prospective employers.[22]

An online interview requires little special preparation for employers, but Career FAQs (www.careerfaqs.com.au) lists things that *interviewees* should keep in mind. It's often the obvious things people overlook (for more on how to take interviews, see Appendix 2 to this chapter, page 217):[23]

- ***Look presentable.*** You might feel silly sitting at home wearing a suit, but it could make a difference.
- ***Clean up the room.*** Do not let the interviewer see you sitting in front of a pile of clutter.
- ***Test first.*** As Career FAQs says, "Five minutes before the video interview is not a good time to realize that your Internet is down, Skype isn't working, or your pet rabbit has chewed through the microphone cord."
- ***Do a dry run.*** Record yourself before the interview to try answering some imaginary questions.
- ***Relax.*** The golden rule with such interviews is to treat them like any face-to-face meeting. Smile, look confident and enthusiastic, try to make eye contact, and don't shout, but do speak clearly.

COMPUTERIZED INTERVIEWS A *computerized selection interview* is one in which a job candidate's oral and/or keyed replies are obtained in response to computerized oral, visual, or written questions and/or situations. Most computerized interviews present the applicant with a series of job-related questions regarding his or her background, experience, education, skills, knowledge, and work attitudes. Some such computerized interviews also confront candidates with realistic scenarios (such as irate customers) to which they must respond online.[24]

Typical computerized interviews present questions in a multiple-choice format, one at a time. A sample interview question for a person applying for a job as a retail store clerk might be:

How would your supervisor rate your customer service skills?

a. Outstanding
b. Above average
c. Average
d. Below average
e. Poor[25]

Questions come in rapid sequence and require concentration.[26] The typical computerized interview program measures the response time to each question. A delay in answering certain questions such as "Can you be trusted?" flags a potential problem. The accompanying HR as a Profit Center feature illustrates the bottom line impact such systems can have.

IMPROVING PERFORMANCE: HR as a Profit Center

Great Western Bank

When Bonnie Dunn tried out for a teller's job at Great Western Bank, she faced a lineup of tough customers.[27] One woman sputtered contradictory instructions about depositing a check and then blew her top when Bonnie wasn't fast enough. Another said, "You people are unbelievably slow."

Both these customers appeared on a computer screen, as part of a 20-minute computerized job interview. Ms. Dunn sat in front of the screen, responding via a touch screen and a microphone. She was tested on making change and on sales skills, and on keeping her cool. When applicants sit down facing the computer, they hear it say, "Welcome to the interactive assessment aid." The computer records their comments for evaluation later. To begin the interview, applicants touch an icon on the screen, eliciting an ominous foreword: "We'll be keeping track of how long it takes you and how many mistakes you make. Accuracy is more important than speed."

Great Western's system dramatically reduced in-person interviewing of unacceptable candidates, saving valuable HR time and resources. And, partly because the candidates see what the job is really like, those hired are reportedly 26% less likely to leave within 90 days of hiring, significantly reducing the bank's employee turnover costs.

Discussion Question 7-1: You have to hire dozens of wait staff every year for a new restaurant on Miami Beach. Explain how you would use a computerized interview, including questions and tasks for candidates.

SPEED DATING For better or worse, some employers use "speed dating" interviewing. One sent e-mails to all applicants for an advertised position. Four hundred (of 800 applicants) showed up. Over several hours, applicants first mingled with employees, and then (in a so-called "speed dating area") had one-on-one contacts with employees for a few minutes. Based on this, the recruiting team chose 68 candidates for follow-up interviews.[28]

BAIN & COMPANY CASE INTERVIEW Bain & Company uses case interviews as part of its candidate selection process. By having candidates explain how they would address the case "client's" problems, the case interview combines elements of behavioral and situational questioning to provide a more realistic assessment of the candidate's consulting skills. The accompanying screen grab shows Bain candidates how to prepare for the case-based interview.

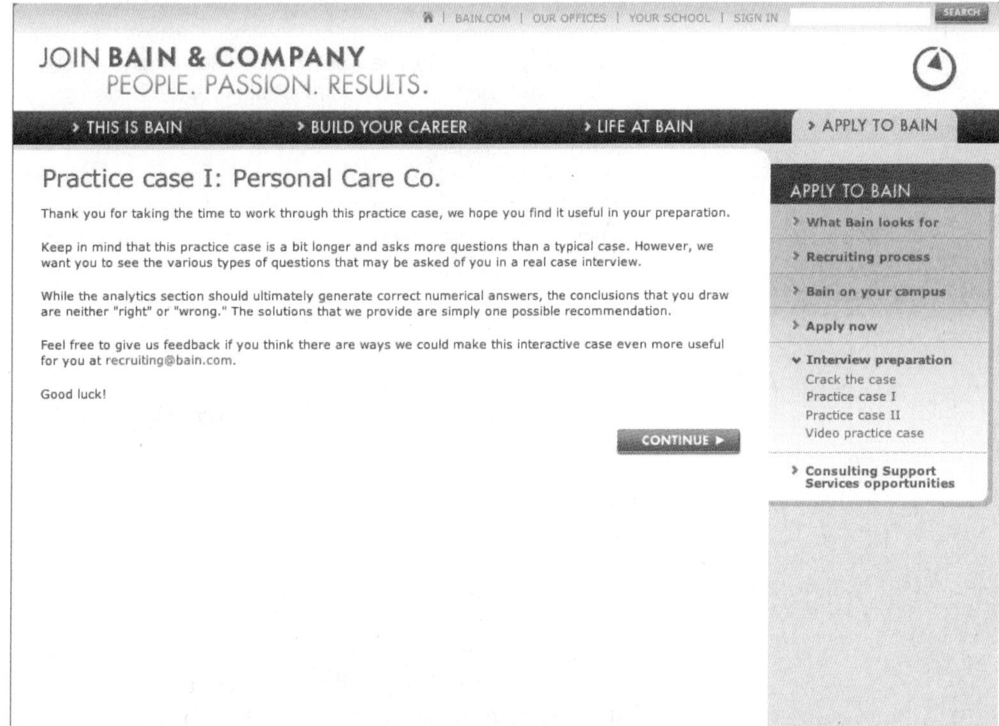

Bain candidates need to prepare for their case-based interviews.

Source: John Bain & Company, www.joinbain.com, accessed September 2011.

Three Ways to Make the Interview More Useful

Interviews hold an ironic place in the hiring process: Everyone uses them, but they're generally not particularly valid. The knack is to do them properly. If you do, then the interview is generally a good predictor of performance and is comparable with many other selection techniques.[29] Keep three things in mind—use structured interviews, know what to ask, and avoid the common interviewing errors.

USE STRUCTURED SITUATIONAL INTERVIEWS First, *structure the interview.*[30] Structured interviews (particularly structured interviews using situational questions) are more valid than unstructured interviews for predicting job performance. They are more valid partly because they are more reliable—for example, the same interviewer administers the interview more consistently from candidate to candidate.[31] Situational structured interviews yield a higher mean validity than do job-related (or behavioral) interviews, which in turn yield a higher mean validity than do "psychological" interviews (which focus more on motives and interests).[32]

KNOW WHAT TO ASK Interviews are better at revealing some things than others. In one study, interviewers were able to size up the interviewee's extraversion and agreeableness. What they could *not* assess accurately were the traits that often matter most on jobs—like conscientiousness and emotional stability.[33] One implication seems to be, focus more on situational and job knowledge questions that help you assess how the candidate will actually respond to typical situations on that job.

KNOW YOUR EMPLOYMENT LAW

Interviewing Candidates

Various EEO laws, including Title VII of the Civil Rights Act of 1964, and the Civil Rights Act of 1991, require employment interviewers to exercise caution. Questions regarding an applicant's race, color, religion, sex, age, national origin, or disability trigger red flags. Again, it's generally not illegal to ask a female job candidate about marital status or an 80-year-old applicant "how old are you?" It certainly is not advisable to do so, but the manager can ask such questions, as long as he or she can show either that the employer does not discriminate or that it can defend the interview question as a BFOQ or business necessity. However, many state and local laws do bar asking them. And the EEOC disapproves of such practices as asking applicants their age.

If a protected group member does bring a charge of discrimination against the employer, what will sway the court in favor of the employer? A study of federal district court cases provides some insights. The most important action seems to be to make sure the interview process is structured and consistently applied. Three aspects of interview structure—(1) having objective/job-related questions, (2) standardizing interview administration, and (3) having multiple interviewers—were related to verdicts in favor of employers.[34] This seems to suggest using panel or series situational or behavioral structured interviews.

Of course, the best approach is to avoid having job candidates file charges in the first place. Here, fairness is important. Endeavor to make it clear to applicants that the interview process is fair, that the interviewer treats the interviewee with courtesy and respect, and that the interviewer is willing to explain the interview process and the nature and rationale for the questions.[35]

BEWARE OF COMMITTING INTERVIEWING ERRORS In addition to structuring the interview and knowing what to ask, effective interviewers understand and avoid the *various errors that can undermine* any interview's usefulness. We turn to these next.

Errors That Can Undermine an Interview's Usefulness

2 List and explain the main errors that can undermine an interview's usefulness.

Effective employment interviewers understand and avoid the following common interview errors.

First Impressions (Snap Judgments)

Probably the most widespread error is that interviewers tend to jump to conclusions—make snap judgments—about candidates during the first few minutes of the interview (or even before the interview starts, based on test scores or résumé data). One researcher estimates that in 85% of the cases, interviewers had made up their minds before the interview even began, based on first impressions the interviewers gleaned from candidates' applications and personal appearance.[36] In one typical study, giving interviewers the candidates' test scores biased the ultimate assessment of the candidates. In another study, interviewers judged candidates who they were told formerly suffered from depression or substance abuse more negatively.[37]

First impressions are especially damaging when the prior information about the candidate is negative. In one study, interviewers who previously received unfavorable reference letters about applicants gave those applicants less credit for past successes and held them more personally responsible for past failures after the interview. And the interviewers' final decisions (to accept or reject those applicants) always reflected what they expected of the applicants based on the references, quite aside from the applicants' actual interview performance.[38]

Add to this two more interviewing facts. First, interviewers are more influenced by unfavorable than favorable information about the candidate. Second, their impressions are much more likely to change from favorable to unfavorable than from unfavorable to favorable. Indeed, many interviewers really search more for negative information, often without realizing it.

The bottom line is that most interviews are loaded against the applicant. One who starts well could easily end up with a low rating because unfavorable information tends to predominate. And for the interviewee who starts out poorly, it's almost impossible to overcome that first bad impression.[39] One psychologist interviewed CEOs of 80 top companies. She concluded that you "don't even get to open your mouth."[40] Instead, the interviewer will size up your posture, handshake, smile, and "captivating aura." It's difficult to overcome that first impression, one way or another.

Not Clarifying What the Job Requires

Interviewers who don't have an accurate picture of what the job entails and what sort of candidate is best for it usually make their decisions based on incorrect impressions or stereotypes of what a good applicant is. They then erroneously match interviewees with their incorrect stereotypes. You should clarify what sorts of traits you're looking for, and why, before starting the interview.

One classic study involved 30 professional interviewers.[41] Half got just this brief job description: "the eight applicants here represented by their application blanks are applying for the position of secretary." The other 15 interviewers got much more explicit job information, including typing speed and bilingual ability, for instance.

More job knowledge translated into better interviews. The 15 interviewers with more job information generally all agreed among themselves about each candidate's potential; those without it did not. The latter also didn't discriminate as well among applicants—they tended to give them all high ratings.

Candidate-Order (Contrast) Error and Pressure to Hire

candidate-order (or contrast) error
An error of judgment on the part of the interviewer due to interviewing one or more very good or very bad candidates just before the interview in question.

Candidate-order (or contrast) error means that the order in which you see applicants affects how you rate them. In one study, managers had to evaluate a sample candidate who was "just average" after first evaluating several "unfavorable" candidates. They scored the average candidate more favorably than they might otherwise because, in contrast to the unfavorable candidates, the average one looked better than he actually was. This contrast effect can be huge: In some early studies, evaluators based only a small part of the applicant's rating on his or her actual potential.[42]

Pressure to hire accentuates this problem. Researchers told one group of managers to assume they were behind in their recruiting quota. They told a second group they were ahead. Those "behind" rated the same recruits more highly.[43]

Nonverbal Behavior and Impression Management

The applicant's nonverbal behavior (smiling, avoiding your gaze, and so on) can also have a surprisingly large impact on his or her rating. In one study, 52 human resource specialists watched videotaped job interviews in which *the applicants' verbal content was identical*, but their nonverbal behavior differed markedly. Researchers told applicants in one group to exhibit minimal eye contact, a low energy level, and low voice modulation. Those in a second group demonstrated the opposite behavior. Twenty-three of the 26 personnel specialists who saw the high-eye-contact, high-energy-level candidate would have invited him or her for a second interview. None who saw the low-eye-contact, low-energy-level candidate would have recommended a second interview.[44] It seems to pay interviewees to "look alive."

Nonverbal behaviors are probably so important because interviewers infer your personality from the way you act in the interview. In one study, 99 graduating college seniors completed questionnaires, which included measures of personality, among other things. The students then reported their success in generating follow-up interviews and job offers. The interviewee's personality, particularly his or her level of extraversion, had a pronounced influence on whether or not he or she received follow-up interviews and job offers.[45] In turn, extraverted applicants seem particularly prone to self-promotion, and self-promotion is strongly related to the interviewer's perceptions of candidate–job fit.[46] Even structuring the interview doesn't seem to cancel out the effects of such nonverbal behavior.[47]

IMPRESSION MANAGEMENT Clever candidates capitalize on that fact. One study found that some used ingratiation to persuade interviewers to like them. For instance, the candidates praised the interviewers or appeared to agree with their opinions, thus signaling they shared similar beliefs. Sensing that a perceived similarity in attitudes may influence how the interviewer rates them, some interviewees try to emphasize (or fabricate) such similarities.[48] Others make self-promoting comments about their accomplishments.[49] Self-promotion means promoting one's own skills and abilities to create the impression of competence.[50] Psychologists call using techniques like ingratiation and self-promotion "impression management." Self-promotion is an effective tactic; however faking or lying generally backfires.[51]

Effect of Personal Characteristics: Attractiveness, Gender, Race

Unfortunately, physical attributes also distort assessments.[52] For example, people usually ascribe more favorable traits and more successful life outcomes to attractive people.[53] Similarly, race can play a role, depending on how you conduct the interview. In one study, for example, the white members of a racially balanced interview panel rated white candidates higher, while the black interviewers rated black candidates higher. (In all cases, *structured* interviews produced less of a difference between minority and white interviewees than did unstructured interviews.)[54]

Interviewers' reactions to minority stereotypes are complex. In one study, the researchers dressed the "applicants" in either traditional Muslim attire (black scarf and full-length black robe) or simple two-piece black pantsuits. Both applicants got the same number of job offers. However, interactions were shorter and more interpersonally negative when applicants wore the Muslim attire.[55]

In general, candidates evidencing various attributes and disabilities (such as child-care demands, HIV-positive status, and being wheelchair-bound) have less chance of obtaining a positive decision, even when the person performed well in the structured interview.[56] The following section expands on this.

Diversity Counts: Applicant Disability and the Employment Interview

Researchers surveyed 40 disabled people from various occupations. The disabled people felt that interviewers tend to avoid directly addressing the disability, and therefore make their decisions without all the facts.[57]

What the disabled people prefer is a discussion that allows the employer to clarify his or her concerns and reach a knowledgeable conclusion. Among the questions they said they would like interviewers to ask were these:

- Is there any kind of setting or special equipment that will facilitate the interview process for you?
- Is there any specific technology that you currently use or have used in previous jobs that assists the way you work?
- What other kind of support did you have in previous jobs? Is there anything that would benefit you?
- Discuss a barrier or obstacle, if any, that you have encountered in any of your previous jobs. How was that addressed?
- Do you anticipate any transportation or scheduling issues with the work schedule expected of this position?

Remember that under the Americans with Disabilities Act, the interviewer must limit his or her questions to whether the applicant has any physical or mental impairment that may interfere with his or her ability to perform the job's essential tasks.[58]

In another study, the researchers manipulated the candidates' appearance, for instance "by placing scar like marks on the cheeks of some of the applicants for some interviews, but not for others." Results revealed that managers who interviewed a facially stigmatized applicant (versus a non-stigmatized applicant) rated the applicant lower [and] recalled less information about the interview" (in part, apparently, because staring at the "scars" distracted the interviewers).[59]

EMPLOYMENT DISCRIMINATION "TESTERS" The use of employment discrimination "testers" makes nondiscriminatory interviewing even more important. As defined by the EEOC, testers are "individuals who apply for employment which they do not intend to accept, for the sole purpose of uncovering unlawful discriminatory hiring practices."[60] Although not really seeking employment, testers have legal standing with the courts and EEOC.[61]

One civil rights group sent four university students—two white, two black—to an employment agency, supposedly in pursuit of a job. The civil rights group gave the four "testers" backgrounds and training to make their qualifications appear almost indistinguishable from each other. The white tester/applicants got interviews and job offers. The black tester/applicants got neither interviews nor offers.[62]

IMPROVING PERFORMANCE: HR Practices Around the Globe

Selection Practices Abroad

In choosing (interview or other) selection criteria abroad, the manager in a multinational subsidiary walks a thin line between using the parent company's selection process and adapting it to local cultural differences. One study focused on Bangladesh.[63] Traditional selection practices there are different from what one might expect in the United States. For example, "age is considered synonymous to wisdom." Therefore, job advertisements for mid- and senior-level positions often set a minimum age as a selection criteria, while " [f]or the entry level positions in public sector organizations, age limit is restricted up to 30 years of age." But managers of multinational subsidiaries there are slowly implementing their corporate headquarters' prescribed HRM practices. As a result, the "traditional" way of doing things is evolving, and the multinationals are thereby affecting local recruitment and selection practices. That said, a manager would still be wise to understand each country's unique cultural demands before holding an interview there.

Discussion Question 7-2: You are interviewing candidates in Bangladesh and you have a great candidate who unfortunately is 25 years old, when the job calls for someone at least 40. List three questions you would ask to see if the person is still qualified.

Interviewer Behavior

Finally, the *interviewer's* behavior also affects the interviewee's performance and rating.

For example, some interviewers inadvertently telegraph the expected answers,[64] as in: "This job involves a lot of stress. You can handle that, can't you?" Even subtle cues (like a smile or nod) can telegraph the desired answer.[65] Some interviewers talk so much that applicants have no time to answer questions. At the other extreme, some interviewers let the applicant dominate the interview, and so don't ask all their questions.[66] When interviewers have favorable pre-interview impressions of the applicant, they tend to act more positively toward that person (smiling more, for instance).[67] Other interviewers play interrogator, forgetting that it's not civil to play "gotcha" by gleefully pouncing on inconsistencies. Some interviewers play amateur psychologist, unprofessionally probing for hidden meanings in what the applicant says. Others ask improper questions, forgetting that discriminatory questions "had a significant negative effect on participant's reactions to the interview and interviewer."[68] Other interviewers are simply unable to conduct interviews.

In summary, interviewing errors to avoid include:

- First impressions (snap judgments)
- Not clarifying what the job involves and requires
- Candidate-order error and pressure to hire
- Nonverbal behavior and impression management
- The effects of interviewees' personal characteristics
- The interviewer's inadvertent behaviors

Social Media and HR

Both employers and job candidates use social media tools as part of the employment interview process. For prospective interviewees, acing the job interview is all about knowing as much as possible about the prospective employer and what it's looking for in employees; and, as one expert at Syracuse University Career Services points out, social media tools are excellent sources of such information.[69] For example, you will find lists of new hires and demographic information about employees on the employer's LinkedIn site. (Similarly, the employers can use LinkedIn to give prospective employees a better insight into "Why you should work for us"). Following the employer's official Twitter accounts and blogs can also reveal important information about things like changes in the company's strategies and business units that show the interviewee did his or her homework. Its executives may also have their own "unofficial" Twitter accounts and blogs. Use these for insights into the issues they face.

How to Design and Conduct an Effective Interview

3 Define a structured situational interview and give examples of situational questions, behavioral questions, and background questions that provide structure.

structured situational interview
A series of job-relevant questions with predetermined answers that interviewers ask of all applicants for the job.

There is little doubt that the **structured situational interview**—a series of job-relevant questions with predetermined answers that interviewers ask of all applicants for the job—produces superior results.[70] Ideally, the basic idea is to (1) write situational (what would you do), behavioral (what did you do), or job knowledge questions, *and* (2) have job experts (like those supervising the job) also write several answers for each of these questions, rating the answers from good to poor. The people who interview the applicants then use rating sheets anchored with these examples of good or bad answers to rate the interviewees' answers.[71]

Designing a Structured Situational Interview

The procedure is as follows.[72]

Step 1. **Analyze the job.** Write a job description with a list of job duties; required knowledge, skills, and abilities; and other worker qualifications.

Step 2. **Rate the job's main duties.** Rate each job duty, say from 1 to 5, based on how important it is to doing the job.

Step 3. **Create interview questions.** Create interview questions for each of the job duties, with more questions for the important duties. Recall that *situational questions* pose a hypothetical job situation, such as "What would you do if the machine suddenly began heating up?" *Job knowledge questions* assess knowledge essential to job performance (such as "What is HTML?"). *Willingness questions* gauge the applicant's willingness and motivation to meet the job's requirements—to do repetitive physical work or to travel, for instance. *Behavioral questions,* of course, ask candidates how they've handled similar situations.

The people who create the questions usually write them as critical incidents. For example, to probe for conscientiousness, the interviewer might ask this situational question:

> Your spouse and two teenage children are sick in bed with colds. There are no relatives or friends available to look in on them. Your shift starts in 3 hours. What would you do?

Step 4. **Create benchmark answers.** Next, *for each question*, develop ideal (benchmark) answers for good (a 5 rating), marginal (a 3 rating), and poor (a 1 rating) answers and a rating sheet. The structured interview guide (pages 214–216) presents an example. Three benchmark answers (from low to high) for the example question above might be, "I'd stay home—my spouse and family come first" (1); "I'd phone my supervisor and explain my situation" (3); and "Since they only have colds, I'd come to work" (5).

Step 5. **Appoint the interview panel and conduct interviews.** Employers generally conduct structured situational interviews using a panel, rather than one-on-one. The panel usually consists of three to six members, preferably the same ones who wrote the questions and answers. It may also include the job's supervisor and/or incumbent, and a human resources representative. The same panel interviews all candidates for the job.[73]

The panel members review the job description, questions, and benchmark answers before the interview. One panel member introduces the applicant, and asks all questions of all applicants in this and succeeding candidates' interviews (to ensure consistency). However, all panel members record and rate the applicant's answers on the rating sheet (as on pages 214–216). They do this by indicating where the candidate's answer to each question falls relative to the benchmark poor, marginal, or good answers. At the end of the interview, someone answers any questions the applicant has.[74]

Web-based programs help interviewers design and organize behaviorally based selection interviews. For example, SelectPro (www.selectpro.net) enables interviewers to create behavior-based selection interviews, custom interview guides, and automated online interviews. The HR Tools feature explains another interviewing approach.

IMPROVING PERFORMANCE: HR Tools for Line Managers and Entrepreneurs

How to Conduct an Effective Interview

You may not have the time or inclination to create a structured situational interview. However, there is still much you can do to make your interviews systematic and productive.

Step 1: **First, make sure you know the job.** Do not start the interview unless you understand the job's duties and what human skills you're looking for. Study the job description.

Step 2: **Structure the interview.** *Any* structuring is better than none. If pressed for time, you can still do several things to ask more consistent and job-relevant questions, without developing a full-blown structured interview.[75] They include:[76]

- Base questions on *actual job duties.* This will minimize irrelevant questions.
- Use *job knowledge, situational, or behavioral questions*, and know enough about the job to be able to evaluate the interviewee's answers. Questions that simply ask for opinions and attitudes, goals and aspirations, and self-descriptions and self-evaluations allow candidates to present themselves in an overly favorable manner or avoid revealing weaknesses.[77] Figure 7-2 illustrates structured questions.
- *Use the same questions* with all candidates. This improves reliability. It also reduces bias by giving all candidates the same opportunity.
- Perhaps use *descriptive rating scales* (excellent, fair, poor) to rate answers. For each question, if possible, have several ideal answers and a score for each. Then rate each candidate's answers against this scale.
- If possible, use a *standardized interview form.* Interviews based on structured guides like the ones in Figure 7-1 (pages 193–194) or Figure 7A-1, "structured interview guide" (pages 214–216), usually result in better interviews.[78] At the very least, list your questions before the interview.

FIGURE 7-2 Examples of Questions That Provide Interview Structure

Job Knowledge Questions

1. What steps would you follow in changing the fan belt on a Toyota Camry?
2. What factors would you consider in choosing a computer to use for work?

Experience Questions

3. What experience have you had actually repairing automobile engines?
4. What experience have you had creating marketing programs for consumer products?

Behavioral (Past Behavior) Questions

5. Tell me about a time when you had to deal with a particularly obnoxious person. What was the situation, and how did you handle it?
6. Tell me about a time when you were under a great deal of stress.What was the situation, and how did you handle it?

Situational (What Would You Do) Questions

7. Suppose your boss insisted that a presentation had to be finished by tonight, but your subordinate said she has to get home early to attend an online class, so she is unable to help you.What would you do?
8. The CEO just told you that he's planning on firing your boss, with whom you are very close, and replacing him with you.What would you do?

Step 3: **Get organized.** Hold the interview in a private room to minimize interruptions (including text messages). Prior to the interview, review the candidate's application and résumé. Note any areas that are vague or that may indicate strengths or weaknesses.

Step 4: **Establish rapport.** The main reason for the interview is to find out about the applicant. Start by putting the person at ease. Greet the candidate and start the interview by asking a noncontroversial question, perhaps about the weather that day.

Step 5: **Ask questions.** Try to follow the situational, behavioral, and job knowledge questions you wrote out ahead of time. You'll find a sampling of other technical questions (such as "What did you most enjoy about your last job?") in Figure 7-3. As a rule,

Don't telegraph the desired answer.
Don't interrogate the applicant as if the person is on trial.
Don't monopolize the interview, nor let the applicant do so.
Do ask open-ended questions.
Do encourage the applicant to express thoughts fully.
Do draw out the applicant's opinions and feelings by repeating the person's last comment as a question (e.g., "You didn't like your last job?").
Do ask for examples.[79]
Do ask, "If I were to arrange for an interview with your boss, what would he or she say are your strengths, weaker points, and overall performance?[80]

Step 6: **Take brief, unobtrusive notes during the interview.** Doing so may help avoid making a snap decision early in the interview, and may also help jog your memory once the interview is complete. Take notes, jotting down just the key points of what the interviewee says.[81]

Step 7: **Close the interview.** Leave time to answer any questions the candidate may have and, if appropriate, to advocate your firm to the candidate.

Try to end the interview on a positive note. Tell the applicant whether there is any interest and, if so, what the next step will be. Make rejections diplomatically—"Although your background is impressive, there are other candidates whose experience is closer to our requirements." Remember, as one recruiter says, "An interview experience should leave a lasting, positive impression of the company, whether the candidate receives and accepts an offer or not."[82] If the applicant is still under consideration but you can't reach a decision now, say so.

In rejecting a candidate, one perennial question is, should you provide an explanation or not? In one study, rejected candidates who received an explanation detailing why the employer rejected them felt that the rejection process was fairer. Unfortunately, doing so may not be practical. Most employers say little, to avoid pushback and legal problems.[83]

Step 8: **Review the interview.** After the candidate leaves, review your interview notes, score the interview answers (if you used a guide), and make a decision.

We'll address what *interviewees* can do to apply these findings and to excel in the interview in Appendix 2 to this chapter.

Discussion Question 7-3: Write a one-paragraph (single-spaced) memo to the people who do your company's recruiting on the topic, "The five most important things an interviewer can do to have a useful selection interview."

Talent Management: Profiles and Employee Interviews

To ensure an integrated, goal-oriented human resource effort, talent management adherents use the same "competency model" or job profile (listing required skills, knowledge, behaviors and other competencies) for creating interview questions as for recruiting, testing, training, appraising, and paying the employee.

The manager can use the job's profile to formulate job-related situational, behavioral, and knowledge interview questions when selecting someone for a job or set of roles. For example, Table 7-1 (page 206) summarizes illustrative skill, knowledge, trait, and experience profile elements for a chemical engineer candidate, along with sample interview questions. Interviewing engineers using questions that are based on the job's required skills and other competencies focuses your questions precisely on those things someone must be proficient at to do this job well.

Organization and Planning Skills

1. Describe a specific situation which illustrates how you set objectives to reach a goal.
2. Tell me about a time when you had to choose between two or more important opportunities. How did you go about deciding which was most important to you?
3. Tell me how you normally schedule your time in order to accomplish your day-to-day tasks.
4. Describe a situation where you had a major role in organizing an important event. How did you do it?
5. Think about a lengthy term paper or report that you have written. Describe how you organized, researched, and wrote that report.
6. Give an example of how you organized notes and other materials in order to study for an important exam.
7. Describe a time when you reorganized something to be more efficient. How did you do it?
8. Think of a time when you made important plans that were fouled up. How did you react? What did you do?

Interaction and Leadership

1. Tell me about an event in your past which has greatly influenced the way you relate to people.
2. Give a specific example that best illustrates your ability to deal with an uncooperative person.
3. Some people have the ability to "roll with the punches." Describe a time when you demonstrated this skill.
4. Tell me when you had to work with someone who had a negative opinion of you. How did you overcome this?
5. Recall a time when you participated on a team. Tell me an important lesson you learned that is useful to you today.
6. Describe an instance when you reversed a negative situation at school, work, or home. How did you do it?
7. Describe a situation which best illustrates your leadership ability.
8. Think about someone whose leadership you admire. What qualities impress you?

Assertiveness and Motivation

1. Describe several work standards that you have set for yourself in past jobs. Why are these important to you?
2. Tell me a time when you have experienced a lack of motivation. What caused this? What did you do about it?
3. Describe a situation where you had to deal with someone whom you felt was dishonest. How did you handle it?
4. Describe a situation that made you extremely angry. How did you react?
5. Tell me about a time that best illustrates your ability to "stick things out" in a tough situation.
6. Describe a time when you motivated an unmotivated person to do something you wanted them to do.
7. Give me an example of a time when you were affected by organizational politics. How did you react?
8. Give me an example of when someone tried to take advantage of you. How did you react?

Decision Making and Problem Solving

1. Give an example that illustrates your ability to make a tough decision.
2. Tell me about a decision you made even though you did not have all the facts.
3. Describe a situation where you have had to "stand up" for a decision you made, even though it was unpopular.
4. Describe a situation where you changed your mind, even after you publicly committed to a decision.
5. Describe a situation that illustrates your ability to analyze and solve a problem.
6. Tell me about a time where you acted as a mediator to solve a problem between two other people.
7. Describe a problem that seemed almost overwhelming to you. How did you handle it?
8. Tell me about a time where you have used a creative or unique approach to solve a tough problem.

The following general questions will also help you prepare for employment interviews:

1. Tell me a little about yourself.
2. Why did you attend Indiana State University?
3. What led you to choose your major or career field?
4. What college subjects did you like best/least? What did you like/dislike about them?
5. What has been your greatest challenge in college?
6. Describe your most rewarding college experience.
7. Do you think that your grades are a good indication of your academic abilities?
8. If you could change a decision you made while at college, what would you change? Why?
9. What campus involvements did you choose? What did you gain/contribute?
10. What are your plans for continued or graduate study?
11. What interests you about this job? What challenges are you looking for in a position?
12. How have your educational and work experiences prepared you for this position?
13. What work experiences have been most valuable to you and why?
14. Why are you interested in our organization? In what way do you think you can contribute to our company?
15. How would you describe yourself?
16. What do you consider to be your greatest strengths? Weaknesses? Give examples.
17. If I asked the people who know you for one reason why I shouldn't hire you, what would they say?
18. What accomplishments have given you the most satisfaction? Why?
19. What are your long-range career objectives? How do you plan to achieve these?
20. How would you describe your ideal job?
21. What two or three things are most important to you in your job?
22. Do you have a geographical preference? Why?

FIGURE 7-3 Suggested Supplementary Questions for Interviewing Applicants

Source: Figure showing "Sample Interview Questions" from Indiana State University Career Center website.

Go into the interview with an accurate picture of the traits of an ideal candidate, know what you're going to ask, and be prepared to keep an open mind about the candidate.

Digital Vision/Thinkstock

TABLE 7-1 Asking Profile-Oriented Interview Questions

Profile Component	Example	Sample Interview Question
Skill	Able to use computer drafting software	Tell me about a time you used CAD Pro computerized design software.
Knowledge	How extreme heat affects hydrochloric acid (HCL)	Suppose you have an application where HCL is heated to 400 degrees Fahrenheit at 2 atmospheres of pressure; what happens to the HCL?
Trait	Willing to travel abroad at least 4 months per year visiting facilities	Suppose you had a family meeting that you had to attend next week and our company informed you that you had to leave for a job abroad immediately, and stay 3 weeks. How would you handle that?
Experience	Designed pollution filter for acid-cleaning facility	Tell me about a time when you designed a pollution filter device for an acid-cleaning facility. How did it work? What particular problems did you encounter? How did you address them?

4 What are the main points to know about developing and extending the actual job offer?

Developing and Extending the Job Offer

After all the interviews, background checks, and tests, the employer decides to whom to make an offer. The *judgmental* approach subjectively weighs all the evidence about the candidate. The *statistical* approach quantifies all the evidence and perhaps uses a formula to predict job success. The *hybrid* approach combines statistical results with judgment. Statistical and hybrid are more defensible; judgmental is better than nothing. It will base the actual offer on, for instance, the candidate's apparent attractiveness as a prospective employee, the level of the position, and pay rates for similar positions. Next the employer extends an actual job offer to the candidate verbally. Here, the employer's point person (who might be the person to whom the new employee will report, or the human resource director, for instance) discusses the offer's main parameters. These include, for instance, pay rates, benefits, and actual job duties. There may be some negotiations. Then, once agreement is reached, the employer will extend a written job offer to the candidate.

There are several issues to consider with the written offer. Perhaps most important, understand the difference between a job offer letter and a contract. In a job offer letter, the employer lists the offer's basic information. This typically starts with a welcome sentence. It then includes job-specific information (such as details on salary and pay), benefits information, paid leave information, and terms of employment (including, for instance, successful completion of job testing and physical exams). There should be a strong statement that the employment relationship is "at will." There is then a closing statement. This again welcomes the employee, mentions who the employer's point person is if any questions arise, and instructs the candidate to sign the letter of offer if it is acceptable. It is prudent to have an attorney review the offer before extending it.[84]

For many positions (such as executive) a contract is in order. In contrast to a letter of offer (which should always be "at will"), an employment contract may have a duration (such as 3 years). Therefore, the contract will also describe grounds for termination or resignation, and severance provisions. The contract will almost always also include terms regarding confidentiality, nondisclosure requirements, and covenants not to compete (although some job offer letters for positions such as engineer may include such provisions as well). See www.Shrm.org/template-tools/toolkits for more information.

Depending upon the position, the employment contract (and, occasionally, the offer letter) may include a relocation provision. This lays out what the employer is willing to pay the new employee to relocate, for instance, in terms of moving expenses. State law generally governs enforcement of individual employment contracts. For letter of offer and employment contract samples, see, for example, http://www.unh.edu/hr/sites/unh.edu.hr/files/pdfs/offer-letter-template-status-staff.pdf, http://jobsearchtech.about.com/od/jobofferletters/a/jobofferletter.htm, and http://office.microsoft.com/en-us/templates/results.aspx?qu=offer+letter&ex=1.

Review

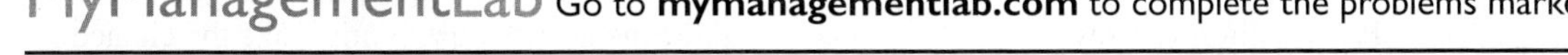

MyManagementLab Go to **mymanagementlab.com** to complete the problems marked with this icon. 

Chapter Section Summaries

1. A selection interview is a selection procedure designed to predict future job performance based on applicants' oral responses to oral inquiries; we discussed several **basic types of interviews**. There are structured versus unstructured interviews. We also distinguished between interviews based on the types of questions (such as situational versus behavioral) and on how you administer the interview, such as one-on-one, sequentially, or even via computer/video/telephone. However you decide to conduct and structure the interview, be careful what sorts of traits you try to assess, and beware of committing the sorts of interviewing errors we touch on next.
2. One reason selection interviews are often less useful than they should be is that managers make predictable **errors that undermine an interview's usefulness**. They jump to conclusions or make snap judgments based on preliminary information, they don't clarify what the job really requires, they succumb to candidate-order error and pressure to hire, and they let a variety of nonverbal behaviors and personal characteristics undermine the validity of the interview.
3. The manager should know how to **design and conduct an effective interview**. The structured situational interview is a series of job-related questions with predetermined answers that interviewers ask of all applicants for the job. Steps in creating a structured situational interview include analyzing the job, rating the job's main duties, creating interview questions, creating benchmark answers, and appointing the interview panel and conducting interviews. Steps in conducting an effective interview include making sure you know the job, structuring the interview, getting organized, asking

questions, taking brief unobtrusive notes during the interview, and reviewing the interview.

4. After choosing which candidate to hire, the employer turns to **developing and extending the job offer**. Things to keep in mind here include understanding the difference between a job offer letter and a contract. A job offer letter lists the offer's basic information, including details on salary and pay, benefits information, paid leave information, and terms of employment. There should be a strong statement specifying that the employment relationship is "at will." In contrast to a letter of offer, it is not unusual for an employment contract to have a duration (such as 3 years).

Discussion Questions

7-4. There are several ways to conduct a selection interview. Explain and illustrate the basic ways in which you can classify selection interviews.

7-5. Briefly describe each of the following types of interviews: unstructured panel interviews, structured sequential interviews, job-related structured interviews.

7-6. For what sorts of jobs do you think unstructured interviews might be most appropriate? Why?

7-7. How would you explain the fact that structured interviews, regardless of content, are generally more valid than unstructured interviews for predicting job performance?

✪ **7-8.** Briefly discuss what an interviewer can do to improve his or her interviewing performance.

✪ **7-9.** What items should a letter of offer definitely contain?

Individual and Group Activities

7-10. Prepare and give a short presentation titled "How to Be Effective as a Selection Interviewer."

7-11. Use the Internet to find employers who now do preliminary selection interviews via the Web. Do you think these interviews are useful? Why? How would you improve them?

7-12. In groups, discuss and compile examples of "the worst interview I ever had." What was it about these interviews that made them so bad? If time permits, discuss as a class.

7-13. In groups, prepare an interview (including a sequence of at least 20 questions) you'll use to interview candidates for the job of teaching a course in human resources management. Each group should present their interview questions in class.

7-14. Some firms swear by unorthodox interview methods. For example, Tech Planet, of Menlo Park, California, uses weekly lunches and "wacky follow-up sessions" as substitutes for first-round job interviews. During the informal meals, candidates are expected to mingle, and the Tech Planet employees they meet at the luncheons then review them. One Tech Planet employee asks candidates to ride a unicycle in her office to see if "they'll bond with the corporate culture or not." Toward the end of the screening process, the surviving group of interviewees has to solve brainteasers, and then openly evaluate their fellow candidates' strengths and weaknesses. What do you think of this screening process? What are its pros and cons? What changes, if any, would you recommend?[85]

7-15. Several years ago, Lockheed Martin Corp. sued the Boeing Corp. in Orlando, Florida, accusing it of using Lockheed's trade secrets to help win a multibillion-dollar government contract. Among other things, Lockheed Martin claimed that Boeing had obtained those trade secrets from a former Lockheed Martin employee who switched to Boeing.[86] But in describing methods companies use to commit corporate espionage, one writer says that hiring away the competitor's employees or hiring people to go through its dumpster are just the most obvious methods companies use to commit corporate espionage. As he says, "one of the more unusual scams—sometimes referred to as 'help wanted'—uses a person posing as a corporate headhunter who approaches an employee of the target company with a potentially lucrative job offer. During the interview, the employee is quizzed about his responsibilities, accomplishments, and current projects. The goal is to extract important details without the employee realizing there is no job."[87]

Assume you own a small high-tech company. What would you do (in terms of employee training, or a letter from you, for instance) to try to minimize the chance that one of your employees will fall into that kind of a trap? Also, compile a list of 10 questions that you think such a corporate spy might ask one of your employees.

7-16. KNOWLEDGE BASE Appendix A, PHR and SPHR Knowledge Base, at the end of this book (pages 580–588) lists the knowledge someone studying for the HRCI certification exam needs to have in each area of human resource management (such as in Strategic Management, Workforce Planning, and Human Resource Development). In groups, do four things: (1) review Appendix A; (2) identify the material in this chapter that relates to the required knowledge Appendix A lists; (3) write four multiple-choice exam questions on this material that you believe would be suitable for inclusion in the HRCI exam; and (4) if time permits, have someone from your team post your team's questions in front of the class, so that students in all teams can answer the exam questions created by the other teams.

Experiential Exercise

The Most Important Person You'll Ever Hire

Purpose: The purpose of this exercise is to give you practice using some of the interview techniques you learned from this chapter.

Required Understanding: You should be familiar with the information presented in this chapter, and read this: For parents, children are precious. It's therefore interesting that parents who hire "nannies" to take care of their children usually do little more than ask several interview questions and conduct what is often, at best, a perfunctory reference check. Given the often questionable validity of interviews, and the (often) relative inexperience of the father or mother doing the interviewing, it's not surprising that many of these arrangements end in disappointment. You know from this chapter that it is difficult to conduct a valid interview unless you know exactly what you're looking for and, preferably, structure the interview. Most parents simply aren't trained to do this.

How to Set Up the Exercise/Instructions:

- Set up groups of five or six students. Two students will be the interviewees, while the other students in the group will serve as panel interviewers. The interviewees will develop an interviewer assessment form, and the panel interviewers will develop a structured situational interview for a "nanny."

7-17. Instructions for the interviewees: The interviewees should leave the room for about 20 minutes. While out of the room, the interviewees should develop an "interviewer assessment form" based on the information presented in this chapter regarding factors that can undermine the usefulness of an interview. During the panel interview, the interviewees should assess the interviewers using the interviewer assessment form. After the panel interviewers have conducted the interview, the interviewees should leave the room to discuss their notes. Did the interviewers exhibit any of the factors that can undermine the usefulness of an interview? If so, which ones? What suggestions would you (the interviewees) make to the interviewers on how to improve the usefulness of the interview?

7-18. Instructions for the interviewers: While the interviewees are out of the room, the panel interviewers will have 20 minutes to develop a short structured situational interview form for a "nanny." The panel interview team will interview two candidates for the position. During the panel interview, each interviewer should be taking notes on a copy of the structured situational interview form. After the panel interview, the panel interviewers should discuss their notes. What were your first impressions of each interviewee? Were your impressions similar? Which candidate would you all select for the position and why?

Video Case

Video Title: Interviewing Candidates (Zipcar)

SYNOPSIS

Zipcar is a company that allows customers to share a car for a fee as small as a short cab ride. Individuals who become Zipcar members are able to reserve a vehicle with as little advance notice as 1 hour through any wireless device, unlock a car with a card that members carry with them, and drive for the reserved period of time. The goal of Zipcar is to reduce the number of cars being driven and thereby reduce environmental pollution.

Zipcar is a fast-growing innovative company that supports the environment and is socially responsible. This makes it an attractive place to work for many who are looking for a company that is doing something new. When selecting new employees, Zipcar aims to find people who are passionate about the brand, professional, courteous, and presentable. It wants someone who understands the value of the organization and the culture within which the company operates.

Discussion Questions

7-19. What makes Zipcar an attractive employer for which to work?

7-20. What do those doing the actual hiring at Zipcar feel are important characteristics to find in potential employees?

7-21. List three behavioral and three situational questions that you would use to interview Zipcar employment applicants.

7-22. According to the video, what practices should you avoid during an interview? How do these compare with those we discussed in this chapter?

Application Case

The Out-of-Control Interview

Maria Fernandez is a bright, popular, and well-informed mechanical engineer who graduated with an engineering degree from State University in June 2013. During the spring preceding her graduation, she went out on many job interviews, most of which she thought were conducted courteously and were reasonably useful in giving both her and the prospective employer a good impression of where each of them stood on matters of importance to both of them. It was, therefore, with great anticipation that she looked forward to an interview with the one firm in which she most wanted to work: Apex Environmental. She had always had a strong interest in the environment and believed that the best use of her training and skills lay in working for a firm like Apex, where she thought she could have a successful career while making the world a better place.

The interview, however, was a disaster. Maria walked into a room where five men—the president of the company, two vice presidents, the marketing director, and another engineer—began throwing questions at her that she felt were aimed primarily at tripping her up rather than finding out what she could offer through her engineering skills. The questions ranged from being unnecessarily discourteous ("Why would you take a job as a waitress in college if you're such an intelligent person?") to being irrelevant and sexist ("Are you planning on starting a family anytime soon?"). Then, after the interview, she met with two of the gentlemen individually (including the president), and the discussions focused on her technical expertise. She thought that these later discussions went fairly well. However, given the apparent aimlessness and even mean-spiritedness of the panel interview, she was astonished when several days later the firm made her a job offer.

The offer forced her to consider several matters. From her point of view, the job itself was perfect. She liked what she would be doing, the industry, and the firm's location. And in fact, the president had been quite courteous in subsequent discussions. She was left wondering whether the panel interview had been intentionally tense to see how she'd stand up under pressure, and, if so, why they would do such a thing?

Questions

7-23. How would you explain the nature of the panel interview Maria had to endure? Specifically, do you think it reflected a well-thought-out interviewing strategy on the part of the firm or carelessness on the part of the firm's management? If it were carelessness, what would you do to improve the interview process at Apex Environmental?

7-24. Would you take the job offer if you were Maria? If you're not sure, what additional information would help you make your decision?

7-25. The job of applications engineer for which Maria was applying requires (a) excellent technical skills with respect to mechanical engineering, (b) a commitment to working in the area of pollution control, (c) the ability to deal well and confidently with customers who have engineering problems, (d) a willingness to travel worldwide, and (e) a very intelligent and well-balanced personality. List 10 questions you would ask when interviewing applicants for the job.

Continuing Case

Carter Cleaning Company

The Better Interview

Like virtually all the other HR-related activities at Carter Cleaning Centers, the company currently has no organized approach to interviewing job candidates. Store managers, who do almost all the hiring, have a few of their own favorite questions that they ask. But in the absence of any guidance from management, they all admit their interview performance leaves something to be desired. Similarly, Jack Carter himself is admittedly most comfortable dealing with what he calls the "nuts and bolts" machinery aspect of his business and has never felt particularly comfortable having to interview management or other job applicants. Jennifer is sure that this lack of formal interviewing practices, procedures, and training account for some of the employee turnover and theft problems. Therefore, she wants to do something to improve her company's performance in this important area.

Questions

7-26. In general, what can Jennifer do to improve her employee interviewing practices? Should she develop interview forms that list questions for management and nonmanagement jobs? If so, how should these look and what questions should be included? Should she initiate a computer-based interview approach? If so, why and how?

7-27. Should she implement an interview training program for her managers, and if so, specifically what should be the content of such a training program? In other words, if she did decide to start training her management people to be better interviewers, what should she tell them and how should she tell it to them?

Translating Strategy into HR Policies and Practices Case*,§

**The accompanying strategy map for this chapter is in the MyManagementLab, and the overall map on the inside back cover of this text outlines the relationships involved.*

IMPROVING PERFORMANCE at The Hotel Paris

The New Interviewing Program

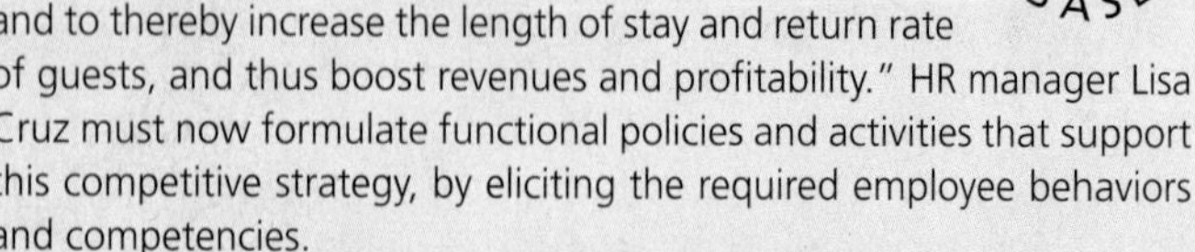

The Hotel Paris's competitive strategy is "To use superior guest service to differentiate the Hotel Paris properties, and to thereby increase the length of stay and return rate of guests, and thus boost revenues and profitability." HR manager Lisa Cruz must now formulate functional policies and activities that support this competitive strategy, by eliciting the required employee behaviors and competencies.

As an experienced HR professional, Lisa knew that the company's new testing program would go only so far. She knew that, at best, employment tests accounted for perhaps 30% of employee performance. It was essential that she and her team design a package of interviews that her hotel managers could use to assess—on an interactive and personal basis—candidates for various positions. It was only in that way that the hotel could hire the sorts of employees whose competencies and behaviors would translate into the kinds of outcomes—such as improved guest services—that the hotel required to achieve its strategic goals.

Lisa receives budgetary approval to design a new employee interview system. She and her team start by reviewing the job descriptions and job specifications for the positions of front-desk clerk, assistant manager, security guard, valet, door person, and housekeeper. Focusing on developing structure valet, door for each position, the team sets about devising interview questions. For example, for the front-desk clerk and assistant manager, they formulate several *behavioral questions*, including, "Tell me about a time when you had to deal with an irate person, and what you did." And, "Tell me about a time when you had to deal with several

§Written by and copyright Gary Dessler, PhD.

conflicting demands at once, such as having to study for several final exams at the same time, while working. How did you handle the situation?" They also developed a number of *situational questions*, including "Suppose you have a very pushy incoming guest who insists on being checked in at once, while at the same time you're trying to process the check-out for another guest who must be at the airport in 10 minutes. How would you handle the situation?" For these and other positions, they also developed several *job knowledge* questions. For example, for security guard applicants, one question her team created was, "What are the local legal restrictions, if any, regarding using products like Mace if confronted by an unruly person on the hotel grounds?" The team combined the questions into structured interviews for each job, and turned to testing, fine-tuning, and finally using the new system.

Questions

7-28. For the jobs of security guard, and valet, develop five additional situational, five behavioral, and five job knowledge questions, with descriptive good/average/poor answers.

7-29. Combine your questions into a complete interview that you would give to someone who must interview candidates for these jobs.

MyManagementLab

Go to **mymanagementlab.com** for Auto-graded writing questions as well as the following Assisted-graded writing questions:

7-30. Briefly discuss and give examples of at least five common interviewing mistakes. What recommendations would you give for avoiding these interviewing mistakes?

7-31. Why do you think situational interviews yield a higher mean validity than do job-related or behavioral interviews, which in turn yield a higher mean validity than do psychological interviews?

7-32. MyManagementLab only—comprehensive writing assignment for this chapter.

Key Terms

unstructured (or nondirective) interview, 192
structured (or directive) interview, 192
situational interview, 193
behavioral interview, 193
job-related interview, 194
stress interview, 195
unstructured sequential interview, 195
structured sequential interview, 195
panel interview, 195
mass interview, 195
candidate-order (or contrast) error, 199
structured situational interview, 202

Endnotes

1. Denis Morin and Denis L. Pascale, "The Structured Interview: Enhancing Staff Selection," *Personnel Psychology* 63, no. 1 (Spring 2010), pp. 250–255.
2. Michael McDaniel et al., "The Validity of Employment Interviews: A Comprehensive Review and Meta-Analysis," *Journal of Applied Psychology* 79, no. 4 (1994), p. 599. See also Laura Graves and Ronald Karren, "The Employee Selection Interview: A Fresh Look at an Old Problem," *Human Resource Management* 35, no. 2 (Summer 1996), pp. 163–180. For an argument against holding selection interviews, see D. Heath et al., "Hold the Interview," *Fast Company*, no. 136 (June 2009), pp. 51–52.
3. Therese Macan, "The Employment Interview: A Review of Current Studies and Directions for Future Research," *Human Resource Management Review* 19 (2009), pp. 203–218.
4. Duane Schultz and Sydney Schultz, *Psychology and Work Today* (Upper Saddle River, NJ: Prentice Hall, 1998), p. 830. A study found that interview structure "was best described by four dimensions: questioning consistency, evaluation standardization, question sophistication, and rapport building." Chapman and Zweig, "Developing a Nomological Network."
5. McDaniel et al., "The Validity of Employment Interviews," p. 602.
6. We'll see later in this chapter that there are other ways to "structure" selection interviews. Many of them have nothing to do with using structured guides like these.
7. Laura Gollub Williamson et al., "Employment Interview on Trial: Linking Interview Structure with Litigation Outcomes," *Journal of Applied Psychology* 82, no. 6 (1996), p. 908. As an example, the findings of one recent study "Demonstrate the value of using highly structured interviews to minimize the potential influence of applicant demographic characteristics on selection decisions." Julie McCarthy, Chad Van Iddekinge, and Michael Campion, "Are Highly Structured Job Interviews Resistant to Demographic Similarity Effects?" *Personnel Psychology* 60, no. 3 (2010), pp. 325–359.
8. Williamson et al., "Employment Interview on Trial."
9. McDaniel et al., "The Validity of Employment Interviews," p. 602.
10. Paul Taylor and Bruce Small, "Asking Applicants What They Would Do Versus What They Did: A Meta-Analytic Comparison of Situational and Past Behavior Employment Interview Questions," *Journal of Occupational and Organizational Psychology* 75, no. 3 (September 2002), pp. 277–295.
11. Margery Weinstein, "You're Hired!" *Training* 48, no. 4, pp. 34-37; http://www.trainingmag.com/article/you%E2%80%99re-hired accessed July 19, 2013.
12. Aparna Nancherla, "Anticipated Growth in Behavioral Interviewing," *Training & Development*, April 2008, p. 20.
13. Bill Stoneman, "Matching Personalities with Jobs Made Easier with Behavioral Interviews," *American Banker*, November 30, 2000, p. 8a.
14. Martha Frase-Blunt, "Games Interviewers Play," *HR Magazine*, January 2001, pp. 104–114.
15. Kevin Murphy and Charles Davidshofer, *Psychological Testing* (Upper Saddle River, NJ: Prentice Hall, 2001), pp. 430–431.
16. Marlene Dixon et al., "The Panel Interview: A Review of Empirical Research and Guidelines for Practice," *Public Personnel Management* 31, no. 3 (Fall 2002), pp. 397–429.
17. Ibid. See also M. Ronald Buckley, Katherine A. Jackson, and Mark C. Bolino, "The Influence of Relational Demography on Panel Interview Ratings: A Field Experiment," *Personnel Psychology* 60, no. 3 (Autumn 2007), pp. 627–646.

18. "Phone Interviews Might Be the Most Telling, Study Finds," *BNA Bulletin to Management*, September 1998, p. 273; and Lisa M. Moynihan, et al., "A Longitudinal Study of the Relationships Among Job Search Self-Efficacy, Job Interviews, and Employment Outcomes," *Journal of Business and Psychology*, 18, no. 2 (Winter 2003), pp. 207–233. For phone interview job search suggestions, see, for example, Janet Wagner, "Can You Succeed in a Phone Interview?" *Strategic Finance* 91, no. 10 (April 2010), pp. 22, 61.
19. Susan Strauss et al., "The Effects of Videoconference, Telephone, and Face-to-Face Media on Interviewer and Applicant Judgments in Employment Interviews," *Journal of Management* 27, no. 3 (2001), pp. 363–381. If the employer records a video interview with the intention of sharing it with hiring managers who don't participate in the interview, it's advisable to first obtain the candidate's written permission. Matt Bolch, "Lights, Camera . . . Interview!" *HR Magazine*, March 2007, pp. 99–102.
20. Job interviewing apps are also available through Apple's App Store. One is from Martin's iPhone Apps. For people seeking technical jobs, this app includes hundreds of potential interview questions, such as brain Teasers and algorithms, www.martinreddy.net/iphone/interview, accessed July 5, 2009.
21. Anjali Athavaley, "A Job Interview You Don't Have to Show Up For," *The Wall Street Journal*, June 20, 2007, http://online.wsj.com/article/SB118229876637841321.html, accessed April 8, 2011.
22. http://interviewstream.com/About, accessed April 1, 2013.
23. These are quoted or adapted from www.careerfaqs.com.au/getthatjob_video_interview.asp, accessed March 2, 2009.
24. Douglas Rodgers, "Computer-Aided Interviewing Overcomes First Impressions," *Personnel Journal*, April 1987, pp. 148–152; see also Linda Thornburg, "Computer-Assisted Interviewing Shortens Hiring Cycle," *HR Magazine*, February 1998, p. 73ff; and http://interviewstream.com/demorequest?gclid=COyxjOqd36sCFUbs7QodMziuOw, accessed October 2, 2011.
25. Rogers, "Computer-Aided Interviewing Overcomes First Impressions."
26. Gary Robins, "Dial-an-Interview," *Stores*, June 1994, pp. 34–35.
27. This is quoted from or paraphrased from William Bulkeley, "Replaced by Technology: Job Interviews," *The Wall Street Journal*, August 22, 1994, pp. B1, B7. For more on careers at Great Western see www.greatwesternbank.com/aboutus/careers/, accessed April 1, 2013.
28. Emily Maltby, "To Find the Best Hires, Firms Become Creative," *The Wall Street Journal*, November 17, 2009, p. B6.
29. For example, structured employment interviews using either situational questions or behavioral questions tend to yield high criterion-related validities (.63 versus .47). This is particularly so where the raters can use descriptively anchored rating scale answer sheets; these use short descriptors to illustrate good, average, or poor performance. Taylor and Small, "Asking Applicants What They Would Do Versus What They Did." See also Julie McCarthy et al., "Are Highly Structured Job Interviews Resistant to Demographic Similarity Effects?" *Personnel Psychology* 63, no. 2 (Summer 2010), pp. 325–359.
30. Williamson et al., "Employment Interview on Trial," p. 900.
31. Frank Schmidt and Ryan Zimmerman, "A Counterintuitive Hypothesis About Employment Interview Validity and Some Supporting Evidence," *Journal of Applied Psychology* 89, no. 3 (2004), pp. 553–561.
32. This validity discussion and these findings are based on McDaniel et al., "The Validity of Employment Interviews," pp. 607–610; the validities for situational, job-related, and psychological interviews were (.50), (.39), and (.29), respectively.
33. Murray Barrick et al., "Accuracy of Interviewer Judgments of Job Applicant Personality Traits," *Personnel Psychology* 53 (2000), pp. 925–951.
34. Richard A. Posthuma, Frederick P. Morgeson, and Michael A. Campion, "Beyond Employment Interview Validity: A Comprehensive Narrative Review of Recent Research and Trends Over Time," *Personnel Psychology* 55, no. 1 (March 2002), pp. 1–81.
35. Ibid.
36. McDaniel et al., "The Validity of Employment Interviews," p. 608.
37. Anthony Dalessio and Todd Silverhart, "Combining Biodata Test and Interview Information: Predicting Decisions and Performance Criteria," *Personnel Psychology* 47 (1994), p. 313; and Nora Reilly et al., "Benchmarks Affect Perceptions of Prior Disability in a Structured Interview," *Journal of Business & Psychology* 20, no. 4 (Summer 2006), pp. 489–500.
38. S. W. Constantin, "An Investigation of Information Favorability in the Employment Interview," *Journal of Applied Psychology* 61 (1976), pp. 743–749. It should be noted that a number of the studies discussed in this chapter involve having interviewers evaluate interviews based on written transcripts (rather than face to face) and that a study suggests that this procedure may not be equivalent to having interviewers interview applicants directly. See Charles Gorman, William Glover, and Michael Doherty, "Can We Learn Anything About Interviewing Real People from 'Interviews' of Paper People? A Study of the External Validity Paradigm," *Organizational Behavior and Human Performance* 22, no. 2 (October 1978), pp. 165–192; and Frederick P. Morgeson, Matthew H. Reider, Michael A. Campion, and Rebecca A. Bull, "Review of Research on Age Discrimination in the Employment Interview," *Journal of Business Psychology* 22 (2008), pp. 223–232.
39. David Tucker and Patricia Rowe, "Relationship Between Expectancy, Causal Attribution, and Final Hiring Decisions in the Employment Interview," *Journal of Applied Psychology* 64, no. 1 (February 1979), pp. 27–34. See also Robert Dipboye, Gail Fontenelle, and Kathleen Garner, "Effect of Previewing the Application on Interview Process and Outcomes," *Journal of Applied Psychology* 69, no. 1 (February 1984), pp. 118–128; and Nora Reilly, et al., "Benchmarks Affect Perceptions of Prior Disability in a Structured Interview," op cit.
40. Anita Chaudhuri, "Beat the Clock: Applying for Job? A New Study Shows That Interviewers Will Make Up Their Minds About You Within a Minute," *The Guardian*, June 14, 2000, pp. 2–6.
41. John Langdale and Joseph Weitz, "Estimating the Influence of Job Information on Interviewer Agreement," *Journal of Applied Psychology* 57 (1973), pp. 23–27.
42. R. E. Carlson, "Effect of Applicant Sample on Ratings of Valid Information in an Employment Setting," *Journal of Applied Psychology* 54 (1970), pp. 217–222.
43. R. E. Carlson, "Selection Interview Decisions: The Effect of Interviewer Experience, Relative Quota Situation, and Applicant Sample on Interview Decisions," *Personnel Psychology* 20 (1967), pp. 259–280.
44. See, for example, Scott T. Fleischmann, "The Messages of Body Language in Job Interviews," *Employee Relations* 18, no. 2 (Summer 1991), pp. 161–166; James Westphal and Ithai Stern, "Flattery Will Get You Everywhere (Especially if You're a Male Caucasian): How Ingratiation, Board Room Behavior, and a Demographic Minority Status Affect Additional Board Appointments at U.S. Companies," *Academy of Management Journal* 50, no. 2 (2007), pp. 267–288.
45. David Caldwell and Jerry Burger, "Personality Characteristics of Job Applicants and Success in Screening Interviews," *Personnel Psychology* 51 (1998), pp. 119–136.
46. Amy Kristof-Brown et al., "Applicant Impression Management: Dispositional Influences and Consequences for Recruiter Perceptions of Fit and Similarity," *Journal of Management* 28, no. 1 (2002), pp. 27–46. See also Lynn McFarland et al., "Impression Management Use and Effectiveness Across Assessment Methods," *Journal of Management* 29, no. 5 (2003), pp. 641–661.
47. Timothy DeGroot and Janaki Gooty, "Can Nonverbal Cues Be Used to Make Meaningful Personality Attributions in Employment Interviews?" *Journal of Business Psychology* 24 (2009), p. 179.
48. Posthuma, Morgeson, and Campion, "Beyond Employment Interview Validity," 1–87.
49. C. K. Stevens and A. L. Kristof, "Making the Right Impression: A Field Study of Applicant Impression Management During Interviews," *Journal of Applied Psychology* 80, pp. 587–606; Schultz and Schultz, *Psychology and Work Today*, p. 82. See also Jay Stuller, "Fatal Attraction," *Across the Board* 42, no. 6 (November/ December 2005), pp. 18–23. See also Allen Huffcutt et al., "Understanding Applicant Behavior in Employment Interviews: A Theoretical Model of Interviewee Performance," *Human Resource Management Review* 20, no. 1 (2011), pp. 350–367.
50. Chad Higgins and Timothy Judge, "The Effect of Applicant Influence Tactics on Recruiter Perceptions of Fit and Hiring Recommendations: A Field Study," *Journal of Applied Psychology* 89, no. 4 (2004), pp. 622–632. Some researchers in this area question results like these. The problem is that much of the interviewing research uses students as raters and hypothetical jobs, so it's not clear that we can apply the findings to the real world. For example, with respect to age bias in interviews, "Laboratory studies may create too much artificiality," in Frederick P. Morgeson, Matthew H. Reider, Michael A. Campion, and Rebecca A. Bull, "Review of Research on Age Discrimination in the Employment Interview," *Journal of Business Psychology* 22 (2008), pp. 223–232.
51. Brian Swider et al., "Managing and Creating an Image in the Interview: The Role of Interviewee Initial Impressions," *Journal of Applied Psychology* 96, no. 6 (2011), pp. 1275–1288.

52. See, for example, Madeline Heilmann and Lois Saruwatari, "When Beauty Is Beastly: The Effects of Appearance and Sex on Evaluations of Job Applicants for Managerial and Nonmanagerial Jobs," *Organizational Behavior and Human Performance* 23 (June 1979), pp. 360–372; and Cynthia Marlowe, Sandra Schneider, and Carnot Nelson, "Gender and Attractiveness Biases in Hiring Decisions: Are More Experienced Managers Less Biased?" *Journal of Applied Psychology* 81, no. 1 (1996), pp. 11–21.
53. Marlowe et al., "Gender and Attractiveness Biases," p. 11.
54. Allen Huffcutt and Philip Roth, "Racial Group Differences in Employment Interview Evaluations," *Journal of Applied Psychology* 83, no. 2 (1998), pp. 179–189.
55. Eden King and Afra Ahmad, "An Experimental Field Study of Interpersonal Discrimination Toward Muslim Job Applicants," *Personnel Psychology* 63, no. 4 (2010), pp. 881–906.
56. N. S. Miceli et al., "Potential Discrimination in Structured Employment Interviews," *Employee Responsibilities and Rights* 13, no. 1 (March 2001), pp. 15–38.
57. Andrea Rodriguez and Fran Prezant, "Better Interviews for People with Disabilities," *Workforce*, www.workforce.com, accessed November 14, 2003.
58. Pat Tammaro, "Laws to Prevent Discrimination Affect Job Interview Process," *The Houston Business Journal*, June 16, 2000, p. 48.
59. Juan Madera and Michele Hebl, "Discrimination Against Facially Stigmatized Applicants in Interviews: An Eye Tracking and Face-to-Face Investigation," *Journal of Applied Psychology* 97, no. 2, pp. 317–330.
60. This is based on John F. Wymer III and Deborah A. Sudbury, "Employment Discrimination: 'Testers'—Will Your Hiring Practices 'Pass'?" *Employee Relations Law Journal* 17, no. 4 (Spring 1992), pp. 623–633.
61. Bureau of National Affairs, *Daily Labor Report*, December 5, 1990, p. D1.
62. Wymer and Sudbury, "Employment Discrimination," p. 629.
63. Monowar Mahmood, "National Culture vs Corporate Culture: Employee Recruitment and Selection Practices of Multinationals in a Developing Country Context," *Journal of International Management Studies* 11, no. 1, (Jan. 2011), p. 110. Published by International Academy of Business and Economics, www.iabe.org/domains/iabeX/journal .aspx?journalid=16, accessed July 19, 2013.
64. Arthur Pell, "Nine Interviewing Pitfalls," *Managers Magazine*, January 1994, p. 20.
65. Thomas Dougherty, Daniel Turban, and John Callender, "Confirming First Impressions in the Employment Interview: A Field Study of Interviewer Behavior," *Journal of Applied Psychology* 79, no. 5 (1994), p. 663.
66. See Pell, "Nine Interviewing Pitfalls," p. 29; Parth Sarathi, "Making Selection Interviews Effective," *Management and Labor Studies* 18, no. 1 (1993), pp. 5–7.
67. Posthuma, Morgeson, and Campion, "Beyond Employment Interview Validity," pp. 1–87.
68. Pell, "Nine Interviewing Pitfalls," p. 30; quote from Alan M. Saks and Julie M. McCarthy, "Effects of Discriminatory Interview Questions and Gender on Applicant Reactions," *Journal of Business and Psychology* 21, No. 2 (Winter 2006), p. 175.
69. Dan Klamm, "3 Ways to Ace Your Job Interview with Social Media," http://mashable .com/2010/06/01/job-interview-social-media/, accessed April 1, 2013.
70. This section is based on Elliot Pursell et al., "Structured Interviewing," *Personnel Journal* 59 (November 1980), pp. 907–912; and G. Latham et al., "The Situational Interview," *Journal of Applied Psychology* 65 (1980), pp. 422–427. See also Michael Campion, Elliott Pursell, and Barbara Brown, "Structured Interviewing: Raising the Psychometric Properties of the Employment Interview," *Personnel Psychology* 41 (1988), pp. 25–42; and Paul R. Bernthal, "Recruitment and Selection," www.ddiworld.com/DDIWorld/media/trend-research/recruitment-and-selection_ere_es_ddi .pdf?ext=.pdf, accessed October 10, 2011. For a recent approach, see K. G. Melchers et. al., "Is More Structure Really Better? A Comparison of Frame-of-Reference Training and Descriptively Anchored Rating Scales to Improve Interviewers' Rating Quality," *Personnel Psychology* 64, no. 1 (2011), pp. 53–87.
71. Taylor and Small, "Asking Applicants What They Would Do Versus What They Did." Structured employment interviews using either situational questions or behavioral questions tend to yield high validities. However, structured interviews with situational question formats yield the higher ratings. This may be because interviewers get more consistent (reliable) responses with situational questions (which force all applicants to apply the same scenario) than they do with behavioral questions (which require each applicant to find applicable experiences). However, there is some evidence that for higher-level positions, situational question–based interviews are inferior to behavioral question–based ones, possibly because the situations are "just too simple to allow any real differentiation among candidates for higher level positions." Allen Huffcutt et al., "Comparison of Situational and Behavioral Description Interview Questions for Higher Level Positions," *Personnel Psychology* 54, no. 3 (2001), p. 619.
72. See Phillip Lowry, "The Structured Interview: An Alternative to the Assessment Center?" *Public Personnel Management* 23, no. 2 (Summer 1994), pp. 201–215. See also Todd Maurer and Jerry Solamon, "The Science and Practice of a Structured Employment Interview Coaching Program," *Personnel Psychology* 59, no. 2 (Summer 2006), pp. 433–456.
73. Pursell et al., "Structured Interviewing," p. 910.
74. From a speech by industrial psychologist Paul Green and contained in *BNA Bulletin to Management*, June 20, 1985, pp. 2–3. For additional practical guidance see, for example, www.state.gov/documents/organization/ 107843.pdf, accessed October 10, 2012.
75. Williamson et al., "Employment Interview on Trial," p. 901; Michael Campion, David Palmer, and James Campion, "A Review of Structure in the Selection Interview," *Personnel Psychology* 50 (1997), pp. 655–702. See also Maurer and Solamon, "The Science and Practice of a Structured Employment Interview."
76. Unless otherwise specified, the following are based on Williamson et al., "Employment Interview on Trial," pp. 901–902.
77. Campion, Palmer, and Campion, "A Review of Structure," p. 668.
78. Carlson, "Selection Interview Decisions."
79. Pamela Kaul, "Interviewing Is Your Business," *Association Management,* November 1992, p. 29. See also Nancy Woodward, "Asking for Salary Histories," *HR Magazine,* February 2000, pp. 109–112. Gathering information about specific interview dimensions such as social ability, responsibility, and independence (as is often done with structured interviews) can improve interview accuracy, at least for more complicated jobs. See also Andrea Poe, "Graduate Work: Behavioral Interviewing Can Tell You If an Applicant Just Out of College Has Traits Needed for the Job," *HR Magazine* 48, no. 10 (October 2003), pp. 95–96.
80. Edwin Walley, "Successful Interviewing Techniques," *The CPA Journal* 63 (September 1993), p. 70; and Randy Myers, "Interviewing Techniques: Tips From the Pros," *Journal of Accountancy* 202, no. 2 (August 2006), pp. 53–55.
81. Catherine Middendorf and Therese Macan, "Note Taking in the Employment Interview: Effects on Recall and Judgment," *Journal of Applied Psychology* 87, no. 2 (2002), pp. 293–303.
82. Weirick, "The Perfect Interview," p. 85.
83. Stephen Gilliland et al., "Improving Applicants' Reactions to Rejection Letters: An Application of Fairness Theory," *Personnel Psychology* 54 (2001), pp. 669–703.
84. www.Shrm.org/template-tools/how-to-guides, accessed March 3, 2012.
85. Kris Maher, "New High-Tech Recruiting Tools: Unicycles, Yahtzee and Silly Putty," *The Wall Street Journal*, June 6, 2000, p. B14; see also Paul McNamara, "Extreme Interview," *Network World*, June 25, 2001, p. 65.
86. Tim Barker, "Corporate Espionage Takes Center Stage with Boeing Revelation," *Knight Ridder/Tribune Business News*, June 15, 2003.
87. Ibid.
88. See, for example, the classic excellent discussion of job-hunting and interviewing in Richard Payne, *How to Get a Better Job Quickly* (New York: New American Library, 1979).

APPENDIX 1 for Chapter 7

Structured Interview Guide

STEP 1—Create a Structured Interview Guide

Instructions:
First, here in step 1, create a structured interview guide like this one (including a competency definition, a lead question, and benchmark examples and answers, for instance) for each of the job's required competencies:

Competency: Interpersonal Skills

Definition:
Shows understanding, courtesy, tact, empathy, concern; develops and maintains relationships; may deal with people who are difficult, hostile, distressed; relates well to people from varied backgrounds and situations; is sensitive to individual differences.

Lead Questions:
Describe a situation in which you had to deal with people who were upset about a problem. What specific actions did you take? What was the outcome or result?

Benchmark Level	Level Definition	Level Examples
5	Establishes and maintains ongoing working relationships with management, other employees, internal or external stakeholders, or customers. Remains courteous when discussing information or eliciting highly sensitive or controversial information from people who are reluctant to give it. Effectively handles situations involving a high degree of tension or discomfort involving people who are demonstrating a high degree of hostility or distress.	Presents controversial findings tactfully to irate organization senior management officials regarding shortcomings of a newly installed computer system, software programs, and associated equipment.
4		Mediates disputes concerning system design/architecture, the nature and capacity of data management systems, system resources allocations, or other equally controversial/sensitive matters.
3	Cooperates and works well with management, other employees, or customers, on short-term assignments. Remains courteous when discussing information or eliciting moderately sensitive or controversial information from people who are hesitant to give it. Effectively handles situations involving a moderate degree of tension or discomfort involving people who are demonstrating a moderate degree of hostility or distress.	Courteously and tactfully delivers effective instruction to frustrated customers. Provides technical advice to customers and the public on various types of IT such as communication or security systems, data management procedures or analysis.
2		Familiarizes new employees with administrative procedures and office systems.
1	Cooperates and works well with management, other employees, or customers during brief interactions. Remains courteous when discussing information or eliciting non-sensitive or non-controversial information from people who are willing to give it. Effectively handles situations involving little or no tension, discomfort, hostility, or distress.	Responds courteously to customers' general inquiries. Greets and assists visitors attending a meeting within own organization.

FIGURE 7A-1 Structured Interview Guide

Source: www.state.gov/documents/organization/107843.pdf, and United States Office of Personnel Management. Structured Interviews: Interview Guide and Evaluation Materials for Structured Interviews.

STEP 2—INDIVIDUAL EVALUATION FORM

Instructions:
Next, in step 2, create a form for evaluating each job candidate on each of the job's competencies:

Candidate to be assessed: ______________________________

Date of Interview: ______________________________

Competency: Problem Solving				
Definition: Identifies problems; determines accuracy and relevance of information; uses sound judgment to generate and evaluate alternatives, and to make the recommendations.				
Question: Describe a situation in which you identified a problem and evaluated the alternatives to make a recommendation or decision. What was the problem and who was affected?				
Probes: How did you generate and evaluate your alternatives? What was the outcome?				
Describe specific behaviors observed: (Use back of sheet, if necessary)				
1-Low	2	3-Average	4	5-Outstanding
Uses logic to identify alternatives to solve routine problems. Reacts to and solves problems by gathering and applying information from standard materials or sources that provide a limited number of alternatives.		Uses logic to identify alternatives to solve moderately difficult problems. Identifies and solves problems by gathering and applying information from a variety of materials or sources that provide several alternatives.		Uses logic to identify alternatives to solve complex or sensitive problems. Anticipates problems and identifies and evaluates potential sources of information and generates alternatives to solve problems where standards do not exist.

Final Evaluation:	Printed Name:	Signature:

FIGURE 7A-1 *Continued*

STEP 3—PANEL CONSENSUS EVALUATION FORM

Instructions:
Finally, in step 3, create a panel consensus evaluation form like this one, which the members of the panel who interviewed the candidate will use to evaluate his or her interview performance.

Candidate: ______________________________

Date: ______________________________

Panel Consensus Evaluation Form

Instructions:
Translate each individual evaluation for each competency onto this form. If all of the individual competency evaluations are within one rating scale point, enter the average of the evaluations in the column labeled Group Evaluation. If more than one point separates any two raters, a consensus discussion must occur with each party justifying his/her evaluation. The lead interviewer or his/her designee should take notes on the consensus discussion in the space provided. Any changes in evaluation should be initialed and a final evaluation entered for each competency.

Competency	Final Individual Evaluations			Group Evaluation
	(1)	(2)	(3)	
Interpersonal Skills				
Self-Management				
Reasoning				
Decision Making				
Problem Solving				
Oral Communication				
Total Score				

Consensus Discussion Notes:

Signature Panel Member 1: ______________________________

Signature Panel Member 2: ______________________________

Signature Panel Member 3: ______________________________

FIGURE 7A-1 ***Continued***

APPENDIX 2 for Chapter 7

Interview Guide for Interviewees

Before managers move into positions where they have to interview others, they usually must navigate some interviews themselves. It's therefore useful to apply some of what we discussed in this chapter to navigating one's own interviews.

Interviewers will tend to use the interview to try to determine what you are like as a person. In other words, how you get along with other people and your desire to work. They will look first at how you behave. Specifically, they will note whether you respond concisely, cooperate fully in answering questions, state personal opinions when relevant, and keep to the subject at hand; these are very important elements in influencing the interviewer's decision.

There are six things to do to get an extra edge in the interview.[88]

1. ***Preparation is essential.*** Before the interview, learn all you can about the employer, the job, and the people doing the recruiting. On the Web, using social media, or looking through business periodicals, find out what is happening in the employer's field. Try to unearth the employer's problems. Be ready to explain why you think you would be able to solve such problems, citing some of your *specific accomplishments* to make your case.
2. ***Uncover the interviewer's real needs.*** Spend as little time as possible answering your interviewer's first questions and as much time as possible getting him or her to describe his or her needs. Determine what the person is expecting to accomplish, and the type of person he or she feels is needed. Use open-ended questions such as, "Could you tell me more about that?"
3. ***Relate yourself to the interviewer's needs.*** Once you know the type of person your interviewer is looking for and the sorts of problems he or she wants solved, you are in a good position to describe your own accomplishments *in terms of the interviewer's needs.* Start by saying something like, "One of the problem areas you've said is important to you is similar to a problem I once faced." Then state the problem, describe your solution, and reveal the results.
4. ***Think before answering.*** Answering a question should be a three-step process: Pause—Think—Speak. *Pause* to make sure you understand what the interviewer is driving at, *think* about how to structure your answer, and then *speak.* In your answer, try to emphasize how hiring you will help the interviewer solve his or her problem.
5. ***Remember that appearance and enthusiasm are important.*** Appropriate clothing, good grooming, a firm handshake, and energy are important. Maintain eye contact. In addition, speak with enthusiasm, nod agreement, and remember to take a moment to frame your answer (pause, think, speak) so that you sound articulate and fluent.
6. ***Make a good first impression.*** Remember that in most cases interviewers make up their minds about the applicant during the early minutes of the interview. A good first impression may turn to bad during the interview, but it is unlikely. Bad first impressions are almost impossible to overcome. Experts suggest paying attention to the following key interviewing considerations:
   - Appropriate clothing
   - Good grooming
   - A firm handshake
   - The appearance of controlled energy
   - Pertinent humor and readiness to smile
   - A genuine interest in the employer's operation and alert attention when the interviewer speaks
   - Pride in past performance
   - An understanding of the employer's needs and a desire to serve them

8 Training and Developing Employees

Source: Amanda Hall/Getty Images

MyManagementLab®

Improve Your Grade!

When you see this icon, visit **www.mymanagementlab.com** for activities that are applied, personalized, and offer immediate feedback.

Training and Development Policies and Practices → The Employee Skills and Performance → Required to Achieve Company's Strategic Goals

For a bird's eye view of how one company created a new training program to improve its strategic performance, read the Hotel Paris case on pages 252–253 and answer the questions after reading the chapter.

WHERE ARE WE NOW . . .

Chapters 6 and 7 explained how to interview and select employees. Once employees are hired, the employer must train them. The purpose of this chapter is to increase your effectiveness in training employees. The main topics we'll cover include orienting and onboarding new employees, overview of the training process, implementing the training program, implementing management development programs, managing organizational change programs, and evaluating the training effort. Then, in Chapter 9, we'll turn to appraising employees.

LEARNING OBJECTIVES

1 Summarize the purpose and process of employee orientation.

2 List and briefly explain each of the steps in the training process.

3 Explain how to use five training techniques.

4 List and briefly discuss four management development methods.

5 List and briefly discuss the importance of the steps in leading organizational change.

6 Explain why a controlled study may be superior for evaluating the training program's effects.

For about 6 years after buying May Department Stores Co., Macy's Inc. stressed consolidation. First, it focused on integrating the regional department stores under one Macy's umbrella. Then the recession hit and Macy's shifted to cutting costs. Meanwhile, Macy's customer service suffered. Many sales associates weren't providing the service level that customers wanted. With the deteriorating service cutting into its sales and profits, the question was, what should Macy's do about it now? We'll see what they did.

1 Summarize the purpose and process of employee orientation.

Orienting and Onboarding New Employees

Carefully selecting employees doesn't guarantee they'll perform effectively. Even high-potential employees can't do their jobs if they don't know what to do or how to do it. Making sure your employees do know what to do and how to do it is the purpose of orientation and training. The human resources department usually designs the orientation and training programs, but the supervisor does most of the day-to-day orienting and training. Every manager therefore should know how to orient and train employees. We will start with orientation.

The Purposes of Employee Orientation/Onboarding

employee orientation
A procedure for providing new employees with basic background information about the firm.

Employee orientation (or "onboarding") involves more than what most people realize.[1] **Employee orientation** provides new employees with the information they need to function (such as computer passwords and company rules); ideally, it should also help new employees start getting emotionally attached to the firm. You want to accomplish four things when orienting new employees:

1. Make the new employee feel welcome and at home and part of the team.
2. Make sure the new employee has the basic information to function effectively, such as e-mail access, personnel policies and benefits, and expectations in terms of work behavior.
3. Help the new employee understand the organization in a broad sense (its past, present, culture, and strategies and vision of the future).
4. Start socializing the person into the firm's culture and ways of doing things.[2]

That last step distinguishes today's *onboarding* programs from traditional orientation.[3] For example, the Mayo Clinic's "heritage and culture" onboarding program emphasizes core Mayo Clinic values such as teamwork, personal responsibility, innovation, integrity, diversity, customer service, and mutual respect.[4]

The Orientation Process

The length of the orientation program depends on what you cover. Most take several hours. The human resource specialist (or, in smaller firms, the office manager) performs the first part of the orientation by explaining basic matters like working hours and benefits. Then the supervisor continues the orientation by explaining (see Figure 8-1) the department's organization, introducing the person to his or her new colleagues, familiarizing him or her with the workplace, and reducing first-day jitters. Supervisors should be vigilant. Follow up on and encourage new employees to engage in activities (such as taking breaks with current employees) that will enable each to "learn the ropes." For new employees with disabilities, integration and socialization is highly influenced by the behavior of coworkers and supervisors.[5]

However at firms like Toyota Motor USA, onboarding-type orientations may take a week and include lectures by company officers, and exercises covering company history and values. At a minimum, as in Figure 8-1, an orientation should provide information on matters such as employee benefits, personnel policies, safety measures and regulations, and a facilities tour.[6] New employees should receive (and sign for) print or Internet-based employee handbooks covering such matters.

KNOW YOUR EMPLOYMENT LAW

The Employee Handbook

Courts may find that the employee handbook's contents are legally binding commitments. Even apparently sensible handbook policies (such as "the company will not retaliate against employees who raise concerns about important issues in the workplace") can backfire without the proper disclaimers. The handbook should include a disclaimer stating "nothing in this handbook should be taken as creating a binding contract between employer and employees, and all employment is on an at will basis."[7] Say that statements of company policies, benefits, and regulations do not constitute the terms and conditions of an employment contract, either expressed or implied. Do not insert statements such as "No employee will be fired without just cause" or statements that imply or state that employees have tenure.

Employers should also adjust their employee handbook contents to the realities of social media. For example, the National Labor Relations Board might take issue with a handbook policy prohibiting employees from badmouthing their employer in social media, arguing that doing so constrains employees' rights to complain about working conditions to coworkers.[8]

UNIVERSITY of CALIFORNIA SAN DIEGO
MEDICAL CENTER

NEW EMPLOYEE DEPARTMENTAL ORIENTATION CHECKLIST

(Return to Human Resources within 10 days of Hire)

NAME:	HIRE DATE:	SSN:	JOB TITLE:
DEPARTMENT:	NEO DATE:	DEPARTMENTAL ORIENTATION COMPLETED BY:	

TOPIC	DATE REVIEWED	N/A
1. HUMAN RESOURCES INFORMATION		
a. Departmental Attendance Procedures and UCSD Medical Center Work Time & Attendance Policy	a. ______	☐
b. Job Description Review	b. ______	☐
c. Annual Performance Evaluation and Peer Feedback Process	c. ______	☐
d. Probationary Period Information	d. ______	☐
e. Appearance/Dress Code Requirements	e. ______	☐
f. Annual TB Screening	f. ______	☐
g. License and/or Certification Renewals	g. ______	☐
2. DEPARTMENT INFORMATION		
a. Organizational Structure-Department Core Values Orientation	a. ______	☐
b. Department/Unit Area Specific Policies & Procedures	b. ______	☐
c. Customer Service Practices	c. ______	☐
d. CQI Effort and Projects	d. ______	☐
e. Tour and Floor Plan	e. ______	☐
f. Equipment/Supplies	f. ______	☐
Keys issued	______	☐
Radio Pager issued	______	☐
Other ______	______	☐
g. Mail and Recharge Codes	g. ______	☐
3. SAFETY INFORMATION		
a. Departmental Safety Plan	a. ______	☐
b. Employee Safety/Injury Reporting Procedures	b. ______	☐
c. Hazard Communication	c. ______	☐
d. Infection Control/Sharps Disposal	d. ______	☐
e. Attendance at annual Safety Fair (mandatory)	e. ______	☐
4. FACILITES INFORMATION		
a. Emergency Power	a. ______	☐
b. Mechanical Systems	b. ______	☐
c. Water	c. ______	☐
d. Medical Gases	d. ______	☐
e. Patient Room	e. ______	☐
Bed	______	☐
Headwall	______	☐
Bathroom	______	☐
Nurse Call System	______	☐
5. SECURITY INFORMATION		
a. Code Triage Assignment	a. ______	☐
b. Code Blue Assignment	b. ______	☐
c. Code Red – Evacuation Procedure	c. ______	☐
d. Code 10 – Bomb Threat Procedure	d. ______	☐
e. Departmental Security Measures	e. ______	☐
f. UCSD Emergency Number 6111 or 911	f. ______	☐

This generic checklist may not constitute a complete departmental orientation or assessment. Please attach any additional unit specific orientation material for placement in the employee's HR file

I have been oriented on the items listed above______________________

D1999(R7-01) **WHITE** – HR Records (8912) **Yellow** – Department Retains

FIGURE 8-1 New Employee Departmental Orientation Checklist

Source: "New Employee Departmental Orientation Checklist" from UCSD *Health Care website*. Used with permission of UC San Diego Medical Center.

ORIENTATION TECHNOLOGY Employers use technology to support orientation. For example, at the University of Cincinnati, new employees spend about 45 minutes online learning about their new employer's mission, organization, and policies and procedures. IBM uses virtual environments like Second Life to support orientation, particularly for employees abroad. The new employees choose virtual avatars, for instance, to learn how to enroll for benefits.[9] ION Geophysical uses an online onboarding portal solution called RedCarpet. It includes a streaming video welcome message, and photos and profiles of new colleagues.[10] With Workday's iPhone app, employers provide their employees with easy mobile access to their employee directories. Users can search their company's worker directory for names, images, and contact information; call or e-mail coworkers directly; and view physical addresses on Google Maps.[11] Some employers place scannable QR codes along the orientation tour's stops, to provide information about each department and its role.[12]

Overview of the Training Process

2 List and briefly explain each of the steps in the training process.

training
The process of teaching new or current employees the basic skills they need to perform their jobs.

Directly after orientation, training should begin. **Training** means giving new or current employees the skills that they need to perform their jobs, such as showing new salespeople how to sell your product. Training might involve having the current jobholder explain the job to the new hire, or multi-week classroom or Internet classes.

Training is important. If even high-potential employees don't know what to do and how to do it, they will improvise or do nothing useful at all. Furthermore, by one estimate, about three-fourths of 30-something age high achievers begin looking for new positions within a year of starting, often due to dissatisfaction with inadequate training.[13]

KNOW YOUR EMPLOYMENT LAW

Training and the Law

Managers should understand the legal implications of their training-related decisions, for instance with respect to discrimination, negligent training, and overtime pay.

With respect to *discrimination*, Title VII of the Civil Rights Act of 1964 and related legislation requires that the employer avoid *discriminatory* actions in all aspects of its human resource management process, and that applies to selecting which employees to train. Employers face much the same consequences for discriminating against protected individuals when selecting candidates for training programs as they would in selecting candidates for jobs, or for promotion or other related decisions. *Harassment training* is another example. The EEOC stresses that if feasible, employers "should provide training to all employees to ensure they understand their [sexual harassment] rights and responsibilities.'"[14] In practice, courts will consider the adequacy of the employer's sexual harassment training to determine whether it exercised reasonable care to prevent harassment.[15]

negligent training
A situation where an employer fails to train adequately, and the employee subsequently harms a third party.

Inadequate training can also expose the employer to liability for **negligent training**. As one expert puts it, "it's clear from the case law that where an employer fails to train adequately and an employee subsequently does harm to third parties, the court will find the employer liable." Among other things, the employer should confirm the applicant/employee's claims of skill and experience, provide adequate training (particularly where employees work with dangerous equipment), and evaluate the training to ensure that it is actually reducing risks.[16]

Given its frequent off-the-job nature, the question may arise, "must we pay the employee for the *time the latter spends in training?*" Often the answer is "no." For example, if the training program is strictly voluntary, and not directly related to the trainee's job, and the trainee does not perform any productive work, then the trainee should not expect to be compensated. Similarly, employers who require job candidates to complete short training sessions as prerequisites for being considered for positions usually do not need to compensate the trainees, as long as several conditions are met. Specifically, the employer should receive no immediate benefit from the training; should not guarantee trainees they'll get jobs at the end of their training; should inform the trainees up front that they will not be paid for the time they spend training; and should make the training similar to what the trainee might expect in a vocational school, even though the employer uses its own facilities.[17] Most other after-hours training requires overtime pay for eligible workers.

Aligning Strategy and Training

The employer's strategic plans should govern its training goals.[18] In essence, the aim is to identify the employee behaviors the firm will need to execute its strategy, and from that deduce what competencies (for instance skills and knowledge) employees will need. Then, put in place training goals and programs to instill these competencies.[19] For example, Caterpillar Inc. created Caterpillar University to oversee all its training and development programs. Company executives set the university's policies and oversee "the alignment of the corporation's learning needs with the enterprises' business strategy."[20] The accompanying HR as a Profit Center feature illustrates how aligning training with strategy helped Macy's boost its revenues.

Training and Performance

Training ranks higher than appraisal and feedback and just below goal setting in its effect on productivity.[21] Companies spend on average $1,103 per employee for training per year and offer each about 28 hours of training.[22] Some experts use the phrase "workplace learning and performance" in lieu of training to emphasize that training aims to boost both employee learning and organizational performance.[23]

What can one do to ensure the training effort translates into improved performance? Define the training effort's purpose in terms of how it should affect organizational performance. Make sure the company's strategies drive the training program's design. Check with your internal "customers" (such as the sales manager who asks for a new salesforce training program) to make sure the program is working for them. View working for these internal customers to improve their performance as your mission. Ask "customers" "how are we doing."[24]

IMPROVING PERFORMANCE: HR as a Profit Center

The Training Program That Turned Macy's Around

For about 6 years after buying May Department Stores Co., Macy's Inc. was in a consolidation/cost-cutting mode. During these years, Macy's customer service suffered. Many sales associates weren't providing the level of service that customers wanted. The question was, what should Macy's do about it now?

Macy's top management turned to a new strategy. As its CEO said, "We are [now] talking about a cultural shift . . . becoming more of a growth company."[25] However, Macy's top management knew that growth would not occur without a big improvement in how its sales associates treated customers.

To produce the improved customer service Macy's needed to achieve its new strategy, Macy's installed a new training program. Rather than just watching a 90-minute interactive video as they previously did, sales associates now attended 3½-hour training sessions aimed at cultivating higher levels of customer service. Macy's management believed the training program and resulting customer service improvement would be the biggest factor in driving their company's sales growth. And indeed, same store sales rose 5.3% in 2011, 3.7% in 2012, and about 3.5% in 2013, well above many competitors'.[26]

Discussion Question 8-1: Show in outline form the strategy map steps that you think would explain how training produced improved sales at Macy's.

The ADDIE Five-Step Training Process

The employer should use a rational training process. The gold standard here is still the basic analysis-design-develop-implement-evaluate (ADDIE) training process model that training experts have used for years.[27] As an example, one training vendor describes its training process as follows:[28]

- *Analyze* the training need.
- *Design* the overall training program.
- *Develop* the course (actually assembling/creating the training materials).

- *Implement* training, by actually training the targeted employee group using methods such as on-the-job or online training.
- *Evaluate* the course's effectiveness.

We'll look at each step next.

Conducting the Training Needs Analysis

The training needs analysis may address the employer's *strategic/longer term* training needs and/or its *current* training needs.

STRATEGIC TRAINING NEEDS ANALYSIS Strategic goals (perhaps to enter new lines of business or to expand abroad) often means the firm will have to fill new jobs. *Strategic training needs analysis* identifies the training employees will need to fill these new future jobs. For example, when Wisconsin-based Signicast Corp. decided to build a new, high-tech plant, the firm's top management knew the plant's employees would need new skills to run the computerized machines. They worked closely with their HR team to formulate hiring policies and training programs to ensure the firm would have the human resources required to populate the new plant.

The results of the strategic training-based needs analysis will also support the employer's succession planning. The latter, recall, means identifying the training and development that employees need to fill the firm's key future positions, and those positions of course will reflect the firm's strategic plans.

CURRENT TRAINING NEEDS ANALYSIS Most training efforts aim to improve current performance—specifically training new employees, and those whose performance is deficient.

How you analyze current training needs depends on whether you're training new or current employees. The main task for *new* employees is to determine what the job entails and to break it down into subtasks, each of which you then teach to the new employee.

Analyzing *current* employees' training needs is more complex, because you must also ascertain whether training is the solution. For example, performance may be down due to poor motivation. Managers use *task analysis* to identify new employees' training needs, and *performance analysis* to identify current employees' training needs.

task analysis
A detailed study of a job to identify the specific skills required.

competency model
A graphic model that consolidates, usually in one diagram, a precise overview of the competencies (the knowledge, skills, and behaviors) someone would need to do a job well.

TASK ANALYSIS: ANALYZING NEW EMPLOYEES' TRAINING NEEDS Particularly with lower-level workers, it's customary to hire inexperienced personnel and train them. The aim here is to give these new employees the skills and knowledge they need to do the job. **Task analysis** is a detailed study of the job to determine what specific skills—like Java (in the case of a Web developer) or interviewing (in the case of a supervisor)—the job requires. For task analysis, job descriptions and job specifications are essential. They list the job's specific duties and skills, which are the basic reference points in determining the training required. Managers also uncover training needs by reviewing performance standards, performing the job, and questioning current job holders and their supervisors.[29]

Some managers supplement the job description and specification with a *task analysis record form*. This form (see Table 8-1) consolidates information regarding required tasks and skills. As Table 8-1 illustrates, the form contains six columns of information, such as "Skills or knowledge required."

TALENT MANAGEMENT: USING COMPETENCY PROFILES AND MODELS Best talent management practice suggests using the same set of job-related competencies for training the employee as for recruiting, selecting, appraising, and paying him or her. We saw that doing so often begins with summarizing the job's required human competencies (required skills, knowledge, and behaviors such as leadership) in a competency model. The **competency model** consolidates, usually in one diagram, a precise overview of the competencies someone would need to do the job well. Figure 4-11 (page 112) was one example.

The employer can then design its training program to foster these competencies. For example, the American Society for Training and Development (ASTD) built a competencies model for

TABLE 8-1 Sample Task Analysis Record Form

	Task List	When and How Often Performed	Quantity and Quality of Performance	Conditions Under Which Performed	Skills or Knowledge Required	Where Best Learned
1.	Operate paper cutter	4 times per day		Noisy pressroom: distractions		
1.1	Start motor	4 times per day				On the job
1.2	Set cutting distance		± tolerance of 0.007 in.		Read gauge	On the job
1.3	Place paper on cutting table		Must be completely even to prevent uneven cut		Lift paper correctly	On the job
1.4	Push paper up to cutter				Must be even	On the job
1.5	Grasp safety release with left hand		100% of time, for safety		Essential for safety	On the job but practice first with no distractions
1.6	Grasp cutter release with right hand				Must keep both hands on releases	On the job but practice first with no distractions
1.7	Simultaneously pull safety release with left hand and cutter release with right hand				Must keep both hands on releases	On the job but practice first with no distractions
1.8	Wait for cutter to retract		100% of time, for safety		Must keep both hands on releases	On the job but practice first with no distractions
1.9	Retract paper				Wait until cutter retracts	On the job but practice first with no distractions
1.10	Shut off		100% of time, for safety			On the job but practice first with no distractions
2.	Operate printing press					
2.1	Start motor					

Note: Task analysis record form showing some of the tasks and subtasks performed by a printing press operator.

the job of training and development professional. It includes 10 core trainer competencies, such as being able to achieve performance improvement, instructional design, and training delivery. As one competency example, the model describes *instructional design* as "designing, creating, and developing formal learning solutions to meet organizational needs; analyzing and selecting the most appropriate strategy, methodologies, and technologies to maximize the learning experience and impact."[30] Training a trainer would thus require, for instance, making sure he or she could, once training is complete, exhibit the skills and knowledge (competence) that enables him or her to design, create, and develop formal learning solutions to meet organizational needs.[31]

performance analysis
Verifying that there is a performance deficiency and determining whether that deficiency should be corrected through training or through some other means (such as transferring the employee).

PERFORMANCE ANALYSIS: ANALYZING CURRENT EMPLOYEES' TRAINING NEEDS For underperforming current employees, you can't assume that training is the solution. In other words, is it lack of training, or something else? **Performance analysis** is the process of verifying that there is a performance deficiency and determining whether the employer should correct such deficiencies through training or some other means (like transferring the employee).

Performance analysis begins with comparing the person's actual performance to what it should be. Doing so helps to confirm that there is a performance deficiency, and (hopefully) helps the manager to identify its cause. Examples of performance deficiencies might be:

I expect each salesperson to make 10 new contracts per week, but John averages only six.

Other plants our size average no more than two serious accidents per month; we're averaging five.

There are several ways to identify how a current employee is doing. These include reviewing:

- Performance appraisals
- Job-related performance data (including productivity, absenteeism and tardiness, grievances, waste, late deliveries, product quality, downtime, repairs, equipment utilization, and customer complaints)
- Observations by supervisors or other specialists
- Interviews with the employee or his or her supervisor
- Tests of things like job knowledge, skills, and attendance
- Attitude surveys
- Individual employee daily diaries
- Assessment center results
- Special performance gap analytical software, such as from Saba Software, Inc.

CAN'T DO/WON'T DO Uncovering why performance is down is the heart of performance analysis. The aim here is to distinguish between can't-do and won't-do problems. First, determine whether it is a *can't-do* problem and, if so, its specific causes. For example: The employees don't know what to do or what your standards are; there are obstacles in the system such as lack of tools or supplies; there are no job aids (such as color-coded wires that show assemblers which wire goes where); you've hired people who haven't the skills to do the job; or there is inadequate training.

Or, it might be a *won't-do* problem. Here employees could do a good job if they wanted to. One expert says, "Perhaps the biggest trap that trainers fall into is [developing] training for problems that training just won't fix."[32] For instance, the better solution might be to change the incentives.

Designing the Training Program

Armed with the needs analysis results, the manager next designs the training program. *Design* means planning the overall training program including training objectives, delivery methods, and program evaluation. Sub-steps include setting performance objectives, creating a detailed training outline (all training program steps from start to finish), choosing a program delivery method (such as lectures or Web), and verifying the overall program design with management. The design should include summaries of how you plan to set a training environment that motivates your

Most employers can build training programs like this one based on existing online and offline content offered by training content providers.

© Kim Kulish/Corbis

trainees both to learn and to transfer what they learn to the job. It is also here that the manager reviews possible training program content (including workbooks, exercises, and activities), and estimates a budget for the training program.[33] If the program is to use technology, the manager should include a review of the technology he or she plans to use as part of the analysis.[34] We'll look more closely next at several specific design issues.

SETTING LEARNING OBJECTIVES[35] Training, development, learning, or (more generally) *instructional objectives* should specify in measurable terms what the trainee should be able to do after successfully completing the training program.[36] For example:

> The technical service representative will be able to adjust the color guidelines on this HP Officejet All-in-One printer copier within 10 minutes according to the device's specifications.

The learning objectives should first address the performance deficiencies that you identified via the needs analysis. Thus, if the sales team's sales are 40% too low, the objectives should focus on ensuring they get the knowledge, skills, and attitudes they need to boost sales. But at the same time, the learning objectives must be practical, given the constraints.

One constraint is financial. The employer will generally want to see and approve a *training budget* for the program. Typical costs include the development costs (of having, say, a human resource specialist working on the program for a week or two), the direct and indirect (overhead) costs of the trainers' time, participant compensation (for the time they're actually being trained), and the cost of evaluating the program. The question, of course, isn't just "Can we afford this program?" but "Does it pay to spend this much, given the benefits we'll devise from the program—will it improve performance, and if so by how much?" Therefore, prepare to defend the program on a benefits-versus-costs basis.

There are also other constraints to consider. For example, time constraints may require reducing three or four desirable learning objectives to one or two.

CREATING A MOTIVATIONAL LEARNING ENVIRONMENT Municipalities running programs for traffic violators know there's often no better way to get someone's attention than by presenting a terrifying video accident. In other words, they know the best training starts not with a lecture but by making the material meaningful.

The same is true at work. Learning requires both ability and motivation, and the training program's design should consider both. In terms of *ability*, the learner–trainee needs (among other things) the required reading, writing, and mathematics skills, and the knowledge base. Trainees are rarely homogeneous, for instance, in terms of intellectual capacity. In setting the learning environment, the manager therefore should address several trainee-ability issues. For example, how will our program accommodate differences in trainee abilities? Do we need to provide remedial training?

Second, the learner must also be motivated. No manager should waste his or her time showing a disinterested employee how to do something (even if he or she has the requisite ability).

Many books exist on how to motivate employees, but several specific observations are pertinent here.[37] The training program's effects will be diminished if trainees return to their jobs to snide comments such as, "I hope you liked your little vacation" from colleagues. Therefore, the low-hanging fruit in motivating trainees is to make sure the trainee's peers and supervisor support the training effort. Ideally, particularly for larger programs, top management should visibly support the program. Beyond that, various motivation theories provide useful guidance. From behavior modification, we know that the training should provide opportunities for positive reinforcement. "Expectancy theory" shows us that the trainees need to know they have the ability to succeed in the program, and that the value to them of completing the program is high. Self-efficacy is crucial—trainees must believe they have the capacity to succeed. We can summarize such motivational points as follows.

MAKE THE LEARNING MEANINGFUL Learners are more motivated to learn something that has meaning for them. Therefore:

1. At the start of training, provide a bird's-eye view of the material that you are going to present. For example, show why it's important, and provide an overview.[38]
2. Use familiar examples.

3. Organize the information so you can present it logically, in meaningful units.
4. Use terms and concepts that are already familiar to trainees.
5. Use visual aids.
6. Create a perceived training need in trainees' minds.[39] In one study, pilots who experienced pretraining, accident-related events subsequently learned more from an accident-reduction training program than did those experiencing fewer such events.[40] Similarly, "before the training, managers need to sit down and talk with the trainee about why they are enrolled in the class, what they are expected to learn, and how they can use it on the job."[41]

MAKE SKILLS TRANSFER OBVIOUS AND EASY Make it easy to transfer new skills and behaviors from the training site to the job site:

1. Maximize the similarity between the training situation and the work situation.
2. Provide adequate practice.
3. Label or identify each feature of the machine and/or step in the process.
4. Direct the trainees' attention to important aspects of the job. For example, if you're training a customer service rep to handle calls, explain the different types of calls he or she will encounter.[42]
5. Provide "heads-up" information. For example, supervisors often face stressful conditions. You can reduce the negative impact of such events by letting supervisory trainees know they might occur.[43]
6. Trainees learn best at their own pace. If possible, let them pace themselves.

REINFORCE THE LEARNING Make sure the learner gets plenty of feedback. In particular:

1. Trainees learn best when the trainers immediately reinforce correct responses, perhaps with a quick "well done."
2. The learning curve goes down late in the day. Partial-day training is generally superior to full day training.
3. Provide follow-up assignments at the close of training, so trainees are reinforced by having to apply back on the job what they've learned.[44]
4. Incentivize. Some companies, such as Hudson Trail outfitters, an outdoor-gear retailer, offer trainees incentives of outdoor gear for completing each training program segment.[45]

ENSURE TRANSFER OF LEARNING TO THE JOB Unfortunately, less than 35% of trainees seem to be transferring what they learned in training to their jobs a year after training. Improving on that sad statistic requires steps at each stage of training. *Prior to training*, get trainee and supervisor input in designing the program, institute a training attendance policy, and encourage employees to participate.

During training, provide trainees with training experiences and conditions (surroundings, equipment) that resemble the actual work environment. Goal-setting is important. In one study, some trainees set goals at the start of the program for the skills they were being taught. After training, they were rated them more highly on these skills than were those who hadn't set goals.[46]

After training, reinforce what trainees learned, for instance, by appraising and rewarding employees for using new skills, and by making sure that they have the tools and materials they need to use their new skills.[47]

OTHER TRAINING DESIGN ISSUES Managers address several other issues during the training design stage. Most importantly, they review relevant alternative training methodologies (lectures, Web-based, and so on) and choose likely methods for their program. They also decide how they will organize the various training content components, choose how to evaluate the program, develop an overall summary plan for the program, and obtain management's approval to move ahead.

Developing the Program

Program development means actually assembling the program's training content and materials. It means choosing the actual content the program will present, as well as designing/choosing the specific instructional methods (lectures, cases, Web-based, etc.) you will use. Training equipment and materials include (for example) iPads, workbooks, lectures, PowerPoint slides, Web- and computer-based activities, course activities, trainer resources (manuals, for instance), and support materials.

Some employers create their own training content, but there's also a vast selection of online and offline content. (See, for example, the American Society for Training and Development's Infoline at www.astd.org, www.trainerswarehouse.com, and www.gneil.com, among thousands of such suppliers.)[48] Turnkey training packages often include a trainer's guide, self-study book, video, and other content.

Once you design, approve, and develop the program, management can implement and then evaluate it. *Implement* means actually provide the training, using one or more of the instructional methods (such as lectures) that we discuss next.

Implementing the Training Program

3 Explain how to use five training techniques.

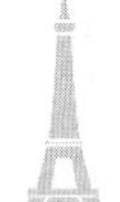

HR in Practice at the Hotel Paris As Lisa and the CFO reviewed measures of the Hotel Paris's current training efforts, it was clear that some changes were in order. Most other service companies provided at least 40 hours of training per employee per year, while the Hotel Paris offered, on average, no more than five or six. To see how they handled this, see the case on pages 252–253.

With objectives set and the program designed and developed, you can turn to implementing the training program. This means actually doing the training, using one or more of the following training methods.

On-the-Job Training

on-the-job training (OJT) Training a person to learn a job while working on it.

On-the-job training (OJT) means having a person learn a job by actually doing it. Every employee, from mailroom clerk to CEO, should get on-the-job training when he or she joins a firm. In many firms, OJT is the only training available.[49]

TYPES OF ON-THE-JOB TRAINING The most familiar on-the-job training is the *coaching or understudy method*. Here, an experienced worker or the trainee's supervisor trains the employee. This may involve simply observing the supervisor, or (preferably) having the supervisor or job expert show the new employee the ropes, step-by-step. On-the-job training is part of multifaceted training at The Men's Wearhouse, which combines on-the-job training with comprehensive initiation programs and continuing-education seminars. Every manager is accountable for developing his or her subordinates.[50] *Job rotation*, in which an employee (usually a management trainee) moves from job to job at planned intervals, is another OJT technique. *Special assignments* similarly give lower-level executives firsthand experience in working on actual problems.

Do not take the on-the-job training effort for granted. Instead, plan out and structure the OJT experience. Train the trainers themselves (often the employees' supervisors), and provide training materials. They should know, for instance, how to motivate learners. Because low expectations may translate into poor trainee performance, supervisor/trainers should emphasize their high expectations.

Many firms use "peer training" for OJT; for instance, expert employees answer calls at selected times during the day or participate in in-house "radio programs" to answer their peers' call-in questions about technical aspects of doing their jobs.[51] Others use employee teams to analyze the jobs and prepare training materials. The employees, already job experts, reportedly conduct task analyses more quickly and effectively than do training experts.[52]

THE OJT PROCESS Here are some steps to help ensure OJT success.

Step 1: Prepare the learner

1. Put the learner at ease.
2. Explain why he or she is being taught.
3. Create interest and find out what the learner already knows about the job.
4. Explain the whole job and relate it to some job the worker already knows.
5. Place the learner as close to the normal working position as possible.
6. Familiarize the worker with equipment, materials, tools, and trade terms.

Step 2: Present the operation

1. Explain quantity and quality requirements.
2. Go through the job at the normal work pace.
3. Go through the job at a slow pace several times, explaining each step. Between operations, explain the difficult parts, or those in which errors are likely to be made.
4. Again, go through the job at a slow pace several times; explain the key points.
5. Have the learner explain the steps as you go through the job at a slow pace.

Step 3: Do a tryout

1. Have the learner go through the job several times, slowly, explaining each step to you. Correct mistakes and, if necessary, do some of the complicated steps the first few times.
2. Run the job at the normal pace.
3. Have the learner do the job, gradually building up skill and speed.
4. Once the learner can do the job, let the work begin, but don't abandon him or her.

Step 4: Follow-up

1. Designate to whom the learner should go for help.
2. Gradually decrease supervision, checking work from time to time.
3. Correct faulty work patterns before they become a habit. Show why the method you suggest is superior.
4. Compliment good work.

Apprenticeship Training

apprenticeship training A structured process by which people become skilled workers through a combination of classroom instruction and on-the-job training.

Apprenticeship training is a process by which people become skilled workers, usually through a combination of formal learning and long-term on-the-job training, often under the tutelage of a master craftsperson. When steelmaker Dofasco discovered that many of their employees would be retiring within 5 to 10 years, the company decided to revive its apprenticeship training. New recruits spend about 32 months in an internal apprenticeship training program, learning various jobs under the tutelage of experienced employees.[53]

The U.S. Department of Labor's National Apprenticeship System promotes apprenticeship programs. More than 460,000 apprentices participate in 28,000 programs, and registered programs can receive federal and state contracts and other assistance.[54] Figure 8-2 lists popular recent apprenticeships.

Informal Learning

Surveys from the American Society for Training and Development estimate that as much as 80% of what employees learn on the job they learn through informal means, including performing their jobs while interacting every day with their colleagues.[55]

FIGURE 8-2 Some Popular Apprenticeships

Source: www.doleta.gov/OA/occupations.cfm, accessed October 12, 2012.

The U.S. Department of Labor's Registered Apprenticeship program offers access to more than 1,000 occupations, such as the following:

- Able seaman
- Carpenter
- Chef
- Child care development specialist
- Construction craft laborer
- Dental assistant
- Electrician
- Elevator constructor
- Fire medic
- Law enforcement agent
- Over-the-road truck driver
- Pipefitter

Employers can facilitate informal learning. For example, one Siemens plant places tools in cafeteria areas to take advantage of the work-related discussions taking place. Even installing whiteboards with markers can facilitate informal learning. Sun Microsystems implemented an informal online learning tool it called Sun Learning eXchange. This evolved into a platform containing more than 5,000 informal learning items/suggestions addressing topics ranging from sales to technical support.[56] Cheesecake Factory employees use VideoCafé, a YouTube-type platform, to let employees "upload and share video snippets on job-related topics, including customer greetings and food preparation."

Job Instruction Training

job instruction training (JIT)
Listing each job's basic tasks, along with key points, in order to provide step-by-step training for employees.

Many jobs (or parts of jobs) consist of a sequence of steps best learned step-by-step. Such step-by-step training is called **job instruction training (JIT)**. First, list the job's required steps (let's say for using a mechanical paper cutter) each in its proper sequence. Then list a corresponding "key point" (if any) beside each step. The steps in such a *job instruction training sheet* show trainees what to do, and the key points show how it's to be done—and why, as follows:

Steps	Key Points
1. Start motor	None
2. Set cutting distance	Carefully read scale—to prevent wrong-sized cut
3. Place paper on cutting table	Make sure paper is even—to prevent uneven cut
4. Push paper up to cutter	Make sure paper is tight—to prevent uneven cut
5. Grasp safety release with left hand	Do not release left hand—to prevent hand from being caught in cutter
6. Grasp cutter release with right hand	Do not release right hand—to prevent hand from being caught in cutter
7. Simultaneously pull cutter and safety releases	Keep both hands on corresponding releases—avoid hands being on cutting table
8. Wait for cutter to retract	Keep both hands on releases—to avoid having hands on cutting table
9. Retract paper	Make sure cutter is retracted; keep both hands away from releases
10. Shut off motor	None

As an example, the steps UPS teaches new drivers include: Shift into the lowest gear or into park; turn off the ignition; apply the parking brake; release the seatbelt with left hand; open the door; place the key on your ring finger.[57]

Lectures

Lecturing is a quick and simple way to present knowledge to large groups of trainees, as when the sales force needs to learn a new product's features.[58] Here are some guidelines for presenting a lecture:[59]

- Don't start out on the wrong foot, for instance, with an irrelevant joke.
- Speak only about what you know well.
- Give your listeners signals. For instance, if you have a list of items, start by saying something like, "There are four reasons why the sales reports are necessary. . . . The first. . . ."
- Use anecdotes and stories to show rather than tell.
- Be alert to your audience. Watch body language for negative signals like fidgeting or boredom.
- Maintain eye contact with the audience.
- Make sure everyone can hear. Repeat questions that you get from trainees.
- Leave hands hanging naturally at your sides.
- Talk from notes or PowerPoint slides, rather than from a script.
- Break a long talk into a series of short talks. Don't give a short overview and then spend a 1-hour presentation going point by point through the material. Break the long talk into a series of 10-minute talks, each with its own introduction. Write brief PowerPoint slides,

and spend about a minute on each. Each introduction highlights what you'll discuss, why it's important to the audience, and why they should listen to you.[60]

- Practice. If possible, rehearse under conditions similar to those under which you will actually give your presentation.

Programmed Learning

programmed learning
A systematic method for teaching job skills, involving presenting questions or facts, allowing the person to respond, and giving the learner immediate feedback on the accuracy of his or her answers.

Whether the medium is a textbook, PC, or the Internet, **programmed learning** is a step-by-step, self-learning method that consists of three parts:

1. Presenting questions, facts, or problems to the learner
2. Allowing the person to respond
3. Providing feedback on the accuracy of answers, with instructions on what to do next

Generally, programmed learning presents facts and follow-up questions frame by frame. What the next question is often depends on how the learner answers the previous question. The built-in feedback from the answers provides reinforcement.

Programmed learning reduces training time. It also facilitates learning by letting trainees learn at their own pace, get immediate feedback, and reduce their risk of error. Some argue that trainees do not learn much more from programmed learning than from a textbook. Yet studies generally support programmed learning's effectiveness. A typical study focused on 40 second year undergraduates in an organic chemistry course. Some studied in a conventional lecture setting and others used programmed learning. The researchers concluded, "The findings suggest that programmed learning could be considered as a better alternative to conventional lecturing in teaching stereochemistry."[61]

Intelligent tutoring systems take programmed learning one step further. In addition to the usual programmed learning, computerized intelligent tutoring systems learn what questions and approaches worked and did not work for the learner, and then adjust the instructional sequence to the trainee's unique needs.

Behavior Modeling

behavior modeling
A training technique in which trainees are first shown good management techniques in a film, are asked to play roles in a simulated situation, and are then given feedback and praise by their supervisor.

Behavior modeling involves (1) showing trainees the right (or "model") way of doing something, (2) letting trainees practice that way, and then (3) giving feedback on the trainees' performance. Behavior modeling training is one of the most widely used, well-researched, and highly regarded psychologically based training interventions.[62] The basic procedure is as follows:

1. ***Modeling.*** First, trainees watch live or video examples showing models behaving effectively in a problem situation. Thus, the video might show a supervisor effectively disciplining a subordinate, if teaching "how to discipline" is the aim of the training program.
2. ***Role-playing.*** Next, the trainees get roles to play in a simulated situation; here they are to practice the effective behaviors demonstrated by the models.
3. ***Social reinforcement.*** The trainer provides reinforcement in the form of praise and constructive feedback.
4. ***Transfer of training.*** Finally, trainees are encouraged to apply their new skills when they are back on their jobs.

Audiovisual-Based Training

Although increasingly replaced by Web-based methods, audiovisual-based training techniques like DVDs, films, PowerPoint, and audiotapes are still popular.[63] The Ford Motor Company uses videos in its dealer training sessions to simulate problems and reactions to various customer complaints, for example.

Vestibule Training

With vestibule training, trainees learn on the actual or simulated equipment but are trained off the job (perhaps in a separate room or *vestibule*). Vestibule training is necessary when it's too costly or dangerous to train employees on the job. Putting new assembly-line workers right to work could slow production, for instance, and when safety is a concern—as with pilots—simulated training may be the only practical alternative. As an example, UPS uses a life-size learning lab to provide a 40-hour, 5-day realistic training program for driver candidates.[64]

Electronic Performance Support Systems (EPSS)

electronic performance support systems (EPSS)
Sets of computerized tools and displays that automate training, documentation, and phone support; integrate this automation into applications; and provide support that's faster, cheaper, and more effective than traditional methods.

job aid
A set of instructions, diagrams, or similar methods available at the job site to guide the worker.

Electronic performance support systems (EPSS) are computerized tools and displays that automate training, documentation, and phone support.[65] When you call a Dell service rep, he or she is probably asking questions prompted by an EPSS; it takes you both, step-by-step, through an analytical sequence. Without the EPSS, Dell would have to train its service reps to memorize an unrealistically large number of solutions. Aetna Insurance cut its 13-week instructor-led training course for new call center employees by about 2 weeks by providing the employees with performance support tools.[66]

Performance support systems are modern job aids. **Job aids** are sets of instructions, diagrams, or similar methods available at the job site to guide the worker.[67] Job aids work particularly well on complex jobs that require multiple steps, or where it's dangerous to forget a step. For example, airline pilots use job aids (a checklist of things to do prior to takeoff).

Videoconferencing

Videoconferencing involves delivering programs over broadband lines, the Internet, or satellite. Vendors such as Cisco offer videoconference products such as Webex and TelePresence (www.cisco.com/en/US/products/ps10352/index.html). Employers typically use videoconferencing technology with other technology. For example, Cisco's Unified Video Conferencing (CUVC) product line combines Cisco group collaboration and decision-making software with videoconferencing, video telephony, and realistic "TelePresence" capabilities.[68]

Computer-Based Training (CBT)

Computer-based training refers to training methods that use interactive computer-based systems to increase knowledge or skills. For example, employers use CBT to teach employees safe methods for avoiding falls. The system lets trainees replay the lessons and answer questions, and are especially effective when paired with actual practice under a trainer's watchful eye.[69]

Computer-based training is increasingly realistic. For example, *interactive multimedia training* integrates the use of text, video, graphics, photos, animation, and sound to create a complex training environment with which the trainee interacts.[70] In training a physician, for instance, such a system lets a medical student take a hypothetical patient's medical history, conduct an examination, and analyze lab tests. The student can then interpret the sounds and draw conclusions for a diagnosis. *Virtual reality training* takes this realism a step further, by putting trainees into a simulated environment.

Simulated Learning

"Simulated learning" means different things to different people. A survey asked training professionals what experiences qualified as simulated learning experiences. The percentages of trainers choosing each experience were:

- Virtual reality-type games, 19%
- Step-by-step animated guide, 8%
- Scenarios with questions and decision trees overlaying animation, 19%
- Online role-play with photos and videos, 14%
- Software training including screenshots with interactive requests, 35%
- Other, 6%[71]

Virtual reality puts the trainee in an artificial three-dimensional environment that simulates events and situations experienced on the job.[72] Sensory devices transmit how the trainee is responding to the computer, and the trainee "sees, feels and hears" what is going on, assisted by special goggles and sensory devices.[73]

The U.S. Armed Forces use simulation-based training programs for soldiers and officers. For example, the army developed video game–type training programs called Full-Spectrum

Command and Full-Spectrum Warrior for training troops in urban warfare. They offer realistic features, and cultivate real-time leadership and decision-making skills.[74]

OTHER EXAMPLES Employers increasingly use computerized simulations (sometimes called *interactive learning*) to inject realism into their training. Orlando-based Environmental Tectonics Corporation created an Advanced Disaster Management simulation for emergency medical response trainees. One simulated scenario involves a plane crash. So realistic that it's "unsettling," trainees including firefighters and airport officials respond to the simulated crash's sights and sounds via pointing devices and radios.[75] Cisco embedded the learning required to train thousands of Cisco trainees for Cisco certification exams within a video game–like program that includes music, graphics, and sound effects.[76] A Novartis pharmaceuticals division runs about 80 or so clinical trials per year, and it must be sure each trial team is trained for this. Novartis uses a custom made simulation as a team training device. For example, the simulation shows trainees "how their decisions affected the quality of the trial and whether their decision saved time or added time to the process."[77] The Cheesecake Factory uses a simulation that shows employees how to build the "perfect hamburger."

ADVANTAGES Training simulations are expensive to create, but for large companies the cost per employee is usually reasonable.[78] In general, interactive and simulated technologies reduce learning time by an average of 50%.[79] Other advantages include mastery of learning (if the trainee doesn't learn it, he or she generally can't move on to the next step), increased retention, and increased trainee motivation (resulting from responsive feedback).

Specialist multimedia software houses such as Graphic Media of Portland, Oregon, produce much of the content for these programs. They produce both custom titles and generic programs such as a $999 package for teaching workplace safety.

Lifelong and Literacy Training Techniques

lifelong learning
Provides employees with continuing learning experiences over their tenure with the firm, with the aims of ensuring they have the opportunity to learn the skills they need to do their jobs and to expand their occupational horizons.

Lifelong learning means providing employees with continuing learning experiences over their tenure with the firm, with the aim of ensuring they have the opportunity to learn the skills they need to do their jobs and to expand their horizons. For example, one senior waiter at the Rhapsody restaurant in Chicago received his undergraduate degree and began work toward a master of social work using the lifelong learning account (LiLA) program his employer offers. Lifelong learning may thus range from basic remedial skills (for instance, English as a second language) to college. Somewhat similar to 401(k) plans, employers and employees contribute to LiLA plans (without the tax advantages of 401(k) plans), and the employee can use these funds to better himself or herself.[80]

LITERACY TRAINING By one estimate, about 39 million people in the United States have learning disabilities. Some call the American workforce ill-prepared.[81] Yet today's emphasis on teamwork and quality requires that employees read, write, and understand numbers.[82]

Employers often turn to private firms like Education Management Corporation to provide the requisite education.[83] Another simple approach is to have supervisors teach basic skills by giving employees writing and speaking exercises.[84] For example, if an employee needs to use a manual to find out how to change a part, teach that person how to use the index to locate the relevant section. Some call in teachers from a local high school.

IMPROVING PERFORMANCE: HR Practices Around the Globe

Diversity Training at ABC Virtual Communications, Inc.

Diversity training aims to improve cross-cultural sensitivity, with the goal of fostering more harmonious working relationships among a firm's employees. Such training typically includes improving interpersonal skills, understanding and valuing cultural differences, improving technical skills, socializing employees into the corporate culture, indoctrinating new workers into the U.S. work ethic, improving English proficiency and basic math skills, and improving bilingual skills for English-speaking employees.[85] For example, IBM has online programs to educate managers regarding diversity, inclusive leadership, and sexual harassment.

Training materials include interactive learning modules that enable trainees to practice what they've learned, testimonials from IBM executives, and self-assessment tools.[86]

Most employers opt for an off-the-shelf diversity training program such as *Just Be F.A.I.R.* from VisionPoint productions. It includes streaming video, a facilitator discussion guide, participant materials and workbook, a DVD with print materials, PowerPoint slides, and two videos (the purchase price for the program is about $1,000). Vignettes illustrate such things as the potential pitfalls of stereotyping people.[87]

ABC Virtual Communications, Inc. (www.abcv.com/) is a Des Moines, Iowa, provider of customized software development and other solutions. It therefore requires qualified personnel, particularly software engineers. Recruiting such employees is difficult anywhere, but particularly in Iowa, where many recent graduates move away. A shortage of qualified personnel would weaken the firm's performance.

ABC therefore recruits foreign-born individuals. However, it was obvious that hiring these skilled employees wasn't enough: ABC needed a diversity management training program that could turn these new employees—and the firm's current employees—into productive colleagues.

Their program consists of several courses. New ABC employees, representing 14 countries and 45 ethnic groups, take a mandatory 8-hour orientation overview for new employees on the American Workplace. All ABC employees take an "effective communications" training course. Conversational English and accent reduction classes for employees and their families are available through Rosetta Stone language learning software. The company also partnered with Des Moines Area Community College to create specialized classes for individual needs. At ABC Virtual, a globally diverse workforce was the key to improved performance, and diversity training helped them manage their diversity.[88]

Discussion Question 8-2: List five competencies that you believe such a diversity program should cultivate.

Team Training

Teamwork does not always come naturally. Companies devote many hours to training new employees to listen to each other and to cooperate. For example, a Baltimore Coca-Cola plant suffered from high turnover and absenteeism.[89] The new plant manager decided to address these problems by reorganizing around teams. He then used team training to support and improve team functioning.

Team training focused on technical, interpersonal, and team management issues. In terms of *technical training*, for instance, management encouraged team employees to learn each other's jobs, to encourage flexible team assignments. **Cross training** means training employees to do different tasks or jobs than their own; doing so facilitates flexibility and job rotation, as when you expect team members to occasionally share jobs.

cross training
Training employees to do different tasks or jobs than their own; doing so facilitates flexibility and job rotation.

Interpersonal problems often undermine team functioning. Team training here therefore included *interpersonal skills* training such as in listening, handling conflict, and negotiating.[90] Effective teams also require team management skills, for instance in problem solving, meetings management, consensus decision making, and team leadership, and the teams received such training as well.

Many employers use team training to build stronger management teams. For example, some use outdoor "adventure" training such as Outward Bound programs to build teamwork. This usually involves taking a firm's management team out into rugged, mountainous terrain.[91] The aim is to foster trust and cooperation among trainees. One chief financial officer for a bank helped organize a retreat for 73 of his firm's financial employees. As he said, "They are very individualistic in their approach to their work. . . . What I have been trying to do is get them to see the power of acting more like a team."[92] Other team training methods include action learning and team building, which we'll address later in this chapter.[93]

Improving Performance Through HRIS

INTERNET-BASED TRAINING Employers use Internet-based learning to deliver almost all the types of training we have discussed to this point. For example, ADP trains new salespeople online, using a Blackboard learning management system similar to one used by college students.[94] The Italian eyewear company Luxottica (whose brands include LensCrafters and Sunglass Hut) provides training to its 38,000 employees worldwide via instant online access to information on new products and regulations.[95] Recently, state-owned postal service China Post had to train about 100,000 employees quickly. It created a new center to manage its online training college, which now delivers about 9,000 hours of training annually, offering over 600 programs.[96]

LEARNING PORTALS A *learning portal* is a section of an employer's website that offers employees online access to training courses. Many employers arrange to have an online training vendor make its courses available via the employer's portal. Most often, the employer contracts with applications service providers (ASPs). Here, when employees go to their firm's learning portal, they actually access the menu of training courses that the ASP offers for the employer. A Google search for e-learning companies reveals many, such as SkillSoft, Plateau Systems, and Employment Law Learning Technologies.

Learning Management Systems Learning management systems (LMS) are special software tools that support Internet training by helping employers identify training needs, and to schedule, deliver, assess, and manage the online training itself. (Blackboard and WebCT are two familiar college-oriented learning management systems). General Motors uses an LMS to help its dealers in Africa and the Middle East deliver training. The Internet-based LMS includes a course catalog, supervisor approved self-enrollment, and pre- and post-course tests. The system then automatically schedules the individual's training.[97]

Many employers integrate the LMS with the company's talent management systems. That way, skills inventories and succession plans automatically update as employees complete their training.[98]

Online learning doesn't necessarily teach individuals faster or better. In one review, Web-based instruction was a bit more effective than classroom instruction for teaching memory of facts and principles; Web-based instruction and classroom instruction were equally effective for teaching information about how to perform a task or action.[99] But, of course, the need to teach large numbers of students remotely, or to enable trainees to study at their leisure, often makes e-learning the logical choice.[100]

Some employers opt for *blended learning*. Here, trainees use multiple delivery methods (such as manuals, in-class lectures, and Web-based seminars or "webinars") to learn the material.[101] Intuit (which makes TurboTax) uses instructor-led classroom training for getting new distributors up to speed. Then they use virtual classroom systems (see the following) for things like monthly meetings with distributors, and for classes on special software features.[102]

The Virtual Classroom

virtual classroom
Teaching method that uses special collaboration software to enable multiple remote learners, using their PCs or laptops, to participate in live audio and visual discussions, communicate via written text, and learn via content such as PowerPoint slides.

A **virtual classroom** uses collaboration software to enable multiple remote learners, using their PCs or laptops, to participate in live audio and visual discussions, communicate via written text, and learn via content such as PowerPoint slides.

The virtual classroom combines the best of Web-based learning offered by systems like Blackboard and WebCT with live video and audio. Thus, Elluminate Live! lets learners communicate with clear, two-way audio; build communities with user profiles and live video; collaborate with chat and shared whiteboards; and learn with shared applications such as PowerPoint slides.[103]

Mobile Learning

A majority of large employers distribute internal communications and training via mobile devices.[104] Employees at CompuCom Systems Inc. access instruction manuals through mobile devices; the company subsidizes employee purchases of smart phones or tablets to facilitate this. Natural user interfaces such as Apple's Siri voice recognition system facilitate such training.[105]

Mobile learning (or "on-demand learning") means delivering learning content, on the learner's demand, via mobile devices like cell phones, laptops, and tablets, wherever and whenever the learner has the time and desire to access it.[106] For example, trainees can take full online courses using dominKnow's (www.dominknow.com) iPhone-optimized Touch Learning Center Portal.[107]

Employers use mobile learning to deliver training and downloads on topics "from how to close an important sales deal to optimizing organizational change."[108] IBM uses mobile learning to deliver just-in-time information (for instance, about new product features) to its sales force. To facilitate this, its training department often breaks up, say, an hour program into easier-to-use 10-minute pieces. Some employers use blogs to communicate learning to trainees.[109] J.P. Morgan encourages employees to use instant messaging, for instance, to update colleagues about new products quickly.

Social Media and HR

Employers use social media, such as LinkedIn, Facebook, and Twitter, and virtual worlds like Second Life to communicate company news and messages and to provide training.[110] For example, British Petroleum uses Second Life to train new gas station employees. The aim here is to show new gas station employees how to use the safety features of gasoline storage tanks. BP built three-dimensional renderings of the tank systems in Second Life. Trainees use these to "see" underground and observe the effects of using the safety devices.[111]

Web 2.0 learing
Training that uses online technologies such as social networks, virtual worlds (such as Second Life), and systems that blend synchronous and asynchronous delivery with blogs, chat rooms, bookmark sharing, and tools such as 3-D simulations.

Web 2.0 learning is learning that utilizes online technologies such as social networks, virtual worlds (such as Second Life), and systems that blend synchronous and asynchronous delivery with blogs, chat rooms, bookmark sharing, and tools such as 3-D simulations.[112] About 40% of learning professionals surveyed said their companies use Web 2.0 learning, and 86% said they anticipated doing so. One large firm uses Web 2.0 to deliver credit card sales training to its service representatives around the country. *Collaborative peer forums* require teams of six to eight trainees to virtually "sell" their sales problem and solution to an executive.[113] The accompanying HR Tools feature shows how managers can create their own training programs.

IMPROVING PERFORMANCE: HR Tools for Line Managers and Entrepreneurs

Creating Your Own Training Program

While it would be nice if supervisors in even the largest firms could tap into their companies' packaged training programs to train the new people that they hire, the fact is that many times they cannot. You often hire and are responsible for the performance of a new employee only to find that your company provides little or no specialized training for this person, beyond the new person's introductory orientation. Without the required training, your team's performance might well suffer.

If so, you have several options. First, for either the individual manager or small business owner there are literally hundreds of suppliers of prepackaged training solutions. These range from self-study programs from the American Management Association, to more elaborate programs, for instance from American Media, or Business Advantage Inc. Similarly, reviewing trade journals such as *EHStoday* (www.ehstoday.com) will provide information on specialized prepackaged training program suppliers (in this case, for occupational safety and health).

outsourced learning
Utilizing a resource outside the company to provide employee training.

Second, small and medium-sized companies may also want to take advantage of the new trend toward **outsourced learning**.[114] Major consulting firms such as Accenture and IBM Global Services can obtain increased returns to scale by providing training solutions to multiple clients. Therefore many employers are now saving training dollars by outsourcing their entire learning functions to them.

Third, you can create your own "costless" training program, using the following process.

Step 1. **Set Training Objectives.** First, write down your training objectives. For example, your objective might be to reduce scrap, or to get new employees up to speed within 2 weeks.

Step 2. **Write a Detailed Job Description.** A detailed job description is the heart of any training program. It should list the daily and periodic tasks of each job, along with a summary of the steps in each task.

Step 3. **Develop an Abbreviated Task Analysis Record Form.** For practical purposes, the individual manager or small business owner can use an abbreviated version of the Task Analysis Record Form (Table 8-1) containing just four columns. In the first, list *tasks* (including what is to be performed in terms of each of the main tasks, and the steps involved in each task). In column B, list *performance standards* (in terms of quantity, quality, accuracy, and so on). In column C, list *trainable skills* required, things the employee must know or do to perform the task. This column provides you with specific knowledge and skills (such as "Keep both hands on the wheel") that you want to stress. In the fourth column, list *aptitudes required*. These are the human aptitudes (such as mechanical comprehension, and so on) that the employee should have to be trainable for the task and for which the employee can be screened ahead of time.

Step 4. **Develop a Job Instruction Sheet.** Next, develop a job instruction sheet for the job. We saw earlier that a job instruction training sheet shows the steps in each task as well as key points for each.

Step 5. **Prepare a Training Package for the Job.** At a minimum, your training package should include the job description, abbreviated Task Analysis Record Form, and job instruction sheet, all collected in a training manual. The latter should also contain a summary of the training program's objectives, and a listing of the trainable skills required for the trainee. The manual might also contain an introduction to the job, and an explanation of how the job fits with other jobs in the plant or office.

You also have to decide which media to use in your training program. A simple but effective on-the-job training program using current employees or supervisors as trainers requires only the materials we just described. However, it could turn out that the nature of the job or the number of trainees requires producing or purchasing special audio or video disks, PowerPoint slide presentations, or more extensive online or printed materials.

Implementing Management Development Programs

4 List and briefly discuss four management development methods.

KNOWLEDGE BASE

management development
Any attempt to improve current or future management performance by imparting knowledge, changing attitudes, or increasing skills.

Management development is any attempt to improve managerial performance by imparting knowledge, changing attitudes, or increasing skills.

Strategy and Development

Like succession planning, management development programs should stem from the employer's strategy and personnel plans. For example, strategies to enter new businesses or expand overseas imply that the employer will need managers with the skills to manage these new businesses.

The management development process consists of (1) *assessing* the company's strategic needs (for instance, for staffing the prospective new businesses), (2) *appraising* managers' current performance and skills (in this case with respect to filling the new business' top positions), and then (3) *developing* the managers (and future managers) to fill these positions.[115] Management development is usually part of the employer's *succession planning process,* the process through which a company plans for and fills senior-level openings.[116]

Some management development programs are company-wide and involve all or most new (or potential) managers. Thus, new MBAs may join GE's management development program and rotate through various assignments and educational experiences. The aims include assessing their management potential and giving them the necessary developmental experience. The firm may then slot superior candidates onto a "fast track," a development program that prepares them more quickly for senior-level commands.

Other development programs aim to fill specific top positions, such as CEO. Firms such as GE spend years developing, testing, and watching several potential replacements before finally choosing one.

Candidate Assessment and the 9-Box Grid

Some high potential managers fail in their jobs, while some (apparently) low potential managers excel. How then does an employer choose who to send through an expensive development program?

The 9-Box Grid is one tool. It shows *Potential* from low to medium to high on the vertical axis, and *Performance* from low to medium to high across the bottom—a total of nine possible boxes.

The grid can simplify, somewhat, the task of choosing development candidates. At the extremes, for instance, low potentials/low performers would not move on. The high potential/high performance stars most assuredly would. Most employers focus their development resources on high performer/high potential stars, and secondarily on those rated high potential/moderate performer, or high performer/moderate potential.[117] Other employers focus development resources on the company's "mission critical employees"—those central to the firm's success and survival. We'll see how later in this section.

In any case, individual assessment should always precede development. At frozen foods manufacturer Schawn, senior executives first whittle 40 or more development candidates down to about 10. Then the program begins with a 1-day assessment by outside consultants of each manager's leadership strengths and weaknesses. This assessment becomes the basis for each manager's individual development plan. Action-learning (practical) projects then supplement individual and group training activities.[118]

It is sensible to adapt the specific development experiences to the stage of the potential leader-trainee's career. Early in the person's career, focus development on cross functional projects, international assignments, and a multiple business situations. After identifying the person as a true potential leader, then a position on a senior management team, experience with external stakeholders (such as the investors), a "Chief of Staff" assignment to an experienced leader, and responsibility for leading an acquisition integration are appropriate. Finally, just before promoting this person to a top-level position, send him or her to a top-tier executive program for advanced training in areas such as organizational design and strategic management.[119]

The most popular development activities include on-the-job training, executive coaching, action learning, 360° feedback, experiential learning, off-site retreats (where managers meet with colleagues for learning), mentoring, and job rotation.[120] We'll look at some of these.

Managerial On-the-Job Training

Managerial on-the-job training methods include job rotation, the coaching/understudy approach, and action learning. **Job rotation** means moving managers from department to department to broaden their understanding of the business and to test their abilities. The trainee may be a recent college graduate; or a senior manager being groomed for further promotion.

job rotation
A management training technique that involves moving a trainee from department to department to broaden his or her experience and identify strong and weak points.

COACHING/UNDERSTUDY APPROACH Here the trainee works directly with a senior manager or with the person he or she is to replace; the latter is responsible for the trainee's coaching. Normally, the understudy relieves the executive of certain responsibilities, giving the trainee a chance to learn the job.

action learning
A training technique by which management trainees are allowed to work full-time analyzing and solving problems in other departments.

ACTION LEARNING **Action learning** programs give managers released time to work analyzing and solving problems in departments other than their own. Its basics include carefully selected teams of 5 to 25 members, assigning the teams real-world business problems that extend beyond their usual areas of expertise, and structured learning through coaching and feedback. The employer's senior managers usually choose the projects and decide whether to accept the teams' recommendations.[121] For example, Pacific Gas & Electric Company's (PG&E) Action-Forum Process has three phases:

1. A 6- to 8-week *framework* phase, during which the team defines and collects data on an issue;
2. The *action forum*—2 to 3 days at PG&E's learning center discussing the issue and developing action-plan recommendations; and
3. *Accountability sessions*, where the teams meet with the leadership group at monthly intervals to review progress.

Off-the-Job Management Training and Development Techniques

There are also many off-the-job techniques for training and developing managers.

case study method
A development method in which the manager is presented with a written description of an organizational problem to diagnose and solve.

THE CASE STUDY METHOD As most everyone knows, the **case study method** has trainees solve realistic problems after studying written or video case descriptions. The person then analyzes the case, diagnoses the problem, and presents his or her findings and solutions in a discussion with other trainees.

Integrated case scenarios create long-term, comprehensive case situations. For example, one FBI Academy integrated case scenario starts with "a concerned citizen's telephone call and ends 14 weeks later with a simulated trial. In between is the stuff of a genuine investigation. . . ." Scriptwriters (often employees in the employer's training group) write the scripts. The scripts include background stories, detailed personnel histories, and role-playing instructions; their aim is to develop specific skills, such as interviewing witnesses.[122]

management game
A development technique in which teams of managers compete by making computerized decisions regarding realistic but simulated situations.

MANAGEMENT GAMES Computerized **management games** enable trainees to learn by making realistic decisions in simulated situations. For example, *Interpret* is a team exercise that "explores team communication, the management of information and the planning and implementation of a strategy. It raises management trainees' communication skills, helps them to better manage the information flow between individuals and the team, and improves planning and problem solving skills."[123] Each team might have to decide how much to spend on advertising, how much to produce, and how much inventory to maintain.

People learn best by being involved, and games gain such involvement. They also help trainees develop their problem-solving skills, and to focus attention on planning rather than just putting out fires. They can also develop leadership skills and foster cooperation and teamwork.

OUTSIDE SEMINARS Numerous companies and universities offer Web-based and traditional classroom management development seminars and conferences. The selection of 1- to 3-day training programs offered by the American Management Association illustrates what's available. Recently, for instance, their offerings ranged from "developing your emotional intelligence" to "assertiveness training," "assertiveness training for managers," "assertiveness training for women in business," "dynamic listening skills for successful communication," and "fundamentals of cost accounting."[124] Specialized groups, such as SHRM, provide specialized seminars for their profession's members.[125]

UNIVERSITY-RELATED PROGRAMS Many universities provide executive education and continuing education programs in leadership, supervision, and the like. These can range from 1- to 4-day programs to executive development programs lasting 1 to 4 months.

The Advanced Management Program of Harvard's Graduate School of Business Administration illustrates.[126] Students are experienced managers. The program uses cases and lectures to provide management skills. In one such program, Hasbro wanted to improve its executives' creativity skills. Dartmouth University's Amos Tuck Business School provided a "custom approach to designing a program that would be built from the ground up to suit Hasbro's specific needs."[127]

role-playing
A training technique in which trainees act out parts in a realistic management situation.

ROLE-PLAYING The aim of **role-playing** is to create a realistic situation and then have the trainees assume the parts (or roles) of specific persons in that situation. Each trainee gets a role, such as:

> You are the head of a crew of telephone maintenance workers, each of whom drives a small service truck to and from the various jobs. Every so often you get a new truck to exchange for an old one, and you have the problem of deciding to which of your crew members you should give the new truck. Often there are hard feelings, so you have a tough time being fair.[128]

When combined with the general instructions and other roles, role-playing can trigger spirited discussions among the trainees. The aim is to develop trainees' skills in areas like leadership and delegating. For example, a supervisor could experiment with both a considerate and an autocratic leadership style, whereas in the real world this isn't so easy. Role-playing may also help someone to be more sensitive to others' feelings.

in-house development center
A company-based method for exposing prospective managers to realistic exercises to develop improved management skills.

CORPORATE UNIVERSITIES Many firms, particularly larger ones, establish **in-house development centers** (often called *corporate universities*). GE, Caterpillar, and IBM are examples. Employers may collaborate with academic institutions, and with training and development program providers and Web-based educational portals, to create packages of programs and materials for their centers. The best corporate universities (1) actively align offerings with corporate goals, (2) focus on developing skills that support business needs, (3) evaluate learning and performance, (4) use technology to support learning, and (5) partner with academia.[129]

Many employers offer virtual—rather than bricks-and-morter—corporate university services. For example, Cerner offers its employees "Cerner KnowledgeWorks." This offers employees three types of knowledge. *Dynamic knowledge* "is real-time content . . . such as e-mails, instant messages, or conference calls." *Moderated content* "includes best practices, such as case studies or wikis that capture information about situations where we did well and how we did it." *Codified content* "is more formal documentation of official company practices, and includes installation guides, help files, and formal training or courses."[130]

executive coach
An outside consultant who questions the executive's associates in order to identify the executive's strengths and weaknesses, and then counsels the executive so he or she can capitalize on those strengths and overcome the weaknesses.

EXECUTIVE COACHES Many firms retain executive coaches to help develop their top managers' effectiveness. An **executive coach** is an outside consultant who questions the executive's boss, peers, subordinates, and (sometimes) family in order to identify the executive's strengths and weaknesses, and to counsel the executive so he or she can capitalize on those strengths and overcome the weaknesses.[131] Executive coaching can cost $50,000 per executive. Experts recommend using formal assessments prior to coaching, to uncover strengths and weaknesses and to provide more focused coaching.[132]

Executive coaching can be effective. Participants in one study included about 1,400 senior managers who had received "360 degree" performance feedback from bosses, peers, and subordinates. About 400 worked with an executive coach to review the feedback. About a year later, these and about 400 managers who didn't receive coaching again received multisource feedback. The managers who received coaching were more likely to set more effective goals for their subordinates, and to have improved ratings from subordinates and supervisors.[133]

The coaching field is unregulated, so managers should do their due diligence. Check references, and consult the International Coach Federation, a trade group.

THE SHRM LEARNING SYSTEM The Society for Human Resource Management (SHRM) encourages HR professionals to qualify for certification by taking examinations. The society offers several preparatory training programs (http://www.shrm.org/Education/educationalproducts/learning/Pages/default.aspx). These include self-study, and a college/university option that includes classroom interaction with instructors and other learners.[134]

Leadership Development at GE

General Electric is known for its success in developing its executive talent. Their current mix of executive development programs illustrate what they offer:[135]

Leadership programs: These multiyear training programs rotate about 3,000 employees per year through various functions with the aim of enabling people to run a large GE business.

Session C: This is GE's intense multi-level performance appraisal process. The CEO personally reviews GE's top 625 officers every year.

Crotonville: This is GE's corporate training campus in New York and offers a mix of conventional classroom learning and team-based training and cultural trips.

Boca Raton: At this annual meeting of GE's top 625 officers, they network, share their best ideas, and get to understand the company's strategy for the coming year.

The next big thing: Whether it's productivity and quality improvement through "Six Sigma" or "innovation," GE focuses its employees on central themes or initiatives.

Monthly dinners: Jeffrey Immelt, GE's CEO, meets periodically at dinners and breakfasts to learn more about his top executives and to "strengthen his connections with his top team."[136]

Talent Management and Differential Development Assignments

In today's competitive environment, the usual HR practice of allocating development opportunities and other scarce resources across the board or based solely on performance makes less sense. It often makes more sense to "actively manage" the process by focusing more of the employer's resources on the "mission-critical employees" who top management deems most crucial to the employer's future growth. Doing so is a characteristic best practice of talent management—oriented firms.

We'll look closer at how employers do this in the following chapter, but several examples follow:

- High potential trainees in Johnson & Johnson's special "LeAD" leadership development program receive advice and regular assessments from coaches brought in from outside the company.[137]
- Some companies share future strategies on a privileged basis with rising leaders. For example, they invite them to quarterly meetings with high-level executives, and let them access an online portal where the rising leaders can review the company's strategy and critical metrics.[138]

5 List and briefly discuss the importance of the steps in leading organizational change.

Managing Organizational Change Programs

Several years ago, Intel Corp. carried out a major reorganization that one writer says, "May have badly damaged employee development, morale and the company's culture of innovation."[139]

We'll see that major organizational changes like these are never easy, but the hardest part may be overcoming the resistance. Individuals, groups, and even entire organizations tend to resist change, because they are accustomed to the usual way of doing things or because of perceived threats to their influence, for instance.[140]

Nokia CEO Stephen Elop.

Simon Dawson/Bloomberg/Getty Images

What to Change

In any case, the first question is, "What should we change?"

Not that many years ago, Nokia was the worldwide leader in handsets and smartphones. When Apple introduced its first iPhone, Nokia's phone market share plummeted. Nokia's board appointed a new CEO with Silicon Valley experience, Stephen Elop.[141] Its smart phone share was down, and it was losing low-cost handset business to Asian competitors. Nokia's Symbian mobile operating system was out of date. Nokia was too slow in executing changes. Elop had to jumpstart Nokia.

Faced with situations like these, managers can change one or more of five aspects of their companies—their *strategy, culture, structure, technologies*, or the *attitudes and skills* of the employees.

STRATEGIC CHANGE Organizational turnarounds often start with a change in the firm's strategy, mission, and vision—with *strategic change*. For example, Elop embarked on a strategy to renew Nokia by streamlining Nokia's product development process and by partnering with Microsoft with the aim of introducing a new Microsoft-based smart phone within a year.

OTHER CHANGES Elop also instituted other changes. In terms of *structure,* Nokia split responsibility for its smart phones and handsets into two new units. He replaced managers in Nokia's mobile phones unit and markets unit. In *technology,* Elop reduced the Symbian operating system's central role, replacing it with Microsoft's mobile operating system. With its *culture*, Elop had his new management team change the firm's culture, for instance, by impressing on Nokia's employees the need to eradicate bureaucratic decision making.

However, strategic, cultural, structural, and technological changes, no matter how logical, will fail without employees' active support.[142] Organizational change therefore also invariably involves bringing about *changes in the employees* themselves and in their attitudes, skills, and behaviors.[143]

Unfortunately, doing so is easier said than done. Many will view the change as negative. Resistance may be formidable. Knowing how to deal with that resistance is the heart of organizational change. (In 2013 Microsoft bought Nokia's mobile phone operations).

Lewin's Change Process

Psychologist Kurt Lewin formulated a model to summarize the basic process for implementing a change with minimal resistance. To Lewin, all behavior in organizations was a product of two kinds of forces: those striving to maintain the status quo and those pushing for change. Implementing change thus means reducing the forces for the status quo or building up the forces for change. Lewin's process consists of three steps:

1. *Unfreezing* means reducing the forces that are striving to maintain the status quo, usually by presenting a provocative problem or event to get people to recognize the need for change and to search for new solutions.
2. *Moving* means developing new behaviors, values, and attitudes. The manager may accomplish this through organizational structure changes, through conventional training and development activities, and sometimes through the other organizational development techniques (such as the team building) we'll discuss later.
3. *Refreezing* means building in the reinforcement to make sure the organization doesn't slide back into its former ways of doing things—for instance, change the incentive system.

Leading Organizational Change[144]

Of course, the challenge is in the details. A CEO such as Nokia's Stephen Elop needs a process for leading such a change. An 8-step process for leading organizational change follows.[145]

Unfreezing Stage

1. ***Establish a sense of urgency.*** Most managers start by creating a sense of urgency. For example, the CEO might present executives with a (fictitious) analyst's report describing the firm's imminent demise.
2. ***Mobilize commitment*** through joint diagnosis of problems. Having established a sense of urgency, the leader may then create one or more task forces to diagnose the problems facing the company. Such teams can produce a shared understanding of what they can and must improve, and thereby mobilize commitment.

Moving Stage

3. ***Create a guiding coalition.*** No one can really implement major organizational change alone. Most CEOs create a guiding coalition of influential people. They work together as a team to act as missionaries and implementers.
4. ***Develop and communicate a shared vision.*** For example, Stephen Elop's vision was of a streamlined Nokia moving fast to build advanced smart phones based on Microsoft's operating system. Vision guidelines are *keep it simple* (for example, "We are going to become faster than anyone else in our industry at satisfying customer needs."), *use multiple forums* (meetings, e-mails, formal and informal interaction), and *lead by example*.[146]
5. ***Help employees make the change.*** Are there impediments to change? Do policies, procedures, or the firm's organization make it difficult to act? Do intransigent managers discourage employees from acting? For example, Elop quickly replaced many of Nokia's top and mid-level managers.
6. Consolidate gains and produce more change. Aim for attainable short-term accomplishments. Use the credibility from these to change the remaining systems, structures, and policies that don't fit well with the company's new vision.[147]

Refreezing Stage

7. Reinforce the new ways of doing things with changes to the company's systems and procedures. For example, use new appraisal standards and incentives to reinforce the desired behaviors.
8. Finally, the leader must *monitor and assess progress*. At Nokia, for instance, "How many new products has the company introduced?" "What is our smart phone and handset market shares?"

Note however that process only takes one so far, because leadership style is critical. Transformational leaders—those who motivate their followers to transcend their personal interests, to enable their followers to identify with the collective goal, to articulate a clear and attainable vision—are far more likely to achieve organizational change.[148]

organizational development
A special approach to organizational change in which employees themselves formulate and implement the change that's required.

Using Organizational Development

There are many ways to reduce resistance to change. Among the many suggestions are that managers impose rewards or sanctions that guide employee behaviors, explain why the change is needed, negotiate with employees, give inspirational speeches, or ask employees to help design the change.[149] Organizational development (OD) taps into the latter. **Organizational development** is a change process through which employees formulate the change that's required and implement it, often with the assistance of trained consultants. OD has several distinguishing characteristics:

1. It usually involves *action research*, which means collecting data about a group, department, or organization, and feeding the information back to the employees so they can analyze it and develop hypotheses about what the problems might be.
2. It applies behavioral science knowledge to improve the organization's effectiveness.
3. It changes the organization in a particular direction—toward empowerment, improved problem solving, responsiveness, quality of work, and effectiveness.

There are four basic categories of OD applications: human process, technostructural, human resource management, and strategic applications (see Table 8-2).

HUMAN PROCESS APPLICATIONS Human process OD techniques aim to give employees the insight and skills required to analyze their own and others' behavior more effectively, so they can then solve interpersonal and intergroup problems. These problems might include, for instance, conflict among employees.

For example, *sensitivity, laboratory*, or *t-group* (the *t* is for "training") training's basic aim is to increase the participant's insight into his or her own behavior by encouraging an open expression of feelings in the trainer-guided t-group. Typically, 10 to 15 people meet, usually away from the job, with no specific agenda. Instead, the focus is on the feelings and emotions in the group at the meeting. The facilitator encourages participants to portray themselves as they feel within the group rather than in terms of past behaviors. The t-group's success depends on the feedback each person gets from the others, and on the participants' willingness to be candid.[150]

T-group training's personal nature suggests that participation should be voluntary. Some view it as unethical because you can't consider participation "suggested" by one's superior as voluntary. Others argue that it can be dangerous if led by an incompetent trainer.

TABLE 8-2 Categories of OD Interventions

Human Process	Human Resource Management
T-groups	Goal setting
Process consultation	Performance appraisal
Third-party intervention	Reward systems
Team building	Career planning and development
Organizational confrontation meeting	Managing workforce diversity
Survey research	Employee wellness
Technostructural	**Strategic**
Formal structural change	Integrated strategic management
Differentiation and integration	Culture change
Cooperative union–management projects	Strategic change
Quality circles	Self-designing organizations
Total quality management	
Work design	

According to experts French and Bell, the typical *team-building* meeting begins with the consultant interviewing each of the group members and the leader before the meeting.[151] They are asked what their problems are, how they think the group functions, and what obstacles are keeping the group from performing better. The consultant then categorizes the interview data into themes (such as "inadequate communications") and presents the themes to the group at the start of the meeting. The group ranks the themes in terms of importance, and the most important ones become the agenda for the meeting. The group then explores and discusses the issues, examines the underlying causes of the problems, and begins devising solutions.

Survey research requires that employees throughout the organization complete attitude surveys. The facilitator then uses those data as a basis for problem analysis and action planning. Surveys are a convenient way to unfreeze a company's management and employees. They provide a comparative, graphic illustration of the fact that the organization does have problems to solve.[152]

TECHNOSTRUCTURAL INTERVENTIONS OD practitioners also help to change firms' structures, methods, and job designs, using an assortment of technostructural interventions. For example, in a *formal structural change* program, the employees collect data on the company's existing organizational structure; they then jointly redesign and implement a new one.

HUMAN RESOURCE MANAGEMENT APPLICATIONS OD practitioners use action research to enable employees to analyze and change their firm's human resources practices. Targets of change here might include the performance appraisal and reward systems, as well as installing diversity programs.

STRATEGIC OD APPLICATIONS *Strategic interventions* aim to use action research to improve a company's strategic management. *Integrated strategic management* is one example. It consists of four steps: managers and employees (1) analyze current strategy and organizational structure, (2) choose a desired strategy and organizational structure, and (3) design a strategic change plan—"an action plan for moving the organization from its current strategy and organizational design to the desired future strategy and design."[153] Finally, (4) the team oversees implementing the strategic change and reviewing the results.[154]

6 Explain why a controlled study may be superior for evaluating the training program's effects.

Evaluating the Training Effort

With today's emphasis on measuring results, it is crucial that the manager evaluate the training program. There are several things you can measure: participants' *reactions* to the program, what (if anything) the trainees *learned* from the program, and to what extent their on-the-job *behavior* or *results* changed as a result of the program. In one survey of about 500 U.S. organizations, 77% evaluated their training programs by eliciting reactions, 36% evaluated learning, and about 10% to 15% assessed the program's behavior and/or results.[155] Computerization facilitates evaluation. For example, Bovis Lend Lease uses learning management system software to monitor which employees are taking which courses, and the extent to which they're improving their skills.[156]

There are two basic issues to address when evaluating training programs. One is the design of the evaluation study and, in particular, whether to use controlled experimentation. The second is, "What should we measure?"

Designing the Study

In deciding how to design the evaluation study, the basic concern is this: How can we be sure that the training caused the results that we're trying to measure? The *time series design* is one option. Here, as in Figure 8-3, you take a series of performance measures before and after the training program. This can provide some insight into the program's effectiveness.[157] However, you can't be sure that the training (rather than, say, a new company-wide pay plan) caused any change.

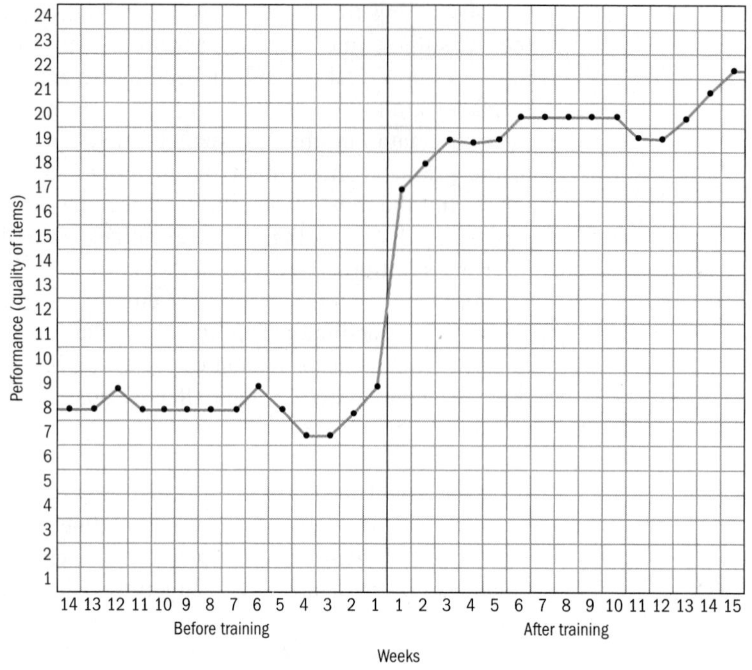

FIGURE 8-3 Using a Time Series Graph to Assess a Training Program's Effects

controlled experimentation
Formal methods for testing the effectiveness of a training program, preferably with before-and-after tests and a control group.

Controlled experimentation is therefore the evaluation process of choice. A controlled experiment uses a training group and a control group that receives no training. Data (for instance, on quantity of sales or quality of service) are obtained both before and after one group is exposed to training and before and after a corresponding period in the control group. This makes it easier to determine the extent to which any change in the training group's performance resulted from the training, rather than from some organization-wide change like a raise in pay. (The pay raise should have affected employees in both groups equally.)[158]

Training Effects to Measure

The manager can measure four basic categories of training outcomes or effects:

1. ***Reaction.*** Evaluate trainees' reactions to the program. Did they like the program? Did they think it worthwhile?
2. ***Learning.*** Test the trainees to determine whether they learned the principles, skills, and facts they were supposed to learn.
3. ***Behavior.*** Ask whether the trainees' on-the-job behavior changed because of the training program. For example, are employees in the store's complaint department more courteous toward disgruntled customers?
4. ***Results.*** Most important, ask, "What results did we achieve, in terms of the training objectives previously set?" For example, did the number of customer complaints diminish? Reactions, learning, and behavior are important. But if the training program doesn't produce measurable performance-related results, then it probably hasn't achieved its goals.[159]

Evaluating these is straightforward. Figure 8-4 presents one page from a sample evaluation questionnaire for assessing *reactions*. Or, you might assess trainees' *learning* by testing their new knowledge. For *behavioral change,* perhaps assess the effectiveness of a supervisory performance appraisal training program by asking that person's subordinates, "Did your supervisor provide you with examples of good and bad performance when he or she appraised your performance most recently?" Finally, directly assess a training program's *results* by measuring, say, the percentage of phone calls that call center trainees subsequently answered correctly. The accompanying HR as a Profit Center feature illustrates measuring a program's impact.

OPM *INSTRUCTOR HANDOUTS* *United States Office of Personnel Management*

TRAINING EVALUATION FORM

TITLE OF COURSE: **"Work and Family Issues — A Module for Supervisors and Managers"**
NAME OF INSTRUCTOR:

DATE OF TRAINING
Started:___________
Ended:___________

NAME: (Optional)	**POSITION TITLE/GRADE:**

AGENCY:	**OFFICE PHONE:** (Optional)	**OFFICE ADDRESS:** (Optional)

Rate Your Knowledge and Skill Level (Circle your rating)	**Overall, how would you rate this course?**
Before this course Low ------------------------------------High 1 2 3 4 5	__ Excellent __Very Good __ Good
After this course Low ------------------------------------High 1 2 3 4 5	__ Fair __ Poor

EVALUATION OF COURSE
(Check appropriate box)

ITEMS OF EVALUATION How did the course sharpen your knowledge or skills in:	Excellent	Very Good	Good	Fair	Poor	Not Applicable
1. What work and family programs are	◦	◦	◦	◦	◦	◦
2. Who uses work and family programs	◦	◦	◦	◦	◦	◦
3. How to recognize/solve work/family issues	◦	◦	◦	◦	◦	◦
4. Helping you take practical steps on the job	◦	◦	◦	◦	◦	◦

RATING OF INSTRUCTOR

1. Presentation, organization, delivery	◦	◦	◦	◦	◦	◦
2. Knowledge and command of the subject	◦	◦	◦	◦	◦	◦
3. Use of audio-visuals or other training aids	◦	◦	◦	◦	◦	◦
4. Stimulation of an open exchange of ideas, participation, & group interaction	◦	◦	◦	◦	◦	◦

STRONG POINTS OF THE COURSE
◦
◦
◦

WEAK POINTS OF THE COURSE
◦
◦
◦

ADDITIONAL DATA YOU WOULD LIKE TO HAVE COVERED IN COURSE
◦
◦
◦

ADDITIONAL COMMENTS/OR RECOMMENDATIONS

FIGURE 8-4 A Training Evaluation Form

IMPROVING PERFORMANCE: HR as a Profit Center

Judging Training's Impact

A careful comparison of the training program's costs and benefits can enable the human resource team to compute the program's return on investment. Online calculators such as the one shown below are available to facilitate such analyses. For some other examples, see for instance, exceltemplates.net/images/2009/trainingcost.jpg, www.tjtaylor.net/resources-tools2.htm, www.redhat.com/resourcelibrary/onlinetools/training-roi-calculator. and www.fastrak-consulting.co.uk/tactix/Features/tngroi/tngroi.htm.

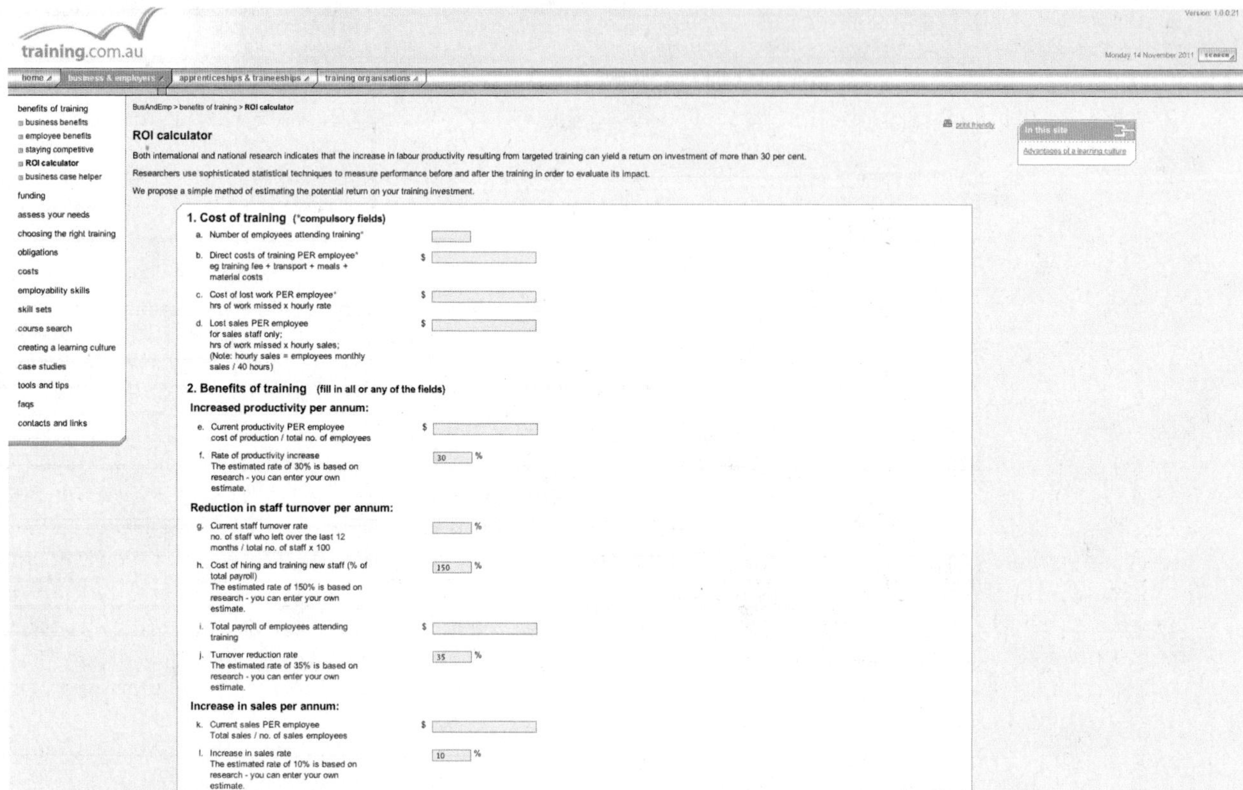

Online Training Evaluation Calculator

Source: www.training.com.au (Department of Education, Employment and Workplace Relations, Australian Government), accessed September 2011.

Review

MyManagementLab Go to **mymanagementlab.com** to complete the problems marked with this icon. 

Chapter Section Summaries

1. Getting your new employee on board and up to speed begins with **orienting and training** him or her. Employee orientation means providing new employees with the information they need to function, and helping them start being emotionally attached to the firm. This may simply involve providing them with brief written orientation materials and an employee handbook, but sometimes involves a formal process aimed at instilling in the employee the company's cherished values. The four-step training process includes needs analysis,

instructional design, implementation, and evaluation. Trainees need to be motivated to learn. Ensuring that they are motivated involves making the learning meaningful, making skills transfers easy, and reinforcing the learning.

2. We can use the acronym **ADDIE** to outline the **training process**: analyze, develop, design, implement, and evaluate. Before training employees, it's necessary to analyze their training needs and design the training program. In training new employees, employers use task analysis—basically, a detailed study of the job—to determine what skills the job requires. For current employees, performance analysis is required, specifically to verify that there is performance efficiency and to determine if training is the solution. Distinguishing between can't do and won't do problems is the main issue here. Once you understand the issues, you can design a training program, which means identifying specific training objectives, clarifying a training budget, and then actually designing the program in terms of the actual content.
3. With this in place, you can turn to **implementing the training program**. Specific training methods include on-the-job training, apprenticeship training, informal learning, job instruction training, lectures, programmed learning, audiovisual-based training, vestibule training, videoconferencing, electronic performance support systems, and computer-based training. Computerized training is increasingly popular, with many packaged programs available. Frequently, programs today are Internet-based, with employees accessing packaged online programs, backed up by learning management systems, through their company's learning portals. Employers also increasingly use mobile learning, for instance, delivering short courses and explanations to employees' smartphoes. With increasing demands for technologically literate employees, lifelong learning can help ensure employees have the basic educational backgrounds they need to succeed on their jobs. Diversity training aims to create better cross-cultural sensitivity with the goal of fostering more harmonious working relationships.
4. Most training methods are useful for all employees, but some are particularly appropriate for **management development programs**. Like all employees, new managers often get on-the-job training, for instance, via job rotation and coaching. In addition, it's usual to supply various off-the-job training and development opportunities—for instance, using the case study method, management games, outside seminars, university-related programs, corporate universities, executive coaches, and (for human resource managers) the SHRM learning system.
5. When facing economic, competitive, or other challenges, managers have to execute **organizational change programs**. These may aim at changing the company's strategy, culture, structure, technologies, or the attitudes and skills of the employees. Often, the trickiest part of organizational change is overcoming employees' resistance to it. With that in mind, steps in an effective organizational change program include establishing a sense of urgency, mobilizing commitment, creating a guiding coalition, developing and communicating a shared vision, helping employees make the change, consolidating gains, reinforcing new ways of doing things, and monitoring and assessing progress. Organizational development is a special approach to organizational change, one that involves action research, which means collecting data about a group and feeding the information back to the employees so they can analyze it and develop hypotheses about what the problems might be.
6. Whatever the training program, it's important to **evaluate the training effort**. You can measure reaction, learning, behavior, or results, ideally using a control group that is not exposed to training, in parallel with the group that you're training.

CHAPTER 8

Discussion Questions

8-3. "A well-thought-out orientation program is essential for all new employees, whether they have experience or not." Explain why you agree or disagree with this statement.

8-4. Explain how you would apply our "motivation points" (pages 227–228) in developing a lecture, say, on orientation and training.

✪ **8-5.** What are some typical on-the-job training techniques? What do you think are some of the main drawbacks of relying on informal on-the-job training for breaking new employees into their jobs?

✪ **8-6.** Describe the pros and cons of five management development methods.

8-7. Do you think job rotation is a good method to use for developing management trainees? Why or why not?

8-8. What is organizational development and how does it differ from traditional approaches to organizational change?

8-9. List and briefly explain each of the steps in the training process.

Individual and Group Activities

8-10. You're the supervisor of a group of employees whose task is to assemble disk drives that go into computers. You find that quality is not what it should be and that many of your group's devices have to be brought back and reworked. Your boss says, "You'd better start doing a better job of training your workers."

a. What are some of the staffing factors that could be contributing to this problem?

b. Explain how you would go about assessing whether it is in fact a training problem.

8-11. Choose a task with which you are familiar—mowing the lawn, making a salad, or studying for a test—and develop a job instruction sheet for it.

8-12. Working individually or in groups, develop a short, programmed learning program on the subject "Guidelines for Giving a More Effective Lecture."

8-13. Find three or four actual examples of employers using social media for training purposes. At what levels of managers are the offerings aimed? What seem to be the most popular types of programs? Why do you think that's the case?

8-14. Working individually or in groups, develop several specific examples to illustrate how a professor teaching human resource management could use at least four of the techniques described in this chapter in teaching his or her HR course.

8-15. Working individually or in groups, develop an orientation program for high school graduates entering your university as freshmen.

8-16. KNOWLEDGE BASE Appendix A, PHR and SPHR Knowledge Base, at the end of this book (pages 580–588) lists the knowledge someone studying for the HRCI certification exam needs to have in each area of human resource management (such as in Strategic Management, Workforce Planning, and Human Resource Development). In groups of four to five students, do four things: (1) review Appendix A; (2) identify the material in this chapter that relates to the required knowledge Appendix A lists; (3) write four multiple-choice exam questions on this material that you believe would be suitable for inclusion in the HRCI exam; and (4) if time permits, have someone from your team post your team's questions in front of the class, so that students in all teams can answer the exam questions created by the other teams.

8-17. Perhaps no training task in Afghanistan was more pressing than that involved in creating the country's new army, which is an ongoing task. These were the people who were to help the coalition bring security to Afghanistan. However, many new soldiers and even officers had no experience. There were language barriers between trainers and trainees. And some trainees found themselves quickly under fire from insurgents when they went as trainees out into the field. Based on what you learned about training from this chapter, list the five most important things you would tell the U.S. officer in charge of training to keep in mind as he designs the training program.

Experiential Exercise

Flying the Friendlier Skies

Purpose: The purpose of this exercise is to give you practice in developing a training program for the job of airline reservation clerk for a major airline.

Required Understanding: You should be fully acquainted with the material in this chapter and should read the following description of an airline reservation clerk's duties:

> Customers contact our airline reservation clerks to obtain flight schedules, prices, and itineraries. The reservation clerks look up the requested information on our airline's online flight schedule systems, which are updated continuously. The reservation clerk must deal courteously and expeditiously with the customer, and be able to find quickly alternative flight arrangements in order to provide the customer with the itinerary that fits his or her needs. Alternative flights and prices must be found quickly, so that the customer is not kept waiting, and so that our reservations operations group maintains its efficiency standards. It is often necessary to look under various routings, since there may be a dozen or more alternative routes between the customer's starting point and destination.

You may assume that we just hired 30 new clerks, and that you must create a 3-day training program.

How to Set Up the Exercise/Instructions: Divide the class into teams of five or six students.

Airline reservation clerks obviously need numerous skills to perform their jobs. JetBlue Airlines has asked you to design quickly the outline of a training program for its new reservation clerks.

8-18. You may want to start by listing the job's main duties and by reviewing any work you may have done for the exercise at the end of Chapter 6.

8-19. In any case, please produce the requested outline, making sure to be very specific about what you want to teach the new clerks, and what methods and aids you suggest using to train them.

Video Case

Video Title: Training (Wilson Learning)

SYNOPSIS

Maxene Raices is a senior manager at Wilson Learning, a company that specializes in developing training programs. She describes the best practices that make training most effective. She explains how training sessions have to be planned carefully with an outcome in mind, and have to consist of more than just lecturing. Good training programs help employees do their jobs, and ideally produce measurable results. Managers can use technology to make training even more effective, giving opportunities for people spread over various locations to attend training sessions.

Discussion Questions

8-20. How does Wilson Learning's "know, show, do" approach fit with the training processes that this chapter described?

8-21. Explain what specific training tools and processes discussed in this chapter you would use to implement a "know, show, do" training approach.

8-22. What do you think of the experimental design Wilson used to assess the call-center training program? How would you suggest the company improve it?

8-23. Discuss four types of technology Wilson could use to deliver training, based on the information in this chapter.

8-24. What are two reasons that Maxene gives for thinking it is important for different learning styles to be recognized?

8-25. How does identifying the intended outcomes of a training shape the training itself?

Video Title: Training and Developing Employees (Witness.org)

SYNOPSIS

Witness.org trains human rights advocacy groups to capture on video the testimonies of survivors and witnesses to human rights abuses all over the world. The company's goal is to empower the people who are directly involved in the situations, by giving them the tools necessary to use the power of video to communicate their stories. Witness.org trains advocacy partners on how to use the video equipment, how to tell a story in such a way that it effects change in those who hear it, and how to get the video in front of the people who are able to make a positive change.

Witness.org is run by a core of 28 people with experience in a variety of areas, including speaking multiple languages, managing a nonprofit organization, producing videos, and working with human rights issues. These employees train advocacy groups on the technical aspects of creating a video, as well as safety and security issues related to producing videos containing sensitive materials. The main goal of Witness.org is to achieve changes in policies, laws, or behaviors that are currently causing human suffering.

Discussion Questions

8-26. Explain how training and development play an important role in Witness.org.

8-27. Describe the challenges incurred in the training and development process at Witness.org.

8-28. Describe the group of experts who conduct the training for Witness.org.

Application Case*

Reinventing the Wheel at Apex Door Company

Jim Delaney, president of Apex Door, has a problem. No matter how often he tells his employees how to do their jobs, they invariably "decide to do it their way," as he puts it, and arguments ensue between Jim, the employee, and the employee's supervisor. One example is the door-design department, where the designers are expected to work with the architects to design doors that meet the specifications. While it's not "rocket science," as Jim puts it, the designers invariably make mistakes—such as designing in too much steel, a problem that can cost Apex tens of thousands of wasted dollars, once you consider the number of doors in, say, a 30-story office tower.

The order processing department is another example. Jim has a very specific and detailed way he wants the order written up, but most of the order clerks don't understand how to use the multipage order form. They simply improvise when it comes to a detailed question such as whether to classify the customer as "industrial" or "commercial."

The current training process is as follows. None of the jobs has a training manual per se, although several have somewhat out-of-date job descriptions. The training for new people is all on the job. Usually, the person leaving the company trains the new person during the 1- or 2-week overlap period, but if there's no overlap, the new person is trained as well as possible by other employees who have filled in occasionally on the job in the past. The training is the same throughout the company—for machinists, secretaries, assemblers, engineers, and accounting clerks, for example.

*Source: Copyright Dr. Gary Dessler.

Questions

8-29. What do you think of Apex's training process? Could it help to explain why employees "do things their way"? If so, how?

8-30. What role should job descriptions play in training at Apex?

8-31. Explain in detail what you would do to improve the training process at Apex. Make sure to provide specific suggestions, please.

Continuing Case

Carter Cleaning Company

The New Training Program

The Carter Cleaning Centers currently have no formal orientation or training policies or procedures, and Jennifer believes this is one reason why the standards to which she and her father would like employees to adhere are generally not followed.

The Carters would prefer that certain practices and procedures be used in dealing with the customers at the front counters. For example, all customers should be greeted with what Jack refers to as a "big hello." Garments they drop off should immediately be inspected for any damage or unusual stains so these can be brought to the customer's attention, lest the customer later return to pick up the garment and erroneously blame the store. The garments are then supposed to be placed together in a nylon sack immediately to separate them from other customers' garments. The ticket also has to be carefully written, with the customer's name and telephone number and the date clearly noted on all copies. The counter person is also supposed to take the opportunity to try to sell the customer additional services such as waterproofing, or simply notify the customer that "Now that people are doing their spring cleaning, we're having a special on drapery cleaning all this month." Finally, as the customer leaves, the counter person is supposed to make a courteous comment like "Have a nice day." Each of the other jobs in the stores—pressing, cleaning and spotting, and so forth—similarly contain certain steps, procedures, and, most importantly, standards the Carters would prefer to see upheld.

The company has had problems, Jennifer feels, because of a lack of adequate employee training and orientation. For example, two new employees became very upset last month when they discovered that they were not paid at the end of the week, on Friday, but instead were paid (as are all Carter employees) on the following Tuesday. The Carters use the extra 2 days in part to give them time to obtain everyone's hours and compute their pay. The other reason they do it, according to Jack, is that "frankly, when we stay a few days behind in paying employees it helps to ensure that they at least give us a few days' notice before quitting on us. While we are certainly obligated to pay them anything they earn, we find that psychologically they seem to be less likely to just walk out on us Friday evening and not show up Monday morning if they still haven't gotten their pay from the previous week. This way they at least give us a few days' notice so we can find a replacement."

There are other matters that could be covered during orientation and training, says Jennifer. These include company policy regarding paid holidays, lateness and absences, health benefits (there are none, other than workers' compensation), substance abuse, eating or smoking on the job (both forbidden), and general matters like the maintenance of a clean and safe work area, personal appearance and cleanliness, time sheets, personal telephone calls, and personal e-mail.

Jennifer believes that implementing orientation and training programs would help to ensure that employees know how to do their jobs the right way. And she and her father further believe that it is only when employees understand the right way to do their jobs that there is any hope their jobs will be accomplished the way the Carters want them to be accomplished.

Questions

8-32. Specifically, what should the Carters cover in their new employee orientation program and how should they convey this information?

8-33. In the HR management course Jennifer took, the book suggested using a job instruction sheet to identify tasks performed by an employee. Should the Carter Cleaning Centers use a form like this for the counter person's job? If so, what should the form look like, say, for a counter person?

8-34. Which specific training techniques should Jennifer use to train her pressers, her cleaner/spotters, her managers, and her counter people? Why should these training techniques be used?

Translating Strategy into HR Policies and Practices Case*,§

**The accompanying strategy map for this chapter is in the MyManagementLab, and the overall map on the inside back cover of this text outlines the relationships involved.*

IMPROVING PERFORMANCE at The Hotel Paris Case

The New Training Program

The Hotel Paris's competitive strategy is "To use superior guest service to differentiate the Hotel Paris properties, and to thereby increase the length of stay and return rate of guests, and thus boost revenues and profitability." HR manager Lisa Cruz must now formulate functional policies and activities that support this competitive strategy, by eliciting the required employee behaviors and competencies.

As she reviewed her company's training processes, Lisa had many reasons to be concerned. For one thing, the Hotel Paris relied almost exclusively on informal on-the-job training. New security guards attended a one-week program offered by a law enforcement agency, but all other new hires, from assistant manager to housekeeping crew, learned the rudiments of their jobs from their colleagues and their supervisors, on the job. Lisa noted that the drawbacks of this informality were evident when she compared the Hotel Paris's performance on various training metrics with those of other hotels and service firms. For example, in terms of number of hours training per employee per year, number of hours training for new employees, cost per trainee hour, and percent of payroll spent on training, the Hotel Paris was far from the norm when benchmarked against similar firms.

§Written by and copyright Gary Dessler, PhD.

As Lisa and the CFO reviewed measures of the Hotel Paris's current training efforts, it was clear that (when compared to similar companies) some changes were in order. Most other service companies provided at least 40 hours of training per employee per year, while the Hotel Paris offered, on average, no more than five or six. Similar firms offered at least 40 hours of training per *new* employee, while the Hotel Paris offered, at most, 10. Even the apparently "good" metrics comparisons simply masked poor results. For example, whereas most service firms spend about 8% of their payrolls on training, the Hotel Paris spent less than 1%. The problem, of course, was that the Hotel Paris's training wasn't more efficient, it was simply nonexistent.

Given this and the commonsense links between (1) employee training and (2) employee performance, the CFO gave his go-ahead for Lisa and her team to design a comprehensive package of training programs for all Hotel Paris employees. They retained a training supplier to design a 1-day training program comprised of lectures and audiovisual material for all new employees. This program covered the Hotel Paris's history, competitive strategy, and its critical employee capabilities and behaviors, including the need to be customer oriented. With a combination of lectures and video examples of correct and incorrect behaviors, the behavior-modeling part of this program aimed to cultivate in new employees the company's essential values, including, "we endeavor to do everything we can to make the guests' stay 100% pleasant."

The team developed separate training programs for each of the hotel's other individual job categories. For example, it retained a special vendor to create computer-based training programs, complete with interactive scenarios, for both the front-desk clerks and telephone operators. As with all the new training programs, they had these translated into the languages of the countries in which the Hotel Paris did business. The team chose to stay with on-the-job training for both the housekeeping and valet/doorperson job categories, but formalized this training with special handbooks for each job category's supervisory staff. For assistant managers, the team developed a new videoconference-based online training and development program. In this way, the new managers could interact with other assistant managers around the chain, even as they were learning the basics of their new jobs. Lisa and the CFO were not at all surprised to find that within a year of instituting the new training programs, scores on numerous employee capabilities and behavior metrics (including speed of check-in/out, percent of employees scoring at least 90% on Hotel Paris's values quiz, and percent room cleaning infractions) improved markedly. They knew from previous analyses that these improvements would, in turn, drive improvements in customer and organizational outcomes, and strategic performance.

Questions

8-35. Based on what you read in this chapter, what would you have suggested Lisa and her team do first with respect to training, particularly in terms of the company's strategy? Why?

8-36. Have Lisa and the CFO sufficiently investigated whether training is really called for? Why? What would you suggest?

8-37. Based on what you read in this chapter and what you may access via the Web, develop a detailed training program for one of these hotel positions: security guard, housekeeper, or door person.

MyManagementLab

Go to **mymanagementlab.com** for Auto-graded writing questions as well as the following Assisted-graded writing questions:

8-38. John Santos is an undergraduate business student majoring in accounting. He just failed the first accounting course, Accounting 101. He is understandably upset. How would you use performance analysis to identify what, if any, are John's training needs?

8-39. One reason for implementing global training programs is the need to avoid business losses "due to cultural insensitivity." What sort of cultural insensitivity do you think is referred to, and how might that translate into lost business? What sort of training program would you recommend to avoid such cultural insensitivity?

8-40. MyManagementLab only—comprehensive writing assignment for this chapter.

Key Terms

Endnotes

1. Marjorie Derven, "Management Onboarding," *Training & Development*, April 2008, pp. 49–52.
2. Sabrina Hicks, "Successful Orientation Programs," *Training & Development*, April 2000, p. 59. See also Howard Klein and Natasha Weaver, "The Effectiveness of an Organizational Level Orientation Program in the Socialization of New Hires," *Personnel Psychology* 53 (2000), pp. 47–66; and Laurie Friedman, "Are You Losing Potential New Hires at Hello?" *Training & Development*, November 2006, pp. 25–27.
3. Charlotte Garvey, "The Whirlwind of a New Job," *HR Magazine*, June 2001, p. 111. See also Talya Bauer et al., "Newcomer Adjustment During Organizational Socialization: A Meta-Analytic Review of Antecedents, Outcomes, and Methods," *Journal of Applied Psychology* 92, no. 3 (2007), pp. 707–721.
4. Sheila Hicks et al., "Orientation Redesign," *Training & Development*, July 2006, pp. 43–46.
5. Mukta Kulkarni and Mark Lengnick-Hall, "Socialization of People with Disabilities in the Workplace," *Human Resource Management* 60, no. 4 (July–August 2011), pp. 521–540.
6. See, for example, John Kammeyer-Mueller and Connie Wanberg, "Unwrapping the Organizational Entry Process: Disentangling Multiple Antecedents and Their Pathways to Adjustments," *Journal of Applied Psychology* 88, no. 5 (2003), pp. 779–794.
7. "Drug Rep Claims Handbook Protection from Retaliation," *BNA Bulletin to Management*, December 18, 2012, p. 8.
8. Steve Taylor, "Employee Handbook Updates for 2013," *HR Magazine*, February 2013, p. 14.
9. Ed Frauenheim, "IBM Learning Programs Get a 'Second Life,'" *Workforce Management*, December 11, 2006, p. 6. See also J. T. Arnold, "Gaming Technology Used to Orient New Hires," *HR Magazine* (2009 HR Trendbook supp), pp. 36, 38.
10. Jennifer Taylor Arnold, "Ramping Up on Boarding," *HR Magazine*, May 2010, pp. 75–78.
11. www.workday.com/company/news/workday-mobility.php, accessed March 24, 2009.
12. "Four Ways to Use QR Codes to Enliven Your Learning Event," *Training & Development*, January 2013, p. 19.
13. "Lack of Training Fuels Desire to Job Search," *Training & Development*, January 2013, p. 23.
14. Mindy Chapman, "The Return on Investment for Training," *Compensation & Benefits Review*, January/February 2003, pp. 32–33.
15. Ibid., p. 33.
16. Ibid., p. 33.
17. Ibid., pp. 216–217.
18. Rita Smith, "Aligning Learning with Business Strategy," *Training & Development*, November 2008, pp. 41–43.
19. Christine Ellis and Sarah Gale, "A Seat at the Table," *Training*, March 2001, pp. 90–96.
20. Christopher Glynn, "Building a Learning Infrastructure," *Training & Development*, January 2008, pp. 38–43. Training and development executives at Kelly Services Inc. meet periodically with the company's senior executives to "identify new priorities and reallocate training dollars as needed, based on the strategic needs of the business." Garry Kranz, "More to Learn," *Workforce Management*, January 2011, p. 27.
21. "Companies Invested More in Training Despite Economic Setbacks, Survey Says," *BNA Bulletin to Management*, March 7, 2002, p. 73; "Employee Training Expenditures on the Rise," *American Salesman* 49, no. 1 (January 2004), pp. 26–28.
22. "Companies Invested More in Training"; Andrew Paradise, "The 2008 ASTD State of the Industry Report Shows Sustained Support for Corporate Learning," *Training & Development*, November 2008, pp. 45–51.
23. Brenda Sugrue et al., "What in the World Is WLP?" *Training & Development*, January 2005, pp. 51–54.
24. Jack Berry, "Transforming HRD into an Economic Value Add," *Training & Development*, September 2011, p. 66.
25. Rachel Dodes, "At Macy's, a Makeover on Service," *The Wall Street Journal*, April 11, 2011, p. B-10.
26. Ibid. See also, "Macy's Earnings, Revenue Edge Above Estimates," www.cnbc.com/id/100491292, accessed April 4, 2013.
27. W. Clayton Allen, "Overview and Evolution of the ADDIE Training System," *Advances in Developing Human Resources* 8, no. 4 (November 2006), pp. 430–441.
28. www.intulogy.com/process//, accessed April 20, 2011.
29. P. Nick Blanchard and James Thacker, *Effective Training: Systems, Strategies and Practices* (Upper Saddle River, NJ: Prentice Hall, 1999), pp. 138–139. See also Matthew Casey and Dennis Doverspike, "Training Needs Analysis and Evaluation for New Technologies Through the Use of Problem Based Inquiry," *Performance Improvement Quarterly* 18, no. 1 (2005), pp. 110–124.
30. Justin Arneson et al., "Training and Development Competencies: We Define to Create Competitive Advantage," *Training & Development*, January 2013, p. 45.
31. See also, for example, Jennifer Salopek, "The Power of the Pyramid," *Training and Development,* May 2009, pp. 70–73.
32. Tom Barron, "When Things Go Haywire," *Training & Development*, February 1999, pp. 25–27; see also, for example, Bill Stetar, "Training: It's Not Always the Answer," *Quality Progress*, March 2005, pp. 44-49, http://performancetechnology.com/ptg_pdfs/qp0305stetar.pdf, accessed October 11, 2012.
33. Employers increasingly utilize learning content management systems (LCMS) to compile an author training content. See, for example, Bill Perry, "Customized Content at Your Fingertips," *Training and Development*, June 2009, pp. 29–30.
34. P. Nick Blanchard and James Thacker, *Effective Training* (Upper Saddle River, NJ: Pearson, 2010), pp. 26–94, 153–199, 285–316; see also Bruno Neal," "e-ADDIE!," *T1D* 65, no. 3 (March 2011), pp. 76–77.
35. Jay Bahlis, "Blueprint for Planning Learning," *Training & Development*, March 2008, pp. 64–67.
36. P. Nick Blanchard and James Thacker, *Effective Training: Systems, Strategies, and Practices* (Upper Saddle River, NJ: Prentice Hall, 2007), p. 8; and G. Sadri, "Boosting Performance Through Self-Efficacy," *T1D* 65 no. 6 (June 2011), pp. 30–31.
37. Ibid.
38. Ibid., p. 90.
39. Kenneth Wexley and Gary Latham, *Developing and Training Human Resources in Organizations* (Upper Saddle River, NJ: Prentice Hall, 2002), p. 305.
40. Ibid.
41. Kathryn Tyler, "Focus on Training," *HR Magazine*, May 2000, pp. 94–102.
42. Janice A. Cannon-Bowers et al., "Framework for Understanding Pre-Practice Conditions and Their Impact on Learning," *Personnel Psychology* 51 (1998), pp. 291–320; see also J. S. Goodman et al., "Feedback Specificity, Information Processing, and Transfer of Training," *Organizational Behavior and Human Decision Processes* 115 no. 2 (July 2011), pp. 253–267.
43. Ibid., p. 305.
44. Ibid., and see Kendra Lee, "Reinforce Training," *Training* 48 no. 3 (May/June 2011), p. 24.
45. Eric Krell, "Get Sold on Training Incentives, " *HR Magazine*, February 2013, p. 57.
46. Stefanie Johnson, "Go for the Goal (as): Relationship Between Goal Setting and Transfer of Training Following Leadership Development," *Academy of Management Learning & Education* 11, no. 4 (2012), pp. 555–569.
47. Alan Saks and Monica Belcourt, "An Investigation of Training Activities and Transfer of Training in Organizations," *Human Resource Management* 45, no. 4 (Winter 2006), pp. 629–648. The percentage of managers transferring behaviors from training to the job may be as low as 10% to 20%. See George Vellios, "On the Level," *Training & Development*, December 2008, pp. 26–29. See also K. Lee, "Implement Training Successfully," *Training* 46, no. 5 (June 2009), p. 16.
48. Large training providers include Element K, Geo Learning, learn.com, Outsmart, Plateau, Saba People Systems, and Sum-Total Systems. "Training Providers," *Workforce Management*, January 2011, p. 8.
49. Wexley and Latham, *Developing and Training Human Resources*, pp. 78–79.
50. Donna Goldwasser, "Me a Trainer?" *Training*, April 2001, pp. 60–66; http://employment.menswearhouse.com/ats/advantageSelector.action;jsessionid=C6EA17158451F5A290 2F7195B678CF6A?type=training, accessed June 1, 2011.
51. See, for example, www.aps-online.net/consulting/structured_ojt.htm, accessed June 1, 2011; and Kathryn Tyler, "15 Ways to Train on the Job," *HR Magazine* 53 no. 9 (September 2008), pp. 105–108.
52. The following four steps in on-the-job training based on William Berliner and William McLarney, *Management Practice and Training* (Burr Ridge, IL: McGraw-Hill, 1974), pp. 442–443. For the discussion of employee

task analysis, see "Eight Steps to Better On-the-Job Training," *HR Focus* 80, no. 7 (July 2003), pp. 11, 13–14.

53. Cindy Waxer, "Steelmaker Revives Apprentice Program to Address Graying Workforce, Forge Next Leaders," *Workforce Management*, January 30, 2006, p. 40.
54. Kermit Kaleba, "New Changes to Apprenticeship Program Could Be Forthcoming," *Training & Development*, February 2008, p. 14.
55. Robert Weintraub and Jennifer Martineau, "The Just in Time Imperative," *Training & Development*, June 2002, p. 52; Andrew Paradise, "Informal Learning: Overlooked or Overhyped?" *Training & Development*, July 2008, pp. 52–53. In one survey, about one-third of respondents said they did not earmark training dollars for informal learning.
56. Aparna Nancherla, "Knowledge Delivered in Any Other Form Is . . . Perhaps Sweeter," *Training & Development*, May 2009, pp. 54–60.
57. Nadira Hira, "The Making of a UPS Driver," *Fortune*, November 12, 2007, p. 120.
58. Arthur Winfred Jr. et al., "Effectiveness of Training in Organizations: A Meta Analysis of Design and Evaluation Features," *Journal of Applied Psychology* 88, no. 2 (2003), pp. 234–245.
59. Donald Michalak and Edwin G. Yager, *Making the Training Process Work* (New York: Harper & Row, 1979), pp. 108–111. See also Richard Wiegand, "Can All Your Trainees Hear You?" *Training & Development Journal* 41, no. 8 (August 1987), pp. 38–43; and "Dos and Don'ts at the Podium," *Journal of Accountancy* 200, no. 3 (September 2005).
60. Jacqueline Schmidt and Joseph Miller, "The Five-Minute Rule for Presentations," *Training & Development*, March 2000, pp. 16–17; and "Dos and Don'ts at the Podium," op cit.
61. G. N. Nash, J. P. Muczyk, and F. L. Vettori, "The Role and Practical Effectiveness of Programmed Instruction," *Personnel Psychology* 24 (1971), pp. 397–418; Duane Schultz and Sydney Ellen Schultz, *Psychology and Work Today* (Upper Saddle River, NJ: Prentice Hall, 1998), pp. 181–183; chemistry study based on N. Izzet Kurbanoglu, Yavuz Taskesenligil, and Mustafa Sozbilir, "Programmed Instruction Revisited: A Study on Teaching Stereochemistry," *Chemistry Education Research and Practice* 7, no. 1 (2006), pp. 13–21.
62. Paul Taylor et al., "A Meta-Analytic Review of Behavior Modeling Training," *Journal of Applied Psychology* 90, no. 4 (2005), pp. 692–719.
63. Wexley and Latham, *Developing and Training*, pp. 131–133. See also Teri O. Grady and Mike Matthews, "Video . . . Through the Eyes of the Trainee," *Training* 24, no. 7 (July 1987), pp. 57–62; "New ARTBA PPE Video and Laborers' Night Work Suggestions Highlight Construction Safety Advances," *EHS Today* 2, no. 7 (July 2009), p. 51.
64. Paula Ketter, "What Can Training Do for Brown?" *Training & Development*, May 2008, pp. 30–36.
65. Craig Marion, "What Is the EPSS Movement and What Does It Mean to Information Designers?" August 20, 1999.
66. Josh Bersin and Karen O'Leonard, "Performance Support Systems," *Training & Development*, April 2005, p. 68.
67. Blanchard and Thacker, *Effective Training*, p. 163.
68. www.radvision.com/Support/cisco.htm, accessed June 1, 2011.
69. Dina Berta, "Computer-Based Training Clicks with Both Franchisees and Their Employees," *Nation's Restaurant News*, July 9, 2001, pp. 1, 18; and, "Is Online Fall Protection Training Effective?" *EHS Today* 3, no. 7 (July 2010).
70. P. Nick Blanchard and James Thacker, *Effective Training: Systems, Strategies, and Practices* (Upper Saddle River, NJ: Pearson, 2003), p. 247; see also Michael Laff, "Simulations: Slowly Proving Their Worth," *Training & Development*, June 2007, pp. 30–34.
71. Laff, "Simulations."
72. Blanchard and Thacker, *Effective Training*, 2003, p. 248.
73. Ibid., p. 249. See also Kim Kleps, "Virtual Sales Training Scores a Hit," *Training & Development*, December 2006, pp. 63–64.
74. Paul Harris, "Simulation: The Game Is On," *Training & Development*, October 2003, p. 49. See also Jenni Jarventaus, "Virtual Threat, Real Sweat," *Training & Development*, May 2007, pp. 72–78.
75. Jarventaus, "Virtual Threat, Real Sweat."
76. Clark Aldrich, "Engaging Mini-Games Find Niche in Training," *Training & Development*, July 2007, pp. 22–24; and "Cisco's Global Training Machine," *Workforce Management*, November 17, 2008, p. 30.
77. The Drew Robb, "Let the Games Begin," *HR Magazine*, September 2012, p. 96.
78. "What Do Simulations Cost?" *Training & Development*, June 2007, p. 88; see also Paul Harris, "Immersive Learning Seeks a Foothold," *Training & Development*, January 2009, pp. 40–45; and R. S. Polimeni et al., "Using Computer Simulations to Recruit and Train Generation Y Accountants," *The CPA Journal* 79, no. 5 (May 2009), pp. 64–68.
79. Garry Kranz, "More to Learn," *Workforce Management*, January 2011, p. 27; quote is from Ann Pace, "Spurring Innovation and Engaging the Learners of the 2011 Workplace," *T + D* 65, no. 8 (August 2011), pp. 64–69.
80. Susan Ladika, "When Learning Lasts a Lifetime," *HR Magazine*, May 2008, p. 57.
81. Jeremy Smerd, "New Workers Sorely Lacking Literacy Skills," *Workforce Management*, December 10, 2008, p. 6.
82. Paula Ketter, "The Hidden Disability," *Training & Development*, June 2006, pp. 34–40.
83. Jennifer Salopek, "The Growth of Succession Management," *Training & Development*, June 2007, pp. 22–24; and Kermit Kaleba, "Businesses Continue to Push for Lifelong Learning," *Training & Development*, June 2007, p. 14.
84. Rita Zeidner, "One Workforce—Many Languages," *HR Magazine*, January 2009, pp. 33–37.
85. Matthew Reis, "Do-It-Yourself Diversity," *Training & Development*, March 2004, pp. 80–81.
86. www.prismdiversity.com/resources/diversity_training.html, accessed June 1, 2011.
87. Jennifer Salopek, "Trends: Lost in Translation," *Training & Development*, December 2003, p. 15; www.visionpoint.com/training-solutions/title/just-be-fair-basic-diversity-training, accessed June 17, 2011.
88. Paraphrased from "Best Practice: Workforce Diversity Training," The Manufacturing Practices Center of Excellence, www.brmpcoe.org/bestpracticea/internal/abev/abcv_15.html.
89. Blanchard and Thacker, pp. 403–405.
90. Ibid., p. 404.
91. Holly Dolezalek, "Extreme Training," *Training* 47, no. 1 (January 2010), pp. 26–28.
92. Douglas Shuit, "Sound of the Retreat," *Workforce Management,* September 2003, p. 40.
93. As another example, see Max Mihelich, "Bit by Bit: Standup Comedy as a Teambuilding Exercise," *Workforce Management*, February 2013, p. 16.
94. Kevin Alansky, "Blackboard Pays Off for ADP," *T1D* 65, no. 6 (June 2011), pp. 68–69; see also Barbara Carnes, "The Ties That Bind," *Training & Development*, January 2013, pp. 38–40.
95. Greg Wright, "Retailers Buy into Relearning," *HR Magazine*, December 7, 2010, pp. 87–90.
96. Pat Galagan, "Made Fast in China," *Training and Development*, January 2013, p. 30.
97. John Zonneveld, "GM Dealer Training Goes Global," *Training & Development*, December 2006, pp. 47–51. See also "What's Next for the LMS?" *Training & Development*, September 2011, p. 16.
98. "The Next Generation of Corporate Learning," *Training & Development*, June 2003, p. 47.
99. Ibid.
100. For a list of guidelines for using e-learning, see, for example, Mark Simon, "E-Learning No How," *Training & Development*, January 2009, pp. 34–39.
101. "The Next Generation of Corporate Learning," *Training & Development*, June 2004, p. 47; Jennifer Hofmann and Nanatte Miner, "Real Blended Learning Stands Up," *Training & Development*, September 2008, pp. 28–31; J. Hofmann, "Top 10 Challenges of Blended Learning," *Training* (Minneapolis, Minn.) 48, no. 2 (March/April 2011), pp. 12–13; and Lee Salz, "Use Webinars for Training and Revenue," *Training* 48, no. 2 (March/April 2011), p. 14.
102. Ruth Clark, "Harnessing the Virtual Classroom," *Training & Development*, November 2005, pp. 40–46.
103. Traci Sitzmann et al., "The Comparative Effectiveness of Web-Based and Classroom Instruction: A Meta-Analysis," *Personnel Psychology* 59 (2006), pp. 623–664.
104. Bill Roberts, "From IT Learning to Mobile Learning," *HR Magazine*, August 2012, pp. 61–65.
105. Chris Pirie, "Technology Plus Learning Equals Inspiration," *Training & Development*, December 2012, pp. 39–46.
106. Jennifer Taylor Arnold, "Learning On-the-Fly," *HR Magazine*, September 2007, p. 137; see also M. Donahue, "Mobile Learning Is the Next Generation in Training." *Hotel Management* 226, no. 4 (April 4, 2011), p. 17.
107. www.dominknow.com, accessed March 23, 2009.
108. Elizabeth Agnvall, "Just-in-Time Training," *HR Magazine*, May 2006, pp. 67–78.
109. For a similar program at Accenture, see Don Vanthournout and Dana Koch, "Training at Your Fingertips," *Training & Development*, September 2008, pp. 52–57. For a discussion of blogs in training see Becky Livingston,

"Harnessing Blogs for Learning," *T + D* 65, no. 5 (May 2011), pp. 76–77.

110. Catherine Skrzypinski, "Social Media Changes Employee Expectations Regarding Communication," *HR Magazine*, January 2013, p. 14; see also Dan Steer, "Improve Formal Learning with Social Media," *Training & Development*, December 2012, pp. 31–33.
111. Pat Galagan, "Second That," *Training & Development*, February 2008, pp. 34–37.
112. Paraphrased from Manuel London and M. J. Hall, "Unlocking the Value of Web 2.0 Technologies for Training and Development: The Shift from Instructor–Controlled, Adaptive Learning to Learner–Driven, Generative Learning," *Human Resource Management* 50, no. 6 (November–December 2011), p. 761.
113. This is based on ibid., pp. 763–765.
114. David Upton, "What Really Makes Factories Flexible?" *Harvard Business Review*, July–August 1995, p. 75.
115. For a discussion of leadership development tools, see John Beeson, "Building Bench Strength: A Tool Kit for Executive Development," *Business Horizons* 47, no. 6 (November 2004), pp. 3–9. See also Rita Smith and Beth Bledsoe, "Grooming Leaders for Growth," *Training & Development*, August 2006, pp. 47–50.
116. Paula Caligiuri, "Developing Global Leaders," *Human Resource Management Review* 16 (2006), pp. 219–228.
117. Gail Johnson Morris and Kim Rogers, "High Potentials Are Still Your Best Bet," *Training & Development*, February 2013, pp. 58–62.
118. Ann Pomeroy, "Head of the Class," *HR Magazine*, January 2005, p. 57. Of course traits like cognitive ability and personality also mold job success, not just training. See, for example, Lisa Dragoni et al., "Developing Executive Leaders: The Relative Contribution of Cognitive Ability, Personality, and the Accumulation of Work Experience in Predicting Strategic Thinking Competency," *Personnel Psychology* 60, no. 4 (2011), pp. 829–861.
119. Michael Watkins, "How Managers Become Leaders," *Harvard Business Review*, June 2012, p. 69.
120. Mike Czarnowsky, "Executive Development," *Training & Development*, September 2008, pp. 44–45.
121. "Thrown into Deep End, Workers Surface as Leaders," *BNA Bulletin to Management*, July 11, 2002, p. 223. See also Michelle Peters, "Accomplish Two for One with Action Learning," *Training & Development*, February 2013, pp. 52–54.
122. Chris Whitcomb, "Scenario-Based Training at the FBI," *Training & Development*, June 1999, pp. 42–46. See also Michael Laff, "Serious Gaming: The Trainer's New Best Friend," *Training & Development*, January 2007, pp. 52–57.
123. http://teamcommunication.blogspot.com/, accessed June 17, 2011.
124. www.amanet.org/, accessed August 22, 2011.
125. For information on the SHRM learning system, see http://www.shrm.org/Education/educationalproducts/learning/Pages/default.aspx?utm_campaign=LearningSystem_All_2012&utm_medium=mailing&utm_source=brochure, accessed July 21, 2013.
126. For a list of Harvard programs, see http://www.exed.hbs.edu/Pages/default.aspx, accessed July 21, 2013.
127. Ann Pomeroy, "Head of the Class," *HR Magazine*, January 2005, p. 57. See also Michael Laff, "Centralized Training Leads to Nontraditional Universities," *Training & Development*, January 2007, pp. 27–29; Chris Musselwhite, "University Executive Education Gets Real," *Training & Development*, May 2006, p. 57; and Ralph Miller and David Abdow, "Executive Education That Works," Training & Development, December 2012, pp. 28–30.
128. Norman Maier, Allen Solem, and Ayesha Maier, *The Role Play Technique* (San Diego, CA: University Associates, 1975), pp. 2–3. See also Karen Griggs, "A Role Play for Revising Style and Applying Management Theories," *Business Communication Quarterly* 68, no. 1 (March 2005), pp. 60–65.
129. Martha Peak, "Go Corporate U!" *Management Review* 86, no. 2 (February 1997), pp. 33–37; and Jessica Li and Amy Lui Abel, "Prioritizing and Maximizing the Impact of Corporate Universities," *T1D* 65, no. 5 (May 2011), pp. 54–57.
130. Russell Gerbman, "Corporate Universities 101," *HR Magazine*, February 2000, pp. 101–106; Holly Dolezalek, "University 2.0," *Training* 44, no. 8 (September 2007), pp. 22–23.
131. "Executive Coaching: Corporate Therapy," *The Economist*, November 15, 2003, p. 61. See also Steve Gladis, "Executive Coaching Builds Steam in Organizations," *Training & Development*, December 2007, pp. 59–61.
132. "As Corporate Coaching Goes Mainstream, Key Prerequisite Overlooked: Assessment," *BNA Bulletin to Management*, May 16, 2006, p. 153.
133. James Smither et al., "Can Working with an Executive Coach Improve Multisource Feedback Ratings over Time?" *Personnel Psychology* 56, no. 1 (Spring 2003), pp. 23–44.
134. For information on the SHRM learning system, see http://www.shrm.org/Education/educationalproducts/learning/Pages/default.aspx?utm_campaign=LearningSystem_All_2012&utm_medium=mailing&utm_source=brochure, accessed July 21, 2013.
135. This is based on Diane Brady, "Can GE Still Manage?" *Bloomberg Businessweek*, April 25, 2010, p. 29.
136. Ibid.
137. Quoted and abstracted from "Five Rules for Talent Management in the New Economy," May 2010, www.towerswatson.com/viewpoints/1988, accessed August 22, 2011.
138. Ibid.
139. Ed Fraeuenheim, "Lost in the Shuffle," *Workforce Management*, January 14, 2008, p. 13.
140. See, for example, John Austin, "Mapping Out a Game Plan for Change," *HR Magazine*, April 2009, pp. 39–42.
141. Nokia examples based on www.engadget.com/2011/02/05/nokia-reportedly-planning-organizational-changes-mobile-phone/, and http://press.nokia.com/press-release/, accessed June 17, 2011.
142. Gina Gotsill and Meryl Natchez, "From Resistance to Acceptance: How to Implement Change Management," *Training & Development*, November 2007, pp. 24–26.
143. See, for example, ibid.
144. The steps are based on Michael Beer, Russell Eisenstat, and Bert Spector, "Why Change Programs Don't Produce Change," *Harvard Business Review*, November–December 1990, pp. 158–166; Thomas Cummings and Christopher Worley, *Organization Development and Change* (Minneapolis, MN: West Publishing Company, 1993); John P. Kotter, "Leading Change: Why Transformation Efforts Fail," *Harvard Business Review*, March–April 1995, pp. 59–66; and John P. Kotter, *Leading Change* (Boston: Harvard Business School Press, 1996). Change doesn't necessarily have to be painful. See, for example, Eric Abrahamson, "Change Without Pain," *Harvard Business Review*, July–August 2000, pp. 75–79. See also David Herold et al., "Beyond Change Management: A Multilevel Investigation of Contextual and Personal Influences on Employees' Commitment to Change," *Journal of Applied Psychology* 92, no. 4 (2007), p. 949.
145. Ibid.
146. Kotter, "Leading Change," p. 85.
147. Beer, Eisenstat, and Spector, "Why Change Programs Don't Produce Change," p. 164.
148. Shaul Oreg and Yair Berson, "Leadership and Employees' Reactions to Change: The Role of Leader's Personal Attributes and Transformational Leadership Style," *Personnel Psychology* 64, (2011), pp. 627–659. See also Shahron Williams van Roij, "Training Older Workers: Lessons Learned, Unlearned, and Relearned from the Field of Instructional Design," *Human Resource Management* 51, no. 2 (March–April 2012), pp. 281–298.
149. Stacie Furst and Daniel Cable, "Employee Resistance to Organizational Change: Managerial Influence Tactics and Leader Member Exchange," *Journal of Applied Psychology* 3, no. 2 (2008), p. 453.
150. Beer, Eisenstat, and Spector, "Why Change Programs Don't Produce Change," p. 164.
151. Wendell French and Cecil Bell Jr., *Organization Development* (Upper Saddle River, NJ: Prentice Hall, 1995), pp. 171–193. For examples of actual team building programs see, for example, www.teambuildinginc.com/, and www.teamcraft.com/, both accessed October 11, 2012.
152. Benjamin Schneider, Steven Ashworth, A. Catherine Higgs, and Linda Carr, "Design Validity, and Use of Strategically Focused Employee Attitude Surveys," *Personnel Psychology* 49 (1996), pp. 695–705.
153. Cummings and Worley, *Organization Development and Change*, p. 501.
154. For a description of how to make OD a part of organizational strategy, see Aubrey Mendelow and S. Jay Liebowitz, "Difficulties in Making

OD a Part of Organizational Strategy," *Human Resource Planning* 12, no. 4 (1995), pp. 317–329; and Valerie Garrow and Sharon Varney, "What Does OD Do?" *People Management* (June 4, 2009).
155. Wexley and Latham, *Developing and Training Human Resources in Organizations*, p. 128.
156. Todd Raphel, "What Learning Management Reports Do for You," *Workforce*, June 2001, pp. 56–58.
157. Wexley and Latham, *Developing and Training Human Resources in Organizations*, p. 153.
158. See, for example, Jack Phillips and Patti Phillips, "Moving From Evidence to Proof," *T1D* 65, no. 8 (August 2011), pp. 34–39 for a discussion of a process for gathering training assessment data.
159. A recent review concluded that the relationship of training to human resource outcomes and organizational performance is positive, but that training "is only very weakly related to financial outcomes. Given this, managers may want to assess training results not just in terms of employee behavior and performance, but company financial performance as well. See Phyllis Tharenou et al., "A Review and Critique of Research on Training and Organizational Level Outcomes," *Human Resource Management Review* 17 (2007), pp. 251–273.

9 Performance Management and Appraisal

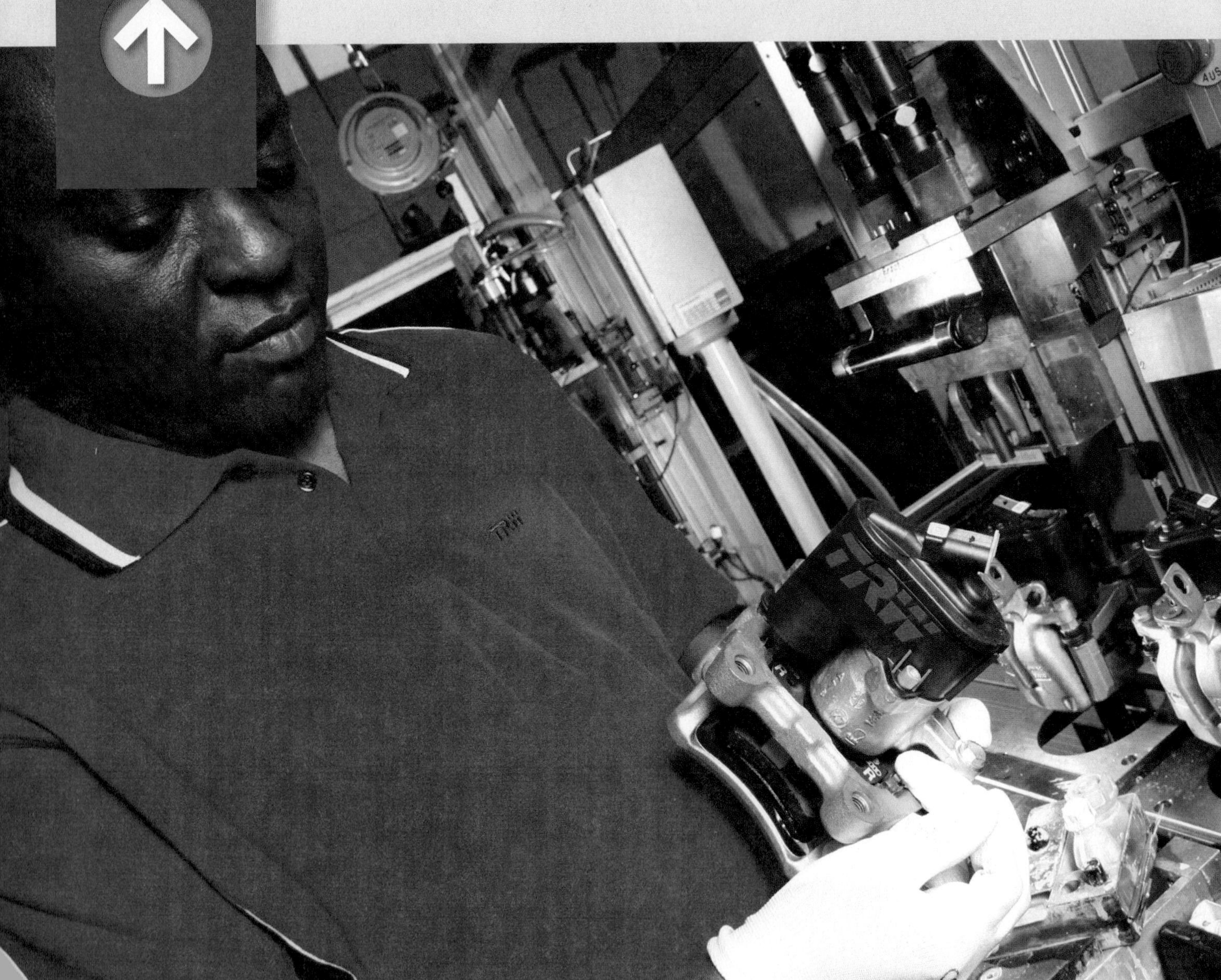

Source: TRW Automotive

MyManagementLab®

Improve Your Grade!

When you see this icon, visit **www.mymanagementlab.com** for activities that are applied, personalized, and offer immediate feedback.

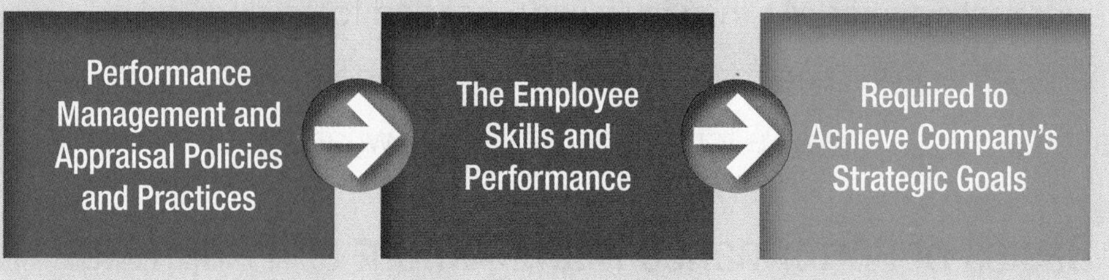

For a bird's eye view of how one company created a performance management system to improve its strategic performance, read the Hotel Paris case on page 288 and answer the questions after reading the chapter.

WHERE ARE WE NOW . . .

Chapters 6 to 8 explained selecting and training employees. Next, the manager appraises how they are doing. The purpose of this chapter is to explain how to do that. The main topics we cover include the basics of performance management and appraisal, techniques for appraising performance, dealing with rater error appraisal problems, managing the appraisal interview, and talent management and employee appraisal. Managing turnover, retention and careers are logical consequences of appraisal: We'll turn to those topics in a later chapter.

LEARNING OBJECTIVES

1. Describe the appraisal process.
2. Define performance management and discuss how it differs from performance appraisal
3. Develop, evaluate, and administer at least four performance appraisal tools.
4. Explain and illustrate the problems to avoid in appraising performance.
5. Perform an effective appraisal interview.
6. Explain how to "segment" employees for appraisal and reward purposes.

With over 100,000 employees in 36 countries on five continents, administering employee appraisals and managing performance is a complicated process in a company like TRW.[1] With global competition, TRW's top management knew it had to take steps to make the firm more competitive and performance driven. At the time, TRW had a traditional, paper-based employee appraisal system, and most of the firm's far-flung departments even used their own appraisal systems. As they reviewed what had to be done next, top management decided that a company-wide performance appraisal/management system was a top priority. We'll see what they did.

The Basics of Performance Management and Appraisal

1 Describe the appraisal process.

Few things supervisors do are fraught with more peril than appraising subordinates' performance. Employees tend to be overly optimistic about what their ratings will be. And they know their raises, careers, and peace of mind may hinge on how you rate them. As if that's not enough, few appraisal processes are as fair as employers think they are. Many obvious and not-so-obvious problems (such as the tendency to rate everyone "average") distort the process. However, the perils notwithstanding, performance appraisal plays a central role in managing people.

The Performance Appraisal Process

performance appraisal
Evaluating an employee's current and/or past performance relative to his or her performance standards.

performance appraisal process
A three-step appraisal process involving (1) setting work standards, (2) assessing the employee's actual performance relative to those standards, and (3) providing feedback to the employee with the aim of helping him or her to eliminate performance deficiencies or to continue to perform above par.

Performance appraisal means evaluating an employee's current and/or past performance relative to his or her performance standards. You may equate appraisal forms like Figure 9-1 with "performance appraisal," but appraisal involves more than forms. It also requires setting performance standards, and assumes that the employee receives the training, feedback, and incentives required to eliminate performance deficiencies. Stripped to its essentials, performance appraisal always involves the three-step **performance appraisal process**: (1) setting work standards; (2) assessing the employee's actual performance relative to those standards (this usually involves some rating form); and (3) providing feedback to the employee with the aim of helping him or her to eliminate performance deficiencies or to continue to perform above par.

Effective appraisals actually begin before the actual appraisal, with the manager defining the employee's job and performance criteria. *Defining the job* means making sure that you and your subordinate agree on his or her duties and job standards and on the appraisal method you will use.

Why Appraise Performance?

There are five reasons to appraise subordinates' performance.

- First, most employers base pay, promotion, and retention decisions on the employee's appraisal.[2]
- Second, appraisals play a central role in the employer's *performance management* process. Performance management means continuously ensuring that each employee's performance makes sense in terms of the company's overall goals.
- Third, the appraisal lets the manager and subordinate develop a plan for correcting any deficiencies, and to reinforce the subordinate's strengths.

FIGURE 9-1 Sample Faculty Evaluation Survey
Source: Copyright Gary Dessler, PhD.

Instructions: Thoughtful evaluations help the faculty member better understand and improve his or her teaching practices. For each of the following eight items, please assign a score, giving your highest score of 7 for Outstanding, a score of 4 for Average, your lowest score of 1 for Needs Improvement, and an NA if the question is not applicable:

Evaluation Items

____ 1. The instructor was prepared for his/her lectures.
____ 2. The course was consistent with the course objectives.
____ 3. The instructor was fair in how he/she graded me.
____ 4. The instructor carefully planned and organized this course.
____ 5. The instructor was available during his/her posted office hours.
____ 6. The instructor responded to online inquiries in a timely manner.
____ 7. In terms of knowledge and/or experience, the instructor was competent to teach this course.
____ 8. Overall how would you rate this course?

- Fourth, appraisals provide an opportunity to review the employee's career plans in light of his or her exhibited strengths and weaknesses. We address career planning in Chapter 10.
- Finally, appraisals enable the supervisor to identify if there is a training need, and the remedial steps required.

2 Define performance management and discuss how it differs from performance appraisal

Performance Management

Performance appraisal is fine in theory, but in practice, appraisals don't always go smoothly. Goals aren't set, the "appraisal" is a form from an office supply store, and the yearly feedback, if any, may be agonizing, with both participants fleeing before any coaching takes place. This runs counter to common sense. Employees should know what their goals are, performance feedback should be useful, and if there is a problem, the time to take action is right away, not 6 months or a year later.

This mismatch between what appraisals should be and what they are prompted the rise of performance management. *Performance management* means different things to different people. Some use "performance management" as a synonym for "performance appraisal." But in fact, performance management involves more than performance appraisal's emphasis on setting work standards, assessing performance, and providing feedback once or twice a year. Performance management involves defining, measuring, motivating, and developing the employee's goal-oriented performance on a continuing basis.[3] This means ensuring that the employee's goals are linked to the strategic and operational goals of the company; giving your subordinates timely feedback about their performance; providing them with the resources and training they need to do their assignments and tasks; rewarding good performance; and continuously checking how your employees are doing.[4] In sum, **performance management** is the "*continuous* process of identifying, measuring, and developing the performance of individuals and teams and *aligning* their performance with the organization's *goals*."[5] Diagrammatically, we can view this process as follows:

performance management
The *continuous* process of identifying, measuring, and developing the performance of individuals and teams and *aligning* their performance with the organization's *goals*.

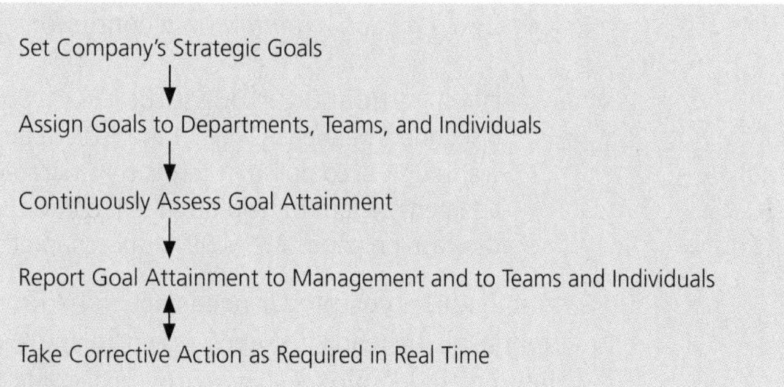

Applying a finer filter, we can summarize performance management's six basic elements as follows:[6]

- *Direction sharing* means communicating the company's goals throughout the company and then translating these into doable departmental, team, and individual goals.
- *Goal alignment* means having a method to help managers and employees to see the link between their goals and those of their department and company.
- *Ongoing performance monitoring* usually includes using computerized systems that measure and then e-mail progress and exception reports based on the person's progress toward meeting his or her performance goals.
- *Ongoing feedback* includes both face-to-face and computerized feedback regarding progress toward goals.
- *Coaching and developmental support* should be an integral part of the feedback process.
- *Recognition and rewards* keep the employee's goal-directed performance on track.

Using Information Technology to Support Performance Management

Many companies use information technology to automate performance management and to monitor, feedback, and correct deviations in real time. (The accompanying HR Practices Around the

FIGURE 9-2 Summary of Performance Management Report

Source: Based on "Personal Goal Management" from the Active Strategy website. Copyright © 2012 by ActiveStrategy, Inc.

PERFORMANCE GOAL MANAGEMENT

Report Card | Link | Edit | Options | Copy

Details - 2013 Performance Goal Scorecard — In Progress (01/01/2013 - 12/31/13)

Goals for Brown, Lisa — Score 4.5

Employee's Individual Performance Goals

Goal	Target	Weight	Score	Date
Achieve 10% Sales Increase	8	45	7.0	June 2013
Improved Customer Satisfaction Rating	4.2	25	4.0	June 2013
Meet Budgetary Constraints	5	15	2.5	June 2013
Improved Leadership Ratings	4.8	15	4.5	June 2013

Departmental Performance Goals

Goal	Target	Weight	Score	Date
Achieve 15% Sales Increase	5	50	3.5	June 2013
Increase Online sales 10%	3.5	25	2.8	June 2013
Meet Budgetary Constraints	5	10	4.2	June 2013
All Employees Cross-Trained on All Products	4.5	15	3.5	June 2013

Globe feature describes an actual application.) A typical IT-supported performance management process does this as follows:

- *Assign financial and nonfinancial goals* to each team's activities along the strategy map chain of activities leading from the team's activities up to the company's overall strategic goals. (For example, an airline measures ground crew aircraft turnaround time in terms of "improve turnaround time from an average of 30 minutes per plane to 26 minutes per plane this year.")
- *Inform all employees* of their goals.
- *Use IT-supported tools* like scorecard software and digital dashboards to continuously display, monitor, and assess each team's and employee's performance. (We discussed these in Chapter 3, Human Resource Management Strategy and Analysis.) Figure 9-2 presents an employee's online performance management report.
- *Take corrective action* on a continuous basis.

HR in Practice at the Hotel Paris Both Lisa and the firm's CFO were concerned by the current disconnect between (1) what the current appraisal process was focusing on and (2) what the company wanted to accomplish in terms of its strategic goals. They wanted the firm's new performance management system to help breathe life into the firm's strategic performance. To see what they did, read the case on pages 288–289 of this chapter.

But again, no employer needs special software to take a performance management approach to appraisal. Instead, it comes down to the manager's behaviors. These behaviors, again, require linking the employees' performance goals to the company's strategic or operational goals and explaining their goals to them, giving your subordinates continuous feedback on how they are doing, providing the necessary resources and coaching, checking the work, and rewarding good performance.[7]

IMPROVING PERFORMANCE: HR Practices Around the Globe

Performance Management at General Dynamics Armament Systems (GDAS)

General Dynamics Armament (GDAS) designs, develops, and produces high performance products for the military, industrial, and commercial markets.[8] GDAS reorganized its various programs around teams. The teams and their team members have individual responsibility for income, sales, deliveries, and customer satisfaction. Organizing its programs around teams meant GDAS needed a better way to track the teams' performances and monitor and manage the company's performance.

Its *Performance Measures Reporting System* uses a standard set of performance metrics processed and reported through a special Business Metrics Scorecard. The Scorecard displays the performance metrics for each team in three ways (Actual, Baseline Plan, and Current Plan). It then calculates and displays a variance between the actual and the planned performances.

GDAS uses multiple Scorecards to display performance metrics, such as for team and for divisional performance. The Scorecards allow GDAS to maintain all of its crucial performance data in one system so managers can easily access the information anytime via the Intranet. The Scorecards provide GDAS with approximately 450 performance reports and charts. To produce these charts manually would require 13 full-time employees. Instead, the Performance Measures Reporting System, at a cost of $1 million, generates the reports and charts automatically.

Discussion Question 9-1: Describe three examples of scorecard displays GDAS might show on their performance management system's digital dashboard-type display.

Source: "Best Practice: Performance Measures Reporting System," Best Manufacturing Practices Center of Excellence, www.bmpcoe.org/bestpractices/internal/gdas/gdas_11.html, accessed April 5, 2013.

Defining the Employee's Goals and Performance Standards

Both performance appraisal and performance management function by comparing "what should be" with "what is." Managers use one or more of three bases—goals, job dimensions, and competencies—to establish ahead of time what the appraisee's end results "should be." Whichever you use, remember that employees need and expect to know ahead of time on what basis their managers will appraise them.[9]

First, the manager can assess to what extent *the employee is attaining his or her numerical goals*. Such goals should derive from the company's overall goals. For example, a company-wide goal of reducing costs by 10% should translate into goals for how individual employees or teams will cut costs. The HR as a Profit Center feature shows an example.

IMPROVING PERFORMANCE: HR as a Profit Center

Setting Performance Goals at Ball Corporation

Few HR practices have as big an impact on a company's performance as does setting and measuring goals. For example, Ball Corporation supplies metal packaging to customers such as food and paint manufacturers worldwide.[10] The management team at one Ball plant concluded that it could improve plant performance by instituting an improved process for setting goals and for ensuring that the plant's employees' behaviors were in synch with these goals.[11] The new program began by training plant leaders on how to improve performance, and on setting and communicating daily performance goals. They in turn communicated and tracked daily goal attainment by distributing team scorecards to the plant's work teams. Plant employees received special coaching and training to ensure they had the skills required for achieving the goals. According to management, within 12 months the plant increased production by 84 million cans, reduced customer complaints by 50%, and obtained a return-on-investment of more than $3 million.[12]

Discussion Question 9-2: Explain what performance management behaviors the Ball program included.

Managers often say that effective goals should be "SMART." They are *specific*, and clearly state the desired results. They are *measurable*, and answer the question "how much?" They are *attainable*. They are *relevant*, and clearly derive from what the manager and company want to achieve. And they are *timely*, with deadlines and milestones.[13] Research provides insights into setting motivational goals. The accompanying HR Tools feature summarizes these findings.

IMPROVING PERFORMANCE: HR Tools for Line Managers and Entrepreneurs

How to Set Effective Goals

Behavioral science research studies suggest four guidelines for setting performance goals:

1. **Assign specific goals.** Employees who receive specific goals usually perform better than those who do not.
2. **Assign measurable goals.** Put goals in quantitative terms and include target dates or deadlines. If measurable results will not be available, then "satisfactory completion"—such as "satisfactorily attended workshop"—is the next best thing.

3. **Assign challenging but doable goals.** Goals should be challenging, but not so difficult that they appear unrealistic.
4. **Encourage participation.** Managers often face this question: Should I tell my employees what their goals are, or let them participate with me in setting their goals? The evidence suggests that participatively set goals do not consistently result in higher performance than assigned goals, nor do assigned goals consistently result in higher performance than participative ones. It is only when the participatively set goals are set higher than the assigned ones that the participatively set goals produce higher performance. Because it tends to be easier to set higher standards when your employees participate, participation tends to lead to improved performance.[14]

Discussion Question 9-3: Write a short paragraph that addresses the question: "Why is it not a good idea to simply tell employees to 'do their best' when assigning a task?"

A *second* familiar basis upon which to appraise someone is to use a form with *basic job dimensions* (such as "Quality" and "Quantity"). Thus, an instructor's appraisal form might include criteria such as, "The instructor is well prepared." The assumption is that "being prepared" is a useful guiding standard for "what should be."

COMPETENCIES AND BEHAVIORAL STANDARDS A third option is to appraise employees based *on their mastery of the competencies* (generally the skills, knowledge, and/or personal behaviors) performing the job requires.

Consider an example. We saw in Chapter 4 that BP's exploration division appraises employees' skills using a skills matrix (see Figure 4-12, page 114). This matrix shows the basic skills to be assessed (such as "technical expertise"), and the minimum level of each skill the job requires (what the minimum skill level "should be"). Employees appraised as having the requisite level of each skill are qualified to fill the position.

Who Should Do the Appraising?

Appraisals by the immediate supervisor are still the heart of most appraisal processes. Getting a supervisor's appraisal is relatively straightforward and makes sense. The supervisor is usually in the best position to observe and evaluate the subordinate's performance, and is responsible for that person's performance.

The human resources department serves an advisory role. Generally, they provide the advice on what appraisal tool to use, but leave final decisions on procedures to operating managers. The human resource team should also train supervisors to improve their appraisal skills, monitor the appraisal system's effectiveness, and ensure that it complies with EEO laws.

However, relying only on supervisors' appraisals isn't advisable. For example, an employee's supervisor may not appreciate how customers and colleagues see the employee's performance. There is also always some danger of bias for or against the employee. If so, managers have several options.

PEER APPRAISALS With more firms using self-managing teams, appraisal of an employee by his or her peers—peer appraisal—is popular. Typically, an employee due for an annual appraisal chooses an appraisal chairperson. The latter then selects one supervisor and three peers to evaluate the employee's work.

Peer appraisals can be effective. One study involved undergraduates placed into self-managing work groups. The researchers found that peer appraisals had "an immediate positive impact on [improving] perception of open communication, task motivation, social loafing, group viability, cohesion, and satisfaction."[15]

RATING COMMITTEES A rating committee usually consists of the employee's immediate supervisor and three or four other supervisors.[16]

Using multiple raters is advantageous. It helps cancel out problems such as bias on the part of individual raters.[17] It can also provide a way to include in the appraisal the different facets of an employee's performance observed by different appraisers. Studies often find that the ratings obtained from different sources rarely match.[18] It's therefore advisable to obtain ratings from the supervisor, his or her boss, and at least one other manager who is familiar with the employee's work.[19] At a minimum, employers require that the supervisor's boss sign off on any appraisals the supervisor does.

Many employers use rating committees to appraise employees.

iStockphoto/Thinkstock

SELF-RATINGS Some employers obtain employees' self-ratings, usually in conjunction with supervisors' ratings. The basic problem, of course, is that employees usually rate themselves higher than do their supervisors or peers.[20] One study found that, when asked to rate their own job performances, 40% of employees in jobs of all types placed themselves in the top 10%, and virtually all remaining employees rated themselves at least in the top 50%.[21] In another study, subjects' self-ratings correlated negatively with their subsequent performance in an assessment center—the higher they appraised themselves, the worse they did in the center. In contrast, an average of the person's supervisor, peer, and subordinate ratings predicted the subjects' assessment center performance.[22]

APPRAISAL BY SUBORDINATES Many employers have subordinates rate their managers, usually for developmental rather than for pay purposes. Anonymity affects the feedback. Managers who receive feedback from subordinates who identify themselves view the upward feedback process more positively. However, subordinates who identify themselves tend to give inflated ratings.[23]

The evidence suggests that upward feedback improves managers' performance. One study focused on 252 managers during five annual administrations of an upward feedback program. Managers who were initially rated poor or moderate "showed significant improvements in [their] upward feedback ratings over the five-year period."[24] And, managers who met with their subordinates to discuss their upward assessment improved more than the managers who did not.[25]

Recently, the American military, concerned about numerous misconduct allegations, began requiring generals and admirals to be evaluated by their peers and subordinates.[26]

360-DEGREE FEEDBACK With 360-degree feedback, the employer collects performance information all around an employee—from his or her supervisors, subordinates, peers, and internal or external customers—generally for developmental rather than pay purposes.[27] The usual process is to have the raters complete online ratee appraisal surveys. Computerized systems then compile this feedback into individualized reports to ratees (see the sample in Figure 9-3).

Results are mixed. Participants seem to prefer this approach, but one study concluded that multisource feedback led to "generally small" improvements in subsequent ratings by supervisors, peers, and subordinates.[28] Such appraisals are more candid when subordinates know rewards or promotions are not involved.

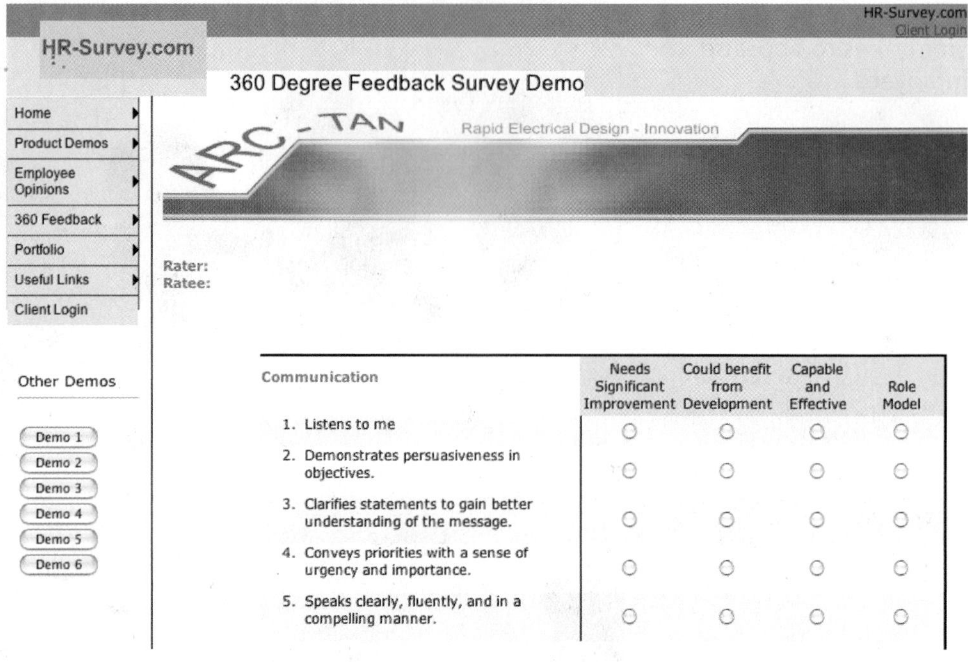

FIGURE 9-3 Online 360-Degree Feedback

Source: "Online 360-Degree Feedback," from HR-SURVEY .COM. Copyright © 2012 by HR-Survey, LLC. Reprinted with permission. www.hr-survey.com/sd3609q.htm.

There are several ways to improve 360-degree appraisals.

- Anchor the 360-degree rating dimensions (such as "listens to me") with specific behavioral examples (such as "stops what he's doing when I speak to her").[29]
- Make sure the feedback the person receives is productive, unbiased, and development oriented.[30]
- Reduce the administrative costs associated with collecting multisource feedback by using a Web-based system such as that in Figure 9-3. This one lets the rater rate the person along a series of dimensions with ratings such as "capable and effective."[31]

Social Media and HR

More employers are turning to social media-based appraisals. Workforce Rypple (http://work.com/) is one such "social performance management platform."[32] Basically, Rypple supplements traditional appraisals. Employees and managers use it to set goals, and to provide feedback and recognition.[33]

For example, employees at Washington-based LivingSocial use Rypple to comment on each other's work. LivingSocial then uses these comments as an input to its formal employee appraisals.[34] Solar energy company Sunrun also uses Rypple. A spokesman says "It's great for putting ideas out there, you can unveil objectives to the whole team, ask for opinions and suggestions and then work on them together. We do 360 feedback each week . . .,"[35] Saba Social Performance Management Software is another such tool.[36] Employers often combine such ongoing reviews with sites such as Globoforce (www.globoforce.com/), which automate the process of instantaneously rewarding and recognizing colleagues.

Techniques for Appraising Performance

3 Develop, evaluate, and administer at least four performance appraisal tools.

As explained earlier, many employers use information technology scorecard tools (such as Figure 9-2, page 262,) to automate performance management. These tools, with their digital dashboards, monitor, report, and correct performance deviations in real time. However many (or most) employers still use traditional performance appraisal tools like one or more of those described next.

Sample Performance Rating Form

Employee's Name ______________________ Level: Entry-level employee

Manager's Name ______________________

Key Work Responsibilities	Results/Goals to Be Achieved
1. ______	1. ______
2. ______	2. ______
3. ______	3. ______
4. ______	4. ______

Communication

1 2 3 4 5

Below Expectations	Meets Expectations	Role Model
Even with guidance, fails to prepare straightforward communications, including forms, paperwork, and records, in a timely and accurate manner; products require minimal corrections. Even with guidance, fails to adapt style and materials to communicate straightforward information.	With guidance, prepares straightforward communications, including forms, paperwork, and records, in a timely and accurate manner; products require minimal corrections. With guidance, adapts style and materials to communicate straightforward information.	Independently prepares communications, such as forms, paperwork, and records, in a timely, clear, and accurate manner; products require few, if any, corrections. Independently adapts style and materials to communicate information.

Organizational Know-How

1 2 3 4 5

Below Expectations	Meets Expectations	Role Model
<performance standards appear here>	<performance standards appear here>	<performance standards appear here>

Personal Effectiveness

1 2 3 4 5

Below Expectations	Meets Expectations	Role Model
<performance standards appear here>	<performance standards appear here>	<performance standards appear here>

Teamwork

1 2 3 4 5

Below Expectations	Meets Expectations	Role Model
<performance standards appear here>	<performance standards appear here>	<performance standards appear here>

Achieving Business Results

1 2 3 4 5

Below Expectations	Meets Expectations	Role Model
<performance standards appear here>	<performance standards appear here>	<performance standards appear here>

FIGURE 9-4 Sample Graphic Performance Rating Form with Behavioral Examples

Source: "Sample Performance Rating Form from Performance Management: A Roadmap for Developing, Implementing and Evaluating Performance Management Systems" by Elaine D. Pulakos from *SHRM Effective Practice Guidelines*. Copyright © 2004 by SHRM Foundation. Reprinted with permission. All rights reserved.

Graphic Rating Scale Method

The **graphic rating scale** is the simplest and most popular method for appraising performance. The graphic rating scale (Figure 9-4) lists several job dimensions (such as "communication" or "teamwork") and a range of performance values (from "below expectations" to "role model" or "unsatisfactory" to "outstanding") for each trait. The supervisor rates each subordinate by

graphic rating scale
A scale that lists a number of traits and a range of performance for each. The employee is then rated by identifying the score that best describes his or her level of performance for each trait.

circling or checking the score that best describes the subordinate's performance for each trait, and totals the ratings. Employers can design the graphic rating scale to evaluate job dimensions, competencies, or goals.

As in Figure 9-4, some rating scales focus on basic *job dimensions* such as quantity, communications, teamwork, and know-how.

Competency based graphic rating forms are another option. Figure 9-5 shows a partial rating form for a pizza chef. It focuses on specific required job-related skills, one of which is "Be able to maintain adequate inventory of pizza dough." Here you would assess how well the employee did in developing and exercising each of these skills. Similarly, one may focus on the extent to which the employee exhibits the sorts of behavioral competencies needed to perform the job. Section I of Figure 9-6 illustrates this.[37] Here "Effectively leads and motivates nurses" is one required behavioral competency for a nurse supervisor.

Or, the manager might rate (as in Section II of Figure 9-6) how well the employee did with respect to achieving specific *goals*. "Nursing unit experienced zero patient medication errors in period" would be one example.

Alternation Ranking Method

alternation ranking method
Ranking employees from best to worst on a particular trait, choosing highest, then lowest, until all are ranked.

Ranking employees from best to worst on a trait or traits is another option. Since it is usually easier to distinguish between the worst and best employees, an **alternation ranking method** is most popular. First, list all subordinates to be rated, and then cross out the names of any not known well enough to rank. Then, on a form like that in Figure 9-7, indicate the employee who is the highest on the performance dimension being measured and the one who is the lowest. Then choose the next highest and the next lowest, alternating between highest and lowest until all employees have been ranked.

Paired Comparison Method

paired comparison method
Ranking employees by making a chart of all possible pairs of the employees for each trait and indicating which is the better employee of the pair.

The **paired comparison method** makes the ranking method more precise. For every trait (quantity of work, quality of work, and so on), you compare every employee with every other employee. With, say, five employees to rate, you use a chart as in Figure 9-8 of all possible pairs of employees for each trait. Then choose who the better employee of the pair is. In Figure 9-8, Maria ranked highest (has the most + marks) for quality of work, whereas Art was ranked highest for creativity.

Forced Distribution Method

forced distribution method
Similar to grading on a curve; predetermined percentages of ratees are placed in various performance categories.

The **forced distribution method** is similar to grading on a curve. With this method, the manager places predetermined percentages of ratees into performance categories. At Lending Tree, the top 15% ratees are "1's," the middle 75% are "2's," and the bottom 10% are "3's" and the "first to go." GE used top 20%, middle 70%, and bottom 10% for its managers, and most of the bottom 10% lost their jobs.[38] (GE no longer strictly adheres to its famous 20/70/10 split.)[39]

Forced distribution's big advantage is that it prevents supervisors from rating all or most employees "satisfactory" or "high." Forced distribution makes some sense. It reflects the fact that top employees often outperform average or poor ones by as much as 100%.[40] About a fourth of *Fortune* 500 companies use versions of it.[41]

But as students know, forced grading systems are unforgiving. With it, you're either in the top 5% or 10% (and get that "A"), or you're not. One survey found that 77% of responding

FIGURE 9-5 One Item from an Appraisal Form Assessing Employee Performance on Specific Job-Related Skills

Position: Pizza Cheif			
Skill 1: Be able to maintain adequate inventory of pizza dough		Rating	
Each round pizza dough must be between 12 and 14 ounces each, kneaded at least 2 minutes before being placed in the temperature and humidity-controlled cooler, and kept there for at least 5 hours prior to use. There should be enough, but no more for each day's demand.	Needs improvement	Satisfactory	Excellent

Section I: Competencies: Does this employee exhibit the core competencies the job requires?

Exhibits Leadership Competency

Effectively leads and motivates nurses: Builds a culture that is open and receptive to improved clinical care; Sets clear goals for nurses; Is supportive of nurses; Motivates nurses to achieve their goals.

Generally exceeds expectations	Generally meets expectations	Generally fails to meet expectations
________	________	________

Exhibits Technical Supervisory Competency

Effectively supervises nurses' technical activities: Exhibits the command of technical nursing knowledge and skills required to supervise nurses effectively, such as, assuring that nurses accurately administer medications, treat patients, intervene effectively to patients' expressions of symptoms, and accurately carry out physicians' instructions.

Generally exceeds expectations	Generally meets expectations	Generally fails to meet expectations
________	________	________

Exhibits Managerial Supervisory Competency

Effectively manages unit: Develops annual, monthly, weekly, and daily plans within context of hospital's plans; effectively organizes and assigns nurses' work; maintains required nursing staffing levels and trains nurses; effectively monitors and controls nursing unit performance using hospital-approved metrics.

Generally exceeds expectations	Generally meets expectations	Generally fails to meet expectations
________	________	________

Exhibits Communications Competency

Effectively communicates: Actively listens to and understands what others say; effectively conveys facts and ideas in writing and orally.

Generally exceeds expectations	Generally meets expectations	Generally fails to meet expectations
________	________	________

Exhibits Decision-Making Competency

Effectively recognizes and solves problems and makes decisions: uses data to analyze alternatives and support conclusions; able to solve problems even of moderate to high complexity.

Generally exceeds expectations	Generally meets expectations	Generally fails to meet expectations
________	________	________

Section II: Goals: Did this employee achieve his or her goals for the period you are appraising?

Primary goals employee was to achieve for this period *(Note: list specific goals)*	Rating 5 Exceeded goal 3 Met goal 1 Did not achieve goal	Explanations and/or examples
Goal 1	5 4 3 2 1	
Goal 2	5 4 3 2 1	
Goal 3	5 4 3 2 1	
Goal 4	5 4 3 2 1	
Goal 5	5 4 3 2 1	

Employee name and signature	Person doing appraisal	Date of appraisal

FIGURE 9-6 Pearson Pennsylvania Hospital Competencies and Goals-Based Appraisal Form for a Nurse-Supervisor

Source: Copyright Gary Dessler, PhD.

FIGURE 9-7 Alternation Ranking Method

ALTERNATION RANKING SCALE

Trait: ____________________

For the trait you are measuring, list all the employees you want to rank. Put the highest-ranking employee's name on line 1. Put the lowest-ranking employee's name on line 20. Then list the next highest ranking on line 2, the next lowest ranking on line 19, and so on. Continue until all names are on the scale.

Highest-ranking employee

1. ____________	11. ____________
2. ____________	12. ____________
3. ____________	13. ____________
4. ____________	14. ____________
5. ____________	15. ____________
6. ____________	16. ____________
7. ____________	17. ____________
8. ____________	18. ____________
9. ____________	19. ____________
10. ____________	20. ____________

Lowest-ranking employee

employers were at least "somewhat satisfied" with forced ranking, while the remaining 23% were dissatisfied. The biggest complaints: 44% said it damages morale.[42] Some writers refer unkindly to it as "Rank and Yank."[43] Therefore, appoint a committee to review any employee's low ranking. And remember that distinguishing between top and bottom performers is usually not even the problem: "The challenge is to differentiate meaningfully between the other 80%."[44]

critical incident method
Keeping a record of uncommonly good or undesirable examples of an employee's work-related behavior and reviewing it with the employee at predetermined times.

Critical Incident Method

With the **critical incident method**, the supervisor keeps a log of positive and negative examples (critical incidents) of a subordinate's work-related behavior. Every 6 months or so, supervisor and subordinate meet to discuss the latter's performance, using the incidents as examples.

FIGURE 9-8 Paired Comparison Method

Note: 1 means "better than." − means "worse than." For each chart, add up the number of +'s in each column to get the highest ranked employee.

Note: + means "better than." – means "worse than." For each chart, add up the number of +'s in each column to get the highest ranked employee.

FOR THE TRAIT "QUALITY OF WORK"

Employee rated:

As Compared to:	A Art	B Maria	C Chuck	D Diane	E José
A Art		+	+	−	−
B Maria	−		−	−	−
C Chuck	−	+		+	−
D Diane	+	+	−		+
E José	+	+	+	−	

Maria ranks highest here

FOR THE TRAIT "CREATIVITY"

Employee rated:

As Compared to:	A Art	B Maria	C Chuck	D Diane	E José
A Art		−	−	−	−
B Maria	+		−	+	+
C Chuck	+	+		−	+
D Diane	+	−	+		−
E José	+	−	−	+	

Art ranks highest here

TABLE 9-1 Examples of Critical Incidents for Assistant Plant Manager

Continuing Duties	Targets	Critical Incidents
Schedule production for plant	90% utilization of personnel and machinery in plant; orders delivered on time	Instituted new production scheduling system; decreased late orders by 10% last month; increased machine utilization in plant by 20% last month
Supervise procurement of raw materials and inventory control	Minimize inventory costs while keeping adequate supplies on hand	Let inventory storage costs rise 15% last month; overordered parts "A" and "B" by 20%; underordered part "C" by 30%
Supervise machinery maintenance	No shutdowns due to faulty machinery	Instituted new preventative maintenance system for plant; prevented a machine breakdown by discovering faulty part

Compiling incidents is useful. It provides examples the supervisor can use to explain the person's rating. It makes the supervisor think about the subordinate's appraisal all during the year (so the rating doesn't just reflect the employee's most recent performance). The downside is that it doesn't produce relative ratings for pay raise purposes. In Table 9-1, one of the assistant plant manager's duties was to supervise procurement and minimize inventory costs. The critical incident log shows that he or she let inventory storage costs rise 15%; this provides an example of what performance to improve.

Narrative Forms

All or part of the written appraisal may be in narrative form, as in Figure 9-9. Here the person's supervisor assesses the employee's past performance and required areas of improvement.

FIGURE 9-9 Sample Narrative Appraisal Form

Source: Copyright Gary Dessler, PhD.

Supervisory Appraisal of Employee: Narrative Form		
Employee's Name	Department	Present Position
Appraisal Date	Supervisor Name/Title	Performance Period

Supervisor-Appraiser: First, briefly describe results for each of this employee's goals this year. Then, preferably using specific examples, describe the level of the employee's job knowledge, skills, and abilities. Then, jointly set goals for the coming period and describe required employee training and development in each area. Finally, describe your overall assessment of this employee's work this period.

Appraisal Criteria	Narrative Appraisal	Goals, Training, & Development
Job-Related Goals 1. ____ 2. ____ 3. ____	 ____ ____ ____	 ____ ____ ____
Employee Job Knowledge		
Employee Job Skills		
Employee Job Abilities		
Overall Assessment		

The supervisor's narrative assessment helps the employee understand where his or her performance was good or bad, and how to improve that performance.

Behaviorally Anchored Rating Scales

behaviorally anchored rating scale (BARS)
An appraisal method that aims at combining the benefits of narrative critical incidents and quantified ratings by anchoring a quantified scale with specific narrative examples of good and poor performance.

A **behaviorally anchored rating scale (BARS)** is an appraisal tool that anchors a numerical rating scale with specific illustrative examples of good or poor performance. Its proponents say it provides better, more equitable appraisals than do the other tools we've discussed.[45]

Developing a BARS typically requires five steps:

1. ***Write critical incidents.*** Ask the job's jobholders and/or supervisors to write specific illustrations (critical incidents) of effective and ineffective performance on the job.
2. ***Develop performance dimensions.*** Have these people cluster the incidents into 5 or 10 performance dimensions, such as "salesmanship skills."
3. ***Reallocate incidents.*** To verify these groupings, have another team who also know the job reallocate the original critical incidents to the cluster they think it fits best. Retain a critical incident if most of this second team assigns it to the same cluster as did the first.
4. ***Scale the incidents.*** This second group then rates the behavior described by the incident as to how effectively or ineffectively it represents performance on the dimension (7- to 9-point scales are typical).
5. ***Develop a final instrument.*** Choose about six or seven of the incidents as the dimension's behavioral anchors.[46] We'll look at an example.

Figure 9-10 shows a BARS for one performance dimension for a car salesperson—the dimension "automobile salesmanship skills."

RESEARCH INSIGHT Three researchers developed a BARS for grocery checkout clerks.[47] They collected many checkout clerk critical incidents, and then grouped or clustered these into eight performance dimensions:

Knowledge and Judgment
Conscientiousness
Skill in Human Relations
Skill in Operation of Register
Skill in Bagging
Organizational Ability of Checkstand Work
Skill in Monetary Transactions
Observational Ability

They then developed behaviorally anchored rating scales for each of these eight dimensions. Each contained a vertical scale (ranging from 1 to 9) for rating performance from "extremely poor" to "extremely good." Then they inserted specific critical incidents (such as "by knowing the price of items, this checker would be expected to look for mismarked and unmarked items") to anchor or illustrate each level of performance. Figure 9-10 shows a similar BARS, but for a car salesperson.

ADVANTAGES The critical incidents along the scale *illustrate* what to look for in terms of superior performance, average performance, and so forth. The critical incidents make it *easier to explain* the ratings to appraisees. Clustering the critical incidents into five or six performance dimensions (such as "salesmanship skills") helps make the performance dimensions more *independent of one another*. (For example, a rater should be less likely to rate an employee high on all dimensions simply because he or she was rated high in "salesmanship skills.") Finally, BARS seem to be relatively *reliable:* different raters' appraisals of the same person tend to be similar.[48]

Mixed Standard Scales

Mixed standard scales are somewhat similar to behaviorally anchored scales. They are called mixed scales because the employer "mixes" together all the good or poor behavioral example statements when listing them. The aim is to reduce rating errors by making it less obvious to the person doing the appraising (1) what performance dimensions he or she is rating; and (2) whether the behavioral example statements represent high, medium, or low performance. The supervisor rates the employee by indicating whether the latter's performance is better than, the same, or worse than the statement.

FIGURE 9-10 Behaviorally Anchored Rating Scale

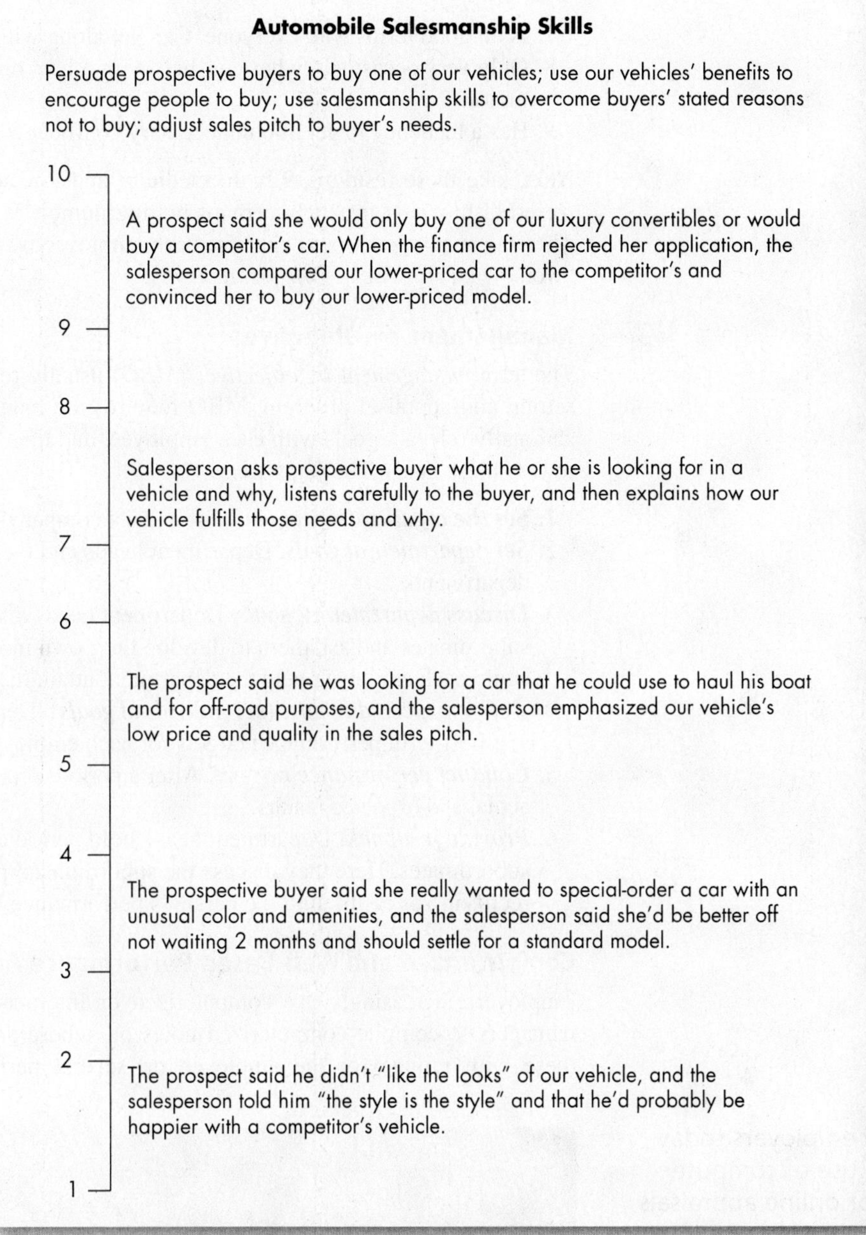

Automobile Salesmanship Skills

Persuade prospective buyers to buy one of our vehicles; use our vehicles' benefits to encourage people to buy; use salesmanship skills to overcome buyers' stated reasons not to buy; adjust sales pitch to buyer's needs.

Suppose you want to appraise employees on the dimensions Quality of Work, Conscientiousness, and Gets Along with Others. You write three "high, medium, low" behavioral examples for each of these three dimensions, as follows.[49]

For *Quality of Work*

1. Employee's work is striking in its accuracy, there is never any evidence of carelessness in it.
2. The accuracy of employee's work is satisfactory; it is not often that you find clear evidence of carelessness.
3. Frequent careless errors in this employee's work.

For *Conscientiousness*

4. Is quick and efficient, able to keep work on schedule.
5. Is efficient enough, usually getting through assignments and work in a reasonable time.
6. There is some lack of efficiency on employee's part. Employee may take too much time to complete assignments, and sometimes does not really finish them.

For *Gets Along with Others*

7. Is on good terms with everyone. Can get along with people even when they disagree.
8. Only very occasionally has conflicts with others on the job, and these are likely to be minor.
9. Has a tendency to get into unnecessary conflicts with people.

Next, take these resulting 9 high, medium, and low statements, and list them randomly, in a mixed fashion, for instance, perhaps putting number 9 above first, then 4, then 2, and so forth. Then the supervisor would appraise each employee by rating him or her "better," "the same" or "worse than" *for each of the 9 statements.*

Management by Objectives

The term *management by objectives (MBO)* usually refers to a multistep company-wide goal-setting and appraisal program. MBO requires the manager to set specific measurable, organizationally relevant goals with each employee, and then periodically discuss the latter's progress toward these goals. The steps are:

1. ***Set the organization's goals.*** Establish a company-wide plan for next year and set goals.
2. ***Set departmental goals.*** Department heads and their superiors jointly set goals for their departments.
3. ***Discuss departmental goals.*** Department heads discuss the department's goals with their subordinates and ask them to develop their own individual goals. They should ask, "How could each employee help the department attain its goals?"
4. ***Define expected results (set individual goals).*** Department heads and their subordinates set short-term performance targets for each employee.
5. ***Conduct performance reviews.*** After a period, department heads compare each employee's actual and expected results.
6. ***Provide feedback.*** Department heads hold periodic performance review meetings with subordinates. Here they discuss the subordinates' performance and make any plans for rectifying or continuing the person's performance.

Computerized and Web-Based Performance Appraisal

Employers increasingly use computerized or Internet-based appraisal systems. These enable managers to compile computerized notes on subordinates during the year, and then to merge these with ratings for the employee on several performance traits. The software presents

Many employers today make use of computerized or online appraisals for evaluating employee performance.

Jupiterimages/Thinkstock

FIGURE 9-11 Online Appraisal Tool

Source: "Online Appraisal Tool," from HRONLINE.COM website. Copyright © 2012 by HRN Performance Solutions. Reprinted with permission. All rights reserved. http://www.hronline.com/Screenshots-1128.html accessed September 13, 2013.

written examples to support part of the appraisal. Most such appraisals combine several appraisal methods, usually graphic ratings anchored by critical incidents.[50]

For example, *Employee Appraiser* (developed by the Austin-Hayne Corporation, San Mateo, California) presents a menu of evaluation dimensions, including dependability, initiative, communication, decision making, leadership, judgment, and planning and productivity.[51] Within each dimension (such as "Communication") are separate performance factors for things like writing, verbal communication, and receptivity to criticism. When the user clicks on a performance factor, he or she is presented with a graphic rating scale. However, instead of numerical ratings,

"Employee Appraiser" uses behaviorally anchored examples. Thus, for *verbal communication* there are six choices, ranging from "presents ideas clearly" to "lacks structure." The manager chooses the phrase that most accurately describes the worker. Then "Employee Appraiser" generates an appraisal with sample text.

Seagate Technology uses "Enterprise Suite" for managing the performance of its 39,000 employees.[52] Early in Seagate's first fiscal quarter, employees enter the system and set goals and development plans for themselves that make sense in terms of Seagate's corporate objectives. Employees update their plans quarterly, and then do self-evaluations at the end of the year, with follow-up reviews by their supervisors. Figure 9-11 illustrates another good online appraisal tool, in this case from PerformancePro.

Electronic Performance Monitoring

electronic performance monitoring (EPM)
Having supervisors electronically monitor the amount of computerized data an employee is processing per day, and thereby his or her performance.

Electronic performance monitoring (EPM) systems use computer network technology to allow managers to monitor their employees' computers. They allow managers to monitor the employees' rate, accuracy, and time spent working online.[53]

EPM can improve productivity, but also seems to raise employee stress. However, one researcher concludes that "Electronic Performance Monitoring (EPM) represents the future of performance feedback where supervisors can electronically monitor the amount and quality of work an employee is producing and have objective indicators of employee performance immediately available and visible."[54]

Conversation Days

When employees at Juniper Networks Inc. expressed concerns about their annual performance reviews and the lack of positive feedback, Juniper changed the process. Instead of once a year performance reviews, there are now semiannual "conversation days." The stress in these manager-employee conversations is on areas for improvement and growth, and on setting stretch goals that align with the employee's career interests. There are no explicit performance ratings.

Using Multiple Methods

Rating forms often merge several approaches. Thus, Figure 9-4 (page 267) has a numerical graphic rating scale anchored with behavioral incidents such as "Even with guidance, fails to. . . ." The HR Practices Around the Globe feature illustrates setting up a system to appraise employees abroad.

IMPROVING PERFORMANCE: HR Practices Around the Globe

TRW's New Global Performance Management System

As a global competitor facing stiff competition, TRW needed a performance management system that was consistent and comprehensive.[55] It had to be *consistent* in that employees in all of TRW's far-flung organization could use the same system. It had to be *comprehensive* in that it consolidated the various components of performance management into a single common system. For TRW, these components included goal setting, performance appraisal, professional development, and succession planning.

TRW's team created an online system, one in which most TRW employees and supervisors worldwide could input and review their data electronically. (The team subsequently created an equivalent paper-based system, for use by certain employees abroad who didn't have easy access to the Web.) The Web-based performance management system included data such as biographical data, previous year's professional development activities, overall performance, and future potential/positions.

To facilitate filling out the online form, the team created a wizard that leads the user from step to step. The system also includes pull-down menus. For example, in the "demonstrated strengths" area, the pull-down menus allow the user to select specific competencies such as "financial acumen."

In practice, either the employee or the manager can trigger the performance management process by completing the appraisal and sending it to the other (the employee usually begins the process). Once the employee finishes the online form, a system-generated e-mail notifies the manager that the form is ready for review. Then the two fine-tune the appraisal by meeting in person, and by interacting online.

The new system produced benefits well beyond systematizing TRW's performance management process. It focuses everyone's attention on goal-oriented performance. It identifies development needs that are important to both TRW and the employee. It gives managers instantaneous access to employee performance-related data (by clicking the "managing employees" function, a manager sees an overview of the assessment status of each of his or her direct reports). It gives all managers access to an employee database so that, for instance, a search for a mechanical engineer with Chinese language skills takes just a few minutes. And, the system lets the manager quickly review the development needs of all his or her employees. The result is an integrated, goal-oriented employee development and appraisal "Performance Management Process."

Discussion Question 9-4: TRW wanted a "consistent" system it could use globally. A study similarly found that large multinational companies from the United States, Holland, Japan, Korea, and Taiwan used the same performance management forms and procedures abroad that they do at headquarters.[56] Discuss two cultural differences between the United States and any one other country that you might have thought would make having a single system less than feasible.

4 Explain and illustrate the problems to avoid in appraising performance.

unclear standards
An appraisal that is too open to interpretation.

halo effect
In performance appraisal, the problem that occurs when a supervisor's rating of a subordinate on one trait biases the rating of that person on other traits.

central tendency
A tendency to rate all employees the same way, such as rating them all average.

Dealing with Rater Error Appraisal Problems

In a perfect world, all employers would use performance management systems with clear goals, fair appraisals, swift feedback, and useful coaching. Alas, that is rarely the case.[57] Graphic-type rating forms in particular are susceptible to several "rater error" problems; in other words, systematic errors in judgment that occur when people evaluate each other: unclear standards, halo effect, central tendency, leniency or strictness, and bias.

Potential Rating Problems

UNCLEAR STANDARDS Table 9-2 illustrates the **unclear standards** problem. This graphic rating scale seems objective. However, it might well result in unfair appraisals, because the traits and degrees of merit are ambiguous. For example, different supervisors might define "good" performance, "fair" performance, and so on, differently. The same is true of traits such as "quality of work."[58]

The way to fix this problem is to include descriptive phrases that define or illustrate each trait, as in Figure 9-4. That form spells out what measures like "Role Model" or "Below Expectations" mean. This specificity results in more consistent and more easily explained appraisals.

Stockbyte/Getty Images

Supervisors must be familiar with appraisal techniques, understand and avoid problems that can cripple appraisals, and know how to conduct appraisals fairly.

HALO EFFECT Experts define **halo effect** as "the influence of a rater's general impression on ratings of specific ratee qualities."[59] For example, supervisors often rate unfriendly employees lower on all traits, rather than just on "gets along well with others." Being aware of this problem is a step toward avoiding it. Supervisory training can also alleviate the problem, as can using a BARS (on which, recall, the performance dimensions are usually independent of each other).

CENTRAL TENDENCY **Central tendency** means rating all employees average. For example, if the rating scale ranges from 1 to 7, raters tend to avoid the highs (6 and 7) and lows (1 and 2) and rate most of their people between 3 and 5. Doing so distorts the evaluations, making them less useful for promotion, salary, or counseling purposes. Ranking employees instead of using graphic rating scales can reduce this problem, since ranking means you can't rate them all average.

TABLE 9-2 A Graphic Rating Scale with Unclear Standards

	Excellent	Good	Fair	Poor
Quantity of work				
Quality of work				
Creativity				
Integrity				

Note: For example, what exactly is meant by "good," "quantity of work," and so forth?

strictness/leniency
The problem that occurs when a supervisor has a tendency to rate all subordinates either high or low.

LENIENCY OR STRICTNESS Other supervisors tend to rate all their subordinates high or low, just as some instructors are notoriously high or low graders. This **strictness/leniency** problem is especially severe with graphic rating scales. *Ranking* forces supervisors to distinguish between high and low performers.

There are other solutions. One is for the employer to recommend that supervisors avoid giving all their employees high (or low) ratings. A second is to require a distribution—that, say, about 10% of the people should be rated "excellent," 20% "good," and so forth. (But remember it may not be an error at all, as when all subordinates really are superior.)[60]

RECENCY EFFECTS Recency means letting what the employee has done recently blind you to what his or her performance has been over the year. The main solution is to accumulate critical incidents all year long.

bias
The tendency to allow individual differences such as age, race, and sex to affect the appraisal ratings employees receive.

Diversity Counts: The Problem of Bias

Biased appraisals have a variety of causes. One study of **bias** focused on the rater's personality. Raters who scored higher on "conscientiousness" tended to give their peers lower ratings—they were stricter, in other words; those more "agreeable" gave higher ratings—they were more lenient.[61] Managers also tend to be more lenient when appraising subordinates for administrative purposes like pay raises then for development purposes.[62] Furthermore, "performance ratings amplify the quality of the personal relationship between boss and employee. Good relationships tend to create good [appraisal] experiences, bad relationships bad ones."[63]

Unfortunately, subordinates' demographic traits (age, race, gender, and so on) also affect ratings. A 36-year-old supervisor ranked a 62-year-old subordinate at the bottom of the department's rankings, and then fired him. The court held that the younger boss's discriminatory motives might have prejudiced the dismissal decision.[64] In one study, promoted women had to have received higher performance ratings than promoted men to be promoted, "suggesting that women were held to stricter standards for promotion."[65] In another study, raters penalized successful women for their success.[66]

The bottom line is that the appraisal often says more about the appraiser than about the appraisee.[67] (Or as one researcher said, "rater idiosyncratic biases account for the largest percentage of the observed variances in performance ratings.")[68] Potential bias is one reason to use multiple raters, have the supervisor's boss review the rating, and/or have "calibration" meetings where supervisors discuss among themselves their reasons for the appraisals they gave each of their subordinates.[69]

Guidelines for Effective Appraisals

Problems like strictness and bias can make an appraisal worse than none at all. Would an employee not be better off with no appraisal than with a seemingly objective but actually biased one?

The best prescription is to remember that it's not performance *appraisal* but performance *management*. As noted earlier, this means linking the employee's performance goals to the company's strategic or operational goals, giving timely feedback, providing the necessary resources and coaching, checking the work, and rewarding good performance.[70]

But, appraisals are still mostly interpersonal, and so are subject to human frailties (like bias). To minimize this, consider the following guidelines.

KEEP IN MIND THE GRAPHIC RATING PROBLEMS Understand the potential appraisal problems (such as central tendency). Doing so can help you avoid it.

USE THE RIGHT APPRAISAL TOOL Each has pros and cons. For example, the ranking method avoids central tendency but can cause bad feelings when employees' performances are in fact all "high." In practice, employers choose an appraisal tool based on several criteria. Accessibility and ease-of-use is probably first. That is why graphic rating scales are popular; Table 9-3 summarizes each tool's pros and cons.

KEEP A DIARY Keep a diary of employees' performances.[71] One study involved 112 first-line supervisors. The conclusion of this and similar studies is that compiling critical incidents as they occur anchors the eventual appraisal in reality and thus improves appraisal outcomes.[72]

GET AGREEMENT ON A PLAN The aim of the appraisal should be to improve unsatisfactory performance (and/or to reinforce exemplary performance). The appraisal should therefore result in a plan for what the employee must do to improve his or her efforts.

TABLE 9-3 Important Advantages and Disadvantages of Appraisal Tools

Tool	Advantages	Disadvantages
Graphic rating scale	Simple to use; provides a quantitative rating for each employee.	Standards may be unclear; halo effect, central tendency, leniency, bias can also be problems.
BARS	Provides behavioral "anchors." BARS is very accurate.	Difficult to develop.
Alternation ranking	Simple to use (but not as simple as graphic rating scales). Avoids central tendency and other problems of rating scales.	Can cause disagreements among employees and may be unfair if all employees are, in fact, excellent.
Forced distribution method	End up with a predetermined number or % of people in each group.	Employees' appraisal results depend on your choice of cutoff points.
Critical incident method	Helps specify what is "right" and "wrong" about the employee's performance; forces supervisor to evaluate subordinates on an ongoing basis.	Difficult to rate or rank employees relative to one another.
MBO	Tied to jointly agreed-upon performance objectives.	Time-consuming.

BE A FAIR AND EFFECTIVE SUPERVISOR For better or worse, the quality of the interpersonal interactions between the supervisor and employee will shape the appraisal's impact and worth. Supervisors (and particularly new supervisors) must therefore manage their interpersonal relations with their employees and be trained in both the technical and interpersonal aspects of appraising employees and giving them feedback.[73] Supervisors should understand how to build trust through open relationships, engage in continuous performance conversations, diagnose and productively address performance issues, and deliver and react to feedback conversations constructively.[74] To facilitate this, the employer should formally evaluate and reward supervisors partly based on their effectiveness in managing performance.[75]

Either due to the supervisor's ineptitude or inherent unfairness, many appraisals are unfair. Some managers ignore accuracy and honesty, and instead, use appraisals for political purposes (such as encouraging employees with whom they don't get along to leave the firm).[76] The employees' standards should be clear, employees should understand the basis on which you're going to appraise them, and the appraisals should be objective and fair.[77] Best practices for ensuring this are in the checklist in Figure 9-12.

FIGURE 9-12 Checklist of Best Practices for Administering Fair Performance Appraisals

Source: Based on Richard Posthuma, "Twenty Best Practices for Just Employee Performance Reviews," *Compensation and Benefits Review*, January/February 2008, pp. 47–54; www.employeeperformance.com/PerformanceManagementResources/BestPracticesforPerformanceAppraisals.php, accessed July, 2010; and www.successfactors.com/articles/optimize-performance-management, accessed July, 2010. Reprinted with permission of the Society for Human Resource Management (www.shrm.com), Alexandria, VA, Publisher of *HR Magazine*, © SHRM.

- Base the performance review on duties and standards from a job analysis.
- Try to base the performance review on observable job behaviors or objective performance data.
- Make it clear ahead of time what your performance expectations are.
- Use a standardized performance review procedure for all employees.
- Make sure whoever conducts the reviews has frequent opportunities to observe the employee's job performance.
- Either use multiple raters or have the rater's supervisor evaluate the appraisal results.
- Include an appeals mechanism.
- Document the appraisal review process and results.
- Discuss the appraisal results with the employee.
- Let the employees know ahead of time how you're going to conduct the reviews.
- Let the employee provide input regarding your assessment of him or her.
- Indicate what the employee needs to do to improve.
- Train the supervisors who will be doing the appraisals. Make sure they understand the procedure to use, how problems (like leniency and strictness) arise, and how to deal with them.

KNOW YOUR EMPLOYMENT LAW

Appraising Performance

Since passage of Title VII in 1964, courts have addressed the link between appraisals and personnel actions. They have often found that an inadequate appraisal system lay at the root of illegal discriminatory actions, particularly in cases concerning layoffs, promotions, discharges, or merit pay.[78] For example, one court held that the firm had violated Title VII when it laid off several Hispanic-surnamed employees based on poor performance ratings. The court concluded that the practice was illegal because: the firm based the appraisals on subjective supervisory observations; it did not administer and score the appraisals in a standardized fashion; and two of the three supervisory evaluators did not have daily contact with the employees they appraised. Personal bias, unreasonably rating everyone high (or low), and relying just on recent events are some other reasons courts gave for deciding that firms' appraisal processes and subsequent personnel actions were unfair.[79]

Steps to ensure your appraisals are legally defensible include:

- Base the duties and criteria you appraise on a job analysis.
- At the start of the period, communicate performance standards to employees in writing.
- Using a single overall rating of performance is not acceptable to the courts, which often characterize such systems as vague.[80] Courts generally require combining separate ratings for each performance dimension (quality, quantity, and so on) with some formal weighting system to yield a summary score.
- Include an employee appeals process. Employees should have the opportunity to review and make comments, written or verbal, about their appraisals before they become final, and should have a formal appeals process to appeal their ratings.
- One appraiser should never have absolute authority to determine a personnel action.
- Document all information bearing on a personnel decision in writing. "Without exception, courts condemn informal performance evaluation practices that eschew documentation."[81]
- Train supervisors. If formal rater training is not possible, at least provide raters with written instructions on how to use the rating scale.[82]

If such a case gets to court, what will judges look for? A review of about 300 U.S. court decisions is informative. Actions reflecting fairness and due process were most important. Figure 9-13 presents a checklist (including the steps above) for developing a legally defensible appraisal process.[83]

FIGURE 9-13 Checklist for a Legally Defensible Appraisal

- Preferably, conduct a job analysis to establish performance criteria and standards.
- Communicate performance standards to employees and to those rating them, in writing.
- When using graphic rating scales, avoid undefined abstract trait names (such as "loyalty" or "honesty").
- Use subjective narratives as only one component of the appraisal.
- Train supervisors to use the rating instrument properly.
- Allow appraisers daily contact with the employees they're evaluating.
- Don't use a single overall rating of performance.
- Have more than one appraiser, and conduct all such appraisals independently.
- One appraiser should never have absolute authority to determine a personnel action.
- Give employees the opportunity to review and make comments.
- Have a formal appeals process.
- Document everything.
- Provide corrective guidance to assist poor performers in improving.

Managing the Appraisal Interview

5 Perform an effective appraisal interview.

appraisal interview
An interview in which the supervisor and subordinate review the appraisal and make plans to remedy deficiencies and reinforce strengths.

The traditional periodic appraisal typically culminates in an **appraisal interview**. Here the manager and the subordinate review the appraisal and make plans to remedy deficiencies and reinforce strengths. These interviews are often uncomfortable. Few people like to receive—or give—negative feedback. Adequate preparation and effective implementation are essential. Supervisors face four types of appraisal situations, each with its unique objectives:[84]

Satisfactory—Promotable is the easiest interview: The person's performance is satisfactory and promotion looms. Your objective is to discuss the person's career plans and to develop specific development plans.

Satisfactory—Not promotable is for employees whose performance is satisfactory but for whom promotion is not possible. The objective here is to maintain satisfactory performance. The best option is usually to find incentives that are important to the person and sufficient to maintain performance. These might include extra time off, a small bonus, or recognition.

When the person's performance is *unsatisfactory but correctable*, the interview objective is to lay out an action/development plan (see Figure 9-14) for correcting the unsatisfactory performance.

Finally, the interview where the employee is *unsatisfactory* and the situation is *uncorrectable* may be particularly tense. Dismissal is often the preferred approach.

How to Conduct the Appraisal Interview

Useful interviews begin before the interview. Beforehand, review the person's job description, compare performance to the standards, and review the previous appraisals. Give the employee at least a week's notice to review his or her work. Set a time for the interview. Interviews with lower-level personnel like clerical workers should take less than an hour. Interviews with management employees often take 1 or 2 hours. Conduct the interview privately with no interruptions.

An effective interview requires effective coaching skills. Coaching doesn't mean telling someone what to do. Instead, it is a process.[85] *Preparation* means understanding the problem and the employee. Here the manager will watch the employee to see what he or she is doing, review productivity data, and observe the workflow.

FIGURE 9-14 Sample Employee Development Plan

Source: www.career-change-mentor.com/support-files/sampleemployeedevelopmentplan.pdf, accessed April 28, 2009.

Sample Employee Development Plan

Employee Name: J. Citizen Position Title: HR Analyst Date Developed: ____________ Date Last Revised: ____________

A. Key objectives and core competencies

List top 3-5 business objectives for this year:	List core competencies for position:	
1. Implement revised employee development system	1. Employee Development	4. Communication
2. Provide organization development support	2. Recruitment	5. Conflict Management
3. Reduce employee turnover by 5%	3. Organization Development	6. Grievance Management

B. Competency gaps and action plan

List top 2-3 core competencies that need development	List key gaps for each core competency	Briefly state how you will close each gap	Target completion date	Status R/Y/G
1. Employee Dev.	1. Succession Plng.	1. Participate in succession planning reviews in sister company to learn about process		G
2. Grievance Mgmt.	2. Elevation Process	2. Attend refresher training. Develop draft process. Pilot draft process and review.		Y
3.	3.	3.		

C. Comments/Notes – to be noted during Manager & Employee progress review of development plan

Succession Planning – good progress made on understanding process. Next step is to improve working knowledge of process by implementing it. Keep in close contact with mentor from sister company for advice and direction.
Elevation Process – refresher training attended but was inadequate. Plan in place to get assistance from HR Manager.

Status: Green – completed; Yellow – incomplete/plan in place to achieve objective; Red – not achieved/no plan in place

Manager's Name: ________________ Signature: __________ Date Reviewed: __________

Planning the solution is next. This requires reaching agreement on the problem, and laying out a change plan in the form of *steps to take, measures of success,* and *date to complete.*

With agreement on a plan, the manager can start the *actual coaching*. One writer says, "[a]n effective coach offers ideas and advice in such a way that the subordinate can hear them, respond to them, and appreciate their value."[86] Useful guidelines include:

1. ***Talk in terms of objective work data.*** Use examples such as absences, tardiness, and productivity.
2. ***Don't get personal.*** Don't say, "You're too slow producing those reports." Instead, compare the person's performance to a standard. ("These reports should normally be done within 10 days.") Similarly, don't compare the person's performance to that of other people. ("He's quicker than you are.")
3. ***Encourage the person to talk.*** Stop and listen to what the person is saying; ask open-ended questions (such as, "What do you think we can do to improve the situation?"). Use a command such as "Go on." Restate the person's last point as a question, as in, "You don't think you can get the job done?"
4. ***Get agreement.*** Make sure the person leaves knowing specifically what he or she is doing right and doing wrong and with agreement on how things will be improved, and has an action plan (Figure 9-14) with targets and dates.

Whether subordinates express satisfaction with their appraisal interview will depend on several things. These include not feeling threatened, having an opportunity to present their ideas and feelings and to influence the course of the interview, and having a helpful and constructive supervisor conduct the interview.

Figure 9-15 provides an appraisal interview checklist.

How to Handle a Defensive Subordinate

When a supervisor tells someone his or her performance is poor, the first reaction is often denial. Denial is a defense mechanism. By denying the fault, the person avoids having to question his or her own competence.

Therefore, dealing with defensiveness is an important appraisal skill. In his book *Effective Psychology for Managers*, psychologist Mortimer Feinberg suggests the following:

1. Recognize that defensive behavior is normal.
2. Never attack a person's defenses. Don't try to "explain someone to themselves" (as in, "You know the reason you're using that excuse is that you can't bear to be blamed."). Instead, concentrate on the fact ("sales are down").

FIGURE 9-15 Appraisal Interview Checklist

Source: Copyright Gary Dessler, PhD.

Appraisal Interview Checklist

Interview Item: Did you	Yes	No
1. Review the employee's job description, previous appraisals, goals, and current job standards prior to the interview?		
2. Provide adequate time and a private, cordial, non-threatening environment for the interview?		
3. Focus your discussion and comments on objective work data?		
4. Encourage the appraisee to talk (restate last comment as a question, etc.), and make it clear you are listening (nod, etc.)?		
5. Give the appraisee an opportunity to fully present his or her ideas and feelings?		
6. Consciously avoid attacking the appraisee's defenses?		
7. Criticize in a way that allowed the appraisee to maintain his or her dignity?		
8. Discuss your evaluation of each of the appraisee's job duties and/or goals?		
9. Reach agreement on the training and development required to improve the appraisee's performance?		
10. Discuss, as appropriate, the steps the employer may take if improvement goals are not met?		
11. Discuss the appraisee's performance in light of his or her career aspirations?		

3. Postpone action. Sometimes it's best to do nothing. Employees may react to sudden threats by hiding behind their defenses. Given sufficient time, a more rational reaction takes over.
4. Recognize your limitations. The supervisor is (probably) not a psychologist. Offering understanding is one thing; trying to deal with psychological problems is another.

How to Criticize a Subordinate

When necessary, criticize in a manner that lets the person maintain his or her dignity—in private, and constructively. Provide examples of critical incidents and specific suggestions. Avoid once-a-year "critical broadsides" by giving feedback periodically, so that the formal review contains no surprises. Never say the person is "always" wrong. Criticism should be objective and free of personal bias.

When the employee is not doing well, the manager will have to decide how candid to be. GE's former CEO Jack Welch once called it cruel to tell someone who's doing a mediocre job that their work is satisfactory.[87] Someone who might have changed course may instead spend years in a dead-end job, only to be dismissed when a more demanding boss arrives.

How to Handle a Formal Written Warning

The employee's performance may be so weak that it requires a formal written warning. Such warnings serve two purposes: (1) To shake your employee out of his or her bad habits, and (2) to help you defend your rating to your own boss and (if needed) to the courts.

Written warnings should list the employee's standards, make it clear that the employee was aware of the standard, specify any deficiencies relative to the standard, and show the employee had an opportunity to correct his or her performance.

Talent Management and Employee Appraisal

6 Explain how to "segment" employees for appraisal and reward purposes.

In Chapter 4, we defined talent management as the goal-oriented and integrated process of planning, recruiting, developing, appraising, and compensating employees. *Actively managing* how employees are appraised and rewarded is one best talent management practice.

Appraising and Actively Managing Employees

How does this apply to appraisal and rewards? By modifying the basis on which the company allocates rewards. Perhaps with the exception of selected "fast-track" employees, managers tend to allocate rewards (such as compensation and development opportunities) either across-the-board, or based on the employee's appraisal ratings (or both). They don't sufficiently "actively manage" the process.

Talent management-oriented employers do use performance appraisal to evaluate how their employees are performing. However, they also segment their employees based on how critical the employees are to the company's success. Then they focus more effort and resources on the company's "mission-critical" employees.

Figure 9-16 illustrates this. Accenture uses a 4 × 4 strategic role assessment matrix to plot employees by *Performance* (exceptional, high, medium, low) and *Value to the Organization* (mission-critical, core, necessary, non-essential). Consider a chemical engineering company that designs pollution control equipment. Here, the firm's experienced engineers may be "mission-critical," engineer-trainees "core," sales, accounting, and HR "necessary," and outsourceable employees such as those in maintenance "non-essential." The company would then tie pay, development, dismissal, and other personnel decisions to each employee's position in the matrix, not just to their performance ratings.

Segmenting and Actively Managing Employees in Practice

Several examples can illustrate how this works in practice.

- McKinsey & Co. recommends limiting the "high potential group in whom the company invests heavily to no more than 10 to 20% of managerial and professional staff."[88]
- Unilever includes 15% of employees per management level in its high potential list each year, and expects these people to move to the next management level within five years.[89]
- GE prioritizes jobs and focuses on what it calls its employee "game changers."[90]
- Shell China appoints "career stewards" to meet regularly with "emerging leaders." They make sure they're getting the right development opportunities.[91]

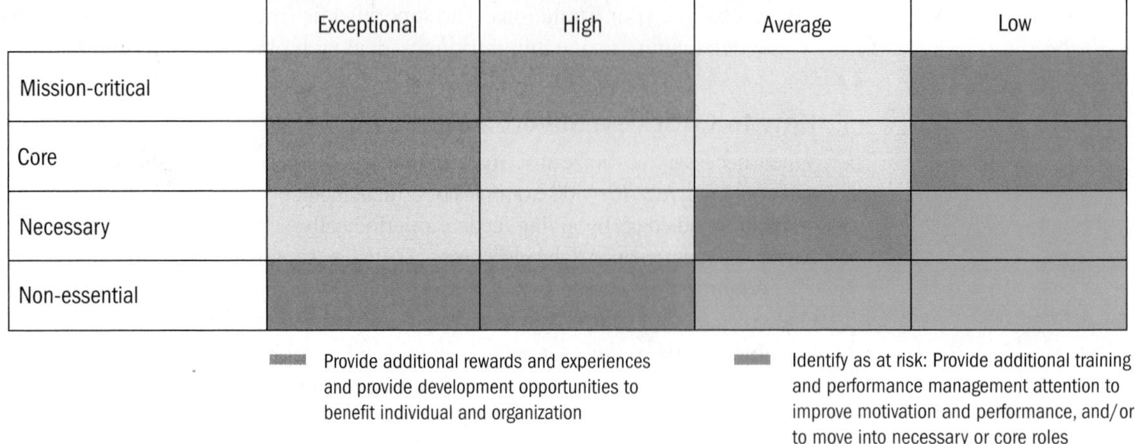

FIGURE 9-16 Accenture's Strategic Role Assessment Matrix

Source: "The New Talent Equation" *Outlook*, June 2009. Copyright © 2009 by Accenture. Reprinted by permission. All rights reserved.

Review

MyManagementLab Go to **mymanagementlab.com** to complete the problems marked with this icon. 

Chapter Section Summaries

1. Before appraising performance, managers should understand certain **basic concepts in performance management and appraisal**. Stripped to its essentials, performance appraisal involves setting work standards, assessing the employee's actual performance relative to those standards, and providing feedback to the employee. Managers should appraise employees based on the criteria previously assigned, and the actual standards should be specific, measurable, attainable, relevant, and timely.
2. More employers are moving from traditional performance appraisals to *performance management*.
   - Performance management is the continuous process of identifying, measuring, and developing the performance of individuals and teams and aligning their performance with the organization's goals.
   - Its basic building blocks include direction (goals) sharing, goal alignment, ongoing performance monitoring, ongoing feedback, coaching, and rewards and recognition.
   - The performance management approach reflects a total quality philosophy toward performance. More importantly, it focuses on aligning and monitoring the link between the company's overall strategic goals and what each individual employee and team are supposed to accomplish.
   - In practice, employers use information technology to support performance management, for instance, using digital dashboards to monitor and correct each team's performance on a real-time basis.
3. There are several basic **techniques managers use for appraising performance**.
   - Whichever tool you use, the appraisal should provide information on which to base pay and promotional decisions, clarify for the employee important company-relevant goals, develop a plan for correcting deficiencies, and support career planning.
   - In terms of specific techniques, the graphic rating scale lists a number of traits and a range of performance for each. Managers use generic job dimensions such as quantity, or focus on the job's goals, or required competencies.
   - With the alternation ranking method, you rank employees from best to worst on a particular trait.
   - The paired comparison method means ranking employees by making a chart of all possible pairs of the employees and indicating which is the better employee of the pair.

- Many employers use the forced distribution method, which is similar to grading on a curve. Here you place predetermined percentages of appraisees in various performance categories.
- Regardless of the specific methods used, the manager may want to maintain a record of critical incidents—uncommonly good or undesirable examples of employees' work behavior—to review with the employee.
- A behaviorally anchored rating scale anchors a quantified scale with specific narrative examples of good and poor performance.
- In practice, many employers use computerized and/or Web-based performance appraisal methods.

4. Many supervisors find appraisals difficult to administer, and it's important to understand **how to deal with performance appraisal rater error problems**. Particularly with graphic rating scales, potential appraisal problems include unclear standards, halo effect, central tendency, leniency/strictness, recency effects, and bias. Guidelines for effective appraisals include knowing the problems (such as bias), using the right appraisal tool, keeping a diary of incidents, getting agreement on a plan, and being fair. Appraisals also need to be legally defensible, for instance, based on a job analysis and on defined rather than subjective standards. The appraisal may be administered by the immediate supervisor or by the employee's peers, a rating committee, via self-appraisal, by subordinates, or by 360-degree feedback. In any case, it's advisable to have at least the supervisor of the person completing the appraisal reviewing and approving it.
5. The supervisor needs to keep several points in mind during the **appraisal interview**. Preparation is essential, talk in terms of objective work, don't get personal, encourage the person to talk, and get agreement on how things will be improved. Minimize defensive reactions, for instance, by avoiding attacking the employee's defenses. Criticize objectively, in private, and constructively.
6. **Talent management** argues for focusing management's attention and resources on the company's mission-critical employees, those who are critical to the firm's strategic needs. They segment their employees based on how critical the employees are to the company's success.

Discussion Questions

✪ **9-5.** What is the purpose of a performance appraisal?

9-6. Answer the question, "Who should do the appraising?"

9-7. Discuss the pros and cons of four performance appraisal tools.

9-8. Explain how you would use the alternation ranking method, the paired comparison method, and the forced distribution method.

9-9. Explain in your own words how you would go about developing a behaviorally anchored rating scale.

✪ **9-10.** Explain the problems to be avoided in appraising performance.

9-11. Compare and contrast performance management and performance appraisal.

Individual and Group Activities

9-12. Working individually or in groups, develop a graphic rating scale for the following jobs: secretary, professor, bus driver.

9-13. Working individually or in groups, describe the advantages and disadvantages of using the forced distribution appraisal method for college professors.

9-14. Working individually or in groups, develop, over the period of a week, a set of critical incidents covering the classroom performance of one of your instructors.

9-15. Appendix A, PHR and SPHR Knowledge Base, at the end of this book (pages 580–588) lists the knowledge someone studying for the HRCI certification exam needs to have in each area of human resource management (such as in Strategic Management, Workforce Planning, and Human Resource Development). In groups of four to five students, do four things: (1) review Appendix A; (2) identify the material in this chapter that relates to the required knowledge Appendix A lists; (3) write four multiple-choice exam questions on this material that you believe would be suitable for inclusion in the HRCI exam; and (4) if time permits, have someone from your team post your team's questions in front of the class, so that students in all teams can answer the exam questions created by the other teams.

9-16. Just about every week, Donald Trump tells another "apprentice," "You're fired!" Review recent (or archived) episodes of Donald Trump's *Apprentice* show and answer this: What performance appraisal system did Mr. Trump use, and do you think it resulted in valid appraisals? What techniques discussed in this chapter did he seem to apply? How would you suggest he change his appraisal system to make it more effective?

Experiential Exercise

Grading the Professor

Purpose: The purpose of this exercise is to give you practice in developing and using a performance appraisal form.

Required Understanding: You are going to develop a performance appraisal form for an instructor and should therefore be thoroughly familiar with the discussion of performance appraisals in this chapter.

How to Set Up the Exercise/Instructions: Divide the class into groups of four or five students.

9-17. First, based on what you now know about performance appraisal, do you think Figure 9-1 is an effective scale for appraising instructors? Why? Why not?

9-18. Next, your group should develop its own tool for appraising the performance of an instructor. Decide which of the appraisal tools (graphic rating scales, alternation ranking, and so on) you are going to use, and then design the instrument itself.

9-19. Next, have a spokesperson from each group post his or her group's appraisal tool on the board. How similar are the tools? Do they all measure the same factors? Which factor appears most often? Which do you think is the most effective tool on the board?

9-20. The class should select the top 10 factors from all of the appraisal tools presented to create what the class perceives to be the most effective tool for appraising the performance of the instructor.

Video Case

Video Title: Performance Management (California Health Foundation)

SYNOPSIS

Kim Galvin, the human resources director of the California Health Foundation, explains the nature of the company's performance management system. The employee appraisal system is open-ended and includes just a few general categories, covering the employees' past performance with respect to their objectives set at the previous year's appraisal, and their future goals in the company.

Discussion Questions

9-21. Specifically what type of appraisal tool does the company seem to be using, based on what you read in this chapter? How would you modify it?

9-22. What do you think of the idea of getting anonymous third-party feedback on the employee? Why?

9-23. Why does Kim Galvin think that, besides the human resources director, only an employee and his or her manager should review the employee's performance review? What (if any) is the drawback of not having the supervisor's own manager review the appraisal? Would you require some type of review, and why?

9-24. Suppose, as Kim Galvin says, you have an employee who is very well liked but not meeting the job expectations. What would you do?

9-25. How does the California Health Foundation handle employees who may be candidates for future promotion?

Video Title: Appraising (Hautelook)

SYNOPSIS

Performance appraisal can be performed both by employees and by their supervisors. The online clothing retail company Hautelook conducts evaluations by both a formal and an informal process. Informal evaluations can happen at any time during the year, whereas formal evaluations are in January, with an informal mid-year review in July. Hautelook has an informal culture, where managers have an open-door policy and employees are encouraged to have regular discussions with managers as to their performance, as well as to self-evaluate their own performance continually. Hautelook rewards employees in various ways, such as by recognition, raises, bonuses, and promotions. Filling positions by internal promotion is strongly emphasized, and employees are encouraged to think about how they might advance their position in the company in the future.

Discussion Questions

9-26. What appraisal tool or tools would you recommend using at Hautelook, and why?

9-27. What do you think of how Hautelook handled its attendance problem? Was this an appraisal or a discipline problem? What difference would it make in how you handle the problem?

9-28. Which appraisal problems from this chapter would help to explain the "fairness and accuracy" issues that sometimes arise in the company's appraisals?

9-29. From what you've seen in this video, what exactly would you do to turn Hautelook's appraisal process into more of a performance management process?

Video Title: Appraising (The Weather Channel)

SYNOPSIS

Employee appraisals at The Weather Channel are recommended to be done on an ongoing, continual basis so that an employee always knows where he or she stands as far as what is expected and how well he or she is doing. This way, the employee can look forward to performance reviews instead of dreading them. The idea is that the appraisals will be a confirmation of the progress the employee has been making.

An employee is recognized not just for what he or she has achieved during the appraisal year, but for the ways in which his or her goals were accomplished. The employee can thereby have opportunities identified for building on his or her previous performance and better progress within the company.

Discussion Questions

9-30. From what Ms. Taylor says, does The Weather Channel really use a "performance management" process? Why do you conclude that?

9-31. How, specifically, does a firm's performance management process support its training process?

9-32. How would you reduce the anxiety and stress of an appraisal, based on what you read in this chapter?

9-33. How exactly would you appraise the employees' "competencies"? What tools would you use specifically, and why?

Application Case

Appraising the Secretaries at Sweetwater U

Rob Winchester, newly appointed vice president for administrative affairs at Sweetwater State University, faced a tough problem shortly after his university career began. Three weeks after he came on board in September, Sweetwater's president, Rob's boss, told Rob that one of his first tasks was to improve the appraisal system used to evaluate secretarial and clerical performance at Sweetwater U. The main difficulty was that the performance appraisal was traditionally tied directly to salary increases given at the end of the year. Therefore, most administrators were less than accurate when they used the graphic rating forms that were the basis of the clerical staff evaluation. In fact, what usually happened was that each administrator simply rated his or her clerk or secretary as "excellent." This cleared the way for them to receive a maximum pay raise every year.

But the current university budget simply did not include enough money to fund another "maximum" annual raise for every staffer. Furthermore, Sweetwater's president felt that the custom of providing invalid feedback to each secretary on his or her year's performance was not productive, so he had asked the new vice president to revise the system. In October, Rob sent a memo to all administrators, telling them that in the future no more than half the secretaries reporting to any particular administrator could be appraised as "excellent." This move, in effect, forced each supervisor to begin ranking his or her secretaries for quality of performance. The vice president's memo met widespread resistance immediately—from administrators, who were afraid that many of their secretaries would begin leaving for more lucrative jobs, and from secretaries, who felt that the new system was unfair and reduced each secretary's chance of receiving a maximum salary increase. A handful of secretaries had begun picketing outside the president's home on the university campus. The picketing, caustic remarks by disgruntled administrators, and rumors of an impending slowdown by the secretaries (there were about 250 on campus) made Rob Winchester wonder whether he had made the right decision by setting up forced ranking. He knew, however, that there were a few performance appraisal experts in the School of Business, so he decided to set up an appointment with them to discuss the matter.

He met with them the next morning. He explained the situation as he had found it: The current appraisal system had been set up when the university first opened 10 years earlier. A committee of secretaries had developed it. Under that system, Sweetwater's administrators filled out forms similar to the one shown in Table 9-2. This once-a-year appraisal (in March) had run into problems almost immediately, since it was apparent from the start that administrators varied widely in their interpretations of job standards, as well as in how conscientiously they filled out the forms and supervised their secretaries. Moreover, at the end of the first year it became obvious to everyone that each secretary's salary increase was tied directly to the March appraisal. For example, those rated "excellent" received the maximum increases, those rated "good" received smaller increases, and those given neither rating received only the standard across-the-board cost-of-living increase. Since universities in general—and Sweetwater, in particular—have paid secretaries somewhat lower salaries than those prevailing in private industry, some secretaries left in a huff that first year. From that time on, most administrators simply rated all secretaries excellent in order to reduce staff turnover, thus ensuring each a maximum increase. In the process, they also avoided the hard feelings aroused by the significant performance differences otherwise highlighted by administrators.

Two Sweetwater experts agreed to consider the problem, and in 2 weeks they came back to the vice president with the following recommendations. First, the form used to rate the secretaries was grossly insufficient. It was unclear what "excellent" or "quality of work" meant, for example. They recommended instead a form like that in Figure 9-4. In addition, they recommended that the vice president rescind his earlier memo and no longer attempt to force university administrators to arbitrarily rate at least half their secretaries as something less than excellent. The two consultants pointed out that this was unfair, since it was quite possible that any particular administrator might have staffers who were all or virtually all excellent—or conceivably, although less likely, all below standard. The experts said that the way to get all the administrators to take the appraisal process more seriously was to stop tying it to salary increases. In other words, they recommended that every administrator fill out a form as in Figure 9-4 for each secretary at least once a year and then use this form as the basis of a counseling session. Salary increases would have to be made on some basis other than the performance appraisal, so that administrators would no longer hesitate to fill out the rating forms honestly.

Rob thanked the two experts and went back to his office to ponder their recommendations. Some of the recommendations (such as substituting the new rating form for the old) seemed to make sense. Nevertheless, he still had serious doubts as to the efficacy of any graphic rating form, particularly compared with his original, preferred forced ranking approach. The experts' second recommendation—to stop tying the appraisals to automatic salary increases—made sense but raised at least one very practical problem: If salary increases were not to be based on performance appraisals, on what were they to be based? He began wondering whether the experts' recommendations weren't simply based on ivory tower theorizing.

Questions

9-34. Do you think that the experts' recommendations will be sufficient to get most of the administrators to fill out the rating forms properly? Why? Why not? What additional actions (if any) do you think will be necessary?

9-35. Do you think that Vice President Winchester would be better off dropping graphic rating forms, substituting instead one of the other techniques we discussed in this chapter, such as a ranking method? Why?

9-36. What performance appraisal system would you develop for the secretaries if you were Rob Winchester? Defend your answer.

Continuing Case

Carter Cleaning Company

The Performance Appraisal

After spending several weeks on the job, Jennifer was surprised to discover that her father had not formally evaluated any employee's performance for all the years that he had owned the business. Jack's position was that he had "a hundred higher-priority things to attend to," such as boosting sales and lowering costs, and, in any case, many employees didn't stick around long enough to be appraisable anyway. Furthermore, contended Jack, manual workers such as those doing the pressing and the cleaning did periodically get positive feedback in terms of praise from Jack for a job well done, or criticism, also from Jack, if things did not look right during one of his swings through the stores. Similarly, Jack was never shy about telling his managers about store problems so that they, too, got some feedback on where they stood.

This informal feedback notwithstanding, Jennifer believes that a more formal appraisal approach is required. She believes that there are criteria such as quality, quantity, attendance, and punctuality that should be evaluated periodically even if a worker is paid on piece rate. Furthermore, she feels quite strongly that the managers need to have a list of quality standards for matters such as store cleanliness, efficiency, safety, and adherence to budget on which they know they are to be formally evaluated.

Questions

9-37. Is Jennifer right about the need to evaluate the workers formally? The managers? Why or why not?

9-38. Develop a performance appraisal method for the workers and managers in each store.

Translating Strategy into HR Policies and Practices Case*,§

**The accompanying strategy map for this chapter is in the MyManagementLab, and the overall map on the inside back cover of this text outlines the relationships involved.*

IMPROVING PERFORMANCE at the Hotel Paris

The New Performance Management System

The Hotel Paris's competitive strategy is "To use superior guest service to differentiate the Hotel Paris properties, and to thereby increase the length of stay and return rate of guests, and thus boost revenues and profitability." HR manager Lisa Cruz must now formulate appraisal policies and activities that support this competitive strategy, by eliciting the required employee behaviors and competencies.

Lisa knew that the Hotel Paris's performance appraisal system was inadequate. When the founders opened their first hotel, they went to an office-supply store and purchased a pad of performance appraisal forms. The hotel chain uses these. Each form is a two-sided page. Supervisors indicate whether the employee's performance in terms of various standard traits including quantity of work, quality of work, and dependability was excellent, good, fair, or poor. Lisa knew that, among other flaws, this appraisal tool did not force either the employee or the supervisor to focus the appraisal on the extent to which the employee was helping the Hotel Paris to achieve its strategic goals. She wanted a system that focused the employee's attention on taking those actions that would contribute to helping the company achieve its goals, for instance, in terms of improved customer service.

Both Lisa and the firm's CFO were concerned by the current disconnect between (1) what the current appraisal process was focusing on and (2) what the company wanted to accomplish in terms of its strategic goals. They wanted the firm's new performance management system to help breathe life into the firm's strategic performance, by focusing employees' behavior specifically on the performances that would help the Hotel Paris achieve its strategic goals.

Lisa and her team created a performance management system that focused on both competencies and objectives. In designing the new system, their starting point was the job descriptions they had created for the hotel's employees. These descriptions each included required competencies. Consequently, using a form similar to Figure 9-5, the front-desk clerks' appraisals now focus on competencies such as "able to check a guest in or out in five minutes or less." Most service employees' appraisals include the competency, "able to exhibit patience and guest support of this even when busy with other activities." There were other required competencies. For example, the Hotel Paris wanted all service employees to show initiative in helping guests, to be customer oriented, and to be team players (in terms of sharing information and best practices). Each of these competencies derives from the Hotel's aim of becoming more service-oriented. Each employee now also receives one or more strategically relevant objectives for the coming year. (One, for a housecleaning crewmember, said, "Martha will have no more than three room cleaning infractions in the coming year," for instance.)

In addition to the goals and competencies-based appraisals, other Hotel Paris performance management forms laid out the development efforts that the employee would undertake in the coming year. Instructions also reminded the supervisors that, in addition to the annual and semiannual appraisals, they should continuously interact with and update their employees. The result was a comprehensive performance management system: The supervisor appraised the employee based on goals and competencies that were driven by the company's strategic needs. And, the actual appraisal resulted in new goals for the coming year, as well as in specific development plans that made sense in terms of the company's and the employees' needs and preferences.

Questions

9-39. Choose one job, such as front-desk clerk. Based on any information you have (including job descriptions you may have created in other chapters), write a list of duties, competencies, and performance standards for that chosen job.

9-40. Based on that, create a performance appraisal form for appraising that job.

MyManagementLab

Go to **mymanagementlab.com** for Auto-graded writing questions as well as the following Assisted-graded writing questions:

9-41. Discuss the pros and cons of using different potential raters to appraise a person's performance.

9-42. Answer the question, "How would you avoid defensiveness during an appraisal interview?"

9-43. MyManagementLab only—comprehensive writing assignment for this chapter.

Key Terms

performance appraisal, 260
performance appraisal process, 260
performance management, 261
graphic rating scale, 267
alternation ranking method, 268
paired comparison method, 268
forced distribution method, 268
critical incident method, 270
behaviorally anchored rating scale (BARS), 272
electronic performance monitoring (EPM), 276
unclear standards, 277
halo effect, 277
central tendency, 277
strictness/leniency, 278
bias, 278
appraisal interview, 280

Endnotes

1. D. Bradford Neary, "Creating a Company-Wide, Online, Performance Management System: A Case at TRW, Inc.," *Human Resource Management* 41, no. 4 (Winter 2002), pp. 491–498. See also http://trw.com/, accessed April 5, 2013.
2. Experts debate the pros and cons of tying appraisals to pay decisions. One side argues that doing so distorts the appraisals. A recent study concludes the opposite. Based on an analysis of surveys from over 24,000 employees in more than 6,000 workplaces in Canada, the researchers concluded: (1) linking the employees' pay to their performance appraisals contributed to improved pay satisfaction; (2) even when appraisals are *not* directly linked to pay, they apparently contributed to pay satisfaction, "probably through mechanisms related to perceived organizational justice"; and (3) whether or not the employees received performance pay, "individuals who do not receive performance appraisals are significantly less satisfied with their pay." Mary Jo Ducharme et al., "Exploring the Links Between Performance Appraisals and Pay Satisfaction," *Compensation and Benefits Review,* September/October 2005, pp. 46–52. See also Robert Morgan, "Making the Most of Performance Management Systems," *Compensation and Benefits Review,* September/October 2006, pp. 22–27.
3. Angelo Kinicki, Kathryn Jacobson, Suzanne Peterson, and Gregory Prussia, "Development and Validation of the Performance Management Behavior Questionnaire," *Personnel Psychology* 60, no. 6 (2013), p. 4.
4. Ibid., p. 45.
5. Peter Glendinning, "Performance Management: Pariah or Messiah," *Public Personnel Management* 31, no. 2 (Summer 2002), pp. 161–178. See also Herman Aguinis, *Performance Management* (Upper Saddle River, NJ: Prentice Hall 2007), p. 2.
6. These are quoted or paraphrased from Howard Risher, "Getting Serious About Performance Management," *Compensation and Benefits Review,* November/December 2005, p. 19.
7. Ibid., p. 45.
8. www.gdatp.com/about/, accessed April 5, 2013.
9. Vesa Suutari and Marja Tahbanainen, "The Antecedents of Performance Management Among Finnish Expatriates," *Journal of Human Resource Management* 13, no. 1 (February 2002), pp. 53–75.
10. www.ball.com/page.jsp?page=1, accessed June 1, 2011.
11. "Aligning People and Processes for Performance Improvement," *T1D* 65, no. 3 (March 2011), p. 80.
12. Ibid.
13. "Get SMART About Setting Goals," *Asia Africa Intelligence Wire,* May 22, 2005.
14. See, for example, E. A. Locke and G. P. Latham, "Building a Practically Useful Theory of Goal Setting and Task Motivation. A 35-Year Odyssey," *American Psychologist* 57, no. 9 (2002), pp. 705–717.
15. Vanessa Druskat and Steven Wolf, "Effects and Timing of Developmental Peer Appraisals in Self-Managing Work-Groups," *Journal of Applied Psychology* 84, no. 1 (1999), pp. 58–74. For a recent review, see Erich Dierdorff and Eric Surface, "Placing Peer Ratings in Context: Systematic Influences beyond Ratee Performance," *Personnel Psychology* 60, no. 1 (Spring 2007), pp. 93–126.
16. See, for example, Brian Hoffman and David Woehr, "Disentangling the Meaning of Multisource Performance Rating Source and Dimension Factors," *Personnel Psychology* 62 (2009), pp. 735–765.
17. As one study recently concluded, "Far from being a source of non-meaningful error variance, the discrepancies among ratings from multiple perspectives can in fact capture meaningful variance in multilevel managerial performance." In-Sue Oh and Christopher Berry, "The Five Factor Model of Personality and Managerial Performance: Validity Gains Through the Use of 360° Performance Ratings," *Journal of Applied Psychology* 94, no. 6 (2009), p. 1510.
18. Jeffrey Facteau and S. Bartholomew Craig, "Performance Appraisal Ratings from Different Rating Scores," *Journal of Applied Psychology* 86, no. 2 (2001), pp. 215–227.
19. See also Kevin Murphy et al., "Raters Who Pursue Different Goals Give Different Ratings," *Journal of Applied Psychology* 89, no. 1 (2004), pp. 158–164.
20. Such findings may be culturally related. One study compared self and supervisor ratings in "other-oriented" cultures (as in Asia, where values tend to emphasize teams). It found that self and supervisor ratings were related. M. Audrey Korsgaard et al., "The Effect of Other Orientation on Self: Supervisor Rating Agreement," *Journal of Organizational Behavior* 25, no. 7 (November 2004), pp. 873–891. See also Heike Heidemeier and Klaus Mosar, "Self Other Agreement in Job Performance Ratings: A Meta-Analytic Test of a Process Model," *Journal of Applied Psychology* 94, no. 2 (2009), pp. 353–370.
21. Forest Jourden and Chip Heath, "The Evaluation Gap in Performance Perceptions: Illusory Perceptions of Groups and Individuals," *Journal of Applied Psychology* 81, no. 4 (August 1996), pp. 369–379. See also Sheri Ostroff, "Understanding Self-Other Agreement: A Look at Rater and Ratee Characteristics, Context, and Outcomes," *Personnel Psychology* 57, no. 2 (Summer 2004), pp. 333–375.
22. Paul Atkins and Robert Wood, "Self Versus Others Ratings as Predictors of Assessment Center Ratings: Validation Evidence for 360 Degree Feedback Programs," *Personnel Psychology* 55, no. 4 (Winter 2002), pp. 871–904.

23. David Antonioni, "The Effects of Feedback Accountability on Upward Appraisal Ratings," *Personnel Psychology* 47 (1994), pp. 349–355. For an anonymous online appraisal method see, for example, http://work.com/perform, accessed October12, 2012.
24. Alan Walker and James Smither, "A Five-Year Study of Upward Feedback: What Managers Do with Their Results Matters," *Personnel Psychology* 52 (1999), pp. 393–423, and Austin F. R. Smith and Vincent J. Fortunato, "Factors Influencing Employee Intentions to Provide Honest Upward Feedback Ratings," *Journal of Business Psychology* 22 (2008), pp. 191–207.
25. The evidence from another study suggests also that "upward and peer 360-degree ratings may be biased by rater affect [whether the rater likes the ratee]; therefore, at this point, these ratings should be used for the sole purpose of providing ratees with developmental feedback." David Antonioni and Heejoon Park, "The Relationship Between Rater Affect and Three Sources of 360-Degree Feedback Ratings," *Journal of Management* 27, no. 4 (2001), pp. 479–495.
26. Thom Shanker, "Conduct at Issue As Subordinates Review Officers," *The New York Times*, April 14, 2013, pp A1, A4.
27. See, for example, "360-Degree Feedback on the Rise Survey Finds," *BNA Bulletin to Management,* January 23, 1997, p. 31; Leanne Atwater et al., "Multisource Feedback: Lessons Learned and Implications for Practice," *Human Resource Management* 46, no. 2 (Summer 2007), p. 285. However, a small number of employers are beginning to use 360-degree feedback for performance appraisals, rather than just development. See, for example, Tracy Maylett, "360° Feedback Revisited: The Transition from Development to Appraisal," *Compensation & Benefits Review,* September/October 2009, pp. 52–59.
28. James Smither et al., "Does Performance Improve Following Multi-Score Feedback? A Theoretical Model, Meta Analysis, and Review of Empirical Findings," *Personnel Psychology* 58 (2005), pp. 33–36.
29. Christine Hagan et al., "Predicting Assessment Center Performance with 360 Degree, Top-Down, and Customer-Based Competency Assessments," *Human Resource Management* 45, no. 3 (Fall 2006), pp. 357–390.
30. Jim Meade, "Visual 360: A Performance Appraisal System That's 'Fun,'" *HR Magazine,* July 1999, pp. 118–119. www.halogensoftware.com/landing/leading-solution/e360.php?source=msn&c=Search-e360&kw=360%20evaluations, accessed October 11, 2012.
31. www.sumtotalsystems.com/performance/index.html?e=001&sitenbr=156896193&keys=visual+360&submit.x=11&submit.y=11&submit=submit, accessed April 20, 2008.
32. Leena Rao, "Salesforce Debuts Rypple-Powered Work.com to Help Companies Manage Talent, Partners With Facebook," September 19th, 2012, http://techcrunch.com/2012/09/19/salesforce-debuts-rypple-powered-work-com-to-help-companies-manage-talent/, accessed April 5, 2013.
33. Ibid.
34. Rachel Silverman and Leslie Kwoh, "Performance Reviews Facebook Style," *The Wall Street Journal*, August 1, 2012, p. B6.
35. Jenny Hill, "Could Social Media Revolutionise the Performance Appraisal Process?" www.hrmagazine.co.uk/hro/features/1073216/could-social-media-revolutionise-performance-appraisal-process, accessed April 5, 2013.
36. www.saba.com/blogs/2011/03/24/what-is-social-performance-management/, accessed July 20, 2013.
37. Howard Risher, "Getting Serious About Performance Management," *Compensation & Benefits Review*, November/December 2005, pp. 18–26.
38. Leslie Kwoh, "Rank and Yank Retains Vocal Fans," *The Wall Street Journal*, January 31, 2012, p. B12.
39. Jena McGregor, "The Struggle to Measure Performance," *BusinessWeek*, January 9, 2006, p. 26.
40. Steve Bates, "Forced Ranking," *HR Magazine*, June 2003, pp. 63–68.
41. Steven Cullen et al., "Forced Distribution Rating Systems and the Improvement of Workforce Potential: A Baseline Simulation," *Personnel Psychology* 58 (2005), p. 1.
42. "Survey Says Problems with Forced Ranking Include Lower Morale and Costly Turnover," *BNA Bulletin to Management*, September 16, 2004, p. 297.
43. Steve Bates, "Forced Ranking: Why Grading Employees on a Scale Relative to Each Other Forces a Hard Look at Finding Keepers, Losers May Become Weepers," *HR Magazine* 48, no. 6 (June 2003), p. 62. See also D. J. Schleicher et al., "Rater Reactions to Forced Distribution Rating Systems," *Journal of Management* 35, no. 4 (August 2009), pp. 899–927.
44. Clinton Wingrove, "Developing an Effective Blend of Process and Technology in the New Era of Performance Management," *Compensation & Benefits Review*, January/February 2003, p. 26.
45. See, for example, Timothy Keaveny and Anthony McGann, "A Comparison of Behavioral Expectation Scales and Graphic Rating Scales," *Journal of Applied Psychology* 60 (1975), pp. 695–703. See also Neil Hauenstein et al., "BARS and Those Mysterious, Missing Middle Anchors," *Journal of Business & Psychology* 25, no. 4 (December 2010), pp. 663–672.
46. Based on Donald Schwab, Herbert Heneman III, and Thomas DeCotiis, "Behaviorally Anchored Scales: A Review of the Literature," *Personnel Psychology* 28 (1975), pp. 549–562. For a discussion, see also Uco Wiersma and Gary Latham, "The Practicality of Behavioral Observation Scales, Behavioral Expectation Scales, and Trait Scales," *Personnel Psychology* 30, no. 3 (Autumn 1986), pp. 619–689, and Neil Hauenstein et al., "BARS and Those Mysterious, Missing Middle Anchors," op cit.
47. Lawrence Fogli, Charles Hulin, and Milton Blood, "Development of First Level Behavioral Job Criteria," *Journal of Applied Psychology* 55 (1971), pp. 3–8. See also Joseph Maiorca, "How to Construct Behaviorally Anchored Rating Scales (BARS) for Employee Evaluations," *Supervision*, August 1997, pp. 15–19; and Neil Hauenstein et al., "BARS and Those Mysterious, Missing Middle Anchors," op cit.
48. Kevin R. Murphy and Joseph Constans, "Behavioral Anchors as a Source of Bias in Rating," *Journal of Applied Psychology* 72, no. 4 (November 1987), pp. 573–577; Aharon Tziner, "A Comparison of Three Methods of Performance Appraisal with Regard to Goal Properties, Goal Perception, and Ratee Satisfaction," *Group & Organization Management* 25, no. 2 (June 2000), pp. 175–191.
49. www.explorehr.org/articles/home/performance_appraisal_methods.html and http://jobsin.build-reciprocal-links.com/section-for-recruiters/performance-appraisal-management/2519110-performance-appraisal-method-mixed-standard-scales.html, accessed April 21, 2011.
50. However, one study concludes that Web-based performance management systems don't seem to improve performance management system effectiveness. Edward Lawler III et al., "What Makes Performance Appraisals Effective?" *Compensation & Benefits Review* 44, no. 4 (2012), p. 196.
51. www.employeeappraiser.com/index.php, accessed January 10, 2008.
52. Drew Robb, "Building a Better Workforce," *HR Magazine*, October 2004, pp. 87–94.
53. See, for example, Stoney Alder and Maureen Ambrose, "Towards Understanding Fairness Judgments Associated with Computer Performance Monitoring: An Integration of the Feedback, Justice, and Monitoring Research," *Human Resource Management Review* 15, no. 1 (March 2005), pp. 43–67. For a recent analysis of EPM, see Katherine J. S. Rogers, Michael J. Smith, and Pascale C. Sainfort, "Electronic Performance Monitoring, Job Design and Psychological Stress," Paper available at www.igi-global.com/chapter/electronic-performance-monitoring-job-design/45284, accessed October 12, 2012.
54. Ibid., and David T. Goomas, "Electronic Performance Self Monitoring and Engineered Labor Standards for 'Man-Up' Drivers in a Distribution Center," *Journal of Business and Psychology* 21 no. 4 (Summer 2007), pp. 541–558.
55. D. Bradford Neary, "Creating a Company-Wide, Online, Performance Management System: A Case Study at TRW Inc.," *Human Resource Management* 41, no. 4 (Winter 2002), p. 495.
56. Hsi-An Shih, Yun-Hwa Chiang, and In-Sook Kim, "Expatriate Performance Management from MNEs of Different National Origins," *International Journal of Manpower* 26, no. 2 (February 2005), pp. 157–175.
57. See, for example, Jonathan Segal, "Performance Management Blunders," *HR Magazine*, November 2010, pp. 75–77.
58. See, for example, Adrienne Fox, "Curing What Ails Performance Reviews," *HR Magazine*, January 2009, pp. 52–55.
59. Andrew Solomonson and Charles Lance, "Examination of the Relationship Between True Halo and Halo Effect in Performance Ratings," *Journal of Applied Psychology* 82, no. 5 (1997), pp. 665–674.
60. Manuel London, Edward Mone, and John C. Scott, "Performance Management and Assessment: Methods for Improved Rater Accuracy and Employee Goal Setting," *Human Resource Management* 43, no. 4 (Winter 2004), pp. 319–336.
61. Ted Turnasella, "Dagwood Bumstead, Will You Ever Get That Raise?" *Compensation & Benefits Review*, September–October 1995, pp. 25–27. See also Solomonson and Lance, "Examination of the Relationship Between True Halo and Halo Effect," pp. 665–674.
62. I. M. Jawahar and Charles Williams, "Where All the Children Are Above Average: The Performance Appraisal Purpose Effect," *Personnel Psychology* 50 (1997), p. 921.

63. Annette Simmons, "When Performance Reviews Fail," *Training & Development* 57, no. 9 (September 2003), pp. 47–53.
64. "Flawed Ranking System Revives Workers' Bias Claim," *BNA Bulletin to Management*, June 28, 2005, p. 206.
65. Karen Lyness and Madeline Heilman, "When Fit Is Fundamental: Performance Evaluations and Promotions of Upper-Level Female and Male Managers," *Journal of Applied Psychology* 91, no. 4 (2006), pp. 767–775.
66. Madeleine Heilman et al., "Penalties for Success: Reactions to Women Who Succeed at Male Gender Type Tasks," *Journal of Applied Psychology* 89, no. 3 (2004), pp. 416–427. Managers may not rate successful female managers negatively (for instance, in terms of likability and boss desirability) when they see the woman as supportive, caring, and sensitive to their needs. Madeleine Heilmann and Tyler Okimoto, "Why Are Women Penalized for Success at Male Tasks? The Implied Communality Deficit," *Journal of Applied Psychology* 92, no. 1 (2007), pp. 81–92.
67. Wingrove, "Developing an Effective Blend of Process and Technology," pp. 25–30.
68. Gary Greguras et al., "A Field Study of the Effects of Rating Purpose on the Quality of Multisource Ratings," *Personnel Psychology* 56 (2003), pp. 1–21.
69. Joanne Sammer, "Calibrating Consistency," *HR Magazine*, January 2008, pp. 73–74. As one study recently concludes, "Far from being a source of non-meaningful error variance, the discrepancies among ratings from multiple perspectives can in fact capture meaningful variance in multilevel managerial performance." In-Sue Oh and Christopher Berry, "The Five Factor Model of Personality and Managerial Performance: Validity Gains Through the Use of 360° Performance Ratings," *Journal of Applied Psychology* 94, no. 6 (2009), p. 1510.
70. Ibid., p. 45.
71. Angelo DeNisi and Lawrence Peters, "Organization of Information in Memory and the Performance Appraisal Process: Evidence from the Field," *Journal of Applied Psychology* 81, no. 6 (1996), pp. 717–737. See also A. Fox, "Curing What Ails Performance Reviews," *HR Magazine* 54, no. 1 (January 2009), pp. 52–56.
72. Juan Sanchez and Phillip De La Torre, "A Second Look at the Relationship Between Rating and Behavioral Accuracy in Performance Appraisal," *Journal of Applied Psychology* 81, no. 1 (1996), p. 7. See also "How to . . . Improve Appraisals," *People Management* 15, no. 3 (January 29, 2009), p. 57.
73. This is based on Howard Risher, "Getting Performance Management on Track," *Compensation & Benefits Review* 43, no. 5 (2011), pp. 273–281.
74. E. Pulakos and R. O'Leary, "Why Is Performance Management Broken? *Industrial and Organizational Psychology* 4 (2011), pp. 146–164.
75. Ibid.
76. M. Ronald Buckley et al., "Ethical Issues in Human Resources Systems," *Human Resource Management Review* 11 (2001), pp. 11, 29. See also Ann Pomeroy, "The Ethics Squeeze," *HR Magazine,* March 2006, pp. 48–55; "10 Tips for Avoiding Liability in Conducting Evaluations." *The Legal Intelligencer* May 12, 2010. Academic OneFile, accessed October 13, 2012.
77. G. R Weaver and L. K. Treviño, "The Role of Human Resources in Ethics/Compliance Management: A Fairness Perspective," *Human Resource Management Review*, 2001, pp. 113–134. Researchers recently conducted studies of 490 police officers undergoing standardized promotional exams. Among their conclusions was that "Organizations should strive to ensure that candidates perceived justice both in the content of personnel assessments and in the way they are treated during the assessment process." Julie McCarthy et al., "Progression Through the Ranks: Assessing Employee Reactions to High Stakes Employment Testing," *Personnel Psychology* 62 (2009), p. 826.
78. David Martin et al., "The Legal Ramifications of Performance Appraisal: The Growing Significance," *Public Personnel Management* 29, no. 3 (Fall 2000), pp. 381–383.
79. This is based on Kenneth L. Sovereign, *Personnel Law* (Upper Saddle River, NJ: Prentice Hall, 1994), pp. 113–114. See also "Avoiding HR Lawsuits," *Credit Union Executive*, November–December 1999, p. 6.
80. James Austin, Peter Villanova, and Hugh Hindman, "Legal Requirements and Technical Guidelines Involved in Implementing Performance Appraisal Systems," in Gerald Ferris and M. Ronald Buckley (eds.), *Human Resources Management*, 3rd ed. (Upper Saddle River, NJ: Prentice Hall, 1996), pp. 271–288.
81. Austin et al., op. cit., p. 282.
82. But beware: One problem with training raters to avoid rating errors is that, sometimes, what appears to be an error—such as leniency—isn't an error at all, as when all subordinates really are superior performers. Manuel London, Edward Mone, and John Scott, "Performance Management and Assessment: Methods for Improved Rater Accuracy and Employee Goal Setting," *Human Resource Management* 43, no. 4 (Winter 2004), pp. 319–336.
83. Wayne Cascio and H. John Bernardin, "Implications of Performance Appraisal Litigation for Personnel Decisions," *Personnel Psychology*, Summer 1981, pp. 211–212; Gerald Barrett and Mary Kernan, "Performance Appraisal and Terminations: A Review of Court Decisions Since *Brito v. Zia* with Implications for Personnel Practices," *Personnel Psychology* 40, no. 3 (Autumn 1987), pp. 489–504; Elaine Pulakos, *Performance Management*, SHRM Foundation, 2004.
84. Based on Robert Johnson, *The Appraisal Interview Guide* (New York: AMACOM, 1979) pp. 5–50; Judy Block, *Performance Appraisal on the Job: Making It Work for You* (New York: Executive Enterprises Publications, 1981) pp. 58–62.
85. This is based on Richard Luecke, *Coaching and Mentoring* (Boston: Harvard Business School Press, 2004), pp. 8–9.
86. Ibid., p. 9.
87. Jack Welch, broadcast interview at Fairfield University, C-Span, May 5, 2001.
88. Adapted or quoted from Gunter Stahl et al., "Global Talent Management: How Leading Multinationals Build and Sustain Their Talent Pipelines," Faculty and Research Working Paper, INSEAD, 2007.
89. Ibid.
90. Adapted or quoted from "Next Generation Talent Management," Hewitt.com, accessed June 2010.
91. Ibid.

10

Managing Employee Retention, Engagement, and Careers

Source: Bloomberg/Getty Images

MyManagementLab®

Improve Your Grade!

When you see this icon, visit **www.mymanagementlab.com** for activities that are applied, personalized, and offer immediate feedback.

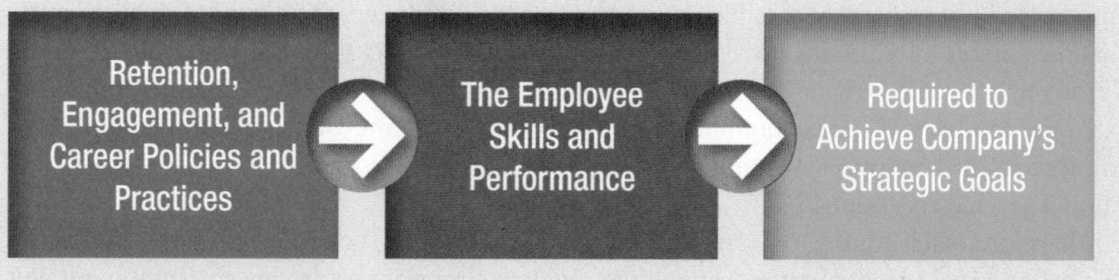

For a bird's eye view of how one company created a retention plan to improve its strategic performance, read the Hotel Paris case on pages 317–318 and answer the questions after reading the chapter.

WHERE ARE WE NOW . . .

Having invested time and resources in selecting, training, and appraising employees, the employer of course wants its employees to stay with the firm. Unfortunately, keeping good employees can be challenging. The main purpose of this chapter is to help you be more effective at improving employee retention, engagement, and careers. The main topics we'll address are managing employee turnover and retention, managing employee engagement, career management, employee life-cycle career management, and managing dismissals.

LEARNING OBJECTIVES

1 Describe a comprehensive approach to retaining employees.

2 Explain why employee engagement is important, and how to foster such engagement.

3 Discuss what employers and supervisors can do to support employees' career development needs.

4 List and briefly explain the main decisions employers should address in reaching promotion and other employee life-cycle career decisions.

5 Explain each of the main grounds for dismissal.

IBM recently celebrated 100 years since its creation.[1] Few companies stay in business that long. Most credit IBM's longevity to its ability to adapt to changing customer needs. Today, for instance, technology is changing so fast that IBM will soon need a workforce with dramatically different skills than its current employees have. In many companies, that would signal impending turnover and huge turnover costs, as new employees replace old. What should IBM do to build that new workforce, and to retain the employees it needs to move ahead? We'll see what they did.

Managing Employee Turnover and Retention

1 Describe a comprehensive approach to retaining employees.

Having invested time and resources hiring and training the employee, the manager wants to make sure that the person stays. Doing so requires understanding the forces driving employees to leave.

Turnover—the rate at which employees leave the firm—varies markedly among industries. For example, turnover in the accommodation and food services industry is very high, with over half the industry's employees voluntarily leaving each year. In contrast, voluntary turnover in educational services is about 12%.[2]

Furthermore, such figures only reflect employees who leave voluntarily, such as for better jobs. They don't include involuntary separations, such as for poor performance.[3] Combining voluntary and involuntary turnover produces some astounding statistics. For example, the turnover in many food service firms is around 100% per year. In other words, many restaurants need to replace just about all their employees every year! Turnover is expensive, as the HR as a Profit Center feature shows.

IMPROVING PERFORMANCE: HR as a Profit Center

Turnover and Performance

What is the link between turnover rates and organizational performance? Perhaps surprisingly, the issue is a matter of debate (although it would seem obvious that firing an incompetent employee would be a positive).[4] The problem is that what might be a positive in individual cases becomes a negative when the employer repeatedly loses employees. One study concludes that *all* turnover, voluntary or involuntary, is associated with reduced organizational performance. The researchers say, "Organizations must recognize that when turnover rates rise, their workforce and financial performances are at risk. They should search for strategies to mitigate and eliminate turnover, recognizing that lower turnover [of all types] is always better."[5]

One study analyzed the tangible and intangible costs of turnover in a call center with 31 agents and 4 supervisors.[6] Tangible costs associated with an agent's leaving included the costs of recruiting, screening, interviewing, and testing applicants, as well as the cost of wages while the new agent was oriented and trained. Intangible costs included the cost of lost productivity for the new agent (who is less productive at first), the cost of rework for the new agent's errors, and the supervisory cost for coaching the new agent. The researchers' calculations estimated the cost of an agent leaving at about $21,551. This call center averaged 18.6 vacancies per year (about a 60% turnover rate). Therefore, the researchers estimated the total annual cost of agent turnover at $400,853. Taking steps to cut this turnover rate in, say, half could save this firm about $200,000 per year. How to cut turnover? Another study focused on turnover intentions among government technology workers. It concluded that human resource managers could influence turnover through practices such as promotion opportunities, training and development, pay and reward satisfaction, and family-friendly policies.[7] The bottom line is that HR practices can have a big influence on employee turnover, and thereby on the company's profitability.

Discussion Question 10-1: Discuss three steps you would take to reduce the need to dismiss employees.

Reducing turnover requires identifying and managing the reasons for both voluntary and involuntary turnover.[8] We address managing voluntary turnover here, and managing involuntary turnover later in the chapter.

Managing Voluntary Turnover

Managing voluntary turnover requires identifying its causes and then addressing them.

The logical place to start is by measuring the number of employees (particularly top performers and high potentials) who leave the company.[9] SHRM recommends computing turnover as follows: "First calculate turnover for each month by dividing the number of [voluntary] separations during the month by the average number of employees during that month and multiplying by 100. Then calculate the annual turnover rate by adding the 12 months of turnover percentages together."[10]

However, identifying *why* employees voluntarily leave is not so easy. People who are dissatisfied with their jobs are more likely to leave, but the sources of dissatisfaction are many and varied. Figure 10-1 provides an example.[11] The consultants collected survey data from 262 U.S. organizations having a minimum of 1,000 employees. In this survey, the five top

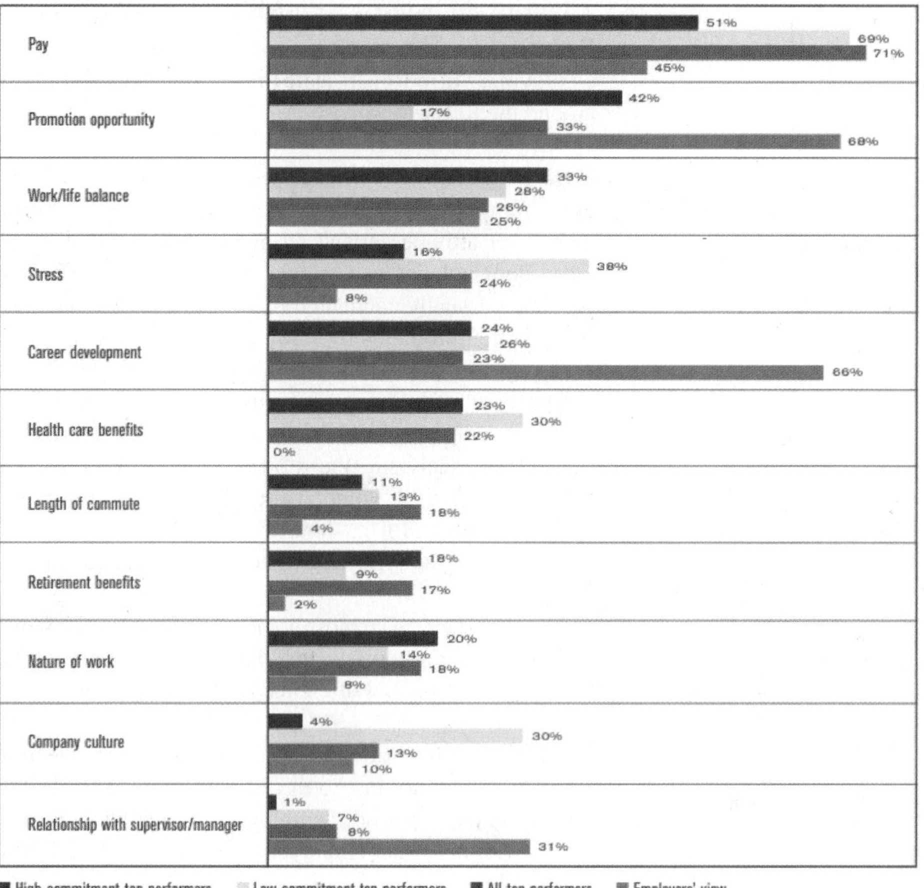

FIGURE 10-1 Reasons Top-Performing Employees Leave an Organization

Source: Figure from "Aligning Rewards with the Changing Employment Deal" from *Strategic Rewards Report*, 2006–2007. Copyright © 2006 by Watson Wyatt Worldwide. Reprinted with permission of Towers Watson. All rights reserved.

reasons high commitment/top-performing employees gave for leaving (ranked from high to low) were pay, promotional opportunities, work–life balance, career development, and health care benefits. (In contrast, *employers* ranked the top five reasons employees left as promotion, career development, pay, relationship with supervisor, and work–life balance). Other reasons employees voluntarily leave include unfairness, not having their voices heard, and a lack of recognition.[12] Sometimes simply asking, "All things considered, how satisfied are you with your job?" can be as effective as soliciting employees' attitudes toward various facets of the job (such as supervision and pay).[13] Practical considerations affect turnover. For example, high unemployment reduces voluntary turnover, and some locales have fewer job opportunities (and thus turnover) than do others.

Of course, losing low-performing employees isn't as problematic as losing high-performing ones. The restaurant chain Applebee's incentivizes their managers differentially, with higher incentives for reducing turnover among top-performing employees.[14]

Retention Strategies for Reducing Voluntary Turnover

In any case, given the variety of things prompting employees to leave voluntarily, what can one do to manage voluntary turnover? We'll list some tactics next, but there is no silver bullet. The manager should understand that retaining employees is a talent management issue, and that the best retention strategies are therefore multifunctional. For example, employees who aren't interested in their jobs, sense that they're not suited for their jobs, or who feel under-compensated are more likely to leave. Employers can only address such issues by instituting effective and coordinated talent management (recruitment, selection, training, appraisal, and compensation) practices. Put another way, turnovers (both voluntary and involuntary) often start with poor selection decisions, compounded by inadequate training, insensitive appraisals, and inequitable pay. Trying to formulate a "retention strategy" without considering all of one's HR practices is futile.

A Comprehensive Approach to Retaining Employees

Experts from the consulting company Development Dimensions International (DDI) and the employment firm Robert Half International suggest building comprehensive retention programs around the following steps.

IDENTIFY THE ISSUES Identifying the issues is an important first step. Effectively conducted exit interviews provide useful insights into turnover problem areas. Many employers routinely administer attitude surveys to monitor employees about matters such as supervision and pay. Open door policies and anonymous "hotlines" help management identify and remedy morale problems. Usually conducted by the employee's manager, the aim of a *stay interview* is to head off retention problems by finding out "how the employee is doing." Typical questions include "When you travel to work each day, what are you looking forward to?", and "How can I best support you?" Unlike anonymous group engagement surveys, stay interviews are one on one, and reportedly provide useful information for reducing turnover and improving engagement.[15] Sometimes, analyzing the situation leads to simple solutions. Walmart discovered it could significantly reduce voluntary turnover by providing aggressively *realistic previews* about the job's demands and work hours.[16] Then, having identified potential problems, the employer can take steps like the following to boost employee retention.

COMPENSATION The most obvious explanation for why employees quit is often also the correct one: low pay. Particularly for high performers and key employees, enhanced pay has recently been the retention tool of choice for many employers.[17]

SELECTION "Retention starts up front, with the selection and hiring of the right employees."[18] Selection refers not just to the worker but also to choosing the right supervisors. For example, FedEx conducts periodic employee attitude surveys. The supervisor then meets to review the results with his or her employees to address any leadership problems the surveys raise.

PROFESSIONAL GROWTH One expert says, "Professionals who feel their company cares about their development and progress are much more likely to stay."[19] Periodically discuss with employees their career preferences and prospects, and help them lay out career plans. Furthermore, "don't wait until performance reviews to remind top employees how valuable they are to your company."[20]

MEANINGFUL WORK AND OWNERSHIP OF GOALS People can't do their jobs if they don't know what to do or what their goals are. Therefore, retaining employees requires making it clear what your expectations are regarding their performance and what their responsibilities are.

PROMOTE WORK–LIFE BALANCE In one survey conducted by Robert Half and careerbuilder .com, workers identified "flexible work arrangements" and "telecommuting" as the two top benefits that would encourage them to choose one job or another.

USE HIGH-PERFORMANCE WORK SYSTEM PRACTICES High-performance HR practices reduce employee turnover. In one study, call center employers that made greater use of high involvement work practices (for instance, in terms of employee empowerment, problem-solving groups, and self-directed teams) had significantly lower rates of quits, dismissals, and total turnover. So did those that "invested" more in employees (for instance, in terms of promotion opportunities, high relative pay, pensions, and full-time jobs).[21]

USE DATA ANALYTICS Alliant Techsystems Inc. uses business analytics to sift through employee data in order to calculate, in terms of a "flight-risk model," the likelihood that any particular employee will leave.[22] Google uses analytics to crunch through employee data on metrics such as absence rates and morale to identify potential leavers. Nationwide Mutual Insurance Co. managers receive monthly "scorecards" with turnover data.

COUNTEROFFERS If a valued employee says he or she is leaving for another job, should you make a counteroffer? Many argue against doing so, calling it a "Band-Aid for a head wound."[23]

Employers who do allow counteroffers need a policy that specifies what people and positions are eligible for counteroffers, allowable compensation enhancements, and how to determine the offer.[24]

Social Media and HR

Social media tools have changed the engagement/retention process. For example, websites such as globoforce.com (www.globoforce.com/) facilitate social recognition by enabling each employee's colleagues to comment on and to recognize and reward the person's contributions. Vendors assert this leads to "dramatic improvements in employee engagement, retention and measurable adoption of corporate culture."[25]

Social media also enables an otherwise muted layoff to go viral. When UBS bank dismissed 10,000 employees recently, former employees quickly took to Twitter. Some claimed they discovered they were fired when they arrived to work and found their passes deactivated.[26]

WORKFORCE PLANNING Identifying and preparing for skills gaps can help reduce the turnover that unexpected skills gaps can trigger. The accompanying Improving Performance feature explains how.

IMPROVING PERFORMANCE: HR Practices Around the Globe

IBM Dodges an Employee Turnover Problem

Technological change means IBM will soon need a workforce with dramatically different skills than its workforce has now. IBM could merely assess its employees periodically and let go those who don't measure up. Instead, IBM put in place an "on-demand" staffing strategy. This aims to ensure that its current employees get the training and coaching they need to play roles in IBM's future.[27] To do this, IBM budgeted $700 million per year to identify needed skills, spot gaps for skills that are in short supply, and train and assess its executives, managers, and rank-and-file employees. IBM's on-demand staffing effort is supporting IBM's strategy, which depends on offering the fast-evolving technological services its customers need, at once, on demand. The program is also improving employee retention, by minimizing the layoffs, resignations, and turnover costs that might occur if employees' skills were inconsistent with IBM's new needs.

Discussion Question 10-2: Discuss how IBM could be saving money by spending $700 million per year on this program.

Talent Management and Employee Retention

Talent management best practice suggests focusing augmented retention efforts on the company's most important employees. For example, Accenture's 4 × 4 matrix (discussed in Chapter 9, page 284) plots employees by performance and by value to the organization. Accenture then ties pay, development, dismissal, and other personnel decisions to each employee's position in the matrix.

Job Withdrawal

Unfortunately, voluntary turnover is just one way that employees withdraw. Withdrawal in general means separating oneself from one's current situation—it's a means of escape for someone who is dissatisfied or fearful. At work, *job withdrawal* has been defined as "actions intended to place physical or psychological distance between employees and their work environments."[28]

Absences and voluntary turnover are two obvious types of job withdrawal. Others can be less obvious if no less corrosive. Some examples include "taking undeserved work breaks, spending time in idle conversation and neglecting aspects of the job one is obligated to perform."[29] Other employees stop "showing up" mentally ("psychological withdrawal"), perhaps daydreaming at their desks while productivity suffers.[30] The employee is there, but mentally absent. In fact, the *job withdrawal process* tends to be incremental, often evolving from daydreaming to absences to quitting: "[W]hen an employee perceives that temporary withdrawal will not resolve his/her problems, then the employee is apt to choose a more permanent form of withdrawal (i.e., turnover, assuming that alternative work opportunities are available)."[31]

DEALING WITH JOB WITHDRAWAL Studies confirm the high costs of job withdrawal behavior, so understanding its causes is important.[32] Many people have experienced the desire to withdraw—to "get away" from some situation—so it's perhaps not difficult to empathize with those who feel they must escape. Some think of it in terms of pain versus pleasure. People tend to move toward situations that make them feel good, and away from those that make them feel bad.[33] People are repelled by situations that produce unpleasant, uncomfortable emotions, and are attracted to those that produce pleasant, comfortable ones.[34]

The manager can therefore think of withdrawal-reducing strategies in terms of reducing the job's negative effects, and/or of raising its positive effects. Because potential negatives and positives are virtually limitless, addressing withdrawal problems again requires a comprehensive human resource management approach. Illustrative potential negatives include, for instance, boring jobs, poor supervision, low pay, bullying, lack of career prospects, and poor working conditions. Potential positives include job enrichment, supportive supervision, equitable pay/family-friendly benefits, disciplinary/appeals processes, career development opportunities, safe and healthy working conditions, and having high-morale colleagues.[35] Interviews, surveys, and observation can help identify issues to address.

With more employees taking their jobs home via smart phones and iPads, employee detachment (not withdrawal) isn't always a bad thing. Two researchers found detaching oneself from work improves family life. They advise working out a system for ensuring some quality family time. For example, the employee and his or her partner might "agree on certain rules such as keeping the weekend free of work, or switching off the mobile phone after dinner."[36]

Managing Employee Engagement

2 Explain why employee engagement is important, and how to foster such engagement.

Withdrawal and turnover often reflect diminished employee engagement. *Engagement* refers to being psychologically involved in, connected to, and committed to getting one's jobs done. Engaged employees "experience a high level of connectivity with their work tasks," and therefore work hard to accomplish their task-related goals.[37]

Employee Engagement and Performance

Employee engagement is important because both employee behavior (including turnover) and organizational performance reflect whether employees are "engaged." For example, based on Gallup surveys, business units with the highest levels of employee engagement have an 83% chance of performing above the company median, while those with the lowest employee engagement have only a 17% chance.[38] A survey by Watson Wyatt Worldwide concluded that companies with highly engaged employees have 26% higher revenue per employee.[39] The director of recruiting at the nonprofit Fair Trade USA believes boosting engagement helps to explain the firm's subsequent 10% drop in turnover. One report said the earnings growth rate per share of companies with highly engaged employees is almost 4 times that of others.[40] Starwood Hotels measure engagement and find it relates to important outcomes such as customer satisfaction and financial results. Other relevant outcome measures might include absenteeism, safety, sales, turnover, and profitability.[41] The Improving Performance feature presents another example.

Yet studies, including one by Towers Watson, conclude that only about 21% of the global workforce is engaged, while almost 40% is disengaged.[42] In one large survey, 57% of respondents were disengaged within 2 years after hiring.[43]

IMPROVING PERFORMANCE: HR Practices Around the Globe

Employee Engagement at Rio Tinto

Rio Tinto is a global mining corporation with operations in 43 countries. Seeking to better understand the links in its company between employee engagement and organizational performance, Rio Tinto partnered with the consulting firm Towers Watson to conduct an employee engagement survey and to analyze the results. They began by collecting extensive employee engagement survey data from Rio Tinto employees around the world. The Towers Watson consultants then used a statistical process they called *linkage analysis* to analyze how employee engagement measures related to dozens of performance and maintenance measures in Rio Tinto's plants and mines around the world. The analysis compared Rio Tinto's employee engagement scores with benchmark scores from other companies in Towers Watson's database. The engagement metrics focused on things like understanding and support for the vision of the company, support for company values, and "willingness to go the extra mile to ensure business success." Rio Tinto concluded that the employee engagement data related to performance outcomes across its many facilities around the world.[44] The bottom line is that by analyzing the links between (1) various employee engagement metrics and (2) measures of the company's performance, Rio Tinto was better able to understand how taking specific steps to improve employee engagement would translate into improved organizational performance.

Actions That Foster Engagement

The same Towers Watson findings illustrate how employers can improve employee engagement. Figure 10-2 summarizes these findings.[45] Important engagement-supporting actions include making sure employees (1) understand how their departments contribute to the company's success, (2) see how their own efforts contribute to achieving the company's goals, and (3) get a sense of accomplishment from working at the firm. Employers should also hold managers responsible for employee engagement. For example, the lubricant company WD-40 conducts periodic opinion surveys containing engagement measures, and has supervisors and managers meet with their employees to discuss how to improve the results.[46]

Employee participation also improves engagement. For example, Milliken & Co. uses employee participation safety teams at one plant. The safety process consists of 16 employees on the plant's safety steering committee, which in turn governs 8 employee safety subcommittees. The program appears to produce high levels of safety engagement among employees, and significant improvements in the plant accident rates.[47]

Perhaps the best way to improve engagement is to remember that engagement is a two-way street. Employees tend to be committed to and engaged in companies that are committed to them. Such companies demonstrate what psychologists call "perceived organizational support," wherein the employee perceives that the employer values his or her contribution and cares about his or her well being.[48] Researchers measure such organizational support with survey items such as, "The organization values my contribution to its well-being"; "The organization would understand a long absence due to my illness"; and "The organization really cares about my well being."[49] Companies such as software supplier SAS therefore go to extraordinary lengths to provide

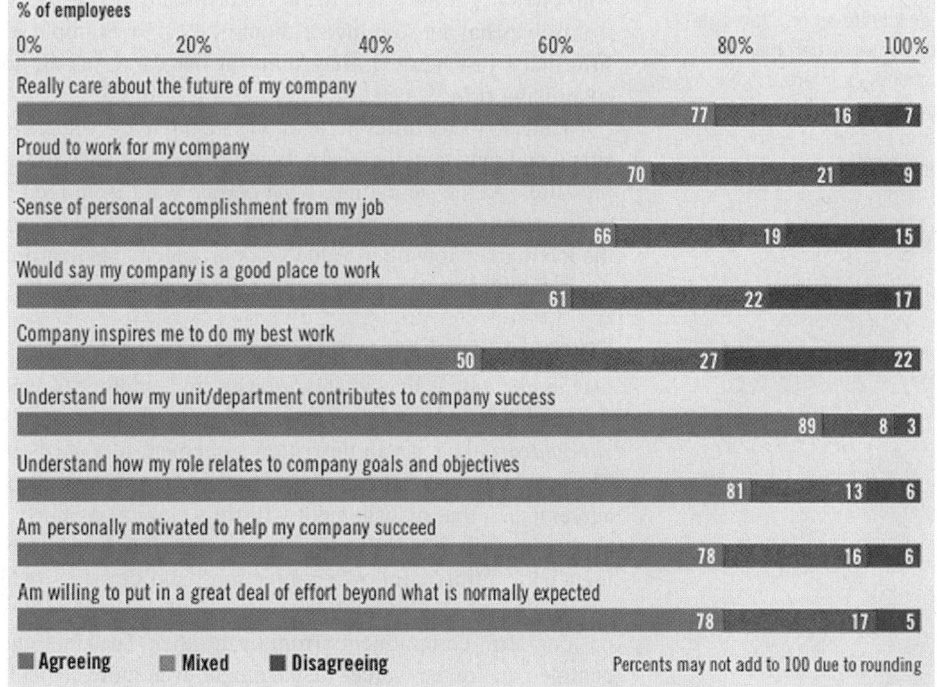

FIGURE 10-2 Employer Actions That Make Employees Feel More Engaged

Source: "Working Today: Understanding What Drives Employee Engagement," from *The 2003 Towers Perrin Talent Report*. Copyright © Towers Perrin. Reprinted with permission of Towers Watson.

the family-friendly benefits and support that their employees correctly perceive as meaning "the company cares about me." They also work hard to make sure their employees have happy and fulfilling careers. We turn to this next.

3 Discuss what employers and supervisors can do to support employees' career development needs.

Career Management

Employers recognize that career management plays an important role in engaging and retaining employees. For example, one survey found that employers planned to use both compensation and career development to retain and engage the right talent.[50]

Offering career support is generally a win-win situation. The employees, armed with better insights about their occupational strengths, should be better equipped to serve the company and less likely to leave.[51] The employer should benefit from higher engagement and lower turnover.

HR in Practice at the Hotel Paris If the Hotel Paris wanted satisfied guests, they had to have engaged employees who did their jobs as if they owned the company, even when the supervisor was nowhere in sight. But for the employees to be engaged, Lisa knew the Hotel Paris had to make it clear that the company was also committed to its employees. To see what they did, see the case on pages 317–318 of this chapter.

Careers Terminology

career
The occupational positions a person has had over many years.

career management
The process for enabling employees to better understand and develop their career skills and interests, and to use these skills and interests more effectively.

career development
The lifelong series of activities that contribute to a person's career exploration, establishment, success, and fulfillment.

career planning
The deliberate process through which someone becomes aware of personal skills, interests, knowledge, motivations, and other characteristics and establishes action plans to attain specific goals.

We may define **career** as the occupational positions a person holds over the years. **Career management** is a process for enabling employees to better understand and develop their career skills and interests and to use these skills and interests most effectively both within the company and after they leave the firm. **Career development** is the lifelong series of activities (such as workshops) that contribute to a person's career exploration, establishment, success, and fulfillment. **Career planning** is the deliberate process through which someone becomes aware of personal skills, interests, knowledge, motivations, and other characteristics; acquires information about opportunities and choices; identifies career-related goals; and establishes action plans to attain specific goals.

We'll see that the employee's manager and employer should play roles in guiding and developing the employee's career. However, the employee must always accept full responsibility for his or her own career development and career success.

Careers Today

People once viewed careers as a sort of upward stairway from job to job, more often than not with one or at most a few firms. Today, many people do still move up but many (or most) find themselves having to reinvent themselves. For example, the sales rep, laid off by a publishing firm that's just merged, may reinvent her career as an account executive at a media-oriented advertising firm.[52]

Careers today differ in other ways from a few years ago. With more women pursuing professional and managerial careers, families must balance the challenges associated with dual career pressures. At the same time, what people want from their careers is changing. Baby boomers—those retiring in the next few years—tended to be job- and employer-focused. People entering the job market now often value work arrangements that provide more opportunities for balanced work–family lives.

Psychological Contract

One implication is that what employers and employees expect from each other is changing. What the employer and employee expect of each other is part of what psychologists call a *psychological contract.* This is "an unwritten agreement that exists between employers and employees."[53] The psychological contract identifies each party's mutual expectations. For example, the unstated agreement is that management will treat employees fairly and provide satisfactory work conditions, hopefully in a long-term relationship. Employees are expected to respond "by demonstrating a good attitude, following directions, and showing loyalty to the organization."[54]

But with today's tumultuous labor markets, neither the employer nor the employee can count on long-term commitments from each other. That fact changes the terms of the psychological contract, and makes career management even more critical for the employee.

The Employee's Role in Career Management

The employer and manager have roles in guiding employees' careers, but no employee should abandon this task to others. Career planning means matching individual strengths and weaknesses with occupational opportunities and threats. The person wants to pursue occupations, jobs, and a career that capitalize on his or her interests, aptitudes, values, and skills. He or she also wants to choose occupations, jobs, and a career that make sense in terms of projected future demand for various types of occupations. The consequences of a bad choice are too severe to leave to others. There is a wealth of sources to turn to.

As one example of a career planning aid, career-counseling expert John Holland says that personality (including values, motives, and needs) is one career choice determinant. Thus, a person with a strong social orientation might be attracted to careers that entail interpersonal rather than intellectual or physical activities and to occupations such as social work. Holland found six basic personality types or orientations. Individuals can use his Self-Directed Search (SDS) test (available online at www.self-directed-search.com) to assess their occupational orientations and preferred occupations.

The SDS has an excellent reputation, but the career seeker needs to be wary of some of the other online career assessment sites. One study of 24 no-cost online career assessment websites concluded that they were easy to use, but suffered from insufficient validation and confidentiality. However, a number of online career assessment instruments such as Career Key (www.careerkey.org) do reportedly provide validated and useful information.[55] O*NET offers a free comprehensive online "My Next Move" occupations and career assessment system (www.onetcenter.org/mynextmove.html). You will find other examples at http://associationdatabase.com/aws/NCDA/pt/sp/resources, and in the following exercises, and a more in-depth discussion of career planning and job search tools in the appendix on pages 321–327.

EXERCISE 1 One useful exercise for identifying occupational skills is to head a page "The School or Occupational Tasks Most Enjoyed Doing." Then write a short essay describing the tasks. Provide as much detail as you can about your duties and responsibilities, and what you found enjoyable

As noted in the accompanying text, O*NET offers a free comprehensive online "My Next Move" occupation and career assessment system for building your future career (www.onetcenter.org/mynextmove.html).

Source: Screenshot of O*NET website, www.onetonline.org/.

about each task. (It's not necessarily the most enjoyable *job* you've had, but the most enjoyable *task* you've had to perform within your jobs.) Next, on other pages, do the same thing for two other tasks. Now scrutinize the three essays. Underline the skills that you mentioned the most often. For example, did you especially enjoy the hours you spent in the library doing research for your boss when you worked one summer as an intern?[56]

EXERCISE 2 Another exercise can prove enlightening. On a page, answer the question: "If you could have any kind of job, what would it be?" Invent your own job if need be, and don't worry about what you *can* do—just what you want to do.[57]

The Employer's Role in Career Management

The employer's career development roles depend on how long the employee has been with the firm. For example, *before hiring*, realistic job interviews can help prospective employees more accurately gauge if the job is a good fit.

Especially for recent college graduates, *the first job* can be crucial for building confidence and a more realistic picture of what he or she can and cannot do: Providing challenging first jobs and having an experienced mentor who can help the person learn the ropes are important. Some refer to this as preventing **reality shock**, a phenomenon that occurs when a new employee's high expectations and enthusiasm confront the reality of a boring, unchallenging job.

reality shock
Results of a period that may occur at the initial career entry when the new employee's high job expectations confront the reality of a boring or otherwise unattractive work situation.

After the person has been *on the job* for a while, periodic job rotation can help the person develop a more realistic picture of what he or she is (and is not) good at. Perhaps more importantly, *career-oriented appraisals*—in which the manager doesn't just appraise the employee but also gives him or her honest feedback on the realities of the person's career aspirations—are crucial.

Employer Career Management Options

Most employers do not provide a wide range of expensive career development options. However, career development systems needn't be complicated. Even just receiving performance feedback from supervisors, having individual development plans, and having access to training is enough for many employees. Beyond that, job postings, formal career-oriented performance appraisals, formal counseling and mentoring with managers, and individual succession planning for high-potential employees are valuable.[58] Yet only about a fourth of the respondents in one survey even had individual development plans.[59] Figure 10-3 illustrates a simple employee career planning form.[60]

CAREER MANAGEMENT PROGRAMS Other options are more comprehensive. Some employers create Web-based or offline libraries of career development materials, and offer career workshops and perhaps individual career coaches for career guidance. First USA Bank has its "Opportunity Knocks" program. In addition to career development training and follow-up support, the program includes career development centers at work sites that employees use on company time. The latter contain materials such as career assessment and planning tools.[61] WorkforceVision from Criterion, Inc., supplies online systems that help the employer analyze an employee's training needs. Clicking on the employee's name launches his or her work history, competencies, career path, and other information. For each competency (such as leadership), a bar chart graphically shows a "gap analysis" highlighting the person's strengths and weaknesses. The firm can then organize developmental activities around the person's needs.[62]

CAREER PLANNING WORKSHOPS AND CAREER COACHES A career planning workshop is "a planned learning event in which participants are expected to be actively involved, completing career planning exercises and inventories and participating in career skills practice sessions."[63] A typical workshop includes self-assessment exercises (skills, interests, values, and so on), an assessment of important occupational trends, and goal-setting and action-planning segments.

Career coaches generally help employees create 1- to 5-year plans showing where their careers with the firm may lead. Then, the employer and employee base the latter's development plans on what he or she will need to move up.[64] The coaches help individual employees identify their development needs and obtain the training, professional development, and networking opportunities that they require to satisfy those needs.[65]

FIGURE 10-3 Employee Career Development Plan

Source: "Employee Career Development Plan" Copyright © 2012 by BLR-Business & Legal Resources (www.HR.BLR.com). Reprinted with permission.

Employee Career Development Plan

Employee: ______________ **Position:** __________

Manager: ______________ **Department:** __________

Date of Appraisal: ______________

1. What is the next logical step up for this employee, and when do you think he or she will be ready for it?

Probable Next Job:	When Ready:			
	Now	6 Months	1 Year	2 Years
1.	☐	☐	☐	☐
2.	☐	☐	☐	☐
3.	☐	☐	☐	☐

2. What is the highest probable promotion within five years?

3. What does this employee need to prepare for promotion?

- Knowledge: ______________

  Action Plan: ______________

- Still Training: ______________

  Action Plan: ______________

- Management Training: ______________

  Action Plan: ______________

The Manager's Role

It's hard to overstate the impact that a supervisor can have on his or her employee's career development. With little or no additional effort than realistic performance reviews and candid career advice, a competent supervisor can help the employee get on and stay on the right career track. At the other extreme, an uncaring or unsupportive supervisor may look back on years of having inhibited his or her employees' career development.

The manager can do several things to support his or her subordinates' career development needs. When the subordinate first starts, make sure he or she develops the skills required to get off to a good start. Schedule regular performance appraisals; at these reviews, cover the extent to which the employee's current skills and performance are consistent with the person's career aspirations. Provide the employee with an informal development plan like that in Figure 10-4. Keep subordinates informed about how they can utilize the firm's current career-related benefits, and encourage them to do so.[66]

mentoring
Advising, counseling, and guiding.

Mentoring means having experienced senior people advising, counseling, and guiding employees' longer-term career development. An employee who agonizes over which career to pursue or how to navigate office politics may need mentoring.

Mentoring may be formal or informal. Informally, mid- and senior-level managers may voluntarily help less-experienced employees—for instance, by giving them career advice and

HR Management Checklists

A. Employee's Major Strengths
1. ______
2. ______
3. ______

B. Areas for Improvement/Development
1. ______
2. ______
3. ______

C. Development Plans: Areas for Development
1. ______
2. ______
3. ______
4. ______

Development Strategy:
______

D. Employee's Comments on This Review: ______

E. Reviewer's Comments: ______

Growth potential in present position and future growth potential for increased responsibilities: ______

Employer's Signature: ______ Date: ______
Reviewer's Signature: ______ Date: ______
Reviewer's Manager's Signature: ______ Date: ______

FIGURE 10-4 Sample Performance Review Development Plan

Source: "Sample Performance Review Development Plan" Copyright © 2012 by BLR-Business & Legal Resources (www.HR.BLR.com). Reprinted with permission.

helping them to navigate office politics. Many employers also have formal mentoring programs. For instance, the employer may pair protégés with potential mentors, and provide training to help mentor and protégé better understand their respective responsibilities. Either formal or informal, studies show that having a mentor give career-related guidance and act as a sounding board can significantly enhance one's career satisfaction and success.[67]

For the supervisor, mentoring is both valuable and dangerous. It is valuable insofar as you can influence, in a positive way, the careers and lives of your less experienced subordinates and colleagues. The danger is it can backfire. **Coaching** focuses on daily tasks that you can easily relearn, so coaching's downside is usually limited. *Mentoring* focuses on relatively hard-to-reverse longer-term issues, and often touches on the person's psychology (motives, and how one gets along with others, for instance). Because the supervisor is usually not a psychologist or trained career advisor, he or she must be extra cautious in the mentoring advice he or she gives.

coaching
Educating, instructing, and training subordinates.

THE EFFECTIVE MENTOR Research on what supervisors can do to be better mentors reveals few surprises. Effective mentors *set high standards*, are willing to *invest the time* and effort the mentoring relationship requires, and actively *steer protégés* into important projects, teams, and jobs.[68] Effective mentoring requires *trust*, and the level of trust reflects the mentor's *professional competence*, *consistency*, *ability to communicate*, and readiness to *share control*.[69]

However, studies suggest that traditional mentoring is less effective for women than it is for men. For example, in one survey of employees who had "active mentoring relationships" in one recent year, 72% of the men received one or more promotions in the ensuing 2 years, compared with 65% of the women. A CEO or other senior executive mentored 78% of the men, compared with 69% of the women.[70]

Figures like these are prompting employers to assign women to "mentor/sponsors" who have more organizational clout. For example, when Deutsche Bank discovered that several female managing directors had left the firm for better jobs at competitors, it began pairing them with mentor/sponsors from the bank's executive committee. The latter were in a position to advocate the women for promotion.

Improving Performance Through HRIS: Integrating Talent Management and Career and Succession Planning

In keeping with best talent management practice, the employer should endeavor to coordinate (integrate) its career planning efforts. As one example, the employee's career planning and development plans should reflect his or her performance appraisal ratings. Similarly, as explained in Chapter 5 (pages 128–129), the firm's succession plans should reflect its employees' career interests and appraisal ratings.

Integrated talent management software helps to achieve such ongoing integration. For example, the company that manages the trans-Alaska pipeline has an online portal that lets employees "see their full training history, development plans and upcoming deadlines, register for courses, or do career planning—usually without having to ask for help."[71] At the same time, "managers can get a quick picture of the training needs for a particular group, or see all the employees who have a specific qualification."[72] Halogen eSuccession enables the employer to "identify the skills and competencies required to support your 3–5 year strategic plans and cultivate these in your high—potential employees with career and development planning. . . ."[73] Cornerstone Succession integrates employee skills profiles, career management, and internal recruiting.[74] Sum-Total Succession Planning supports "a holistic, end-to-end talent management strategy" including:[75]

- ***360 feedback.*** Competency reviews by peers are inputs into succession gap analysis;
- ***Career development.*** As employees map out their career progress, plans can be established that address skill, knowledge, and other competencies gaps;
- ***Compensation management.*** Financial plans can be tied to future succession plans so that their financial impact can be modeled;
- ***Career progression.*** Historical information regarding past positions and career progress can be used to guide future succession decisions;
- ***Learning management.*** Learning paths and courses can be set for projected future positions;
- ***Performance management.*** Performance reviews can identify consistent high performers and top talent in the organization; and
- ***Recruiting & hiring.*** The Sum-Total system compares current job profiles with succession plans; external candidates can then be recruited as needed.[76]

4 List and briefly explain the main decisions employers should address in reaching promotion and other employee life-cycle career decisions.

Employee Life-Cycle Career Management

An employee's tenure with a firm tends to follow a life-cycle, from employment interview to first job, promotion, transfer, and perhaps retirement. We'll look here at the latter three.

Making Promotion Decisions

promotion
Advancement to a position of increased responsibility.

Promotions traditionally refer to advancements to positions of increased responsibility.

Most people crave promotions, which usually mean more pay, responsibility, and (often) job satisfaction. For employers, promotions can provide opportunities to reward exceptional performance, and to fill open positions with tested and loyal employees. Yet the promotion process isn't always a positive experience. Unfairness or secrecy can diminish the process. Furthermore, with more employers downsizing, some "promotions" take the form of more challenging but not necessarily higher-ranked or better-paid jobs. Several decisions, therefore, loom large in any firm's promotion process.

KNOW YOUR EMPLOYMENT LAW

Establish Clear Guidelines for Managing Promotions

In general, the employer's promotion processes must comply with all the same anti-discrimination laws as do procedures for recruiting and selecting employees or any other HR actions. For example, Title VII of the 1964 Civil Rights Act covers any "terms, conditions, or privileges of employment." Similarly, the Age Discrimination in Employment Act of 1967 made it unlawful to discriminate against older employees or applicants for employment in any manner, including promotion.

The employer should establish safeguards to ensure that the promotion decision doesn't prompt a discrimination claim, or a claim of retaliation, as it often does. For example, the Fifth U.S. Circuit Court of Appeals allowed a woman's claim of retaliation to proceed when she provided evidence that she was turned down for promotion because a supervisor she had previously accused of sexual harassment persuaded her current supervisor not to promote her.[77]

One way to defend against such claims is to make sure promotion procedures are clear and objective. For example, the Eighth U.S. Circuit Court of Appeals held that a company's failure to set objective guidelines and procedures for promoting current employees may suggest employment discrimination.[78] (In this case, the court found that the organization, a community college, did not consistently use the same procedures for hiring and promotions, did not clarify when and under what conditions vacant positions were announced, or whether or not there were application deadlines.) In another case, the employer turned down the 61-year-old employee for a promotion because of his interview performance; the person who interviewed him said he did not "get a real feeling of confidence" from the candidate.[79] In this case, "the court made it clear that while subjective reasons can justify adverse employment decisions, an employer must articulate any clear and reasonably specific factual bases upon which it based its decision." In other words, have objective evidence supporting your subjective assessment for promotion.

DECISION 1: IS SENIORITY OR COMPETENCE THE RULE? In setting promotion policies, one decision is whether to base promotion on seniority or competence, or some combination of the two.

Today's focus on performance favors competence. However, this depends on several things. Union agreements sometimes contain clauses that emphasize seniority. Civil service regulations that stress seniority rather than competence often govern promotions in many public-sector organizations.

DECISION 2: HOW SHOULD WE MEASURE COMPETENCE? If the firm opts for competence, it must define and measure competence. Defining and measuring *past* performance is relatively straightforward. But promotions should rest on procedures for predicting the candidate's future performance.

For better or worse, most employers use prior performance as a guide, and assume that (based on exemplary prior performance) the person will do well on the new job. Many others use tests or assessment centers, or tools such as the 9-Box Grid (Chapter 8, page 238), to evaluate promotable employees and identify those with executive potential.

For example, given the public safety issues involved, police departments and the military tend to be very systematic when evaluating candidates for promotion to command positions. For the police, traditional promotional reviews include a written knowledge test, an assessment center, credit for seniority, and a score based on recent performance appraisal ratings. Most include a personnel records review. This includes evaluation of job-related influences such as supervisory-related education and experience, ratings from multiple sources, and systematic evaluation of behavioral evidence.[80]

DECISION 3: IS THE PROCESS FORMAL OR INFORMAL? Many firms have informal promotion processes. They may or may not post open positions, and key managers may use their own unpublished promotion criteria. Here employees may (reasonably) conclude that factors like "who you know" are more important than performance, and that working hard to get ahead—at least in this firm—is futile.

Other employers set formal, published promotion policies and procedures. Employees receive a *formal promotion policy* describing the criteria by which the firm awards promotions. A *job posting policy* states the firm will post open positions and their requirements, and circulate these to all employees. As explained in Chapter 5 (Personnel Planning and Recruiting), many employers also maintain *employee qualification databanks* and use replacement charts and computerized employee information systems to assist in such planning.

DECISION 4: VERTICAL, HORIZONTAL, OR OTHER? Promotions aren't necessarily upwards. Thus some employees, such as engineers, may have little or no interest in promotion to managerial roles.

Several options are available. Some firms, such as the exploration division of British Petroleum (BP), create two parallel career paths, one for managers and another for "individual contributors" such as high-performing engineers. At BP, individual contributors can move up to nonsupervisory senior positions, such as "senior engineer." These jobs have most of the financial rewards attached to management-track positions at that level.

Another option is to move the person horizontally. For instance, a production employee may move to human resources to develop his or her skills and to test and challenge his or her aptitudes. In a sense, "promotions" are possible even when leaving the person in the same job. For example, you might enrich the job and provide training to enhance the opportunity for assuming more responsibility.

Practical Considerations

In any case, there are practical steps to take in formulating promotion policies.[81] Establish eligibility requirements, for instance, in terms of minimum tenure and performance ratings. Require the hiring manager to review the job description, and revise if necessary. Vigorously review all candidates' performance and history. Preferably hire only those who meet the job's requirements.

Diversity Counts: The Gender Gap

Women still don't reach the top of the career ladder in numbers proportionate to their numbers in U.S. industry. Women constitute more than 40% of the workforce, but hold less than 2% of top management positions. Blatant or subtle discrimination may account for much of this. In one study, promoted women had to receive higher performance ratings than promoted men to get promoted, "suggesting that women were held to stricter standards for promotion."[82] Women report greater barriers (such as being excluded from informal networks) than do men, and more difficulty getting developmental assignments. Women have to be more proactive than men to get such assignments.

Minority women seem particularly at risk. Women of color hold only a small percentage of professional and managerial private-sector positions. One survey asked minority women what they saw as the barriers to a successful career. The minority women reported that the main barriers to advancement included not having an influential mentor (47%), lack of informal networking with influential colleagues (40%), lack of company role models for members of the same racial or ethnic group (29%), and a lack of high-visibility assignments (28%).[83]

Unfortunately, many career development programs are inconsistent with the needs of minority and non-minority women. For example, many such programs underestimate the role played by family responsibilities in many women's (and men's) lives. Similarly, some programs assume that career paths are continuous; yet the need to stop working for a time to attend to family needs often punctuates the career paths of many people of color and women (and perhaps men).[84] Many refer to this totality of subtle and not-so-subtle barriers to women's career progress as the *glass ceiling*. Employers need to eliminate the barriers that impede women's career progress. Some specific steps include the following.

ELIMINATE INSTITUTIONAL BARRIERS Many practices (such as required late-night meetings) may seem gender neutral but in fact disproportionately affect women.

IMPROVE NETWORKING AND MENTORING To improve female employees' networking opportunities, Marriott International instituted a series of leadership conferences for women.

Speakers offered practical tips for career advancement, and shared their experiences. More important, the conferences provided informal opportunities—over lunch, for instance—for the Marriott women to meet and forge business relationships.

BREAK THE GLASS CEILING Eliminating glass ceiling barriers requires more than an order from the CEO, because the problem is usually systemic. As one expert puts it, "The roots of gender discrimination are built into a platform of work practices, cultural norms and images that appear unbiased. . . . People don't even notice them, let alone question them." These range from the late meetings mentioned earlier to golf course memberships.

ADOPT FLEXIBLE CAREER TRACKS Inflexible promotional ladders (such as "You must work 8 years of 50-hour weeks to apply for partner") can put women—who often have more responsibility for child-raising chores—at a disadvantage. In many large accounting firms, for instance, "more men successfully logged the dozen or so years normally needed to apply for a position as partner. But fewer women stuck around, so fewer applied for or earned these prized positions."[85] One solution is to institute career tracks (including reduced hours and more flexible year-round work schedules) that enable women to periodically reduce their time at work, but remain on a partner track. For example, when the accounting firm Deloitte & Touche noticed it was losing good female auditors, it instituted a new flexible/reduced work schedule. This enabled many working mothers who might otherwise have left to stay with the firm.[86]

Managing Transfers

transfer
Reassignments to similar positions in other parts of the firm.

A **transfer** is a move from one job to another, usually with no change in salary or grade. Employers may transfer a worker to vacate a position where he or she is no longer needed, to fill one where he or she is needed, or more generally to find a better fit for the employee within the firm. Many firms today boost productivity by consolidating positions. Transfers are a way to give displaced employees a chance for another assignment or, perhaps, some personal growth. Employees seek transfers for many reasons, including personal enrichment, more interesting jobs, greater convenience—better hours, location of work, and so on—or to jobs offering greater advancement possibilities.

Managing Retirements

Retirement planning is a significant long-term issue for employers. In the United States, the number of 25- to 34-year-olds is growing relatively slowly, and the number of 35- to 44-year-olds

iStockphoto/Thinkstock

Employers are transferring employees less often, partly because of family resistance.

is declining. So, with many employees in their 60s approaching retirement age, employers face a problem: "companies have been so focused on downsizing to contain costs that they largely neglected a looming threat to their competitiveness . . . a severe shortage of talented workers."[87]

Many have wisely chosen to fill their staffing gaps in part with current or soon-to-be retirees. Fortuitously, 78% of employees in one survey said they expect to continue working in some capacity after normal retirement age (64% said they want to do so part-time). Only about a third plan to continue work for financial reasons; about 43% just want to stay active.[88]

The bottom line is that "retirement planning" is no longer just about helping current employees slip into retirement.[89] It should also help the employer to retain, in some capacity, the skills and brain power of those who would normally retire and leave the firm.

WORKFORCE RETIREMENT PLANNING A reasonable first step is to conduct numerical analyses of pending retirements. This should include a demographic analysis (including a census of the company's employees), a determination of the average retirement age for the company's employees, and a review of how retirement is going to affect the employer's health care and pension benefits. The employer can then determine the extent of the "retirement problem," and take fact-based steps to address it.[90]

Employers seeking to attract and/or retain retirees should take several steps. The general idea is to institute human resource policies that encourage and support older workers. Not surprisingly, studies show that employees who are more committed and loyal to the employer are more likely to stay beyond their normal retirement age.[91] It helps to create a culture that honors experience. For example, the CVS pharmacy chain knows that traditional recruiting media might not attract older workers; CVS thus works through The National Council on Aging, city agencies, and community organizations to find new employees. They also welcome older workers: "I'm too young to retire. [CVS] is willing to hire older people. They don't look at your age but your experience," said one dedicated older worker.[92] Others modify selection procedures. For example, one British bank stopped using psychometric tests, replacing them with role-playing exercises to gauge how candidates deal with customers.

Other techniques employers use to keep older workers include offering them part-time positions, hiring them as consultants or temporary workers, offering them flexible work arrangements, encouraging them to work past traditional retirement age, providing training to upgrade skills, and instituting a phased retirement program. The latter lets senior workers ease into retirement with gradually reduced work schedules.[93]

Sometimes financial exigencies require encouraging employees to retire early. One experienced human resource manager says planning for such an early retirement program should include attention to the business rationale for the program, the benefits to be offered, the expected benefits and costs to the employer, the offer's impact on workforce morale and productivity, legal implications, and how to communicate the offer.[94]

5 Explain each of the main grounds for dismissal.

dismissal
Involuntary termination of an employee's employment with the firm.

Managing Dismissals

Not all employee separations are voluntary. Some career plans and appraisals end not in promotion or graceful retirement but in **dismissal**—involuntary termination of an employee's employment with the firm. Many dismissals are avoidable. For example, many dismissals flow from bad hiring decisions. Using assessment tests, background checks, drug testing, and clearly defined jobs can reduce such dismissals.[95]

Grounds for Dismissal

There are four bases for dismissal: unsatisfactory performance, misconduct, lack of qualifications for the job, and changed requirements of (or elimination of) the job.

Unsatisfactory performance refers to a persistent failure to perform assigned duties or to meet prescribed standards on the job.[96] Specific reasons include excessive absenteeism, tardiness, a persistent failure to meet normal job requirements, or an adverse attitude.

Misconduct is deliberate and willful violation of the employer's rules and may include stealing and rowdy behavior.

Lack of qualifications for the job is an employee's inability to do the assigned work, although he or she is diligent. Because this employee may be trying to do the job, it is reasonable to try to salvage him or her—perhaps by assigning the employee to another job.

Changed requirements of the job is an employee's incapability of doing the job after the nature of the job has changed. Similarly, you may have to dismiss an employee when his or her job is eliminated. Again, the employee may be industrious, so it is reasonable to retrain or transfer this person, if possible.

insubordination
Willful disregard or disobedience of the boss's authority or legitimate orders; criticizing the boss in public.

Insubordination, a form of misconduct, is sometimes the grounds for dismissal. The two basic categories of insubordination are unwillingness to carry out the manager's orders, and disrespectful behavior toward the manager. (This assumes that the orders were legitimate, and that the manager did not incite the reaction through his or her own extreme behavior). Examples of insubordination include:[97]

1. Direct disregard of the boss's authority
2. Direct disobedience of, or refusal to obey, the boss's orders, particularly in front of others
3. Deliberate defiance of clearly stated company policies, rules, regulations, and procedures
4. Public criticism of the boss
5. Blatant disregard of reasonable instructions
6. Contemptuous display of disrespect
7. Disregard for the chain of command
8. Participation in (or leadership of) an effort to undermine and remove the boss from power

FAIRNESS SAFEGUARDS Dismissals are never easy. However, the manager can take steps to make them fair.[98] First, allow the employee to explain why he (or she) did what he did. It could turn out, for instance, that the employee "disobeyed" the order because he or she did not understand it. Similarly, people who get *full explanations* of why and how termination decisions were made "were more likely to perceive their layoff as fair . . . and indicate that they did not wish to take the past employer to court."

Second, have a formal *multistep procedure* (including warning) and an appeal process.

Third, *the person who actually does the dismissing* is important. Employees in one study whose managers informed them of an impending layoff viewed the dismissal fairer than did those told by, say, a human resource manager. Some employers take a less diplomatic approach. About 10% of respondents in one survey said they've used e-mail to fire employees.[99] When JCPenney dismissed thousands of employees in 2012, many were fired in groups of a few dozen to over 100 in an auditorium.[100] Use the right person, and do the dismissal humanely.

Fourth, dismissed employees who feel they've been treated unfairly financially are more likely to sue. Many employers use severance pay to blunt a dismissal's sting.[101] Figure 10-5 summarizes typical severance policies.

KNOW YOUR EMPLOYMENT LAW

Termination at Will

terminate at will
In the absence of a contract, either the employer or the employee can terminate at will the employment relationship.

For more than 100 years, the prevailing rule in the United States has been that without an employment contract, either the employer or the employee can **terminate at will** the employment relationship. In other words, the employee could resign for any reason, at will, and the employer could similarly dismiss an employee for any reason, at will. Today, however, dismissed employees increasingly take their cases to court, and employers are finding that they no longer have a blanket right to fire.

Termination-at-Will Exceptions

Three main protections against wrongful discharge eroded the termination-at-will doctrine—*statutory exceptions, common law exceptions,* and *public policy exceptions.*

First, *statutory exceptions* include federal and state equal employment and workplace laws that prohibit certain dismissals. For example, Title VII of the Civil Rights Act of 1964 prohibits discharging employees based on race, color, religion, sex, or national origin.[102]

Second, numerous *common law exceptions* exist. Courts create these exceptions based on precedents. For example, courts have held that employee handbooks promising termination only "for just cause" may create an exception to the at-will rule.[103]

Finally, under the *public policy exception,* courts have held a discharge to be wrongful when it was against a well-established public policy. Thus, a public policy exception might prohibit an employer from firing an employee for refusing to break the law.

FIGURE 10-5 Median Weeks of Severance Pay by Job Level

Source: "Severance Pay: Current Trends and Practices," from Culpepper Compensation Surveys & Services website, July 2007. Copyright © 2012 Culpepper and Associates, Inc. All Rights Reserved. Reprinted with permission.

Severance Calculation Method	Median Weeks of Severance		
	Executives	**Managers**	**Professionals**
Fixed	26	6	4
Variable Amount by Employment Tenure			
1 year	4	2	2
3 years	7	5	5
5 years	10	7	7
10 years	20	12	10
15 years	26	16	15
Maximum	39	26	24

Avoiding Wrongful Discharge Suits

Wrongful discharge (or *termination*) occurs when an employee's dismissal does not comply with the law or with the contractual arrangement stated or implied by the employer. (In a *constructive discharge* claim, the plaintiff argues that he or she quit, but had no choice because the employer made the work situation so intolerable.[104])

Avoiding wrongful discharge suits requires several things.[105] *First*, have employment policies including grievance procedures that help show you treat employees fairly. Here employers can also use severance pay to blunt a dismissal's sting.[106] No termination is pleasant, but the first line of defense is to handle it justly.[107]

Second, review and refine all employment-related policies, procedures, and documents to limit challenges. Procedural steps include:[108]

- Have applicants sign the employment application. Make sure it contains a statement that "the employer can terminate at any time."
- Review your employee manual to delete statements that could undermine your defense in a wrongful discharge case. For example, delete "employees can be terminated only for just cause."
- Have written rules listing infractions that may require discipline and discharge.
- If a rule is broken, get the worker's side of the story in front of witnesses, and preferably get it signed. Then check out the story.
- Be sure that employees get a written appraisal at least annually. If an employee shows evidence of incompetence, give that person a warning. Provide an opportunity to improve.
- Keep careful confidential records of all actions such as employee appraisals, warnings or notices, and so on.
- Finally, ask the questions in Figure 10-6.

Is the employee covered by any type of written agreement, including a collective bargaining agreement? ____________

Is a defamation claim likely? ____________

Is there a possible discrimination allegation? ____________

Is there any workers' compensation involvement? ____________

Have reasonable rules and regulations been communicated and enforced? ____________

Has the employee been given an opportunity to explain any rule violations or to correct poor performance? ____________

Have all monies been paid within 24 hours after separation? ____________

Has the employee been advised of his or her rights under COBRA? ____________

FIGURE 10-6 Questions to Ask Before Making the Dismissal Final

Source: Personal Law, 4th Edition, by Kenneth L. Sovereign. Copyright © 1999 by Pearson Education, Inc. Reprinted by permission of Pearson Education, Inc., Upper Saddle River, New Jersey.

SECURITY MEASURES Common sense suggests both using a checklist to ensure that dismissed employees return all keys and company property, and (often) accompanying them out of the building. The employer should disable Internet-related passwords and accounts of former employees, plug holes that could allow an ex-employee to gain illegal online access, and have rules for return of company laptops and handhelds. "Measures range from simply disabling access and changing passwords to reconfiguring the network and changing IP addresses, remote access procedures, and telephone numbers," says one chief technology officer.[109]

Supervisor Liability

Courts sometimes hold managers personally liable for their supervisory actions.[110] For example, the Fair Labor Standards Act defines *employer* to include "any person acting directly or indirectly in the interest of an employer in relation to any employee." This can mean the individual supervisor.

STEPS TO TAKE There are several ways to avoid having personal liability become an issue.

- *Follow company policies and procedures.* An employee may initiate a claim against a supervisor who he or she alleges did not follow policies and procedures.
- Administer the dismissal in a manner that does not add to the employee's *emotional hardship* (as would having the employee publicly collect his or her belongings and leave the office).
- *Do not act in anger,* since doing so undermines the appearance of objectivity.
- Finally, *utilize the HR department* for advice regarding how to handle difficult dismissal situations.

The Exit Process and Termination Interview

termination interview
The interview in which an employee is informed of the fact that he or she has been dismissed.

Dismissing an employee is one of the most difficult tasks you can face at work.[111] The dismissed employee, even if warned many times in the past, may still react with disbelief or even violence. Guidelines for the **termination interview** itself are as follows:

1. ***Plan the interview carefully.*** According to experts at Hay Associates, this includes:
   - Make sure the employee keeps the appointment time.
   - Never inform an employee over the phone.
   - Allow 10 minutes as sufficient time for the interview.
   - Use a neutral site, not your own office.
   - Have employee agreements, the human resource file, and a release announcement prepared in advance.
   - Be available at a time after the interview in case questions or problems arise.
   - Have phone numbers ready for medical or security emergencies.
2. ***Get to the point.*** When the employee enters the office, give the person a moment to get comfortable and then inform him or her of your decision.
3. ***Describe the situation.*** Briefly, in three or four sentences, explain why the person is being let go. For instance, "Production in your area is down 4%, and we are continuing to have quality problems. We have talked about these problems several times in the past 3 months, and the solutions are not being followed through on. We have to make a change." Don't personalize the situation as in, "Your production is just not up to par." Emphasize the decision is irrevocable. Preserving the employee's dignity is crucial.[112]
4. ***Listen.*** Continue the interview until the person appears to be talking freely and reasonably calmly.
5. ***Review the severance package.*** Describe severance payments, benefits, access to office support people, and the way references will be handled. However, under no conditions make any promises of benefits beyond those already in the support package.
6. ***Identify the next step.*** The terminated employee may be disoriented and unsure what to do next. Explain where the employee should go next, upon leaving the interview.

outplacement counseling
A formal process by which a terminated person is trained and counseled in the techniques of self-appraisal and securing a new position.

OUTPLACEMENT COUNSELING With **outplacement counseling** the employer arranges for an outside firm to provide terminated employees with career planning and job search skills. *Outplacement firms* usually provide such outplacement services. Employees (usually managers or professionals) who are let go typically have office space and secretarial services they can use at local offices of such firms, plus the counseling services. The outplacement counseling is part of the terminated employee's support or severance package.

exit interviews
Interviews with employees who are leaving the firm, conducted for obtaining information about the job or related matters, to give the employer insight about the company.

EXIT INTERVIEW Many employers conduct **exit interviews** with employees leaving the firm. These are interviews, usually conducted by a human resource professional just prior to the employee leaving, that elicit information aimed at giving employers insights into their companies. Exit interview questions include: How were you recruited? Was the job presented correctly and honestly? What was your supervisor's management style like? How do the employees on the team get along?[113]

The assumption is that because the employee is leaving he or she will be candid, but this is debatable.[114] Researchers found that at the time of separation, 38% of those leaving blamed salary and benefits, and 4% blamed supervision. Followed up 18 months later, 24% blamed supervision and 12% blamed salary and benefits.

Yet these interviews can be useful. When Blue Cross of Northeastern Pennsylvania laid off employees, many said, in exit interviews, "This is not a stable place to work." The firm took steps to address that concern for those who stayed with Blue Cross.

THE EXIT PROCESS The exit interview is just one part of a rational exit process. The employer should follow a checklist. Ensure, for example, that the employee returns all keys and company equipment, that all computer and database password access is terminated, that proper communications are sent internally (for instance, to other employees if appropriate, and to payroll) and externally, that the employee leaves the premises in a timely fashion, and that if necessary precautions are followed to ensure security.

Layoffs and the Plant Closing Law

Nondisciplinary separations may be initiated by either employer or employee. For the *employer*, reduced sales or profits or the desire for more productivity may require layoffs. *Employees* (as we've seen) may leave for better jobs, to retire, or for other reasons. The Worker Adjustment and Retraining Notification Act (WARN Act, or the plant closing law) requires employers of 100 or more employees to give 60 days' notice before closing a facility or starting a layoff of 50 or more people.[115]

layoff
An employer sending employees home due to a lack of work; this is typically a temporary situation.

A **layoff**, in which the employer sends workers home for a time for lack of work, is usually not a permanent dismissal (although it may turn out to be). Rather, it is a temporary one, which the employer expects will be short term. However, some employers use the term *layoff* as a euphemism for discharge or termination. In the deep recession years of 2008 and 2009 combined, employers carried out a total of about 51,000 mass layoffs, idling over 5 million workers.[116]

THE LAYOFF PROCESS A study illustrates one firm's layoff process. Senior management first met to make strategic decisions about the size and timing of the layoffs. They also debated the relative importance of the skills the firm needed going forward. Supervisors then assessed their subordinates, rating their nonunion employees either A, B, or C (union employees were covered by a union agreement making layoffs dependant on seniority). The supervisors then informed each of their subordinates about his or her A, B, or C rating, and told each that those with C grades were most likely to be laid off.[117]

LAYOFF'S EFFECTS It's not surprising that layoffs often result in "deleterious psychological and physical health outcomes" for those losing their jobs as well as for survivors.[118]

But not just the "victims" and "survivors" suffer. In one study, researchers "found that the more managers were personally responsible for handing out WARN notices to employees . . . the more likely they were to report physical health problems, to seek treatment for these problems, and to complain of disturbed sleep."[119]

Given all this, many employers try to minimize layoffs and dismissals during downturns. Reducing everyone's work hours and mandating vacations are two options. Others reduce layoffs by offering financial bonuses for improved productivity.[120]

Ironically, when some employees most need employee assistance programs (such as counseling)—after they're laid off—they lose them. More firms are therefore extending these program benefits for a month or two to former employees. For example, Florida's Sarasota County extended employee assistance program benefits for two months after it laid off some employees.[121]

Adjusting to Downsizings and Mergers

downsizing
The process of reducing, usually dramatically, the number of people employed by a firm.

Downsizing means reducing, usually dramatically, the number of people employed by a firm. The basic idea is to cut costs and raise profitability. Downsizings (some call them "productivity transformation programs")[122] require careful consideration of several matters.

1. First is making sure *the right people* are let go; this requires having an effective appraisal system in place.
2. Second is *compliance with all applicable laws,* including WARN.
3. Third is executing the dismissals in a manner that is *just and fair*.
4. Fourth is *security,* for instance, retrieving keys and ensuring that those leaving don't take prohibited items with them.
5. Fifth is reducing the remaining *employees' uncertainty* and addressing their concerns. This typically involves a post-downsizing announcement and program, including meetings where senior managers field questions from the remaining employees.

Providing advanced notice regarding the layoff can help cushion the otherwise negative effects. So can interpersonal sensitivity (in terms of the manager's demeanor during layoffs).[123] Layoffs can be more challenging abroad due to special legal obligations, such as requirements for a year's notice in some countries.

Supportiveness and creativity is especially important in high-performance-work-system-type firms. These rely heavily on employee engagement and teamwork.[124] Here, turnover is especially disruptive, so it may be particularly important to avoid layoffs. Options here include: implement pay freezes or cuts; introduce a hiring freeze before reducing the workforce; provide candid communications about the need for the downsizing; give employees an opportunity to express their opinions about the downsizing; and be fair and compassionate in implementing the downsizing.[125]

Review

MyManagementLab Go to **mymanagementlab.com** to complete the problems marked with this icon. 

Chapter Section Summaries

1. Managing voluntary turnover requires identifying its causes and then addressing them. A comprehensive approach to **retaining employees** should be multifaceted, and include improved selection, a well-thought-out training and career development program, assistance in helping employees lay out potential career plans, providing employees with meaningful work and recognition and rewards, promoting work–life balance, acknowledging employees' achievements, and providing all this within a supportive company culture.
2. **Employee engagement** is important. Numerous employee outcomes including turnover and performance reflect the degree to which employees are engaged. For example, business units with the highest levels of employee engagement have an 83% chance of performing above the company median, while those with the lowest employee engagement have only a 17% chance. Engagement-supporting actions include making sure employees (1) understand how their departments contribute to the company's success, (2) see how their own efforts contribute to achieving the company's goals, and (3) get a sense of accomplishment from working at the firm.
3. Employees ultimately need to take responsibility for their own careers, but employers and managers should also understand what **career management methods** are available. These include establishing company-based

career centers, offering career planning workshops, providing employee development budgets, and offering online career development workshops and programs. Perhaps the simplest and most direct is to make the appraisal itself career-oriented, insofar as the appraisal feedback is a link to the employee's aspirations and plans. Supervisors can play a major role in their employee's career development. For example, make sure the employee gets the training he or she requires, and make sure appraisals are discussed in the context of the employee's career aspirations.

4. Employers need to address employee **lifecycle career management** issues. Most notably, promotions can provide opportunities to reward exceptional performance, and to fill open positions with tested and loyal employees. Several decisions loom large in any firm's promotion process: Is seniority or competence the rule? How should we measure competence? Is the process formal or informal? Vertical, horizontal, or other? Women and people of color still experience relatively less career progress in organizations, and bias and more subtle barriers are often the cause. In general, the employer's promotion processes must comply with all the same antidiscrimination laws as do procedures for recruiting and selecting employees or any other HR actions. Transfers and retirements are other important career lifecycle issues.
5. **Managing dismissals** is an important part of any supervisor's job. Among the reasons for dismissal are unsatisfactory performance, misconduct, lack of qualifications, changed job requirements, and insubordination. In dismissing one or more employees, however, remember that termination at will as a policy has been weakened by exceptions in many states. Furthermore, great care should be taken to avoid wrongful discharge suits.

Discussion Questions

✪ **10-3.** Why is it advisable for an employee retention effort to be comprehensive? To what extent does IBM's on-demand program fit that description, and why?

10-4. What is the employee's role in the career development process? The manager's role? The employer's role?

✪ **10-5.** What are the main decisions employers should address in reaching promotion decisions?

10-6. Discuss at least four procedural suggestions for managing dismissals effectively.

10-7. What would you as a supervisor do to avoid someone accusing you of wrongful dismissal?

Individual and Group Activities

CHAPTER 10

10-8. Many rightfully offer IBM as an example of an employer that works hard to improve employee retention and engagement. Browse through the employment pages of IBM.com's Web site (such as www-03.ibm.com/employment/build_your_career.html). In this chapter, we discussed actions employers can take to improve employee retention and engagement. From the information on IBM's Web pages, what is IBM doing to support retention and engagement?

10-9. In groups of four or five students, meet with one or two administrators and faculty members in your college or university and, based on this, write a 2-page paper on the topic "the faculty promotion process at our college." What do you think of the process? Based on our discussion in this chapter, could you make any suggestions for improving it?

10-10. Working individually or in groups, choose two occupations (such as management consultant, HR manager, or salesperson) and use sources such as O*NET to size up the future demand for this occupation in the next 10 years or so. Does this seem like a good occupation to pursue? Why or why not?

10-11. In groups of four or five students, interview a small business owner or an HR manager with the aim of writing a 2-page paper addressing the topic "steps our company is taking to reduce voluntary employee turnover." What is this employer's turnover rate now? How would you suggest it improve its turnover rate?

10-12. Appendix A, PHR and SPHR Knowledge Base, at the end of this book (pages 580–588) lists the knowledge someone studying for the HRCI certification exam needs to have in each area of human resource management (such as in Strategic Management, Workforce Planning, and Human Resource Development). In groups of four to five students, do four things: (1) review Appendix A; (2) identify the material in this chapter that relates to the required knowledge Appendix A lists; (3) write four multiple-choice exam questions on this material that you believe would be suitable for inclusion in the HRCI exam; and (4) if time permits, have someone from your team post your team's questions in front of the class, so that students in all teams can answer the exam questions created by the other teams.

10-13. Several years ago, a survey of college graduates in the United Kingdom found that although many hadn't found their first jobs, most were already planning "career breaks" and to keep up their hobbies and interests outside work. As one report of the findings put it, "the next generation of workers is determined not to wind up on the hamster wheel of long hours with no play."[126] Part of the problem seems to be that many already see their friends "putting in more than 48 hours a week" at work. Career experts reviewing the results concluded that many of these recent college grads "are not looking for high-pay, high-profile jobs anymore."[127] Instead, they seem to be looking to "compartmentalize" their lives. They want to keep the number of hours they spend at work down, so they can maintain their hobbies and outside interests. If you were mentoring one of these people at work, what three bits of career advice would you give him or her? Why? What (if anything) would you suggest their employers do to accommodate these graduates' stated career wishes?

10-14. *The Sporting News* (http://aol.sportingnews.com/ncaa-basketball/story/2009-07-29/sporting-news-50-greatest-coaches-all-time) ran a story listing what they called the 50 greatest basketball coaches. Look at this list, and pick out two of the names. Then research these people online to determine what behaviors they exhibited that seem to account for why they were great coaches. How do these behaviors compare with what this chapter had to say about effective mentoring and coaching?

Experiential Exercise

Where Am I Going . . . and Why?

Purpose: The purpose of this exercise is to provide you with experience in analyzing your career preferences.

Required Understanding: Students should be thoroughly familiar with the "Employee's Role in Career Management" section in this chapter, as well as using O*NET (which we discussed in Chapter 4).

How to Set Up the Exercise/Instructions: Using O*NET and the "Employee's Role in Career Management" section in this chapter, analyze your career-related inclinations (you can also take the Self-Directed Search for about $10 at www.self-directed-search.com). Based on this analysis, answer the following questions (if you wish, you may do this analysis in teams of three or four students).

10-15. What does your research suggest to you about what would be your preferable occupational options?

10-16. What are the prospects for these occupations?

10-17. Given these prospects and your own occupational inclinations, outline a brief, 1-page career plan for yourself, including current occupational inclinations, career goals, and an action plan listing four or five development steps you will need to take in order to get from where you are now career-wise to where you want to be, based on your career goals.

Video Case

Video Title: Employee Engagement (PTC)

SYNOPSIS

PTC is one of the world's largest software companies and employee engagement is one of its primary corporate goals. The company strives to appreciate and recognize employees by making sure that their jobs are meaningful and aligned with the company's corporate goals. PTC offers career development, for instance, in terms of management development, coaching, and team building. A corporate framework allows employees to see where they are in their current job and what they need to do to be in the job they aspire to, creating visible and viable career paths within the organization. In addition, employees receive ongoing feedback from the organization, so the employee is always kept in the information and decision-making loop.

Discussion Questions

10-18. Based on this video, what is PTC doing to manage employee engagement? What other suggestions would you make for further improving employee engagement?

10-19. To what extent do you think what PTC is doing will improve employee retention and turnover? Why? What else would you suggest they do? Why?

10-20. Do you think based on the video that PTC has an effective career planning program? Why? What (if anything) would you suggest they do to improve the program?

Video Title: Employee Separation (Gordon Law Group)

SYNOPSIS

At some point in your career, you may be separated from the company you work for, either by your choice or the company's choice. Employee separation is, in all simplicity, where an employer and employee separate their relationship. The Gordon Law Group is a law firm that represents employees in all aspects of employment, from the start to the end. This law group strives to help employees understand and negotiate the relationship between themselves and their companies; and if an employee is separated from his or her company, understanding what happens next.

Discussion Questions

10-21. How would you summarize employees' top concerns when they're separated, based on this video? Do you agree with the lawyer?

10-22. Summarize the impact of a termination on the employee.

10-23. What will the employee's lawyer look at in terms of building "leverage" to get the dismissed employee a better deal?

Application Case

Google Reacts

On the face of it, Google would seem to be the last company that one would expect to have an employee retention problem. Google usually shows up in "Best Employers to Work for" lists; it's famous for full benefits, from dry-cleaning to free Web-enabled transportation from San Francisco to great pensions; it offers great stock options; and as a fast-growing company, it usually has many job applicants. So when its employee turnover began creeping up a few years ago, Google's human resource team had to decide what to do. Part of the problem is that as attractive as Google is to work for, Silicon Valley is filled with attractive employers, from Apple to Facebook. One of Google's first steps was to boost compensation. It gave all 23,000 Google employees a 10% raise, plus a $1,000 tax-free holiday bonus.[128] But still, Google management knew that pay was just part of the solution. It had to take other steps.

Questions

10-24. Without doing any further research than what you learned in this chapter, what other steps would you suggest Google take to improve employee retention?

10-25. Was there any information in previous chapters of this book that would help to illustrate other steps Google took to improve retention?

10-26. Use other Internet sources, including Google.com, to finalize an answer to the question: What other steps should Google take to improve employee retention?

Continuing Case

Carter Cleaning Company

The Career Planning Program

Career planning has always been a pretty low-priority item for Carter Cleaning, since "just getting workers to come to work and then keeping them honest is enough of a problem," as Jack likes to say. Yet Jennifer thought it might not be a bad idea to give some thought to what a career planning program might involve for Carter. Many of their employees had been with them for years in dead-end jobs, and she frankly felt a little badly for them: "Perhaps we could help them gain a better perspective on what they want to do," she thought. And she definitely believed that career support would have an effect on improving Carter's employee retention.

Questions

10-27. What would be the advantages to Carter Cleaning of setting up a career planning program?

10-28. Who should participate in the program? All employees? Selected employees?

10-29. Outline and describe the career development program you would propose for the cleaners, pressers, counter people, and managers at the Carter Cleaning Centers.

Translating Strategy into HR Policies and Practices Case*,§

**The accompanying strategy map for this chapter is in the MyManagementLab, and the overall map on the inside back cover of this text outlines the relationships involved.*

IMPROVING PERFORMANCE at The Hotel Paris

The New Career Management System

The Hotel Paris's competitive strategy is "To use superior guest service to differentiate the Hotel Paris properties, and to thereby increase the length of stay and return rate of guests, and thus boost revenues and profitability." HR manager Lisa Cruz must now formulate functional policies and activities that support this competitive strategy, by eliciting the required employee behaviors and competencies.

Lisa Cruz knew that as a hospitality business, the Hotel Paris was uniquely dependent upon having engaged, high-morale employees. In a factory or small retail shop, the employer might be able to rely on direct supervision to make sure that the employees were doing their jobs. But in a hotel, just about every employee is "on the front line." There is usually no one there to supervise the limousine driver when he or she picks up a guest at the airport, or when the valet takes the guest's car, or the front-desk clerk signs the guest in, or the housekeeping clerk needs to handle a guest's special request. If the hotel wanted satisfied guests, they had to have engaged employees who did their jobs as if they owned the company, even when the supervisor was nowhere in sight. But for the employees to be engaged, Lisa knew the Hotel Paris had to make it clear that the company was also committed to its employees.

From her experience, she knew that one way to do this was to help her employees have successful and satisfying careers, and she was therefore concerned to find that the Hotel Paris had no career management process at all. Supervisors weren't trained to discuss employees' developmental needs or promotional options during the performance appraisal interviews. Promotional processes were informal. And the firm made no attempt to provide any career development services that might help its employees to develop a better understanding of what their career options were, or should be. Lisa was sure that engaged employees were key to improving the experiences of its guests, and that she couldn't boost employee engagement without doing a better job of attending to her employees' career needs. In two hotels she began encouraging supervisors to at least engage in career-oriented appraisals with their subordinates, on a pilot project basis.

For Lisa Cruz and the CFO, their preliminary research left little doubt about the advisability of instituting a new career management system at the Hotel Paris. Based on their pilot project, employees in those Hotel Paris hotels who had been working under the new career management directive were more engaged, received more complimentary letters from guests, and received higher performance appraisal ratings than did employees who did not have career plans. The CFO therefore gave the go-ahead to design and institute a new Hotel Paris career management program.

Lisa and her team knew that they already had most of the building blocks in place, thanks to the new performance management system they had instituted just a few weeks earlier. For example, the new performance management system already required that the supervisor

§Written by and copyright Gary Dessler, PhD.

appraise the employee based on goals and competencies that were driven by the company's strategic needs; and the appraisal itself produced new goals for the coming year and specific development plans for the employee. These development plans had to make sense in terms of both the company's and the employee's needs and preferences.

In addition to the new performance management elements already in place, Lisa and her team created an online "Hotel Paris Career Center." With links to a choice of career assessment tools such as the Self-Directed Search, www.self-directed-search.com, and wizard-based templates for developing one's own career plan, the site went far toward providing the Hotel Paris's employees with the career assistance that they required. Also on the site, a new "International Job Openings" link made it easier for Hotel Paris employees to identify positions for which they might be qualified. The results exceeded Lisa and the CFO's expectations. Virtually every employee produced a career plan within the first 6 months. The appraisal interviews often turned into animated, career-oriented development sessions, and soon the various measures of employee commitment and guest service were trending up.

Questions

10-30. "Many hotel jobs are inherently 'dead end'; for example, maids, laundry workers, and valets either have no great aspirations to move up, or are just using these jobs temporarily, for instance, to help out with household expenses." First, do you agree with this statement—why, or why not? Second, list three more specific career activities you would recommend Lisa implement for these employees.

10-31. Build on the company's new system by recommending two more specific career development activities the hotel should implement.

10-32. What other specific career development activities would you recommend in light of the fact that the Paris's hotels and employees are disbursed around the world?

MyManagementLab

Go to **mymanagementlab.com** for Auto-graded writing questions as well as the following Assisted-graded writing questions:

10-33. Explain why employee engagement is important, and how to foster such engagement. What exactly would you as a supervisor do to increase your employees' engagement?

10-34. List and discuss the four steps in effectively coaching an employee. How could (and would) a professional football coach apply these steps?

10-35. MyManagementLab only—comprehensive writing assignment for this chapter.

Key Terms

career, 300
career management, 300
career development, 300
career planning, 300
reality shock, 302
mentoring, 303
coaching, 304
promotion, 305
transfers, 308
dismissal, 309
insubordination, 310
terminate at will, 310
termination interview, 312
outplacement counseling, 312
exit interview, 313
layoff, 313
downsizing, 314

Endnotes

1. "IBM's Centenary: The Test of Time," *The Economist*, June 11, 2011, p. 20; "IBM Is Founded," www.ibm.com/ibm100/us/en/icons/founded/, accessed August 28, 2011.
2. See, for example, www.nobscot.com/survey/index.cfm, and www.bls.gov/jlt/, accessed April 27, 2011. For computing turnover see SHRM, "Executive Brief: Differences in Employee Turnover Across Key Industries," www.shrm.org, accessed August 30, 2012.
3. Jean Phillips and Stanley Gulley, *Strategic Staffing* (Upper Saddle River, NJ: Pearson Education, 2012).
4. Tae–Youn Park and Jason Shaw, "Turnover Rates and Organizational Performance: A Meta-analysis," *Journal of Applied Psychology* 98, no. 2 (2013), pp. 268–309.
5. Ibid., p. 283. See also Jolivette Wallace and Kristena Gaylor, "A Study of the Dysfunctional and Functional Aspects of Voluntary Employee Turnover," *SAM Advanced Management Journal* 77, no. 3 (Summer 2012), p. 27.
6. The following example is based on Barbara Hillmer, Steve Hillmer, and Gale McRoberts, "The Real Costs of Turnover: Lessons from a Call Center," *Human Resource Planning* 27, no. 3 (2004), pp. 34–41.
7. Kim Soonhee, "The Impact of Human Resource Management on State Government IT Employee Turnover Intentions," *Public Personnel Management* 41, no. 2 (Summer 2012), p. 257.
8. Tae–Youn Park and Jason Shaw, "Turnover Rates and Organizational Performance: A Meta-analysis," *Journal of Applied Psychology* 98, no. 2 (2013), pp. 268–309.
9. Adrienne Fox, "Drive Turnover Down," *HR Magazine*, July 2012, pp. 23–27.
10. SHRM, "Executive Brief: Differences in Employee Turnover Across Key Industries," www.shrm.org, accessed August 30, 2012.
11. www.worldatwork.org/waw/adimLink?id=17180, accessed April 27, 2011.
12. Phillips and Gulley, *Strategic Staffing*, p. 329.
13. Stephen Robbins and Timothy Judge, *Organizational Behavior* (Upper Saddle River, NJ: Pearson Education, 2011), p. 81.
14. Phillips and Gulley, *Strategic Staffing*, p. 328.
15. Katherine Tyler, "Who Will Stay and Who Will Go?" *HR Magazine*, December 2011, pp. 101–103.
16. See also David Ernest, David Allen, and Ronald Landis, "Mechanisms Linking Realistic Job Previews with Turnover: A Meta-analytic Path Analysis," *Personnel Psychology* 60, no. 4 (2011), pp. 865–897.

17. "Employers Using Cash to Retain Key Talent," *BNA Bulletin to Management*, June 26, 2012, p. 202.
18. Max Messmer, "Employee Retention: Why It Matters Now," *CPA Magazine*, June/July 2009, p. 28; and "The Employee Retention Challenge," Development Dimensions International, 2009.
19. Messmer, "Employee Retention."
20. Ibid. See also Eric Krell, "Five Ways to Manage High Turnover," *HR Magazine*, April 2012, pp. 63–65.
21. Rosemary Batt and Alexander Colvin, "An Employment Systems Approach to Turnover: Human Resources Practices, Quits, Dismissals, and Performance," *Academy of Management Journal* 54, no. 4 (2011), pp. 695–717.
22. Ed Frauenheim, "Numbers Game," *Workforce Management*, March 2011, pp. 20–21.
23. "Counteroffers: Smart Move to Keep a Star or Waste of Time?", *BNA Bulletin to Management*, November 6, 2012, p. 358.
24. Ibid.
25. www.globoforce.com/, accessed April 7, 2013.
26. "Shocked UBS Staff Take to Twitter," www.CNBC.com/ID/49617998/, accessed October 21, 2012.
27. Jessica Marquez, "IBM Cuts Costs and Reduces Layoffs as It Prepares Workers for an 'On Demand' World," *Workforce Management* 84, no. 5 (May 2005), pp. 84–85.
28. David Wilson, "Comparative Effects of Race/Ethnicity and Employee Engagement on Withdrawal Behavior," *Journal of Managerial Issues* 21, no. 2 (Summer 2009), pp. 165–166, 195–215.
29. Paul Eder and Robert Eisenberger, "Perceived Organizational Support: Reducing the Negative Influence of Coworker Withdrawal Behavior," *Journal of Management* 34, no. 1 (February 2008), pp. 55–68.
30. Wilson, "Comparative Effects of Race/Ethnicity and Employee Engagement."
31. Lisa Hope Pelled and Katherine R. Xin, "Down and Out: An Investigation of the Relationship Between Mood and Employee Withdrawal Behavior," *Journal of Management* 25, no. 6 (1999), pp. 875–895.
32. Ibid.
33. Pelled and Xin, "Down and Out."
34. Ibid.
35. See, for example, Margaret Shaffer and David Harrison, "Expatriates' Psychological Withdrawal from International Assignments: Work, Nonwork, and Family Influences," *Personnel Psychology* 51, no. 1 (Spring 1998), pp. 87–118; Karl Pajo, Alan Coetzer, and Nigel Guenole, "Formal Development Opportunities and Withdrawal Behaviors by Employees in Small and Medium-Sized Enterprises," *Journal of Small Business Management* 48, no. 3 (July 2010), pp. 281–301; and P. Eder et al., "Perceived Organizational Support: Reducing the Negative Influence of Coworker Withdrawal Behavior," *Journal of Management* 34 no. 1 (February 2008), pp. 55–68.
36. Verena Hahn and Christian Dormann, "The Role of Partners and Children for Employees' Psychological Detachment from Work and Well-Being," *Journal of Applied Psychology* 98, no. 1 (2013), pp. 26–36.
37. Michael Christian, Adela Garza, and Jerel Slaughter, "Work Engagement: A Quantitative Review and Test of Its Relations with Task and Contextual Performance," *Personnel Psychology* 60, no. 4 (2011), pp. 89–136.
38. Adrienne Fox, "Raising Engagement," *HR Magazine*, May 2010, pp. 35–40.
39. Except as noted, this is based on Kathryn Tyler, "Prepare for Impact," *HR Magazine* 56, no. 3 (March 2011), pp. 53–56.
40. Bob Kelleher, "Engaged Employees Equal High-Performing Organizations," *Financial Executive* 27, no. 3 (April 2011), p. 51.
41. Kathryn Tyler, "Prepare for Impact," *HR Magazine*, March 2011, pp. 53–56.
42. As another example, one recent study distinguished among physical engagement ("I work with intensity on my job, I exert my full effort to my job," and so on), emotional engagement ("I am enthusiastic in my job, I feel energetic at my job," and so on), and cognitive engagement ("at work, my mind is focused on my job," and "at work, I pay a lot of attention to my job"). Bruce Louis Rich et al., "Job Engagement: Antecedents and Effects on Job Performance," *Academy of Management Journal* 53, no. 3 (2010), pp. 617–635.
43. Tamara Lytle, "When the Honeymoon's Over," *HR Magazine*, August 2012, pp. 47–48.
44. "Providing a Rock Solid Link Between Employee Engagement and Business Performance: A Towers Watson and Rio Tinto Case Study," www.towerswatson.com/en-AU/Insights/IC-Types/Case-Studies/2011/Providing-a-Rock-Solid-Link-Between-Employee-Engagement-and-Business-Performance-A-Towers-Watson-a, accessed April 9, 2013.
45. Rich, "Job Engagement."
46. Michael Tucker, "Make Managers Responsible," *HR Magazine*, March 2012, pp. 75–78.
47. Carly Tebbetts and Robert Allen, "Milliken's Keys to Employee Engagement, Increased Workplace Safety and Productivity," *EHS Today*, January 2013, pp. 39–40.
48. http://eisenberger.psych.udel.edu/POS.html, accessed April 8, 2013.
49. Eisenberger, R., Huntington, R., Hutchison, S., & Sowa, D., "Perceived Organizational Support," *Journal of Applied Psychology* 71 (1986), p. 502.
50. "Organizations Focus on Employee Engagement to Attract and Retain Top Talent," www.Mercer.com, accessed July 24, 2010.
51. Barbara Greene and Liana Knudsen, "Competitive Employers Make Career Development Programs a Priority," *San Antonio Business Journal* 15, no. 26 (July 20, 2001), p. 27.
52. For example, see Phyllis Moen and Patricia Roehling, *The Career Mystique* (Boulder, CO: Rowman & Littlefield Publishers, 2005).
53. Robbins and Judge, *Organizational Behavior*, p. 285.
54. Ibid., p. 284.
55. Edward Levinson et al., "A Critical Evaluation of the Web-Based Version of the Career Key," *Career Development Quarterly* 50, no. 1 (September 1, 2002), pp. 26–36.
56. Richard Bolles, *What Color Is Your Parachute?* (Berkeley, CA: Ten Speed Press, 2003), pp. 5–6.
57. This example is based on Richard Bolles, *The Three Boxes of Life* (Berkeley, CA: Ten Speed Press, 1976). Richard Bolles updates his famous career book *What Color Is Your Parachute* annually. It contains this and many other career exercises. The 2013 edition is published by Ten Speed Press in Berkeley, California.
58. Yehuda Baruch, "Career Development in Organizations and Beyond: Balancing Traditional and Contemporary Viewpoints," *Human Resource Management Review* 16 (2006), p. 131.
59. Carla Joinson, "Employee, Sculpt Thyself with a Little Help," *HR Magazine*, May 2001, pp. 61–64.
60. Bright, "Career Development."
61. Patrick Kiger, "First USA Bank, Promotions and Job Satisfaction," *Workforce*, March 2001, pp. 54–56.
62. Jim Meade, "Boost Careers and Succession Planning," *HR Magazine*, October 2000, pp. 175–178. www.halogensoftware.com/products/halogen-eappraisal/development-planning/?source=msn&c=Search-eApp&kw=career%20planning%20tools, accessed October 14, 2012. Separately, About.com lists several free online career planning tools. See http://careerplanning.about.com/od/careertests/Free_Self_Assessment_Tools_Online.htm, accessed October 14, 2012.
63. Fred Otte and Peggy Hutcheson, *Helping Employees Manage Careers* (Upper Saddle River, NJ: Prentice Hall, 1992), p. 143.
64. David Foote, "Wanna Keep Your Staff Happy? Think Career," *Computerworld*, October 9, 2000, p. 38. For an example, the U.S. Homeland Security Department's TSA has a career coaching/planning program. See http://tsacareercoaching.tsa.dhs.gov/index.php/faq-tsa-career-plan/, accessed October 14, 2012.
65. Julekha Dash, "Coaching to Aid IT Careers, Retention," *Computerworld*, March 20, 2000, p. 52.
66. Bill Hayes, "Helping Workers with Career Goals Boosts Retention Efforts," *Boston Business Journal* 21, no. 11 (April 20, 2001), p. 38.
67. Michael Doody, "A Mentor Is a Key to Career Success," *Health-Care Financial Management* 57, no. 2 (February 2003), pp. 92–94.
68. Luecke, *Coaching and Mentoring*, pp. 100–101.
69. Ferda Erdem and Janset Özen Aytemur, "Mentoring—A Relationship Based on Trust: Qualitative Research," *Public Personnel Management* 37, no. 1 (Spring 2008), pp. 55–65.
70. Herminia Ibarra, Nancy Carter, and Christine Silva, "Why Men Still Get More Promotions Than Women," *Harvard Business Review*, September 2010, pp. 80–85.
71. Tim Harvey, "Enterprise Training System Is Trans Alaska Pipeline's Latest Safety Innovation," *Pipeline and Gas Journal* 229, no. 12 (December 2002), pp. 28–32.
72. Ibid.
73. www.halogensoftware.com/products/halogen-esuccession/, accessed August 27, 2012.
74. www.cornerstoneondemand.com/leadership-development-and-succession, accessed August 27, 2012.
75. Quoted from www.sumtotalsystems.com/products/career-succession-planning.html, accessed August 28, 2011.
76. Ibid.
77. *Gee v. Pincipi*, 5th Cir., number 01-50159, April 18, 2002, "Alleged Harasser's Comments Tainted Promotion Decision," www.shrm.org, accessed March 2, 2004.
78. Maria Danaher, "Unclean Promotion Procedures Smack of Discrimination," www.shrm.org, accessed March 2, 2004.

79. Elaine Herskowitz, "The Perils of Subjective Hiring and Promotion Criteria," www.shrm.org, accessed January 1, 2009.
80. George Thornton III and David Morris, "The Application of Assessment Center Technology to the Evaluation of Personnel Records," *Public Personnel Management* 30, no. 1 (Spring 2001), p. 55.
81. Pamela Babcock, quoting Terry Henley, SPHR, in "Promotions: Is There a 'New Normal'?" www.shrm.org/hrdisciplines/employeereltions/articles/Pages/PromotionsIsThereaNewNormal.aspx, accessed June 1, 2011.
82. Karen Lyness and Madeline Heilman, "When Fit Is Fundamental: Performance Evaluations and Promotions of Upper-Level Female and Male Managers," *Journal of Applied Psychology* 91, no. 4 (2006), pp. 777–785.
83. "Minority Women Surveyed on Career Growth Factors," *Community Banker* 9, no. 3 (March 2000), p. 44.
84. In Ellen Cook et al., "Career Development of Women of Color and White Women: Assumptions, Conceptualization, and Interventions from an Ecological Perspective," *Career Development Quarterly* 50, no. 4 (June 2002), pp. 291–306.
85. Kathleen Melymuka, "Glass Ceilings & Clear Solutions," *Computerworld*, May 29, 2000, p. 56.
86. Robin Shay, "Don't Get Caught in the Legal Wringer When Dealing with Difficult to Manage Employees," www.shrm.org http://moss07.shrm.org/Publications/hrmagazine/EditorialContent/Pages/0702toc.aspx, accessed July 28, 2009.
87. Ken Dychtwald et al., "It's Time to Retire Retirement," *Harvard Business Review*, March 2004, p. 49.
88. "Employees Plan to Work Past Retirement, But Not Necessarily for Financial Reasons," *BNA Bulletin to Management*, February 19, 2004, pp. 57–58. See also Mo Wang, "Profiling Retirees in the Retirement Transition and Adjustment Process: Examining the Longitudinal Change Patterns of Retirees' Psychological Well-Being," *Journal of Applied Psychology* 92, no. 2 (2007), pp. 455–474.
89. See, for example, Matt Bolch, "Bidding Adieu," *HR Magazine*, June 2006, pp. 123–127; and Claudia Deutsch, "A Longer Goodbye," *The New York Times*, April 20, 2008, pp. H1, H10.
90. Luis Fleites and Lou Valentino, "The Case for Phased Retirement," *Compensation & Benefits Review*, March/April 2007, pp. 42–46.
91. Andrew Luchak et al., "When Do Committed Employees Retire? The Effects of Organizational Commitment on Retirement Plans Under a Defined Benefit Pension Plan," *Human Resource Management* 47, no. 3 (Fall 2008), pp. 581–599.
92. Dychtwald et al., "It's Time to Retire Retirement," p. 52.
93. Eric Krell, "Ways to Phased Retirement," *HR Magazine*, October 2010, p. 90.
94. Eric Krell, "Make It Easier to Say Goodbye," *HR Magazine*, October 2012, p. 41.
95. Andrea Poe, "Make Foresight 20/20," *HR Magazine*, February 20, 2000, pp. 74–80. See also Nancy Hatch Woodward, "Smoother Separations," *HR Magazine*, June 2007, pp. 94–97.
96. Joseph Famularo, *Handbook of Modern Personnel Administration* (New York: McGraw Hill, 1982), pp. 65.3–65.5. See also Carolyn Hirschman, "Off Duty, Out of Work," *HR Magazine*, www.shrm.org/hrmagazine/articles/0203/0203hirschman.asp, accessed January 10, 2008.
97. Kenneth Sovereign, *Personnel Law* (Upper Saddle River, NJ: Prentice Hall, 1999), p. 148; "Disciplinary Issues: What constitutes Insubordination?," www.shrm.org/TemplatesTools/hrqa/Pages/CMS_020144.aspx , accessed September 11, 2013.
98. Wanberg et al., "Perceived Fairness of Layoffs"; Brian Klass and Gregory Dell'omo, "Managerial Use of Dismissal: Organizational Level Determinants," *Personnel Psychology* 50 (1997), pp. 927–953; Nancy Hatch Woodward, "Smoother Separations," *HR Magazine*, June 2007, pp. 94–97.
99. "E-Mail Used for Layoffs, Humiliation," *BNA Bulletin to Management*, October 2, 2007, p. 315.
100. Donna Mattioli et al., "Penney Wounded by Deep Staff Cuts," *The Wall Street Journal*, April 15, 2013.
101. "Fairness to Employees Can Stave Off Litigation."
102. Robert Lanza and Morton Warren, "United States: Employment at Will Prevails Despite Exceptions to the Rule," *Society for Human Resource Management Legal Report*, October/November 2005, pp. 1–8.
103. Ibid.
104. Paul Falcon, "Give Employees the (Gentle) Hook," *HR Magazine*, April 2001, pp. 121–128.
105. James Coil III and Charles Rice, "Three Steps to Creating Effective Employee Releases," *Employment Relations Today*, Spring 1994, pp. 91–94; Richard Bayer, "Termination with Dignity," *Business Horizons* 43, no. 5 (September 2000), pp. 4–10; Betty Sosnin, "Orderly Departures," *HR Magazine* 50, no. 11 (November 2005), pp. 74–78; "Severance Pay: Not Always the Norm," *HR Magazine*, May 2008, p. 28.
106. See, for example, Richard Hannah, "The Attraction of Severance," *Compensation & Benefits Review*, November/December 2008, pp. 37–44.
107. Jonathan Segal, "Severance Strategies," *HR Magazine*, July 2008, pp. 95–96.
108. James Coil III and Charles Rice, "Three Steps to Creating Effective Employee Releases," *Employment Relations Today*, Spring 1994, pp. 91–94; "Fairness to Employees Can Stave Off Litigation," *BNA Bulletin to Management*, November 27, 1999, p. 377; Richard Bayer, "Termination with Dignity," *Business Horizons* 43, no. 5 (September 2000), pp. 4–10; Betty Sosnin, "Orderly Departures," *HR Magazine* 50, no. 11 (November 2005), pp. 74–78; "Severance Pay: Not Always the Norm," *HR Magazine*, May 2008, p. 28.
109. Jaikumar Vijayan, "Downsizings Leave Firms Vulnerable to Digital Attacks," *Computerworld* 25 (2001), pp. 6–7.
110. Edward Isler et al., "Personal Liability and Employee Discipline," *Society for Human Resource Management Legal Report*, September/October 2000, pp. 1–4.
111. Based on Coil III and Rice, "Three Steps to Creating Effective Employee Releases." See also Martha Frase-Blunt, "Making Exit Interviews Work," *HR Magazine*, August 2004, pp. 9–11.
112. William J. Morin and Lyle York, *Outplacement Techniques* (New York: AMACOM, 1982), pp. 101–131; F. Leigh Branham, "How to Evaluate Executive Outplacement Services," *Personnel Journal* 62 (April 1983), pp. 323–326; Sylvia Milne, "The Termination Interview," *Canadian Manager*, Spring 1994, pp. 15–16; and Matthew S. Wood and Steven J. Karau, "Preserving Employee Dignity During the Termination Interview: An Empirical Examination," *Journal of Business Ethics* 86, no. 4 (2009), pp. 519–534.
113. Marlene Piturro, "Alternatives to Downsizing," *Management Review*, October 1999, pp. 37–42; "How Safe Is Your Job?" *Money*, December 1, 2001, p. 130.
114. Joseph Zarandona and Michael Camuso, "A Study of Exit Interviews: Does the Last Word Count," *Personnel* 62, no. 3 (March 1981), pp. 47–48. For another point of view, see "Firms Can Profit from Data Obtained from Exit Interviews," *Knight-Ridder/Tribune Business News*, February 13, 2001, Item 0104 4446.
115. See Rodney Sorensen and Stephen Robinson, "What Employers Can Do to Stay Out of Legal Trouble When Forced to Implement Layoffs," *Compensation & Benefits Review*, January/February 2009, pp. 25–32.
116. "Mass Layoffs at Lowest Level Since July 2008, BLS Says," *BNA Bulletin to Management*, January 12, 2010, p. 13.
117. Leon Grunberg, Sarah Moore, and Edward Greenberg, "Managers' Reactions to Implementing Layoffs: Relationship to Health Problems and Withdrawal Behaviors," *Human Resource Management* 45, no. 2 (Summer 2006), pp. 159–178.
118. Ibid.
119. Ibid.
120. "Adopting Laid-Off Alternatives Could Help Employers Survive, Even Thrive, Analysts Say," *BNA Bulletin to Management*, February 24, 2009, p. 57.
121. Joann Lublin, "Employers See Value in Helping Those Laid Off," *The Wall Street Journal*, September 24, 2007, p. B3.
122. "Calling a Layoff a Layoff," *Workforce Management*, April 21, 2008, p. 41.
123. "Communication Can Reduce Problems, Litigation After Layoffs, Attorneys Say," *BNA Bulletin to Management*, April 14, 2003, p. 129.
124. Roderick Iversen and Christopher Zatzick, "The Effects of Downsizing of Labor Productivity: The Value of Showing Consideration for Employees' Morale and Welfare and High Performance Work Systems," *Human Resource Management* 50, no. 1 (January/February 2011), pp. 29–44.
125. Ibid., p. 40. For a discussion of the Global feature's EU employment contractual issues, see Phillips Taft and Cliff Powell, "The European Pensions and Benefits Environment: A Complex Ecology," *Compensation and Benefits Review*, January/February 2005, pp. 37–50.
126. "New Trend in Career Hunt," *Europe Intelligence Wire*, February 10, 2004.
127. Ibid.
128. http://abclocal.go.com/kgo/story?section=news/business&id=7775524, accessed June 1, 2011.
129. John Holland, *Making Vocational Choices: A Theory of Careers* (Upper Saddle River, NJ: Prentice Hall, 1973).
130. Ibid., p. 5. Researchers and career specialists are working with the U.S. government's

O*NET to devise a methodology that will enable individuals to make better use of O*NET in identifying and choosing career paths. See, for example, Patrick Converse et al., "Matching Individuals to Occupations Using Abilities and the O*NET: Issues and an Application in Career Guidance," *Personnel Psychology* 57 (2004), pp. 451–47.

131. Quoted or paraphrased from www.onetcenter.org/mynextmove.html, accessed April 8, 2013.

132. This is based on Edgar Schein, *Career Dynamics* (Reading, MA; Addison Wesley, 1978), pp. 128–129; and Edgar Schein, "Career Anchors Revisited: Implications for Career Development in the 21st Century," *Academy of Management Executive* 10, no. 4 (1996), pp. 80–88.

133. Ibid., pp. 257–262. For a recent test of Schein's career anchor concept, see Yvon Martineau et al., "Multiple Career Anchors of Québec Engineers: Impact on Career Path and Success," *Relations Industrielles/Industrial Relations* 60, no. 3, Summer 2005, p. 45; pp. 455–482.

134. This example is based on Richard Bolles, *The Three Boxes of Life* (Berkely, CA: Ten Speed Press, 1976). See also Richard Bolles, *What Color Is Your Parachute?*

135. Deb Koen, "Revitalize Your Career," *Training and Development*, January 2003, pp. 59–60.

136. See John Wareham, "How to Make a Headhunter Call You," *Across-the-Board* 32, no. 1 (January 1995), pp. 49–50, and Deborah Wright Brown and Alison Konrad, "Job Seeking in a Turbulent Environment: Social Networks and the Importance of Cross-Industry Ties to an Industry Change," *Human Relations* 54, no. 8 (August 2001), p. 1018.

137. Based on Phyllis Korkke, "How to Say 'Look at Me!' to an Online Recruiter," *The New York Times*, January 20, 2013, p. 8; and Eilene Zimmerman, "Recruiting a Recruiter for Your Next Job," *The New York Times*, April 7, 2013, p. 10.

138. Sheryl Jean, "Say Goodbye to Paper, Hello to Social Resume," *The Miami Herald*, March 4, 2013, p. 19.

139. "Resume Banks Launched," *Financial Executives* 17, no. 6 (September 2001), p. 72; James Siegel, "The ACCA Launches Online Career Center," *A/C, Heating & Refrigeration News*, June 16, 2003, p. 5.

140. See, for example, "Job Search Tips" *The America's Intelligence Wire*, May 17, 2004; and "What to Do When Your Job Search Stalls," *BusinessWeek* online, March 16, 2004.

141. A classic but still one of the most useful job search guides available: Richard Payne, *How to Get a Better Job Quicker* (New York, Mentor, 1987), pp. 54–87.

142. Sara Needleman, "Posting a Job Profile Online? Keep It Polished," August 29, 2006, *The Wall Street Journal*, p. B7.

143. "Read This Before You Put a Resume Online," *Fortune*, May 24, 1999, pp. 290–291.

144. Richard Payne, *How to Get a Better Job Quicker* (New York, Mentor, 1987)

APPENDIX for Chapter 10

Managing Your Career and Finding a Job

The individual must be responsible for creating and managing his or her own career. And, in today's job marketplace, knowing how to find and get a job is crucial.

Making Career Choices

It is unfortunate but true that many people don't put much thought into their careers. Some choose majors based on class scheduling preferences, favorite professors, or unstated psychological motives. Others stumble into jobs because "that's all that was available." If there was ever anything that cried out for fact-based decisions, it is choosing your career. The first and essential step here is to learn as much as possible about your interests, aptitudes, and skills.

Identify Your Occupational Orientation Career-counseling expert John Holland says that personality (including values, motives, and needs) is one career choice determinant. For example, a person with a strong social orientation might be attracted to careers that entail interpersonal rather than intellectual or physical activities and to occupations such as social work. Based on research with his Vocational Preference Test (VPT), Holland found six basic personality types or orientations (see www.self-directed-search.com).[129]

1. **Realistic orientation.** These people are attracted to occupations that involve physical activities requiring skill, strength, and coordination. Examples include forestry, farming, and agriculture.
2. **Investigative orientation.** Investigative people are attracted to careers that involve cognitive activities (thinking, organizing, understanding) rather than affective activities (feeling, acting, or interpersonal and emotional tasks). Examples include biologist, chemist, and college professor.
3. **Social orientation.** These people are attracted to careers that involve interpersonal rather than intellectual or physical activities. Examples include clinical psychology, foreign service, and social work.
4. **Conventional orientation.** A conventional orientation favors careers that involve structured, rule-regulated activities, as well as careers in which it is expected that the employee subordinate his or her personal needs to those of the organization. Examples include accountants and bankers.
5. **Enterprising orientation.** Verbal activities aimed at influencing others characterize enterprising personalities. Examples include managers, lawyers, and public relations executives.
6. **Artistic orientation.** People here are attracted to careers that involve self-expression, artistic creation, expression of emotions, and individualistic activities. Examples include artists, advertising executives, and musicians.

Most people have more than one occupational orientation (they might be social, realistic, and investigative, for example), and Holland believes that the more similar or compatible these orientations are, the less internal conflict or indecision a person will face in making a career choice. To help illustrate this, Holland suggests placing each orientation in one corner of a hexagon, as in Figure 10A-1. As you can see, the model has

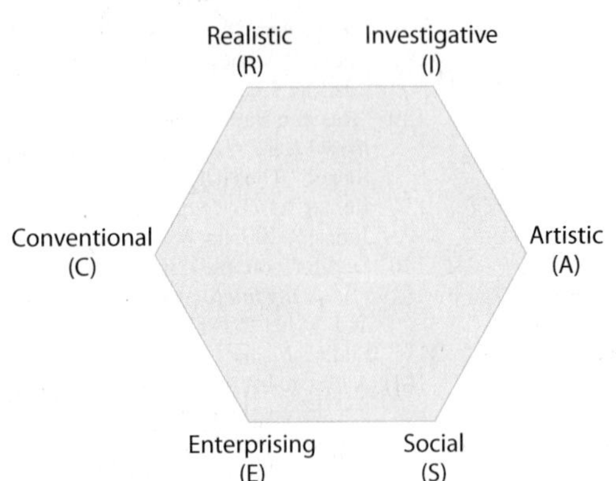

FIGURE 10A-1 Choosing an Occupational Orientation

six corners, each of which represents one personal orientation (for example, enterprising). According to Holland's research, the closer two orientations are in this figure, the more compatible they are. If your number-one and number-two orientations fall side by side, you will have an easier time choosing a career. However, if your orientations turn out to be opposite (such as realistic and social), you may experience more indecision in making a career choice because your interests are driving you toward very different types of careers. You can take Holland's SDS online for a small fee (see www.self-directed-search.com).

Identify Your Skills You may have a conventional orientation, but whether you have *the skills* to be an accountant, banker, or credit manager will largely determine which occupation you ultimately choose. Therefore, you have to identify your skills. We presented some exercises for this earlier in this chapter, on pages 301–302.

Aptitudes and Special Talents For career planning purposes, a person's aptitudes are usually measured with a test battery such as the general aptitude test battery (GATB), which most state one-stop career centers make available. This instrument measures various aptitudes including intelligence and mathematical ability. You can also use specialized tests, such as for mechanical comprehension. Holland's Self-Directed Search will also provide some insights into your aptitudes, as will O*NET.[130]

O*NET O*NET offers a free online "My Next Move" occupation and career assessment system (www.onetcenter.org/mynextmove.html). It includes *O*NET Interest Profiler*, a tool that offers customized career suggestions on over 900 different careers based on a person's interests and level of education and work experience. Users obtain important information including skills, tasks, salaries, and employment outlook for occupations.[131]

Identify Your Career Anchors Edgar Schein says that career planning is a continuing process of discovery—one in which a person slowly develops a clearer occupational self-concept in terms of what his or her talents, abilities, motives, needs, attitudes, and values are. Schein also says that as you learn more about yourself, it becomes apparent that you have a dominant *career anchor*, a concern or value that you will not give up if a [career] choice has to be made.

Career anchors, as their name implies, are the pivots around which a person's career swings; a person becomes conscious of them because of learning, through experience, about his or her talents and abilities, motives and needs, and attitudes and values. Based on his research at the Massachusetts Institute of Technology, Schein believes that career anchors are difficult to predict because they are evolutionary and a product of a process of discovery. Some people may never find out what their career anchors are until they have to make a major choice—such as whether to take the promotion to the headquarters staff or strike out on their own by starting a business. It is at this point that all the person's past work experiences, interests, aptitudes, and orientations converge into a meaningful pattern that helps show what (career anchor) is the most important factor in driving the person's career choices. Based on his study of MIT graduates, Schein identified five career anchors.[132]

Technical/Functional Competence People who had a strong technical/functional career anchor tended to avoid decisions that would drive them toward general management. Instead, they made decisions that would enable them to remain and grow in their chosen technical or functional fields.

Managerial Competence Other people showed a strong motivation to become managers and their career experience enabled them to believe they had the skills and values required. A management position of high responsibility is their ultimate goal. When pressed to explain why they believed they had the skills necessary to gain such positions, many in Schein's research sample answered that they were qualified because of what they saw as their competencies in a combination of three areas: (1) *analytical competence* (ability to identify, analyze, and solve problems under conditions of incomplete information and uncertainty); (2) *interpersonal competence* (ability to influence, supervise, lead, manipulate, and control people at all levels); and (3) *emotional competence* (the capacity to be stimulated by emotional and interpersonal crises rather than exhausted or debilitated by them, and the capacity to bear high levels of responsibility without becoming paralyzed).

Creativity Some of the graduates had become successful entrepreneurs. To Schein these people seemed to have a need "to build or create something that was entirely their own product—a product or process that bears their name, a company of their own, or a personal fortune that reflects their accomplishments." For example, one graduate had become a successful purchaser, restorer, and renter of townhouses in a large city; another had built a successful consulting firm.

Autonomy and Independence Some seemed driven by the need to be on their own, free of the dependence that can arise when a person elects to work in a large organization where promotions, transfers, and salary decisions make them subordinate to others. Many of these graduates also had a strong technical/functional orientation. Instead of pursuing this orientation in an organization, they had decided to become consultants, working either alone or as part of a relatively small firm. Others had become professors of business, freelance writers, and proprietors of a small retail business.

Security A few of the graduates were mostly concerned with long-run career stability and job security. They seemed willing to do what was required to maintain job security, a decent income, and a stable future in the form of a good retirement program and benefits. For those interested in *geographic security*, maintaining a stable, secure career in familiar surroundings was generally more important than pursuing superior career choices, if choosing the latter meant injecting instability or insecurity into their lives by forcing them to pull up roots and move to another city. For others, security meant *organizational security*. They might today opt for government jobs, where tenure still tends to be a way of life. They were much more willing to let their employers decide what their careers should be.

Assessing Career Anchors To help you identify career anchors, take a few sheets of blank paper and write out your answers to the following questions:[133]

1. What was your major area of concentration (if any) in high school? Why did you choose that area? How did you feel about it?
2. What is (or was) your major area of concentration in college? Why did you choose that area? How did you feel about it?
3. What was your first job after school? (Include military if relevant.) What were you looking for in your first job?
4. What were your ambitions or long-range goals when you started your career? Have they changed? When? Why?
5. What was your first major change of job or company? What were you looking for in your next job?
6. What was your next major change of job, company, or career? Why did you initiate or accept it? What were you looking for? (Do this for each of your major changes of job, company, or career.)
7. As you look back over your career, identify some times you have especially enjoyed. What was it about those times that you enjoyed?
8. As you look back, identify some times you have not especially enjoyed. What was it about those times you did not enjoy?
9. Have you ever refused a job move or promotion? Why?
10. Now review all your answers carefully, as well as the descriptions for the five career anchors (technical/functional competence, managerial competence, creativity and independence, autonomy, security). Based on your answers to the questions, rate, for yourself, each of the anchors from 1 to 5. 1 equals low importance, 5 equals high importance.
    Technical/functional competence _____
    Managerial competence _____
    Creativity and independence _____
    Autonomy _____
    Security _____

What Do You Want to Do?

We have explained occupational orientations, skills, and career anchors and the role these play in choosing a career. Now, another exercise can prove enlightening. On a sheet of paper, answer the question: "If you could have any kind of job, what would it be?" Invent your own job if need be, and don't worry about what you can do—just what you want to do.[134]

Identify High-Potential Occupations Learning about your skills and interests is only half the job of choosing an occupation. You also have to identify those occupations that are right (given your occupational orientations, skills, career anchors, and occupational preferences) as well as those that will be in high demand in the years to come.

Not surprisingly, the most efficient way to learn about, compare, and contrast occupations is through the Internet. The U.S. Department of Labor's online *Occupational Outlook Handbook* (www.bls.gov/oco/) is updated each year, and provides detailed descriptions and information on hundreds of occupations Figure 10A-2). O*NET similarly provides occupational demand updates. The New York State Department of Labor (http://nycareerzone.org) similarly provides excellent information on careers categorized in clusters, such as Arts and Humanities, Business and Information Systems, and Engineering and Technology. All these sites include information regarding demand for and employment prospects for the occupations they cover. Figure 10A-3 lists some other sites to turn to both for occupational information and for information on where to turn to when searching for a job—the subject to which we ourselves now turn.

The states' one-stop career centers are another excellent source. In them, job seekers can now apply for unemployment benefits, register with the state job service, talk to career counselors, use computers to write résumés and access the Internet, take tests, and use career libraries, which offer books and videos on various employment topics. In some centers job hunters can even make use of free telephones, fax machines, and photocopiers to facilitate job searches.

Finding the Right Job

You have identified your occupational orientation, skills, and career anchors and have picked out the occupation you want and made plans for a career. If necessary, you have embarked on the required education and training. Your next step is to find a job that you want in the company and locale in which you want to work.

Before leaving a current job, however, make sure leaving is what you want. Many people make the mistake of changing jobs or occupations when a smaller change would suffice. Dissatisfied at work, they assume it must be the job or the occupation. But, why decide to switch from being a lawyer to a teacher, when it's not the profession but that law firm's 80-hour week that's the problem?

The person needs to use a process of elimination. For example, you may like your occupation and employer, but not how your specific job is structured. Others may find their employers' ways of doing things are the problem. Or, it may in fact be the occupation. In any case, the solution should fit the cause. For example, if, after thinking it through, you are satisfied with your occupation and where you work, but not with your job as it's organized now, try reconfiguring it. For example, consider alternative work arrangements such as flexible hours or telecommuting; delegate or eliminate the job functions you least prefer; and seek

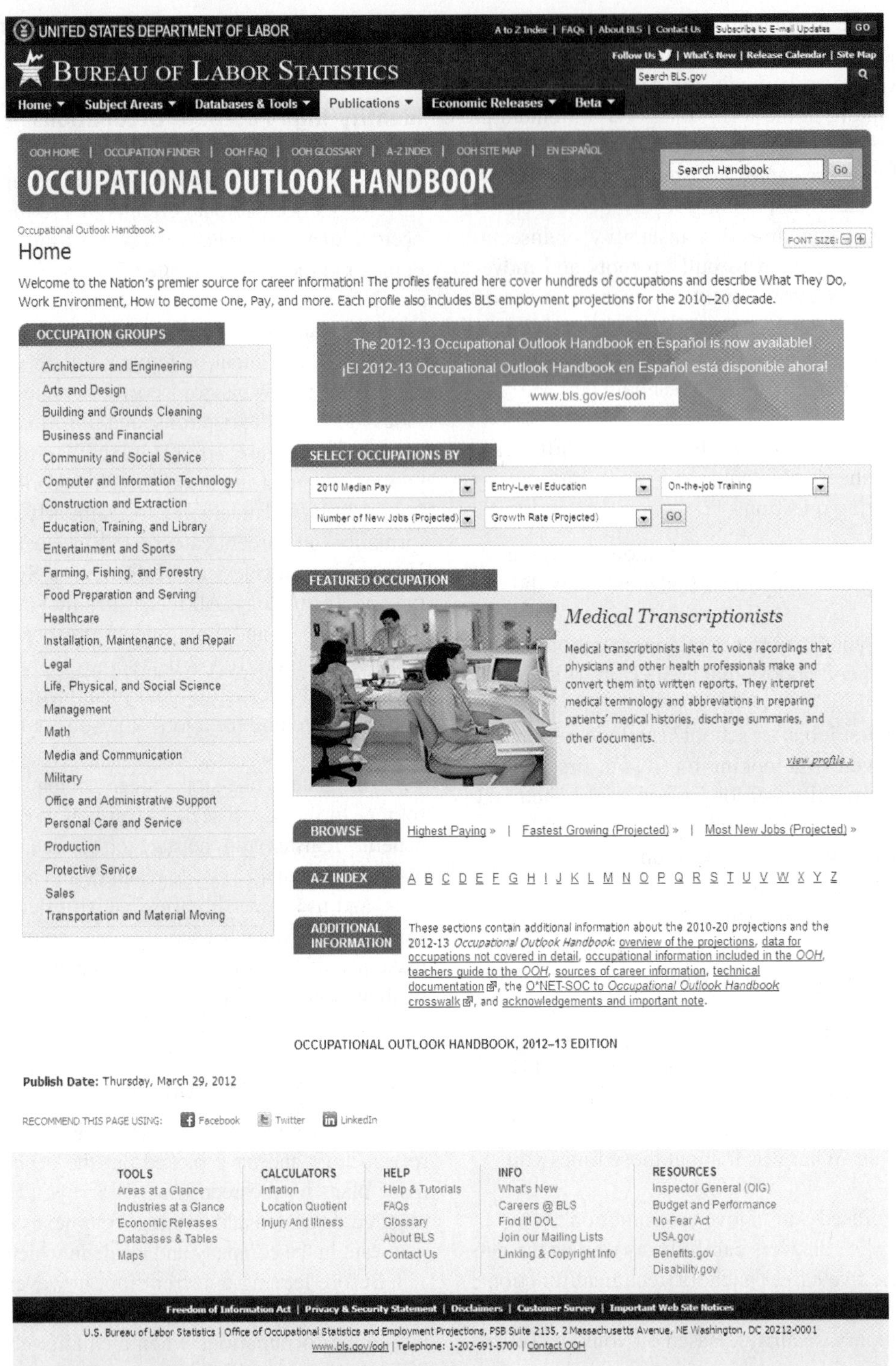

FIGURE 10A-2 ***Occupational Outlook Handbook*** **Online**

Source: www.bls.gov//oco, accessed September 19, 2013.

out a "stretch assignment" that will let you work on something you find more challenging.[135]

Job Search Techniques In Chapter 5 (Personnel Planning and Recruiting) we saw that employers use various tools to find recruits, so it should not be surprising that jobseekers should use pretty much the same tools.

Personal Contacts Generally, the most popular way to seek job leads and interviews is to rely on personal contacts such as friends and relatives.[136] So, let as many responsible people as possible know that you are looking for a job and also what kind of job you want. (Beware, though, if you are currently employed and don't want your job search getting back to your current boss. If that is the case, then just pick out two or three

Selected Online Sources of Occupational Information

- All Star Jobs
- CampusCareeerCenter
- CareerBliss.com
- CareerOneSto
- CareerExplorer
- CareerOverview
- CityTownInfo
- College Central Network
- CollegeGrad.com
- Construct My Future (information about construction careers)
- Cool Works
- EducationPlanner
- eMedicalAssistants
- Explore Health Careers
- Green Jobs Ready
- hotjobs.com
- International Jobs
- Job Search Intelligence
- MyArtsCareer
- Occupational Outlook Handbook
- Professional Development for Teachers
- Quintessential Careers
- ResumeINDEX
- SalaryList
- Science Buddies—Careers
- Simply Hired
- Snag a Job

FIGURE 10A-3 Selected Online Sources of Occupational Information

Source: http://mappingyourfuture.org/planyourcareer/careerresources.htm Accessed June 13, 2013.

very close friends and tell them to please be discreet in seeking a job for you.)

No matter how close your friends or relatives are to you, by the way, you do not want to impose too much on them. It is usually best to ask them for the name of someone they think you should talk to in the kind of firm in which you'd like to work, and then do the digging yourself.

Social Media and HR Employers scour social media for recruits, and job seekers should therefore make sure their names stand out. For example, job seekers can enhance their professional reputations by creating a Twitter presence. Those "Liking" a company on Facebook may receive early notice of job openings. Spend a few minutes every day on LinkedIn making new connections, and share links and advice with those in your LinkedIn network.[137] Join LinkedIn industry groups to build visibility. Make sure your résumé is in PDF format and readable on a smart phone screen. To bring yourself to recruiters' attention, follow up on comments they make on their blogs or in industry websites. Fewer job searchers are using paper résumés and are instead using social résumés. *Social résumés* provide snapshots of who the job searcher is by combining text material, photos, and samples of a person's work in info-graphic résumés posted on social media such as Twitter, LinkedIn, and blogs.[138]

Finally, remember that the prospective employer will probably Google you before extending the offer, and may well ask for access to your Facebook and LinkedIn pages.

Online Job Boards and Employer Websites Most of the large online job search sites such as monster.com (and those in Figure 10A-3) have local-area search capabilities. Use *The Wall Street Journal*'s career website (www.careerjournal.com/) to search for jobs by occupation and location. Most big-city newspapers also have their own (or links to) online local job listings. In addition to job boards like Monster and specialized ones (like www.theladder.com), virtually all large companies, industries, and crafts have their own specialized sites.[139] For example, the Air Conditioning Contractors in America (www.acca.org/careers/) and Financial Executives International (www.fei.org) make it easy for industry employers and prospective employees to match their needs. Remember to use mobile services, for instance, accessing jobs via the Careerbuilder iPhone portal.

Answering Advertisements Most experts agree that answering ads is a low-probability way to get a job, and it becomes increasingly less likely that you will get a job this way as the level of jobs increases. Furthermore, automated applicant tracking services now crunch through thousands of résumés in seconds, making it even harder to stand out by answering ads. Nevertheless, good sources of classified ads for professionals and managers include the *New York Times*, *The Wall Street Journal*, and specialized journals in your field that list job openings. All these sources also post the positions online, of course.

Many employers don't even accept application letters anymore. For those who do, however, be sure to create the right impression with the materials you submit; check the typing, style, grammar, neatness, and so forth, and check your résumé to make sure it is geared to the job for which you are applying. In your cover letter, be sure to have a paragraph or so in which you specifically address why your background and accomplishments are appropriate to the advertised position; you must respond clearly to the company's identified needs.[140]

Be very careful in replying to blind ads, however (such as those with just a post office box). Some executive search firms and companies will run ads even when no position exists just to gauge the market, and there is always the chance that you blunder into responding to your own firm.

Employment Agencies Agencies are especially good at placing people in jobs paying up to about $80,000, but they can be useful for higher-paying jobs as well. The employer usually pays the fees for professional and management jobs. Assuming you know the job you want, review a few back issues of your paper's Sunday classified ads to identify the agencies that consistently handle the positions you want. Approach three or four initially, preferably in response to specific ads, and avoid signing any contract that gives an agency the exclusive right to place you.

Executive Recruiters We've seen that employers retain executive recruiters to seek out top talent for their clients;

employers always pay any fees. They do not do career counseling, but if you know the job you want, it pays to contact a few. Send your résumé and a cover letter summarizing your objective in precise terms, including job title and the size of company desired, work-related accomplishments, current salary, and salary requirements. However, beware, because some firms today call themselves executive search or career consultants but do no searches: They just charge a (often hefty) fee to help you manage your search. Remember that with a search firm you never pay a fee.

Career Counselors Career counselors will not help you find a job per se; rather, they specialize in aptitude testing and career counseling. They are listed under "Career Counseling" or "Vocational Guidance." Their services usually cost $400 or so and include psychological testing and interviews with an experienced career counselor. Check the firm's services, prices, and history as well as the credentials of the person you will be dealing with.

Executive Marketing Consultants Executive marketing consultants manage your job-hunting campaign. They generally are not recruiters and do not have jobs to fill. Depending on the services you choose, your cost will range from $600 to $5,000 or more. The process may involve months of weekly meetings. Services include résumé and letter writing, interview skill building, and developing a full job-hunting campaign. Before approaching a consultant, though, you should definitely do an in-depth self-appraisal (as explained in this appendix) and read books like Richard Bolles's *What Color Is Your Parachute?*

Make sure to do your due diligence, and remember these consultants are not recruiters and will not get you a job—you must do the legwork. Then check out three or four of these firms (they are listed under "Executive Search Consultants") by visiting each and asking: What exactly is your program? How much does each service cost? Are there any extra costs, such as charges for printing and mailing résumés? What does the contract say? After what point will you get no rebate if you're unhappy with the services? Then check the Better Business Bureau, and decide which of these firms (if any) is for you.

Employers' Websites With more companies listing job openings on their websites, any serious job hunter should be using this valuable source. Doing so requires some special résumé preparations, as we'll see next.

Writing Your Résumé Your résumé is often still an important selling document, one that can determine whether you get offered a job interview. Of course, you should not produce a slipshod résumé: Avoid overcrowded pages, difficult-to-read copies, typographical errors, and other problems of this sort. And do not use a make-do résumé. Produce a new résumé for each job you are applying for, gearing your job objective and accomplishments to the job you want. Here are some résumé pointers, as offered by employment counselor Richard Payne and other experts.[141]

Introductory Information Start your résumé with your name, home and e-mail address, and your home or cell phone number.

Job Objective Next, state your job objective. This should summarize in one sentence the specific position you want, where you want to do it (type and size of company), and a special reason an employer might have for wanting you to fill the job. For example, "Marketing manager in a medium-size e-commerce company in a situation in which strong creative skills would be valuable."

Job Scope For each of your previous jobs, write a paragraph that shows job title, whom you reported to directly and indirectly, who reported to you, how many people reported to you, the operational and human resource budgets you controlled, and what your job entailed (in one sentence).

Your Accomplishments This is the heart of your résumé. It shows for each of your previous jobs: (1) a concrete action you took and why you took it and (2) the specific result of your action—the "payoff." For example, "As production supervisor, I introduced a new process to replace costly hand soldering of component parts. The new process reduced assembly time per unit from 30 to 10 minutes and reduced labor costs by over 60%." Use several of these statements for each job.

Length Keep your résumé to two pages or less, and list education, military service (if any), and personal background (hobbies, interests, associations) on the last page.

Make Your Résumé Scannable For many job applications, it's important to write a scannable résumé, in other words, one that is electronically readable by a computer system. Many medium- and larger-sized firms that do extensive recruiting and hiring—especially online and with the aid of applicant tracking systems—use software to review large numbers of résumés, screening out those that don't seem to match (often based on the absence of certain key words that the employer is looking for). Make sure to present your qualifications using powerful key words appropriate to the job or jobs for which you are applying. For example, a trainer might use key words and phrases such as: *computer-based training*, *interactive video*, and *group facilitator*.

Online Bios Today, employers often encourage or require their professionals and managers to post brief biographies on corporate intranets or websites. These bios let other employees know about their colleagues' expertise; they can also attract recruiters' inquiries. Tips for writing such bios include:[142]

Fill it with details. "The more information you enter, the more likely a person seeking someone with your background will find you. . . ."

Avoid touchy subjects. For example, avoid discussing religion and politics.

Look the part. Your profile may require posting photos. If so, dress in professional attire.

Make it search friendly. Make sure your profile contains the key words you think someone searching for someone with your background and expertise would be looking for, such as *manager*, *supervisor*, or *engineer*.

Use abbreviations. Abbreviations are important. For example, someone searching the site might more readily punch in "MBA" than "Masters in Business Administration."

Say it with numbers. Describe specifically how your work has contributed to your current employer's and past employer's bottom lines.

Proofread. Carefully proofread your online profile, as you would your résumé.

A Caveat If you post your résumé on the Web, experts suggest taking precautions. At a minimum, date your résumé (in case it lands on your boss's desk 2 years from now). Also insert a disclaimer forbidding unauthorized transmission by headhunters; check ahead of time to see who has access to the database on which you're posting your résumé; and try to cloak your identity by listing your capabilities but not your name or employer—just an anonymous e-mail account to receive inquiries.[143]

Handling the Interview

You have done all your homework; now the big day is almost here; you have an interview scheduled with the person who is responsible for hiring for the job you want. What must you do to excel in the interview? Here are some suggestions.

Prepare, Prepare, Prepare. First, remember that preparation is essential. Before the interview, learn all you can about the employer, the job, and the people doing the recruiting. Search the Internet (or your library) to find out what is happening in the employer's field. Who is the competition? How are they doing?

Uncover the Interviewer's Needs Spend as little time as possible answering your interviewer's first questions and as much time as possible getting the person to describe his or her needs—what the person is looking to get accomplished and the type of person needed. Use open-ended questions, such as "Could you tell me more about that?"

Relate Yourself to the Person's Needs Once you understand the type of person your interviewer is looking for and the sorts of problems he or she wants solved, you are in a good position to describe your own accomplishments in terms of the interviewer's needs.[144] Start by saying something like, "One of the problem areas you've indicated is important to you is similar to a problem I once faced." Then state the problem, describe your solution, and reveal the results.

Make a Good Appearance and Show Enthusiasm Appearance, a firm handshake, and visual cues such as looking the interviewer in the eyes are crucial. Remember that studies of interviews show that in almost 80% of the cases, interviewers make up their minds about the applicant during the first few moments of the interview. A good first impression may turn bad during the interview, but it is unlikely. Bad first impressions, however, are almost impossible to overcome.

PART FOUR Compensation

11 Establishing Strategic Pay Plans

Source: Purestock/Thinkstock

MyManagementLab®

Improve Your Grade!

When you see this icon, visit **www.mymanagementlab.com** for activities that are applied, personalized, and offer immediate feedback.

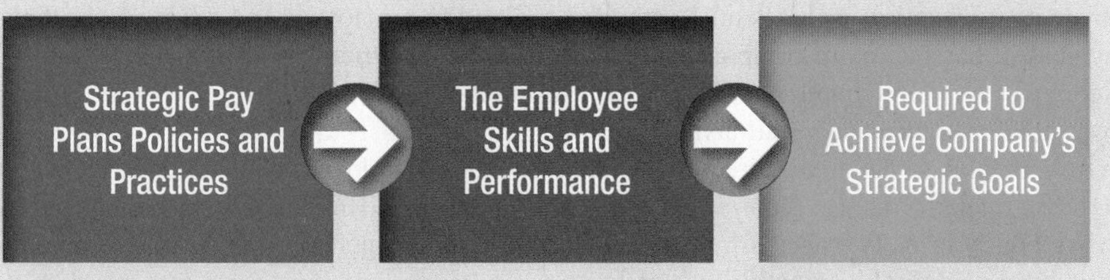

For a bird's eye view of how one company created a new pay plan to improve its strategic performance, read the Hotel Paris case on page 361 and answer the questions after reading the chapter.

WHERE ARE WE NOW . . .

Once you've appraised and coached your employees, they of course expect to be paid. Prudent employers don't set pay rates arbitrarily. Each employee's pay should make sense in terms of what other employees earn, and this requires a pay plan. The main purpose of this chapter is to show you how to establish a pay plan. The main topics we cover are basic factors in determining pay rates; job evaluation methods; how to create a market-competitive pay plan; pricing managerial and professional jobs; and contemporary topics in compensation. The next chapter focuses specifically on pay-for-performance and incentive plans.

LEARNING OBJECTIVES

1 List the basic factors determining pay rates.

2 Define and give an example of how to conduct a job evaluation.

3 Explain in detail how to establish a market-competitive pay plan.

4 Explain how to price managerial and professional jobs.

5 Explain the difference between competency-based and traditional pay plans.

In the grocery business, when Walmart opens a store, the other stores' usual reaction is to cut costs, particularly wages and benefits. So as Wegman's Food Markets, Inc., adds more stores and increasingly competes with Walmart, its management needs to decide this: Should we cut pay to better compete based on cost, or pursue a different compensation policy?[1] We'll see how they boosted profits by raising pay.

Basic Factors in Determining Pay Rates

1 List the basic factors determining pay rates.

employee compensation
All forms of pay or rewards going to employees and arising from their employment.

direct financial payments
Pay in the form of wages, salaries, incentives, commissions, and bonuses.

indirect financial payments
Pay in the form of financial benefits such as insurance.

Employee compensation includes all forms of pay going to employees and arising from their employment. It has two main components, **direct financial payments** (wages, salaries, incentives, commissions, and bonuses) and **indirect financial payments** (financial benefits like employer-paid insurance and vacations).

In turn, employers can make direct financial payments to employees based on increments of time or based on performance. Time-based pay still predominates. Blue-collar and clerical workers receive hourly or daily wages, for instance. Others, like managers or Web designers, tend to be salaried and paid weekly, monthly, or yearly.

The second direct payment option is to pay for performance. For example, piecework ties compensation to the amount of production (or number of "pieces") the worker turns out. Sales commissions tie pay to sales. Many employers' pay plans combine time-based pay and incentives.

In this chapter, we explain how to formulate plans for paying employees a time-based wage or salary. Subsequent chapters cover performance-based financial incentives and bonuses (Chapter 12) and employee benefits (Chapter 13).

Several factors should influence any pay plan's design. These include strategic policy considerations, as well as equity, legal, and union considerations.

Aligning Total Rewards with Strategy

The compensation plan should first advance the firm's strategic aims—management should produce an *aligned reward strategy*. This means creating a compensation package (including wages, incentives, and benefits) that produces the employee behaviors the firm needs to achieve its competitive strategy.[2]

We will see that many employers formulate a total rewards strategy to support their broader strategic aims. *Total rewards* encompass the traditional pay, incentives, and benefits, but also things such as more challenging jobs (job design), career development, and recognition programs.

Table 11-1 lists illustrative questions to ask when crafting a strategy-oriented pay policy.

HR in Practice at the Hotel Paris Even the most casual review by Lisa Cruz and the CFO made it clear that the Hotel Paris's compensation plan wasn't designed to support the firm's new strategic goals. To see how they handled this, see the case on page 361 of this chapter.

Equity and Its Impact on Pay Rates

In studies at Emory University, researchers investigated how capuchin monkeys reacted to inequitable pay. Some monkeys got sweet grapes in return for trading pebbles; others got cucumber slices. If a monkey receiving a cucumber slice saw a neighbor get grapes, it slammed down the pebble or refused to eat.[3] The moral may be that even lower primates demand fair treatment in pay.

EQUITY THEORY OF MOTIVATION Amongst humans too, *the equity theory of motivation* postulates that people are motivated to maintain a balance between what they perceive as their contributions and their rewards. Equity theory states that if a person perceives an inequity, a tension or drive will develop that motivates him or her to reduce the tension and perceived inequity. Research tends to support equity theory, particularly as it applies to those underpaid.[4] For example, in one study turnover of retail buyers was significantly lower when the buyers perceived fair treatment in rewards and in how employers allocated rewards.[5] Overpaying can sometimes backfire too, perhaps "due to feelings of guilt or discomfort."[6]

TABLE 11-1 Do Our Compensation Policies Support Our Strategic Aims?

- What are our strategic aims?
- What employee behaviors and skills do we need to achieve our strategic aims?
- What compensation policies and practices—salary, incentive plans, and benefits—will help to produce the employee behaviors we need to achieve our strategic aims?

In compensation, one can address *external, internal, individual*, and *procedural* equity.[7]

- *External equity* refers to how a job's pay rate in one company compares to the job's pay rate in other companies.
- *Internal equity* refers to how fair the job's pay rate is when compared to other jobs within the same company (for instance, is the sales manager's pay fair, when compared to what the production manager earns?).
- *Individual equity* refers to the fairness of an individual's pay as compared with what his or her coworkers are earning for the same or very similar jobs within the company, based on each person's performance.
- *Procedural equity* refers to the "perceived fairness of the processes and procedures used to make decisions regarding the allocation of pay."[8]

ADDRESSING EQUITY ISSUES Managers use various means to address such equity issues. For example, they use salary surveys (surveys of what other employers are paying) to monitor and maintain external equity. They use job analysis and comparisons of each job ("job evaluation") to maintain internal equity. They use performance appraisal and incentive pay to maintain individual equity. And they use communications, grievance mechanisms, and employees' participation to help ensure that employees view the pay process as procedurally fair. Some firms administer surveys to monitor employees' pay satisfaction. Questions typically include, "How satisfied are you with your pay?" and "What factors do you believe are used when your pay is determined?"[9]

To head off discussions that might prompt feelings of internal inequity, some firms maintain strict secrecy over pay rates, with mixed results.[10] However, "open pay" policies can backfire. In one firm, employees vigorously opposed paying a high salary to a great candidate unless everyone else's pay went up too, for instance.[11] And for external equity, online pay sites like Salary .com make it easy to see what one could earn elsewhere.

Legal Considerations in Compensation

Employers do not have free reign in designing pay plans. Various laws specify things like minimum wages, overtime rates, and benefits.[12] For example, the 1931 **Davis-Bacon Act** lets the secretary of labor set wage rates for laborers and mechanics employed by contractors working for the federal government. The 1936 **Walsh-Healey Public Contract Act** sets basic labor standards for employees working on any government contract that amounts to more than $10,000. It contains minimum wage, maximum hour, and safety and health provisions, and requires time-and-a-half pay for work over 40 hours a week. **Title VII of the 1964 Civil Rights Act** makes it unlawful for employers to discriminate against any individual with respect to hiring, compensation, terms, conditions, or privileges of employment because of race, color, religion, sex, or national origin.[13] We'll look next at other important compensation-related laws.

Davis-Bacon Act
A 1931 law that sets wage rates for laborers employed by contractors working for the federal government.

Walsh-Healey Public Contract Act
A 1936 law that requires minimum wage and working conditions for employees working on any government contract amounting to more than $10,000.

Title VII of the 1964 Civil Rights Act
This act makes it unlawful for employers to discriminate against any individual with respect to hiring, compensation, terms, conditions, or privileges of employment because of race, color, religion, sex, or national origin.

Fair Labor Standards Act
This 1938 act provides for minimum wages, maximum hours, overtime pay, and child labor protection. The law, amended many times, covers most employees.

THE 1938 FAIR LABOR STANDARDS ACT The **Fair Labor Standards Act**, originally passed in 1938 and since amended many times, contains minimum wage, maximum hours, overtime pay, equal pay, record-keeping, and child labor provisions that are familiar to most working people.[14] It covers virtually all U.S. workers engaged in the production and/or sale of goods for interstate and foreign commerce. In addition, agricultural workers and those employed by certain larger retail and service companies are included. State fair labor standards laws cover most employers not covered by the Fair Labor Standards Act (FLSA).[15]

One familiar provision governs *overtime pay.* It says employers must pay overtime at a rate of at least one-and-a-half times normal pay for any hours worked over 40 in a workweek. Thus, if a worker covered by the act works 44 hours in one week, he or she must be paid for 4 of those hours at a rate equal to one-and-a-half times the hourly or weekly base rate the person would have earned for 40 hours. For example, if the person earns $12 an hour (or $480 for a 40-hour week), he or she would be paid at the rate of $18 per hour ($12 times 1.5) for each of the 4 overtime hours worked, or $72 ($18 times 4) for the extra 4 hours. If the employee instead receives time off for the overtime hours, the employer must compute the number of hours granted off at the one-and-a-half-times rate (6 hours off for the 4 hours of overtime in our case), in lieu of overtime pay. Employers need to monitor when employees clock in and out, lest they become obligated for additional demands for overtime pay.[16] Vendors such as Pacific

Timesheet (www.pacifictimesheet.com) provide mobile payroll time sheets. Employees who work outside the office can access and fill these in via their iPhones or similar devices. This improves attendance and payroll accuracy, and helps eliminate overpaying overtime.[17] Newer time clocks have iPad-like touch screens and reduce "buddy punching" with instant photos and biometric sensors.[18]

KNOW YOUR EMPLOYMENT LAW

The Workday

Employers need to be vigilant about employees who arrive early or leave late, lest the extra time spent on the employer's property obligate the employer to compensate the employee for that time. For example, a diligent employee may get dropped off at work early and spend, say, 20 minutes before his or her day actually starts doing work-related chores such as compiling a list of clients to call that day. While there is no hard and fast rule, some courts follow the rule that employees who arrive 15 or more minutes early are presumed to be working unless the employer can prove otherwise.[19] If using time clocks, employers should always instruct employees not to clock in more than 5–10 minutes early (or out 5–10 minutes late). Smart phones give employers further reason to meticulously record workers' hours. An app from the Department of Labor lets employees track their work hours.[20] The Chicago Police Department distributed smart phones to its officers in the field. One police officer subsequently sued, claiming that he wasn't paid overtime for the hours he spent using his smart phone off the clock. Even giant firms make errors. Walmart agreed to pay up to $640 million to settle 63 wage and hour suits alleging infractions, such as failing to pay overtime and not providing required meal breaks.[21]

The FLSA also sets a *minimum wage*. This sets a floor for employees covered by the act (and usually bumps up wages for practically all workers when Congress raises the minimum). The minimum wage was $7.25 in 2013.[22] Many states have their own minimum wage. For example, the minimum wage is $8.00 in Massachusetts and California, $8.25 in Illinois, and $9.04 in Washington State.[23] About 80 localities, including Boston and Chicago, require businesses that have contracts with the city to pay employees wages ranging from $8 to $12 an hour.[24]

FLSA *child labor provisions* prohibit employing minors between 16 and 18 years old in hazardous occupations, and carefully restrict employment of those under 16.

A great many employers today pay people as "independent contractors" rather than as employees. Strictly speaking, these people are like consultants, and therefore are not covered by the FLSA. The accompanying Know Your Employment Law feature explains about paying this type of worker.

EXEMPT/NONEXEMPT Specific categories of employees are *exempt* from the FLSA or certain provisions of the act, and particularly from the act's overtime provisions. They are "exempt employees." A person's exemption depends on his or her responsibilities, duties, and salary. Bona fide executive, administrative (like office managers), and professional employees (like architects) are generally exempt from the minimum wage and overtime requirements of the act.[25] A white-collar worker earning more than $100,000 and performing any one exempt administrative, executive, or professional duty is automatically ineligible for overtime pay. Other employees can generally earn up to $23,660 per year and still automatically get overtime pay (so most employees earning less than $455 per week are nonexempt and earn overtime).[26] Figure 11-1 lists some examples of typically exempt and nonexempt jobs.

If an employee is exempt from the FLSA's minimum wage provisions, then he or she is also exempt from its overtime pay provisions. However, certain employees are *always* exempt from overtime pay provisions. They include, among others, agricultural employees, live-in household employees, taxi drivers, and motion picture theater employees.[27]

Identifying exemptions is tricky. As noted, some jobs—for example, top managers and lawyers—are clearly exempt, while others—such as office workers earning less than

FIGURE 11-1 Some Typical Exempt, Nonexempt Job Titles

Source: Based on www.flsa.com/coverage.html, accessed August 5, 2011; and www.dol.gov/elaws/esa/flsa/screen75.asp, accessed October 15, 2012.

EXEMPT	NONEXEMPT
Lawyers	Paralegals
Medical doctors	Accounting clerks
Dentists	Bookkeepers
Engineers (with degrees)	Licensed practical nurses
Teachers	Clerical employees
Scientists	Most secretaries (although some, such as the CEO's secretary, might be exempt)
Registered nurses	Lab technicians
General managers	
Pharmacists	
Administrative employees*	

* The administrative exemption is designed for relatively high-level employees whose main job is to "keep the business running." Examples of administrative functions, whose high level employees may typically be exempt, include labor relations and personnel (human resources employees), payroll and finance (including budgeting and benefits management), records maintenance, accounting and tax, marketing and advertising (as differentiated from direct sales), quality control, public relations (including shareholder or investment relations, and government relations), legal and regulatory compliance, and some computer-related jobs (such as network, internet and database administration).

$23,660 per year—are clearly nonexempt. But beyond that, one should review the job before classifying it as exempt or nonexempt. Figure 11-2 presents a procedure for making this decision. Make sure, for instance, that the job currently does in fact require, say, an exempt-type supervisory duty.[28]

FLSA exemption lawsuits are on the rise. "Supervisors" are saying they don't really supervise two or more employees.[29] And the U.S. Supreme Court held that drug company sales reps that call on doctors are FLSA-exempt outside salespersons.[30]

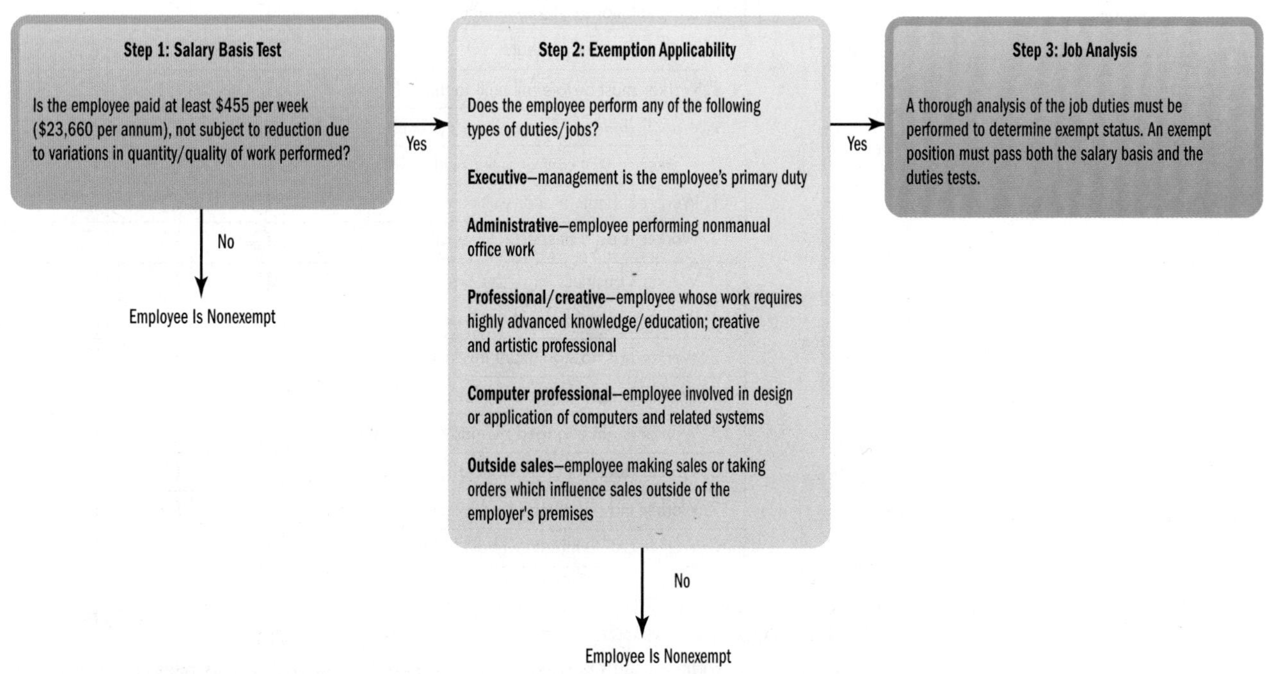

FIGURE 11-2 Who Is Exempt? Who Is Not Exempt?

KNOW YOUR EMPLOYMENT LAW

The Independent Contractor

Whether someone is an employee or an *independent contractor* is a continuing issue for employers.[31] For example, a federal court ruled that most of FedEx's roughly 15,000 owner-operator delivery people were independent contractors, not employees.[32]

Why claim someone is an independent contractor? Because the FLSA's overtime and most other requirements do not apply, and the employer need not pay unemployment compensation; payroll taxes; Social Security taxes; or city, state, and federal income taxes or compulsory workers' compensation for that worker.

The problem is that many so-called independent contractor relationships aren't independent contractor relationships. There is no single rule or test. Instead, the courts will look at the total situation. The major consideration is this: The more the employer controls what the worker does and how he or she does it, the more likely it is that the courts will find the worker to be an employee. Figure 11-3 lists some factors courts will consider. The IRS lists rules at www.irs.gov/Businesses/Small-Businesses-&-Self-Employed/Independent-Contractor-%28Self-Employed%29-or-Employee%3F.

To minimize the risks of independent contractor misclassification, employers should execute written agreements (see for instance http://www.uschambersmallbusinessnation.com/toolkits/tool/indcon_m) with all independent contractors. Furthermore, they should not impose work rules on or attempt to prohibit independent contractors from working for others. They should require independent contractors to provide their own tools and to be separately incorporated business entities.[33]

Independent Contractor

Managers are to use the following checklist to classify individuals as independent contractors. If more than three questions are answered "yes," the manager will confer with human resources regarding the classification. (EE = Employees, IC = Independent Contractors)

Factors which show control :

	Yes/EE	No/IC	N/A
1. Worker must comply with instructions.	☐	☐	☐
2. Worker is trained by person hired.	☐	☐	☐
3. Worker's services are integrated in business.	☐	☐	☐
4. Worker must personally render services.	☐	☐	☐
5. Worker cannot hire or fire assistants.	☐	☐	☐
6. Work relationship is continuous or indefinite.	☐	☐	☐
7. Work hours are present.	☐	☐	☐
8. Worker must devote full time to this business.	☐	☐	☐
9. Work is done on the employer's premises.	☐	☐	☐
10. Worker cannot control order or sequence.	☐	☐	☐
11. Worker submits oral or written reports.	☐	☐	☐
12. Worker is paid at specific intervals.	☐	☐	☐
13. Worker's business expenses are reimbursed.	☐	☐	☐
14. Worker is provided with tools or materials.	☐	☐	☐
15. Worker has no significant investment.	☐	☐	☐
16. Worker has no opportunity for profit/loss.	☐	☐	☐
17. Worker is not engaged by many different firms.	☐	☐	☐
18. Worker does not offer services to public.	☐	☐	☐
19. Worker may be discharged by employer.	☐	☐	☐
20. Worker can terminate without liability.	☐	☐	☐

FIGURE 11-3 Independent Contractor

Source: Form reproduced with permission from the publisher BLR—Business & Legal Resources (www.HR.BLR.com)

Equal Pay Act
A 1963 amendment to the Fair Labor Standards Act designed to require equal pay for women doing the same work as men.

1963 EQUAL PAY ACT The **Equal Pay Act**, an amendment to the Fair Labor Standards Act, states that employees of one sex may not be paid wages at a rate lower than that paid to employees of the opposite sex for doing roughly equivalent work. Specifically, if the work requires equal skills, effort, and responsibility and involves similar working conditions, employees of both sexes must receive equal pay, unless the differences in pay stem from a seniority system, a merit system, the quantity or quality of production, or "any factor other than sex."

Employee Retirement Income Security Act (ERISA)
The 1974 law that provides government protection of pensions for all employees with company pension plans. It also regulates vesting rights (employees who leave before retirement may claim compensation from the pension plan).

1974 EMPLOYEE RETIREMENT INCOME SECURITY ACT Aimed at protecting employees' pensions, the **Employee Retirement Income Security Act (ERISA)** provides for the creation of government-run, employer-financed corporations to protect employees against the failure of their employers' pension plans. It also sets regulations regarding vesting rights (*vesting* refers to the equity or ownership the employees build up in their pension plans should their employment terminate before retirement). ERISA also regulates *portability rights* (the transfer of an employee's vested rights from one organization to another). It also contains fiduciary standards to prevent dishonesty in pension plan funding.

OTHER LEGISLATION AFFECTING COMPENSATION Various other laws influence compensation decisions. For example, the *Age Discrimination in Employment Act* prohibits age discrimination against employees who are 40 years of age and older in all aspects of employment, including compensation.[34] The *Americans with Disabilities Act* prohibits discrimination against qualified persons with disabilities in all aspects of employment. The *Family and Medical Leave Act* aims to entitle eligible employees, both men and women, to take up to 12 weeks of unpaid, job-protected leave for the birth of a child or for the care of a child, spouse, or parent. And various executive orders require employers that are federal government contractors or subcontractors to not discriminate in certain employment areas, including compensation.

Each state has its own *workers' compensation laws*. Among other things, these aim to provide prompt, sure, and reasonable income to victims of work-related accidents. The *Social Security Act of 1935* (as amended) provides for unemployment compensation for workers unemployed through no fault of their own for up to 26 weeks (and recently extended), and for retirement benefits. (We'll discuss Social Security benefits in a later chapter.) The federal wage garnishment law limits the amount of an employee's earnings that employers can withhold (garnish) per week, and protects the worker from discharge due to garnishment.

Digital vision/Thinkstock

Two executives discuss a print layout; one happens to be in a wheelchair. Federal law mandates that the wheelchair-bound employee not suffer discrimination in compensation.

Union Influences on Compensation Decisions

Unions and labor relations laws also influence pay plan design. The National Labor Relations Act of 1935 (Wagner Act) granted employees the right to unionize and to bargain collectively. Historically, the wage rate has been the main issue in collective bargaining. However, unions also negotiate other pay-related issues, including time off with pay, income security (for those in industries with periodic layoffs), cost-of-living adjustments, and health care benefits.

The Wagner Act created the National Labor Relations Board (NLRB) to oversee employer practices and ensure that employees receive their rights. For example, the NLRB says that employers must give the union a written explanation of the employer's "wage curves"—the graph that relates job to pay rate. The union is also entitled to know members' salaries.[35]

Pay Policies

The employer's compensation strategy will manifest itself in *pay policies*. For example, a top hospital like Johns Hopkins might have a policy of paying nurses 20% above the prevailing market wage. Pay policies can influence the employer's performance and profitability, as the accompanying feature on Wegmans Foods illustrates.

Managers need pay policies on a range of issues. One is whether to emphasize *seniority* or *performance*. For example, it takes 18 years for a U.S. federal employee to progress from step 1 to step 9 of the government's pay scale. Such seniority-based pay may be advantageous to the extent that seniority is an objective standard. One disadvantage is that top performers may get the same raises as poor ones. Seniority-based pay might seem to be a relic reserved for some government agencies and unionized firms. However, one survey found that 60% of employees responding thought high-seniority employees got the most pay. Only about 35% said their companies paid high performers more.[36]

How to distinguish between *high and low performers* is another policy issue. For example, for many years Payless ShoeSource gave everyone the same raise. However, after seeing its market share drop over several years, management decided on a turnaround strategy. This necessitated revising the firm's compensation policies, to differentiate more aggressively between top performers and others.[37] Other pay policies cover how to award salary increases and promotions, overtime pay, probationary pay, leaves for military service, jury duty, and holidays.

IMPROVING PERFORMANCE: HR as a Profit Center

Wegmans Foods

Strategic compensation management means formulating a total rewards package that produces the employee skills and behaviors that the company needs to achieve its strategic goals.

Wegmans exemplifies this. It competes in the retail food sector, where profit margins are thin and where online competitors and giants like Walmart drive costs and prices down. The usual reaction is to cut employee benefits and costs.[38] Wegmans takes a different approach. It views its workforce as an integral part of achieving Wegmans' strategic aims of *optimizing service while controlling costs by improving systems and productivity*. For example, one dairy department employee designed a new way to organize the cooler, thus improving ordering and inventory control.[39]

Wegmans' compensation policies aim to elicit just this sort of employee dedication. The firm offers above-market pay rates, affordable health insurance, and a full range of employee benefits. Wegmans hasn't laid off employees in 96 years.[40] Wegmans' pay policies thus aim to produce exactly the sorts of employee behaviors the company needs to achieve its strategic aims.

It is likely that its pay policies are one reason for the firm's exceptional profitability. For example, Wegmans employee turnover (from 38% for part-timers to 6%–7% for full timers) is well below the industry's overall average of about 47%.[41] Its stores (which at about 120,000 square feet are much larger than competitors') average about $950,000 a week in sales (compared to a national average of $361,564), or about $49 million in sales annually, compared with a typical Walmart store's grocery sales of $23.5 million in sales.[42] As Wegmans' human resource head has said, good employees assure higher productivity, and that translates into better bottom-line results.[43]

Discussion Question 11-1: If Wegmans does so well with a high-pay policy, why don't more employers do this as well?

GEOGRAPHY How to account for geographic differences in cost of living is another big pay policy issue. For example, the average base pay for an office supervisor ranges from about $49,980 in Florida to $60,980 in New York.[44]

Employers handle cost-of-living differentials for transferees in several ways. One is to pay a differential for ongoing costs in addition to a one-time allocation. For example, one employer pays a differential of $6,000 per year to people earning $35,000 to $45,000 whom it transfers from Atlanta to Minneapolis. Others simply raise the employee's base salary. The accompanying feature on Compensating Expatriate Employees expands on this.

IMPROVING PERFORMANCE: HR Practices Around the Globe

Compensating Expatriate Employees

The question of cost-of-living differentials has particular significance to multinational firms, where pay rates range widely from, say, France to Zambia.

How should multinationals compensate expatriate employees—those it sends overseas? Two basic international compensation policies are popular: home-based and host-based plans.[45]

With a *home-based salary plan*, an international transferee's base salary reflects his or her home country's salary. The employer then adds allowances for cost-of-living differences—housing and schooling costs, for instance. This is a reasonable approach for short-term assignments, and avoids the problem of having to change the employee's base salary every time he or she moves.

In the *host-based plan*, the firm ties the international transferee's base salary to the host country's salary structure. In other words, the manager from New York who is sent to France would have his or her base salary changed to the prevailing base salary for that position in France, rather than keep the New York base salary. The firm usually tacks on cost-of-living, housing, schooling, and other allowances here as well.

Most multinational enterprises set expatriates' salaries according to the *home-based salary plan*. (Thus, a French manager assigned to Kiev by a U.S. multinational will generally have a base salary that reflects the salary structure in the manager's home country, in this case France.) In addition, the person typically gets allowances including cost-of-living, relocation, housing, education, and hardship allowances (for more challenging countries). The employer also usually pays any extra tax burdens resulting from taxes the manager is liable for over and above those he or she would have to pay in the home country.

Discussion Question 11-2: Why do you think most employers opt for the home-based salary plan?

Job Evaluation Methods

2 Define and give an example of how to conduct a job evaluation.

job evaluation
A systematic comparison done in order to determine the worth of one job relative to another.

Employers use two basic approaches to setting pay rates: *market-based approaches* and *job evaluation methods*. Many firms, particularly smaller ones, simply use a *market-based* approach. Doing so involves conducting formal or informal salary surveys to determine what others in the relevant labor markets are paying for particular jobs. They then use these figures to price their own jobs. *Job evaluation methods* involve assigning values to each of the company's jobs. This helps to produce a pay plan in which each job's pay is equitable based on its value to the employer. However, we'll see that even with the job evaluation approach, managers must adjust pay rates to fit the market.[46]

Job evaluation is a formal and systematic comparison of jobs to determine the worth of one job relative to another. Job evaluation aims to determine a job's relative worth. Job evaluation eventually results in a *wage* or *salary structure* or hierarchy (this shows the pay rate for various

iStockphoto/Thinkstock

The job evaluation committee typically includes at least several employees, and has the important task of evaluating the worth of each job using compensable factors.

jobs or groups of jobs). The basic principle of job evaluation is this: Jobs that require greater qualifications, more responsibilities, and more complex job duties should receive more pay than jobs with lesser requirements.[47] The basic job evaluation procedure is to compare jobs in relation to one another—for example, in terms of required effort, job complexity, and skills. Suppose you know (based on your job evaluation) the relative worth of the key jobs in your firm. You then conduct a salary survey to see what others are paying for similar jobs. You are then well on your way to being able to price *all* the jobs in your company equitably, by slotting them in around the key jobs.

Compensable Factors

You can use two basic approaches to compare the worth of several jobs. First, you might decide that one job is more important than another is, and not dig any deeper. As an alternative, you could compare the jobs by focusing on certain basic factors the jobs have in common. Compensation management specialists call these **compensable factors**. They are the factors that establish how the jobs compare to one another, and that determine the pay for each job.

compensable factor
A fundamental, compensable element of a job, such as skills, effort, responsibility, and working conditions.

Some employers develop their own compensable factors. However, most use factors popularized by packaged job evaluation systems or by federal legislation. For example, the Equal Pay Act uses four compensable factors—skills, effort, responsibility, and working conditions. The method popularized by the Hay consulting firm emphasizes three factors: know-how, problem solving, and accountability. Walmart uses knowledge, problem-solving skills, and accountability requirements.

Identifying compensable factors plays a central role in job evaluation. You usually compare each job with all comparable jobs using the same compensable factors. However, the compensable factors you use depend on the job and the job evaluation method. For example, "decision making" might make sense for a manager's job, but not for a cleaner's job.[48]

Preparing for the Job Evaluation

Job evaluation is a judgmental process and demands close cooperation among supervisors, HR specialists, and employees and union representatives. The initial steps include identifying the need for the program, getting cooperation, and then choosing an evaluation committee. The committee then performs the actual evaluation.

Identifying the need for job evaluation should not be difficult. For example, dissatisfaction reflected in high turnover, work stoppages, or arguments may result from paying employees different rates for similar jobs. Managers may express uneasiness with an informal way of assigning pay rates.

Employees may fear that a systematic evaluation of their jobs may reduce their pay rates, so *getting employees to cooperate* in the evaluation is important. For example, you can tell employees that because of the impending job evaluation program, pay rate decisions will no longer be made just by management whim, and that no current employee's rate will be adversely affected because of the job evaluation.

Finally, *choose a job evaluation committee.* The committee usually consists of about five members, most of whom are employees. Management has the right to serve on such committees, but employees may view this with suspicion. However, a human resource specialist can usually be justified to provide expert assistance. Union representation is possible. In most cases, though, the union's position is that it is accepting the results of the job evaluation only as an initial decision and is reserving the right to appeal actual job pricing decisions through grievance or bargaining channels.[49] Once appointed, each committee member should receive a manual explaining both the job evaluation process and how to conduct the job evaluation.

The evaluation committee then performs three main functions. First, it usually identifies 10 or 15 key **benchmark jobs**. These will be the first jobs they'll evaluate and will serve as the anchors or benchmarks against which the relative importance or value of all other jobs is compared. Next, the committee may select *compensable factors* (although the human resources department will usually choose these). Finally, the committee performs its most important function—actually *evaluating the worth of each job.* For this, the committee will probably use one of the following methods: ranking, job classification, or point method.

benchmark job
A job that is used to anchor the employer's pay scale and around which other jobs are arranged in order of relative worth.

Job Evaluation Methods: Ranking

ranking method
The simplest method of job evaluation that involves ranking each job relative to all other jobs, usually based on overall difficulty.

The simplest job evaluation method ranks each job relative to all other jobs, usually based on some overall factor like "job difficulty." There are several steps in the job **ranking method**.

1. ***Obtain job information.*** Job analysis is the first step. Here job descriptions for each job are prepared, and the information they contain about the job's duties is usually the basis for ranking jobs. (Sometimes job specifications are also prepared. However, the ranking method usually ranks jobs based on the whole job, rather than on several compensable factors. Therefore, job specifications, which tend to list job demands in terms of compensable factors such as problem solving, decision making, and skills, are not as important with this method as they are for other job evaluation methods.)
2. ***Select and group jobs.*** It is usually not practical to make a single ranking for all jobs in an organization. The usual procedure is to rank jobs by department or in clusters (such as factory workers or clerical workers). This eliminates the need for direct comparison of, say, factory jobs and clerical jobs.
3. ***Select compensable factors.*** In the ranking method, it is common to use just one factor (such as job difficulty) and to rank jobs based on the whole job. Regardless of the number of factors you choose, it's advisable to explain the definition of the factor(s) to the evaluators carefully so that they all evaluate the jobs consistently.
4. ***Rank jobs.*** For example, give each rater a set of index cards, each of which contains a brief description of a job. Then they rank these cards from lowest to highest. Some managers use an "alternation ranking method" for making the procedure more accurate. Here you take the cards, first choosing the highest and the lowest, then the next highest and next lowest, and so forth, until you've ranked all the cards. Table 11-2 illustrates a job ranking. Jobs in this small health facility rank from orderly up to office manager. The corresponding pay scales are on the right. After ranking, it is possible to slot additional jobs between those already ranked and to assign an appropriate wage rate. Online programs, as at www.hr-guide.com/data/G909.htm, can help you rank (and check the rankings of) your positions.
5. ***Combine ratings.*** Usually, several raters rank the jobs independently. Then the rating committee (or the employer) can simply average the raters' rankings.

This is the simplest job evaluation method, as well as the easiest to explain. And it usually takes less time than other methods.

Drawbacks derive more from how managers use ranking than from the method itself. For example, there's a tendency to rely too heavily on "guesstimates" (of things like overall difficulty), since ranking usually does not use compensable factors. Similarly, ranking provides no yardstick for quantifying the value of one job relative to another. For example, job number 4 may in fact be five times "more valuable" than job number 5, but with the ranking method all you know is that one job ranks higher than the other. Ranking is usually more appropriate for small employers that can't afford the time or expense of developing a more elaborate system.

TABLE 11-2 Job Ranking at Jackson Hospital

Ranking Order	Annual Pay Scale
1. Office manager	$43,000
2. Chief nurse	42,500
3. Bookkeeper	34,000
4. Nurse	32,500
5. Cook	31,000
6. Nurse's aide	28,500
7. Orderly	25,500

Note: After ranking, it becomes possible to slot additional jobs (based on overall job difficulty, for instance) between those already ranked and to assign each an appropriate wage rate.

The *factor comparison method* is a special ranking method. It requires ranking each of a job's "factors" (such as education required, experience, and complexity), and then adding up the points representing the number of "degrees" of each factor each job has. Employers seldom use it today.

Job Evaluation Methods: Job Classification

job classification (or job grading)
A method for categorizing jobs into groups.

classes
Grouping jobs based on a set of rules for each group or class, such as amount of independent judgment, skill, physical effort, and so forth, required. Classes usually contain similar jobs.

grades
A job classification system like the class system, although grades often contain dissimilar jobs, such as secretaries, mechanics, and firefighters. Grade descriptions are written based on compensable factors listed in classification systems.

grade definition
Written descriptions of the level of, say, responsibility and knowledge required by jobs in each grade. Similar jobs can then be combined into grades or classes.

Job classification (or job grading) is a simple, widely used job evaluation method in which raters categorize jobs into groups; all the jobs in each group are of roughly the same value for pay purposes. We call the groups **classes** if they contain similar jobs, or **grades** if they contain jobs that are similar in difficulty but otherwise different. Thus, in the federal government's pay grade system, a "press secretary" and a "fire chief" might both be graded "GS-10" (GS stands for "General Schedule"). On the other hand, in its job class system, the state of Florida might classify all "secretary IIs" in one class, all "maintenance engineers" in another, and so forth.

In practice, there are several ways to categorize jobs. One is to write class or grade descriptions or summaries (similar to job descriptions); you then place jobs into classes or grades based on how well they fit these descriptions. Another to write a set of compensable factor-based rules for each class (for instance, how much independent judgment, skill, and physical effort does the class of jobs require?). Then categorize the jobs according to these rules.

The usual procedure is to choose compensable factors and then develop short class or grade descriptions that describe each class (or grade) in terms of the amount or level of the factors in those jobs. For example, the U.S. government's classification system uses the following compensable factors: (1) difficulty and variety of work, (2) supervision received and exercised, (3) judgment exercised, (4) originality required, (5) nature and purpose of interpersonal work relationships, (6) responsibility, (7) experience, and (8) knowledge required. Based on these compensable factors, raters write a **grade definition** like that in Figure 11-4. This one shows one grade description (GS-7) for the federal government's pay grade system. Then the evaluation committee reviews all job descriptions and slots each job into its appropriate grade, by comparing each job description to the rules in each grade description. Thus, the federal government system classifies the positions *automotive mechanic*, *welder*, *electrician*, and *machinist* in grade GS-10.

The classification method has several advantages. The main one is that most employers usually end up grouping jobs into classes or grades anyway, regardless of the evaluation method they use. They do this to avoid having to price separately dozens or hundreds of jobs. Of course, the job classification automatically groups the employer's jobs into classes. The disadvantages are that it is difficult to write the class or grade descriptions, and considerable judgment is required to apply them. Yet many employers use this method with success.

Job Evaluation Methods: Point Method

point method
The job evaluation method in which a number of compensable factors are identified and then the degree to which each of these factors is present on the job is determined.

The **point method**'s overall aim is to determine the degree to which the jobs you're evaluating contain selected compensable factors. It involves identifying several compensable factors for the jobs, as well as the degree to which each factor is present in each job. Assume there are five degrees of the compensable factor "responsibility" a job could contain. Further, assume you assign a different number of points to each degree of each compensable factor. Once the evaluation committee determines the degree to which each compensable factor (like

FIGURE 11-4 Example of a Grade Definition

Source: "Grade Level Guide for Clerical and Assistance Work" from U.S. Office of Personnel Management, June 1989.

Grade	Nature of Assignment	Level of Responsibility
GS-7	Performs specialized duties in a defined functional or program area involving a wide variety of problems or situations; develops information, identifies interrelationships, and takes actions consistent with objectives of the function or program served.	Work is assigned in terms of objectives, priorities, and deadlines; the employee works independently in resolving most conflicts; completed work is evaluated for conformance to policy; guidelines, such as regulations, precedent cases, and policy statements require considerable interpretation and adaptation.

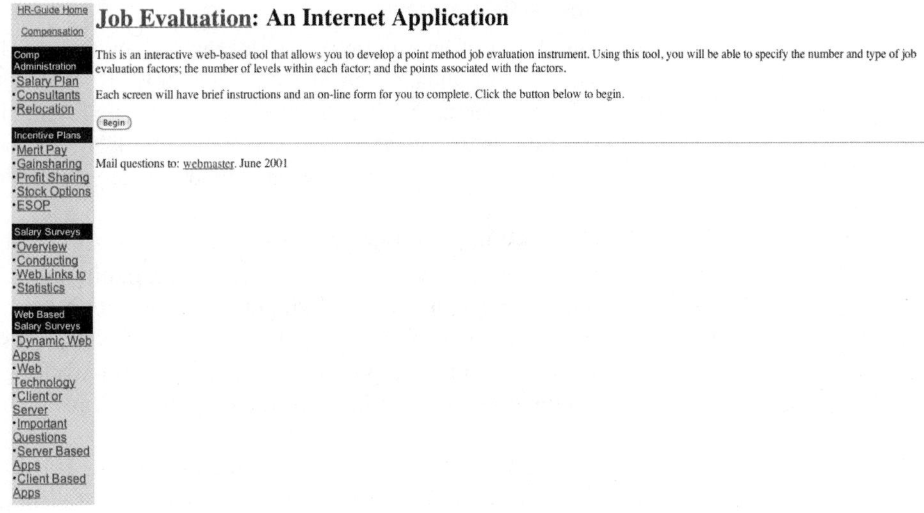

Computer-aided job evaluation can streamline the job evaluation process
Source: Screen capture: www.hr-software.netcgi/JobEvaluation.cgi. Used by permission.

"responsibility" and "effort") is present in a job, it can calculate a total point value for the job by adding up the corresponding degree points for each factor. The result is a quantitative point rating for each job. The point method of job evaluation is the most popular job evaluation method today.[50]

"PACKAGED" POINT PLANS A number of groups (such as the Hay Group, the National Electrical Manufacturer's Association, and the National Trade Association) have developed standardized point plans. Many thousands of employers use these systems. They contain ready-made factor and degree definitions and point assessments for a wide range of jobs. Employers can often use them with little or no modification.

Computerized Job Evaluations

Using job evaluation methods such as the point method can be time-consuming. Accumulating the information about "how much" of each compensable factor the job contains is a tedious process. The evaluation committees must debate the level of each compensable factor in each job. They then write down their consensus judgments and compute each job's point values or rankings.

Computer-aided job evaluation can streamline the job evaluation process. The accompanying screen grab illustrates one. Most of these computerized systems have two main components. There is, first, a structured questionnaire. This contains items such as "enter total number of employees who report to this position." Second, all such systems use statistical models. These allow the computer program to evaluate jobs more or less automatically, by assigning points.

3 Explain in detail how to establish a market-competitive pay plan.

How to Create a Market-Competitive Pay Plan

As we said, many firms simply price their jobs based on what other employers are paying—they use a market-based approach. However, most employers also base their pay plans on job evaluations. These evaluations assign values (such as point values) to each job. This helps to produce a pay plan in which each job's pay is internally equitable, based, as it is, on the job's value to the employer (as measured, for instance, by how many points it warrants). However, even with the job evaluation approach, managers must adjust pay rates to fit the market.[51] After all, you want employees' pay to be equitable internally—relative to what their colleagues in the firm are earning—but also competitive to what *other* employers are paying. In a *market-competitive pay plan* a job's compensation reflects the job's value in the company, as well as what other employers are paying for similar jobs in the marketplace. Because the point method (or "point-factor method") is so popular, we'll use it as the centerpiece of our step-by-step example for creating a market-competitive pay plan.[52] The 16 steps in creating a market-competitive pay plan begin with choosing benchmark jobs.

1. Choose Benchmark Jobs

Particularly when an employer has dozens or hundreds of different jobs, it's impractical and unnecessary to evaluate each of them separately. Therefore, the first step in the point method is to select benchmark jobs. Benchmark jobs are representative of the entire range of jobs the employer needs to evaluate. Like "accounting clerk" they should be common among employers (thus making it easier to survey what competitors are paying for similar jobs).[53]

2. Select Compensable Factors

The choice of compensable factors depends on tradition (as noted, the Equal Pay Act of 1963 uses four compensable factors: skill, effort, responsibility, and working conditions), and on strategic and practical considerations. For example, if your firm's competitive advantage is quality, you might substitute "responsibility for quality" for working conditions, or simply add it as a fifth factor.[54] Similarly, using "working conditions" makes little practical sense for evaluating executive jobs.

The employer should carefully define each factor. This is to ensure that the evaluation committee members will each apply the factors with consistency. Figure 11-5 shows (on top) one such definition, in this case for the factor job complexity. The human resource specialist often draws up the definitions.

3. Assign Weights to Compensable Factors

Having selected compensable factors, the next step is to determine the relative importance (or weighting) of each factor (for instance, how much more important is "skill" than "effort"?). This is important because for each cluster of jobs some factors are bound to be more important than others are. Thus, for executive jobs the "mental requirements" factor

FIGURE 11-5 Illustrative Point Values and Degree Definitions for the Factor Job Complexity

Source: Copyright Gary Dessler, PhD.

Factor Definition: What Is Job Complexity? Job complexity generally refers to the amount of judgment, initiative, ingenuity, and complex data analysis that doing the job requires. To what extent does the person doing this job confront unfamiliar problems, deal with complex decisions, and have to exercise discretion?

Degree	Points	Job Complexity Degree Definitions: What to Look for in the Job
First	120	Here the job is routine and consists of repetitive operations requiring little or no choice of action and the automatic application of easily understood rules and procedures. For example, a filing clerk.
Second	240	Here the employee follows detailed instructions but may have to make limited decisions based on previously prescribed instructions which lay our prescribed alternatives. For example, a billing clerk or a receptionist.
Third	360	Here the employee again follows detailed instructions but because the number of matters to consider is more varied the employee needs to exhibit initiative and independent judgment, under direct supervision. For example, a nurse's aide.
Fourth	480	Here the employee can generally follow standard practices but the presence of nonroutine problems requires that the employee be able to use initiative and judgment to analyze and evaluate situations, possibly modifying the standard procedures to adjust to the new situations. For example, a nurse.
Fifth	600	On this job, the employee needs to use independent judgment and plan and perform complex work under only general supervision, often working independently toward achieving overall results. For example, medical intern.

would carry far more weight than would "physical requirements." To assign weights, we assume we have a total 100 percentage points to allocate for each job. Then (as an illustration), assign percentage weights of 60% for the factor job complexity, 30% for effort, and 10% for working conditions.[55]

4. Convert Percentages to Points for Each Factor

Next, we want to convert the percentage weights assigned to each compensable factor into point values for each factor (this is, after all, the point method). It is traditional to assume we are working with a total number of 1,000 points (although one could use some other figure). To convert percentages to points for each compensable factor, *multiply the percentage weight for each compensable factor (from the previous step) by 1,000.*[56] This will tell you the *maximum number of points* for each compensable factor. Doing so in this case would translate into 1,000 × 0.60 = 600 possible points for job complexity, 1,000 × 0.30 = 300 points for effort, and 1,000 × 0.10 = 100 points for working conditions.

5. Define Each Factor's Degrees

Next, split each factor into degrees, and define (write degree definitions for) each degree so that raters may judge the amount or degree of a factor existing in a job. Thus, for a factor such as "job complexity" you might choose to have five degrees, ranging from "here the job is routine" to "uses independent judgment." (Our definitions for each degree are shown in Figure 11-5 under "Job Complexity Degree Definitions: What to Look for in the Job"). The number of degrees usually does not exceed five or six, and the actual number depends mostly on judgment. Thus, if all employees work either in a quiet, air-conditioned office or in a noisy, hot factory, then two degrees would probably suffice for the factor "working conditions." You need not have the same number of degrees for each factor, and you should limit degrees to the number necessary to distinguish among jobs.

6. Determine for Each Factor Its Factor Degrees' Points

The evaluation committee must be able to determine the number of points each job is worth. To do this, the committee must be able to examine each job and (from each factor's degree definitions) determine what degree of each compensable factor that job has. For them to do this, we must first assign points to *each degree of each compensable factor*. For example, in our illustration, we have five possible degrees of job complexity, and the job complexity compensable factor is worth up to 600 points maximum. In our case, we simply decide that the first degree level of job complexity is worth 120 (or one-fifth of 600) points, the second degree level is worth 240 points, the third degree level is worth 360 points, the fourth degree level is worth 480 points, and the fifth degree is worth the maximum 600 points (see Figure 11-5).[57] Do this for each factor (as in Table 11-3).

7. Review Job Descriptions and Job Specifications

The heart of job *evaluation* involves determining the amount or degree to which the job contains the selected compensable factors such as effort, job complexity, and working conditions. The team conducting the job evaluation will frequently do so by first reviewing each job's job description and job specification. As we explained in Chapter 4 (Job Analysis), it is through the job analysis that the manager identifies the job's duties and responsibilities and writes the job

TABLE 11-3 Points Assigned to Factors and to Their Degrees (Revised)

Factors	First-Degree Points	Second-Degree Points	Third-Degree Points	Fourth-Degree Points	Fifth-Degree Points
Job complexity (Total maximum points equal 600)	120	240	360	480	600
Effort (Total maximum points equal 300)	60	120	180	240	300
Working conditions (Total maximum points equal 100 points)	20	40	60	80	100

description and job specification. Ideally, the job analysis should therefore have included information about the compensable factors (such as job complexity) around which the employer plans to build its compensation plan.[58]

8. Evaluate the Jobs

Steps 1-7 provide us with the information, (for instance on points and degrees,) based on which we can evaluate the jobs. The committee now gathers the job descriptions and job specifications for the benchmark jobs they will focus on.

Then, from their review of each job description and job specification the committee *determines the degree to which each compensable factor is present in each job*. Thus for, say, a job of master mechanic, the team might conclude (after studying the job description and job specification) that the master mechanic's job deserves the third degree level of *job complexity* points, the first degree level of *effort*, and the first degree level of *working conditions*.

Knowing the job complexity, effort, and working conditions degrees for each job, *and knowing the number of points we previously assigned to each degree* of each compensable factor, we can now determine how many job complexity, effort, and working conditions points each benchmark job should contain. (We know the degree level for each factor for each job, so we merely check the corresponding points (see Table 11-3) that we previously assigned to each of these degrees.)

Finally, we add up these degree points for each job to determine each job's total number of points.[59] The master mechanic job gets 360 + 60 + 20 = 440 points from Table 11-3. This enables us to list a hierarchy of jobs, based upon each job's points. We can soon turn to assigning wage rates to each job (step 9). But first, we should define market-competitive pay plan and wage curve.

WHAT IS A MARKET-COMPETITIVE PAY PLAN? What should the pay rate be for each job? Of course, jobs with more points should command higher pay. The question is what pay rate to use. Our company's current, "internal" pay rates? Or pay rates based on what the "external" market is paying?[60]

market-competitive pay system
A pay system in which the employer's actual pay rates are competitive with those in the relevant labor market.

With a **market-competitive pay system**, the employer's actual pay rates are competitive with those in the relevant labor market, as well as equitable internally.[61] Put simply, the basic approach is to compare what the employer is *currently* paying for each job ("internal pay") with what the market is paying for the same or similar job ("external pay"), and then to combine this information to produce a market-competitive pay system.

wage curve
Shows the relationship between the value of the job and the average wage paid for this job.

WHAT ARE WAGE CURVES? **Wage curves** play a central role in assigning wage rates to jobs. The wage curve typically shows the pay rates paid for jobs, relative to the points or rankings assigned to each job by the job evaluation. Figure 11-6 presents an example. Note that it shows pay rates for jobs on the vertical axis, and point values for these jobs along the horizontal axis.

FIGURE 11-6 **Plotting a Wage Curve**

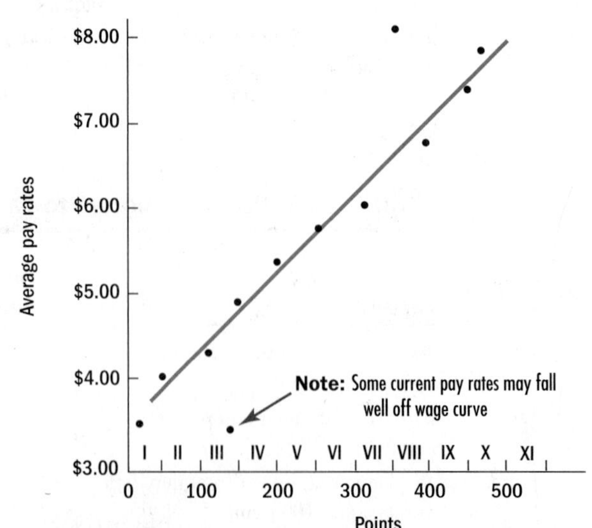

The purpose of the wage curve is to show the relationships between (1) the value of the job (expressed in points) as determined by one of the job evaluation methods and (2) the pay rates for the job. (We'll see that many employers may combine jobs into classes or grades. Here the wage curve would show the relationship between average pay rates for each grade, and each grade's average point value.) The pay rates on the wage curve are traditionally those now paid by the employer. However, if there is reason to believe the current pay rates are out of step with the market rates for these jobs, the employer will have to adjust them. One way to do this is to compare a wage curve that shows the jobs' *current* wage rates relative to the jobs' points, with a second curve that shows *market* wage rates relative to points. We do this as follows.

9. Draw the Current (Internal) Wage Curve

First, to study how each job's points relates to its current pay rate, we start by drawing an *internal wage curve.* Plotting each job's points and the wage rate the employer is now paying for each job (or wage rates, if there are several for each job) produces a scatter plot as in Figure 11-7 (left). We now draw a wage curve (on the right) through these plots that shows how point values relate to current wage rates. We can draw this wage line by just estimating a line that best fits the plotted points (by minimizing the distances between the plots and the curve). Or we can use regression, a statistical technique. Using the latter will produce a current/internal wage curve that best fits the plotted points. In any case, we show the results in Figure 11-7 (right).[62]

10. Conduct a Market Analysis: Salary Surveys

salary survey
A survey aimed at determining prevailing wage rates. A good salary survey provides specific wage rates for specific jobs. Formal written questionnaire surveys are the most comprehensive, but telephone surveys and newspaper ads are also sources of information.

Next, we must compile the information needed to draw an *external wage curve* for our jobs, based on what other employers are paying for similar jobs. **Salary surveys**—surveys of what others are paying—play a big role in pricing jobs.[63] Employers use salary surveys in three ways. First, they use survey data to price benchmark jobs. Benchmark jobs are the anchor jobs around which they slot their other jobs, based on each job's relative worth to the firm. Second, employers typically price 20% or more of their positions directly in the marketplace (rather than relative to the firm's benchmark jobs), based on a survey of what comparable firms are paying for comparable jobs. (Google might do this for jobs like systems engineer, whose salaries fluctuate widely and often.) Third, surveys also collect data on benefits like insurance, sick leave, and vacations for decisions regarding employee benefits.

Salary surveys can be formal or informal. *Informal* phone or Internet surveys are good for checking specific issues, such as when a bank wants to confirm the salary at which to advertise a newly open teller's job, or whether some banks are really paying tellers an incentive. Some large employers can afford to send out their own *formal* surveys to collect compensation information from other employers. These ask about things like number of employees, overtime policies, starting salaries, and paid vacations.

COMMERCIAL, PROFESSIONAL, AND GOVERNMENT SALARY SURVEYS Many employers use surveys published by consulting firms, professional associations, or government agencies. For example, the U.S. Department of Labor's Bureau of Labor Statistics' (BLS) *National Compensation Survey (NCS)* provides comprehensive reports of occupational earnings, compensation cost trends, and benefits (www.bls.gov/bls/wages.htm).

Detailed occupational earnings are available from the national compensation survey for over 800 occupations in the United States, calculated with data from employers in all industry sectors in every State and the District of Columbia (http://stats.bls.gov/oes/current/oes_nat.htm). The *Current Employment Statistics Survey* is a monthly survey of the payroll records of business

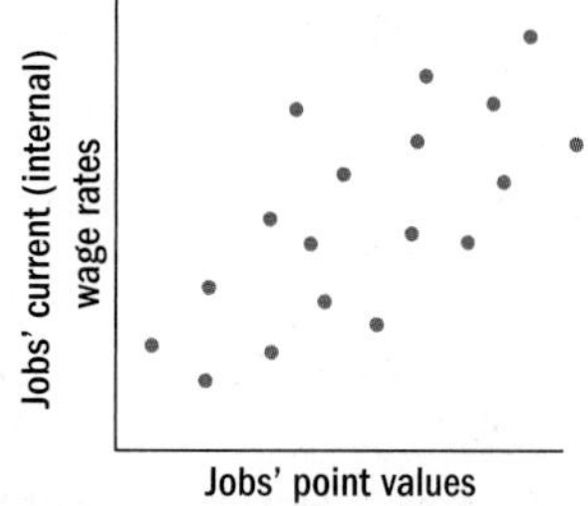

FIGURE 11-7 **The Current/Internal Wage Curve**

establishments that provides data on earnings of production and nonsupervisory workers at the national level. This provides information about earnings as well as production bonuses, commissions, and cost-of-living increases. The *National Compensation Survey—Benefits* provides information on the share of workers who participate in specified benefits, such as health care, retirement plans, and paid vacations. These data also show the details of those benefits, such as amounts of paid leave. Internationally, the BLS reports comparative hourly compensation costs in local currencies and U.S. dollars for production workers and all employees in manufacturing in its international labor comparisons tables.

Private consulting and/or executive recruiting companies like Hay Associates, Towers Watson Global Data Services, and Aon (www.aon.com) publish data covering compensation for top and middle management and members of boards of directors. Professional organizations like the Society for Human Resource Management and the Financial Executives Institute publish surveys of compensation practices among members of their associations.[64]

USING THE INTERNET TO DO COMPENSATION SURVEYS An expanding array of Internet-based options makes it easy for anyone to access published compensation survey information. Table 11-4 shows some popular salary survey websites.

Many of these sites, such as Salary.com, provide national salary levels for jobs that the site then arithmetically adjusts to each locale based on cost-of-living formulas. To get a real-time picture of what employers in your area are actually paying for, say, accounting clerks, it's useful to access the online Internet sites of one or two of your local newspapers. For example, the *South Florida Sun-Sentinel* (and many papers) uses a site called careerbuilder.com. It lists just about all the job opportunities listed in the newspaper by category and, in many instances, their wage rates (http://www.careerbuilder.com/).

11. Draw the Market (External) Wage Curve

The current/internal wage curve from step 9 is helpful. For example, showing, as it does, how a job's current pay rate compares with its points helps the employer identify jobs for which pay rates are currently too high or too low, relative to others in the company. (For example, if a job's current wage rate is well above the internal wage curve, it suggests that the present wage rate for that job is inequitably high, given the number of points we've assigned to that job.)

What the current (internal) wage curve does *not* reveal is whether our pay rates are too high, too low, or just right relative to what other firms are paying. For this, we need to draw a *market* or ex*ternal wage* curve.

To draw the market/external wage curve, we produce a scatter plot and wage curve as in Figure 11-8 (left and right). However, instead of using our firm's current wage rates, we use market wage rates (obtained from salary surveys). The market/external wage curve compares our jobs' points with market pay rates for our jobs.

TABLE 11-4 Some Pay Data Web Sites

Sponsor	Internet Address	What It Provides	Downside
Salary.com	Salary.com	Salary by job and zip code, plus job and description, for hundreds of jobs	Adapts national averages by applying local cost-of-living differences
U.S. Office of Personnel Management	www.opm.gov/oca/09Tables/index.asp	Salaries and wages for U.S. government jobs, by location	Limited to U.S. government jobs
Job Star	http://jobstar.org/tools/salary/sal-prof.php	Profession-specific salary surveys	Necessary to review numerous salary surveys for each profession
cnnmoney.com	cnnmoney.com	Input your current salary and city; for comparable salary in destination city	Based on national averages adapted to cost-of-living differences

FIGURE 11-8 The Market/External Wage Curve

FIGURE 11-9 Plotting Both the Market and Internal Wage Curves

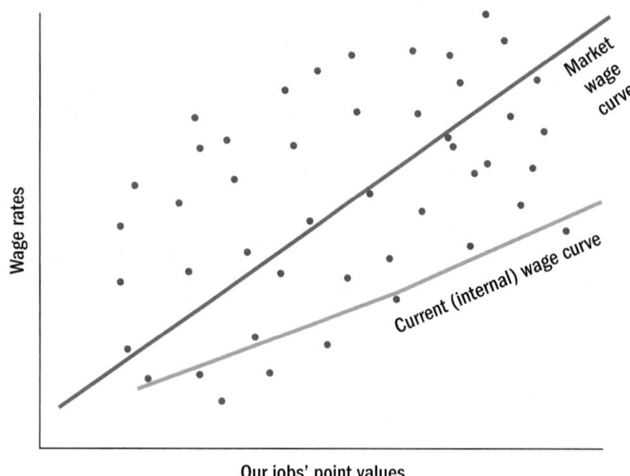

12. Compare and Adjust Current and Market Wage Rates for Jobs

How different are the market rates others are paying for our jobs and the current rates we are now paying for our jobs? To determine this, we can draw both the current/internal and market/external wage curves on one graph, as in Figure 11-9. The market wage curve might be higher than our current wage curve (suggesting that our current pay rates may be too low), or below our current wage curve (suggesting that our current wage rates might be too high). Or perhaps market wage rates are higher for some of our jobs and lower for others.[65]

Based on comparing the current/internal wage curve and market/external wage curve in Figure 11-9, we must decide whether to adjust the current pay rates for our jobs, and if so how. This calls for a policy decision by management. Strategic considerations influence this decision. Do our strategic aspirations suggest we should pay more, the same, or less than competitors? For example, we might decide to move our current internal wage curve up (and thereby give everyone a raise), or down (and thereby perhaps withhold pay increases for some time), or adjust the slope of the internal wage curve to increase what we pay for some jobs and decrease what we pay for others. In any case, the wage curve we end up with (the orange line in Figure 11-10 on page 348) should now be equitable internally (in terms of the point value of each job) and equitable externally (in terms of what other firms are paying).[66]

13. Develop Pay Grades

Employers typically group similar jobs (in terms of points) into grades for pay purposes. Then, instead of having to deal with hundreds of job rates, you might only have to focus on, say, pay rates for 10 or 12 pay grades. For example, Serco, a services firm which operates a London, England, light railway system, set up pay grades after ranking jobs using a point system based on knowledge, management complexity, and the job's magnitude and impact on the organization.[67]

pay (or wage) grade
A pay grade is comprised of jobs of approximately equal difficulty.

A **pay (or wage) grade** is comprised of jobs of approximately equal difficulty or importance as determined by job evaluation. If you used the point method of job evaluation, the pay grade

FIGURE 11-10 **Wage Structure**

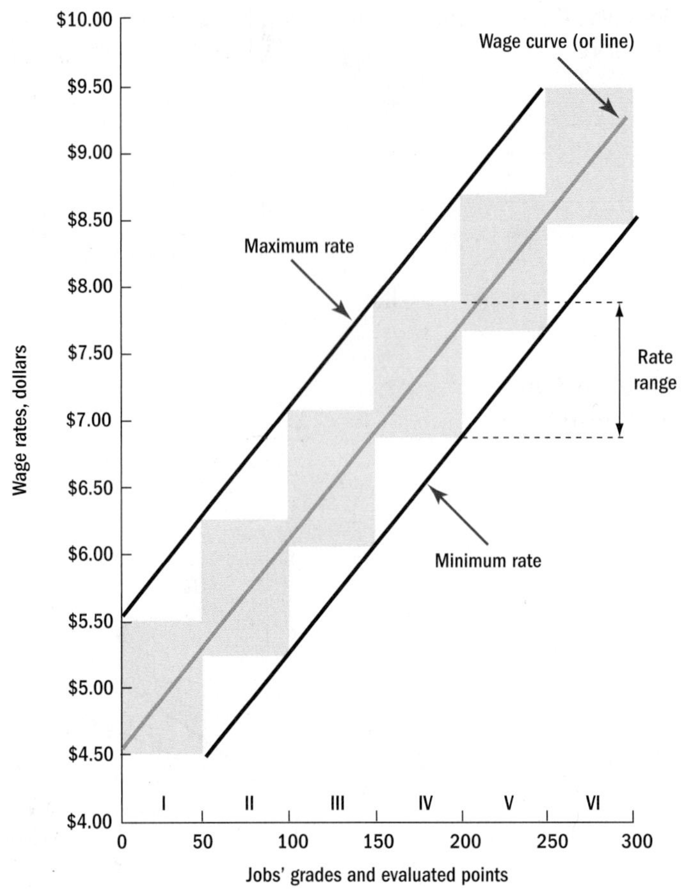

consists of jobs falling within a range of points. If the ranking method was used, the grade consists of a specific number of ranks. If you use the classification system, then your jobs are already categorized into classes (or grades).

DETERMINING THE NUMBER OF PAY GRADES It is standard to establish grades of equal point spread. (In other words, each grade might include all those jobs falling between 50 and 100 points, 100 and 150 points, 150 and 200 points, etc.) Since each grade is the same width, the main issue involves determining how many grades to have. There doesn't seem to be any optimal number, although 10 to 16 grades for a given job cluster (shop jobs, clerical jobs, etc.) seems to be common. You need more pay grades if there are, say, 1,000 jobs to be graded than if there are only 100.

14. Establish Rate Ranges

Most employers do not pay just one rate for all jobs in a particular pay grade. For example, GE Medical won't want to pay all its accounting clerks, from beginners to long tenure, at the same rate, even though they may all be in the same pay grade. Instead, employers develop vertical pay (or "rate") ranges for each of the horizontal pay grades (or pay classes). These **pay (or rate) ranges** often appear as vertical boxes within each grade, showing minimum, maximum, and midpoint pay rates for that grade, as in Figure 11-10. (Specialists call this graph a *wage structure.* Figure 11-10 graphically depicts the range of pay rates—in this case, per hour—paid for each pay grade.) Alternatively, you may depict the pay range for each class or grade as steps in a table, as in Table 11-5, on page 349. Here you will have specific corresponding pay rates for each step within each grade in tabular form. Thus Table 11-5 shows the pay rates and steps for most federal government grades. As of the time of this pay schedule, for instance, employees in positions classified in grade GS-10 could be paid annual salaries between $56,857 and $73,917, depending on the level or step at which they were hired into the grade, the amount of time they were in the grade, and any merit increases they've received.

pay (or rate) ranges
A series of steps or levels within a pay grade, usually based upon years of service.

TABLE 11-5 Federal Government Salary Table, Effective January 2011

For the Locality Pay Area of Washington-Baltimore-Northern Virginia, DC-MD-VA-WV-I/M Annual Rates by Grade and Step

Grade	Step 1	Step 2	Step 3	Step 4	Step 5	Step 6	Step 7	Step 8	Step 9	Step 10
1	22115	22854	23589	24321	25056	25489	26215	26948	26977	27663
2	24865	25456	26279	26977	27280	28082	28885	29687	30490	31292
3	27130	28034	28938	29843	30747	31651	32556	33460	34364	35269
4	30456	31471	32486	33501	34516	35531	36546	37560	38575	39590
5	34075	35210	36346	37481	38616	39752	40887	42022	43158	44293
6	37983	39249	40514	41780	43046	44312	45578	46843	48109	49375
7	42209	43616	45024	46431	47838	49246	50653	52061	53468	54875
8	46745	48303	49861	51418	52976	54534	56092	57649	59207	60765
9	51630	53350	55070	56791	58511	60232	61952	63673	65393	67114
10	56857	58752	60648	62544	64439	66335	68230	70126	72022	73917
11	62467	64548	66630	68712	70794	72876	74958	77040	79122	81204
12	74872	77368	79864	82359	84855	87350	89846	92341	94837	97333
13	89033	92001	94969	97936	100904	103872	106839	109807	112774	115742
14	105211	108717	112224	115731	119238	122744	126251	129758	133264	136771
15	123758	127883	132009	136134	140259	144385	148510	152635	155500	155500

* Rate limited to the rate for level IV of the Executive Schedule (5 U.S.C. 5304 (g) (1)).

Source: www.opm.gov/policy-data-oversight/pay-leave/salaries-wages/2011/general-schedule/washington-baltimore-northern-virginia-dc-md-va-wv-pa-annual-rates-by-grade-and-step/, accessed September 12, 2013.

DEVELOPING RATE RANGES As in Figure 11-10 the wage curve usually anchors the average pay rate for each vertical pay range. The firm might then arbitrarily decide on a maximum and minimum rate for each grade, such as 15% above and below the wage curve. As an alternative, some employers allow the pay range for each grade to become taller (they include more pay rates) for the higher pay ranges, reflecting the greater demands and performance variability inherent in more complex jobs. As in Figure 11-10, most employers structure their rate ranges to overlap a bit, so an employee in one grade who has more experience or seniority may earn more than would someone in an entry-level position in the next higher pay grade.[68]

There are several reasons to use pay ranges for each pay grade. First, it lets the employer take a more flexible stance in the labor market. For example, it makes it easier to attract experienced, higher-paid employees into a pay grade at the top of the range, since the starting salary for the pay grade's lowest step may be too low to attract them. Pay ranges also let companies provide for performance differences between employees within the same grade or between those with different seniorities.

compa ratio
Equals an employee's pay rate divided by the pay range midpoint for his or her pay grade.

Compensation experts sometimes use *compa ratios.* The **compa ratio** equals an employee's pay rate divided by the pay range midpoint for his or her pay grade. A compa ratio of 1 means the employee is being paid exactly at the pay range midpoint. If the compa ratio is above 1 then the person's pay rate exceeds the midpoint pay for the job. If it is below then the pay rate is less than the midpoint. The compa ratio can help reveal how many jobs in each pay grade are paid above and below competitive market pay rates.[69]

15. Address Remaining Jobs

To this point, we have focused our job evaluation on a limited number of benchmark jobs, as is traditional. We now want to add our remaining jobs to the wage structure. We can do this in two ways. We can evaluate each of the remaining jobs using the same process we just went through. Or we can simply slot the remaining jobs into the wage structure where we feel they belong, without formally evaluating and assigning points to these jobs. Jobs similar enough to our benchmark jobs we can easily slot into the wage structure. Jobs we're not sure about should undergo the same job evaluation process; we assign points to them and precisely slot them into the wage structure.[70]

16. Correct Out-of-Line Rates

Finally, the wage rate the firm is now paying for a particular job may fall well off the wage curve or well outside the rate range for its grade, as illustrated in Figure 11-6 (page 344). This means that the average pay for that job is currently too high or too low, relative to other jobs in the firm. For underpaid jobs, the solution is clear: Raise the wages of underpaid employees to the minimum of the rate range for their pay grade.

Current pay rates falling above the rate range are a different story. These are "red circle," "flagged," or "overrates." There are several ways to cope with this problem. One is to freeze the rate paid to these employees until general salary increases bring the other jobs into line. A second option is to transfer or promote the employees involved to jobs for which you can legitimately pay them their current pay rates. The third option is to freeze the rate for 6 months, during which time you try to transfer or promote the overpaid employees. If you cannot, then cut the rate you pay these employees to the maximum in the pay range for their pay grade. The accompanying HR Tools feature explains a streamlined pay plan procedure for small businesses.

IMPROVING PERFORMANCE: HR Tools for Line Managers and Entrepreneurs

Developing a Workable Pay Plan

Developing a pay plan is as important in a small firm as in a large one. Pay that is too high wastes money; too low triggers turnover; and internally inequitable causes endless badgering by employees demanding raises. The president who wants to concentrate on major issues like sales should institute a rational pay plan.

Market rates come first. Sites like LinkedIn and Salary.com will show localized average pay rates for jobs in your geographic area. The Sunday newspaper classified ads (on-and–offline) will yield useful information on wages offered for jobs similar to those you are trying to price. Local Job Service "One Stop" offices can provide a wealth of information, as they compile extensive information on pay ranges and averages for many of the jobs listed on O*NET. Employment agencies, always anxious to establish ties with employers, will provide good data. Local college and university career centers will reveal prevailing pay rates for many jobs. Professional associations (such as the careers link for civil engineers at www.asce.org/) are good sources of professionals' pay rates.

Smaller firms are making use of the Internet in other ways. StockHouse Media Corp (www.stockhouse.com/) is an international provider of online financial content and community development products with employees around the world. It uses the Web for determining salaries for all the firm's personnel. For example, the HR manager uses e-mail to request salary data from professional groups like the Society for Human Resource Management, and surfs the Internet to monitor rates and trends by periodically checking job boards, company websites, and industry associations.[71]

If you employ more than 20 employees or so, conduct at least a rudimentary job evaluation. You will need job descriptions, since these will be the source of data regarding the nature and worth of each job. Checking websites like O*Net or JobDescription.com can be useful here.

You may find it easier to split your employees into three clusters—say, managerial/professional, office/clerical, and plant personnel. For each of the three groups, choose several compensable factors. Then rank (or assign points to) each job in that cluster based on (say,) a ranking job evaluation. For each job you will then want to create a pay range. In general, you might choose as the midpoint of that range the average market salary for that job, or an average of the market rate and what you are currently paying. Then produce a range of about 30% around this average, broken into five steps. (Thus, assemblers, one of the plant personnel jobs, might earn from $8.00 to $12.60 per hour, in five steps.)

Required compensation policies will include amount of holiday and vacation pay (as we explain in Chapter 13), overtime pay policy, method of pay (weekly, biweekly, monthly), garnishments, and time card or sign-in sheet procedures. For sources of sample policies see, for example, sites such as http://hr.blr.com/timesavers?type=54 and the HR systems discussion on pages 572–574.

Discussion Question 11-3: What type of job evaluation method would you use in a company with 15 employees? Why?

Pricing Managerial and Professional Jobs

4 Explain how to price managerial and professional jobs.

Developing compensation plans for managers or professionals is similar in many respects to developing plans for any employee. The basic aim is the same: to attract, motivate, and retain good employees. And job evaluation is about as applicable to managerial and professional jobs (below the top executive levels) as to production and clerical ones.

There are some big differences, though. Managerial jobs tend to stress harder-to-quantify factors like judgment and problem solving more than do production and clerical jobs. There is also more emphasis on paying managers and professionals based on their performance or on what they can do, rather than on static job demands like working conditions. And one must compete in the marketplace for executives who sometimes have rock star pay. So, job evaluation, although still important for management jobs, usually plays a secondary role to issues like bonuses, incentives, market rates, and benefits.

What Determines Executive Pay?

For top executive jobs (especially the CEO), job evaluation typically has less relevance. The traditional wisdom is that company size and performance significantly affect top managers' salaries. Yet studies from the early 2000s showed that size and performance explained only about 30% of CEO pay: "In reality, CEO pay is set by the board taking into account a variety of factors such as the business strategy, corporate trends, and most importantly where they want to be in a short and long term."[72] One study concluded that three main factors, *job complexity* (span of control, the number of functional divisions over which the executive has direct responsibility, and management level), the employer's *ability to pay* (total profit and rate of return), and the executive's *human capital* (educational level, field of study, work experience) accounted for about two-thirds of executive compensation variance.[73] In practice, CEOs exercise influence over their boards of directors. So, their pay sometimes doesn't reflect strictly arms-length negotiations.[74]

Shareholder activism and government oversight have tightened the restrictions on what companies pay top executives. For example, the banking giant HSBC shelved plans to raise its CEO's pay by over a third after shareholders rejected the proposals.[75]

MANAGERIAL JOB EVALUATION Many employers do use job evaluation for pricing managerial jobs (at least, below the top jobs). The basic approach is to classify executive and management positions into a series of grades, each with a salary range.

As with nonmanagerial jobs, one alternative is to rank the executive and management positions in relation to each other, then grouping into classes those of similar value. However, firms also use the job classification and point methods, with compensable factors like position scope, complexity, and difficulty. As with any jobs, job analysis, salary surveys, and the fine-tuning of salary levels around wage curves also play roles.

Compensating Executives and Managers

Compensation for a company's top executives usually consists of four main elements.[76] *Base pay* includes the person's fixed salary as well as, often, guaranteed bonuses such as "10% of pay at the end of the fourth fiscal quarter, regardless of whether or not the company makes a profit." *Short-term incentives* are usually cash or stock bonuses for achieving short-term goals, such as year-to-year increases in sales revenue. *Long-term incentives* aim to encourage the executive to take actions that drive up the value of the company's stock and include things like stock options; these generally give the executive the right to purchase stock at a specific price for a specific period. Finally, *executive benefits and perks* include things such as supplemental executive retirement pension plans. With so many complicated elements, employers must also be alert to the tax and securities law implications of their executive compensation decisions.[77]

ELEMENTS OF EXECUTIVE PAY Salary is traditionally the cornerstone of executive compensation. On it, employers layer benefits, incentives, and perquisites—all normally conferred in proportion to base pay. Procter & Gamble Co.'s CEO was paid $15.2 million in 2012, including a base salary of $1.6 million, a cash-based bonus of $2.4 million, stock options valued at $4.4 million, stock awards of $6.45 million, plus perks such as air travel.[78] Top executive compensation packages can be whoppers. The CEO of Oracle earned just over $96 million in one recent year, and the CEO of Walt Disney Corporation $37.1 million.[79] But overpaid as many critics may think they are, one expert says CEOs with the highest 20% of compensation produced stock returns 60% greater than those of other firms in their industries.[80]

Executive compensation emphasizes performance (discussed in Chapter 12) more than do other employees' pay plans, since organizational results reflect executives' contributions more directly than those of lower-echelon employees.[81] Indeed, boards are boosting the emphasis on performance-based pay (in part due to shareholder activism). The big issue here is identifying the appropriate performance measures. Typical short-term measures include revenue growth and operating profit margin. Long-term measures include rate of return above some predetermined base.

Compensating Professional Employees

In compensating professionals, employers should first ensure that each employee is actually a "professional" under the law. The Fair Labor Standards Act "provides an exemption from both minimum wage and overtime pay for employees employed as bona fide executive, administrative, professional and outside sales employees."[82] However, calling someone a professional doesn't make him or her one. In addition to earning at least $455 per week, the person's main duty must "be the performance of work requiring advanced knowledge," and "the advanced knowledge must be customarily acquired by a prolonged course of specialized intellectual instruction."[83] One company hired a high school graduate as an exempt "product design specialist II," earning $62,000 per year. The job required 12 years of relevant experience, but no particular education. The court ruled the job was nonexempt.[84]

Beyond that, compensating professional employees like engineers presents unique problems.[85] Analytical jobs emphasize compensable factors such as creativity and problem solving, ones not easily compared or measured. Furthermore, how do you measure performance? For example, the success of an engineer's invention depends on how the firm develops and markets it.

Employers can use job evaluation for professional jobs. Compensable factors here tend to focus on problem solving, creativity, job scope, and technical knowledge and expertise. Firms use the point method and job classification.

Yet in practice, firms rarely rely on just job evaluation for pricing professional jobs. Factors like creativity are hard to measure, and non-pay issues often influence professionals' job decisions. For example, Google recently raised its employees' salaries by 10% in the face of defections by even their highest paid professionals, such as the head of its Chrome OS team, to Facebook.[86] Many of these Google professionals, although well paid by most standards, still felt underpaid. Some moved to jobs they hoped would have more challenges. Others may have sought younger firms with new stock options.

Most employers therefore emphasize a market-pricing approach for these jobs. They price professional jobs in the marketplace as best they can, to establish the values for benchmark jobs. Then they slot these benchmark jobs and their other professional jobs into a salary structure. Each professional discipline usually ends up having four to six grade levels, each with a broad salary range. This helps employers remain competitive when bidding for professionals who literally have global employment possibilities.[87]

Improving Performance Through HRIS: Payroll Administration

Payroll administration is one of the first functions most employers computerize or outsource, and for good reason. Administering the payroll system—keeping track of each employee's worker status, wage rate, dependents, benefits, overtime, tax status, and so on; computing each paycheck; and then directing the actual printing of checks or direct deposits is a time-consuming task, one complicated by the need to comply with many federal, state, and local wage, hour, and other laws.

Many employers do perform this function in-house, usually with a payroll processing software package. Intuit's *Basic Payroll* lets the employer, "[e]nter hours worked and get instant paycheck calculations, including earnings, payroll taxes, and deductions. Then print paychecks yourself. *Basic Payroll* calculates federal and state payroll taxes for you, so you can easily e-pay federal taxes and write a check for state taxes."[88] Kronos's *Workforce Payroll* automates the payroll process, and offers self-service features. For example (see www.kronos.com/HR/Payroll-Software/Payroll-Software.aspx), *Workforce Payroll* will "[l]et your employees see pay stubs and earning histories, make changes to direct deposit and W-4 forms, print W-2s, and even check out how changes to their deductions will affect their paychecks."

On the other hand, many employers do outsource payroll administration to vendors such as ADP. These vendors offer a range of payroll processing options. For instance, smaller employers may opt to call in their payroll data to the vendor's specialists, while larger ones may have this data processed automatically online. In deciding which vendor to use, the employer should consider its goals and the potential economic benefits, as well as factors such as the vendor's reputation. SHRM recommends evaluating the initial list of prospective vendors based on the employer's goals for the relationship. Don't just consider the relative economic benefits of outsourcing the function (rather than doing it in-house), but also the desirability of integrating the employer's internal systems with the vendor's, streamlining tax compliance and filings, and increasing employee self-service.[89]

Contemporary Topics in Compensation

5 Explain the difference between competency-based and traditional pay plans.

How employers pay employees is evolving. In this final section, we'll look at six important contemporary compensation topics: competency-based pay, broadbanding, talent management, comparable worth, board oversight of executive pay, and total rewards.

Competency-Based Pay

Some managers question whether job evaluations that slot jobs into narrow cubbyholes ("Machinist I," "Machinist II," and so on) might not actually be counterproductive. For example, high-performance work systems depend on flexible multiskilled job assignments and on teamwork, and there's no place here for employees to say "That's not my job."

competency-based pay
Where the company pays for the employee's range, depth, and types of skills and knowledge, rather than for the job title he or she holds.

Competency-based pay (and broadbanding, explained later) aims to avoid that problem.[90] With competency- generally skill or knowledge-based pay, you pay the employee for the skills and knowledge he or she is capable of using rather than for the responsibilities or title of the job currently held.[91] Experts variously call this competence-, knowledge-, or skill-based pay. With competency-based pay, an employee in a class I job who could (but may not have to at the moment) do class II work gets paid as a class II worker, not a class I. *Competencies* are demonstrable personal characteristics such as knowledge, skills, and personal behaviors such as leadership. Why pay employees based on the skill levels they achieve, rather than based on the jobs they're assigned to? With more companies organizing around teams, you want to encourage employees to get and to use the skills required to rotate among jobs.

In practice, competency-based pay usually comes down to pay for knowledge or skill based pay.[92] Most such pay programs generally contain five elements. The employer *defines* specific required skills and chooses a *method* for basing the person's pay on his or her skills. A *training* system lets employees acquire skills. There is a formal competency *testing* system. And, the work is *designed* so that employees can easily move among jobs of varying skill levels. As an example, review Chapter 4's Figure 4-12 on page 114. For this job, BP lists the minimum level for each skill (such as Technical Expertise and Problem Solving) someone holding this job must attain. As an employee achieves each level of each skill, he or she would receive a bump in pay. The accompanying JLG program feature shows another example.

A recent survey found that only about 12% use what they call skill-based pay and 13% use competency-based pay.[93] In challenging economic times, perhaps the efficiencies of job evaluation sometimes outweigh the flexibility that comes with competency-based pay.

Many employers, such as General Mills, pay certain workers based on attained skill levels.

IMPROVING PERFORMANCE: HR Practices Around the Globe

JLG's Skill-Based Pay Program

JLG industries supplies access equipment such as aerial work platforms and mast booms.[94] The firm instituted a skill-based pay program to reward employees for the number of basic skills they can perform rather than for the jobs to which they are assigned.[95] JLG integrated the skill pay program into its existing payroll system, and supported it with a computerized reporting system.

As an employee acquires and masters a new skill, JLG increases his or her pay on a scheduled basis. Pay increases are directly proportional to employee "value" based on skill acquisition. Pay adjustment increments are $0.30 per hour and can be in addition to regularly scheduled merit increases. Qualified employees are eligible to receive a skill-based wage adjustment at three times. The first increase is available at the completion of an initial 6-month probationary employment period. An additional skill-based adjustment may come in conjunction with the employee's annual merit review. Other skill-based adjustments are allowed yearly and 6 months after the annual merit review.

JLG assigns all hourly production and maintenance workers to a particular Job Family. A Job Family consists of a group of employees performing similar activities and requiring similar skills. *Each Job Family has a set of required skills,* including certain job-related skills as well as skills related to quality and safety.

Skill assessment is ongoing. Formal evaluation begins at the end of the 6-month probationary period, at which time the employee is tested for mastery of *the minimum skills* required for the Job Family. (A 100% mastery of these minimum skills is required for successful completion of the probationary period.) Then, twice a year, the company analyzes the employee's progress towards more *advanced skills*, and sets training objectives. Careful consideration is given to the employee's interests, capabilities, limitations, and cross-training requirements. Overall responsibility for skills acquisition and career development rests with the employee. The employee determines his/her level of participation in acquiring new or additional skills. Supervisors assist by helping the employee identify and plan for new skills to be acquired, and by creating opportunities for cross training and certifying the skills training.

To determine if an employee is qualified for a skill based pay raise, a comparison is made between the employee's current wage rate and the target rate within the Job Family to which the employee is assigned. Target pay rates are based on the degree of mastery of the complete skill set required for a Job Family. If the current wage rate is equal to or greater than the target rate, no pay adjustment is made. If the current rate is below the target rate, a skill-based adjustment is authorized for employees who mastered the Job Family's skills.

In place since the 1990s, JLG reports that the program is producing benefits. The greater skill base it fosters permits faster adaptation to technology and product mix changes. With a greater skill range, workers are better able to focus on problem areas and avoid idle time waiting for problems to be fixed, or for work done by others. Employees can participate more actively in problem-solving because of their wider perspective on total work flow. The program permits lower overall staffing levels by incorporating specialized tasks others might otherwise be hired to perform into Job Family skill requirements. The company has been able to raise minimum hiring qualifications. Overall increases in productivity have enabled expansion of capacity.

Discussion Question 11-4: Review our discussion of competencies in Chapter 4; then write three competency statements for one job you believe they would have at a company such as JLG. A useful competency statement includes three elements: the *name and a brief description* of the competency, a *description of the observable behaviors* that represent proficiency in the competency, and *proficiency levels*.

Broadbanding

Most firms end up with pay plans that slot jobs into classes or grades, each with its own vertical pay rate range. For example, the U.S. government's pay plan consists of 15 main grades (GS-1 to GS-15), each with its own pay range. For an employee whose job falls in one of these grades, the pay range for that grade dictates his or her minimum and maximum salary.

The question is, "How wide should the salary grades be, in terms of the number of job evaluation points they include?" (For example, the U.S. government could collapse its 15 salary grades into 5 or 6 broader bands.) There is a downside to having (say, 15) narrow grades. For instance, if you want someone whose job is in grade 2 to fill in for a time in a job that happens to be in grade 1, it's difficult to reassign that person without lowering his or her salary. Similarly, if you want the person to learn about a job that happens to be in grade 3, the employee might first want a corresponding raise to grade 3 pay. Traditional grade pay plans thus may tend to breed inflexibility.

broadbanding
Consolidating salary grades and ranges into just a few wide levels or "bands," each of which contains a relatively wide range of jobs and salary levels.

That is why some firms are broadbanding their pay plans.[96] **Broadbanding** means collapsing salary grades into just a few wide levels or bands, each of which contains a relatively wide range of jobs and pay levels. Figure 11-11 illustrates this. Here, the company's previous six pay grades are consolidated into two broad grades or "broadbands."

A company may create broadbands for all its jobs, or for specific groups such as managers or professionals. The (vertical) pay rate range of each broadband is relatively large, since it ranges from the minimum pay of the lowest grade the firm merged into the broadband up to the maximum pay of the highest merged grade. Thus, for example, instead of having 10 salary grades, each of which contains a salary range of $15,000, the firm might collapse the 10 grades into three broadbands, each with a set of jobs such that the difference between the lowest- and highest-paid jobs might be $40,000 or more. For the jobs that fall in this broadband, there is therefore a much wider range of pay rates. You can move an employee from job to job within the broadband more easily, without worrying about the employee's moving outside the relatively narrow rate range associated with a traditional narrow pay grade. Broadbanding therefore facilitates flexibility.

PROS AND CONS Broadbanding injects greater flexibility into employee pay.[97] The broader salary bands can include both supervisors and subordinates and also facilitate moving employees into higher or lower skilled jobs temporarily, without bumping the person into a new pay range. Thus, "the employee who needs to spend time in a lower-level job to develop a certain skill set can receive higher-than-usual pay for the work, a circumstance considered impossible under traditional pay systems."[98] Conversely, employees assigned to traditional narrowly defined pay grades may take a "that's not my job" attitude and focus on their usual assigned duties.[99] It also provides more flexibility in what new employees can be paid.

FIGURE 11-11
Broadbanded Structure and How It Relates to Traditional Pay Grades and Ranges

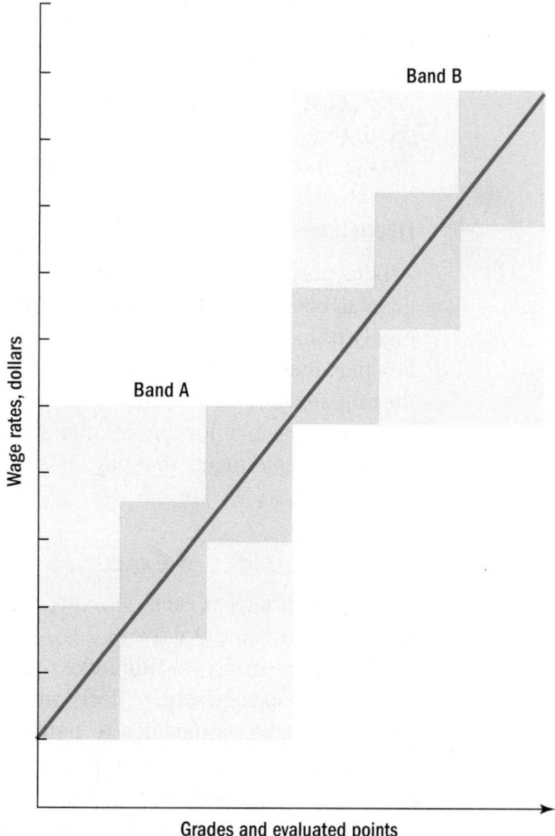

However, broadbanding can be unsettling. "There's a sense of permanence in the set of job responsibilities often attached to job titles," one manager says. That sense of permanence isn't as clear when employees move frequently from project to project and job to job.[100]

Talent Management and Actively Managing Compensation Allocations

Employers are becoming more selective about how they allocate pay raises and other rewards. Probably the most notable example here is the trend to allocating rewards not just based on merit or seniority but on the employee's importance to the company's mission. For example, we saw that one telecommunications firm previously spread development money and compensation evenly over its 8,000 employees. When the recession came, it segmented its employees into business impact, high performers, high potentials, and critical skills. Then they shifted their dollars from low performers and those not making an impact to high performers, high potentials, and those with critical skills.[101]

Comparable Worth

comparable worth
The concept by which women who are usually paid less than men can claim that men in comparable rather than in strictly equal jobs are paid more.

Comparable worth refers to the requirement to pay men and women equal wages for jobs that are dissimilar but of comparable value (for instance measured in points) to the employer. This may mean comparing dissimilar jobs, such as nurses to truck mechanics. The question "comparable worth" seeks to address is this: Should you pay women who are performing jobs *equal* to men's or just *comparable* to men's the same as men? If you only pay women who are doing the same jobs (equal jobs) as men the same as men, then the result may be to limit women's pay rates to that of the lower-paid jobs in which women tend to predominate.

County of Washington v. Gunther (1981) was a pivotal case. It involved Washington County, Oregon, prison matrons who claimed sex discrimination. The county had evaluated roughly comparable (but different) men's jobs as having 5% more "job content" (based on a point evaluation system) than the women's jobs, but paid the men 35% more.[102] Why should there be such a pay discrepancy for roughly comparable jobs? After moving through the courts to the U.S. Supreme Court, Washington County finally agreed to pay 35,000 employees in female-dominated jobs almost $500 million in pay raises over 7 years to settle.

Comparable worth has implications for job evaluation. Virtually every comparable worth case that reached a court involved the point method of job evaluation. By assigning points to dissimilar jobs, point plans facilitate comparability ratings among different jobs. Should employers still use point plans? Perhaps the wisest approach is for employers to price their jobs as they see fit (with or without point plans), but to also ensure that women have equal access to all jobs. In other words, eliminate sex-segregated jobs.

Diveristy Counts: The Pay Gap

All this notwithstanding, women in the United States earn only about 80% as much as men.[103] In general, education may reduce the wage gap somewhat.[104] But gaps remain, even among the most highly trained. For example, new female medical doctors recently earned about $17,000 per year less than their male counterparts did.[105] Reasons put forward for the male-female gap range from the outdated notion that employers view women as having less leverage, to the fact that professional men change jobs more often (gaining more raises in the process) and that women tend to end up in departments that pay less.[106] In any case, it's a problem employers need to recognize and address.

Board Oversight of Executive Pay

There are various reasons why boards are scrutinizing their executives' pay more than in the past. The Dodd-Frank Law of 2010 requires that American companies give shareholders a "say on pay." Law firms are filing class-action suits demanding information from companies about their senior executive pay decisions.[107] The Financial Accounting Standards Board requires that most public companies recognize as an expense the fair value of the stock options they grant.[108] The Sarbanes-Oxley Act makes executives personally liable, under certain conditions, for corporate financial oversight lapses. The chief justice of Delaware's Supreme Court said that governance issues, shareholder activism, and other changes have "created a new set of expectations for directors."[109] The Securities and Exchange Commission (SEC) requires filing detailed compensation-related information, including a listing of all individual "perks" or benefits if they total more than $100,000.[110]

The net result is that lawyers specializing in executive pay suggest that boards of directors (whose compensation committees usually make these pay decisions in large firms) ask themselves these questions:[111]

- Has our compensation committee identified its duties and processes?
- Is our compensation committee using the appropriate compensation advisors?
- Are there particular executive compensation issues that our committee should address?[112]
- Do our procedures demonstrate diligence and independence (including careful deliberations and records)?
- Is our committee appropriately communicating its decisions? How will shareholders react?[113]

Total Rewards, Recognition, and Employee Performance

Financial and competitive pressures are shifting employers' attention from purely financial pay packages to what they call total rewards. As noted earlier, *total rewards* encompass the traditional financial compensation components. However, they also include recognition programs and redesigned jobs (discussed in Chapter 4), telecommuting programs, health and well-being programs, and training and career development. Some employers distribute annual total rewards statements to employees to help them appreciate the full range of rewards that they are receiving.[114]

Non-cash rewards such as gift cards, merchandise, and recognition therefore play a rising role in compensation, because they are cost-effective and improve performance.[115] After installing an online system that enabled employees at a West Virginia DuPont plant to award each other recognition, 95% were soon using it.[116] International Fitness Holdings lets employees use a Facebook-type application to recognize peers by posting messages and sending private e-mails.[117] Employers contract with sites like Globoforce.com to provide online recognition systems. As one consulting company says,

> "In the next generation of talent management, organizations will . . . customize total rewards packages. Through personalized Web portals, organizations will offer rewards menus and associated dollar credits that are tailored to groups of workers and even individual workers. Dollar amounts will be tied to role and performance as opposed to age or seniority. Options offered will go beyond the traditional flexible benefits fare to include choice in work assignments and location, time and money for training, and working time flexibility. For example, AstraZeneca PLC offers workers customized rewards menus, allowing them to design the specifics of their rewards packages."[118]

Review

MyManagementLab Go to **mymanagementlab.com** to complete the problems marked with this icon. 

Chapter Section Summaries

1. In establishing strategic pay plans, managers first need to understand some **basic factors in determining pay rates**. Employee compensation includes both direct financial payments and indirect financial statements. The factors determining the design of any pay plan include legal, union, company strategy/policy, and equity. Legal considerations include, most importantly, the Fair Labor Standards Act, which governs matters such as minimum wages and overtime pay. Specific categories of employees are exempt from the act or certain provisions of the act, particularly its overtime provisions. The Equal Pay Act of 1963 and

the Employee Retirement Income Security Act are other important laws.

2. Employers use two basic approaches to setting pay rates: *market-based approaches* and **job evaluation methods**. Many firms, particularly smaller ones, simply use a *market-based* approach. Job evaluation methods involve assigning values to each of the company's jobs. This helps to produce a pay plan in which each job's pay is equitable based on its value to the employer.
   - Job evaluation is a systematic comparison done in order to determine the worth of one job relative to another based on compensable factors.
   - Compensable factors refer to compensable elements of a job such as skills and efforts.
   - Popular job evaluation methods include ranking, job classification, the point method, and factor comparison.
   - With ranking, for instance, you conduct a job analysis, group jobs by department, and have raters rank jobs.
3. We said the process of **creating a market-competitive pay plan** while ensuring external, internal, and procedural equity consists of 16 steps as follows: 1. Choose Benchmark Jobs; 2. Select Compensable Factors; 3. Assign Weights to Compensable Factors; 4. Convert Percentages to Points for Each Factor; 5. Define Each Factor's Degrees; 6. Determine for Each Factor Its Factor Degrees' Points; 7. Review Job Descriptions and Job Specifications; 8. Evaluate the Jobs; 9. Draw the Current (Internal) Wage Curve; 10. Conduct a Market Analysis: Salary Surveys; 11. Draw the Market (External) Wage Curve; 12. Compare and Adjust Current and Market Wage Rates for Jobs; 13. Develop Pay Grades; 14. Establish Rate Ranges; 15. Address Remaining Jobs; 16. Correct Out-of-Line Rates
   - Salary surveys may be informal phone or Internet surveys, or formal surveys conducted by the employer or utilizing commercial, professional, and/or government salary surveys.
   - Once the committee uses job evaluation to determine the relative worth of each job, it can turn to the task of assigning pay rates to each job; it would usually first want to group jobs into pay grades to streamline the process.
   - The team can then use wage curves to price each grade and then fine-tune pay rates.
4. **Pricing managerial and professional jobs** involves some special issues. Managerial pay typically consists of base pay, short-term incentives, long-term incentives, and executive benefits and, particularly at the top levels, doesn't lend itself to job evaluation but rather to understanding the job's complexity, the employer's ability to pay, and the need to be competitive in attracting top talent.
5. We addressed several important **special topics in compensation**. More employers are moving from paying jobs based on their intrinsic duties toward paying jobs based on the competencies the job requires. The main reason for doing so is to encourage employees to develop the competencies they need to move seamlessly from job to job. Broadbanding means consolidating several rates and ranges into a few wide levels or "bands," each of which contains a relatively wide range of jobs in salary levels. Broadbanding encourages employees to move freely from job to job and facilitates implementing team-based high-performance management systems. Comparable worth refers to the requirement to pay men and women equal pay for jobs that are of comparable rather than strictly equal value to the employee. With many stockholders concerned with excessive executive remuneration, board oversight of executive pay has become an important issue, and boards of directors should use qualified advisors and exercise diligence and independence in formulating executive pay plans. Total rewards encompass the traditional compensation components, but also things such as recognition and redesigned more challenging jobs.

Discussion Questions

✪ **11-5.** What is the difference between exempt and nonexempt jobs?

✪ **11-6.** Should the job evaluation depend on an appraisal of the jobholder's performance? Why? Why not?

11-7. What is the relationship between compensable factors and job specifications?

11-8. Define and give an example of how to conduct a job evaluation.

11-9. The average pay for most university presidents is around $300,000 per year, but many earn much more. For example, the president of NYU received about $1 million in 1 year. Discuss why you would (or would not) pay university presidents as much or more than many corporate CEOs.

11-10. Do small companies need to develop a pay plan? Why or why not?

Individual and Group Activities

11-11. Working individually or in groups, conduct salary surveys for the following positions: entry-level accountant and entry-level chemical engineer. What sources did you use, and what conclusions did you reach? If you were the HR manager for a local engineering firm, what would you recommend that you pay for each job?

11-12. Working individually or in groups, develop compensation policies for the teller position at a local bank. Assume that there are four tellers: two were hired in May and the other two were hired in December. The compensation policies should address the following: appraisals, raises, holidays, vacation pay, overtime pay, method of pay, garnishments, and time cards.

11-13. Working individually or in groups, access relevant Web sites to determine what equitable pay ranges are for these jobs: chemical engineer, marketing manager, and HR manager, all with a bachelor's degree and 5 years' experience. Do so for the following cities: New York, New York; San Francisco, California; Houston, Texas; Denver, Colorado; Miami, Florida; Atlanta, Georgia; Chicago, Illinois; Birmingham, Alabama; Detroit, Michigan; and Washington, D.C. For each position in each city, what are the pay ranges and the average pay? Does geographical location impact the salaries of the different positions? If so, how?

11-14. Appendix A, PHR and SPHR Knowledge Base, at the end of this book (pages 580–588) lists the knowledge someone studying for the HRCI certification exam needs to have in each area of human resource management (such as in Strategic Management, Workforce Planning, and Human Resource Development). In groups of four to five students, do four things: (1) review Appendix A; (2) identify the material in this chapter that relates to the required knowledge Appendix A lists; (3) write four multiple-choice exam questions on this material that you believe would be suitable for inclusion in the HRCI exam; and (4) if time permits, have someone from your team post your team's questions in front of the class, so that students in all teams can answer the exam questions created by the other teams.

11-15. Working individually or in groups, use the point system described in steps 1 to 16 in this chapter. Do so for a job description that you find online—the list at http://hiring.monster.com/hr/hr-best-practices/recruiting-hiring-advice/job-descriptions/sample-job-descriptions.aspx is useful. To simplify things, assume there is only one factor you have to use, and that it is Job Complexity, so that you can use Figure 11-5.

Experiential Exercise

Ranking the College's Administrators

Purpose: The purpose of this exercise is to give you experience in performing a job evaluation using the ranking method.

Required Understanding: You should be thoroughly familiar with the ranking method of job evaluation and obtain job descriptions for your college's dean, department chairperson, director of admissions, library director, registrar, and your professor.

How to Set Up the Exercise/Instructions: Divide the class into groups of four or five students. The groups will perform a job evaluation of the positions of dean, department chairperson, and professor using the ranking method.

- Perform a job evaluation by ranking the jobs. You may use one or more compensable factors.

11-16. If time permits, a spokesperson from each group can put his or her group's rankings on the board. Did the groups end up with about the same results? How did they differ? Why do you think they differed?

Video Case

Video Title: Planning (TWZ Role-Play)

SYNOPSIS

This video details a team meeting at Eco Threads, a company that is facing a financial challenge of cutting $2 million out of their budget over 2 years. This meeting is between some of the management of the company and how they are approaching the budget-planning process and weighing the pros and cons of cutting jobs versus cutting hours worked. Susan and Dean share their ideas for trimming the budget with Mitch. Susan is for cutting jobs and potentially investigating outsourcing jobs to other countries. Dean would prefer not to cut jobs or outsource, but rather cut employees' hours and institute job sharing. Mitch then explains the sensitive nature of budgetary planning and the conflicts that may arise during this process.

Discussion Questions

11-17. Although cutting jobs, cutting hours, and/or outsourcing are traditional ways to deal with budgetary crises, they're not the only ways. Some employers (and even many employees) prefer maintaining "full employment" and instead cutting pay rates to make up the financial shortfall. Would this be a sensible alternative for Eco Threads to consider? Why?

11-18. Suppose Eco Threads does decide to keep everyone fully employed and instead cuts pay rates to obtain the required budget savings. Based on what you learned here, specifically what concerns would you have about cutting pay rates? What steps would you suggest they take to make sure that the resulting post-cut pay rates are equitable?

Application Case

Salary Inequities at AstraZeneca

More than 50 years after passage of the Equal Pay Act, women in America still earn about 80 cents for every dollar earned by a man. That adds up to a loss for the average female worker of about $380,000 over a lifetime.

Recently, the U.S. Department of Labor's Office of Federal Contract Compliance Programs (OFCCP) entered into an agreement with AstraZeneca, a large international pharmaceuticals firm, for the company to pay some of its female sales associates a total of $250,000.[119] AstraZeneca had a contract valued at over $2 billion with the U.S. Department of Veterans Affairs to provide drugs to hospitals around the country. That made it subject to Executive Order 11246, which aims to ensure that employees of U.S. contractors and subcontractors with federal contracts pay their employees fairly without regard to sex, race, color, religion, and national origin.

After conducting a compliance review, the OFCCP concluded that AstraZeneca violated Executive Order 11246 by failing to ensure certain women employees were paid fairly. According to the OFCCP lawsuit, an AstraZeneca Business Center had routinely paid some of its female "primary care" and "specialty care" level III pharmaceutical sales specialists an average of $1,700 less than men with the same positions.

Because of the company's pay secrecy policies, many of the women didn't know they were being paid less. In addition to the financial settlement, AstraZeneca and OFCCP will review records of the firm's female employees in 14 states. If they find additional statistical evidence of wage discrimination, the company must remedy it.

Questions

AstraZeneca has brought you in as a compensation consultant. Here are the questions they would like you to answer for them:

11-19. Although the case with OFCCP is closed, we wonder if there are any less discriminatory explanations possible for why our women sales reps on average earned less than men. If so, what are they?

11-20. Our own company now uses a point method to evaluate jobs for pay purposes, and each resulting job class also has a rate range associated with it. Sales associates are now paid a salary that is not based on incentive pay. List three specific things we can do to ensure that a similar problem (inequitable pay based on gender) does not arise again, assuming they continue using the point plan.

11-21. What sort of compensation plan would you recommend for us, and why?

Continuing Case

Carter Cleaning Company

The New Pay Plan

Carter Cleaning Centers does not have a formal wage structure nor does it have rate ranges or use compensable factors. Wage rates are based mostly on those prevailing in the surrounding community and are tempered with an attempt on the part of Jack Carter to maintain some semblance of equity between what workers with different responsibilities in the stores are paid.

Carter does not make any formal surveys when determining what his company should pay. He peruses the want ads almost every day and conducts informal surveys among his friends in the local chapter of the laundry and cleaners trade association. While Jack has taken a "seat-of-the-pants" approach to paying employees, his salary schedule has been guided by several basic pay policies. Although many of his colleagues adhere to a policy of paying minimum rates, Jack has always followed a policy of paying his employees about 10% above what he feels are the prevailing rates, a policy that he believes reduces turnover while fostering employee loyalty. Of somewhat more concern to Jennifer is her father's informal policy of paying men about 20% more than women for the same job. Her father's explanation is, "They're stronger and can work harder for longer hours, and besides they all have families to support."

Questions

11-22. Is the company at the point where it should be setting up a formal salary structure based on a complete job evaluation? Why?

11-23. Is Jack Carter's policy of paying 10% more than the prevailing rates a sound one, and how could that be determined?

11-24. Similarly, is Carter's male–female differential wise? If not, why not?

11-25. Specifically, what would you suggest Jennifer do now with respect to her company's pay plan?

Translating Strategy into HR Policies and Practices Case*,§

**The accompanying strategy map for this chapter is in the MyManagementLab; and the overall map on the inside back cover of this text outlines the relationships involved.*

IMPROVING PERFORMANCE at The Hotel Paris

The New Compensation Plan

The Hotel Paris's competitive strategy is "To use superior guest service to differentiate the Hotel Paris properties, and to thereby increase the length of stay and return rate of guests, and thus boost revenues and profitability." HR manager Lisa Cruz must now formulate functional policies and activities that support this competitive strategy by eliciting the required employee behaviors and competencies.

Like several other HR systems at the Hotel Paris, the compensation program was unplanned and unsophisticated. The company has a narrow target range for what it will pay employees in each job category (front-desk clerk, security guard, and so forth). Each hotel manager decides where to start a new employee within that narrow pay range. The company has given little thought to tying general pay levels or individual employees' pay to the company's strategic goals. For example, the firm's policy is simply to pay its employees a "competitive salary," by which it means about average for what other hotels in the city are paying for similar jobs. Lisa knows that pay policies like these may actually run counter to what the company wants to achieve strategically, in terms of creating an extraordinarily service-oriented workforce. How can you hire and retain a top workforce, and channel their behaviors toward high-quality guest services, if you don't somehow link performance and pay? She and her team therefore turn to the task of assessing and redesigning the company's compensation plan.

Even the most casual review by Lisa Cruz and the CFO made it clear that the company's compensation plan wasn't designed to support the firm's new strategic goals. For one thing, they knew that they should pay somewhat more on average than did their competitors if they expected employees to exceed expectations when it came to serving guests. Yet their review of a variety of metrics (including the Hotel Paris's salary/competitive salary ratios, the total compensation expense per employee, and the target percentile for total compensation) suggested that in virtually all job categories the Hotel Paris paid no more than average, and, occasionally, paid somewhat less.

The current compensation policies had also bred what one hotel manager called an "I don't care" attitude on the part of most employees. What she meant was that most Hotel Paris employees quickly learned that regardless of what their performance was, they always ended up getting paid about the same as employees who performed better and worse than they did. So, the firm's compensation plan actually created a disconnect between pay and performance: It was not channeling employees' behaviors toward those required to achieve the company's goals. In some ways, it was doing the opposite.

Lisa and the CFO knew they had to institute a new, strategic compensation plan. They wanted a plan that improved employee morale, contributed to employee engagement, reduced employee turnover, and rewarded (and thus encouraged) the sorts of service-oriented behaviors that boosted guest satisfaction. After meeting with the company's CEO and the Board, the CFO gave Lisa the go-ahead to redesign the company's compensation plan, with the overall aim of creating a new plan that would support the company's strategic aims.

Lisa and her team (which included a consulting compensation expert) set numerous new measurable compensation policies for the Hotel Paris, and these new policies formed the heart of the new compensation plan. A new job evaluation study provided a more rational and fair basis upon which the company could assign pay rates. A formal compensation survey by the consultant established, for the first time at the Hotel Paris, a clear picture of what competitive hotels and similar businesses were paying in each geographic area, and enabled the Hotel Paris team to more accurately set targets for what each position at the hotel should be paying. Rather than just paying at the industry average, or slightly below, the new policy called for the Hotel Paris to move all its salaries into the 75th percentile over the next 3 years.

As they instituted the new compensation policies, Lisa and the CFO were pleased to learn from feedback from the hotel managers that they were already noting several positive changes. The number of applicants for each position had increased by over 50% on average, turnover dropped by 80%, and surveys of morale and commitment were producing higher results. Lisa and her team now began to consider how to inject more of a "pay for performance" element into the company's compensation plan, perhaps by instituting new bonuses and incentives. We will see what she did in Chapter 12.

Questions

11-26. Lisa knew little about setting up a new compensation plan. What would you tell her if she asked, "How do I set up a new compensation plan for the Hotel Paris?"

11-27. Would you suggest that Hotel Paris implement a competency-based pay plan for its nonmanagerial staff? Why or why not? If so, outline what they need to do.

11-28. Devise a ranking job evaluation system for the Hotel Paris's nonmanagerial employees (housekeepers, valets, front-desk clerks, phone operators, waitstaff, groundskeepers, and security guards) and use it to show the worth of these jobs relative to one another.

§Written and copyright by Gary Dessler, PhD.

MyManagementLab

Go to **mymanagementlab.com** for Auto-graded writing questions as well as the following Assisted-graded writing questions:

11-29. What are the pros and cons of broadbanding, and would you recommend an employer you're familiar with use it? Why or why not?

11-30. Compare and contrast the following methods of job evaluation: ranking, classification, factor comparison, and point method.

11-31. MyManagementLab only—comprehensive writing assignment for this chapter.

Key Terms

employee compensation, 330
direct financial payments, 330
indirect financial payments, 330
Davis-Bacon Act (1931), 331
Walsh-Healey Public Contract Act (1936), 331
Title VII of the 1964 Civil Rights Act, 331
Fair Labor Standards Act (1938), 331
Equal Pay Act, 335
Employee Retirement Income Security Act (ERISA), 335
job evaluation, 337
compensable factor, 338
benchmark job, 338
ranking method, 339
job classification (or grading), 340
classes, 340
grades, 340
grade definition, 340
point method, 340
market-competitive pay system, 344
wage curve, 344
salary survey, 345
pay (or wage) grade, 347
pay (or rate) ranges, 348
compa ratio, 349
competency-based pay, 353
broadbanding, 355
comparable worth, 356

Endnotes

1. Elayne Robertson Demby, "Two Stores Refused to Join the Race to the Bottom for Benefits and Wages," *Workforce Management*, February 2004, pp. 57–59; www.wegmans.com/webapp/wcs/stores/servlet/CategoryDisplay?langId=1&storeId=10052&catalogId=10002&categoryId=256548, accessed March 25, 2009.
2. Richard Henderson, *Compensation Management* (Reston, VA: Reston Publishing, 1980), pp. 101–127; and Stacey L. Kaplan, "Total Rewards in Action: Developing a Total Rewards Strategy," *Benefits & Compensation Digest* 42, no. 8 (August 2005), pp. 32–37.
3. Nicholas Wade, "Play Fair: Your Life May Depend on It," *The New York Times*, September 12, 2003, p. 12.
4. Robert Bretz and Stephen Thomas, "Perceived Inequity, Motivation, and Final Offer Arbitration in Major League Baseball," *Journal of Applied Psychology*, June 1992, pp. 280–282; Reginald Ell, "Addressing Employees' Feelings of Inequity: Capitalizing on Equity Theory in Modern Management," *Supervision* 72, no. 5 (May 2011), pp. 3–6.
5. James DeConinck and Duane Bachmann, "An Analysis of Turnover Among Retail Buyers," *Journal of Business Research* 58, no. 7 (July 2005), pp. 874–882.
6. Michael Harris et al., "Keeping Up with the Joneses: A Field Study of the Relationships Among Upward, Lateral, and Downward Comparisons and Pay Level Satisfaction," *Journal of Applied Psychology* 93, no. 3 (2008), pp. 665–673.
7. David Terpstra and Andre Honoree, "The Relative Importance of External, Internal, Individual, and Procedural Equity to Pay Satisfaction," *Compensation & Benefits Review*, November/December 2003, pp. 67–74.
8. Ibid., p. 68.
9. Millicent Nelson et al., "Pay Me More: What Companies Need to Know About Employee Pay Satisfaction," *Compensation & Benefits Review*, March/April 2008, pp. 35–42.
10. Pay inequities manifest in unexpected ways. In one study, the researchers studied the impact of keeping pay rates secret, rather than publicizing them on individual employees' test performance. They found that individuals with lower levels of tolerance for inequity reacted particularly harshly to pay secrecy in terms of weaker individual test performance. Peter Bamberger and Elena Belogolovsky, "The Impact of Pay Secrecy on Individual Test Performance," *Personnel Psychology* 60, no. 3 (2010), pp. 965–996.
11. Rachel Emma Silverman, "Psst. . . . This Is What Your Coworker Is Paid," *The Wall Street Journal*, January 30, 2013, p. B6.
12. Henderson, *Compensation Management*; see also Barry Gerhart and Sara Rynes, *Compensation: Theory, Evidence, and Strategic Implications* (Thousand Oaks, CA: Sage Publications, 2003); and Joseph Martocchio, *Strategic Compensation* (Upper Saddle River, NJ: Prentice Hall, 2006), pp. 67–94.
13. In a recent case, *Ledbetter v. Goodyear Tire & Rubber Co.*, the U.S. Supreme Court notably restricted the amount of time (to 180 or 300 days) after each allegedly discriminatory pay decision under Title VII to file or forever lose the claim. Congress subsequently passed and President Obama assigned a new law significantly expanding the amount of time to file such claims. See, for example, "Following *Ledbetter* Ruling, Issue of Workers Sharing Pay Information Takes Center Stage," *BNA Bulletin to Management*, July 17, 2007, p. 225.
14. The recently approved Genetic Information Nondiscrimination Act amended the Fair Labor Standards Act to increase penalties for the death or serious injury of employees under age 18. Allen Smith, "Penalties for Child Labor Violations Increase," *HR Magazine*, July 2008, p. 19.
15. Also note that 18 states have their own rules governing overtime. The states are Alaska, Arkansas, California, Colorado, Connecticut, Hawaii, Illinois, Kentucky, Maryland, Minnesota, Montana, New Jersey, North Dakota, Oregon, Pennsylvania, Washington, West Virginia, and Wisconsin. "DOL's Final Rule Is Not the Final Word on Overtime for Employers in 18 States," *BNA Bulletin to Management*, June 3, 2004, pp. 55, 177.
16. One company, Healthcare Management Group, estimates that "clock creep"—employees regularly clocking in a bit earlier—costs as much as $250,000 per year in overtime. The company remedied the situation by installing an automated time and attendance system. These systems help provide real-time labor data to line managers, and automatically update timing systems

for changes such as daylight savings time. Jennifer Arnold, "Reining in Overtime Costs," *HR Magazine*, April 2009, pp. 74–76.
17. www.pacifictimesheet.com/timesheet_products/pacific_timesheet_handheld_pda_field_data_entry_software.htm, accessed March 23, 2009.
18. Dave Zielinski, "On the Clock," *HR Magazine*, April 2012, pp. 67–68.
19. Ibid., p. 215.
20. James Coleman, "App Provides Reminder to Ensure Recordkeeping Is in Order," *BNA Bulletin to Management*, June 14, 2011, p. 191.
21. "Wal-Mart to Settle 63 Wage and Hour Suits, Paying Up to $640 Million to Resolve Claims," *BNA Bulletin to Management*, January 13, 2009, p. 11.
22. "Senate Passes Minimum Wage Increase That Includes Small-Business Tax Provisions," *BNA Bulletin to Management*, February 6, 2007, p. 41; www.dol.gov/esa/whd/flsa, accessed August 12, 2007.
23. Stephen Greenhouse, "Raising the Floor on Pay," *The New York Times*, April 10, 2012, p. B1.
24. Society for Human Resource Management, "The Evolution of Compensation," *Workplace Visions*, 2002, p. 2; www.dol.gov/esa/minwage/america.htm, accessed June 3, 2004.
25. For a description of exemption requirements, see Jeffrey Friedman, "The Fair Labor Standards Act Today: A Primer," *Compensation*, January/February 2002, pp. 51–54. See also www.shrm.org/issues/FLSA, accessed August 12, 2007; and www.dol.gov/esa/whd/flsa, accessed August 12, 2007.
26. "Employer Ordered to Pay $2 Million in Overtime," *BNA Bulletin to Management*, September 26, 1996, pp. 308–309. See also "Restaurant Managers Awarded $2.9 Million in Overtime Wages for Nonmanagement Work," *BNA Bulletin to Management*, August 30, 2001, p. 275.
27. Because the overtime and minimum wage rules only changed in 2004, exactly how to apply these rules is still in a state of flux. If there's doubt about exemption eligibility, it's probably best to check with the local Department of Labor Wage and Hour office. See, for example, "Attorneys Say FLSA Draws a Fine Line Between Exempt/Nonexempt Employees," *BNA Bulletin to Management*, July 5, 2005, p. 219; "DOL Releases Letters on Administrative Exemption, Overtime," *BNA Bulletin to Management*, October 18, 2005, p. 335. The U.S. Labor Department occasionally changes its positions. For example, in 2010 it concluded that mortgage loan officers are subject to the administrative exemption from federal overtime pay, although several years previously IT had ruled the opposite. Tim Watson and Barry Miller, "Tightening a White Collar Exemption," *HR Magazine*, December 2010, p. 95.
28. See, for example, Jeffrey Friedman, "The Fair Labor Standards Act Today: A Primer," *Compensation*, January/ February 2002, p. 53; Andre Honoree, "The New Fair Labor Standards Act Regulations and the Sales Force: Who Is Entitled to Overtime Pay?" *Compensation & Benefits Review*, January/February 2006, p. 31; www.shrm.org/issues/FLSA, accessed August 12, 2007; www.dol.gov/esa/whd/flsa, accessed August 12, 2007. One U.S. District Court recently held that 359 former loan officers at Quicken Loans Inc. were not misclassified as "administrative" employees, and therefore were not eligible for back overtime compensation. Matthew Heller, "Quicken Verdict Gives Employers Hope on Overtime," *Workforce Management*, May 2011, p. 6.
29. Diane Cadrain, "Guard Against FLSA Claims," *HR Magazine*, April 2008, pp. 97–100.
30. "Justices 5-4 Reject Labor Department View, Find Pharmaceutical Sales Reps FLSA-Exempt." *BNA Bulletin to Management*, June 19, 2012, p. 193.
31. Recently, several state legislatures have moved to tighten regulations regarding misclassifying workers as independent contractors, some going so far as adding criminal penalties for violations. "Misclassification Cases Draw More Attention, Attorneys Say," *BNA Bulletin to Management*, December 15, 2009, p. 399. Eleven states recently joined with the U.S. Labor Department and Internal Revenue Service to coordinate efforts in fighting misclassification. "Agencies, 11 States Join Forces to Fight Misclassification; IRS Launches Program," *BNA Bulletin to Management*, September 20, 2011, p. 305. The U.S. Department of Labor is now working closely with state agencies to proceed with challenges to independent contractor worker misclassifications. "DOL, State Agencies, and Litigants Proceed with Challenges to Worker Misclassification," *BNA Bulletin to Management*, August 14, 2012, p. 257.
32. "Federal Court Mostly Rules for FedEx Ground in Driver Lawsuits Alleging Misclassification," *BNA Bulletin to Management*, December 21, 2010, p. 403. Different countries classify independent contractors in different ways, so retaining such contractors abroad requires knowledge of the specific local requirements. Eric Krell, "Status Check," *HR Magazine*, November 2011, pp. 63–66.
33. This is based on Matthew Simpson, "Five Steps to Reduce the Risks of Miscalculation," *BNA Bulletin to Management*, February 21, 2012, p. 63.
34. Robert Nobile, "How Discrimination Laws Affect Compensation," *Compensation & Benefits Review*, July/August 1996, pp. 38–42.
35. See, for example, www.bls.gov/opub/cwc/cm20030124ar01p1.htm, accessed October 9, 2011. See also Barry Hirsch and Edward Schumacher, "Unions, Wages, and Skills," *Journal of Human Resources* 33, no. 1 (Winter 1998), p. 115.
36. Peg Buchenroth, "Driving Performance: Making Pay Work for the Organization," *Compensation & Benefits Review*, May/June 2006, pp. 30–35.
37. Jessica Marquez, "Raising the Performance Bar," *Workforce Management*, April 24, 2006, pp. 31–32.
38. Demby, "Two Stores Refused to Join the Race."
39. Ibid.
40. www.wegmans.com, accessed June 1, 2011.
41. Demby, "Two Stores Refuse to Join the Race," www.hoovers.com/company/Wegmans_Food_Markets_Inc/cfhtji-1.Html, accessed June 1, 2011.
42. Ibid.
43. Demby, "Two Stores Refuse to Join the Race."
44. http://www.bls.gov/oes/current/oes431011.htm, accessed July 27, 2013.
45. This is based on compensation management.
46. Joseph Martocchio, *Strategic Compensation* (Upper Saddle River, NJ: Pearson Education, 2011), p. 140.
47. Martocchio, *Strategic Compensation*, p. 138. See also Nona Tobin, "Can Technology Ease the Pain of Salary Surveys?" *Public Personnel Management* 31, no. 1 (Spring 2002), pp. 65–78.
48. You may have noticed that job analysis as discussed in Chapter 4 can be a useful source of information on compensable factors, as well as on job descriptions and job specifications. For example, a quantitative job analysis technique like the position analysis questionnaire generates quantitative information on the degree to which the following five basic factors are present in each job: having decision-making/communication/social responsibilities, performing skilled activities, being physically active, operating vehicles or equipment, and processing information. As a result, a job analysis technique like the PAQ is actually as (or some say, more) appropriate as a job evaluation technique (than for job analysis) in that jobs can be quantitatively compared to one another on those five dimensions and their relative worth thus ascertained. Another point worth noting is that you may find that a single set of compensable factors is not adequate for describing all your jobs. This is another reason why many managers therefore divide their jobs into job clusters. For example, you might have a separate job cluster for factory workers, for clerical workers, and for managerial personnel. You would then probably have a somewhat different set of compensable factors for each job cluster.
49. Michael Carrell and Christina Heavrin, *Labor Relations and Collective Bargaining* (Upper Saddle River, NJ: Prentice Hall, 2004), pp. 300–303.
50. John Kilgour, "Job Evaluation Revisited: The Point Factor Method," *Compensation & Benefits Review*, July/August 2008, p. 40.
51. Martocchio, *Strategic Compensation*, p. 140.
52. For a discussion, see Roger Plachy, "The Point Factor Job Evaluation System: A Step-by-Step Guide, Part I," *Compensation & Benefits Review*, July/August 1987, pp. 12–27; Roger Plachy, "The Case for Effective Point-Factor Job Evaluation, Viewpoint I," *Compensation & Benefits Review*, March/April 1987, pp. 45–48; Roger Plachy, "The Point-Factor Job Evaluation System: A Step-by-Step Guide, Part II," *Compensation & Benefits Review*, September/October 1987, pp. 9–24; and particularly John Kilgour, "Job Evaluation Revisited: The Point Factor Method," *Compensation & Benefits Review*, July/August 2008, pp. 37–46.
53. Martocchio, *Strategic Compensation*, p. 141.
54. Kilgour, "Job Evaluation Revisited," pp. 37–46.
55. Ibid.
56. Ibid.
57. Ibid.
58. Ibid.
59. Ibid.
60. Ibid. Of course, the level of economic activity influences compensation expectations. For instance, salary increases were lower than expected in 2010 due to a lackluster economy, but were predicted to increase significantly

for 2011. Fay Hansen, "Currents in Compensation and Benefits," *Compensation & Benefits Review* 42, no. 6 (2010), p. 435.

61. Martocchio, *Strategic Compensation*, p. 151.
62. Kilgour, "Job Evaluation Revisited," pp. 37–46.
63. Henderson, *Compensation Management*, pp. 260–269. See also "Web Access Transforms Compensation Surveys," *Workforce Management*, April 24, 2006, p. 34.
64. For more information on these surveys, see the company's brochure, "Domestic Survey References," Watson Wyatt Data Services, 218 Route 17 North, Rochelle Park, NJ 07662. See www.watsonwyatt.com/search/publications.asp?ArticleID=21432, accessed October 29, 2009.
65. Kilgour, "Job Evaluation Revisited," pp. 37–46.
66. Ibid.
67. David W. Belcher, *Compensation Administration* (Englewood Cliffs, NJ: Prentice Hall, 1974), pp. 257–276; and Nicola Sulliva, "Serco Introduces Pay Grade Structure for Senior Staff," *Employee Benefits*, July 2010, p. 5.
68. Martocchio, *Strategic Compensation*, p. 185.
69. Ibid., p. 189.
70. Kilgour, "Job Evaluation Revisited," pp. 37–46.
71. Susan Marks, "Can the Internet Help You Hit the Salary Mark?" *Workforce*, January 2001, pp. 86–93.
72. James Reda, "Executive Pay Today and Tomorrow," *Corporate Board* 22, no. 126 (January 2001), p. 18.
73. Syed Tahir Hijazi, "Determinants of Executive Compensation and Its Impact on Organizational Performance," *Compensation & Benefits Review* 39, no. 2 (March–April 2007), p. 58(9).
74. For example, one book argues that executives of large companies use their power to have themselves compensated in ways that are not sufficiently related to performance. Lucian Bebchuk and Jesse Fried, *Pay Without Performance: The Unfulfilled Promise of Executive Compensation* (Boston: Harvard University Press, 2004).
75. http://uk.reuters.com/article/2010/02/23/uk-hsbc-idUKTRE61M6FT20100223, accessed June 23, 2011.
76. Mark Meltzer and Howard Goldsmith, "Executive Compensation for Growth Companies," *Compensation & Benefits Review*, November/December 1997, pp. 41–50; Martocchio, *Strategic Compensation*, pp. 421–428. See also Martin J. Conyon, "Executive Compensation and Incentives," *The Academy of Management Perspectives* 20, no. 1 (February 2006), p. 25(20); and "Realities of Executive Compensation—2006/2007 Report on Executive Pay and Stock Options," www.watsonwyatt.com/research/resrender.asp?id=2006-US-0085&page=1, accessed May 20, 2007.
77. Douglas Tormey, "Executive Compensation: Creating a 'Legal' Checklist," *Compensation & Benefits Review*, July/August 1996, pp. 12–36. See also Bruce Ellig, "Executive Pay: A Primer," *Compensation & Benefits Review*, January/February 2003, pp. 44–50.
78. http://finance.yahoo.com/news/p-gs-ceo-pay-slips-200307540.html, accessed February 8, 2013.
79. "At the Top of Their Industries," *The New York Times*, April 7, 2013, business page 8.
80. "American Chief Executives Are Not Overpaid," *The Economist*, September 8, 2012, p. 67.
81. See, for example, Fay Hansen, "Current Trends in Compensation and Benefits," *Compensation & Benefits Review* 36, no. 2 (March/April 2004), pp. 7–8.
82. www.dol.gov/whd/regs/compliance/fairpay/fs17d_professional.pdf, accessed June 1, 2011.
83. Ibid.
84. Roger S. Achille, "FLSA Requires Education for Professional Exemption," www.shrm.org/LegalIssues/FederalResources/Pages/2ndFLSAProfessionalExemption.Aspx, accessed August 28, 2011.
85. See, for example, Martocchio, *Strategic Compensation*; and Patricia Zingheim and Jay Schuster, "Designing Pay and Rewards in Professional Services Companies," *Compensation & Benefits Review*, January/February 2007, pp. 55–62.
86. Farhad Manjoo, "Engineers to the Valley: Pay Up," *Fast Company* 153, no. 38 (March 2011).
87. Dimitris Manolopoulos, "What Motivates Research and Development Professionals? Evidence from Decentralized Laboratories in Greece," *International Journal of Human Resource Management* 17, no. 4 (April 2006), pp. 616–647.
88. http://www.bing.com/shopping/quickbooks-basic-payroll-2012-complete-package/p/F0EBDFF1F6F276B60004?q=payroll+software&lpf=0&lpq=payroll%2bsoftware&FORM=ENCA&lppc=16, accessed May 20, 2012.
89. www.shrm.org/HRdisciplines/pages/CMS_012013.aspx, accessed May 20, 2012.
90. See, for example, Robert Heneman and Peter LeBlanc, "Development of and Approach for Valuing Knowledge Work," *Compensation & Benefits—Review*, July/August 2002, p. 47. A recent survey found that only about 12% of employers use skill-based pay, and 13% use competency-based pay. Frank Giancola, "Skill-Based Pay: Fad or Classic?" *Compensation & Benefits Review* 43, no. 4 (2011), pp. 220–226.
91. Gerald Ledford Jr., "Paying for the Skills, Knowledge, and Competencies of Knowledge Workers," *Compensation & Benefits Review*, July/August 1995, p. 56; see also P. K. Zingheim et al.,"Competencies and Rewards: Substance or Just Style?" *Compensation and Benefits Review* 35, no. 5 (September/October 2003), pp. 40–44.
92. Joseph Martocchio, *Strategic Compensation*, p. 168.
93. Frank Giancola, "Skill-Based Pay: Fad or Classic?" *Compensation & Benefits Review* 43, no. 4 (2011), pp. 220–226.
94. http://www.jlg.com/en-US/Industries.html, accessed April 9, 2013.
95. Quoted or paraphrased from "JLG Industries, Inc., "Information: Skill-Based Pay Program," www.bmpcoe.org/bestpractices/internal/jlg/jlg_14.html, accessed April 9, 2013.
96. See, for example, www.shrm.org/hrdisciplines/compensation/articles/pages/salarystructures.aspx, accessed September 27, 2013.
97. David Hofrichter, "Broadbanding: A 'Second Generation' Approach," *Compensation & Benefits Review*, September/October 1993, pp. 53–58. See also "The Future of Salary Management," *Compensation & Benefits Review*, July/August 2001, pp. 7–12.
98. Ibid., p. 55.
99. For example, see Sandra Emerson, "Job Evaluation: A Barrier to Excellence?" *Compensation & Benefits Review*, January/February 1991, pp. 39–52; Nan Weiner, "Job Evaluation Systems: A Critique," *Human Resource Management Review* 1, no. 2 (Summer 1991), pp. 119–132; and Brian Klaas, "Compensation in the Jobless Organization," *Human Resource Management Review* 12, no. 1 (Spring 2002), pp. 43–62.
100. Dawne Shand, "Broadbanding the IT Worker," *Computerworld* 34, no. 41 (October 9, 2000).
101. "Five Rules for Talent Management in the New Economy," www.towerswatson.com/viewpoints/2606, accessed November 9, 2010.
102. *County of Washington v. Gunther*, U.S. Supreme Court, no. 80–426, June 8, 1981.
103. Laura Fitzpatrick, "Why Do Women Still Earn Less Than Men?" www.time.com/time/nation/article/0,8599,1983185,00.html, accessed May 21, 2011.
104. Christopher Dougherty, "Why Are the Returns to Schooling Higher for Women Than for Men?" *Journal of Human Resources* 40, no. 4 (Fall 2005), pp. 969–988.
105. Rachel Silverman, "Women Doctors Face Pay Disparity," *The Wall Street Journal*, February 8, 2011, p. D4.
106. "Women Still Earned Less Than Men, BLS Data Show," *BNA Bulletin to Management*, June 8, 2000, p. 72. However, there is some indication that there is less gender-based pay gap among full-time workers ages 21 to 35 living alone. Kent Hoover, "Study Finds No Pay Gap for Young, Single Workers," *Tampa Bay Business Journal* 20, no. 19 (May 12, 2000), p. 10. See also E. Frazier, "Raises for Women Executives Match Those for Men, but Pay Gap Persists," *The Chronicle of Philanthropy* 20, no. 24 (October 2, 2008), p. 33.
107. "The Say on Pay Payday," *The Economist*, February 16, 2013, p. 65.
108. Mark Poerio and Eric Keller, "Executive Compensation 2005: Many Forces, One Direction," *Compensation & Benefits Review*, May/June 2005, pp. 34–40.
109. Ibid., p. 38.
110. Jennifer Dudley, "The New Executive Compensation Rule: The Tough Disclosures," *Compensation & Benefits Review*, July/August 2007, pp. 28–34.
111. Society for Human Resource Management, "Changing Leadership Strategies," *Workplace Visions*, no. 1 (2008), p. 3.
112. For a discussion of some of the issues that go into hammering out an executive employment agreement, see, for example, Jonathan Cohen and Laura Clark, "Is the Executive Employment Agreement Dead?" *Compensation & Benefits Review*, July/August 2007, pp. 50–55.
113. Ibid. See also Brent Longnecker and James Krueger, "The Next Wave of Compensation Disclosure," *Compensation & Benefits Review*, January/February 2007, pp. 50–54.

114. Frank L. Giancola, "A Framework for Understanding New Concepts in Compensation Management," op cit.; and Georgina Fuller, "Total Reward Statements," *Employee Benefits*, January 2011, p. 47. See also "Report: Recruiting, Keeping Critical Employees Remains Challenge," *BNA Bulletin to Management*, October 2, 2012, p. 319.
115. Melissa Van Dyke and Mike Ryan, "Changing the Compensation Conversation on the Growing Utility of Non-Cash Rewards and Recognition," *Compensation & Benefits Review* 44, no. 5 (2013), pp. 276–279.
116. Meg Breslin, "Solid Rewards Program Can Be Rewarding for Businesses," *Workforce Management*, January 2013, p. 8.
117. Dave Zielinski, "Giving Praise," *HR Magazine*, October 2012, p. 77.
118. "Next Generation Talent Management," www.hewittassociates.com/_MetaBasicCMAssetCache_/Assets/Articles/next_generation.pdf, accessed November 9, 2010.
119. This case based on www.nature.com/scitable/forums/women-in-science/astro-zeneca-settles-women-s-pay-inequality-20334719; www.dol.gov/opa/media/press/ofccp/OFCCP20110829.htm; http://social.dol.gov/blog/astrazeneca-what-we-learned/, all accessed August 31, 2012.

CHAPTER 11

12 Pay for Performance and Financial Incentives

Source: PRILL / Shutterstock

MyManagementLab®

Improve Your Grade!

When you see this icon, visit **www.mymanagementlab.com** for activities that are applied, personalized, and offer immediate feedback.

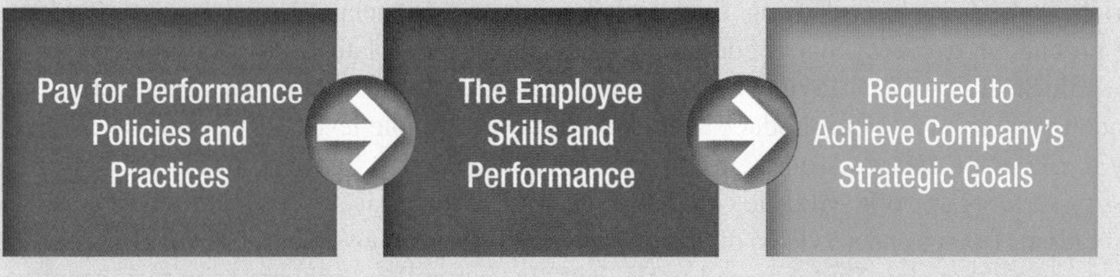

For a bird's eye view of how one company created a pay for performance system to improve its strategic performance, read the Hotel Paris case on page 391, and answer the questions after reading the chapter.

WHERE ARE WE NOW . . .

Chapter 11 focused on developing the total pay plan and on salaries and wages. Incentives are important components in any pay plan. The main purpose of this chapter is to explain how managers use incentives to motivate employees. The main topics we'll discuss are money's role in motivation, individual employee incentive and recognition programs, incentives for salespeople, incentives for managers and executives, and team and organization-wide incentive plans. In Chapter 13 we'll turn to financial and nonfinancial benefits and services, which comprise the third component of employee compensation packages.

LEARNING OBJECTIVES

1. Explain how you would apply four motivation theories in formulating an incentive plan.
2. Discuss the main incentives for individual employees.
3. Discuss the pros and cons of commissions versus straight pay for salespeople.
4. Describe the main incentives for managers and executives.
5. Name and describe the most popular organization-wide incentive plans.

The owners of a 21-store fast-food franchise in the Midwest knew that their stores' performance and profits depended on their employees' performance. They hoped a new employee incentives program could boost their employees' and their stores' performance. We'll see that it did, and what exactly the new program entailed.

Money's Role in Motivation

1 Explain how you would apply four motivation theories in formulating an incentive plan.

financial incentives
Financial rewards paid to workers whose production exceeds some predetermined standard.

productivity
The ratio of outputs (goods and services) divided by the inputs (resources such as labor and capital).

fair day's work
Output standards devised based on careful, scientific analysis.

scientific management movement
Management approach based on improving work methods through observation and analysis.

variable pay
Any plan that ties pay to productivity or profitability, usually as one-time lump payments.

Frederick Taylor popularized using **financial incentives**—financial rewards paid to workers whose production exceeds some predetermined standard—in the late 1800s. As a supervisor at the Midvale Steel Company, Taylor was concerned with what he called "systematic soldiering"—the tendency of employees to produce at the minimum acceptable level. Some workers had the energy to run home and work on their houses after a 12-hour day. Taylor knew that if he could harness this energy at work, Midvale could achieve huge productivity gains. **Productivity** "is the ratio of outputs (goods and services) divided by the inputs (resources such as labor and capital)."[1]

In pursuing that aim, Taylor turned to financial incentives. At the time, primitive incentive plans were in use, but were generally ineffective (because employers arbitrarily changed incentive rates).

He made three contributions. He saw the need for formulating a **"fair day's work,"** namely precise output standards for each job. He spearheaded the **scientific management movement**, which emphasized improving work through observation and analysis. And he popularized using incentive pay to reward employees who produced over standard.

Incentive Pay Terminology

Managers often use two terms synonymously with incentive plans.[2] Traditionally, all incentive plans are *pay-for-performance* plans. They all tie employees' pay to the employees' performance. **Variable pay** is more specific: It is usually an incentive plan that ties a group or team's pay to some measure of the firm's (or the unit's) overall profitability;[3] *profit-sharing plans* (discussed later) are one example.[4] However, confusing as it may be, some experts use the term *variable pay* to include incentive plans for individual employees.[5]

Linking Strategy, Performance, and Incentive Pay

In any case, incentive pay—tying workers' pay to their performance—is widely popular.[6] The problem is that linking pay to performance is easier said than done. One plan, at Levi Strauss, is widely assumed to have been the last nail in the coffin of Levi's U.S.-based production. As logical as it seems to link pay to performance, about 83% of companies with such programs say their programs are at best somewhat successful. One study found that just 28% of the 2,600 U.S. workers it surveyed said their companies' incentive plans motivated them. "Employees don't see a strong connection between pay and performance, and their performance is not particularly influenced by the company's incentive plan," said one expert.[7] Equally problematical is the fact that some incentives incentivize the wrong behavior.[8] Thus, incentivizing "number of cars sold" in a dealership might produce high performance (in numbers of cars sold) but a low per-car profit.

There are other reasons for incentive plans' often-dismal results. For example, many employers ignore the fact that incentives that may motivate some people won't motivate others.[9] Compensation experts therefore argue that managers should understand the motivational bases of incentive plans.[10] We'll review some motivation background next, and then go on to explain various incentive plans.

Motivation and Incentives

Several motivation theories have particular relevance to designing incentive plans.

MOTIVATORS AND FREDERICK HERZBERG Frederick Herzberg said the best way to motivate someone is to organize the job so that doing it provides the challenge and recognition we all need to help satisfy "higher-level" needs for things like accomplishment and recognition. These needs are relatively insatiable, says Herzberg, so challenging work provides a sort of built-in motivation generator. Doing things to satisfy a worker's "lower level" needs for things like better pay and working conditions just keeps the person from becoming dissatisfied.

Herzberg says the factors ("hygienes") that satisfy lower-level needs are different from those ("motivators") that satisfy or partially satisfy higher-level needs. If *hygiene* factors (factors outside the job itself, such as working conditions, salary, and incentive pay) are inadequate, employees become dissatisfied. However, adding more of these hygienes (like incentives) to the job (supplying what Herzberg calls "extrinsic motivation") is an inferior way to try to motivate someone, because lower-level needs are quickly satisfied. Inevitably the person says, in effect, "I want another raise."

Instead of relying on hygienes, says Herzberg, managers interested in creating a self-motivated workforce should emphasize "job content" or *motivator* factors. Managers do this by enriching workers' jobs so that the jobs are more challenging, and by providing feedback and recognition—they make doing the job intrinsically motivating, in other words. In organizational psychology, **intrinsic motivation** is motivation that derives from the pleasure someone gets from doing the job or task. It comes from "within" the person, rather than from externally, such as a financial incentive plan. Intrinsic motivation means that just doing the task provides the motivation. Herzberg makes the point that relying exclusively on financial incentives is risky. The employer should also provide the recognition and challenging work that most people desire.

intrinsic motivation
Motivation that derives from the pleasure someone gets from doing the job or task.

DEMOTIVATORS AND EDWARD DECI Psychologist Edward Deci's work highlights another potential downside to relying too heavily on extrinsic rewards: They may backfire. Deci found that extrinsic rewards could at times actually detract from the person's intrinsic motivation.[11] The point may be stated thusly: Be cautious in devising incentive pay for highly motivated employees, lest you inadvertently demean and detract from the desire they have to do the job out of a sense of responsibility.

EXPECTANCY THEORY AND VICTOR VROOM In general, people won't pursue rewards they find unattractive, or where the odds of success are very low. Psychologist Victor Vroom's expectancy motivation theory echoes these commonsense observations. He says a person's motivation to exert some level of effort depends on three things: the person's **expectancy** (in terms of probability) that his or her effort will lead to performance;[12] **instrumentality**, or the perceived connection (if any) between successful performance and actually obtaining the rewards; and **valence**, which represents the perceived value the person attaches to the reward.[13] In Vroom's theory:

expectancy
A person's expectation that his or her effort will lead to performance.

instrumentality
The perceived relationship between successful performance and obtaining the reward.

valence
The perceived value a person attaches to the reward.

$$\text{Motivation} = (E \times I \times V),$$

where E represents expectancy, I instrumentality, and V valence. If E or I or V is zero or inconsequential, there will be no motivation.

Vroom's theory has three implications for how managers design incentive plans.

- First, if employees don't *expect* that effort will produce performance, no motivation will occur. So, managers must ensure that their employees have the skills to do the job, and believe they can do the job. Thus training, job descriptions, and confidence building and support are important in using incentives.
- Second, Vroom's theory suggests that employees must see the *instrumentality* of their efforts—they must believe that successful performance will in fact lead to getting the reward. Managers can accomplish this, for instance, by creating easy to understand incentive plans.
- Third, the reward itself must be of *value* to the employee. Ideally, the manager should take into account individual employee preferences.

BEHAVIOR MODIFICATION/REINFORCEMENT AND B. F. SKINNER Using incentives also assumes the manager understands how consequences affect behavior.[14] Psychologist B.F. Skinner's findings are useful here. Managers apply Skinner's principles by using *behavior modification.* **Behavior modification** means changing behavior through rewards or punishments that are contingent on performance. For managers, behavior modification boils down to two main principles. First, that behavior that appears to lead to a positive consequence (reward) tends to be repeated, whereas behavior that appears to lead to a negative consequence (punishment) tends not to be repeated; and second, that managers can therefore get someone to change his or her behavior by providing the properly scheduled rewards (or punishment).

behavior modification
Using contingent rewards or punishment to change behavior.

To arrange our discussion, we will organize the following sections around individual employee incentive and recognition programs, sales compensation programs, management and executive incentive compensation programs, and team and organization-wide incentive programs. First, however, see the Know Your Employment Law feature to see how legal issues affect incentive plan design.

KNOW YOUR EMPLOYMENT LAW

Employee Incentives and the Law

Various laws affect incentive pay. Under the Fair Labor Standards Act, if the incentive the worker receives is in the form of a prize or cash award, the employer generally must *include the value of that award* when calculating the worker's overtime pay for that pay period.[15] So, unless you structure the incentive bonuses properly, the bonus itself becomes part of the week's wages. For example, suppose someone who earns $10 per hour for a 40-hour week also earns, in one week, performance incentive pay (a performance bonus) of $80 for the week, or $480 total pay for the week. Further, assume she *also* works 2 hours overtime that week. The overtime rate for each of the 2 hours she works overtime is not simply 1.5 times her regular $10 per hour pay. Instead it is 1.5 times $12 per hour. Why? Because with her performance bonus she earned $480 for the 40 hour week, and $480 divided by 40 hours is $12 per hour. Therefore she actually earned in total that week $480 plus the overtime pay of $12 per hour for the two extra hours, or $480 + $24 = $504 total for the week.

Certain bonuses are excludable from overtime pay calculations. For example, Christmas and gift bonuses that are not based on hours worked, or are so substantial that employees don't consider them a part of their wages, do not have to be included in overtime pay calculations. Similarly, purely discretionary bonuses in which the employer retains discretion over how much if anything to pay are excludable.

However other types of incentive pay *must* be included. Under the Fair Labor Standards Act (FLSA), bonuses to include in overtime pay computations include those promised to newly hired employees; those provided for in union contracts or other agreements; and those announced to induce employees to work more productively or efficiently or to induce them to remain with the company. Such bonuses would include many of those we turn to next, such as individual and group production bonuses.

Individual Employee Incentive and Recognition Programs

Several incentive plans are particularly suited for use with individual employees.

2 Discuss the main incentives for individual employees.

Piecework

piecework
A system of pay based on the number of items processed by each individual worker in a unit of time, such as items per hour or items per day.

Piecework is the oldest incentive plan and still the most commonly used. Earnings are tied directly to what the worker produces; the person is paid a piece rate for each unit he or she produces. Thus, if Tom Smith gets $0.40 apiece for stamping out doorjambs, then he would get, say, $80 for stamping out 200.

Developing a workable piece rate plan requires both job evaluation and (strictly speaking) industrial engineering. Job evaluation enables you to assign an hourly wage rate to the job in question. But the crucial issue in piece rate planning is the production standard, and this standard is often developed by industrial engineers. The engineers state production standards in terms of a standard number of minutes per unit or a standard number of units per hour. In Tom Smith's case, the job evaluation indicated that his doorjamb stamping job was worth $8.00 an hour. The industrial engineer determined that 20 jambs per hour was the standard production rate. Therefore, the engineered piece rate (for each doorjamb) was $8.00 divided by 20, which equals $0.40 per doorjamb.

straight piecework
An incentive plan in which a person is paid a sum for each item he or she makes or sells, with a strict proportionality between results and rewards.

With a **straight piecework** plan, Tom Smith would be paid based on the number of door jambs he produced; there would be no guaranteed minimum wage. However, today most employers must guarantee their workers a minimum wage. With a guaranteed piecework plan, Tom Smith would be paid $7.25 per hour (the minimum wage) whether or not he stamped out 18 door jambs per hour (at $0.40 each). But he would also get $0.40 for each unit over 18.

Piecework generally implies straight piecework, a strict proportionality between results and rewards regardless of the level of output. Thus, in Smith's case, he continues to get $0.40 apiece for stamping out door jambs, even if he stamps out more than planned, say, 500 per day. However, certain types of piecework plans call for a sharing of productivity gains between worker and employer. Typically, the worker here receives reduced credit for all production above standard—perhaps $0.35 per piece over 400 units per day, for instance.[16] Conversely, some such plans boost the employee's share once a threshold is met—such as paying Tom $0.45 each once he reached 400 units per day.

standard hour plan
A plan by which a worker is paid a basic hourly rate but is paid an extra percentage of his or her rate for production exceeding the standard per hour or per day. Similar to piecework payment but based on a percent premium.

The **standard hour plan** is like the piecework plan, with one difference. Instead of getting a rate per piece, the worker gets a pay premium equal to the percent by which his or her performance exceeds the standard. So if Tom's standard is 160 door jambs per day ($64 per day), and he brings in 200 jambs, he'd get an extra 25% (40/160), or $80. Using this approach may reduce workers' tendency to link their production standard (18 jambs per hour) to pay. This makes it easier to change the standard.

ADVANTAGES AND DISADVANTAGES Piecework incentive plans have several advantages. They are simple to calculate and easily understood by employees. Piecework plans appear equitable in principle, and their incentive value can be powerful since they tie pay directly to performance.

Piecework also has disadvantages. The main one is its unsavory reputation, based on some employers' habit of arbitrarily raising production standards whenever they found their workers earning "excessive" wages. A more subtle disadvantage is that since piece rates are quoted on a per piece basis, in worker's minds the production standard (in pieces per hour) become tied inseparably to the amount of money earned.

Piecework systems thus risk engendering rigidity. When the employer tries to revise production standards, resistance ensues.[17] Employees become preoccupied with producing the number of units needed. They can become less focused on quality and may resist switching jobs (since doing so could reduce productivity). Attempts to introduce innovative processes may more likely fail, insofar as they require adjusting engineered standards. Equipment maintenance tends to decline as employees focus on maximizing machine input.[18]

For such reasons, more employers are moving to other plans, such as those on the following pages.[19]

Merit Pay as an Incentive

merit pay (merit raise)
Any salary increase awarded to an employee based on his or her individual performance.

KNOWLEDGE BASE

Merit pay or a **merit raise** is a salary increase the firm awards to an individual employee based on individual performance. It is different from a bonus in that it usually becomes part of the employee's base salary, whereas bonuses are generally one-time payments. Although the term *merit pay* can apply to the incentive raises given to any employee, the term is more often used for professional, office, and clerical employees.

Merit pay is the subject of much debate. Advocates argue that awarding pay raises across the board (without regard to individual merit) may detract from performance by showing employees they'll be rewarded regardless of how they perform.

Detractors present good reasons why merit pay can backfire. Most notably, since many appraisals are unfair, so too are the merit decisions you base them on.[20]

The evidence, while mixed, tends to support using merit pay. One study focused on 218 workers in a nuclear waste facility. The researchers found a "very modest relationship between merit pay increase and performance rating."[21] Research into tying merit pay increases to teachers' or faculty members' research and/or teaching performance suggest that merit pay is more clearly linked with research productivity than with teaching effectiveness.[22]

When they're not working, the solution is not to throw out merit raises, but to improve them. This starts with establishing effective appraisal procedures and ensuring that managers do in fact tie merit pay awards to performance.

Merit plan effectiveness also depends on differentiating among employees. In one survey, the highest-paid office clerical employees got short-term incentive payouts of about 13%, the lowest rated got 3%, and mid-rated employees got 8%.[23]

Employers are experimenting with using crowdsourcing for awarding bonuses. For example, one small San Francisco-based company asked each employee to distribute 1,200 stock options among coworkers however they chose.[24] Allowing everyone to "vote" on each other's performance can help identify employees who are helpful team contributors but might otherwise slip under management's radar.

HR in Practice at the Hotel Paris Based on their analysis, Lisa Cruz and the CFO concluded that by any measure, their company's incentive plan was inadequate. The percentage of the workforce whose merit increase is tied to performance is effectively zero, because managers awarded merit pay across the board. To see how they handled this, see the case on page 391.

MERIT PAY OPTIONS Two adaptations of merit pay plans are popular. One awards merit raises in a lump sum once a year and does *not* make the raise part of the employee's salary (making them, in effect, short-term bonuses for lower-level workers). Traditional merit increases are cumulative, but these *lump-sum merit raises* are not. This produces two potential benefits. First, the merit raise is not baked into the employee's salary, so you need not pay it year after year. Lump-sum merit increases can also be more dramatic motivators than a traditional merit raise. For example, a 5% lump-sum merit payment to a $30,000 employee is $1,500 cash, as opposed to a weekly merit payout of $29 for 52 weeks.

The other adaptation ties merit awards to both individual and organizational performance. Table 12-1 presents an example. In this example, you might measure the company's performance by, say, profits. Here, company performance and the employee's performance (using his or her performance appraisal) receive equal weight in computing the merit pay. In Table 12-1 an outstanding performer would receive 70% of his or her maximum lump-sum award even when the organization's performance was marginal. However, employees with marginal or unacceptable performance would get no lump-sum awards even when the firm's performance was outstanding. The bonus plan at Discovery Communications is an example. Executive assistants can receive bonuses of up to a maximum of 10% of their salaries. The boss's evaluation of the assistant's individual performance accounts for 80% of the potential bonus; 10% is based on how the division does, and 10% on how the company does.[25]

Diversity Counts

We saw in Chapter 10 that women typically earn only about 85% as much as men. It turns out that in some cases, women may also not have access to the same bonus plans as men do.[26] In the English town of Sheffield, for instance, town employees such as gardeners and street cleaners, mostly male, were eligible to receive "productivity improvement" bonuses, which raised their pay by up to 38%. Care workers, primarily female, could not participate in the bonus plan, and thus earned much less than the men did. Successful employers know that "diversity counts," and that in designing all their total pay components, it's important to consider the plan's affect on female employees.

Incentives for Professional Employees

Professional employees are those whose work involves the application of learned knowledge to the solution of the employer's problems, such as lawyers and engineers.

Making incentive pay decisions for professional employees is challenging. For one thing, firms usually pay professionals well anyway. For another, they're already driven by the desire to produce high-caliber work.

However, it is unrealistic to assume that people like Google engineers work only for professional gratification. Few firms, therefore, work harder to maintain competitive incentives for professionals. For example, Google reportedly pays higher incentives to engineers working on important projects. Those who choose the intrinsic motivation of working on more theoretical long-term projects are rewarded if their research pays off.[27] As at most Silicon Valley firms,

TABLE 12-1 Merit Award Determination Matrix (an Example)

The Employee's Performance Rating (Weight = 0.50)	*The Company's Performance (Weight = 0.50)*				
	Outstanding	Excellent	Good	Marginal	Unacceptable
Outstanding	1.00	0.90	0.80	0.70	0.00
Excellent	0.90	0.80	0.70	0.60	0.00
Good	0.80	0.70	0.60	0.50	0.00
Marginal	—	—	—	—	—
Unacceptable	—	—	—	—	—

Note: To determine the dollar value of each employee's award: (1) multiply the employee's annual, straight-time wage or salary as of June 30 times his or her maximum incentive award (as determined by management or the board—such as, "10% of each employee's pay") and (2) multiply the resultant product by the appropriate percentage figure from this table. For example, if an employee had an annual salary of $40,000 on June 30 and a maximum incentive award of 7% and if her performance and the organization's performance were both "excellent," the employee's award would be $2,240: ($40,000 × 0.07 × 0.80 = $2,240).

Google's professionals also bask in the light of potentially millionaire-making stock option grants.

Dual-career ladders are another way to manage professionals' pay. At many employers, a bigger salary and bonus requires rerouting from, say, engineering into management. However, not all professionals want management. Therefore, many employers institute dual-career ladders, such as one for managers and another for engineers. The latter offer professionals the prospect of using advanced technical skills and earning higher pay without switching to management.[28]

Nonfinancial and Recognition-Based Awards

Employers often supplement financial incentives with various nonfinancial and recognition-based awards. The term *recognition program* usually refers to formal programs, such as employee-of-the-month programs. *Social recognition program* generally refers to informal manager–employee exchanges such as praise, approval, or expressions of appreciation for a job well done. *Performance feedback* means providing quantitative or qualitative information on task performance so as to change or maintain performance; showing workers a graph of how their performance is trending is an example.[29]

Recognition has a positive impact on performance, either alone or in conjunction with financial rewards.[30] In one survey, 89% of surveyed companies reported having recognition programs in place, for things ranging from exceptional performance to attendance, safety, sales, and major life events.[31]

Employers are bulking up their recognition programs. For example, Baudville, a workplace recognition vendor, offers an e-card service called ePraise. Employers use this to remind employees of how much they're appreciated. Intuit shifted its employee recognition, years of service, patent awards, and wellness awards programs to Globoforce, an awards vendor, several years ago. The move "allowed us to build efficiencies and improved effectiveness" into the programs' management, says Intuit's vice president of performance, rewards, and workplace.[32] Management consultant Hewitt Associates uses www.bravanta.com to help its managers more easily recognize exceptional employee service with special awards. Other sites include www.premierechoiceaward.com/secure/home.asp, www.giveanything.com, www.incentivecity.com, and www.kudoz.com.

Social Media and HR[33]

Various new apps let employees showcase their awards, contributions, and praise from coworkers. Apps like those at http://blog.intuit.com/employees/6-mobile-apps-for-recognizing-and-rewarding-employees/ also facilitate employees praising each other. For example, one lets employees "Give recognition by picking out a badge and typing in a quick note to thank the people who matter most. . . ." Others let users post the positive feedback they receive to their LinkedIn profiles.

Most employers combine financial and nonfinancial awards. At American Skandia, which provides insurance and financial planning products and services, customer service reps who exceed standards receive a plaque, a $500 check, their photo and story on the firm's internal website, and a dinner for themselves and their teams.[34] One survey of 235 managers found that the most-used rewards to motivate employees (top–down, from most used to least) were:[35]

- Employee recognition
- Gift certificates
- Special events
- Cash rewards
- Merchandise incentives
- E-mail/print communications
- Training programs
- Work/life benefits
- Variable pay
- Group travel
- Individual travel
- Sweepstakes

The HR Tools feature elaborates.

IMPROVING PERFORMANCE: HR Tools for Line Managers and Entrepreneurs

The individual line manager should not rely just on the employer's financial incentive plans for motivating subordinates. Those plans may not be very complete, and there are simply too many opportunities to motivate employees every day to let those opportunities pass. What to do?

First, the best option for motivating an employee is also the simplest—*make sure the employee has a doable goal* and that he or she agrees with it. It makes little sense to try to motivate employees with financial incentives if they don't know their goals or don't agree with them. Psychologist Edwin Locke and his colleagues have consistently found that specific, challenging goals lead to higher task performance than do specific, unchallenging goals; vague goals; or no goals.

Second, *recognizing an employee's contribution* is a powerful motivation tool. Studies (and theories like those of Herzberg) show that recognition has a positive impact on performance, either alone or in combination with financial rewards. For example, in one study, combining financial rewards with recognition produced a 30% performance improvement in service firms, almost twice the effect of using each reward alone.

Third, use *social recognition* (such as compliments) as positive reinforcement on a day-to-day basis. Figure 12-1 presents a list.[36]

- Challenging work assignments
- Freedom to choose own work activity
- Having fun built into work
- More of preferred task
- Role as boss's stand-in when he or she is away
- Role in presentations to top management
- Job rotation
- Encouragement of learning and continuous improvement
- Being provided with ample encouragement
- Being allowed to set own goals
- Compliments
- Expression of appreciation in front of others
- Note of thanks
- Employee-of-the-month award
- Special commendation
- Bigger desk
- Bigger office or cubicle

FIGURE 12-1 Social Recognition and Related Positive Reinforcement Managers Can Use

Source: Bob Nelson, *1001 Ways to Reward Employees* (New York: Workman Pub, 1994), p. 19; Sunny C. L. Fong and Margaret A. Shaffer, "The Dimensionality and Determinants of Pay Satisfaction: A Cross-Cultural Investigation of a Group Incentive Plan," *International Journal of Human Resource Management* 14, no. 4 (June 2003), p. 559.

Discussion Question 12-1: You have decided to verify that recognition does in fact improve performance. To that end, you will use an honest observation to praise someone's performance today. What was the effect of your experiment?

Job Design

Although not usually considered an "incentive," job design (discussed more fully in Chapter 4, Job Analysis and the Talent Management Process) can have a significant impact on employee motivation and retention. A study by Harvard Business School researchers concluded that job design is a primary driver of employee engagement. A study by Sibson Consulting concluded that job responsibility and feedback were the fifth and seventh most important drivers of employee engagement. A study by Towers Watson concluded that challenging work ranked as the seventh most important driver for attracting employees.[37] Job design is thus a useful part of an employer's total rewards program.

The Profit Center feature illustrates how employers combine incentives to boost profits.

IMPROVING PERFORMANCE: HR as a Profit Center

Can Financial and Nonfinancial Incentives Boost Performance in a Fast-Food Chain?

Two researchers studied the impact of financial and nonfinancial incentives on business performance in 21 stores of a fast-food franchise in the Midwest.[38] The researchers compared performance over time in stores that did and did not use financial and nonfinancial incentives. Each store had about 25 workers and two managers. The researchers trained the managers to identify measurable employee behaviors that were currently deficient but that could influence store performance. Example behaviors included "keeping both hands moving at the drive-through window" and "repeating the customer's order back to him or her."[39] Then the researchers instituted financial and nonfinancial incentive plans. They measured store performance in terms of gross profitability (revenue minus expenses), drive-through time, and employee turnover.

Financial Incentives

Some employees in some of the stores received financial incentives for exhibiting the desired behaviors. The financial incentives consisted of lump-sum bonuses in the workers' paychecks. For example, if the manager observed a work team exhibiting up to 50 behaviors (such as "working during idle time") during the observation period, he or she added $25 to the paychecks of all store employees that period; 50 to 100 behaviors added $50 per paycheck, and more than 100 behaviors added $75 per paycheck. Payouts eventually rose over time as the employees learned to enact the behaviors they were to exhibit.

Nonfinancial Incentives

The researchers trained the managers in some stores to use nonfinancial incentives such as feedback and recognition. For example, for *performance feedback* managers maintained charts showing the drive-through times at the end of each day. They placed the charts by the time clocks. Thus, these store employees could keep track of their store's performance on measures like drive-through times. The researchers also trained managers to administer *recognition* to employees. For instance, "I noticed that today the drive-through times were really good."[40]

Results

The program was successful. Both the financial and nonfinancial incentives improved employee and store performance.[41] For example, store profits rose 30% for those units where managers used financial rewards. Store profits rose 36% for those units where managers used nonfinancial rewards. During the same 9-month period, drive-through times decreased 19% for the financial incentives group, and 25% for the nonfinancial incentives groups. Turnover improved 13% for the financial incentives group, and 10% for the nonfinancial incentives group.

Implications for Managers

Here is what these findings mean for managers designing an incentive plan:[42]

1. **Ask: Does it make sense to use incentives?**[43] It makes more sense to use an incentive plan when:
   - Motivation (not ability) is the problem.
   - Employee effort and results are directly related.
   - The employees can control the behavior you plan to incentivize.
2. **Link the incentive with your strategy.** Link the incentive to behavior that is critical for achieving strategic goals.[44] For example, the fast-food restaurant chain's owners wanted to boost the stores' performance and profits. Incentivizing employees to work faster and smarter accomplished that.
3. **Design the program to be motivational.** Victor Vroom would say there should be a clear link between *effort and performance*, and between *performance and reward*, and that the reward must be *attractive* to the employee. Employees must have the skills and training to do the job. Employers should support the incentive plan with performance feedback, as in the form of performance graphs.
4. **Don't forget feedback and recognition.** They can be as influential as financial incentives.
5. **Set complete standards.** For example, don't just pay for "repeating the customer's order" if speeding up processing time is important too.
6. **Be scientific.** Don't waste money on incentives that seem logical but that may not be contributing to performance. As in this study, *gather evidence* and analyze the effects of the incentive plan over time. Ascertain whether it is indeed influencing the measures (such as employee turnover) that you want to improve.[45]

Discussion Question 12-2: The dean has asked you to design an incentive plan for your professor. How would you apply what you learned in this feature to do so?

Incentives for Salespeople

3 Discuss the pros and cons of commissions versus straight pay for salespeople.

Sales compensation plans typically rely heavily on sales commissions, and should aim to achieve the company's strategic and sales goals. As one survey said, "the performance metrics given to the sales team must drive behaviors that will help the company's . . . strategy to be successful."[46]

Unfortunately, the same survey also found that "30% of respondents believe their sales compensation program rewarded the right behaviors 'not well' or 'very poorly.'"[47] Employers are therefore moving to align the measures they use to reward their salespeople with their firms' strategies.[48]

Salary Plan

Some firms pay salespeople fixed salaries (perhaps with occasional incentives in the form of bonuses, sales contest prizes, and the like).[49] Why do this? Straight salary makes sense when the main task involves prospecting (finding new clients) or account servicing. Turnover is another reason. Faced with the difficulty of attracting and keeping good salespeople, a Buick-GMC dealership in Lincolnton, North Carolina, offers straight salary as an option to salespeople who sell an average of at least eight vehicles a month.[50]

The straight salary approach also makes it easier to switch territories or to reassign sales people, and it can foster sales staff loyalty. The main disadvantage, of course, is that straight salary may not motivate potentially high-performing salespeople.[51]

Commission Plan

Straight commission plans pay salespeople for results, and only for results. Commission plans tend to attract high-performing salespeople who see that effort clearly produces rewards. Sales costs are proportionate to sales rather than fixed, and the company's fixed sales costs are thus lower. Such plans are easy to understand and compute. Commission plan alternatives include straight commissions, quota bonuses (for meeting particular quotas), management by objectives programs (pay is based on specific metrics), and ranking programs (these reward high achievers but pay little or no bonuses to the lowest performing salespeople).[52]

However, problems abound. In poorly designed plans, salespeople may focus on making the sale, and neglect nonselling duties such as servicing small accounts and pushing hard-to-sell items. Wide variations in pay may occur; this can make some feel the plan is inequitable. Misjudging sales potential can lead to excessively high commissions and to the need to cut commission rates. Salespersons' pay may be excessive in boom times and low in recessions. Furthermore, sales performance—like any performance—reflects not just motivation, but ability. If the person hasn't the sales skills, commissions won't produce sales.[53]

Combination Plan

Most companies pay salespeople a combination of salary and commissions, usually with a sizable salary component. An incentive mix of about 70% base salary/30% incentive seems typical; this cushions the salesperson's downside risk (of earning nothing), while limiting the risk that the commissions could get out of hand from the firm's point of view.[54]

Combination plans have pros and cons.[55] They give salespeople a floor to their earnings, let the company specify what services the salary component is for (such as servicing current accounts), and still provide an incentive for superior performance. However, the salary component isn't tied to performance, so the employer trades away some incentive value.

Combination plans also tend to become complicated, and misunderstandings can result. This might not be a problem with a simple salary-plus-commission plan, but most plans are not so simple. For example, in a "commission-plus-drawing-account" plan, the salesperson is paid based on commissions. However, he or she can draw on future earnings during low sales periods. In the "commission-plus-bonus" plan, the firm pays its salespeople mostly based on commissions. However, they also get a small bonus for directed activities like selling slow-moving items.

Maximizing Sales Results

In setting sales quotas and commission rates, the goal is to motivate sales activity but avoid excessive commissions. Unfortunately, the tendency to set commission rates informally often reduces plans' effectiveness.[56]

Setting effective quotas is an art. Questions to ask include: Are quotas communicated to the sales force within 1 month of the start of the period? Does the sales force know how their quotas are set? Do you combine bottom–up information (like account forecasts) with top–down requirements (like the company business plan)? Are returns and de-bookings reasonably low?[57]

One expert suggests the following rule as to whether the sales incentive plan is effective: 75% or more of the sales force achieving quota or better, 10% of the sales force achieving higher performance level (than previously), and 5% to 10% of the sales force achieving below-quota performance and receiving performance development coaching.[58] The employer should also consider the effect of sales carryover. In most firms, a significant portion of the sales in one year reflects a "carryover" (sales that would repeat even without any efforts by the sales force) of sales from the prior year. Paying the sales force a commission on all the current year's sales means the employer has paid a commission on last year's carryover sales, which the sales force had little or no role in bringing in this year.[59]

A survey of sales effectiveness reveals that salespeople at high-performing companies:

- Receive 38% of their total cash compensation in the form of *sale incentive pay* (compared with 27% for salespeople at low-performing companies)
- Are twice as likely to receive stock, *stock options*, or other equity pay as their counterparts at low-performing companies (36% versus 18%)
- Spend 264 more hours per year on *high-value sales activities* (e.g., prospecting, making sales presentations, and closing) than salespeople at low-performing companies
- Spend 40% more time each year with their *best potential customers*—qualified leads and prospects they know—than salespeople at low-performing companies
- Spend nearly 25% *less time on administration*, allowing them to allocate more time to core sales activities, such as prospecting leads and closing sales[60]

Distinguishing among performers is also important. For example, some companies distinguish among stars, laggards, and core performers. Some companies limit how much their salespeople can earn in commissions, but doing so can perversely encourage star salespeople to quit selling when they reach their quotas. Laggards seem to do better with more frequent, quarterly bonuses and social pressure to improve their performance. Core performers—the vast midrange of the sales force—should have multitier targets. The first tier target is what sales agents historically attain. The second-tier reflects what a small percentage of the sales force attains. The third tier target is usually only attained by the company's star salespeople.[61]

Sales Incentives in Action

Car salespersons' compensation ranges from 100% commission to a small base salary with commission accounting for most of total compensation. Traditionally, the car salesperson's commission is based on a percentage of the difference between the dealer's invoice cost and the amount the car is sold for, minus an amount to cover the "pack" or dealer overhead (the pack being perhaps $300 for a new car to $800 for a used car, and rising for pricier cars).[62]

This approach encourages the salesperson to hold firm on the retail price, and to push "after-sale products" like floor mats and side moldings. There may also be extra incentives to sell packages such as rustproofing. For selling slow-moving vehicles, the salesperson may get a "spiff"—an extra incentive bonus over commission. And there are bonuses, such as Salesperson of the Month (perhaps $300 for most cars sold).[63]

Commission plans like these still dominate, but not as much. Many dealerships are substituting salary plus bonus plans for commissions. This reflects the growing emphasis on "one price no hassle" pricing.[64] But in either case, the pay plan's aim is to produce the salesperson behaviors the dealership needs to support its strategic aims.

Improving Performance Through HRIS: How Effective Are Your Incentives?

Somewhat astonishingly, given the amount of money employers pay out in commissions, about 60% of employers track sales performance and sales commissions much as they did decades ago, using spreadsheets.[65] But to maximize performance, the sales manager typically needs evidence, such as: Do the salespeople understand the compensation plans? Do they know how we measure and reward performance? Are quotas fair? Is there a correlation between performance and commissions? And, does our commission plan maximize sales of our most profitable products?[66] Spreadsheets don't easily support these types of analyses.

Conducting these analyses requires special enterprise incentive management software applications.[67] Several vendors supply these. One is VUE Software™, which supplies VUE Compensation Management®.[68] With the aid of VUE Compensation Management® the sales

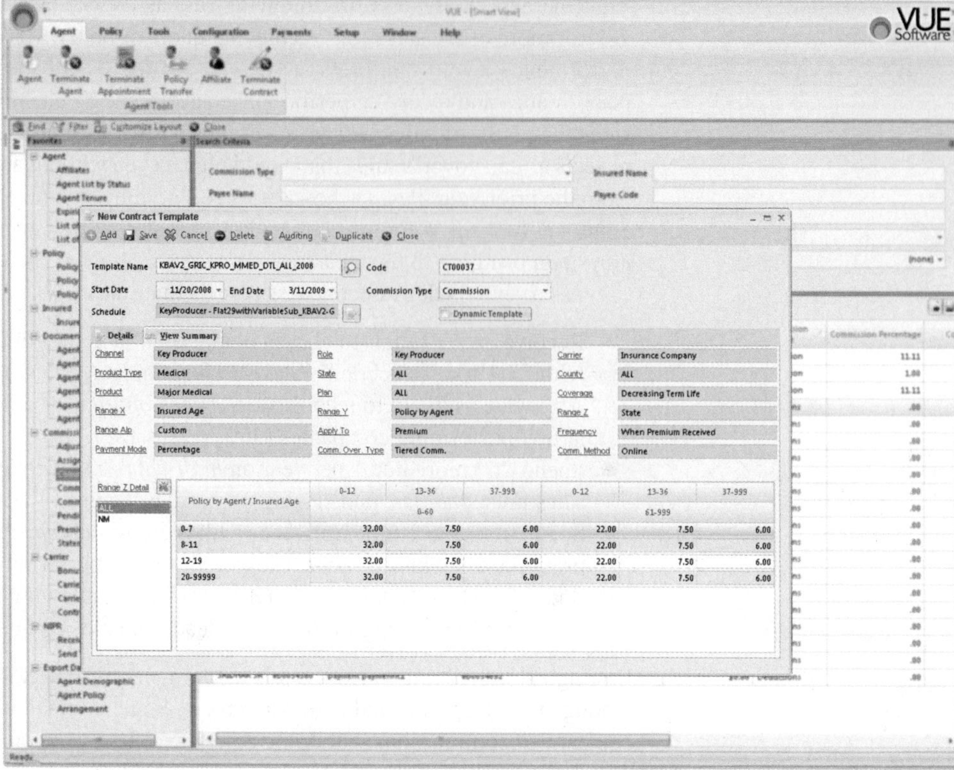

With the aid of VUE Compensation Management® the sales manager can analyze compensation and performance data, conduct "what-if" analyses and reports, and do trend analyses.

Source: Computer Solutions & Software. Used by permission of Stephen Bruno.

manager can analyze compensation and performance data, conduct "what-if" analyses and reports, and do trend analyses.[69] For example, with more than 1,000 sales representatives, First Tennessee Bank was having problems managing its sales incentive programs.[70] Bank employees had to enter by hand sales information for each of the 1,000 sales reps onto Excel spreadsheets. The process "had begun to spiral out of control." Switching to an enterprise incentive management system solved the problem.[71]

4 Describe the main incentives for managers and executives.

Incentives for Managers and Executives

Managers play a crucial role in divisional and company-wide profitability, and most firms therefore put considerable thought into how to reward them. Most managers get short-term and long-term incentives in addition to salary.[72] For firms offering short-term incentive plans, virtually all—96%—in one study provided those incentives in cash. For those offering long-term incentives, about 48% offer them as stock options. These aim to motivate and reward management for long-term growth in shareholder value.[73]

Strategy and the Executive's Long-Term and Total Rewards Package

Few human resource practices have as profound an influence on strategic success as the executive's long-term incentives. Whether consolidating operations, or pursuing growth, firms can't fully implement strategies in just 1 or 2 years. Therefore, the long-term signals you send managers regarding what you reward can affect whether the firm's strategy succeeds.

In turn, the executives' total reward components—base salary, short- and long-term incentives, and benefits—must align with each other and with achieving the company's strategic aims. Compensation experts suggest first defining the strategic aims for the executive compensation plan—"What is our strategy and what are our strategic goals?"—then decide what long-term behaviors (boosting sales, cutting costs, and so on) the executives must exhibit to achieve the firm's strategic goals. The next step is to shape each component of the executive total compensation package (base salary, short- and long-term incentives, and benefits) and group them into a balanced plan that makes sense in terms of motivating the executive to achieve these aims.

The rule then is this: Each pay component should help focus the manager's attention on the behaviors required to achieve the company's strategic goals.[74]

Therefore, using multiple, strategy-based performance criteria for incentivizing executives is best. Criteria include financial performance, number of strategic goals met, employee productivity measures, customer satisfaction surveys, and employee morale surveys. The bottom line is that the top executive's pay package should direct his or her attention toward accomplishing the company's strategic goals.[75] One expert estimates that the typical CEO's salary accounts for about one-fifth of his or her pay. A bonus based on explicit performance standards accounts for another fifth, and long-term incentive awards such as stock options and long-term performance plans account for the remaining three-fifths.[76] Ideally, the executive compensation plan's performance standards should include a combination of market benchmarks (such as performance against competitors) as well as business performance standards (such as earnings per share growth).

SARBANES-OXLEY The Sarbanes-Oxley Act of 2002 affects how employers formulate their executive incentive programs. Congress passed Sarbanes-Oxley to inject a higher level of responsibility into executives' and board members' decisions. It makes them personally liable for violating their fiduciary responsibilities to their shareholders. The act also requires CEOs and CFOs of a public company to repay any bonuses, incentives, or equity-based compensation received from the company during the 12-month period following the issuance of a financial statement that the company must restate due to material noncompliance with a financial reporting requirement stemming from misconduct.[77]

We'll now look at short- and long-term management incentives.

Short-Term Incentives and the Annual Bonus

annual bonus
Plans that are designed to motivate short-term performance of managers and which are tied to company profitability.

For better or worse, employers are shifting away from long-term incentives to put more emphasis on short-term performance and incentives.[78] Most firms have **annual bonus** plans for motivating managers' short-term performance. Such short-term incentives can easily produce plus or minus adjustments of 25% or more to total pay. Three factors influence one's bonus: eligibility, fund size, and individual performance.

ELIGIBILITY Employers first decide eligibility. Most traditionally based annual bonus eligibility on job level/title, base salary, and/or officer status. Some simply based eligibility on job level or job title, or salary.[79] Recently, more employers are offering a broader range of employees annual incentive plans ". . . in which both executives and other employees participate."[80] The change reflects the fact that more employees—not just top managers—are now responsible for measurable contributions.

The trend is evident from surveys of what determines bonus plan eligibility. Rather than job title or officer status, s*alary grade or band* is now the most common eligibility determinant, reported by 42% of employers in one survey. This was followed by *title/reporting relationship* (24%), *officer status* (13%), *compensation committee approval* (11%), *discretionary* (6%), and *base salary* (2%).[81]

The percentage size of any bonus is typically greater for top-level executives. Thus, an executive earning $250,000 in salary may be able to earn another 80% of his or her salary as a bonus, while a manager in the same firm earning $100,000 can earn only another 30%. Recently, Microsoft's CEO was eligible for an annual bonus of up to 100% of his salary (but he collected only half). A typical bonus percentage might be executives, 45% of base salary; managers, 25%; and supervisory personnel, 12%.

FUND SIZE Second, one must determine how big the annual bonus fund should be. Most employers (33% in one survey) traditionally use the Sum of Targets approach.[82] Specifically, they estimate the likely bonus for each eligible ("target") employee, and total these to arrive at the bonus pool's size.

However, more employers are funding the short-term bonus fund based on financial results. Here there are no fixed rules about the proportion of profits to pay out. One alternative is to reserve a minimal amount of the profits, say, 10%, for safeguarding stockholders' investments. Then establish a fund for bonuses equal to, say, 20% of the operating profit before taxes in excess of this safeguard amount. Suppose the operating profits were $200,000 (after putting away 10% to

Even in retail stores, it's not unusual to compensate store managers partly based on short-term sales and profits.

Baerbel Schmidt/Getty Images

safeguard stockholders). Then the management bonus fund might be 20% of $200,000 or $40,000. Most employers use more than one financial measure on which to base the bonus fund, with sales, earnings per share, and cash flow the most popular.[83] Other illustrative formulas include:

- Twelve percent of net earnings after deducting 6% of net capital
- Ten percent of the amount by which net income exceeds 5% of stockholders' equity

The employer may also use a formula to base the bonus pool on other measures the employer wishes to emphasize. For example, Transocean Ltd., the firm that managed the Deepwater Horizon Gulf oil rig that sank in 2010, uses a formula that includes "safety" as 25% of the formula. After the Gulf explosion, senior Transocean executives donated any safety bonuses to the victims' families.[84]

Some firms don't use a formula to determine fund size at all, but make that decision on a discretionary basis.[85] Others, again, determine fund size by simply summing up the likely awards.

THE INDIVIDUAL AWARDS Finally, one must have a way to decide the actual individual awards. Typically, the employer sets a target bonus (as well as maximum bonus, perhaps double the target bonus) for each eligible position. The actual bonus then reflects the manager's performance. For example, having previously decided which financial performance measures (return on assets, revenue growth, and so on) to use to measure each manager's performance, the employer computes preliminary total company bonus estimates, and compares the total amount of money required with the bonus fund available.[86] If necessary, it then adjusts the individual bonus estimates. In any case, outstanding managers should receive at least their target bonuses, and marginal ones should receive at best below-average awards. Use what you save on the marginal employees to supplement the outstanding employees. Yet a study of CEOs of Standard & Poor's 1500 companies for a recent 3-year period found that 57% of the CEOs received pay increases although company performance (in terms of total shareholder return) did not improve.[87]

One question is whether managers will receive bonuses based on individual performance, corporate performance, or both. Firms usually tie top-level executive bonuses mostly to overall corporate results (or divisional results if the executive heads a major division). But as one moves farther down, corporate profits become a less accurate gauge of a manager's contribution. For supervisors or the heads of functional departments, it often makes more sense to base the bonus more closely to individual performance.

Many firms therefore end up tying short-term bonuses to both organizational and individual performance. Perhaps the simplest method is the *split-award plan.* This makes the manager

TABLE 12-2 Multiplier Approach to Determining Annual Bonus

Individual Performance (Based on Appraisal, Weight = 0.50)	*Company Performance (Based on Sales Targets, Weight = 0.50)*			
	Excellent	Good	Fair	Poor
Excellent	1.00	0.90	0.80	0.70
Good	0.80	0.70	0.60	0.50
Fair	0.00	0.00	0.00	0.00
Poor	0.00	0.00	0.00	0.00

Note: To determine the dollar amount of a manager's award, multiply the maximum possible (target) bonus by the appropriate factor in the matrix.

eligible for two bonuses, one based on his or her individual effort and one based on the organization's overall performance. Thus, a manager might be eligible for an individual performance bonus of up to $10,000, but receive only $2,000 at the end of the year, based on his or her individual performance evaluation. But the person might also receive a second bonus of $3,000, based on the firm's profits for the year.

One drawback to this approach is that it may give marginal performers too much—for instance, someone could get a company-based bonus, even if his or her own performance is mediocre. One way to avoid this is to use the *multiplier method.* As Table 12-2 illustrates, multiply the person's target bonus by 1.00, 0.80, or zero (if the firm's performance is excellent, and the person's performance is excellent, good, fair, or poor). A manager whose own performance is poor does not even receive the company-based bonus.

Strategic Long-Term Incentives

Employers use long-term incentives to inject a long-term perspective into their executives' decisions. With only short-term criteria to shoot for, a manager could conceivably boost profitability by reducing plant maintenance, for instance; this tactic might catch up with the company 2 or 3 years later.

Long-term incentives such as stock options, if well-designed, should only pay off if the firm achieves its strategic goals (such as "double our rate of return"), at which point the owners and investors should also benefit from the executives' efforts. Long-term incentives may also be "golden handcuffs," motivating executives to stay by letting them accumulate capital (usually options to buy company stock) that they can only cash in after a certain period. Popular long-term incentives include cash, stock, stock options, stock appreciation rights, and phantom stock. We'll look at each.

stock option
The right to purchase a stated number of shares of a company stock at today's price at some time in the future.

STOCK OPTIONS A **stock option** is the right to purchase a specific number of shares of company stock at a specific price during a specific period. The executive thus hopes to profit by exercising his or her option to buy the shares in the future but at today's price. This assumes the stock will go up. Unfortunately, this depends partly on considerations outside the manager's control.[88] When stock markets dropped a few years ago, many employers including Intel and Google modified option plans to boost the likely payout.[89] The HR Practices Around the Globe feature addresses one aspect of this.

IMPROVING PERFORMANCE: HR Practices Around the Globe

"International human resource management" is important because cultural, political, legal, and economic differences mean that employees in one country often react differently to an HR practice than would employees in other countries.

For example, until January 2006, China basically prohibited publicly listed companies from offering stock incentive plans to their managers. At that point improving economic conditions and an evolving political philosophy led to new regulations. Soon 42 Chinese listed companies were permitting such plans.

A recent study focused on those 42 companies. It sought to determine how the new incentive plans affected company performance. To understand the findings it's important to know that managing in China still has unique characteristics. For example, prior to becoming publicly listed firms, the big firms are usually owned by the government. Furthermore, the government may well continue to retain certain ownership control rights even after the firms go on the stock market. In such cases, a company's owners may have goals different from that of management. For example, government owners might want to maximize employment, rather than profitability. The question is, given such cultural and political realities, do management stock option plans in China translate into improved company performance, as they often do in the United States?

The researchers compared the performance of the 42 Chinese companies that did adopt management stock-option plans with a control group of firms without such plans. One thing they found was that the stock-option plans did improve firm performance *in companies controlled by private shareholders*, but not in companies controlled by the government. In the latter, goals such as maximizing employment may have outweighed boosting profits, thus limiting managers' profit-boosting efforts.

The findings highlight why managing globally is challenging. In this case, a stock option plan that might improve financial performance in the United States might fail in China, where the government owners' goals may well differ from the desire of managers to boost profits.

Discussion Question 12-3: Given these findings, would it make sense for managers in government-controlled companies to receive stock options tied to something other than profitability, such as "no employees lose their jobs in this company"? Why?

Source: Robert Boylan, Maggie Foley, and Yu-Jun Lian, "Are Equity Incentives Effective in Chinese Listed Firms? New Evidence from Propensity Score Matching (PSN)," *International Journal of Business Strategy* 10, no. 3, September 2010.

STOCK OPTION PROBLEMS The chronic problem with stock options is that they often reward even managers who have lackluster performance, but there are also other issues. In some cases, executives allegedly lied about the dates they received their options to boost their returns. Options may also encourage executives to take perilous risks in pursuit of higher (at least short-term) profits.[90] Stock options provide an incentive to go for spectacular results, but since the managers haven't actually bought the stock yet, they don't risk their own money. One solution is to simply draft the option plan so it forces recipients to convert their options to stock more quickly.[91]

OTHER STOCK PLANS Beyond that, the trend is toward tying rewards more explicitly to performance goals. Instead of stock options, more firms are granting various types of performance-based shares. With *performance-contingent restricted stock* the executive receives his or her shares only if he or she meets the preset performance targets.[92] With (time-based) *restricted stock plans*, the firm usually awards rights to the shares without cost to the executive but the employee is restricted from acquiring (and selling) the shares for, say, 5 years. The employer's aim is to retain the employee's services during that time.[93] With *indexed options*, the option's exercise price fluctuates with the performance of, say, a market index. Then, if the company's stock does no better than the index, the manager's options are worthless. With *premium priced options*, the exercise price is higher than the stock's closing price on the date of the grant, so the executive can't profit from the options until the stock makes significant gains.[94]

Stock appreciation rights (SARs) permit the recipient to exercise the stock option (by buying the stock) or to take any appreciation in the stock price in cash, stock, or some combination of these. Under *phantom stock plans*, executives receive not shares but "units" that are similar to shares of company stock. Then at some future time, they receive value (usually in cash) equal to the appreciation of the "phantom" stock they own. Both SARs and phantom stock essentially "are bonus plans that grant not stock but rather the right to receive an award based on the value of the company's stock."[95] A *performance achievement plan* awards shares of stock for the achievement of predetermined financial targets, such as profit or growth in earnings per share. Most employees seem to prefer cash bonuses to either stock options or restricted stocks. Due to differences in employee preferences, when possible, enable each employee to choose whether to receive stock options or restricted stock.[96]

ETHICS AND INCENTIVES Anyone designing a long-term incentive plan should keep in mind the management truism "People put their efforts where they know they'll be rewarded." The problem is that simplistic incentives that focus on just one factor (such as cost-cutting) may inadvertently encourage managers to ignore other important factors (such as long-term investment). Similarly, in the absence of strong ethical standards, incentives may breed unethical behavior. One article even notes that "in today's cash focused culture, where new research suggests that money may have similar influences on individual actions as drugs or sex, the unexpected impact of plans that reward certain behaviors with cash is perhaps more than first thought."[97] Examples are depressingly familiar. For example, *Forbes* recently alleged that one firm's culture now "rewards hard-nosed aggressiveness and doesn't put the client's interests before those of the firm."[98] For stock option plan designers, the solution is to include a sufficient array of bonus-able criteria in the incentive plan, while fostering an ethical culture.

Some Other Executive Incentives

Companies also offer a range of other executive incentives. Some incentivize executives to stay with the firm. This is especially important when executives might flee because another company is stalking the firm with intentions to buy it. **Golden parachutes** are extraordinary payments companies make to executives in connection with a change in company ownership or control. For example, a company's "golden parachute" clause might state that, with a change in ownership of the firm, the executive would receive a one-time payment of $2 million.[99]

golden parachute
A payment companies make in connection with a change in ownership or control of a company.

Some firms use loans as incentives, for example by guaranteeing large loans to directors and officers to buy company stock. Thus, directors and officers of Conseco owed the company more than $500 million in hard-to-repay loans when company shares tanked.[100]

Team and Organization-Wide Incentive Plans

5 Name and describe the most popular organization-wide incentive plans.

We've focused so far on individual employee incentives (such as piecework, commissions, and executive bonuses). Let's look now at incentives for teams, and for all employees company-wide.

How to Design Team Incentives

Firms increasingly rely on teams to manage their work. They therefore need incentive plans that encourage teamwork and focus team members on performance. **Team (or group) incentive plans** pay incentives to the team based on the team's performance.

team (or group) incentive plan
A plan in which a production standard is set for a specific work group, and its members are paid incentives if the group exceeds the production standard.

The main question here is how to reward the team's performance, and the wrong choice can prove lethal. Levi Strauss switched from an individual to a team incentive plan, one that rewarded the team as a whole for its output. Unfortunately, they neglected the fact that some employees worked harder than others did. The slower ones (economists sometimes call them "free riders" because they take a free ride on others' efforts) were paid the same as the faster ones. The faster ones, no longer individually incentivized, slowed down, production declined, and Levi's closed its U.S. factories.

So, the main aim is to have all your team pulling together. Free riders notwithstanding, the usual approach is still to tie rewards to some overall standard (goal) of group performance,

Baerbel Schmidt/Getty Images

Team incentives can foster a sense of cooperation and unanimity.

such as "20 total labor hours per car."[101] One company established such an overall standard for its teams. If the firm reached 100% of its goal, the employees would share in about 5% of the improvement (in labor costs saved). The firm divided the resulting bonus pool by the number of employees to compute the value of a "share." If the firm achieved less than 100% of its goal, the bonus pool was less. The results of this plan in terms of focusing teams on the firm's strategic goals were reportedly "extraordinary."[102] Firms such as Toyota that use such team plans rely on employee selection, training and peer pressure to minimize free riding.

ENGINEERED STANDARDS While most employers just use experience to estimate what the team goal or standard should be ("20 total labor hours per car) others carefully engineer their production standards. If so, the employer will typically base the team incentive on either the piece rate or standard hour plan. All team members then typically receive the same share of the team's incentive pay. Thus the team might receive say, $5 for each wheel installed above the industrially engineered "standard" 10 wheels per hour.

Occasionally, the employer may want to pay team members according to some other formula. For instance, instead of paying each team member based on how well the team as a whole does, pay everyone based on how well the *best* team member does. This counterintuitive option may make sense when an employer has reason to believe the new team incentive plan might demotivate high-performing team members. That's what happened at Levi's, for instance.

PROS AND CONS OF TEAM INCENTIVES Team incentives often make sense. They reinforce team planning and problem solving, and can help ensure cooperation. Team incentives also facilitate training, since each member has an interest in getting new members trained fast. The main disadvantage is the demotivating effects of workers who share in the team-based pay but who don't put their hearts into it (free riders).

Evidence-Based HR: Inequities That Undercut Team Incentives

Although about 85% of large employers reportedly use some type of group- or team-based incentives, studies suggest that team incentives are often counterproductive. Why?

A researcher studied business students enrolled in a graduate online MBA program.[103] She devised a method for systematically categorizing how they said they reacted to the team incentives they'd experienced in the past.

She found that inequity was the big problem.[104] Each team member's financial compensation was often the same, although one or two people "did the lion's share of the work." In other cases, the employer chose one or two team members for promotion, leaving others to feel they'd worked hard to support someone else's career. The bottom line seems to be that unless you minimize inequities, it's probably best to pay employees based on their individual contributions, rather than on collective team performance.

The other thing to keep in mind is that successful teamwork reflects more than team incentives. Again, companies such as Toyota screen, hire, train, and cultivate workers to be team members, so the incentives are just one component.

organization-wide incentive plan
Incentive plan in which all or most employees can participate.

Many employers take the team incentive idea to the next logical level and institute incentive plans in which all or most employees participate. **Organization-wide incentive plans** are plans in which all or most employees can participate, and which generally tie the reward to some measure of company-wide performance. Also called *variable pay plans*, they include profit sharing, Scanlon/gainsharing plans, and employee stock ownership (ESOP) plans. We'll look at them next.

Profit-Sharing Plans

profit-sharing plan
A plan whereby employees share in the company's profits.

Profit-sharing plans are plans in which all or most employees receive a share of the firm's annual profits. Research is sketchy. One study concludes that there is ample evidence that profit-sharing plans boost productivity and morale, but that their effect on profits is insignificant, once you factor in the costs of the plans' payouts.[105] A recent study, conducted in Spain, concluded that profit-sharing plans enhance employees' organizational commitment.[106]

There are several types of profit-sharing plans. With *current profit-sharing* or cash plans, employees share in a portion of the employer's profits quarterly or annually. Here the firm simply distributes a percentage of profits (usually 15% to 20%) as profit shares to employees at regular intervals. The Home Depot instituted such a cash program for all its store workers. It started paying store associates a bonus if their stores met certain financial goals. In one recent year, The Home Depot distributed a total of $90 million under that company-wide incentive plan.[107]

With *deferred profit-sharing* plans, the employer puts cash awards into trust accounts for the employees' retirement.[108] Employees' income taxes on the distributions are deferred until the employee retires or withdraws funds from the plan (thus "deferred profit sharing-plans"). Such plans are essentially pension plans "in which the employer has discretion to determine when and how much the company pays into the plan."[109] The employer generally distributes such awards based on a percentage of the employee's salary, or some measure of the employee's contribution to company profits.[110]

Scanlon Plans

Scanlon plan
An incentive plan developed in 1937 by Joseph Scanlon and designed to encourage cooperation, involvement, and sharing of benefits.

Few would argue with the idea that the most powerful way of ensuring employee commitment is to synchronize the company's goals with those of its employees—in other words, to ensure that by pursuing his or her goals, the worker pursues the employer's goals as well. Experts have proposed many ways to attain this. However, few have been as successful as the **Scanlon plan**, developed in 1937 by Joseph Scanlon, a United Steel Workers Union official.[111] It is still popular today.

The Scanlon plan is remarkably progressive, considering that it is now more than 75 years old. Scanlon plans have five basic features.[112] The first is Scanlon's *philosophy of cooperation.* This philosophy assumes that managers and workers must rid themselves of the "us" and "them" attitudes that normally inhibit employees from developing a sense of ownership in the company.

A second feature is what its practitioners call *identity.* This means that in order to focus employee involvement, the company must articulate its mission or purpose, and employees must understand how the business operates in terms of customers, prices, and costs. *Competence* is a third basic feature. The program, say three experts, "explicitly recognizes that a Scanlon plan demands a high level of competence from employees at all levels."[113] This suggests careful selection and training.

The fourth feature of the plan is the *involvement system.* Employees present improvement suggestions to the appropriate departmental-level committees, which transmit the valuable ones to the executive-level committee. It then decides whether to implement the suggestion.

The fifth element of the plan is the *sharing of benefits formula.* If a suggestion is implemented and successful, all employees usually share in 75% of the savings. For example, assume that the normal monthly ratio of payroll costs to sales is 50%. (Thus, if sales are $600,000, payroll costs should be $300,000.) Assume the firm implements suggestions that result in payroll costs of $250,000 in a month when sales were $550,000 and payroll costs therefore should have been $275,000 (50% of sales). The savings attributable to these suggestions is $25,000 ($275,000 minus $250,000). Workers would typically split 75% of this ($18,750), while $6,250 would go to the firm. In practice, the firm sets aside about one-quarter of the $18,750, for months when payroll costs exceed the standard.

Other Gainsharing Plans

gainsharing plan
An incentive plan that engages employees in a common effort to achieve productivity objectives and share the gains.

The Scanlon plan is one early version of today's **gainsharing plans**. Gainsharing is an incentive plan that engages many or all employees in a common effort to achieve a company's productivity objectives, with any resulting cost-savings gains shared among employees and the company.[114] In addition to the Scanlon plan, other popular gainsharing plans include the Lincoln, Rucker, and Improshare plans.

The basic difference among these plans is how employers determine employee bonuses. The Scanlon formula divides payroll expenses by total sales (or, sometimes, by total sales plus increases in inventory). In one version of the *Lincoln incentive system*, first instituted at the Lincoln Electric Company of Ohio, employees work on a guaranteed piecework basis. The company then distributes total annual profits (less taxes, 6% dividends to stockholders, and a reserve) each year among employees based on their merit rating. Most firms implement customized gainsharing plans.

Results—from efforts in hospitals, as well as manufacturing plants—suggest that gainsharing can improve productivity and patient care, and reduce grievances, but may also entail considerable implementation costs.[115] Based on positive results, the U.S. Department of Health and Human Services approved certain hospital gainsharing plans. Here the hospital pays physicians a share of any cost savings attributable in part to the physicians' efforts. In any case, there are eight basic steps in implementing a gainsharing plan:[116]

1. Establish general plan objectives, such as boosting productivity or lowering labor costs.
2. Choose specific performance measures, such as labor hours per unit produced.
3. Decide the portion of gains employees will receive. In the Scanlon example mentioned earlier, employees receive about 75% of the gains.
4. Decide on a method for distributing the employees' share of the gains. Popular methods include equal percentage of pay or equal shares.
5. Choose the form of payment, usually cash.
6. Decide how often to pay bonuses. Firms tend to pay based on financial performance measures annually and on labor productivity measures quarterly or monthly.
7. Develop the involvement system. The most commonly used systems include steering committees, update meetings, suggestion systems, and problem-solving teams.
8. Implement the plan.

earnings-at-risk pay plan
Plan that puts some portion of employees' normal pay at risk if they don't meet their goals, in return for possibly obtaining a much larger bonus if they exceed their goals.

At-Risk Pay Plans

In an **earnings-at-risk pay plan**, employees agree to put some portion of their normal pay (say, 6%) at risk (forego) if they don't meet their goals, in return for possibly obtaining a much larger bonus (say, 12%) if they exceed their goals. Suppose the at-risk employees' base pay will be 94% of their counterparts' working in a not-at-risk department. If the former department then achieves its goals, employees get a bonus bringing them up to full pay; if it exceeds its goals, they receive a 12% bonus.

employee stock ownership plan (ESOP)
A corporation contributes shares of its own stock to a trust in which additional contributions are made annually. The trust distributes the stock to employees on retirement or separation from service.

Employee Stock Ownership Plans

Employee stock ownership plans (ESOPs) are company-wide plans in which the employer contributes shares of its own stock (or cash to be used to purchase such stock) to a trust established to purchase shares of the firm's stock for employees. The firm generally makes these contributions annually in proportion to total employee compensation, with a limit of 15% of compensation. The trust holds the stock in individual employee accounts. It then distributes the stock to employees upon retirement (or other separation from service), assuming the person has worked long enough to earn ownership of the stock. (*Stock options*, as discussed earlier in this chapter, go directly to the employees individually to use as they see fit, rather than into a retirement trust.)

ESOPs are popular. The company receives a tax deduction equal to the fair market value of the shares it transfers to the trustee, and can claim an income tax deduction for dividends paid on ESOP-owned stock. Employees, as noted, aren't taxed until they receive a distribution from the trust, usually at retirement. The Employee Retirement Income Security Act (ERISA) allows a firm to borrow against employee stock held in trust and then repay the loan in pretax rather than after-tax dollars, another tax incentive for using such plans.[117]

ESOPs can also help the shareholders of closely held corporations (for instance, a family owns all the shares) to diversify their assets. They place some of their own shares of the company's stock into the ESOP trust and (with the company compensating them for the shares they put in the trust) then purchase other marketable securities for themselves in their place.[118]

Research suggests that ESOPs probably do encourage employees to develop a sense of ownership in and commitment to the firm, but their effects on motivation and performance are questionable. In any case, those responsible for the funds—usually, the firm's top executives—must be fastidious in executing their fiduciary responsibilities for the fund.[119]

BROAD-BASED STOCK OPTIONS Some companies offer "broad-based stock option plans" in which all or most employees can participate. The basic thinking is that sharing ownership in the company with employees makes motivational and practical sense.[120]

Employers seem to be cutting back on these. For example, Time Warner, Microsoft, Aetna, and Charles Schwab discontinued distributing stock options to most employees. Some of them, including Microsoft, are instead awarding stock. With current tax laws, companies must show the options as an expense when awarded, reducing their attractiveness as a "costless" reward. Microsoft and others apparently feel awarding stock instead of stock options is a more direct and immediate way to link pay to performance.[121]

Incentive Plans in Practice: Nucor

Nucor Corp. is the largest steel producer in the United States. It also has the highest productivity and lowest labor cost per ton.[122] Employees can earn bonuses of 100% or more of base salary, and all Nucor employees participate in one of four performance-based incentive plans. With the *production incentive plan*, operating and maintenance employees and supervisors get weekly bonuses based on their work groups' productivity. The *department manager incentive plan* pays department managers annual incentive bonuses based mostly on the ratio of net income to dollars of assets employed for their division. With the *professional and clerical bonus plan*, employees who are not in one of the two previous plans get bonuses based on their divisions' net income return on assets.[123] Finally, under the *senior officer incentive plan*, Nucor senior managers (whose base salaries are lower than those in comparable firms) get bonuses based on Nucor's annual overall percentage of net income to stockholders equity.[124] Nucor also divides 10% of its operating profits yearly among all employees (except senior officers). Depending on company performance, this may be from 1% to over 20% of an employee's pay.

Review

MyManagementLab Go to **mymanagementlab.com** to complete the problems marked with this icon. 

Chapter Section Summaries

1. In designing an effective financial incentive plan, it's important to understand the relationship between **money and motivation**.
   - Frederick Hertzberg said the best way to motivate someone is to organize the job so that it provides the feedback and challenge that helps satisfy the person's higher-level needs.
   - Edward Deci found that extrinsic rewards may actually detract from a person's intrinsic motivation.
   - Victor Vroom's expectancy motivation theory says a person's motivation depends on expectancy, instrumentality, and valence.
   - Psychologist B. F. Skinner's behavior modification–based approach means changing behavior through rewards or punishments that are contingent on performance.
2. Several incentive plans are particularly suited for **individual employee incentives and recognition programs**. Piecework is an incentive plan in which a person is paid a sum for each item he or she makes. Merit pay refers to any salary increase awarded to an employee based on his or her individual performance. Nonfinancial and recognition-based awards are increasingly important and include awards in the form of employee recognition, gift certificates, and individual travel. Many employers use enterprise incentive management systems to automate the planning, analysis, and management of their incentive plans.
3. **Incentives for salespeople** are typically sales commissions. Although the percentage of pay in the form of sales commission may vary from zero to 100%, a survey found that salespeople at high-performing companies receive about 38% of their total cash compensation in the form of sales-related variable pay.
4. Managers take many things into consideration when formulating **incentives for managers and executives**. Most firms have annual bonus plans aimed at motivating managers' short-term performance. The actual award often depends on some combination of individual performance and organizational performance, so that, for instance, high-performing managers get a bonus even if the company itself underperforms. Long-term incentives include stock options, "golden parachutes," and stock appreciation rights.
5. With more employers organizing their efforts around teams, **team and organization-wide incentive plans are more important**. With team incentive plans, the main question is whether to reward members based on individual or team performance; both have pros and cons. Organization-wide incentive plans are plans in which all or most employees can participate. These include profit-sharing plans in which employees share in the company's profits; gainsharing plans, including the Scanlon plan, engage employees in a common effort to achieve productivity objectives and thereby share the gains. Employee stock ownership plans are company-wide plans in which the employer contributes shares of its own stock to a trust established to purchase shares of the firm's stock for employees.

Discussion Questions

12-4. Compare and contrast six types of incentive plans.

12-5. Explain five reasons why incentive plans fail.

12-6. Describe the nature of some important management incentives.

12-7. You are applying for a job as a manager and are at the point of negotiating salary and incentives. What questions would you ask your prospective employer concerning incentives? Describe the incentives package you would try to negotiate for yourself.

12-8. In this chapter, we listed a number of guidelines for instituting a pay-for-performance plan. Do you think these points make sense in terms of motivation theory? Why or why not?

12-9. What is merit pay? Do you think it's a good idea to award employees merit raises? Why or why not?

12-10. Give four examples of when you would suggest using team or group incentive programs rather than individual incentive programs.

Individual and Group Activities

12-11. Working individually or in groups, create an incentive plan for the following positions: chemical engineer, plant manager, used-car salesperson. What factors did you have to consider in reaching your conclusions?

12-12. A state university system in the Southeast instituted a "Teacher Incentive Program" (TIP) for its faculty. Faculty committees within each university's colleges were told to award $5,000 raises (not bonuses) to about 40% of their faculty members based on how good a job they did teaching undergraduates, and how many courses they taught per year. What are the potential advantages and pitfalls of such an incentive program? How well do you think it was accepted by the faculty? Do you think it had the desired effect?

12-13. Appendix A, PHR and SPHR Knowledge Base, at the end of this book (pages 580–588) lists the knowledge someone studying for the HRCI certification exam needs to have in each area of human resource management (such as in Strategic Management, Workforce Planning, and Human Resource Development). In groups of four to five students, do four things: (1) review Appendix A; (2) identify the material in this chapter that relates to the required knowledge Appendix A lists; (3) write four multiple-choice exam questions on this material that you believe would be suitable for inclusion in the HRCI exam; and (4) if time permits, have someone from your team post your team's questions in front of the class, so that students in all teams can answer the exam questions created by the other teams.

KNOWLEDGE BASE

12-14. Several years ago, the pension plan of the Utility Workers Union of America proposed that shareholders change the corporate bylaws of Dominion Resources, Inc., so that in the future management had to get shareholder approval of executive pay exceeding $1 million, as well as detailed information about the firm's executive incentive plans. Many unions—most of which have pension funds with huge investments in U.S. companies—are taking similar steps. They point out that, usually, under Internal Revenue Service regulations, corporations can't deduct more than $1 million in pay for any of a company's top five paid executives. Under the new rules the unions are pushing, boards of directors will no longer be able to approve executive pay above $1 million; instead, shareholders would have to vote on it. In terms of effectively running a company, what do you think are the pros and cons of the unions' recommendations? Would you vote for or against the unions' recommendation? Why?

Experiential Exercise

Motivating the Sales Force at Express Auto

Purpose: The purpose of this exercise is to give you practice developing an incentive plan.

Required Understanding: Be thoroughly familiar with this chapter, and read the following:

Express Auto, an automobile mega-dealership with more than 600 employees that represents 22 brands, has just received a very discouraging set of survey results. Customer satisfaction scores have fallen for the ninth straight quarter. Customer complaints include:

- It was hard to get prompt feedback from mechanics by phone.
- Salespeople often did not return phone calls.
- The finance people seemed "pushy."
- New cars were often not properly cleaned or had minor items that needed immediate repair or adjustment.
- Cars often had to be returned to have repair work redone.

Table 12-3 describes Express Auto's current compensation system.

How to Set Up the Exercise/Instructions: Divide the class into groups of four to five students. One or more groups should

TABLE 12-3 Express Auto Compensation System

Express Auto Team	Responsibility of Team	Current Compensation Method
1. Sales force	Persuade buyer to purchase a car.	Very small salary (minimum wage) with commissions. Commission rate increases with every 20 cars sold per month.
2. Finance office	Help close the sale; persuade customer to use company finance plan.	Salary, plus bonus for each $10,000 financed with the company.
3. Detailing	Inspect cars delivered from factory, clean, and make minor adjustments.	Piecework paid on the number of cars detailed per day.
4. Mechanics	Provide factory warranty service, maintenance, and repair.	Small hourly wage, plus bonus based on (1) number of cars completed per day and (2) finishing each car faster than the standard estimated time to repair.
5. Receptionists/phone service personnel	Primary liaison between customer and sales force, finance, and mechanics.	Minimum wage.

analyze each of the five teams in column one. Each student group should analyze the compensation package for its Express Auto team. Each group should address these questions:

12-15. In what ways might your team's compensation plan contribute to the customer service problems?

12-16. What recommendations would you make to improve the compensation system in a way that would likely improve customer satisfaction?

Video Case

Video Title: Motivation (TWZ Role-Play)

SYNOPSIS

During a rough economy, companies struggle with rewarding employees when they can't afford to give raises. This video examines some incentives that employees may accept in lieu of money, at least temporarily. In this video, David is meeting with his supervisor, Linda, to discuss a potential raise. Their company could not afford to give raises the previous year and David understood that since it was a bad economy; as a company, they needed to pull together. Since the company has seemed to be doing better, David feels the time is right to ask for a raise. While Linda agrees that David is a valuable employee and she appreciates everything he has done for the company, she is not able to increase his salary. Linda does suggest some other options to David other than a raise, such as a flexible schedule, being a leader of a new project, or some training that he has been interested in taking. This video conveys the importance of communicating openly and equitably with each employee and knowing each employee as an individual in order to provide options of interest and value to him or her. It also discusses ways to create a collective spirit among workers.

Discussion Questions

12-17. What do you think Dr. Fred Herzberg would tell Linda about the potential problem of not giving David his well-earned raise?

12-18. How effective do you think the incentives Linda suggested will be? What other suggestions would you make to Linda for keeping David motivated? Why?

12-19. On the whole, how good a job do you think Linda has done in dealing with David's concerns to this point? Why do you say that?

Video Title: Motivating Employees Through Company Culture (Zappos)

SYNOPSIS

Zappos is an online store that sells shoes, clothing, accessories, housewares, and beauty products. They are known throughout the industry for excellent customer service. Zappos CEO Tony Hsieh is also committed to making Zappos a fun loving and energetic place to work. Hsieh's passion is to create a culture where he would be excited about going to work every day. He aims to motivate and inspire his employees with a commitment to 10 Core Values, including create fun and a little weirdness; be adventurous, creative, and open-minded; and build positive and family spirit.

Discussion Questions

12-20. Motivation is fine, but what companies need is performance. How does the Zappos approach seem to be doing in terms of improving employee performance?

12-21. Make a list of five specific financial and nonfinancial rewards you would recommend for Zappos. Next to each, indicate why you chose it.

Application Case

Inserting the Team Concept into Compensation—or Not

In his new position at Hathaway Manufacturing, one of the first things Sandy Caldwell wanted to do was improve productivity through teamwork at every level of the firm. As the new human resource manager for this plant, Sandy set out to change the culture to accommodate the team-based approach he had become so enthusiastic about in his most recent position.

Sandy started by installing the concept of team management at the highest level, to oversee the operations of the entire plant. The new management team consisted of manufacturing, distribution, planning, technical, and human resource plant managers. Together they developed a new vision for the 500-employee facility, which they expressed in the simple phrase "Excellence Together." They drafted a new mission statement for the firm that focused on becoming customer driven and team based, and that called upon employees to raise their level of commitment and begin acting as "owners" of the firm.

The next step was to convey the team message to employees throughout the company. The communication process went surprisingly well, and Sandy was happy to see his idea of a "workforce of owners" begin to take shape. Teams trained together, developed production plans together, and embraced the technique of 360-degree feedback, in which an employee's performance evaluation is obtained from supervisors, subordinates, peers, and internal or external customers. Performance and morale improved, and productivity began to tick upward. The company even sponsored occasional celebrations to reward team achievements, and the team structure seemed firmly in place.

Sandy decided to change one more thing. Hathaway's longstanding policy had been to give all employees the same annual pay increase. But Sandy felt that in the new team environment, outstanding performance should be the criterion for pay raises. After consulting with CEO Regina Cioffi, Sandy sent a memo to all employees announcing the change to team-based pay for performance.

The reaction was immediate and 100% negative. None of the employees was happy with the change, and among their complaints, two stood out. First, because the 360-degree feedback system made everyone responsible in part for someone else's performance evaluation, no one was comfortable with the idea that pay raises might also be linked to peer input. Second, there was a widespread perception that the way the change was decided upon, and the way it was announced, put the firm's commitment to team effort in doubt. Simply put, employees felt left out of the decision process.

Sandy and Regina arranged a meeting for early the next morning. Sitting in her office, they began a painful debate. Should the new policy be rescinded as quickly as it was adopted, or should it be allowed to stand?

Questions

12-22. Does the pay-for-performance plan seem like a good idea? Why or why not?

12-23. What advice would you give Regina and Sandy as they consider their decision?

12-24. What mistakes did they make in adopting and communicating the new salary plan? How might Sandy have approached this major compensation change a little differently?

12-25. Assuming the new pay plan is eventually accepted, how would you address the fact that in the new performance evaluation system, employees' input affects their peers' pay levels?

Note: The incident in this case is based on an actual event at Frito-Lay's Kirkwood, New York, plant, as reported in C. James Novak, "Proceed with Caution When Paying Teams," *HR Magazine*, April 1997, p. 73.

Continuing Case

Carter Cleaning Company

THE INCENTIVE PLAN

The question of whether to pay Carter Cleaning Center employees an hourly wage or an incentive of some kind has always intrigued Jack Carter.

His basic policy has been to pay employees an hourly wage, except that his managers do receive an end-of-year bonus depending, as Jack puts it, "on whether their stores do well or not that year."

However, he is considering using an incentive plan in one store. Jack knows that a presser should press about 25 "tops" (jackets, dresses, blouses) per hour. Most of his pressers do not attain this ideal standard, though. In one instance, a presser named Walt was paid $8 per hour, and Jack noticed that regardless of the amount of work he had to do, Walt always ended up going home at about 3:00 P.M., so he earned about $300 at the end of the week. If it was a holiday week, for instance, and there were a lot of clothes to press, he might average 22 to 23 tops per hour (someone else did pants) and so he'd earn perhaps $300 and still finish each day in time to leave by 3:00 P.M. so he could pick up his children at school. But when things were very slow in the store, his productivity would drop to perhaps 12 to 15 pieces an hour, so that at the end of the week he'd end up earning perhaps $280, and in fact not go home much earlier than he did when it was busy.

Jack spoke with Walt several times, and while Walt always promised to try to do better, it gradually became apparent to Jack that Walt was simply going to earn his $300 per week no matter what. Though Walt never told him so directly, it dawned on Jack that Walt had a family to support and was not about to earn less than his "target" wage, regardless of how busy or slow the store was. The problem was that the longer Walt kept pressing each day, the longer the steam boilers and compressors had to be kept on to power his machines, and the fuel charges alone ran close to $6 per hour. Jack clearly needed some way short of firing Walt to solve the problem, since the fuel bills were eating up his profits.

His solution was to tell Walt that, instead of an hourly $8 wage, he would henceforth pay him $0.33 per item pressed. That way, said Jack to himself, if Walt presses 25 items per hour at $0.33 he will in effect get a small raise. He'll get more items pressed per hour and will therefore be able to shut the machines down earlier.

On the whole, the experiment worked well. Walt generally presses 25 to 35 pieces per hour now. He gets to leave earlier and, with the small increase in pay, he generally earns his target wage. Two problems have arisen, though. The quality of Walt's work has dipped a bit, plus his manager has to spend a minute or two each hour counting the number of pieces Walt pressed that hour. Otherwise, Jack is fairly pleased with the results of his incentive plan, and he's wondering whether to extend it to other employees and other stores.

Questions

12-26. Should this plan be extended to pressers in the other stores?

12-27. Should other employees (cleaner/spotters, counter people) be put on a similar plan? Why? Why not? If so, how, exactly?

12-28. Is there another incentive plan you think would work better for the pressers? Describe it.

12-29. A store manager's job is to keep total wages to no more than 30% of sales and to maintain the fuel bill and the supply bill at about 9% of sales each. Managers can also directly affect sales by ensuring courteous customer service and by ensuring that the work is done properly. What suggestions would you make to Jennifer and her father for an incentive plan for store managers or front-desk clerks?

Translating Strategy into HR Policies and Practices Case*,§

**The accompanying strategy map for this chapter is in MyManagementLab; the overall map in the inside back cover of this text outlines the relationships involved.*

IMPROVING PERFORMANCE at The Hotel Paris

The New Incentive Plan

The Hotel Paris's competitive strategy is "To use superior guest service to differentiate the Hotel Paris properties, and to thereby increase the length of stay and return rate of guests, and thus boost revenues and profitability." HR manager Lisa Cruz must now formulate functional policies and activities that support this competitive strategy by eliciting the required employee behaviors and competencies.

One of Lisa Cruz's biggest pay-related concerns is that the Hotel Paris compensation plan does not link pay to performance in any effective way. Because salaries were historically barely competitive, supervisors tended to award merit raises across the board. So, employees who performed well got only about the same raises as did those who performed poorly. Similarly, there was no bonus or incentive plan of any kind aimed at linking employee performance to strategically relevant employee capabilities and behaviors such as greeting guests in a friendly manner or providing expeditious check-ins and check-outs. The bottom line for Lisa and the CFO was that the company's financial rewards system—potentially, the single biggest tool they had for channeling employee performance toward accomplishing the Hotel Paris's goals—was totally inadequate. She and her team thus turned to the job of deciding what sort of incentive-based reward systems to install.

Based on their analysis, Lisa Cruz and the CFO concluded that by any metric, their company's incentive plan had to be changed. The percentage of the workforce whose merit increase or incentive pay was tied to performance was effectively zero, because managers awarded merit pay across the board. No more than 5% of the workforce (just the managers) was eligible for incentive pay. And, the percentage difference in incentive pay between a low-performing and a high-performing employee was less than 2%. Lisa knew from industry studies that in top firms, over 80% of the workforce had merit pay or incentive pay tied to performance. She also knew that in high-performing firms, there was at least a 5% or 6% difference in incentive pay between a low-performing and a high-performing employee. The CFO authorized Lisa to design a new strategy-oriented incentive plan for the Hotel Paris's employees. Their overall aim was to incentivize the pay plans of just about all the company's employees.

Lisa and the company's CFO laid out three measurable criteria that the new incentive plan had to meet. First, at least 90% (and preferably all) of the Hotel Paris's employees must be eligible for a merit increase or incentive pay that is tied to performance. Second, there must be at least a 10% difference in incentive pay between a low-performing and high-performing employee. Third, the new incentive plan had to include specific bonuses and evaluative mechanisms that linked employee behaviors in each job category with strategically relevant employee capabilities and behaviors. For example, front-desk clerks were to be rewarded in part based on the friendliness and speed of their check-ins and check-outs, and the housecleaning crew was to be evaluated and rewarded in part based on the percentage of room cleaning infractions.

With these criteria in mind, Lisa and her team turned to designing the new merit and incentive pay plan. They created a larger merit pay pool, and instructed supervisors that employees scoring in the lower 10% of performance were to receive no merit pay, while the difference in merit pay between the top category and medium category employees was to be 10%. They contracted with an online employee recognition firm and instituted a new "Hotel Paris instantaneous thank you award program." Under this program, any guest or any supervisor could recommend any hotel employee for an instantaneous recognition award; if approved by the department manager, the employee could choose the recognition award by going to the company's website. The incentive structure for all the company's managers, including hotel managers, assistant managers, and departmental managers, now ties at least 10% of each manager's annual pay to the degree to which his or her hotel achieves its strategic aims. The plan measures this in terms of ratings on the guest satisfaction index, average length of guest stay, and frequency of guest returns. Ratings on all these metrics soon began to rise.

Questions

12-30. Discuss what you think of the measurable criteria that Lisa and the CFO set for their new incentive plan.

12-31. Given what you know about the Hotel Paris's strategic goals, list three or four specific behaviors you would incentivize for each of the following groups of employees: front-desk clerks, hotel managers, valets, housekeepers.

12-32. Lay out a complete incentive plan (including all long- and short-term incentives) for the Hotel Paris's hotel managers.

§Written and copyright by Gary Dessler, PhD.

MyManagementLab

Go to **mymanagementlab.com** for Auto-graded writing questions as well as the following Assisted-graded writing questions:

12-33. When and why would you pay a salesperson a combined salary and commission?

12-34. What is a Scanlon plan? Based on what you've read in this chapter, what features of an effective incentive program does the Scanlon plan include?

12-35. MyManagementLab only—comprehensive writing assignment for this chapter.

Key Terms

financial incentives, 368
productivity, 368
fair day's work, 368
scientific management movement, 368
variable pay, 368
intrinsic motivation, 369
expectancy, 369
instrumentality, 369
valence, 369
behavior modification, 369
piecework, 370
straight piecework, 370
standard hour plan, 370
merit pay (merit raise), 371
annual bonus, 379
stock option, 381
golden parachute, 383
team (or group) incentive plan, 383
organization-wide incentive plan, 384
profit-sharing plan, 384
Scanlon plan, 385
gainsharing plan, 385
earnings-at-risk pay plan, 386
employee stock ownership plan (ESOP), 386

Endnotes

1. Jay Heizer and Barry Render, *Operations Management* (Upper Saddle River, NJ: Pearson, 2001), p. 15.
2. See, for example, Mary Ducharme and Mark Podolsky, "Variable Pay: Its Impact on Motivation and Organisation Performance," *International Journal of Human Resources Development and Management* 6 (May 9, 2006), p. 68.
3. Ibid.
4. "Employers Use Pay to Lever Performance," *BNA Bulletin to Management*, August 21, 1997, p. 272; and "Variable Pay Is Superior to Bonus," *People Management*, February 24, 2011, p. 14.
5. See, for example, Kenan Abosch, "Variable Pay: Do We Have the Basics in Place?" *Compensation & Benefits Review*, July/August 1998, pp. 2–22.
6. Even the traditional holiday bonus is being replaced by performance-based pay. A survey by consultants Hewitt Associates found that only about 5% of employers surveyed would distribute holiday cash bonuses. About 78% said they were offering performance-based awards, up from 51% about 15 years previously. "Cash Bonuses Are Ghosts of Holidays Past, Survey Says," *BNA Bulletin to Management*, December 13, 2005, p. 396. See also "Aligning Rewards with the Changing Employment Deal: 2006/2007 Strategic Rewards® Report," www.watsonwyatt.com/research/resrender.asp?id=2006-US-0038&page=1, accessed May 20, 2007.
7. "Few Employees See the Pay for Performance Connection," *Compensation & Benefits Review* 17, no. 2 (June 2003); "Most Workers Not Motivated by Cash," *Incentive Today*, July–August 2004, p. 19; and "Pay-for-Performance Plans' Impact Uncertain: Study," *Modern Healthcare*, May 24, 2004, p. 34.
8. Kathy Chu, "Employers See Lackluster Results Linking Salary to Performance," *The Wall Street Journal*, June 15, 2004, p. D2.
9. Ted Turnasella, "Pay and Personality," *Compensation & Benefits Review*, March/April 2002, pp. 45–59.
10. Jason Shaw et al., "Reactions to Merit Pay Increases: A Longitudinal Test of a Signal Sensitivity Perspective," *Journal of Applied Psychology* 88, no. 3 (2003), pp. 538–544.
11. See, for example, Edward Deci, *Intrinsic Motivation* (New York: Plenum, 1975).
12. Ruth Kanfer, "Motivation Theory," in Harry C. Triandis, Marvin D. Dunnette, and Leaetta M. Hough, *Handbook of Industrial and Organizational Psychology* (Palo Alto, CA: Consulting Psychologists Press, 1994), p. 113. For a recent discussion about applying Vroom's principles, see B. Schaffer, "Leadership and Motivation." *Supervision* 69, no. 2 (February 2008), pp. 6–9.
13. For a discussion, see John P. Campbell and Robert Prichard, "Motivation Theory in Industrial and Organizational Psychology," in Marvin Dunnette (ed.), *Industrial and Organizational Psychology* (Chicago: Rand McNally, 1976), pp. 74–75; Kanfer, "Motivation Theory," pp. 115–116; and B. Schaffer, "Leadership and Motivation," op cit.
14. See, for example, Aubrey Daniels et al., "The Leader's Role in Pay Systems and Organizational Performance," *Compensation & Benefits Review*, May/June 2006, pp. 58–60; and Suzanne Peterson and Fred Luthans, "The Impact of Financial and Non-Financial Incentives on Business Unit Outcomes Over Time," *Journal of Applied Psychology* 91, no. 1 (2006), pp. 156–165.
15. See, for example, Diane Cadrain, "Cash Versus Non-Cash Rewards," *HR Magazine*, April 2003, pp. 81–87.
16. Richard Henderson, compensation management, Reston Virginia, Reston, 1979, page 363.
17. David Belcher, compensation administration (Englewood Cliffs New Jersey: Prentice Hall, 1973), page 314.
18. These problems have been long known. See, for example, Thomas Wilson, "Is It Time to Eliminate the Piece Rate Incentive System?" *Compensation and Benefits Review*, March–April 1992, pages 43–49.
19. William Atkinson, "Incentive Pay Programs That Work in Textile," *Textile World* 151, no. 2 (February 2001), pp. 55–57.
20. See, for example, "Bias Creeps into Bonus Process, MIT Study Finds," *Workforce Management*, September 20, 2008, pp. 8–9.
21. The average uncorrected cross-sectional correlation was 17. Michael Harris et al., "A Longitudinal Examination of a Merit Pay System: Relationships Among Performance Ratings, Merit Increases, and Total Pay Increases," *Journal of Applied Psychology* 83, no. 5 (1998), pp. 825–831. See also H. Risher, "Add Merit Pay for Performance," *Compensation and Benefits Review* 40, no. 6 (November/December 2008), pp. 22–29.
22. Eric R. Schulz and Denise Marie Tanguay, "Merit Pay in a Public Higher Education Institution: Questions of Impact and Attitudes," *Public Personnel Management* 35, no. 1 (Spring 2006), p. 71(18); Thomas S. Dee and Benjamin J. Keys, "Does Merit Pay Reward Good Teachers? Evidence from a Randomized Experiment," *Journal of Policy Analysis & Management* 23, no. 3 (Summer 2004), pp. 471–488. See also Sanghee Park and Michael Sturman, "How and What You Pay Matters: The Relative Effectiveness of Merit Pay, Bonuses and Long-Term Incentives on Future Job Performance," *Compensation & Benefits Review* 44, no. 2 (2012), pp. 80–85.
23. Fay Hansen, "Wage and Salary Trends," *Compensation & Benefits Review* 40, no. 5 (November/December 2008), p. 5.

24. Rachel Silverman, "My Colleague, My Paymaster," *The Wall Street Journal*, April 4, 2012, pages B1, B8.
25. Jonathan Glater, "Varying the Recipe Helps TV Operations Solve Morale Problem," *The New York Times*, March 7, 2001, p. C1.
26. "News." *Community Care* 8 Sept. 2011. *Academic OneFile*. Web. 17 Mar. 2013.
27. Steve Yegge, quoted in http://glinden.blogspot.com/2006/09/management-and-incentives-at-google.html, accessed June 1, 2011.
28. Brian Skelton, "Dual-Career Tracks: Rewarding and Maintaining Technical Expertise," www.todaysengineer.org/2003/May/dual-ladder.asp, accessed June 1, 2011.
29. Peterson and Luthans, "The Impact of Financial and Nonfinancial Incentives."
30. See, for example, ibid., pp. 156–165.
31. "Employee Recognition," *WorldatWork*, April 2008, at www.worldatwork.org/waw/adimLink?id=25653, accessed November 3, 2009.
32. Michelle V. Rafter, "Back in a Giving Mood," *Workforce Management* 88, no. 10 (September 14, 2009), pp. 25–29.
33. "WorkSimple 'praise' app boosts employee recognition," *T+D* Jan. 2012: 21. *Academic OneFile*. Web. 17 Mar. 2013.
34. See, for example, Leslie Yerkes, *Fun Works: Creating Places Where People Love to Work* (San Francisco, CA: Berrett-Koehler Publishers, 2007).
35. Charlotte Huff, "Recognition That Resonates," *Workforce Management*, September 11, 2006, pp. 25–29. See also Scott Jeffrey and Victoria Schaffer, "The Motivational Properties of Tangible Incentives," *Compensation & Benefits Review*, May/June 2007, pp. 44–50. A survey of executives concluded that three nonfinancial incentives—praise and commendation from immediate managers, attention from leaders, and opportunities to lead project or task forces—all ranked higher in motivational effectiveness than did financial incentives including stock options. Daniel Morrell, "Employee Perceptions and the Motivation of Non-Monetary Incentives," *Compensation & Benefits Review* 43, no. 5 (September/October 2011), pp. 318–323.
36. Bob Nelson, *1001 Ways to Reward Employees* (New York: Workman Pub., 1994), p. 19. See also Sunny C. L. Fong and Margaret A. Shaffer, "The Dimensionality and Determinants of Pay Satisfaction: A Cross-Cultural Investigation of a Group Incentive Plan," *International Journal of Human Resource Management* 14, no. 4 (June 2003), p. 559(22).
37. www.deloitte.com/assets/Dcom-UnitedStates/Local%20Assets/Documents/us_consulting_2010StrategicSalesCompensationSurvey_072910.pdf, accessed June 1, 2011.
38. Suzanne Peterson and Fred Luthans, "The Impact of Financial and Nonfinancial Incentives on Business Unit Outcomes Over Time," *Journal of Applied Psychology* 91, no. 1 (2006), pp. 156–165.
39. Ibid., p. 159.
40. Ibid., p. 159.
41. Ibid., p. 162. See also "Delivering Incentive Compensation Plans That Work," *Financial Executive* 25, no. 7 (September 2009), pp. 52–54.
42. For a checklist for determining when pay for performance is advisable, see Myron Glassman et al., "Evaluating Pay for Performance Systems: Critical Issues for Implementation," *Compensation & Benefits Review* 42, no. 4 (2010), p. 236.
43. Reed Taussig, "Managing Cash Based Incentives," *Compensation & Benefits Review*, March/April 2002, pp. 65–68. See also Nigel Nicholson, "How to Motivate Your Problem People," *Harvard Business Review*, January 2003, pp. 57–65; and "Incentives, Motivation and Workplace Performance," Incentive Research Foundation, www.incentivescentral.org/employees/whitepapers, accessed May 19, 2007.
44. "Two Frameworks for a More ROI-Minded Rewards Plan," *Pay for Performance Report*, February 2003, p. 1, www.ioma.com/issues/PFP/2003_02/518132-1.html, accessed November 3, 2009; and Alan Robinson and Dean Schroeder, "Rewards That Really Work," *Security Management*, July 2004, pp. 30–34. See also Patricia Zingheim and Jay Schuster, "What Are Key Pay Issues Right Now?" *Compensation & Benefits Review*, May/June 2007, pp. 51–55.
45. Theodore Weinberger, "Evaluating the Effectiveness of an Incentive Plan Design Within Company Constraints," *Compensation & Benefits Review*, November/December 2005, pp. 27–33; and Howard Risher, "Adding Merit to Pay for Performance," *Compensation & Benefits Review*, November/December 2008, pp. 22–29.
46. www.deloitte.com/assets/Dcom-UnitedStates/Local%20Assets/Documents/us_consulting_2010StrategicSalesCompensationSurvey_072910.pdf, accessed June 1, 2011.
47. Ibid.
48. Deloitte Varicent, 2010 Strategic Sales Compensation Survey, p. 6, at http://www.deloitte.com/assets/Dcom-UnitedStates/Local%20Assets/Documents/us_consulting_2010StrategicSalesCompensationSurvey_072910.pdf, accessed August 29, 2011.
49. Straight salary by itself is not, of course, an incentive compensation plan as we use the term in this chapter.
50. Donna Harris, "Dealers Rethink How They Pay Salespeople," *Automotive News*, June 14, 2010, www.autonews.com/apps/pbcs.dll/article?AID=/20100614/RETAIL07/306149932m, accessed June 1, 2011.
51. Sonjun Luo, "Does Your Sales Incentive Plan Pay for Performance?" *Compensation & Benefits Review*, January/ February 2003, pp. 18–24.
52. Scott Ladd, "May the Sales Force Be with You," *HR Magazine*, September 2010, p. 105.
53. Luo, "Does Your Sales Incentive Plan Pay for Performance," pp. 331–345. See also James M. Pappas and Karen E. Flaherty, "The Moderating Role of Individual-Difference Variables in Compensation Research," *Journal of Managerial Psychology* 21, no. 1 (January 2006), pp. 19–35; and T. B. Lopez, C. D. Hopkins, and M. A. Raymond, "Reward Preferences of Salespeople: How Do Commissions Rate?" *Journal of Personal Selling & Sales Management* 26, no. 4 (Fall 2006), p. 381(10).
54. Bill O'Connell, "Dead Solid Perfect: Achieving Sales Compensation Alignment," *Compensation & Benefits Review*, March/April 1996, pp. 46–47. See also C. Albrech, "Moving to a Global Sales Incentive Compensation Plan," *Compensation & Benefits Review* 41, no. 4 (July/August 2009), p. 52.
55. See, for example, Pankaj Madhani, "Realigning Fixed and Variable Pay in Sales Organizations: An Organizational Lifestyle Approach," *Compensation & Benefits Review* 42, no. 6, pp. 488–498.
56. Leslie Stretch, "From Strategy to Profitability: How Sales Compensation Management Drives Business Performance," *Compensation & Benefits Review*, May/June 2008, pp. 32–37.
57. S. Scott Sands, "Ineffective Quotas: The Hidden Threat to Sales Compensation Plans," *Compensation & Benefits Review* (March/April 2000), pp. 35–42. See also "Driving Profitable Sales Growth: 2006/2007 Report on Sales Effectiveness," www.watsonwyatt.com/research/resrender.asp?id=2006-US-0060&page=1, accessed May 20, 2007.
58. Peter Gundy, "Sales Compensation Programs: Built to Last," *Compensation & Benefits Review* (September/October 2002), pp. 21–28. See also T. B. Lopez, C. D. Hopkins, and M. A. Raymond, "Reward Preferences of Salespeople: How Do Commissions Rate?" *Journal of Personal Selling & Sales Management* 26, no. 4 (Fall 2006), p. 381(10).
59. Pankaj Madhani, "Reallocating Fixed and Variable Pay in Sales Organizations: a Sales Carryover Perspective," *Compensation & Benefits Review* 43, no. 6, (2011) pp. 346–360.
60. "Driving Profitable Sales Growth: 2006/2007 Report on Sales Effectiveness," www.watsonwyatt.com/research/resrender.asp?id=2006-US-0060&page=1, accessed May 20, 2007.
61. Thomas Steenburgh and Michael Ahearne, "Motivating Salespeople: What Really Works," *The Harvard Business Review*, July–August 2012, pp. 71–75.
62. "Car Salesman Commission the Way It Works," http://carsalesprofessional.com/car-salesman-commission/, accessed June 26, 2011.
63. Ibid.
64. Peter Glendinning, "Kicking the Tires of Automotive Sales Compensation," *Compensation & Benefits Review*, September/October 2000, pp. 47–53; and Michele Marchetti, "Why Sales Contests Don't Work," *Sales and Marketing Management* 156 (January 2004), p. 19. See also "Salary and Bonus Gain Favor in Sales Pay (for Motor Vehicle Salespeople)," *Automotive News* 75, no. 5915 (February 5, 2001), p. 50.
65. Varicent, "2010 Strategic Sales."
66. Bob Conlin, "Best Practices for Designing New Sales Compensation Plans," *Compensation & Benefits Review*, March/April 2008, p. 51.
67. Ibid., p. 53.
68. www.vuesoftware.com/Product/Compensation_Management.aspx, accessed June 1, 2011.
69. Ibid.
70. Jeremy Wuittner, "Plenty of Incentives to Use E.I.M. Software Systems," *American Banker* 168, no. 129 (July 8, 2003), p. 680.
71. Nina McIntyre, "Using EIM Technology to Successfully Motivate Employees," *Compensation & Benefits Review*, July/August 2001, pp. 57–60.
72. Mark Meltzer and Howard Goldsmith, "Executive Compensation for Growth Companies," *Compensation & Benefits Review*, November/December 1997, pp. 41–50; and Barbara Kiviat, "Everyone into the Bonus Pool," *Time* 162, no. 24 (December 15, 2003), p. A5.
73. www.mercer.com/pressrelease/details.jhtml/dynamic/idContent/1263210, accessed January 2, 2007.

74. Meltzer and Goldsmith, "Executive Compensation for Growth Companies," pp. 41–50. See also Patricia Zingheim and Jay Schuster, "Designing Pay and Rewards in Professional Companies," *Compensation & Benefits Review*, January/February 2007, pp. 55–62; and Ronald Bottano and Russell Miller, "Making Executive Compensation Count: Tapping into the New Long-Term Incentive Portfolio," *Compensation & Benefits Review*, July/August 2007, pp. 43–47.
75. George Yancey, "Aligning the CEO's Incentive Plan with Criteria That Drive Organizational Performance," *Compensation & Benefits Review* 42, no. 3 (2010), pp. 190–196.
76. Richard Ericson, "Benchmarking for Executive Incentive Pay: The Importance of Performance Standards," *Compensation & Benefits Review* 43, no. 2, (2010), pp. 92–99.
77. See "The Impact of Sarbanes-Oxley on Executive Compensation," www.thelenreid.com, accessed December 11, 2003. See also Brent Longnecker and James Krueger, "The Next Wave of Compensation Disclosure," *Compensation & Benefits Review*, January/February 2007, pp. 50–54.
78. James Reda, "Executive Compensation: Balancing Risk, Performance and Pay," *Financial Executive* 25, no. 9 (November 2009), pp. 46–50. See also Bruce Ellig, "Short-Term Incentives: Top-Down or Bottom-Up?" *Compensation & Benefits Review* 43, no 3, (May/June 2011), pp. 179–183.
79. Meltzer and Goldsmith, "Executive Compensation for Growth Companies," pp. 44–45; See also Jennifer Wynter-Palmer, "Is the Use of Short-Term Incentives Good Organization Strategy?" *Compensation & Benefits Review* 44, no. 5, 2013, pp. 254–265.
80. Max Smith and Ben Stradley, "New Research Tracks the Evolution of Annual Incentive Plans," *Executive Compensation*, Towers Watson, 2010, Towerswatson.com, accessed August 28, 2011.
81. Ibid.
82. Ibid.
83. Ibid.
84. Dionne Searcey, "Transocean Executives to Donate Bonuses," *The Wall Street Journal*, April 6, 2011, p. B1.
85. Meltzer and Goldsmith, "Executive Compensation for Growth Companies," p. 44. Fay Hansen, "Salary and Wage Trends," *Compensation & Benefits Review*, March/April 2004, pp. 9–10.
86. Bruce Ellig, "Executive Pay Financial Measurements," *Compensation & Benefits Review*, September/October 2008, pp. 42–49.
87. "Study: CEO Compensation Not Tied to Company Performance," *BNA Bulletin to Management*, March 22, 2011, p. 92.
88. Benjamin Dunford et al., "Underwater Stock Options and Voluntary Executive Turnover: A Multidisciplinary Perspective Integrating Behavioral and Economic Theories," *Personnel Psychology* 61 (2008), pp. 687–726.
89. Phred Dvorak, "Slump Yields Employee Rewards," *The Wall Street Journal*, October 10, 2008, p. B2; Don Clark and Jerry DiColo, "Intel to Let Workers Exchange Options," *The Wall Street Journal*, March 24, 2009, p. B3.
90. Wm. Gerard Sanders and Donald Hambrick, "Swinging for the Fences: The Effects of CEO Stock Options on Company Risk-Taking and Performance," *Academy of Management Journal* 50, no. 5 (2007), pp. 1055–1078.
91. "Study Finds That Directly Owning Stock Shares Leads to Better Results," *Compensation & Benefits Review*, March/April 2001, p. 7. See also Ira Kay, "Whither the Stock Option? While Stock Options Lose More Luster as Executive Motivators, Compensation Committees Face Challenges, Including Selecting Other Forms of Stock Incentives," *Financial Executive* 20, no. 2 (March–April 2004), p. 46(3); and Lucian A. Bebchuk and Jesse M. Fried, "Pay Without Performance: Overview of the Issues," *Academy of Management Perspective* 20, no. 1 (February 2006), p. 5(20).
92. www.mercer.com/pressrelease/details.jhtml/dynamic/idContent/1263210, accessed January 2, 2007.
93. www.nceo.org/main/article.php/id/43/, accessed June 1, 2011.
94. Louis Lavelle, "How to Halt the Options Express," *BusinessWeek*, September 9, 2002.
95. www.nceo.org/main/article.php/id/43/, accessed June 1, 2011.
96. Menahchem Abudy and Efrat Shust, "Employee's Attitudes Toward Equity-Based Compensation," *Compensation & Benefits Review* 44, no. 5, 2013, pages 246–253.
97. Christine Bevilacqua and Parbudyal Singh, "Pay for Performance—Panacea or Pandora's Box? Revisiting an Old Debate in the Current Economic Environment," *Compensation & Benefits Review*, September/October 2009, pp. 21–26.
98. www.forbes.com/2010/06/14/goldman-sachs-paulson-markets-lloyd-blankfein.html, accessed May 21, 2011.
99. Under IRS regulations, companies cannot deduct all golden parachute payments made to executives, and the executive must pay a 20% excise tax on the golden parachute payments. "Final Regs Issued for Golden Parachute Payments," *Executive Tax and Management Report* 66, no. 17 (September 2003), p. 1.
100. "Conseco Not Alone on Executive Perks," *Knight-Ridder/Tribune Business News*, August 28, 2003, item 03240015. See also "Realities of Executive Compensation—2006/2007 Report on Executive Pay and Stock Options," www.watsonwyatt.com/research/resrender.asp?id=2006-US-0085&page=1, accessed May 20, 2007.
101. Other suggestions are as follows: equal payments to all members on the team; differential payments to team members based on their contributions to the team's performance; and differential payments determined by a ratio of each group member's base pay to the total base pay of the group. See Kathryn Bartol and Laura Hagmann, "Team Based Pay Plans: A Key to Effective Team Work," *Compensation & Benefits Review*, November–December 1992, pp. 24–29. See also Charlotte Garvey, "Steer Teams with the Right Pay," *HR Magazine*, May 2002, pp. 70–71; and K. Merriman, "On the Folly of Rewarding Team Performance, While Hoping for Teamwork," *Compensation & Benefits Review* 41, no. 1 (January/February 2009), pp. 61–66.
102. Richard Seaman, "The Case Study: Rejuvenating an Organization with Team Pay," *Compensation & Benefits Review*, September/October 1997, pp. 25–30. See also Peter Wright, Mark Kroll, Jeffrey A. Krug, and Michael Pettus, "Influences of Top Management Team Incentives on Firm Risk Taking," *Strategic Management Journal* 28, no. 1 (January 2007), pp. 81–89.
103. K. Merriman, "On the Folly of Rewarding Team Performance, While Hoping for Teamwork," *Compensation & Benefits Review*, January/February 2009, pp. 61–66.
104. As another example, see Bernd Irlenbusch and Gabriele K. Lünser, "Relative Rewards within Team-Based Compensation," November 2006. IZA Discussion Paper No. 2423. Available at SSRN: http://ssrn.com/abstract=947075, accessed May 21, 2011.
105. Seongsu Kim, "Does Profit Sharing Increase Firms' Profits?" *Journal of Labor Research*, Spring 1998, pp. 351–371. See also Jacqueline Coyle-Shapiro et al., "Using Profit-Sharing to Enhance Employee Attitudes: A Longitudinal Examination of the Effects on Trust and Commitment," *Human Resource Management* 41, no. 4 (Winter 2002), pp. 423–449.
106. Alberto Bayo-Moriones and Martin Larraza-Kintana, "Profit Sharing Plans and Effective Commitment: Does the Context Matter?" *Human Resource Management* 48, no. 2 (March–April 2009), pp. 207–226.
107. Kaja Whitehouse, "More Companies Offer Packages Linking Pay Plans to Performance," *The Wall Street Journal*, December 13, 2005, p. B4.
108. Under the U.S. tax code, "any arrangement that provides for the deferral of compensation in a year later than the year in which the compensation was earned may be considered a deferred compensation arrangement." Steven Friedman, "2008 Compliance Strategies for Employers in Light of Final 409A Regulations," *Compensation & Benefits Review*, March/April 2008, p. 27.
109. www.axa-equitable.com/retirement/how-do-company-profit-sharing-plans-work.html, accessed June 1, 2011.
110. Joseph Martocchio, *Strategic Compensation* (Upper Saddle River, NJ: Prentice Hall, 2006), pp. 163–165.
111. Brian Graham-Moore and Timothy Ross, *The Scanlon Way to Improved Productivity: A Practical Guide* (New York: Wiley, 1978), p. 2. For a review of potential problems, see Denis Collins, "Death of a Gainsharing Plan: Power Politics and Participatory Management," *Organizational Dynamics* 24 (Summer 1995), pp. 23–37. For an historical perspective on gainsharing's effectiveness, see Alexander Gardner, "Goal Setting and Gainsharing: The Evidence of Effectiveness," *Compensation & Benefits Review* 43, no 4 (July/August 2011), pp. 236–244.
112. These are based in part on Steven Markham, K. Dow Scott, and Walter Cox Jr., "The Evolutionary Development of a Scanlon Plan," *Compensation & Benefits Review*, March/April 1992, pp. 50–56. See also Woodruff Imberman, "Are You Ready to Boost Productivity with a Gainsharing Plan? To Survive and Prosper in Our Hyper-competitive Environment, Board Converters Must Motivate Employees at All Levels," *Official Board Markets* 82, no. 47 (November 25, 2006), p. 5(2); and James Reynolds and Daniel Roble, "Combining Pay for Performance with Gainsharing," *Healthcare Financial Management* 60, no. 11 (November 2006), p. 50(6).
113. Markham et al., "The Evolutionary Development of a Scanlon Plan," p. 51.
114. Barry W. Thomas and Madeline Hess Olson, "Gainsharing: The Design Guarantees Success," *Personnel Journal*, May 1998,

pp. 73–79; and A. C. Gardner, "Goal Setting and Gainsharing: The Evidence on Effectiveness," *Compensation and Benefits Review* 43, no. 4 (July/August 2011), pp. 236–244.

115. Paraphrased from Woodruff Imberman, "Boosting Plant Performance with Gainsharing," *Business Horizons*, November–December 1992, p. 77. See also Max Reynolds and Joane Goodroe, "The Return of Gainsharing: Gainsharing Appears to Be Enjoying a Renaissance," *Healthcare Financial Management* 59, no. 11 (November 2005), p. 114(6); and Dong-One Kim, "The Benefits and Costs of Employee Suggestions Under Gainsharing," *Industrial and Labor Relations Review* 58, no. 4 (July 2005), p. 631(22); and hospital gainsharing discussion in Anjana Patel, "Gainsharing: Past, Present, and Future," *Healthcare Financial Management* 60, no. 9 (September 2006), pp. 124–128, 130.

116. Paul Rossler and C. Patrick Koelling, "The Effect of Gainsharing on Business Performance at a Paper Mill," *National Productivity Review*, Summer 1993, pp. 365–382; and hospital gainsharing discussion in Anjana Patel, "Gainsharing: Past, Present, and Future," *Healthcare Financial Management* 60, no. 9 (September 2006), pp. 124–128, 130.

117. See for example, http://www.dol.gov/dol/topic/health-plans/erisa.htm, accessed October 2, 2011.

118. Steven Etkind, "ESOPs Create Liquidity for Share Holders and Help Diversify Their Assets," *Estate Planning* 24, no. 4 (May 1998), pp. 158–165. See also S. Coomes, "Employee Stock Plans Can Save Taxes, Attract Talent," *Nation's Restaurant News* 42, no. 36 (September 15, 2008), p. 12.

119. William Smith, Harold Lazarus, and Harold Murray Kalkstein, "Employee Stock Ownership Plans: Motivation and Moral Issues," *Compensation & Benefits Review*, September/October 1990, pp. 37–46. See also "ESOP Trustees Breached Their Fiduciary Duties Under ERISA by Failing to Make Prudent Investigation into Value of Stock Purchased by ESOP," *Tax Management Compensation Planning Journal* 30, no. 10 (October 4, 2002), p. 301(1); and J. D. Mamorsky, "Court Approves ERISA Action Against ENRON Executives, Trustee, and Plan Auditor for Retirement Plan Losses," *Journal of Compensation and Benefits* 20, no. 1 (January–February 2004), p. 46(7); G. Ledford et al., "The Effects of Stock Ownership on Employee Attitudes and Behavior: Evidence from the Rewards of Work Studies," *Journal of Compensation & Benefits* 20, no. 2 (March/April 2004), pp. 24–30.

120. James Sesil et al., "Broad-Based Employee Stock Options in U.S. New Economy Firms," *British Journal of Industrial Relations* 40, no. 2 (June 2002), pp. 273–294.

121. Eric Dash, "Time Warner Stops Granting Stock Options to Most of Staff," *The New York Times*, February 19, 2005, item 128921996.

122. Janet Wiscombe, "Can Pay for Performance Really Work?" *Workforce*, August 2001, p. 30.

123. Susan Marks, "Incentives That Really Reward and Motivate," *Workforce*, June 2001, pp. 108–114.

124. Although not an issue at Nucor, the employer needs to beware of instituting so many incentive plans (cash bonuses, stock options, recognition programs, and so on) tied to so many different behaviors that employees don't have a clear priority of the employer's priorities. See, for example, Stephen Rubenfeld and Jannifer David, "Multiple Employee Incentive Plans: Too Much of a Good Thing?" *Compensation & Benefits Review*, March/ April 2006, pp. 35–43.

13 Benefits and Services

Source: Peathegee Inc/Getty Images

MyManagementLab®

Improve Your Grade!

When you see this icon, visit **www.mymanagementlab.com** for activities that are applied, personalized, and offer immediate feedback.

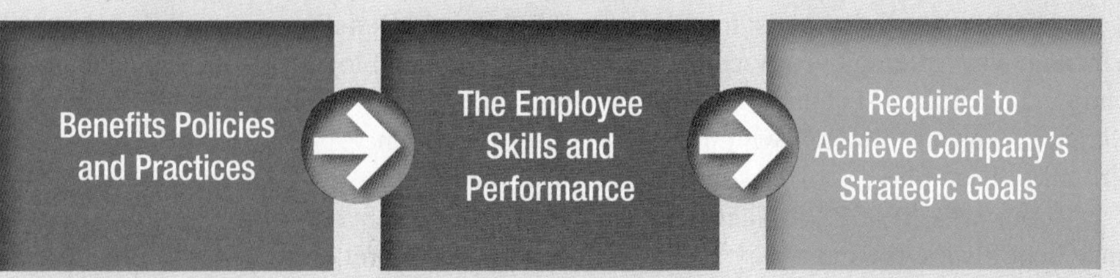

For a bird's eye view of how one company created a new benefits plan to improve its strategic performance, read the Hotel Paris case on pages 423–424 and answer the questions after reading the chapter.

WHERE ARE WE NOW . . .

We've now covered two compensation components, salaries (or wages), and incentives. The main purpose of this chapter is to explain the third major component, employee benefits. The main topics we discuss are pay for time not worked; insurance benefits; retirement benefits; personal services and family-friendly benefits; and flexible benefits programs. This chapter completes our discussion of employee compensation. The next chapter starts a new part of this book, and focuses on another important human resource task—managing employee relations.

LEARNING OBJECTIVES

1. Name and define each of the main pay for time not worked benefits.
2. Describe each of the main insurance benefits.
3. Discuss the main retirement benefits.
4. Outline the main employees' services benefits.
5. Explain the main flexible benefit programs.

When she took over as director of the government driving agency, the new director knew she had to address her agency's employee absence rate.[1] The rate had peaked at 14 days out per employee, at a cost of about $20 million per year. She knew that employee benefits such as sick leave were important. But she also knew her agency had to control those costs. We'll see what she did.

Introduction: The Benefits Picture Today

benefits
Indirect financial and nonfinancial payments employees receive for continuing their employment with the company.

"What are your benefits?" is the first thing many applicants ask. **Benefits**—indirect financial and nonfinancial payments employees receive for continuing their employment with the company—are an important part of just about everyone's compensation.[2] They include things like health and life insurance, pensions, time off with pay, and child-care assistance.

Virtually all employers offer some health insurance coverage.[3] Employee benefits account for about 33% to 40% of wages and salaries (or about 28% of total payrolls). Health insurance benefits are the most expensive, followed by legally required benefits (like unemployment insurance). Figure 13-1 summarizes the breakdown of benefits as a percentage of employee compensation.

Health-care benefit costs are rising. For example, health insurance costs rose about 4% in one recent year, to a total of $15,745 for family coverage. And employers are racing to deal with the cost implications of the new Patient Protection and Affordable Care Act, as we will see.[4]

Employees understand the value of health benefits. In one survey, 78% of employees cited health-care benefits as most crucial to retaining them; 75% cited compensation. But the same survey found that only 34% are satisfied with their health-care benefits.[5] Even human resource managers sometimes underestimate benefits' attractiveness. One survey concluded that many human resource managers erroneously assume that things like job security, autonomy and independence, and opportunities to use skills are more important to employees than are benefits.[6]

Policy Issues

Employers therefore need to design benefits packages carefully. The list of policy issues includes what benefits to offer, who receives coverage, whether to include retirees in the plan, whether to deny benefits to employees during initial "probationary" periods, how to finance benefits, cost-containment procedures, and how to communicate benefits options to employees.[7]

Legal issues loom large. Federal laws mandate some benefits (such as Social Security) while other benefits are at the employer's discretion (see Table 13-1). However, federal law also affects discretionary benefits such as vacation leave. And employers must adhere to the laws of the states in which they do business. For example, California requires most state contractors to provide domestic partner benefits for employees.[8]

There are many benefits and ways to classify them. We will classify them as (1) pay for time not worked (such as vacations), (2) insurance benefits, (3) retirement benefits, (4) personal services benefits, and (5) flexible benefits. We will start our discussion with pay for time not worked.

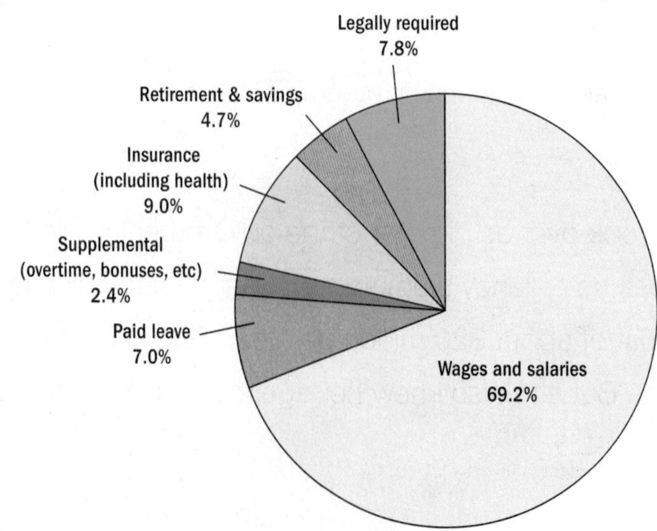

FIGURE 13-1 Relative Importance of Employer Costs for Employee Compensation, June, 2013

Source: www.bls.gov/news.release/ecec.nr0.htm, accessed September 16, 2013.

TABLE 13-1 Some Required and Discretionary Benefits

Benefits Required by Federal or Most State Laws	Benefits Discretionary on Part of Employer*
Social Security	Disability, health, and life insurance
Unemployment insurance	Pensions
Workers' compensation	Paid time off for vacations, holidays, sick leave, personal leave, jury duty, etc.
Leaves under Family Medical Leave Act	Employee assistance and counseling programs, "family-friendly" benefits for child care, elder care, flexible work schedules, etc., executive perquisites

Note: *Although not required under federal law, all these benefits are regulated in some way by federal law, as explained in this chapter.

HR in Practice at the Hotel Paris As they reviewed the benefits numbers, Lisa Cruz and the CFO became increasingly concerned. They computed several benefits-related metrics for their firm, including *benefits costs as a percentage of payroll* and *sick days per full-time equivalent employee per year.* The results were not what they should have been. They had to change their benefits plan. To see how they handled this, read the case on pages 423–424.

1 Name and define each of the main pay for time not worked benefits.

supplemental pay benefits
Benefits for time not worked such as unemployment insurance, vacation and holiday pay, and sick pay.

unemployment insurance (or compensation)
Provides benefits if a person is unable to work through some fault other than his or her own.

Pay for Time Not Worked

Pay for time not worked—also called **supplemental pay benefits**—is a very costly benefit, because of the large amount of time off most employees receive. Common specific time-off-with-pay benefits include holidays, vacations, jury duty, funeral leave, military duty, personal days, sick leave, sabbatical leave, maternity leave, and unemployment insurance payments for laid-off or terminated employees.

Unemployment Insurance

All states have their own **unemployment insurance (or compensation)** laws. These provide benefits to eligible workers who become unemployed through no fault of their own. The benefits derive from a tax on employers that can range from 0.1% to 5% of taxable payroll in most states. An employer's unemployment tax rate reflects its rate of employee terminations. Unemployment tax rates are rising in many states. For example, prior to the recent recession, Maryland's unemployment insurance tax rate was 0.3% or lower, but now averages 2.2% to 13.5% per employee.[9] All states follow federal unemployment insurance guidelines.

Greta Pratt/Corbis Images

Unemployment insurance/compensation laws provide short-term benefits to people who lose their jobs through no fault of their own.

Firms aren't required to let everyone they dismiss receive unemployment benefits—only those released through no fault of their own. Thus, strictly speaking, a worker fired for chronic lateness can't legitimately claim benefits. But many managers are lackadaisical in protecting their employers. Employers therefore spend thousands of dollars on unemployment taxes unnecessarily.

The main rule is to keep a list of written warnings to demonstrate that poor performance caused the dismissal. The checklist in Table 13-2 can help. (Those fired during their initial "90-day probation" *are* eligible for unemployment, so follow that checklist for them, too.)

Vacations and Holidays

Most firms offer vacation and holiday benefits. About 90% of full-time workers and 40% of part-time workers get an average of 8 paid holidays off.[10] Common U.S. paid holidays include New Year's Day, Memorial Day, Independence Day, Labor Day, Thanksgiving Day, and Christmas Day.[11] On average, American workers get about 9 days of vacation leave after 1 year's employment, 14 days after 5 years, and 17 after 10 years.[12]

Firms should address several holiday- and vacation-related policy issues, such as how many vacation days employees get, and which days (if any) are paid holidays. Other vacation policy decisions include:

- Are employees paid for accrued vacation time if they quit before taking their vacations?
- Will you pay employees for a holiday if they don't come to work the day before and the day after the holiday?
- And, should we pay some premium—such as time and a half—when employees must work on holidays?

More firms are taking a more flexible vacation leave approach. For example, IBM gives each employee at least 3 weeks' vacation, but doesn't track how much vacation each takes. Employees just make informal arrangements with supervisors.[13]

In contrast, some employers emphasize centralized absence oversight (called "integrated absence management"). This starts with collecting data. For instance, how many people are on leave; how many days of work is the employer losing; how much is the employer spending to replace absent workers; and what units have the attendance problems?[14] These employers then closely monitor all aspects of their employees' leaves and absences.

Wage surveys and websites like www.insperity.com/products/performance-management/policies-now provide sample vacation policies for inclusion in the firm's employee manual.

TABLE 13-2 An Unemployment Insurance Cost-Control Checklist

Do You:

- Keep documented history of lateness, absence, and warning notices
- Warn chronically late employees before discharging them
- Have a rule that 3 days' absence without calling in is reason for automatic discharge
- Request doctor's note on return to work after absence
- Make written approval for personal leave mandatory
- Stipulate date for return to work from leave
- Obtain a signed resignation statement
- Mail job abandonment letter if employee fails to return on time
- Document all instances of poor performance
- Require supervisors to document the steps taken to remedy the situation
- Document employee's refusal of advice and direction
- Require all employees to sign a statement acknowledging acceptance of firm's policies and rules
- File the protest against a former employee's unemployment claim on time (usually within 10 days)
- Use proper terminology on claim form and attach documented evidence regarding separation
- Attend hearings and appeal unwarranted claims
- Check every claim against the individual's personnel file
- Routinely conduct exit interviews to produce information for protesting unemployment claims

KNOW YOUR EMPLOYMENT LAW

Some Legal Aspects of Vacations and Holidays

Although federal law doesn't require vacation benefits, the employer must still formulate its vacation policy with care. As an example, many employers' vacation policies say vacation pay accrues, say, on a biweekly basis. By doing so, these employers obligate themselves to pay new employees pro rata vacation pay if they leave the firm during their first year. But if the employer's vacation policy requires that a new employee pass his or her first employment anniversary *before becoming entitled* to a vacation, the employee gets no vacation pay if he or she leaves during that first year.

Another frequent question is whether the employer can cancel an employee's scheduled vacation, for instance, due to a rush of orders. Here it's important that the employer formulate its vacation policy so it's clear that the employer reserves the right to require vacation cancellation and rescheduling if production so demands.

Sick Leave

sick leave
Provides pay to an employee when he or she is out of work because of illness.

Sick leave provides pay to employees when they're out of work due to illness. Most policies grant full pay for a specified number of sick days—perhaps 12 per year, usually accumulating at the rate of, say, 1 day per month of service.

The problem is that while many employees use their sick days only when sick, others use it whether they're sick or not. In one survey, personal illnesses accounted for about 45% of unscheduled sick leave absences. Family issues (27%), personal needs (13%), and "entitlement" (9%) were other reasons cited.[15] Such absenteeism costs U.S. employers perhaps $100 billion per year, with personal illness accounting for about a third of the absences.[16]

Social Media and HR

Social media sites can get sick leave workers in trouble. In one case, an employee took a sick day, saying that chronic pain prevented her from coming to work. Unfortunately, she posted pictures of herself drinking at a festival the day she was supposed to be home sick. One of her Facebook "friends" got the photo and showed it to a company supervisor. The company fired her for absence, and an appeals court upheld the employer's decision.[17]

COST-REDUCTION TACTICS Employers use several tactics to reduce excessive sick leave absence. Some repurchase unused sick leave at the end of the year by paying their employees a sum for each unused sick day. The problem is that legitimately sick employees may come to work. Others hold monthly lotteries in which only employees with perfect monthly attendance are eligible for a cash prize. At Marriott, employees can trade the value of some sick days for other benefits. Others aggressively investigate all absences, calling absent employees at home.[18]

Many employers use *pooled paid leave plans* (or *"banks"*).[19] These plans lump together sick leave, vacation, and personal days into a single leave pool. For example, one hospital previously granted new employees 25 days off per year (10 vacation days, 3 personal days, and 12 sick days). Employees used, on average, 5 of those 12 sick days (as well as all vacations and personal days).[20] The pooled paid leave plan allowed new employees to accrue 18 days to use as they saw fit. (Special absences like serious short-term illnesses and bereavement leave were handled separately.) The pooled plan reduced absences. Most firms don't include federal holidays in their paid time off "banks."[21] The accompanying Profit Center feature shows how one employer cut costs.

IMPROVING PERFORMANCE: HR as a Profit Center

Controlling Sick Leave

Sick leave often gets out of control because employers don't measure it. In one survey, only 57% of employers formally tracked sick days for their exempt employees.[22] Three-fourths of the employers couldn't provide an estimate of what sick pay was costing them. Therefore, the employer should first have a system in place for monitoring sick leaves and for measuring their financial impact.[23]

Effective HR practices can then help reduce absence problems. When she became director of the United Kingdom's Driver and Vehicle Licensing Agency, the new director knew steps were needed to address its absence rate.[24] The rate had peaked at 14 days out per employee in 2005, at a cost of about $20 million per year (£10.3 million).

The new director organized a human resource absence initiative.[25] The agency set a goal of reducing absences by 30% by 2010. Agency directors received absence-reduction goals, and their progress was tracked. The agency introduced new policies on special leave, rehabilitation support, and monitoring absentees. They made it easier for employees to swap work shifts, and introduced a guaranteed leave day policy.

By 2010, the sickness absence rate was down to 7.5 days per employee and productivity was up, for multi-year savings of about $48 million dollars (£24.4 million).

Discussion Question 13-1: A note on this agency in Wikipedia refers to "amazingly high" levels of sick leave among staff at the DVLA [around 2007], with employees having an average of three weeks a year sick leave."[26] What sorts of inaction on the part of previous managers could help explain such poor attendance?

Leaves and the Family and Medical Leave Act

Parental leave is an important benefit. About half of workers are women, about 80% will become pregnant during their work lives, and many workers are single parents. Under the Pregnancy Discrimination Act, employers must treat women applying for pregnancy leave as they would any other employee requesting a leave under the employer's sick leave policies. Furthermore, the Family and Medical Leave Act of 1993 (FMLA) (see Figure 13-2) stipulates that:[27]

1. Private employers of 50 or more employees must provide eligible employees (women or men) up to 12 weeks of unpaid leave for their own serious illness, the birth or adoption of a child, or the care of a seriously ill child, spouse, or parent.
2. Employers may require employees to take their paid sick leave or annual leave as part of the 12-week leave provided in the law.
3. Employees taking leave are entitled to receive health benefits while they are on unpaid leave, under the same terms and conditions as when they were on the job.
4. Employers must guarantee most employees the right to return to their previous or equivalent position with no loss of benefits at the end of the leave.

In a survey of 416 human resource professionals, about half said they approved FMLA leaves they believed were not legitimate, due to vague interpretations of the law.[28] Others find tracking leaves problematic.[29] Furthermore, though usually unpaid, the costs associated with hiring and training temporary replacements are high.

Other laws govern sick leaves. For example, under the Americans with Disabilities Act (ADA), a qualified employee with a disability may be eligible for a leave if it's necessary to accommodate the employee.[30]

KNOW YOUR EMPLOYMENT LAW

FMLA Guidelines

Managers who want to avoid granting nonrequired FMLA leaves need to understand the FMLA. For example, to be eligible for leave under the FMLA, the employee must have worked for the employer for at least a total of 12 months and have worked (not just been paid, as someone might be if on leave) for 1,250 or more hours in the past 12 consecutive months.[31] If these conditions do not apply, no leave is required.

Employers should have procedures for all leaves of absence (including those under the FMLA). In particular:

- Give no employee a leave until the reason for the leave is clear.
- If the leave is for medical or family reasons, the employer should obtain medical certification.

- Use a standard form to record both the employee's expected return date and the fact that, without an authorized extension, the firm may terminate his or her employment (see Figure 13-3).
- One employment lawyer says employers should "kind of bend over backward" when deciding if an employee is eligible for leave based on an FMLA situation.[32] However, employers can require independent medical assessments before approving paid FMLA disability leaves.[33]

FIGURE 13-2 Your Rights under the Family and Medical Leave Act of 1993

Your Rights under the Family and Medical Leave Act of 1993

FMLA requires covered employers to provide up to 12 weeks of unpaid, job-protected leave to "eligible" employees for certain family and medical reasons. Employees are eligible if they have worked for their employer for at least one year, and for 1,250 hours over the previous 12 months, and if there are at least 50 employees within 75 miles. The FMLA permits employees to take leave on an intermittent basis or to work a reduced schedule under certain circumstances.

Reasons for Taking Leave:

Unpaid leave must be granted for *any* of the following reasons:

- to care for the employee's child after birth, or placement for adoption or foster care;
- to care for the employee's spouse, son or daughter, or parent who has a serious health condition; or
- for a serious health condition that makes the employee unable to perform the employee's job.

At the employee's or employer's option, certain kinds of *paid* leave may be substituted for unpaid leave.

Advance Notice and Medical Certification:

The employee may be required to provide advance leave notice and medical certification. Taking of leave may be denied if requirements are not met.

- The employee ordinarily must provide 30 days advance notice when the leave is "foreseeable."
- An employer may require medical certification to support a request for leave because of a serious health condition, and may require second or third opinions (at the employer's expense) and a fitness for duty report to return to work.

Job Benefits and Protection:

- For the duration of FMLA leave, the employer must maintain the employee's health coverage under any "group health plan."
- Upon return from FMLA leave, most employees must be restored to their original or equivalent positions with equivalent pay, benefits, and other employment terms.
- The use of FMLA leave cannot result in the loss of any employment benefit that accrued prior to the start of an employee's leave.

Unlawful Acts by Employers:

FMLA makes it unlawful for any employer to:

- interfere with, restrain, or deny the exercise of any right provided under FMLA.
- discharge or discriminate against any person for opposing any practice made unlawful by FMLA or for involvement in any proceeding under or relating to FMLA.

Enforcement:

- The U.S. Department of Labor is authorized to investigate and resolve complaints of violations.
- An eligible employee may bring a civil action against an employer for violations.

FMLA does not affect any Federal or State law prohibiting discrimination, or supersede any State or local law or collective bargaining agreement which provides greater family or medical leave rights.

For Additional Information:

If you have access to the Internet visit our FMLA website: **http://www.dol.gov.** To locate your nearest Wage-Hour Office, telephone our Wage-Hour toll-free information and help line at 1-866-4USWAGE (1-866-487-9243); a customer service representative is available to assist you with referral information from 8am to 5pm **in your time zone;** or log onto our Home Page at **http://www.wagehour.dol.gov.**

U.S. Department of Labor
Employment Standards Administration
Wage and Hour Division
Washington, D.C. 20210

WH Publication 1420
Revised August 2001

Many employers are enriching their parental leave plans to make it more attractive for mothers to return from maternity leave. Tactics include keeping in touch during maternity leave, offering flexible jobs with reduced travel and hours, and longer leaves.[34]

Severance Pay

severance pay
A one-time payment some employers provide when terminating an employee.

Many employers provide **severance pay**, a one-time separation payment when terminating an employee. Most managers expect employees to give them 1 or 2 weeks' notice if they plan to quit, so it seems appropriate to provide severance pay when dismissing an employee. Reducing the chances of litigation from disgruntled former employees is another reason. Severance pay also helps reassure employees who stay on after a downsizing that they'll receive some financial help if they're let go, too.

FIGURE 13-3 Online Request for Leave Form

Source: www.opm.gov/FORMS/PDF_FILL/opm71.pdf, accessed October 17, 2012.

Request for Leave or Approved Absence

1. Name *(Last, first, middle)*

2. Employee or Social Security Number

3. Organization

4. Type of Leave/Absence

Check appropriate box(es) and enter date and time below)	Date From	Date To	Time From	Time To	Total Hours
☐ Accrued annual leave					
☐ Restored annual leave					
☐ Advance annual leave					
☐ Accrued sick leave					
☐ Advance sick leave					

Purpose:
☐ Illness/injury/incapacitation of requesting employee
☐ Medical/dental/optical examination of requesting employee
☐ Care of family member, including medical/dental/optical examination of family member, or bereavement
☐ Care of family member with a serious health condition
☐ Other

☐ Compensatory time off					
☐ Other paid absence (specify in remarks)					
☐ Leave without pay					

5. **Family and Medical Leave**

If annual leave, sick leave, or leave without pay will be used under the Family and Medical Leave Act of 1993 (FMLA), please provide the following information:

☐ I hereby invoke my entitlement to family and medical leave for:
☐ Birth/Adoption/Foster care
☐ Serious health condition of spouse, son, daughter, or parent
☐ Serious health condition of self

Contact your supervisor and/or your personnel office to obtain additional information about your entitlements and responsibilities under the FMLA. Medical certification of a serious health condition may be required by your agency.

6. Remarks

7. **Certification:** I certify that the leave/absence requested above is for the purpose(s) indicated. I understand that I must comply with my employing agency's procedures for requesting leave/approved absence (and provide additional documentation, including medical certification, if required) and that falsification of information on this form may be grounds for disciplinary action, including removal.

7a. Employee signature

7b. Date signed

8a. Official action on request ☐ Approved ☐ Disapproved *(If disapproved, give reason. If annual leave, initiate action to reschedule.)*

8b. Reason for disapproval

8c. Signature

8d. Date signed

Privacy Act Statement

Section 6311 of title 5, United States Code, authorizes collection of this information. The primary use of this information is by management and your payroll office to approve and record your use of leave. Additional disclosures of the information may be: To the Department of Labor when processing a claim for compensation regarding a job connected injury or illness; to a State unemployment compensation office regarding a claim; to Federal Life Insurance or Health Benefits carriers regarding a claim; to a Federal, State, or local law enforcement agency when your agency becomes aware of a violation or possible violation of civil or criminal law; to a Federal agency when conducting an investigation for employment or security reasons; to the Office of Personnel Management or the General Accounting Office when the information is required for evaluation of leave administration; or the General Services Administration in connection with its responsibilities for records management.

Public Law 104-134 (April 26, 1996) requires that any person doing business with the Federal Government furnish a social security number or tax identification number. This is an amendment to title 31, Section 7701. Furnishing the social security number, as well as other data, is voluntary, but failure to do so may delay or prevent action on the application. If your agency uses the information furnished on this form for purposes other than those indicated above, it may provide you with an additional statement reflecting those purposes.

Office of Personnel Management 5 CFR 630 | Local Reproduction Authorized | OPM Form 71 June 2001 Formerly Standard Form (SF) 71

Print Form | Clear Form | Save Form

The reason for the dismissal affects the employer's severance pay policy. About 95% of employees dismissed due to downsizings got severance pay, but only about a third of employers offer severance when terminating for poor performance. It is uncommon to pay when employees quit. The average maximum severance is 39 weeks for executives and about 30 weeks for other downsized employees.[35] About half of employers surveyed give white-collar and exempt employees 1 week of severance pay per year of service, and about one-third do the same for blue-collar workers.[36] If the employer obligates itself (for instance, in its employee handbook) to pay severance, then its "voluntary" plan must comply with additional rules under ERISA.[37]

GUIDELINES In any event, keep several things in mind when designing the severance plan:

- List the situations for which the firm will pay severance, such as layoffs resulting from reorganizations.
- Require signing of a knowing and voluntary waiver/general release prior to remittance of any severance pay, absolving the employer from employment-related liability.

- Reserve the right to terminate or alter the severance policy.
- Make it clear that any continuing severance payments continue until only the stated deadline or until the employee gets a new job, whichever occurs first.
- Remember that, as with all personnel actions, employers must make severance payments, if any, equitably.[38]

supplemental unemployment benefits
Provide for a "guaranteed annual income" in certain industries where employers must shut down to change machinery or due to reduced work. These benefits are paid by the company and supplement unemployment benefits.

Supplemental Unemployment Benefits

In some industries such as auto making, shutdowns to reduce inventories or change machines are common. **Supplemental unemployment benefits** are cash payments that supplement the employee's unemployment compensation, to help the person maintain his or her standard of living while out of work.

2 Describe each of the main insurance benefits.

Insurance Benefits

Most employers also provide a number of required or voluntary insurance benefits, such as workers' compensation and health insurance.

workers' compensation
Provides income and medical benefits to work-related accident victims or their dependents regardless of fault.

Workers' Compensation

Workers' compensation laws aim to provide sure, prompt income and medical benefits to work-related accident victims or their dependents, regardless of fault. Every state has its own workers' compensation law and commission, and some run their own insurance programs. However, most require employers to carry workers' compensation insurance with private, state-approved insurance companies. Neither the state nor the federal government contributes any funds for workers' compensation.

HOW BENEFITS ARE DETERMINED Workers' compensation can be monetary or medical. In the event of a worker's death or disablement, the person's dependents receive a cash benefit based on prior earnings—usually one-half to two-thirds the worker's average weekly wage, per week of employment. Most states have a time limit—such as 500 weeks—for which benefits can be paid. If the injury causes a specific loss (such as an arm), the employee may receive additional benefits based on a statutory list of losses, even though he or she may return to work. In addition to these cash benefits, employers must furnish medical, surgical, and hospital services as required for the employee.

For workers' compensation to cover an injury or work-related illness, one must only prove that it arose while the worker was on the job. It doesn't matter that he or she may have been at fault. Suppose you instruct employees to wear safety goggles at their machines. One worker doesn't and has an eye injury on the job. The company must still provide workers' compensation benefits.

Keep in mind that ADA provisions generally prohibit employers from inquiring about an applicant's workers' compensation history. Furthermore, failing to let an employee who was on injury-related workers' compensation return to work, or not accommodating him or her, could lead to ADA lawsuits.

CONTROLLING WORKERS' COMPENSATION COSTS It is important to control workers' compensation claims (and therefore costs). The employer's insurance company usually pays the claim, but the employer's premiums reflect the amount of claims.[39] Fewer claims also imply fewer accidents.

There are several ways to reduce workers' compensation claims. For example, screen out accident-prone workers. Reduce accident-causing conditions. And reduce the health problems that sometimes trigger these claims—for instance, by instituting effective safety and health programs, and complying with safety standards laws. Furthermore, some workers' compensation claims are not legitimate. Supervisors should watch for red flags. These include vague accident details, minor accidents resulting in major injuries, lack of witnesses, injuries occurring late Friday, and late reporting.[40]

Case management is a popular cost-control method. It is "the treatment of injured workers on a case-by-case basis by an assigned manager, usually a registered nurse, who coordinates with the physician and health plan to determine which care settings are the most effective for quality care and cost."[41]

Moving aggressively to support the injured employee and to get him or her back to work quickly is important too. The involvement of an attorney and the duration of the claim both influence the workers claim cost.[42] Many firms have programs such as physical therapy nursing assistance to help reintegrate claim recipients. Also, monitor health-care providers to confirm they're complying with their fee schedules.[43]

Hospitalization, Health, and Disability Insurance

Health insurance looms large in many people's choice of employer, because it's so expensive.[44] Hospitalization, health, and disability insurance helps protect employees against hospitalization costs and the income loss arising from off-the-job accidents or illness. Many employers purchase insurance from life insurance companies, casualty insurance companies, or Blue Cross (for hospital expenses) and Blue Shield (for physician expenses) organizations. Others contract with health maintenance organizations or preferred provider organizations. The employer and employee usually both contribute to the plan. Table 13-3 illustrates the prevalence of health-related benefits.

COVERAGE Most employer health plans provide at least basic hospitalization and surgical and medical insurance for all eligible employees at group rates. Insurance is generally available to all employees—including new nonprobationary ones—regardless of health or physical condition. Most basic plans pay for hospital room and board, surgery charges, and medical expenses (such as doctors' visits to the hospital). Some also provide "major medical" coverage to meet the medical expenses resulting from serious illnesses.

Most employers' health plans also cover health-related expenses like doctors' visits, eye care, and dental services. Other plans pay for general and diagnostic visits to the doctor's office, vision care, hearing aids, and prescription drugs. *Disability insurance* provides income protection for salary loss due to illness or accident, and may continue until age 65 or beyond. Disability benefits usually range from 50% to 75% of the employee's base pay if he or she is disabled.

health maintenance organization (HMO)
A prepaid health-care system that generally provides routine round-the-clock medical services as well as preventive medicine in a clinic-type arrangement for employees, who pay a nominal fee in addition to the fixed annual fee the employer pays.

HMOS Many employers offer membership in a **health maintenance organization (HMO)**, a medical organization consisting of specialists (surgeons, psychiatrists, and so on), often operating out of a health-care center. It provides routine medical services to employees who pay a nominal fee. Employees often have "gatekeeper" doctors who must approve appointments with specialist doctors. The HMO receives a fixed annual fee per employee from the employer (or employer and employee), regardless of whether it provides that person service.

TABLE 13-3 Percentage of Employers Offering Some Popular Health Benefits—Change over Time

	Yes (%) 2005	Yes (%) 2011
Prescription drug program coverage	97	96
Dental insurance	95	94
Mail order prescription program	90	91
PPO (preferred provider organization)	87	84
Chiropractic coverage	56	83
Mental health insurance	72	82
Vision insurance	80	76
Employee assistance program	73	75
Medical/Flexible spending account	80	73
HMO (health maintenance organization)	53	33

Source: Adapted from 2011 SHRM Employee Benefits Survey Report, p. 2. www.shrm.org/Research/SurveyFindings/Articles/Documents/Emp_Benefits_Tables.pdf, accessed, June 1, 2011. Reprinted with permission from the Society for Human Resource Management. All rights reserved. See the 2012 survey report at www.shrm.org/Research/SurveyFindings/Articles/Documents/2012_EmpBenefits_Report.pdf, accessed September 17, 2013.

preferred provider organizations (PPOs)
Groups of health-care providers that contract with employers, insurance companies, or third-party payers to provide medical care services at a reduced fee.

PPOS **Preferred provider organizations (PPOs)** are a cross between HMOs and the traditional doctor–patient arrangement: They are "groups of health care providers that contract with employers, insurance companies, or third-party payers to provide medical care services at a reduced fee."[45] Unlike HMOs, PPOs let employees select providers (such as doctors) from a relatively wide list, and see them in their offices, often without gatekeeper doctor approval. Providers agree to discounts and to certain controls, for example, on testing.[46]

MENTAL HEALTH BENEFITS The World Health Organization estimated that more than 34 million people in the United States between the ages of 18 and 64 suffer from mental illness.[47] Mental illnesses represent about 24% of all reported disabilities, more than disabling injuries, cardiovascular diseases, and cancer combined.

Mental health costs are rising. Reasons include widespread drug and alcohol problems, an increase in states that require employers to offer minimum mental health benefits, and the fact that mental health claims tend to trigger other health-care claims. The Mental Health Parity Act of 1996 (as amended in 2008) sets minimum mental health-care benefits; it also prohibits employer group health plans from adopting mental health benefits limitations without comparable limitations on medical and surgical benefits.[48]

KNOW YOUR EMPLOYMENT LAW

The Legal Side of Health Benefits

With the United States introducing new health insurance laws, federal influence over health benefits will increase substantially in the next few years.

Patient Protection and Affordable Care Act of 2010

As originally enacted, under the Patient Protection and Affordable Care Act employers with at least 50 full-time equivalent employees were to offer minimum levels of affordable health-care coverage or pay a penalty, as of 2014. To be eligible, an employee must work at least 30 hours per week or a total of 130 hours in a calendar month.[49] Signed into law by President Obama in 2010, employers faced a number of other deadlines under the Act. For example, employers must begin reporting the value of health-care benefits on employee's W-2 statements, and contributions to flexible spending arrangements were limited to $2,500 as of January 1, 2013.[50] By 2018, employers with health-care plans that cost more than the threshold the law sets (for instance, $27,500 for family coverage) have to pay a 40% tax on the amount of coverage over $27,500. Individual and group health plans that already provide dependent coverage must expand eligibility up to age 26.[51]

Under the law, each state (or when necessary, the federal government) will run public health insurance exchanges; in effect, marketplaces for buying and selling insurance. In part to discourage employers from dropping their health-care plans and sending employees to the new health exchanges, the law imposes fines of $2,000 per worker on any employer with more than 50 workers who don't offer health insurance plans.

However, the act's deadlines are changing. In 2013 the administration put several Affordable Care Act elements on hold. It postponed the employer mandate to offer insurance to workers by a year, until 2014. And it issued new rules allowing states that planned to offer insurance exchanges to have two extra years, until 2015, to verify the eligibility of the people they insure.

Employers in one survey by the consulting firm Mercer expected this act to raise their health-care expenses.[52] As the act phases in over the next few years (assuming no further changes), the excise tax on high-cost plans was the employers' main cost concern. Other cost-raisers, the employers said, include the expanded coverage for older children, the ban on lifetime benefit dollar limits, the requirement that employers auto-enroll new hires into a health plan, and the rule that employers must offer coverage to employees including those working less than 30 hours per week (many of whom now have no health benefits).[53] Reports indicate that some employers are considering eliminating their health plans, or turning more full-time workers into workers working less than 30 hours per week. About 43% of employers surveyed say their workers will have to pay more for their health-care plans.[54] Some employers are considering reducing their coverage.[55] Other employers calculate that it may be cheaper to pay the penalty than supply the insurance.[56]

(Continued)

COBRA

COBRA—the Consolidated Omnibus Budget Reconciliation Act—requires most private employers to continue to make health benefits available to separated employees and their families for a time, generally 18 months after separation.[57] The former employee must pay for the coverage.

Employers ignore COBRA's regulations at their peril. The employer does not want separated employees to leave and be injured, and then claim it never told them they could have continued their insurance coverage. Therefore, when a new employee first becomes eligible for the company's insurance plan, the person *must* receive (and acknowledge receiving) an explanation of his or her COBRA rights. And all employees separated from the company should sign a form acknowledging that they received and understand those rights. (See Figure 13-4 for a checklist.)

Detailed record keeping is crucial for COBRA compliance. The following checklist is designed to ensure that the proper records are maintained for problem-free COBRA compliance.

	Yes	No
• Do you maintain records so that it is easily determined who is covered by your group health care plan?	☐	☐
• Do you record terminations of covered employees as soon as terminations occur?	☐	☐
• Do you track reduction of hours of employees covered by group health care plans?	☐	☐
• Do you track deaths of employees covered by group health care plans?	☐	☐
• Do you track leaves of absence of employees covered by group health care plans?	☐	☐
• Do you track Medicare eligibility of employees covered by group health care plans?	☐	☐
• Do you track the disability status of employees covered by group health care plans?	☐	☐
• Do you track retirees covered by group health care plans?	☐	☐
• Do you maintain current addresses of employees?	☐	☐
• Do you maintain current addresses of individuals receiving COBRA benefits?	☐	☐
• Do you require employees to provide a written acknowledgment that they have received notice of their COBRA rights?	☐	☐
• Do you have a system to determine who has paid COBRA premiums on time?	☐	☐
• Do you have a system to determine who has obtained other group health coverage so that they are no longer eligible for COBRA under your plan?	☐	☐
• Do you maintain a telephone log of calls received about COBRA?	☐	☐
• Do you maintain a record of changes in your plan?	☐	☐
• Do you maintain a record of how premiums are calculated?	☐	☐
• Do you maintain a log of those employees who are denied COBRA coverage?	☐	☐
• Do you maintain a log of why employees are denied COBRA coverage?	☐	☐

FIGURE 13-4 COBRA Record-Keeping Compliance Checklist

Source: "COBRA Record Keeping Compliance Checklist." Copyright © 2012 by BLR–Business & Legal Resources (www.HR.BLR.com). Reprinted with permission.

Other Laws

Other federal laws are pertinent. For example, among other things, the *Employee Retirement Income Security Act* of 1974 (ERISA) sets minimum standards for most voluntarily established pension and health plans in private industry.[58] *The Newborn Mother's Protection Act of 1996* prohibits employers' health plans from using incentives to encourage employees to leave the hospital after childbirth after less than the legislatively determined minimum stay. Employers who provide health-care services must follow the privacy rules of the *Health Insurance Portability and Accountability Act of 1996 (HIPAA)*.[59] Employers must provide the same health-care benefits to employees over the age of 65 that they do to younger workers, even though the older workers are eligible for federal Medicare health insurance. Under the *Americans with Disabilities Act,* the health plan generally shouldn't make distinctions based on disability. Under the *Genetic Information Nondiscrimination Act* of 2008 (GINA), even innocent actions can be problems. For example, if a health plan administrator writes down that a member's mother passed away from breast cancer, making the note could conceivably violate the act.[60] States such as California have their own FLMAs.[61]

Global HR

Global employers must account for multinational legal, cultural, and programmatic differences. For example, the most prevalent supplemental employee benefits in the United States are pension, medical, and life and long-term disability insurance, while in the United Kingdom (with its national health program) they are pension, car benefit, and life and long-te[illegible]n disability.[62]

Improving Performance: Trends in Employer Health-Care Cost Control

A business with 50 employees might pay $1 million or more just for insurance coverage, before accounting for things like sick days. Health-care cost control is therefore one big way the HR department can improve profits.

Employers are endeavoring to rein in health-care costs. Perhaps most notably, employers are incentivizing workers to make better lifestyle choices, as a way to lower health-care costs.[63] For example, the top three health-care priorities of employers in a recent Aon Hewitt Health Care Survey report were, "Offer incentives or disincentives to motivate sustained health-care behavior change"; "Promote a culture of health in the workplace (e.g., healthy cafeteria, flexible schedules to allow time for physical activity)"; and "Move to rewarding improved health results or outcomes."[64] Many others retain *cost-containment specialists* to help reduce such costs. And most negotiate more aggressively with their health care insurance providers.[65] Most cost-control efforts necessarily start by instituting methods for measuring and tracking health-care costs.[66]

For many employers, deductibles and co-pays are the low-hanging fruit in health-care cost control. For example, 22% of employers imposed deductibles of at least $1,000 recently.[67] *Consumer-driven health plans (CDHPs)* are increasingly popular. These are high-deductible plans that give employees access to, for instance, a health savings account. (The Medicare Modernization Act of 2003 allows employers to establish tax-free health savings accounts (HSA).)[68] After the employer, employee, or both deposit pretax (and thus tax-sheltered) pay in the employees' HSAs, employees or their families can use their HSA funds to pay for "low dollar" (not catastrophic) medical expenses.[69] The assumption is that this will motivate employees to utilize less expensive health-care options, and thus avoid big deductibles.[70] In 2013 IBM moved retirees from their company-supported plan, substituting a *stipend* to buy insurance at *private exchange* insurance marketplaces.[71] We'll address other important cost-control tools next.

COMMUNICATION AND EMPOWERMENT Most importantly, *make sure employees know the costs* of their medical benefits.[72] So, for example, periodically send a statement to each employee listing the employer's costs for each health benefit. *Online selection* lets employees choose the best of the employer's health-care offerings, based on input from other employees concerning matters like doctor visits and specialists.

WELLNESS PROGRAMS Many illnesses are preventable. In one study "employers who undertook prevention programs aimed at cardiovascular disease . . . reported an average 28% reduction in sick leave, [and] a 26% reduction in direct health-care costs."[73] As noted, many employers therefore offer preventive services and incentives.[74] Some link each employee's health-care premiums to his or her healthy behaviors.[75] *Clinical prevention* programs include things like mammograms and routine checkups. Walgreens owns companies that provide *on-site health-care services* such as mammograms for employers.[76] *Health promotion and disease prevention* programs include seminars and incentives aimed at improving unhealthy behaviors.[77] Other wellness program trends include obesity management, stress management, senior health improvement, and tobacco cessation programs.[78] Incentives, for instance, \$50–\$100, can boost wellness program participation, but may backfire.[79] Whirlpool gives nonsmoker discounts on health-care premiums worth about \$500. It suspended 39 workers it caught smoking outside the plant after claiming on their benefits enrollment forms that they were not tobacco users.

On site clinics About 34% of employers with over 500 employees offer some type of on-site or nearby health clinics, sometimes managed through third parties.[80]

CLAIM AUDITS It makes little sense to initiate cost cuts when employers are paying out thousands or millions of dollars in erroneous claims. Unfortunately, with health-care plans increasingly complicated, it's easier for errors to occur. One survey found that although the industry standard for percentage of claims errors is 3%, the *actual* percentage of claims with errors was about 6.3%. The industry standard for percentage of claims dollars actually paid in error was 1%; the *actual* percentage of claims dollars paid in error were 3.4%. So, setting standards for errors and then auditing all claims may be the most direct way to reduce employer health-care expenses.[81]

LIMITED PLANS More employers are offering limited-benefit health-care insurance plans. Unlike health-care plans that may have lifetime coverage limits of \$1 million or more, these "mini" medical plans have annual caps of about \$2,000–\$10,000 per year, and correspondingly lower premiums.[82]

OUTSOURCING Benefits management ranks high on HR activities that employers outsource.[83] In one survey, 94% outsourced management of flexible spending accounts, 89% outsourced defined contribution plans, 72% outsourced defined benefit plans, and 68% outsourced the auditing of dependents.[84]

OTHER COST-CONTROL OPTIONS Employers are taking other steps as well. Some are moving to *defined contribution health insurance plans*. Like 401(k) pension plans, these defined contribution health insurance plans tie each employee's health-care benefits to what he or she and the employer contributes, rather than providing health-care benefits (for instance, hospital care limits) that are defined in advance.[85] Many employers are reducing health benefits for their future *retirees*.[86] Small firms are joining *benefits purchasing alliances,* banding together to purchase health-care benefits. Other employers encourage *medical tourism*, which means asking employees to have non-urgent medical procedures abroad, where costs are lower.[87] Some, such as Viking Range Corp., have *self-funded* or self-insured health plans. Rather than paying premiums to insurance carriers, Viking pays employees' medical claims directly.[88] About 19% of almost 600 employers surveyed had some form of health-care plan *spousal exclusion policies*, such as excluding a spouse when similar coverage was available from the spouse's employer.[89] Employers are demanding insurers use *accountable care organizations* (ACO), special vendors who help insurers, health-care providers, and others with the goal of improving costs and outcomes.[90] One simple way to cut costs is just to ensure that any *dependents* enrolled are actually eligible for coverage.[91] The accompanying Profit Center feature shows how one employer cut costs.

IMPROVING PERFORMANCE: HR as a Profit Center

The Doctor Is on the Phone

With more than 12,000 employees in its health plan, Rent A Center was looking for a better way to get its employees the medical advice they required, while also reducing health plan costs. The company signed an agreement with Teladoc.Inc. Teladoc's doctors provide medical consultations over the phone. In the first 16 months the new telemedicine program was in effect, Rent A Center saved more than \$770,000 in doctor and hospital visits and in employee productivity that would have been lost.

The program seems to be win-win. The Teladoc consultation is free to employees, compared to a $20 office co-payment, and the doctors are available 24 hours per day, usually within 30 minutes. If necessary, they call in antibiotics prescriptions. And for Rent A Center, there's that extra $770,000 in their bottom line.[92]

Discussion Question 13-2: Would you recommend this program to your employer? Why?

PPAA Finally, employers are planning to make substantial changes to their health-care programs in response to the Patient Protection and Affordable Care Act. For example, 68% plan to boost employee contributions for dependents; 26% plan to end employer sponsorship of retiree medical coverage; and 33% plan to reward or penalize employees based on measurable criteria such as cholesterol levels.[93]

Long-Term Care

Long-term care insurance—for things like nursing assistance to former employees in their old age—is a key employee benefit. The Health Insurance Portability and Accountability Act of 1996 lets employers and employees deduct the cost of long-term care insurance premiums from their annual income taxes, making this benefit more attractive.[94] Employers can also provide insurance benefits for several types of long-term care, such as adult day care, assisted living, and custodial care.

Life Insurance

group life insurance
Provides lower rates for the employer or employee and includes all employees, including new employees, regardless of health or physical condition.

In addition to hospitalization and medical benefits, most employers provide **group life insurance** plans. Such plans generally offer lower rates than individual plans, and usually accept all employees regardless of health or physical condition.

In general, there are three key personnel policies to address: the benefits-paid schedule (the amount of life insurance benefits is usually tied to the employee's annual earnings), supplemental benefits (continued life insurance coverage after retirement, for instance), and financing (the amount and percent the employee contributes).

Accidental death and dismemberment coverage provides a lump-sum benefit in addition to life insurance benefits when death is accidental. It also provides benefits in case of accidental loss of limbs or sight.

Benefits for Part-Time and Contingent Workers

About 19 million people work part-time (less than 35 hours a week).[95] The recession, more phased retirements, and a desire to better balance work and family life help explain this phenomenon. In any case, many firms provide holiday, sick leave, and vacation benefits to part-timers, and more than 70% offer some form of health-care benefits to them.[96]

The accompanying HR Practices Around the Globe feature shows how some global employers cut their employee insurance costs.

IMPROVING PERFORMANCE: HR Practices Around the Globe

Multinational Insurance Benefits Risk Pooling[97]

An employer with employees in just one country can take advantage of discounts and economies of scale when buying insurance. But what does an employer do when its employees are spread among several countries? Because of licensing issues among countries, the employer can't just buy insurance from one company. It therefore often ends up using locally licensed insurance carriers in each country to get its employees in each country group life, medical, and retirement and other insurance.

That means higher insurance costs. The solution, for many global employers, is an insurance pool. Basically, the employer places its insurance business with a vendor that has affiliates (an "insurance network") in the countries where the employer has employees. By doing so, the vendor may be able to "pool" the employer's and employees' risks together, producing a dividend that can reduce the global employer's health and other employee insurance costs.

Discussion Question 13-3: Google search *multinational insurance licensing laws*, check a few sites, and make a list of four specific ways insurance licensing laws differ among countries.

3 Discuss the main retirement benefits.

Retirement Benefits

The first contingent of baby-boomers turned 65 a few years ago. This presents two challenges for employers. First (as we explained in Chapter 10 (Managing Employee Retention, Engagement, and Careers), employers are taking steps to entice older workers to keep working in some capacity.[98] Second, retirement benefits such as federal Social Security and employer pension/ retirement plans like the 401(k) are big issues.

Social Security

Social Security
Federal program that provides three types of benefits: retirement income at the age of 62 and thereafter, survivor's or death benefits payable to the employee's dependents regardless of age at time of death, and disability benefits payable to disabled employees and their dependents. These benefits are payable only if the employee is insured under the Social Security Act.

Most people assume that **Social Security** provides income only when they are older than 62, but it actually provides three types of benefits. The familiar *retirement benefits* provide an income if you retire at age 62 or thereafter and are insured under the Social Security Act. Second are *survivor's* or *death benefits.* These provide monthly payments to your dependents regardless of your age at death (assuming you're insured under Social Security). Finally, *disability payments* provide monthly payments to employees who become disabled totally (and to their dependents) if they meet certain requirements. The Social Security system also administers the Medicare program, which provides health services to people age 65 or older. "Full retirement age" for non-discounted Social Security benefits traditionally was 65—the usual age for retirement. It is now 67 for those born 1960 or later.[99]

A tax on the employee's wages funds Social Security (technically, "Federal Old Age and Survivor's Insurance"). As of 2013, the maximum amount of earnings subject to Social Security tax was $113,700; the employer and employee each pay 7.65%.[100]

Pension Plans

pension plans
Plans that provide a fixed sum when employees reach a predetermined retirement age or when they can no longer work due to disability.

defined benefit pension plan
A plan that contains a formula for determining retirement benefits.

defined contribution pension plan
A plan in which the employer's contribution to employees' retirement savings funds is specified.

portability
Instituting policies that enable employees to easily take their accumulated pension funds when they leave an employer.

401(k) plan
A defined contribution plan based on section 401(k) of the Internal Revenue Code.

savings and thrift plan
Plan in which employees contribute a portion of their earnings to a fund; the employer usually matches this contribution in whole or in part.

Pension plans provide income to individuals in their retirement, and just over half of full-time workers participate in some type of pension plan at work.

We can classify pension plans as contributory versus noncontributory plans, qualified versus nonqualified plans, and defined contribution versus defined benefit plans.[101] The employee contributes to the contributory pension plan, while the employer makes all contributions to the noncontributory pension plan. Employers derive certain tax benefits (such as tax deductions) for contributing to qualified pension plans (they are "qualified" for preferred tax treatment by the IRS); nonqualified pension plans get less favorable tax treatment. As with all pay plan components, employers should ensure retirement benefits support their strategic needs. For example, set guiding principles such as "assist in attracting employees."[102]

With **defined benefit pension plans**, the employee's pension is specified ("defined"), in that the person knows in advance his or her pension benefits. A formula usually ties the pension to a percentage of the person's pre-retirement pay (for example, to an average of his or her last 5 years of employment), multiplied by the years he or she worked for the company. Due to tax law changes and other reasons, defined benefit plans now represent a minority of pension benefit plans.[103] However, even younger employees now express a strong preference for defined benefit plans.[104] Some companies, such as Union Pacific, offer them as employee retention tools.[105]

Defined contribution pension plans specify ("define") what *contribution* the employee and employer will make to the employee's retirement or savings fund. Here the contribution is defined, not the pension. With a *defined benefit* plan, the employee can compute what his or her retirement *benefits* will be upon retirement. With a *defined contribution* plan, the actual pension will depend on the amounts contributed to the fund *and* on the success of the fund's investment earnings. Defined contribution plans are popular among employers due to their relative ease of administration, favorable tax treatment, and other factors. **Portability**—making it easier for employees who leave the firm prior to retirement to take their accumulated pension funds with them—is easier with defined contribution plans.

deferred profit-sharing plan
A plan in which a certain amount of profits is credited to each employee's account, payable at retirement, termination, or death.

401(K) PLANS The most popular defined contribution plans are based on section 401(k) of the Internal Revenue Code, and called **401(k) plans**. The employee authorizes the employer to deduct a sum from his or her paycheck before taxes, and to invest it in the bundle of investments in his or her 401(k) account. The deduction is pretax, so the employee pays no tax on those dollars until after he or she retires (or removes the money from the 401(k) plan). The person can deduct annually an amount up to the IRS maximum (about $15,000). The employer arranges, usually with an investment company such as Fidelity Investments, to administer the 401(k) plan

iStockphoto/Thinkstock

Firms such as Vanguard, Fidelity, and others can establish online, fully Web-based 401(k) plans even for small firms with 10 to 50 employees.

and to make investment options (typically mutual stock funds and bond funds) available to the plan. In the recent downturn, more employees made "hardship withdrawals" from their 401(k) plans.[106]

Employers must choose 401(k) providers with care. The employer has a fiduciary responsibility to its employees and must monitor the fund and its administration.[107] In addition to trustworthiness, the 401(k) plan provider should make it easy to enroll and participate in the plan.[108] Firms such as Vanguard, Fidelity, and others establish Web-based 401(k) plans with online tools—such as an "asset allocation planner"—even for small firms. Employers must also monitor 401(k) housekeeping issues such as late deposits and incorrect employer matching contributions.[109]

Under the Pension Protection Act of 2006, employers who sponsor plans that facilitate both *automatic enrollment* and allocation to *default investments* (such as age-appropriate "lifestyle funds") reduce their compliance burdens.[110]

OTHER PLANS The 401(k) plan is one example of a **savings and thrift plan.**[111] In any savings and thrift plan, employees contribute a portion of their earnings to a fund, and the employer usually matches this contribution completely or in part.

As discussed in Chapter 12 (Incentives), employers use a **deferred profit-sharing plan** to contribute a portion of their profits in cash to a pension fund, regardless of the level of employee contribution (personal income taxes on those contributions are deferred until the employee retires or leaves the employer). An **employee stock ownership plan (ESOP)** is a qualified, tax-deductible defined contribution plan in which employers contribute stock to a trust for eventual use by employees who retire.

employee stock ownership plan (ESOP)
A qualified, tax-deductible stock bonus plan in which employers contribute stock to a trust for eventual use by employees.

CASH BALANCE PENSION PLANS With *defined benefits* plans, to get your maximum pension, you generally must stay with your employer until you retire—the formula takes the number of years you work into consideration. With *defined contribution* plans, your pension is more portable—you can leave with it at any time, perhaps rolling it over into your next employer's pension plan. Without delving into the details, **cash balance plans** are a hybrid; they have defined benefit plans' more predictable benefits, but the portability advantages of defined contribution plans.[112] The employer contributes a percentage of employees' current pay to the employees' pension plans every year, and employees earn interest on this amount.[113]

cash balance plans
Plans under which the employer contributes a percentage of employees' current pay to employees' pension plans every year, and employees earn interest on this amount.

Employee Retirement Income Security Act of 1975 (ERISA)
Signed into law by President Ford to require that pension rights be vested and protected by a government agency, the PBGC.

Pension Benefits Guarantee Corporation (PBGC)
Established under ERISA to ensure that pensions meet vesting obligations; also insures pensions should a plan terminate without sufficient funds to meet its vested obligations.

KNOW YOUR EMPLOYMENT LAW

Pension Planning and the Law

Federal law regulates pension planning and administration. As a rule, pension planning requires expert help.[114]

The **Employee Retirement Income Security Act of 1975 (ERISA)** is the basic law. It requires that employers have written pension plan documents and adhere to certain guidelines, such as regarding eligibility.[115] ERISA protects the employer's pension or health plans' assets by requiring that those who control the plans act responsibly. The *fiduciary's* responsibility is to run the plan solely in the interest of participants and beneficiaries.

Employers (and employees) also want their pension contributions to be "qualified," or tax deductible, so they must adhere to the *income tax codes.* Under *labor relations laws,* the employer must let its unions participate in pension plan administration. The *Job Creation and Worker Assistance Act* provides guidelines regarding what rates of return employers should use in computing their pension plan values.

PBGC ERISA established the **Pension Benefits Guarantee Corporation (PBGC)** to oversee and insure a pension if a plan terminates without sufficient funds. The PBGC guarantees only defined benefit plans, not defined contribution plans. And it will only pay a pension of up to about $54,000 per year for someone 65 years of age with a plan terminating recently.[116] So, high-income workers still face reduced pensions if their employers go bankrupt.

MEMBERSHIP REQUIREMENTS When does the employee become eligible for a pension? Under the Tax Reform Act of 1986, an employer can require that an employee complete a period of no more than 2 years' service to the company before becoming eligible to participate in the plan. However, if it requires more than 1 year of service before eligibility, the plan must grant employees full and immediate vesting rights at the end of that period.

VESTING *Vested funds* are the money employer and employee have placed in the latter's pension fund that cannot be forfeited for any reason. The employees' contributions are always theirs, of course. However, until ERISA, the *employers'* contribution in many pension plans didn't vest until the employee retired. Someone could have worked for a company for 30 years and been left with no pension if the company went bust 1 year before the person retired.

Employers can choose one of two minimum vesting schedules (employers can allow funds to vest faster if they wish). With *cliff vesting*, the period for acquiring a nonforfeitable right to employer matching contributions (if any) is 3 years. So, the employee must have nonforfeitable rights to these funds by the end of 3 years. With the second (*graded vesting*) option, pension plan participants must receive nonforfeitable rights to the matching contributions as follows: 20% after 2 years, and then 20% for each succeeding year, with a 100% nonforfeitable right by the end of 6 years.

Pensions and Early Retirement

early retirement window
A type of offering by which employees are encouraged to retire early, the incentive being liberal pension benefits plus perhaps a cash payment.

To trim their workforces or for other reasons, some employers encourage employees to retire early. Many such plans take the form of **early retirement window** arrangements for specific employees (often age 50+). The "window" means that for a limited time, the employees can retire early, generally with a combination of improved or liberalized pension benefits plus a cash payment.

Early retirement programs can backfire, however. When Verizon offered enhanced pension benefits to encourage what it hoped would be 12,000 employees to retire, more than 21,000 took the plan. Verizon had to replace 16,000 managers.[117]

Furthermore, unless structured properly, older employees can challenge early retirement programs as de facto ways for forcing them to retire against their will. Although it is generally legal to use incentives to encourage individuals to choose early retirement, the employee's decision must be voluntary. Under the Older Workers' Benefit Protection Act (OWBPA), the employee's waiver must be knowing and voluntary, and give the employee ample time to consider the agreement and to seek legal advice.

Improving Performance Through HRIS: Online Benefits Management Systems

Benefits administration can require devoting hundreds of hours to answering employees' questions about benefits and updating employees' benefits information.[118] Typical employee questions include, "If I retire in 2 years, what will be my monthly retirement income?" Tasks like that cry out for online self-service benefits management applications.

BENELOGIC For example, when the organization that assists Pennsylvania school districts with their insurance needs decided to help the school boards automate their benefits administration, they chose a company called Benelogic.[119] The solution, called the "Employee Benefit Electronic Service Tool," lets users manage all aspects of benefits administration, including enrollment, plan descriptions, eligibility, and premium reconciliation, via their browsers.[120]

Benelogic hosts and maintains the Web application on its servers, and creates customized, Web-based applications for each school district. The system facilitates online employee benefit enrollment, and provides centralized call center support for benefit-related questions. It even handles benefits-related payroll and similar functions by collaborating with companies like ADP (for payroll). Each school board employee accesses the Benelogic site via a link on his or her own board's website.

BENEFITS WEBSITES Employers are also adding new services to their own benefits websites. In addition to offering things like self-enrollment, the insurance company USAA's website (www.usaa.com) helps employees achieve better work–life balance. For example, employees can respond to a list of words (such as *stressed*), and see suggestions for dealing with stress.[121] Boeing's Pay & Benefits Profile site gives employees real-time information about their salary and bonuses, benefits, pension, and even special services such as child-care referrals.[122]

To facilitate employee benefits self-management, other employers are providing workers with mobile Apps (see, for example, http://appfinder.lisisoft.com/tag/employee-benefits.html). For example, clients of Discovery Benefits Inc., a benefits administrator, reportedly logged in through its App about 25,000 times in one recent year, saving Discovery the time it would have spent dealing with call- ins.[123]

4 Outline the main employees' services benefits.

Personal Services and Family-Friendly Benefits

Although time off, insurance, and retirement benefits account for the lion's share of benefits costs, most employers also provide various services benefits. These include personal services (such as legal and personal counseling), "family-friendly" services (such as child-care facilities), educational subsidies, and executive perquisites (such as company cars for its executives).

Tough economic times mean employers are revamping the personal services benefits they offer. Among the most-*dropped* benefits recently were educational assistance, long-term care insurance, and job sharing. "Most-added" benefits included legal counseling, lactation rooms, work-at-home policies, and paid or subsidized off-site fitness.[124] For example, when the Dallas-Fort Worth Airport found that its employee fitness and wellness facility wasn't producing the expected health cost savings, it instituted incentives to get employees to use it more regularly.[125]

Personal Services

Personal services benefits include credit unions, legal services, counseling, and social and recreational opportunities. (Some employers use the term *voluntary benefits* to cover personal services benefits that range from things like pet insurance to automobile insurance.[126]) We'll look at some of these.

employee assistance program (EAP)
A formal employer program for providing employees with counseling and/or treatment programs for problems such as alcoholism, gambling, or stress.

EMPLOYEE ASSISTANCE PROGRAMS **Employee assistance programs (EAPs)** provide counseling and advisory services, such as personal legal and financial services, child and elder care referrals, adoption assistance, mental health counseling, and life event planning.[127] EAPs are popular, with more than 60% of larger firms offering them. One study found that personal mental health was the most common problem addressed by employee assistance programs, followed by family problems.[128]

Software giant SAS Institute, Inc., offers generous employee benefits. The North Carolina firm keeps turnover at 4% in an industry where 20% is typical, partly by offering family-friendly benefits like paid maternity leave, day care on site, lunchtime piano concerts, massages, and yoga classes like this one.

For employers, EAPs produce advantages, not just costs. For example, sick family members and problems like depression account for many sick days employees take. Employee assistance programs can reduce such absences by providing expert advice on issues like elder care referrals.[129] Few but the largest employers establish their own EAPs. Most contract with vendors such as Magellan Health Services and CIGNA Behavioral Health.[130]

In either case, employers and managers should keep several issues in mind. Everyone involved including supervisors and EAP staff must respect *confidentiality.* Also, keep files locked, limit access, and minimize identifying information. *Be aware of legal issues.* For example, in most states counselors must disclose suspicions of child abuse to state agencies. *Define* the program's purpose, employee eligibility, the roles and responsibilities of EAP and employer personnel, and procedures for using the plan. Ensure your EAP vendors fulfill *professional and state licensing requirements.*

Family-Friendly (Work–Life) Benefits

Several trends have changed the benefits landscape. There are more households where both adults work, more one-parent households, more women in the workforce, and more workers over age 65.[131]

family-friendly (or work–life) benefits
Benefits such as child care and fitness facilities that make it easier for employees to balance their work and family responsibilities.

Such trends lead many employers to bolster their **family-friendly (or "work–life") benefits.**[132] These include child care, elder care, fitness facilities, and flexible work schedules—benefits that help employees balance their family and work lives.[133] We'll look at some examples.

SUBSIDIZED CHILD CARE Most working people make private provisions to take care of their children. Organized day care centers accounted for about 30% of child-care arrangements, and relatives or nonrelatives accounted for most of the remaining arrangements.

Employers who want to reduce the distractions associated with finding reliable child care can help. Some employers simply investigate the day care facilities in their communities and recommend certain ones to employees. Others set up company-sponsored and subsidized day care facilities. For example, Abbott Laboratories built a $10 million child-care center at its headquarters north of Chicago, daytime home to about 400 children of Abbott employees.[134]

By establishing subsidized day care, employers assumedly can benefit in several ways. These include improved recruiting results, lower absenteeism, improved morale, favorable publicity, and lower turnover. But, good planning is required. This often starts with a questionnaire to employees to answer questions like, "What would you be willing to pay for care for one child in a child-care center near work?"

SICK CHILD BENEFITS Unexpected absences accounted for a cost per absence to employers of about $700 per episode (for temp employees and reduced productivity, for instance). More employers are thus offering emergency child-care benefits, for example, when a young child's regular babysitter is a no-show. Texas Instruments built a Web database its employees use to find last-minute child-care providers. Others, like Canadian financial company CIBC, are expanding their on-site child-care centers to handle last-minute emergencies.[135]

ELDER CARE The responsibility for caring for aging relatives can affect employee performance.[136] One study found that, to care for an older relative, 64% of employees took sick days or vacation time, 33% decreased work hours, 22% took leaves of absence, 20% changed their job status from full- to part-time, 16% quit their jobs, and 13% retired early.

More employers are therefore providing elder care services. For example, the United Auto Workers and Ford provide elder care referral services for Ford's salaried employees, including assessments and recommendations on the best care.[137] The National Council on Aging has a website to help find benefit programs: www.benefitscheckup.org.

FAMILY-FRIENDLY BENEFITS AND THE BOTTOM LINE It's not easy to evaluate the "profitability" of such programs. A recent analysis of family-friendly benefits found little evidence that they improve performance.[138]

However, measuring performance isn't easy. "Family-friendly" firms such as SAS routinely turn up on "best companies to work for" lists. This probably makes it easier to recruit and retain good employees. Employees probably forego some pay for services like built-in day care.

And some advantages are indirect. For example, work–family conflict may affect performance, which family-type benefits may improve.[139]

The bottom line is that employers are reviewing (and often reducing) these benefits. Even Google, long known for offering benefits that blow most other employers away (free buses from the city, on-campus day care, and restaurants) has cut back a bit of late.

Other Personal Services Benefits

Employers provide other personal services benefits.[140] Google, perennially a "100 best companies to work for," still offers an on-campus bowling alley, cafés company wide, adoption assistance, the Google Child Care Center, free shuttle service from San Francisco, and on-site dry cleaning (for instance).[141] Home Depot offers a "nose to tail coverage" pet health insurance program. Ben & Jerry's gives employees three pints of ice cream to take home daily. CVS Caremark, seeking to retain older employees, offers various elder-friendly benefits. Its "snowbird" program lets pharmacists winter in Florida and work in the Northeast when it's warmer, for instance.[142]

EDUCATIONAL SUBSIDIES Based on one survey, the percentage of employers offering education benefits dropped from 68% in 2007 to 58% in 2011.[143] Such programs are expensive. The employer may also be paying its best employees to leave. Researchers studied how the U.S. Navy's part-time college education reimbursements influenced job mobility. Taking tuition assistance decreased the probability the person stayed in the Navy.[144]

Payments may range from all tuition and expenses down to a fixed several hundred dollars per year. Many employers also reimburse non–job-related courses (such as a Web designer taking an accounting class) that pertain to company business.[145] Many employers provide college programs on the employer's premises, or remedial work in basic literacy.

Diversity Counts: Domestic Partner Benefits

When employers provide *domestic partner benefits* to employees, the employees' same-sex or opposite-sex domestic partners are eligible to receive the same benefits (health care, life insurance, and so forth) as do the husband, wife, or legal dependent of one of the firm's employees. Many employers offer domestic partner benefits. For instance, Northrop Grumman Corp. extends domestic partner benefits to the 9,500 salaried workers at its Newport News shipyard.[146]

With the passage of the Defense of Marriage Act, Congress provided that employers may not treat same-sex domestic partners the same as employees' spouses for purposes of federal law. There was therefore some doubt as to whether the benefits extended to domestic partners would be federal tax free, as they generally are under IRS guidelines for "dependents" including the taxpayer's spouse or son or daughter, or parent or aunt.[147]

However in 2013 the U.S. Supreme Court struck down part of the Defense of Marriage Act. Under this ruling, gay couples married in states where it is legal must receive the same federal health, tax, Social Security and other benefits heterosexual couples receive.[148]

Executive Perquisites

When you reach the pinnacle of the organizational pyramid—or close to the top—you will find, waiting for you, the Executive Perk. Perquisites (perks for short) are special benefits for top executives. They range from company planes to private bathrooms.

Most fall between these extremes. Perks include *management loans* (typically to exercise executives' stock options); *financial counseling*; and *relocation benefits*, often including subsidized mortgages, purchase of the executive's current house, and payment for the move. Publicly traded companies must itemize all executives' perks (if they total more than $100,000).

Flexible Benefits Programs

5 Explain the main flexible benefit programs.

Employees prefer choice in their benefits plans. In one survey of working couples, 83% took advantage of flexible hours (when available); 69% took advantage of the flexible-style benefits we'll discuss next; and 75% said that they prefer flexible benefits plans.[149]

FIGURE 13-5 One Page from Online Survey of Employees' Benefits Preferences

Source: http://data.grapevinesurveys.com/survey.asp?sid=20062143964099, accessed September 16, 2013.

Your Logo Here. 125 px

300 px

Human Resources - Employee Benefits Survey

Please take a moment to tell us your thoughts on the Company benefits plan. Your input is valued and will help us make this better.

Health care

1 **Please rate the following.**
1-Very Satisfied, 5-Very Dissatisfied

	1	2	3	4	5
Medical plan	1	2	3	4	5
Dental plan	1	2	3	4	5
Vision plan	1	2	3	4	5

Retirement and Savings Plan

Given this, it is prudent to survey employees' benefits preferences, perhaps using a form like that in Figure 13-5. In any case, employers should provide for choice when designing benefits plans.

The Cafeteria Approach

flexible benefits plan/cafeteria benefits plan
Individualized plans allowed by employers to accommodate employee preferences for benefits.

One way to provide a choice is with an aptly named *cafeteria benefits plan.* (Pay specialists use **flexible benefits plan** and **cafeteria benefits plan** synonymously.) A *cafeteria plan* is one in which the employer gives each employee a benefits fund budget, and lets the person spend it on the benefits he or she prefers, subject to two constraints. First, the employer must of course limit the total cost for each employee's benefits package. Second, each employee's benefits plan must include certain required items such as Social Security, workers' compensation, and unemployment insurance. Employees can often make midyear changes to their plans if, for instance, their dependent care costs rise and they want to divert contributions.[150] IRS regulations require formal written plans describing the employer's cafeteria plan, including benefits and procedures for choosing them.[151]

TYPES OF PLANS Cafeteria plans come in several varieties. To give employees more flexibility in what benefits they use, about 70% of employers offer *flexible spending accounts* for medical and other expenses. This option lets employees pay for certain benefits expenses with pretax dollars (so the IRS, in effect, subsidizes some of the employee's expense). To encourage employees to use this option, some firms are offering *debit cards* that employees can use at their medical provider or pharmacy.[152] *Core plus option plans* establish a core set of benefits (such as medical insurance), which are usually mandatory for all employees. Beyond the core, employees can then choose various benefits options.[153]

The accompanying HR Tools feature explains how many smaller employers manage the costs of their various benefits.

IMPROVING PERFORMANCE: HR Tools for Line Managers and Entrepreneurs

Benefits and Employee Leasing

Many businesses—particularly smaller ones—don't have the resources or employee base to support the cost of many of the benefits we've discussed in this chapter. That's one big reason they turn to "employee leasing."

In brief, employee leasing firms (also called *professional employer organizations* or *staff leasing firms*) assume all or most of the employer's human resources chores. In doing so, they also become the employer of record for the employer's employees, by transferring them all to the employee leasing firm's payroll. The leasing firm thus becomes the employees' legal employer, and usually handles employee-related activities such as recruiting, hiring (with client firms' supervisors' approvals), and paying taxes (Social Security payments, unemployment insurance, and so on).

Insurance and benefits are usually the big attraction. Even group rates for life or health insurance can be quite high when only 20 or 30 employees are involved. That's where leasing comes in. Remember that the leasing firm is now the legal employer. The employees are thus part of a larger insurable group, along with other employers' former employees. The small business owner may get insurance it couldn't otherwise afford.

As in dealing with all vendors, the employer should have a detailed negotiated agreement with the employee leasing firm. Define what the services will be; include priorities, responsibilities, and warranties.[154] Understand that if the leasing firm merges into another firm, the new parent may require you to change your systems once the contract period expires.[155]

Discussion Question 13-4: Explain how you believe you'd react to having your employer switch you to a leasing firm, and why.

Flexible Work Schedules

Flexible work schedules are popular.[156] Single parents use them for balancing work and family responsibilities. And for many millennial employees, flexible work schedules provide a way to pursue their careers without surrendering the quality of life they desire. There are several flexible work schedule options.

flextime
A work schedule in which employees' workdays are built around a core of midday hours, and employees determine, within limits, what other hours they will work.

FLEXTIME **Flextime** is a plan whereby employees' workdays are built around a core of midday hours, such as 11:00 A.M. to 2:00 P.M. Thus, workers may opt to work from 7:00 A.M. to 3:00 P.M. or from 11:00 A.M. to 7:00 P.M. The number of employees in formal flextime programs—from 4% of operators to 17% of executive employees—doesn't tell the whole story. Many more employees take advantage of informal flexible work schedules.[157] The effect of flextime for most employees is about 1 hour of leeway before 9:00 A.M. or after 5:00 P.M.[158]

TELECOMMUTING Telecommuting—using technology to work away from the office—is popular. About 48% of employers offer ad hoc telecommuting options, while 17% offer them on a full-time basis.[159] Some jobs have much higher rates. For example, almost 45% of medical transcription is reportedly work from home.[160] Just over 13 million Americans work from home at least one day per week, with Fridays and Mondays the favorite days to stay home.[161]

On the other hand, Yahoo famously said it needed its employees "working side by side" and brought them back to the office from telecommuting.[162]

Employers that offer telecommuting must calculate the program's benefits and costs. Thus, Delta Airlines spends an initial $2,500 for each home-based reservation agent for computer and software licenses, but pays each such agent $1.50 per hour less than call center counterparts. Less obvious expenses include having IT answer telecommuters' technical questions.[163] A telecommuting program at Capital One Bank apparently led to about a 41% increase in workplace satisfaction, and a 53% increase in those who say their workplace enhances group productivity.[164] The accompanying HR Practices Around the Globe feature shows another example of how telecommuting cuts costs.

IMPROVING PERFORMANCE: HR Practices Around the Globe

NES Rentals

Seeking to cut costs while maintaining its reputation for great products and service, NES Rentals sent their employees home. Today, three-fourths of their customer support, collections, finance, and other back-office workers at their Chicago office work from home at least part of the week.[165] They no longer have dedicated desks, but share space in the office. The CEO says productivity has increased 20%. Employee turnover dropped from 7% in 2009 to "virtually non-existent" in 2010. NES is leasing 40% less office space, saving $100,000 in real estate expenses. He estimates NES's total savings from instituting this new telecommuting benefit at about $350,000 annually.[166]

Discussion Question 13-5: Why do you think some firms, such as NES, like telecommuting, while others, such as Yahoo, shun it?

compressed workweek
Schedule in which employee works fewer but longer days each week.

COMPRESSED WORKWEEKS Many employees, like airline pilots, do not work conventional 5-day, 40-hour workweeks. Workers like these typically have **compressed workweek** schedules—they work fewer days each week, but each day they work longer hours. Some firms have four 10-hour day workweeks. Some workers—in hospitals, for instance—work three 12-hour shifts, and then take off for 4 days.[167]

EFFECTIVENESS OF FLEXIBLE WORK SCHEDULE ARRANGEMENTS Studies show that flexible work schedules have positive effects on employee productivity, job satisfaction, and employee absenteeism; the effect on absenteeism is generally greater than on productivity. Highly flexible programs were less effective than less flexible ones.[168]

Some experts argue that 12-hour shifts increase fatigue and accidents. To reduce potential side effects, some employers install treadmills and exercise bikes, and special lights that mimic daylight.

job sharing
Allows two or more people to share a single full-time job.

work sharing
Refers to a temporary reduction in work hours by a group of employees during economic downturns as a way to prevent layoffs.

OTHER FLEXIBLE WORK ARRANGEMENTS **Job sharing** allows two or more people to share a single full-time job. For example, two people may share a 40-hour-per-week job, with one working mornings and the other working afternoons. About 22% of the firms questioned in one survey indicated that they allow job sharing.[169] Job sharing can be particularly useful for retirement-aged employees. It allows them to reduce their hours while the company retains their expertise.[170] **Work sharing** refers to a temporary reduction in work hours by a group of employees during economic downturns as a way to prevent layoffs. Thus, 400 employees may all agree to work (and be paid for) only 35 hours per week, to avoid a layoff of 30 workers.

Review

MyManagementLab Go to **mymanagementlab.com** to complete the problems marked with this icon.

Chapter Section Summaries

1. Because benefits are so important to employees, it's important that all managers understand the benefits picture today. In addition to the fact that benefits are very important to employees, the other big issue, of course, is that benefits in general and health care costs in particular are rising very fast. About 78% of employees cite health care benefits as most crucial to retaining them.
2. Employers provide numerous **pay for time not worked benefits**.
   - Unemployment insurance provides benefits to eligible workers who become unemployed through no fault of their own. The main rule is to keep a list of written warnings.
   - American workers tend to get about 9 days of leave after 1 year of employment.
   - Sick pay provides pay to an employee when he or she is out of work because of illness. Minimizing sick leave pay is important, and here cost reduction tactics include repurchasing unused sick leave or simply using paid leave plans that lump sick leave, vacation, and holidays into one leave pool.

- The Family and Medical Leave Act requires larger employers to provide up to 12 weeks of unpaid leave for family-related issues.
- Severance pay is a one-time payment some employers provide when terminating an employee.

3. Most employers also provide a number of required or voluntary **insurance benefits**. Workers' compensation laws aim to provide sure, prompt medical benefits to work-related accident victims or their dependents, regardless of fault. Most employer health plans provide at least basic hospitalization and surgical and medical insurance for eligible employees. When an employee is terminated or terminates his or her employment, it is essential that the employer make the person aware of his or her COBRA rights. The basic overall trend in health-care cost control is to take steps (for instance, in terms of communication and empowerment, health savings accounts, and claims audits) to keep the rising cost of health-care insurance under control.
4. Particularly with stock markets volatile, **retirement benefits** are important to employees today. Social Security is a federal program that provides retirement income at the age of 62 and thereafter, as well as other benefits. Many employers make available pension plans; these provide an income when employees reach retirement age or when they can no longer work due to disability. Defined benefit plans contain a formula for determining retirement benefits, while defined contribution plans are plans in which the contribution to employees' retirement savings plans is specified. 401(k) plans are the most well-known of the latter. The Employee Retirement Income Security Act of 1975 requires that employers have written pension plan documents, and established the Pension Benefits Guarantee Corporation to oversee employers' pension plans. Key pension policy issues include membership requirements and testing.
5. Most employers also provide various **personal services and family-friendly benefits**. These include credit unions, employee assistance programs, and subsidized child care and elder care.
6. Employees prefer choice in their benefits plans, so **flexible benefits programs** are important. Flexible benefits or cafeteria benefits plans are individual plans that accommodate employee preferences for benefits. Some employers turn to employee leasing companies to capitalize on the advantage of the leasing firm's large employee base to get better employee benefits for their employees. Employers also are implementing various types of flexible work schedules, including flextime, compressed workweeks, and other flexible work arrangements such as job sharing.

CHAPTER 13

Discussion Questions

13-6. What is unemployment insurance? Is an organization required to pay unemployment benefits to all dismissed employees? Explain how you would go about minimizing your organization's unemployment insurance tax.

13-7. Explain how ERISA protects employees' pension rights.

13-8. Describe the main retirement benefits.

13-9. What are the main provisions of the FMLA?

Individual and Group Activities

13-10. Working individually or in groups, research the unemployment insurance rate and laws of your state. Write a summary detailing your state's unemployment laws. Assuming Company X has a 30% rate of annual personnel terminations, calculate Company X's approximate unemployment tax rate in your state.

13-11. Assume you run a small business. Working individually or in groups, visit the website www.dol.gov/elaws. See the Small Business Retirement Savings Advisor. Write a 2-page summary explaining: (1) the various retirement savings programs available to small business employers, and (2) which retirement savings program you would choose for your small business and why.

13-12. You are the HR consultant to a small business with about 40 employees. Now the firm offers only 5 days of vacation, 5 paid holidays, and legally mandated benefits such as unemployment insurance payments. Develop a list of other benefits you believe it should offer, along with your reasons for suggesting them.

13-13. Appendix A, PHR and SPHR Knowledge Base, at the end of this book (pages 580–588) lists the knowledge someone studying for the HRCI certification exam needs to have in each area of human resource management (such as in Strategic Management, Workforce Planning, and Human Resource Development). In groups of four to five students, do four things: (1) review Appendix A; (2) identify the material in this chapter that relates to the required knowledge Appendix A lists; (3) write four multiple-choice exam questions on this material that you believe would be suitable for inclusion in the HRCI exam; and (4) if time permits, have someone from your team post your team's questions in front of the class, so that students in all teams can answer the exam questions created by the other teams.

KNOWLEDGE BASE

CHAPTER 13

Experiential Exercise

Revising the Benefits Package

Purpose: The purpose of this exercise is to provide practice in developing a benefits package for a small business.

Required Understanding: Be very familiar with the material presented in this chapter. In addition, review Chapter 11 to reacquaint yourself with sources of compensation survey information, and come to class prepared to share with your group the benefits package for the small business in which you work or in which someone with whom you're familiar works.

How to Set Up the Exercise/Instructions: Divide the class into groups of four or five students. Your assignment is as follows: Maria Cortes runs a small personnel recruiting office in Miami and has decided to start offering an expanded benefits package to her 25 employees. At the current time, the only benefits are 7 paid holidays per year and 5 sick days per year. In her company, there are 2 other managers, as well as 17 full-time recruiters and 5 secretarial staff members. Your assignment is as follows:

- In the time allotted, your group should create a benefits package in keeping with the size and requirements of this firm.

Video Case

Video Title: Pay for Performance and Financial Incentives (Joie de Vivre Hospitality)

SYNOPSIS

Chip Conley is the founder of Joie de Vivre Hospitality (JDV), a collection of boutique hotels, restaurants, and spas in California. Conley aims to foster employee motivation using Maslow's Hierarchy of Needs and has written books and lectured on the subject. Joie de Vivre pays average wages, but experiences low turnover due to the nature of the relationships it has formed with each employee.

Discussion Questions

13-14. Chip Conley, founder of Joie de Vivre Hospitality, believes that most companies frame their financial incentives in the wrong way. Explain what he means. What does JDV do differently?

13-15. Why does Joie de Vivre offer free hotel stays to all employees as part of its incentive plan?

13-16. According to the video, what separates a world-class organization is its ability to care for its employees in good times and in bad. How did JDV accomplish this during the dot-com crash and post-9/11 industry recession?

13-17. Of the compensation, benefits, and incentives practices we discussed in Chapters 11, 12, and 13, which would you recommend JDV implement, and why?

Application Case

Striking for Benefits

A few years ago, the strike by Southern California grocery workers against the state's major supermarket chains was almost 5 months old. The main issue was employee benefits, and specifically how much (if any) of the employees' health-care costs the employees should pay themselves. Based on their existing contract, Southern California grocery workers had unusually good health benefits. For example, they paid nothing toward their health insurance premiums, and paid only $10 co-payments for doctor visits. However, supporting these excellent health benefits cost the big Southern California grocery chains over $4 per hour per worker.

The big grocery chains were not proposing cutting health-care insurance benefits for their existing employees. Instead, they proposed putting any new employees hired after the new contract went into effect into a separate insurance pool, and contributing $1.35 per hour for their health insurance coverage. That meant new employees' health insurance would cost each new employee perhaps $10 per week. And, if that $10 per week weren't enough to cover the cost of health care, then the employees would have to pay more, or do without some of their benefits.

It was a difficult situation for all involved. For the grocery chain employers, skyrocketing health-care costs were undermining their competitiveness; the current employees feared any step down the slippery slope that might eventually mean cutting their own health benefits. The unions didn't welcome a situation in which they'd end up representing two classes of employees, one (the existing employees) who had excellent health insurance benefits, and another (newly hired employees) whose benefits were relatively meager, and who might therefore be unhappy from the moment they took their jobs and joined the union.

Questions

13-18. Assume you are mediating this dispute. Discuss five creative solutions you would suggest for how the grocers could reduce the health insurance benefits and the cost of their total benefits package without making any employees pay more.

13-19. From the grocery chains' point of view, what is the downside of having two classes of employees, one of which has superior health insurance benefits? How would you suggest they handle the problem?

13-20. Similarly, from the point of view of the union, what are the downsides of having to represent two classes of employees, and how would you suggest handling the situation?

Source: Based on "Settlement Nears for Southern California Grocery Strike," *Knight-Ridder/Tribune Business News*, February 26, 2004, item 04057052.

Continuing Case

Carter Cleaning Company

The New Benefit Plan

Carter Cleaning Centers has traditionally provided only legislatively required benefits for its employees. These include unemployment compensation, Social Security, and workers' compensation (which is provided through the same insurance carrier that insures the stores for such hazards as theft and fire). The principals of the firm—Jack, Jennifer, and their families—have individual, family-supplied health and life insurance.

Jennifer can see several potential problems with the company's policies regarding benefits and services. One is turnover. She wants to study whether similar companies' experiences with providing health and life insurance benefits enable these firms to reduce employee turnover and perhaps pay lower wages. Jennifer is also concerned that her company has no formal vacation or paid days off or sick leave policies. Informally, at least, it is understood that employees get 1 week's vacation after 1 year's work, but in the past the policy regarding paid vacations for days such as New Year's Day and Thanksgiving Day has been very inconsistent. Sometimes employees who had been on the job only 2 or 3 weeks were paid fully for one of these holidays, while at other times employees who had been with the firm for 6 months or more had been paid for only half a day.

She also wonders whether it would be advisable to establish some type of day care center for the employees' children. Many of them have no place to go during the day (they are preschoolers) or have no place to go after school; she wonders whether a day care benefit would be in the best interests of the company.

Questions

13-21. Draw up a policy statement regarding vacations, sick leave, and paid days off for Carter Cleaning Centers.

13-22. What would you tell Jennifer are the advantages and disadvantages to Carter Cleaning Centers of providing its employees with health, hospitalization, and life insurance programs?

13-23. Would you advise establishing some type of day care center for the Carter Cleaning employees? Why or why not?

Translating Strategy into HR Policies and Practices Case*,§

**The accompanying strategy map for this chapter is in the MyManagementLab; and the overall map on the inside back cover of this text outlines the relationships involved.*

IMPROVING PERFORMANCE at The Hotel Paris

The New Benefits Plan

The Hotel Paris's competitive strategy is "To use superior guest service to differentiate the Hotel Paris properties, and to thereby increase the length of stay and return rate of guests, and thus boost revenues and profitability." HR manager Lisa Cruz must now formulate functional policies and activities that support this competitive strategy by eliciting the required employee behaviors and competencies.

While the Hotel Paris's benefits (in terms of things like holidays and health care) were comparable to other hotels', Lisa Cruz knew they weren't good enough to support the high-quality service behaviors her company sought. Indeed, the fact that they were roughly comparable to those of similar firms didn't seem to impress the Hotel Paris's employees. Sixty percent of them consistently said they were dissatisfied with their benefits. Lisa's concern (with which the CFO concurred) was that dissatisfaction with benefits contributed to low morale and engagement, and thus to inhibiting the Hotel Paris from achieving its strategic aims. Lisa therefore turned to the task of assessing and redesigning the company's benefits plans.

As they reviewed the benefits numbers, Lisa Cruz and the CFO became concerned. They computed several benefits-related metrics for their firm, including benefits costs as a percentage of payroll, sick days per full-time equivalent employee per year, benefits cost/competitor's benefits cost ratio, and workers' compensation experience ratings. The results, said the CFO, offered a "good news–bad news" situation. On the good side, as noted, the ratios were similar to most competing hotels'. The bad news was that the measures were well below those for high-performing service businesses. The CFO authorized Lisa to design and propose a new benefits plan.

Lisa knew there were several things she wanted to accomplish. She wanted a plan that contributed to improved employee morale and engagement. And, she wanted the plan to include elements that made it easier for her employees to do their jobs—so that, as she put it, "they could come to work and give their full attention to giving our guests great service, without worrying about child care and other family distractions."

The new plan's centerpiece was a proposal for much better family-friendly benefits. Because so many of each hotel's employees were single parents, and because each hotel had to run 24 hours a day, Lisa's team proposed, and the Board approved, setting aside a room in each hotel for an on-site child-care facility and for hiring a trained professional attendant. They considered instituting a flexible work schedule program, but for most of the jobs, this was impractical, because each front-line employee simply had to be there at his or her appointed hour. However, they did institute a new job-sharing program. Now two people could share one housekeeping or front-desk clerk job, as long as the job was covered.

One of the metrics Lisa and her team specifically wanted to address was the relatively high absence rate at the Hotel Paris. Because so many of these jobs are front-line jobs—valets, limousine drivers, and front-desk clerks, for instance—absence had a particularly serious effect on metrics like overtime pay and temporary help costs. Here, at the urging of her compensation consultant, Lisa decided to opt for a

§Written by and copyright Gary Dessler, PhD.

system similar to Marriott's "BENETRADE." With this benefit program, employees can trade the value of some sick days for other benefits. As Lisa put it, "I'd rather see our employees using their sick day pay for things like additional health-care benefits, if it means they'll think twice before taking a sick day to run a personal errand."

After just less than a year, Lisa and the CFO believe the new program is successful. Their studies suggest that the improved benefits are directly contributing to improved employee morale and commitment, sick days have diminished by 40%, and employee turnover is down 60%. And when they advertise for open positions, over 60% of the applicants cite "family-friendly benefits" as a top reason for applying to work at the Hotel Paris.

Questions

13-24. What is your opinion of the new Hotel Paris benefits plan?

13-25. Because employers typically make benefits available to all employees, they may not have the motivational effects of incentive plans. Given this, list five employee behaviors you believe Hotel Paris could try to improve through an enhanced benefits plan, and explain why you chose them.

13-26. Given your answer to question 13-20, explain specifically what other benefits you would recommend the Hotel Paris implement to achieve these behavioral improvements.

MyManagementLab

Go to **mymanagementlab.com** for Auto-graded writing questions as well as the following Assisted-graded writing questions:

13-27. You are applying for a job as a manager and are at the point of negotiating salary and benefits. What questions would you ask your prospective employer concerning benefits? Describe the benefits package you would try to negotiate for yourself.

13-28. What is "portability"? Why do you think it is (or isn't) important to a recent college graduate?

13-29. MyManagementLab only—comprehensive writing assignment for this chapter.

Key Terms

benefits, 398
supplemental pay benefits, 399
unemployment insurance (or compensation), 399
sick leave, 401
severance pay, 403
supplemental unemployment benefits, 405
workers' compensation, 405
health maintenance organization (HMO), 406
preferred provider organizations (PPOs), 407
group life insurance, 411
Social Security, 412
pension plans, 412
defined benefit pension plan, 412
defined contribution pension plan, 412
portability, 412
401(k) plan, 412
savings and thrift plan, 413
deferred profit-sharing plan, 413
employee stock ownership plan (ESOP), 413
cash balance plans, 413
Employee Retirement Income Security Act (ERISA), 413
Pension Benefits Guarantee Corporation (PBGC), 413
early retirement window, 414
employee assistance program (EAP), 415
family-friendly (or work–life) benefits, 416
flexible benefits plan/cafeteria benefits plan, 418
flextime, 419
compressed workweek, 420
job sharing, 420
work sharing, 420

Endnotes

1. Judith Whitaker, "How HR Made a Difference," *People Management* 27 (October 28, 2010).
2. Based on Frederick Hills, Thomas Bergmann, and Vida Scarpello, *Compensation Decision Making* (Fort Worth, TX: The Dryden Press, 1994), p. 424. See also Fay Hansen, "The Cutting Edge of Benefit Cost Control," *Workforce*, March 2003, pp. 36–42; Crain's Benefits Outlook 2009, www.crainsbenefit.com/news/survey-finds-nearly-20-percent-of-employers-plan-to-drop-health-benefits.php, accessed July 28, 2009.
3. "Survey Finds 99 Percent of Employers Providing Health-Care Benefits," *Compensation & Benefits Review*, September/October 2002, p. 11. See also "National Compensation Survey: Employee Benefits in Private Industry in the United States, March 2006," U.S. Department of Labor, U.S. Bureau of Labor Statistics, August 2006.
4. Emily Jane Fox, "Health Insurance Premiums Climb 4% in 2012," http://money.cnn.com/2012/09/11/pf/insurance/health-insurance-premiums/index.html, accessed April 12, 2013. See also "Costs This Year Increased at Highest Rate Since 2004, Survey Reveals," *HR Focus* 88, no. 1 (January 10, 2011); "Employee Medical Costs Expected to Increase by 8.5 Percent in 2012, According to PwC," www.pwc.com/us/en/pressreleases/2011/employer-medical-costs-expected-to-increase.jhtml, accessed September 14, 2011.
5. "Trouble Ahead? Dissatisfaction with Benefits, Compensation," *HR Trendbook*, 2008, p. 16.
6. Frank Giancola, "Are Employee Benefit Programs Being Given Enough Credit for Their Effect on Employee Attitudes?" *Compensation & Benefits Review* 44, no. 5 (2012), pp. 291–297.
7. Joseph Martocchio, *Strategic Compensation* (Upper Saddle River, NJ: Prentice Hall, 2001), p. 262.
8. "California Domestic Partner Benefits Mandate Carries Likely Impact Beyond State's

Borders," *BNA Bulletin to Management*, November 6, 2003, p. 353.

9. "HR Plays a Major Role in Curbing Company Unemployment Insurance Costs, Analysts Say," *BNA Bulletin to Management*, August 3, 2010, pp. 241–242.
10. www.bls.gov/opub/perspectives/issue2.pdf, accessed June 1, 2011.
11. Ibid.
12. www.bls.gov/opub/perspectives/issue2.pdf, accessed June 1, 2011.
13. Ken Belson, "At IBM, a Vacation Anytime, or Maybe No Vacation at All," *The New York Times*, August 31, 2007, pp. A1–A18.
14. Robert Grossman, "Gone But Not Forgotten," *HR Magazine*, September 2011, p. 44; then put in place solutions such as rigorous absenteeism claims reviews.
15. "National Compensation Survey: Employee Benefits in Private Industry in the United States, March 2006," U.S. Bureau of Labor Statistics, August 2006, p. 116. See also "Spurious Sick-Notes Spiral Upwards," *The Safety and Health Practitioner* 22, no. 6 (June 2004), p. 3.
16. "Unscheduled Employee Absences Cost Companies More Than Ever," *Compensation & Benefits Review*, March/April 2003, p. 19; Robert Grossman, "Gone but Not Forgotten," *HR Magazine* 56, no. 9 (September 2011), pp. 34–46.
17. "Employee Who's Facebook Photos Suggested Fraud Lacks FMLA Claims, Sixth Circuit Rules," *BNA Bulletin to Management*, November 20, 2012, p. 371.
18. "Making Up for Lost Time: How Employers Can Curb Excessive Unscheduled Absences," *BNA Human Resources Report*, October 20, 2003, p. 1097. See also W. H. J. Hassink et al., "Do Financial Bonuses Reduce Employee Absenteeism? Evidence from a Lottery," *Industrial and Labor Relations Review* 62, no. 3 (April 2009), pp. 327–342.
19. "SHRM Benefits Survey Finds Growth in Employer Use of Paid Leave Pools," *BNA Bulletin to Management*, March 21, 2002, p. 89.
20. See M. Michael Markowich and Steve Eckberg, "Get Control of the Absentee-Minded," *Personnel Journal*, March 1996, pp. 115–120; "Exploring the Pluses, Minuses, and Myths of Switching to Paid Time Off Banks," *BNA Bulletin to Management* 55, no. 25 (June 17, 2004), pp. 193–194.
21. Society for Human Resource Management 2009 Employee Benefits Survey, quoted in Martha Frase, "Taking Time Off to the Bank," *HR Magazine*, March 2010, p. 42.
22. "Creating Holistic Time Off Programs Can Significantly Reduce Expenses," *Compensation & Benefits Review*, July/August 2007, pp. 18–19.
23. See, for example, Rita Zeidner, "Strategies for Saving in a Down Economy," *HR Magazine*, February 2009, p. 28.
24. Judith Whitaker, "How HR Made a Difference," *People Management* 27 (October 28, 2010).
25. Ibid.
26. http://en.wikipedia.org/wiki/Driver_and_Vehicle_Licensing_Agency, accessed April 13, 2013.
27. The Department of Labor updated its regulations for administering the Family and Medical Leave Act in November 2008. See "DOL Issues Long-Awaited Rules; Address a Serious Health Condition, Many Other Issues," *BNA Bulletin to Management*, November 18, 2008, p. 369. In 2008, Congress amended the family and medical leave act to include, among other things, leave rights particularly for military families. See Sarah Martin, "FMLA Protection Recently Expanded to Military Families: Qualifying Exigency and Service Member Family Leave," *Compensation & Benefits Review*, September/October 2009, pp. 43–51.
28. "Ten Years After It Was Signed into Law, FMLA Needs Makeover, Advocates Contend," *BNA Bulletin to Management*, February 20, 2003, p. 58.
29. "HR Professionals Face Sundry Challenges Administering FMLA Leave, Survey Asserts," *BNA Bulletin to Management*, July 20, 2007, p. 233.
30. Jill Fisher, "Reconciling the Family Medical Leave Act with Overlapping or Conflicting State Leave Laws," *Compensation & Benefits Review*, September/October 2007, pp. 39–44.
31. Based on Dennis Grant, "Managing Employee Leaves: A Legal Primer," *Compensation & Benefits Review* 35, no. 4 (2003), p. 41. There are several unresolved issues in what "12 months' employment" means. For example, several courts recently held that an employee *can* count previous periods of employment with the employer to satisfy the 12-month requirement. See Daniel Ritter et al., "Recent Developments Under the Family and Medical Leave Act," *Compensation & Benefits Review*, September/October 2007, p. 33.
32. Gillian Flynn, "Employers Need an FMLA Brush-Up," *Workforce*, April 1997, pp. 101–104. See also "Worker Who Was Employee for Less Than One Year Can Pursue FMLA Claim, Federal Court Determines," *BNA Fair Employment Practices*, April 26, 2001, p. 51.
33. "Workers Who Come and Go Under FMLA Complicate Attendance Policies, Lawyer Says," *BNA Bulletin to Management*, March 16, 2000, p. 81.
34. Sue Shellenbarger, "The Mommy Drain: Employers Beef Up Perks to Lure New Mothers Back to Work," *The Wall Street Journal*, September 28, 2006, p. D1.
35. "Severance Pay," July 2007, *Culpepper Compensation & Benefits Surveys*.
36. Terry Baglieri, "Severance Pay," www.shrm.org, accessed December 23, 2006.
37. Ibid.
38. Ibid.
39. "Workers' Compensation Costs Are Rising Faster Than Wages," *BNA Bulletin to Management*, July 31, 2003, p. 244.
40. "Workers' Comp Claims Rise with Layoffs, But Employers Can Identify, Prevent Fraud," *BNA Bulletin to Management*, October 4, 2001, p. 313.
41. "Using Case Management in Workers' Compensation," *BNA Bulletin to Management*, June 6, 1996, p. 181; for other tactics, see, for example, H. Jorgensen, "Overhauling Claims Management." *Risk Management* 54, no. 7 (July 2007), p. 50. See also Donna Owens, "Back to Work," *HR Magazine*, November 2012, pp. 49–51.
42. "Workers Comp Research Provides Insight into Curbing Health Care Costs," *EHS Today*, February 2010, p. 18.
43. "Firms Cite Own Efforts as Key to Controlling Costs," *BNA Bulletin to Management*, March 21, 1996, p. 89. See also "Workers' Compensation Outlook: Cost Control Persists," *BNA Bulletin to Management*, January 30, 1997, pp.33–44; and Annmarie Lipold, "The Soaring Costs of Workers' Comp," *Workforce*, February 2003, p. 42ff.
44. In one recent survey, 53% of workers said they would trade some pay for better retirement benefits: "Employees Willing to Trade Pay for More Benefits, Survey Finds," *BNA Bulletin to Management,* March 6, 2012, p. 78.
45. Hills, Bergmann, and Scarpello, *Compensation Decision Making*, p. 137.
46. "Costs This Year Increased at Highest Rate Since 2004, Survey Reveals," *HR Focus* 88, no. 1 (January 10, 2011).
47. Society for Human Resource Management, "Mental Health Trends," *Workplace Visions,* no. 2, http://moss07.shrm.org/Research/FutureWorkplaceTrends/Pages/0303.aspx, accessed July 28, 2009.
48. "Mental-Health Parity Measure Enacted as Part of Financial Rescue Signed by Bush," *BNA Bulletin to Management*, October 7, 2008, p. 321. Because the act requires employers who offer mental health coverage to make that coverage similar to their medical and surgical health coverage benefits, many employers are dropping health care coverage. Alice Andors, "This Parity Pay Off?" *HR Magazine*, September 2012, pp. 45–46.
49. "IRS Unveils Proposed Rules of 'Shared Responsibility,'" *BNA Bulletin to Management*, January 18, 2013, p. 12.
50. "Deadlines Vary for Implementing Provisions of Health Care Law," *BNA Bulletin to Management*, May 4, 2010, p. 143; "Ruling Means Employers Now Face Various PPACA Deadlines," *BNA Bulletin to Management*, August 10, 2012, p. 222.
51. "Regulation Will Allow Young Adults Up to Age 26 to Retain Dependent Coverage," *BNA Bulletin to Management,* May 18, 2010, p. 153.
52. www.mercer.com/press-releases/1380755, accessed July 25, 2011.
53. Ibid.
54. "The Insured and the Unsure," *The Economist* 6 (January 20, 2013), p. 59.
55. Mark Lutes and Adam Solander, "Cadillac Tax Could Jeopardize Viability of Employer-Based Plans," *BNA Bulletin to Management*, November 27, 2012, p. 382.
56. Joanne Sammer, "How to Choose Health Insurance Exchanges," *HR Magazine*, October 2012, pp. 47–52.
57. See, for example, Karli Dunkelberger, "Avoiding COBRA's Bite: Three Keys to Compliance," *Compensation & Benefits Review*, March/April 2005, pp. 44–48. See also, Patrick Muldowney, "Cobra and the Stimulus Act: A Sign of Things to Come?" *Compensation & Benefits Review* 42, no. 1 (January/February 2010), pp. 24–49.
58. www.DOL.gov, accessed December 23, 2006.
59. Larri Short and Eileen Kahanar, "Unlocking the Secrets of the New Privacy Rules," *Occupational Hazards*, September 2002, pp. 51–54.
60. Kevin Maroney, "Prognosis Negative? GINA's Interim Incentives Ruling a Concern for Wellness Programs," *Compensation & Benefits Review* 42, no. 2 (2010), pp. 94–101.

61. Joanne Deschenaux, "Managing Leaves of Absence in California Is Complicated," *HR Magazine*, June 2011, p. 23.
62. David Tobenkin, "Learn the Landscape," *HR Magazine*, May 2011, pp. 51–53.
63. Katie Thomas, "Companies Get Straight on Health of Workers," *The New York Times* (March 20, 2013), p. B1.
64. http://insight.aon.com/?elqPURLPage=6567, accessed April 11, 2013.
65. "Hewitt Says Employer Measures to Control Increases in Health Care Costs Are Working," *BNA Bulletin to Management*, October 7, 2008, p. 323.
66. James Curcio, "Creating Standardized Metrics and Benchmarking for Health, Absence and Productivity Management Programs: The EMPAQ Initiative," *Compensation & Benefits Review* 42, no. 2 (2010), pp. 109–126.
67. Jerry Geisel, "Employers Accelerate Health Care Cost-Shifting," *Business Insurance* 45, no. 21 (May 23, 2011), pp. 3, 21.
68. Christine Keller and Christopher Condeluci, "Tax Relief and Health Care Act Should Prompt Re-Examination of HSAs," *SHRM Legal Report*, July–August 2007, p. 1.
69. In contrast, with health reimbursement arrangements (HRA) only the employer makes contributions. See "Types of Tax Favored Health Accounts," *HR Magazine*, August 2008, p. 76.
70. Michael Bond et al., "Using Health Savings Accounts to Provide Low-Cost Health-Care," *Compensation & Benefits Review*, March/April 2005, pp. 29–32.
71. Kathleen McGrory, "Big shift may come in retirees' coverage," *Miami Herald*, September 16, 2013, pp. 1B, 6B.
72. Alan Cohen, "Decision-Support in the Benefits Consumer Age," *Compensation & Benefits Review*, March/April 2006, pp. 46–51.
73. Ron Finch, "Preventive Services: Improving the Bottom Line for Employers and Employees," *Compensation & Benefits Review*, March/April 2005, p. 18. Note that prevention/wellness programs can run afoul of the Americans with Disabilities Act. So, for instance, employers should not make participation in such plans mandatory or use information obtained in such programs in such a way that violates ADA confidentiality requirements or discriminates against employees who are not physically fit. See "Despite Good Intentions, Wellness Plans Can Run Afoul of ADA, Attorney Cautions," *BNA Bulletin to Management* 56, no. 51 (December 20, 2005), p. 41.
74. "Employer Partners to Launch a Three-Year Wellness Initiative," *BNA Bulletin to Management*, August 7, 2007, p. 255. See also Drew Robb, "Benefits Choices: Educating the Consumer," *HR Magazine*, March 2011, pp. 29–30.
75. Susan Wells, "Wellness Rewards," *HR Magazine*, February 2012, pp. 67–69.
76. "On-Site Clinics Aimed at Cutting Costs, Promoting Wellness," *BNA Bulletin to Management*, March 25, 2008, p. 103. See also Susan Wells, "Navigating the Expanding Wellness Industry," *HR Magazine*, March 2011, pp. 45–50.
77. Ibid. See also Josh Cable, "The Road to Wellness," *Occupational Hazards*, April 2007, pp. 23–27.
78. George DeVries, "The Top 10 Wellness Trends for 2008 and Beyond," *Compensation & Benefits Review*, July/August 2008, pp. 60–63.
79. Susan Wells, "Getting Paid for Staying Well," *HR Magazine*, February 2010, p. 59.
80. Susan Ladika, "Some Firms Find In-House Clinics Just What the Doctor Ordered," *Workforce Management,* March 2011, pp. 6–7.
81. Vanessa Fuhrmanns, "Oops! As Health Plans Become More Complicated, They're Also Subject to a Lot More Costly Mistakes," *The Wall Street Journal*, January 24, 2005, p. R4.
82. Martha Frase, "Minimalist Health Coverage," *HR Magazine*, June 2009, pp. 107–112.
83. "HR Outsourcing: Managing Costs and Maximizing Provider Relations," *BNA, Inc.* 21, no. 11 (Washington, DC: November 2003), p. 10.
84. Bill Roberts, "Outsourcing in Turbulent Times," *HR Magazine*, November 2009, p. 45.
85. "To Cut Costs, Employers Considering Defined Contribution Health Insurance Plans," *BNA Bulletin to Management,* November 20, 2011, p. 377.
86. "One in Five Big Firms May Drop Coverage for Future Retirees, Health Survey Finds," *BNA Bulletin to Management*, December 12, 2002, p. 393. Reducing retiree benefits requires a preliminary legal review. See James McElligott Jr., "Retiree Medical Benefit Developments in the Courts, Congress, and EEOC," *Compensation & Benefits Review*, March/April 2005, pp. 23–28; Natalie Norfus, "Retiree Benefits: Does an Employer's Obligation to Pay Ever End?" *Compensation & Benefits Review*, January/February 2008, pp. 42–45; and Joanne Sammer, "Exit Strategy: Ending Retiree Medical Benefits," *HR Magazine*, September 2011, pp. 57–62.
87. Robert Christadore, "Benefits Purchasing Alliances: Creating Stability in an Unstable World," *Compensation & Benefits Review*, September/October 2001, pp. 49–53; Betty Liddick, "Going the Distance for Health Savings," *HR Magazine*, March 2007, pp. 51–55; J. Wojcik, "Employers Consider Short-Haul Medical Tourism," *Business Insurance* 43, no. 29 (August 24, 2009), pp. 1, 20.
88. Rita Pyrillis, "Self-Thought: Companies Ponder Bringing Insurance In-House," *Workforce Management,* April 2012, pp. 3–4.
89. David Tobenkin, "Spousal Exclusions on the Rise," *HR Magazine*, November 2011, pp. 55–56.
90. Rebecca Vesely, "A New Remedy Emerges for Spiraling Health Costs," *Workforce Management*, June 2012, p. 14.
91. "Dependent Eligibility Audits Can Help Rein in Health Care Costs, Analysts Say," *BNA Bulletin to Management*, September 9, 2008, p. 289.
92. Susan Galactica, "There's a Doctor on the Phone? Employers Dial-Up Telemedicine," *Workforce Management*, September 2012, p. 8.
93. Susan Wells, "Big Changes Considered," *HR Magazine*, June 2011, pp. 63–64.
94. Carolyn Hirschman, "Will Employers Take the Lead in Long-Term Care?" *HR Magazine*, March 1997, pp. 59–66. For recent perspective, see A. D. Postal, "Industry Ramps Up Opposition to LTC Program in Senate Health Bill," *National Underwriter* (Life & Health/Financial Services Edition) 113, no. 14 (July 20, 2009), pp. 10, 32.
95. See, for example, Nancy Woodward, "Part-Time Benefits: A Moving Target," *HR Magazine*, November 2012, pp. 61–64.
96. Bill Leonard, "Recipes for Part-Time Benefits," *HR Magazine*, April 2000, pp. 56–62.
97. Summarized from Stephen G. Barry, "Multinational Pooling: Financing Global Employee Benefits More Efficiently," *Benefits & Compensation Digest*, July 2009, Vol. 46 Issue 7, p40; www.insurope.com/MPooling.asp, accessed September 29, 2013.
98. Brenda Paik Sunoo, "Millions May Retire," *Workforce*, December 1997, p. 48. See also "Many Older Workers Choose to 'Un-Retire' or Not Retire at All," *Knight Ridder/ Tribune Business News*, September 28, 2003, item 03271012; Patrick Purcell, "Older Workers: Recent Trends in Employment and Retirement," *Journal of Deferred Compensation* 8, no. 3 (Spring 2003), pp. 30–54; and "For Many Seniors, a Job Beats Retirement," *Knight Ridder/Tribune Business News*, February 9, 2003, item 3040001.
99. The U.S. Treasury has reportedly spent most of the trust fund on other government programs, so that changes (for instance, in terms of reducing benefits, making people wait longer for benefits, or making some people pay more for benefits) will be necessary. John Kilgour, "Social Security in the 21st Century," *Compensation & Benefits Review* 42, no. 6 (2010), pp. 459–469.
100. http://www.ssa.gov/pressoffice/factsheets/colafacts2013.htm, accessed April 13, 2013.
101. Martocchio, *Strategic Compensation,* pp. 245–248; and Lin Grensing-Pophal, "A Pension Formula That Pays Off," *HR Magazine* (February 2003), pp. 58–62.
102. For one recent example of how to do this, see Gail Nichols, "Reviewing and Redesigning Retirement Plans," *Compensation & Benefits Review*, May/June 2008, pp. 40–47.
103. Many employers are considering terminating their plans but most employers are considering instead either ceasing benefits accruals for all participants or just for future participants. Michael Cotter, "The Big Freeze: The Next Phase in the Decline of Defined Benefit Plans," *Compensation & Benefits Review*, March/April 2009, pp. 44–53.
104. Patty Kujawa, "The Young and Not So Restless," *Workforce Management*, May 2012, p. 6). See also Joanne Sammer, "Are Defined Benefit Plans Dead?" *HR Magazine*, July 2012, pp. 29–32.
105. Patty Kujawa, "Young Workers Craving Defined Benefit Plans," *Workforce Management*, March 2011, p. 16.
106. Jessica Marquez, "More Workers Yanking Money Out of 401(k)s," *Workforce Management*, August 11, 2008, p. 4.
107. Nancy Pridgen, "The Duty to Monitor Appointed Fiduciaries Under ERISA," *Compensation & Benefits Review*, September/October 2007, pp. 46–51; "Individual 401(k) Plan Participant Can Sue Plan Fiduciary for Losses, Justices Rule," *BNA Bulletin to Management*, February 20, 2008, p. 65.
108. "Benefit Trends: Automatic Enrollment Takes Off," *Compensation & Benefits Review*, September/October 2008, p. 14.
109. For a discussion, see Jewel Esposito, "Avoiding 401(k) ERISA Disasters," *Compensation & Benefits Review* 42, no. 1 (January/February 2010), pp. 39–45.
110. Jack VanDerhei, "The Pension Protection Act and 401(k)s," *The Wall Street Journal*, April 20, 2008, p. 12.

111. Wyatt, "401(k) Conversion," p. 20.
112. "New Pension Law Plus a Recent Court Ruling Doom Age-Related Suits, Practitioners Say," *BNA Bulletin to Management* 57, no. 36 (September 5, 2006), pp. 281–282; and www.dol.gov/ebsa/FAQs/faq_consumer_cashbalanceplans.html, accessed January 9, 2010.
113. Harold Burlingame and Michael Gulotta, "Cash Balance Pension Plan Facilitates Restructuring the Workforce at AT&T," *Compensation & Benefits Review*, November/December 1998, pp. 25–31; Eric Lekus, "When Are Cash Balance Pension Plans the Right Choice?" *BNA Bulletin to Management*, January 28, 1999, p. 7; Jerry Geisel, "IRS Releases Long-Awaited Cash Balance Guidance," *Pensions & Investments* 38, no. 22 (November 1 2010), p. 22.
114. Rita Pyrillis, "Picking a PBM for '13," *Workforce Management*, June 2012, p. 8.
115. This is based on Eric Parmenter, "Employee Benefit Compliance Checklist," *Compensation & Benefits Review*, May/June 2002, pp. 29–38.
116. http://www.pbgc.gov/wr/benefits/payments/if-you-are-not-yet-receiving-benefits.html, accessed April 13, 2013.
117. Patrick Kiger, "Early-Retirement Plans Backfire, Driving Up Costs Instead of Cutting Them," *Workforce Management*, January 2004, pp. 66–68.
118. "Benefits Cost Control Solutions to Consider Now," *HR Focus* 80, no. 11 (November 2003), p. 1.
119. Johanna Rodgers, "Web Based Apps Simplify Employee Benefits," *Insurance and Technology* 28, no. 11 (November 2003), p. 21. See also www.benelogic.com/, accessed June 28, 2011.
120. Ibid.
121. Scott Harper, "Online Resources System Boosts Worker Awareness," *BNA Bulletin to Management*, April 10, 2007, p. 119.
122. Drew Robb, "A Total View of Employee Records," *HR Magazine*, August 2007, pp. 93–96.
123. Michelle Rafter, "Mobile Apps for Benefits Go from Luxury to Necessity," *Workforce Management*, June 2012, p. 3.
124. Brad Reagan, "Perks with a Payoff," *The Wall Street Journal*, October 24, 2011, p. r3.
125. Ibid.
126. Carolyn Hirschman, "Employees' Choice," *HR Magazine*, February 2006, pp. 95–99.
127. Joseph O'Connell, "Using Employee Assistance Programs to Avoid Crises," *Long Island Business News*, April 19, 2002, p. 10.
128. See Scott MacDonald et al., "Absenteeism and Other Workplace Indicators of Employee Assistance Program Clients and Matched Controls," *Employee Assistance Quarterly* 15, no. 3 (2000), pp. 51–58. See also Paul Courtis et al., "Performance Measures in the Employee Assistance Program," *Employee Assistance Quarterly* 19, no. 3 (2005), pp. 45–58.
129. See, for example, Donna Owens, "EAPs for a Diverse World," *HR Magazine*, October 2006, pp. 91–96.
130. "EAP Providers," *Workforce Management*, July 14, 2008, p. 16.
131. "Fathers Fighting to Keep Work–Life Balance Are Finding Employers Firmly in their Corner," *BNA Bulletin to Management* 56, no. 24 (June 14, 2005), p. 185.
132. Susan Wells, "Are You Too Family-Friendly?" *HR Magazine*, October 2007, pp. 35–39.
133. Maureen Hannay and Melissa Northam, "Low-Cost Strategies for Employee Retention," *Compensation & Benefits Review*, July/August 2000, pp. 65–72. See also Roseanne Geisel, "Responding to Changing Ideas of Family," *HR Magazine*, August 2004, pp. 89–98.
134. Patrick Kiger, "A Case for Childcare," *Workforce Management*, April 2004, pp. 34–40.
135. www.shrm.org/rewards/library, accessed December 23, 2006. See also Kathy Gurchiek, "Give Us Your Sick," *HR Magazine*, January 2007, pp. 91–93.
136. Kelli Earhart, R. Dennis Middlemist, and Willie Hopkins, "Elder Care: An Emerging Assistance Issue," *Employee Assistance Quarterly* 8, no. 3 (1993), pp. 1–10. See also "Finding a Balance Between Conflicting Responsibilities: Work and Caring for Aging Parents," *Monday Business Briefing*, July 7, 2004; and "Employers Feel Impact of Eldercare: Some Expanded Benefits for Workers," *Knight Ridder/Tribune Business News*, June 13, 2004, item 04165011.
137. Rudy Yandrick, "Elder Care Grows Up," *HR Magazine*, November 2001, pp. 72–77.
138. Marcus Butts et al., "How Important Are Work-Family Support Policies? A Meta-Analytic Investigation of Their Effects on Employee Outcomes," *Journal of Applied Psychology* 98, no. 1 (2013), pp. 1–25.
139. Susan Lambert, "Added Benefits: The Link Between Work Life Benefits and Organizational Citizenship Behavior," *Academy of Management Journal* 43, no. 5 (2000), pp. 801–815. Timothy Judge et al., "Work Family Conflict and Emotions: Effects at Work and Home," *Personnel Psychology* 59 (2006), pp. 779–814.
140. "Rising Gas Prices Prompting Employers to Consider Varied Computer Benefit Options," *BNA Bulletin to Management*, June 20, 2008, p. 201.
141. See "The 100 Best Companies to Work For," *Fortune*, February 6, 2012, p. 117.
142. Tamera Lionel, "Benefits for Older Workers," *HR Magazine*, March 2012, pp. 53–58.
143. Jennifer Schramm, "Undereducated," *HR Magazine*, September 2011, p. 136.
144. Richard Buddin and Kanika Kapur, "The Effect of Employer-Sponsored Education on Job Mobility: Evidence from the U.S. Navy," *Industrial Relations* 44, no. 2 (April 2005), pp. 341–363.
145. Mary Burke, Euren Esen, and Jessica Collison, "2003 Benefits Survey," SHRM/SHRM Foundation, 1800 Duke Street, Alexandria VA, 2003, p. 30. See also Michael Laff, "U.S. Employers Tighten Reins on Tuition Reimbursement," *Training & Development*, July 2006, p. 18.
146. Carolyn Shapiro, "More Companies Cover Benefits for Employee's Domestic Partners," *Knight-Ridder/Tribune Business News*, July 20, 2003.
147. "What You Need to Know to Provide Domestic Partner Benefits," *HR Focus* 80, no. 3 (August 2003), p. 3.
148. http://articles.washingtonpost.com/2013-06-26/politics/40195683_1_gay-couples-edith-windsor-doma Accessed August 1, 2013.
149. "Couples Want Flexible Leave, Benefits," *BNA Bulletin to Management*, February 19, 1998, p. 53; SHRM, "2003 Benefits Survey," p. 14. See also Paul Harris, "Flexible Work Policies Mean Business," *Training & Development*, April 2007, pp. 32–36.
150. Carolyn Hirshman, "Kinder, Simpler Cafeteria Rules," *HR Magazine*, January 2001, pp. 74–79.
151. "Employers Should Update Cafeteria Plans Now Based on Proposed Regs, Experts Say," *BNA Bulletin to Management*, September 4, 2007, pp. 281–282.
152. "Debit Cards for Health-Care Expenses Receive Increased Employer Attention," *BNA Bulletin to Management*, September 25, 2003, p. 305.
153. Martocchio, *Strategic Compensation*, p. 263.
154. Bill Roberts, "Good Vendor Relations," *HR Magazine*, September 2011, p. 110.
155. Ibid.
156. Elka Maria Torpey, "Flexible Work: Adjusting the When and Where of Your Job," *Occupational Outlook Quarterly*, Summer 2007, pp. 14–27.
157. "Slightly More Workers Are Skirting 9–5 Tradition," *BNA Bulletin to Management*, June 20, 2002, p. 197.
158. The percentage of employers with flextime programs actually dropped from 2007 to 2011, from 58% to 53%. Joseph Coombs, "Flexibility Still Meeting Resistance," *HR Magazine*, July 2011, p. 72.
159. Dori Meinert, "Make Telecommuting Pay Off," *HR Magazine*, June 2011, pp. 33–37. See also Donna Dennis et al., "Effective Leadership in a Virtual Workforce," *Training & Development*, February 2013, pp. 47–49.
160. "Telework Among Full-Time Employees Almost Doubled in the Last Decade, Study Says," *BNA Bulletin to Management*, June 12, 2012, p. 187.
161. "13.4 Million Work from Home in 2010, Census Bureau Reports," *BNA Bulletin to Management*, October 16, 2012, p. 330.
162. Martha White, "One Part Gone: Yahoo Says No to Telecommuting," www.CNBC.com/ID/100492123/, accessed February 25, 2013.
163. Dori Meinert, "Make Telecommuting Pay Off," *HR Magazine*, June 2011, pp. 33–37.
164. Ann Pomeroy, "The Future Is Now," *HR Magazine*, September 2007, pp. 46–52. Whether called telecommuting or telework, the proportion of all employees doing some portion of their work from home about doubled in the last decade to 2.1%. However, some jobs have much higher rates. For example, almost 45% of medical transcription is reportedly work from home. "Telework Among Full-Time Employees Almost Doubled in the Last Decade, Study Says," *BNA Bulletin to Management*, June 12, 2012, p. 187.
165. John Pletz, "Workers, Go Home," *Crain's Chicago Business* 34, no. 8 (February 21, 2011), pp. 2, 14.
166. Ibid.
167. See, for example, "Compressed Workweeks Gain Popularity, but Concerns Remain About Effectiveness," *BNA Bulletin to Management*, September 16, 2008, p. 297.
168. Boris Baltes et al., "Flexible and Compressed Workweek Schedules: A Meta-Analysis of Their Effects on Work-Related Criteria," *Journal of Applied Psychology* 84, no. 4 (1999), pp. 496–513. See also Charlotte Hoff, "With Flextime, Less Can Be More," *Workforce Management*, May 2005, pp. 65–66.
169. SHRM, "2003 Benefits Survey," p. 2.
170. "With Job Sharing Arrangements, Companies Can Get Two Employees for the Price of One," *BNA Bulletin to Management* 56, no. 47 (November 22, 2005), pp. 369–370.

PART FIVE Enrichment Topics in Human Resource Management

14 Ethics, Employee Relations, and Fair Treatment at Work

Source: Bloomberg/Getty Images

MyManagementLab®

Improve Your Grade!

When you see this icon, visit **www.mymanagementlab.com** for activities that are applied, personalized, and offer immediate feedback.

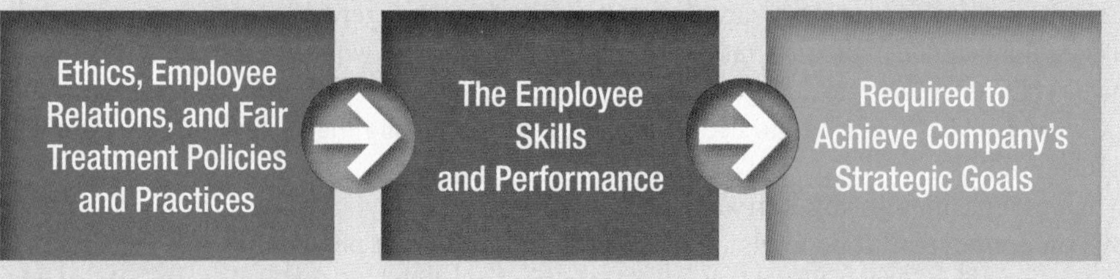

For a bird's eye view of how one company created a new discipline program to improve its strategic performance, read the Hotel Paris case on page 451 and answer the questions after reading the chapter.

WHERE ARE WE NOW . . .

Although many view the topics in Chapters 1–13 (recruitment, selection, appraisal, training, and compensation) as the heart of human resource management, most employees expect something more. For example, they expect their employers to treat them fairly, and to have a safe work environment. Now, in Part Five, we therefore turn to ethics, employee fairness, safety, and union relations. The main purpose of this chapter is to explain ethics, employee rights, and fair treatment, all building blocks for positive employee relations. Our topics include basics of ethics and fair treatment at work; what shapes ethical behavior at work?; using human resource management tools to promote ethics and fair treatment; managing employee discipline; and managing employee relations.

LEARNING OBJECTIVES

1. Explain what is meant by ethical behavior at work.
2. Discuss important factors that shape ethical behavior at work.
3. Describe at least four specific ways in which HR management can influence ethical behavior at work.
4. Employ fair disciplinary practices.
5. Explain what is meant by employee relations and what employers can do to improve it.

After a worker uprising over pay and work rules at Apple Inc.'s Foxconn iPhone assembly plant in Shenzhen, China, Apple asked the plant's owner to have the Fair Labor Association (FLA) survey the plant's workers. The FLA found "tons of issues."[1] We'll see what they found and what Foxconn's management did to save the situation.

Basics of Ethics and Fair Treatment at Work

1 Explain what is meant by ethical behavior at work.

Managers face ethical issues every day. As an example, one manager had a proposal on her desk from a firm that supplies software monitoring tools. These tools would enable her company to scrutinize what its employees and job candidates said and did on social networking sites like Facebook and LinkedIn. She had to decide if purchasing and using the monitoring software was a good idea.[2]

Is using such monitoring software acceptable, or would you view it as unethical—as "spying" on employees? It depends in part on what your ethical perspective is.

Since most everyone reading this book rightfully views himself or herself as an ethical person, why include ethics in this book? For three reasons. First, ethics is not theoretical. Instead, it greases the wheels that make businesses work. Managers who promise raises but don't deliver, salespeople who say "the order's coming" when it's not, production managers who take kickbacks from suppliers—they all corrode the trust that day-to-day business transactions depend on. According to one lawsuit, marketers for Pfizer Inc. influenced the company to suppress unfavorable studies about one of its drugs; now plaintiffs are suing for billions.[3]

Second, human resource decisions are loaded with ethical consequences (which is why the HRCI includes HR Ethics in its Knowledge Base).[4] For example, "My team shouldn't work on the machine until I've checked it for safety, but my boss is in a hurry: What should I do?"

Third, most employers strive to maintain positive employee relations between themselves and their employees. Doing so is impossible if employees view the company or its managers as unethical.

Let's look first at what *ethics* means.

The Meaning of Ethics

ethics
The principles of conduct governing an individual or a group; specifically, the standards you use to decide what your conduct should be.

Ethics are "the principles of conduct governing an individual or a group"—the principles people use to decide what their conduct should be.[5] However, ethical decisions don't include just any type of conduct. Deciding which car to buy generally won't involve ethics. Instead, ethical decisions are always rooted in morality. *Morality* means society's accepted standards of behavior, and always involves basic questions of right and wrong such as stealing, murder, and how to treat other people. How to treat employees is therefore usually as much of an ethical question as a legal one.[6]

Ethics and the Law

In fact, the law is a far-from-perfect guide to what is ethical, because something may be legal but not right, or right but not legal. Firing a 38-year-old employee with 20 years' tenure without reason or notice may be unethical, but still legal, for instance. A vice president for business practices at United Technologies Corp. (and a former trial lawyer) put it this way: "*Ethics* means making decisions that represent what you stand for, not just what the laws are."[7]

The law may not be a foolproof guide to what's ethical, but some managers treat it as if it is. Businesses exist to produce a profit, so profitability tends to be the initial screen managers use to make decisions. After profits comes, "Is it legal?" Unfortunately, they may then ask "Is it ethical" only as an afterthought, if at all.

KNOWLEDGE BASE

Ethics, Public Policy, and Employee Rights

Societies don't rely on employers' ethics or sense of fairness or morality to ensure that they do what's right. Societies also institute laws. These lay out what employers can and cannot do; for instance, in terms of their hiring. In so doing, these laws also carve out explicit rights for employees. For example, Title VII of The Civil Rights Act gives an employee the right to bring legal charges against an employer if he or she believes it discriminated against him or her due to race. Figure 14-1 lists some legal areas under which workers have rights.

UNALIENABLE RIGHTS However, not all rights derive from laws. Many rights flow from broader unwritten "human" or "unalienable rights," broad, unwritten beliefs that people hold.[8] For example, the U.S. Declaration of Independence famously states, "*We hold these truths to be self-evident, that all men are created equal, that they are endowed by their Creator with certain unalienable Rights, that among these are Life, Liberty and the pursuit of Happiness.*"

FIGURE 14-1 Partial List of Legal Areas under Which Workers Have Legal Rights

- Leave of absence and vacation rights
- Injuries and illnesses rights
- Noncompete agreement rights
- Employees' rights on employer policies
- Discipline rights
- Rights on personnel files
- Employee pension rights
- Employee benefits rights
- References rights
- Rights on criminal records
- Employee distress rights
- Defamation rights
- Employees' rights on fraud
- Rights on assault and battery
- Employee negligence rights
- Rights on political activity
- Union/group activity rights
- Whistleblower rights
- Workers' compensation rights

PUBLIC POLICY Although many laws, such as Title VII, aim to guarantee rights that some people view as unalienable, reasonable people may differ over what the exact laws should be.

Most laws therefore also reflect public policy. In other words, governments enact laws so as to further their public policy aims. Thus, if New York City decides that it's in its' citizens' best interests to require all its businesses to provide employee sick leaves, it may pass a law to do that. *Public policy* "consists of political decisions for implementing programs to achieve societal goals."[9] As with sick leave laws, governments express their chosen public policies in the laws and regulations they set.

So, for example, the National Labor Relations Act established the right of employees to engage in collective bargaining. The Landrum Griffin Act contained a "Bill of Rights" for union members, protecting them from mistreatment from their unions. The Fair Labor Standards Act gave employees the right to a minimum wage and overtime pay. The Occupational Safety and Health Act gave employees the right to refuse to work under unsafe conditions. The bottom line is that although ethics, fairness, and morality do help govern how employers treat their employees, the enforceable rights embedded in employment and other laws also govern what employers do.

Workplace Unfairness

One way a company's ethics manifest themselves is in how fairly it treats its employees. Anyone who's suffered unfair treatment at work knows it is demoralizing. Unfair treatment reduces morale, increases stress, and has negative effects on performance.[10] Employees of abusive supervisors are more likely to quit, and to report lower job and life satisfaction and higher stress.[11] The effects on employees of such abusiveness are particularly pronounced where the abusive supervisors seem to have support from higher-ups.[12]

Sometimes workplace unfairness is subtle. For example, unstated policies requiring CPA associates to work and travel 7 days per week may unfairly eliminate working mothers from partner tracks. Other unfairness is more blatant. For example, one survey of 1,000 U.S. employees concluded that about 45% said they had worked for abusive bosses.[13] At work, *fair treatment* reflects concrete actions such as "employees are treated with respect," and "employees are treated fairly" (see Figure 14-2).[14]

Why Treat Employees Fairly?

There are many reasons why managers should be fair. The golden rule is one obvious reason. What may not be so obvious is that supervisory unfairness can backfire on the company. For example, victims of unfairness exhibit more workplace deviance, such as theft and sabotage.[15] Perceptions of fairness relate to enhanced employee commitment; enhanced satisfaction with the organization, jobs, and leaders; and enhanced organizational citizenship behaviors.[16] People who view themselves as victims of unfairness also suffer a range of ill effects including poor health, strain, and psychological conditions.[17] Unfairness leads to increased tensions between the employee and his or her family or partner.[18] Aggressive supervisors undermine their subordinates' effectiveness and may prompt them to act destructively.[19]

EXAMPLE A study illustrates how unfairness works. College instructors first completed surveys concerning the extent to which they saw their colleges as treating them with *procedural* and

FIGURE 14-2 Perceptions of Fair Interpersonal Treatment Scale

Source: "The Perceptions of Their Interpersonal Treatment Scale: Development and Validation of a Measure of Interpersonal Treatment in the Workplace" by Michelle A. Donovan, from *Journal of Applied Psychology*, 1998, Volume 83(5).

What is your organization like most of the time? Circle yes if the item describes your organization, No if it does not describe your organization, and ? if you cannot decide.

IN THIS ORGANIZATION:

1. Employees are praised for good work	Yes	?	No
2. Supervisors yell at employees (R)	Yes	?	No
3. Supervisors play favorites (R)	Yes	?	No
4. Employees are trusted	Yes	?	No
5. Employees' complaints are dealt with effectively	Yes	?	No
6. Employees are treated like children (R)	Yes	?	No
7. Employees are treated with respect	Yes	?	No
8. Employees' question and problems are responded to quickly	Yes	?	No
9. Employees are lied to (R)	Yes	?	No
10. Employees' suggestions are ignored (R)	Yes	?	No
11. Supervisors swear at employees (R)	Yes	?	No
12. Employees' hard work is appreciated	Yes	?	No
13. Supervisors threaten to fire or lay off employees (R)	Yes	?	No
14. Employees are treated fairly	Yes	?	No
15. Coworkers help each other out	Yes	?	No
16. Coworkers argue with each other (R)	Yes	?	No
17. Coworkers put each other down (R)	Yes	?	No
18. Coworkers treat each other with respect	Yes	?	No

Note: R = the item is reverse scored

procedural justice
The fairness of the process.

distributive justice
The fairness and justice of a decision's result.

distributive justice. (**Procedural justice** refers to fair processes; **distributive justice** refers to fair outcomes.) Procedural justice items included, for example, "In general, the department/college's procedures allow for requests for clarification or for additional information about a decision." Distributive justice items included, "I am fairly rewarded considering the responsibilities I have." Then the instructors completed organizational commitment questionnaires, with items such as "I am proud to tell others that I am part of this department/college." Their students then completed surveys, with items such as "The instructor was sympathetic to my needs," and "The instructor treated me fairly."

The results were impressive. Instructors who perceived high distributive and procedural justice were more committed. Furthermore, these instructors' students reported higher levels of instructor effort, prosocial behaviors, and fairness, and had more positive reactions to their instructors.[20] The accompanying HR Practices around the Globe feature shows how one employer in China improved its treatment of employees.

IMPROVING PERFORMANCE: HR Practices Around the Globe

The Foxconn Plant in Shenzhen, China

social responsibility
The extent to which companies should and do channel resources toward improving one or more segments of society other than the firm's owners or stockholders.

The phrase *social responsibility* tends to trigger images of charitable contributions and helping the homeless, but it actually refers to much more. For example, it refers to the honesty of the company's ads, to the quality of the parts it builds into its products; and to the honesty, ethics, fairness, and "rightness" of its dealings with customers, suppliers, and, of course, employees. The basic question is always whether the company is serving all its constituencies (or "stakeholders") fairly and honestly. Corporate **social responsibility** thus refers to the extent to which companies should and do channel resources toward improving one or more segments of society other than the firm's owners or stockholders.[21]

The worker uprising at Apple's Foxconn iPhone assembly plant in Shenzhen, China, shows that workers around the globe want their employers to treat them in a fair and socially responsible manner.

After the walkouts, Apple Inc. asked the Fair Labor Association (FLA) to survey the plant's workers. The FLA found "tons of issues."[22] For example, employees faced "overly strict" product-quality demands without adequate training: "Every job is tagged to time, there are targets on how many things must be completed within an hour," said Xie Xiaogang, 22, who worked at Foxconn's Shenzhen plant. ". . . In this environment, many people cannot take it."[23] Heavy overtime work requirements and having to work through a holiday week were other examples.

Hon Hai, the Foxconn plant's owner, soon changed its plant human resource practices, for instance, raising salaries and cutting mandatory overtime. Those changes were among 284 made by Foxconn after the audits uncovered violations of Chinese regulations.[24] The changes show that fair treatment is a global obligation.

Discussion Question 14-1: How would you explain the fact that workers in such diverse cultures as America and China seem to covet fair treatment?

Bullying and Victimization

Some unfairness is blatant. Bullying—singling out someone to harass and mistreat—is an increasingly serious problem. The U.S. government (www.stopbullying.gov/#) points out that while definitions of bullying vary, most would agree that bullying involves three things:

- ***Imbalance of power.*** People who bully use their power to control or harm, and the people being bullied may have a hard time defending themselves.
- ***Intent to cause harm.*** Actions done by accident are not bullying; the person bullying has a goal to cause harm.
- ***Repetition.*** Incidents of bullying happen to the same person over and over by the same person or group, and that bullying can take many forms, such as:
  - ***Verbal:*** name-calling, teasing
  - ***Social:*** spreading rumors, leaving people out on purpose, breaking up friendships
  - ***Physical:*** hitting, punching, shoving
  - ***Cyberbullying:*** using the Internet, mobile phones, or other digital technologies to harm others

Employers must have systems in place (such as grievance procedures and policies to monitor employees' harassing use of social media websites) to ensure that the company can and does deal with such unfair treatment.[25]

Undoubtedly, the perpetrator is to blame for bullying. However, how some people behave and their personalities do make them more likely victims.[26] Those "more likely" include submissive victims (who seem more anxious, cautious, quiet, and sensitive), provocative victims (who show more aggressive behavior), and victims low in self-determination (who seem to leave it to others to make decisions for them).

RESEARCH INSIGHT A study illustrates the interpersonal dynamics involved. Research suggests that people with higher intellectual capability often suffer bullying at school—for instance, derogatory names such as *geek* and *nerd.* In this study, 217 employees of a health-care organization completed a survey that measured cognitive ability, victimization, and how the person behaved at work.[27] The researchers found that it wasn't just whether the person was smart that determined if he or she was victimized. Instead, people with high cognitive ability who *also* behaved more independently were more likely to be bullied. Smart team players were less likely to be victimized. In any case, punishing those who engage in workplace aggression is essential.[28]

What Shapes Ethical Behavior at Work?

2 Discuss important factors that shape ethical behavior at work.

Why do people do bad things? It's complicated. However one review of over 30 years of ethics research concluded that three factors combine to determine the ethical choices we make.[29] The authors titled their paper "Bad Apples, Bad Cases, and Bad Barrels." This title highlighted their conclusion that when

> "Bad apples" (people who are inclined to make unethical choices), must deal with "Bad cases" (ethical situations that are ripe for unethical choices), while working in
>
> "Bad barrels" (company environments that foster or condone unethical choices), . . . then this brew combines to determine whether or not someone acts ethically.

Here's a closer look at what they found.

The Person (What Makes Bad Apples?)

Because people bring to their jobs their own ideas of what is morally right and wrong, each person must shoulder much of the credit (or blame) for his or her ethical choices.

Some people are just more principled. For example, researchers surveyed CEOs to study the CEOs' intentions to engage in two questionable practices: soliciting a competitor's technological secrets, and making illegal payments to foreign officials. The researchers concluded that the CEOs' personal predispositions more strongly affected their decisions than did outside pressures or characteristics of their firms.[30] Most importantly, people differ in their level of "cognitive moral development." The most principled people, with the highest level of cognitive moral development, think through the implications of their decisions and apply ethical principles.

TRAITS We can also draw several conclusions about the traits of ethical or unethical people. "Moral disengagement" is a big factor.[31] People who are "morally disengaged" (more likely to do unethical things without feeling distressed—they might say, for instance that "people who get mistreated have usually done something to bring it on themselves") are much more likely to engage in unethical behavior.

Age may be a factor, too. One study surveyed 421 employees to measure the degree to which various traits correlated with ethical decisions. (Decisions included "doing personal business on company time" and "calling in sick to take a day off for personal use.") Older workers generally had stricter interpretations of ethical standards and made more ethical decisions than did younger ones.

Honesty testing (as we discussed in Chapter 6) also shows that some people are more inclined to make the wrong ethical choice. How would you rate your own ethics? Figure 14-3 presents a short self-assessment survey (you'll find other survey takers' answers on page 452).

Which Ethical Situations Make for Bad (Ethically Dangerous) Situations?

But, it's not just the person but the type of ethical decision that he or she confronts. Perhaps surprisingly, "smaller" ethical dilemmas prompt more bad choices. What determines "small"? Basically, how much harm can befall victims of the choice, or the number of people potentially affected by the choice. So in "less serious" situations it's more likely someone will say, in effect, "It's okay to do this, even though it's wrong."

What Are the "Bad Barrels"?—The Outside Factors That Mold Ethical Choices

Finally, the study concluded that some companies produce more poisonous social environments ("barrels") than do others; these environments in turn influence each employee's ethical choices.[32]

For example, companies that promote an "everyone for him- or herself" culture were more likely to suffer from unethical choices. Those that encouraged employees to consider the well-being of everyone had more ethical choices. Furthermore, a company whose managers put in place "a strong ethical culture that clearly communicates the range of acceptable and unacceptable behavior is associated with fewer unethical decisions in the workplace."[33] What follows are specific steps managers take to create a more ethical environment.

JOB-RELATED PRESSURES If people did unethical things at work solely for personal gain, it perhaps would be understandable (though inexcusable). The scary thing is that it's often not personal interests but the pressures of the job. As one former executive said at his trial, "I took these actions, knowing they were wrong, in a misguided attempt to preserve the company to allow it to withstand what I believed were temporary financial difficulties."[34]

One study illustrates this. It asked employees to list their reasons for taking unethical actions at work.[35] For most of these employees, "meeting schedule pressures," "meeting overly aggressive financial or business objectives," and "helping the company survive" were the three top causes. "Advancing my own career or financial interests" ranked about last.[36] In any case, reducing such "outside" pressures is crucial for heading off ethical lapses.

PRESSURE FROM THE BOSS It's hard to resist even subtle pressure from one's boss. According to one report, for instance, "the level of misconduct at work dropped dramatically when employees

The spread of technology into the workshop has raised a variety of new ethical questions and many old ones still linger. Compare your answers with those of other Americans surveyed, on page 452.

Office Technology

1. Is it wrong to use company e-mail for personal reasons?
   ☐ Yes ☐ No
2. Is it wrong to use office equipment to help your children or spouse do schoolwork?
   ☐ Yes ☐ No
3. Is it wrong to play computer games on office equipment during the workday?
   ☐ Yes ☐ No
4. Is it wrong to use office equipment to do Internet shopping?
   ☐ Yes ☐ No
5. Is it unethical to blame an error you made on a technological glitch?
   ☐ Yes ☐ No
6. Is it unethical to visit pornographic Web sites using office equipment?
   ☐ Yes ☐ No

Gifts and Entertainment

7. What's the value at which a gift from a supplier or client becomes troubling?
   ☐ $25 ☐ $50 ☐ $100
8. Is a $50 gift to a boss unacceptable?
   ☐ Yes ☐ No
9. Is a $50 gift *from* the boss unacceptable?
   ☐ Yes ☐ No
10. Of gifts from suppliers: Is it OK to take a $200 pair of football tickets?
    ☐ Yes ☐ No
11. Is it OK to take a $120 pair of theater tickets?
    ☐ Yes ☐ No
12. Is it OK to take a $100 holiday food basket?
    ☐ Yes ☐ No
13. Is it OK to take a $25 gift certificate?
    ☐ Yes ☐ No
14. Can you accept a $75 prize won at a raffle at a supplier's conference?
    ☐ Yes ☐ No

Truth and Lies

15. Due to on-the-job pressure, have you ever abused or lied about sick days?
    ☐ Yes ☐ No
16. Due to on-the-job pressure, have you ever taken credit for someone else's work or idea?
    ☐ Yes ☐ No

FIGURE 14-3 ***The Wall Street Journal*** **Workplace Ethics Quiz**

Source: Ethics and Compliance Office Association, Waltham, MA and The Ethical Leadership Group, Global Compliance's Expert Advisors, Wilmette, IL. (printed in *The Wall Street Journal,* October 21, 1999: B1–B4). © 1999 by Ethics and Compliance Office Association. Reprinted by permission. All rights reserved.

said their supervisors exhibited ethical behavior."[37] Yet, in another poll, only about 27% of employees strongly agreed that their organizations' leadership is ethical.[38]

Examples of how supervisors lead subordinates astray ethically include:

- Tell staffers to do whatever is necessary to achieve results.
- Overload top performers to ensure that work gets done.
- Look the other way when wrongdoing occurs.
- Take credit for others' work or shift blame.[39]

ETHICS POLICIES AND CODES An ethics policy and code is another "outside force" that employers can use to signal that their companies are serious about ethics. For example, IBM's code of ethics says, in part:

> Neither you nor any member of your family may, directly or through others, solicit or accept from anyone money, a gift, or any amenity that could influence or could reasonably give the appearance of influencing IBM's business relationship with that person or organization. If you or your family members receive a gift (including money), even if the gift was unsolicited, you must notify your manager and take appropriate measures, which may include returning or disposing of what you received.[40]

Some firms also urge employees to apply a quick "ethics test" to evaluate whether what they're about to do fits the company's code of conduct. For example, Raytheon Co. asks employees who face ethical dilemmas to ask:

Is the action legal?
Is it right?
Who will be affected?
Does it fit Raytheon's values?
How will it "feel" afterward?
How will it look in the newspaper?
Will it reflect poorly on the company?[41]

ENFORCEMENT Codifying the rules without enforcing them is futile. As one study of ethics concludes, "strong statements by managers may reduce the risk of legal and ethical violations by their work forces, but enforcement of standards has the greatest impact."[42] More firms, such as Lockheed Martin Corp., therefore appoint chief ethics officers.[43] *Ethics audits* typically address topics like conflicts of interest, giving and receiving gifts, employee discrimination, and access to company information.[44]

WHISTLEBLOWERS Some companies encourage employees to use hotlines and other means to "blow the whistle" on the company when they discover fraud. In complying with the Dodd-Frank Act, the SEC recently established a whistleblower reward for people who report unethical corporate behavior to it.[45] It is also tracking possible incidents of retaliation against whistleblowers.[46]

organizational culture
The characteristic values, traditions, and behaviors a company's employees share.

THE ORGANIZATION'S CULTURE Employees get their signals about what's acceptable not just from what managers say, but from what they do.[47] For instance, a CEO who posts an ethics code and then ignores it in what he or she actually does sends the wrong signal to employees. Those signals then mold the company's **organizational culture**. Culture is the "characteristic values, traditions, and behaviors a company's employees share." A *value* is a basic belief about what is right or wrong, or about what you should or shouldn't do. ("Honesty is the best policy" would be a value.) Values are important because they guide behavior. Managing people and shaping their behavior therefore depends on shaping the values they use as behavioral guides. For example, if management really believes "honesty is the best policy," the actions it takes should reflect this value. Managers therefore have to think through how to send the right signals to their employees—in other words, create the right culture. Doing so includes:

- ***Clarifying expectations.*** First, managers should make clear what values they want subordinates to follow. For example, the IBM ethics statement makes it clear the company takes ethics seriously.
- ***Using signs and symbols.*** *Symbolism* –what the manager actually does and thus the signals he or she sends—ultimately does the most to create and sustain the company's culture. Managers need to "walk the talk." They can't say "don't fudge the financials" and then do so themselves.
- ***Providing physical support.*** The physical manifestations of the manager's values—the firm's incentive plan, appraisal system, and disciplinary procedures, for instance—send strong signals regarding what employees should and should not do. Does the firm reward ethical behavior or penalize it?[48]

FRAUD CONTROLS Fraud controls reduce occupational fraud. For example, the Association of Certified Fraud Examiners found that fraud controls such as hotlines, surprise audits, fraud training for employees, and mandatory vacations can each reduce internal theft by around 50%.[49]

In Summary: Some Guidelines to Keep in Mind When Managing Ethical Behavior at Work

Here in a nutshell is what research findings suggest for managers:[50]

- Ethical behavior starts with *moral awareness*. Does the person even recognize that a moral issue exists in the situation?

- *Managers* should influence employee ethics by carefully cultivating the right norms, leadership, reward systems, and culture.
- Ethics suffer when people undergo *moral disengagement*. For example, you're more likely to harm others when you view the victims as "outsiders."
- The most powerful morality comes from *within*. In effect, when the moral person asks, "Why be moral?" the answer is, "because that is who I am."[51]
- *Highly challenging goals* pursued blindly and job pressures can contribute to unethical behavior.[52] For example, "A sales goal of $147 an hour can lead auto mechanics to 'repair' things that weren't broken."[53]
- Don't reward *bad behavior*. Don't promote someone who got a big sale through devious means.[54]
- *Punish unethical behavior*. Employees expect you to discipline the perpetrators.
- The degree to which employees *openly talk about ethics* is a good predictor of ethical conduct.
- Be aware that people tend to alter their *moral compasses* when they join organizations. They uncritically equate "what's best for this organization (or team, or department)" with "what's the right thing to do?" The accompanying HR Tools feature applies this to the small business.

IMPROVING PERFORMANCE: HR Tools for Line Managers and Entrepreneurs

Small Business Ethics

When people think of unethical corporate behavior, big companies come to mind, because they're usually in the headlines. Yet studies show that small and midsize enterprises are prone to the same unethical corporate behavior as big firms.

For example, one study of 20 small to midsize firms found that bribery, corrupt dealings, payoffs to local gangsters, and a general tone of dishonesty were all "business as usual" at many of these firms.[55] Sometimes, they were clever about their corrupt dealings. When doing business abroad, one U.S. business tried to keep its hands clean by forming a "strategic alliance" with a local firm. The latter then did the dirty work, for example, handling the local bribes, while the U.S. firm's managers looked the other way.

There are several reasons why smaller firms have to be particularly alert to unethical behavior. Small firms don't have the resources for ethics officers, ethics hotlines, or the ethics training that big firms have. Furthermore, having an unethical accountant in a billion-dollar firm embezzle $10 million is a nuisance. Having the sales manager of a $10 million firm walk off with $1 million cash could be the end.

Small business owners can take several steps to establish a useful ethics program. First, *size up your company's current ethics-related activities*. Even a self-audit based on guidelines like those in this chapter (the availability of an ethics code, ethics training, internal controls to monitor ethical behavior, and so on) can be worthwhile, Second, *create a code of conduct (Googling "code of conduct" will reveal thousands of examples)*, and make it clear that you take it seriously. Third, *train your people*. Training needn't be complicated. For example, one expert suggests having your managers develop scenarios, relevant to your business, illustrating which behaviors are ethical and which are not; then meet to discuss these. Fourth, make it easier to *solicit feedback* from your employees, so that they can more easily provide you with suspicions of unethical behavior. ("Open door" polices and anonymous suggestion boxes are examples.) And, perhaps most importantly, *walk the talk*. In a small business, the owner or CEO is so visible that employees will take their ethical signals from him or her.

Discussion Question 14-2: Create a 50-word ethics code for a small business.

Using Human Resource Management Tools to Promote Ethics and Fair Treatment

3 Describe at least four specific ways in which HR management can influence ethical behavior at work.

The manager has various human resource management tools he or she can use to foster ethics and fair treatment. We'll address these next.

HR in Practice at the Hotel Paris As the head of HR for the Hotel Paris, Lisa Cruz was especially concerned about her company maintaining the highest ethical standards. To show how she handled this, see the case on page 451 of this chapter.

Selection Tools

One writer says, "The simplest way to tune up an organization, ethically speaking, is to hire more ethical people."[56] "Screening for ethics" should start before applicants even apply; use recruitment materials that emphasize the firm's commitment to ethics. (Figure 14-4 is an example.) Managers can then use screening tools like honesty tests, background checks, and questions such as "Have you ever observed someone stretching the rules at work? What did you do about it?"[57] Also, treat job applicants fairly. "If prospective employees perceive that the hiring process does not treat people fairly, they may assume that ethical behavior is not important in the company."[58]

Training Tools

Ethics training is basically mandatory. Since 1991, federal sentencing guidelines have prescribed reduced penalties for employers accused of misconduct who implement codes of conduct and ethics training.[59] The Sarbanes-Oxley Act of 2002 makes ethics training even more important.

Ethics training usually involves showing employees how to recognize ethical dilemmas, how to apply codes of conduct to resolve problems, and how to use personnel activities like disciplinary practices in ethical ways.[60] The training should emphasize the moral underpinnings of the ethical choice and the company's deep commitment to integrity and ethics. Include participation by top managers in the program to emphasize that commitment.[61]

Improving Performance Through HRIS: Complying with Sarbanes-Oxley

Particularly in very large companies, managing ethics programs isn't easy or cheap. Doing so requires the almost continuous attention of the company's top managers, as well as investments in setting up and monitoring ethics codes and training employees. The Sarbanes-Oxley Act of 2002 "has added a wide range of new issues to the traditional compliance function."[62]

Larger firms need a cost-effective way of offering the necessary training. Ethics training is therefore often Internet-based. For example, Lockheed Martin's 160,000 employees take ethics and legal compliance training via the firm's intranet. Lockheed's online ethics program software also keeps track of how well the company and its employees are doing in terms of maintaining high ethical standards—monitoring ethics failures, for instance.[63] Online ethics training

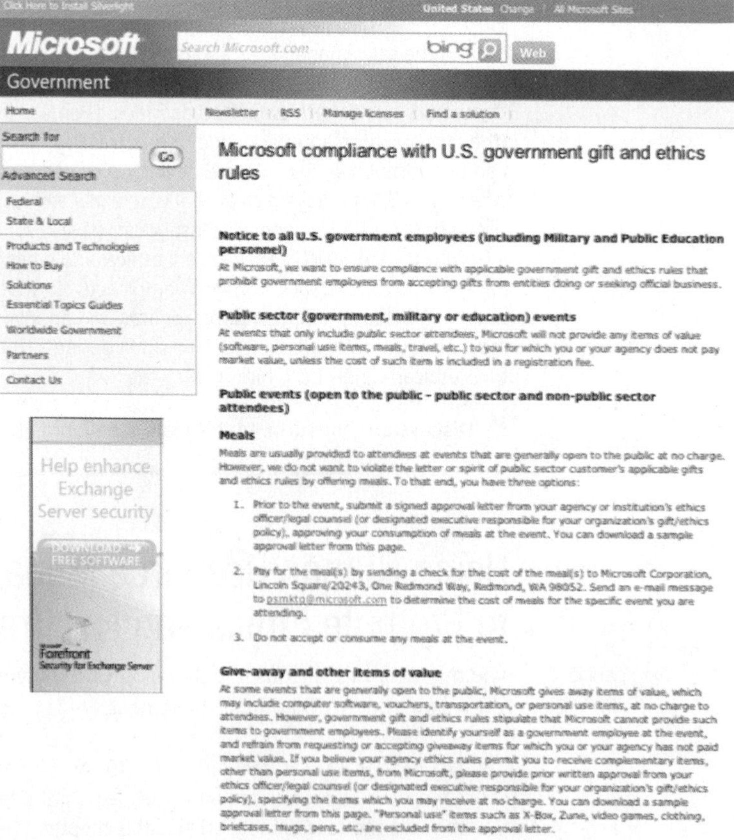

Click Here to Install Silverlight | United States Change | All Microsoft Sites

Microsoft | Search Microsoft.com | bing | Web

Government

Home | Newsletter | RSS | Manage licenses | Find a solution

Search for | Go | Advanced Search

Federal
State & Local
Products and Technologies
How to Buy
Solutions
Essential Topics Guides
Worldwide Government
Partners
Contact Us

Help enhance Exchange Server security
DOWNLOAD FREE SOFTWARE
Forefront Security for Exchange Server

Microsoft compliance with U.S. government gift and ethics rules

Notice to all U.S. government employees (including Military and Public Education personnel)

At Microsoft, we want to ensure compliance with applicable government gift and ethics rules that prohibit government employees from accepting gifts from entities doing or seeking official business.

Public sector (government, military or education) events

At events that only include public sector attendees, Microsoft will not provide any items of value (software, personal use items, meals, travel, etc.) to you for which you or your agency does not pay market value, unless the cost of such item is included in a registration fee.

Public events (open to the public - public sector and non-public sector attendees)

Meals

Meals are usually provided to attendees at events that are generally open to the public at no charge. However, we do not want to violate the letter or spirit of public sector customer's applicable gifts and ethics rules by offering meals. To that end, you have three options:

1. Prior to the event, submit a signed approval letter from your agency or institution's ethics officer/legal counsel (or designated executive responsible for your organization's gift/ethics policy), approving your consumption of meals at the event. You can download a sample approval letter from this page.
2. Pay for the meal(s) by sending a check for the cost of the meal(s) to Microsoft Corporation, Lincoln Square/20243, One Redmond Way, Redmond, WA 98052. Send an e-mail message to psmktg@microsoft.com to determine the cost of meals for the specific event you are attending.
3. Do not accept or consume any meals at the event.

Give-away and other items of value

At some events that are generally open to the public, Microsoft gives away items of value, which may include computer software, vouchers, transportation, or personal use items, at no charge to attendees. However, government gift and ethics rules stipulate that Microsoft cannot provide such items to government employees. Please identify yourself as a government employee at the event, and refrain from requesting or accepting giveaway items for which you or your agency has not paid market value. If you believe your agency ethics rules permit you to receive complementary items, other than personal use items, from Microsoft, please provide prior written approval from your ethics officer/legal counsel (or designated executive responsible for your organization's gift/ethics policy), specifying the items which you may receive at no charge. You can download a sample approval letter from this page. "Personal use" items such as X-Box, Zune, video games, clothing, briefcases, mugs, pens, etc. are excluded from the approval letter.

FIGURE 14-4 Using the Company Website to Emphasize Ethics

Source: Screenshot courtesy of Microsoft Corporation.

tools include *Business Ethics for Managers* from SkillSoft (skillsoft.com).[64] Some employers are switching from packaged ethics training to more company-relevant customized programs. For example, Yahoo! had a vendor produce an animated package containing ethical scenarios set in Yahoo! company offices around the world. The 45-minute program covers Yahoo!'s code of conduct as well as issues like the Foreign Corrupt Practices Act.[65]

Performance Appraisal Tools

Unfair appraisals send the signal that the employer may condone unethical behavior. At a minimum:

- The employees' standards should be clear.
- Employees should understand the basis on which they're going to be appraised.
- The supervisor should perform the appraisal objectively and fairly.[66]
- The employer should include ethics goals in appraisals of its leaders, particularly its senior leaders.[67]

Employee Privacy Policies[68]

Like unfair appraisals, most employees view invasions of their privacy as both unethical and unfair. At work, employee privacy violations include *intrusion* (such as locker room and e-mail surveillance), *publication* of private matters, *disclosure* of medical records, and *appropriation* of an employee's name or likeness for commercial purposes.[69] In practice, background checks, monitoring off-duty conduct and lifestyle, drug testing, workplace searches, and workplace monitoring trigger most privacy violations.[70] We'll focus on workplace monitoring.

THE PROBLEM Workplace privacy is a growing problem due to the proliferation of online and "smart" devices. For example, a New Jersey court found an employer liable when one of its employees used his company computer at work to distribute child pornography. Someone had previously alerted the employer to the suspicious activity and the employer hadn't taken action.[71] Yet taking action might have meant increased monitoring and reduced privacy.

The increased use of blogging and Twitter-type tools further expands the potential for distributing questionable content.[72] And with more employers using their own iPads and smart phones at work, new problems arise.[73] One employer gave employees iPods to use, and found they were now clogging the firm's servers with illegal music downloads.[74] Security is another problem. One "4-gigabyte MP3 player, such as the first generation of iPod Mini . . . can take home a lot of corporate data," said one employer (a process some graphically describe as "podslurping").[75]

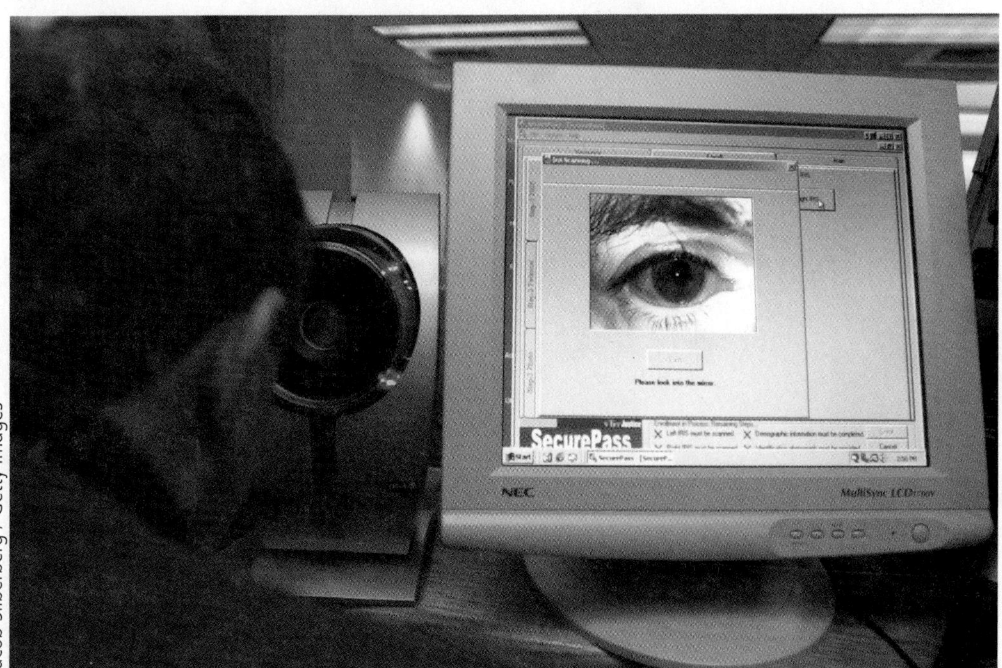

More employers are using iris scanning to verify employee identity.

Jacob Silberberg / Getty Images

One hospital found that, to facilitate working at home, some medical staff were e-mailing patients' confidential records to themselves, violating federal privacy laws. Other employers face demands to produce employee e-mail as part of litigation, as when one employee sues another for sexual harassment.[76] A U.S. Federal Trade Commission decision may even make employers liable for deceptive company endorsements that employees post on their own blogs or on social media sites such as Facebook, even if the employers didn't authorize them.[77] Prudent monitoring and instituting e-mail and privacy policies is therefore an urgent problem.

Social Media and HR

A SHRM survey found that 40% of employers surveyed have a formal policy governing social media used by employees. However, employers need to formulate such policies with care. For example, an overly broad restriction against "making disparaging comments about the company through any media, including online," probably would not be legally defensible under labor laws.[78] On the other hand, prohibiting "plainly egregious conduct" such as obscene, intimidating, or unlawfully discriminatory comments probably would be.

Electronic Communications Privacy Act (ECPA)
Intended in part to restrict interception and monitoring of oral and wire communications, but with two exceptions: employers who can show a legitimate business reason for doing so, and employers who have employees' consent to do so.

KNOW YOUR EMPLOYMENT LAW

Electronic Monitoring

What can the employer do? There are two main restrictions on workplace monitoring: the **Electronic Communications Privacy Act (ECPA)**, and *common-law protections* against invasion of privacy (protections that have evolved from court decisions). The ECPA is a federal law intended to help restrict interception and monitoring of oral and wire communications. It contains two exceptions. The "business purpose exception" permits employers to monitor communications if they can show a legitimate business reason for doing so. The second, "consent exception," lets employers monitor communications if they have their employees' consent to do so.[79]

Electronic eavesdropping is thus legal—up to a point. For example, federal law and most state laws allow employers to monitor employees' phone calls in the ordinary course of business. However, they must stop listening when it becomes clear the conversation is personal. You can also intercept e-mail to protect the property rights of the e-mail provider. However, court cases suggest employers may have fewer rights to monitor e-mail than previously assumed.[80]

To be safe, employers issue e-mail and online service usage policies, which warn employees that those systems should be used for business only. Employers also have employees sign e-mail and telephone monitoring acknowledgment statements like that in Figure 14-5. Many employees probably assume that their communications using the corporate e-mail system are open to review, but that e-mails they send via the employer's system but using personal e-mail accounts such as Gmail aren't. However, that's not necessarily true. An attorney should review the company's e-mail policy, but at a minimum make it clear that employees should have no expectation of privacy in their e-mail and Internet usage.[81] Also emphasize that all messages sent and received on the employer's e-mail system are company property and not confidential.[82]

Videotaped workplace monitoring requires more caution. Continuous video surveillance of employees in an office setting may not be a problem. But a Boston employer had to pay over $200,000 to five workers it secretly videotaped in an employee locker room, after they sued.[83]

I understand that XYZ Company periodically monitors any e-mail communications created, sent, or retrieved using this company's e-mail system. Therefore I understand that my e-mail communications may be read by individuals other than the intended recipient. I also understand that XYZ Company periodically monitors telephone communications, for example to improve customer service quality.

____
Signature | Date

____
Print Name | Department

FIGURE 14-5 Sample E-Mail Monitoring Acknowledgment Statement

It's therefore not surprising that in one survey 41% of employers with more than 20,000 employees had someone reading employee e-mails.[84] Ninety-six percent block access to adult websites, 61% to game sites.[85] Some check employees' personal blogs or Facebook sites to see if they're publicizing work-related matters.[86] Even Twitter is becoming a monitoring issue.[87] But such broad monitoring can be a dilemma for employers, as the Profit Center feature illustrates.

IMPROVING PERFORMANCE: HR as a Profit Center

Monitoring and Profits

Monitoring today obviously goes far beyond listening in on phone lines. New York's Bronx Lebanon Hospital uses biometric scanners to ensure that employees who clock in really are who they say they are.[88] Iris scanning tends to be the most accurate authorization device. Some organizations like the Federal Aviation Administration use it to control employees' access to its network information systems.[89] Employers ranging from United Parcel Service to the City of Oakland, California, use GPS units to monitor their truckers' and street sweepers' whereabouts—and therefore productivity.[90]

Such monitoring of course raises privacy issues.[91] The dilemma is that monitoring may also boost profits. For example, employers routinely use software to monitor (usually secretly) what their employees are doing online. When one employer noticed that employees were piling up overtime claims, they installed new software and discovered many employees were spending hours each day shopping online instead of working. BankAmerica asked about 90 of its workers to wear sensor badges; based on the resulting information the bank concluded that employees who worked in close knit teams and spoke frequently with others were more productive. When the bank took steps to get employees mingling, productivity rose by at least 10%.[92] To keep productivity up, the British grocery chain Tesco has some distribution center employees wear "Motorola arm mounted terminals" (armbands) that keep track of how quickly employees are unloading and scanning goods.[93]

Physicians often say that "every medicine contains a little poison," since anything, even aspirin, becomes dangerous if misused. For employers, the dilemma is to obtain the profit advantages of monitoring, while minimizing the ethical and privacy issues that using it raises.

Discussion Question 14-3: How would you feel if your employer told you to wear an armband monitor? Why? How would you react?

Reward and Disciplinary Systems

Finally, in terms of HR steps the manager can take to promote ethics and fair behavior, employees expect employers to punish unethical conduct and to reward ethical conduct.[94] Furthermore, the employer should discipline executives, not just underlings, who misbehave.[95]

KNOWLEDGE BASE

Managing Employee Discipline

4 Employ fair disciplinary practices.

discipline
A means to encourage employees to adhere to rules and regulations.

Few human resource management practices will poison employees' perceptions of "ethical and fair treatment" or undermine employee-employer relations as will unfair disciplinary processes. The purpose of **discipline** is to encourage employees to adhere to rules and regulations. Discipline is necessary when an employee violates one of the rules.[96] However, the process must be well-thought out and fair.[97]

The Three Pillars

The manager builds a fair discipline process on three pillars: rules and regulations, a system of progressive penalties, and an appeals process.

RULES AND REGULATIONS A set of clear disciplinary rules and regulations is the first pillar. The rules should address issues such as theft, destruction of company property, drinking on the job, and insubordination. Examples of rules include:

Poor performance is not acceptable. Each employee is expected to perform his or her work properly and efficiently and to meet established standards of quality.

Alcohol and drugs do not mix with work. The use of either during working hours and reporting for work under the influence of either are both strictly prohibited.

The purpose of the rules is to inform employees ahead of time what is and is not acceptable behavior. Tell employees, preferably in writing, what is not permitted. This should occur during orientation. The employee orientation handbook should contain the rules and regulations.

PENALTIES A system of progressive penalties is the second pillar of effective discipline. The severity of the penalty usually depends on the offense and the number of times it has occurred. For example, most companies issue warnings for the first unexcused lateness. However, for a fourth offense, discharge is the usual disciplinary action.

APPEALS PROCESS Third, an appeals process should be part of the disciplinary process. The aim here is to ensure that supervisors mete out discipline fairly.

FedEx's *guaranteed fair treatment* multistep program illustrates this. In *step 1, management review,* the complainant submits a written complaint to a middle manager. The department head reviews all relevant information; holds a meeting with the complainant; makes a decision to either uphold, modify, or overturn management's action; and communicates the decision in writing to the complainant and the department's HR representative.

If not satisfied, then in *step 2, officer complaint,* the complainant submits a written appeal to the vice president or senior vice president of the division.

Finally, in *step 3, executive appeals review,* the complainant may submit a written complaint to the employee relations department. The complaint is then investigated and a case file prepared for the executive review appeals board. The appeals board—the CEO, the COO, the chief HR officer, and three senior vice presidents—then reviews the information and makes a decision to uphold, overturn, or initiate a board of review or to take other appropriate action.

Some supervisory behavior may be impossible to overcome. For example, the employer can sometimes mitigate the effects of unfair disciplinary procedures by establishing disciplinary appeals processes. However, behaviors that attack the employee's personal and/or social identity are difficult to remedy.[98]

Diversity Counts: Comparing Males and Females in a Discipline Situation

What several researchers sadly call the "Evil Woman Thesis" argues that when a woman doesn't act the way other men and women think she should act, they tend to treat her more harshly than they might if a man acted unexpectedly.99

While such a thesis might seem ridiculous, the research seems to support it. In one study, 360 graduate and undergraduate business school students reviewed a labor arbitration case. The case involved two employees, one male and one female, with similar work records and tenure with their employers. Both were discharged for violation of company rules related to alcohol and drugs. The case portrays one worker's behavior as a more serious breach of company rules: The more culpable worker (a male in half the study and a female in the other half) had brought the intoxicant to work. The students had to express their agreement with two alternative approaches (tough or not-so-tough) to settling the dispute that arose after the discharge.

The researchers found bias against the female "employee" by both the male and female students. Both the male and female students recommended harsher treatment for the "culpable" female employees in the case than they did for the "culpable" man. As the researchers conclude, "women, as decision makers, appear to be as willing as men to impose harsher discipline on women than upon men."

The accompanying HR Tools feature summarizes fair discipline guidelines.

IMPROVING PERFORMANCE: HR Tools for Line Managers and Entrepreneurs

Disciplining an Employee

Even if you're a manager in a *Fortune* 500 company, you may find yourself without company guidelines when you're thinking of disciplining or discharging an employee for violating company rules. An error could trigger a costly appeal, or even litigation. In such a situation, fair discipline guidelines would include:[100]

- **Make sure the evidence supports the charge of employee wrongdoing.** Arbitrators often cite that "the employer's evidence did not support the charge of employee wrongdoing" when reinstating discharged employees.

- **Make sure to protect the employees' due process rights.** Arbitrators normally reverse discharges and suspensions when the process that led to them is obviously unfair or violates due process.[101]
- **Adequately warn the employee of the disciplinary consequences of his or her alleged misconduct.** Have the employee sign a form as in Figure 14-6.
- **The rule that allegedly was violated should be "reasonably related" to the efficient and safe operation of the particular work environment.**
- **Fairly and adequately investigate the matter before administering discipline.**
- **The investigation should produce substantial evidence of misconduct.**
- **Apply applicable rules, orders, or penalties without discrimination.**
- **Maintain the employee's right to counsel.** For example, all union employees generally have the right to bring a representative to an interview that they reasonably believe might lead to disciplinary action.
- **Don't rob your subordinate of his or her dignity.**
- **Remember that the burden of proof is on you.** In U.S. society, a person is considered innocent until proven guilty.
- **Get the facts.** Don't base your decision on hearsay evidence or on your general impression.
- **Don't act while angry.**
- **Use ombudsmen,** These are neutral counselors outside the chain of command to whom employees who believe they were treated unfairly can turn to for advice.[102]

FIGURE 14-6 Report of Employee Discipline

Apex Telecommunications Corporation
Report of Disciplinary Action and Warning

Employee's Name____________________
Employee's Department__________________
Date of Misconduct________________ Today's Date________________

Description of Incident and misconduct (including witnesses, if any)________________

Witnesses to Incident________________

If the misconduct violated an Apex Co. policy or rule, state the policy or rule________________

Employee's explanation for misconduct, if any________________

Disciplinary action taken, if any________________

The employee was warned today that if misconduct such as this reoccurs at any time during the next_____ weeks, he or she may be subject to the following disciplinary action________________

Supervisor's signature	Employee's signature
Print name	Print name

Discussion Question 14-4: Do you think it would suffice to just say "Do unto others as you would have others do to you," instead of carrying around this guidelines list? Why?

DISCIPLINE WITHOUT PUNISHMENT Traditional discipline has two main drawbacks. First, no one likes being punished. Second, punishment tends to gain short-term compliance, but not long-term cooperation.

nonpunitive discipline
Discipline without punishment, usually involving a system of oral warnings and paid "decision-making leaves" in lieu of more traditional punishment.

Discipline without punishment (or alternative or **nonpunitive discipline**) aims to avoid these drawbacks by reducing the punitive nature of the discipline. Steps include:[103]

1. ***Issue an oral reminder for a first infraction.***
2. ***Should another incident arise within 6 weeks, issue a formal written reminder, and place a copy in the employee's personnel file.*** Also, hold a second private discussion with the employee.
3. ***Give a paid, 1-day "decision-making leave."*** If another incident occurs in the next 6 weeks or so, tell the employee to take a 1-day leave with pay, and to consider whether he or she wants to abide by the company's rules. When the employee returns to work, he or she meets with you and gives you a decision.
4. ***If no further incidents occur in the next year or so, purge the 1-day paid suspension from the person's file.*** If the behavior is repeated, the next step is **dismissal**.

dismissal
Involuntary termination of an employee's employment with the firm.

The process would not apply to exceptional circumstances. Criminal behavior or in-plant fighting might be grounds for immediate dismissal, for instance.

5 Explain what is meant by employee relations and what employers can do to improve it.

Managing Employee Relations

Most employers strive to maintain positive relations between themselves and their employees. However, doing so is impossible if employees believe the company bullies them, spies on them, or (in general) treats them unethically or unfairly. Therefore, policies that foster ethics, fair treatment, and fair discipline form the bedrock of positive employee relations. On that foundation, the employer can then build an effective employee relations program, to which we now turn.

What Is Employee Relations?

employee relations
The activity of establishing and maintaining the positive employee–employer relationships that contribute to satisfactory productivity, motivation, morale, and discipline, as well as maintaining a positive, productive, and cohesive work environment.

Employee relations is the activity that involves establishing and maintaining the positive employee–employer relationships that contribute to satisfactory productivity, motivation, morale, and discipline, and to maintaining a positive, productive, and cohesive work environment.[104] Whether you're recruiting employees, managing union organizing campaigns, asking employees to work overtime, or doing some other task, it obviously makes sense to have employees "on your side." Most employers therefore endeavor to build positive employee relations on the sensible assumption that doing so beats building negative ones. Managing employee relations is usually assigned to HR, and is a topic the SHRM Knowledge Base addresses. In this section, we'll address managing employee relations in terms of three main topics: *improving and assessing employee relations through improved communications, developing employee recognition/relations programs,* and *using employee involvement strategies.*

Improving and Assessing Employee Relations Through Better Communications

Employers use various communications tools to bolster their employee relations efforts. For example, one university's website says, "We believe in keeping our employees fully informed about our policies, procedures, practices and benefits."[105] This employer uses an *open-door policy* to encourage communication between employees and managers, an *employee handbook* covering basic employment information, and "the opportunity to keep abreast of University events and other information of interest through the *website, e-mail* and *hard copy memoranda*."[106] One writer notes that "no one likes to hear complaints, but soliciting them effectively remains critical to an employer's relationship with employees, ethics and employee relations."[107] Doing so may include hosting employee *focus groups*, making available *ombudsman* and *suggestion boxes*, and implementing telephone and Web-based *hotlines*. Some employers use hotline providers to manage their hotlines. The vendor sets up the hotlines, receives the employees' comments, and provides ongoing feedback to the employer

exit interviews
Interviews with employees who are leaving the firm, conducted for obtaining information about the job or related matters, to give the employer insight about the company.

about employees' concerns, as well as periodic summaries of comments and trends. **Exit interviews**, which we discussed in an earlier chapter, provide another opportunity to sample the quality of one's employee relations.[108] Individual supervisors can of course use methods such as open-door policies and "management by walking around" to informally monitor "how things are going."

Other employers use surveys, newsletters, and staff meetings to facilitate communications. The owner of 11 IHOP restaurants reduced its employee turnover with an *online survey*. It lets new employees anonymously report their opinions about the hiring process.[109] Feedback led to recalibrating their firm's training and orientation methods, and reportedly reduced turnover by about a third. In Bonita Springs, Florida, Mel's Gourmet Diner keeps employees informed with a quarterly *newsletter*. It distributes copies at the chain's 10 locations, but also posts it on the company website, and plans to translate it into Spanish.[110] Sea Island Shrimp House in San Antonio, Texas, keeps employees in its seven restaurants communicating with its "cascading huddles" (very quick meetings). At 9 A.M., top management meets in the first daily huddle. The next huddle is a conference call with store managers. Then, store managers meet with hourly employees at each location before the restaurants open, to make sure they've communicated the news of the day. "It's all about alignment and good, timely communications," says the company.[111]

USING ORGANIZATIONAL CLIMATE SURVEYS Employee attitude, morale, or climate surveys play a part in many firms' employee relations efforts. They use the surveys to "take the pulse" of their employees' attitudes toward a variety of organizational issues including leadership, safety, role clarity, fairness, and pay, and to thereby get a sense of whether their employee relations need improvement. The dividing lines between attitude surveys, satisfaction or morale surveys, and climate surveys are somewhat arbitrary; several experts define *organizational climate* as "the shared perceptions organizational members have about their organization and work environment."[112]

Many such surveys are available off the shelf. For instance, one SHRM sample survey has employees use a scale from 1 ("to a very little extent") to 5 ("to a very great extent") to answer survey questions. Questions include, "Are work activities sensibly organized?", "Overall, how satisfied are you with your supervisor?", "Overall, how satisfied are you with your job?", "Do you have confidence and trust in your supervisor?", "Is your work group's work high in quality?", and "Does doing your job well lead to things like recognition and respect from those you work with?"[113] Other employers create their own specialized surveys. Thus, the FedEx Survey Feedback Action (SFA) program lets employees express feelings about the company and their managers and (to some extent) about service, pay, and benefits. Each manager then has an opportunity to discuss the anonymous department results with his or her subordinates, and create an action plan for improving work group commitment. Sample questions include:

"I can tell my manager what I think."

"My manager tells me what is expected."

"My manager listens to my concerns."

"My manager keeps me informed."

Developing Employee Recognition/Relations Programs

Opportunities for two-way communications improve employee relations, but there are also other types of employee relations programs. Most notable here are the sorts of employee recognition and award programs we touched on in Chapter 12, particularly formal companywide programs such as employee-of-the-month awards. For example, one trade journal notes how "Winston–Salem N.C.–based Murray Supply Co. hosted a companywide recognition dinner in March, at which associates received awards based on the length of service, sales achievements and safe driving."[114] Other employees received the "corporate office employee of the year award," "employee of the year for the entire company," "branch employee of the year award," and "manufacturers rep of the year" awards. Employers often distribute such awards with much fanfare at special events such as awards dinners. One SHRM survey found that 76% of organizations surveyed had such employee recognition programs, and another 5% planned to implement one within the next year.[115]

Instituting recognition and service award programs requires some planning.[116] For example, instituting a *service award program* requires reviewing the tenure of existing employees and establishing meaningful award periods (1 year, 5 years, etc.). It then requires establishing a budget, selecting awards, having a procedure for monitoring what awards to actually award, having a process for giving awards (such as special dinners or staff meetings), and periodically assessing program success. Similarly, instituting a *recognition program* requires developing criteria for recognition (such as customer service, cost savings, etc.), creating forms and procedures for submitting and reviewing nominations, selecting meaningful recognition awards, and establishing a process for actually awarding the recognition awards.

Creating Employee Involvement Strategies

Employee relations tend to improve when employees get involved with the company in positive ways, and so *employee involvement* is another useful employee relations strategy.

Getting employees involved in discussing and solving organizational issues provides several benefits. Employees often know more about how to improve their work processes than anyone; therefore asking them is often the simplest way to boost performance. Getting them involved in addressing some issue will hopefully boost their sense of ownership of the process. It may also signal to them that their opinions are valued, thereby contributing to better employee relations.

Employers use various means to encourage employee involvement. Some employers organize focus groups. A *focus group* is comprised of a small sample of employees who are presented with a specific question or issue and who interactively express their opinions and attitudes on that issue with the focus group's assigned facilitator.

Social Media and HR

Some employers use *social media* such as the pinboard-style social photo sharing website Pinterest to encourage involvement.[117] The employer Red Door Interactive used a Pinterest-based project it called "San Diego Office Inspiration" to encourage employees to contribute interior design, architectural, and decor ideas for its new offices.[118]

suggestion teams
Temporary teams whose members work on specific analytical assignments, such as how to cut costs or raise productivity.

problem-solving teams
Semipermanent teams that identify and research work processes and develop solutions to work-related problems.

quality circle
A special type of formal problem-solving team of specially trained employees who meet once a week to solve problems affecting their work area.

self-managing/self-directed work team
A highly trained group of around eight employees who are fully responsible for turning out a well-defined segment of finished work.

USING EMPLOYEE INVOLVEMENT TEAMS Employers also use various types of teams to gain employees' involvement in addressing organizational issues. **Suggestion teams** are temporary teams whose members work on specific analytical assignments, such as how to cut costs or raise productivity. One employer, an airline, split employees such as baggage handlers and ground crew into separate teams, linking team members via its website for brainstorming and voting on ideas.[119] Some employers formalize this process by appointing semipermanent **problem-solving teams**. These teams identify and research work processes and develop solutions to work-related problems.[120] They usually consist of the supervisor and five to eight employees from a common work area.[121]

A **quality circle** is a special type of formal problem-solving team, usually composed of 6 to 12 specially trained employees who meet weekly to solve problems affecting their work area.[122] The team first gets training in problem-analysis techniques (including basic statistics). Then it applies the problem-analysis process (problem identification, problem selection, problem analysis, solution recommendations, and solution review by top management) to solve problems in its work area.[123]

In many facilities, specially trained teams of self-managing employees do their jobs with little or no oversight from supervisory personnel. For many, such teams represent the pinnacle of employee involvement. A **self-managing/self-directed work team** is "a highly trained group of around eight employees, fully responsible for turning out a well-defined segment of finished work."[124] The "well-defined segment" might be an Acura dashboard installed or a fully processed insurance claim. In any case, such teams have two distinguishing features. They are empowered to supervise and do virtually all of their own work; and their work results in a specific item or service.

For example, the GE aircraft engine plant in Durham, North Carolina, is a self-managing team-based facility. The plant's 170 workers work in teams, all of which report to the factory manager.[125] In such teams, employees "train one another, formulate and track their own budgets, make capital investment proposals as needed, handle quality control and inspection, develop their own quantitative standards, improve every process and product, and create prototypes of possible new products."[126] Such autonomy can be highly involving. As the vice president of one company said about organizing his firm around teams, "People on the floor were talking about world markets, customer needs, competitors' products, making process improvements—all the things managers are supposed to think about."[127]

USING SUGGESTION SYSTEMS Most employers understand that employee suggestions can produce significant savings. For example, one study several years ago of 47 companies concluded that the firms had saved more than $624 million in one year from their suggestion programs; more than 250,000 suggestions were submitted, of which employers adopted over 93,000 ideas.[128] Furthermore, employees find it involving to make suggestions. In one recent survey, 54% of the 497 employees surveyed said they made more than 20 suggestions per year, while another 24% said they made between 10 and 20 suggestions per year.[129] The accompanying Profit Center feature provides an example.

IMPROVING PERFORMANCE: HR as a Profit Center

The Cost-Effective Suggestion System[130]

A Lockheed Martin unit in Oswego, New York, developed what it called its "Cost-Effectiveness Plus" suggestion program to encourage and recognize employees for streamlining processes. With the Cost-Effectiveness Plus program, employees electronically submit their ideas. These are then evaluated and approved by the local manager and the program's coordinator (and by higher management when necessary). This particular program reportedly saves this facility about $77,000 per implemented idea, or more than $100 million each year.

Today's suggestion systems are more sophisticated than the "suggestion boxes" of years ago.[131] The main improvements are in how the manager formalizes and communicates the suggestion process. The head of one company that designs and installs suggestion systems for employers lists the essential elements of an effective employee suggestion system as follows:[132]

- Senior staff support
- A simple, easy process for submitting suggestions
- A strong process for evaluating and implementing suggestions
- An effective program for publicizing and communicating the program
- A program focus on key organizational goals

Discussion Question 14-5: Based on this, write a one-page outline describing an employee suggestion system for a small department store.

Review

MyManagementLab Go to **mymanagementlab.com** to complete the problems marked with this icon. 

Chapter Section Summaries

1. **Ethics and fair treatment** play important roles in managing employees at work. Ethics refers to the principles of conduct governing an individual or a group. Few societies rely solely on managers' ethics or sense of fairness, and therefore legislate employee rights, such as regarding employee pension rights, references rights, defamation rights, and union activity rights.

2. Many things **influence ethical behavior at work**. One study concluded that ethical behavior reflects "Bad Apples, Bad Cases, and Bad Barrels." From research, we know that moral awareness, the managers themselves, moral engagement, morality, unmet goals, and rewards all influence ethical behavior. The person is important, in that people bring to their jobs their own ideas of what is morally right or wrong. The boss

and how he or she molds the organizational culture have a prevailing effect on ethical behavior, because it's difficult to resist even subtle pressure from your boss. Employers themselves can take steps to support ethical behavior, for instance via training, whistle-blower programs, and ethics codes.

3. Managers can use **HR methods to promote ethics and fair treatment**. For example, in selection, hire ethical people and emphasize the fairness of selection procedures. Similarly, ethics training, conducting fair and just performance appraisals, rewarding ethical behavior, and generally treating employees fairly all promote ethics and the perception of fair treatment.
4. Managing **employee discipline and privacy** are important management skills. The basics of a fair and just disciplinary process include clear rules and regulations, a system of progressive penalties, and an appeals process. Some employers use nonpunitive discipline, which usually involves a system of oral warnings and paid "decision-making leaves." With more employers using Internet monitoring and technologies such as biometrics, monitoring is widespread. The Electronic Communications Privacy Act and common law protections against invasion of privacy limit, somewhat, workplace monitoring. Employers should have employees sign e-mail and telephone monitoring acknowledgment statements.
5. **Employee relations** is the activity that involves establishing and maintaining the positive employee–employer relationships that contribute to satisfactory productivity, motivation, morale, and discipline, and to maintaining a positive, productive, and cohesive work environment.

Discussion Questions

14-6. Explain how you would ensure fairness in disciplining, discussing particularly the prerequisites to disciplining, disciplining guidelines, and the discipline without punishment approach.

✪14-7. Why is it important in our litigious society to manage electronic monitoring properly?

14-8. Provide two examples of behaviors that would probably be unethical but legal, and three that would probably be illegal but ethical.

14-9. List 10 things your college or university does to encourage ethical behavior by students and/or faculty.

14-10. You need to select a nanny for your or a relative's child, and want someone ethical. What would you do to help ensure you ended up hiring someone ethical?

✪14-11. You believe your coworker is being bullied. How would you verify this and what would you do about it if it is true?

14-12. Define *employee relations* and discuss at least four methods for managing it.

Individual and Group Activities

14-13. Working individually or in groups, interview managers or administrators at your employer or college in order to determine the extent to which the employer or college endeavors to build two-way communication, and the specific types of programs used. Do the managers think they are effective? What do the employees (or faculty members) think of the programs in use at the employer or college?

14-14. Working individually or in groups, obtain copies of the student handbook for your college and determine to what extent there is a formal process through which students can air grievances. Based on your contacts with other students, has it been an effective grievance process? Why or why not?

14-15. Working individually or in groups, determine the nature of the academic discipline process in your college. Do you think it is effective? Based on what you read in this chapter, would you recommend any modifications?

14-16. Appendix A, PHR and SPHR Knowledge Base, at the end of this book (pages 550–558) lists the knowledge someone studying for the HRCI certification exam needs to have in each area of human resource management (such as in Strategic Management, Workforce Planning, and Human Resource Development). In groups of four to five students, do four things: (1) review Appendix A; (2) identify the material in this chapter that relates to the required knowledge Appendix A lists; (3) write four multiple-choice exam questions on this material that you believe would be suitable for inclusion in the HRCI exam; and (4) if time permits, have someone from your team post your team's questions in front of the class, so that students in all teams can answer the exam questions created by the other teams.

KNOWLEDGE BASE

14-17. In a research study at Ohio State University, a professor found that even honest people, left to their own devices, would steal from their employers.[133] In this study, the researchers gave financial services workers the opportunity to steal a small amount of money after participating in an after-work project for which the pay was inadequate. Would the employees steal to make up for the underpayment? In most cases, yes. Employees who scored low on an honesty test stole whether or not their office had an ethics program that said stealing from the company was illegal. Employees who scored high on the honesty test also stole, but only if their office did not have such an employee ethics program—the "honest" people didn't steal if there was an ethics policy.

Individually or in groups, answer these questions: Do you think findings like these are generalizable? In other words, would they apply across the board to employees in other types of companies and situations? If your answer is yes, what do you think this implies about the need for and wisdom of having an ethics program?

Experiential Exercise

Discipline or Not?

Purpose: The purpose of this exercise is to provide you with some experience in analyzing and handling an actual disciplinary action.

Required Understanding: Students should be thoroughly familiar with the facts of the following incident, titled "Botched Batch." **Do not read the "award" or "discussion" sections until after the groups have completed their deliberations.**

How to Set Up the Exercise/Instructions: Divide the class into groups of four or five students. Each group should take the arbitrator's point of view and assume that they are to analyze the case and make the arbitrator's decision. Review the case again at this point, but please do not read the award and discussion sections.

Each group should answer the following questions:

14-18. Based on what you read in this chapter, including all relevant guidelines, what would your decision be if you were the arbitrator? Why?

14-19. Do you think that after their experience in this arbitration the parties involved will be more or less inclined to settle grievances by themselves without resorting to arbitration?

Botched Batch

Facts: A computer department employee made an entry error that botched an entire run of computer reports. Efforts to rectify the situation produced a second set of improperly run reports. Because of the series of errors, the employer incurred extra costs of $2,400, plus a weekend of overtime work by other computer department staffers. Management suspended the employee for 3 days for negligence, and revoked a promotion for which the employee had previously been approved.

Protesting the discipline, the employee stressed that she had attempted to correct her error in the early stages of the run by notifying the manager of computer operations of her mistake. Maintaining that the resulting string of errors could have been avoided if the manager had followed up on her report and stopped the initial run, the employee argued that she had been treated unfairly because the manager had not been disciplined even though he compounded the problem, whereas she was severely punished. Moreover, citing her "impeccable" work record and management's acknowledgment that she had always been a "model employee," the employee insisted that the denial of her previously approved promotion was "unconscionable."

(Please do **not** *read beyond this point until after you have answered the two questions.)*

Award: The arbitrator upholds the 3-day suspension, but decides that the promotion should be restored.

Discussion: "There is no question," the arbitrator notes, that the employee's negligent act "set in motion the train of events that resulted in running two complete sets of reports reflecting improper information." Stressing that the employer incurred substantial cost because of the error, the arbitrator cites "unchallenged" testimony that management had commonly issued 3-day suspensions for similar infractions in the past. Thus, the arbitrator decides, the employer acted with just cause in meting out an "evenhanded" punishment for the negligence.

Turning to the denial of the already approved promotion, the arbitrator says that this action should be viewed "in the same light as a demotion for disciplinary reasons." In such cases, the arbitrator notes, management's decision normally is based on a pattern of unsatisfactory behavior, an employee's inability to perform, or similar grounds. Observing that management had never before reversed a promotion as part of a disciplinary action, the arbitrator says that by tacking on the denial of the promotion in this case, the employer substantially varied its disciplinary policy from its past practice. Because this action on management's part was not "evenhanded," the arbitrator rules, the promotion should be restored.[134]

Video Case

Video Title: Whistleblower on the NSA (Ethics and Social Responsibility of Business)

SYNOPSIS

Whistleblowing is an ethical issue that has been the subject of much debate, especially recently. Whistleblower laws exist in many forms to protect employees from retaliation when they blow the whistle. Both legal and ethical scholars have more or less agreed that it's more ethical to protect the public from harm than to be loyal to an employer. This video is about Mark Klein, a retired AT&T phone and Internet technician, who blew the whistle on the federal government. Klein discovered that the National Security Agency (NSA), which is in charge of intercepting electronic communications around the world and tracking the foreign enemies of the United States, had a secret room in an AT&T building and was recording all of the domestic and foreign Internet traffic of 16 other major phone and Internet companies. According to Klein, the NSA was blindly vacuuming up huge amounts of data across those links. Believing Americans had the right to know what the NSA was doing, Klein went public with what he knew.

Discussion Questions

14-20. Of course, this is not the only instance of someone "going public"; the former NSA employee Edward Snowden allegedly did something much more serious recently. Do you agree that it is more ethical to protect the public than one's employer? Why?

14-21. Based on what you read in this chapter, what steps should AT&T take to make sure that one of its employees doesn't find it necessary to blow the whistle on them again?

14-22. What rights (if any) do you think employers violate when they try to silence whistleblowers?

14-23. If Mr. Klein were still an AT&T employee, what discipline (if any) do you think would be appropriate for his whistleblowing, and why?

Application Case

Enron, Ethics, and Organizational Culture

For many people, a company called Enron Corp. still ranks as one of history's classic examples of ethics run amok. During the 1990s and early 2000s, Enron was in the business of wholesaling natural gas and electricity. Enron made its money as the intermediary (wholesaler) between suppliers and customers. Without getting into all the details, the nature of Enron's business—and the fact that Enron didn't actually own the assets—meant that its profit statements and balance sheets listing the firm's assets and liabilities were unusually difficult to understand.

It turned out that the lack of accounting transparency enabled the company's managers to make Enron's financial performance look much better than it actually was. Outside experts began questioning Enron's financial statements in 2001. In fairly short order, Enron collapsed, and courts convicted several of its top executives of things like manipulating Enron's reported assets and profitability. Many investors (including former Enron employees) lost all or most of their investments in Enron. In Enron's case this breakdown is perhaps more perplexing than usual. As one writer said,

> Enron had all the elements usually found in comprehensive ethics and compliance programs: a code of ethics, a reporting system, as well as a training video on vision and values led by [the company's top executives].[135]

Experts subsequently put forth many explanations for how a company that was apparently so ethical outwardly could actually have been making so many bad ethical decisions without other managers (and the board of directors) noticing. The explanations ranged from a "deliberate concealment of information by officers," to more psychological explanations (such as employees not wanting to contradict their bosses) and the "surprising role of irrationality in decision-making."[136]

But perhaps the most persuasive explanation of how an apparently ethical company could go so wrong concerns organizational culture. The reasoning here is that it's not the rules but what employees feel they should do that determines ethical behavior. For example (speaking in general, not specifically about Enron), the executive director of the Ethics Officer Association put it this way:

> [W]e're a legalistic society, and we've created a lot of laws. We assume that if you just knew what those laws meant that you would behave properly. Well, guess what? You can't write enough laws to tell us what to do at all times every day of the week in every part of the world. We've got to develop the critical thinking and critical reasoning skills of our people because most of the ethical issues that we deal with are in the ethical gray areas.

Questions

14-24. Based on what you read in this chapter, summarize in one page or less how you would explain Enron's ethical meltdown.

14-25. It is said that when one securities analyst tried to confront Enron's CEO about the firm's unusual accounting statements, the CEO publicly used vulgar language to describe the analyst, and that Enron employees subsequently thought doing so was humorous. If true, what does that say about Enron's ethical culture?

14-26. This case and chapter had something to say about how organizational culture influences ethical behavior. What role do you think culture played at Enron? Give five specific examples of things Enron's CEO could have done to create a healthy ethical culture.

Continuing Case

Carter Cleaning Company

Guaranteeing Fair Treatment

Being in the laundry and cleaning business, the Carters feel strongly about not allowing employees to smoke, eat, or drink in their stores. Jennifer was therefore surprised to walk into a store and find two employees eating lunch at the front counter. There was a large pizza in its box, and the two of them were sipping colas and eating slices of pizza and submarine sandwiches off paper plates. Not only did it look messy, but there were grease and soda spills on the counter and the store smelled from onions and pepperoni, even with the exhaust fan pulling air out through the roof. In addition to being a turnoff to customers, the mess on the counter meant that a customer's order might actually become soiled in the store.

Although this was a serious matter, Jennifer didn't feel that what the counter people were doing was grounds for dismissal (partly because the store manager had apparently condoned their actions). It seemed to her that the matter called for more than just a warning but less than dismissal.

Questions

14-27. What would you do if you were Jennifer, and why?

14-28. Should a disciplinary system be established at Carter Cleaning Centers?

14-29. If so, what should it cover? How would you suggest it deal with a situation such as the one with the errant counter people?

14-30. How would you deal with the store manager?

Translating Strategy into HR Policies and Practices Case*,§

**The accompanying strategy map for this chapter is in the MyManagementLab and the overall map in the inside back cover of this text outlines the relationships involved.*

IMPROVING PERFORMANCE at The Hotel Paris

The Hotel Paris's New Ethics, Justice, and Fair Treatment Process

The Hotel Paris's competitive strategy is "To use superior guest service to differentiate the Hotel Paris properties, and to thereby increase the length of stay and return rate of guests, and thus boost revenues and profitability." HR manager Lisa Cruz must now formulate functional policies and activities that support this competitive strategy, by eliciting the required employee behaviors and competencies.

As the head of HR for the Hotel Paris, Lisa Cruz was especially concerned about her company maintaining the highest ethical standards. Her concerns were twofold. First, there are, in any single hotel each day, at least a dozen people (including housekeepers, front-desk clerks, security guards, and so on) with easy access to guests' rooms, and to their personal belongings. Guests—many younger, and many unwary—are continually walking the halls unprotected. So, in a service company like this, there is simply no margin for ethical errors.

But she was concerned about ethics for a second reason. She knew that employees do not like being treated unfairly, and that unfairness in any form could manifest itself in low morale and in diminished performance. She wondered if her employees' low morale and engagement—as measured by her firm's attitude surveys—stemmed, in part, from what they perceived as unjust treatment. Lisa therefore turned to the task of assessing and redesigning the Hotel Paris's ethics, justice, and fair treatment practices.

When she sat with the CFO to discuss her proposal for the Hotel Paris's fairness, justice, and ethics system, Lisa came armed with some research. In 2003, the *Journal of Applied Psychology* published a study that showed how improving the level of interpersonal and procedural justice in a service company can lead to improved employee attitudes and performance and thus to improved hotel performance.[137] And the study was done in a hotel chain.

In this study, the researchers collected employee survey data from a hotel chain's 111 different hotels in the United States and Canada. The employee services department of this hotel chain obtained completed surveys from 8,832 of the hotel's employees. The researchers also obtained data on employee turnover as well as on the employees' commitment, employees' intentions to remain with the organization, and guest satisfaction.

Clearly, having fair and just procedures in place effected these hotels' employee morale and behavior, and thus company performance—they could even measure the links. For example, procedural justice and interpersonal justice were related to increased levels of employees' satisfaction with supervision. Procedural justice and satisfaction with supervision were both related to improved employee commitment. And employee commitment was related to intention to remain with the hotel, and therefore to reducing employee turnover. Furthermore, procedural and interpersonal justice led to improved employee satisfaction with supervision and commitment, and thus to improved employee discretionary service behaviors, and ultimately to higher guest service satisfaction.

For Lisa and the CFO, these results provided a concrete and measurable rationale for moving ahead with improving the Hotel Paris's fairness, justice, and ethics practices. The researchers' results supported, in a measurably defensible way, the idea that spending the money required to improve procedural and interpersonal justice would likely improve employee attitudes and behaviors (employee commitment, discretionary service behavior, and employee turnover), and, thereby, improve guest satisfaction and company performance. The results even suggested by "how much" improving morale and justice might boost guest satisfaction.

Lisa and her HR team took a number of steps to institute new ethics, justice, and fair treatment practices at the Hotel Paris. Working with the company's general counsel, they produced and presented to the CEO a new Hotel Paris code of ethics, as well as a more complete set of ethical guidelines. These now appear on the Hotel Paris's careers website link, and are part of each new employee's orientation packet. They contracted with a vendor to provide a customized, Web-based ethics training program, and made it clear that the first employees to participate in it were the company's top executives.

Lisa and her team then proceeded methodically through the company's entire HR process, starting with recruitment and selection. The selection process now includes an honesty test. New guidelines ensure an open and fair performance appraisal process. The team completely revamped the hotel's disciplinary process. They instituted a new appeals process that included appeals to each hotel's manager, and then to Lisa Cruz, and finally to a top management executive appeals committee. They instituted a new discipline without punishment system. They instituted new guidelines outlining grounds for dismissal. The new procedure requires that someone from HR approve any dismissal before it is final, and be present when any employee who's been with the firm for more than a year is dismissed.

After 6 months of operating under the new system, several changes are evident. Surveys Lisa took before the new program, and now, indicate a significant upward movement in the employees' perceptions of "consistent and equitable treatment of all employees." Grievances are down by 80%, 95% of employees are able to quote the ethics code, employee morale and commitment are up, and, in general, employee service type behaviors (such as greeting guests in a friendly manner) have increased, too. Lisa and the CFO are pleased with the new system, and are optimistic it will also help to improve customer service satisfaction.

Questions

14-31. What do you think of the adequacy and effectiveness of the steps Lisa has taken so far?

14-32. List three more specific steps Hotel Paris should take with respect to each individual human research function (selection, training, and so on) to improve the level of ethics in the company.

14-33. Based on what you learned in this chapter, write a short (less than one page) explanation Lisa can use to sell to top management the need to further improve the hotel chain's fairness and justice processes.

§Written by and copyright Gary Dessler, PhD.

CHAPTER 14

MyManagementLab

Go to **mymanagementlab.com** for Auto-graded writing questions as well as the following Assisted-graded writing questions:

14-34. What techniques would you use as alternatives to traditional discipline? Why do you think alternatives like these are important, given industry's need today for highly committed employees?

14-35. Several years ago Walmart instituted a new employee scheduling system that makes it more difficult for its employees to know for sure what hours they would be working. Basically, the store supervisor calls them at the last minute if there's an opening that day. Based on what you read in this chapter, is the new system ethical? Why or why not? Is it fair? What would you do if you were a Walmart employee?

14-36. MyManagementLab only—comprehensive writing assignment for this chapter.

Key Terms

ethics, 430
procedural justice, 432
distributive justice, 432
social responsibility, 432
organizational culture, 436
Electronic Communications Privacy Act (ECPA), 440
discipline, 441
nonpunitive discipline, 444
dismissal, 444
employee relations, 444
exit interviews, 445
suggestion teams, 446
problem-solving teams, 446
quality circle, 446
self-managed/self-directed work teams, 446

Ethics Quiz Answers

Quiz is on page 435.

1. 34% said personal e-mail on company computers is wrong.
2. 37% said using office equipment for schoolwork is wrong.
3. 49% said playing computer games at work is wrong.
4. 54% said Internet shopping at work is wrong.
5. 61% said it's unethical to blame your error on technology.
6. 87% said it's unethical to visit pornographic sites at work.
7. 33% said $25 is the amount at which a gift from a supplier or client becomes troubling, while 33% said $50, and 33% said $100.
8. 35% said a $50 gift to the boss is unacceptable.
9. 12% said a $50 gift from the boss is unacceptable.
10. 70% said it's unacceptable to take the $200 football tickets.
11. 70% said it's unacceptable to take the $120 theater tickets.
12. 35% said it's unacceptable to take the $100 food basket.
13. 45% said it's unacceptable to take the $25 gift certificate.
14. 40% said it's unacceptable to take the $75 raffle prize.
15. 11% reported they lie about sick days.
16. 4% reported they take credit for the work or ideas of others.

Endnotes

1. "When the Jobs Inspector Calls," *The Economist*, March 31, 2012, p. 73.
2. For a discussion of the software, see Ed Frauenheim, "The Thought Police?" *Workforce Management*, March 2011, pp. 28–30.
3. Keith Winstein, "Suit Alleges Pfizer Spun Unfavorable Drug Studies," *The Wall Street Journal*, October 8, 2008, p. B1.
4. "What Role Should HR Play in Corporate Ethics?" *HR Focus* 81, no. 1 (January 2004), p. 3. See also Dennis Moberg, "Ethics Blind Spots in Organizations: How Systematic Errors in Person Perception Undermine Moral Agency," *Organization Studies* 27, no. 3 (2006), pp. 413–428.
5. Manuel Velasquez, *Business Ethics: Concepts and Cases* (Upper Saddle River, NJ: Prentice Hall, 1992), p. 9. See also O. C. Ferrell, John Fraedrich, and Linda Ferrell, *Business Ethics* (Boston: Houghton Mifflin, 2008).
6. For further discussion of ethics and morality, see Tom Beauchamp and Norman Bowie, *Ethical Theory and Business* (Upper Saddle River, NJ: Prentice Hall, 2001), pp. 1–19.
7. Richard Osborne, "A Matter of Ethics," *Industry Week* 49, no. 14 (September 4, 2000), pp. 41–42.
8. See http://archives.gov/exhibits/charters/bill_of_rights.html, accessed May 31, 2011.
9. http://focus.illinoisstate.edu/modules/policy/publicpolicy.shtml, accessed September 14, 2011.
10. See, for example, Chris Long et al., "Fairness Monitoring: Linking Managerial Controls and Fairness Judgments in Organizations," *Academy of Management Journal* 54, no 3 (2012), pp. 1045–1068.
11. Bennett Tepper, "Consequences of Abusive Supervision," *Academy of Management Journal* 43, no. 2 (2000), pp. 178–190. See also Samuel Aryee et al., "Antecedents and Outcomes of Abusive Supervision: A Test of a Trickle-Down Model," *Journal of Applied Psychology* 92, no. 1 (2007), pp. 191–201.
12. Mindy Shoss et al., "Blaming the Organization for Abusive Supervision: The Roles of Perceived Organizational Support and Supervisors Organizational Embodiment," *Journal of Applied Psychology* 98, no. 1 (2013), pp. 158–168.
13. Teresa Daniel, "Tough Boss or Workplace Bully?" *HR Magazine* (June 2009), pp. 83–86.

14. Michelle Donovan et al., "The Perceptions of Fair Interpersonal Treatment Scale: Development and Validation of a Measure of Interpersonal Treatment in the Workplace," *Journal of Applied Psychology* 83, no. 5 (1998), pp. 683–692.
15. Bennett Tepper et al., "Abusive Supervision and Subordinates Organization Deviance," *Journal of Applied Psychology* 93, no. 4 (2008), pp. 721–732.
16. Gary Weaver and Linda Treviño, "The Role of Human Resources in Ethics/Compliance Management: A Fairness Perspective," *Human Resource Management Review* 11 (2001), p. 117.
17. Jordan Robbins et al., "Perceived Unfairness and Employee Health: A Meta-Analytic Integration," *Journal of Applied Psychology* 97, no. 2 (2012), pp. 235–272.
18. Dawn Carlson et al., "The Fallout from Abusive Supervision: An Examination of Subordinates and Their Partners," *Personnel Psychology* 60, no. 4 (2011), pp. 937–961.
19. Marie Mitchell and Maureen Ambrose, "Employees Behavioral Reactions to Supervisor Aggression: An Examination of Individual and Situational Factors," *Journal of Applied Psychology* 97, no. 6 (2012), pp. 1148–1170.
20. Suzanne Masterson, "A Trickle-Down Model of Organizational Justice: Relating Employees' and Customers' Perceptions of and Reactions to Fairness," *Journal of Applied Psychology* 86, no. 4 (2001), pp. 594–601.
21. Based on Daniel Denison, *Corporate Culture and Organizational Effectiveness* (New York: Wiley, 1990), p. 155.
22. "When the Jobs Inspector Calls," *The Economist*, March 31, 2012, p. 73.
23. Alexandra Ho and Tim Culpan, with assistance from Jun Yang in Seoul, Andrea Wong in Taipei, Tian Ying in Beijing, and Jasmine Wang in Hong Kong. "Foxconn Labor Disputes Disrupt IPhone Output for 2nd Time," *By Bloomberg News*, Oct 8, 2012 5:26 A.M, ET, www.bloomberg.com/news/2012-10-07/foxconn-labor-disputes-disrupt-iphone-output-for-2nd-time.html, accessed April 14, 2013.
24. Ibid.
25. "Facebook Harassment: Social Websites May Prompt Need for New Policies, Procedures," *BNA Bulletin to Management*, July 20, 2010, p. 225.
26. Eugene Kim and Teresa Glomb, "Get Smarty-Pants: Cognitive Ability, Personality, and Victimization," *Journal of Applied Psychology* 95, no. 3 (2010), pp. 889–901.
27. Ibid.
28. Ibid., p. 1166.
29. Jennifer Kish-Gephart, David Harrison, and Linda Trevino, "Bad Apples, Bad Cases, and Bad Barrels: Meta-Analytic Evidence About Sources of Unethical Decisions That Work," *Journal of Applied Psychology* 95, no. 1 (2010), pp. 1–31.
30. Sara Morris et al., "A Test of Environmental, Situational, and Personal Influences on the Ethical Intentions of CEOs," *Business and Society*, August 1995, pp. 119–147. See also Dennis Moberg, "Ethics Blind Spots in Organizations: How Systematic Errors in Person's Perception Undermine Moral Agency," *Organization Studies* 27, no. 3 (2006), pp. 413–428; and Scott Reynolds et al., "Automatic Ethics: The Effects of Implicit Assumptions and Contextual Cues on Moral Behavior," *Journal of Applied Psychology* 95, no. 5 (2010), pp. 752–760.
31. Celia Moore et al., "Why Employees Do Bad Things," *Personnel Psychology* 60, no. 5 (2012), pp. 1–48.
32. Ibid., p. 21.
33. Ibid.
34. "Former CEO Joins WorldCom's Indicted," *Miami Herald*, March 3, 2004, p. 4C.
35. Ferrell and Fraedrich, *Business Ethics*, p. 28; adapted from Rebecca Goodell, *Ethics in American Business: Policies, Programs, and Perceptions*, Washington, D.C.: Ethics Resource Center, 1994, p. 54. For other insights into unethical behavior's causes see, for example, F. Gino et al., "Nameless + Harmless = Blameless: When Seemingly Irrelevant Factors Influence Judgment of (Un)ethical Behavior," *Organizational Behavior and Human Decision Processes* 111, no. 2 (March 2010), pp. 93–101; and J. Camps et al., "Learning Atmosphere and Ethical Behavior, Does It Make Sense?" *Journal of Business Ethics* 94, no. 1 (June 2010), pp. 129–147.
36. A recent study suggests that people may not be so selfless. People who were more prone to take unethical actions were also more likely to expect reciprocity. Elizabeth Umphress, John Bingham, and Marie Mitchell, "Unethical Behavior in the Name of the Company: The Moderating Effect of Organizational Identification and Positive Reciprocity Beliefs on Unethical Pro-organizational Behavior," *Journal of Applied Psychology* 95, no. 4 (2010), pp. 769–770.
37. "Ethics Policies Are Big with Employers, But Workers See Small Impact on the Workplace," *BNA Bulletin to Management*, June 29, 2000, p. 201.
38. Jennifer Schramm, "Perceptions on Ethics," *HR Magazine*, November 2004, p. 176.
39. From Guy Brumback, "Managing Above the Bottom Line of Ethics," *Supervisory Management*, December 1993, p. 12. See also E. E. Umphress et al., "The Influence of Distributive Justice on Lying for and Stealing from a Supervisor," *Journal of Business Ethics* 86, no. 4 (June 2009), pp. 507–518; and S. Chen, "The Role of Ethical Leadership Versus Institutional Constraints: A Simulation Study of Financial Misreporting by CEOs," *Journal of Business Ethics* 93 part supplement 1 (June 2010), pp. 33–52.
40. IBM Business Conduct Guidelines, www.ibm.com/investor/pdf/BCG2012.pdf, accessed August 2, 2013.
41. Dayton Fandray, "The Ethical Company," *Workforce* 79, no. 12 (December 2000), pp. 74–77.
42. Richard Beatty et al., "HR's Role in Corporate Governance: Present and Prospective," *Human Resource Management* 42, no. 3 (Fall 2003), p. 268.
43. Dale Buss, "Corporate Compasses," *HR Magazine*, June 2004, pp. 127–132.
44. Eric Krell, "How to Conduct an Ethics Audit," *HR Magazine*, April 2010, pp. 48–51.
45. www.sec.gov/news/press/2011/2011-116.htm, accessed September 6, 2012.
46. "SEC Actively Tracking Conduct That Might Constitute Retaliation," *BNA Bulletin to Management*, October 23, 2012, p. 342.
47. David Mayer et al., "Who Displays Ethical Leadership, and Why Does It Matter? An Examination of Antecedents and Consequences of Ethical Leadership," *Academy of Management Journal* 55, no. 1 (2012), p. 167.
48. Sometimes the most straightforward way of changing a company's culture is to move fast to change its top management. For example, some observers believe that General Motors' board fired CEO Fritz Henderson in part because he hadn't moved fast enough to telegraph the need for change in the company by changing the company's top management. Jeremy Smerd, "A Stalled Culture Change?" *Workforce Management*, December 14, 2009, pp. 1, 3.
49. Betsy Shepherd, "Occupational Fraud," *Workforce Management*, April 2012, p. 18.
50. This list based on Linda K. Treviño, Gary R. Weaver, and Scott J. Reynolds, "Behavioral Ethics in Organizations: A Review," *Journal of Management* 32, no. 6 (2006), pp. 951–990.
51. R. Bergman, "Identity as Motivation: Toward a Theory of the Moral Self," in *Moral Development, Self and Identity*, ed. D. K. Lapsley and D. Narvaez (Mahwah, NJ: Erlbaum, 2004), pp. 21–46.
52. M. E. Schweitzer, L. Ordonez, and B. Douma, "Goal Setting as a Motivator of Unethical Behavior," *Academy of Management Journal* 47, no. 3 (2004), pp. 422–432.
53. Max Bazerman and Ann Tenbrunsel, "Ethical Breakdowns," *Harvard Business Review*, April 2011, p. 60.
54. N. M. Ashkanasy, C. A. Windsor, and L. K. Treviño, "Bad Apples in Bad Barrels Revisited: Cognitive Moral Development, Just World Beliefs, Rewards, and Ethical Decision Making," *Business Ethics Quarterly* 16 (2006), pp. 449–474.
55. "Ethics: It Isn't Just the Big Guys," *The American Intelligence Wire*, July 28, 2003, p. 10.
56. J. Krohe Jr., "The Big Business of Business Ethics," *Across the Board* 34 (May 1997), pp. 23–29; Deborah Wells and Marshall Schminke, "Ethical Development and Human Resources Training: An Integrator Framework," *Human Resource Management Review* 11 (2001), pp. 135–158.
57. "Ethical Issues in the Management of Human Resources," *Human Resource Management Review* 11 (2001), p. 6; Joel Lefkowitz, "The Constancy of Ethics Amidst the Changing World of Work," *Human Resource Management Review* 16 (2006), pp. 245–268; William Byham, "Can You Interview for Integrity?" *Across the Board* 41, no. 2 (March/April 2004), pp. 34–38. For a description of how the United States Military Academy uses its student admission and socialization processes to promote character development, see Evan Offstein and Ronald Dufresne, "Building Strong Ethics and Promoting Positive Character Development: The Influence of HRM at the United States Military Academy at West Point," *Human Resource Management* 46, no. 1 (Spring 2007), pp. 95–114.
58. Gary Weaver and Linda Treviño, "The Role of Human Resources in Ethics/Compliance Management: A Fairness Perspective," *Human Resource Management Review* 11 (2001), p. 123. See also Linda Andrews, "The Nexus of Ethics," *HR Magazine*, August 2005, pp. 53–58.
59. Kathryn Tyler, "Do the Right Thing: Ethics Training Programs Help Employees Deal with Ethical Dilemmas," *HR Magazine*, February 2005, pp. 99–102.
60. "Ethical Issues in the Management of Human Resources," p. 6.

61. Weaver and Treviño, "The Role of Human Resources in Ethics/Compliance Management," p. 123.
62. Michael Burr, "Corporate Governance: Embracing Sarbanes-Oxley," *Public Utilities Fortnightly*, October 15, 2003, pp. 20–22.
63. M. Ronald Buckley et al., "Ethical Issues in Human Resources Systems," *Human Resource Management Review* 11, nos. 1–2 (2001), pp. 11, 29. See also Ann Pomeroy, "The Ethics Squeeze," *HR Magazine*, March 2006, pp. 48–55.
64. Tom Asacker, "Ethics in the Workplace," *Training & Development*, August 2004, p. 44; http://skillsoft.com/catalog/search.asp?title=Business+Ethics&type=Courses&submit.x=45&submit.y=15, accessed August 11, 2009.
65. Ed Finkel, "Yahoo Takes New Road on Ethics Training," *Workforce Management*, July 2010, p. 2.
66. Weaver and Treviño, "The Role of Human Resources in Ethics/Compliance Management," pp. 113–134.
67. "Fortune 500 Firms Face Unique Pressures Leading to Ethical Lapses, Report Reveals," *BNA Bulletin to Management*, July 31, 2012, p. 242.
68. Milton Zall, "Employee Privacy," *Journal of Property Management* 66, no. 3 (May 2001), p. 16.
69. Morris Attaway, "Privacy in the Workplace on the Web," *Internal Auditor* 58, no. 1 (February 2001), p. 30.
70. Declam Leonard and Angela France, "Workplace Monitoring: Balancing Business Interests with Employee Privacy Rights," *Society for Human Resource Management Legal Report* (May–June 2003), pp. 3–6.
71. "After Employer Found Liable for Worker's Child Porn, Policies May Need to Be Revisited," *BNA Bulletin to Management* (March 21, 2006), p. 89.
72. "Twitter Is Latest Electronic Tool to Pose Challenges and Opportunities for Employers," *BNA Bulletin to Management*, June 16, 2009, p. 185. See also Sean Valentine et al., "Exploring the Ethicality of Firing Employees Who Blog," *Human Resource Management* 49, no. 1 (January/February 2010), pp. 87–108.
73. Dave Zielinski, "Bring Your Own Device," *HR Magazine*, February 2012, pp. 71–74.
74. Kathy Gurchiek, "iPods Can Hit Sour Note in the Office," *HR Magazine*, April 2006; www.highbeam.com/doc/1G1-144992472.html.
75. Ibid.
76. Rita Zeidner, "Keeping E-Mail in Check," *HR Magazine*, June 2007, pp. 70–74.
77. "FTC Rules May Make Employers Liable for Worker Web Conduct," *BNA Bulletin to Management*, January 19, 2010, p. 23.
78. "Attorneys Advise Reconsidering Social Media Policies Based on NLRB Counsel's Report," *BNA Bulletin to Management*, February 21, 2012, p. 58.
79. *Vega-Rodriguez v. Puerto Rico Telephone Company*, CA1, #962061, 4/8/97, discussed in "Video Surveillance Withstands Privacy Challenge," *BNA Bulletin to Management*, April 17, 1997, p. 121. Also see, J. Greenwald, "Monitoring Communications? Know Legal Pitfalls," *Business Insurance* 45, no. 6 (February 7, 2011), pp. 1, 17.
80. *Quon v. Arch Wireless Operating Co.*, 529 F.3d 892 (9th Cir. 2008); "Employers Should Re-Examine Policies in Light of Ruling," *BNA Bulletin to Management*, August 12, 2008, p. 263.
81. Searcey, "Some Courts Raise Bar on Reading Employee Email," p. A17.
82. "When Can an Employer Access Private E-Mail on Its System?" *BNA Bulletin to Management*, July 14, 2009, p. 224; one employment lawyer says that courts look to whether the employer's process is reasonable when determining if the employer's monitoring practices are acceptable. Electronic monitoring is generally reasonable "where there is a legitimate business purpose, where policies exist to set the privacy expectations of employees, and where employees are informed of the rules and understand the methods used to monitor the workplace." Nicole Kamm, "I Got Electronic Information," *HR Magazine*, January 2010, pp. 57–58.
83. Bill Roberts, "Are You Ready for Biometrics?" *HR Magazine*, March 2003, pp. 95–96.
84. Fredric Leffler and Lauren Palais, "Filter Out Perilous Company E-Mails," *Society for Human Resource Management Legal Report*, August 2008, p. 3. A recent survey of 220 large U.S. firms suggests that about 38% of them have people reading or otherwise analyzing employees' outgoing e-mail. Dionne Searcey, "Some Courts Raise Bar on Reading Employee Email," *The Wall Street Journal*, November 19, 2009, p. A17.
85. Bill Roberts, "Stay Ahead of the Technology Use Curve," *HR Magazine*, October 2008, pp. 57–61.
86. One attorney notes that problems can arise with the Federal Stored Communications Act if the employer uses illicit or coercive means to access the employee's private social media accounts. *BNA Bulletin to Management*, July 21, 2009, p. 225.
87. See also "Twitter Is Latest Electronic Tool to Pose Challenges and Opportunities for Employers," *BNA Bulletin to Management*, June 16, 2009, p. 185.
88. "Time Clocks Go High Touch, High Tech to Keep Workers from Gaming the System," *BNA Bulletin to Management*, March 25, 2004, p. 97.
89. Andrea Poe, "Make Foresight 20/20," *HR Magazine*, February 2000, pp. 74–80.
90. Gundars Kaupin et al., "Recommended Employee Location Monitoring Policies," www.shrm.org, accessed January 2, 2007.
91. Rita Zeidner, "New Face in the C-Suite," *HR Magazine*, January 2010, p. 39.
92. Rachel Emma Silverman, "Tracking Sensors Invade the Workplace," *The Wall Street Journal*, March 7, 2013, pp. B1, B2.
93. Claire Suddath, "Tesco Monitors Employees with Motorola on Bands," www.BusinessWeek.com/articles/2013-02-13/Tesco-monitors-employees-with-Motorola-arm–bands, accessed February 14, 2013.
94. Ibid., p. 125.
95. Grossman, "Executive Discipline," pp. 46–51. See also Jean Thilmany, "Supporting Ethical Employees," *HR Magazine* 52, no. 9 (September 2007), pp. 105–106, 108, 110, 112.
96. Lester Bittel, *What Every Supervisor Should Know* (New York: McGraw-Hill, 1974), p. 308; Paul Falcone, "Fundamentals of Progressive Discipline," *HR Magazine*, February 1997, pp. 90–92; Thomas Salvo, "Practical Tips for Successful Progressive Discipline," SHRM White Paper, July 2004, www.shrm.org/hrresources/whitepapers_published/CMS_009030.asp, accessed January 5, 2008.
97. For fair discipline guidelines, see Bittel, *What Every Supervisor Should Know*, p. 308; Paul Falcone, "Fundamentals of Progressive Discipline," *HR Magazine*, February 1997, pp. 90–92; and *How to Discipline and Fire Employees*, www.entrepreneur.com/article/79928, accessed May 3, 2012.
98. David Mayer et al., "When Do Fair Procedures Not Matter? A Test of the Identity Violation Effect," *Journal of Applied Psychology* 94, no. 1 (2009), pp. 142–161.
99. Grossman, "Executive Discipline," pp. 46–51; "The Evil Women Theses," based on Sandra Hartman et al., "Males and Females in a Discipline Situation Exploratory Research on Competing Hypotheses," *Journal of Managerial Issues* 6, no. 1 (Spring 1994), pp. 57, 64–68; "A Woman's Place," *The Economist* 356, no. 8184 (August 19, 2000), p. 56.
100. For fair discipline guidelines, see Bittel, *What Every Supervisor Should Know*, p. 308; Falcone, "Fundamentals of Progressive Discipline," pp. 90–92; and *How to Discipline and Fire Employees*.
101. George Bohlander, "Why Arbitrators Overturn Managers in Employee Suspension and Discharge Cases," *Journal of Collective Negotiations* 23, no. 1 (1994), pp. 76–77.
102. "Employers Turn to Corporate Ombuds to Defuse Internal Ticking Time Bombs," *BNA Bulletin to Management*, August 9, 2005, p. 249.
103. Dick Grote, "Discipline Without Punishment," *Across the Board* 38, no. 5 (September 2001), pp. 52–57.
104. "Workforce Compensation and Performance Service, Office of Performance and Compensation Systems Design, Classification Programs Division, July 1999, HRCD-7; "Employee Relations," *HR Magazine* 55, no. 7 (July 2010), p. SS-4.
105. http://view.fdu.edu/default.aspx?id=3529, accesssed September 6, 2012.
106. Ibid.
107. Carolyn Hirschman, "Giving Voice to Employee Concerns: Encouraging Employees to Speak Out Requires Respectful Treatment and Appropriate Action," *HR Magazine* 53, no. 8 (August 2008), pp. 50–54.
108. Tschanen Niederkohr, "Employee Relations: Use the Exit Interview to Gain Valuable Insight," *Aftermarket Business* 117, no. 11 (November 2007), p. 8.
109. Dina Berta, "IHOP Franchisee Employs Post-Hiring Surveys to Get Off Turnover 'Treadmill,'" *Nation's Restaurant News* 41, no. 39 (October 1, 2007), p. 6.
110. Kate Leahy, "The 10 Minute Manager's Guide to . . . Communicating with Employees," *Restaurants & Institutions* 116, no. 11 (June 1, 2006), pp. 22–23.
111. Ibid.
112. J. G. Carr, A. M. Schmidt, J. K. Ford, and R. P. DeShon, "Climate Perceptions Matter: A Meta-Analytic Path Analysis Relating Molar Climate, Cognitive and Affective States, and Individual Level Work Outcomes," *Journal of Applied Psychology* 88 (2003), pp. 605–619; quoted in Stephen Robbins and Timothy Judge, *Organizational Behavior* (Upper Saddle River, NJ: Prentice Hall, 2011), p. 524.
113. Survey: Employee Survey Number One, www.shrm.org/templatestools/samples/HRforms, accessed April 11, 2012.
114. Pat Lenius, "Murray Supply Host Recognition Dinner," *Supply House Times*, May 2011, p. 70.

115. SHRM Survey Findings: Employee Recognition Programs, Winter 2012. In collaboration with and commissioned by Globoforce (www.globoforce.com/).
116. This is based on Recognition: Service Award Checklist, www.shrm.org/templatestools/samples/HRforms, November 5, 2010, accessed April 14, 2012.
117. http://mashable.com/follow/topics/pinterest, accessed April 15, 2012.
118. http://mashable.com/2012/04/06/pinterest-employee-engagement/, accessed April 15, 2012.
119. Tamara Lytle, "Giving Employees a Say: Getting—and Acting on—Ideas Offered by Employees Can Save Employers Money and Build a Sense of Ownership Among Workers," *HR Magazine* 56, no. 10 (October 2011), pp. 69–74.
120. James H. Shonk, *Team-Based Organizations* (Chicago: Irwin, 1997), pp. 27–33.
121. Ibid., p. 28.
122. John Katzenbach and Douglas Smith, "The Discipline of Teams," *Harvard Business Review* (March/April 1993), pp. 116–118.
123. Everett Adams Jr., "Quality Circle Performance," *Journal of Management* 17, no. 1 (1991), pp. 25–39.
124. Jack Orsburn et al., *Self-Directed Teams* (Homewood, Il: Business One Irwin, 1990), p. 8.
125. Charles Fishman, "Engines of Democracy," *Fast Company*, October 1999, pp. 173–202.
126. Tom Peters, *Liberation Management* (New York: Alfred A. Knopf, 1992), pp. 238–239.
127. Orsburn et al., *Self-Directed Teams*, pp. 22–23.
128. Susan Wells, "From Ideas to Results: To Get the Most from Your Company's Suggestion System, Move Ideas Up the Ladder Through a Formal Process," *HR Magazine* 50, no. 2 (February 2005), pp. 54–59.
129. Rebecca Hastings, "Survey: Employees Have Plenty of Suggestions," www.shrm.org/HRdisciplines/employeerelations/articles, February 29, 2012, accessed April 15, 2012.
130. Based on Wells, "From Ideas to Results."
131. Ibid.
132. This is quoted from ibid.
133. Based on "Theft Is Unethical," *HR Solutions* 34 (October 2002), p. 66.
134. Bureau of National Affairs, *Bulletin to Management*, September 13, 1985, p. 3.
135. David Gebler, "Is Your Culture a Risk Factor?" *Business and Society Review* 111, no. 3 (Fall 2006), pp. 337–362.
136. John Cohan, "'I Didn't Know' and 'I Was Only Doing My Job': Has Corporate Governance Careened Out of Control? A Case Study of Enron's Information Myopia," *Journal of Business Ethics* 40, no. 3 (October 2002), pp. 275–299.
137. Tony Simons and Quinetta Roberson, "Why Managers Should Care about Fairness. The Effects of Aggregate Justice Perceptions on Organizational Outcomes," *Journal of Applied Psychology* 88, no. 3 (2003), p. 432

15 Labor Relations and Collective Bargaining

Source: Bloomberg/Getty Images

MyManagementLab®

Improve Your Grade!

When you see this icon, visit **www.mymanagementlab.com** for activities that are applied, personalized, and offer immediate feedback.

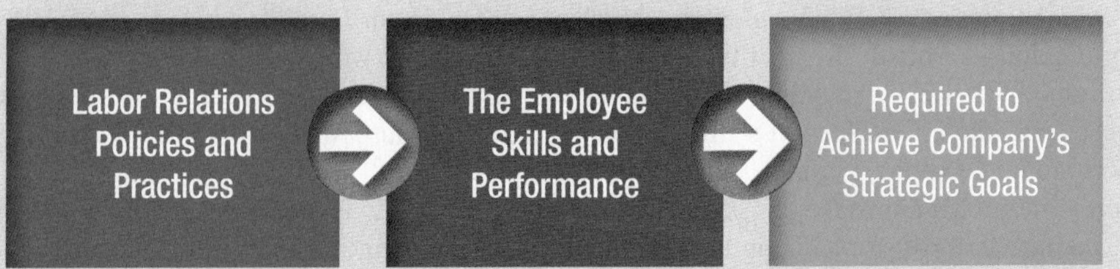

For a bird's eye view of how one company created a new labor relations program to improve its strategic performance, read the Hotel Paris case on pages 484–485 and answer the questions after reading the chapter.

WHERE ARE WE NOW . . .

The topics we discussed earlier, such as discipline and fair treatment, are among those that influence whether employees join unions. Now, the main purpose of this chapter is to help you deal effectively with unions and grievances. The main topics we discuss are the labor movement; unions and the law; the union drive and election; the collective bargaining process; dealing with disputes and grievances; and the union movement today and tomorrow.

LEARNING OBJECTIVES

1 Give a brief history of the American labor movement.

2 Discuss the main features of at least three major pieces of labor legislation.

3 Present examples of what to expect during the union drive and election.

4 Illustrate with examples of bargaining that is not in good faith.

5 Develop a grievance procedure.

6 Describe a strategy for cooperative labor relations.

Some people call Costco "The Anti-Walmart," because Costco treats its workers and unions so well.[1] Whereas Walmart is known for difficult labor relations (it recently said it was eliminating health insurance for future employees working under 24 hours per week),[2] Costco actually keeps profits up in part with positive labor relations policies. We'll see how they do it.

The Labor Movement

1 Give a brief history of the American labor movement.

Unions are still important. While union membership is down, about 14 million U.S. workers still belong to unions—around 11.3% of the total number of men and women working in America.[3] And in some industries—including transportation and public utilities, where more than 26% of employees are union members—it's still hard to get a job without joining a union.[4] Most union members are in the public sector, as opposed to the private sector.[5]

Furthermore, it's a mistake to assume that unions affect employers only negatively. For example, perhaps by professionalizing the staff and/or systematizing practices, heart attack mortality among patients in hospitals with unionized registered nurses was 5% to 9% lower than in nonunion hospitals.[6] The accompanying Profit Center feature provides another example of the potential benefits of good union-management relations.

IMPROVING PERFORMANCE: HR as a Profit Center

The "Anti-Walmart"

It's not easy competing with Walmart's low prices, but Walmart Stores' Sam's Club is actually second in sales to Costco. How does Costco stay ahead? In part with "strong labor relations, low employee turnover and liberal benefits."[7] For example, Costco pays about 90% of the health insurance costs of its over 90,000 domestic employees.[8] And its relations with labor unions are comparatively gentle. For example, when California grocery store workers picketed several chains a few years ago, "Costco Wholesale Corp. avoided the fray, quietly renegotiating a separate contract with its union employees there." The new contract boosted Costco workers' wages and the firm's contribution to their pension plans.

Costco's HR strategy is to fend off Walmart's low wages and labor costs by eliciting higher productivity and better service from its employees. The strategy seems to be working. Costco's sales per employee are about $500,000 a year versus $340,000 at Sam's Club.[9] Turnover is far below the retail industry average.[10] Having a positive labor relations strategy that supports Costco's overall aim of boosting profits through better productivity and service is working for Costco.

Discussion Question 15-1: If supportive labor relations works so well for Costco, why do you think Walmart doesn't use it too?

Support for unions has always ebbed and flowed in America, and today pressures are building against unions. For example, critical budget problems following the recent recession prompted several states to reduce public employees' numbers, pensions, and pay.

We'll look at unions and dealing with them in this chapter.

Library of Congress

Making fenders at an early Ford factory in Ypsilanti, Michigan. In addition to heavy physical labor, workers faced health hazards—poor lighting, dust, and dangerous machinery.

Why Do Workers Organize?

Experts have spent much time and money trying to discover why workers unionize, and they've proposed many theories. Yet there is no simple answer.

It's not just about better pay or working conditions, though these are important. For example, recent median weekly wages for union workers was $943, versus $742 for nonunion workers.[11] Union workers also generally receive more holidays, sick leave, unpaid leave, insurance plan benefits, long-term disability benefits, and other benefits. Unions also somewhat reduced the impact of downsizings and wage cuts in many industries.[12]

Two other factors—employer unfairness and the union's power—are also important. In one Australia-based firm, researchers found that "individuals who believe that the company rules or policies were administered unfairly or to their detriment were more likely to turn to unions."[13] But, to vote pro-union, the employees also had to believe the union could actually improve their wages, benefits, and treatment.

THE BOTTOM LINE The bottom line is that the urge to unionize often boils down to the workers' belief that it's only through unity that they can protect themselves from management whims. When Kaiser Permanente cut back on vacation and sick leave for its pharmacists, the Guild for Professional Pharmacists won back the lost vacation days. Said one, "Kaiser is a pretty benevolent employer, but there's always the pressure to squeeze a little."[14] One labor relations lawyer says, "The one major thing unions offer is making you a 'for cause' instead of an 'at will' employee, which guarantees a hearing and arbitration if you're fired."[15] So, in practice, low morale, fear of job loss, and arbitrary management actions help foster unionization.

In some respects, things have not changed in years. Here is how one writer describes the motivation behind the early (1900s) unionization of automobile workers:

> In the years to come, economic issues would make the headlines when union and management met in negotiations. But in the early years, . . . the principal grievances of the autoworkers were the speed-up of production and the lack of any kind of job security. As production tapered off, the order in which workers were laid off was determined largely by the whim of foremen and other supervisors. . . . Generally, what the workers revolted against was the lack of human dignity and individuality, and a working relationship that was massively impersonal, cold, and nonhuman. They wanted to be treated like human beings—not like faceless clock card numbers.[16]

What Do Unions Want?

We can generalize by saying that unions have two sets of aims, for *union security* and for *improved wages, hours, working conditions*, and *benefits* for their members.

UNION SECURITY First and probably foremost, unions seek security for themselves. They fight hard for the right to represent a firm's workers, and to be the exclusive bargaining agent for all employees in the unit. (As such, they negotiate contracts for all employees, including those not members of the union.) Five types of union security are possible:

1. **Closed shop.**[17] The company can hire only current union members. Congress outlawed closed shops in interstate commerce, but they still exist in some states for particular industries (such as printing). They account for fewer than 5% of union contracts.
2. **Union shop.** The company can hire nonunion people, but they must join the union after a prescribed period and pay dues. (If not, they can be fired.) These account for about 73% of union contracts.
3. **Agency shop.** Employees who do not belong to the union still must pay the union an amount equal to union dues (on the assumption that the union's efforts benefit *all* the workers).
4. **Preferential shop.** Union members get preference in hiring, but the employer can still hire nonunion members.
5. ***Maintenance of membership arrangement.*** Employees do not have to belong to the union. However, union members employed by the firm must maintain membership in the union for the contract period. These account for about 4% of union agreements.

closed shop
A form of union security in which the company can hire only union members. This was outlawed in 1947 but still exists in some industries (such as printing).

union shop
A form of union security in which the company can hire nonunion people, but they must join the union after a prescribed period of time and pay dues. (If they do not, they can be fired.)

agency shop
A form of union security in which employees who do not belong to the union must still pay union dues on the assumption that union efforts benefit all workers.

preferential shop
Union members get preference in hiring, but the employer can still hire nonunion members.

right to work
A term used to describe state statutory or constitutional provisions banning the requirement of union membership as a condition of employment.

Not all states give unions the right to require union membership as a condition of employment. **Right to work** is a term used to describe "state statutory or constitutional provisions banning the requirement of union membership as a condition of employment."[18] *Right-to-work laws* don't outlaw unions. They do outlaw (within those states) any form of union security. There are 23 right-to-work states.[19] Right to work adversely affects union membership levels.[20]

IMPROVED WAGES, HOURS, AND BENEFITS Once the union ensures its security at the employer, it fights to improve its members' wages, hours, working conditions and benefits. The typical labor agreement also gives the union a role in other human resource activities, including recruiting, selecting, compensating, promoting, training, and discharging employees.

The AFL-CIO and the SEIU

The American Federation of Labor and Congress of Industrial Organizations (AFL-CIO) is a voluntary federation of about 57 national and international labor unions in the United States. The separate AFL and CIO merged in 1955. For many people in the United States, the AFL-CIO is synonymous with the word *union*.

There are three layers in the AFL-CIO and most other U.S. unions. The worker joins the local union, to which he or she pays dues. The local is in turn a single chapter in the national union. For example, if you were a teacher in Detroit, you would belong to the local union there, which is one of hundreds of local chapters of the American Federation of Teachers, their national union (most unions actually call themselves international unions). The third layer is the national federation, in this case, the AFL-CIO.

The Service Employees International Union (SEIU) is a federation of more than 2.2 million members. It includes the largest health-care union, with more than 1.1 million members, including nurses, LPNs, and doctors, and the second largest public employees union, with more than 1 million local and state government workers.[21]

Union federation membership is in flux. Several years ago, the SEIU, the International Brotherhood of Teamsters, and UNITE HERE left the AFL-CIO and established their own federation, called the Change to Win Coalition. Together, the departing unions represented over one-quarter of the AFL-CIO's membership and budget. Change to Win plans to be more aggressive about organizing workers than they say the AFL-CIO was.[22] Then the UNITE HERE union left Change to Win and rejoined the AFL-CIO, possibly slowing Change to Win's momentum.

Unions and the Law

2 Discuss the main features of at least three major pieces of labor legislation.

Norris-LaGuardia Act of 1932
This law marked the beginning of the era of strong encouragement of unions and guaranteed to each employee the right to bargain collectively "free from interference, restraint, or coercion."

National Labor Relations (or Wagner) Act
This law banned certain types of unfair practices and provided for secret-ballot elections and majority rule for determining whether a firm's employees want to unionize.

National Labor Relations Board (NLRB)
The agency created by the Wagner Act to investigate unfair labor practice charges and to provide for secret-ballot elections and majority rule in determining whether or not a firm's employees want a union.

The history of the American labor movement is one of expansion and contraction, in response to public policy changes. Until about 1930, there were no special labor laws. Employers were not required to engage in collective bargaining with employees and were virtually unrestrained in their behavior toward unions; the use of spies and firing of union agitators were widespread. "Yellow dog" contracts, whereby management could require nonunion membership as a condition for employment, were widely enforced. Most union weapons—even strikes—were illegal.

This situation lasted until the Great Depression (around 1930).[23] Since then, in response to changing public attitudes and economic conditions, labor law has gone through three clear periods: from "strong encouragement" of unions, to "modified encouragement coupled with regulation," and finally to "detailed regulation of internal union affairs."[24]

Period of Strong Encouragement: The Norris-LaGuardia (1932) and National Labor Relations (or Wagner) Acts (1935)

The **Norris-LaGuardia Act of 1932** set the stage for a new era in which union activity was encouraged. It guaranteed to each employee the right to bargain collectively "free from interference, restraint, or coercion." It declared yellow dog contracts unenforceable. And it limited the courts' abilities to issue injunctions (stop orders) for activities such as peaceful picketing and payment of strike benefits.

Yet this act did little to restrain employers from fighting labor organizations. So, in 1935, Congress passed the **National Labor Relations (or Wagner) Act** to add teeth to Norris-LaGuardia. It did this by (1) banning certain unfair labor practices, (2) providing for secret-ballot elections and majority rule for determining whether a firm's employees would unionize, and (3) creating the **National Labor Relations Board (NLRB)** to enforce these two provisions.

UNFAIR EMPLOYER LABOR PRACTICES The Wagner Act deemed "statutory wrongs" (but not crimes) five unfair labor practices used by employers:

1. It is unfair for employers to "interfere with, restrain, or coerce employees" in exercising their legally sanctioned right of self-organization.
2. It is unfair for company representatives to dominate or interfere with either the formation or the administration of labor unions. Among other specific management actions found to be unfair under these first two practices are bribing employees, using company spy systems, moving a business to avoid unionization, and black-listing union sympathizers.
3. Employers are prohibited from discriminating in any way against employees for their legal union activities.
4. Employers are forbidden to discharge or discriminate against employees simply because the latter file unfair practice charges against the company.
5. Finally, it is an unfair labor practice for employers to refuse to bargain collectively with their employees' duly chosen representatives.

FIGURE 15-1 NLRB Form 501: Filing an Unfair Labor Practice

Source: National Labor Relations Board, www.nlrb.gov/.

FORM NLRB 501
(2 81)

FORM EXEMPT UNDER
44 U.S.C. 3512

UNITED STATES OF AMERICA
NATIONAL LABOR RELATIONS BOARD
CHARGE AGAINST EMPLOYER

INSTRUCTIONS: File an original and 4 copies of this charge with NLRB Regional Director for the region in which the alleged unfair labor practice occurred or is occurring.	DO NOT WRITE IN THIS SPACE	
	CASE NO.	DATE FILE

1. EMPLOYER AGAINST WHOM CHARGE IS BROUGHT

a. NAME OF EMPLOYER	b. NUMBER OF WORKERS EMPLOYED	
c. ADDRESS OF ESTABLISHMENT (*street and number, city, State, and ZIP code*)	d. EMPLOYER REPRESENTATIVE TO CONTACT	e. PHONE NO.
f. TYPE OF ESTABLISHMENT (*factory, mine, wholesaler, etc.*)	g. IDENTIFY PRINCIPAL PRODUCT OR SERVICE	

h. THE ABOVE-NAMED EMPLOYER HAS ENGAGED IN AND IS ENGAGING IN UNFAIR LABOR PRACTICES WITHIN THE MEANING OF SECTION 8(a), SUBSECTIONS (1) AND ________ (*list subsections*) OF THE NATIONAL LABOR RELATIONS ACT, AND THESE UNFAIR LABOR PRACTICES ARE UNFAIR LABOR PRACTICES AFFECTING COMMERCE WITHIN THE MEANING OF THE ACT.

2. BASIS OF THE CHARGE (*be specific as to facts, names, addresses, plants involved, dates, places, etc.*)

BY THE ABOVE AND OTHER ACTS, THE ABOVE-NAMED EMPLOYER HAS INTERFERED WITH, RESTRAINED, AND COERCED EMPLOYEES IN THE EXERCISE OF THE RIGHTS GUARANTEED IN SECTION 7 OF THE ACT.

3. FULL NAME OF PARTY FILING CHARGE (*if labor organization, give full name, including local name and number*)

4a. ADDRESS (*street and number, city, State, and ZIP code*)	4b. TELEPHONE NO.

5. FULL NAME OF NATIONAL OR INTERNATIONAL LABOR ORGANIZATION OF WHICH IT IS AN AFFILIATE OR CONSTITUENT UNIT (*to be filled in when charge is filed by a labor organization*)

6. DECLARATION

I declare that I have read the above charge and that the statements therein are true to the best of my knowledge and belief.

By ________
(signature of representative or person filing charge) (title, if any)

Address ________
(telephone number) (date)

WILLFULLY FALSE STATEMENTS ON THIS CHARGE CAN BE PUNISHED BY FINE AND IMPRISONMENT
(*U.S. CODE, TITLE 18, SECTION 1001*)

Unions file an unfair labor practice charge (see Figure 15-1) with the National Labor Relations Board. (For example, the American Guild of Musical Artists said it would file an unfair labor charge against the New York City Opera if it cut staff and moved.) The board then decides whether to take action. Possible actions include dismissal of the complaint, request for an injunction against the employer, or an order that the employer cease and desist.

FROM 1935 TO 1947 Union membership increased quickly after passage of the Wagner Act. Other factors such as an improving economy and aggressive union leadership contributed to this rise. But by the mid-1940s, largely due to massive postwar strikes, public policy began to shift against what many viewed as union excesses. The stage was set for passage of the Taft-Hartley Act.

Period of Modified Encouragement Coupled with Regulation: The Taft-Hartley Act (1947)

Taft-Hartley Act of 1947
Also known as the *Labor Management Relations Act*, this law prohibited unfair union labor practices and enumerated the rights of employees as union members. It also enumerated the rights of employers.

The **Taft-Hartley** *(or Labor Management Relations)* **Act of 1947** reflected the public's less enthusiastic attitude toward unions. It amended the National Labor Relations (Wagner) Act by limiting unions in four ways: (1) prohibiting unfair union labor practices, (2) enumerating the rights of employees as union members, (3) enumerating the rights of employers, and (4) allowing the President of the United States to bar temporarily national emergency strikes.

Unfair Union Labor Practices

The Taft-Hartley Act enumerated several labor practices that unions were prohibited from engaging in:

1. First, it banned *unions* from *restraining or coercing employees* from exercising their guaranteed bargaining rights. (Some union actions that courts have held illegal include telling an anti-union employee that he or she will lose his or her job once the union gains recognition, and issuing patently false statements during union organizing campaigns.)
2. It is also an unfair labor practice for a union to *cause an employer to discriminate* in any way against an employee so as to encourage or discourage his or her union membership. For example, the union cannot try to force an employer to fire a worker because he or she doesn't attend union meetings or refuses to join a union. There is one exception: Suppose a closed or union shop prevails (and union membership is therefore a prerequisite to employment). Then the union may demand the discharge of someone who fails to pay his or her initiation fees and dues.
3. It is an unfair labor practice for a union to *refuse to bargain in good faith* with the employer about wages, hours, and other employment conditions.
4. It is an unfair labor practice for a union to engage in *featherbedding* (requiring an employer to pay an employee for services not performed).

RIGHTS OF EMPLOYEES The Taft-Hartley Act protected the rights of employees against their unions in other ways. For example, many people felt that compulsory unionism violated the right of freedom of association. Legitimized by Taft-Hartley, new right-to-work laws sprung up in 19 (now 23) states (mainly in the South and Southwest). In New York, for example, in many printing firms you can't work as a press operator unless you belong to a printers' union. In Florida, a right-to-work state, printing shops typically employ both union and nonunion operators. Even today, union membership varies widely by state, from a high of 26.8% in New York to a low of 3.2% in North Carolina.[25] The Taft-Hartley act also required the employee's authorization before the union could subtract dues from his or her paycheck.

In general, the Labor Relations (Taft-Hartley) Act does not restrain unions from unfair labor practices to the extent that the law does employers. It says unions may not restrain or coerce employees. However, "violent or otherwise threatening behavior or clearly coercive or intimidating union activities are necessary before the NLRB will find an unfair labor practice."[26] Examples include physical assaults or threats, economic reprisals, and mass picketing that restrains lawful entry or leaving.

RIGHTS OF EMPLOYERS The Taft-Hartley Act also explicitly gave *employers* certain rights. First, it gave them full freedom to express their views concerning union organization. For example, as a manager you can tell your employees that in your opinion unions are worthless, dangerous to the economy, and immoral. You can even (generally) hint that unionization and high-wage demands might result in the permanent closing of the plant (but not its relocation). Employers can set forth the union's record concerning violence and corruption, if appropriate. In fact, the only major restraint is that employers must avoid threats, promises, coercion, and direct interference with workers who are trying to reach a decision. There can be no threat of reprisal or force or promise of benefit.[27]

Furthermore, the employer (1) cannot meet with employees on company time within 24 hours of an election or (2) suggest to employees that they vote against the union while they are at home or in the employer's office (although he or she can do so while in their work area or where they normally gather).

national emergency strikes
Strikes that might "imperil the national health and safety."

NATIONAL EMERGENCY STRIKES The Taft-Hartley Act also allows the U.S. president to intervene in **national emergency strikes**. These are strikes (for example, by railroad workers) that might "imperil the national health and safety." The president may appoint a board of inquiry and, based on its report, apply for an injunction restraining the strike for 60 days. If the parties don't reach a settlement during that time, the president can have the injunction extended for another 20 days. During this last period, employees take a secret ballot to ascertain their willingness to accept the employer's last offer.

Landrum-Griffin Act of 1959
Also known as the *Labor Management Reporting and Disclosure Act*, this law aimed at protecting union members from possible wrongdoing on the part of their unions.

PERIOD OF DETAILED REGULATION OF INTERNAL UNION AFFAIRS: THE LANDRUM-GRIFFIN ACT (1959) In the 1950s, Senate investigations revealed unsavory practices on the part of some unions, and the result was the **Landrum-Griffin Act** (officially, the *Labor Management Reporting and Disclosure Act*) **of 1959.** An overriding aim of this act was to protect union members from possible union wrongdoing. Like Taft-Hartley, it also amended the National Labor Relations (Wagner) Act.

First, the Act contains a *bill of rights* for union members. It provides for certain rights in the nomination of candidates for union office. It also affirms a member's right to sue his or her union and ensures that the union cannot fine or suspend a member without due process.

This act also laid out rules regarding union elections. For example, national and international unions must elect officers at least once every 5 years, using a secret-ballot mechanism. And the Act regulates the kind of person who can serve as a union officer. For example, it bars for a time persons convicted of felonies from holding union officer positions.

Senate investigators also discovered flagrant examples of employer wrongdoing. Employers and their "labor relations consultants" had bribed union agents and officers, for example. Landrum-Griffin therefore expanded the list of unlawful employer actions. For example, companies can no longer pay their own employees to entice them not to join the union.

LABOR LAW TODAY As we'll see toward the end of this chapter, it isn't quite clear whether the pressures toward a more encouraging or a more discouraging climate for labor law will prevail for the next few years. On the one hand, we'll see that unions are pushing for new legislation that would substantially improve unions' efforts. On the other hand, economic realities (shrinking state budgets, and increased competitive pressures, for instance) have undoubtedly reduced union membership.

The Union Drive and Election

3 Present examples of what to expect during the union drive and election.

It is through the union drive and election that a union tries to be recognized to represent employees. To protect themselves and their employers, supervisors need to understand this process. It has five basic steps.[28]

Step 1. Initial Contact

During the initial contact stage, the union determines the employees' interest in organizing, and establishes an organizing committee.

The initiative for the first contact between the employees and the union may come from the employees, from a union already representing other employees of the firm, or from another union. In any case, there is an initial contact.

Once an employer becomes a target, a union official usually assigns a representative to assess employee interest. The representative visits the firm to determine if enough employees are interested in a campaign, identifies employees who would make good leaders in the organizing campaign, and creates an organizing committee. The aim is to educate the committee about the benefits of forming a union and the law and procedures for forming a local union.

The union must follow certain rules when it starts contacting employees. The law allows organizers to solicit employees for membership as long as the effort doesn't endanger the performance or safety of the employees. Therefore, much contact takes place off the job, perhaps at home or at places near work. Organizers can also safely contact employees on company grounds during off hours (such as lunch or break time). Yet, in practice, there will be much informal organizing going on at the workplace as employees debate organizing. Sometimes the first inkling management has is the distribution of handbills soliciting union membership.

Much soliciting will be via e-mail, but prohibiting employees from sending pro-union e-mail messages using company e-mail isn't easy. You can't discriminate against union activities.

Therefore, prohibiting only union e-mail may violate NLRB rules. And barring workers from using e-mail for all non–work-related topics may be futile if the company actually does little to stop it.

LABOR RELATIONS CONSULTANTS Both management and unions typically use "labor relations consultants." These may be law firms, researchers, psychologists, labor relations specialists, or public relations firms. Some are former union organizers.[29]

For the employer, the consultant's services may range from ensuring that the firm properly fills out routine labor relations forms to managing the union campaign. Unions may use public relations firms to improve their image, or specialists to manage corporate campaigns. (These pressure shareholders and creditors to get management to agree to the union's demands.)

Some say consultants encourage questionable tactics. One tactic is to delay the union vote with lengthy hearings at the NLRB. The longer the delay in the vote, they argue, the more time the employer has to drill anti-union propaganda into the employees.

union salting
A union organizing tactic by which workers who are in fact employed full-time by a union as undercover organizers are hired by unwitting employers.

UNION SALTING Unions are not without creative ways to win elections. The National Labor Relations Board defines **union salting** as "placing of union members on nonunion job sites for the purpose of organizing." Critics claim that "salts" interfere with business operations and harass employees.[30] The U.S. Supreme Court ruled that union salts are "employees" under the National Labor Relations Act; the NLRB will require that employers pay salts if they fire them for trying to organize.[31] The solution is to know whom you're hiring. However, not hiring someone solely because he or she might be pro-union or a union salt would be discriminatory.[32]

Step 2. Obtaining Authorization Cards

authorization cards
In order to petition for a union election, the union must show that at least 30% of employees may be interested in being unionized. Employees indicate this interest by signing authorization cards.

For the union to petition the NLRB for the right to hold an election, it must show that a sizable number of employees may be interested in organizing. Therefore, the next step for union organizers is to try to get the employees to sign **authorization cards** (see Figure 15-2). Among other things, these usually authorize the union to seek a representation election and state that the employee has applied to join the union. Thirty percent of the eligible employees in an appropriate bargaining unit must sign before the union can petition the NLRB for an election (although in Figure 15-2 this employer has agreed with SEIU to recognize the union without a follow-up vote if a majority of employees sign the authorization cards).

FIGURE 15-2 Sample Authorization Card

SAMPLES UNIONS of AMERICA

Authorization for Representation

I hereby authorize Local 409 of the SAMPLES union to be my exclusive representative for the purposes of collective bargaining with my employer. I understand that my signature on this card may be used to obtain certification of Local 409 as our exclusive bargaining representative without an election.

This card will verify that I have applied for union membership and that effective ________________ I hereby authorize you to deduct each pay period from my earnings an amount equal to the regular current rate of monthly union dues and initiation fee.

Employer: ____________________ **Worksite:** ____________________

Date: ______________ **Name:** ________________________________

Street Address: __________________ **City:** ___________ **Zip code:** __________

Home Phone: ___________ **Cell Phone:** ____________ **Home E-mail:** ___________

Department: ____________________

Job Title/Classification: ____________________

Signature: ______________________________

You must print and mail in this authorization card for it to be recognized. Only original cards are valid and should be submitted. Mail to:

SAMPLES Unions of America, Local 409
301 Samples Way
Miami,FL 33101

This is a dangerous time for supervisors. During this stage, both union and management use propaganda. The union claims it can improve working conditions, raise wages, increase benefits, and generally get the workers better deals. Management can attack the union on ethical and moral grounds and cite the cost of union membership. Management can also explain its accomplishments, express facts and opinions, and explain the law applicable to organizing campaigns. However, neither side can threaten, bribe, or coerce employees. And an employer (or supervisor) may not make promises of benefits to employees or make unilateral changes in terms and conditions of employment that were not planned to be implemented prior to the onset of union organizing activity.

STEPS TO TAKE Management can take several steps with respect to the authorization cards. For example, the NLRB ruled an employer might lawfully inform employees of their right to revoke their authorization cards, even when employees have not asked for such information. The employer can also distribute pamphlets that explain just how employees can revoke their cards. However, the law prohibits any material assistance to employees such as postage or stationery.

Similarly, it is an unfair labor practice to tell employees they can't sign a card. What you *can* do is prepare supervisors so they can explain what the card actually authorizes the union to do—including subjecting the employee to union rules. The union, for instance, may force the employee to picket and fine any member who does not comply. Such explanations can be an effective weapon.

One thing managers should *not* do is look through signed authorization cards if confronted with them by union representatives. The NLRB could construe that as an unfair labor practice, as spying on those who signed. Doing so could also later form the basis of a charge alleging discrimination due to union activity, if the firm subsequently disciplines someone who signed a card.

During this stage, unions can picket the company, subject to three constraints: (1) The union must file a petition for an election within 30 days after the start of picketing; (2) the firm cannot already be lawfully recognizing another union; and (3) there cannot have been a valid NLRB election during the past 12 months.

Step 3. Hold a Hearing

Once the union collects the authorization cards, one of three things can occur. If the employer chooses *not to contest union recognition* at all, then the parties need no hearing, and a special "consent election" is held. If the employer chooses not to contest the union's *right to an election*, and/or the scope of the bargaining unit, and/or which employees are eligible to vote in the election, no hearing is needed and the parties can stipulate an election. If an employer *does* wish to contest the union's right, it can insist on a hearing to determine those issues. An employer's decision about whether to insist on a hearing is a strategic one. Management bases it on the facts of each case, and on whether it feels it needs more time to try to persuade employees not to elect a union.

Most companies do contest the union's right to represent their employees, claiming that a significant number don't really want the union. It is at this point that the National Labor Relations Board gets involved. The union usually contacts the NLRB, which requests a hearing. It then sends a hearing officer to investigate. The examiner sends both management and union a notice of representation hearing (NLRB Form 852; see Figure 15-3) that states the time and place of the hearing.

The hearing addresses several issues. First, does the record indicate there is enough evidence to hold an election? (For example, did 30% or more of the employees in an appropriate bargaining unit sign the authorization cards?) Second, the examiner decides what the bargaining unit will be. The **bargaining unit** is the group of employees that the union will be authorized to represent and bargain for collectively. If the entire organization is the bargaining unit, the union will represent all nonsupervisory, nonmanagerial, and nonconfidential employees, even though the union may be oriented mostly toward blue-collar workers. (Professional and nonprofessional employees can be included in the same bargaining unit only if the professionals agree.) If your firm disagrees with the examiner's bargaining unit decision, it can challenge the decision. This will require a separate NLRB ruling.

bargaining unit
The group of employees the union will be authorized to represent.

The NLRB hearing addresses other issues. These include, "Does the employer qualify for coverage by the NLRB?" and "Is the union a labor organization within the meaning of the National Labor Relations Act?"

FIGURE 15-3 NLRB Form 852: Notice of Representation Hearing

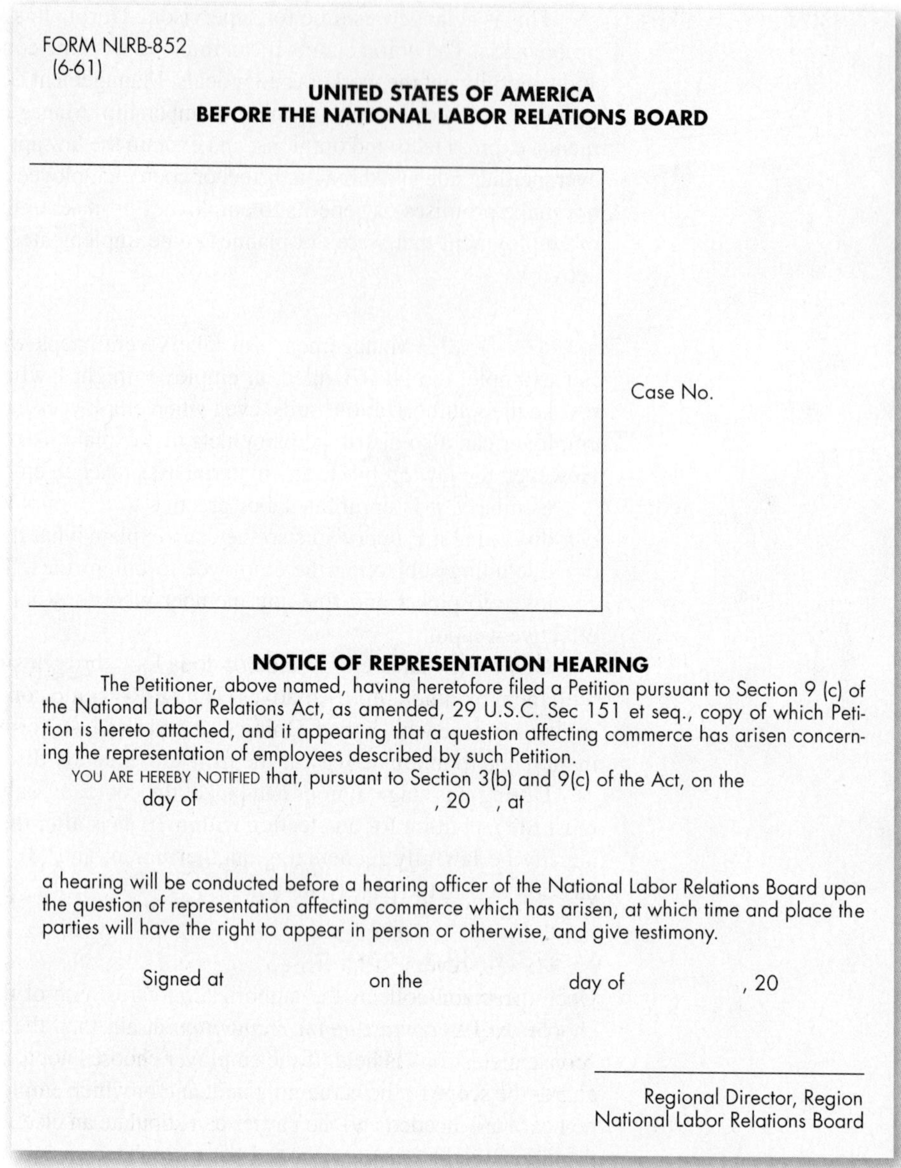

FORM NLRB-852
(6-61)

UNITED STATES OF AMERICA
BEFORE THE NATIONAL LABOR RELATIONS BOARD

Case No.

NOTICE OF REPRESENTATION HEARING

The Petitioner, above named, having heretofore filed a Petition pursuant to Section 9 (c) of the National Labor Relations Act, as amended, 29 U.S.C. Sec 151 et seq., copy of which Petition is hereto attached, and it appearing that a question affecting commerce has arisen concerning the representation of employees described by such Petition.

YOU ARE HEREBY NOTIFIED that, pursuant to Section 3(b) and 9(c) of the Act, on the day of , 20 , at

a hearing will be conducted before a hearing officer of the National Labor Relations Board upon the question of representation affecting commerce which has arisen, at which time and place the parties will have the right to appear in person or otherwise, and give testimony.

Signed at on the day of , 20

Regional Director, Region
National Labor Relations Board

If the results of the hearing are favorable for the union, the NLRB will order holding an election. It will issue a Notice of Election (NLRB Form 707) to that effect for the employer to post.

Step 4. The Campaign

During the campaign that precedes the election, union and employer appeal to employees for their votes. The union will emphasize that it will prevent unfairness, set up grievance and seniority systems, and improve wages. Union strength, they'll say, will give employees a greater voice in disciplinary matters and in determining wages and working conditions. Management will stress that improvements like those don't require unions and that wages are equal to or better than with a union. Management will also emphasize the cost of union dues; the fact that the union is an "outsider"; and that if the union wins, a strike may follow. It can even attack the union on ethical and moral grounds, while insisting that employees will not be as well off and may lose freedom. But neither side can threaten, bribe, or coerce employees.

Step 5. The Election

The election occurs within 30 to 60 days after the NLRB issues its Decision and Direction of Election. The election is by secret ballot; the NLRB provides the ballots (see Figure 15-4), voting booth, and ballot box, and counts the votes and certifies the results.

FIGURE 15-4 Sample NLRB Ballot

UNITED STATES OF AMERICA
National Labor Relations Board

OFFICIAL SECRET BALLOT

FOR CERTAIN EMPLOYEES OF

Do you wish to be represented for purposes of collective bargaining by —

MARK AN "S" IN THE SQUARE OF YOUR CHOICE

YES ☐ NO ☐

DO NOT SIGN THIS BALLOT. Fold and drop in ballot box.
If you spoil this ballot return it to the Board Agent for a new one.

The union becomes the employees' representative if it wins the election, and winning means getting a majority of the votes *cast*, not a majority of the total workers in the bargaining unit. (Also keep in mind that if an employer commits an unfair labor practice, the NLRB may reverse a "no union" election. Supervisors must therefore be careful not to commit unfair practices.)

Several things influence whether the union wins the certification election. Unions have a higher probability of success in geographic areas with a higher percentage of union workers. High unemployment seems to lead to poorer results for the union, perhaps because employees fear that unionization efforts might result in reduced job security or employer retaliation. Unions usually carefully pick the size of their bargaining unit (all clerical employees in the company, only those at one facility, and so on) because the larger the bargaining unit, the smaller the probability of union victory. The more workers vote, the less likely a union victory, probably because more workers who are not strong supporters vote. The union is important, too: The Teamsters union is less likely to win a representation election than other unions, for instance.[33]

How to Lose an NLRB Election

Over the years, unions typically won about 55% of elections held each year.[34] According to expert Matthew Goodfellow, there is no sure way employers can win elections, but several sure ways to lose one.[35]

REASON 1. ASLEEP AT THE SWITCH In one study, in 68% of the companies that lost to the union, executives were caught unaware. In these companies, turnover and absenteeism had increased, productivity was erratic, and safety was poor. Grievance procedures were rare. When the first reports of authorization cards began trickling in, they usually responded with letters describing the company as "one big family" and calling for a "team effort."[36]

REASON 2. APPOINTING A COMMITTEE Of the losing companies, 36% formed a committee to manage the campaign. The problems here are that: (1) Promptness is essential in an election situation, and committees move slowly. (2) Most committee members are NLRB neophytes, whose views reflect hope rather than experience. (3) A committee's decision is usually a compromise decision, not necessarily the most effective one.

This expert suggests giving full responsibility to one decisive executive. A human resource director and a consultant or advisor with broad experience in labor relations should assist this person.

REASON 3. CONCENTRATING ON MONEY AND BENEFITS In 54% of the elections studied, the company lost because top management concentrated on money and benefits. As Goodfellow says:

> Employees may want more money, but quite often, if they feel the company treats them fairly, decently, and honestly, they are satisfied with reasonable, competitive rates and benefits. It is only when they feel ignored, uncared for, and disregarded that money becomes a major issue to express their dissatisfaction.[37]

REASON 4. DELEGATING TOO MUCH TO DIVISIONS For companies with plants scattered around the country, unionizing one plant tends to lead to unionizing others. The solution is, don't abdicate all personnel and industrial relations decisions to plant managers.[38] Dealing effectively with unions—monitoring employees' attitudes, reacting properly when the union appears, and so on—requires centralized guidance from the main office and its human resources staff.

HR in Practice at the Hotel Paris The CFO and Lisa agreed that it was important that she and her team develop and institute a new set of policies and practices that would enable the Hotel Paris to deal more effectively with unions. Read the case on pages 484–485 to see how they handled this.

Evidence-Based HR: What to Expect the Union to Do to Win the Election

The other side of the coin is this: What can unions do to boost their chances they'll win the election? A researcher analyzed data from 261 NLRB elections. She found that the best way for unions to win is a "rank-and-file strategy." It includes union tactics such as the following:[39]

1. "Reliance on a slow, underground, person-to-person campaign using house calls, small group meetings, and pre-union associations to develop leadership and union commitment, and prepare workers for employer anti-union strategies before the employer becomes aware of the campaign."
2. The union will focus on building active rank-and-file participation, including an organizing committee reflecting the different interest groups in the bargaining unit.
3. The union will press for a first contract early in the organizing process.
4. The union will use "inside and outside pressure tactics to build worker commitment and compel the employer to run a fair campaign."
5. There will be an emphasis during the organizing campaign on issues such as respect, dignity, and fairness, not just traditional bread-and-butter issues like wages.

The Supervisor's Role

Target recently won a unionization election at a New York store, but a federal judge overturned it and required a new election. The judge found that Target managers had violated labor law by telling employees they couldn't wear union buttons or distribute flyers, and by threatening to discipline workers who discussed union matters.[40]

Supervisors are an employer's first line of defense in the unionizing effort. They are often in the best position to sense employee attitude problems, and to discover the first signs of union activity. However, supervisors can also inadvertently undermine their employer's union efforts. Supervisory unfair labor practices could then (1) cause the NLRB to hold a new election after your company has won a previous election, or (2) cause your company to forfeit the second election and go directly to contract negotiation.

For example, one plant superintendent reacted to a union's initial organizing attempt by prohibiting distribution of union literature in the plant's lunchroom. Since solicitation of off-duty workers in nonwork areas is generally legal, the company subsequently allowed the union to post literature on the company's bulletin board and to distribute literature in nonworking areas inside the plant. However, the NLRB still ruled that the initial act of prohibiting distribution of the literature was an unfair labor practice, one not "made right" by the company's subsequent efforts. The NLRB used the superintendent's action as one reason for invalidating an election that the company had won.[41]

SOME TIPS Supervisors can use the acronym TIPS to remember what *not* to do during the campaigns.[42] *Do not* Threaten, Interrogate, make Promises to, or Spy on employees (for instance, do not threaten that you will close or move the business, cut wages, reduce overtime, or lay off employees). FORE outlines what you may do. *You may* give employees Facts (like what signing the authorization card means), express your Opinion about unions, explain factually correct Rules (such as that the law permits permanently replacing striking employees), and share your Experiences about unions. The Know Your Employment Law feature expands on this.

KNOW YOUR EMPLOYMENT LAW

Rules Regarding Literature and Solicitation

Managers and employers can generally take steps to legally restrict union organizing activity.[43]

1. Employers can always bar nonemployees from soliciting employees when the employee is on duty and not on a break.
2. Employers can usually stop employees from soliciting other employees for any purpose if one or both employees are on paid-duty time and not on a break.
3. Most employers (generally not including retail stores, shopping centers, and certain other employers) can bar nonemployees from the building's interiors and work areas as a right of private property owners.[44]
4. Employers can deny on- or off-duty employees access to interior or exterior areas only if they can show the rule is required for reasons of production, safety, or discipline.

Again, such restrictions are valid only if the employer doesn't discriminate against the union. Thus, if the employer lets employees collect money for baby gifts, to sell Avon products or Tupperware, or to engage in other solicitation during their working time, it may not be able lawfully to prohibit them from union soliciting during work time. Here is one example of a specific rule aimed at limiting union organizing or activity:

> Solicitation of employees on company property during working time interferes with the efficient operation of our business. Nonemployees are not permitted to solicit employees on company property for any purpose. Except in break areas where both employees are on break or off the clock, no employee may solicit another employee during working time for any purpose.[45]

Decertification Elections: Ousting the Union

Winning an election and signing an agreement don't necessarily mean that the union is in the company to stay. The same law that grants employees the right to unionize also gives them a way to terminate legally (decertify) their union's right to represent them. There are around 450 to 500 **decertification** elections each year, of which unions usually win around 30%.[46] That's actually a more favorable win rate for management than the rate for the original, representation elections.

decertification
Legal process for employees to terminate a union's right to represent them.

Decertification campaigns are similar to certification campaigns.[47] The union organizes membership meetings and house-to-house visits, mails literature into the homes, and uses phone calls, e-mails, NLRB appeals, and (sometimes) threats and harassment to win the election. Employers can't legally start the decertification process, but once started management uses meetings—including one-on-one meetings, small-group meetings, and meetings with entire units—as well as legal or expert assistance, letters, improved working conditions, and subtle or not-so-subtle threats to try to influence the votes.[48]

Globalization complicates the employer's union relations challenges, as the accompanying HR Practices around the Globe feature shows.

IMPROVING PERFORMANCE: HR Practices Around the Globe

France Comes to the Workers' Aid

Employers planning to expand abroad should consider the recent experience of drug maker Sanofi SA, in France. Because of the relatively high cost of running its research facility in southwestern France, Sanofi told its researchers there it intended to close their facility.[49] Employees began staging weekly protests, supported by the French government, which opposes profitable companies slashing jobs. After 9 months, the company was still waiting for a government report on the situation so it could finish negotiating with its unions and try to get some of them other jobs elsewhere. As one Sanofi manager said, "In France, the politics, the labor laws are extremely different than in any other regions. . . . It means that for sites like Toulouse . . . anything you want to do differently gets to be a confrontational issue."[50]

Discussion Question 15-2: With government policies like this, how do you think French companies remain competitive with those, say, in the United States?

The Collective Bargaining Process

What Is Collective Bargaining?

4 Illustrate with examples of bargaining that is not in good faith.

collective bargaining
The process through which representatives of management and the union meet to negotiate a labor agreement.

When and if the union becomes your employees' representative, a day is set for management and labor to meet and negotiate a labor agreement. This agreement will contain specific provisions covering wages, hours, and working conditions.

What exactly is **collective bargaining**? According to the National Labor Relations Act:

> For the purpose of [this act,] to bargain collectively is the performance of the mutual obligation of the employer and the representative of the employees to meet at reasonable times and confer in good faith with respect to wages, hours, and terms and conditions of employment, or the negotiation of an agreement, or any question arising thereunder, and the execution of a written contract incorporating any agreement reached if requested by either party, but such obligation does not compel either party to agree to a proposal or require the making of a concession.

In plain language, this means that both management and labor are required by law to negotiate wage, hours, and terms and conditions of employment "in good faith."

What Is Good Faith?

good faith bargaining
Both parties are making every reasonable effort to arrive at agreement; proposals are being matched with counterproposals.

Good faith bargaining is the cornerstone of effective labor–management relations. It means that both parties communicate and negotiate, match proposals with counterproposals, and make a reasonable effort to arrive at an agreement. It does not mean that one party compels another to agree. Nor does it require that either party make any specific concessions (although some may be necessary).[51]

How can you tell if bargaining is *not* in good faith? Here are some examples.[52]

Surface bargaining. Going through the motions of bargaining without any real intention of completing an agreement.

Inadequate concessions. Unwillingness to compromise.

Inadequate proposals and demands. The NLRB considers the advancement of proposals to be a positive factor in determining overall good faith.

Dilatory tactics. The law requires that the parties meet and "confer at reasonable times and intervals." Obviously, refusal to meet with the union does not satisfy the positive duty imposed on the employer.

Imposing conditions. Attempts to impose conditions that are so onerous or unreasonable as to indicate bad faith.

Making unilateral changes in conditions. This is a strong indication that the employer is not bargaining with the required intent of reaching an agreement.

Bypassing the representative. The duty of management to bargain in good faith involves, at a minimum, recognition that the union representative is the one with whom the employer must deal in conducting negotiations.

Withholding information. An employer must supply the union with information, upon request, to enable it to discuss the collective bargaining issues intelligently.

Of course, requiring good faith bargaining doesn't mean that negotiations can't grind to a halt. For example, a few years ago the National Football League accused the Players Association of not bargaining in good faith, using delays to "run out the clock" so that the players could bring suit against the NFL.[53]

The Negotiating Team

Both union and management send negotiating teams to the bargaining table, and both go into the bargaining sessions having "done their homework."

First, they acquire data on which to build their bargaining positions.[54] From compensation surveys they compile data on pay and benefits, including comparisons with local pay rates and to rates for similar jobs in the industry. Data on the distribution of the workforce (in terms of age, sex, and seniority, for instance) are important, because it determines benefits. Internal economic data regarding benefits, earnings, and the cost of overtime are important too. Union representatives will have sounded out union members on their desires and conferred with representatives of related unions.

Management will also "cost" the current labor contract and determine the increased cost—total, per employee, and per hour—of the union's demands. It will use information from grievances and feedback from supervisors to determine what the union's demands might be, and prepare counteroffers and arguments.[55] Other popular tactics include attitude surveys to test employee reactions to various sections of the contract that management may feel require change, and informal conferences with local union leaders to discuss the operational effectiveness of the contract and to send up trial balloons on management ideas for change.

Costing the Contract

Collective bargaining experts emphasize the need to cost the union's demands carefully. One says,

> The mistake I see most often is [HR professionals who] enter the negotiations without understanding the financial impact of things they put on the table. For example, the union wants three extra vacation days. That doesn't sound like a lot, except that in some states, if an employee leaves, you have to pay them for unused vacation time. [So] now your employer has to carry that liability on their books at all times.[56]

voluntary (or permissible) bargaining items
Items in collective bargaining over which bargaining is neither illegal nor mandatory—neither party can be compelled against its wishes to negotiate over those items.

illegal bargaining items
Items in collective bargaining that are forbidden by law; for example, a clause agreeing to hire "union members exclusively" would be illegal in a right-to-work state.

mandatory bargaining items
Items in collective bargaining that a party must bargain over if they are introduced by the other party—for example, pay.

Bargaining Items

Labor law sets out categories of specific items that are subject to bargaining: These are mandatory, voluntary, and illegal items.

Voluntary (or permissible) bargaining items are neither mandatory nor illegal; they become a part of negotiations only through the joint agreement of both management and union. Neither party can compel the other to negotiate over voluntary items. You cannot hold up signing a contract because the other party refuses to bargain on a voluntary item, such as benefits for retirees.

Illegal bargaining items are forbidden by law. A clause agreeing to hire union members exclusively would be illegal in a right-to-work state, for example.

Table 15-1 presents some of the 70 or so **mandatory bargaining items** over which bargaining is mandatory under the law. They include wages, hours, rest periods, layoffs, transfers, benefits, and severance pay. Others, such as drug testing, are added as the law evolves.

Building Negotiating Skills

Hammering out a satisfactory labor agreement requires negotiating skills. Experienced negotiators use *leverage, desire, time, competition, information, credibility,* and *judgment* to improve their bargaining positions. *Leverage* means factors that help or hinder the negotiator.[57] Things

TABLE 15-1 Bargaining Items

Mandatory	Permissible	Illegal
Rates of pay	Indemnity bonds	Closed shop
Wages	Management rights as to union affairs	Separation of employees based on race
Hours of employment	Pension benefits of retired employees	Discriminatory treatment
Overtime pay	Scope of the bargaining unit	
Shift differentials	Including supervisors in the contract	
Holidays	Additional parties to the contract such as the international union	
Vacations	Use of union label	
Severance pay	Settlement of unfair labor charges	
Pensions	Prices in cafeteria	
Insurance benefits	Continuance of past contract	
Profit-sharing plans	Membership of bargaining team	
Christmas bonuses	Employment of strikebreaker	
Company housing, meals, and discounts		
Employee security		
Job performance		
Union security		
Management–union relationship		
Drug testing of employees		

Source: Michael R. Carrell and Christina Heavrin, *Labor Relations and Collective Bargaining: Cases, Practices, And Law*, 6th Edition, © 2001. Reprinted by permission of Pearson Education, Inc. Upper Saddle River, NJ.

you can leverage include *necessity, desire, competition*, and *time*.[58] For example, the union knows that an employer who needs to fill a big order fast (*necessity*) is at a disadvantage.

Similarly, the employer who makes its *desires* too obvious undercuts its position. *Competition* is important too. There is no more convincing ploy than subtly hinting you've got an alternative (like shifting services abroad). *Time* (particularly deadlines) can also tilt things for or against you.

"Knowledge is power" when negotiating, so having *information* is advantageous, as is *credibility*. Finally, good negotiators need *judgment:* the ability to "strike the right balance between gaining advantages and reaching compromises, in the substance as well as in the style of [their] negotiating technique."[59]

Bargaining Hints

Expert Reed Richardson has the following advice for bargainers:

1. Be sure to set clear objectives for every bargaining item, and be sure you understand the reason for each.
2. Do not hurry.
3. When in doubt, caucus with your associates.
4. Be well prepared with firm data supporting your position.
5. Strive to keep some flexibility in your position.
6. Don't concern yourself just with what the other party says and does; find out why.
7. Respect the importance of face saving for the other party.
8. Be alert to the real intentions of the other party—not only for goals, but also for priorities.
9. Be a good listener.
10. Build a reputation for being fair but firm.
11. Learn to control your emotions and use them as a tool.
12. As you make each bargaining move, be sure you know its relationship to all other moves.
13. Measure each move against your objectives.
14. Remember that collective bargaining is a compromise process. There is no such thing as having all the pie.

impasse
Collective bargaining situation that occurs when the parties are not able to move further toward settlement, usually because one party is demanding more than the other will offer.

15. Try to understand the people and their personalities.[60]
16. Remember that excessive bargainer transparency and openness can backfire.[61]

Impasses, Mediation, and Strikes

In collective bargaining, an **impasse** occurs when the parties are not able to move further toward settlement. This usually occurs because one party is demanding more than the other will offer. Sometimes a third party, such as a mediator, can resolve an impasse. If the impasse is not resolved, the union may call a work stoppage, or strike.[62]

mediation
Intervention in which a neutral third party tries to assist the principals in reaching agreement.

fact finder
A neutral party who studies the issues in a dispute and makes a public recommendation for a reasonable settlement.

arbitration
The most definitive type of third-party intervention, in which the arbitrator usually has the power to determine and dictate the settlement terms.

interest arbitration
Arbitration enacted when labor agreements do not yet exist or when one or both parties are seeking to change the agreement.

rights arbitration
Arbitration that interprets existing contract terms, for instance, when an employee questions the employer's right to have taken some disciplinary action.

strike
A withdrawal of labor.

economic strike
A strike that results from a failure to agree on the terms of a contract that involves wages, benefits, and other conditions of employment.

unfair labor practice strike
A strike aimed at protesting illegal conduct by the employer.

wildcat strike
An unauthorized strike occurring during the term of a contract.

sympathy strike
A strike that takes place when one union strikes in support of the strike of another.

picketing
Having employees carry signs announcing their concerns near the employer's place of business.

THIRD-PARTY INVOLVEMENT Negotiators use three types of third-party interventions to overcome an impasse. With **mediation**, a neutral third party tries to assist the principals in reaching agreement. The mediator meets with each party to determine where each stands, and then uses this information to find common ground for bargaining. When Hostess Brands couldn't reach agreement with its unions, its bankruptcy judge had them join him for a mediation session, where he tried (unsuccessfully) to broker a new contract.[63]

In certain situations, as in a national emergency dispute, a **fact finder** is a neutral party who studies the issues in a dispute and makes a public recommendation for a reasonable settlement.[64] Presidential emergency fact-finding boards resolved impasses in certain critical transportation disputes.

Arbitration is the most definitive third-party intervention, because the arbitrator may have the power to determine and dictate the settlement terms. With *binding arbitration*, both parties are committed to accepting the arbitrator's award. With *nonbinding arbitration*, they are not. Arbitration may also be voluntary or compulsory (imposed by a government agency). In the United States, voluntary binding arbitration is the most prevalent.

There are two main topics of arbitration. **Interest arbitration** centers on working out a labor agreement; the parties use it when such agreements do not yet exist or when one or both parties are seeking to change the agreement. **Rights arbitration** really means "contract interpretation arbitration." It usually involves interpreting existing contract terms, for instance, when an employee questions the employer's right to have taken some disciplinary action.[65]

SOURCES OF THIRD-PARTY ASSISTANCE Various public and professional agencies make arbitrators and mediators available. For example, the American Arbitration Association (AAA) represents and provides the services of thousands of arbitrators and mediators to employers and unions. The U.S. government's Federal Mediation and Conciliation Service provides both arbitrators and mediators (see Figure 15-5).[66] In addition, most states provide arbitrator and mediation services.

STRIKES A **strike** is a withdrawal of labor. There are four main types of strikes. An **economic strike** results from a failure to agree on the terms of a contract. Unions call **unfair labor practice strikes** to protest illegal conduct by the employer. A **wildcat strike** is an unauthorized strike occurring during the term of a contract. A **sympathy strike** occurs when one union strikes in support of the strike of another union.[67] For example, in sympathy with South Korean Hyundai workers, the United Auto Workers organized a rally outside of Hyundai's technical center in Superior Township, Michigan, and took steps to hold other rallies.[68]

The likelihood of and severity of a strike depends partly on the parties' willingness to "take a strike."[69] The number of major work stoppages (strikes involving 1,000 workers or more) peaked at about 400 per year between 1965 and 1975, and today average around 20.

Picketing, or having employees carry signs announcing their concerns near the employer's place of business, is one of the first activities to appear during a strike. Its purpose is to inform the public about the existence of the labor dispute and often to encourage them to refrain from doing business with the struck employer.

Employers have several options when employees strike. One is to temporarily shut down the affected area and halt operations. A second is to contract out work to blunt the effects of the strike. A third is to continue operations, perhaps using supervisors and other nonstriking workers. A fourth alternative is hiring replacements for the strikers.

Diminished union influence plus competitive pressures now prompt more employers to replace (or consider replacing) strikers with permanent replacement workers. One study

FIGURE 15-5 Form to Request Mediation Services

Source: Federal Mediation and Conciliation Service.

FMCS Form F-53
Revised 5-92

Form Approved
OMB No. 3076-0005

FEDERAL SECTOR LABOR RELATIONS
NOTICE TO FEDERAL MEDIATION AND CONCILIATION SERVICE

Mail To:

Notice Processing Unit
FEDERAL MEDIATION AND CONCILIATION SERVICE
2100 K Street, N.W.
Washington, D.C. 20427

THIS NOTICE IS IN REGARD TO: (MARK"X")

① ☐ AN INITIAL CONTRACT — (INCLUDED FLRA CERTIFICATION NUMBER) # ____
☐ A CONTRACT REOPENER — REOPENER DATE ____
☐ THE EXPIRATION OF AN EXISTING AGREEMENT — EXPIRATION DATE: ____

② ☐ ***OTHER REQUESTS FOR THE ASSISTANCE OF FMCS IN BARGAINING*** ***(MARK "X")***
SPECIFY TYPE OF ISSUE(S)

③ ☐ ***REQUEST FOR GRIEVANCE MEDIATION (SEE ITEM #10)*** ***(MARK "X")***
ISSUE(S)

④ NAME OF FEDERAL AGENCY | NAME OF SUBDIVISION OR COMPONENT, IF ANY
STREET ADDRESS OF AGENCY | CITY | STATE | ZIP
AGENCY OFFICIAL TO BE CONTACTED | AREA CODE & PHONE NUMBER

⑤ NAME OF NATIONAL UNION OR PARENT BODY | NAME AND/OR LOCAL NUMBER
STREET ADDRESS | CITY | STATE | ZIP
UNION OFFICIAL TO BE CONTACTED | AREA CODE & PHONE NUMBER

LOCATION OF NEGOTIATIONS OR WHERE MEDIATION WILL BE HELD
⑥ STREET ADDRESS | CITY | STATE | ZIP

⑦ APPROX. # OF EMPLOYEES IN BARGAINING UNIT(S) >> | IN ESTABLISHMENT>>

⑧ THIS NOTICE OR REQUEST IS FILED ON BEHALF OF ***(MARK "X")*** ☐UNION ☐AGENCY

⑨ NAME AND TITLE OF OFFICIAL(S) SUBMITTING THIS NOTICE OR REQUEST | AREA CODE AND PHONE NUMBER
STREET ADDRESS | CITY | STATE | ZIP

FOR GRIEVANCE MEDIATION, THE SIGNATURES OF BOTH PARTIES ARE REQUIRED:*

⑩ SIGNATURE (AGENCY) | DATE | SIGNATURE (UNION) | DATE

*Receipt of this form does not commit FMCS to offer its services. Receipt of this form will not be acknowledged in writing by FMCS. While use of this form is voluntary, its use will facilitate FMCS service to respondents. Public reporting burden for this collection of information is estimated to average 10 minutes per response, including time for reviewing the collection of information. Send comments regarding this burden estimate or any other aspect of this collection of information, including suggestions for reducing this burden, to FMCS Division of Administrative Services, Washington, D.C. 20427, and to the Office of Management and Budget, Paperwork Reduction Project. Washington, D.C. 20603

For Instructions, See Back

of human resource managers found that of respondents, 18% "would not consider striker replacements," 31% called it "not very likely," 23% "somewhat likely," and 21% "very likely."[70] In a labor dispute a few years ago, the NFL implied they might use replacement players.[71]

Employers generally can replace strikers. In one case known as *Mackay*, the U.S. Supreme Court ruled that although the National Labor Relations Act does prohibit employers from interfering with employees' right to strike, employers still have the right to continue their operations and to replace strikers. Subsequent decisions by the National Labor Relations Board put some limitations on *Mackay*. For example, employers cannot permanently replace strikers who are protesting unfair labor practices; they must rehire strikers who unconditionally apply for reinstatement.

STRIKE GUIDELINES FOR EMPLOYERS As negotiations between the Hibbing Taconite Steel Plant in Minnesota and the United Steelworkers of America headed toward a deadline, the firm brought

Picketing is one of the first activities to occur during a strike. The purpose is to inform the public about the labor dispute.

Scott Olson/Getty Images

in security workers and trailers to house them. Two experts say that, with a strike imminent, following these guidelines is advisable:

- Pay all striking employees what you owe them on the first day of the strike.
- Secure the facility. Management should control access to the property. Consider hiring guards to protect replacements coming and going.
- Notify all customers, and prepare a standard official response to all queries.
- Contact all suppliers and others who will have to cross the picket line. Establish alternative methods of obtaining supplies.
- Arrange for overnight stays in the facility, and for delivered meals, if necessary.
- Notify the local unemployment office of your need for replacement workers.
- Photograph the facility before, during, and after picketing. If necessary, install video equipment to monitor picket lines.
- Record all facts concerning strikers' demeanor and activities and such incidents as violence, threats, mass pickets, property damage, or problems.
- Gather the following evidence: number of pickets and their names; time, date, and location of picketing; wording on every sign carried by pickets; and descriptions of picket cars and license numbers.[72]

corporate campaign
An organized effort by the union that exerts pressure on the corporation by pressuring the company's other unions, shareholders, directors, customers, creditors, and government agencies, often directly.

boycott
The combined refusal by employees and other interested parties to buy or use the employer's products.

inside games
Union efforts to convince employees to impede or to disrupt production—for example, by slowing the work pace.

OTHER "WEAPONS" Management and labor each have other weapons to break an impasse. The union, for example, may resort to a corporate campaign. A **corporate campaign** is an organized effort by the union to exert pressure on the employer by pressuring the company's other unions, shareholders, corporate directors, customers, creditors, and government agencies.[73] Thus, the union might surprise members of the board of directors by picketing their homes and organizing a **boycott** of the company's banks.[74] The United Auto Workers recently began trying to organize hourly factory workers at foreign-owned car plants in the United States. The union commenced picketing U.S. Hyundai, Daimler, Toyota, and Nissan dealerships.[75]

Inside games are union efforts to convince employees to impede or to disrupt production—for example, by slowing the work pace or refusing to work overtime.[76] Inside games are basically strikes—albeit "strikes" in which the company continues to pay the employees. In one inside game at a Caterpillar plant, UAW grievances rose from 22 to 336. This tied up workers and management in unproductive endeavors on company time.[77]

Improving Performance Through HRIS: Unions Go High Tech

E-mail and Twitter enable unions to send mass announcements to collective bargaining unit members and use e-mail to reach supporters and government officials for their corporate campaigns. For example, the group trying to organize Starbucks workers (the *Starbucks Workers' Union*) set up their own website (www.starbucksunion.org). It includes notes like "Our hard work has made record profits for Starbucks. It's time to unite for our fair share."[78]

lockout
A refusal by the employer to provide opportunities to work.

For their part, employers can try to break an impasse with lockouts. A **lockout** is a refusal by the employer to provide opportunities to work. It (sometimes literally) locks out employees and prohibits them from doing their jobs (and being paid). Faced with a new contract that might slash their wages by 50%, Canadian Auto Workers Union employees from one Caterpillar plant found themselves locked out after six months of negotiations failed to produce a settlement.[79]

The NLRB views lockouts as an unfair labor practice only when the employer acts for a prohibited purpose. Trying to bring about a settlement on terms favorable to the employer is not a prohibited purpose. Lockouts are not widely used; employers are usually reluctant to cease operations when employees are willing to continue working.

injunction
A court order compelling a party or parties either to resume or to desist from a certain action.

Both employers and unions can seek a court injunction if they believe the other side is causing irreparable harm to the other party. An **injunction** is a court order compelling a party or parties either to resume or to desist from a certain action.[80]

The Contract Agreement

The actual contract agreement may be a 20- or 30-page document, or longer. It may contain just general declarations of policy, or detailed rules and procedures. The tendency today is toward the longer contract.

The main sections of a typical contract cover subjects such as these: (1) management rights; (2) union security and automatic payroll dues deduction; (3) grievance procedures; (4) arbitration of grievances; (5) disciplinary procedures; (6) compensation rates; (7) hours of work and overtime; (8) benefits: vacations, holidays, insurance, pensions; (9) health and safety provisions; (10) employee security seniority provisions; and (11) contract expiration date.

5 Develop a grievance procedure.

Dealing with Disputes and Grievances

Hammering out a labor agreement is not the last step in collective bargaining. No labor contract can cover all contingencies and answer all questions. For example, suppose the contract says you can only discharge an employee for "just cause." You subsequently discharge someone for speaking back to you. Was speaking back to you "just cause"?

grievance procedure
Formal process for addressing any factor involving wages, hours, or conditions of employment that is used as a complaint against the employer.

The labor contract's **grievance procedure** provides an orderly system whereby both employer and union determine whether some action violated the contract.[81] It is the vehicle for administering the contract day-to-day. However, this involves interpretation only, usually not negotiating new terms or altering existing ones.

Sources of Grievances

In practice, it is probably easier to list those items that *don't* precipitate grievances than the ones that do. Employees may use just about anything involving wages, hours, or conditions of employment as the basis of a grievance.

Discipline cases and seniority problems including promotions, transfers, and layoffs would top this list. Others would include grievances growing out of job evaluations and work assignments, overtime, vacations, incentive plans, and holidays.[82] Here are three examples of grievances:

- ***Absenteeism.*** An employer fired an employee for excessive absences. The employee filed a grievance stating that there had been no previous warnings related to excessive absences.
- ***Insubordination.*** An employee on two occasions refused to obey a supervisor's order to meet with him, unless a union representative was present at the meeting. As a result, the employee was discharged and subsequently filed a grievance protesting the discharge.
- ***Plant rules.*** The plant had a posted rule barring employees from eating or drinking during unscheduled breaks. The employees filed a grievance claiming the rule was arbitrary.[83]

Grievances are often symptoms of underlying problems. Sometimes bad relationships between supervisors and subordinates are to blame: This is often the cause of grievances over "fair treatment," for instance. Organizational factors like ambiguous instructions also cause frustration and grievances. Union activism is another cause; the union may solicit grievances from workers to underscore ineffective supervision. Some individuals are by their nature negative, dissatisfied, and prone to complaints. Discipline and dismissal are two major sources of grievances.

The Grievance Procedure

Most collective bargaining contracts contain a grievance procedure. It lists the steps in the procedure, time limits associated with each step, and specific rules such as "all charges of contract violation must be reduced to writing." Nonunionized employers need such procedures, too.

Grievance procedures differ from firm to firm. Some contain simple, two-step procedures. Here, the grievant, union representative, and company representative meet to discuss the grievance. If they don't find a satisfactory solution, the grievance goes before a third-party arbitrator who hears the case, writes it up, and makes a decision. Figure 15-6 shows a grievance record form.

At the other extreme, the grievance procedure may contain six or more steps. The first step might be for the grievant and shop steward to meet informally with the supervisor of the grievant

FIGURE 15-6 Sample Online Grievance Form

Click to Fill in Text or Check a Box
Tab to Next Field

Date Received at Step B *(MM/DD/YYYY)*

UNITED STATES POSTAL SERVICE

USPS-NALC Joint Step A Grievance Form

INFORMAL STEP A — NALC Shop Steward Completes This Section

1. Grievant's Name *(Last, first, middle initial)* | 2. Home Telephone No.
3. Seniority Date *(MM/DD/YYYY)* | 4. Status *(Check one)* ☐ FT ☐ FTF ☐ PTR ☐ PTF ☐ TE | 5. Grievant's SSN
6. Installation/Work Unit | 7. Finance Number
8. NALC Branch No. | 9. NALC Grievance No. | 10. Incident Date *(MM/DD/YYYY)* | 11. Date Discussed with Supervisor *(Filing Date)*
12a. Companion MSPB Appeal? ☐ Yes ☐ No | 12b. Companion EEO Appeal? ☐ Yes ☐ No
13a. Supervisor's Printed Name and Initials *(Completed by Supervisor)* | 13b. Steward's Printed Name and Initials *(Completed by Steward)*

FORMAL STEP A — Formal Step A Parties Complete This Section

14. USPS Grievance No.
15. Issue Statement/Provide Contract Provision(s) and Frame the Issue(s)
16. Undisputed Facts *(List and Attach All Supporting Documents)* — Attachments? ☐ No ☐ Yes Number____
17. UNION'S full, detailed statement of disputed facts and contentions *(List and Attach All Supporting Documents)* — Attachments? ☐ No ☐ Yes Number____
18. MANAGEMENT'S full, detailed statement of disputed facts and contentions *(List and Attach All Supporting Documents)* — Attachments? ☐ No ☐ Yes Number____
19. Remedy Requested/Offered
20. Disposition and Date *(Check one)* ☐ Resolved ☐ Withdrawn ☐ Not Resolved | Date of Formal Step A Meeting *(MM/DD/YYYY)*
21a. USPS Representative Name | 21b. Telephone No. *(Include Area Code)*
21c. USPS Representative Signature | 21d. Date *(MM/DD/YYYY)*
22a. NALC Representative Name | 22b. Telephone No. *(Include Area Code)*
22c. NALC Representative Signature | 22d. Date *(MM/DD/YYYY)*

PS Form 8190, August 2002 *(Page 1 of 2)*

to try to find a solution. The next steps involve the grievant and union representatives meeting with higher-level managers. Finally, if top management and the union can't reach agreement, the grievance may go to arbitration.

Guidelines for Handling Grievances

The best way for a supervisor to handle a grievance is to develop a work environment in which grievances don't arise in the first place. Hone your ability to avoid, recognize, diagnose, and correct the causes of potential employee dissatisfaction (such as unfair appraisals or poor communications) before they become grievances.

Given that many factors including union pressures prompt grievances, it would be naïve to think that grievances arise only due to supervisor unfairness. However, there's little doubt that the quality of the interpersonal relations among you and your subordinates will influence your team's grievance rate. The supervisor is on the firing line and must steer a course between treating employees fairly and maintaining management's rights and prerogatives. The HR Tools feature presents some guidelines.

IMPROVING PERFORMANCE: HR Tools for Line Managers and Entrepreneurs

How to Handle a Grievance Situation

Grievances cost money, in terms of lost work time, productivity, and (possibly) arbitrators' fees. One expert has developed a list of supervisor do's and don'ts as useful guides in handling grievances.[84] Some critical ones include:

Do:

1. Investigate and handle each case as though it may eventually result in arbitration.
2. Talk with the employee about his or her grievance; give the person a full hearing.
3. Require the union to identify specific contractual provisions allegedly violated.
4. Comply with the contractual time limits for handling the grievance.
5. Visit the work area of the grievance.
6. Determine whether there were any witnesses.
7. Examine the grievant's personnel record.
8. Fully examine prior grievance records.
9. Treat the union representative as your equal.
10. Hold your grievance discussions privately.
11. Fully inform your own supervisor of grievance matters.

Don't:

1. Discuss the case with the union steward alone—the grievant should be there.
2. Make arrangements with individual employees that are inconsistent with the labor agreement.
3. Hold back the remedy if the company is wrong.
4. Admit to the binding effect of a past practice.
5. Relinquish to the union your rights as a manager.
6. Settle grievances based on what is "fair." Instead, stick to the labor agreement.
7. Bargain over items not covered by the contract.
8. Treat as subject to arbitration claims demanding the discipline or discharge of managers.
9. Give long written grievance answers.
10. Trade a grievance settlement for a grievance withdrawal.
11. Deny grievances because "your hands have been tied by management."
12. Agree to informal amendments in the contract.

Discussion Question 15-3: Write a 30-word guide that summarizes the essence of these do's and don'ts.

Social Media and HR

Labor–management attorneys often counsel employers to have social media policies aimed at managing employees' use of such media. Such policies typically require that employees state that any postings are their own and don't represent the company's positions, that they should not use such media during work time, and that disparaging comments about the employer or its employees are prohibited.[85]

However, recent NLRB decisions state that such policy restrictions may violate the rights employees have under the National Labor Relations Act (such as to take "concerted activity" by discussing working conditions with coworkers). At first, the NLRB seemed to suggest that simply restricting employees from making disrespectful comments about the company or its employees would be acceptable to it. However, subsequent NLRB decisions put even this in doubt.[86] At least one labor–management attorney now actually advises against publishing any such social media policy at all.[87]

The Union Movement Today and Tomorrow

6 Describe a strategy for cooperative labor relations.

Several factors contributed to the decline in union membership over the past 50 or so years. Unions traditionally appealed mostly to blue-collar workers, and the proportion of blue-collar jobs has been decreasing. Globalization increased competition and pressures on employers to cut costs and boost productivity, further squeezing unions. Other factors pressuring employers and unions include the deregulation of trucking, airlines, and communications; outdated equipment and factories; mismanagement; new technology; and laws (such as occupational safety) that somewhat substituted for and reduced the need for unions. As noted, the recent recession triggered budget cuts in both the public and private sectors, prompting anti-union public policy attitudes, and the loss of about one million public sector union jobs. Bankruptcies, such as those that swept the U.S. airline industry, often end with courts imposing less favorable contract terms on union employees.[88]

The net effect has been the permanent layoff of hundreds of thousands of union members, the permanent closing of company plants, the relocation of companies to nonunion settings (either in the United States or abroad), and mergers and acquisitions that eliminated union jobs and affected collective bargaining agreements. Union membership as a percentage of people working has dropped by about two-thirds over 50 years, to 11.3%.[89]

Card Check and Other New Union Tactics

Unions are not sitting idly by.[90] The priorities of the Change to Win Coalition (whose members broke off from the AFL-CIO) illustrate the new union strategies to

> make it our first priority to help millions more workers form unions so we can build a strong movement for rewarding work in America [and] unite the strength of everyone who works in the same industry so we can negotiate with today's huge global corporations for everyone's benefit.[91]

Unions are making inroads into traditionally hard-to-organize worker segments like professionals and white-collar workers.

Scott Olson/Getty Images

In practice, this means Change to Win will be very aggressive about organizing workers, will focus on organizing women and minority workers, will focus more on organizing temporary or contingent workers, and will target specific multinational companies for international campaigns.[92]

RECENT TRENDS IN LABOR LAWS First, several recent NLRB decisions will, in effect, support union efforts. In one case,[93] it approved "micro bargaining units," small groups of workers who share interests, a step which should make it easier for unions to win elections. The NLRB also called for speeded-up elections, which cut the time from petition until election from about 38 days to 20 days.[94] It expanded the amount of time that employees who organized under a card check process (see below) had to wait to start a decertification process. And after being exempted for many years from having to disclose their participation with each other in a union campaign, employers and their union campaign-related consultants and attorneys now must report their relationship.[95]

MORE AGGRESSIVE Unions are also becoming more aggressive. They are pushing Congress to pass the *Employee Free Choice Act*. This would make it easier for employees to unionize. Instead of secret-ballot elections, the act would institute a "card check" system. Here the union would win recognition when a majority of workers signed authorization cards saying they want the union. Several large companies, including Cingular Wireless, have already agreed to the card check process.[96] The act would also require binding arbitration to set a first contract's terms if the company and union can't negotiate an agreement within 120 days.[97] Unions are also using *class action lawsuits* to support employees in nonunionized companies, to pressure employers. For example, unions recently used class action lawsuits to support workers' claims under the Fair Labor Standards Act and the Equal Pay Act.[98]

EXAMPLE The steps that the Union of Needletrades, Industrial and Textile Employees (UNITE) took against Cintas Corp. illustrate some unions' new tactics. In their effort against Cintas, UNITE (which later merged with another union to form UNITE HERE) didn't petition for an NLRB election. Instead, UNITE proposed using the card check process. They also filed a $100 million class action suit against the company. Then, Cintas workers in California filed a lawsuit claiming that the company was violating a nearby municipality's "living wage" law. UNITE then joined forces with the teamsters union, which in turn began targeting Cintas's delivery people.[99]

COORDINATION Unions are becoming more proactive in terms of coordinating their efforts.[100] For example, in its "Union Cities" campaigns, AFL-CIO planners work with local labor councils and individual unions to gain the support of a target city's elected officials. In Los Angeles, this helped the service workers' union organize janitors in that city.

GLOBAL CAMPAIGNS Walmart recently agreed to let the workers in its stores in China join unions. Walmart's China experience stems in part from efforts by SEIU. SEIU's global campaigns reflect the belief that "huge global service sector companies routinely cross national borders and industry lines as they search for places where they can shift operations to exploit workers with the lowest possible pay and benefits."

SEIU is therefore strengthening its ties with unions in other countries.[101] SEIU worked with China's All China Federation of Trade Unions (ACFTU) to help the latter organize China's Walmart stores.[102] And recently, America's United Steelworkers merged with the largest labor union in Britain to create "Workers Uniting" to better deal with multinational employers.[103] The UAW is training activists and sending them abroad to help organize workers at car plants overseas.[104] Any company that thinks it can avoid unions by sending jobs abroad may be surprised.

Cooperative Clauses

When AT&T's workers threatened recently to strike if the company insisted on raising workers' health-care premiums, AT&T began training managers to fill in for workers.[105]

However, labor–management relations history is also sprinkled with cooperation. For example, more than 50 years ago, General Motors and Toyota created a joint venture they called New United Motor Manufacturing Inc. (NUMMI). The partners hoped to merge GM's marketing expertise with Toyota's famous team-based management system.[106] NUMMI and the United Auto

Workers (UAW) agreed that management and labor would work together as a team, give workers a voice in decision making, and build high-quality cars at low cost. NUMMI and the UAW installed a new labor–management system in their plant. NUMMI's 2,400 hourly workers were organized around teams of 5 to 10 members. NUMMI reduced the number of supervisors.[107] The plant was soon very successful (although both parties eventually ended their joint venture).

Since then, many labor–management agreements have included so-called cooperative agreements. These agreements generally commit union and management to adopt one or more cooperative themes. For example, one analysis of labor contracts expiring between 1997 and 2007 found that roughly half of the 1,041 contracts studied contained cooperative clauses. Parties commit to adhere to one or more of these cooperative themes (in descending order of frequency-of-mention in the agreements):[108]

- Intent to cooperate
- A statement of commitment to cooperate
- Committees to review mutual concerns that arise
- Decisions on traditional issues
- Guarantees of employment security
- Commitments to high-performance practices
- Decisions on strategic issues
- Full cooperation

At one extreme, for example, Alcoa's agreement contained a full "Cooperative Partnership Clause." This included provisions for joint management–labor decision-making committees, and a commitment to maintain employee security under catastrophic market conditions.[109] At the other extreme, many contain only a statement of intent to cooperate, such as on traditional issues like drug abuse, health care, and safety.

STRATEGIES FOR COOPERATIVE LABOR–MANAGEMENT RELATIONS The question is, "What management strategy does an employer follow to foster cooperation?" In brief, one that emphasizes the sorts of fairness and openness we discussed earlier in this book. As two researchers conclude, "perceptions of a cooperative labor relations climate are positively influenced by procedural justice, the union's willingness to adopt an integrative [cooperative] approach to bargaining, and management willingness to share information with the union."[110] There's little doubt, as another study argues, that unions "that have a cooperative relationship with management can play an important role in overcoming barriers to the effective adoption of practices that have been linked to organizational competitiveness."[111] But employers who want to capitalize on that potential must change how they think, by emphasizing a cooperative partnership.[112]

Review

MyManagementLab Go to **mymanagementlab.com** to complete the problems marked with this icon. 

Chapter Section Summaries

1. The **labor movement** is important. About 14 million U.S. workers belong to unions—around 11.3% of the total. Workers unionize not just to get more pay or better working conditions; employer unfairness and the union's power are also important. Unions aim for union security, and then for improved wages, hours, and working conditions and benefits for their members. Union security options include the closed shop, union shop, agency shop, preferential shop, and maintenance of membership arrangement. The AFL-CIO plays an important role in the union movement as a voluntary federation of about 56 national and international labor unions in the United States.
2. To understand unions and their impact, it's necessary to understand the interplay between **unions and the law**. In brief, labor law has gone through periods of strong encouragement of unions, to modified encouragement coupled with regulation, and finally to detailed regulation of internal union affairs. Today, the legal environment seems to be moving toward increased

encouragement of unions. Historically, the laws encouraging the union movement included the Norris-LaGuardia and National Labor Relations (Wagner) Acts of the 1930s. These outlawed certain unfair employer labor practices and made it easier for unions to organize. The Taft-Hartley or Labor Management Relations Act of 1947 addressed keeping unions from restraining or coercing employees, and listed certain unfair union labor practices. In the 1950s, the Landrum-Griffin Act (technically, the Labor Management Reporting and Disclosure Act) further protected union members from possible wrongdoing on the part of their unions.

3. When unions begin organizing, all managers and supervisors usually get involved, so it's essential to understand the mechanics of **the union drive and election**. The main steps include initial contact, obtaining authorization cards, holding a hearing, the campaign itself, and the election. Supervisors need to understand their role at each step in this process. Follow the acronym TIPS—do not Threaten, Interrogate, make Promises, or Spy. And follow FORE—provide Facts, express your Opinions, explain factually correct Rules, and share your Experiences. Managers need to understand rules regarding literature and solicitation. For example, employers can always bar nonemployees from soliciting employees during their work time, and can usually stop employees from soliciting other employees when both are on duty time and not on a break.
4. The employer and union hammer out an agreement via the **collective bargaining process**. The heart of collective bargaining is good faith bargaining, which means both parties must make reasonable efforts to arrive at agreement, and proposals are matched with counterproposals. Both negotiating teams will work hard to understand their respective clients' needs and to quantify their demands. In the actual bargaining sessions, there are mandatory bargaining items such as pay, illegal bargaining items, and voluntary bargaining items such as benefits for retirees. If things don't go smoothly during collective bargaining, the parties may utilize third-party intermediaries, including mediators, fact finders, and arbitrators. Strikes represent a withdrawal of labor. There are economic strikes resulting from a failure to agree on the terms of the contract, as well as unfair labor practice strikes, wildcat strikes, and sympathy strikes. During strikes, picketing may occur. Other tactics include a corporate campaign by the union, boycotting, inside games, or (for employers) lockouts.
5. Most managers become involved with **disputes and grievances** during their careers. Most collective bargaining agreements contain a specific grievance procedure listing the steps in the procedure. In general, the best way to handle a grievance is to create an environment in which grievances don't occur. However, if a grievance does occur, things to do include investigate, handle each case as though it may eventually result in arbitration, talk with the employee about the grievance, and comply with the contractual time limits for handling the grievance. On the other hand, don't make arrangements with individual employees that are inconsistent with the labor agreement or hold back the remedy if the company is wrong.
6. Membership is down but in some ways unions are becoming more influential today, so it's important to understand the **union movement today and tomorrow**. For example, unions are becoming more aggressive in terms of pushing Congress to pass the Employee Free Choice Act, which, among other things, would enable employees to vote for the union by signing authorization cards, rather than going through a formal union election. New union federations, such as Change to Win, are being more aggressive about organizing workers, and unions are going global, for instance, by helping employees in China organize local Walmart stores.

Discussion Questions

15-4. Why do employees join unions? What are the advantages and disadvantages of being a union member?

15-5. Discuss four sure ways to lose an NLRB election.

15-6. Briefly illustrate how labor law has gone through a cycle of repression and encouragement.

15-7. Explain in detail each step in a union drive and election.

15-8. Define impasse, mediation, and strike, and explain the techniques that are used to overcome an impasse.

Individual and Group Activities

15-9. You are the manager of a small manufacturing plant. The union contract covering most of your employees is about to expire. Working individually or in groups, discuss how to prepare for union contract negotiations.

15-10. Working individually or in groups, use Internet resources to find situations where company management and the union reached an impasse at some point during their negotiation process, but eventually resolved the impasse. Describe the issues on both sides that led to the impasse. How did they move past the impasse? What were the final outcomes?

15-11. Appendix A, PHR and SPHR Knowledge Base, at the end of this book (pages 580–588) lists the knowledge someone studying for the HRCI certification exam needs to have in each area of human resource management (such as in Strategic Management, Workforce Planning, and Human Resource Development). In groups of four to five students, do four things: (1) review Appendix A; (2) identify the material in this chapter that relates to the required knowledge Appendix A lists; (3) write four multiple-choice exam questions on this material that you believe would be suitable for inclusion in the HRCI exam; and (4) if time permits, have someone from your team post your team's questions in front of the class, so that students in all teams can answer the exam questions created by the other teams.

15-12. Several years ago, 8,000 Amtrak workers agreed not to disrupt service by walking out, at least not until a court hearing was held. Amtrak had asked the courts for a temporary restraining order, and the Transport Workers Union of America was actually pleased to postpone its walkout. The workers were apparently not upset at Amtrak, but at Congress for failing to provide enough funding for Amtrak. What, if anything, can an employer do when employees threaten to go on strike, not because of what the employer did, but what a third party—in this case, Congress—has done or not done? What laws would prevent the union from going on strike in this case?

Experiential Exercise

The Union-Organizing Campaign at Pierce U

Purpose: The purpose of this exercise is to give you practice in dealing with some of the elements of a union-organizing campaign.[113]

Required Understanding: You should be familiar with the material covered in this chapter, as well as the following incident, "An Organizing Question on Campus."

Incident an Organizing Question on Campus: Art Tipton is human resource director of Pierce University, a private university located in a large urban city. Ruth Zimmer, a supervisor in the maintenance and housekeeping services division of the university, has just come into Art's office to discuss her situation. Zimmer's division is responsible for maintaining and cleaning physical facilities of the university. Zimmer is one of the department supervisors who supervise employees who maintain and clean on-campus dormitories.

In the next several minutes, Zimmer proceeds to express her concerns about a union-organizing campaign that has begun among her employees. According to Zimmer, a representative of the Service Workers Union has met with several of her employees, urging them to sign union authorization cards. She has observed several of her employees "cornering" other employees to talk to them about joining the union and to urge them to sign union authorization (or representation) cards. Zimmer even observed this during working hours as employees were going about their normal duties in the dormitories. Zimmer reports that a number of her employees have come to her asking for her opinions about the union. They told her that several other supervisors in the department had told their employees not to sign any union authorization cards and not to talk about the union at any time while they were on campus. Zimmer also reports that one of her fellow supervisors told his employees that anyone who was caught talking about the union or signing a union authorization card would be disciplined and perhaps dismissed.

Zimmer says that her employees are very dissatisfied with their wages and with the conditions that they have endured from students, supervisors, and other staff people. She says that several employees told her that they had signed union cards because they believed that the only way university administration would pay attention to their concerns was if the employees had a union to represent them. Zimmer says that she made a list of employees who she felt had joined or were interested in the union, and she could share these with Tipton if he wanted to deal with them personally. Zimmer closed her presentation with the comment that she and other department supervisors need to know what they should do in order to stomp out the threat of unionization in their department.

How to Set Up the Exercise/Instructions: Divide the class into groups of four or five students. Assume that you are labor relations consultants the university retained to identify the problems and issues involved and to advise Art Tipton on the university's rights and what to do next. Each group will spend the time allotted discussing the issues. Then, outline those issues, as well as an action plan for Tipton. What should he do next?

If time permits, a spokesperson from each group should list on the board the issues involved and the group's recommendations. What should Art do?

Video Case

Video Title: Union-Management Relations (UPS)

SYNOPSIS

The former human resources head for UPS describes what it's like (for both an employer and an employee) to work with a labor union. The roles and functions of labor unions are discussed, and the advantages and disadvantages that can accrue to both employees and management are explained. The future of unions, and other arrangements that fulfill some of the same roles, are also discussed.

Discussion Questions

15-13. From what you know about UPS, what do you think would make the union believe that the company was ripe for being organized?

15-14. Do you agree that unions "stifle creativity"? Why or why not?

15-15. Do you agree that employees who excel in nonunion environments earn more than they would in unionized companies? Why?

15-16. What other "replacements" for unions have helped reduce union membership, according to the chapter?

Application Case

Negotiating with the Writers Guild of America

The talks between the Writers Guild of America (WGA) and the Alliance of Motion Picture & Television Producers (producers) began tense, and then got tenser.[114]

The biggest issue was how to split revenue from new media, such as when television shows move to the Internet. The producers said they wanted a profit-splitting system rather than the current residual system. Under the residual system, writers continue to receive "residuals" or income from shows they write every time they're shown (such as when *Seinfeld* appears in reruns). Writers Guild executives argued producers' revenues from advertising and subscription fees had recently jumped by about 40%.[115]

The situation grew tenser.[116] Even after meeting six times, it seemed that "the parties' only apparent area of agreement is that no real bargaining has yet to occur."[117]

Soon, the Writers Guild asked its members for strike authorization, and the producers were claiming that the guild was just trying to delay negotiations until the current contract expired (at the end of October). As the president of the producers' group said, "We have had six across-the-table sessions and there was only silence and stonewalling from the WGA leadership. . . . The WGA leadership apparently has no intention to bargain in good faith."[118] As evidence, the producers claimed that the WGA negotiating committee left one meeting after less than an hour.

Both sides knew timing was very important. During the fall and spring, television series production is in full swing. So, a writers' strike now would have a bigger impact than waiting until, say, the summer to strike. Perhaps not surprisingly, some movement was soon discernible.[119] Then the WGA and producers reached agreement. The new contract was "the direct result of renewed negotiations between the two sides, which culminated Friday with a marathon session including top WGA officials and the heads of the Walt Disney Co. and News Corp."[120]

Questions

15-17. The producers said the WGA was not bargaining in good faith. What did they mean by that, and do you think the evidence is sufficient to support the claim?

15-18. The WGA did eventually strike. What tactics could the producers have used to fight back once the strike began? What tactics do you think the WGA used?

15-19. This was a conflict between professional and creative people (the WGA) and TV and movie producers. Do you think the conflict was therefore different in any way than are the conflicts between, say, the Autoworkers or Teamsters unions against auto and trucking companies? Why?

15-20. What role (with examples) did negotiating skills seem to play in the WGA producers' negotiations?

Continuing Case

Carter Cleaning Company

The Grievance

On visiting one of Carter Cleaning Company's stores, Jennifer was surprised to be taken aside by a long-term Carter employee, who met her as she was parking her car. "Murray (the store manager) told me I was suspended for 2 days without pay because I came in late last Thursday," said George. "I'm really upset, but around here the store manager's word seems to be law, and it sometimes seems like the only way anyone can file a grievance is by meeting you or your father like this in the parking lot." Jennifer was very disturbed by this revelation and promised the employee she would look into it and discuss the situation with her father. In the car heading back to headquarters, she began mulling over what Carter Cleaning Company's alternatives might be.

Questions

15-21. Do you think it is important for Carter Cleaning Company to have a formal grievance process? Why or why not?

15-22. Based on what you know about the Carter Cleaning Company, outline the steps in what you think would be the ideal grievance process for this company.

15-23. In addition to the grievance process, can you think of anything else that Carter Cleaning Company might do to make sure grievances and gripes like this one are expressed and are heard by top management?

Translating Strategy into HR Policies and Practices Case*,§

**The accompanying strategy map for this chapter is in the MyManagementLab; and the overall map on the inside back cover of this text outlines the relationships involved.*

IMPROVING PERFORMANCE at The Hotel Paris

The Hotel Paris's New Labor Relations Practices

The Hotel Paris's competitive strategy is "To use superior guest service to differentiate the Hotel Paris properties, and to thereby increase the length of stay and return rate of guests, and thus boost revenues and profitability." HR manager Lisa Cruz must now formulate functional policies and activities that support this competitive strategy and boost performance by eliciting the required employee behaviors and competencies.

Lisa Cruz's parents were both union members, and she had no strong philosophical objections to unions, per se. However, as the head of HR for the Hotel Paris, she did feel very strongly that her employer should do everything legally possible to remain union-free. She knew that this is what the hotel chain's owners and top executives wanted, and that achieving their strategic goals would be best accomplished by staying union free. Furthermore, the evidence seemed to support their position. At least one study that she'd seen concluded that firms with 30% or more of their eligible workers in unions were in the bottom 10% in terms of performance, while those with 8% to 9% of eligible workers in unions scored in the top 10%.[121] The problem was that the Hotel Paris really had no specific policies and procedures in place to help its managers and supervisors deal with union activities. With all the laws regarding

§Written by and copyright Gary Dessler, PhD.

what employers and their managers could and could not do to respond to a union's efforts, Lisa knew her company was "a problem waiting to happen." She turned her attention to deciding what steps she and her team should take with regard to labor relations and collective bargaining.

Lisa and the CFO knew that unionization was a growing reality for the Hotel Paris. About 5% of the hotel chain's U.S. employees were already unionized, and unions in this industry were quite active. For example, as they were surfing the Internet to better gauge the situation, Lisa and the CFO came across the website from the Hotel Employees Restaurant Union, local 26. It describes their success in negotiating a contract at several local hotels including ones managed by the Westin and Hilton chains. The CFO and Lisa agreed that it was important that she and her team develop and institute a new set of policies and practices that would enable the Hotel Paris to deal more effectively with unions.

Together with a labor–management attorney, the team developed a 20-page "What You Need to Know When the Union Calls" manual for Hotel Paris managers and supervisors. This contained three sets of information. First, it provided a succinct outline of *labor relations law*, particularly as it relates to the company's managers. Second, it laid a *detailed set of guidelines* regarding what supervisors could and could not do with respect to union organizing activities. Third, it identified all line supervisors as the company's *"front-line eyes and ears"* with respect to union organizing activity. Here, the manual provided examples of activities that might suggest that a union was trying to organize the hotel's employees, and whom the supervisor should notify.

Lisa and her team also decided to ensure that the company was responsive to its employees' concerns. Lisa and her team believed that many of the steps they'd taken earlier should help. For example, improving salaries and wages, providing financial incentives, and instituting the new ethics, justice, and fairness programs already seemed to be having a measurable effect on employee morale. One year after the hotel's new labor relations efforts went into effect, the percentage of eligible employees in unions was down to 3%.

Questions

15-24. List and briefly describe what you believe are the three most important steps Hotel Paris management can take now to reduce the likelihood unions will organize more of its employees.

15-25. Write a detailed 2-page outline for a "What You Need to Know When the Union Calls" manual. Lisa will distribute this manual to her company's supervisors and managers, telling them what they need to know about looking out for possible unionizing activity, and how to handle actual organizing process–related supervisory tasks.

MyManagementLab

Go to **mymanagementlab.com** for Auto-graded writing questions as well as the following Assisted-graded writing questions:

15-26. Describe important tactics you would expect the union to use during the union drive and election.

15-27. What is meant by good faith bargaining? Using examples, explain when bargaining is not in good faith.

15-28. MyManagementLab only—comprehensive writing assignment for this chapter.

Key Terms

closed shop, 459
union shop, 459
agency shop, 459
preferential shop, 459
right to work, 459
Norris-LaGuardia Act of 1932, 460
National Labor Relations (or Wagner) Act, 460
National Labor Relations Board (NLRB), 460
Taft-Hartley Act of 1947, 462
national emergency strikes, 463
Landrum-Griffin Act of 1959, 463
union salting, 464
authorization cards, 464
bargaining unit, 465
decertification, 469
collective bargaining, 470
good faith bargaining, 470
voluntary (or permissible) bargaining items, 471
illegal bargaining items, 471
mandatory bargaining items, 471
impasse, 473
mediation, 473
fact finder, 473
arbitration, 473
interest arbitration, 473
rights arbitration, 473
strike, 473
economic strike, 473
unfair labor practice strike, 473
wildcat strike, 473
sympathy strike, 473
picketing, 473
corporate campaign, 475
boycott, 475
inside games, 475
lockout, 476
injunction, 476
grievance procedure, 476

Endnotes

1. For example, see http://articles.moneycentral.msn.com/Investing/Extra/CostcoTheAntiWalMart.aspx?page=1, accessed June 29, 2011; and, Hamilton Nolan, "The Anti-Wal-Mart," http://gawker.com/costco-the-anti-wal-mart-511739135, accessed August 7, 2013.
2. Christine Frey, "Costco's Love of Labor: Employees' Well-Being Key to Its Success," www.seattlepi.com/default/article/Costco-s-love-of-labor-Employees-well-being-key-1140722.php, accessed June 29, 2011; Steven Greenhouse and Reed Abelson, "Wal-Mart Cuts Some Health Care Benefits," *The New York Times*, (October 21, 2011), pp. B1,B5.

3. Stephen Greenhouse, "Share of the Workforce in a Union Falls to a 97 Year Low, 11.3%," *The New York Times*, January 24, 2013, B1;] http://www.bls.gov/news.release/union2.nr0.htm, accessed August 7. 2013.
4. Ibid.
5. Stephen Greenhouse, "Most US Union Members Are Working for the Government, New Data Shows," *The New York Times*, January 23, 2010, pp. B1–B5.
6. Michael Ash and Jean Seago, "The Effect of Registered Nurses' Unions on Heart Attack Mortality," *Industrial and Labor Relations Review* 57, no. 3 (April 2004), pp. 422–442.
7. http://articles.moneycentral.msn.com/Investing/Extra/CostcoTheAntiWalMart.aspx?page=1, accessed September 15, 2011; and, Hamilton Nolan, "The Anti-Wal-Mart," http://gawker.com/costco-the-anti-wal-mart-511739135, accessed August 7, 2013.
8. Ibid.
9. Ibid.
10. Ibid.
11. http://www.bls.gov/news.release/union2.nr0.htm, accessed August 7. 2013.
12. Dale Belman and Paula Voos, "Changes in Union Wage Effects by Industry: A Fresh Look at the Evidence," *Industrial Relations* 43, no. 3 (July 2004), pp. 491–519.
13. Donna Buttigieg et al., "An Event History Analysis of Union Joining and Leaving," *Journal of Applied Psychology* 92, no. 3 (2007), pp. 829–839.
14. Kris Maher, "The New Union Worker," *The Wall Street Journal*, September 27, 2005, pp. B1, B11.
15. Robert Grossman, "Unions Follow Suit," *HR Magazine*, May 2005, p. 49.
16. Warner Pflug, *The UAW in Pictures* (Detroit: Wayne State University Press, 1971), pp. 11–12.
17. Arthur Sloane and Fred Witney, *Labor Relations* (Upper Saddle River, NJ: Prentice Hall, 2007)), pp. 335–336.
18. Benjamin Taylor and Fred Witney, *Labor Relations Law* (Upper Saddle River, NJ: Prentice Hall, 1992), pp. 170–171; www.dol.gov/whd/state/righttowork.htm, accessed June 5, 2010.
19. www.dol.gov/whd/state/righttowork.htm, accessed June 5, 2010. (Indiana applicable only to school employees.)
20. "Research Inconclusive About Effective Right to Work on Economy," *BNA Bulletin to Management*, January 8, 2013, p. 14.
21. www.seiu.org/our-union/, accessed June 1, 2011.
22. Steven Greenhouse, "4th Union Quits AFL-CIO in a Dispute Over Organizing," *The New York Times*, September 15, 2005, p. A14.
23. Some trace early U.S. labor relations legislation back to a fire at the Triangle Shirtwaist factory in 1911. Following that tragedy, in which 146 people died, New York State passed a number of legal reforms covering not only safety but also issues such as low wages, child labor, and long hours. New York City and New York State soon adopted 36 new laws, and many view these laws as the basis for and precursor to the U.S. labor legislation efforts that began in earnest in the 1930s. "The Birth of the New Deal," *The Economist*, March 19, 2011, p. 39.
24. The following material is based on Arthur Sloane and Fred Witney, *Labor Relations* (Upper Saddle River, NJ: Prentice Hall, 2001), pp. 46–124.
25. www.bls.gov/news.release/union2.nr0.htm, accessed June 1, 2011.
26. Michael Carrell and Christina Heavrin, *Labor Relations and Collective Bargaining* (Upper Saddle River, NJ: Prentice Hall, 2004), p. 180.
27. Sloane and Witney, *Labor Relations*, p. 121.
28. For organizing examples from the unions' point of view, see www.twu.org/international/steps, accessed June 29, 2011; www.opeiu.org/NeedAUnion/StepstoCreatingaUnion-Workplace/tabid/71/Default.aspx, accessed June 29, 2011; and particularly http://ufcwone.org/steps-form-union, accessed August 7, 2013. See also http://www.nlrb.gov/nlrb-process, and http://www.nlrb.gov/what-we-do/conduct-elections, both accessed August 7, 2013.
29. Kris Maher, "Unions' New Foe: Consultants," *The Wall Street Journal*, August 15, 2005, p. B1.
30. "Some Say Salting Leaves Bitter Taste for Employers," *BNA Bulletin to Management*, March 4, 2004, p. 79; and www.nlrb.gov/global/search/index.aspx?mode=s&qt=salting&col=nlrb&gb=y, accessed January 14, 2008. For a management lawyer's perspective, see www.fklaborlaw.com/union_salt-objectives.html, accessed May 25, 2007.
31. "Spurned Union Salts Entitled to Back Pay, D.C. Court Says, Affirming Labor Board," *BNA Bulletin to Management*, June 21, 2001, p. 193.
32. D. Diane Hatch and James Hall, "Salting Cases Clarified by NLRB," *Workforce*, August 2000, p. 92. See also www.fklaborlaw.com/union_salt-objectives.html, accessed May 25, 2007.
33. Edwin Arnold et al., "Determinants of Certification Election Outcomes in the Service Sector," *Labor Studies Journal* 25, no. 3 (Fall 2000), p. 51.
34. "Number of Elections, Union Wins Increased in 2002," *BNA Bulletin to Management*, June 19, 2003, p. 197.
35. This section is based on Matthew Goodfellow, "How to Lose an NLRB Election," *Personnel Administrator* 23 (September 1976), pp. 40–44. See also Matthew Goodfellow, "Avoid Unionizing: Chemical Company Union Election Results for 1993," *Chemical Marketing Reporter* 246 (July 18, 1994), p. SR14; Gillian Flynn, "When the Unions Come Calling," *Workforce*, November 2000, pp. 82–87.
36. Ibid.
37. Ibid.
38. Harry Katz, "The Decentralization of Collective Bargaining: A Literature Review and Comparative Analysis," *Industrial and Labor Relations Review* 47, no. 1 (October 1993), p. 11; and F. Traxler, "Bargaining (De)centralization, Macroeconomic Performance and Control Over the Employment Relationship," *British Journal of Industrial Relations*, 41, no. 1 (March 2003), pp. 1–27.
39. The following are adapted and/or quoted from Kate Bronfenbrenner, "The Role of Union Strategies in NLRB Certification Elections," *Industrial and Labor Relations Review* 50 (January 1997), pp. 195–212; see also J. Fiorito et. al., "Understanding Organising Activity Among US National Unions," *Industrial Relations Journal* 41, no. 1 (January 2010), pp. 74–92.
40. Stephen Greenhouse, "Union Gets New Election at a Target," *The New York Times*, May 22, 2012, B3.
41. Frederick Sullivan, "Limiting Union Organizing Activity Through Supervisors," *Personnel* 55 (July/August 1978), pp. 55–65. See also Edward Young and William Levy, "Responding to a Union-Organizing Campaign: Do You and Your Supervisors Know the Legal Boundaries in a Union Campaign?" *Franchising World* 39, no. 3 (March 2007), pp. 45–49.
42. Ibid., pp. 167–168.
43. Jonathan Segal, "Unshackle Your Supervisors to Stay Union Free," *HR Magazine*, June 1998, pp. 62–65. See also www.nlrb.gov/workplace_rights/nlra_violations.aspx, accessed January 14, 2008.
44. Whether employers must give union representatives permission to organize on employer-owned property at shopping malls is a matter of legal debate. The U.S. Supreme Court ruled in *Lechmere, Inc. v. National Labor Relations Board* that employers may bar nonemployees from their property if the nonemployees have reasonable alternative means of communicating their message to the intended audience. However, if the employer lets other organizations like the Salvation Army set up at their workplaces, the NLRB may view discriminating against the union organizers as an unfair labor practice. See, for example, "Union Access to Employer's Customers Restricted," *BNA Bulletin to Management*, February 15, 1996, p. 49; "Workplace Access for Unions Hinges on Legal Issues," *BNA Bulletin to Management*, April 11, 1996, p. 113.
45. "Union Access to Employer's Customers Restricted," pp. 4–65. The appropriateness of these sample rules may be affected by factors unique to an employer's operation, and they should therefore be reviewed by the employer's attorney before implementation.
46. Clyde Scott and Edwin Arnold, "Deauthorization and Decertification Elections: An Analysis and Comparison of Results," *Working USA* 7, no. 3 (Winter 2003), pp. 6–20; www.nlrb.gov/nlrb/shared_files/brochures/rpt_september2002.pdf, accessed January 14, 2008.
47. Carrell and Heavrin, *Labor Relations and Collective Bargaining*, pp. 120–121.
48. See, for example, David Meyer and Trevor Bain, "Union Decertification Election Outcomes: Bargaining Unit Characteristics and Union Resources," *Journal of Labor Research* 15, no. 2 (Spring 1994), pp. 117–136; Arthur Sloane and Fred Witney, *Labor Relations* (Upper Saddle River, NJ: Prentice Hall, 2007), p. 96.
49. Mimosa Spencer and Jeanne Whalen, "Change France? Sanofi Find It Can't," *The Wall Street Journal*, April 11, 2013, pp. B1, D5.
50. Ibid., B1.
51. www.nlrb.gov/nlrb/shared_files/brochures/basicguide.pdf, accessed January 14, 2008.
52. Carrell and Heavrin, *Labor Relations and Collective Bargaining*, pp. 176–177.
53. www.bloomberg.com/news/2011-02-14/nfl-files-unfair-labor-practice-charge-against-union.html, accessed June 1, 2011.
54. John Fossum, *Labor Relations* (Dallas: BPI, 1982), pp. 246–250; Arthur Sloane and Fred Witney, *Labor Relations*, op cit., pp. 197–205.
55. *Boulwareism* is the name given to a strategy, now generally held in disfavor, by which the company, based on an exhaustive study of what it believed its employees wanted, made but one offer at the bargaining table and then refused to bargain any further unless convinced by the union on the basis of new facts that its original position was wrong. The NLRB subsequently found that the practice of offering the same settlement to all units, insisting that certain parts of the package could not differ among agreements, and communicating to the employees about how negotiations were going amounted

to an illegal pattern. Fossum, *Labor Relations*, p. 267.

56. Kathryn Tyler, "Good-Faith Bargaining," *HR Magazine*, January 2005, p. 52.
57. These are based on James C. Freund, *Smart Negotiating* (New York: Simon & Schuster, 1992), pp. 42–46.
58. James C. Freund, *Smart Negotiating* (New York: Simon & Schuster, 1992), pp. 42–46.
59. Ibid., 33. One interesting observation: Communicating threats is more effective than communicating anger. See Marwan Sineceure et al., "Hot or Cold: Is Communicating Anger or Threats More Effective in Negotiation?" *Journal of Applied Psychology* 96, no. 5 (2011), pp. 1019–1032.
60. Reed Richardson, *Collective Bargaining by Objectives* (Upper Saddle River, NJ: Prentice Hall, 1977), p. 150. Both sides will try to manipulate the media to jockey for better positions; for example, see J. McCafferty, "Labor-Management Dispute Resolution & the Media," *Dispute Resolution Journal* 56, no. 3 (August/October 2001), pp. 40–47.
61. Many negotiators pride themselves on being open, honest, and straightforward in their negotiations, but at least one study suggests that this can backfire. Specifically, people who are inclined to be straightforward may also develop a greater concern for their counterpart's interest, which in turn can lead to greater concession making during the negotiation. D. Scott DeRue et al., "When Is Straightforwardness a Liability in Negotiations? The Role of Integrative Potential and Structural Power," *Journal of Applied Psychology* 94, no. 4 (2009), pp. 1032–1047.
62. With or without reaching a solution, impasses and union–management conflict can leave union members demoralized. See, for example, Jessica Marquez, "Taking Flight," *Workforce*, June 9, 2008, pp. 1, 18.
63. Jacqueline Palank et al., "Last Chance to Save the Twinkie," *The Wall Street Journal*, November 20, 2012, p. B1.
64. Fossum, *Labor Relations*, p. 312.
65. Carrell and Heavrin, *Labor Relations and Collective Bargaining*, p. 501.
66. http://fmcs.gov/assets/files/annual%20reports/FY2006_Annual_Report.pdf, accessed January 14, 2008.
67. Fossum, *Labor Relations*, p. 317.
68. www.autoblog.com/2010/12/06/report-uaw-to-hold-sympathy-strike-for-hyundai-workers-in-korea/, accessed June 1, 2011.
69. This is based on Arthur Sloane and Fred Whitney, *Labor Relations* (Upper Saddle River, NJ: Prentice Hall, 2010), p. 213.
70. "Striker Replacements," *BNA Bulletin to Management*, February 6, 2003, p. S7.
71. http://profootballtalk.nbcsports.com/2011/03/21/league-doesnt-rule-out-replacement-players-during-lockout/, accessed June 29, 2011.
72. Stephen Cabot and Gerald Cuerton, "Labor Disputes and Strikes: Be Prepared," *Personnel Journal* 60 (February 1981), pp. 121–126. See also Brenda Sunoo, "Managing Strikes, Minimizing Loss," *Personnel Journal* 74, no. 1 (January 1995), p. 50ff.
73. Some labor lawyers report an increase in the use by unions of corporate campaigns. Janet Walthall, "Unions Increasingly Using Corporate Campaigns," *BNA Bulletin to Management*, February 16, 2010, p. 55.
74. For a discussion, see Herbert Northrup, "Union Corporate Campaigns and Inside Games as a Strike Form," *Employee Relations Law Journal* 19, no. 4 (Spring 1994), pp. 507–549.
75. Matthew Dolan, "UAW Targets Foreign Car Plants in US," *The Wall Street Journal*, December 23, 2010, p. B3. See also Rachel Feintzeig, "Teamsters Act Tough with Twinkies Maker," *The Wall Street Journal*, February 14, 2012, p. B-4.
76. Northrup, "Union Corporate Campaigns and Inside Games," p. 513.
77. Ibid., p. 518.
78. www.starbucksunion.org, accessed August 7, 2013.
79. James Hagerty and Caroline Van Hasselt, "Lockout Tests Union's Clout," *The Wall Street Journal,* January 30, 2012, p. B-1.
80. Clifford Koen Jr., Sondra Hartman, and Dinah Payne, "The NLRB Wields a Rejuvenated Weapon," *Personnel Journal*, December 1996, pp. 85–87; and D. Silverman, "The NLRA at 70: A New Approach to Processing 10(j)s [NLRA at Seventy conference in New York City, 2005]," *Labor Law Journal*, 56, no. 3 (Fall 2005), pp. 203–206.
81. Sloane and Witney, *Labor Relations*, 10th ed., pp. 221–227.
82. Carrell and Heavrin, *Labor Relations and Collective Bargaining*, pp. 417–418.
83. Richardson, *Collective Bargaining by Objectives.*
84. M. Gene Newport, *Supervisory Management* (St. Paul, MN: West Group, 1976), p. 273; see also Walter Baer, "Grievance Handling: 101 Guides for Supervisors" (New York: American Management Association, 1970); and Mark Lurie, "The Eight Essential Steps in Grievance Processing," *Dispute Resolution Journal* 54 no. 4 (November 1999), pp. 61–65.
85. "An Employer Prohibits Social Media Use During Workday?" *BNA Bulletin to Management*, October 23, 2012, p. 344.
86. Nonunion Employers Should Heed Recent NLRB Rulings, Speakers Say," *BNA Bulletin to Management*, December 4, 2012, p. 385.
87. David Rubin, "Get Antisocial," *HR Magazine*, February 2013, pp. 69–70.
88. Susan Carey and Jack Nicas, "AMR Will Ask the Judge to Toss Labor Pacts," *The Wall Street Journal,* March 23, 2012, p. B3.
89. www.bls.gov/news.release/union2.nr0.htm, accessed April 2, 2009.
90. See, for example, Jo Blandon et al., "Have Unions Turned the Corner? New Evidence on Recent Trends in Union Recognition in UK Firms," *British Journal of Industrial Relations* 44, no. 2 (June 2006), pp. 169–190.
91. Jennifer Schramm, "The Future of Unions," *Society for Human Resource Management, Workplace Visions* 4 (2005), pp. 1–8.
92. Ibid. See also www.changetowin.org/about-us.html, accessed February 13, 2010.
93. Specialty health care and rehabilitation center of mobile, 357 NLRB number 83, 2011.
94. Robert Grossman, "Five Labor Relations Battlefronts," *HR Magazine*, August 2012, pp. 34–36.
95. Ibid.
96. "The Limits of Solidarity," *The Economist*, September 23, 2006, p. 34.
97. Chris Maher, "Specter Won't Support Union-Backed Bill," *The Wall Street Journal*, March 25, 2009, p. A3.
98. "Unions Using Class Actions to Pressure Nonunion Companies," *BNA Bulletin to Management*, August 22, 2006, p. 271. Some believe that today, "long-term observers see more bark than bite in organized labors efforts to revitalize." See, for example, Robert Grossman, "We Organized Labor and Code," *HR Magazine,* January 2008, pp. 37–40.
99. Andy Meisler, "Who Will Fold First?" *Workforce Management,* January 2004, pp. 28–38.
100. Dean Scott, "Unions Still a Potent Force," *Kiplinger Business Forecasts*, March 26, 2003.
101. Schramm, "The Future of Unions," p. 6.
102. Fong and Maher, "US Labor Chief Moves into China," p. 1.
103. Steven Greenhouse, "Steelworkers Merge with British Union," *The New York Times*, July 3, 2008, p. C4.
104. Matthew Dolan and Neil Boudette, "UAW to Send Activists Abroad," *The Wall Street Journal,* March 23, 2011, p. B2.
105. Shalini Rankchandran and Anton Troianovski, "AT&T's Strike Camp," *The Wall Street Journal,* April 5, 2012, pp. B1–B2.
106. Michael Carroll and Christina Heavrin, *Labor Relations and Collective Bargaining* (Upper Saddle River, NJ: Pearson, 2004), pp. 62–63.
107. Carrell and Heavrin, *Labor Relations and Collective Bargaining*.
108. George Gray, Donald Myers, and Phyllis Myers, "Cooperative Provisions in Labor Agreements: A New Paradigm?" *Monthly Labor Review,* January 1, 1999. See also Mark Schoeff Jr., "Labor on the March," *Workforce Management*, February 2010, pp. 1, 18–19.
109. Gray et al., "Cooperative Provisions in Labor Agreements."
110. Stephen Deery and Roderick Iverson, "Labor–Management Cooperation: Antecedents and Impact on Organizational Performance," *Industrial & Labor Relations Review* 58, no. 4 (July 2005), pp. 588–609.
111. Carol Gill, "Union Impact on the Effective Adoption of High Performance Work Practices," *Human Resource Management Review* 19 (2009), pp. 39–50.
112. See also Thomas Kochan, "A Jobs Compact for America's Future," *Harvard Business Review*, March 2012, pp. 64–70.
113. Raymond Hilgert and Cyril Ling, *Cases and Experiential Exercises in Management* (Upper Saddle River, NJ: Prentice Hall, 1996), pp. 201–203.
114. Chris Pursell, "Rhetoric Flying in WGA Talks," *TelevisionWeek,* July 23, 2007, pp. 3, 35; Peter Sanders, "In Hollywood, a Tale of Two Union Leaderships," *The Wall Street Journal*, January 7, 2008, p. B2.
115. Pursell, "Rhetoric Flying in WGA Talks."
116. Ibid.
117. James Hibberd, "Guild Talks Break with No Progress," *TVWeek* 26, no. 38 (October 8, 2007), pp. 1, 30.
118. Ibid.
119. "DGA Deal Sets the Stage for Writers," *TelevisionWeek,* January 21, 2008, pp. 3, 33.
120. "WGA, Studios Reach Tentative Agreement," *UPI NewsTrack*, February 3, 2008.
121. Brian Becker et al., *The HR Scorecard* (Boston: Harvard Business School Press, 2001), p. 16.

16 Employee Safety and Health

Source: © Bloomberg/Getty Images

MyManagementLab®

Improve Your Grade!

When you see this icon, visit **www.mymanagementlab.com** for activities that are applied, personalized, and offer immediate feedback.

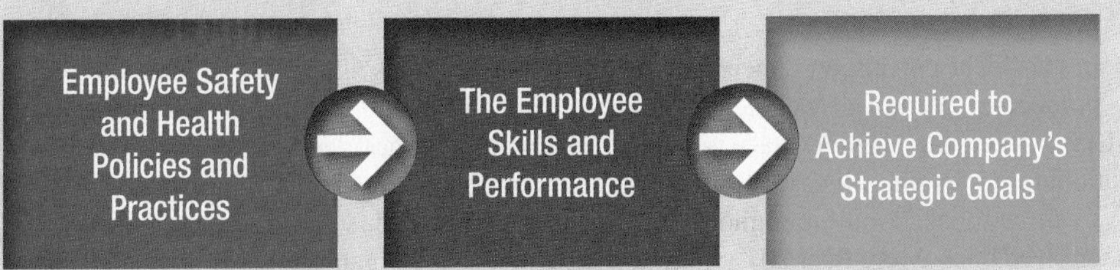

For a bird's eye view of how one company created a new safety program to improve its strategic performance, read the Hotel Paris case on page 526 and answer the questions after reading the chapter.

WHERE ARE WE NOW . . .

Along with fairness and labor relations, safety is an important issue in employee relations, and in the quality of employees' lives and the employer's performance. The main purpose of this chapter is to provide you with knowledge managers need to deal with workplace safety and health issues. The main topics we discuss are introduction: safety and the manager; manager's briefing on occupational safety law; what causes accidents?; how to prevent accidents; workplace health hazards: problems and remedies; and occupational security and risk management.

LEARNING OBJECTIVES

1 Explain the supervisor's role in safety.

2 Explain the basic facts about safety law and OSHA.

3 Answer the question, "What causes accidents?"

4 List and explain five ways to prevent accidents.

5 List five workplace health hazards and how to deal with them.

6 Discuss the prerequisites for a security plan and how to set up a basic security program.

The bakery plant manager knew that her plant's accident rate was too high, and that accidents were harming employees, boosting the plant's costs, and reducing its performance. We'll see what they did.

Introduction: Safety and the Manager

Why Safety Is Important

1 Explain the supervisor's role in safety.

Safety and accident prevention concern managers for several reasons, one of which is the staggering number of workplace accidents. While accident rates are falling, in one recent year, 4,609 U.S. workers died in workplace incidents,[1] and workplace accidents caused about 3 million occupational injuries and illnesses.[2] Such figures probably underestimate injuries and illnesses by two or three times.[3] And they ignore the hardships the accidents cause to the employee and his or her loved ones. More than 80% of the workers in one survey ranked workplace safety more important than minimum wages, sick days, and maternity leave.[4] Safety also affects costs and profits, as the accompanying Profit Center feature illustrates.

Injuries aren't just a problem in dangerous industries like construction. For example, new computers contribute to airtight "sick building" symptoms like headaches. And office work is susceptible to things like repetitive trauma injuries.

IMPROVING PERFORMANCE: HR as a Profit Center

Improving Safety Boosts Profits

Many people assume that when employers economize on safety programs the money they save improves profits, but that's not the case. Poor safety and the injuries and illnesses they beget actually drive up many costs, including medical expenses, workers' compensation, and lost productivity.[5] Poor safety practices even raise wage rates, because wage rates are higher on jobs with riskier working conditions, other things equal.[6]

For example, one study found a 9.4% drop in injury claims and a 26% average savings on workers' compensation costs in inspected companies over 4 years (inspections were conducted by California's occupational safety and health agency,) with no apparent adverse effect on the companies' sales, credit rating, or employment.[7] A survey of chief financial officers concluded that for every one dollar invested in injury prevention, the employer earns two dollars. Forty percent of the chief financial officers said "productivity" was the top benefit of effective workplace safety.[8] One forest products company saved over $1 million over 5 years by investing only about $50,000 in safety improvements and employee training. In the United States, work-related hearing loss costs employers about $242 million a year in workers' compensation claims alone, costs that are probably avoidable through earmuffs, earplugs, and training.[9] So ironically, one of the easiest ways to cut costs and boost profits is to improve one's safety programs.

Discussion Question 16-1: Assuming this is true, why do so many employers apparently cut corners on safety?

Management's Role in Safety

We will see that reducing accidents often boils down to reducing accident-causing conditions and accident-causing acts. However, telling employees to "work safely" is futile unless everyone knows management is serious about safety.[10] Management's attitude is crucial.

Historically, for instance, DuPont's accident rate has been much lower than that of the chemical industry as a whole. This good safety record is partly due to an organizational commitment to safety, which is evident in the following description:

> One of the best examples I know of in setting the highest possible priority for safety takes place at a DuPont Plant in Germany. Each morning at the DuPont Polyester and Nylon Plant, the director and his assistants meet at 8:45 to review the past 24 hours. The first matter they discuss is not production, but safety. Only after they have examined reports of accidents and near misses and satisfied themselves that corrective action has been taken do they move on to look at output, quality, and cost matters.[11]

Safety therefore starts at the top.[12] The employer should institutionalize its commitment with a safety policy, publicize it, and give safety matters high priority. Louisiana-Pacific Corp. starts all meetings with a brief safety message.[13] Georgia-Pacific reduced its workers' compensation costs by requiring that managers halve accidents or forfeit 30% of their bonuses. ABB Inc. requires its top executives to make safety observation tours of the company's facilities, sites, and projects at least quarterly.[14] The HR Tools feature illustrates the supervisor' role.

IMPROVING PERFORMANCE: HR Tools for Line Managers and Entrepreneurs

The Supervisor's Role in Accident Prevention

After inspecting a work site in which workers were installing sewer pipes in a 4-foot trench, the OSHA inspector cited the employer for violating the OSHA rule requiring employers to have a "stairway, ladder, ramp or other safe means of egress."[15] In the event the trench caved in, workers needed a quick way out.

As in most such cases, the employer had the primary responsibility for safety, but the local supervisor was responsible for day-to-day inspections. Here, the supervisor did not properly do his daily inspection. The trench did cave in, injuring workers (and, secondarily, costing his company many thousands of dollars).

Whether you're the manager in the IT department of a *Fortune* 500 company or managing an excavation or dry cleaning store, daily safety inspections should always be part of your routine. As one safety recommendation recently put it, "a daily walk-through of your workplace—whether you are working in outdoor construction, indoor manufacturing, or any place that poses safety challenges—is an essential part of your work."[16]

What to look for depends on the workplace for which you're responsible. For example, construction sites and dry cleaning stores have hazards all their own. But in general you can use a checklist of unsafe conditions such as the one in Figure 16-7 (page 500–502) to spot problems. We present another, more extensive checklist in Figure 16-9 (page 521–524) at the end of this chapter.

Discussion Question 16-2: Please stop what you are doing and look around the immediate area where you are now: List four potential safety hazards.

2 Explain the basic facts about safety law and OSHA.

Occupational Safety and Health Act of 1970
The law passed by Congress in 1970 "to assure so far as possible every working man and woman in the nation safe and healthful working conditions and to preserve our human resources."

Occupational Safety and Health Administration (OSHA)
The agency created within the Department of Labor to set safety and health standards for almost all workers in the United States.

Manager's Briefing on Occupational Safety Law

Congress passed the **Occupational Safety and Health Act of 1970** "to assure so far as possible every working man and woman in the nation safe and healthful working conditions and to preserve our human resources."[17] The only employers it doesn't cover are self-employed persons, farms in which only immediate members of the employer's family work, and some workplaces already protected by other federal agencies or under other statutes. The act covers federal agencies, but usually not state and local governments.

The act created the **Occupational Safety and Health Administration (OSHA)** within the Department of Labor. OSHA's basic purpose is to administer the act and to set and enforce the safety and health standards that apply to almost all workers in the United States. The Department of Labor enforces the standards, and OSHA has inspectors working out of branch offices to ensure compliance.

OSHA Standards and Record Keeping

OSHA operates under the "general" standard clause that each employer:

> . . . shall furnish to each of his [or her] employees employment and a place of employment which are free from recognized hazards that are causing or are likely to cause death or serious physical harm to his [or her] employees.

To carry out this basic mission, OSHA promulgates detailed legally enforceable standards. (Figure 16-1 presents a small part of the standard governing guardrails for scaffolds.) The regulations don't just list standards to which employers should adhere, but "how." For example, OSHA's respiratory protection standard also covers employee training.

FIGURE 16-1 OSHA Standards Example
Source: Occupational Safety and Hazard Administration (OSHA).

Guardrails not less than 2″ × 4″ or the equivalent and not less than 36″ or more than 42″ high, with a midrail, when required, of a 1″ × 4″ lumber or equivalent, and toeboards, shall be installed at all open sides on all scaffolds more than 10 feet above the ground or floor. Toeboards shall be a minimum of 4″ in height. Wire mesh shall be installed in accordance with paragraph [a] (17) of this section.

occupational illness
Any abnormal condition or disorder caused by exposure to environmental factors associated with employment.

Under OSHA, employers with 11 or more employees must maintain records of and report certain occupational injuries and occupational illnesses. An **occupational illness** is any abnormal condition or disorder caused by exposure to environmental factors associated with employment. This includes acute and chronic illnesses caused by inhalation, absorption, ingestion, or direct contact with toxic substances or harmful agents.

WHAT THE EMPLOYER MUST REPORT As in Figure 16-2, employers must report all occupational illnesses.[18]

They must also report most occupational injuries, specifically those that result in medical treatment (other than first aid), loss of consciousness, restriction of work (one or more lost workdays), restriction of motion, or transfer to another job.[19] If an on-the-job accident results in the death of an employee or in the hospitalization of five or more employees, all employers, regardless of size, must report the accident to the nearest OSHA office.

OSHA's current record-keeping rules allow the employer to conclude that an event needn't be reported if the facts so warrant—such as if a worker slips and falls after catching his foot on his car's seat belt when not at work on the company lot.[20]

However, OSHA's record-keeping requirements are still broad.[21] Examples of recordable conditions include food poisoning suffered by an employee in the employer's cafeteria and ankle sprains that occur during voluntary participation in a company softball game at a picnic the employee was required to attend. Figure 16-3 shows the OSHA form for reporting occupational injuries or illness.

Inspections and Citations

OSHA enforces its standards through inspections and (if necessary) citations. The inspection is usually unannounced. OSHA may not conduct warrantless inspections without an employer's consent. It may inspect with an authorized search warrant or its equivalent.[22] With a limited number of inspectors, OSHA recently has focused on "fair and effective enforcement," combined with outreach, education and compliance assistance, and various OSHA–employer cooperative programs (such as its "Voluntary Protection Programs").[23]

FIGURE 16-2 What Accidents Must Be Reported under the Occupational Safety and Health Act (OSHA)?

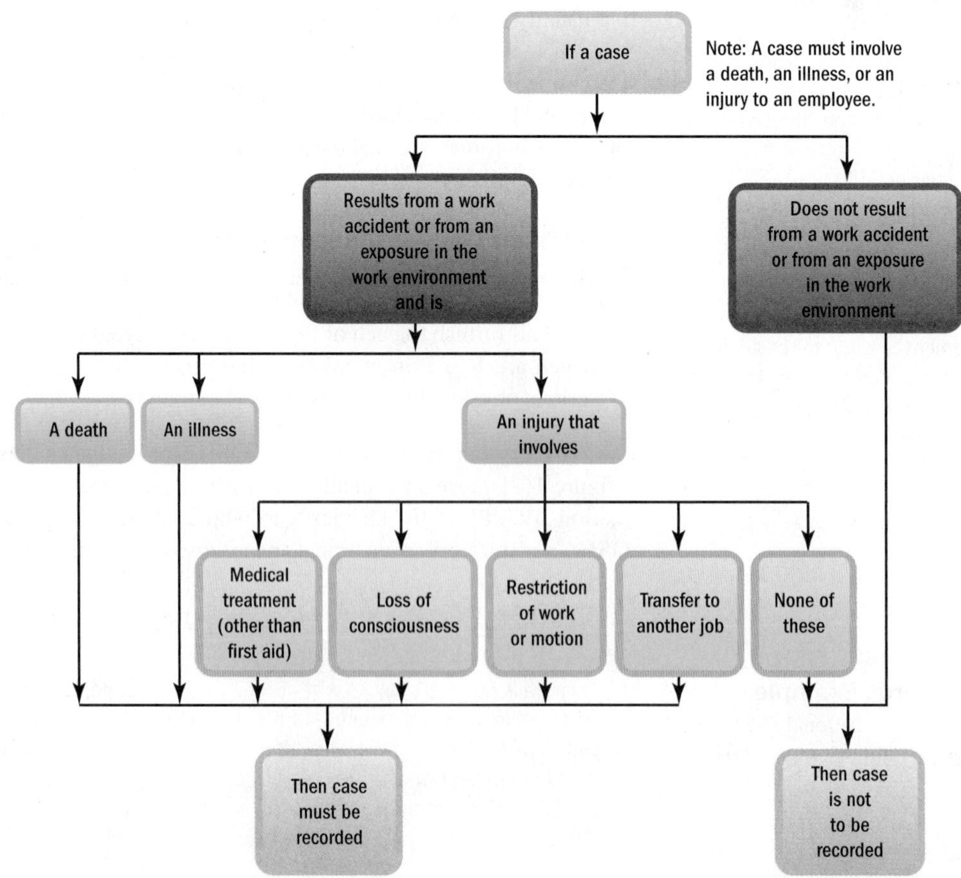

OSHA's FORM 301

Injury and Illness Incident Report

Attention: This form contains information relating to employee health and must be used in a manner that protects the confidentiality of employees to the extent possible while the information is being used for occupational safety and health purposes.

U.S. Department of Labor
Occupational Safety and Health Administration

Form approved OMB no. 1218-0176

This *Injury and Illness Incident Report* is one of the first forms you must fill out when a recordable work-related injury or illness has occurred. Together with the *Log of Work-Related Injuries and Illnesses* and the accompanying *Summary*, these forms help the employer and OSHA develop a picture of the extent and severity of work-related incidents.

Within 7 calendar days after you receive information that a recordable work-related injury or illness has occurred, you must fill out this form or an equivalent. Some state workers' compensation, insurance, or other reports may be acceptable substitutes. To be considered an equivalent form, any substitute must contain all the information asked for on this form.

According to Public Law 91-596 and 29 CFR 1904, OSHA's recordkeeping rule, you must keep this form on file for 5 years following the year to which it pertains.

If you need additional copies of this form, you may photocopy and use as many as you need.

Completed by ______________________

Title ______________________

Phone (_____)_____-_______ **Date** ___/___/___

Information about the employee

1) Full name ______________________

2) Street ______________________

City ______________ State ________ ZIP ______

3) Date of birth ____/____/____

4) Date hired ____/____/____

5) ☐ Male
☐ Female

Information about the physician or other health care professional

6) Name of physician or other health care professional ______________________

7) If treatment was given away from the worksite, where was it given?

Facility ______________________

Street ______________________

City ______________ State ________ ZIP ______

8) Was employee treated in an emergency room?
☐ Yes
☐ No

9) Was employee hospitalized overnight as an in-patient?
☐ Yes
☐ No

Information about the case

10) Case number from the *Log* ______________ *(Transfer the case number from the Log after you record the case.)*

11) Date of injury or illness ____/____/____

12) Time employee began work ____________ AM/PM

13) Time of event ____________ AM/PM
☐ Check if time cannot be determined

14) ***What was the employee doing just before the incident occurred?*** Describe the activity, as well as the tools, equipment, or material the employee was using. Be specific. *Examples:* "climbing a ladder while carrying roofing materials"; "spraying chlorine from hand sprayer"; "daily computer key-entry."

15) ***What happened?*** Tell us how the injury occurred. *Examples:* "When ladder slipped on wet floor, worker fell 20 feet"; "Worker was sprayed with chlorine when gasket broke during replacement"; "Worker developed soreness in wrist over time."

16) ***What was the injury or illness?*** Tell us the part of the body that was affected and how it was affected; be more specific than "hurt," "pain," or sore." *Examples:* "strained back"; "chemical burn, hand"; "carpal tunnel syndrome."

17) ***What object or substance directly harmed the employee?*** *Examples:* "concrete floor"; "chlorine"; "radial arm saw," *If this question does not apply to the incident, leave it blank.*

18) ***If the employee died, when did death occur?***
Date of death ____/____/____

Public reporting burden for this collection of information is estimated to average 22 minutes per response, including time for reviewing instructions, searching existing data sources, gathering and maintaining the data needed, and completing and reviewing the collection of information. Persons are not required to respond to the collection of information unless it displays a current valid OMB control number. If you have any comments about this estimate or any other aspects of this data collection, including suggestions for reducing this burden, contact: US Department of Labor, OSHA Office of Statistical Analysis, Room N-3644, 200 Constitution Avenue, NW, Washington, DC 20210. Do not send the completed forms to this office.

FIGURE 16-3 Form Used to Record Occupational Injuries and Illnesses
Source: U.S. Department of Labor.

INSPECTION PRIORITIES OSHA takes a "worst-first" approach in setting inspection priorities. Priorities include, from highest to lowest, imminent dangers, catastrophes and fatal accidents, employee complaints, high-hazard industries inspections, and follow-up inspections.[24] In one recent year, OSHA conducted about 40,600 inspections.[25]

OSHA conducts an inspection within 24 hours when a complaint indicates an immediate danger, and within 3 working days when a serious hazard exists. For a "nonserious" complaint filed in writing by a worker or a union, OSHA will respond within 20 working days. OSHA handles other nonserious complaints by writing to the employer and requesting corrective action. OSHA recently told almost 15,000 U.S. employers that because of their higher-than-average injury and illness rates, they may be subject to inspections.[26]

THE INSPECTION The inspection begins when the OSHA officer arrives at the workplace.[27] He or she displays credentials and asks to meet an employer representative. (The credentials must include photograph and serial number.) The officer explains the visit's purpose, the scope of the inspection, and the standards that apply. An authorized employee representative accompanies the officer during the inspection. The inspector can also stop and question workers (in private, if necessary). The act protects each employee from discrimination for exercising his or her disclosure rights.[28]

OSHA inspectors look for all types of violations, but some areas grab more attention. The five most frequent OSHA inspection violation areas are scaffolding, fall protection, hazard communication, lockout/tagout (electrical disengagement), and respiratory problems.[29]

Finally, the inspector holds a closing conference with the employer's representative. Here the inspector discusses apparent violations for which OSHA may issue or recommend a **citation** and penalty. At this point, the employer can produce records to show compliance efforts. Figure 16-4 lists a manager's inspection guidelines.

citation
Summons informing employers and employees of the regulations and standards that have been violated in the workplace.

PENALTIES OSHA can impose penalties. These generally range from $5,000 up to $150,000 for willful or repeat serious violations but can be far higher—$13 million after a tragedy at BP's Texas City plant, for instance.[30] The parties settle many OSHA cases before litigation, in "precitation settlements."[31] Non-serious violations may carry no penalties.

FIGURE 16-4 OSHA Inspection Tips for Managers

Initial Contact

- Refer the inspector to your OSHA coordinator.
- Check the inspector's credentials.
- Ask why he or she is inspecting. Is it a complaint? Programmed visit? Fatality or accident follow-up? Imminent danger investigation?
- If the inspection is the result of a complaint, the inspector won't identify the complainant, but you are entitled to know whether the person is a current employee.
- Notify your OSHA counsel, who should review all requests from the inspector for documents and information. Your counsel also should review the documents and information you provide to the inspector.

Opening Conference

- Establish the focus and scope of the planned inspection: Does the inspector want to inspect the premises or simply study your records?
- Discuss the procedures for protecting trade-secret areas, conducting employee interviews, and producing documents.
- Show the inspector that you have safety programs in place. He or she may not go to the work floor if paperwork is complete and up-to-date.

Walk-Around Inspection

- Accompany the inspector and take detailed notes.
- If the inspector takes a photo or video, you should too.
- Ask the inspector for duplicates of all physical samples and copies of all test results.
- Be helpful and cooperative, but don't volunteer information.
- To the extent possible, immediately correct any violation the inspector identifies.

Employees have rights and responsibilities under OSHA standards, such as to wear their hard hats, but OSHA can't cite them if they violate their responsibilities.

Stockbyte/Thinkstock

In general, OSHA calculates penalties based on the gravity of the violation and usually takes into consideration things like the size of the business, the firm's compliance history, and the employer's good faith.[32] In practice, OSHA must have a final order from the independent Occupational Safety and Health Review Commission (OSHRC) to enforce a penalty.[33] An employer who files a notice of contest can drag out an appeal for years. Many do.[34] OSHA publicizes its inspection results online. Its website (www.osha.gov) provides easy access to most companies' (or competitors') OSHA enforcement history.[35]

Responsibilities and Rights of Employers and Employees

Both employers and employees have responsibilities and rights under the Occupational Safety Health Act. *Employers* are responsible for providing "a workplace free from recognized hazards," for being familiar with mandatory OSHA standards, and for examining workplace conditions to make sure they conform to OSHA standards.[36] Employers have the right to seek advice and off-site consultation from OSHA, request and receive proper identification of the OSHA compliance officer before inspection, and to be advised by the compliance officer of the reason for an inspection.

Employees also have rights and responsibilities, but OSHA can't cite them for violations of their responsibilities. Employees are responsible, for example, for complying with all applicable OSHA standards, for following all employer safety and health rules and regulations, and for reporting hazardous conditions to the supervisor. They have the right to demand safety and health on the job without fear of punishment. Retaliating against employees for reporting injuries or safety problems is illegal (see the OSHA safety poster in Figure 16-5).[37] The HR Tools feature explains one OSHA service for small businesses.

FIGURE 16-5 OSHA Safety Poster

You Have a Right to a Safe and Healthful Workplace.

IT'S THE LAW!

- You have the right to notify your employer or OSHA about workplace hazards. You may ask OSHA to keep your name confidential.
- You have the right to request an OSHA inspection if you believe that there are unsafe and unhealthful conditions in your workplace. You or your representative may participate in the inspection.
- You can file a complaint with OSHA within 30 days of discrimination by your employer for making safety and health complaints or for exercising your rights under the *OSH Act*.
- You have a right to see OSHA citations issued to your employer. Your employer must post the citations at or near the place of the alleged violation.
- Your employer must correct workplace hazards by the date indicated on the citation and must certify that these hazards have been reduced or eliminated.
- You have the right to copies of your medical records or records of your exposure to toxic and harmful substances or conditions.
- Your employer must post this notice in your workplace.

The *Occupational Safety and Health Act of 1970 (OSH Act)*, P.L. 91-596, assures safe and healthful working conditions for working men and women throughout the Nation. The Occupational Safety and Health Administration, in the U.S. Department of Labor, has the primary responsibility for administering the *OSH Act*. The rights listed here may vary depending on the particular circumstances. To file a complaint, report an emergency, or seek OSHA advice, assistance, or products, call 1-800-321-OSHA or your nearest OSHA office: • Atlanta (404) 562-2300 • Boston (617) 565-9860 • Chicago (312) 353-2220 • Dallas (214) 767-4731 • Denver (303) 844-1600 • Kansas City (816) 426-5861 • New York (212) 337-2378 • Philadelphia (215) 861-4900 • San Francisco (415) 975-4310 • Seattle (206) 553-5930. Teletypewriter (TTY) number is 1-877-889-5627. To file a complaint online or obtain more information on OSHA federal and state programs, visit OSHA's website at www.osha.gov. If your workplace is in a state operating under an OSHA-approved plan, your employer must post the required state equivalent of this poster.

1-800-321-OSHA

www.osha.gov

U.S. Department of Labor • Occupational Safety and Health Administration • OSHA 3165

DEALING WITH EMPLOYEE RESISTANCE Although employees are responsible to comply with OSHA standards, they often resist; the employer usually remains liable for any penalties. The refusal of some workers to wear hard hats typifies this problem.

Employers have attempted to defend themselves by citing worker intransigence. In most cases, courts still hold employers liable for workplace safety violations. The independent three-member Occupational Safety and Health Review Commission that reviews OSHA decisions says employers must make "a diligent effort to discourage, by discipline if necessary, violations of safety rules by employees."[38] However, the only sure way to eliminate liability is to make sure that no accidents occur.

IMPROVING PERFORMANCE: HR Tools for Line Managers and Entrepreneurs

Free On-Site Safety and Health Services

Small businesses have unique challenges when it comes to managing safety. Without HR or safety departments, they often don't know where to turn for safety advice.[39]

OSHA provides free on-site safety and health services for small businesses. This service uses safety experts from state agencies and provides consultations, usually at the employer's workplace. According to OSHA, this safety and health consultation program is completely separate from the OSHA inspection effort, and no citations are issued or penalties proposed.

The employer triggers the process by requesting a voluntary consultation. There is then an opening conference with a safety expert, a walk-through, and a closing conference at which the employer and safety expert discuss the latter's observations. The consultant provides a detailed report explaining the findings. The employer's only obligation is to commit to correcting serious job safety and health hazards in a timely manner.

OSHA also has a website called "OSHA's $afety Pays Program" www.osha.gov/dcsp/smallbusiness/safetypays/estimator.html. Use its pull-down window and choose a potential injury or illness such as "Burns." After entering some other data (such as potential number of injuries) this tool will reveal the estimated cost of the specific occupational injury or illness, and the estimated impact on your company's profits.

Discussion Question 16-3: Write a short description on this theme: "How a small business owner can make use of OSHA's $afety Pays website."

3 Answer the question, "What causes accidents?"

What Causes Accidents?

There are three basic causes of workplace accidents: chance occurrences, unsafe conditions, and employees' unsafe acts. Chance occurrences (such as walking past a tree just when a branch falls) are more or less beyond management's control. We will therefore focus on unsafe conditions and unsafe acts.

What Causes Unsafe Conditions?

unsafe conditions
The mechanical and physical conditions that cause accidents.

Unsafe conditions are a main cause of accidents. They include:

- Improperly guarded equipment
- Defective equipment
- Hazardous procedures around machines or equipment
- Unsafe storage—congestion, overloading
- Improper illumination—glare, insufficient light
- Improper ventilation.[40]

The solution here is to identify and eliminate the unsafe conditions. The main aim of the OSHA standards is to address these mechanical and physical accident-causing conditions. The employer's safety department (if any) and its human resource managers and top managers should take responsibility for identifying unsafe conditions.

While accidents can happen anywhere, there are some high-danger zones. About one-third of industrial accidents occur around forklift trucks, wheelbarrows, and other handling and lifting areas. The most serious accidents usually occur by metal and woodworking machines and saws, or around transmission machinery like gears, pulleys, and flywheels.[41]

SAFETY CLIMATE Work schedules and fatigue also affect accident rates. Accident rates usually don't increase too noticeably during the first 5 or 6 hours of the workday. But after that, the accident rate increases faster. This is due partly to fatigue and partly to the fact that accidents occur more often during night shifts. In part due to reduced headcount and more people with second jobs, employee fatigue is a growing problem today.[42] Many employers are therefore taking steps to reduce employee fatigue, such as banning mandatory overtime.

The workplace "climate" or psychology is very important. One researcher reviewed the fatal accidents offshore oil workers suffered in the British North Sea.[43] A strong pressure to complete the work as quickly as possible, employees who are under stress, and a poor safety climate—for instance, supervisors who never mentioned safety—were some of the psychological conditions leading to accidents. Similarly, accidents occur more frequently in plants with high seasonal layoff rates, hostility among employees, many garnished wages, and blighted living conditions.

What Causes Unsafe Acts?

Unsafe employee acts (such as not wearing hard hats) will undo your efforts to banish unsafe conditions, but there are no easy answers to what causes people to act that way.

It may seem obvious that some people are simply accident prone, but the research isn't clear.[44] On closer inspection it turns out some "accident repeaters" were just unlucky, or may have been more meticulous about reporting their accidents.[45] However, there is evidence that people with specific traits may indeed be accident prone. For example, people who are impulsive, sensation seeking, extremely extroverted, and less conscientious (in terms of being less fastidious and dependable) have more accidents.[46]

Furthermore, the person who is accident prone on one job may not be so on another. For example, personality traits that correlate with filing vehicular insurance claims include *entitlement* ("think there's no reason they should not speed"), *impatience* ("were 'always in a hurry'"), *aggressiveness* ("the first to move when the light turns green"), and *distractibility* ("frequently distracted by cell phones, eating, and so on").[47]

HR in Practice at the Hotel Paris Lisa and the CFO reviewed their company's safety records, and what they found disturbed them deeply. In terms of every safety-related metric they could find, including accident costs per year, lost time due to accidents, workers compensation per employee, and number of safety training programs per year, the Hotel Paris compared unfavorably with most other hotel chains and service firms. To see how they handled this, see the case on page 526 of this chapter.

4 List and explain five ways to prevent accidents.

How to Prevent Accidents

In practice, accident prevention boils down to: (1) reducing unsafe conditions and (2) reducing unsafe acts. In large firms, the chief safety officer (often called the "environmental health and safety officer") is responsible for this.[48] In smaller firms, managers, including those from human resources, plant management, and first-line managers, share these responsibilities.

Reducing Unsafe Conditions

Reducing unsafe conditions is the employer's first line of defense in accident prevention. Safety engineers should design jobs to remove or reduce physical hazards. Supervisors play a role here. Checklists like those in Figures 16-6 and 16-7, or the self-inspection checklist in Figure 16-9 (pages 521–524), can help identify and remove potential hazards.

Employers use computerized tools to design safer equipment. For example, Designsafe (from Designsafe Engineering, Ann Arbor, Michigan) helps to automate hazard analysis, risk assessment, and safety options identification. Designsafe helps the safety designer choose the most appropriate safety control device for keeping the worker safe, such as adjustable enclosures, presence-sensing devices, and personal protective equipment.[49]

Sometimes the solution for an unsafe condition is obvious, and sometimes it's not. For example, slippery floors often cause slips and falls.[50] Obvious remedies include floor mats and better lighting. Perhaps less obviously, personal safety gear, like slip-resistant footwear with grooved soles, can also reduce slips and falls. Cut-resistant gloves reduce the hazards of working with sharp objects.[51] (Hand injuries account for about 1 million emergency department visits annually by U.S. workers.[52])

job hazard analysis
A systematic approach to identifying and eliminating workplace hazards before they occur.

JOB HAZARD ANALYSIS A Yale University science student, working late in a lab, was critically injured when her hair became caught in a spinning lathe. **Job hazard analysis** involves a systematic approach to identifying and eliminating such hazards before they cause accidents. According to OSHA, job hazard analysis "focuses on the relationship between the worker, the task, the tools, and the work environment," and ends by reducing the potential risks to acceptable levels.[53]

Consider a safety analyst looking at the Yale science lab, with the aim of identifying potential hazards. Performing a job hazard analysis here might involve looking at the situation and asking these questions:

- ***What can go wrong?*** A student's hair or clothing could become caught in the lathe, a rotating object that "catches" it and pulls it into the machine.
- ***What are the consequences?*** The student could receive a severe injury as his or her body part or hair is caught and drawn into the spinning lathe.
- ***How could it happen?*** The accident could happen as a result of the student leaning too close to the lathe while working at the bench, or walking too close to the lathe, or bending to reach for an article that fell close to the lathe.
- ***What are other contributing factors?*** Speed is one contributing factor. The problem would occur so quickly that the student would be unable to take evasive action once the lathe ensnarled the hair.

I. GENERAL HOUSEKEEPING

Adequate and wide aisles—no materials protruding into aisles
Parts and tools stored safely after use—not left in hazardous positions that could cause them to fall
Even and solid flooring—no defective floors or ramps that could cause falling or tripping accidents
Waste cans and sand pails—safely located and properly used
Material piled in safe manner—not too high or too close to sprinkler heads
Floors—clean and dry
Firefighting equipment—unobstructed
Work benches orderly
Stockcarts and skids safely located, not left in aisles or passageways
Aisles kept clear and properly marked; no air lines or electric cords across aisles

II. MATERIAL HANDLING EQUIPMENT AND CONVEYANCES

On all conveyances, electric or hand, check to see that the following items are all in sound working conditions:
Brakes—properly adjusted
Not too much play in steering wheel
Warning device—in place and working
Wheels—securely in place; properly inflated
Fuel and oil—enough and right kind
No loose parts
Cables, hooks, or chains—not worn or otherwise defective
Suspended chains or hooks conspicuous
Safely loaded
Properly stored

III. LADDERS, SCAFFOLD, BENCHES, STAIRWAYS, ETC.

The following items of major interest to be checked:
Safety feet on straight ladders
Guardrails or handrails
Treads, not slippery
Not cracked, or rickety
Properly stored
Extension ladder ropes in good condition
Toeboards

IV. POWER TOOLS (STATIONARY)

Point of operation guarded
Guards in proper adjustment
Gears, belts, shafting, counterweights guarded
Foot pedals guarded
Brushes provided for cleaning machines
Adequate lighting
Properly grounded
Tool or material rests properly adjusted
Adequate work space around machines
Control switch easily accessible
Safety glasses worn
Gloves worn by persons handling rough or sharp materials
No gloves or loose clothing worn by persons operating machines

V. HAND TOOLS AND MISCELLANEOUS

In good condition—not cracked, worn, or otherwise defective
Properly stored
Correct for job
Goggles, respirators, and other personal protective equipment worn where necessary

VI. WELDING

Arc shielded
Fire hazards controlled
Operator using suitable protective equipment
Adequate ventilation
Cylinder secured
Valves closed when not in use

VII. SPRAY PAINTING

Explosion-proof electrical equipment
Proper storage of paints and thinners in approved metal cabinets
Fire extinguishers adequate and suitable; readily accessible
Minimum storage in work area

VIII. FIRE EXTINGUISHERS

Properly serviced and tagged
Readily accessible
Adequate and suitable for operations involved

FIGURE 16-6 Checklist of Mechanical or Physical Accident-Causing Conditions

Source: Courtesy of the American Insurance Association. From "A Safety Committee Man's Guide," pp. 1–64.

FIGURE 16-7 Supervisor's Safety Checklist

Source: Office of the Chief Information Officer, United States Department of Commerce. http://ocio.os.doc.gov/s/groups/public/@doc/@os/@ocio/@oitpp/documents/content/dev01_002574.pdf assessed October 15, 2013.

FORM **CD-574**
(9/02)

U.S. Department of Commerce
Office Safety Inspection Checklist for Supervisors and Program Managers

Name:	**Division:**
Location:	**Date:**
Signature:	

This checklist is intended as a guide to assist supervisors and program managers in conducting safety and health inspections of their work areas. It includes questions relating to general office safety, ergonomics, fire prevention, and electrical safety. Questions which receive a "**NO**" answer require corrective action. If you have questions or need assistance with resolving any problems, please contact your safety office. More information on office safety is available through the Department of Commerce Safety Office website at http://ohrm.doc.gov/safetyprogram/safety.htm.

Work Environment

Yes	No	N/A	
○	○	⊙	Are all work areas clean, sanitary, and orderly?
○	○	⊙	Is there adequate lighting?
○	○	⊙	Do noise levels appear high?
○	○	⊙	Is ventilation adequate?

Walking / Working Surfaces

Yes	No	N/A	
○	○	⊙	Are aisles and passages free of stored material that may present trip hazards?
○	○	⊙	Are tile floors in places like kitchens and bathrooms free of water and slippery substances?
○	○	⊙	Are carpet and throw rugs free of tears or trip hazards?
○	○	⊙	Are hand rails provided on all fixed stairways?
○	○	⊙	Are treads provided with anti-slip surfaces?
○	○	⊙	Are step ladders provided for reaching overhead storage areas and are materials stored safely?
○	○	⊙	Are file drawers kept closed when not in use?
○	○	⊙	Are passenger and freight elevators inspected annually and are the inspection certificates available for review on-site?
○	○	⊙	Are pits and floor openings covered or otherwise guarded?
○	○	⊙	Are standard guardrails provided wherever aisle or walkway surfaces are elevated more than 48 inches above any adjacent floor or the ground?
○	○	⊙	Is any furniture unsafe or defective?
○	○	⊙	Are objects covering heating and air conditioning vents?

Ergonomics

Yes	No	N/A	
○	○	⊙	Are employees advised of proper lifting techniques?
○	○	⊙	Are workstations configured to prevent common ergonomic problems? (Chair height allows employees' feet to rest flat on the ground with thighs parallel to the floor, top of computer screen is at or slightly below eye level, keyboard is at elbow height. Additional information on proper configuration of workstations is available through the Commerce Safety website at http://ohrm.doc.gov/safetyprogram/safety.htm)
○	○	⊙	Are mechanical aids and equipment, such as; lifting devices, carts, dollies provided where needed?
○	○	⊙	Are employees surveyed annually on their ergonomic concerns?

FIGURE 16-7 (Continued)

FORM **CD-574**
(9/02)

Emergency Information (Postings)

Yes	No	N/A	
○	○	⦿	Are established emergency phone numbers posted where they can be readily found in case of an emergency?
○	○	⦿	Are employees trained on emergency procedures?
○	○	⦿	Are fire evacuation procedures/diagrams posted?
○	○	⦿	Is emergency information posted in every area where you store hazardous waste?
○	○	⦿	Is established facility emergency information posted near a telephone?
○	○	⦿	Are the OSHA poster, and other required posters displayed conspicuously?
○	○	⦿	Are adequate first aid supplies available and properly maintained?
○	○	⦿	Are an adequate number of first aid trained personnel available to respond to injuries and illnesses until medical assistance arrives?
○	○	⦿	Is a copy of the facility fire prevention and emergency action plan available on site?
○	○	⦿	Are safety hazard warning signs/caution signs provided to warn employees of pertinent hazards?

Fire Prevention

Yes	No	N/A	
○	○	⦿	Are flammable liquids, such as gasoline, kept in approved safety cans and stored in flammable cabinets?
○	○	⦿	Are portable fire extinguishers distributed properly (less than 75 feet travel distance for combustibles and 50 feet for flammables)?
○	○	⦿	Are employees trained on the use of portable fire extinguishers?
○	○	⦿	Are portable fire extinguishers visually inspected monthly and serviced annually?
○	○	⦿	Is the area around portable fire extinguishers free of obstructions and properly labeled ?
○	○	⦿	Is heat-producing equipment used in a well ventilated area?
○	○	⦿	Are fire alarm pull stations clearly marked and unobstructed?
○	○	⦿	Is proper clearance maintained below sprinkler heads (i.e., 18" clear)?

Emergency Exits

Yes	No	N/A	
○	○	⦿	Are doors, passageways or stairways that are neither exits nor access to exits and which could be mistaken for exits, appropriately marked "NOT AN EXIT," "TO BASEMENT," "STOREROOM," etc.?
○	○	⦿	Are a sufficient number of exits provided?
○	○	⦿	Are exits kept free of obstructions or locking devices which could impede immediate escape?
○	○	⦿	Are exits properly marked and illuminated?
○	○	⦿	Are the directions to exits, when not immediately apparent, marked with visible signs?
○	○	⦿	Can emergency exit doors be opened from the direction of exit travel without the use of a key or any special knowledge or effort when the building is occupied?
○	○	⦿	Are exits arranged such that it is not possible to travel toward a fire hazard when exiting the facility?

(Continued)

FIGURE 16-7 (Continued)

FORM **CD-574**
(9/02)

Electrical Systems
(Please have your facility maintenance person or electrician accompany you during this part of the inspection)

Yes	No	N/A	
○	○	⊙	Are all cord and cable connections intact and secure?
○	○	⊙	Are electrical outlets free of overloads?
○	○	⊙	Is fixed wiring used instead of flexible/extension cords?
○	○	⊙	Is the area around electrical panels and breakers free of obstructions?
○	○	⊙	Are high-voltage electrical service rooms kept locked?
○	○	⊙	Are electrical cords routed such that they are free of sharp objects and clearly visible?
○	○	⊙	Are all electrical cords grounded?
○	○	⊙	Are electrical cords in good condition (free of splices, frays, etc.)?
○	○	⊙	Are electrical appliances approved (Underwriters Laboratory, Inc. (UL), etc)?
○	○	⊙	Are electric fans provided with guards of not over one-half inch, preventing finger exposures?
○	○	⊙	Are space heaters UL listed and equipped with shutoffs that activate if the heater tips over?
○	○	⊙	Are space heaters located away from combustibles and properly ventilated?
○	○	⊙	In your electrical rooms are all electrical raceways and enclosures securely fastened in place?
○	○	⊙	Are clamps or other securing means provided on flexible cords or cables at plugs, receptacles, tools, equipment, etc., and is the cord jacket securely held in place?
○	○	⊙	Is sufficient access and working space provided and maintained about all electrical equipment to permit ready and safe operations and maintenance? (This space is 3 feet for less than 600 volts, 4 feet for more than 600 volts)

FORM **CD-574**
(9/02)

Material Storage

Yes	No	N/A	
○	○	⊙	Are storage racks and shelves capable of supporting the intended load and materials stored safely?
○	○	⊙	Are storage racks secured from falling?
○	○	⊙	Are office equipment stored in a stable manner, not capable of falling?

The job hazard analysis should provide the basis for creating countermeasures. Given the speed with which any such accident would occur, it's unlikely that training by itself would suffice. Instead, the lathe area here should be ensconced in its own protective casing, and changes made to ensure that the lathe can't spin unless the student takes action via a foot pedal to keep the lathe power on.

operational safety reviews
Reviews conducted by agencies to ascertain whether units under their jurisdiction are complying with all the applicable safety laws, regulations, orders, and rules.

OPERATIONAL SAFETY REVIEWS After Japan's Fukushima nuclear power plant exploded in 2011, many wondered if the International Atomic Energy Agency (IAEA) had conducted the necessary operational safety reviews. **Operational safety reviews** (or safety operations reviews) are conducted by agencies to ascertain whether units under their jurisdiction are complying with all the applicable safety laws, regulations, orders, and rules. For example, under IAEA's Operational Safety Review Program, "international teams of experts conduct in-depth reviews of operational safety performance at a nuclear power plant."[54]

PERSONAL PROTECTIVE EQUIPMENT Getting employees to wear personal protective equipment (PPE) like hard hats is a famously difficult chore.[55] Wearability is important. In addition to providing reliable protection, protective gear should fit properly; be easy to care for, maintain, and repair; be flexible and lightweight; provide comfort and reduce heat stress; have rugged construction; be relatively easy to put on and take off; and be easy to clean, dispose of, and recycle.[56] Many employers, such as Kimberly-Clark and MCR Safety, are tapping into the new fibers and fabrics to design easier wearing high-tech solutions.[57] Including employees in planning the safety program and addressing comfort issues contribute to employees' willingness to use the protective gear.[58]

Of course, the manager should require wearing the protective equipment before the accident, not just after it. For example, a combustible dust explosion at a sugar refinery killed 14 employees and burned many others. The employer subsequently required that all employees wear fire resistant clothing, unfortunately too late for the victims.[59]

But again, reducing unsafe conditions is always the first line of defense. Then use administrative controls (such as job rotation to reduce long-term exposure to the hazard). Only then turn to PPE.[60]

Diversity Counts: Protecting Vulnerable Workers

In designing safe and healthy environments, employers should pay special attention to vulnerable workers, such as young, immigrant, aging, and women workers.[61] (The Fair Labor Standards Act strictly limits young people's exposure to dangerous jobs, but about 64 workers under age 18 died from work-related injuries in one recent year.[62]) For example, as the CEO of one safety engineering company said, "For decades, women essentially were ignored when it came to designing eye and face protection." Today, more products are available in smaller sizes.[63]

Similarly, with more workers postponing retirement, older workers are doing more manufacturing jobs.[64] They can do these jobs effectively. However, there are numerous potential physical changes associated with aging, including loss of strength, loss of muscular flexibility, and reduced reaction time.[65] This means that employers should make special provisions such as designing jobs to reduce heavy lifting, and boosting lighting levels.[66] The fatality rate for older workers is about three times that of younger workers.[67]

Reducing Unsafe Acts

While reducing unsafe conditions is the first line of defense, human misbehavior will short-circuit even the best safety efforts. Sometimes the misbehavior is intentional, but often it's not. For example, distractions contribute to at least half of all car accidents. The National Safety Council recently estimated that cell phone use was involved in 24% of all motor vehicle crashes.[68] (Drivers of commercial motor vehicles on interstate routes are banned from using handheld mobile telephones while driving.)[69] At work, not noticing moving or stationary objects or that a floor is wet often causes accidents.[70] And, ironically, "making a job safer with machine guards or PPE lowers people's risk perceptions and thus can lead to an increase in at-risk behavior."[71]

Unfortunately, just telling employees to "pay attention" usually isn't enough. First, identify and try to eliminate potential risks, such as unguarded equipment. Next, reduce potential distractions, such as noise, heat, and stress. Then, carefully screen and train employees, as we explain next.

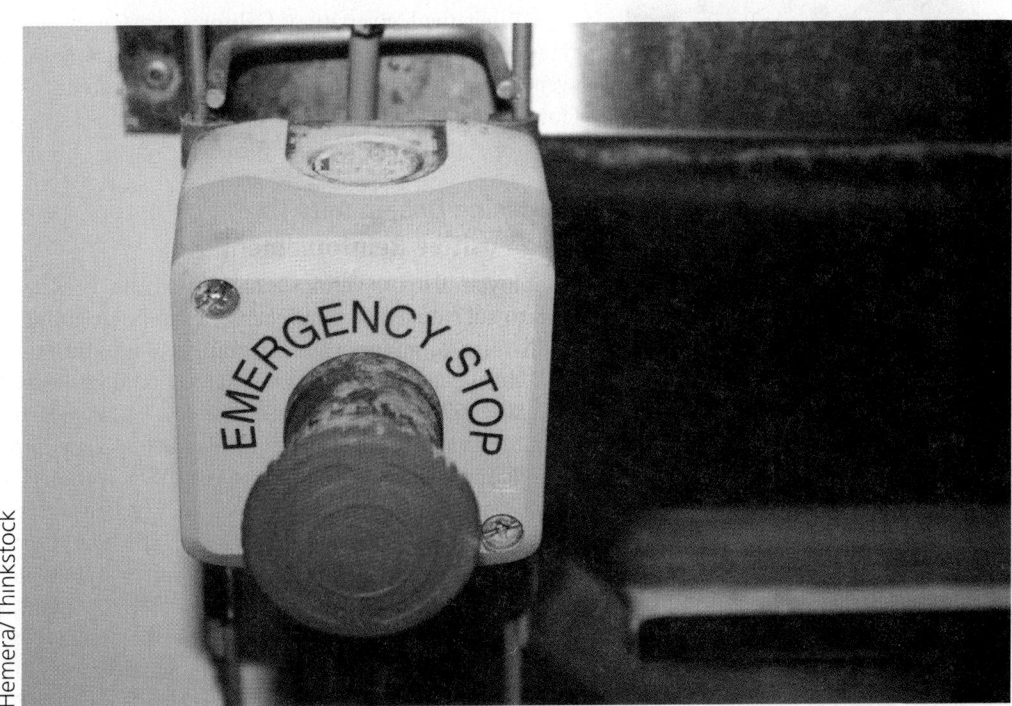

Emergency stop devices, such as buttons, override other machine controls to remove power from hazardous machine motion.

Hemera/Thinkstock

Reducing Unsafe Acts Through Screening

Proper employee screening and placement reduces unsafe acts. Here, the employer's aim is to identify the traits that might predict accidents on the job in question, and then screen candidates for this trait. For example, the Employee Reliability Index (ERI) (see www.ramsaycorp.com/catalog/view/?productid=208) measures reliability dimensions such as emotional maturity, conscientiousness, and safe job performance.[72] Though not definitive, using the ERI in selection did seem to be associated with reductions in work-related accidents in one study. Others use *job simulation tests* (which attempt to measure the applicant by simulating physically demanding work activities) and *physical capabilities tests* (which measure muscle strength and motion) to predict who will have more accidents.[73]

Similarly, behavioral interview questions can be revealing. For example, ask, "What would you do if you saw another employee working in an unsafe way?" and "What would you do if your supervisor gave you a task, but didn't provide any training on how to perform it safely?"[74]

Reducing Unsafe Acts Through Training

Safety training reduces unsafe acts, especially for new employees. You should instruct employees in safe practices and procedures, warn them of potential hazards, and work on developing a safety-conscious attitude. OSHA's standards require more than training. Employees must demonstrate that they actually learned what to do. (For example, OSHA's respiratory standard requires that each employee demonstrate how to inspect, put on, and remove respirator seals.[75] OSHA has two booklets, *Training Requirements Under OSHA* and *Teaching Safety and Health in the Workplace*.)

However, the main aim of safety training is not to meet OSHA training standards; it is to impart the knowledge and skills required to reduce accidents. OSHA, the National Institute for Occupational Safety and Health (NIOSH), and numerous private vendors provide online safety training solutions.[76]

The nature of the safety training is important. One study found that the most effective safety training demanded high employee engagement.[77] In this study, the "least engaging" programs included lectures, films, reading materials, and video-based training. Moderately engaging programs included computer interface instruction with feedback. "Engaging" ones included behavioral modeling, simulation, and hands-on training.

Improving Performance Through HRIS Online Safety Training

Employers also turn to the Web to support their safety training programs.[78] For example, PureSafety (www.ulworkplace.com) enables firms to create their own training websites, complete with a "message from the safety director." Once an employer installs the PureSafety website, it can populate the site with courses from companies that supply health and safety courses via that site.[79]

When the University of California system wanted to deliver mandated safety training to its 50,000 employees on 10 different campuses, it developed a program with the vendor Vivid Learning Systems to deliver online. The 2-hour custom online lab safety fundamentals course covers OSHA regulations as well as interactive exercises and feedback opportunities for participants.[80]

John Panella/Shutterstock

One way to motivate and encourage safety in a factory is to tell employees how much management values it: This safety poster on an exterior factory wall tells employees how well they are doing.

Reducing Unsafe Acts Through Posters, Incentives, and Positive Reinforcement

Employers also use various tools to motivate worker safety.[81] Safety posters are one, but are no substitute for comprehensive safety programs. Employers should combine them with other techniques (like screening and training) to reduce unsafe conditions and acts, and change the posters often. Posters should be easily visible, legible, and well-lit.[82]

Incentive programs are also useful.[83] Management at Tesoro Corporation's Golden Eagle refinery in California instituted one such plan. Employees earn "WINGS" (an acronym for Willing Involvement Nurtures Greater Safety) points for engaging in one or more specific safety activities, such as taking emergency response training. Employees can each earn up to $20 per month by accumulating points.[84] The Profit Center feature shows another example.

OSHA has argued that such programs don't cut down on actual injuries or illnesses, but only on injury and illness *reporting*. OSHA might question any safety incentive payment that is so high that the award might dissuade reasonable workers from reporting safety problems.[85] One option is to emphasize nontraditional incentives, like recognition.[86] In any case, the incentive program needs to be part of a comprehensive safety program.[87]

IMPROVING PERFORMANCE: HR as a Profit Center

Using Positive Reinforcement

Many employers successfully use *positive reinforcement programs* to improve safety. Such programs provide workers with continuing positive feedback, usually in the form of graphical performance reports and supervisory support, to shape the workers' safety-related behavior.

Researchers introduced one program in a wholesale bakery.[88] The new safety program included training and positive reinforcement. The researchers set and communicated a reasonable safety goal (in terms of observed incidents performed safely). Next, employees participated in a 30-minute training session by viewing pairs of slides depicting scenes that the researchers staged in the plant. One slide, for example, showed the supervisor climbing over a conveyor; the parallel slide showed the supervisor walking around the conveyor. After viewing an unsafe act, employees had to describe, "What's unsafe here?" Then the researchers demonstrated the same incident again but performed in a safe manner, and explicitly stated the safe-conduct rule ("go around, not over or under, conveyors").

At the conclusion of the training phase, supervisors showed employees a graph with their pretraining safety record (in terms of observed incidents performed safely) plotted. Supervisors then encouraged workers to consider increasing their performance to the new safety goal for their own protection, to decrease costs, and to help the plant get out of its last place safety ranking. Then the researchers posted the graph and a list of safety rules.

Whenever observers walked through the plant collecting safety data, they posted on the graph the percentage of incidents they had seen performed safely by the group as a whole, thus providing the workers with positive feedback. Workers could compare their current safety performance with both their previous performance and their assigned goal. In addition, supervisors praised workers when they performed selected incidents safely. Safety in the plant subsequently improved markedly.

Discussion Question 16-4: List six more unsafe incidents you believe might occur in a bakery, and a "safe manner" for doing each.

Reducing Unsafe Acts by Fostering a Culture of Safety

Employers and supervisors should create a safety-conscious culture by showing that they take safety seriously. One study measured safety culture in terms of questions like "my supervisor says a good word whenever he sees the job done according to the safety rules" and "my supervisor approaches workers during work to discuss safety issues."[89]

According to one safety expert, a workplace with a safety-oriented culture exhibits:

1. *Teamwork,* in the form of management and employees both involved in safety;
2. Highly visible and interactive *communication and collaboration* on safety matters;
3. A *shared vision* of safety excellence (specifically, an overriding attitude that all accidents and injuries are preventable);
4. *Assignment* of critical safety functions to specific individuals or teams;
5. A *continuous effort* toward identifying and correcting workplace safety problems and hazards;[90] and,
6. *Encouragement* of incident reporting.[91]

Reducing Unsafe Acts by Creating a Supportive Environment

Supportive supervisors' teams seem to have better safety records. "Organizations can develop a supportive environment by training supervisors to be better leaders, emphasizing the importance of teamwork and social support, and establishing the value of safety."[92]

Reducing Unsafe Acts by Establishing a Safety Policy

The company's written safety policy should emphasize that accident prevention is of the utmost importance at your firm, and that the firm will do everything practical to eliminate or reduce accidents and injuries.

Reducing Unsafe Acts by Setting Specific Loss Control Goals

Set specific safety goals to achieve. For example, set safety goals in terms of frequency of lost-time injuries per number of full-time employees.

Reducing Unsafe Acts Through Behavior-Based and Safety Awareness Programs

behavior-based safety
Identifying the worker behaviors that contribute to accidents and then training workers to avoid these behaviors.

Behavior-based safety means identifying the worker behaviors that contribute to accidents and then training workers to avoid these behaviors. Tenneco Corporation (which manufactures Monroe brand suspensions) implemented a behavior-based safety program. The firm selected internal consultants from among its quality managers, training managers, engineers, and production workers. After training, the internal consultants identified five critical behaviors for Tenneco's first safety program, such as *Eyes on task: Does the employee watch his or her hands while performing a task?* The consultants made observations and collected data on the behaviors. Then they instituted training programs to get employees to perform these five behaviors properly.[93]

safety awareness program
Program that enables trained supervisors to orient new workers arriving at a job site regarding common safety hazards and simple prevention methods.

Employers also use *safety awareness* programs to improve employee safe behavior. A **safety awareness program** means trained supervisors orient new workers arriving at a job site regarding common safety hazards and simple prevention methods. For example, the Roadway Safety Awareness Program covers trucker safety issues such as stopping distances required at various speeds (see the accompanying screen grab).

Reducing Unsafe Acts Through Employee Participation

Employees are an excellent source of insights about safety problems and solutions. For example, when the International Truck and Engine Corp. began designing a new robot-based plant, management appointed joint labor–management safety teams for each department.[94] The teams worked with project engineers to design safeguards for the robot equipment. The company sent one safety team to Japan to watch the robot machines in action, and to identify items teams needed to address. This team worked with employees to identify possible hazards and to develop new devices (such as color-coded locks) to protect the employees.[95]

Conducting Safety and Health Audits and Inspections

Managers should routinely inspect for problems using safety audit/checklists (as in Figure 16-7, page 500–502) as aids. Also, investigate all accidents and "near misses." Set up employee safety committees to evaluate safety adequacy, conduct and monitor safety audits, and suggest ways for improving safety.[96] Managers expedite safety audits by using personal digital assistants.[97] For

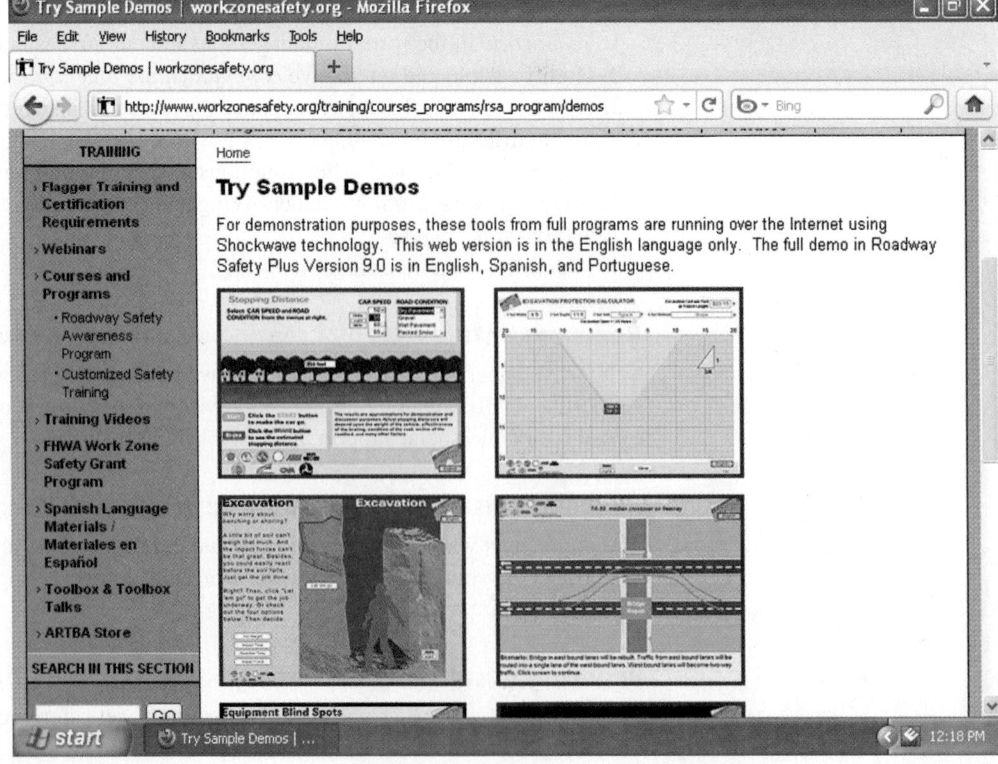

The Roadway Safety Awareness Program covers trucker safety issues such as stopping distances required at various speeds.

Source: National Work Zone Safety Information Clearinghouse, a project of the American Road & Transportation Builders Association—Transportation Development Foundation.

TABLE 16-1 Reducing Unsafe Conditions and Acts: A Summary

Reduce Unsafe Conditions
Identify and eliminate unsafe conditions.
Use administrative means, such as job rotation.
Use personal protective equipment.
Reduce Unsafe Acts
Emphasize top management commitment.
Emphasize safety.
Establish a safety policy.
Reduce unsafe acts through selection.
Provide safety training.
Use posters and other propaganda.
Use positive reinforcement.
Use behavior-based safety programs.
Encourage worker participation.
Conduct safety and health inspections regularly.

example, Process and Performance Measurement (PPM) is a Windows application for designing and completing safety audit questionnaires. To use this application, the manager gives the safety audit a name, enters the audit questions, and lists possible answers. Typical questions for a fire extinguisher audit might include, "Are fire extinguishers clearly identified and accessible?" and "Are only approved fire extinguishers used in the workplace?"[98] The supervisor or employee then uses his or her PDA to record the audit and transmit it to the firm's safety office.

Evidence-based safety and security-related metrics to audit would include, for instance, injury and illness rates, workers' compensation cost per employee, at-risk behavior reduction, and safety training exercises.[99] To ensure that the audit results in improvements, *trend the audit data* (for instance, to see if accident rates are rising or falling or steady), and *track the corrective actions* through to completion.[100]

Table 16-1 summarizes suggestions for reducing unsafe conditions and acts.[101] The accompanying HR Practices Around the Globe feature shows one safety program abroad.

IMPROVING PERFORMANCE: HR Practices Around the Globe

Safety at Saudi Petrol Chemical

The industrial safety and security manager for the Saudi Petrol Chemical Co., in Jubail City, Saudi Arabia, says that his company's excellent safety record results from the fact that "our employees are champions of safety."[102] Employees are involved in every part of the safety process. They serve on safety committees, develop and lead daily and monthly safety meetings, and conduct job safety analyses, for instance.

Safety begins with the company's top management. Senior management representatives serve on the company's Management Health and Safety Committee. This committee meets monthly to review incident reports, establish health and safety goals, review safety statistics, and endorse and sponsor safety programs.

The firm cultivates its "safety first" culture from the day a new employee arrives at work. For example, new employees are encouraged to participate in the safety process during orientation. Then (about 6 weeks later) they attend a one-day orientation where company officials emphasize the importance of the company's health, safety, and environmental policies and programs. Employees also participate in monthly departmental training sessions to discuss departmental safety issues and safety suggestions. They work with their departmental committees to conduct monthly safety audits, to review and document departmental job safety, and to submit safety suggestions (about 60 suggestions are submitted per month). Employees are required to report every safety incident and near miss, and more than 600 reports are submitted each year.

Discussion Question 16-5: Answer this: "Based on what I read so far in this chapter, here is why I think this facility has a good safety record."

Controlling Workers' Compensation Costs

In the event an accident does occur, the employee may turn to the employer's workers' compensation insurance to cover his or her expenses and losses.[103] We addressed workers' compensation in the *Benefits* chapter, but address several safety-related points here.

The time to start "controlling" workers' compensation claims is before the accident happens.[104] For example, LKL Associates, Inc., of Orem, Utah, cut its workers' compensation premiums in half by communicating written safety and substance abuse policies to workers and then strictly enforcing those policies.[105] Monitoring workers' compensation claims is also important. The Profit Center feature explains.

IMPROVING PERFORMANCE: HR as a Profit Center

Reducing Workers' Compensation Claims

Claims-tracking software helps employers understand and reduce their workers' compensation claims. For example, a health services agency in Bangor, Maine, purchased CompWatch, a workers' compensation claims management and tracking program. The agency entered all its previous claims, and used CompWatch to analyze trends. The agency discovered some of its auto accidents were apparently due to its drivers' need for training, so the agency introduced a driver safety program. In one department, this apparently led to a 42% reduction in auto accidents from one year to the next.[106]

Discussion Question 16-6: Explain briefly how using CompWatch illustrates a scientific approach.

Workplace Health Hazards: Problems and Remedies

5 List five workplace health hazards and how to deal with them.

Most workplace hazards aren't as obvious as unguarded equipment or slippery floors. Many are unseen hazards (such as mold) that the company inadvertently produces as part of its production processes. Typical workplace exposure hazards include chemicals and other hazardous materials, temperature extremes, biohazards (including those that are naturally occurring, such as mold, and man-made, such as anthrax), and ergonomic hazards (such as uncomfortable equipment).[107]

Chemicals and Industrial Hygiene

OSHA standards list exposure limits for about 600 chemicals. Table 16-2 lists some of these. Hazardous substances like these require air sampling and other preventive and precautionary measures.

Managing such hazards comes under the area of *industrial hygiene* and involves recognition, evaluation, and control. First, the facility's health and safety officers (possibly working with teams of supervisors and employees) must *recognize* possible exposure hazards. This typically

Exposure to asbestos is a major potential source of occupational respiratory disease. This worker wears protective clothing and a respirator to remove asbestos from ceiling panels in a classroom.

TABLE 16-2 OSHA Substance-Specific Health Standards

Substance	Permissible Exposure Limits*
Asbestos	.1001
Vinyl chloride	.1017
Inorganic arsenic	.1018
Lead	.1025
Cadmium	.1027
Benzene	.1028
Coke oven emissions	.1029
Cotton dust	.1043
1,2-Dibromo-3-chloropropane	.1044
Acrylonitrile	.1045
Ethylene oxide	.1047
Formaldehyde	.1048
4,4'-Methylenedianiline	.1050
Methylene chloride	.1051

Note: *The actual measurement yardstick is substance-specific. For example, the yardstick for asbestos is permissible fiber per cubic centimeter, and for formaldehyde it is parts formaldehyde per million parts of air

Source: John F. Rekus, "If You Thought Air Sampling Was Too Difficult to Handle, This Guide Can Help You Tackle Routine Sampling with Confidence, Part I," *Occupational Hazards*, May 2003, p. 43. See also www.osha.gov/SLTC/pel/, accessed June 30, 2011.

involves conducting plant/facility walk-around surveys, employee interviews, records reviews, and reviews of government (OSHA) and nongovernmental standards.

Having identified a possible hazard, *evaluation* involves determining how severe the hazard is. This requires measuring the exposure, comparing the measure to some benchmark (as in Table 16-2), and determining if the risk is within standard.[108]

Hazard *control* involves eliminating or reducing the hazard. Note that personal protective gear is generally the *last* option for dealing with such problems. The employer must first install engineering controls (such as process enclosures or ventilation) and administrative controls (including training and improved housekeeping).

KNOW YOUR EMPLOYMENT LAW

Hazard Communication

In, say, a dry cleaning store, it might not be apparent just by looking at it that the clear cleaning chemical hydrofluoric acid will eat through glass and blind an unsuspecting worker. Under OSHA's regulations, employers must communicate the presence and nature of hazards to which workers might be exposed. OSHA's *hazard communication standard,* recently revised, states that "in order to ensure chemical safety in the workplace, information about the identities and hazards of the chemicals must be available and understandable to workers." In line with this, says OSHA, chemical manufacturers and importers must label and provide hazard safety data sheets to their customers. All employers must have labels and safety data sheets available for their exposed workers, and train workers to handle the chemicals appropriately.[109]

More generally, the employer should make provision for communicating the full range of safety and security issues. These include safety policies, facilities security procedures, violence reduction policies and procedures, hazards communication, and plans to deal with natural or human-made disasters.[110]

Asbestos Exposure at Work and Air Quality

Asbestos is a major source of occupational respiratory disease. Efforts are still underway to rid old buildings of the substance.

OSHA standards require several actions with respect to asbestos. Employers must monitor the air whenever they expect the level of asbestos to rise to one-half the allowable limit

(0.1 fibers per cubic centimeter). Engineering controls—walls, special filters, and so forth—are required to maintain an asbestos level that complies with OSHA standards. Only then can employers use respirators if additional efforts are required to achieve compliance.

One downside of environmentally "green" office buildings is that sealed buildings can produce illnesses such as itchy eyes ("sick building syndrome"). The problem is that emissions from printers and photocopiers and other chemical pollutants can reduce air quality.[111] One solution is continuous monitoring.

Alcoholism and Substance Abuse

Alcoholism and substance abuse are problems at work. About two-thirds of people with an alcohol disorder work full-time.[112] Some estimate that almost 13 million workers use drugs illicitly.[113] About 15% of the U.S. workforce (just over 19 million workers) "has either been hung over at work, been drinking shortly before showing up for work, or been drinking or impaired while on the job at least once during the previous year."[114] Employee alcoholism may cost U.S. employers about $226 billion per year, for instance in higher absenteeism and accidents.[115]

TESTING For many employers, dealing with substance abuse begins with substance abuse testing.[116] It's unusual to find employers who don't at least test job candidates for substance abuse before formally hiring them. And many states are instituting mandatory random drug testing for high-hazard workers. For example, New Jersey now requires random drug testing of electrical workers.[117]

DEALING WITH SUBSTANCE ABUSE Ideally, a drug-free workplace program includes five components:

1. A drug-free workplace policy
2. Supervisor training
3. Employee education
4. Employee assistance
5. Drug testing

The policy should state, at a minimum, "The use, possession, transfer, or sale of illegal drugs by employees is prohibited." It should also explain the policy's rationale, and the disciplinary consequences. Supervisors should be trained to monitor employees' performance, and to stay alert to drug-related performance problems.

Several tools are available to screen for alcohol or drug abuse. The most widely used self-reporting screening instruments for alcoholism are the 4-item CAGE and the 25-item Michigan Alcoholism Screening Test (MAST). The former asks questions like these: Have you ever (1) attempted to Cut back on alcohol, (2) been Annoyed by comments about your drinking, (3) felt Guilty about drinking, (4) had an Eye-opener first thing in the morning to steady your nerves?[118] As in Table 16-3, alcohol-related symptoms range from tardiness in the earliest stages of alcohol abuse to prolonged, unpredictable absences in its later stages.[119]

Preemployment drug testing discourages those on drugs from applying for jobs or coming to work for employers who do testing.[120] (For instance, one study found that over 30% of regular drug users employed full-time said they were less likely to work for a company that conducted preemployment screening.)[121] Some applicants or employees may try to evade the test, for instance, by purchasing "clean" specimens. Several states—including New Jersey, North Carolina, Virginia, Oregon, South Carolina, Pennsylvania, Louisiana, Texas, and Nebraska—have laws making drug-test fraud a crime.[122] The newer oral fluid drug test eliminates the "clean specimen" problem and is much less expensive to administer.[123]

Preemployment tests pick up only about half the workplace drug users, so ongoing random testing is advisable. One study concluded that preemployment drug testing had little effect on workplace accidents. However, a combination of preemployment and random ongoing testing was associated with a significant reduction in workplace accidents.[124]

Disciplining, discharge, in-house counseling, and referral to an outside agency are the four traditional prescriptions when a *current* employee tests positive. Most professionals seem to counsel treatment rather than outright dismissal, at least initially. Employers often make available employee assistance programs (EAPs) to provide the counseling necessary to support employees with alcohol or drug abuse problems.

TABLE 16-3 Observable Behavior Patterns Indicating Possible Alcohol-Related Problems

Alcoholism Stage	Some Possible Signs of Alcoholism Problems	Some Possible Alcoholism Performance Issues
Early	Arrives at work late	Reduced job efficiency
	Untrue statements	Misses deadlines
	Leaves work early	
Middle	Frequent absences, especially Mondays	Accidents
	Colleagues mentioning erratic behavior	Warnings from boss
	Mood swings	Noticeably reduced performance
	Anxiety	
	Late returning from lunch	
	Frequent multi-day absences	
Advanced	Personal neglect	Frequent falls, accidents
	Unsteady gait	Strong disciplinary actions
	Violent outbursts	Basically incompetent performance
	Blackouts and frequent forgetfulness	
	Possible drinking on job	

Source: Gopal Patel and John Adkins Jr., "The Employer's Role in Alcoholism Assistance," *Personnel Journal* 62, no. 7 (July 1983), p. 570; Mary-Anne Enoch and David Goldman, "Problem Drinking and Alcoholism: Diagnosis and Treatment," *American Family Physician*, February 1, 2002, www.aafp.org/afp/20020201/441.html, accessed July 20, 2008; and Ken Pidd et al., "Alcohol and Work: Patterns of Use, Workplace Culture, and Safety," www.nisu.flinders.edu.au/pubs/reports/2006/injcat82.pdf, accessed July 20, 2008.

Whether the alcohol abuse reflects a "disability" under the ADA depends on several things.[125] In general, employers can hold alcohol dependent employees to the same performance standards as they hold nonalcoholics. However, there are legal risks. Employees have sued for invasion of privacy, wrongful discharge, defamation, and illegal searches. Therefore, before implementing a drug control program employers should use employee handbooks, bulletin board/intranet postings, and the like to publicize their substance abuse plans. Make sure to explain the conditions under which testing might occur and what accommodations you made for employees who voluntarily seek treatment.

Stress, Burnout, and Depression

Problems such as alcoholism and drug abuse sometimes reflect stress and depression. In turn, a variety of workplace factors can lead to stress. These include work schedule, pace of work, job security, route to and from work, workplace noise, poor supervision, and the number and nature of customers or clients.[126]

Personal factors also influence stress. For example, Type A personalities—workaholics who feel driven to be on time and meet deadlines—normally place themselves under greater stress. Add to job stress the stress caused by nonjob problems like divorce, and many workers are problems waiting to happen.

Human consequences of job stress include anxiety, depression, anger, cardiovascular disease, headaches, accidents, and even early onset Alzheimer's disease.[127] A Danish study found that nurses working under excessive pressure had double the risk for heart attacks.[128]

For the employer, consequences include diminished performance and increased absenteeism and turnover. A study of 46,000 employees concluded that high-stress workers' health care costs were 46% higher than those of their less-stressed coworkers.[129] Yet only 5% of surveyed U.S. employers say they're addressing workplace stress.[130]

REDUCING JOB STRESS There are a number of ways to alleviate dysfunctional stress. These range from commonsense remedies (getting more sleep) to remedies like biofeedback and meditation. Finding a more suitable job, getting counseling, and planning and organizing each day's activities are other sensible responses.[131] In his book *Stress and the Manager*, Dr. Karl Albrecht suggests the following ways for a person to reduce job stress:[132]

- Build rewarding, pleasant, cooperative relationships with colleagues and employees.
- Don't bite off more than you can chew.
- Build an especially effective and supportive relationship with your boss.
- Negotiate with your boss for realistic deadlines on important projects.
- Learn as much as you can about upcoming events and get as much lead time as you can to prepare for them.
- Find time every day for detachment and relaxation.
- Take a walk around the office to keep your body refreshed and alert.
- Find ways to reduce unnecessary noise.
- Reduce the amount of trivia in your job; delegate routine work when possible.
- Limit interruptions.
- Don't put off dealing with distasteful problems.
- Make a constructive "worry list" that includes solutions for each problem.
- Get more and better quality sleep.[133]

Meditation is an option. Choose a quiet place with soft light and sit comfortably. Then meditate by focusing your thoughts (for example, count breaths or visualize a calming location such as a beach). When your mind wanders, bring it back to focusing your thoughts on your breathing or the beach.[134]

WHAT THE EMPLOYER CAN DO The employer and its supervisors play roles in reducing stress. Supportive supervisors and fair treatment are important. Other steps include reducing personal conflicts on the job and encouraging open communication between management and employees. Huntington Hospital in Pasadena, California, introduced an on-site concierge service to help its employees reduce work-related stress. It takes care of tasks like making vacation plans for the employees.[135] Some employers use "resilience training" to help employees deal with stress. As one example, "participants consider previous stressful situations in their lives that they have overcome and identify factors that made the situations manageable."[136]

One British firm has a three-tiered employee stress-reduction program.[137] First is *primary prevention.* This focuses on ensuring that things like job designs and workflows are correct. Second is *intervention.* This includes individual employee assessment, attitude surveys to find sources of stress, and supervisory intervention. Third is *rehabilitation*, which includes employee assistance programs and counseling.

burnout
The total depletion of physical and mental resources caused by excessive striving to reach an unrealistic work-related goal.

BURNOUT Experts define **burnout** as the total depletion of physical and mental resources caused by excessive striving to reach an unrealistic work-related goal. Burnout builds gradually, manifesting itself in symptoms such as irritability, discouragement, exhaustion, cynicism, entrapment, and resentment.[138]

Employers can head off burnout, for instance, by monitoring employees in potentially high-stress jobs.[139] What can a burnout candidate do? In his book *How to Beat the High Cost of Success*, Dr. Herbert Freudenberger suggests:

- ***Break your patterns.*** First, the more well-rounded your life is, the better protected you are against burnout.
- ***Get away from it all periodically.*** Schedule occasional periods of introspection where you can get away from your usual routine.
- ***Reassess your goals in terms of their intrinsic worth.*** Are the goals you've set for yourself attainable? Are they really worth the sacrifices?
- ***Think about your work.*** Could you do as good a job without being so intense?
- ***Stay active.*** A recent study concluded that "the increase in job burnout and depression was strongest among employees who did not engage in physical activity and weakest to the point of non-significance among those engaging in high physical activity."[140]

Another way to reduce burnout is to (try to) put your job aside once you go home. For example, researchers measured psychological detachment from work during nonwork time with items such as "during after-work hours, I forget about work."[141]

EMPLOYEE DEPRESSION *Employee depression* is a serious problem at work. Experts estimate that depression results in more than 200 million lost workdays in the United States annually, and may cost U.S. businesses $24 billion or more per year just in absenteeism and lost productivity.[142] Depressed people also tend to have worse safety records.[143]

Employers should work harder to ensure that depressed employees utilize available support services. One survey found that while about two-thirds of large firms offered employee assistance programs covering depression, only about 14% of employees with depression said they ever used one.[144]

Employers therefore need to train supervisors to identify depression's warning signs and to counsel those who may need such services to use the firm's employee assistance program.[145] Depression is a disease. It does no more good to tell a depressed person to "snap out of it" than it would to tell someone with a heart condition to stop acting tired. Typical depression warning signs (if they last for more than 2 weeks) include persistent sad, anxious, or "empty" moods; sleeping too little; reduced appetite; loss of interest in activities once enjoyed; restlessness or irritability; and difficulty concentrating.[146]

Solving Computer-Related Ergonomic Problems

OSHA has no specific standards for computer workstations. It does have general standards that might apply, regarding, for instance, radiation, noise, and electrical hazards.[147]

NIOSH provided general recommendations regarding computer screens. Most relate to *ergonomics* or design of the worker–equipment interface. These include:

- Employees should take a 3- to 5-minute break from working at the computer every 20–40 minutes, and use the time for other tasks.
- Design maximum flexibility into the workstation so it can be adapted to the individual operator. For example, use adjustable chairs with midback supports. Don't stay in one position for long periods.
- Reduce glare with devices such as shades over windows and indirect lighting.
- Give workers a complete preplacement vision exam to ensure properly corrected vision for reduced visual strain.[148]
- Allow the user to position his or her wrists at the same level as the elbow.
- Put the screen at or just below eye level, at a distance of 18 to 30 inches from the eyes.
- Let the wrists rest lightly on a pad for support.
- Put the feet flat on the floor or on a footrest.[149]

Repetitive Motion Disorders

Repetitive motion disorders include disorders such as carpal tunnel syndrome and tendonitis, and result from too many uninterrupted repetitions of an activity or motion, or from unnatural motions such as twisting the arm or wrist. It affects people who perform repetitive tasks such as assembly line or computer work. Employers can reduce the problem, for instance, with programs to help workers adjust their pace of work.[150]

Infectious Diseases

With many employees traveling to and from international destinations, monitoring and controlling infectious diseases is an important safety issue.[151]

Employers can take steps to prevent the entry or spread of infectious diseases. These steps include:

1. Closely monitor the Centers for Disease Control and Prevention (CDC) travel alerts. Access this information at www.cdc.gov.
2. Provide daily medical screenings for employees returning from infected areas.
3. Deny access for 10 days to employees or visitors who have had contact with suspected infected individuals.
4. Tell employees to stay home if they have a fever or respiratory system symptoms.
5. Clean work areas and surfaces regularly. Make sanitizers containing alcohol easily available.
6. Stagger breaks. Offer several lunch periods to reduce overcrowding. Special situations prompt special requirements. For example, a few years ago, the CDC advised employers that health-care workers working with H1N1 patients should use special respirators to reduce virus inhalation risks.[152]

Workplace Smoking

Smoking is a serious health and cost problem. For employers, these costs derive from higher health and fire insurance, increased absenteeism, and reduced productivity (as when a smoker takes a 10-minute break behind the store). The California Environmental Protection Agency estimated that each year in the United States, secondhand smoke causes 3,000 deaths due to lung cancer and 35,000 to 62,000 illnesses due to heart problems (not all work related).[153]

The manager can probably deny a job to a smoker as long as smoking isn't used as a surrogate for other discrimination.[154] Federal laws don't expressly prohibit discrimination against smokers. However, if a majority of a company's smokers also happen to be minorities, anti-smoking activities could be viewed as discriminatory. Furthermore, 17 states and the District of Columbia ban discriminating against smokers.[155]

Most employers these days ban indoor smoking, often designating small outdoor areas where smoking is permitted. Many states and municipalities now ban indoor smoking in public areas (see http://en.wikipedia.org/wiki/List_of_smoking_bans#United_States for a list).

Some firms take a hard-line approach. WEYCO Inc., a benefits services company in Michigan, first gave employees 15 months' warning and offered smoking secession assistance. Then they began firing or forcing out all its workers who smoke, including those who do so in their homes.[156]

Occupational Security and Risk Management

6 Discuss the prerequisites for a security plan and how to set up a basic security program.

Workplace *safety* relates to risks of injury or illness to employees. Workplace *security* relates to protecting employees from internal and external security risks such as criminal acts by outside perpetrators and threats of terrorism.[157] According to SHRM, workplace security plans should address tasks such as establishing a formal security function, protecting the firm's intellectual property (for instance, through noncompete agreements), developing crisis management plans, establishing theft and fraud prevention procedures, preventing workplace violence, and installing facility security systems.[158]

Most employers have security arrangements.[159] A SHRM survey found that about 85% of responding organizations now have some type of formal disaster plan.[160] Many firms also instituted special handling procedures for suspicious mail packages and hold regular emergency evacuation drills.

Enterprise Risk Management

Enterprise risk management is "the process of assessing exposures to loss within an operation and determining how best to eliminate, manage or otherwise reduce the risk of an adverse event from having a negative impact on the business."[161]

Companies face a variety of risks, only some of which are direct risks to employees' health and safety. Specific risks include, for instance, natural disaster risks, financial risks, and risks to the firm's computer systems. *Human capital risks* would rank high. These include safety risks like those we discussed in this chapter as well as, for instance, risks from unionization and from inadequate staffing plans.[162]

How the employer manages a specific risk depends on the class of risk it falls in. *Internal preventable* risks arise from actions within the company and include things like employees' illegal conduct or workplace accidents.[163] Employers manage these risks with methods such as ethical codes of conduct, disciplinary procedures, and safety rules. *Strategy risks* are risks that managers accept as part of executing their strategies, such as the risk a banker takes that a borrower might default. Employers manage strategy risks with independent experts (like those who assess insurance risks) and with internal experts, like the risk managers who help to oversee banks' loan portfolios. *External risks* come from outside the company and include things like political and natural disasters, terrorism, and sudden economic shifts. Managing external risks involves methods like scenario planning, in which the company endeavors to identify, analyze, and plan for unpredictable eventualities.

Preventing and Dealing with Violence at Work

Violence against employees is one such (internal preventable) enterprise risk, and a huge problem.[164] On average, 20 workers are murdered and 18,000 assaulted each week at work. By one

FIGURE 16-8 How to Heighten Security in Your Workplace

- Improve external lighting.
- Use drop safes to minimize cash on hand.
- Post signs noting that only a limited amount of cash is on hand.
- Install silent alarms and surveillance cameras.
- Increase the number of staff on duty.
- Provide staff training in conflict resolution and nonviolent response.
- Close establishments during high-risk hours late at night and early in the morning.
- Issue a weapons policy; for instance, "firearms or other dangerous or deadly weapons cannot be brought onto the facility either openly or concealed."

Source: see "Creating a Safer Workplace: Simple Steps Bring Results," *Safety Now, September 2002,* pp. 1–2. See also www.osha.gov/SLTC/etools/hospital/hazards/workplaceviolence/checklist.html, and www.osha.gov/Publications/osha3153.pdf, both accessed September 6, 2013.

early estimate, workplace violence costs employers about $4 billion a year.[165] One report called bullying the "silent epidemic" of the workplace, "where abusive behavior, threats, and intimidation often go unreported."[166] Customers, not coworkers, are often the perpetrators.[167] However, many assaults involve a current or former partner or spouse.[168] Other workplace violence manifests itself in sabotage, rather than personal attacks.

Workplace violence incidents by employees are predictable and avoidable. According to one recent survey, 29% of workers who knew about or experienced workplace violence said nothing about it.[169] *Risk Management Magazine* estimates that about 86% of past workplace violence incidents were anticipated by coworkers, who had brought them to management's attention prior to the incidents actually occurring. Yet management usually did little or nothing.[170] Human resource managers can take several steps to reduce the incidence of workplace violence:

HEIGHTEN SECURITY MEASURES Heightened security measures are the first line of defense, whether the violence derives from coworkers, customers, or outsiders. According to OSHA, measures should include those in Figure 16-8.

IMPROVE EMPLOYEE SCREENING With about 30% of workplace attacks committed by coworkers, screening out potentially violent applicants is the employer's next line of defense.

Personal and situational factors correlate with workplace aggression. Men, and individuals scoring higher on "trait anger" (the predisposition to respond to situations with hostility), are more likely to exhibit workplace aggression. In terms of the situation, interpersonal injustice and poor leadership predict aggression against supervisors.[171]

Employers can screen out potentially violent workers before they're hired. Obtain an employment application, and check the applicant's employment history, education, and references.[172] Sample interview questions include "What frustrates you?" and "Who was your worst supervisor and why?"[173] Certain background circumstances, such as the following, may call for a more in-depth background checking:[174]

- An unexplained gap in employment
- Incomplete or false information on the résumé or application
- A negative, unfavorable, or false reference
- Prior insubordinate or violent behavior on the job[175]
- A criminal history involving harassing or violent behavior
- A prior termination for cause with a suspicious (or no) explanation
- History of drug or alcohol abuse
- Strong indications of instability in the individual's work or personal life as indicated, for example, by frequent job changes or geographic moves
- Lost licenses or accreditations[176]

USE WORKPLACE VIOLENCE TRAINING You can also train supervisors to identify the clues that typify potentially violent current employees. Common clues include:[177]

- An act of violence on or off the job
- Erratic behavior evidencing a loss of perception or awareness of actions

- Overly confrontational or antisocial behavior
- Sexually aggressive behavior
- Isolationist or loner tendencies
- Insubordinate behavior with a threat of violence
- Tendency to overreact to criticism
- Exaggerated interest in war, guns, violence, mass murders, catastrophes, and so on
- Commission of a serious breach of security
- Possession of weapons, guns, knives, or like items in the workplace
- Violation of privacy rights of others, such as searching desks or stalking
- Chronic complaining and the raising of frequent, unreasonable grievances
- A retributory or get-even attitude

The U.S. Postal Service took steps to reduce workplace assaults. These include more background checks, drug testing, a 90-day probationary period for new hires, more stringent security (including a hotline that lets employees report threats), and training for managers to create a healthier culture.[178] The HR Tools feature lists guidelines for firing high-risk employees.

IMPROVING PERFORMANCE: HR Tools for Line Managers and Entrepreneurs

Guidelines for Firing a High-Risk Employee

When firing a high-risk employee:

- Plan all aspects of the meeting, including its time, location, the people to be present, and agenda.
- Involve security enforcement personnel.
- Advise the employee that he or she is no longer permitted onto the employer's property.
- Conduct the meeting in a room with a door leading to the outside of the building.
- Keep the termination brief and to the point.
- Make sure he or she returns all company-owned property at the meeting.
- Don't let the person return to his or her workstation.
- Conduct the meeting early in the week and early in the morning so he or she has time to meet with employment counselors or support groups.
- Offer as generous a severance package as possible.
- Protect the employee's dignity by not advertising the event.[179]

Discussion Question 16-7: Discuss how taking this approach might save the employer money (as well as protecting the one doing the firing.)

VIOLENCE TOWARD WOMEN AT WORK Men have more fatal occupational injuries than do women, but the proportion of women who are victims of assault is much higher. The Gender-Motivated Violence Act (part of the Violence Against Women Act) imposes liabilities on employers whose women employees become violence victims.[180] Of all females murdered at work, more than three-fourths are victims of random criminal violence carried out by an assailant unknown to the victim. Family members, coworkers, or acquaintances commit the rest. Tangible security improvements including better lighting, cash-drop boxes, and similar steps can help. Women (and men) should have access to domestic crisis hotlines, such as www.womenshealth.gov/violence-against-women/get-help-for-violence/violence-help-hotlines.html, and to employee assistance programs.

Setting Up a Basic Security Program

As noted, workplace *security* relates to protecting employees from internal and external security risks. This often starts with facilities security.

In simplest terms, instituting a basic facility security program requires four steps: analyzing the current *level* of risk, and then installing *mechanical, natural*, and *organizational* security systems.[181] Many organizations establish cross-functional threat assessment teams.[182] At one university, for instance, "The team meets regularly to discuss issues relating to violence, security and potential threats directed at students, faculty and staff at the Metropolitan Campus."[183]

Security programs ideally start with an analysis of the facility's *current level of risk.* Here, start with the obvious. For example, what is the neighborhood like? Does your facility (such as

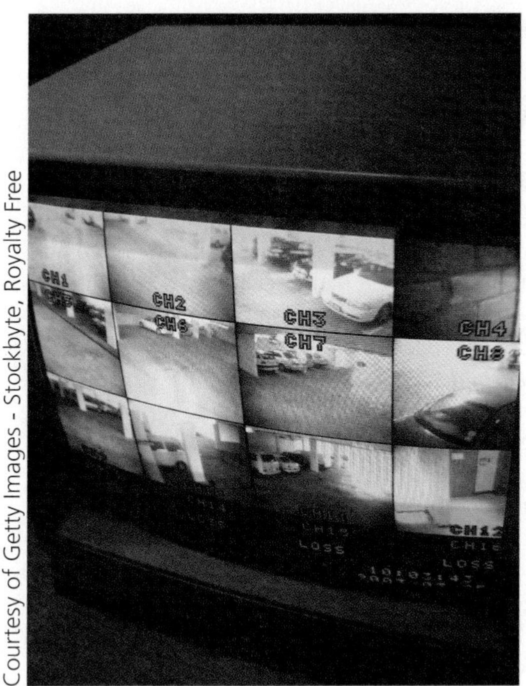

Courtesy of Getty Images - Stockbyte, Royalty Free

Many employers install video security cameras to monitor areas in and around their premises.

the office building you're in) house other businesses or individuals that might bring unsafe activities to your doorstep? As part of this initial threat assessment, also review these six matters:

1. **Reception area access,** including need for a "panic button";
2. **Interior security,** including secure restrooms, and better identification of exits;
3. **Authorities' involvement,** in particular emergency procedures developed with local law enforcement;
4. **Mail handling,** including screening and opening mail;
5. **Evacuation,** including evacuation procedures and training; and
6. **Backup systems,** such storing data off site.

Having assessed the potential current level of risk, the employer then turns its attention to assessing and improving natural, mechanical, and organizational security.[184]

NATURAL SECURITY *Natural security* means capitalizing on the facility's natural or architectural features to minimize security problems. For example, do too many entrances hamper controlling facility access?

MECHANICAL SECURITY *Mechanical security* is the utilization of security systems such as locks, intrusion alarms, access control systems, and surveillance systems to reduce the need for continuous human surveillance.[185] Many mail rooms use scanners to check incoming mail. Biometric scanners that read thumb or palm prints or retina or vocal patterns make it easier to enforce plant security.[186]

ORGANIZATIONAL SECURITY Finally, *organizational security* means using good management to improve security. For example, it means properly training and motivating security staff and lobby attendants. Similarly, ensure that the security staff has written orders that define their duties, especially in situations such as fire, elevator entrapment, hazardous materials spills, medical emergencies, hostile intrusions, suspicious packages, civil disturbances, and workplace violence.[187] Also ask, "Are you properly investigating the backgrounds of new hires and contractors?"

Basic Prerequisites for a Crime Prevention Plan

As one corporate security summary put it, "workplace security involves more than . . . installing an alarm system."[188] Ideally, a comprehensive corporate anticrime program should start with the following:[189]

1. ***Company philosophy and policy on crime.*** Make sure employees understand that the employer has a zero-tolerance policy with respect to workers who commit any crimes.
2. ***Investigations of job applicants.*** Always conduct full background checks.
3. ***Crime awareness training.*** Make it clear during training and orientation that the employer is tough on workplace crime.
4. ***Crisis management.*** Establish and communicate what to do in the event of a bomb threat, fire, or other emergency.

Company Security and Employee Privacy

Security programs often entail monitoring employee communications and workplace activities. But as noted earlier in this text, monitoring encroaches on employee privacy. Ideally, employers should get employees' consent for monitoring. However, the employer may also monitor if it's clear from existing policies and notices that employees should have known monitoring might take place.

The employer can make it easier to legally investigate employees for potential security breaches. Steps include:[190]

1. Distribute a policy that (a) says the company reserves the right to inspect and search employees as well as their personal property, electronic media, and files; and (b) that lockers and desks remain the property of the company and are subject to search.

2. Train investigators to focus on the facts and avoid making accusations.
3. Remember that employees can request that an employee representative be present during the investigative interview.
4. Make sure all investigations and searches are evenhanded and nondiscriminatory.

Business Continuity and Emergency Plans

The possibility of emergencies prompted by fires, attacks, and similar issues means that employers need facility continuity and emergency plans.[191] One source estimates that 40% of companies never reopen after suffering business disruptions from a major catastrophe, so putting a disaster plan in place is imperative. Emergency preparedness resources include www.ready.gov and The National Institute for Occupational Safety and Health (www.CD3.GOP/NIOSH/topics/emergency.html).[192] Such plans should cover *early detection of a problem, methods for communicating the emergency externally*, and *communications plans for initiating an evacuation.* The initial alarm should come first. The employer should then follow the initial alarm with an announcement providing specific information about the emergency and letting employees know what action they should take. Many use social networks or text messaging.[193]

Social Media and HR

Social media such as Twitter are obvious choices for quickly communicating emergency information to large numbers of dispersed individuals. When a tornado hit Bridgeport, Connecticut, a few years ago, the city's administrators used Twitter to let citizens know about things like power outages and blocked roads. The Canadian Red Cross uses social media to publicize preparedness information and respond to questions from affected communities. And emergency managers, utility companies, and the public used social media to share updates on things like shelter locations when Hurricane Sandy struck the northeast.[194]

One should also have plans for dealing with health issues.[195] Thus, in the case of a cardiac arrest emergency, early CPR and an automated external defibrillator are essential. These devices should be available and one or more local employees trained in their use.[196]

Plans are also required for *business continuity* in the event of a disaster. The employer can designate a secure area of the company website for employee communications, listing such things as expected hours of operation, facilities opening schedules, and alternative work locations.[197] The disaster plans should include establishing a command center and identifying employees considered essential in the event of a disaster, including responsibilities for each. The SBA provides business continuity information at www.preparemybusiness.org.

Terrorism

The employer can take several steps to protect its employees and physical assets from terrorist attack. These steps, now familiar at many workplaces, include:

- Screen the identities of everyone entering the premises.[198]
- Check mail carefully.
- Identify ahead of time a lean "crisis organization" that can run the company on an interim basis after a terrorist threat.
- Identify in advance under what conditions you will close the company down, as well as the shutdown process.
- Institute a process to put the crisis management team together.
- Prepare evacuation plans and make sure exits are well marked and unblocked.
- Designate an employee who will communicate with families and off-site employees.
- Identify an upwind, off-site location near your facility to use as a staging area for all evacuated personnel.
- Designate in advance several employees who will do headcounts at the evacuation staging area.
- Establish an emergency text-messaging policy and procedure to notify affected individuals that an emergency may exist.[199]

Review

MyManagementLab Go to **mymanagementlab.com** to complete the problems marked with this icon. ✪

Chapter Section Summaries

1. The subject **safety and the manager** concerns managers for several reasons, one of which is the number of workplace accidents. Reducing accidents often boils down to reducing accident-causing conditions and accident-causing acts. However, safety always starts at the top. Telling employees to "work safely" is futile unless everyone knows management is serious about safety.
2. Because of this, all managers need to be familiar with **occupational safety law**. The Occupational Safety and Health Act was passed by Congress in 1972 to assure so far as possible every working man and woman in the nation has safe and healthful working conditions, and to preserve human resources. The act created the Occupational Safety and Health Administration (OSHA). OSHA, in turn, promulgates thousands of specific policies and standards with which employers must comply. It enforces these standards via a system of inspections, citations, and, where necessary, penalties. Inspectors cannot make warrantless inspections, and managers need to make sure a designated OSHA coordinator is present if an inspector demands admittance.
3. There are three basic **causes of workplace accidents**: chance occurrences, unsafe conditions, and employees' unsafe acts. Unsafe conditions include things like improperly guarded equipment and hazardous procedures. Unsafe acts sometimes reflect personality traits such as impatience and distractibility.
4. In practice, **how to prevent accidents** boils down to reducing unsafe conditions and reducing unsafe acts. Reducing unsafe conditions is always the first line of defense and includes using checklists and following OSHA standards. Once all necessary steps are taken, employers need to encourage employees to use personal protective equipment. There are then several basic approaches to reducing unsafe acts, for instance, through proper selection and placement, training, motivation and positive reinforcement, behavior-based safety, employee participation, and conducting safety and health audits.
5. Most **workplace health hazards** aren't obvious, like unguarded equipment.
   - Typical exposure hazards include, for instance, chemicals, biohazards, and improperly designed equipment.
   - Managing exposure hazards like these comes under the area of industrial hygiene, and involves recognition, evaluation, and control. Obvious areas of concern include asbestos exposure and infectious diseases.
   - Managers need to be familiar with alcoholism, substance abuse, and their manifestations at work and particularly be familiar with signs of these problems and how to deal with them.
   - Stress, burnout, and depression are more serious at work than many people realize, and both the employee and employer can take steps to deal with them. Employers especially need to train supervisors to identify depression's warning signs and to counsel those who may need special services.
6. Most employers today have **occupational security and risk management programs**. Violence against employees is an enormous problem. Heightened security measures are an employer's first line of defense and include, for instance, improving external lighting and using drop boxes to minimize cash on hand. Improved employee screening can reduce the risk of hiring potentially violent employees. However, employers also need to provide workplace violence training (for instance, including what to watch for such as verbal threats) and enhanced attention to employee retention and dismissal processes. Instituting a basic facility security program involves analyzing the current level of risk, and then installing mechanical, natural, and organizational security systems.

CHAPTER 16

Discussion Questions

16-8. Explain how to reduce the occurrence of unsafe acts on the part of your employees.

✪ **16-9.** Explain the supervisor's role in safety.

16-10. Explain what causes unsafe acts.

16-11. Describe at least five techniques for reducing accidents.

✪ **16-12.** Explain how you would reduce stress at work.

Individual and Group Activities

16-13. Working individually or in groups, answer the question, "Is there such a thing as an accident-prone person?" Develop your answer using examples of actual people you know who seemed to be accident prone on some endeavor.

16-14. Working individually or in groups, compile a list of the factors at work or in school that create dysfunctional stress for you. What methods do you use for dealing with the stress?

16-15. Appendix A, PHR and SPHR Knowledge Base, at the end of this book (pages 580–588) lists the knowledge someone studying for the HRCI certification exam needs to have in each area of human resource management (such as in Strategic Management, Workforce Planning, and Human Resource Development). In groups of four to five students, do four things: (1) review Appendix A; (2) identify the material in this chapter that relates to the required knowledge Appendix A lists; (3) write four multiple-choice exam questions on this material that you believe would be suitable for inclusion in the HRCI exam; and (4) if time permits, have someone from your team post your team's questions in front of the class, so that students in all teams can answer the exam questions created by the other teams.

16-16. A safety journal presented some information about what happens when OSHA refers criminal complaints about willful violations of OSHA standards to the U.S. Department of Justice (DOJ). In one 20-year period, OSHA referred 119 fatal cases allegedly involving willful violations of OSHA to the DOJ for criminal prosecution. The DOJ declined to pursue 57% of them, and some were dropped for other reasons. Of the remaining 51 cases, the DOJ settled 63% with pretrial settlements involving no prison time. So, counting acquittals, of the 119 cases OSHA referred to the DOJ, only 9 resulted in prison time for at least one of the defendants. "The Department of Justice is a disgrace," charged the founder of an organization for family members of workers killed on the job. One possible explanation for this low conviction rate is that the crime in cases like these is generally a misdemeanor, not a felony, and the DOJ generally tries to focus its attention on felony cases. Given this information, what implications do you think this has for how employers and their managers should manage their safety programs, and why do you take that position?

16-17. A 315-foot-tall, 2-million-pound crane collapsed on a construction site in East Toledo, Ohio, killing four ironworkers. Do you think catastrophic failures like this are avoidable? If so, what steps would you suggest the general contractor take to avoid a disaster like this?

Experiential Exercise

How Safe Is My University?

Purpose: The purpose of this exercise is to give you practice in identifying unsafe conditions.

Required Understanding: You should be familiar with material covered in this chapter, particularly that on unsafe conditions and that in Figures 16-6, 16-7, and 16-9.

How to Set Up the Exercise/Instructions: Divide the class into groups of four. Assume that each group is a safety committee retained by your college's or university's safety engineer to identify and report on any possible unsafe conditions in and around the school building. Each group will spend about 45 minutes in and around the building you are now in for the purpose of identifying and listing possible unsafe conditions. (Make use of the checklists in Figures 16-6, 16-7, and 16-9.)

Return to the class in about 45 minutes. A spokesperson for each group should list on the board the unsafe conditions you have identified. How many were there? Do you think these also violate OSHA standards? How would you go about checking?

GENERAL

	OK	ACTION NEEDED
1. Is the required OSHA workplace poster displayed in your place of business as required where all employees are likely to see it?	☐	☐
2. Are you aware of the requirement to report all workplace fatalities and any serious accidents (where five or more are hospitalized) to a federal or state OSHA office within 48 hours?	☐	☐
3. Are workplace injury and illness records being kept as required by OSHA?	☐	☐
4. Are you aware that the OSHA annual summary of workplace injuries and illnesses must be posted by February 1 and must remain posted until March 1?	☐	☐
5. Are you aware that employers with 10 or fewer employees are exempt from the OSHA record-keeping requirements, unless they are part of an official BLS or state survey and have received specific instructions to keep records?	☐	☐
6. Have you demonstrated an active interest in safety and health matters by defining a policy for your business and communicating it to all employees?	☐	☐
7. Do you have a safety committee or group that allows participation of employees in safety and health activities?	☐	☐
8. Does the safety committee or group meet regularly and report, in writing, its activities?	☐	☐
9. Do you provide safety and health training for all employees requiring such training, and is it documented?	☐	☐
10. Is one person clearly in charge of safety and health activities?	☐	☐
11. Do all employees know what to do in emergencies?	☐	☐
12. Are emergency telephone numbers posted?	☐	☐
13. Do you have a procedure for handling employee complaints regarding safety and health?	☐	☐

WORKPLACE

ELECTRICAL WIRING, FIXTURES, AND CONTROLS

	OK	ACTION NEEDED
1. Are your workplace electricians familiar with the requirements of the National Electrical Code (NEC)?	☐	☐
2. Do you specify compliance with the NEC for all contract electrical work?	☐	☐
3. If you have electrical installations in hazardous dust or vapor areas, do they meet the NEC for hazardous locations?	☐	☐
4. Are all electrical cords strung so they do not hang on pipes, nails, hooks, etc.?	☐	☐
5. Is all conduit, BX cable, etc., properly attached to all supports and tightly connected to junction and outlet boxes?	☐	☐
6. Is there no evidence of fraying on any electrical cords?	☐	☐
7. Are rubber cords kept free of grease, oil, and chemicals?	☐	☐
8. Are metallic cable and conduit systems properly grounded?	☐	☐
9. Are portable electric tools and appliances grounded or double insulated?	☐	☐
10. Are all ground connections clean and tight?	☐	☐
11. Are fuses and circuit breakers the right type and size for the load on each circuit?	☐	☐
12. Are all fuses free of "jumping" with pennies or metal strips?	☐	☐
13. Do switches show evidence of overheating?	☐	☐
14. Are switches mounted in clean, tightly closed metal boxes?	☐	☐
15. Are all electrical switches marked to show their purpose?	☐	☐
16. Are motors clean and kept free of excessive grease and oil?	☐	☐
17. Are motors properly maintained and provided with adequate overcurrent protection?	☐	☐
18. Are bearings in good condition?	☐	☐
19. Are portable lights equipped with proper guards?	☐	☐
20. Are all lamps kept free of combustible material?	☐	☐
21. Is your electrical system checked periodically by someone competent in the NEC?	☐	☐

Develop your own checklist.

These are only sample questions.

(Continued)

FIGURE 16-9 Self-Inspection Safety and Health Checklist

Note: For a much more extensive checklist, see "Self-Inspection Checklists," www.osha.gov/Publications/smallbusiness/small-business.html#check, accessed September 6, 2013.

Develop your own checklist.

These are only sample questions.

EXITS AND ACCESS

	OK	ACTION NEEDED
1. Are all exits visible and unobstructed?	☐	☐
2. Are all exits marked with a readily visible sign that is properly illuminated?	☐	☐
3. Are there sufficient exits to ensure prompt escape in case of emergency?	☐	☐
4. Are areas with restricted occupancy posted and is access/egress controlled by persons specifically authorized to be in those areas?	☐	☐
5. Do you take special precautions to protect employees during construction and repair operations?	☐	☐

FIRE PROTECTION

	OK	ACTION NEEDED
1. Are portable fire extinguishers provided in adequate number and type?	☐	☐
2. Are fire extinguishers inspected monthly for general condition and operability and noted on the inspection tag?	☐	☐
3. Are fire extinguishers recharged regularly and properly noted on the inspection tag?	☐	☐
4. Are fire extinguishers mounted in readily accessible locations?	☐	☐
5. If you have interior standpipes and valves, are these inspected regularly?	☐	☐
6. If you have a fire alarm system, is it tested at least annually?	☐	☐
7. Are employees periodically instructed in the use of extinguishers and fire protection procedures?	☐	☐
8. If you have outside private fire hydrants, were they flushed within the last year and placed on a regular maintenance schedule?	☐	☐
9. Are fire doors and shutters in good operating condition?	☐	☐
Are they unobstructed and protected against obstruction?	☐	☐
10. Are fusible links in place?	☐	☐
11. Is your local fire department well acquainted with your plant, location, and specific hazards?	☐	☐
12. Automatic sprinklers:		
Are water control valves, air, and water pressures checked weekly?	☐	☐
Are control valves locked open?	☐	☐
Is maintenance of the system assigned to responsible persons or a sprinkler contractor?	☐	☐
Are sprinkler heads protected by metal guards where exposed to mechanical damage?	☐	☐
Is proper minimum clearance maintained around sprinkler heads?	☐	☐

HOUSEKEEPING AND GENERAL WORK ENVIRONMENT

	OK	ACTION NEEDED
1. Is smoking permitted in designated "safe areas" only?	☐	☐
2. Are NO SMOKING signs prominently posted in areas containing combustibles and flammables?	☐	☐
3. Are covered metal waste cans used for oily and paint-soaked waste?	☐	☐
Are they emptied at least daily?	☐	☐
4. Are paint spray booths, dip tanks, etc., and their exhaust ducts cleaned regularly?	☐	☐
5. Are stand mats, platforms, or similar protection provided to protect employees from wet floors in wet processes?	☐	☐
6. Are waste receptacles provided and are they emptied regularly?	☐	☐
7. Do your toilet facilities meet the requirements of applicable sanitary codes?	☐	☐
8. Are washing facilities provided?	☐	☐
9. Are all areas of your business adequately illuminated?	☐	☐
10. Are floor load capacities posted in second floors, lofts, storage areas, etc.?	☐	☐
11. Are floor openings provided with toe boards and railings or a floor hole cover?	☐	☐
12. Are stairways in good condition with standard railings provided for every flight having four or more risers?	☐	☐
13. Are portable wood ladders and metal ladders adequate for their purpose, in good condition, and provided with secure footing?	☐	☐
14. If you have fixed ladders, are they adequate, and are they in good condition and equipped with side rails or cages or special safety climbing devices, if required?	☐	☐
15. For loading docks:		
Are dockplates kept in serviceable condition and secured to prevent slipping?	☐	☐
Do you have means to prevent car or truck movement when dockplates are in place?	☐	☐

FIGURE 16-9 (Continued)

MACHINES AND EQUIPMENT

	OK	ACTION NEEDED
1. Are all machines or operations that expose operators or other employees to rotating parts, pinch points, flying chips, particles, or sparks adequately guarded?	☐	☐
2. Are mechanical power transmission belts and pinch points guarded?	☐	☐
3. Is exposed power shafting less than 7 feet from the floor guarded?	☐	☐
4. Are hand tools and other equipment regularly inspected for safe condition?	☐	☐
5. Is compressed air used for cleaning reduced to less than 30 psi?	☐	☐
6. Are power saws and similar equipment provided with safety guards?	☐	☐
7. Are grinding wheel tool rests set to within 1/8 inch or less of the wheel?	☐	☐
8. Is there any system for inspecting small hand tools for burred ends, cracked handles, etc.?	☐	☐
9. Are compressed gas cylinders examined regularly for obvious signs of defects, deep rusting, or leakage?	☐	☐
10. Is care used in handling and storing cylinders and valves to prevent damage?	☐	☐
11. Are all air receivers periodically examined, including the safety valves?	☐	☐
12. Are safety valves tested regularly and frequently?	☐	☐
13. Is there sufficient clearance from stoves, furnaces, etc., for stock, woodwork, or other combustible materials?	☐	☐
14. Is there clearance of at least 4 feet in front of heating equipment involving open flames, such as gas radiant heaters, and fronts of firing doors of stoves, furnaces, etc.?	☐	☐
15. Are all oil and gas fired devices equipped with flame failure controls that will prevent flow of fuel if pilots or main burners are not working?	☐	☐
16. Is there at least a 2-inch clearance between chimney brickwork and all woodwork or other combustible materials?	☐	☐
17. For welding or flame cutting operations:		
Are only authorized, trained personnel permitted to use such equipment?	☐	☐
Have operators been given a copy of operating instructions and asked to follow them?	☐	☐
Are welding gas cylinders stored so they are not subjected to damage?	☐	☐
Are valve protection caps in place on all cylinders not connected for use?	☐	☐
Are all combustible materials near the operator covered with protective shields or otherwise protected?	☐	☐
Is a fire extinguisher provided at the welding site?	☐	☐
Do operators have the proper protective clothing and equipment?	☐	☐

Develop your own checklist.

These are only sample questions.

MATERIALS

	OK	ACTION NEEDED
1. Are approved safety cans or other acceptable containers used for handling and dispensing flammable liquids?	☐	☐
2. Are all flammable liquids that are kept inside buildings stored in proper storage containers or cabinets?	☐	☐
3. Do you meet OSHA standards for all spray painting or dip tank operations using combustible liquids?	☐	☐
4. Are oxidizing chemicals stored in areas separate from all organic material except shipping bags?	☐	☐
5. Do you have an enforced NO SMOKING rule in areas for storage and use of hazardous materials?	☐	☐
6. Are NO SMOKING signs posted where needed?	☐	☐
7. Is ventilation equipment provided for removal of air contaminants from operations such as production grinding, buffing, spray painting and/or vapor degreasing, and is it operating properly?	☐	☐
8. Are protective measures in effect for operations involved with x-rays or other radiation?	☐	☐
9. For lift truck operations:		
Are only trained personnel allowed to operate forklift trucks?	☐	☐
Is overhead protection provided on high lift rider trucks?	☐	☐
10. For toxic materials:		
Are all materials used in your plant checked for toxic qualities?	☐	☐
Have appropriate control procedures such as ventilation systems, enclosed operations, safe handling practices, proper personal protective equipment (such as respirators, glasses or goggles, gloves, etc.) been instituted for toxic materials?	☐	☐

(Continued)

FIGURE 16-9 (Continued)

Develop your own checklist.

These are only sample questions.

EMPLOYEE PROTECTION	OK	ACTION NEEDED
1. Is there a hospital, clinic, or infirmary for medical care near your business?	☐	☐
2. If medical and first-aid facilities are not nearby, do you have one or more employees trained in first aid?	☐	☐
3. Are your first-aid supplies adequate for the type of potential injuries in your work-place?	☐	☐
4. Are there quick water flush facilities available where employees are exposed to corrosive materials?	☐	☐
5. Are hard hats provided and worn where any danger of falling objects exists?	☐	☐
6. Are protective goggles or glasses provided and worn where there is any danger of flying particles or splashing of corrosive materials?	☐	☐
7. Are protective gloves, aprons, shields, or other means provided for protection from sharp, hot, or corrosive materials?	☐	☐
8. Are approved respirators provided for regular or emergency use where needed?	☐	☐
9. Is all protective equipment maintained in a sanitary condition and readily available for use?	☐	☐
10. Where special equipment is needed for electrical workers, is it available?	☐	☐
11. When lunches are eaten on the premises, are they eaten in areas where there is no exposure to toxic materials, and not in toilet facility areas?	☐	☐
12. Is protection against the effect of occupational noise exposure provided when the sound levels exceed those shown in the OSHA noise standard?	☐	☐

FIGURE 16-9 (Continued)

Video Case

Video Title: Safety (California Health Foundation)

SYNOPSIS

Company initiatives to promote safety and emergency preparedness are discussed. These include proactive measures to encourage employee health and to prevent injuries, especially ergonomic ones. Different methods of preventing injuries are discussed, including employee health programs that reimburse employees for gym memberships, smoking cessation, weight loss, and other programs. When the company helps foster better employee health, they are more likely to perform well and remain free of injuries.

Discussion Questions

16-18. What are some ways of lowering stress that the California Health Foundation emphasizes?

16-19. How are the employees at the California Health Foundation involved in ensuring an adequate response to an emergency?

16-20. Why are proactive measures the most appropriate for addressing ergonomic injuries?

16-21. Based on what you've seen to this point, how comprehensive would you say that the company's safety program is? What suggestions would you make for additional steps it should take?

16-22. What are the other economic side effects of accidents?

16-23. Do you agree that "safety in the office is a matter of attitude"? Why or why not?

16-24. What other steps would you suggest the company take to boost safety? For instance, what would you have supervisors do to improve the company's safety and accident record?

Video Title: Safety (City of Los Angeles)

SYNOPSIS

In this video, Randall Macfarlane says, among other things, that they use four methods to ensure safety and health: training, providing personal protective equipment, providing a special 8-hour training course for their staff, and holding biweekly safety meetings. He also says they train supervisors to recognize behaviors or other things that may be warning signs. Furthermore, an in-house review every year aims to make sure all information, videos, and so on, are current. He also focuses on ergonomics in order to prevent problems like carpal tunnel syndrome. The company has periodic reviews from California's Occupational Safety and Health Administration.

Discussion Questions

16-25. What should the city do prior to issuing personal protective equipment, according to this chapter?

16-26. What do you think of the safety program? What else would you suggest, and why?

16-27. What are some of the issues and caveats the employer and its supervisors should follow when dealing with a visit from the Occupational Safety and Health Administration?

16-28. If you were asked to put together a list of items that supervisors should keep in mind with respect to supervising safety and health at work, what would you include on your list?

Application Case

The New Safety and Health Program

At first glance, a dot-com company is one of the last places you'd expect to find potential safety and health hazards—or so the owners of LearnInMotion.com thought. There's no danger of moving machinery, no high-pressure lines, no cutting or heavy lifting, and certainly no forklift trucks. However, there are safety and health problems.

In terms of accident-causing conditions, for instance, the one thing dot-com companies have are cables and wires. Even with extensive use of wifi and Bluetooth, there are cables connecting computers to screens and to servers, and in many cases cables running from some computers to separate printers. There are 10 telephones in this particular office, all on 15-foot power lines that always seem to be snaking around chairs and tables. There is, in fact, an astonishing amount of cable considering this is an office with so-called wireless connections and with fewer than 10 employees. When the installation specialists wired the office (for electricity, high-speed cable, phone lines, burglar alarms, and computers), they estimated they used well over 5 miles of cables of one sort or another. Most of these are hidden in the walls or ceilings, but many of them snake their way from desk to desk, and under and over doorways. Several employees have tried to reduce the nuisance of having to trip over wires whenever they get up by putting their plastic chair pads over the wires closest to them. However, that still leaves many wires unprotected. In other cases, they brought in their own packing tape and tried to tape down the wires in those spaces where they're particularly troublesome, such as across doorways.

The cables and wires are only one of the more obvious potential accident-causing conditions. The firm's programmer, before he left the firm, had tried to repair the main server while the unit was still electrically alive. To this day, they're not sure exactly where he stuck the screwdriver, but the result was that he was "blown across the room," as one manager put it. He was all right, but it was still a scare. And while they haven't received any claims yet, every employee spends hours at his or her computer, so carpal tunnel syndrome is a risk, as are a variety of other problems such as eyestrain and strained backs.

One recent accident particularly scared the owners. The firm uses independent contractors to deliver the firm's books and DVD-based courses in New York and two other cities. A delivery person was riding his bike east at the intersection of Second Avenue and East 64th Street in New York when he was struck by a car going south on Second Avenue. Luckily, he was not hurt, but the bike's front wheel was wrecked, and the narrow escape got the firm's two owners, Mel and Maria, thinking about their lack of a safety program.

It's not just the physical conditions that concern the two owners. They also have some concerns about potential health problems such as job stress and burnout. Although the business may be (relatively) safe with respect to physical conditions, it is also relatively stressful in terms of the demands it makes in hours and deadlines. It is not unusual for employees to get to work by 7:30 or 8 o'clock in the morning and to work through until 11 or 12 o'clock at night, at least 5 and sometimes 6 or 7 days per week.

The bottom line is that both Maria and Mel feel quite strongly that they need to do something about implementing a health and safety plan. Now, they want you, their management consultants, to help them do it. Here's what they want you to do for them.

Questions

16-29. Based upon your knowledge of health and safety matters and your actual observations of operations that are similar to theirs, make a list of the potential hazardous conditions employees and others face at LearnInMotion.com. What should they do to reduce the potential severity of the top five hazards?

16-30. Would it be advisable for them to set up a procedure for screening out stress-prone or accident-prone individuals? Why or why not? If so, how should they screen them?

16-31. Write a short position paper on the subject, "What should we do to get all our employees to behave more safely at work?"

16-32. Based on what you know and on what other dot-coms are doing, write a short position paper on the subject, "What can we do to reduce the potential problems of stress and burnout in our company?"

Continuing Case

Carter Cleaning Company

The New Safety Program

Employees' safety and health are very important matters in the laundry and cleaning business. Each facility is a small production plant in which machines, powered by high-pressure steam and compressed air, work at high temperatures washing, cleaning, and pressing garments, often under very hot, slippery conditions. Chemical vapors are produced continually, and caustic chemicals are used in the cleaning process. High-temperature stills are almost continually "cooking down" cleaning solvents in order to remove impurities so that the solvents can be reused. If a mistake is made in this process—like injecting too much steam into the still—a boilover occurs, in which boiling chemical solvent erupts out of the still and over the floor, and on anyone who happens to be standing in its way.

As a result of these hazards and the fact that chemically hazardous waste is continually produced in these stores, several government agencies (including OSHA and the Environmental Protection Agency) have instituted strict guidelines regarding the management of these plants. For example, posters have to be placed in each store notifying employees of their right to be told what hazardous chemicals they are dealing with and what the proper method for handling each chemical is. Special waste-management firms must be used to pick up and properly dispose of the hazardous waste.

A chronic problem the Carters (and most other laundry owners) have is the unwillingness on the part of the cleaning/spotting workers to wear safety goggles. Not all the chemicals they use require safety goggles, but some—like the hydrofluoric acid used to remove rust stains from garments—are very dangerous. The latter is kept in special plastic containers, since it dissolves glass. The problem is that wearing safety goggles can be troublesome. They are somewhat uncomfortable, and they become smudged easily and thus cut down on visibility.

As a result, Jack has always found it almost impossible to get these employees to wear their goggles.

Questions

16-33. How should the firm go about identifying hazardous conditions that should be rectified? Use checklists such as those in Figures 16-6 and 16-9 to list at least 10 possible dry-cleaning store hazardous conditions.

16-34. Would it be advisable for the firm to set up a procedure for screening out accident-prone individuals? How should they do so?

16-35. How would you suggest the Carters get all employees to behave more safely at work? Also, how would you advise them to get those who should be wearing goggles to do so?

Translating Strategy into HR Policies and Practices Case*,§

**The accompanying strategy map for this chapter is in the MyManagementLab; and the overall map on the inside back cover of this text outlines the relationships involved.*

IMPROVING PERFORMANCE at The Hotel Paris

The New Safety and Health Program

The Hotel Paris's competitive strategy is "To use superior guest service to differentiate the Hotel Paris properties, and to thereby increase the length of stay and return rate of guests, and thus boost revenues and profitability." HR manager Lisa Cruz must now formulate functional policies and activities that support this competitive strategy and boost performance, by eliciting the required employee behaviors and competencies.

While "hazardous conditions" might not be the first thing that comes to mind when you think of hotels, Lisa Cruz knew that hazards and safety were in fact serious issues for the Hotel Paris. Indeed, everywhere you look—from the valets leaving car doors open on the driveways to slippery areas around the pools, to thousands of pounds of ammonia, chlorine, and other caustic chemicals that the hotels use each year for cleaning and laundry, hotels provide a fertile environment for accidents. Obviously, hazardous conditions are bad for the Hotel Paris. They are inhumane for the workers. High accident rates probably reduce employee morale and thus service. And accidents raise the company's costs and reduce its profitability, for instance in terms of workers' compensation claims and absences. Lisa knew that she had to clean up her firm's occupational safety and health systems, for its employees' well-being, and to achieve the company's strategic goals.

Lisa and the CFO reviewed their company's safety records, and what they found disturbed them deeply. In terms of every safety-related metric they could find, including accident costs per year, lost time due to accidents, workers' compensation per employee, and number of safety training programs per year, the Hotel Paris compared unfavorably with most other hotel chains and service firms. "Why, just in terms of extra workers' compensation costs, the Hotel Paris must be spending $500,000 a year more than we should be," said the CFO. And that didn't include lost time due to accidents, or the negative effect accidents had on employee morale, or the cost of litigation (as when, for instance, one guest accidentally burned himself with chlorine that a pool attendant had left unprotected). The CFO authorized Lisa to develop a new safety and health program.

Lisa and her team began by hiring a safety and health consultant, someone who had been an inspector and then manager with OSHA. Based on their analysis, the team then took numerous steps, including the following. First, specially trained teams consisting of someone from Lisa's HR group, the local hotel's assistant manager, and three local hotel employees went through each local hotel "with a fine tooth comb," as Lisa put it. They used an extensive checklist to identify and eliminate unsafe conditions.

Lisa's team took other steps. They convinced the Hotel Paris's board of directors and chairman and CEO to issue a joint statement emphasizing the importance of safety, and the CEO, during a one-month period, visited each hotel to meet with all employees and emphasize safety. The Hotel Paris also contracted with a safety training company. This firm created special online safety programs for the company's managers, and developed five-day training seminars for the hotels' staffs.

The new programs seem to be effective. Lisa and the CFO were pleased to find, after about a year, that accident costs per year, lost time due to accidents, and workers' compensation expenses were all down at least 40%. And anecdotal evidence from supervisors suggested that employees feel better about the company's commitment to them, and were providing better service as a result.

Questions

16-36. Based on what you read in this chapter, what's the first step you would have advised the Hotel Paris to take as part of its new safety and health program, and why?

16-37. List 10 specific high-risk areas in a typical hotel you believe Lisa and her team should look at now, including examples of the safety or health hazards that they should look for there.

16-38. Give three specific examples of how Hotel Paris can use HR practices to improve its safety efforts.

16-39. Write a one-page summary addressing the topic, "How improving safety and health at the Hotel Paris will contribute to us achieving our strategic goals."

CHAPTER 16

MyManagementLab

Go to **mymanagementlab.com** for Auto-graded writing questions as well as the following Assisted-graded writing questions:

16-40. Discuss the basic facts about OSHA—its purpose, standards, inspections, and rights and responsibilities.

16-41. Describe the steps employers can take to reduce workplace violence.

16-42. MyManagementLab only—comprehensive writing assignment for this chapter.

Key Terms

Occupational Safety and Health Act of 1970, 491
Occupational Safety and Health Administration (OSHA), 491
occupational illness, 492
citation, 494
unsafe conditions, 497
job hazard analysis, 498
operational safety reviews, 502
behavior-based safety, 506
safety awareness program, 506
burnout, 512

Endnotes

1. Figures for 2011. https://www.osha.gov/oshstats/commonstats.html, accessed August 8, 2013.
2. Figures for 2011. http://www.bls.gov/news.release/archives/osh_10252012.pdf, accessed April 18, 2013.
3. "BLS Likely Underestimating Injury and Illness Estimates," *Occupational Hazards*, May 2006, p. 16; Tahira Probst et al., "Organizational Injury Rate Underreporting: The Moderating Effect of Organizational Safety Climate," *Journal of Applied Psychology* 93, no. 5 (2008), pp. 1147–1154.
4. "Workers Rate Safety Most Important Workplace Issue," *EHS Today*, October 2010, p. 17.
5. www.osha.gov/dcsp/products/topics/businesscase/, accessed April 16, 2013.
6. Russell Sobel, "Occupational Safety and Profit Maximization: Friends or Foes?", *The Journal of Socioeconomics* 30, no. 9 (2010), pp. 429–433.
7. David Levine et al., "Randomized Government Safety Inspections Reduce Worker Injuries with No Detectable Job Loss," *Science* 336 (May 18, 2012), pp. 907–911.
8. Chief Financial Officer Survey, Liberty Mutual Insurance Co., 2005.
9. Mike Rich, "Preventing Hearing Loss," www.adhesivesmag.com, January 2012, pp. 40–41.
10. One study recently concluded that, "employee perceptions of the extent to which managers and supervisors are committed to workplace safety likely influence employee safety behavior and, subsequently, injuries." Jeremy Beus et al., "Safety Climate and Juries: An Examination of Theoretical and Empirical Relationships," *Journal of Applied Psychology* 95, no. 4 (2010), pp. 713–727.
11. Willie Hammer, *Occupational Safety Management and Engineering* (Upper Saddle River, NJ: Prentice Hall, 1985), pp. 62–63. See also "DuPont's 'STOP' Helps Prevent Workplace Injuries and Incidents," *Asia Africa Intelligence Wire*, May 17, 2004.
12. F. David Pierce, "Safety in the Emerging Leadership Paradigm," *Occupational Hazards*, June 2000, pp. 63–66. See also, for example, Josh Williams, "Optimizing the Safety Culture," *Occupational Hazards*, May 2008, pp. 45–49.
13. Sandy Smith, "Louisiana-Pacific Corp. Builds Safety into Everything It Does," *Occupational Hazards*, November 2007, pp. 41–42.
14. Sandy Smith, "ABB Inc. Relies on Leadership and Accountability for Safety Performance," *EHS Today*, November 2012, p. 38.
15. "Did This Supervisor Do Enough to Protect Trench Workers?" *Safety Compliance Letter*, October 2003, p. 9.
16. Ibid.
17. Based on "All About OSHA" (Washington, DC: U.S. Department of Labor, 1980), www.OSHA.gov, accessed January 19, 2008.
18. "OSHA Hazard Communication Standard Enforcement," *BNA Bulletin to Management*, February 23, 1989, p. 13. See also William Kincaid, "OSHA vs. Excellence in Safety Management," *Occupational Hazards*, December 2002, pp. 34–36. Flow diagram based on *What Every Employer Needs to Know About OSHA Recordkeeping* (Washington, DC: U.S. Department of Labor, 1978), p. 3.
19. *What Every Employer Needs to Know About OSHA Record Keeping*, U.S. Department of Labor, Bureau of Labor Statistics (Washington, DC), Report 412–3, p. 3.
20. Arthur Sapper and Robert Gombar, "Nagging Problems Under OSHA's New Record-Keeping Rule," *Occupational Hazards*, March 2002, p. 58.
21. Brian Jackson and Jeffrey Myers, "Just When You Thought You Were Safe: OSHA Record-Keeping Violations," *Management Review*, May 1994, pp. 62–63; www.osha.gov/recordkeeping/index.html, accessed October 26, 2011.
22. "Supreme Court Says OSHA Inspectors Need Warrants," *Engineering News Record*, June 1, 1978, pp. 9–10; W. Scott Railton, "OSHA Gets Tough on Business," *Management Review* 80, no. 12 (December 1991), pp. 28–29; Steve Hollingsworth, "How to Survive an OSHA Inspection," *Occupational Hazards*, March 2004, pp. 31–33.
23. http://osha.gov/as/opa/oshafacts.html, accessed January 19, 2008; Edwin Foulke Jr., "OSHA's Evolving Role in Promoting Occupational Safety and Health," *EHS Today*, November 2008, pp. 44–49; https://www.osha.gov/dcsp/compliance_assistance/index_programs.html, accessed August 8, 2013.
24. www.osha.gov/Publications/osha2098.pdf+OSHA+inspection+priorities&hl=en&ct=clnk&cd=1&gl=us, accessed January 19, 2008.
25. http://www.osha.gov/oshstats/commonstats.html, accessed April 18, 2013.
26. See "Site-Specific Targeting Program Letters Mailed to High Injury/Illness Rate Employers," *BNA Bulletin to Management*, April 10, 2012, p. 113.
27. This section is based on "All About OSHA," pp. 23–25. See also "OSHA Final Rule Expands Employees' Role in Consultations, Protects Employer Records," *BNA Bulletin to Management*, November 2, 2000, p. 345.
28. D. Diane Hatch and James Hall, "A Flurry of New Federal Regulations," *Workforce*, February 2001, p. 98.
29. www.osha.gov/dcsp/compliance_assistance/frequent_standards.html, accessed May 28, 2012.
30. It was not until July 12, 2012, that British Petroleum and the U.S. government agreed on $13 million in OSHA fines and resolving outstanding citations against the company for the Texas City explosion. "BP to Pay $13 Million in OSHA Penalties," *EHS Today*, August 2012, p. 12.
31. www.osha.gov/Publications/osha2098.pdf+OSHA+inspection+priorities&hl=en&ct=clnk&cd=1&gl=us, accessed January 19, 2008.
32. "Enforcement Activity Increased in 1997," *BNA Bulletin to Management*, January 29, 1998, p. 28. See also www.osha.gov/as/opa/osha-faq.html, accessed May 26, 2007.
33. "Enforcement Activity Increased."
34. For a discussion of how to deal with citations and proposed penalties, see, for example, Michael Taylor, "OSHA Citations and Proposed Penalties: How to Beat the Rap," *EHS Today*, December 2008, pp. 34–36.
35. Employers with high injury rates may also be subject to additional monitoring. For example, OSHA recently sent about 15,000 letters to employers telling them that their injury and illness rates were much higher than the national average. ("OSHA Sends 15,000 Letters to Employers with High Injury Rates and Offers Assistance," *BNA Bulletin to Management*, March 16, 2010, p. 83.
36. Knowing OSHA's rules is not enough. The employer should develop and communicate its own written safety and health rules to employees, monitor violations, and discipline employees who violate the rules. Michael Taylor, "OSHA Compliance Mistakes," *EHS Today*, July 2012, pp. 29–31.
37. "New OSHA Enforcement Memo Target Safety Incentive Programs, Retaliation," *BNA Bulletin to Management*, March 27, 2012, p. 99.
38. Arthur Sapper, "The Oft-Missed Step: Documentation of Safety Discipline," *Occupational Hazards*, January 2006, p. 59.
39. Sean Smith, "OSHA Resources Can Help Small Businesses with Hazards," *Westchester County Business Journal*, August 4, 2003, p. 4.
40. "A Safety Committee Man's Guide," Aetna Life and Casualty Insurance Company, Catalog 87684. See also Dan Petersen, "The Barriers to Safety Excellence," *Occupational Hazards*, December 2000, pp. 37–39.
41. "Did This Supervisor Do Enough to Protect Trench Workers?" *Safety Compliance Letter*, October 2003, p. 9.
42. "The Dawning of a New Era," *Workforce Management*, December 2010, p. 3.
43. For a discussion of this, see David Hofmann and Adam Stetzer, "A Cross-Level Investigation of Factors Influencing Unsafe Behaviors and Accidents," *Personnel Psychology* 49 (1996), pp. 307–308. See also David Hofman and Barbara Mark, "An Investigation of the

Relationship Between Safety Climate and Medication Errors as Well as Other Nurse and Patient Outcomes," *Personnel Psychology* 50, no. 9 (2006), pp. 847–869.

44. Duane Schultz and Sydney Schultz, *Psychology and Work Today* (Upper Saddle River, NJ: Prentice Hall, 2002), p. 332.
45. Robert Pater and Robert Russell, "Drop That 'Accident Prone' Tag: Look for Causes Beyond Personal Issues," *Industrial Safety and Hygiene News* 38, no. 1 (January 2004), p. 50, http://findarticles.com/p/articles/mi_hb5992/is_200401/ai_n24195869/, accessed August 11, 2009.
46. Discussed in Douglas Haaland, "Who's the Safest Bet for the Job? Find Out Why the Fun Guy in the Next Cubicle May Be the Next Accident Waiting to Happen," *Security Management* 49, no. 2 (February 2005), pp. 51–57.
47. "Thai Research Points to Role of Personality in Road Accidents," www.driveandstayalive.com/info%20section/news/individual%20news%20articles/x_050204_personality-in-crash-causation_thailand.htm, February 2, 2005, accessed August 11, 2009; Donald Bashline et al., "Bad Behavior: Personality Tests Can Help Underwriters Identify High-Risk Drivers," *Best's Review* 105, no. 12 (April 2005), pp. 63–64.
48. Todd Nighswonger, "Threat of Terror Impacts Workplace Safety," *Occupational Hazards*, July 2002, pp. 24–26.
49. Michael Blotzer, "Safety by Design," *Occupational Hazards*, May 1999, pp. 39–40; and www.designsafe.com/dsesoftware.php, accessed May 26, 2007.
50. Susannah Figura, "Don't Slip Up on Safety," *Occupational Hazards*, November 1996, pp. 29–31. See also Russ Wood, "Defining the Boundaries of Safety," *Occupational Hazards*, January 2001, pp. 41–43.
51. See, for example, Laura Walter, "What's in a Glove?" *Occupational Hazards*, May 2008, pp. 35–36.
52. Donald Groce, "Keep the Gloves On!" *Occupational Hazards*, June 2008, pp. 45–47.
53. www.osha.gov/Publications/osha3071.pdf, accessed April 21, 2011.
54. www-ns.iaea.org/reviews/op-safety-reviews.asp, accessed April 21, 2011.
55. For example, when asked what accounted for injuries such as cuts and lacerations, contusions, and chemical exposure at their facilities, most employees concluded either that workers were not wearing the proper protective equipment or had been given the wrong protection for the task. Brian Perry, "Don't Invite an OSHA Citation with Lower Quality PPE," *EHS Today*, January 2011, p. 23.
56. James Zeigler, "Protective Clothing: Exploring the Wearability Issue," *Occupational Hazards*, September 2000, pp. 81–82. See also Judy Smithers, "Use OSHA's Compliance Directive to evaluate Your PPE Program," *EHS Today*, January 2012, pp. 43–45.
57. Sandy Smith, "Protective Clothing and the Quest for Improved Performance," *Occupational Hazards*, February 2008, pp. 63–66. Note that the vast array of available personal protective equipment makes choosing the appropriate equipment what one expert calls "complex and sometimes confusing." See Scott Larsen, "Integrated Use of Personal Protective Equipment," *EHS Today*, June 2012, p. 31.
58. Tim Andrews, "Getting Employees Comfortable with PPE," *Occupational Hazards*, January 2000, pp. 35–38. Note that personal protective equipment can backfire. As one expert says, "Making a job safer with machine guards or PPE lowers people's risk perceptions and thus can lead to an increase in at-risk behavior." Therefore, also train employees not to let their guard down. E. Scott Geller, "The Thinking and Seeing Components of People-Based Safety," *Occupational Hazards*, December 2006, pp. 38–40.
59. Laura Walter, "FR Clothing: Leaving Hazards in the Dust," *EHS Today*, January 2010, pp. 20–22.
60. "The Complete Guide to Personal Protective Equipment," *Occupational Hazards*, January 1999, pp. 49–60. See also Edwin Zalewski, "Noise Control: It's More Than Just Earplugs: OSHA Requires Employers to Evaluate Engineering and Administrative Controls Before Using Personal Protective Equipment," *Occupational Hazards* 68, no. 9 (September 2006), p. 48(3). You can find videos about personal protective products at "SafetyLive TV" at www.occupationalhazards.com, accessed March 14, 2009.
61. Sandy Smith, "Protecting Vulnerable Workers," *Occupational Hazards*, April 2004, pp. 25–28.
62. Katherine Torres, "Challenges in Protecting a Young Workforce," *Occupational Hazards*, May 2006, pp. 24–27.
63. J. P. Sankpill, "A Clear Vision for Eye and Face Protection," *EHS Today*, November 2010, p. 29.
64. See, for instance, Laura Walter, "Training the Older Worker," *EHS Today*, February 2011, p. 39.
65. Robert Pater, "Boosting Safety with an Aging Workforce," *Occupational Hazards*, March 2006, p. 24.
66. Michael Silverstein, M.D., "Designing the Age Friendly Workplace," *Occupational Hazards*, December 2007, pp. 29–31.
67. Elizabeth Rogers and William Wiatrowski, "Injuries, Illnesses, and Fatalities Among Older Workers," *Monthly Labor Review* 128, no. 10 (October 2005), pp. 24–30.
68. "Cell Phone Use Contributes to 24% of Crashes," *EHS Today*, May 2012, p. 22.
69. "DOT Final Rule Bans Cell Phone Use by Commercial Bus Drivers, Truckers," *BNA Bulletin to Management*, December 6, 2011, p. 387.
70. Robert Pater and Ron Bowles, "Directing Attention to Boost Safety Performance," *Occupational Hazards*, March 2007, pp. 46–48.
71. E. Scott Geller, "The Thinking and Seeing Components of People-Based Safety," *Occupational Hazards*, December 2006, pp. 38–40.
72. Gerald Borofsky, Michelle Bielema, and James Hoffman, "Accidents, Turnover, and the Use of a Preemployment Screening Inventory: Further Contributions to the Validation of the Employee Reliability Inventory," *Psychological Reports*, 1993, pp. 1067–1076; www.ramsaycorp.com/catalog/view/?productid=208, accessed October 26, 2011.
73. Ibid., p. 1072. See also Keith Rosenblum, "The Companion Solution to Ergonomics: Pretesting for the Job," *Risk Management* 50, no 11 (November 2003), p. 26(6).
74. Dan Hartshorn, "The Safety Interview," *Occupational Hazards*, October 1999, pp. 107–111.
75. John Rekus, "Is Your Safety Training Program Effective?" *Occupational Hazards*, August 1999, pp. 37–39; see also www.osha.gov/Publications/osha2254.pdf, accessed October 25, 2011.
76. Laura Walter, "Surfing for Safety," *Occupational Hazards*, July 2008, pp. 23–29.
77. Michael Burke et al., "The Dread Factor: How Hazards and Safety Training Influence Learning and Performance," *Journal of Applied Psychology* 96, no. 1 (2011), pp. 46–70.
78. See, for example, Ron Bruce, "Online from Kazakhstan to California," *Occupational Hazards*, June 2008, pp. 61–65.
79. Michael Blotzer, "PDA Software Offers Auditing Advances," *Occupational Hazards*, December 2001, p. 11. See also Erik Andersen "Automating Health & Safety Processes Creates Value," *Occupational Hazards*, April 2008, pp. 53–63.
80. Dave Zielinski, "Putting Safety Training Online," *HR Magazine*, January 2013, p. 51.
81. In a survey of about 2,600 employees, roughly one-fourth said they would not intervene if they saw a coworker acting unsafely, for fear the coworker would be defensive or angry. Phillip Ragain et al., "The Causes and Consequences of Employees' Silence," *EHS Today*, July 2011, pp. 36–38.
82. Jack Rubinger, "Signs, Labels and Lighting for a Safe and Productive Workplace," *EHS Today*, October 2012, p. 67.
83. See, for example, Cable, "Seven Suggestions for a Successful Safety Incentive Program." See also J. M. Saidler, "Gift Cards Make Safety Motivation Simple," *Occupational Health & Safety* 78, no. 1 (January 2009), pp. 39–40.
84. Don Williamson and Jon Kauffman, "From Tragedy to Triumph: Safety Grows Wings at Golden Eagle," *Occupational Hazards*, February 2006, pp. 17–25; and www.tsocorp.com/TSOCorp/SocialResponsibility/HealthandSafety/HealthandSafety, accessed June 30, 2011.
85. "Are Traditional Incentive Programs Illegal?" *EHS Today*, April 2012, p. 12. See also Howard Mavity, "OSHA: Don't Get Caught in the Trap of Rewarding Employees for Reducing Recordables!", *EHS Today*, September 2012, pp. 39–41; and James Stanley, "OSHA's Warning on Safety Incentive Programs Are Wide of the Mark," *EHS Today*, October 2012, p. 63.
86. James Nash, "Construction Safety: Best Practices in Training Hispanic Workers," *Occupational Hazards*, February 2004, pp. 35–38.
87. Ibid., p. 37.
88. Judi Komaki, Kenneth Barwick, and Lawrence Scott, "A Behavioral Approach to Occupational Safety: Pinpointing and Reinforcing Safe Performance in a Food Manufacturing Plant," *Journal of Applied Psychology* 63 (August 1978), pp. 434–445. See also Anat Arkin, "Incentives to Work Safely," *Personnel Management* 26, no. 9 (September 1994), pp. 48–52; Peter Makin and Valerie Sutherland, "Reducing Accidents Using a Behavioral Approach," *Leadership and*

Organizational Development Journal 15, no. 5 (1994), pp. 5–10; Sandy Smith, "Why Cash Isn't King," *Occupational Hazards*, March 2004, pp. 37–38.

89. Dov Zohar, "A Group Level Model of Safety Climate: Testing the Effect of a Group Climate on Students in Manufacturing Jobs," *Journal of Applied Psychology* 85, no. 4 (2000), pp. 587–596. See also Steven Yule, Rhona Flin, and Andy Murdy, "The Role of Management and Safety Climate in Preventing Risk-Taking at Work," *International Journal of Risk Assessment and Management* 7, no. 2 (December 20, 2006), p. 137; and Judy Agnew, "Building the Foundation for a Sustainable Safety Culture," *EHS Today*, February 2013, pp. 41–43.
90. Quoted from Sandy Smith, "Breakthrough Safety Management," *Occupational Hazards*, June 2004, p. 43. For a discussion of developing a safety climate survey, see also Sara Singer et al., "Workforce Perceptions of Hospital Safety Culture: Development and Validation of the Patient Safety Climate in Healthcare Organizations Survey," *Health Services Research* 42, no. 5 (October 2007), pp. 19–23.
91. "Encourage Incident Reporting to Improve Safety Culture," *EHS Today*, December 2012, p. 16.
92. Jennifer Nahrgang et al., "Safety at Work: A Meta-Analytic Investigation of the Link Between Job Demands, Job Resources, Burnout, Engagement, and Safety Outcomes," *Journal of Applied Psychology* 96, no. 1 (2011), p. 86.
93. Stan Hodson and Tim Gordon, "Tenneco's Drive to Become Injury Free," *Occupational Hazards*, May 2000, pp. 85–87. For another example, see Terry Mathis, "Lean Behavior-Based Safety," *Occupational Hazards*, May 2005, pp. 33–34.
94. Tim McDaniel, "Employee Participation: A Vehicle for Safety by Design," *Occupational Hazards*, May 2002, pp. 71–76.
95. For another good example, see Christopher Chapman, "Using Kaizen to Improve Safety and Ergonomics," *Occupational Hazards*, February 2006, pp. 27–29.
96. Lisa Cullen, "Safety Committees: A Smart Business Decision," *Occupational Hazards*, May 1999, pp. 99–104. See also www.osha.gov/Publications/osha2098.pdf, accessed May 26, 2007; and D. Kolman, "Effective Safety Committees," *Beverage Industry* 100, no. 3 (March 2009), pp. 63–65.
97. www.aihaaps.ca/palm/occhazards.html, accessed April 26, 2009.
98. Michael Blotzer, "PDA Software Offers Auditing Advances," *Occupational Hazards*, December 2001, p. 11.
99. John Garber, "Introduction to the Human Resource Discipline of Safety and Security," www.shrm.org/templates_tools/toolkits, accessed May 27, 2012.
100. Mike Powell, "Sustaining Your Safety Sweep Audit Process," *EHS Today*, December 2012, pp. 35–36.
101. Note that the vast majority of workers' injury-related deaths occur not at work, but when the employees are off the job, often at home. More employers, including Johnson & Johnson, are therefore implementing safety campaigns encouraging employees to apply safe practices at home, as well as at work. Katherine Torres, "Safety Hits Home," *Occupational Hazards*, July 2006, pp. 19–23.
102. S. L. Smith, "Sadaf Drives for Safety Excellence," *Occupational Hazards*, November 1998, p. 41. For further discussion, see also Kathy Seabrook, "10 Strategies for Global Safety Management," *Occupational Hazards*, June 1999, pp. 41–43.
103. Michele Campolieti and Douglas Hyatt, "Further Evidence on the 'Monday Effect' in Workers' Compensation," *Industrial and Labor Relations Review* 59, no. 3 (April 2006), pp. 438–450.
104. See, for example, Rob Wilson, "Five Ways to Reduce Workers' Compensation Claims," *Occupational Hazards*, December 2005, pp. 43–46.
105. "Strict Policies Mean Big Cuts in Premiums," *Occupational Hazards*, May 2000, p. 51.
106. Donna Clendenning, "Taking a Bite Out of Workers' Comp Costs," *Occupational Hazards*, September 2000, pp. 85–86.
107. This is based on Paul Puncochar, "The Science and Art to Identifying Workplace Hazards," *Occupational Hazards*, September 2003, pp. 50–54.
108. Ibid., p. 52.
109. "Hazard Communication," www.OSHA.gov/dsg/hazcom/index.HTML, accessed May 26, 2012.
110. Garber, "Introduction to the Human Resource Discipline of Safety and Security."
111. Gareth Evans, "Wireless Monitoring for a Safe Indoor Environment," *EHS Today*, December 2010, pp. 35–39.
112. Based on the report "Workplace Screening and Brief Intervention: What Employers Can and Should Do About Excessive Alcohol Use," www.ensuringsolutions.org/resources/resources_show.htm?doc_id=673239, accessed August 11, 2009.
113. "Employers Can Play Key Role in Preventing Painkiller Abuse, but Many Remain Reluctant," *BNA Bulletin to Management*, February 15, 2011, p. 49.
114. "15% of Workers Drinking, Drunk, or Hungover While at Work, According to New University Study," *BNA Bulletin to Management*, January 24, 2006, p. 27.
115. Samuel Bacharach et al., "Alcohol Consumption and Workplace Absenteeism: The Moderating Effect of Social Support," *Journal of Applied Psychology* 95, no. 2 (2010), pp. 334–348.
116. See, for example, L. Claussen, "Can You Spot the Meth Addict?" *Safety & Health* 179, no. 4 (April 2009), pp. 48–52.
117. "New Jersey Union Takes on Mandatory Random Drug Tests," *Record* (Hackensack, NJ), January 2, 2008.
118. www.dol.gov/asp/programs/drugs/workingpartners/sab/screen.asp, accessed April 27, 2008.
119. Gopal Pati and John Adkins Jr., "The Employer's Role in Alcoholism Assistance," *Personnel Journal* 62, no. 7 (July 1983), p. 570. See also Commerce Clearing House, "How Should Employers Respond to Indications an Employee May Have an Alcohol or Drug Problem?" *Ideas and Trends*, April 6, 1989, pp. 53–57; "The Employer's Role in Alcoholism Assistance," *Personnel Journal* 62, no. 7 (July 1983), pp. 568–572.
120. William Current, "Pre-Employment Drug Testing," *Occupational Hazards*, July 2002, p. 56. See also William Current, "Improving Your Drug Testing ROI," *Occupational Health & Safety* 73, no. 4 (April 2004), pp. 40, 42, 44.
121. William Current, "Pre-Employment Drug Testing," *Occupational Hazards*, July 2002, p. 56. See also William Current, "Improving Your Drug Testing ROI," *Occupational Health & Safety* 73, no. 4 (April 2004), pp. 40, 42, 44.
122. Diane Cadrain, "Are Your Employees' Drug Tests Accurate?" *HR Magazine*, January 2003, pp. 41–45.
123. Roberts, "Random Drug Testing Can Help Reduce Accidents for Construction Companies," p. 6.
124. Frank Lockwood et al., "Drug Testing Programs and Their Impact on Workplace Accidents: A Time Series Analysis," *Journal of Individual Employment Rights* 8, no. 4 (2000), pp. 295–306; and Sally Roberts, "Random Drug Testing Can Help Reduce Accidents for Construction Companies; Drug Abuse Blamed for Heightened Risk in the Workplace," *Business Insurance* 40 (October 23, 2006), p. 6.
125. Beth Andrus, "Accommodating the Alcoholic Executive," *Society for Human Resource Management Legal Report*, January 2008, pp. 1, 4.
126. Eric Sundstrom et al., "Office Noise, Satisfaction, and Performance," *Environment and Behavior*, no. 2 (March 1994), pp. 195–222; and "Stress: How to Cope with Life's Challenges," *American Family Physician* 74, no. 8 (October 15, 2006).
127. "Failing to Tackle Stress Could Cost You Dearly," *Personnel Today*, September 12, 2006; www.sciencedaily.com/releases/2007/06/070604170722.htm, accessed November 3, 2009.
128. Tara Parker-Pope, "Time to Review Workplace Reviews?" *The New York Times*, May 18, 2010, p. D5.
129. "Drug-Free Workplace: New Federal Requirements," *BNA Bulletin to Management*, February 9, 1989, pp. 1–4. Note that the Drug-Free Workplace Act does not mandate or mention testing employees for illegal drug use. See also www.dol.gov/elaws/drugfree.htm and www.dot.gov/ost/dapc (this site contains detailed guidelines on urine sampling, who's covered, etc.), both accessed May 26, 2007.
130. "Few Employers Addressing Workplace Stress, Watson Wyatt Surveys Find," *Compensation & Benefits Review*, May/June 2008, p. 12.
131. See, for example, Elizabeth Bernstein, "When a Coworker Is Stressed Out," *The Wall Street Journal*, August 26, 2008, pp. B1, B2.
132. Karl Albrecht, *Stress and the Manager* (Englewood Cliffs, NJ: Spectrum, 1979). For a discussion of the related symptoms of depression, see James Krohe Jr., "An Epidemic of Depression?" *Across-the-Board*, September 1994, pp. 23–27; and Todd Nighswonger, "Stress Management," *Occupational Hazards*, September 1999, p. 100.
133. Sabine Sonnentag et al., "'Did You Have a Nice Evening?' A Day-Level Study on Recovery Experiences, Sleep, and Affect," *Journal of Applied Psychology* 93, no. 3 (2008), pp. 674–684.
134. "Meditation Gives Your Mind Permanent Working Holiday; Relaxation Can Improve Your Business Decisions and Your Overall Health," discussed in *Investors Business Daily*,

March 24, 2004, p. 89. See also "Meditation Helps Employees Focus, Relieve Stress," *BNA Bulletin to Management*, February 20, 2007, p. 63.

135. Kathryn Tyler, "Stress Management," *HR Magazine*, September 2006, pp. 79–82.
136. William Atkinson, "Turning Stress into Strength," *HR Magazine*, January 2011, p. 51.
137. "Going Head to Head with Stress," *Personnel Today*, April 26, 2005, p. 1.
138. See, for example, Christina Maslach and Michael Leiter, "Early Predictors of Job Burnout and Engagement," *Journal of Applied Psychology* 93, no. 3 (2008), pp. 498–512.
139. Christina Maslach and Michael Leiter, "Early Predictors of Job Burnout and Engagement," *Journal of Applied Psychology* 93, no. 3 (2008), pp. 498–512.
140. Sharon Toker and Michael Biron, "Job Burnout and Depression: Unraveling Their Temporal Relationship and Considering the Role of Physical Activity," *Journal of Applied Psychology* 97, no. 3 (2012), p. 699.
141. Sabine Sonnentag et al., "Staying Well and Engaged When Demands Are High: The Role of Psychological Detachment," *Journal of Applied Psychology* 95, no. 5 (2010), pp. 965–976.
142. Todd Nighswonger, "Depression: The Unseen Safety Risk," *Occupational Hazards*, April 2002, pp. 38–42.
143. Ibid., p. 40.
144. "Employers Must Move from Awareness to Action in Dealing with Worker Depression," *BNA Bulletin to Management*, April 29, 2004, p. 137.
145. See, for example, Felix Chima, "Depression and the Workplace: Occupational Social Work Development and Intervention," *Employee Assistance Quarterly* 19, no. 4 (2004), pp. 1–20.
146. Ibid.
147. www.OSHA.gov, downloaded May 28, 2005.
148. Anne Chambers, "Computer Vision Syndrome: Relief Is In Sight," *Occupational Hazards*, October 1999, pp. 179–184; and www.OSHA.gov/ETOOLS/computerworkstations/index.html, downloaded May 28, 2005.
149. Sandra Lotz Fisher, "Are Your Employees Working Ergosmart?," *Personnel Journal*, December 1996, pp. 91–92. See also www.cdc.gov/od/ohs/Ergonomics/compergo.htm, accessed May 26, 2007.
150. www.ninds.nih.gov/disorders/repetitive_motion/repetitive_motion.htm, accessed February 28, 2010.
151. Sandy Smith, "SARS: What Employers Need to Know," *Occupational Hazards*, July 2003, pp. 33–35.
152. "CDC Recommends Respirators in Revised H1N1 Flu Guidance for Healthcare Workers," *BNA Bulletin to Management*, October 20, 2009, pp. 329–336; Pamela Ferrante, "H1N1: Spreading the Message," *EHS Today*, January 2010, pp. 25–27.
153. Ronald Davis, "Exposure to Environmental Tobacco Smoke: Identifying and Protecting Those at Risk," *Journal of the American Medical Association*, December 9, 1998, pp. 147–148; see also Al Karr, "Lighting Up," *Safety and Health* 162, no. 3 (September 2000), pp. 62–66.
154. However, note that some experts believe that in some circumstances the EEOC might see a smoking addiction as similar to use of illegal drugs, and thus possibly covered by the ADA. "Policies to Not Hire Smokers Raise Privacy, Bias Issues," *BNA Bulletin to Management*, December 14, 2010, p. 399.
155. Joan Deschenauxh, "Is a 'Smoker–Free' Workplace Right for You? *HR Magazine*, July 2011, pp. 43–45.
156. Steve Bates, "Where There Is Smoke, There Are Terminations: Smokers Fired to Save Health Costs," *HR Magazine* 50, no. 3 (March 2005), pp. 28–29.
157. Garber, "Introduction to the Human Resource Discipline of Safety and Security."
158. Ibid.
159. This is based on "New Challenges for Health and Safety in the Workplace," *Workplace Visions* (Society for Human Resource Management), no. 3 (2003), pp. 2–4. See also J. L. Nash, "Protecting Chemical Plants from Terrorists: Opposing Views," *Occupational Hazards*, February 2004, pp. 18–20.
160. "Survey Finds Reaction to September 11 Attacks Spurred Companies to Prepare for Disasters," *BNA Bulletin to Management*, November 29, 2005, p. 377.
161. John Garber, "Introduction to the Human Resource Discipline of Safety and Security," www.shrm.org/templates_tools/toolkits, accessed May 27, 2012.
162. "Study: Don't Silo Human Capital Risk," www.shrm.org/hrdisciplines/ethics/articles, accessed May 27, 2012.
163. Robert Kaplan and Anette Mikes, "Managing Risks: A New Framework," *Harvard Business Review*, June 2012, pp. 48–60.
164. "Workplace Violence Takes a Deadly Toll," *EHS Today*, December 2009, p. 17.
165. "Violence in Workplace Soaring, New Study Says," *Baltimore Business Journal* 18, no. 34 (January 5, 2001), p. 24.
166. "Bullies Trigger 'Silent Epidemic' at Work, but Legal Cures Remain Hard to Come By," *BNA Bulletin to Management*, February 24, 2000, p. 57.
167. Jerry Hoobler and Jennifer Swanberg, "The Enemy Is Not Us," *International Personnel Management Association for HR* 35, no. 3 (Fall 2006), pp. 229–246.
168. www.cdc.gov/ncipc/dvp/ipv_factsheet.pdf, accessed August 8, 2013.
169. Ibid.
170. Paul Viollis and Doug Kane, "At-Risk Terminations: Protecting Employees, Preventing Disaster," *Risk Management Magazine* 52, no. 5 (May 2005), pp. 28–33.
171. M. Sandy Hershcovis et al., "Predicting Workplace Aggression: A Meta-Analysis," *Journal of Applied Psychology* 92, no. 1 (2007), pp. 228–238.
172. Alfred Feliu, "Workplace Violence and the Duty of Care: The Scope of an Employer's Obligation to Protect Against the Violent Employee," *Employee Relations Law Journal* 20, no. 3 (Winter 1994/95), p. 395.
173. Dawn Anfuso, "Deflecting Workplace Violence," *Personnel Journal*, October 1994, pp. 66–77.
174. Feliu, "Workplace Violence and the Duty of Care," p. 395.
175. See, for example, James Thelan, "Is That a Threat?" *HR Magazine*, December 2009, pp. 61–63.
176. Feliu, "Workplace Violence and the Duty of Care."
177. Ibid., pp. 401–402.
178. "Employers Battling Workplace Violence Might Consider Postal Service Plan," *BNA Bulletin to Management*, August 5, 1999, p. 241.
179. Viollis and Kane, "At-Risk Terminations," pp. 28–33.
180. Kenneth Diamond, "The Gender-Motivated Violence Act: What Employers Should Know," *Employee Relations Law Journal* 25, no. 4 (Spring 2000), pp. 29–41; "Bush Signs 'Violence Against Women Act'; Funding Badly Needed Initiatives to Prevent Domestic & Sexual Violence, Help Victims," *The America's Intelligence Wire*, January 5, 2006.
181. Unless otherwise noted, the following including the six matters to address is based on Richard Maurer, "Keeping Your Security Program Active," *Occupational Hazards*, March 2003, pp. 49–52.
182. Ibid.
183. http://view.fdu.edu/default.aspx?id=3705, accessed February 28, 2010.
184. Maurer, "Keeping Your Security Program Active," p. 50.
185. Ibid.
186. Bill Roberts, "Are You Ready for Biometrics?" *HR Magazine*, March 2003, pp. 95–99.

187. Maurer, "Keeping Your Security Program Active," p. 52.
188. "Focus on Corporate Security," *BNA HR Executive Series*, Fall 2001, p. 4.
189. Ibid.
190. Louis Obdyke, "Investigating Security Breaches, Workplace Theft, and Employee Fraud," *Society for Human Resource Management Legal Report*, January/February 2003, pp. 1–2.
191. Craig Schroll, "Evacuation Planning: A Matter of Life and Death," *Occupational Hazards*, June 2002, pp. 49–51. See also "Thorough Preparation for Natural Disasters Is Most Effective Way to Reduce Risks, Costs," *BNA Bulletin to Management*, November 20, 2012, p. 369.
192. Sandy Smith, "Are You Prepared?" *EHS Today*, March 2012, pp. 33–36.
193. Maurer, "Keeping Your Security Program Active," p. 52; Li Yuan et al., "Texting When There's Trouble," *The Wall Street Journal*, April 18, 2007, p. B1.
194. *PR Newswire*, April 2, 2013 pNA; "Get Tips on Using Social Media for Disaster Recovery." *The Public Manager* 42, no. 1 (Spring 2013), p. 35(3); *Joseph Porcelli* "How FEMA Drove 23,000 People to Join its Online Community," *The America's Intelligence Wire*, Oct 28, 2012 pNA; "Officials Take to Social Media to Share Emergency Information: Canadians Tapped into Social Networks, Expect Emergency Responders to Use Social Media: New Red Cross Survey," *CNW Group*, Oct 9, 2012 pNA.
195. "Swine Flu Tests Employer Emergency Plan; Experts Urge Communicating Best Practices," *BNA Bulletin to Management*, May 5, 2009, pp. 137–144.
196. Sandy Devine, "Are You Ready for a Sudden Cardiac Arrest Emergency?" *EHS Today*, April 2009, pp. 26–29.
197. "Business Continuity: What Is the Best Way to Plan for Disasters That May Affect Our Business, Like the Gulf Oil Spill?", www.shrm.org/templates_tools, accessed May 27, 2012.
198. See also Shari Lau, "Terrorist Screening, Bonus Pay, Labor Department Audits," *HR Magazine*, October 2012, page 28
199. Lloyd Newman, "Terrorism: Is Your Company Prepared?" *Business and Economic Review* 48, no. 2 (February 2002), pp. 7–10; Yuan et al., "Texting When There's Trouble," p. B1.

17

Managing Global Human Resources

Source: ChinaFotoPress/Getty Images

MyManagementLab®

Improve Your Grade!

When you see this icon, visit **www.mymanagementlab.com** for activities that are applied, personalized, and offer immediate feedback.

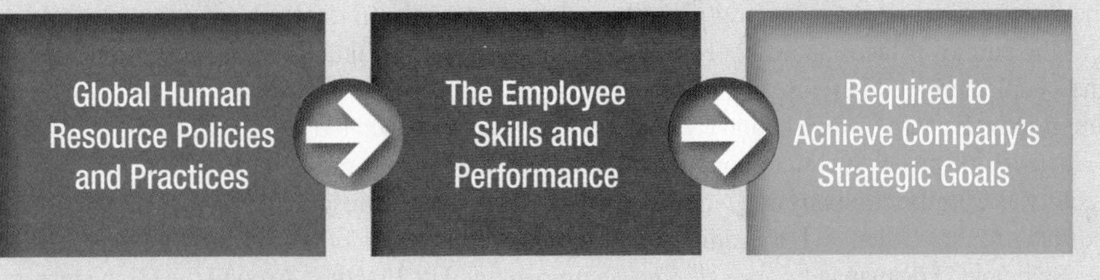

For a bird's eye view of how one company created a global HR program to improve its strategic performance, read the Hotel Paris case on page 554 and answer the questions after reading the chapter.

WHERE ARE WE NOW . . .

More managers today find themselves managing people internationally. The purpose of this chapter is to improve your effectiveness at applying your human resource knowledge and skills when global issues are involved. The topics we'll discuss include the manager's global challenge; adapting human resource activities to intercountry differences; staffing the global organization; training and maintaining employees abroad; and managing HR locally: how to put into practice a global HR system.

LEARNING OBJECTIVES

1 List the HR challenges of international business.

2 Illustrate with examples how intercountry differences affect HRM.

3 List and briefly describe the main methods for staffing global organizations.

4 Discuss some important issues to keep in mind in training, appraising, and compensating international employees.

5 Explain with examples how to implement a global human resource management program.

Walmart Stores, always resistant to unions, had a surprise in China. Opening stores there at a fast clip, it tried to dissuade the local unions from organizing Walmart employees. However, the All China Federation of Trade Unions (ACFTU), with strong government backing, quickly established itself in several Walmart stores. Walmart's strategy has long embraced avoiding unions as one means of reducing costs, so the company was vigorously resisting.[1] We'll see what happened.

The Manager's Global Challenge

1 List the HR challenges of international business.

The challenging thing about managing globally is that what works in one country may not work in another. The employer faces an array of political, social, legal, and cultural differences among countries and people abroad. Therefore, for instance, an incentive plan may work in the United States, but backfire in some Eastern Europe country where workers need a predictable weekly wage to buy necessities. However in spite of such intercountry differences, the employer must create, for each country's local facility and for the company as a whole, a workable set of human resource policies and practices.[2] Distance adds to the challenge. For example, how should Starbucks' chief HR officer, based in Seattle, monitor Starbucks' HR managers abroad? The accompanying HR Practices Around the Globe feature shows how Walmart's HR strategy collided with intercountry differences, in this case in China.

IMPROVING PERFORMANCE: HR Practices Around the Globe

Unionizing Walmart Stores in China

Walmart Stores is retailing's low-cost leader, and avoiding unions is one of its main tactics for keeping costs down and profits up. With more than 2.1 million employees,[3] Walmart wants to keep a tight reign on employee staffing, performance, wages, and benefits. Unions probably would drive up Walmart's labor costs, and impede its ability to make personnel changes.

With its powerful government-backed All China Federation of Trade Unions, China's cultural, political, and labor relations and legal systems are a world away from what Walmart dealt with in America. Not surprisingly, therefore, several years ago the first Walmart China union formed, followed by unions in the firm's other China stores.[4] Walmart China soon experienced the difference unions can make. The company offered three options—transfers to outlets in other cities, demotions, or leaving the company—to 54 local managers it wanted to transfer.[5] Not wanting to change, the China managers sprang into action. One led 11 colleagues to the local union for assistance. Whatever the managers did, it worked. Walmart apparently halted its planned reshuffle. Walmart would definitely have to revise its HR strategy for China, with consequences for its labor costs and pricing and profits.

Discussion Question 17-1: What other non-union surprises do you think Walmart should be planning its HR practices for in China?

What Is International Human Resource Management?

international human resource management (IHRM)
The human resource management concepts and techniques employers use to manage the human resource challenges of their international operations.

Employers rely on **international human resource management (IHRM)** to deal with global HR challenges like these. We can define IHRM as the human resource management concepts and techniques employers use to manage the human resource challenges of their international operations. IHRM generally focuses on three main topics:[6]

1. ***Managing human resources in global companies*** (for example, selecting, training, and compensating employees who work abroad)
2. ***Managing expatriate employees*** (those the employer sends abroad)
3. ***Comparing human resource management practices*** in different countries

Adapting Human Resource Activities to Intercountry Differences

2 Illustrate with examples how intercountry differences affect HRM.

How Intercountry Differences Affect Human Resource Management

As we said, the challenges of international human resource management don't just stem from the distances involved (though this is important). The bigger issue is dealing with the cultural, political, legal, and economic differences among countries and their people. The result is that what works in one country might fail in another.

Companies operating only within the United States generally have the luxury of dealing with a relatively limited set of economic, cultural, and legal variables. The United States is a capitalist, competitive society. And while the U.S. workforce reflects a multitude of cultural and ethnic backgrounds, shared values (such as an appreciation for democracy) help to blur cultural

FIGURE 17-1 Critical Intercountry Differences That Influence International HR Practices

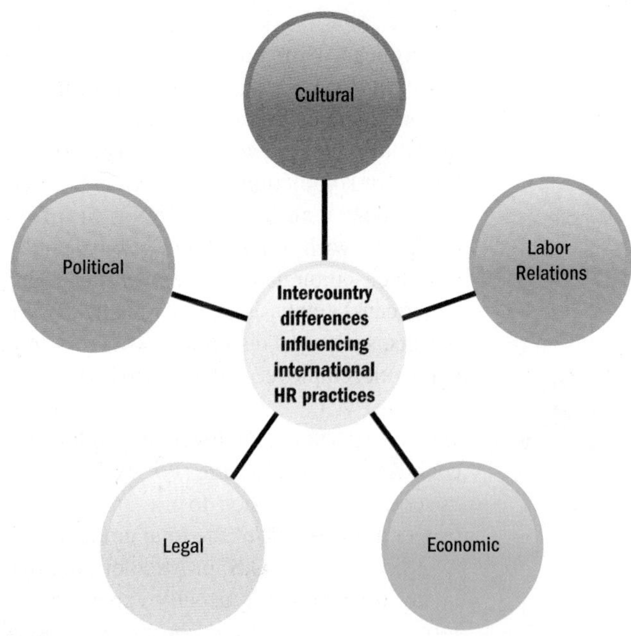

differences. Different states and municipalities certainly have their own employment laws. However, a basic federal framework helps produce a predictable set of legal guidelines regarding matters such as employment discrimination and labor relations.

A company operating multiple units abroad doesn't face such homogeneity. For example, minimum legally mandated holidays range from none in the United Kingdom to 5 weeks in Luxembourg. Italy has no formal requirements for employee representatives on boards of directors, but they're usually required in Denmark. The point is that managers have to adapt their human resource policies and practices to the countries in which they're operating. Figure 17-1 sums up critical intercountry differences.

Cultural Factors

Countries differ widely in their *cultures*—in other words, in the basic values their citizens adhere to, and in how these values manifest themselves in the nation's arts, social programs, and ways of doing things.[7] Cultural differences manifest themselves in differences in how people from different countries think, act, and expect others to act. For example, one study surveyed about 330 managers from Hong Kong, Mainland China, and the United States. The U.S. managers tended to be most concerned with getting the job done. Chinese managers were most concerned with maintaining harmony. Hong Kong managers fell between these two.[8]

Felipe Dupouy/Thinkstock

Employers need to adapt their HR practices to the cultures of the countries where they do business.

THE HOFSTEDE STUDY Studies by Professor Geert Hofstede illustrate international cultural differences. Hofstede says societies differ in five values, which he calls *power distance, individualism, masculinity, uncertainty avoidance,* and *long-term orientation.* For example, power distance represents the degree to which less powerful people accept the unequal distribution of power in society.[9] He concluded that acceptance of such inequality was higher in some countries (such as Mexico) than in others (such as Sweden).[10] In turn, such differences manifest themselves in different behaviors. To see how your country's culture compares with others, go to www.geert-hofstede.com/hofstede_dimensions.php.

Such cultural differences influence human resource policies and practices. For example, Americans' emphasis on individuality may help explain why European managers have more constraints, such as in dismissing workers.[11] As another example, in countries with a history of autocratic rule, employees often had to divulge information. Here, whistleblower rules are less popular.[12]

LEGAL FACTORS Employers expanding abroad must also be familiar with the labor laws in the countries they're entering. For example, in India, companies with more than 100 workers need government permission to fire anyone.[13] In Brazil, firing someone without "just cause" could trigger a fine of 4% of the total amount the worker ever earned.[14]

Similarly, the U.S. practice of employment at will doesn't exist in Europe, where firing or laying off workers is usually expensive. And in many European countries, **works councils**—formal, employee-elected groups of worker representatives—meet monthly with managers on topics ranging from no-smoking policies to layoffs.[15]

works councils
Formal, employee-elected groups of worker representatives.

codetermination
Employees have the legal right to a voice in setting company policies.

Codetermination is the rule in Germany and several other countries. **Codetermination** means employees have the legal right to a voice in setting company policies. Workers elect their own representatives to the supervisory board of the employer.[16]

Economic Systems

Similarly, differences in *economic systems* translate into differences in intercountry HR practices. In *market* economies (such as the United States), governments play a relatively restrained role in deciding what will be produced and sold at what prices. In *planned* economies (such as North Korea), the government decides and plans what to produce and sell at what price. In *mixed* economies (such as China), many industries are still state-owned, while others make decisions based on market demand.

Differences in economic systems tend to translate into differences in human resource management policies. For instance, dismissing employees in China or Europe is more difficult than in the United States. Labor costs also vary widely. For example, hourly compensation costs (in U.S. dollars) for production workers range from $2.01 in the Philippines to $9.34 in Taiwan, $35.53 in the United States, $47.38 in Germany, to $64.15 in Norway.[17]

HR Abroad Example: The European Union

To appreciate the employment effects of cultural, economic, and legal differences like these, consider Europe and China. The separate countries of the former European Community (EC) unified into a common market for goods, services, capital, and even labor called the *European Union (EU).* Tariffs for goods moving across borders from one EU country to another generally disappeared, and employees generally move freely between jobs in EU countries. The introduction of a single currency (the euro) further blurred differences.

Companies doing business in Europe must adjust their human resource policies and practices to EU directives (laws), as well as to country-specific employment laws. The directives' are binding on all member countries, but each country can implement them as they wish. For example, the EU directive on confirmation of employment requires employers to provide employees with written terms and conditions of their employment.[18] In England, a detailed written statement is required, including things like rate of pay, date employment began, and hours of work. Germany doesn't require a written contract.

This interplay of EU directives and country laws means that an employer's human resource practices must vary from country to country. For example:[19]

- ***Minimum EU wages.*** Most EU countries have minimum wage systems. Some set national limits. Others allow employers and unions to work out their own minimum wages.

- ***Working hours.*** The EU sets the workweek at 48 hours, but most EU countries set it at 40 hours.
- ***Termination of employment.*** Required notice periods when dismissing employees in Europe range from none in Spain to 2 months in Italy.

HR Abroad Example: China

For years, employers relied on China's huge workforce to provide products and services at low cost. Part of the reason for the low labor cost was the dearth of labor laws on things like severance pay, minimum wages, and benefits.

But things are changing. For one thing, China's workforce, while still huge, is growing less quickly. For another, China has a new labor contract law. This adds many new employment protections for employees, and makes it more expensive for employers in China to implement personnel actions such as layoffs. Multinational companies doing business in China argue that the new law will raise labor costs and make it difficult to lay off employees, by instituting new severance package rules.[20] Local firms, including the remaining state-owned enterprises, tend to use fewer modern human resource management tools than do private Chinese multinationals like Lenova, but must also deal with the fallout of the new labor law. There are therefore wide variations in how companies in China deal with HR issues such as the following.[21]

RECRUITING Compared to some Western countries, it is relatively difficult to recruit, hire, and retain good employees. China's Employment Contract Law requires, among many other things, that employers report the names, sexes, identification numbers, and contract terms for all employees they hire within 30 days of hiring to local labor bureaus.[22]

In China, recruiting effectiveness depends on nonrecruitment human resource management issues. Employees gravitate toward employers that provide the best career advancement training and opportunities.[23] Firms like Siemens China, with impressive training and development programs, have the least difficulty attracting good candidates. Poaching employees is a serious matter in China. The employer must verify that the applicant is free to sign a new employment agreement.

SELECTION The dominant employee selection method involves analyzing the applicant's résumé and then interviewing him or her. The ideal way to do this is to institute a structured interview process, as many of the foreign firms in China have done.

COMPENSATION Although many managers endorse performance-based pay in China, other employers, to preserve group harmony, make incentive pay a small part of the pay package. And, as in other parts of Asia, team incentives are advisable.[24]

The accompanying HR Tools feature focuses on how smaller U.S. and Chinese employers deal with various HR issues.

IMPROVING PERFORMANCE: HR Tools for Line Managers and Entrepreneurs

Comparing Small Businesses, HR Practices in the United States and China

Cross-country differences tend to manifest themselves in small businesses, too. For example, one study compared practices in 248 small U.S. companies with those in 148 small Chinese companies. (The researchers defined "small companies" as those with 500 or fewer employees.)[25] First, in terms of *job analysis*, jobs in small Chinese companies tend to be more narrowly defined and set in stone than those in small U.S. businesses. For example, the small Chinese firms have more up-to-date job descriptions, their employees deviate from their assigned job duties less frequently, their job descriptions tend to cover all the job's duties, and the job descriptions shape what the worker does.

Similarly, the researchers found significant differences in *performance appraisal practices* between U.S. and Chinese firms. In Chinese firms, compared to the United States, performance appraisals more often focus on the bottom line; appraisal feedback is evaluative rather than developmental; the appraisal focuses on objective, quantifiable results; and the main objective is to improve performance (rather than to develop the employee). Perhaps surprisingly, therefore, performance appraisals in small Chinese companies tend to be more hard-nosed than are those in the United States.

Finally (perhaps surprisingly given China's communist roots), there's more emphasis on incentive pay than guaranteed salaries in China's small businesses. Employees in the Chinese firms are more likely to receive bonuses based on the company's profits, to receive bonuses based on companywide gainsharing plans, to get stock or stock options as incentives, and to be paid based mostly on an incentive plan rather than on a guaranteed income plan. On the other hand, there tends to be less variation among Chinese employees in pay, and more emphasis on seniority.

Discussion Question 17-2: Why do you think appraisal in these Chinese firms seems to be tougher than in the United States?

Staffing the Global Organization

3 List and briefly describe the main methods for staffing global organizations.

Employers' focus today is increasingly on managing human resource activities locally. In other words, their main concern is on selecting, training, appraising, and managing the in-country employees where they do business.

However, deciding whether to fill local positions with local versus expatriate ("imported") employees has been and continues to be a major concern.

HR in Practice at the Hotel Paris On reviewing the data, it was apparent to Lisa and the CFO that the company's global human resource practices were probably inhibiting the Hotel Paris from being the world-class guest services company that it sought to be. To see how they handled this, see the case on page 554 of this chapter.

International Staffing: Home or Local?

expatriates (expats)
Noncitizens of the countries in which employees are working.

home-country nationals
Citizens of the country in which the multinational company has its headquarters.

locals
Citizens of the countries in which employees are working; also called *host-country nationals*.

third-country nationals
Citizens of a country other than the parent or the host country.

In general, we can classify an international company's employees as *expatriates, home-country nationals, locals (host-country nationals),* or *third-country nationals*.[26] **Expatriates (expats)** are noncitizens of the countries in which they are working. Expatriates may also be **home-country nationals**, citizens of the country in which the company is headquartered. **Locals** (also known as *host-country nationals*) work for the company abroad and are citizens of the countries where they are working. **Third-country nationals** are citizens of a country other than the parent or the host country—for example, a French executive working in the Shanghai branch of a U.S. multinational bank.[27]

USING LOCALS Most employees will be locals, for good reason. First, the cost of using expatriates is usually far greater than the cost of using local workers.[28] Some companies are surprised at the cost of posting someone abroad. Agilent Technologies estimated that it cost about three times the expatriate's annual salary to keep the person abroad for 1 year. When it outsourced its expatriate program, it discovered the costs were much higher. The firm then dramatically reduced the number it sent abroad, from about 1,000 to 300 per year.[29]

There are other reasons. In one survey, employers reported a 21% attrition rate for expatriate employees, compared with 10% for their general employee populations.[30] Local people may view the multinational as a "better citizen" if it uses local management talent; some governments even press for staffing with local management.[31] Some expatriates overemphasize short-term results (knowing they will soon move on).[32] It's also more difficult to bring workers into the United States from abroad. U.S. employers must vigorously recruit U.S. workers before filing foreign labor certification requests with the Department of Labor.[33]

USING EXPATS Yet there are also reasons for using expatriates—either home-country or third-country nationals. Employers often can't find local candidates with the required qualifications. Multinationals also view a successful stint abroad as a required step in developing top managers. Furthermore, the assumption is that home-country managers are already steeped in the firm's policies and culture, and thus more likely to apply headquarters' ways of doing things.

However, the trend has been toward using locals or other (non-expat) solutions. Posting expatriates abroad is expensive, security problems give potential expatriates' pause, returning expatriates often leave for other employers within a year or two, and educational facilities are turning out top-quality candidates abroad. As a result, new expatriate postings tend to be down, and many employers are bringing them home early.[34] A survey found that about 47% of U.S. multinationals were maintaining the size of their expat workforces; 18% were increasing it, and 35% were decreasing it.[35] However about half the global companies in one recent survey said they were doubling the number of expats they send to countries like China in the next few years.[36] The human resource team needs to control expat expenses, as the accompanying Profit Center feature explains.

IMPROVING PERFORMANCE: HR as a Profit Center

Reducing Expatriate Costs

Given the expense of sending employees (often, dozens or hundreds of employees) abroad for overseas assignments, the employer's human resource team plays a big role in controlling and reducing expatriate costs. A survey by Mercer shows some of the steps HR managers are taking to reduce these expenses. (Mercer provides consulting, outsourcing, and investment services to employers worldwide.)[37] First, companies are upping the numbers of short-term assignments they make. This lets them use short-term expats to replace some long-term expats (and their families) who the company must maintain abroad for extended periods. Fifty percent of the companies Mercer surveyed are also replacing some expatriate postings with local hires. With an eye on cutting costs, many employers were also reviewing their firms' policies regarding such things as housing, education, and home leave, along with expatriate allowances and premiums (cost-of-living allowance and mobility/quality-of-living premiums).[38] The bottom line is that there's a lot human resource managers can do to cut costs and boost profits by better managing expat assignments.

Discussion Question 17-3: Might not some of these policies make it harder to get employees to move abroad? Why?

OTHER SOLUTIONS The choice is not just between expatriate versus local employees. For example, there are "commuter" solutions, involving frequent international travel but no formal relocation.[39]

One survey found that about 78% of surveyed employers had some form of "localization" policy. This is a policy of transferring a home-country national employee to a foreign subsidiary as a "permanent transferee."[40] For example, U.S. IBM employees originally from India eventually filled many of the 5,000 jobs that IBM recently shifted from the United States to India. These employees elected to move back to India, albeit at local India pay rates. Other firms use Internet-based video technologies and group decision-making software to enable global virtual teams to do business without either travel or relocation.[41]

OFFSHORING As we explained in Chapter 5, *offshoring*—moving business processes such as manufacturing or call-center operations abroad, and thus having local employees abroad do jobs that the firm's domestic employees previously did in-house—is another globalization option.[42] The HR Practices Around the Globe feature shows how human resource managers help employers optimize their offshoring activities.

IMPROVING PERFORMANCE: HR Practices Around the Globe

What Human Resource Management Can Do to Facilitate Offshoring Operations

Human resource managers play a central role in offshoring decisions. IBM Business Consulting Services surveyed employers to see exactly what roles HR was actually playing in these decisions. Here's what they found.[43]

HR's Role in Choosing the Offshoring Site

For example, HR helps top management:[44]

- To determine *total labor costs*. These include direct wages and benefits, as well as potential costs such as severance payments.
- To understand the *local labor markets*, for example, in terms of their size, education levels, unions, and language skills.
- To understand how the firm's current *employment-related reputation* in the locale may affect outsourcing to this locale.
- To decide how much the firm should *integrate the local workforce* into the parent firm's corporate organization. For example, employees performing strategic customer-related tasks (such as engineering) might best become employees. Others (such as call centers) might best remain independent contractors or employees of vendor firms.

HR's Role in Offshoring Recruitment and Selection

In IBM's discussions with offshoring employers, the latter emphasized three recruitment issues:

- Skill shortages. "Despite large candidate pools for entry-level workers, there is an ongoing 'war for talent' in many of these [low-wage] labor markets."[45] This often requires getting employees from other local firms using signing bonuses, higher wages, and improved employee retention policies (for instance, improved promotion opportunities).
- In-bulk hiring. The need to hire hundreds or thousands of employees at once complicates hiring. Employers turn to employment agencies, employee referrals, and college recruiting.
- Screening. The large number of potential candidates often overwhelmed the firms' capacity to screen and evaluate candidates.[46]

HR's Role in Offshoring Employee Retention

IBM found that "perhaps the greatest HR challenge facing globally distributed back-office and customer care centers is the retention of talented employees."[47] The high-pressure nature of these jobs combines with skill shortages to produce high attrition rates. To reduce high attrition, HR managers are taking steps such as:

- Deciding what is an acceptable *target attrition rate*, to measure the employer's retention performance.
- Identifying what *"levers"* reduce attrition. These include more training and development, better compensation and benefits, and improved career opportunities.

Discussion Question 17-4: Discuss two factors that a manufacturer abroad, such as China's Lenovo, might encounter when "offshoring" jobs to the U.S.

USING TRANSNATIONAL AND VIRTUAL TEAMS Managing internationally may require using a "transnational" team, a team composed of employees whose locations span several countries.[48] For example, a European beverage manufacturer formed a 13-member "European Production Task Force," with members from its facilities in five countries, to analyze what factories the firm should operate in Europe.[49]

virtual teams
Groups of geographically dispersed coworkers who interact using a combination of telecommunications and information technologies to accomplish an organizational task.

Such teams often work in virtual environments. **Virtual teams** are groups of geographically dispersed coworkers who interact using a combination of telecommunications and information technologies to accomplish an organizational task.

Virtual teams are popular. Strategic partnerships and joint ventures often require employees of partner companies to act together as a team.[50] To facilitate the merger of Marion Laboratories and Merrell Dow Pharmaceuticals, the companies created a transnational virtual team comprised of members from production sites in Asia, Europe, and North America. The team helped overcome potential merger integration problems, and produced improved productivity and profits.[51]

Virtual teams use information technology. Using desktop videoconferencing systems, communication among team members can embrace the body language and nuances of face-to-face communications.[52] Teams also use collaborative software systems. Microsoft offers a NetMeeting conference system. When combined with products like Framework Technologies Corp.'s ActiveProject 5.0, virtual team members can hold live project reviews and discussions and then store the sessions on the project's website.[53]

The main challenges virtual teams face are often people related. Challenges include building trust, cohesion, and team identity, and overcoming the isolation among team members. Success therefore depends on human resource management actions. In particular, *train* virtual team members in leadership, conflict management, and meetings management, and to respond swiftly to virtual teammates.[54] *Select* virtual team members using behavioral and situational interviews, where they describe how they'd respond to illustrative virtual team situations. And, use current virtual team members to help *recruit* and select new team members.[55]

Management Values and International Staffing Policy

It's not just hard facts that influence international staffing decisions. The top executives' personal inclinations and values also play a role. Some executives are just more "expat-oriented." Experts classify top executives' values as *ethnocentric*, *polycentric*, or *geocentric*.

ETHNOCENTRIC PRACTICES In an ethnocentrically oriented corporation, "the prevailing attitude is that home-country attitudes, management style, knowledge, evaluation criteria, and managers are superior to anything the host country might have to offer."[56]

ethnocentric
The notion that home-country attitudes, management style, knowledge, evaluation criteria, and managers are superior to anything the host country has to offer.

Such values translate into employment practices. With an **ethnocentric** staffing policy, the firm fills key management jobs with parent-country nationals.[57] Reasons given for ethnocentric staffing policies include lack of qualified host-country management talent, a desire to maintain a unified corporate culture and tighter control, and the desire to transfer the parent company's core competencies (such as a specialized manufacturing skill) to a foreign subsidiary more expeditiously.[58]

polycentric
A conscious belief that only the host-country managers can ever really understand the culture and behavior of the host-country market.

POLYCENTRIC PRACTICES In the **polycentric** corporation, "there is a conscious belief that only host-country managers can ever really understand the culture and behavior of the host-country market; therefore, the foreign subsidiary should be managed by local people."[59]

A polycentric-oriented firm staffs its foreign subsidiaries with host-country nationals, and its home office with parent-country nationals. Such policies may reduce the local cultural misunderstandings that might occur if it used expatriate managers, and be less expensive.[60]

geocentric
The belief that the firm's whole management staff must be scoured on a global basis, on the assumption that the best manager of a specific position anywhere may be in any of the countries in which the firm operates.

GEOCENTRIC PRACTICES A **geocentric** staffing policy "seeks the best people for key jobs throughout the organization, regardless of nationality."[61] This global firm will transfer the best person to the open job, wherever he or she may be. This can optimize placements and help build a more consistent culture among the global management team members.

Ethics and Codes of Conduct

Employers also need to make sure their employees abroad are adhering to their firm's ethics codes. However, exporting a firm's ethics rules requires more than giving employees abroad versions of a U.S. employee handbook. For example, few countries abroad adhere to "employment at will." Therefore, even handbooks that say, "We can fire employees at will" won't enable one to dismiss employees.[62] Instead of exporting the employee handbook, some create and distribute a global code of conduct.

Often, the employer's main concern is establishing global standards for adhering to U.S. laws that have cross-border impacts. For example, IBM paid $10 million to settle accusations that it had bribed Chinese and South Korean officials to get $54 million in government contracts.[63] Global employers need global codes of conduct on things like discrimination, harassment, bribery, and Sarbanes-Oxley.

Selecting International Managers

In most respects, screening managers for jobs abroad is similar to screening them for domestic jobs. For either assignment, candidates need the technical knowledge and skills to do the job, and the intelligence and people skills to be successful managers.[64] Testing, interviewing, and background checks are as applicable for selecting expatriates as for domestic assignments.

However, selection for foreign assignments is different. For example, there is the being alone in a foreign land. Furthermore, the person's adaptability is important. Some people adapt anywhere; others fail to adapt anywhere.[65]

How do firms select global managers? Analyses of expatriate practices suggest several things. Traditionally, most selection of expatriates was done ". . . solely on the basis of successful records of job performance in the home country."[66] Today, however, best practices in international assignee selection include providing *realistic previews* to prospective assignees, facilitating *self-selection* to enable expatriate candidates to decide for themselves if the assignments are right for them, and using *traditional selection procedures* focusing on personal traits such as openness.[67] Employers now also use more expatriate selection criteria. Selection criteria include technical/professional skills, expatriates' willingness to go, experience in the country, personality factors (including flexibility), leadership skills, the ability to work with teams, and previous performance appraisals in the selection process. There has been a corresponding decline in U.S. companies' premature return rates, suggesting that employers are more successful at sending expatriates abroad.[68]

TESTING As noted, employers can take steps to improve the expat selection process, and testing is an obvious tool. For example, Brookfield Global Relocation Services Intercultural Group has used its Overseas Assignment Inventory (OAI) for over 40 years to help employers do a better job of selecting candidates for assignments abroad. It says, "Proper assessment and selection of employees for international assignments can mean the difference between success and a missed opportunity. The Overseas Assignment Inventory (OAI—our proprietary assessment tool—can be used for: assessment and selection of candidates, development of chosen expatriates, self-assessment, and building candidate pools." The OAI is an online assessment that measures nine attributes and six context factors crucial for successful adaptation to another culture. Brookfield

FIGURE 17-2 Sample excerpt from the Overseas Assignment Inventory

Source: Brookfield Global Relocation Services, 150 Harvester Drive, Suite 201, Burr Ridge, IL 60527.

Initiative

Why this is important

Initiative refers to a willingness to address new and challenging situations and a confidence in taking action even when situations are unclear. Everyday responsibilities and working well with people can be more complicated in a new country. Those taking the initiative to manage unfamiliar situations are likely to minimize the frustrations associated with getting things done in a new culture. For non-working spouses, taking the initiative to meet people, structure their lives and find meaningful activities is critical to a successful adjustment.

Your score is below the average range, indicating that you:

- ☑ may wait for others to approach you in developing relationships
- ☑ may wait for others to lead in a situation that requires attention
- ☑ may hesitate to seek information in unfamiliar circumstances

What your score means

Your responses suggest that you prefer to wait until a situation is clear before taking action. You may not feel confident about approaching new people, preferring to wait till they approach you. This tendency may be exaggerated in a new culture, where situations are often ambiguous and everyday tasks may be more complex and take more time. It will be important for you to make a special effort to take initiative to get information about how to manage issues that you may be struggling with; and you may need to be more personally assertive to meet people and make new friends. You will need to stretch your comfort level in this area as you adjust to the new culture.

Global Relocation Services establishes global norms and conducts ongoing validation studies of the OAI.[69] See Figure 17-2.

In terms of personality, successful expatriate employees tend to be extroverted, agreeable, and emotionally stable.[70] Not surprisingly, sociable, outgoing, conscientious people seem more likely to fit into new cultural settings.[71]

Intentions are important, too: For example, people who want expatriate careers try harder to adjust to such a life.[72] Similarly, expatriates who are more satisfied with their jobs abroad are more likely to adapt to the foreign assignment.[73]

REALISTIC PREVIEWS Even in familiar foreign postings there will be language barriers, bouts of homesickness, and new friends. Realistic previews about the problems as well as about the country's cultural benefits are thus an important part of screening. The rule is always "spell it all out" ahead of time.[74]

adaptability screening
A process that aims to assess the assignees' (and spouses') probable success in handling a foreign transfer.

ADAPTABILITY SCREENING With flexibility and adaptability very important, **adaptability screening** should be part of the screening process. Adaptability screening aims to assess the assignee's (and spouse's) probable success in handling the foreign transfer, and to alert them to issues (such as the impact on children) the move may involve. Employers often use specially trained psychologists for this.

Here, companies often look for overseas candidates whose work and nonwork experience, education, and language skills already demonstrate ability for living and working with different cultures. Even several successful summers spent traveling overseas or in foreign student programs might provide some basis to believe the potential transferee can adjust abroad.

SELECTION TRENDS As noted, the expat selection situation is improving. Over the past two decades there's been an increase in the number of selection criteria companies use to select expatriates. Employers now regularly use selection criteria such as technical/professional skills, expatriates' willingness to go, experience in the country, personality factors (including flexibility), leadership skills, the ability to work with teams, and previous performance appraisals in the selection process.[75]

Diversity Counts: Sending Women Managers Abroad

While women represent about 50% of the middle management talent in U.S. companies, they represent only 21% of managers sent abroad.[76] What accounts for this?

Many misperceptions still exist.[77] Line managers make these assignments, and many assume that women don't want to work abroad, are reluctant to move their families abroad, or can't get their spouses to move.[78] In fact, this survey found, women do want international assignments, they are not less inclined to move their families, and their male spouses are not necessarily reluctant.

Safety is another issue. Employers tend to assume that women abroad are more likely to become crime victims. However, most surveyed women expats said that safety was no more an issue with women than it was with men.[79]

Fear of cultural prejudices against women is another issue. In some cultures, women do have to follow different rules, for instance, in terms of attire. But as one expat said, "Even in the more harsh cultures, once they recognize that the women can do the job . . . it becomes less of a problem."[80]

Employers take several steps to overcome the misperceptions, and to identify more women to assign abroad. For example, *formalize a process* for identifying employees who are willing to take assignments abroad. (At Gillette, for instance, supervisors use the performance review to identify the subordinate's career interests, including for assignments abroad.) *Train managers* to understand how employees really feel about going abroad, and what the real safety and cultural issues are. Let successful female expats *help recruit* prospective female expats. And provide the expat's spouse with *employment assistance*.[81]

LEGAL ISSUES In selecting employees for international assignments, managers should consider the legal issues. As we explained in Chapter 2 (Equal Opportunity), American equal employment opportunity laws, including Title VII, the ADEA, and the ADA, affect qualified employees of U.S. employers doing business abroad, and foreign firms doing business in the United States or its territories.[82] If equal employment opportunity laws conflict with the laws of the country in which the U.S. employer is operating, the laws of the local country generally take precedence.[83]

Avoiding Early Expatriate Returns

You know the expatriate's assignment probably failed when he or she makes an early, unplanned return. Systematizing the entire expatriate management process is one step in avoiding an early return. For example, employers should have an expatriate policy covering matters such as compensation and travel costs. Include procedures, for instance, requiring that the manager responsible for the expat's costs obtain all chain of command approvals.[84] Another step in avoiding early returns is to test and select people who have the necessary traits and adaptability (as discussed earlier). Finally, because family pressures loom large, employers must attend to them.

FAMILY PRESSURES In one study, U.S. managers listed, in descending order of importance, reasons for expatriates leaving early: inability of spouse to adjust, managers' inability to adjust, other family problems, managers' personal or emotional immaturity, and inability to cope with larger overseas responsibility.[85]

Such findings underscore a truism about selecting international assignees: The problem is usually not incompetence, but family and personal problems. Yet, many employers still often select expatriates mostly based on technical competence.[86]

Given the role of family problems in expatriate failures, the employer should understand just how unhappy and cut off the expatriate manager's spouse can feel abroad. As one spouse said,[87]

> It's difficult to make close friends. So many expats have their guard up, not wanting to become too close. Too many have been hurt, too many times already, becoming emotionally dependent on a friend only to have the inevitable happen—one or the other gets transferred. It's also difficult to watch your children get hurt when their best friend gets transferred.[88]

Three things make it easier. First is *language fluency*, since spouses will feel even more cut off if they can't communicate. Second, having *preschool-age children* seemed to make it easier for the spouse to adjust. "This suggests that younger children, perhaps because of their increased dependency, help spouses retain that part of their social identities . . ."[89] Third, it helps if there is a *strong bond of closeness* between spouse and expat partner. This provides the continuing emotional support many spouses find lacking abroad.

Keep in mind that it's usually not how different culturally the host country is from the person's home country that causes problems; it's the person's ability to adapt.[90] Some people are so culturally at ease that they're fine transferred anywhere; others will fail anywhere.[91] The HR Tools feature sums up some suggestions.

IMPROVING PERFORMANCE: HR Tools for Line Managers and Entrepreneurs

Some Practical Solutions to the Expatriate Challenge

Expat failure is expensive; managers can take several practical steps to improve the expat's success abroad.

- *Provide realistic previews* of what to expect abroad, *careful screening* (of both the prospective expat and his or her spouse), *improved orientation,* and *improved benefits* packages.
- *Shorten the length* of the assignment.
- Use Internet-based *video technologies* and group decision-making software to enable global virtual teams to conduct business without relocation.[92]
- Form "*global buddy*" programs. Here local managers assist new expatriates with advice on things such as office politics, norms of behavior, and where to receive emergency medical assistance.[93]
- *Use executive coaches* to mentor and work with expatriate managers.[94]

Discussion Question 17-5: Choose one country abroad and write 200 words on this topic: "Here is what we should cover in our realistic preview to someone we are sending to this country."

Training and Maintaining Employees Abroad

Orienting and Training Employees on International Assignment

4 Discuss some important issues to keep in mind in training, appraising, and compensating international employees.

When it comes to the orientation and training required for expatriate success overseas, the practices of most U.S. employers reflect more talk than substance. Executives tend to agree that international assignees do best when they receive the special training (in things like language and culture) that they require. Few provide it.

Many vendors offer packaged pre-departure training. In general, the programs use lectures, simulations, videos, and readings to prepare trainees. Their offerings illustrate the aim and content of such programs. One program aims to provide the trainee with (1) the basics of the new country's history, politics, business norms, education system, and demographics; (2) an understanding of how cultural values affect perceptions, values, and communications; and (3) examples of why moving to a new country can be difficult, and how to manage these challenges.[95] Another aims to boost self-awareness and cross-cultural understanding, and to reduce stress and provide coping strategies.[96] A third prepares individuals and their families "to interact successfully in daily life and business situations abroad; understand the impact various factors have on cultural behaviors and attitudes to make the most of the living abroad experience; and to raise awareness of the challenges of moving abroad, culture shock and how to deal with exposure to new cultural experiences."[97]

Some employers use returning managers to cultivate the global mind-sets of those departing. For example, Bosch holds regular seminars, where new arrived returnees pass on their experience to managers and their families going abroad.

ONGOING TRAINING Beyond such pre-departure training, more firms provide continuing, in-country cross-cultural training during the early stages of an overseas assignment.

For example, managers abroad (both expats and locals) continue to need traditional skills-oriented development. At many firms, including IBM, such development includes rotating assignments to help overseas managers grow professionally. IBM and other firms also have management development centers around the world where executives can hone their skills. And classroom programs (such as those at the London Business School or at INSEAD in France) provide overseas executives the educational opportunities (to acquire MBAs, for instance) that stateside colleagues have.

International development activities hopefully have other, less tangible benefits. For example, rotating assignments can help managers form bonds with colleagues around the world. These can help the managers form the informal networks they need to make cross-border decisions more expeditiously.

PepsiCo encourages expatriates to engage in local social activities, such as Latin dance lessons in Mexico City and table tennis tournaments in China, to help them become acclimated faster to local cultures.[98]

Performance Appraisal of International Managers

Several things complicate appraising an expatriate's performance. Cultural differences are one. For example, a candid exchange is often the norm in the United States, but sometimes less so in China, where "face" is a concern.

Furthermore, who does the appraisal? Local management must have some input, but, again, cultural differences may distort the appraisals. (Thus, host-country bosses in Peru might evaluate a U.S. expatriate manager there somewhat negatively if they find his or her use of participative decision making culturally inappropriate.) On the other hand, home-office managers may be so out of touch that they can't provide useful appraisals. In one survey, the managers knew that having appraisers from both the host and home countries produced the best appraisals. But, in practice, most didn't. Instead, they had raters from the host or the home countries do them.[99]

Suggestions for improving the expatriate appraisal process include:

1. Adapt the performance criteria to the local job and situation.
2. Weigh the evaluation more toward the on-site manager's appraisal than toward the home-site manager's.
3. If the home-office manager does the actual written appraisal, have him or her use a former expatriate from the same overseas location for advice.

Anton Gvozdikov/Shutterstock

Many global employers bring their international managers together periodically for training seminars.

Compensating Managers Abroad

The whole area of international compensation presents some thorny problems. On the one hand, there is logic in maintaining company-wide pay scales and policies so that, for instance, you pay divisional marketing directors throughout the world within the same range. This simplifies the job of keeping track of country-by-country wage rates.

Yet not adapting pay scales to local markets will produce more problems than it solves. The fact is it can be enormously more expensive to live in some countries (like Japan) than others (like India); if these cost-of-living differences aren't considered, it will be almost impossible to get managers to take "high-cost" assignments. One way to handle this problem is to pay a similar base salary company-wide, and then add on various allowances according to individual market conditions.[100]

However setting rates abroad isn't always easy. Although there is a wealth of "packaged" compensation survey data available in the United States, such data are not so easy to come by overseas. As a result, one of the greatest difficulties in managing multinational compensation is obtaining consistent compensation measures between countries.

Some multinational companies conduct their own local annual compensation surveys. For example, Kraft conducts one of total compensation in Belgium, Germany, Italy, Spain, and the United Kingdom. It focuses on all forms of compensation paid to each of 10 senior management positions held by local nationals in these firms.

Multiple-nation taxation is another problem. Respondents recently listed "tax compliance" as the top challenge in sending employees abroad.[101]

THE BALANCE SHEET APPROACH The most common approach to formulating expatriate pay is to equalize purchasing power across countries, a technique known as the *balance sheet approach.*[102] More than 85% of North American companies reportedly use this approach.

The basic idea is that each expatriate should enjoy the same standard of living he or she would have had at home. The balance sheet approach addresses four groups of expenses—income taxes, housing, goods and services, and discretionary expenses (child support, car payments, and the like). The employer estimates each of these four expenses in the expat's home country, and in the host country. The employer then pays any differences—such as additional income taxes or housing expenses.

The base salary will normally be in the same range as the manager's home-country salary. In addition, however, there might be an overseas or foreign service salary premium. The executive receives this as a percentage of base salary, to compensate for the adjustments he or she will have to make.[103] There may also be several allowances, including a housing allowance and an education allowance for the expatriate's children. To help the expatriate manage his or her home and foreign financial obligations, most employers use a *split pay* approach; they pay, say, half a person's actual pay in home-country currency and half in the local currency.[104]

Table 17-1 illustrates the balance sheet approach. The U.S. Government State Department estimates the cost of living in Shanghai at 128% of the U.S. cost of living.[105] In this case, the manager's base salary is $160,000, and she faces a U.S. income tax rate of 28%. Other costs are based on the index of living costs abroad published in the "U.S. Department of State Indexes of Living Costs Abroad, Quarters Allowances, and Hardship Differentials," available at http://aoprals.state.gov/content.asp?content_id=186&menu_id=81.

Employers also pay their expatriates and local managers abroad performance incentives. Executive compensation systems around the world are becoming more similar.[106] U.S. firms that

TABLE 17-1 The Balance Sheet Approach (Assumes U.S. Base Salary of $160,000)

Annual Expense	Chicago, U.S.	Shanghai, China (US$ Equivalent)	Allowance
Housing & utilities	$35,000	$44,800	$9,800
Goods & services	6,000	7,680	1,680
Taxes	44,800	57,344	12,544
Discretionary income	10,000	12,800	2,800
Total	$95,800	$122,624	$26,824

offer overseas managers long-term incentives often use overall corporate performance criteria (like worldwide profits) when awarding incentive pay.

EXPATRIATE PAY EXAMPLE As an example, expats working for the company CEMEX:

> . . . get foreign service premium equal to a 10% increase in salary. Some get a hardship premium, depending on the country; it ranges from zero in a relatively comfortable posting to, for example, 30% in Bangladesh. We pay for their housing. We pay for their children's schooling up to college. There's home leave—a ticket back to their home country for the entire family once a year. There are language lessons for the spouse. And we gross up the pay of all expats, to take out the potential effects of local tax law. Say you have an executive earning $150,000. This person would cost close to $300,000 as an ex-pat.[107]

foreign service premiums
Financial payments over and above regular base pay, typically ranging between 10% and 30% of base pay.

hardship allowances
Payments that compensate expatriates for exceptionally hard living and working conditions at certain locations.

mobility premiums
Typically, lump-sum payments to reward employees for moving from one assignment to another.

INCENTIVES As noted, employers pay various incentives to encourage the employee to take the job abroad. For example, **foreign service premiums** are financial payments over and above regular base pay. These typically range from 10% to 30% of base pay, and appear as weekly or monthly salary supplements. **Hardship allowances** compensate expatriates for hard living and working conditions at certain foreign locations. (U.S. diplomats posted to Iraq receive about a 70% boost in base salary, among other incentives.[108]) **Mobility premiums** are typically lump-sum payments to reward employees for moving from one assignment to another.

In terms of buying power, American managers don't rank near the top. "Companies are operating in an increasingly open and competitive global economy, and emerging markets are offering managers higher disposable incomes than established countries." Average disposable income for managers ranges from about $72,000 in Indonesia to $105,000 in the United States; $124,000 in Brazil; and $229,000 in Saudi Arabia.[109]

STEPS IN ESTABLISHING A GLOBAL PAY SYSTEM Balancing global consistency in compensation with local considerations starts with establishing a rewards program that makes sense in terms of the employer's strategic aims.[110] Then the employer turns to more micro issues, such as, is how we're paying our employees abroad competitive?[111] Steps to follow in creating a global pay system include these:[112]

Step 1. **Set strategy.** First, formulate strategic goals for the next 5 years, for instance, in terms of improving productivity or boosting market share.

Step 2. **Identify crucial executive behaviors.** Then, list the actions you expect your executives to exhibit in order to achieve these strategic goals.

Step 3. **Global philosophy framework.** Next, step back and ask how you want *each pay component* to contribute to prompting those executive actions.

Step 4. **Identify gaps.** Next, ask, "To what extent do our pay plans around the world support these actions and what changes if any are required?"

Step 5. **Systematize pay systems.** Next, create more consistent performance assessment practices, and establish consistent job requirements and performance expectations for similar jobs worldwide.

Step 6. **Adapt pay policies.** Finally, review your global pay policies (for setting salary levels, incentives, and so forth). Conduct surveys and analyses to assess local pay practices. Then, fine-tune the firm's global pay policies so they make sense for each location.

Labor Relations Abroad

Firms opening subsidiaries abroad face differing labor relations practices among countries and regions. Walmart successfully neutralized unionization attempts in the United States, but had to accept unions in China.

As another example, unions in Europe are influential, and labor–management bargaining and relations reflect this fact. In general, four issues characterize European labor relations:

- ***Centralization.*** Collective bargaining in Western Europe tends to be industry-wide, whereas in the United States it generally occurs at the enterprise or plant level.

- ***Employer organization.*** Due to the prevalence of industry-wide bargaining in Europe, employers tend to bargain via employer associations, rather than as individual employers.
- ***Union recognition.*** Union recognition is less formal than in the United States. For example, even if a union represents 80% of an employer's workers, another union can try to organize the other 20%.
- ***Content and scope of bargaining.*** U.S. labor–management agreements specify wages, hours, and working conditions. European agreements tend to be brief and to leave individual employers free to institute more generous terms.

Terrorism, Safety, and Global HR

TERRORISM Whether it's off the coast of Somalia or walking down a Brazil street, businesspeople may suffer "express kidnapping," wherein they're kidnapped, hopefully just long enough to get a ransom payment.[113]

Even stationing employees in assumedly safe countries is no guarantee. A few years ago workers in French factories of Sony Corp. and 3M Co. took their managers hostage to negotiate better benefits.[114]

TAKING PROTECTIVE MEASURES Legally, employers have a duty of care for protecting international assignees and their dependents and international business travelers.[115] Many employers use intelligence services for monitoring potential terrorist threats abroad. The head of one intelligence firm estimates such services cost $6,000–$10,000 per year.[116] Some employers retain crisis management teams' services. They then call on these teams, for instance, when criminals kidnap one of their managers. As one executive said, "When you have a specialist, there's a better chance to get the person back."[117]

Retaining risk management companies as a precautionary move can prove valuable. For example, when the protests erupted in Egypt in February 2011, Medex Global Solutions evacuated more than 500 client employees from Egypt, and had already been advising their employer clients about the possibilities for political unrest.[118]

KIDNAPPING AND RANSOM (K&R) INSURANCE Hiring crisis teams and paying ransoms can be prohibitively expensive for all but the largest firms, so many employers buy kidnapping and ransom (K&R) insurance. Various events may trigger payments under such policies. The obvious ones are kidnapping (for instance, the employee is a hostage until the employer pays a ransom), extortion (threatening bodily harm), and detention (holding an employee without any ransom demand).

The insurance typically covers several costs associated with kidnappings, abductions, or extortion. These include hiring a crisis team, the actual ransom payment, insuring the ransom money in transit, legal expenses, and employee death or dismemberment.[119]

Keeping business travelers safe is a specialty, but suggestions here include:[120]

- Provide expatriates with general training about traveling, living abroad, and the destination, so they're oriented when they arrive.
- Tell them not to draw attention to the fact that they're Americans—by wearing flag emblems, for instance.
- Have travelers arrive at airports close to departure time and wait in areas away from the main traffic.
- Equip the expatriate's car and home with security systems.
- Tell employees to vary their departure and arrival times and take different routes to and from work.
- Keep employees current on crime and other problems by regularly checking the State Department's travel advisory service (click on Country Specific Information at http://travel.state.gov/).
- Advise employees to look confident: Body language can attract perpetrators, and those who look like victims often become victimized.[121]

Repatriation: Problems and Solutions

One of the most worrisome facts about sending employees abroad is that 40% to 60% of them will probably quit within 3 years of returning home.[122] Given the investment the employer makes in training and sending these high-potential people abroad, it makes sense to try to retain them.

For this, formal repatriation programs can be useful.[123] One study found that about 5% of returning employees resigned if their firms had formal repatriation programs, while about 22% of those left if their firms had no such programs.[124]

M. Thatcher/Shutterstock

AT&T makes sure that the employee always feels that he or she is still "in the loop" with what's happening back at the home office.

Probably the simplest way to improve retention is to value their experience. As one returnee put it: "My company was, in my view, somewhat indifferent to my experience in China as evidenced by a lack of monetary reward, positive increase, or leverage to my career in any way."[125]

The guiding principle of any repatriation program is this: Make sure the expatriate and his or her family don't feel the company has forgotten them. To that end, AT&T has a three-part repatriation program.[126] First, AT&T *matches the expat and his or her family with a psychologist* trained in repatriation issues. The psychologist meets with the family before they go abroad. The psychologist discusses the challenges they will face, assesses with them how well he or she thinks they will adapt, and stays in touch with them throughout their assignment.

Second, AT&T makes sure *the employee always feels that he or she is still "in the loop"* with the home office. For example, AT&T assigns the expatriate a mentor. It also periodically brings the expat back to the home office to meet with and to socialize with colleagues.

Third, AT&T *provides formal repatriation services.* About 6 months before the overseas assignment ends, the psychologist and an HR representative meet with the expat and the family, to start preparing them. For example, they help plan the employee's next career move, help the person update his or her résumé, and begin putting the person in contact with supervisors back home. They work with the person's family on the logistics of the move back. Then, about a month after returning home, the expat and family attend a "welcome home" seminar to discuss matters like the stress of repatriation.[127]

Social Media and HR

Social media such as LinkedIn are excellent sources of information, suggestions, support, and employment leads and connections for expats or for those considering a job abroad. Among the links you'll find there are: www.linkedin.com/groups/Global-Expat-Professional-Network-4763493, www.expatfinder.com/, www.linkedin.com/groups/Forum-Expatriate-Management-1056387, and www.linkedin.com/title/expatriate+transfer+advisor/.

Improving Performance Through HRIS: Taking the HRIS Global

For global firms, it makes particular sense to expand the firm's human resource information systems to the firm's operations abroad. For example, when Buildnet, Inc., decided to automate and integrate its separate systems for things like applicant tracking, training, and compensation, it chose a Web-based software package called MyHRIS from NuView, Inc. (www.nuviewinc.com). This Internet-based system includes human resource and benefits administration, applicant tracking and résumé scanning, training administration, and succession planning and development.[128] With MyHRIS, managers at any of the firm's locations around the world can access and update more than 200 built-in reports such as "termination summary" or "open positions."[129] The firm's home-office managers can access data and monitor global human resource activities in real-time.

Employers are also taking their employee self-service portals international. For example, Time Warner's "Employee Connection" portal lets its 80,000 worldwide employees self-manage much of their benefits, compensation planning, merit review, and personal information updating online.[130]

Managing HR Locally: How to Put into Practice a Global HR System

5 Explain with examples how to implement a global human resource management program.

With employers increasingly relying on local rather than expatriate employees, transferring one's selection, training, appraisal, pay, and other human resource practices abroad is a top priority. But, given the cross-cultural and other differences, one could reasonably ask, "Is it realistic for a company to try to institute a standardized human resource management system in its facilities around the world?"

A study suggests "yes." In brief, the study's results show that employers may have to defer to local managers on some specific human resource management policy issues. However, they also suggest that big intercountry HR differences are often not necessary. The important thing is how you implement the global human resource management system.

In this study, the researchers interviewed human resource personnel from six global companies—Agilent, Dow, IBM, Motorola, Procter & Gamble, and Shell Oil Co.—as well as international human resources consultants.[131] The study's overall conclusion was that employers who successfully implement global HR systems do so by applying several best practices. The basic idea is to *develop* systems that are *acceptable* to employees in units around the world, and ones that the employers can *implement* more effectively. Figure 17-3 summarizes this.

Developing a More Effective Global HR System

First, these employers engage in two best practices in developing their worldwide human resource policies and practices.

Form global HR networks. To head off resistance, human resource managers around the world should feel part of the firm's global human resource management team. Treat the local human resource managers as equal partners. For instance, form global teams to develop the new human resources system. Create "an infrastructure of partners around the world that you use for support, for buy-in, for organization of local activities, and to help you better understand their own systems and their own challenges."[132]

Remember that it's more important to standardize ends and competencies than specific methods. For example, IBM uses a basically standardized recruitment and selection process worldwide. However, "details such as who conducts the interview (hiring manager vs. recruiter), or whether the prescreen is by phone or in person, differ by country."[133]

Making the Global HR System More Acceptable

Next, employers engage in three best practices so that the global human resource systems they develop will be *acceptable* to local managers around the world. These practices are:

Remember that truly global organizations find it easier to install global systems. For example, their managers work on global teams, and the firms identify, recruit, and place employees globally. As one Shell manager said, "If you're truly global, then you are hiring here [the United States] people who are going to immediately go and work in the Hague, and vice versa."[134] Doing so makes it easier for managers everywhere to accept the wisdom of having a standardized human resource management system.

FIGURE 17-3 Best Practices for Creating Global HR Systems

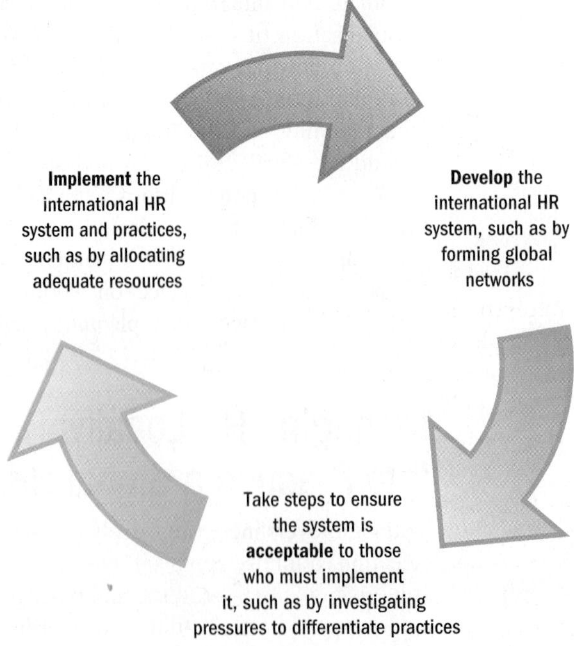

Investigate pressures to differentiate and determine their legitimacy. Local managers will insist, "You can't do that here, because we are different culturally." These "differences" aren't usually persuasive. For example, when Dow wanted to implement an online recruitment and selection tool abroad, the hiring managers there said that their managers would not use it. After investigating the supposed cultural roadblocks, Dow successfully implemented the new system.[135]

However, first carefully assess whether the local culture or other differences might in fact undermine the new system. Be knowledgeable about local legal issues, and be willing to differentiate where necessary.

Try to work within the context of a strong corporate culture. Companies that do so find it easier to obtain agreement among far-flung employees. For example, because of how P&G recruits, selects, trains, and rewards them, its managers have a strong sense of shared values. For instance, new recruits quickly learn to think in terms of "we" instead of "I." They learn to value thoroughness, consistency, self-discipline, and a methodical approach. Having such global unanimity makes it easier to implement standardized human resource practices.

Implementing the Global HR System

Finally, two best practices helped ensure success in actually *implementing* the globally consistent human resource policies and practices.

"You can't communicate enough." "There's a need for constant contact with the decision makers in each country, as well as the people who will be implementing and using the system."[136]

Dedicate adequate resources. For example, don't require the local human resource management offices to implement new job analysis procedures unless the head office provides adequate resources for these additional activities.

Review

MyManagementLab Go to **mymanagementlab.com** to complete the problems marked with this icon. 

Chapter Section Summaries

1. Dealing with **global human resource challenges as a manager** isn't easy. The employer faces an array of political, social, legal, and cultural differences among countries abroad. What works in one country may not work in another:
2. **The need for adapting human resource activities to intercountry differences** influences employers' HR processes. For example, citizens of different countries adhere to different values, and countries have differing economic systems as well as different legal, political, and labor relations systems.
3. **Staffing the global organization** is a major challenge. Companies may use expatriates, home-country nationals, locals, or third-country nationals. Offshoring means having local employees abroad do jobs that domestic employees previously did in-house. Top management values will influence how they staff their operations abroad. Ethnocentric companies tend to emphasize home-country attitudes, polycentric companies focus more on host-country employees, and geocentric employers try to pick the best candidates from wherever they might be. Selecting employees to successfully work abroad depends on several things, most importantly on adaptability screening and on making sure that each employee's spouse and family get the realistic previews and support necessary to make the transition. Successful expatriates tend to be extroverted, agreeable, and emotionally stable individuals.
4. After selecting the employees to send abroad, attention turns to **training and maintaining your expatriate employees**.
   - In terms of pre-departure preparation, training efforts ideally first cover the impact of cultural differences; then, the focus moves to getting participants to

understand how attitudes influence behavior, providing factual knowledge about the target country, and developing skills in areas like language and adjustment.

- In compensating expatriates, most employers use the balance sheet approach; this focuses on four groups of expenses: income taxes, housing, goods and services, and discretionary expenses. This aims to provide supplements to ensure that the employee's standard of living abroad is about what it would have been at home. It's usual to apply incentives such as foreign service premiums and hardship allowances.
- It's prudent to let both the home-office supervisor and the manager's local superior contribute to the appraisal.
- Labor relations tend to be different abroad. For instance, there's a much greater emphasis on centralized bargaining in Europe.
- With terrorism a threat, most employers today take protective measures, including buying kidnapping and ransom insurance.
- It's important to have well-thought-out repatriation programs. These emphasize keeping employees in the loop as far as what's happening in their home offices, bringing them back to the office periodically, and providing formal repatriation services for the expatriate and his or her family to start preparing them for the return.

5. With employers increasingly relying on local rather than expatriate employees, it's important for managers to understand **how to implement a global HR system**. The basic approach involves three steps. (1) Develop a more effective global HR system (by forming global HR networks and remembering that it's more important to standardize ends rather than specific methods). (2) Make the global HR system more acceptable (for instance, by taking a global approach to everything the company does, by investigating pressures to differentiate and determining their legitimacy, and by creating a strong company culture). (3) Implement the global system (by emphasizing continuing communications and by ensuring that adequate resources are available).

Discussion Questions

17-6. You are the president of a small business. What are some of the ways you expect "going international" will affect HR activities in your business?

17-7. What are some of the specific, uniquely international activities an international HR manager typically engages in?

17-8. What intercountry differences affect HRM? Give several examples of how each may affect HRM.

17-9. You are the HR manager of a firm that is about to send its first employees overseas to staff a new subsidiary. Your boss, the president, asks you why such assignments often fail, and what you plan to do to avoid such failures. How do you respond?

17-10. As an HR manager, what program would you establish to reduce repatriation problems of returning expatriates and their families?

Individual and Group Activities

17-11. Working individually or in groups, outline an expatriation and repatriation plan for your professor, whom your school is sending to Bulgaria to teach HR for the next 3 years.

17-12. Give three specific examples of multinational corporations in your area. Check on the Internet or with each firm to determine in what countries these firms have operations. Explain the nature of some of their operations, and summarize whatever you can find out about their international employee selection and training HR policies.

17-13. Choose three traits useful for selecting international assignees, and create a straightforward test to screen candidates for these traits.

17-14. Use a library or Internet source to determine the relative cost of living in five countries as of this year, and explain the implications of such differences for drafting a pay plan for managers being sent to each country.

17-15. Appendix A, PHR and SPHR Knowledge Base, at the end of this book (pages 580–588) lists the knowledge someone studying for the HRCI certification exam needs to have in each area of human resource management (such as in Strategic Management, Workforce Planning, and Human Resource Development). In groups of four to five students, do four things: (1) review Appendix A; (2) identify the material in this chapter that relates to the required knowledge Appendix A lists; (3) write four multiple-choice exam questions on this material that you believe would be suitable for inclusion in the HRCI exam; and (4) if time permits, have someone from your team post your team's questions in front of the class, so that students in all teams can answer the exam questions created by the other teams.

17-16. An issue of *HR Magazine* contained an article titled "Aftershocks of War," which said that soldiers returning to their jobs from Iraq would likely require HR's assistance in coping with "delayed emotional trauma." The term *delayed emotional trauma* refers to the personality changes such as anger, anxiety, or irritability that exposure to the traumatic events of war sometimes triggers in returning veterans. Assume you are the HR manager for the employer of John Smith, who is returning to work next week after 1 year in Iraq. Based on what you read in this chapter, what steps would you take to help smooth John's reintegration into your workforce?

Experiential Exercise

A Taxing Problem for Expatriate Employees

Purpose: The purpose of this exercise is to give you practice identifying and analyzing some of the factors that influence expatriates' pay.

Required Understanding: You should be thoroughly familiar with this chapter and with the website www.irs.gov.

How to Set Up the Exercise/Instructions: Divide the class into teams of four or five students. Each team member should read the following: One of the trickiest aspects of calculating expatriates' pay relates to the question of the expatriate's U.S. federal income tax liabilities. Go to the Internal Revenue Service's website, www.irs.gov. Scroll down to Individuals, and go to Overseas Taxpayers. Your team is the expatriate-employee compensation task force for your company, and your firm is about to send several managers and engineers to Japan, England, and Hong Kong. What information did you find on the site that will help your team formulate expat tax and compensation policies? Based on that, what are the three most important things your firm should keep in mind in formulating a compensation policy for employees you're about to send to Japan, England, and Hong Kong?

Video Case

Video Title: Global HR Management (Joby)

SYNOPSIS

Joby is best known for its line of flexible camera tripods, called Gorillapods, and for its flexible flashlights, called Gorillatorches. Joby has only a few dozen employees, but has offices on three continents. It is often called "the smallest global company in the world."

Discussion Questions

17-17. Describe Joby's approach to managing globally. How does it coordinate design, manufacturing, and distribution in key world markets?

17-18. How does a small company like Joby hire employees to work in its facilities all over the world?

17-19. Based on what you read in this chapter, what suggestions would you make for improving this company's global HR practices?

Application Case*

"Boss, I Think we Have a Problem"

Central Steel Door Corporation has been in business for about 20 years, successfully selling a line of steel industrial-grade doors.[137] The company had gradually increased its presence from the New York City area, first into New England and then down the Atlantic Coast, then through the Midwest and West, and finally into Canada. The company's basic expansion strategy was always the same: Choose an area, open a distribution center, hire a regional sales manager, and then let that regional sales manager help staff the distribution center and hire local sales reps.

Unfortunately, the company's traditional success in finding sales help did not extend to its overseas operations, when Mel Fisher, president of Central Steel Door, decided to expand his company into Europe. He tried for 3 weeks to find a sales manager by advertising in the *International New York Times*, which is read by businesspeople in Europe and by American expatriates living and working in Europe. Although the ads placed in the *Times* also ran for about a month on the *Times*'s website, Mr. Fisher so far has received only five applications. One came from a possibly viable candidate, whereas four came from candidates who Mr. Fisher refers to as "lost souls"—people who seem to have spent most of their time traveling aimlessly from country to country, sipping espresso in sidewalk cafés. When asked what he had done for the last 3 years, one told Mr. Fisher he'd been on a "walkabout."

Other aspects of his international HR activities have been equally problematic. Fisher alienated two of his U.S. sales managers by sending them to Europe to temporarily run the European operations, but neglecting to work out a compensation package that would cover their relatively high living expenses in Germany and Belgium. One ended up staying the better part of the year, and Mr. Fisher was rudely surprised to be informed by the Belgian government that his sales manager owed thousands of dollars in local taxes. The two managers had hired about 10 local people to staff each of the two distribution centers. However, the level of sales was disappointing, so Fisher decided to fire about half the distribution center employees. That's when he got an emergency phone call from his temporary sales manager in Germany: "I've just been told that all these employees should have had written employment agreements and that in any case we can't fire anyone without at least 1 year's notice, and the local authorities here are really up in arms. Boss, I think we have a problem."

Questions

17-20. Based on this chapter and the case incident, compile a list of 10 international HR mistakes Mr. Fisher has made so far.

17-21. How would you have gone about hiring a European sales manager? Why?

17-22. What would you do now if you were Mr. Fisher?

Continuing Case

Carter Cleaning Company

Going Abroad

Jack Carter decided to take his first long vacation in years and go to Mexico for a month in January 2013. What he found surprised him: He spent time in Mexico City and was surprised at the dearth of cleaning stores, particularly considering the amount of air pollution. Traveling north, he passed through Juarez, Mexico, and was similarly surprised at the relatively few cleaning stores he found there. As he drove back into Texas, and back toward home, he began to think about whether it would be advisable to consider expanding his chain of stores into Mexico.

Aside from the possible economic benefits, he liked what he saw in Mexico. Starting a new business again also appealed to him. "I guess entrepreneurship is in my blood," is the way he put it.

As he drove home to have dinner with Jennifer, he began to formulate the questions he would have to ask before deciding whether to expand abroad.

Questions

17-23. Assuming they began by opening just one or two stores in Mexico, what do you see as the main HR-related challenges Jack and Jennifer would have to address?

17-24. How would you go about choosing a manager for a new Mexican store if you were Jack or Jennifer? For instance, would you hire someone locally or send someone from one of your existing stores? Why?

17-25. The cost of living in Mexico is substantially below that of where Carter is now located: How would you go about developing a pay plan for your new manager if you decided to send an expatriate to Mexico?

17-26. Present a detailed explanation of the factors you would look for in your candidate for expatriate manager to run the stores in Mexico.

Translating Strategy into HR Policies and Practices Case*,§

**The accompanying strategy map for this chapter is in the MyManagementLab; and the overall map on the inside back cover of this text outlines the relationships involved.*

IMPROVING PERFORMANCE at The Hotel Paris

Managing Global Human Resources

The Hotel Paris's competitive strategy is, "To use superior guest service to differentiate the Hotel Paris properties, and to thereby increase the length of stay and return rate of guests, and thus boost revenues and profitability." HR manager Lisa Cruz must now formulate functional policies and activities that support this competitive strategy and boost performance by eliciting the required employee behaviors and competencies.

With hotels in 11 cities in Europe and the United States, Lisa knew that the company had to do a better job of managing its global human resources. For example, there was no formal means of identifying or training management employees for duties abroad (either for those going to the United States or to Europe). As another example, recently, after spending upwards of $200,000 on sending a U.S. manager and her family abroad, they had to return her abruptly when the family complained of missing their friends back home. Lisa knew this was no way to run a multinational business. She turned her attention to developing the HR practices her company required to do business more effectively internationally.

On reviewing the data, it was apparent to Lisa and the CFO that the company's global human resource practices were probably inhibiting the Hotel Paris from being the world-class guest services company that it sought to be. For example, high-performing service and hotel firms had formal departure training programs for at least 90% of the employees they sent abroad; the Hotel Paris had no such programs. Similarly, with each city's hotel operating its own local hotel HR information system, there was no easy way for Lisa, the CFO, or the company's CEO to obtain reports on metrics like turnover, absences, or workers' compensation costs across all the different hotels. As the CFO summed it up, "If we can't measure how each hotel is doing in terms of human resource metrics like these, there's really no way to manage these activities, so there's no telling how much lost profits and wasted efforts are dragging down each hotel's performance." Lisa received approval to institute new global human resources programs and practices.

In instituting these new programs and practices, Lisa had several goals in mind. She wanted an integrated human resource information system (HRIS) that allowed her and the company's top managers to monitor and assess, on an ongoing basis, the company's global performance on strategically required employee competencies and behaviors such as attendance, morale, commitment, and service-oriented behavior. To address this need, she received approval to contract with a company that integrated, via the Internet, the separate hotels' HR systems, including human resource and benefits administration, applicant tracking and résumé scanning, and employee morale surveys and performance appraisals.

She also contracted with an international HR training company to offer expatriate training for Hotel Paris employees and their families before they left for their foreign assignments, and to provide short-term support after they arrived. That training company also helped create a series of weeklong "Managers' Seminars." Held once every 6 months at a different hotel in a different city, these gave selected managers from throughout the Hotel Paris system an opportunity to meet and to learn more about the numerous new HR programs and practices that Lisa and her team had been instituting for the purpose of supporting the company's strategic aims. With the help of their compensation specialist, Lisa and her team also instituted a new incentive program for each of the company's local managers, to focus their attention more fully on the company's service-oriented strategic aims. By the end of the year, the Hotel Paris's performance on metrics such as percent of expatriates receiving pre-departure screening, training, and counseling were at or above those of high-performing similar companies. She and the CFO believed, rightly, that they had begun to get their global HR system under control.

Questions

17-27. Provide a one-page summary of what individual hotel managers should know in order to make it more likely incoming employees from abroad will adapt to their new surroundings.

17-28. In previous chapters you recommended various human resource practices Hotel Paris should use. Choose one of these, and explain why you believe they could take this program abroad, and how you suggest they do so.

17-29. Choose one Hotel Paris human resources practice that you believe is essential to the company specifically for achieving its high-quality-service goal, and explain how you would implement that practice in the firm's various hotels worldwide.

§Written by and copyright Gary Dessler, PhD.

CHAPTER 17

MyManagementLab

Go to **mymanagementlab.com** for Auto-graded writing questions as well as the following Assisted-graded writing questions:

17-30. What special training do overseas candidates need? In what ways is such training similar to and different from traditional diversity training?

17-31. How does appraising an expatriate's performance differ from appraising that of a home-office manager? How would you avoid some of the unique problems of appraising the expatriate's performance?

17-32. MyManagementLab only—comprehensive writing assignment for this chapter.

Key Terms

international human resource management (IHRM), 534
works councils, 536
codetermination, 536
expatriates (expats), 538
home-country nationals, 538
locals, 538
third-country nationals, 538
virtual teams, 540
ethnocentric, 541
polycentric, 541
geocentric, 541
adaptability screening, 543
foreign service premiums, 547
hardship allowances, 547
mobility premiums, 547

Endnotes

1. http://talkingunion.wordpress.com/2008/09/27/is-union-reform-possible-in-china, accessed March 25, 2009; "First Wal-Mart Union Begins in China," www.huffingtonpost.com/2008/08/03/first-wal-mart-union-begi_n_116629.html, accessed June 30, 2011.
2. Nancy Wong, "Mark Your Calendar! Important Task for International HR," *Workforce,* April 2000, pp. 72–74.
3. www.hoovers.com/company/Wal-Mart_Stores_Inc/rrjiff-1.html, accessed June 1, 2011.
4. "First Wal-Mart Union Begins in China," www.huffingtonpost.com/2008/08/03/first-wal-mart-union-begi_n_116629.html, accessed June 30, 2011.
5. Based on "Wal-Mart's Reshuffle Plan in China Falters," www.chinadaily.com.cn/china/2009-04/21/content_7699105.htm, accessed June 30, 2011.
6. Anne Marie Francesco and Barry Gold, *International Organizational Behavior,* (Upper Saddle River, NJ: Prentice Hall), 2004, p. 145.
7. A. L. Lytle, J. M. Brett, Z. Barsness, C. H. Tinsley, and M. Janssens, "A Paradigm for Quantitative Cross-Cultural Research in Organizational Behavior," in B. M. Staw and L. L. Cummings (Eds), *Research in Organizational Behavior* 17 (1995), pp. 167–214.
8. David Ralston, David Gustafson, Priscilla Elsass, Fannie Cheung, and Robert Terpstra, "Eastern Values: A Comparison of Managers in the United States, Hong Kong, and the People's Republic of China," *Journal of Applied Psychology* 71, no. 5 (1992), pp. 664–671. See also P. Christopher Earley and Elaine Mosakowski, "Cultural Intelligence," *Harvard Business Review,* October 2004, pp. 139–146.
9. www.geert-hofstede.com/, accessed August 12, 2013.
10. See Vas Taras, Bradley Kirkman, and Piers Steel, "Examining the Impact of Culture's Consequences: A Three-Decade, Multilevel, Multi-Analytic Review of Hofstadter's Cultural Value Dimensions," *Journal of Applied Psychology* 95, no. 3 (2010), pp. 405–439.
11. Chris Brewster, "European Perspectives on Human Resource Management," *Human Resource Management Review* 14 (2004), pp. 365–382.
12. "SOX Compliance, Corporate Codes of Conduct Can Create Challenges for U.S. Multinationals," *BNA Bulletin to Management,* March 28, 2006, p. 97.
13. "In India, 101 Employees Pose Big Problems," *Bloomberg Businessweek,* January 17–23, 2011, p. 13.
14. "Employer Beware," *The Economist,* March 12, 2011, p. 43.
15. See, for example, www.fedee.com/ewc1.html, accessed August 12, 2013.
16. This is discussed in Eduard Gaugler, "HR Management: An International Comparison," *Personnel* 65, no. 8 (1988), p. 28. See also E. Poutsma et al., "The Diffusion of Calculative and Collaborative HRM Practices in European Firms," *Industrial Relations* 45, no. 4 (October 2006), pp. 513–546.
17. 2011 figures, www.bls.gov/news.release/pdf/ichcc.pdf, accessed August 12, 2013.
18. Phillips Taft and Cliff Powell, "The European Pensions and Benefits Environment: A Complex Ecology," *Compensation & Benefits Review,* January/February 2005, pp. 37–50.
19. Ibid.
20. Lisbeth Claus, "What You Need to Know About the New Labor Contract Law of China," SHRM Global Law Special Report, October to November 2008.
21. See, for example, Syed Akhtar et al., "Strategic HRM Practices and Their Impact on Company Performance in Chinese Enterprises," *Human Resource Management* 47, no. 1 (Spring 2008), pp. 15–32.
22. Andreas Lauffs, "Chinese Law Spurs Reforms," *HR Magazine,* June 2008, pp. 92–98.
23. See, for example, Kathryn King-Metters and Richard Metters, "Misunderstanding the Chinese Worker," *The Wall Street Journal,* July 7, 2008, p. R11.
24. Gary Dessler, "Expanding into China? What Foreign Employers Entering China Should Know About Human Resource Management Today," *SAM Advanced Management Journal,* August 2006. See also Joseph Gamble, "Introducing Western-Style HRM Practices to China: Shop Floor Perceptions in a British Multinational," *Journal of World Business* 41, no. 4 (December 2006), pp. 328–340; and Adrienne Fox, "China: Land of Opportunity and Challenge," *HR Magazine,* September 2007, pp. 38–44.
25. Robert Heneman et al., "Compensation Practices in Small Entrepreneurial and High-Growth Companies in the United States and China," *Compensation and Benefits Review,* July/August 2002, pp. 15–16.
26. Francesco and Gold, *International Organizational Behavior,* p. 145.
27. Ibid., p. 106.
28. Ibid., p. 769; Phatak, *International Dimensions of Management,* p. 106.
29. Leslie Klass, "Fed Up with High Costs, Companies Winnow the Ranks of Career Expats," *Workforce Management,* October 2004, pp. 84–88.
30. "Survey Says Expatriates Twice as Likely to Leave Employer as Home-Based Workers," *BNA Bulletin to Management,* May 9, 2006, p. 147.
31. Phatak, *International Dimensions of Management,* p. 108.
32. Daniels and Radebaugh, *International Business,* p. 769.

33. "DOL Releases Final Rule Amending Filing, Processing of Foreign Labor Certifications," *BNA Bulletin to Management*, January 11, 2005, p. 11.
34. Michelle Rafter, "Return Trip for Expats," *Workforce*, March 16, 2009, pp. 1, 3.
35. See "Workforce Trends: Companies Continue to Deploy Ex-Pats," *Compensation & Benefits Review* 42, no. 1 (January/February 2010), p. 6.
36. "Expatriate Assignments in Growth Markets to Soar," *HR Magazine*, January 2013, p. 20.
37. "Mercer's International Assignments Survey 2010," www.imercer.com/products/2010/intl-assignments-survey.aspx, accessed June 2, 2011; "Companies Juggle Cost Cutting with Maintaining Competitive Benefits for International Assignments," www.amanet.org/training/articles/Companies-Juggle-cost-cutting-with-Maintaining-Competitive-Benefits-for-International-Assignments.aspx, accessed June 2, 2011.
38. "Mercer's International Assignments Survey 2010," "Companies Juggle Cost Cutting with Maintaining Competitive Benefits for International Assignments."
39. Helene Mayerhofer et al., "Flexpatriate Assignments: A Neglected Issue in Global Staffing," *International Journal of Human Resource Management* 15, no. 8 (December 2004), pp. 1371–1389; and Martha Frase, "International Commuters," *HR Magazine*, March 2007, pp. 91–96.
40. Timothy Dwyer, "Localization's Hidden Costs," *HR Magazine*, June 2004, pp. 135–144.
41. Michael Harvey et al., "Global Virtual Teams: A Human Resource Capital Architecture," *International Journal of Human Resource Management* 16, no. 9 (September 2005), pp. 1583–1599.
42. Based on Pamela Babcock, "America's Newest Export: White Collar Jobs," *HR Magazine,* April 2004, pp. 50–57.
43. The following is based on "Back-Office and Customer Care Centers in Emerging Economies: A Human Capital Perspective," IBM Business Consulting Services, www-05.ibm.com/nl/topmanagement/pdfs/back_office_and_customer_care.pdf, accessed April 29, 2008.
44. Ibid., pp. 3, 4.
45. Ibid., pp. 5, 6.
46. Ibid., pp. 5, 6.
47. Ibid., p. 10.
48. Charles Snow, Scott Snell, Sue Canney Davison, and Donald Hambrick, "Use Transnational Teams to Globalize Your Company," *Organizational Dynamics*, Spring 1996, pp. 50–67.
49. Ibid.
50. Anthony Townsend, Samuel DiMarie, and Anthony Hendrickson, "Virtual Teams: Technology and the Workplace of the Future," *Academy of Management Executive* 12, no. 3 (1998), pp. 17–29; Christina Gibson and Susan Cohen, *Virtual Teams That Work: Creating Conditions for Virtual Team Effectiveness* (Jossey-Bass: San Francisco, 2004), provides practicing managers with valuable insights into organizing and managing virtual teams. Many companies use international virtual teams to coordinate research and development type projects. Bjorn Ambos and Bodo Schlemglmich, "The Use of International R&D Teams: An Empirical Investigation of Selected Contingency Factors," *Journal of World Business* 39, no. 1 (February 2004), pp. 37–48.
51. Michael Harvey et al., "Challenges to Staffing Global Virtual Teams," *Human Resource Management Review* 14 (2004), p. 281.
52. Ibid., p. 20.
53. Christa Degnan, "ActiveProject Aids Teamwork," *PC Week*, May 31, 1999, p. 35.
54. Except as noted, this is based on information in Bradley Kirkman et al., "Five Challenges to Virtual Team Success: Lessons from Sabre, Inc.," *Academy of Management Executive* 16, no. 3 (2002), p. 70.
55. This item is based on Bradley Kirkman et al., "The Impact of Team Empowerment on Virtual Team Performance: The Moderating Role of Face-To-Face Interaction," *Academy of Management Journal* 47, no. 2 (2004), pp. 175–192
56. Phatak, *International Dimensions of Management*, p. 129.
57. Charles Hill, *International Business: Competing in the Global Marketplace* (Burr Ridge, IL: Irwin, 1994), p. 507.
58. Ibid., pp. 507–510.
59. Ibid.
60. Ibid., p. 509.
61. Ibid. See also M. Harvey et al., "An Innovative Global Management Staffing System: A Competency-Based Perspective," *Human Resource Management* 39, no. 4 (Winter 2000), pp. 381–394.
62. Donald Dowling Jr., "Export Codes of Conduct, Not Employee Handbooks," *Society for Human Resource Management Legal Report*, January/February 2007, pp. 1–4.
63. www.nytimes.com/2011/03/19/business/global/19blue.html, accessed June 30, 2011.
64. Mason Carpenter et al., "International Assignment Experience at the Top Can Make a Bottom-Line Difference," *Human Resource Management* 30, no. 223 (Summer–Fall 2000), pp. 277–285. See also Gunter Stahl and Paula Caligiuri, "The Effectiveness of Expatriate Coping Strategies: The Moderating Role of Cultural Distance, Position Level, and Time on the International Assignment," *Journal of Applied Psychology* 90, no. 4 (2005), pp. 603–615.
65. Sunkyu Jun and James Gentry, "An Exploratory Investigation of the Relative Importance of Cultural Similarity and Personal Fit in the Selection and Performance of Expatriates," *Journal of World Business* 40, no. 1 (February 2005), pp. 1–8. See also Jan Selmer, "Cultural Novelty and Adjustment: Western Business Expatriates in China," *International Journal of Human Resource Management* 17, no. 7 (2006), pp. 1211–1222.
66. Mary G. Tye and Peter Y. Chen, "Selection of Expatriates: Decision-Making Models Used by HR Professionals," *Human Resource Planning* 28, no. 4 (December 2005), p. 15(6).
67. Paula Caligiuri et al., "Selection for International Assignments," *Human Resource Management Review* 19 (2009), pp. 251–262.
68. Zsuzsanna Tungli and Maury Peiperl, "Expatriate Practices in German, Japanese, UK and US Multinational Companies: A Comparative Survey of Changes," *Human Resource Management* 48, no. 1 (January–February 2009), pp. 153–171.
69. http://www.brookfieldgrs.com/intercultural/ accessed Sepetember 7, 2013.
70. P. Caligiuri, "The Big Five Personality Characteristics as Predictors of Expatriates' Desire to Terminate the Assignment and Supervisor-Rated Performance," *Personnel Psychology* 53, no. 1 (Spring 2000), pp. 67–88. See also Margaret A. Shaffer et al., "You Can Take It with You: Individual Differences and Expatriate Effectiveness," *Journal of Applied Psychology* 91, no. 1 (January 2006), pp. 109–125.
71. Quoted in Meredith Downes, Iris I. Varner, and Luke Musinski, "Personality Traits as Predictors of Expatriate Effectiveness: A Synthesis and Reconceptualization," *Review of Business* 27, no. 3 (Spring/Summer 2007), p. 16.
72. Jan Selmer, "Expatriation: Corporate Policy, Personal Intentions and International Adjustment," *International Journal of Human Resource Management* 9, no. 6 (December 1998), pp. 997–1007. See also Barbara Myers and Judith K. Pringle, "Self-Initiated Foreign Experience as Accelerated Development: Influences of Gender," *Journal of World Business* 40, no. 4 (November 2005), pp. 421–431.
73. Hung-Wen Lee and Ching-Hsing, "Determinants of the Adjustment of Expatriate Managers to Foreign Countries: An Empirical Study," *International Journal of Management* 23, no. 2 (2006), pp. 302–311.
74. P. Blocklyn, "Developing the International Executive," *Personnel,* March 1989, p. 45. See also Paula M. Caligiuri and Jean M. Phillips, "An Application of Self-Assessment Realistic Job Previews to Expatriate Assignments," *International Journal of Human Resource Management* 14, no. 7 (November 2003), pp. 1102–1116.
75. Zsuzsanna Tungli and Maury Peiperl, "Expatriate Practices in German, Japanese, UK and US Multinational Companies: A Comparative Survey of Changes," *Human Resource Management* 48, no. 1 (January/February 2009), pp. 153–171.
76. "More Women, Young Workers on the Move," *Workforce Management,* August 20, 2007, p. 9.
77. For a good discussion of this see Yochanan Altman and Susan Shortland, "Women and International Assignments: Taking Stock—A 25 Year Review," *Human Resource Management* 47, no. 2 (Summer 2008), pp. 199–216.
78. Kathryn Tyler, "Don't Fence Her In," *HR Magazine* 46, no. 3 (March 2001), pp. 69–77.
79. Ibid.
80. Ibid.
81. See Nancy Napier and Sully Taylor, "Experiences of Women Professionals Abroad," *International Journal of Human Resource Management* 13, no. 5 (August 2002), pp. 837–851; Iris Fischlmayr, "Female Self-Perception as a Barrier to International Careers?" *International Journal of Human Resource Management* 13, no. 5 (August 2002), pp. 773–783; Wolfgang Mayrhofer and Hugh Scullion, "Female Expatriates in International Business: Evidence from the German Clothing Industry," *International Journal of Human Resource Management* 13, no. 5 (August 2002), pp. 815–836; and Altman and Shortland, "Women and International Assignments."
82. "The Equal Employment Opportunity Responsibilities of Multinational Employers," The U.S. Equal Employment Opportunity Commission, www.EEOC.gov/facts/

multi-employers.html, accessed February 9, 2004.
83. See Donald Dowling Jr., "Choice of Law Contract Clauses May Not Fly Abroad," Society for Human Resource Management Legal Report, October–November 2008, pp. 1–2.
84. Chuck Csizmar, "Does Your Expatriate Program Follow the Rules of the Road?" *Compensation & Benefits Review*, January/February 2008, pp. 61–69.
85. Discussed in Hill, *International Business*, pp. 511–515.
86. Barbara Anderson, "Expatriate Selection: Good Management or Good Luck?" *International Journal of Human Resource Management* 16, no. 4 (April 2005), pp. 567–583.
87. Margaret Shaffer and David Harrison, "Forgotten Partners of International Assignments: Development and Test of a Model of Spouse Adjustment," *Journal of Applied Psychology* 86, no. 2 (2001), pp. 238–254.
88. Ibid., p. 251.
89. Ibid., p. 250.
90. Deresky, *International Management*, p. 90.
91. Sunkyu Jun and James Gentry, "An Exploratory Investigation of the Relative Importance of Cultural Similarity and Personal Fit in the Selection and Performance of Expatriates," *Journal of World Business* 40, no. 1 (February 2005), pp. 1–8. See also Jan Selmer, "Cultural Novelty and Adjustment: Western Business Expatriates in China," *International Journal of Human Resource Management* 17, no. 7 (2006), pp. 1211–1222.
92. M. Harvey et al., "Global Virtual Teams: A Human Resource Capital Architecture," *International Journal of Human Resource Management* 16, no. 9 (September 2005), pp. 1583–1599.
93. Eric Krell, "Budding Relationships," *HR Magazine* 50, no. 6 (June 2005), pp. 114–118. See also Jill Elswick, "Worldly Wisdom: Companies Refine Their Approach to Overseas Assignments, Emphasizing Cost-Cutting and Work–Life Support for Expatriates," *Employee Benefit News,* June 15, 2004, Item 0416600B.
94. Geoffrey Abbott et al., "Coaching Expatriate Managers for Success: Adding Value Beyond Training and Mentoring," *Asia-Pacific Journal of Human Resources* 44, no. 3 (December 2006), pp. 295–317.
95. Adapted from www.interchangeinstitute.org/html/cross_cultural.htm, accessed July 1, 2011.
96. Adapted from www.kwintessential.co.uk/cultural-services/articles/expat-cultural-training.html, accessed July 1, 2011.
97. www.global-lt.com/en/us/cultural-training/cultural-training-expatriate-training-courses.html#60Countries, accessed July 1, 2011.
98. Lynette Clemetson, "The Pepsi Challenge: Helping Ex-Pats Feel at Home," *Workforce Management*, December 2010, p. 36.
99. Hal Gregersen et al., "Expatriate Performance Appraisal in U.S. Multinational Firms," *Journal of International Business Studies* 27, no. 4 (Winter 1996), pp. 711–739. See also Hsi-An Shih, Yun-Hwa Chiang, and In-Sook Kim, "Expatriate Performance Management from MNEs of Different National Origins," *International Journal of Manpower* 26, no. 2 (February 2005), pp. 157–175; and Francesco and Gold, *International Organizational Behavior,* pp. 152–153.
100. See, for example, Victor Infante, "Three Ways to Design International Pay: Headquarters, Home Country, Host," *Workforce*, January 2001, pp. 22–24; and Gary Parker and Erwin Janush, "Developing Expatriate Remuneration Packages," *Employee Benefits Journal* 26, no. 2 (June 2001), pp. 3–51.
101. "Expatriate Assignments in Growth Markets to Soar," *HR Magazine*, January 2013, p. 20.
102. Stephenie Overman, "Focus on International HR," *HR Magazine*, March 2000, pp. 87–92; Sheila Burns, "Flexible International Assignee Compensation Plans," *Compensation & Benefits Review*, May/June 2003, pp. 35–44; Thomas Shelton, "Global Compensation Strategies: Managing and Administering Split Pay for an Expatriate Workforce," *Compensation & Benefits Review*, January/February 2008, pp. 56–59.
103. Phatak, *International Dimensions of Management*, p. 134. See also "China to Levy Income Tax on Expatriates," Asia Africa Intelligence Wire, August 3, 2004, Item A120140119.
104. Thomas Shelton, "Global Compensation Strategies: Managing and Administering Split Pay for an Expatriate Workforce," *Compensation & Benefits Review*, January/February 2008, pp. 56–59.
105. http://aoprals.state.gov/content.asp?content_id=186&menu_id=81, accessed July 1, 2011.
106. See, for example, "More Multinational Organizations Are Taking a Global Approach to Compensation," *Compensation & Benefits Review*, May/June 2008, p. 5.
107. Luis Hernandez, "On Why Ex-Pat Assignments Succeed—or Fail," *Harvard Business Review*, March 2011, p. 73.
108. Mark Schoeff Jr., "Danger and Duty," *Workforce*, November 19, 2007, pp. 1, 3.
109. "Managers Are Paid More in Emerging Economies," *Compensation & Benefits Review*, September/October 2007, p. 19.
110. Robin White, "A Strategic Approach to Building a Consistent Global Rewards Program," *Compensation & Benefits Review*, July/August 2005, p. 25.
111. "Recommendations for Managing Global Compensation Clause in a Changing Economy," Hewitt Associates, www.hewittassociates.com/_MetaBasicCMAssetCache_/Assets/Articles/2009/hewitt_pov_globalcomp_0109.pdf, accessed March 22, 2009.
112. White, "A Strategic Approach," pp. 23–40.
113. "For Employers Conducting Business Abroad, Kidnappings Remain an Ongoing Concern," *BNA Bulletin to Management*, November 23, 2010, p. 369.
114. Jessica Marquez, "Hostage-Taking in France has U.S. Observers on Their Guard," *Workforce Management*, April 20, 2009, p. 10.
115. Lisbeth Claus, "International Assignees at Risk," *HR Magazine*, February 2010, p. 73.
116. Fay Hansen, "Skirting Danger," *Workforce Magazine*, January 19, 2009, pp. 1, 3.
117. Frank Jossi, "Buying Protection from Terrorism," *HR Magazine*, June 2001, pp. 155–160.
118. "Unrest in Egypt Highlights Importance of Crisis Management Plans, Experts Say," *BNA Bulletin to Management*, February 8, 2011, pp. 41–42.
119. Frank Jossi, "Buying Protection from Terrorism," op cit.
120. These are based on or quoted from Samuel Greengard, "Mission Possible: Protecting Employees Abroad," *Workforce*, August 1997, pp. 30–32. See also Z. Phillips, "Global Firms Consider Additional Cover for Overseas Execs," *Business Insurance* 43, no. 23 (June 15–22, 2009), pp. 4, 22.
121. Ibid., p. 32.
122. Carla Joinson, "Save Thousands Per Expatriate," *HR Magazine*, July 2002, p. 77. A survey by accountants KPMG found that only about 4% of the 430 human resource executives surveyed believed they were effectively managing the repatriation process. Tanya Mohn, "The Long Trip Home," *The New York Times*, March 10, 2009, //www.nytimes.com/2009/03/10/business/worldbusiness/10iht-10home.20715091.html, accessed October 15, 2013.
123. Kathryn Tyler, "Retaining Repatriates," *HR Magazine*, March 2006, pp. 97–102.
124. Quoted in Leslie Klaff, "The Right Way to Bring Expats Home," *Workforce*, July 2002, p. 43.
125. Maria Kraimer et al., "The Influence of Expatriate and Repatriate Experiences on Career Advancement and Repatriate Retention," *Human Resource Management* 48, no. 1 (January–February 2009), pp. 27–47.
126. Ibid., p. 43.
127. Ibid.
128. Diane Turner, "NuView Brings Web-Based HRIS to Buildnet," *Workforce*, December 2000, p. 90.
129. Jim Meade, "Web-Based HRIS Meets Multiple Needs," *HR Magazine*, August 2000, pp. 129–133. See also "Dynamic HR: Global Applications from IBM," *Human Resource Management* 48, no. 4 (July/August 2009), pp. 641–648.
130. Drew Robb, "Unifying Your Enterprise with a Global HR Portal," *HR Magazine*, March 2006, pp. 119–120.
131. Ann Marie Ryan et al., "Designing and Implementing Global Staffing Systems: Part 2—Best Practices," *Human Resource Management* 42, no. 1 (Spring 2003), pp. 85–94.
132. Ibid., p. 89.
133. Ibid., p. 90.
134. Ibid., p. 86. See also M. Schoeff, "Adopting an HR Worldview," *Workforce Management* 87, no. 19 (November 17, 2008), p. 8.
135. Ryan, "Designing and Implementing Global Staffing Systems," p. 87.
136. Ibid., p. 92.
137. Written by and copyrighted by Gary Dessler, PhD.

18

Managing Human Resources in Small and Entrepreneurial Firms

Source: David McNew/Getty Images

MyManagementLab®

Improve Your Grade!

When you see this icon, visit **www.mymanagementlab.com** or activities that are applied, personalized, and offer immediate feedback.

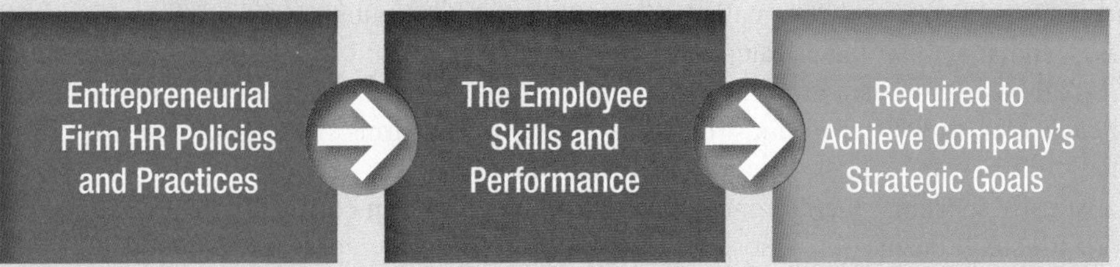

For a bird's eye view of how one company created a new HR information system to improve its strategic performance, read the Hotel Paris case on pages 577–578 and answer the questions after reading the chapter.

WHERE ARE WE NOW . . .

Most people work for small businesses (or create and manage small firms of their own), and such businesses have special human resource management needs. The main purpose of this chapter is to help you apply what you know about human resource management to running a small business. The main topics we'll address include the small business challenge; using Internet and government tools to support the HR effort; leveraging small size with familiarity, flexibility, fairness, and informality; using professional employer organizations; and managing HR systems, procedures, and paperwork.

LEARNING OBJECTIVES

1. Explain why HRM is important to small businesses and how small business HRM is different from that in large businesses.
2. Give four examples of how entrepreneurs can use Internet and government tools to support the HR effort.
3. List five ways entrepreneurs can use their small size to improve their HR processes.
4. Discuss how you would choose and deal with a professional employee organization.
5. Describe how you would create a start-up human resource system for a new small business.

His high school teacher told him he might not make it in business. But today Carlos Ledezma owns two Chevrolet dealerships in Kansas City.[1] Those dealerships are more profitable than most, something Mr. Ledezma attributes in part to his human resource management practices. His business strategy was to boost profits by building repeat business from customers who like dealing with friendly, long-term employees. HR management helped him achieve those goals. We'll see how he did it.

The Small Business Challenge

1 Explain why HRM is important to small businesses and how small business HRM is different from that in large businesses.

In some respects, there's nothing small about *small business*. About 99% of U.S. firms are small businesses, and about half the private-sector people working in the United States work for small firms.[2] Small businesses as a group also account for most of the 600,000 or so new businesses created each year, as well as for most business growth (small firms grow faster than big ones). And small firms create most of the new jobs in the United States.[3]

Statistically speaking, therefore, most people graduating from college in the next few years will work for small businesses—those with less than about 200 employees. So, most everyone reading this book should know something about human resource management in small businesses.

How Small Business Human Resource Management Is Different

Managing human resources in small firms is different for four main reasons: *size, priorities, informality*, and the nature of the *entrepreneur*.

SIZE For one thing, it's very unusual to find a business under 90 or so employees with a dedicated human resource management professional.[4] As a rule, it's not until a company reaches the 100-employee milestone that it can afford an HR specialist. Yet even five- or six-person retail shops must recruit, select, train, and compensate employees. So it's the owner or his or her assistant that does the HR paperwork and tasks. SHRM found that even firms with under 100 employees often spend the equivalent of two-or-so people's time each year addressing human resource management issues.[5] That time usually comes out of the owner's long workday.

PRIORITIES It's not just size but business realities that drive many small business managers and entrepreneurs (the men and women who provide the vision and "spark" that starts a new business) to focus on non-HR issues. After studying small e-commerce firms in the United Kingdom, one researcher concluded that, as important as human resource management is, it just wasn't a high priority for these firms:

> Given their shortage of resources in terms of time, money, people and expertise, a typical SME [small- and medium-size enterprise] manager's organizational imperatives are perceived elsewhere, in finance, production and marketing, with HR of diminished relative importance.[6]

INFORMALITY One effect of this is that human resource management tends to be more informal in smaller firms. Thus, one study analyzed training practices in about 900 family and non-family small companies.[7] Training tended to be informal, with an emphasis on methods like coworker and supervisory on-the-job training.

Such informality isn't just due to a lack of resources, it's a "matter of survival." Entrepreneurs must react fast to changing competitive conditions. So, there's logic in keeping things like compensation policies flexible. The need for small businesses to adapt quickly often means handling matters like raises, appraisals, and time off "on an informal, reactive basis with a short time horizon."[8]

THE ENTREPRENEUR *Entrepreneurs* are people who create businesses under risky conditions. Researchers believe that small firms' relative informality partly stems from entrepreneurs' tendency to want to control things. "Owners tend to want to impose their stamp and personal management style on internal matters, including the primary goal and orientation of the firm, its working conditions and policies, and the style of internal and external communication and how this is communicated to the staff."[9]

IMPLICATIONS What does this mean for the typical SME's human resource management practices?

- First, their rudimentary human resource practices may put small business owners at a *competitive disadvantage*. A small business owner not using tools like Web-based recruiting is accumulating unnecessary costs, and probably deriving inferior results.
- Second, there is a *lack of specialized HR expertise*.[10] Even in larger small businesses, there are at most one or two human resource management people. This makes it likely they'll miss problems in specific areas, such as equal employment law. For example, the smaller firm often hasn't the time or specialized expertise to understand the legal implications—for instance, of inappropriately asking a female job candidate if she's thinking of "starting a family."

- Third, the small business owner may not be fully complying with *compensation regulations and laws*. Examples include paying for overtime hours worked, and distinguishing between employees and independent contractors.
- Fourth, paperwork duplication creates *data entry errors*. Small businesses often don't use human resource information systems, so employee data (name, address, marital status, and so on) often appears on multiple human resource forms (medical enrollment forms, W-4 forms, and so on). Any personal data change then requires manually changing all forms. This is inefficient, and triggers errors.

Diversity Counts

More men than women start new businesses, but according to one study, about 100 million women in 59 countries still started new businesses in one recent year.[11] Interestingly, most of the women who did start businesses were not in the developed world. The most likely countries for women to start businesses were in Latin America and sub-Saharan Africa. This may be because in developed economies, women have more career options. In developing economies such as Ghana, necessity infuses a confidence that drives more women to make it on their own.

Why HRM Is Important to Small Businesses

Small firms that have effective HR practices do better than those that do not.[12] For example, researchers studied 168 family-owned high-growth SMEs. They concluded that successful high-growth SMEs placed more stress on training and development, performance appraisals, recruitment packages, maintaining morale, and setting competitive compensation levels than did less successful ones: "These findings suggest that these human resource activities do in fact have a positive impact on performance [in smaller businesses]."[13]

For many small firms, effective human resource management is also mandatory for getting and keeping big customers. For example, to comply with international ISO-9000 quality standards, many large customers check that their small vendors have and follow certain HR policies.[14] The accompanying Profit Center feature provides another example.

IMPROVING PERFORMANCE: HR as a Profit Center

The Dealership

Auto dealer Carlos Ledezma's strategy was to boost profits by building repeat business from customers who like dealing with friendly, long-term employees.[15] He knew his success therefore depended on building a dedicated and customer-oriented staff, and getting them to stay. To achieve that, he follows a well thought out customer-oriented human resource management strategy. He tests each job candidate to make sure the job is the right fit. There's a weeklong new-employee orientation that introduces them to their jobs and to the firm's mission and culture. Then each new employee gets a senior employee mentor for 90 days.[16] He or she teaches by example. For the first 90 days, mentors receive $50 to $100 for each vehicle their trainee sells. In one recent year, Ledezma spent $150,000 on training.

Ledezma's HR strategy pays off in profits that are well above average. Customers like dealing with his dedicated long-term employees. His annual employee turnover is about 28%, and the average employee stays about 8 years, both much better than the industry average.

Discussion Question 18-1: Write a short note on this topic: "What Carlos Ledezma is doing right with respect to HR management, based on what I've read about HR in the other chapters of this book."

We devote this chapter to methods small business managers can use to improve their human resource management practices, starting with Internet and government tools.

Using Internet and Government Tools to Support the HR Effort

2 Give four examples of how entrepreneurs can use Internet and government tools to support the HR effort.

City Garage is an expanding car service company in Texas.[17] The firm's managers needed mechanics who were comfortable interacting directly with customers in City Garage's "open service area" format (where customers could watch and interact with their mechanics). The old hiring

iStockphoto/Thinkstock

City Garage's managers knew they would never implement their firm's growth strategy without changing how they tested and hired employees.

process was a paper-and-pencil application and one interview, followed by a hire/don't hire decision. The process ate up management time and was ineffective. City Garage's solution was to purchase the Personality Profile Analysis (PPA) online test from Thomas International USA. Now, after a quick application and background check, candidates take the 10-minute, 24-question PPA. City Garage staff then enter the answers into the PPA Software system, and receive test results almost at once. These show whether the applicant is right for the job, based on four personality characteristics.

Like City Garage, no small business need cede the "HR advantage" to big competitors. Knowledgeable small business managers can level the terrain by using Internet-based HR resources, including free online resources from the U.S. government. We'll look at how.

Complying with Employment Laws

Complying with federal (and state and local) employment law is a thorny issue for entrepreneurs. For example, the entrepreneur needs to know, "Must I pay this person overtime?" and, "Must I report this injury?"

Start by knowing which federal employment laws apply. For example, Title VII of the 1964 Civil Rights Act applies to employers with 15 or more employees, while the Age Discrimination in Employment Act of 1967 applies to those with 20 or more.[18] Small business owners will find the legal answers they need to answer questions like these online at federal agencies' websites like the following.

THE DOL The U.S. Department of Labor's "*FirstStep* Employment Law Advisor" (see www.DOL.gov/elaws/firststep/) helps small business managers determine which laws apply to their businesses. First, the elaws wizard takes the owner through questions such as "What is the maximum number of employees your business or organization employs or will employ during the calendar year?" (See Figure 18-1.)

Further on, the "results" page says, "Based on the information you provided in response to the questions in the Advisor, the following employment laws administered by the Department of Labor (DOL) may apply to your business or organization."[19] For a typical small firm, these laws might include the Consumer Credit Protection Act, Employee Polygraph Protection Act, Fair Labor Standards Act, Immigration and Nationality Act, Occupational Safety and Health Act, Uniformed Services Employment and Reemployment Rights Act, and Whistleblower Act.

FIGURE 18-1 *FirstStep* Employment Law Advisor

Source: U.S. Department of Labor, www.dol.gov/elaws/firststep, accessed October 26, 2012.

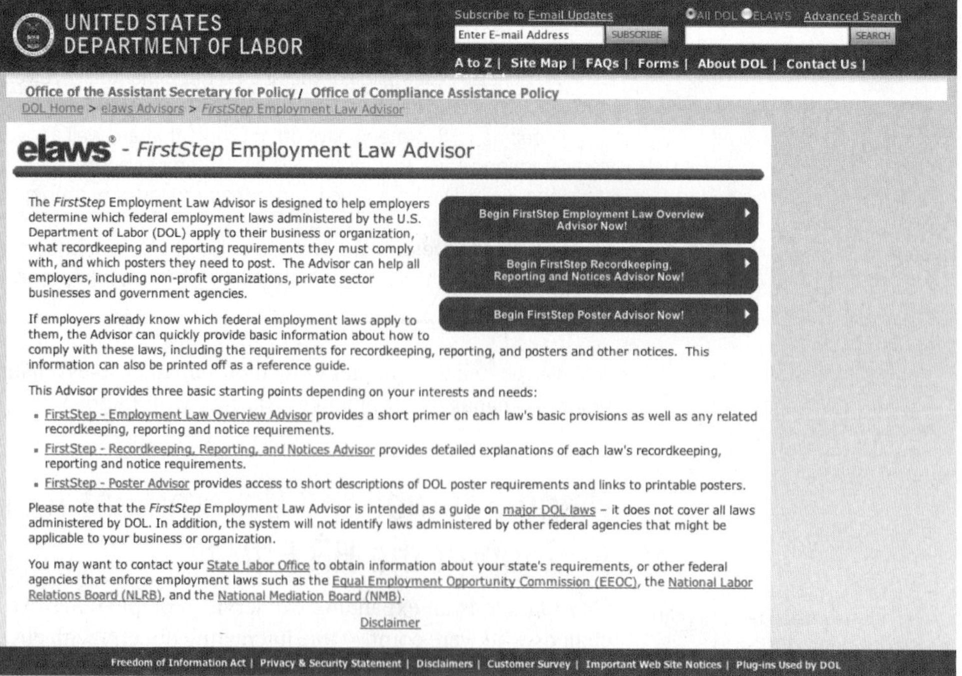

UNITED STATES DEPARTMENT OF LABOR

Subscribe to E-mail Updates | Enter E-mail Address | SUBSCRIBE | All DOL | ELAWS | Advanced Search | SEARCH

A to Z | Site Map | FAQs | Forms | About DOL | Contact Us |

Office of the Assistant Secretary for Policy / Office of Compliance Assistance Policy

DOL Home > elaws Advisors > *FirstStep* Employment Law Advisor

elaws® - *FirstStep* Employment Law Advisor

The *FirstStep* Employment Law Advisor is designed to help employers determine which federal employment laws administered by the U.S. Department of Labor (DOL) apply to their business or organization, what recordkeeping and reporting requirements they must comply with, and which posters they need to post. The Advisor can help all employers, including non-profit organizations, private sector businesses and government agencies.

Begin FirstStep Employment Law Overview Advisor Now!

Begin FirstStep Recordkeeping, Reporting and Notices Advisor Now!

Begin FirstStep Poster Advisor Now!

If employers already know which federal employment laws apply to them, the Advisor can quickly provide basic information about how to comply with these laws, including the requirements for recordkeeping, reporting, and posters and other notices. This information can also be printed off as a reference guide.

This Advisor provides three basic starting points depending on your interests and needs:

- FirstStep - Employment Law Overview Advisor provides a short primer on each law's basic provisions as well as any related recordkeeping, reporting and notice requirements.
- FirstStep - Recordkeeping, Reporting, and Notices Advisor provides detailed explanations of each law's recordkeeping, reporting and notice requirements.
- FirstStep - Poster Advisor provides access to short descriptions of DOL poster requirements and links to printable posters.

Please note that the *FirstStep* Employment Law Advisor is intended as a guide on major DOL laws – it does not cover all laws administered by DOL. In addition, the system will not identify laws administered by other federal agencies that might be applicable to your business or organization.

You may want to contact your State Labor Office to obtain information about your state's requirements, or other federal agencies that enforce employment laws such as the Equal Employment Opportunity Commission (EEOC), the National Labor Relations Board (NLRB), and the National Mediation Board (NMB).

Disclaimer

Freedom of Information Act | Privacy & Security Statement | Disclaimers | Customer Survey | Important Web Site Notices | Plug-ins Used by DOL

FIGURE 18-2 Sample DOL Elaws Advisors

Source: www.dol.gov/elaws/, accessed September 10, 2012.

- The *Coverage and Employment Status Advisor helps* identify which workers are employees covered by the FLSA.
- The *Hours Worked Advisor* provides information to help determine which hours spent in work-related activities are considered FLSA "hours worked" and, therefore, must be paid.
- The *Overtime Security Advisor* helps determine which employees are exempt from the FLSA minimum wage and overtime pay requirements under the Part 541 overtime regulations.
- The *Overtime Calculator Advisor* computes the amount of overtime pay due in a sample pay period based on information from the user.
- The *Child Labor Rules Advisor* answers questions about the FLSA's youth employment provisions, including at what age young people can work and the jobs they can perform.
- The *Section 14(c) Advisor* helps users understand the special minimum wage requirements for workers with disabilities.

A linked DOL site (www.dol.gov/whd/flsa/index.htm) provides information on the Fair Labor Standards Act (FLSA). It's "elaws Advisors" provide practical guidance on questions such as when to pay overtime. Figure 18-2 presents, from this website, a list of elaws Advisors.

THE EEOC The U.S. Equal Employment Opportunity Commission administers Title VII of the Civil Rights Act of 1964 (Title VII), the Age Discrimination in Employment Act of 1967 (ADEA), Title I of the Americans with Disabilities Act of 1990 (ADA), and the Equal Pay Act of 1963 (EPA). Its website (www.EEOC.gov/employers/) contains important information regarding matters such as:

- How do I determine if my business is covered by EEOC laws?
- Who may file a charge of discrimination with the EEOC?
- Can a small business resolve a charge without undergoing an investigation or facing a lawsuit?

As the EEOC says, "While the information in this section of our website applies to all employers, it has been specifically designed for small businesses which may not have a human resources department or a specialized EEO staff" (www.eeoc.gov/employers). The site provides small business owners with practical advice. For example, "What should I do when someone files a charge against my company?"

OSHA The DOL's Occupational Safety and Health Administration site (www.OSHA.gov/) similarly supplies small business guidance (see Figure 18-3). OSHA's site provides, among other things, easy access to the *OSHA Small Business Handbook.* This contains practical information, including industry-specific safety and accident checklists.

Employment Planning and Recruiting

Online tools can make small business owners as effective as their large competitors at writing job descriptions and recruiting applicants. As we saw in Chapter 4 (Job Analysis), the Department of Labor's O*NET (http://online.onetcenter.org) illustrates this. It enables business owners to create accurate job descriptions and job specifications quickly.

WEB-BASED RECRUITING Similarly, small business owners can use the online recruiting tools we discussed in Chapter 5. For example, it's easy to scour LinkedIn.com, and to post jobs on Careerbuilder.com, and on professional associations' job boards.

SOCIAL MEDIA and HR[20]

Many small businesses use social media to recruit applicants. For example, LinkedIn lets employers post job openings and facilitates business networking; one recruiter looks for Linked In members with compelling summaries, excellent recommendations, and memberships in industry groups. On Twitter, recruiters can quickly see if a potential candidate has an appropriate username and photos. But also check Twitter for things like the person's status updates and retweets, to see (for instance) if he or she shares useful information. Small businesses'

FIGURE 18-3 OSHA Website

Source: U.S. Department of Labor, www.osha.gov/dcsp/smallbusiness/index.html.

recruiters should also focus on the social media that makes sense for them. For example, if you're looking for a Facebook marketing expert, look on Facebook. Or look for a photographer on Instagram. And on Facebook and LinkedIn, focus recruiting efforts on industry groups that make sense for your company. Check to see how your competitors use social media, and which communities they use.

Social media recruiting entails risks. For example, conversing with someone whose Facebook profile reveals ethnic background could expose the employer to a discrimination suit if that applicant isn't hired. And many agree that at the end of the day, social media recruiting can't substitute for in-person interactions.

Employment Selection

As with the earlier City Garage example, some tests are so easy to use they are particularly good for smaller firms. An example is the *Wonderlic Personnel Test*, which measures general mental ability. With questions somewhat similar to the SAT, it takes less than 15 minutes to administer the four-page booklet. The tester reads the instructions, and then keeps time as the candidate works through the 50 problems. The tester scores the test by totaling the number of correct answers. Comparing the person's score with the minimum scores recommended for various occupations shows whether the person achieved the minimally acceptable score for the job in question.

The *Predictive Index* is another example. It measures work-related personality traits, drives, and behaviors—in particular dominance, extroversion, patience, and blame avoidance. A template makes scoring simple. The Predictive Index program includes 15 standard benchmark personality patterns. For example, there is the "social interest" pattern, for a person who is generally unselfish, congenial, persuasive, patient, and unassuming. This person would be a good personnel interviewer, for instance.

Many vendors, including Wonderlic and the Predictive Index, offer online applicant testing and screening services. Wonderlic's service (which costs about $8,500 per year for a small firm) first provides job analyses for the employer's jobs. Wonderlic then provides a website the small businesses' applicants can log into to take one or several selection tests (including the Wonderlic Personnel Test).

©michaeljung/Fotolia

Use online tests, for instance, to test an applicant's typing speed, proficiency at QuickBooks, or even ability to sell over the phone.

The following are suggestions from *Inc.* magazine for supercharging a small business's recruiting and screening processes.

- ***Keep it in the industry.*** Use online job boards that target a particular industry or city to minimize irrelevant applicants.[21] For example, Jobing.com maintains 41 city-specific job sites in 19 states. Beyond.com hosts more than 15,000 industry-specific communities.
- ***Automate the process.*** Automated applicant processing systems are inexpensive enough for small employers. For example, systems from Taleo, NuView Systems, and Accolo accept résumés and help automate the screening process. NuView, which costs about $6 to $15 per month per user, asks applicants questions, and bumps out those without, for instance, the required education.[22]
- ***Test online.*** Use online tests, for instance, to test an applicant's typing speed, proficiency at QuickBooks, or even ability to sell over the phone. For example, PreVisor and Kenexa offer close to 1,000 online assessments, charging from several dollars to $50 per test.[23]
- ***Poll your inner circle.*** Tap friends and employees for recommendations and use social networking sites such as LinkedIn, Facebook, and Twitter. Many employers announce job openings through LinkedIn. One says, "I get people vouching for each applicant, so I don't have to spend hours sorting through résumés," he says.[24]
- ***Send a recording.*** InterviewStream, in Bethlehem, Pennsylvania, records online video interviews for about $30 to $60. It sends the candidate an e-mail invitation with a link. When he or she clicks the link, a video interviewer asks the company's prerecorded questions. A Webcam captures the candidate's answers. Employers can allow candidates to rerecord their answers. Hiring managers can review the videos at their leisure.[25]

COMPLYING WITH THE LAW Unfortunately, given the time pressures facing most small business owners, confirming the validity of tests one buys online or through office supply stores is probably the exception, not the rule. As we've seen, there is no rational basis upon which to use invalid tests or devices. Many test providers will assist the employer in establishing a testing procedure. For example, as we noted, Wonderlic will review your job descriptions as part of its process.

Employment Training

Online training can provide employee training that used to be beyond most small employers' reach.

PRIVATE VENDORS The small business owner can tap hundreds of suppliers of prepackaged training solutions. These range from self-study programs from the American Management Association (www.amanet.org) and SHRM (www.shrm.org), to specialized programs. For example, the employer might arrange with PureSafety to have its employees take occupational safety courses from www.puresafety.com.

SkillSoft is another example (http://skillsoft.com/catalog/default.asp). Its courses include business strategy and operations, professional effectiveness, and computer skills. For example, the course "interviewing effectively" is for managers, team leaders, and human resource professionals. About 2½ hours long, it shows trainees how to use behavioral questioning to interview candidates.[26]

The buyer's guide from the American Society of Training and Development (www.astd.org/) is a good place to start to find a vendor (check under Resources).

THE SBA The federal government's Small Business Administration (www.SBA.gov/training/) virtual campus offers online courses, workshops, publications, and learning tools aimed at supporting entrepreneurs.[27] For example, under "Small Business Planner" link to "Writing Effective Job Descriptions," "Employees versus Contractors: What's the Difference?" and "How to Select the Right Person" (see Figure 18-4).

NAM The National Association of Manufacturers (NAM) is the largest industrial trade organization in the United States. It represents about 14,000 member manufacturers, including 10,000 small and mid-sized companies.

NAM's Virtual University (www.namvu.com) helps employees maintain and upgrade their work skills and continue their professional development. It offers almost 650 courses.[28] There are no long-term contracts to sign. Employers simply pay about $10–$30 per course taken by each employee. The catalog includes OSHA, quality, and technical training as well as courses in areas like business and finance, personal development, and customer service.

FIGURE 18-4 Some Online Courses Offered by the Small Business Administration's Virtual Campus for Small Business Training

Source: www.sba.gov/category/navigation-structure/starting-managing-business/managing-business/running-business/human-resources, accessed September 18, 2011.

Employment Appraisal and Compensation

Small employers have easy access to computerized and online appraisal and compensation services. For example, Oracle Corporation's ePerformance (www.oracle.com/us/products/applications/peoplesoft-enterprise/hcm-resource-library/051027.pdf) facilitates performance management by enabling managers to formalize the employee's goals and then assess progress toward meeting those goals.

The eAppraisal system from Halogen Software (www.halogensoftware.com/products/halogen-eappraisal/) is another example.[29]

Similarly, lack of easy access to high-priced salary surveys once made it difficult and time-consuming for smaller businesses to fine-tune their pay scales. Today, sites like www.salary.com makes it easy to determine local pay rates.

Employment Safety and Health

Safety is an important issue for small employers. One European study found that the majority of all serious workplace accidents occur in firms with less than 50 employees.[30] OHSA provides several free services for small employers.

OSHA CONSULTATION[31] First, it provides free on-site safety and health services for small businesses. Employers can contact their nearest OSHA area office to speak to the compliance assistance specialist.

OSHA SHARP The OSHA Sharp program (https://www.osha.gov/dcsp/smallbusiness/sharp.html) is a certification process. OSHA certifies that small employers have achieved commendable levels of safety awareness.[32] Employers request a consultation and visit, and undergo a complete hazard identification survey. The employer agrees to correct identified hazards, and to maintain a safety and health management system. OSHA's on-site project manager may then recommend that OSHA exempt the Sharp employer for 2 years from scheduled inspections.

Leveraging Small Size with Familiarity, Flexibility, Fairness, and Informality

3 List five ways entrepreneurs can use their small size to improve their HR processes.

Because small businesses need to capitalize on their strengths, it makes sense for them to capitalize on their smallness when dealing with employees. For example, smallness can mean more personal *familiarity* with each employee's strengths, needs, and family situation. And it can mean being *flexible* and *informal* in its human resource management policies and practices.[33]

Simple, Informal Employee Selection Procedures

In addition to relatively high-tech online recruitment and selection tools,[34] small business managers shouldn't forget simple, low-tech selection aids. For example, the Work Sampling Test we explained in Chapter 6 involves having the candidate show how he or she would actually do one of the job's tasks—such as a marketing candidate spending 30 minutes outlining an ad for a product. The accompanying HR Tools feature presents a relatively informal selection interview procedure the small business manager may find useful.

IMPROVING PERFORMANCE: HR Tools for Line Managers and Entrepreneurs

A Streamlined Interviewing Process

The small business owner, pressed for time, may use the following practical, streamlined employment interview process:[35]

Preparing for the Interview

One way to do so is to focus on four basic required factors—knowledge and experience, motivation, intellectual capacity, and personality. To proceed this way, ask the following questions:

- **Knowledge and experience.** What must the candidate know to perform the job? What experience is necessary to perform the job?

- **Motivation.** What should the person like doing to enjoy this job? Is there anything the person should not dislike? Are there any essential goals or aspirations the person should have?
- **Intellectual capacity.** Are there any specific intellectual aptitudes required (mathematical, mechanical, and so on)? How complex are the problems the person must solve? What must a person be able to demonstrate intellectually?
- **Personality factor.** What are the critical personality qualities needed for success on the job (ability to withstand boredom, decisiveness, stability, and so on)? How must the job incumbent handle stress, pressure, and criticism? What kind of interpersonal behavior is required in the job?

Knowing How to Probe in the Interview

Next, ask a combination of situational questions plus open-ended questions to probe the candidate's suitability for the job. For example:

- **Knowledge and experience factor.** Probe with situational questions such as "How would you organize such a sales effort?" or "How would you design that kind of website?"
- **Motivation factor.** Probe such areas as the person's likes and dislikes (for each thing done, what he or she liked or disliked about it), aspirations (including the validity of each goal in terms of the person's reasoning about why he or she chose it), and energy level, perhaps by asking what he or she does on, say, a "typical Tuesday."
- **Intellectual factor.** Ask questions that judge such things as complexity of tasks the person has performed, grades in school, test results (including scholastic aptitude tests, and so on), and how the person organizes his or her thoughts and communicates.
- **Personality factor.** Probe by looking for self-defeating behaviors (aggressiveness, compulsive fidgeting, and so on) and by exploring the person's past interpersonal relationships. Ask questions about the person's past interactions (working in a group at school, working with fraternity brothers or sorority sisters, leading the work team on the last job, and so on). Also, try to judge the person's behavior in the interview itself—Is the candidate personable? Shy? Outgoing?

Organizing the Interview

- **Have a plan.** Devise and use a plan to guide the interview. According to interviewing expert John Drake, significant areas to touch on include the candidate's
  - College experiences
  - Work experience—summer, part-time
  - Work experience—full-time (one by one)
  - Goals and ambitions
  - Reactions to the job you are interviewing for
  - Self-assessments (by the candidate of his or her strengths and weaknesses)
  - Military experiences
  - Present outside activities[36]
- **Follow your plan.** Start with an open-ended question for each topic, such as "Could you tell me about what you did in college?" Then probe for information about the person's knowledge and experience, motivation, intelligence, and personality.

Match the Candidate to the Job

You should now be able to draw conclusions about the person's knowledge and experience, motivation, intellectual capacity, and personality, and to summarize the candidate's strengths and limits. Next, compare your conclusions to the job description and the list of requirements you developed when preparing for the interview. This should provide a rational basis for matching the candidate to the job—one based on the traits and aptitudes the job actually requires.

Discussion Question 18-2: List two situation questions (what would you do . . .?) and two behavioral questions (what did you do . . .?) that you might ask to unearth insights into the candidate's motivation.

Flexibility in Training

One study of 191 small and 201 large firms in Europe found that the small firms were relatively informal in their training and development.[37] Many didn't systematically monitor their managers' skill needs, and fewer than 50% (as opposed to 70% of large firms) had career development programs. The smaller firms also tended to focus any management development they did on teaching specific firm-related competencies (such as how to sell the firm's products).[38] The simplified training process we explained on pages 237–238 (Chapter 8) is one good option for the small business. Informal methods such as the following work well, too.

INFORMAL TRAINING METHODS Training expert Stephen Covey says small businesses can do many things to provide job-related training without establishing expensive formal training programs. His suggestions include:[39]

- Offer to cover the tuition for special classes
- Identify online training opportunities
- Provide a library of tapes and DVDs for systematic, disciplined learning during commute times
- Encourage the sharing of best practices among associates
- When possible, send people to special seminars and association meetings for learning and networking
- Create a learning ethic by having everyone teach each other what they are learning

Flexibility in Benefits and Rewards

The Family and Work Institute surveyed the benefits practices of about 1,000 small and large companies.[40] Not surprisingly, they found that large firms offer more *extensive* benefits packages than do smaller ones. However, many small firms overcame this by offering more flexibility. "They've discovered how to turn tiny into tight-knit, earning employees' trust by keeping them in the loop on company news and financials, and their loyalty by providing frequent feedback on performance."[41] At ID Media, with 90 employees, CEO Lynn Fantom gives all new employees a welcome breakfast on their first day. Internet start-up appssavvy Inc.'s CEO foregoes PowerPoint presentations in favor of humorous YouTube videos.[42]

A CULTURE OF FLEXIBILITY Basically, the study found that small business owners, by personally interacting with all employees each day, did a better job of "understanding when work/life issues emerge."[43] Wards Furniture in Long Beach, California, exemplifies this. Many of its 17 employees have been with the firm for 10 to 20 years. Brad Ward, an owner, attributes this partly to his firm's willingness to adapt to its workers' needs. For example, workers can share job responsibilities and work part-time from home.

WORK–LIFE BENEFITS Here are other examples of what Wards and other small employers can offer:[44]

- ***Extra time off.*** For example, Friday afternoons off in the summer.
- ***Compressed workweeks.*** For example, compressed summer workweeks.
- ***Bonuses at critical times.*** Small business owners are more likely to know what's happening in their employees' lives. Use this knowledge to provide special bonuses, for instance, if an employee has a new baby.
- ***Flexibility.*** For example, "If an employee is having a personal problem, help create a work schedule that allows the person to solve problems without feeling like they're going to be in trouble."[45]

At Wards Furniture, workers can share job responsibilities and work part-time from home.

- ***Sensitivity to employees' strengths and weaknesses.*** The small business owner should stay attuned to his or her employees' strengths, weaknesses, and aspirations. For example, give them an opportunity to train for and move into the jobs they desire.
- ***Help them better themselves.*** For example, pay employees to take a class to help them develop their job skills.
- ***Feed them.*** Provide free meals occasionally, perhaps by taking your employees to lunch.
- ***Make them feel like owners.*** For example, give employees input into major decisions, let them work directly with clients, get them client feedback, share company performance data with them, and let them share in the company's financial success.
- ***Make sure they have what they need to do their jobs.*** Having motivated employees is only half the challenge. Also ensure they have the necessary training, procedures, computers, and so on.
- ***Constantly recognize a job well done.*** Capitalize on your day-to-day interactions with employees to "never miss an opportunity to give your employees the recognition they deserve."[46]

SIMPLE RETIREMENT BENEFITS Access to retirement benefits is more prevalent in large firms than small ones. About 75% of large firms offer them, while only about 35% of small ones do.[47]

There are several ways for small firms to provide retirement plans. The Pension Protection Act of 2006 provides for a retirement benefit that combines traditional defined benefit and 401(k) (defined contribution) plans.[48] Only available to employers with less than 500 employees, it exempts employers from the complex pension rules to which large employers must adhere. The employees get a retirement plan that blends a defined pension, plus returns on the part of the investment that plan participants contributed.[49]

The easiest way for small businesses to provide retirement benefits is through a SIMPLE IRA plan. With the SIMPLE (for Savings Incentive Match Plan for Employees) IRA, employers must (and employees may) make contributions to traditional employee IRAs. These plans are for employers or small businesses with 100 or fewer employees and no other retirement plan.

SIMPLE IRAs are inexpensive and simple. The owner contacts an eligible financial institution and fills out several IRS forms. Most banks, mutual funds, and insurance companies that issue annuity contracts are generally eligible.[50] The plan has very low administrative costs. Employer contributions are tax-deductible.[51] A typical employer contribution might match employee contributions dollar for dollar up to 3% of pay. The financial institution usually handles the IRS paperwork and reporting.

Fairness and the Family Business

Most small businesses are "family businesses," since the owner (and often one or more employees) are family members.

Being a non-family employee here isn't easy. The tendency is to treat family and non-family employees differently. If so, as one writer puts it, "It's a sure bet that their lower morale and simmering resentments are having a negative effect on your operations and sapping your profits."[52] Reducing such "fairness" problems involves several steps, including:[53]

- ***Set the ground rules.*** One family business consultant says,

  During the hiring process the [management] applicant should be informed as to whether he or she will be essentially a placeholder, or whether there will be potential for promotion. At a minimum, make the expectations clear, regarding matters such as the level of authority and decision-making the person can expect to attain.[54]
- ***Treat people fairly.*** Work hard to avoid "any appearance that family members are benefiting unfairly from the sacrifice of others."[55]
- ***Confront family issues.*** Discord and tension among family members distracts and demoralizes employees. Family members must confront and work out their differences.
- ***Erase privilege.*** Family members "should avoid any behavior that would lead people to the conclusion that they are demanding special treatment in terms of assignments or responsibilities."[56] Family employees should come in earlier, work harder, and stay later than other employees stay.

Using Professional Employer Organizations

4 Discuss how you would choose and deal with a professional employee organization.

As we explained in Chapter 13 (Benefits and Services), many small business owners look at the issues involved with managing personnel, and decide to outsource most of their human resource functions to vendors.[57] These vendors go by the names *professional employer organizations* (PEOs), *human resource outsourcers* (HROs), or sometimes *employee* or *staff leasing firms*.

How Do PEOs Work?

These vendors range from specialized payroll companies to those that handle all an employer's human resource management requirements.[58] At a minimum, these firms take over the employer's payroll tasks.[59] Usually, however, PEOs assume most of the employer's human resources chores. By transferring the client firm's employees to the PEO's payroll, PEOs become co-employers of record for the employer's employees. The PEO can then fold the client's employees into the PEO's insurance and benefits program, usually at a lower cost. The PEO usually handles employee-related activities such as recruiting, hiring (with client firms' supervisors' approvals), and payroll and taxes. Most PEOs focus on employers with under 100 employees, and charge fees of 2% to 4% of a company's payroll. HROs usually handle these functions on an "administrative services only"—they're basically your "HR office," but your employees still work for you.[60]

Why Use a PEO?

Employers turn to PEOs for several reasons:

LACK OF SPECIALIZED HR SUPPORT Small firms with fewer than about 100 employees typically have no dedicated HR managers. The owner has most of the human resource management burden on his or her shoulders.

PAPERWORK The Small Business Administration estimates that small business owners spend up to 25% of their time on personnel-related paperwork, such as background checks and benefits sign-ups.[61] Because the PEO takes over most of this, many small businesses conclude that it's cheaper for them just to pay the employee leasing firm's fees.

LIABILITY Legally, PEOs generally "contractually share liability with clients and have a vested interest in preventing workplace injuries and employee lawsuits."[62] The PEO should thus help ensure the small business fulfills its Title VII, OSHA, COBRA, and Fair Labor Standards Act responsibilities.[63]

BENEFITS Insurance and benefits are often the big PEO attraction. Getting health and other insurance is a problem for smaller firms. That's where leasing comes in. Leasing may get a small business insurance for its people that it couldn't otherwise.[64]

PERFORMANCE Finally, the professionalism that the PEO brings to recruiting, screening, training, compensating, and maintaining employee safety and welfare will hopefully translate into improved employee and business results.

Caveats

There are several potential downsides. "If your PEO is poorly managed, or goes bankrupt, you could find yourself with an office full of uninsured workers."[65] Many employers view their human resource management practices (like training new engineers) as strategic, and aren't inclined to turn over such tasks to outsiders. Another potential problem is determining who's responsible. For example, who is responsible for an employee's injuries, the PEO or the employer? The contract should address this.[66]

WARNING SIGNS Several things may signal problems with the prospective PEO. One is *lax due diligence*. For example, because they share liability with the employer, they should question you extensively about your firm's workplace safety and human resource policies and practices.[67] Figure 18-5 summarizes guidelines for finding and working with PEOs.

FIGURE 18-5 Guidelines for Finding and Working with PEOs

Source: Based on Robert Beck and J. Starkman, "How to Find a PEO That Will Get the Job Done," *National Underwriter* 110, no. 39 (October 16, 2006), pp. 39, 45; Lyle DeWitt, "Advantages of Human Resource Outsourcing," *The CPA Journal* 75, no. 6 (June 2005), p. 13; www.peo.com/dmn/, accessed April 28, 2008; and Layne Davlin, "Human Resource Solutions for the Franchisee," *Franchising World* 39, no. 10 (October 2007), p. 27.

Employers should choose and manage the PEO relationship carefully. Guidelines for doing so include:

- *Conduct a needs analysis.* Know ahead of time exactly what human resource concerns your company wants to address.
- *Review the services* of all PEO firms you're considering. Determine which can meet all your requirements.
- *Determine if the PEO is accredited.* There is no rating system. However, the Employer Services Assurance Corporation of Little Rock, Arkansas (www.Escorp.org), imposes higher financial, auditing, and operating standards on its members. Also check the National Association of Professional Employer Organizations (www.NAPEO.org), and www.PEO.com.
- Check the provider's bank, credit, insurance, and professional references.
- Understand how the *employee benefits will be funded.* Is it fully insured or partially self-funded? Who is the carrier? Confirm that employers will receive first-day coverage.
- See if the contract assumes the *compliance liabilities in the applicable states.*
- *Review the service agreement carefully.* Are the respective parties' responsibilities and liabilities clear?
- Investigate how long the *PEO has been in business.*
- *Check out the prospective* PEO's staff. Do they seem to have the expertise to deliver on its promises?
- Ask, *how will the firm deliver its services?* In person? By phone? Via the Web?
- Ask about upfront fees and how these are determined.
- *Periodically get proof that payroll taxes and insurance premiums are being paid properly* and that any legal issues are handled correctly.

Managing HR Systems, Procedures, and Paperwork

Introduction

5 Describe how you would create a start-up human resource system for a new small business.

Consider the paperwork required to run a five-person retail shop. Just to start with, recruiting and hiring an employee might require a help wanted advertising listing, an employment application, an interviewing checklist, various verifications—of education and immigration status, for instance—and a telephone reference checklist. You then might need an employment agreement, confidentiality and noncompetition agreements, and an employer indemnity agreement. To process the new employee you might need a background verification, a new employee checklist, and forms for withholding tax and to obtain new employee data. And to keep track of the employee once on board, you'd need—just to start—a personnel data sheet, daily and weekly time records, an hourly employee's weekly time sheet, and an expense report. Then come all the performance appraisal forms, a disciplinary notice, an employee orientation record, separation notice, and employment reference response.

In fact, the preceding list barely scratches the surface of the policies, procedures, and paperwork you'll need to run the human resource management part of your business. Perhaps with just one or two employees you could track everything in your head, or just write a separate memo for each HR action, placing it in a folder for each worker. But with more employees, you'll need a human resource system comprised of standardized forms. Then as the company grows, you'll computerize various parts of the HR system—payroll, or appraising, for instance.

Basic Components of Manual HR Systems

Very small employers (say, with 10 employees or less) will probably start with a manual human resource management system. From a practical point of view, this generally means obtaining and organizing a set of standardized personnel forms covering each important aspect of the HR process—recruitment, selection, training, appraisal, compensation, safety—as well as some means for organizing all this information for each of your employees.

BASIC FORMS The number of forms you would conceivably need even for a small firm is quite large, as the illustrative list in Table 18-1 shows.[68] One simple way to obtain the basic forms of a manual HR system is from websites (such as www.hr.com/en/free_forms/) or books or CDs that provide compilations of HR forms. The forms you want can then be adapted from these sources for your particular situation. Office supply stores (such as Office Depot and Office Max) also sell packages of personnel forms. For example, Office Depot sells packages of individual personnel forms as well as a "Human Resource Kit" containing 10 copies of each

TABLE 18-1 Some Important Employment Forms

New Employee Forms	Current Employee Forms	Employee Separation Forms
Application	Employee Status Change Request	Retirement Checklist
New Employee Checklist	Employee Record	Termination Checklist
Employment Interview	Performance Evaluation	COBRA Acknowledgment
Reference Check	Warning Notice	Unemployment Claim
Telephone Reference Report	Vacation Request	Employee Exit Interview
Employee Manual Acknowledgment	Probation Notice	
Employment Agreement	Job Description	
Employment Application Disclaimer	Probationary Evaluation	
Employee Secrecy Agreement	Direct Deposit Acknowledgment	
	Absence Report	
	Disciplinary Notice	
	Grievance Form	
	Expense Report	
	401(k) Choices Acknowledgment	
	Injury Report	

of the following: Application, Employment Interview, Reference Check, Employee Record, Performance Evaluation, Warning Notice, Exit Interview, and Vacation Request, plus a Lawsuit-Prevention Guide.[69] Also available is a package of Employee Record Folders. Use the folders to maintain a file on each individual employee; on the outside of the pocket is printed a form for recording information such as name, start date, company benefits, and so on.

OTHER SOURCES Several direct-mail catalog companies similarly offer HR materials. For example, HRdirect (www.hrdirect.com) offers packages of personnel forms. These include, for instance, Short- and Long-Form Employee Applications, Applicant Interviews, Employee Performance Reviews, and Absentee Calendars and Reports. Also available are various legal-compliance forms, including standardized Harassment Policy and FMLA Notice forms, as well as posters (for instance, covering legally required postings for matters such as the Americans with Disabilities Act).

G. Neil Company, of Sunrise, Florida (www.gneil.com), is another direct-mail personnel materials source. In addition to a complete line of personnel forms, documents, and posters, it also carries manual systems for matters like attendance history, job analyses, and for tracking vacation requests and safety records. It has a complete HR "start-up" kit containing 25 copies of each of the basic components of a manual HR system. These include, for instance, Long-Form Application for Employment, Attendance History, Payroll/Status Change Notice, Absence Report, and Vacation Request & Approval, all organized in a file box.

Automating Individual HR Tasks

As the small business grows, it becomes impractical to rely on manual HR systems. It is at this point that most small- to medium-sized firms begin computerizing individual human resource management tasks.

HR in Practice at the Hotel Paris Lisa had managed to install several separate information systems, such as for performance appraisals. However, as she discussed one day over lunch with the CFO, these systems were not integrated. To see how she handled this, see the case on pages 577–578 of this chapter.

PACKAGED SYSTEMS There are many resources available. For example, various websites contain categorical lists of HR software vendors.[70] These vendors provide software solutions for virtually all personnel tasks, ranging from benefits management to compensation, compliance, employee relations, outsourcing, payroll, and time and attendance systems.

The G. Neil Company sells software packages for monitoring attendance, employee record keeping, writing employee policy handbooks, and conducting computerized employee appraisals. HRdirect offers software for writing employee policy manuals, writing performance reviews, creating job descriptions, tracking attendance and hours worked for each employee,

employee scheduling, writing organizational charts, managing payroll, conducting employee surveys, scheduling and tracking employee training activities, and managing OSHA compliance. *People Manager* (see, for example, www.hrtools.com/products/PeopleManager.aspx) maintains employee records (including name, address, marital status, number of dependents, emergency contact and phone numbers, hire date, and job history). It also enables management to produce 30 standard reports on matters such as attendance, benefits, and ethnic information quickly.

Human Resource Information Systems (HRIS)

As the company grows, a more comprehensive system becomes necessary. We can define an integrated human resource information system (*HRIS)* as interrelated components working together to collect, process, store, and disseminate information to support decision making, coordination, control, analysis, and visualization of an organization's human resource management activities.[71] There are several reasons for installing an HRIS. The first is improved transaction processing.

Improved Transaction Processing

The day-to-day minutiae of maintaining and updating employee records take an enormous amount of time. One study found that 71% of HR employees' time was devoted to transactional tasks like checking leave balances, maintaining address records, and monitoring employee benefits distributions.[72] HRIS packages substitute powerful computerized processing for a wide range of the firm's HR transactions.

Online Self-Processing

HR information systems also facilitate employee self-processing. For example, at Provident Bank, the benefits system Benelogic lets employees self-enroll in all their desired benefits programs over the Internet at a secure site. It also "support[s] employees' quest for 'what if' information relating to, for example, the impact on their take-home pay of various benefits options."[73] That's all work that HR employees would previously have had to do for Provident's employees.

Improved Reporting Capability

By integrating numerous individual HR tasks (training records, appraisals, employee personal data, and so on), the HRIS improves HR's reporting capabilities. For example, reports might be available (company-wide and by department) for health-care cost per employee, pay and benefits as a percent of operating expense, cost per hire, report on training, volunteer turnover rates, turnover costs, time to fill jobs, and return on human capital invested (in terms of training and education fees, for instance).

HR System Integration

Because the HRIS's software components (record keeping, payroll, appraisal, and so forth) are integrated, they enable the employer to reengineer its HR function. For example, PeopleSoft's HRIS electronically routes salary increases, transfers, and other e-forms through the organization to the proper managers for approval. As one person signs off, it's routed to the next. If someone forgets to process a document, a smart agent issues reminders. The HRIS thus automates what might otherwise be a time-consuming manual process.

HRIS Vendors

Many firms today offer HRIS packages. The website for the International Association for Human Resource Information Management (www.ihrim.org/), for instance, lists Automatic Data Processing, Inc., Business Information Technology, Inc., Human Resource Microsystems, Lawson Software, Oracle Corporation, SAP America, Inc., and about 25 other firms as HRIS vendors.

HR and Intranets

Employers increasingly use their internal intranets for processing human resource management tasks. For example, LG&E Energy Corporation does so for benefits communication. Employees can access LG&E's benefits homepage and (among other things) review the company's 401(k) plan investment options, get answers to frequently asked questions about the company's medical and dental plans, and report changes in family status. Other uses for human resource intranets include, for instance, automating job postings and applicant tracking, setting up training registration, providing electronic pay stubs, publishing an electronic employee handbook, and letting employees update their personal profiles and access their accounts, such as 401(k) accounts.

Review

MyManagementLab Go to **mymanagementlab.com** to complete the problems marked with this icon. 

Chapter Section Summaries

1. Many people reading this book will work for or own their own small businesses, so it's important to understand **the small business challenge**. In terms of managing human resources, small businesses are different in terms of size (not enough employees for a dedicated HR manager), priorities (sales come first), informality, and the nature of the entrepreneur. Without effective human resource management, small business owners run the risk that they'll be at a competitive disadvantage or that without the necessary HR expertise they may commit mistakes that lead to litigation.
2. Being small, small businesses can particularly capitalize on freely available **Internet and government tools to support their HR efforts**. For example, you can use Department of Labor elaw advisors to answer overtime questions, the EEOC's websites for answers on questions like "How can we resolve the charge?" and the Department of Labor's OSHA website to review, for instance, your small business handbook. To better compete, small business owners can also use online recruiting tools like those we discussed in Chapter 5 and training programs available online from companies such as puresafety.com, and from the SBA and National Association of Manufacturers.
3. Small businesses need to capitalize on their strengths, and in this case, it means capitalizing on **familiarity, flexibility, and informality**. For example, in many respects it's easier for small businesses to be flexible about extra time off, compressed workweeks, and job enrichment. They can also use relatively informal but still effective employee selection procedures such as the work-sampling test we discussed. Informal training methods include online training opportunities, encouraging the sharing of best practices among associates, and sending employees to seminars. Because small businesses are often family businesses, it's important to make sure that nonfamily members are treated fairly, something that requires setting ground rules (for instance, regarding promotions), treating employees fairly, dealing with family discord and issues, and erasing privilege. Small businesses can also use simple methods for improving communications, for instance, online newsletters.
4. After reviewing all the challenges of managing human resources, many small business owners turn to **using professional employer organizations**. Also called *human resource outsourcers* or *employee or staff leasing firms*, these firms generally transfer the client firm's employees to the PEO's own payroll and thus become the employer of record for the employer's employees. Reasons to turn to the PEOs include a lack of specialized HR support, a desire to reduce the paperwork burden, avoiding HR-related liability, obtaining better benefits for employees, and providing improved employee and business results.
5. Small business managers need to understand how their **HR systems, procedures, and paperwork** will evolve. At first, there may be a simple manual human resource management system, for instance, with employee records compiled on forms from office supply companies and maintained in manual files. The employer then may purchase one or more packaged systems for automating individual HR tasks, for instance, such as applicant tracking and performance appraisal. As companies grow, they will look to integrate the separate systems with a human resource information system (i.e., interrelated components working together to collect, process, store, and disseminate information to support decision making, coordination, control, analysis, and visualization of the company's human resource management activities).

Discussion Questions

18-3. How and why is HR in small businesses different than that in large firms?

✪ **18-4.** Explain why HRM is important to small businesses.

✪ **18-5.** Explain and give at least five examples of ways entrepreneurs can use small size—familiarity, flexibility, and informality—to improve their HR processes.

18-6. Describe with examples how you would create a start-up, paper-based human resource system for a new small business.

Individual and Group Activities

18-7. Form teams of five or six persons, each with at least one person who owns or has worked for a small business. Based on their experiences, make a list of the "inadequate-HR risks" the business endured, in terms of competitive disadvantage, lack of specialized HR expertise, workplace litigation, compensation laws compliance, and paperwork/data-entry errors.

18-8. You own a small business, and you are confused about which of your employees is eligible for overtime pay. The employees in question include your secretary, two accounting clerks, one engineer, and two inside salespeople. Individually or in groups of four or five students, use the DOL's Overtime Security Advisor and DOL's Calculator to determine who gets overtime pay.

18-9. You have about 32 employees working in your factory. Working individually or in teams of four or five students, find and create a list of five online sources you could use to provide training to them, at no cost to you or to them.

18-10. Appendix A, PHR and SPHR Knowledge Base, at the end of this book (pages 580–588) lists the knowledge someone studying for the HRCI certification exam needs to have in each area of human resource management (such as in Strategic Management, Workforce Planning, and Human Resource Development). In groups of four to five students, do four things: (1) review Appendix A; (2) identify the material in this chapter that relates to the required knowledge Appendix A lists; (3) write four multiple-choice exam questions on this material that you believe would be suitable for inclusion in the HRCI exam; and (4) if time permits, have someone from your team post your team's questions in front of the class, so that students in all teams can answer the exam questions created by the other teams.

Experiential Exercise

Building an HRIS

Purpose: The purpose of this exercise is to give you practice in creating a human resource management system (HRIS).

Required Understanding: You should be fully acquainted with the material in this chapter.

How to Set Up the Exercise/Instructions: Divide the class into teams of five or six students. Each team will need access to the Internet.

Assume that the owners of a small business come to you with the following problem. They have a company with less than 40 employees. They have been taking care of all HR paperwork informally, mostly on slips of paper and with memos. They want you to supply them with a human resource management information system—how computerized it is will be up to you, but they can only afford a budget of $5,000 upfront (not counting your consulting), and then about $500 per year for maintenance. You know from your HR training that there are various sources of paper-based and online systems. Write a two-page proposal telling them exactly what your team would suggest, based on its accumulated existing knowledge, and from online research.

Video Case

Video Title: Managing Human Resources in Entrepreneurial Firms (Blackbird Guitars)

SYNOPSIS

With about 10 employees, Blackbird Guitars must rely on cross-training and job rotation and relatively informal HR management. Founder Joe Luttwack uses various online HR information sources, and pays close attention to California labor laws, where the company resides. An interesting question is how the company will manage growth in production and workforce, since they're now thinking of expanding into retail sales.

Discussion Questions

18-11. Based on what you read in this chapter, what other online sources would you suggest Blackbird use to improve its HR practices?

18-12. Outline five other steps Blackbird should be using to have an improved HR function.

18-13. What do you think accounts for the fact that turnover is low?

Application Case

Netflix Breaks the Rules[74]

Why did Netflix survive as a start-up when the dot-com bubble burst in the late 1990s? Probably because, from the day he started Netflix, founder Reed Hastings believed in breaking the rules. His direct-to-consumer mail and video streaming business model certainly helped Netflix to survive. But the firm's unorthodox human resource management practices helped the company to attract and keep the high producers who design the products that are the firm's lifeblood. Hastings knew that top Silicon Valley workers could choose where they worked, and high pay is pretty much standard throughout the Valley's industries. How to set oneself apart? Hastings and his start-up colleagues believed that a culture that balanced a flexible work environment with few constraints and high responsibility was the answer. They called the policy "Freedom and Responsibility."

Just how unorthodox are the Netflix HR practices? Consider this: As a Netflix professional you get unlimited vacations. One engineer takes 5-week vacations to Europe, because he likes (as he says) to take his time off in big chunks. (An HR officer must approve time off in excess of 30 days annually.) As a Netflix employee, your pay isn't tied to performance appraisals, or even to a compensation plan. Frequent market salary surveys and pay hikes keep everyone's pay aligned with Silicon Valley competitors'. Each employee decides whether to take his or her pay in cash or in Netflix stock. Options vest immediately. Netflix doesn't recruit much at college job fairs, instead hiring mostly highly experienced professionals. There's no training, professional development, or career planning at Netflix (except for legally required training, such as diversity training). You're in charge of your own career.

But with freedom like that comes responsibilities. The company expects its salaried employees to work hard—to "do the jobs of three or four people" as one report put it. And Netflix doesn't have the "frat party" free-wheeling atmosphere that many dot-coms do. It's an adult environment. Netflix does not coddle underperformers. Yearly 360-degree performance reviews provide "direct and honest feedback." Those that aren't cutting it are quickly let go, but (whenever possible) amicably. Rather than the sorts of litigiousness that often characterizes dismissals in other firms (having to prove the person was incompetent, for instance), Netflix writes a check. The company believes that a handsome severance payment helps maintain the person's dignity, makes it easier for supervisors to make tough calls with underperformers, and, of course, minimizes blowback from those it dismisses. It's more like a "no-fault divorce," as one observer put it.

Questions

In many respects, the Netflix HR strategy seems like a dream come true for small businesses. You don't need a pay plan; instead, you just update each person's pay every few months based on market surveys. You offer no training and development. And you don't track vacation time, more or less. If someone's not doing well, you just pay him or her to leave, with no hassles. Netflix seems to have hit upon its own version of "Netflix High-Performance Work Practices." Given that, answer the following questions (please be specific).

18-14. What (if anything) is it about Netflix that makes its HR practices work for it?

18-15. Would you suggest using similar practices in other businesses, such as, say, a new restaurant? Why?

18-16. List the criteria you would use for deciding whether another company is right for Netflix-type HR practices.

18-17. What argument would you make in response to the following: "Netflix just lucked out; they'd have done even better with conventional HR practices."

Continuing Case

Carter Cleaning Company

Cleaning in Challenging Times

As the economic downturn worsened a few years ago, revenues at the Carter stores fell steeply. Many of their customers were simply out of work and didn't need (or couldn't afford) dry cleaning. The Carters actually found themselves giving away some free cleaning services. They started a new program wherein existing customers could get one suit or dress cleaned free each month if they needed it for a job interview.

In the midst of this downturn, the Carters knew they had to get their employment costs under control. The problem was that, realistically, there wasn't much room for cutting staffing in a store. Of course, if a store got very slow, they could double up by having a cleaner/spotter spend some time pressing, or having the manager displace the counter person. But if sales only fell 15% to 20% per store, there really wasn't much room for reducing employee head count because each store never employed many people in the first place.

The question therefore naturally arose as to whether the Carters could cut their employment expenses without dismissing too many people. Jennifer Carter has several questions for you.

Questions

18-18. Assume that we don't want to terminate any of our employees. What work-scheduling-related changes could we make that would reduce our payrolls by, say, 20% per week but still keep all our employees on board?

18-19. We are currently handling most of our personnel-related activities, such as sign-ons, benefits administration, and appraisals, manually. What specific suggestions would you have for us in terms of using software systems to automate our HR processes?

18-20. Suggest at least five free Internet-based sources we could turn to for helping us to lower our total employment costs.

Translating Strategy into HR Policies and Practices Case*,§

The accompanying strategy map for this chapter is in the MyManagementLab; and the overall map on the inside back cover of this text outlines the relationships involved.

IMPROVING PERFORMANCE at The Hotel Paris

The New HRIS

The Hotel Paris's competitive strategy is "To use superior guest service to differentiate the Hotel Paris properties, and to thereby increase the length of stay and return rate of guests, and thus boost revenues and profitability." HR manager Lisa Cruz must now formulate functional policies and activities that support this competitive strategy and boost performance by eliciting the required employee behaviors and competencies.

Challenging economic times in the past few years brought the drawbacks of the Hotel Paris's relatively small size into sharp relief. Large chains like Marriott had vast online reservations capabilities with huge centralized systems that easily and economically handled reservations

§Written by and copyright Gary Dessler, PhD.

requests from throughout the world. By comparison, the Hotel Paris still handled reservations much as hotels did 15 years ago, either with separate websites for each of their hotel locations, e-mail, or an 800-number.

Their human resource management information systems were similarly primitive. Lisa had managed to install several separate information systems, such as for performance appraisals. However, as she discussed one day over lunch with the CFO, the HR systems were not integrated. Therefore, if an employee changed his or her name, for instance, through marriage, people in Lisa's office had to execute all those name changes manually on all the various employee rosters and benefits plans.

This lack of integration was bad enough in boom times, but was worse as the economy soured. The CFO pointed out to her that the amount of money they were spending on human resource management administration was about 30% higher than it was at larger chains such as Marriott. He understood that large size brings economies of scale. But he believed there had to be something they could do to reduce the cost of administering human resource management.

Lisa's solution was to get the CFO's approval to have several software consulting firms including IBM, Accenture, and Oracle provide proposals for how to integrate the hotel's HR information systems. After getting the CFO's and CEO's approval, they contracted with one vendor and installed the system.

Questions

18-21. Using any benchmark data that you can find, including information from this textbook, what are some benchmark metrics that Lisa could be using to assess the efficiency of her human resource management operations? To what extent does the Hotel Paris's quality service orientation enter into how Lisa's metrics should compare?

18-22. Throughout this textbook, we've discussed various specific examples of how human resource management departments have been reducing the cost of delivering their services. Keeping in mind the Hotel Paris's service quality orientation, please list and explain with examples how Lisa Cruz could use at least five of these.

18-23. Focusing only on human resource information systems for a moment, what sorts of systems would you suggest Lisa consider recommending for the Hotel Paris? Why?

18-24. Explain with detailed examples how Lisa can use free online and governmental sources to accomplish at least part of what you propose in your previous answers.

18-25. Give three examples of fee-based online tools you suggest Lisa use.

18-26. Do you suggest Lisa use a PEO? Why?

MyManagementLab

Go to **mymanagementlab.com** for Auto-graded writing questions as well as the following Assisted-graded writing questions:

18-27. Explain and give at least four examples of how entrepreneurs can use Internet and government tools to support the HR effort.

18-28. Discuss what you would do to find, retain, and deal with a professional employee organization on an ongoing basis.

18-29. MyManagementLab only—comprehensive writing assignment for this chapter.

Endnotes

1. Based on Donna Harris, "Mentors Cut Turnover Costs, Boost Sales, Loyalty," *Automotive News* 64, no. 18 (June 28, 2010), p. 10.
2. "SBA: Frequently Asked Questions," http://www.sba.gov/sites/default/files/FAQ_Sept_2012.pdf, accessed August 17, 2013; www.bls.gov/news.release/empsit.nr0.htm, accessed September 10, 2012.
3. "Small Business Economic Indicators 2000," Office of Advocacy, U.S. Small Business Administration (Washington, DC, 2001), p. 5. See also "Small Business Laid Foundation for Job Gains," www.sba.gov/advo, accessed March 9, 2006.
4. Studies show that the size of the business impacts human resource activities such as executive compensation, training, staffing, and HR outsourcing. Peter Hausdorf and Dale Duncan, "Firm Size and Internet Recruiting in Canada: A Preliminary Investigation," *Journal of Small-Business Management* 42, no. 3 (July 2004), pp. 325–334.
5. *SHRM Human Capital Benchmarking Study 2007*, Society for Human Resource Management, p. 12.
6. Graham Dietz et al., "HRM Inside UK E-commerce Firms," *International Small Business Journal* 24, no. 5 (October 2006), pp. 443–470.
7. Bernice Kotey and Cathleen Folker, "Employee Training in SMEs: Effect of Size and Firm Type—Family and Nonfamily," *Journal of Small-Business Management* 45, no. 2 (April 2007), pp. 14–39.
8. Dietz et al., "HRM Inside UK E-commerce Firms."
9. Ibid. See also N. Wasserman, "Planning a Start-Up? Seize the Day . . . Then Expect to Work All Night," *Harvard Business Review* 87, no. 1 (January 2009), pp. 27.
10. Points 2–5 based on Kathy Williams, "Top HR Compliance Issues for Small Businesses," *Strategic Finance* (February 2005), pp. 21–23.
11. "Entrepreneurs: The Gender Gap," http://diversitywoman.com/entrepreneurs-the-gender-gap/, accessed April 20, 2013.
12. However, one study concluded that the increased labor costs associated with high-performance work practices offset the productivity increases associated with high-performance work practices. Luc Sels et al., "Unraveling the HRM–Performance Link: Value Creating and Cost Increasing Effects of Small-Business HRM," *Journal of Management Studies* 43, no. 2 (March 2006), pp. 319–342. For supporting evidence of HR's positive effects on small companies, see also Andrea Rauch et al., "Effects of Human Capital and Long-Term Human Resources Development and Utilization on Employment Growth of Small-Scale Businesses: A Causal Analysis," *Entrepreneurship Theory and Practice* 29, no. 6 (November 2005), pp. 681–698; Andre Grip and Inge Sieben, "The Effects of Human Resource Management on Small Firms' Productivity and Employee's Wages," *Applied Economics* 37, no. 9 (May 20, 2005), pp. 1047–1054.
13. Dawn Carlson et al., "The Impact of Human Resource Practices and Compensation Design on Performance: An Analysis of Family-Owned SMEs," *Journal of Small Business Management* 44, no. 4 (October 2006), pp. 531–543. See also Jake Messersmith and James Guthrie, "High Performance Work Systems in Emergent Organizations: Implications for Firm Performance," *Human Resource Management* 49, no. 2 (March–April 2010), pp. 241–264.
14. Dietz et al., "HRM Inside UK E-commerce Firms."
15. Based on Harris, "Mentors Cut Turnover Costs."
16. Ibid.
17. Gilbert Nicholson, "Automated Assessments for Better Hires," *Workforce* (December 2000), pp. 102–107.
18. www.EEOC.gov/employers/overview.html, accessed February 10, 2008.
19. www.DOL.gov/elaws, accessed February 10, 2008.

20. "Six Common Mistakes Small Businesses Make When Incorporating Social Media into Their Recruiting Efforts," www.roberthalf.us/SocialMediaRecruitingMistakes; Rieva Lesonsky, "Find the Perfect Hire by Tapping into Social Media," *Employment Trends*, January 30, 2013, http://smallbiztrends.com/2013/01/3-ways-find-perfect-hire-social-media.html; and Emily Bennington, "Social Media Recruitment: Social Media Platforms and Your Next Hire," http://hiring.monster.com/hr/hr-best-practices/small-business/social-media-trends/social-media-recruitment.aspx, all accessed April 20, 2013.
21. Daren Dahl, "Recruiting: Tapping the Talent Pool . . . without Drowning in Resumes," *Inc.* 31, no. 3 (April 2009), pp. 121–122.
22. Ibid.
23. Ibid.
24. Ibid.
25. Ibid.
26. Paul Harris, "Small Businesses Bask in Training's Spotlight," *T&D* 59, no. 2 (Fall 2005), pp. 46–52.
27. Ibid.
28. www.themanufacturinginstitute.org/Education-Workforce/Skills-Certification-System/Skills-Certification-System.aspx, accessed September 10, 2012.
29. www.halogensoftware.com/products/halogen-eappraisal, accessed August 17, 2013.
30. Jan de Kok, "Precautionary Actions within Small- and Medium-Sized Enterprises," *Journal of Small Business Management* 43, no. 4 (October 2005), pp. 498–516.
31. Sean Smith, "OSHA Resources Can Help Small Businesses Spot Hazards," *Westchester County Business Journal* (August 4, 2003), p. 4. See also www.osha.gov/as/opa/osha-faq.html, accessed May 26, 2007.
32. www.osha.gov/dcsp/smallbusiness/sharp.html, accessed August 17, 2013.
33. Dietz et al., "HRM Inside UK E-commerce Firms."
34. Adrienne Fox, "McMurray Scouts Top Talent to Produce Winning Results," *HR Magazine* 51, no. 7 (July 2006), pp. 57.
35. This is based on John Drake, *Interviewing for Managers: A Complete Guide to Employment Interviewing* (New York, AMACOM, 1982).
36. Ibid.
37. Colin Gray and Christopher Mabey, "Management Development: Key Differences Between Small and Large Businesses in Europe," *International Small Business Journal* 23, no. 5 (October 2005), pp. 467–485.
38. Ibid. See also Essi Saru, "Organizational Learning and HRD: How Appropriate Are They for Small Firms?" *Journal of European Industrial Training* 31, no. 1 (January 2007), pp. 36–52.
39. From Stephen Covey, "Small Business, Big Opportunity," *Training* 43, no. 11 (November 2006), p. 40.
40. Gina Ruiz, "Smaller Firms in Vanguard of Flex Practices," *Workforce Management* 84, no. 13 (November 21, 2005), p. 10.
41. Kira Bindrum, "Little Firms Redefine Culture of Work," *Crain's New York Business* 25, no. 49 (December 7–13, 2009), p. 20.
42. Ibid., pp. 7–13.
43. Ruiz, "Smaller Firms in Vanguard of Flex Practices."
44. These are from Ty Freyvogel, "Operation Employee Loyalty," *Training Media Review*, September–October 2007.
45. Ibid.
46. Ibid.
47. Jeffrey Marshall and Ellen Heffes, "Benefits: Smaller Firm Workers Often Getting Less," *Financial Executive* 21, no. 9 (November 1, 2005), p. 10.
48. www.dol.gov/ebsa/pdf/ppa2006.pdf, accessed February 18, 2008.
49. Bill Leonard, "New Retirement Plans for Small Employers," *HR Magazine* 51, no. 12 (December 2006), p. 30.
50. Kristen Falk, "The Easy Retirement Plan for Small Business Clients," *National Underwriter* 111, no. 45 (December 3, 2007), pp. 12–13.
51. Ibid. http://www.irs.gov/Retirement-Plans/Plan-Sponsor/SIMPLE-IRA-Plan, accessed August 17, 2013.
52. Phillip Perry, "Welcome to the Family," *Restaurant Hospitality* 90, no. 5 (May 2006), pp. 73, 74, 76, 78.
53. Ibid.
54. Ibid.
55. Ibid.
56. Ibid.
57. Jane Applegate, "Employee Leasing Can Be a Savior for Small Firms," *Business Courier Serving Cincinnati–Northern Kentucky* (January 28, 2000), p. 23.
58. Robert Beck and Jay Starkman, "How to Find a PEO That Will Get the Job Done," *National Underwriter* 110, no. 39 (October 16, 2006), pp. 39, 45.
59. Layne Davlin, "Human Resource Solutions for the Franchisee," *Franchising World* 39, no. 10 (October 2007), pp. 27–28.
60. Beck and Starkman, "How to Find a PEO."
61. Lyle DeWitt, "Advantages of Human Resources Outsourcing," *The CPA Journal* 75, no. 6 (June 2005), pp. 13.
62. Max Chafkin, "Fed Up with HR?" *Inc.* 28, no. 5 (May 2006), pp. 50–52.
63. Ibid.
64. Ibid.
65. Ibid.
66. Diana Reitz, "Employee Leasing Breeds Liability Questions," *National Underwriter Property and Casualty Risk and Benefits Management* 104, no. 18 (May 2000), p. 12.
67. Max Chafkin, "Fed Up with HR?".
68. For a more complete list, see, for example, Sondra Servais, *Personnel Director* (Deerfield Beach, FL: Made E-Z Products, 1994); www.hr.com/en/free_forms/, accessed September 10, 2012; and www.entrepreneur.com/formnet/hrcareers.html, accessed September 10, 2012.
69. www.officedepot.com/a/browse/business-forms-tax-forms-and-recordkeeping/N=5+516208/;jsessionid=0000zlVADjXrV18WJcAFM0Pe-d0:13ddq0u44, accessed September 10, 2012.
70. www.ihrim.org, accessed April 28, 2008; www.pmihrm.com/hr_software_vendors.html, accessed September 10, 2012; and www.hr-guide.com/data/206.htm, accessed September 10, 2012.
71. Adapted from Kenneth Laudon and Jane Laudon, *Management Information Systems: New Approaches to Organization and Technology* (Upper Saddle River, NJ: Prentice Hall, 1998), p. G7. See also Michael Barrett and Randolph Kahn, "The Governance of Records Management," *Directors and Boards* 26, no. 3 (Spring 2002), pp. 45–48; and Anthony Hendrickson, "Human Resource Information Systems: Backbone Technology of Contemporary Human Resources," *Journal of Labor Research* 24, no. 3 (Summer 2003), pp. 381–395.
72. "HR Execs Trade Notes on Human Resource Information Systems," *BNA Bulletin to Management* (December 3, 1998), p. 1. See also Brian Walter, "But They Said Their Payroll Program Complied with the FLSA," *Public Personnel Management* 31, no. 1 (Spring 2002), pp. 79–94.
73. "HR Execs Trade Notes on Human Resource Information Systems," *BNA Bulletin to Management* (December 3, 1998), p. 2. See also Ali Velshi, "Human Resources Information," *The Americas Intelligence Wire* (February 11, 2004).
74. Copyright Gary Dessler, PhD, 2011; based on information in Michelle Conlin, "Netflix: Flex to the Max," September 24, 2007, www.businessweek.com/magazine/content/07_39/b4051059.htm, accessed July 3, 2011; Robert J. Grossman, "Tough Love at Netflix," April 1, 2010, www.shrm.org/Publications/hrmagazine/EditorialContent/2010/0410/Pages/0410grossman3.aspx, accessed July 3, 2011; and David F. Larcker, Allan McCall, and Brian Tayan, "Equity on Demand: The Netflix Approach to Compensation," January 15, 2010, http://hbr.org/product/equity-on-demand-the-netflix-approach-to-compensat/an/CG19-PDF-ENG, accessed July 3, 2011.

APPENDIX A

PHR® and SPHR® Knowledge Base*

The PHR® and SPHR® exams are created using the following PHR® and SPHR® Knowledge Base, which outlines the responsibilities and knowledge needed to be a viable HR professional. The PHR® and SPHR® Knowledge Base is created by HR subject matter experts through a rigorous practice analysis study and then validated by HR professionals working in the field through an extensive survey instrument. The PHR® and SPHR® Knowledge Base periodically is updated to ensure it is consistent with current practices in the HR field. All questions appearing on the exams are linked to the responsibility and knowledge statements outlined below.

IF LAWS CHANGE

We [at the HR Certification Institute] realize that employment laws change constantly. Candidates are responsible for knowing the HR laws and regulations that are in effect as of the start of each exam period.

The percentages that follow each functional area heading are the PHR® and SPHR® percentages, respectively.

01 Strategic Business Management (12%, 29%)

Developing, contributing to and supporting the organization's mission, vision, values, strategic goals and objectives; formulating policies; guiding and leading the change process; and evaluating HR's contributions to organizational effectiveness.

RESPONSIBILITIES

01 Interpret information related to the organization's operations from internal sources, including financial/accounting, business development, marketing, sales, operations, and information technology, in order to contribute to the development of the organization's strategic plan.

02 Interpret information from external sources related to the general business environment, industry practices and developments, technological developments, economic environment, labor pool, and legal and regulatory environment, in order to contribute to the development of the organization's strategic plan.

03 Participate as a contributing partner in the organization's strategic planning process.

04 Establish strategic relationships with key individuals in the organization to influence organizational decision-making.

05 Establish relationships/alliances with key individuals and organizations in the community to assist in achieving the organization's strategic goals and objectives.

06 Develop and utilize metrics to evaluate HR's contributions to the achievement of the organization's strategic goals and objectives.

07 Develop and execute strategies for managing organizational change that balance the expectations and needs of the organization, its employees, and all other stakeholders.

08 Develop and align the organization's human capital management plan with its strategic plan.

*As explained elsewhere in this book, the HR Certification Institute refers to the content in this appendix as "A PHR® and SPHR® Body of Knowledge."

09 Facilitate the development and communication of the organization's core values and ethical behaviors.

10 Reinforce the organization's core values and behavioral expectations through modeling, communication, and coaching.

11 Develop and manage the HR budget in a manner consistent with the organization's strategic goals, objectives, and values.

12 Provide information for the development and monitoring of the organization's overall budget.

13 Monitor the legislative and regulatory environment for proposed changes and their potential impact to the organization, taking appropriate proactive steps to support, modify, or oppose the proposed changes.

14 Develop policies and procedures to support corporate governance initiatives (e.g., board of directors training, whistleblower protection, code of conduct).

15 Participate in enterprise risk management by examining HR policies to evaluate their potential risks to the organization.

16 Identify and evaluate alternatives and recommend strategies for vendor selection and/or outsourcing (e.g., human resource information systems [HRIS], benefits, payroll).

17 Participate in strategic decision-making and due diligence activities related to organizational structure and design (e.g., corporate restructuring, mergers and acquisitions [M&A], offshoring, divestitures). **SPHR® ONLY**

18 Determine strategic application of integrated technical tools and systems (e.g., HRIS, performance management tools, applicant tracking, compensation tools, employee self-service technologies).

ADDRESSED IN THIS BOOK IN CHAPTER(S):	KNOWLEDGE OF
1, 3	01 The organization's mission, vision, values, business goals, objectives, plans and processes.
2, 11, 14, 15, 16	02 Legislative and regulatory processes.
1, 3, and Hotel Paris cases in chapters 3–18.	03 Strategic planning process and implementation.
3	04 Management functions, including planning, organizing, directing and controlling.
	05 Techniques to promote creativity and innovation.
12, 14	06 Corporate governance procedures and compliance (e.g., Sarbanes-Oxley Act).
1, 3, 5	07 Transition techniques for corporate restructuring, M&A, offshoring and divestitures. **SPHR® ONLY**

02 Workforce Planning and Employment (26%, 17%)

Developing, implementing and evaluating sourcing, recruitment, hiring, orientation, succession planning, retention, and organizational exit programs necessary to ensure the workforce's ability to achieve the organization's goals and objectives.

RESPONSIBILITIES

01 Ensure that workforce planning and employment activities are compliant with applicable federal, state, and local laws and regulations.

02 Identify workforce requirements to achieve the organization's short- and long-term goals and objectives (e.g., corporate restructuring, M&A activity, workforce expansion or reduction).

03 Conduct job analyses to create job descriptions and identify job competencies.

04 Identify and document essential job functions for positions.

HR Certification Institute

05 Establish hiring criteria based on job descriptions and required competencies.

06 Analyze labor market for trends that impact the ability to meet workforce requirements (e.g., SWOT analysis, environmental scan, demographic scan). **SPHR® ONLY**

07 Assess skill sets of internal workforce and external labor market to determine the availability of qualified candidates, utilizing third-party vendors or agencies as appropriate.

08 Identify internal and external recruitment sources (e.g., employee referrals, online job boards, résumé banks) and implement selected recruitment methods.

09 Evaluate recruitment methods and sources for effectiveness (e.g., return on investment [ROI], cost-per-hire, time to fill).

10 Develop strategies to brand/market the organization to potential qualified applicants.

11 Develop and implement selection procedures, including applicant tracking, interviewing, testing, reference, and background checking, and drug screening.

12 Develop and extend employment offers and conduct negotiations as necessary.

13 Administer post-offer employment activities (e.g., execute employment agreements, complete I-9 verification forms, coordinate relocations, schedule physical exams).

14 Implement and/or administer the process for non-U.S. citizens to legally work in the United States.

15 Develop, implement and evaluate orientation processes for new hires, rehires, and transfers.

16 Develop, implement, and evaluate retention strategies and practices.

17 Develop, implement, and evaluate succession planning process.

18 Develop and implement the organizational exit process for both voluntary and involuntary terminations, including planning for reductions in force (RIF).

19 Develop, implement and evaluate an AAP, as required.

ADDRESSED IN THIS BOOK IN CHAPTER(S):	KNOWLEDGE OF	
2, 4, 5, 6, 7, and Know Your Employment Law features in chapters 1–17.	08	Federal/state/local employment-related laws and regulations related to workforce planning and employment (e.g., Title VII, ADA, ADEA, USERRA, EEOC Uniform Guidelines on Employee Selection Procedures, Immigration Reform and Control Act, Internal Revenue Code).
3, 4, 5, 6, 7, and HR as a Profit Center features in chapters 1–17.	09	Quantitative analyses required to assess past and future staffing effectiveness (e.g., cost-benefit analysis, costs-per-hire, selection ratios, adverse impact).
5	10	Recruitment sources (e.g., Internet, agencies, employee referral) for targeting passive, semi-active and active candidates.
5	11	Recruitment strategies.
5	12	Staffing alternatives (e.g., temporary and contract, outsourcing, job sharing, part-time).
4, 5	13	Planning techniques (e.g., succession planning, forecasting).
2, 6, 7	14	Reliability and validity of selection tests/tools/methods.
6	15	Use and interpretation of selection tests (e.g., psychological/personality, cognitive, motor/physical assessments, performance, assessment center).
7	16	Interviewing techniques (e.g., behavioral, situational, panel).
	17	Relocation practices.

HR Certification Institute

ADDRESSED IN THIS BOOK IN CHAPTER(S):	KNOWLEDGE OF	
5, 10, 11, 12, 13	18	Impact of total rewards on recruitment and retention.
5, 17, and HR Practices Around the Globe features in chapters 4–17.	19	International HR and implications of global workforce for workforce planning and employment. **SPHR® ONLY**
10	20	Voluntary and involuntary terminations, downsizing, restructuring and outplacement strategies and practices.
4, 5, 6, 7, 8, 9, 10	21	Internal workforce assessment techniques (e.g., skills testing, skills inventory, workforce demographic analysis) and employment policies, practices and procedures (e.g., orientation and retention).
5	22	Employer marketing and branding techniques.
15	23	Negotiation skills and techniques.

03 Human Resource Development (17%, 17%)

Developing, implementing and evaluating activities and programs that address employee training and development, performance appraisal, talent and performance management, and the unique needs of employees to ensure that the knowledge, skills, abilities and performance of the workforce meet current and future organizational and individual needs.

RESPONSIBILITIES

01 Ensure that human resource development programs are compliant with all applicable federal, state, and local laws and regulations.

02 Conduct a needs assessment to identify and establish priorities regarding human resource development activities. **SPHR® ONLY**

03 Develop/select and implement employee training programs (e.g., leadership skills, harassment prevention, computer skills) to increase individual and organizational effectiveness. Note that this includes training design and methods for obtaining feedback from training (e.g., surveys, pre- and post-testing).

04 Evaluate effectiveness of employee training programs through the use of metrics (e.g., participant surveys, pre- and post-testing). **SPHR® ONLY**

05 Develop, implement and evaluate talent management programs that include assessing talent, developing talent and placing high-potential employees. **SPHR® ONLY**

06 Develop/select and evaluate performance appraisal process (e.g., instruments, ranking and rating scales, relationship to compensation, frequency).

07 Implement training programs for performance evaluators. **PHR® ONLY**

08 Develop, implement and evaluate performance management programs and procedures (e.g., goal setting, job rotations, promotions).

09 Develop/select, implement and evaluate programs (e.g., flexible work arrangements, diversity initiatives, repatriation) to meet the unique needs of employees. **SPHR® ONLY**

ADDRESSED IN THIS BOOK IN CHAPTER(S):	KNOWLEDGE OF	
2, 8, 9, 10	24	Applicable federal, state and local laws and regulations related to human resources development activities (e.g., Title VII, ADA, ADEA, USERRA, EEOC Uniform Guidelines on Employee Selection Procedures).
8, 9, 10	25	Career development and leadership development theories and applications.

HR Certification Institute

ADDRESSED IN THIS BOOK IN CHAPTER(S):	KNOWLEDGE OF
8	26 Organizational development theories and applications.
8	27 Training program development techniques to create general and specialized training programs.
8	28 Training methods, facilitation techniques, instructional methods and program delivery mechanisms.
4, 8	29 Task/process analysis.
9	30 Performance appraisal methods (e.g., instruments, ranking and rating scales).
9	31 Performance management methods (e.g., goal setting, job rotations, promotions).
HR Practices Around the Globe features in most chapters, + Chapter 17	32 Applicable global issues (e.g., international law, culture, local management approaches/practices, societal norms). **SPHR® ONLY**
8	33 Techniques to assess training program effectiveness, including use of applicable metrics (e.g., participant surveys, pre- and post-testing).
8	34 E-learning.
8	35 Mentoring and executive coaching.

04 Total Rewards (16%, 12%)

Developing/selecting, implementing/administering and evaluating compensation and benefits programs for all employee groups that support the organization's strategic goals, objectives, and values.

RESPONSIBILITIES

01 Ensure that compensation and benefits programs are compliant with applicable federal, state, and local laws and regulations.

02 Develop, implement, and evaluate compensation policies/programs and pay structures based upon internal equity and external market conditions that support the organization's strategic goals, objectives, and values.

03 Administer payroll functions (e.g., new hires, deductions, adjustments, terminations).

04 Conduct benefits programs needs assessments (e.g., benchmarking, employee survey).

05 Develop/select, implement/administer, and evaluate benefits programs that support the organization's strategic goals, objectives, and values (e.g., health and welfare, retirement, stock purchase, wellness, employee assistance programs [EAP], time-off).

06 Communicate and train the workforce in the compensation and benefits programs and policies (e.g., self-service technologies).

07 Develop/select, implement/administer, and evaluate executive compensation programs (e.g., stock purchase, stock options, incentive, bonus, supplemental retirement plans). **SPHR® ONLY**

08 Develop, implement/administer, and evaluate expatriate and foreign national compensation and benefits programs. **SPHR® ONLY**

ADDRESSED IN THIS BOOK IN CHAPTER(S):	KNOWLEDGE OF
2, 11, 12, 13, 15	36 Federal, state and local compensation, benefits and tax laws (e.g., FLSA, ERISA, COBRA, HIPAA, FMLA, FICA).

HR Certification Institute

ADDRESSED IN THIS BOOK IN CHAPTER(S):	KNOWLEDGE OF	
11, 12, 13	37	Total rewards strategies (e.g., compensation, benefits, wellness, rewards, recognition, employee assistance).
3	38	Budgeting and accounting practices related to compensation and benefits.
11	39	Job evaluation methods.
11	40	Job pricing and pay structures.
5, 11	41	External labor markets and/or economic factors.
11, 12	42	Pay programs (e.g., incentive, variable, merit).
11, 12, 13	43	Executive compensation methods. **SPHR® ONLY**
12, 13	44	Non-cash compensation methods (e.g., stock options, ESOPs). **SPHR® ONLY**
13	45	Benefits programs (e.g., health and welfare, retirement, wellness, EAP, timeoff).
11, 12, 13, 17	46	International compensation laws and practices (e.g., expatriate compensation, entitlements, choice of law codes). **SPHR® ONLY**
11, 12, 13	47	Fiduciary responsibility related to total rewards management. **SPHR® ONLY**

05 Employee and Labor Relations (22%, 18%)

Analyzing, developing, implementing/administering, and evaluating the workplace relationship between employer and employee, in order to maintain relationships and working conditions that balance employer and employee needs and rights in support of the organization's strategic goals, objectives, and values.

RESPONSIBILITIES

01 Ensure that employee and labor relations activities are compliant with applicable federal, state, and local laws and regulations.

02 Assess organizational climate by obtaining employee input (e.g., focus groups, employee surveys, staff meetings).

03 Implement organizational change activities as appropriate in response to employee feedback.

04 Develop employee relations programs (e.g., awards, recognition, discounts, special events) that promote a positive organizational culture.

05 Implement employee relations programs that promote a positive organizational culture.

06 Evaluate effectiveness of employee relations programs through the use of metrics (e.g., exit interviews, employee surveys).

07 Establish workplace policies and procedures (e.g., dress code, attendance, computer use) and monitor their application and enforcement to ensure consistency.

08 Develop, administer and evaluate grievance/dispute resolution and performance improvement policies and procedures.

09 Resolve employee complaints filed with federal, state, and local agencies involving employment practices, utilizing professional resources as necessary (e.g., legal counsel, mediation/arbitration specialists and investigators).

10 Develop and direct proactive employee relations strategies for remaining union-free in non-organized locations.

11 Participate in collective bargaining activities, including contract negotiation and administration. **SPHR® ONLY**

HR Certification Institute

ADDRESSED IN THIS BOOK IN CHAPTER(S):	KNOWLEDGE OF	
2, 10, 14, 15	48	Applicable federal, state and local laws affecting employment in union and nonunion environments, such as antidiscrimination laws, sexual harassment, labor relations and privacy (e.g., WARN Act, Title VII, NLRA).
14	49	Techniques for facilitating positive employee relations (e.g., employee surveys, focus groups, dispute resolution, labor/management cooperative strategies and programs).
14	50	Employee involvement strategies (e.g., employee management committees, self-directed work teams, staff meetings).
14	51	Individual employment rights issues and practices (e.g., employment at will, negligent hiring, defamation, employees' rights to bargain collectively).
9, 10, 14, 15	52	Workplace behavior issues/practices (e.g., absenteeism and performance improvement).
15	53	Unfair labor practices (e.g., employee communication strategies and management training).
15	54	The collective bargaining process, strategies and concepts (e.g., contract negotiation and administration). **SPHR® ONLY**
11, 12, 13, 14	55	Positive employee relations strategies and non-monetary rewards.

06 Risk Management (7%, 7%)

Developing, implementing/administering, and evaluating programs, plans and policies that provide a safe and secure working environment and protect the organization from liability.

RESPONSIBILITIES

01 Ensure that workplace health, safety, security, and privacy activities are compliant with applicable federal, state, and local laws and regulations.

02 Identify the organization's safety program needs.

03 Develop/select and implement/administer occupational injury and illness prevention, safety incentives and training programs. **PHR® ONLY**

04 Develop/select, implement, and evaluate plans and policies to protect employees and other individuals and to minimize the organization's loss and liability (e.g., emergency response, evacuation, workplace violence, substance abuse, return-to-work policies).

05 Communicate and train the workforce on the plans and policies to protect employees and other individuals and to minimize the organization's loss and liability.

06 Develop and monitor business continuity and disaster recovery plans.

07 Communicate and train the workforce on the business continuity and disaster recovery plans.

08 Develop internal and external privacy policies (e.g., identity theft, data protection, HIPAA compliance, workplace monitoring).

09 Administer internal and external privacy policies.

ADDRESSED IN THIS BOOK IN CHAPTER(S):	KNOWLEDGE OF	
2, 14, 16	56	Federal, state and local workplace health, safety, security and privacy laws and regulations (e.g., OSHA, Drug-Free Workplace Act, ADA, HIPAA, Sarbanes-Oxley).
13, 16	57	Occupational injury and illness compensation and programs.

HR Certification Institute

ADDRESSED IN THIS BOOK IN CHAPTER(S):	KNOWLEDGE OF
16	58 Occupational injury and illness prevention programs.
16	59 Investigation procedures of workplace safety, health and security enforcement agencies (e.g., OSHA, National Institute for Occupational Safety and Health [NIOSH]).
16	60 Workplace safety risks.
16	61 Workplace security risks (e.g., theft, corporate espionage, asset and data protection, sabotage).
16	62 Potential violent behavior and workplace violence conditions.
16	63 General health and safety practices (e.g., evacuation, hazard communication, ergonomic evaluations).
14, 16	64 Incident and emergency response plans.
	65 Internal investigation, monitoring and surveillance techniques.
12, 13, 16	66 Issues related to substance abuse and dependency (e.g., identification of symptoms, substance-abuse testing, discipline).
16	67 Business continuity and disaster recovery plans (e.g., data storage and backup, alternative work locations and procedures).
	68 Data integrity techniques and technology (e.g., data sharing, firewalls).
	CORE KNOWLEDGE REQUIRED BY HR PROFESSIONALS:
3, 8	69 Needs assessment and analysis.
18	70 Third-party contract negotiation and management, including development of requests for proposals (RFPs).
	71 Communication skills and strategies (e.g., presentation, collaboration, influencing, diplomacy, sensitivity).
2, 4, 6, 9, 15, 16, 18	72 Organizational documentation requirements to meet federal and state requirements.
8	73 Adult learning processes.
8, 12, 13	74 Motivation concepts and applications.
8	75 Training techniques (e.g., computer-based, classroom, on-the-job).
	76 Leadership concepts and applications.
	77 Project management concepts and applications.
2, and Diversity Counts features in many chapters.	78 Diversity concepts and applications.
	79 Human relations concepts and applications (e.g., interpersonal and organizational behavior).
1, 14	80 HR ethics and professional standards.
Features in most chapters, + Chapter 18	81 Technology to support HR activities (e.g., HRIS, employee self-service, e-learning, ATS).
3, and *HR as a Profit Center* features in most chapters.	82 Qualitative and quantitative methods and tools for analysis, interpretation and decision-making purposes (e.g., metrics and measurements, cost/benefit analysis, financial statement analysis).
8	83 Change management methods.
4	84 Job analysis and job description methods.
	85 Employee records management (e.g., electronic/paper, retention, disposal).
3, 4	86 The interrelationships among HR activities and programs across functional areas.

HR Certification Institute

ADDRESSED IN THIS BOOK IN CHAPTER(S):	KNOWLEDGE OF	
	87	Types of organizational structures (e.g., matrix, hierarchy).
3	88	Environmental scanning concepts and applications.
14	89	Methods for assessing employee attitudes, opinions and satisfaction (e.g., opinion surveys, attitude surveys, focus groups/panels).
3	90	Basic budgeting and accounting concepts.
16	91	Risk management techniques.

The HR Certification Institute (HRCI), established in 1976, is an internationally recognized, independent certifying organization for the human resource profession. The HR Certification Institute is the global leader in developing rigorous exams to demonstrate mastery and real-world application of forward-thinking HR practices, policies, and principles. Today, more than 125,000 HR professionals worldwide proudly maintain the HR Certification Institute's credentials as a mark of high professional distinction. The HR Certification Institute awards the following credentials: Professional in Human Resources (PHR®), Senior Professional in Human Resources (SPHR®), Human Resource Management Professional (HRMP™), Human Resource Business Professional (HRBP™), Global Professional in Human Resources (GPHR®), and California Certifications. To learn more visit www.hrci.org.

APPENDIX B

Comprehensive Cases

BANDAG AUTOMOTIVE*

Jim Bandag took over his family's auto supply business in 2012, after helping his father, who founded the business, run it for about 10 years. Based in Illinois, Bandag employs about 300 people, and distributes auto supplies (replacement mufflers, bulbs, engine parts, and so on) through two divisions, one that supplies service stations and repair shops, and a second that sells retail auto supplies through five "Bandag Automotive" auto supply stores.

Jim's father, and now Jim, have always endeavored to keep Bandag's organization chart as simple as possible. The company has a full-time controller, managers for each of the five stores, a manager that oversees the distribution division, and Jim Bandag's executive assistant. Jim (along with his father, working part-time) handles marketing and sales.

Jim's executive assistant administers the firm's day-to-day human resource management tasks, but the company outsources most HR activities to others, including an employment agency that does its recruiting and screening, a benefits firm that administers its 401(k) plan, and a payroll service that handles its paychecks. Bandag's human resource management systems consist almost entirely of standardized HR forms purchased from an HR supplies company. These include forms such as application and performance appraisal forms, as well as an "honesty" test Bandag uses to screen the staff that works in the five stores. The company performs informal salary surveys to see what other companies in the area are paying for similar positions, and use these results for awarding annual merit increases (which in fact are more accurately cost-of-living adjustments).

Jim's father took a fairly paternal approach to the business. He often walked around speaking with his employees, finding out what their problems were, and even helping them out with an occasional loan—for instance, when he discovered that one of their children was sick, or for part of a new home down payment. Jim, on the other hand, tends to be more abrupt, and does not enjoy the same warm relationship with the employees as did his father. Jim is not unfair or dictatorial. He's just very focused on improving Bandag's financial performance, and so all his decisions, including his HR-related decisions, generally come down to cutting costs. For example, his knee-jerk reaction is usually to offer fewer days off rather than more, fewer benefits rather than more, and to be less flexible when an employee needs, for instance, a few extra days off because a child is sick.

It's therefore perhaps not surprising that over the past few years Bandag's sales and profits have increased markedly, but that the firm has found itself increasingly enmeshed in HR/equal employment–type issues. Indeed, Jim now finds himself spending a day or two a week addressing HR problems. For example, Henry Jaques, an employee at one of the stores, came to Jim's executive assistant and told her he was "irate" about his recent firing and was probably going to sue. Henry's store manager stated on his last performance appraisal that Henry did the technical aspects of his job well, but that he had "serious problems interacting with his coworkers." He was continually arguing with them, and complaining to the store manager about working conditions. The store manager had told Jim that he had to fire Henry because he was making "the whole place poisonous," and that (although he felt sorry because he'd heard rumors that Henry suffered from some mental illness) he felt he had to go. Jim approved the dismissal.

---

*© Gary Dessler, PhD.

Gavin was another problem. Gavin had worked for Bandag for 10 years, the last two as manager of one of the company's five stores. Right after Jim Bandag took over, Gavin told him he had to take a Family and Medical Leave Act medical leave to have hip surgery, and Jim approved the leave. When Gavin returned from leave, Jim told him that his position had been eliminated. Bandag had decided to close his store and open a new, larger store across from a shopping center about a mile away, and had appointed a new manager in Gavin's absence. However, the company did give Gavin a (nonmanagerial) position in the new store as a counter salesperson, at the same salary and with the same benefits as he had before. Even so, "This job is not similar to my old one," Gavin insisted. "It doesn't have nearly as much prestige." His contention is that the FMLA requires that the company bring him back in the same or equivalent position, and that this means a supervisory position, similar to what he had before he went on leave. Jim said no, and they seem to be heading toward litigation.

In another sign of the times at Bandag, the company's controller, Miriam, who had been with the company for about 6 years, went on pregnancy leave for 12 weeks in 2012 (also under the FMLA), and then received an additional 3 weeks' leave under Bandag's extended illness days program. Four weeks after she came back, she asked Jim Bandag if she could arrange to work fewer hours per week, and spend about a day per week working out of her home. He refused, and about 2 months later fired her. Jim Bandag said, "I'm sorry, it's not anything to do with your pregnancy-related requests, but we've got ample reasons to discharge you—your monthly budgets have been several days late, and we've got proof you may have forged documents." She replied, "I don't care what you say your reasons are; you're really firing me because of my pregnancy, and that's illegal."

Jim felt he was on safe ground as far as defending the company for these actions, although he didn't look forward to spending the time and money that he knew it would take to fight each. However, what he learned over lunch from a colleague undermined his confidence about another case that Jim had been sure would be a "slam dunk" for his company. Jim was explaining to his friend that one of Bandag's truck maintenance service people had applied for a job driving one of Bandag's distribution department trucks, and that Jim had turned him down because the worker was deaf. Jim (whose wife has occasionally said of him, "No one has ever accused Jim of being politically correct") was mentioning to his friend the apparent absurdity of a deaf person asking to be a truck delivery person. His friend, who happens to work for UPS, pointed out that the U.S. Court of Appeals for the Ninth Circuit had recently decided that UPS had violated the Americans with Disabilities Act by refusing to consider deaf workers for jobs driving the company's smaller vehicles.

Although Jim's father is semiretired, the sudden uptick in the frequency of such EEO-type issues troubled him, particularly after so many years of labor peace. However, he's not sure what to do about it. Having handed over the reins of the company to his son, he was loath to inject himself back into the company's operational decision making. On the other hand, he was afraid that in the short run these issues were going to drain a great deal of Jim's time and resources, and that in the long run they might be a sign of things to come, with problems like these eventually overwhelming Bandag Automotive. He comes to you, who he knows consults in human resource management, and asks you the following questions.

Questions

B-1. Given Bandag Automotive's size, and anything else you know about it, should we reorganize the human resource management function, and if so, why and how?

B-2. What, if anything, would you do to change and/or improve upon the current HR systems, forms, and practices that we now use?

B-3. Do you think that the employee whom Jim fired for creating what the manager called a poisonous relationship has a legitimate claim against us, and if so, why and what should we do about it?

B-4. Is it true that we really had to put Gavin back into an equivalent position, or was it adequate to just bring him back into a job at the same salary, bonuses, and benefits as he had before his leave?

B-5. Miriam, the controller, is basically claiming that the company is retaliating against her for being pregnant, and that the fact that we raised performance issues was just a smokescreen. Do you think the EEOC and/or courts would agree with her, and, in any case, what should we do now?

B-6. An employee who is deaf has asked us to be one of our delivery people and we turned him down. He's now threatening to sue. What should we do, and why?

B-7. In the previous 10 years, we've had only one equal employment complaint, and now in the last few years we've had four or five. What should I do about it? Why?

Based generally on actual facts, but Bandag is a fictitious company. Bandag source notes: "The Problem Employee: Discipline or Accommodation?" *Monday Business Briefing*, March 8, 2005; "Employee Says Change in Duties After Leave Violates FMLA," *BNA Bulletin to Management*, January 16, 2007, p. 24; "Manager Fired Days After Announcing Pregnancy," *BNA Bulletin to Management*, January 2, 2007, p. 8; "Ninth Circuit Rules UPS Violated ADA by Barring Deaf Workers from Driving Jobs," *BNA Bulletin to Management*, October 17, 2006, p. 329.

ANGELO'S PIZZA*

Angelo Camero was brought up in the Bronx, New York, and basically always wanted to be in the pizza store business. As a youngster, he would sometimes spend hours at the local pizza store, watching the owner knead the pizza dough, flatten it into a large circular crust, fling it up, and then spread on tomato sauce in larger and larger loops. After graduating from college as a marketing major, he made a beeline back to the Bronx, where he opened his first Angelo's Pizza store, emphasizing its clean, bright interior; its crisp green, red, and white sign; and his all-natural, fresh ingredients. Within 5 years, Angelo's store was a success, and he had opened three other stores and was considering franchising his concept.

Eager as he was to expand, his 4 years in business school had taught him the difference between being an entrepreneur and being a manager. As an entrepreneur/small business owner, he knew he had the distinct advantage of being able to personally run the whole operation himself. With just one store and a handful of employees, he could make every decision and watch the cash register, check in the new supplies, oversee the takeout, and personally supervise the service.

When he expanded to three stores, things started getting challenging. He hired managers for the two new stores (both of whom had worked for him at his first store for several years) and gave them only minimal "how to run a store"–type training, on the assumption that, having worked with him for several years, they already knew pretty much everything they needed to know about running a store. However, he was already experiencing human resource management problems, and he knew there was no way he could expand the number of stores he owned, or (certainly) contemplate franchising his idea, unless he had a system in place that he could clone in each new store to provide the manager (or the franchisee) with the necessary management knowledge and expertise to run their stores. Angelo had no training program in place for teaching his store managers how to run their stores. He simply (erroneously, as it turned out) assumed that by working with him they would learn how to do things on the job. Since Angelo had no system in place, the new managers were, in a way, starting off below zero when it came to how to manage a store.

There were several issues that particularly concerned Angelo. Finding and hiring good employees was number one. He'd read the new National Small Business Poll from the National Federation of Independent Business Education Foundation. It found that 71% of small business owners believed that finding qualified employees was "hard." Furthermore, "the search for qualified employees will grow more difficult as demographic and education factors" continue to make it more difficult to find employees. Similarly, reading *The Kiplinger Letter* one day, he noticed that just about every type of business couldn't find enough good employees to hire. Small firms were particularly in jeopardy; the *Letter* said: Giant firms can outsource many (particularly entry-level) jobs abroad, and larger companies can also afford to pay better benefits and to train their employees. Small firms rarely have the resources or the economies of scale to allow outsourcing or to install the big training programs that would enable them to take untrained new employees and turn them into skilled ones.

Although finding enough employees was his biggest problem, finding enough honest ones scared him even more. Angelo recalled from one of his business school courses that companies in the United States are losing a total of well over $400 billion a year in employee theft. As a rough approximation, that works out to about $9 per employee per day and about $12,000 lost annually for a typical company. Furthermore, it was small companies like Angelo's that were particularly in the crosshairs, because companies with fewer than 100 employees are particularly prone to employee theft. Why are small firms particularly vulnerable? Perhaps they lack experience dealing with the problem. More importantly: Small firms are more likely to have a single person doing several jobs, such as ordering supplies and paying the delivery person. This undercuts the checks and balances managers often strive for to control theft. Furthermore, the risk of stealing goes up dramatically when the business is largely based on cash. In a pizza store, many people come in and buy just one or two slices and a cola for lunch, and almost all pay with cash, not credit cards.

And, Angelo was not just worried about someone stealing cash. They can steal your whole business idea, something he learned from painful experience. He had been planning to open a store in what he thought would be a particularly good location, and was thinking of having one of his current employees manage the store. Instead, it turned out that this employee was, in a manner of speaking, stealing Angelo's brain—what Angelo knew about customers, suppliers, where to buy pizza dough, where to buy tomato sauce, how much everything should cost, how to furnish the store, where to buy ovens, store layout—everything. This employee soon quit and opened up his own pizza store, not far from where Angelo had planned to open his new store.

That he was having trouble hiring good employees, there was no doubt. The restaurant business is particularly brutal when it comes to turnover. Many restaurants turn over their employees at a rate of 200% to 300% per year—so every year, each position might have a series of two to three employees filling it. As Angelo said, "I was losing two to three employees a month." As he said, "We're a high-volume store, and while we should have [to fill all the hours in a week] about six employees per store, we were down to only three or four, so my managers and I were really under the gun."

The problem was bad at the hourly employee level: "We were churning a lot at the hourly level," said Angelo. "Applicants would come in, my managers or I would hire them and not spend much time training them, and the good ones would leave in frustration after a few weeks, while often it was the bad ones who'd stay behind." But in the last 2 years, Angelo's three company-owned stores also went through a total of three store managers—"They were just blowing through the door," as Angelo put it, in part because, without good employees, their workday was brutal. As a rule, when a small business owner or manager can't find enough employees (or an employee doesn't show up for work), about 80% of the time the owner or manager does the job himself or herself. So, these managers often ended up working 7 days a week, 10 to 12 hours a day, and many just burned out in the end. One night, working three jobs himself with customers leaving in anger, Angelo decided he'd never just hire someone because he was desperate again, but would start doing his hiring more rationally.

Angelo knew he should have a more formal screening process. As he said, "If there's been a lesson learned, it's much better to spend time up front screening out candidates that don't fit than to hire them and have to put up with their ineffectiveness." He also knew that he could identify many of the traits that his employees needed. For example, he knew that not everyone has the temperament to be a waiter (he has a small pizza/Italian restaurant in the back of his main store). As Angelo said, "I've seen personalities that were off the charts in assertiveness or overly introverted, traits that obviously don't make a good fit for a waiter or waitress."

As a local business, Angelo recruits by placing help wanted ads in two local newspapers, and he's been "shocked" at some of the responses and experiences he's had in response to the ads. Many of the applicants left voicemail messages (Angelo or the other workers in the store were too busy to answer), and some applicants Angelo "just axed" on the assumption that people without good telephone manners wouldn't have very good manners in the store, either. He also quickly learned that he had to throw out a very wide net, even if only hiring one or two people. Many people, as noted, he eliminated from consideration because of the messages they left, and about half the people he scheduled to come in for interviews didn't show up. He'd taken courses in human resource management, so (as he said) "I should know better," but he hired people based almost exclusively on a single interview (he occasionally made a feeble attempt to check references). In total, his HR approach was obviously not working. It wasn't producing enough good recruits, and the people he did hire were often problematic.

What was he looking for? Service-oriented courteous people, for one. For example, he'd hired one employee who used profanity several times, including once in front of a customer. On that employee's third day, Angelo had to tell her, "I think Angelo's isn't the right place for you," and he fired her. As Angelo said, "I felt bad, but also knew that everything I have is on the line for this business, so I wasn't going to let anyone run this business down." Angelo wants reliable people (who'll show up on time), honest people, and people who are flexible about switching jobs and hours as required. He calls his management style "trust and track." "I coach them and give them goals, and then carefully track results."

Angelo's Pizza business has only the most rudimentary human resource management system. Angelo bought several application forms at a local Office Depot, and rarely uses other forms of any sort. He uses his personal accountant for reviewing the company's books, and Angelo himself computes each employee's paycheck at the end of the week and writes the checks. Training is entirely on-the-job. Angelo personally trained each of his employees. For those employees who go on to be store managers, he assumes that they are training their own employees the way that Angelo trained them (for better or worse, as it turns out). Angelo pays "a bit above" prevailing wage rates (judging by other help wanted ads), but probably not enough to make a significant difference in the quality of employees that he attracts. If you asked Angelo what his reputation is as an employer, Angelo, being a candid and forthright person, would probably tell you that he is a supportive but hard-nosed employer who treats people fairly, but whose business reputation may suffer from disorganization stemming from inadequate organization and training. He approaches you to ask you several questions.

Questions

B-8. My strategy is to (hopefully) expand the number of stores and eventually franchise, while focusing on serving only high-quality fresh ingredients. What are three specific human resource management implications of my strategy (including specific policies and practices)?

B-9. Identify and briefly discuss five specific human resource management errors that I'm currently making.

B-10. Develop a structured interview form that we can use for hiring (1) store managers, (2) wait staff, and (3) counter people/pizza makers.

B-11. Based on what you know about Angelo's, and what you know from having visited pizza restaurants, write a one-page outline showing specifically how you think Angelo's should go about selecting employees.

Based generally on actual facts, but Angelo's Pizza is a fictitious company. Angelo's Pizza source notes: Dino Berta, "People Problems: Keep Hiring from Becoming a Crying Game," *Nation's Business News* 36, no. 20 (May 20, 2002), pp. 72–74; Ellen Lyon, "Hiring, Personnel Problems Can Challenge Entrepreneurs," *Patriot-News*, October 12, 2004; Rose Robin Pedone, "Businesses' $400 Billion Theft Problem," *Long Island Business News* 27 (July 6, 1998), pp. 1B–2B; "Survey Shows Small-Business Problems with Hiring, Internet," *Providence Business News* 16 (September 10, 2001), pp. 1B; "Finding Good Workers Is Posing a Big Problem as Hiring Picks Up," *The Kiplinger Letter* 81 (February 13, 2004). Ian Mount, "A Pizzeria Owner Learns the Value of Watching the Books," *The New York Times*, October 25, 2012, p. B8.

GOOGLE*

Fortune magazine named Google the best of the 100 best companies to work for, and there is little doubt why. Among the benefits it offers are free shuttles equipped with Wi-Fi to pick up and drop off employees from San Francisco Bay Area locations, unlimited sick days, annual all-expense-paid ski trips, free gourmet meals, five on-site free doctors, $2,000 bonuses for referring a new hire, free flu shots, a giant lap pool, on-site oil changes, on-site car washes, volleyball courts, TGIF parties, free on-site washers and dryers (with free detergent), Ping-Pong and foosball tables, and free famous people lectures. For many people, it's the gourmet meals and snacks that make Google stand out. For example, human resources director Stacey Sullivan loves the Irish oatmeal with fresh berries at the company's Plymouth Rock Cafe, near Google's "people operations" group. "I sometimes dream about it," she says. Engineer Jan Fitzpatrick loves the raw bar at Google's Tapis restaurant, down the road on the Google campus. Then, of course, there are the stock options—each new employee gets about 1,200 options to buy Google shares (recently worth about $480 per share). In fact, dozens of early Google employees ("Googlers") are already multimillionaires thanks to Google stock. The recession that began around 2008 did prompt Google and other firms to cut back on some of these benefits (cafeteria hours are shorter today, for instance), but Google still pretty much leads the benefits pack.

For their part, Googlers share certain traits. They tend to be brilliant, team oriented (teamwork is the norm, especially for big projects), and driven. *Fortune* describes them as people who "almost universally" see themselves as the most interesting people on the planet, and who are happy-go-lucky on the outside, but type A—highly intense and goal directed—on the inside. They're also super-hardworking (which makes sense, since it's not unusual for engineers to be in the hallways at 3 A.M. debating some new mathematical solution to a Google search problem). They're so team oriented that when working on projects, it's not unusual for a Google team to give up its larger, more spacious offices and to crowd into a small conference room, where they can "get things done." Historically, Googlers generally graduate with great grades from the best universities, including Stanford, Harvard, and MIT. For many years, Google wouldn't even consider hiring someone with less than a 3.7 average—while also probing deeply into the why behind any B grades. Google also doesn't hire lone wolves, but wants people who work together and people who also have diverse interests (narrow interests or skills are a turnoff at Google). Google also wants people with growth potential. The company is expanding so fast that it needs to hire people who are capable of being promoted five or six times—it's only, the company says, by hiring such overqualified people that it can be sure that the employees will be able to keep up as Google and their own departments expand.

The starting salaries are highly competitive. Experienced engineers start at about $130,000 a year (plus about 1,200 shares of stock options, as noted), and new MBAs can expect between $80,000 and $120,000 per year (with smaller option grants). Most recently, Google had about 10,000 staff members, up from its beginnings with just three employees in a rented garage.

Of course, in a company that's grown from 3 employees to 10,000 and from zero value to hundreds of billions of dollars, it may be quibbling to talk about "problems," but there's no doubt that such rapid growth does confront Google's management, and particularly its "people operations" group, with some big challenges. Let's look at these.

For one, Google, as noted earlier, is a 24-hour operation, and with engineers and others frequently pulling all-nighters to complete their projects, the company needs to provide a package of services and financial benefits that supports that kind of lifestyle, and that helps its employees maintain an acceptable work–life balance.

As another challenge, Google's enormous financial success is a two-edged sword. Although Google usually wins the recruitment race when it comes to competing for new employees against competitors like Microsoft or Yahoo!, Google does need some way to stem a rising tide of retirements. Most Googlers are still in their twenties and thirties, but many have become so wealthy from their Google stock options that they can afford to retire. One 27-year-old engineer received a million-dollar founder's award for her work on the program for searching desktop computers, and wouldn't think of leaving "except to start her own company." Similarly, a former engineering vice president retired (with his Google stock profits) to pursue his love of astronomy. The engineer who dreamed up Gmail recently retired (at the age of 30).

Another challenge is that the work not only involves long hours but can also be very tense. Google is a very numbers-oriented environment. For example, consider a typical weekly Google user interface design meeting. Marisa Meyer, the company's vice president of search products and user experience, runs the meeting, where her employees work out the look and feel of Google's products. Seated around a conference table are about a dozen Googlers, tapping on laptops. During the 2-hour meeting, Meyer needs to evaluate various design proposals, ranging from minor tweaks to a new product's entire layout. She's previously given each presentation an allotted amount of time, and a large digital clock on the wall ticks off the seconds. The presenters must quickly present their ideas, but also handle questions such as "what do users do if the tab is moved from the side of the page to the top?" Furthermore, it's all about the numbers—no one at Google would ever say, for instance, "the tab looks better in red"—you need to prove your point. Presenters must come armed with usability experiment results, showing, for instance, that a certain percentage preferred red or some other color. While the presenters are answering these questions as quickly as possible, the digital clock is ticking, and when it hits the allotted time, the presentation must end, and the next team steps up to present. It is a tough and tense environment, and Googlers must have done their homework.

Growth can also undermine the "outlaw band that's changing the world" culture that fostered the services that made Google famous. Even cofounder Sergi Brin agrees that Google risks becoming less "zany" as it grows. To paraphrase one of its top managers, the hard part of any business is keeping that original innovative, small business feel even as the company grows.

Creating the right culture is especially challenging now that Google is truly global. For example, Google works hard to provide the same financial and service benefits every place it does business around the world, but it can't exactly match its benefits in every country because of international laws and international taxation issues. Offering the same benefits everywhere is more important than it might initially appear. All those benefits make life easier for Google staff, and help them achieve a work–life balance. Achieving the right work–life balance is the centerpiece of Google's culture, but this also becomes more challenging as the company grows. On the one hand, Google does expect all of its employees to work super hard; on the other hand, it realizes that it needs to help them maintain some sort of balance. As one manager says, Google acknowledges "that we work hard but that work is not everything."

Recruitment is another challenge. While Google certainly doesn't lack applicants, attracting the right applicants is crucial if Google is to continue to grow successfully. Working at Google requires a special set of traits, and screening employees is easier if it recruits the right people to begin with. For instance, Google needs to attract people who are super-bright, love to work, have fun, can handle the stress, and who also have outside interests and flexibility.

As the company grows internationally, it also faces the considerable challenge of recruiting and building staff overseas. For example, Google now is introducing a new vertical market–based structure across Europe to attract more business advertisers to its search engine. (By vertical market–based structure, Google means focusing on key vertical industry sectors such as travel, retail, automotive, and technology.) To build these industry groupings abroad from scratch, Google promoted its former head of its U.S. financial services group to be the vertical markets director for Europe;

he moved there recently. Google is thus looking for heads for each of its vertical industry groups for all of its key European territories. Each of these vertical market heads will have to educate their market sectors (retailing, travel, and so on) so Google can attract new advertisers. Google already has offices across Europe, and its London office had tripled in size to 100 staff in just 2 years.

However, probably the biggest challenge Google faces is gearing up its employee selection system, now that the company must hire thousands of people per year. When Google started in business, job candidates typically suffered through a dozen or more in-person interviews, and the standards were so high that even applicants with years of great work experience often got turned down if they had just average college grades. But recently, even Google's cofounders have acknowledged to security analysts that setting such an extraordinarily high bar for hiring was holding back Google's expansion. For Google's first few years, one of the company's cofounder's interviewed nearly every job candidate before he or she was hired, and even today one of them still reviews the qualifications of everyone before he or she gets a final offer.

The experience of one candidate illustrates what Google is up against. A 24-year-old was interviewed for a corporate communications job at Google. Google first made contact with the candidate in May, and then, after two phone interviews, invited him to headquarters. There he had separate interviews with about six people and was treated to lunch in a Google cafeteria. They also had him turn in several "homework" assignments, including a personal statement and a marketing plan. In August, Google invited the candidate back for a second round, which it said would involve another four or five interviews. In the meantime, he decided he'd rather work at a start-up, and accepted another job at a new Web-based instant messaging provider.

Google's new head of human resources, a former GE executive, says that Google is trying to strike the right balance between letting Google and the candidate get to know each other while also moving quickly. To that end, Google recently administered a survey to all Google's current employees in an effort to identify the traits that correlate with success at Google. In the survey, employees responded to questions relating to about 300 variables, including their performance on standardized tests, how old they were when they first used a computer, and how many foreign languages they speak. The Google survey team then went back and compared the answers against the 30 or 40 job performance factors they keep for each employee. They thereby identified clusters of traits that Google might better focus on during the hiring process. Google is also moving from the free-form interviews it used in the past to a more structured process.

Questions

B-12. What do you think of the idea of Google correlating personal traits from the employees' answers on the survey to their performance, and then using that as the basis for screening job candidates? In other words, is it or is it not a good idea? Please explain your answer.

B-13. The benefits that Google pays obviously represent an enormous expense. Based on what you know about Google and on what you read in this text, how would you defend all these benefits if you're making a presentation to the security analysts who were analyzing Google's performance?

B-14. If you wanted to hire the brightest people around, how would you go about recruiting and selecting them?

B-15. To support its growth and expansion strategy, Google wants (among other traits) people who are super-bright and who work hard, often round-the-clock, and who are flexible and maintain a decent work–life balance. List five specific HR policies or practices that you think Google has implemented or should implement to support its strategy, and explain your answer.

B-16. What sorts of factors do you think Google will have to take into consideration as it tries transferring its culture and reward systems and way of doing business to its operations abroad?

B-17. Given the sorts of values and culture Google cherishes, briefly describe four specific activities you suggest they pursue during new-employee orientation.

Source notes for Google: "Google Brings Vertical Structure to Europe," *New Media Age*, August 4, 2005, p. 2; Debbie Lovewell, "Employer Profile—Google: Searching for Talent," *Employee Benefits*, October 10, 2005, p. 66; "Google Looking for Gourmet Chefs," *Internet Week*, August 4, 2005; Douglas Merrill, "Google's 'Googley' Culture Kept Alive by Tech," *eWeek*, April 11, 2006; Robert Hof, "Google Gives Employees Another Option," *BusinessWeek Online*, December 13, 2005; Kevin Delaney, "Google Adjusts Hiring Process as Needs Grow," *The Wall Street Journal*, October 23, 2006, pp. B1, B8; Adam Lishinsky, "Search and Enjoy," *Fortune*, January 22, 2007, pp. 70–82; www.nypost.com/seven/10302008/business/frugal_google_cuts_perks_136011.htm, accessed July 12, 2009; Adam Bryant, "The Quest to Build a Better Boss," *The New York Times*, March 13, 2011, pp. 1, 7.

MUFFLER MAGIC*

Muffler Magic is a fast-growing chain of 25 automobile service centers in Nevada. Originally started 20 years ago as a muffler repair shop by Ronald Brown, the chain expanded rapidly to new locations, and as it did so Muffler Magic also expanded the services it provided, from muffler replacement to oil changes, brake jobs, and engine repair. Today, one can bring an automobile to a Muffler Magic shop for basically any type of service, from tires to mufflers to engine repair.

Auto service is a tough business. The shop owner is basically dependent upon the quality of the service people he or she hires and retains, and the most qualified mechanics find it easy to pick up and leave for a job paying a bit more at a competitor down the road. It's also a business in which productivity is very important. The single largest expense is usually the cost of labor. Auto service dealers generally don't just make up the prices that they charge customers for various repairs; instead, they charge based on standardized industry rates for jobs like changing spark plugs or repairing a leaky radiator. Therefore, if someone brings a car in for a new alternator and the standard number of hours for changing the alternator is an hour, but it takes the mechanic 2 hours, the service center's owner may end up making less profit on the transaction.

Quality is a persistent problem as well. For example, "rework" has recently been a problem at Muffler Magic. A customer recently brought her car to a Muffler Magic to have the car's brake pads replaced, which the service center did for her. Unfortunately, when she left she drove only about two blocks before she discovered that she had no brake power at all. It was simply fortuitous that she was going so slowly she was able to stop her car by slowly rolling up against a parking bumper. It subsequently turned out that the mechanic who replaced the brake pads had failed to properly tighten a fitting on the hydraulic brake tubes and the brake fluid had run out, leaving the car with no braking power. In a similar problem the month before that, a (different) mechanic replaced a fan belt, but forgot to refill the radiator with fluid; that customer's car overheated before he got four blocks away, and Muffler Magic had to replace the whole engine. Of course problems like these not only diminish the profitability of the company's profits, but, repeated many times over, have the potential for ruining Muffler Magic's word-of-mouth reputation.

Organizationally, Muffler Magic employs about 300 people, and Ron runs his company with eight managers, including himself as president, a controller, a purchasing director, a marketing director, and the human resource manager. He also has three regional managers to whom the eight or nine service center managers in each area of Nevada report. Over the past 2 years, as the company has opened new service centers, company-wide profits have diminished rather than increased. In part, these diminishing profits probably reflect the fact that Ron Brown has found it increasingly difficult to manage his growing operation. ("Your reach is exceeding your grasp" is how Ron's wife puts it.)

The company has only the most basic HR systems in place. It uses an application form that the human resource manager modified from one that he downloaded from the Web, and the standard employee status change request forms, sign-on forms, I-9 forms, and so on, that it purchased from a human resource management supply house.

---

*© Gary Dessler, PhD.

Training is entirely on-the-job. Muffler Magic expects the experienced technicians that it hires to come to the job fully trained; to that end, the service center managers generally ask candidates for these jobs basic behavioral questions that hopefully provide a window into these applicants' skills. However, most of the other technicians hired to do jobs like rotating tires, fixing brake pads, and replacing mufflers are untrained and inexperienced. They are to be trained by either the service center manager or by more experienced technicians, on-the-job.

Ron Brown faces several HR-type problems. One, as he says, is that he faces the "tyranny of the immediate" when it comes to hiring employees. Although it's fine to say that he should be carefully screening each employee and checking his or her references and work ethic, from a practical point of view, with 25 centers to run, the centers' managers usually just hire anyone who seems to be breathing, as long as he or she can answer some basic interview questions about auto repair, such as, "What do you think the problem is if a 2001 Camry is overheating, and what would you do about it?"

Employee safety is also a problem. An automobile service center may not be the most dangerous type of workplace, but it is potentially dangerous. Employees are dealing with sharp tools, greasy floors, greasy tools, extremely hot temperatures (for instance, on mufflers and engines), and fast-moving engine parts including fan blades. There are some basic things that a service manager can do to ensure more safety, such as insisting that all oil spills be cleaned up immediately. However, from a practical point of view, there are a few ways to get around many of the problems—such as when the technician must check out an engine while it is running.

With Muffler Magic's profits going down instead of up, Brown's human resource manager has taken the position that the main problem is financial. As he says, "You get what you pay for" when it comes to employees, and if you compensate technicians better than your competitors do, then you get better technicians, ones who do their jobs better and stay longer with the company—and then profits will rise. So, the HR manager scheduled a meeting between himself, Ron Brown, and a professor of business who teaches compensation management at a local university. The HR manager has asked this professor to spend about a week looking at each of the service centers, analyzing the situation, and coming up with a compensation plan that will address Muffler Magic's quality and productivity problems. At this meeting, the professor makes three basic recommendations for changing the company's compensation policies.

Number one, she says that she has found that Muffler Magic suffers from what she calls "presenteeism"—in other words, employees drag themselves into work even when they're sick, because the company does not pay them if they are out; the company offers no sick days. In just a few days the professor couldn't properly quantify how much Muffler Magic is losing to presenteeism. However, from what she could see at each shop, there are typically one or two technicians working with various maladies like the cold or flu, and it seemed to her that each of these people was probably really only working about half of the time (although they were getting paid for the whole day). So, for 25 service centers per week, Muffler Magic could well be losing 125 or 130 personnel days per week of work. The professor suggests that Muffler Magic start allowing everyone to take 3 paid sick days per year, a reasonable suggestion. However, as Ron Brown points out, "Right now, we're only losing about half a day's pay for each employee who comes in and who works unproductively; with your suggestion, won't we lose the whole day?" The professor says she'll ponder that one.

Second, the professor recommends putting the technicians on a skill-for-pay plan. Basically, she suggests the following. Give each technician a letter grade (A through E) based upon that technician's particular skill level and abilities. An "A" technician is a team leader and needs to show that he or she has excellent diagnostic troubleshooting skills, and the ability to supervise and direct other technicians. At the other extreme, an "E" technician would typically be a new apprentice with little technical training. The other technicians fall in between those two levels, based on their individual skills and abilities.

In the professor's system, the "A" technician or team leader would assign and supervise all work done within his or her area but generally not do any mechanical repairs himself or herself. The team leader does the diagnostic troubleshooting, supervises and trains the other technicians, and test drives the car before it goes back to the customer. Under this plan, every technician receives a guaranteed hourly wage within a certain range, for instance:

A tech = \$25–\$30 an hour
B tech = \$20–\$25 an hour
C tech = \$15–\$20 an hour
D tech = \$10–\$15 an hour
E tech = \$8–\$10 an hour

Third, to directly address the productivity issue, the professor recommends that each service manager calculate each technician-team's productivity at the end of each day and at the end of each week. She suggests posting the running productivity total conspicuously for daily viewing. Then, the technicians as a group get weekly cash bonuses based upon their productivity. To calculate productivity, the professor recommends dividing the total labor hours billed by the total labor hours paid to technicians; in other words, total labor hours billed *divided by* total hours paid to technicians.

Having done some homework, the professor says that the national average for labor productivity is currently about 60%, and that only the best-run service centers achieve 85% or greater. By her rough calculations, Muffler Magic was attaining about industry average (about 60%—in other words, they were billing for only about 60 hours for each 100 hours that they actually had to pay technicians to do the jobs). (Of course, this was not entirely the technicians' fault. Technicians get time off for breaks and for lunch, and if a particular service center simply didn't have enough business on a particular day or during a particular week, then several technicians may well sit around idly waiting for the next car to come in.) The professor recommends setting a labor efficiency goal of 80% and posting each team's daily productivity results in the workplace to provide them with additional feedback. She recommends that if at the end of a week the team is able to boost its productivity ratio from the current 60% to 80%, then that team would get an additional 10% weekly pay bonus. After that, for every 5% boost of increased productivity above 80%, technicians would receive an additional 5% weekly bonus. So, if a technician's normal weekly pay is \$400, that employee would receive an extra \$40 at the end of the week when his team moves from 60% productivity to 80% productivity.

After the meeting, Ron Brown thanked the professor for her recommendations and told her he would think about it and get back to her. After the meeting, on the drive home, Ron was pondering what to do. He had to decide whether to institute the professor's sick leave policy, and whether to implement the professor's incentive and compensation plan. Before implementing anything, however, he wanted to make sure he understood the context in which he was making his decision. For example, did Muffler Magic really have an incentive pay problem, or were the problems more broad? Furthermore, how, if at all, would the professor's incentive plan impact the quality of the work that the teams were doing? And should the company really start paying for sick days? Ron Brown had a lot to think about.

Questions

B-18. Write a one-page summary outline listing three or four recommendations you would make with respect to each HR function (recruiting, selection, training, and so on) that you think Ron Brown should be addressing with his HR manager.

B-19. Develop a 10-question structured interview form Ron Brown's service center managers can use to interview experienced technicians.

B-20. If you were Ron Brown, would you implement the professor's recommendation addressing the presenteeism problem—in other words, start paying for sick days? Why or why not?

B-21. If you were advising Ron Brown, would you recommend that he implement the professor's skill-based pay and incentive pay plan as is? Why? Would you implement it with modifications? If you would modify it, please be specific about what you think those modifications should be, and why.

Based generally on actual facts, but Muffler Magic is a fictitious company. This case is based largely on information in Drew Paras, "The Pay Factor: Technicians' Salaries Can Be the Largest Expense in a Server Shop, as Well as the Biggest Headache. Here's How One Shop Owner Tackled the Problem," *Motor Age*, November 2003, pp. 76–79; see also Jennifer Pellet, "Health Care Crisis," *Chief Executive*, June 2004, pp. 56–61; "Firms Press to Quantify, Control Presenteeism," *Employee Benefits*, December 1, 2002.

BP TEXAS CITY*

When British Petroleum's (BP) Horizon oil rig exploded in the Gulf of Mexico in 2010, it triggered tragic reminders for experts in the safety community. In March 2005, an explosion and fire at BP's Texas City, Texas, refinery killed 15 people and injured 500 people in the worst U.S. industrial accident in more than 10 years. That disaster triggered three investigations: one internal investigation by BP, one by the U.S. Chemical Safety Board, and an independent investigation chaired by former U.S. Secretary of State James Baker and an 11-member panel that was organized at BP's request.

To put the results of these three investigations into context, it's useful to understand that under its current management, BP had pursued, for the past 10 or so years before the Texas City explosion, a strategy emphasizing cost-cutting and profitability. The basic conclusion of the investigations was that cost-cutting helped compromise safety at the Texas City refinery. It's useful to consider each investigation's findings.

The Chemical Safety Board's (CSB) investigation, according to Carol Merritt, the board's chair, showed that "BP's global management was aware of problems with maintenance, spending, and infrastructure well before March 2005." Apparently, faced with numerous earlier accidents, BP did make some safety improvements. However, it focused primarily on emphasizing personal employee safety behaviors and procedural compliance, and thereby reducing safety accident rates. The problem (according to the CSB) was that "catastrophic safety risks remained." For example, according to the CSB, "unsafe and antiquated equipment designs were left in place, and unacceptable deficiencies in preventive maintenance were tolerated." Basically, the CSB found that BP's budget cuts led to a progressive deterioration of safety at the Texas City refinery. Said Merritt, "In an aging facility like Texas City, it is not responsible to cut budgets related to safety and maintenance without thoroughly examining the impact on the risk of a catastrophic accident."

Looking at specifics, the CSB said that a 2004 internal audit of 35 BP business units, including Texas City (BP's largest refinery), found significant safety gaps they all had in common, including, for instance, a lack of leadership competence, and "systemic underlying issues" such as a widespread tolerance of noncompliance with basic safety rules and poor monitoring of safety management systems and processes. Ironically, the CSB found that BP's accident prevention effort at Texas City had achieved a 70% reduction in worker injuries in the year before the explosion. Unfortunately, this simply meant that individual employees were having fewer accidents. The larger, more fundamental problem was that the potentially explosive situation inherent in the depreciating machinery remained.

The CSB found that the Texas City explosion followed a pattern of years of major accidents at the facility. In fact, there had apparently been an average of one employee death every 16 months at the plant for the last 30 years. The CSB found that the equipment directly involved in the most recent explosion was an obsolete design already phased out in most refineries and chemical plants, and that key pieces of its instrumentation were not working. There had also been previous instances where flammable vapors were released from the same unit in the 10 years prior to the explosion. In 2003, an external audit had referred to the Texas City refinery's infrastructure and assets as "poor" and found what it referred to as a "checkbook mentality," one in which budgets were not sufficient to manage all the risks. In particular, the CSB found that BP had implemented a 25% cut on fixed costs between 1998 and 2000 and that this adversely impacted maintenance expenditures and net expenditures, and refinery infrastructure. Going on, the CSB found that in 2004, there were three major accidents at the refinery that killed three workers.

BP's own internal report concluded that the problems at Texas City were not of recent origin, and instead were years in the making. It said BP was taking steps to address them. Its investigation found "no evidence of anyone consciously or intentionally taking actions or making decisions that put others at risk." Said BP's report, "The underlying reasons for the behaviors and actions displayed during the incident are complex, and the team has spent much time trying to understand them—it is evident that they were many years in the making and will require concerted and committed actions to address." BP's report concluded that there were five underlying causes for the massive explosion:

- A working environment had eroded to one characterized by resistance to change, and a lack of trust.
- Safety, performance, and risk reduction priorities had not been set and consistently reinforced by management.
- Changes in the "complex organization" led to a lack of clear accountabilities and poor communication.
- A poor level of hazard awareness and understanding of safety resulted in workers accepting levels of risk that were considerably higher than at comparable installations.
- Adequate early warning systems for problems were lacking, and there were no independent means of understanding the deteriorating standards at the plant.

The report from the BP-initiated but independent 11-person panel chaired by former U.S. Secretary of State James Baker contained specific conclusions and recommendations. The Baker panel looked at BP's corporate safety oversight, the corporate safety culture, and the process safety management systems at BP at the Texas City plant as well at BP's other refineries.

Basically, the Baker panel concluded that BP had not provided effective safety process leadership and had not established safety as a core value at the five refineries it looked at (including Texas City).

Like the CSB, the Baker panel found that BP had emphasized personal safety in recent years and had in fact improved personal safety performance, but had not emphasized the overall safety process, thereby mistakenly interpreting "improving personal injury rates as an indication of acceptable process safety performance at its U.S. refineries." In fact, the Baker panel went on, by focusing on these somewhat misleading improving personal injury rates, BP created a false sense of confidence that it was properly addressing process safety risks. It also found that the safety culture at Texas City did not have the positive, trusting, open environment that a proper safety culture required. The Baker panel's other findings included the following.

- BP did not always ensure that adequate resources were effectively allocated to support or sustain a high level of process safety performance.
- BP's refinery personnel are "overloaded" by corporate initiatives.
- Operators and maintenance personnel work high rates of overtime.
- BP tended to have a short-term focus and its decentralized management system and entrepreneurial culture delegated substantial discretion to refinery plant managers "without clearly defining process safety expectations, responsibilities, or accountabilities."
- There was no common, unifying process safety culture among the five refineries.
- The company's corporate safety management system did not make sure there was timely compliance with internal process safety standards and programs.

- BP's executive management either did not receive refinery-specific information that showed that process safety deficiencies existed at some of the plants, or did not effectively respond to any information it did receive.[1]
- These findings and the following suggestions are based on "BP Safety Report Finds Company's Process Safety Culture Ineffective," *Global Refining & Fuels Report*, January 17, 2007.

The Baker panel made several safety recommendations for BP, including the following.

1. The company's corporate management must provide leadership on process safety.
2. The company should establish a process safety management system that identifies, reduces, and manages the process safety risks of the refineries.
3. The company should make sure its employees have an appropriate level of process safety knowledge and expertise.
4. The company should involve "relevant stakeholders" in developing a positive, trusting, and open process safety culture at each refinery.
5. BP should clearly define expectations and strengthen accountability for process safety performance.
6. BP should better coordinate its process safety support for the refining line organization.
7. BP should develop an integrated set of leading and lagging performance indicators for effectively monitoring process safety performance.
8. BP should establish and implement an effective system to audit process safety performance.
9. The company's board should monitor the implementation of the panel's recommendations and the ongoing process safety performance of the refineries.
10. BP should transform into a recognized industry leader in process safety management.

In making its recommendations, the panel singled out the company's chief executive at the time, Lord Browne, by saying, "In hindsight, the panel believes if Browne had demonstrated comparable leadership on and commitment to process safety [as he did for responding to climate change] that would have resulted in a higher level of safety at refineries."

Overall, the Baker panel found that BP's top management had not provided "effective leadership" on safety. It found that the failings went to the very top of the organization, to the company's chief executive, and to several of his top lieutenants. The Baker panel emphasized the importance of top management commitment, saying, for instance, that "it is imperative that BP leadership set the process safety tone at the top of the organization and establish appropriate expectations regarding process safety performance." It also said BP "has not provided effective leadership in making certain its management and U.S. refining workforce understand what is expected of them regarding process safety performance."

Lord Browne, the chief executive, stepped down about a year after the explosion. About the same time, some BP shareholders were calling for the company's executives and board directors to have their bonuses more closely tied to the company's safety and environmental performance in the wake of Texas City. In October 2009, OSHA announced it was filing the largest fine in its history for this accident, for $87 million, against BP. One year later, BP's Horizon oil rig in the Gulf of Mexico exploded, taking 11 lives.

Questions

B-22. The text defines ethics as "the principles of conduct governing an individual or a group," and specifically as the standards one uses to decide what his or her conduct should be. To what extent do you believe that what happened at BP is as much a breakdown in the company's ethical systems as it is in its safety systems, and how would you defend your conclusion?

B-23. Are the Occupational Safety and Health Administration's standards, policies, and rules aimed at addressing problems like the ones that apparently existed at the Texas City plant? If so, how would you explain the fact that problems like these could have continued for so many years?

B-24. Since there were apparently at least three deaths in the year prior to the major explosion, and an average of about one employee death per 16 months for the previous 10 years, how would you account for the fact that mandatory OSHA inspections missed these glaring sources of potential catastrophic events?

B-25. The text lists numerous suggestions for "how to prevent accidents." Based on what you know about the Texas City explosion, what do you say Texas City tells you about the most important three steps an employer can take to prevent accidents?

B-26. Based on what you learned in Chapter 14, would you make any additional recommendations to BP over and above those recommendations made by the Baker panel and the CSB? If so, what would those recommendations be?

B-27. Explain specifically how strategic human resource management at BP seems to have supported the company's broader strategic aims. What does this say about the advisability of always linking human resource strategy to a company's strategic aims?

Source notes for BP Texas City: Sheila McNulty, "BP Knew of Safety Problems, Says Report," *The Financial Times*, October 31, 2006, p. 1; "CBS: Documents Show BP Was Aware of Texas City Safety Problems," *World Refining & Fuels Today*, October 30, 2006; "BP Safety Report Finds Company's Process Safety Culture Ineffective," *Global Refining & Fuels Report*, January 17, 2007; "BP Safety Record Under Attack," *Europe Intelligence Wire*, January 17, 2007; Mark Hofmann, "BP Slammed for Poor Leadership on Safety, Oil Firm Agrees to Act on Review Panel's Recommendations," *Business Intelligence*, January 22, 2007, p. 3; "Call for Bonuses to Include Link with Safety Performance," *The Guardian*, January 18, 2007, p. 24; www.bp.com/genericarticle.do?categoryId=9005029&contentId=7015905, accessed July 12, 2009; Steven Greenhouse, "BP Faces Record Fine For '05 Blast," *The New York Times*, October 30, 2009, pp. 1, 6; Kyle W. Morrison, "Blame to Go Around," *Safety & Health* 183, no. 3 (March 2011), p. 40; Ed Crooks, "BP had tools to end spill sooner, court told," www.ft.com/cms/s/0/40d7b076-2ae8-11e3-8fb8-00144feab7de.html?ftcamp=published_links%2Frss%2Fhome_uk%2Ffeed%2F%2Fproduct#axzz2gZshHFOc, accessed October 2, 2013.

GLOSSARY

4/5ths rule Federal agency rule that a minority selection rate less than 80% (4/5ths) of that for the group with the highest rate is evidence of adverse impact.

401(k) plan A defined contribution plan based on section 401(k) of the Internal Revenue Code.

action learning A training technique by which management trainees are allowed to work full-time analyzing and solving problems in other departments.

adaptability screening A process that aims to assess the assignees' (and spouses') probable success in handling a foreign transfer.

adverse impact The overall impact of employer practices that result in significantly higher percentages of members of minorities and other protected groups being rejected for employment, placement, or promotion.

affirmative action Steps that are taken for the purpose of eliminating the present effects of past discrimination.

Age Discrimination in Employment Act of 1967 (ADEA) The act prohibiting arbitrary age discrimination and specifically protecting individuals over 40 years old.

agency shop A form of union security in which employees who do not belong to the union must still pay union dues on the assumption that union efforts benefit all workers.

alternation ranking method Ranking employees from best to worst on a particular trait, choosing highest, then lowest, until all are ranked.

alternative dispute resolution or ADR program Grievance procedure that provides for binding arbitration as the last step.

alternative staffing The use of nontraditional recruitment sources.

Americans with Disabilities Act (ADA) The act requiring employers to make reasonable accommodations for disabled employees; it prohibits discrimination against disabled persons.

annual bonus Plans that are designed to motivate short-term performance of managers and which are tied to company profitability.

applicant tracking systems Online systems that help employers attract, gather, screen, compile, and manage applicants.

application form The form that provides information on education, prior work record, and skills.

appraisal interview An interview in which the supervisor and subordinate review the appraisal and make plans to remedy deficiencies and reinforce strengths.

apprenticeship training A structured process by which people become skilled workers through a combination of classroom instruction and on-the-job training.

arbitration The most definitive type of third-party intervention, in which the arbitrator usually has the power to determine and dictate the settlement terms.

Authority The right to make decisions, direct others' work, and give orders.

authorization cards In order to petition for a union election, the union must show that at least 30% of employees may be interested in being unionized. Employees indicate this interest by signing authorization cards.

bargaining unit The group of employees the union will be authorized to represent.

behavior modeling A training technique in which trainees are first shown good management techniques in a film, are asked to play roles in a simulated situation, and are then given feedback and praise by their supervisor.

behavior modification Using contingent rewards or punishment to change behavior.

behavior-based safety Identifying the worker behaviors that contribute to accidents and then training workers to avoid these behaviors.

behavioral interview A series of job-related questions that focus on how the candidate reacted to actual situations in the past.

behaviorally anchored rating scale (BARS) An appraisal method that aims at combining the benefits of narrative critical incidents and quantified ratings by anchoring a quantified scale with specific narrative examples of good and poor performance.

benchmark job A job that is used to anchor the employer's pay scale and around which other jobs are arranged in order of relative worth.

benefits Indirect financial and nonfinancial payments employees receive for continuing their employment with the company.

bias The tendency to allow individual differences such as age, race, and sex to affect the appraisal ratings employees receive.

bona fide occupational qualification (BFOQ) Requirement that an employee be of a certain religion, sex, or national origin where that is reasonably necessary to the organization's normal operation. Specified by the 1964 Civil Rights Act.

boycott The combined refusal by employees and other interested parties to buy or use the employer's products.

broadbanding Consolidating salary grades and ranges into just a few wide levels or "bands," each of which contains a relatively wide range of jobs and salary levels.

burnout The total depletion of physical and mental resources caused by excessive striving to reach an unrealistic work-related goal.

business process reengineering Redesigning business processes, usually by combining steps, so that small multifunction process teams using information technology do the jobs formerly done by a sequence of departments.

candidate-order (or contrast) error An error of judgment on the part of the interviewer due to interviewing one or more very good or very bad candidates just before the interview in question.

career The occupational positions a person has had over many years.

career development The lifelong series of activities that contribute to a person's career exploration, establishment, success, and fulfillment.

career management The process for enabling employees to better understand and develop their career skills and interests, and to use these skills and interests more effectively.

career planning The deliberate process through which someone becomes aware of personal skills, interests, knowledge, motivations, and other characteristics and establishes action plans to attain specific goals.

case study method A development method in which the manager is presented with a written description of an organizational problem to diagnose and solve.

cash balance plans Plans under which the employer contributes a percentage of employees' current pay to employees' pension plans every year, and employees earn interest on this amount.

central tendency A tendency to rate all employees the same way, such as rating them all average.

citation Summons informing employers and employees of the regulations and standards that have been violated in the workplace.

Civil Rights Act of 1991 (CRA 1991) The act that places the burden of proof back on employers and permits compensatory and punitive damages.

classes Grouping jobs based on a set of rules for each group or class, such as amount of independent judgment, skill, physical effort, and so forth, required. Classes usually contain similar jobs.

closed shop A form of union security in which the company can hire only union members. This was outlawed in 1947 but still exists in some industries (such as printing).

coaching Educating, instructing, and training subordinates.

codetermination Employees have the legal right to a voice in setting company policies.

collective bargaining The process through which representatives of management and the union meet to negotiate a labor agreement.

college recruiting Sending an employer's representatives to college campuses to prescreen applicants and create an applicant pool from the graduating class.

compa ratio Equals an employee's pay rate divided by the pay range midpoint for his or her pay grade.

comparable worth The concept by which women who are usually paid less than men can claim that men in comparable rather than in strictly equal jobs are paid more.

compensable factor A fundamental, compensable element of a job, such as skills, effort, responsibility, and working conditions.

competency model A graphic model that consolidates, usually in one diagram, a precise overview of the competencies (the knowledge, skills, and behaviors) someone would need to do a job well.

Competency-based job analysis Describing the job in terms of measurable, observable, behavioral competencies (knowledge, skills, and/or behaviors) that an employee doing that job must exhibit to do the job well.

competency-based pay Where the company pays for the employee's range, depth, and types of skills and knowledge, rather than for the job title he or she holds.

competitive advantage Any factors that allow an organization to differentiate its product or service from those of its competitors to increase market share.

competitive strategy A strategy that identifies how to build and strengthen the business's long-term competitive position in the marketplace.

compressed workweek Schedule in which employee works fewer but longer days each week.

construct validity A test that is construct valid is one that demonstrates that a selection procedure measures a construct and that construct is important for successful job performance.

content validity A test that is content valid is one that contains a fair sample of the tasks and skills actually needed for the job in question.

controlled experimentation Formal methods for testing the effectiveness of a training program, preferably with before-and-after tests and a control group.

corporate campaign An organized effort by the union that exerts pressure on the corporation by pressuring the company's other unions, shareholders, directors, customers, creditors, and government agencies, often directly.

corporate-level strategy Type of strategy that identifies the portfolio of businesses that, in total, comprise the company and the ways in which these businesses relate to each other.

criterion validity A type of validity based on showing that scores on the test (predictors) are related to job performance (criterion).

critical incident method Keeping a record of uncommonly good or undesirable examples of an employee's work-related behavior and reviewing it with the employee at predetermined times.

cross training Training employees to do different tasks or jobs than their own; doing so facilitates flexibility and job rotation.

Davis-Bacon Act A 1931 law that sets wage rates for laborers employed by contractors working for the federal government.

decertification Legal process for employees to terminate a union's right to represent them.

deferred profit-sharing plan A plan in which a certain amount of profits is credited to each employee's account, payable at retirement, termination, or death.

defined benefit plan A plan that contains a formula for determining retirement benefits.

defined contribution plan A plan in which the employer's contribution to employees' retirement savings funds is specified.

diary/log Daily listings made by workers of every activity in which they engage along with the time each activity takes.

digital dashboard Presents the manager with desktop graphs and charts, and so a computerized picture of where the company stands on all those metrics from the HR scorecard process.

direct financial payments Pay in the form of wages, salaries, incentives, commissions, and bonuses.

discipline A means to encourage employees to adhere to rules and regulations.

discrimination Taking specific actions toward or against a person based on the person's group.

dismissal Involuntary termination of an employee's employment with the firm.

disparate rejection rates A test for adverse impact in which it can be demonstrated that there is a discrepancy between rates of rejection of members of a protected group and of others.

distributive justice The fairness and justice of a decision's result.

diversity The variety or multiplicity of demographic features that characterize a company's workforce, particularly in terms of race, sex, culture, national origin, handicap, age, and religion.

downsizing The process of reducing, usually dramatically, the number of people employed by a firm.

early retirement window A type of offering by which employees are encouraged to retire early, the incentive being liberal pension benefits plus perhaps a cash payment.

earnings-at-risk pay plan Plan that puts some portion of employees' normal pay at risk if they don't meet their goals, in return for possibly obtaining a much larger bonus if they exceed their goals.

economic strike A strike that results from a failure to agree on the terms of a contract that involves wages, benefits, and other conditions of employment.

Electronic Communications Privacy Act (ECPA) Intended in part to restrict interception and monitoring of oral and wire communications, but with two exceptions: employers who can show a legitimate business reason for doing so, and employers who have employees' consent to do so.

electronic performance monitoring (EPM) Having supervisors electronically monitor the amount of computerized data an employee is processing per day, and thereby his or her performance.

electronic performance support systems (EPSS) Sets of computerized tools and displays that automate training, documentation, and phone support; integrate this automation into applications; and provide support that's faster, cheaper, and more effective than traditional methods.

employee assistance program (EAP) A formal employer program for providing employees with counseling and/or treatment programs for problems such as alcoholism, gambling, or stress.

employee compensation All forms of pay or rewards going to employees and arising from their employment.

employee orientation A procedure for providing new employees with basic background information about the firm.

employee recruiting Finding and/or attracting applicants for the employer's open positions.

employee relations The activity of establishing and maintaining the positive employee–employer relationships that contribute to satisfactory productivity, motivation, morale, and discipline, as well as maintaining a positive, productive, and cohesive work environment.

Employee Retirement Income Security Act (ERISA) The 1974 law that provides government protection of pensions for all employees with company pension plans. It also regulates vesting rights (employees who leave before retirement may claim compensation from the pension plan).

employee stock ownership plan (ESOP) A qualified, tax-deductible stock bonus plan in which employers contribute stock to a trust for eventual use by employees.

Equal Employment Opportunity Commission (EEOC) The commission, created by Title VII, empowered to investigate job discrimination complaints and sue on behalf of complainants.

Equal Pay Act A 1963 amendment to the Fair Labor Standards Act designed to require equal pay for women doing the same work as men.

ethics The standards someone uses to decide what his or her conduct should be.

ethnocentric The notion that home-country attitudes, management style, knowledge, evaluation criteria, and managers are superior to anything the host country has to offer.

ethnocentrism The tendency to view members of other social groups less favorably than members of one's own group.

executive coach An outside consultant who questions the executive's associates in order to identify the executive's strengths and weaknesses, and then counsels the executive so he or she can capitalize on those strengths and overcome the weaknesses.

exit interviews Interviews with employees who are leaving the firm, conducted for obtaining information about the job or related matters, to give the employer insight about the company.

expatriates (expats) Noncitizens of the countries in which employees are working.

expectancy chart A graph showing the relationship between test scores and job performance for a group of people.

expectancy A person's expectation that his or her effort will lead to performance.

fact finder A neutral party who studies the issues in a dispute and makes a public recommendation for a reasonable settlement.

fair day's work Output standards devised based on careful, scientific analysis.

Fair Labor Standards Act This 1938 act provides for minimum wages, maximum hours, overtime pay, and child labor protection. The law, amended many times, covers most employees.

family-friendly (or work–life) benefits Benefits such as child care and fitness facilities that make it easier for employees to balance their work and family responsibilities.

Federal Violence Against Women Act of 1994 The act that provides that a person who commits a crime of violence motivated by gender shall be liable to the party injured.

financial incentives Financial rewards paid to workers whose production exceeds some predetermined standard.

flexible benefits plan/cafeteria benefits plan Individualized plans allowed by employers to accommodate employee preferences for benefits.

flextime A work schedule in which employees' workdays are built around a core of midday hours, and employees determine, within limits, what other hours they will work.

forced distribution method Similar to grading on a curve; predetermined percentages of ratees are placed in various performance categories.

foreign service premiums Financial payments over and above regular base pay, typically ranging between 10% and 30% of base pay.

functional authority The authority exerted by an HR manager as coordinator of personnel activities.

functional strategy A strategy that identifies the broad activities that each department will pursue in order to help the business accomplish its competitive goals.

gainsharing plan An incentive plan that engages employees in a common effort to achieve productivity objectives and share the gains.

gender-role stereotypes The tendency to associate women with certain (frequently nonmanagerial) jobs.

geocentric The belief that the firm's whole management staff must be scoured on a global basis, on the assumption that the best manager of a specific position anywhere may be in any of the countries in which the firm operates.

globalization The tendency of firms to extend their sales, ownership, and/or manufacturing to new markets abroad.

golden parachute A payment companies make in connection with a change in ownership or control of a company.

good faith bargaining Both parties are making every reasonable effort to arrive at agreement; proposals are being matched with counterproposals.

good-faith effort strategy An affirmative action strategy that emphasizes identifying and eliminating the obstacles to hiring and promoting women and minorities, and increasing the minority or female applicant flow.

grade definition Written descriptions of the level of, say, responsibility and knowledge required by jobs in each grade. Similar jobs can then be combined into grades or classes.

grades A job classification system like the class system, although grades often contain dissimilar jobs, such as secretaries, mechanics, and firefighters. Grade descriptions are written based on compensable factors listed in classification systems.

graphic rating scale A scale that lists a number of traits and a range of performance for each. The employee is then rated by identifying the score that best describes his or her level of performance for each trait.

grievance procedure Formal process for addressing any factor involving wages, hours, or conditions of employment that is used as a complaint against the employer.

group life insurance Provides lower rates for the employer or employee and includes all employees, including new employees, regardless of health or physical condition.

halo effect In performance appraisal, the problem that occurs when a supervisor's rating of a subordinate on one trait biases the rating of that person on other traits.

hardship allowances Payments that compensate expatriates for exceptionally hard living and working conditions at certain locations.

health maintenance organization (HMO) A prepaid health-care system that generally provides routine round-the-clock medical services as well as preventive medicine in a clinic-type arrangement for employees, who pay a nominal fee in addition to the fixed annual fee the employer pays.

high-performance work system (HPWS) A set of human resource management policies and practices that promote organizational effectiveness.

home-country nationals Citizens of the country in which the multinational company has its headquarters.

HR audit An analysis by which an organization measures where it currently stands and determines what it has to accomplish to improve its HR functions.

HR scorecard A process for assigning financial and nonfinancial goals or metrics to the human resource management–related chain of activities required for achieving the company's strategic aims and for monitoring results.

human capital The knowledge, education, training, skills, and expertise of a firm's workers.

human resource management (HRM) The process of acquiring, training, appraising, and compensating employees, and of attending to their labor relations, health and safety, and fairness concerns.

human resource metrics The quantitative gauge of a human resource management activity, such as employee turnover, hours of training per employee, or qualified applicants per position.

illegal bargaining items Items in collective bargaining that are forbidden by law; for example, a clause agreeing to hire "union members exclusively" would be illegal in a right-to-work state.

impasse Collective bargaining situation that occurs when the parties are not able to move further toward settlement, usually because one party is demanding more than the other will offer.

in-house development center A company-based method for exposing prospective managers to realistic exercises to develop improved management skills.

indirect financial payments Pay in the form of financial benefits such as insurance.

injunction A court order compelling a party or parties either to resume or to desist from a certain action.

inside games Union efforts to convince employees to impede or to disrupt production—for example, by slowing the work pace.

instrumentality The perceived relationship between successful performance and obtaining the reward.

insubordination Willful disregard or disobedience of the boss's authority or legitimate orders; criticizing the boss in public.

interest arbitration Arbitration enacted when labor agreements do not yet exist or when one or both parties are seeking to change the agreement.

interest inventory A personal development and selection device that compares the person's current interests with those of others now in various occupations so as to determine the preferred occupation for the individual.

international human resource management (IHRM) The human resource management concepts and techniques employers use to manage the human resource challenges of their international operations.

intrinsic motivation Motivation that derives from the pleasure someone gets from doing the job or task.

job aid A set of instructions, diagrams, or similar methods available at the job site to guide the worker.

job analysis The procedure for determining the duties and skill requirements of a job and the kind of person who should be hired for it.

job classification (or job grading) A method for categorizing jobs into groups.

job descriptions A list of a job's duties, responsibilities, reporting relationships, working conditions, and supervisory responsibilities—one product of a job analysis.

job enlargement Assigning workers additional same-level activities.

job enrichment Redesigning jobs in a way that increases the opportunities for the worker to experience feelings of responsibility, achievement, growth, and recognition.

job evaluation A systematic comparison done in order to determine the worth of one job relative to another.

job hazard analysis A systematic approach to identifying and eliminating workplace hazards before they occur.

job instruction training (JIT) Listing each job's basic tasks, along with key points, in order to provide step-by-step training for employees.

job posting Publicizing an open job to employees (often by literally posting it on bulletin boards) and listing its attributes, like qualifications, supervisor, working schedule, and pay rate.

job requirements matrix A more complete description of what the worker does and how and why he or she does it; it clarifies each task's purpose and each duty's required knowledge, skills, abilities, and other characteristics.

job rotation A management training technique that involves moving a trainee from department to department to broaden his or her experience and identify strong and weak points.

job sharing Allows two or more people to share a single full-time job.

job specifications A list of a job's "human requirements," that is, the requisite education, skills, personality, and so on—another product of a job analysis.

job-related interview A series of job-related questions that focus on relevant past job-related behaviors.

Landrum-Griffin Act (1959) Also known as the *Labor Management Reporting and Disclosure Act*, this law aimed at protecting union members from possible wrongdoing on the part of their unions.

layoff An employer sending employees home due to a lack of work; this is typically a temporary situation.

lifelong learning Provides employees with continuing learning experiences over their tenure with the firm, with the aims of ensuring they have the opportunity to learn the skills they need to do their jobs and to expand their occupational horizons.

line authority The authority exerted by an HR manager by directing the activities of the people in his or her own department and in service areas (like the plant cafeteria).

line manager A manager who is authorized to direct the work of subordinates and is responsible for accomplishing the organization's tasks.

locals Citizens of the countries in which employees are working; also called *host-country nationals*.

lockout A refusal by the employer to provide opportunities to work.

management assessment center A simulation in which management candidates are asked to perform realistic tasks in hypothetical situations and are scored on their performance. It usually also involves testing and the use of management games.

management development Any attempt to improve current or future management performance by imparting knowledge, changing attitudes, or increasing skills.

management game A development technique in which teams of managers compete by making computerized decisions regarding realistic but simulated situations.

management process The five basic functions of planning, organizing, staffing, leading, and controlling.

manager The person responsible for accomplishing the organization's goals, and who does so by managing (planning, organizing, staffing, leading, and controlling) the efforts of the organization's people.

managing diversity Maximizing diversity's potential benefits while minimizing its potential barriers.

mandatory bargaining items Items in collective bargaining that a party must bargain over if they are introduced by the other party—for example, pay.

market-competitive pay system A pay system in which the employer's actual pay rates are competitive with those in the relevant labor market.

mass interview A panel interviews several candidates simultaneously.

mediation Intervention in which a neutral third party tries to assist the principals in reaching agreement.

mentoring Advising, counseling, and guiding.

merit pay (merit raise) Any salary increase awarded to an employee based on his or her individual performance.

miniature job training and evaluation Training candidates to perform several of the job's tasks, and then evaluating the candidates' performance prior to hire.

mission statement Summarizes the answer to the question, "What business are we in?"

"mixed-motive" case A discrimination allegation case in which the employer argues that the employment action taken was motivated not by discrimination, but by some nondiscriminatory reason such as ineffective performance.

mobility premiums Typically, lump-sum payments to reward employees for moving from one assignment to another.

national emergency strikes Strikes that might "imperil the national health and safety."

National Labor Relations (or Wagner) Act This law banned certain types of unfair practices and provided for secret-ballot elections and majority rule for determining whether a firm's employees want to unionize.

National Labor Relations Board (NLRB) The agency created by the Wagner Act to investigate unfair labor practice charges and to provide for secret-ballot elections and majority rule in determining whether or not a firm's employees want a union.

negligent hiring Hiring workers with questionable backgrounds without proper safeguards.

negligent training A situation where an employer fails to train adequately, and the employee subsequently harms a third party.

nonpunitive discipline Discipline without punishment, usually involving a system of oral warnings and paid "decision-making leaves" in lieu of more traditional punishment.

Norris-LaGuardia Act (1932) This law marked the beginning of the era of strong encouragement of unions and guaranteed to each employee the right to bargain collectively "free from interference, restraint, or coercion."

occupational illness Any abnormal condition or disorder caused by exposure to environmental factors associated with employment.

Occupational Safety and Health Act of 1970 The law passed by Congress in 1970 "to assure so far as possible every working man and woman in the nation safe and healthful working conditions and to preserve our human resources."

Occupational Safety and Health Administration (OSHA) The agency created within the Department of Labor to set safety and health standards for almost all workers in the United States.

Office of Federal Contract Compliance Programs (OFCCP) This office is responsible for implementing the executive orders and ensuring compliance of federal contractors.

on-demand recruiting services (ODRS) Services that provide short-term specialized recruiting to support specific projects without the expense of retaining traditional search firms.

on-the-job training Training a person to learn a job while working on it.

operational safety reviews Reviews conducted by agencies to ascertain whether units under their jurisdiction are complying with all the applicable safety laws, regulations, orders, and rules.

organization chart A chart that shows the organization-wide distribution of work, with titles of each position and interconnecting lines that show who reports to and communicates with whom.

organization People with formally assigned roles who work together to achieve the organization's goals.

organizational culture The characteristic values, traditions, and behaviors a company's employees share.

organizational development A special approach to organizational change in which employees themselves formulate and implement the change that's required.

organization-wide incentive plan Incentive plan in which all or most employees can participate.

outplacement counseling A formal process by which a terminated person is trained and counseled in the techniques of self-appraisal and securing a new position.

outsourced learning Utilizing a resource outside the company to provide employee training.

paired comparison method Ranking employees by making a chart of all possible pairs of the employees for each trait and indicating which is the better employee of the pair.

panel interview An interview in which a group of interviewers questions the applicant.

pay (or rate) ranges A series of steps or levels within a pay grade, usually based upon years of service.

pay (or wage) grade A pay grade is comprised of jobs of approximately equal difficulty.

Pension Benefits Guarantee Corporation (PBGC) Established under ERISA to ensure that pensions meet vesting obligations; also insures pensions should a plan terminate without sufficient funds to meet its vested obligations.

pension plans Plans that provide a fixed sum when employees reach a predetermined retirement age or when they can no longer work due to disability.

performance analysis Verifying that there is a performance deficiency and determining whether that deficiency should be corrected through training or through some other means (such as transferring the employee).

performance appraisal Evaluating an employee's current and/or past performance relative to his or her performance standards.

performance appraisal process A three-step appraisal process involving (1) setting work standards, (2) assessing the employee's actual performance relative to those standards, and (3) providing feedback to the employee with the aim of helping him or her to eliminate performance deficiencies or to continue to perform above par.

performance management The *continuous* process of identifying, measuring, and developing the performance of individuals and teams and *aligning* their performance with the organization's *goals*.

personnel replacement charts Company records showing present performance and promotability of inside candidates for the most important positions.

picketing Having employees carry signs announcing their concerns near the employer's place of business.

piecework A system of pay based on the number of items processed by each individual worker in a unit of time, such as items per hour or items per day.

point method The job evaluation method in which a number of compensable factors are identified and then the degree to which each of these factors is present on the job is determined.

polycentric A conscious belief that only the host-country managers can ever really understand the culture and behavior of the host-country market.

portability Instituting policies that enable employees to easily take their accumulated pension funds when they leave an employer.

position analysis questionnaire (PAQ) A questionnaire used to collect quantifiable data concerning the duties and responsibilities of various jobs.

position replacement card A card prepared for each position in a company to show possible replacement candidates and their qualifications.

preferential shop Union members get preference in hiring, but the employer can still hire nonunion members.

preferred provider organizations (PPOs) Groups of health care providers that contract with employers, insurance companies, or third-party payers to provide medical care services at a reduced fee.

Pregnancy Discrimination Act An amendment to Title VII of the Civil Rights Act that prohibits sex discrimination based on "pregnancy, childbirth, or related medical conditions."

problem-solving teams Semipermanent teams that identify and research work processes and develop solutions to work-related problems.

procedural justice The fairness of the process.

process chart A workflow chart that shows the flow of inputs to and outputs from a particular job.

productivity The ratio of outputs (goods and services) divided by the inputs (resources such as labor and capital).

profit-sharing plan A plan whereby employees share in the company's profits.

programmed learning A systematic method for teaching job skills, involving presenting questions or facts, allowing the person to respond, and giving the learner immediate feedback on the accuracy of his or her answers.

promotion Advancement to a position of increased responsibility.

protected class Persons such as minorities and women protected by equal opportunity laws, including Title VII.

qualifications (or skills) inventories Manual or computerized records listing employees' education, career and development interests, languages, special skills, and so on, to be used in selecting inside candidates for promotion.

qualified individuals Under ADA, those who can carry out the essential functions of the job.

quality circle A special type of formal problem-solving team of specially trained employees who meet once a week to solve problems affecting their work area.

ranking method The simplest method of job evaluation that involves ranking each job relative to all other jobs, usually based on overall difficulty.

ratio analysis A forecasting technique for determining future staff needs by using ratios between, for example, sales volume and number of employees needed.

reality shock Results of a period that may occur at the initial career entry when the new employee's high job expectations confront the reality of a boring or otherwise unattractive work situation.

recruiting yield pyramid The historical arithmetic relationships between recruitment leads and invitees, invitees and interviews, interviews and offers made, and offers made and offers accepted.

reliability The consistency of scores obtained by the same person when retested with the identical tests or with alternate forms of the same test.

restricted policy Another test for adverse impact, involving demonstration that an employer's hiring practices exclude a protected group, whether intentionally or not.

reverse discrimination Claim that due to affirmative action quota systems, white males are discriminated against.

right to work A term used to describe state statutory or constitutional provisions banning the requirement of union membership as a condition of employment.

rights arbitration Arbitration that interprets existing contract terms, for instance, when an employee questions the employer's right to have taken some disciplinary action.

role-playing A training technique in which trainees act out parts in a realistic management situation.

safety awareness program Program that enables trained supervisors to orient new workers arriving at a job site regarding common safety hazards and simple prevention methods.

salary survey A survey aimed at determining prevailing wage rates. A good salary survey provides specific wage rates for specific jobs. Formal written questionnaire surveys are the most comprehensive, but telephone surveys and newspaper ads are also sources of information.

savings and thrift plan Plan in which employees contribute a portion of their earnings to a fund; the employer usually matches this contribution in whole or in part.

Scanlon plan An incentive plan developed in 1937 by Joseph Scanlon and designed to encourage cooperation, involvement, and sharing of benefits.

scatter plot A graphical method used to help identify the relationship between two variables.

scientific management Management approach based on improving work methods through observation and analysis.

self-managing/self-directed work team A highly trained group of around eight employees who are fully responsible for turning out a well-defined segment of finished work.

severance pay A one-time payment some employers provide when terminating an employee.

sexual harassment Harassment on the basis of sex that has the purpose or effect of substantially interfering with a person's work performance or creating an intimidating, hostile, or offensive work environment.

sick leave Provides pay to an employee when he or she is out of work because of illness.

situational interview A series of job-related questions that focus on how the candidate would behave in a given situation.

situational test A test that requires examinees to respond to situations representative of the job.

social responsibility The extent to which companies should and do channel resources toward improving one or more segments of society other than the firm's owners or stockholders.

Social Security Federal program that provides three types of benefits: retirement income at the age of 62 and thereafter, survivor's or death benefits payable to the employee's dependents regardless of age at time of death, and disability benefits payable to disabled employees and their dependents. These benefits are payable only if the employee is insured under the Social Security Act.

staff authority Staff authority gives the manager the right (authority) to advise other managers or employees.

staff manager A manager who assists and advises line managers.

standard hour plan A plan by which a worker is paid a basic hourly rate but is paid an extra percentage of his or her rate for production exceeding the standard per hour or per day. Similar to piecework payment but based on a percent premium.

Standard Occupational Classification (SOC) Classifies all workers into one of 23 major groups of jobs that are subdivided into minor groups of jobs and detailed occupations.

stereotyping Ascribing specific behavioral traits to individuals based on their apparent membership in a group.

stock option The right to purchase a stated number of shares of a company stock at today's price at some time in the future.

straight piecework An incentive plan in which a person is paid a sum for each item he or she makes or sells, with a strict proportionality between results and rewards.

strategic human resource management Formulating and executing human resource policies and practices that produce the employee competencies and behaviors the company needs to achieve its strategic aims.

strategic management The process of identifying and executing the organization's strategic plan by matching the company's capabilities with the demands of its environment.

strategic plan The company's plan for how it will match its internal strengths and weaknesses with external opportunities and threats in order to maintain a competitive advantage.

strategy A course of action the company can pursue to achieve its strategic aims.

strategy map A strategic planning tool that shows the "big picture" of how each department's performance contributes to achieving the company's overall strategic goals.

strategy-based metrics Metrics that specifically focus on measuring the activities that contribute to achieving a company's strategic aims.

stress interview An interview in which the applicant is made uncomfortable by a series of often rude questions. This technique helps identify hypersensitive applicants and those with low or high stress tolerance.

strictness/leniency The problem that occurs when a supervisor has a tendency to rate all subordinates either high or low.

strike A withdrawal of labor.

structured (or directive) interview An interview following a set sequence of questions.

structured sequential interview An interview in which the applicant is interviewed sequentially by several persons; each rates the applicant on a standard form.

structured situational interview A series of job-relevant questions with predetermined answers that interviewers ask of all applicants for the job.

succession planning The ongoing process of systematically identifying, assessing, and developing organizational leadership to enhance performance.

suggestion teams Temporary teams whose members work on specific analytical assignments, such as how to cut costs or raise productivity.

supplemental pay benefits Benefits for time not worked such as unemployment insurance, vacation and holiday pay, and sick pay.

supplemental unemployment benefits Provide for a "guaranteed annual income" in certain industries where employers must shut down to change machinery or due to reduced work. These benefits are paid by the company and supplement unemployment benefits.

sympathy strike A strike that takes place when one union strikes in support of the strike of another.

Taft-Hartley Act (1947) Also known as the *Labor Management Relations Act*, this law prohibited unfair union labor practices and enumerated the rights of employees as union members. It also enumerated the rights of employers.

talent management The goal-oriented and integrated process of planning, recruiting, developing, managing, and compensating employees.

task analysis A detailed study of a job to identify the specific skills required.

task statement Written item that shows *what* the worker does on one particular job task; *how* the worker does it; the *knowledge, skills, and aptitudes required* to do it; and the *purpose of the task*.

team (or group) incentive plan A plan in which a production standard is set for a specific work group, and its members are paid incentives if the group exceeds the production standard.

terminate at will In the absence of a contract, either the employer or the employee can terminate at will the employment relationship.

termination interview The interview in which an employee is informed of the fact that he or she has been dismissed.

test validity The accuracy with which a test, interview, and so on measures what it purports to measure or fulfills the function it was designed to fill.

third-country nationals Citizens of a country other than the parent or the host country.

Title VII of the 1964 Civil Rights Act This act makes it unlawful for employers to discriminate against any individual with respect to hiring, compensation, terms, conditions, or privileges of employment because of race, color, religion, sex, or national origin.

tokenism When a company appoints a small group of women or minorities to high-profile positions, rather than more aggressively seeking full representation for that group.

training The process of teaching new or current employees the basic skills they need to perform their jobs.

transfer Reassignments to similar positions in other parts of the firm.

trend analysis Study of a firm's past employment needs over a period of years to predict future needs.

unclear standards An appraisal that is too open to interpretation.

unemployment insurance (or compensation) Provides benefits if a person is unable to work through some fault other than his or her own.

unfair labor practice strike A strike aimed at protesting illegal conduct by the employer.

Uniform Guidelines Guidelines issued by federal agencies charged with ensuring compliance with equal employment federal legislation explaining recommended employer procedures in detail.

union salting A union organizing tactic by which workers who are in fact employed full-time by a union as undercover organizers are hired by unwitting employers.

union shop A form of union security in which the company can hire nonunion people, but they must join the union after a prescribed period of time and pay dues. (If they do not, they can be fired.)

unsafe conditions The mechanical and physical conditions that cause accidents.

unstructured (or nondirective) interview An unstructured conversational-style interview in which the interviewer pursues points of interest as they come up in response to questions.

unstructured sequential interview An interview in which each interviewer forms an independent opinion after asking different questions.

valence The perceived value a person attaches to the reward.

variable pay Any plan that ties pay to productivity or profitability, usually as one-time lump payments.

video-based simulation A situational test in which examinees respond to video simulations of realistic job situations.

virtual classroom Teaching method that uses special collaboration software to enable multiple remote learners, using their PCs or laptops, to participate in live audio and visual discussions, communicate via written text, and learn via content such as PowerPoint slides.

virtual teams Groups of geographically dispersed coworkers who interact using a combination of telecommunications and information technologies to accomplish an organizational task.

Vocational Rehabilitation Act of 1973 The act requiring certain federal contractors to take affirmative action for disabled persons.

voluntary (or permissible) bargaining items Items in collective bargaining over which bargaining is neither illegal nor mandatory—neither party can be compelled against its wishes to negotiate over those items.

wage curve Shows the relationship between the value of the job and the average wage paid for this job.

Walsh-Healey Public Contract Act A 1936 law that requires minimum wage and working conditions for employees working on any government contract amounting to more than $10,000.

Web 2.0 learing Training that uses online technologies such as social networks, virtual worlds (such as Second Life), and systems that blend synchronous and asynchronous delivery with blogs, chat rooms, bookmark sharing, and tools such as 3-D simulations.

wildcat strike An unauthorized strike occurring during the term of a contract.

work samples Actual job tasks used in testing applicants' performance.

work sampling technique A testing method based on measuring performance on actual basic job tasks.

work sharing Refers to a temporary reduction in work hours by a group of employees during economic downturns as a way to prevent layoffs.

workers' compensation Provides income and medical benefits to work-related accident victims or their dependents regardless of fault.

workflow analysis A detailed study of the flow of work from job to job in a work process.

workforce (or employment or personnel) planning The process of deciding what positions the firm will have to fill, and how to fill them.

works councils Formal, employee-elected groups of worker representatives.

NAME/ORGANIZATION INDEX

Note: Page numbers with *f* indicate figures; those with *n* indicate endnotes; those with *t* indicate tables

C

M

N

O

P

Q

R

S

SUBJECT INDEX

Note: Page numbers with *f* indicate figures; those with *n* indicate endnotes; those with *t* indicate tables

F

Q